WebSphere V3.5 Handbook

KEN UENO

AND THE WEBSPHERE CONSULTING TEAM

PRENTICE HALL PTR
UPPER SADDLE RIVER, NEW JERSEY 07458
www.phptr.com

First Edition (January 2001)

This edition applies to:

- IBM WebSphere Application Server Standard and Advanced Editions V3.5.2 for AIX and Windows
- IBM HTTP Server V1.3.6.12 for AIX and Windows
- IBM Java Development Kit V1.2.2 for AIX and Windows
- IBM DB2 UDB V7.1 FP1 for AIX and Windows
- Lotus Domino R5.0.4 for AIX
- Oracle 8i (8.1.6) for AIX and Windows
- Sybase 12 for AIX

for use with the AIX V4.3.3, Windows NT 4.0 SP6a, and Windows 2000 operating systems.

Comments may be addressed to:

IBM Corporation, International Technical Support Organization
Dept. HZ8 Building 678
P.O. Box 12195
Research Triangle Park, NC 27709-2195

When you send information to IBM, you grant IBM a non-exclusive right to use or distribute the information in any way it believes appropriate without incurring any obligation to you.

Published by Prentice Hall PTR
Prentice-Hall, Inc.
Upper Saddle River, NJ 07458

Take Note!
Before using this information and the product it supports, be sure to read the general information in Appendix H, "Special Notices," on page 1131.

Printed in the United States of America
10 9 8 7 6 5 4 3 2 1

ISBN 0-13-041656-8

Prentice-Hall International (UK) Limited, *London*
Prentice-Hall of Australia Pty. Limited, *Sydney*
Prentice-Hall Canada Inc., *Toronto*
Prentice-Hall Hispanoamericana, S.A., *Mexico*
Prentice-Hall of India Private Limited, *New Delhi*
Prentice-Hall of Japan, Inc., *Tokyo*
Pearson Education Asia Pte. Ltd.
Editora Prentice-Hall do Brasil, Ltda., *Rio de Janeiro*

Contents

Preface

WebSphere Application Server V3.5 is the latest version of the IBM open standards-based e-business application deployment environment. This redbook will show you how to install and use the product. It provides detailed insights into the product's architecture and gives a wealth of practical advice about how best to exploit the features of WebSphere.

At the heart of the book are detailed step-by-step descriptions of the tasks you will carry out to deploy and execute your applications. These descriptions include not only the use of the improved V3.5 GUI administration console but also examples of how to exploit the new command line administration facilities.

The redbook places these task descriptions in a broader context by providing discussions of possible application architectures, deployment topologies, best practices and problem determination when using WebSphere Application Server.

These discussions are founded on clear descriptions of concepts and technologies that provide the framework for WebSphere Application Server. These include the Servlet, JSP and EJB APIs, security, transactions, JDBC, and JNDI.

The redbook also contains details of the support for the Servlet API V2.2 and JSP V1.1 APIs introduced by WebSphere V3.5 Fix Pack 2 and examples of using these new facilities.

The team that wrote this redbook

This redbook was produced by a team of specialists from around the world working at the International Technical Support Organization, Raleigh Center.

Ken Ueno is an Advisory IT Specialist in the WebSphere Performance group, which is a part of WebSphere development in RTP. Previously, he managed residencies and produced Redbooks, which included *WebSphere V3 Performance Tuning Guide* and *WebSphere Scalability: WLM and Clustering* at the International Technical Support Organization, Raleigh Center. Before joining the ITSO, he worked in Internet Systems, IBM Japan Systems Engineering Co., Ltd. in Japan as an IT Specialist.

David Artus is a Consulting IT Specialist in the London Solutions Group, part of IBM EMEA Software Services. He has 20 years of experience in IT, most recently specializing in consulting for the WebSphere product family. His areas of expertise include object technologies and transaction processing.

Larry Brown is a Senior Software Engineer for IBM in the USA. He has over 15 years of experience in the computing field including development, customer consulting, and teaching. His areas of expertise include distributed systems, transaction processing, and fault-tolerant systems.

Larry Clark is an Advisory Software Engineer and a member of the WebSphere Enablement Team in Research Triangle Park, NC, USA. His various development roles have included programming, project management, advanced design, strategy, and architecture.

Chris Gerken is a Senior Programmer for IBM based in the USA. He has nine years of experience in object-oriented programming and design. He represented IBM in the discussions leading to the JSP 1.0 and JSP 1.1 specifications and has since developed workshops on the design and use of JSP custom tags.

Geoff Hambrick is an Executive Consultant on the IBM WebSphere Enablement Team in Austin, Texas. His areas of expertise include object-oriented analysis and design methodologies specializing in distributed object and Web-based applications.

Ashok Iyengar is an Advisory Software Engineer at the IBM Transarc Lab's Customer Solutions Center in San Diego, USA. He has 18 years of IT experience mainly in software development and has worked exclusively with the WebSphere platform for the past couple of years.

Stacy Joines is an IBM Senior Software Engineer at Research Triangle Park, NC. She has four years of experience in WebSphere and the Web application field. She assists customers with proof of concepts regarding WebSphere Application Server, with a focus on WebSphere performance engagements.

Simon Kapadia is an Advisory IT Specialist at the London Solutions Group, part of IBM EMEA Software Services (North Region). His work involves going out to customer sites and implementing solutions, specializing in WebSphere Application Server and Edge Server. He has 10 years of UNIX experience.

Mohamed Ramdani is an IBM IT Specialist in France. He has two years' experience in WebSphere-related technologies. He has worked on a number of projects concerning the design and architecture of an application based on WebSphere and VisualAge for Java using EJB.

James Roca is an IBM-certified AIX Technical Expert working at the UK RS/6000 Technical Support Center. His areas of expertise include multi-vendor UNIX support, AIX network tuning, and firewall (VPN) consulting.

Sung-Ik Son is an Advisory Software Engineer at IBM, Raleigh. He has 14 years of experience in system and application software development. His current areas of expertise are enabling and consulting for WebSphere products.

Lorrie Tomek is an IBM WebSphere consultant in Research Triangle Park, North Carolina. Her areas of expertise include architecture, design, performance and reliability analysis, and object-oriented programming.

Jim VanOosten is a Senior Software Engineer at the IBM Rochester Lab. He has over eight years of experience in object-oriented system design and has worked on the WebSphere Solutions Integration Team for the past year.

Chenxi Zhang is an IBM IT specialist in China. She has four years of experience in the IT field. She currently provides level 1 support for WebSphere in China, helping customers with Web solutions.

Thanks to the following people for their invaluable contributions to this project:

Chris Pentleton, Pentleton Consulting Inc.

Thanks to the following IBM employees:

Jerry Cuomo, Manager, WebSphere Development, Raleigh
Jason R McGee, WebSphere Architect, Raleigh
Michael Fraenkel, WebSphere Architect, Raleigh
Michael Morton, WebSphere Architect, Raleigh
Raj Nagratnam, WebSphere Development, Raleigh
Jamison Wilfred, WebSphere Development, Raleigh
Gabe Montero, WebSphere Development, Raleigh
Subodh Vinchurkar, WebSphere Development, Raleigh
JJ Kahrs, WebSphere Development, Raleigh
Chris Mitchell, WebSphere Development, Raleigh
Thomas Bitonti, WebSphere Development, Raleigh
Richard Bachouse, WebSphere Development, Raleigh
Nabeel Abdallah, WebSphere Development, Raleigh
Scott Johnson, WebSphere Development, Raleigh
Eric Jenney, Manager, WebSphere Development, Rochester
Pete Schommer, WebSphere Development, Rochester
Deb Erickson, WebSphere Development, Rochester
Ken Lawrence, WebSphere Development, Rochester
Joe Bockhold, WebSphere Development, Rochester
John Koehler, WebSphere Development, Rochester
Douglas Berg, WebSphere Development, Rochester
Russ Newcombe, WebSphere Naming Architect, Austin
Stephen Cocks, WebSphere ORB Architect, Austin
Fred Stock, Manager, WebSphere Development, IBM Transarc Lab
Tim Burt, WebSphere Development, IBM Transarc Lab
Amber Roy-Chowdhury, WebSphere Development, IBM Transarc Lab
Mike Young, WebSphere Development, IBM Transarc Lab
Samar Choudhary, WebSphere Development, IBM Transarc Lab
Dongfeng Li, WebSphere Development, IBM Transarc Lab
Daniel Julin, Websphere Development, IBM Transarc Lab
Hany Salem, WebSphere Serviceability Architect, Austin
Eric Labadie, Object Level Trace Architect, IBM Toronto Lab
Kris Kobylinski, Object Level Trace Development, IBM Toronto Lab
Xing Xue, Object Level Trace Development, IBM Toronto Lab
Ron Bostick, WebSphere Performance, Raleigh
Steve Roma, WebSphere Test, Raleigh
Laura Yen, WebSphere Test, Raleigh

Loc Dang, WebSphere Test, Raleigh
Venu Rao, WebSphere Test, Raleigh
Trish York, WebSphere Documentation, Raleigh
Jim Stetor, Manager, Websphere Solutions Integration
Dave Cai, Websphere Solutions Integration
Melissa Modjeski, Websphere Solutions Integration
Barbara Ballard, Websphere Solutions Integration
Ken McCauley, Manager, Websphere Enablement Team, Raleigh
Ken Hygh, Websphere Enablement Team, Raleigh
Keys Botzum, WebSphere Consulting Services, IBM Transarc Lab
Kyle Brown, WebSphere Consulting Services, Raleigh
Lisa Tomita, WebSphere Consulting Services, Raleigh
Vess Ivanov, WebSphere Consulting Services, IBM Toronto Lab
Jeff Blight, EMEA Technical Sales
Kenji Kojima, IBM Japan
Alexander Koutsoumbos, IBM Australia
Ken Klingensmith, Worldwide WebSphere Technical Sales Support
Gail Christensen, ITSO Raleigh Center
Margaret Ticknor, ITSO Raleigh Center
John Ganci, ITSO Raleigh Center
Bill Moore, ITSO Raleigh Center
Tetsuya Shirai, ITSO San Jose Center
Uei Wahli, ITSO San Jose Center

and especially...
Tom Alcott, Worldwide WebSphere Technical Sales Support

Comments welcome

Your comments are important to us!

We want our Redbooks to be as helpful as possible. Please send us your comments about this or other Redbooks in one of the following ways:

- Fax the evaluation form found in "IBM Redbooks review" on page 1155 to the fax number shown on the form.
- Use the online evaluation form found at **ibm.com**/redbooks
- Send your comments in an Internet note to redbook@us.ibm.com

Chapter 1. Overview of WebSphere Application Server V3.5

This redbook is a detailed exploration of WebSphere Application Server V3.5, Standard Edition and WebSphere Application Server V3.5, Advanced Edition. In this introductory chapter we give an overview of the purpose of these two products and the differences between them.

You should note that in this redbook we will not address, WebSphere Application Server, Enterprise Edition. Enterprise Edition builds on the Advanced Edition by including two further products, Component Broker and TXSeries.

1.1 What is WebSphere Application Server?

IBM WebSphere Application Server provides a scalable, industrial-strength deployment platform for your e-business applications.

The Standard Edition supports the standard Java APIs that you can use for developing dynamic Web content: Servlets, JavaServer Pages (JSP) and eXtensible Markup Language (XML).

The Advanced Edition adds support for presenting your business logic as Enterprise JavaBeans (EJB) components. It also provides the capability to scale your application by distributing it across multiple physical machines, and the administrative tools you need to manage your distributed site.

By using WebSphere and its supported technologies you can rapidly build sophisticated applications that are well structured and hence maintainable and extensible at e-business space. This redbook shows you how to use WebSphere facilities and also gives practical advice on how best to exploit them.

1.2 WebSphere Application Server architecture overview

When you install and run either Standard or Advanced editions of WebSphere on a single machine you will see certain key processes running. In this section we give a brief introduction to these processes and their purpose. In later chapters we will give more details and describe other optional facilities.

Figure 1 gives a high-level overview of the major components that comprise a WebSphere instance.

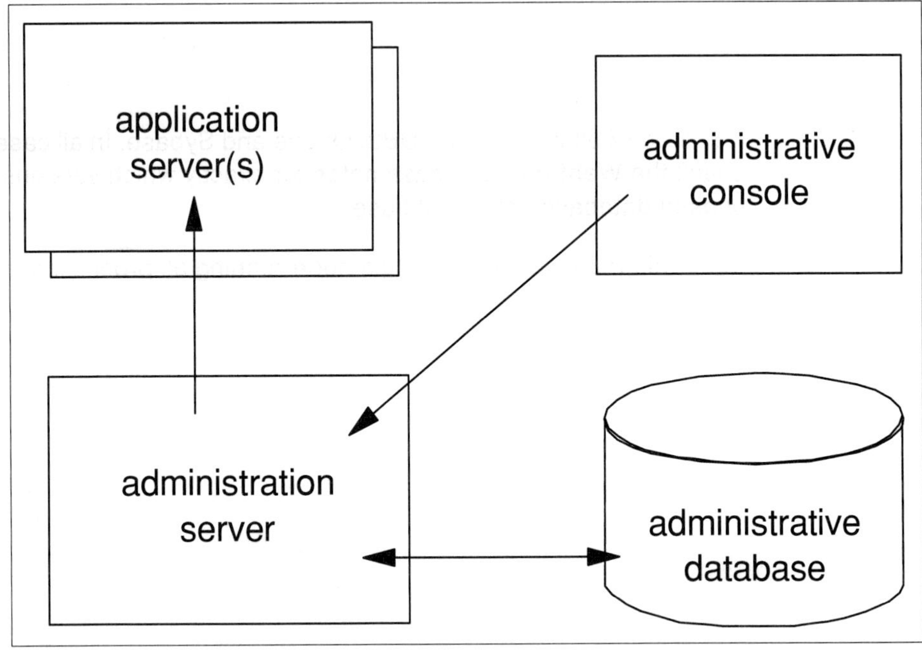

Figure 1. WebSphere components

The following sections describe the components shown in this figure.

1.2.1 Administration server

The administrative server is the systems management runtime component of WebSphere. The administrative server is responsible for runtime management, security, transaction coordination, and workload management. In most cases (exceptions will be outlined later), the administrative server runs on all nodes in a WebSphere administrative domain and controls the interaction between each node and application server process in the domain.

1.2.2 Application server

Your code, servlets, JSPs, EJBs and their supporting classes run in an application server. You can define multiple application servers, each of which has its own Java Virtual Machine (JVM).

You decide which of your servlets, JSPs and EJBs run in which of your application servers.

1.2.3 Administrative database

WebSphere stores all runtime configuration information for a domain in a single persistent repository. In Standard Edition this repository can be stored in InstantDB (which ships with the Standard Edition), DB2 or Oracle. Advanced Edition supports DB2, Oracle and Sybase. In all cases you need to check the WebSphere release notes for exactly which versions of your chosen database you should use.

In our diagram we show a single node running all processes, and this is common in small-scale development situations. It is entirely reasonable to configure the database on a remote server, and in production environments we recommend that you do so.

1.2.4 Administrative console

The administrative console is the graphical user interface used for administration of a WebSphere administrative domain. The administrative console can run on one of the nodes that the administrative server is running on, or it can be a remote node that attaches to a running administrative server.

1.3 Standard Edition

WebSphere Standard Edition is a single system, extremely easy-to-use Web Application Server. You can use Standard Edition for applications producing both static and dynamic Web pages containing:

- Static HTML (HTML, .gif, .wav, etc.)
- HTML with imbedded client-side scripts, for example JavaScript

You can develop applications producing dynamic content with servlets and JSPs.

WebSphere Standard Edition's objective is to be a simple, easy-to-use but complete solution for building an active Web site and basic Web applications that integrate with databases.

WebSphere Standard Edition does not provide the workload management (WLM) functionality that is available in WebSphere Advanced Edition, but does allow for multiple JVMs on a single physical server. WebSphere

Standard Edition is also limited to a single node/machine unlike WebSphere Advanced Edition. These JVMs can be mapped to multiple virtual hosts on a single HTTP server to provide support for hosting multiple Web sites on a single application server.

1.4 Advanced Edition

WebSphere Advanced Edition extends the WebSphere Standard Edition's functions across multiple machines to provide complete support for developing new high-performance, scalable and available, transactional Web-driven applications. WebSphere Advanced Edition focuses on new applications (JSPs and EJBs) that access relational databases for persistent state data.

WebSphere Advanced Edition also supports distributed system management across the nodes in your distributed WebSphere Advanced Edition systems. The set of nodes that are administered collectively comprise a WebSphere administrative domain. You can administer an entire WebSphere domain from a single administrative console.

The distributed WebSphere Advanced Edition architecture also requires other fundamental services. We briefly outline their purpose in the following sections.

1.4.1 Naming

In an object-oriented distributed computing environment, clients must have a mechanism to locate and identify the objects as if the clients and objects were all on the same machine. A naming service provides this mechanism. WebSphere uses the Java Naming and Directory Interface (JNDI) to provide a common front end to the naming service. We describe these features, and the underlying use of Lightweight Directory Access Protocol (LDAP) in Chapter 9, "Using JNDI to access LDAP" on page 347.

1.4.2 Security

WebSphere Advanced Edition allows you to control access to Web resources such as HTML pages and JSPs, and also to control access to EJBs and the business methods they provide. Authorization to access a resource is permission-based. You can grant access permissions to users/groups and control which users/groups can access the resource.

We describe the WebSphere security architecture in Chapter 15, "WebSphere security" on page 651.

1.4.3 Transactions

A transaction is a set of operations that transforms data from one consistent state to another. Any realistic business application will have operations that require several updates be made to a database, and that either all these operations should complete or none should complete. For example, a money transfer should debit one bank account and credit another; it would be a serious error if only one of the two updates were to occur.

Traditional implementations of such business process would require the programmer to place explicit transaction BEGIN and COMMIT statements in the application code. One benefit of the EJB programming model is that you specify your transactional requirements when you configure the EJB, not in the code. So the code is much simpler to write.

WebSphere Advanced Edition in supporting EJBs provides full transactional capabilities. These are implemented using the mechanism defined in the Java Transaction API (JTA).

In Chapter 12, "Transactions" on page 503 gives a detailed explanation of transactions, their support in WebSphere and implementation considerations that developers need to take into account.

1.4.4 Workload management

The workload management (WLM) functionality in WebSphere Advanced Edition introduces the notion of modelling of application server processes. Clones, which are instances of a model, can be created either on a single machine or across multiple machines in a cluster. In either case the WebSphere Advanced Edition WLM provides workload distribution and failover.

We describe these features in Chapter 17, "Workload management" on page 791.

1.5 Open standards

Both WebSphere Standard and Advanced are based on and support key open-industry standards such as HyperText Transfer Protocol (HTTP), HyperText Markup Language (HTML), eXtensible Markup Language (XML), Secure Sockets Layer (SSL), Java, JavaBeans, Common Object Request Broker Architecture (CORBA), Lightweight Directory Access Protocol (LDAP), and most importantly the following Enterprise Java APIs:

- Enterprise JavaBeans (EJB) technology is a reusable Java component for connectivity and transactions (EJB support is provided only in the Advanced Edition).
- JavaServer Pages (JSP) represent inline Java code scripted within Web pages.
- Java Servlets are used in building and deploying server-side Java applications.
- Java Interface Definition Language (JIDL) supports objects whose interfaces are defined in CORBA IDL.
- JDBC is for connections to relational databases. WebSphere supports JDBC within its connection manager and within EJBs, for distributed database interactions and transactions.
- Java Messaging Service (JMS) is to be supported via MQSeries for asynchronous messaging and queuing and for providing an interface.
- Java Transaction Service (JTS) and Java Transaction API (JTA) are low-level APIs for interacting with transaction-capable resources such as relational databases. WebSphere uses these within EJBs for supporting distributed transactions.
- Java Naming and Directory Interface (JNDI) is for communicating with directories and naming systems and is used in WebSphere Application Server to look up existing EJBs and interact with directories.
- Java Remote Method Invocation over Internet Inter-ORB Protocol (RMI/IIOP) is for communicating with Java objects in remote application servers.

Chapter 2. What's new in WebSphere V3.5?

This chapter describes in brief the improvements and additions to IBM WebSphere Application Server V3.5 from the previous release, namely V3.0.2.x. Some changes are very obvious, such as the new look and feel of the WebSphere Administrative Console. Other changes are subtle and affect the runtime, such as performance enhancements to connection manager.

The list of new/improved features in WebSphere V3.5.x includes:

1. Installation
2. InfoCenter (Documentation)
3. Migration
4. JDK1.2
5. Security
6. Administration Tools
7. Connection Pooling
8. Resource Analyzer
9. Log Analyzer
10. New Platform support
11. New Database support
12. New Web Server support

The above feature list is based on WebSphere V3.5 PTF 2 (V3.5.2) and will be discussed in the following sections.

2.1 Installation

The popular GUI installation has three options - Quick, Full, Custom. In addition to that, there is a native installer. This command line feature has two modes - silent (or non-interactive) and interactive. This is useful for remote and multi-node installations.

Other installation enhancements:

- Enhanced prerequisite checking for Custom Installation option
- Quick Installation option installs prerequisites (Web server, database, JDK, etc.)
- Increased support for granting read/write authorities for deployment directories during installation
- Intelligent starting and stopping of services (on Windows-based systems)
- Easier Web downloads of installation image
- Support for organization-wide roll-outs of custom installs

For various installation scenarios and details, please see Appendix A, "Installation steps" on page 1049.

2.2 InfoCenter

Complementing the Help file, ReadMe file, Getting Started Guide, and the Release Notes is a preview version of InfoCenter. It provides a single point of search and navigation among the many pieces of information available for the WebSphere product. From one interface, the user has access to planning and configuration information, installation guides, softcopy books, help files, documentation articles, and other technical supplements.

The Information Center basically replaces the Documentation Center, help frame set, and the Troubleshooter.

WebSphere V3.5 ships with a starter version of InfoCenter. It is normally installed under <WAS_HOME>/web. View it in a browser by pointing to the following file: .../WebSphere/AppServer/web/InfoCenter/index.html.

Note

The complete InfoCenter can be viewed at or downloaded from:

`http://www.ibm.com/software/webservers/appserv/infocenter.html`

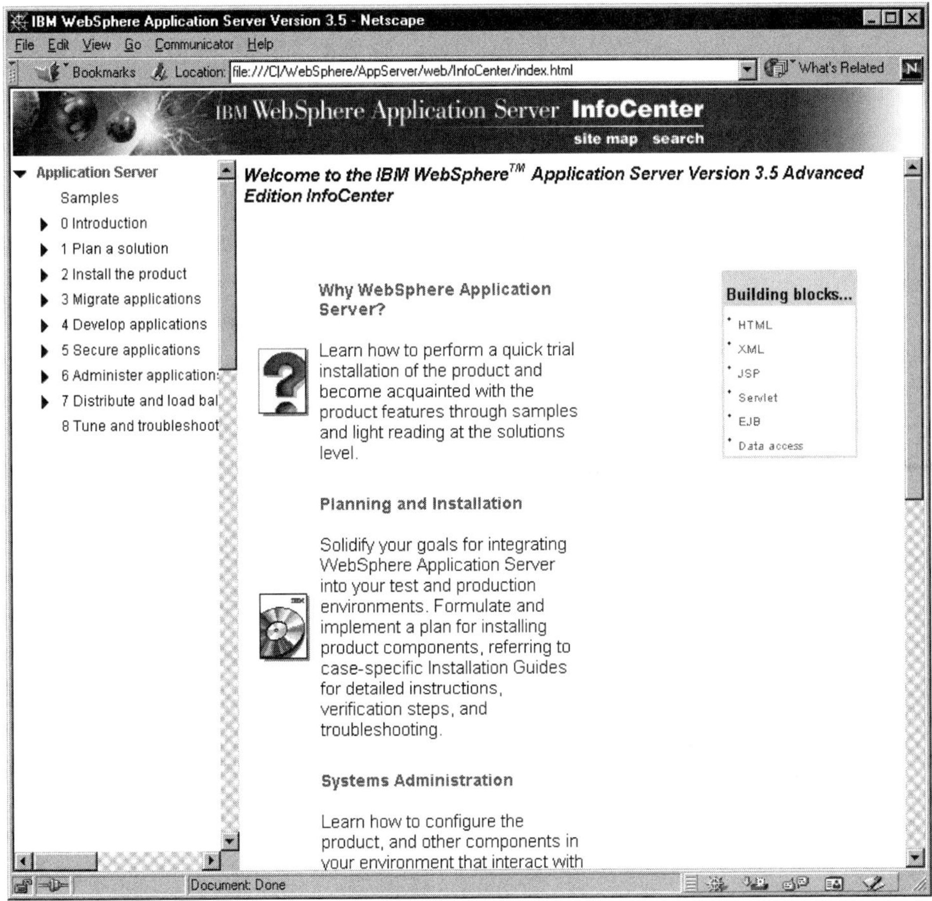

Figure 2. Top-level window of WebSphere V3.5 InfoCenter

Other documentation level enhancements:

- New, all-inclusive InfoCenter with search and print capabilities
- Expanded step-by-step installation and configuration documentation
- New planning documentation for single and multiple machine topologies
- Expanded and better organized migration documentation
- New sections devoted to security and workload management (Advanced Edition)
- Excellent problem determination documentation

2.3 Migration

WebSphere V3.5 comes with a migration assistant. This GUI-based tool is helpful in migrating WebSphere V3.0.2 installations to WebSphere V3.5. The Migration Assistant leads users through the upgrade process. During installation of WebSphere V3.5 on the Windows NT platform, if there is an existing WebSphere V3.0.2 installation, the Migration Assistant automatically detects it and runs. On UNIX platforms it has to be manually started.

The Migration Assistant backs up existing configuration files and all the user files. Only EJBs need to be redeployed and package name changes related to transaction and datasource need to be manually configured.

There are other tools also available that allow database migration. There is also an easier migration facility to migrate from InstantDB to a production level database such as DB2, and JDK migration.

WebSphere migration is discussed in detail in Chapter 26, "Migration" on page 1033.

2.4 Java 2 support

With support for JDK 1.2.2 (Java 2 SE) the following Java APIs are supported with WebSphere Advanced Edition (AE) V3.5 (specific support that exists only in the Enterprise Edition (EE) is noted):

- EJB 1.0 (plus extensions to support RMI/IIOP, transactions, and CMP)
- Java Servlet Specification 2.2
  - WAR files support for deployment
  - Multiple error page support
  - Request dispatchers by name and by relative path
- JavaServer Pages (JSP) 1.1 including Tag Library support
- JDBC 2.0
- Java Naming and Directory Interface (JNDI)1.2
- RMI/IIOP 1.0
- Java Transaction Service (JTS)/Java Transaction API (JTA)1.0
- Java Messaging Service (JMS)1.0 (in conjunction with MQSeries)
- JavaIDL and CORBA (EE only)

2.5 Security

Performance is significantly improved when security is enabled in WebSphere V3.5. One of the new features within security is Client Certificate based authentication.

Microsoft's Active Directory is now supported along with other LDAP servers such as IBM SecureWay, iPlanet, Domino, and Novell Directory Services.

Other security enhancements:

- A Custom Login option
- The ability to enable Domino Single Sign On
- GSKIT 4.0 GUI-based key generation tool

For a detailed discussion on WebSphere Security please see Chapter 15, "WebSphere security" on page 651.

2.6 New and improved administration tools

WebSphere V3.5 improved the administration tools: the WebSphere Administrative Console, the WebSphere Control Program (WSCP), XMLConfig, and Web console.

2.6.1 WebSphere Administrative Console

New functionality has been added while some old confusing functionality has been deleted. The top level console menu has been consolidated and simplified. A couple of new icons were added to the console tool bar. Context-sensitive actions menus are displayed upon right-clicking items.

Other enhancements with administration:

- Enhanced Java console performance
- Improved user interface conventions
  - Eliminated need to explicitly start and stop wizards
  - Standardized wizards, toolbars, and property dialogs
  - Provided toggle between topology and types views
  - Improved progress indicators

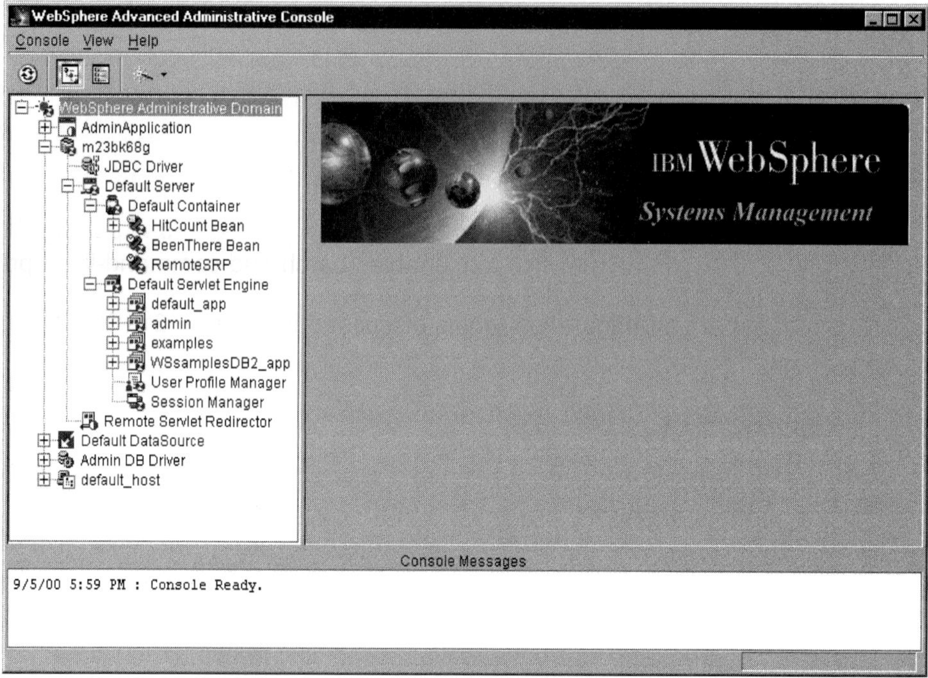

Figure 3. WebSphere V3.5 Advanced administrative console

The Help menu has been improved upon with better context-sensitive topics. New wizards walk you through the tasks of creating a data source, deploying EJBs, and setting security.

For more details, please see Chapter 18, “Administrative console” on page 811.

2.6.2 WSCP

The WebSphere Control Program, WSCP, is a command-line and scripting interface for administering resources in WebSphere AE. It is based on Tcl (tool command language). Tcl is a portable command language that provides programming facilities, such as variables, procedures, and list-processing functions. The WSCP interface extends Tcl by providing a set of commands for manipulating WebSphere objects.

Among other things, WSCP allows you to:

- Define, configure, and manage repository objects from any node
- Import and export configuration data

- Perform diagnostic operations such as enabling trace

For more details, please see Chapter 20, "The WebSphere Control Program (WSCP)" on page 855.

2.6.3 XMLConfig

XMLConfig which was technology previewed in WebSphere V3.0.2 is now fully functional. It is very useful for exporting and importing WebSphere configurations. The tool enables batch and command-line updates.

XML Configuration tool is discussed in Chapter 21, "XMLConfig" on page 877.

2.6.4 Web console

HTTPAdmin runs as a Web application (WebApp) under the Default Server in a WebSphere Administration domain. It basically uses XMLConfig as the underlying tool. Since it uses HyperText Transfer Protocol (HTTP), it works through firewalls and is especially good for managing WebSphere that runs within a DMZ (the secure area between two Internet firewalls).

See Chapter 19, "Web console" on page 843 for a discussion on Web console.

2.7 New and improved connection pooling

The connection manager has been optimized for faster performance. It can handle broken connections, for example. When the database goes down WebSphere does not have to be restarted.

From a coding perspective Table 1 shows you the differences between WebSphere V3.02 and V3.5:

Table 1. Code changes related to the connection manager

	WebSphere V3.02	**WebSphere V3.5**
import package/s	com.ibm.ejs.dbm.jdbcext.*;	com.ibm.ejs.cm.*; com.ibm.ejs.cm.pool.*;
Exception	ConnectionTimeoutException	ConnectionWaitTimeoutException (ConnectionPreemptedException is not supported)

	WebSphere V3.02	WebSphere V3.5
DataSource	Indexed by database URL + user name + passwd. One pool for every unique combination of URL+user+passwd.	Indexed by name. DataSource name corresponds to database URL. One connection pool associated with one DataSource. A pool can have connections for different database users/password.
Recovery from DB failure	Mark connection stale and destroy on application's connection.close().	Destroy the connection.

2.8 New Resource Analyzer

Resource Analyzer is now a separate tool replacing the old one. It is a stand-alone Java client that monitors the performance of WebSphere Application Server, Standard and Advanced Edition. The Resource Analyzer can be invoked via the command line and has a GUI to retrieve and view data in a table or chart form. The new version of Resource Analyzer is a technology preview.

Resource Analyzer is discussed in detail in Chapter 25, "Resource Analyzer" on page 1009.

2.9 New Log Analyzer

A new problem determination tool, the Log Analyzer, is available from the product Web site as a Technical Preview. This GUI-based tool permits the customer to view a log file, named activity.log. It also logs errors which can be filtered based on severity, process ID, thread ID, etc. More importantly, this tool stores all the log information in a simple XML database which permits the customer to analyze the errors and offers additional information such as why the error occurred and how to recover from it.

Details about Log Analyzer can be found in Chapter 24, "Log Analyzer" on page 975.

2.10 New platform support

- HP-UX

  WebSphere V3.5 can be installed on the HP-UX operating system V11.0.

  National Language Support (NLS) has been added to Solaris and HP-UX.

- Windows 2000

  WebSphere V3.5 can easily be installed on the Windows 2000 server platform in a manner similar to that on Windows NT.

2.11 New database support

- Sybase

  Sybase's Adaptive Server Enterprise Edition R12.0 can now be used as the WebSphere administrative database and with container-managed persistence (CMP) EJBs. This support is available of the AIX, Solaris, and Windows NT platforms.

- Oracle 8.1.6

  Additionally Oracle 8.1.6, both thin and thick JDBC drivers, are supported.

  WebSphere V3.5 also supports Distributed Transaction Support for Sybase and Oracle.

2.12 New Web Server support

There is now support for the iPlanet Web Server Enterprise Edition 4.0. The iPlanet Server is a product of Sun and Netscape's alliance. WebSphere continues to support Netscape Server 4.0.

2.13 Conclusion

The latest release of WebSphere has definitely raised the bar on Web application servers. With all the new features it is no wonder that WebSphere is the most popular application server in the world.

Some other new/improved features in WebSphere V3.5.x are:

- Updated samples for use on all supported databases and respective platforms
- New Session Affinity algorithm maximizes session caching

- Client device detection support for pervasive computing
- Domino DSAPI plug-in support

Chapter 3. WebSphere programming model

This chapter outlines the programming model used to develop applications targeted for the IBM WebSphere Application Server Advanced Edition V3.5.

For a programming model to be compelling, we must be able to use it to develop applications that exhibit the following qualities[1]:

- Functional - satisfies user requirements
- Reliable - performs under changing conditions
- Usable - enables easy access to application functions
- Efficient - uses system resources wisely
- Maintainable - can be modified easily
- Portable - can be moved from one environment to another

Further more, the programming model must support a development process that has the following characteristics:

- Repeatable - has well-defined steps
- Measurable - has well-defined work products that result
- Toolable - has well-defined mapping of inputs to outputs
- Predictable - can make reliable estimates of task times
- Scalable - works with varying project sizes
- Flexible - can be varied to minimize risks

The challenge is to balance both sets of requirements while developing an application.

To help make the discussion of the programming model more meaningful and concrete, we will trace the development of an example application from analysis through architecture and design. During the process of developing an application to support order entry ("online buying"), you will see first-hand how the programming model can be employed to meet the challenges outlined above.

3.1 Analysis of an example application

It is not within the scope of this section to describe (or endorse) a specific analysis method, because the WebSphere programming model can be used

[1] These characteristics are derived from ISO 9126 Software Quality Characteristics, now out of print.

with any method. However, we are partial to the Unified Modeling Language (UML) as a notation to describe important analysis work products.

We recommend capturing both the static and dynamic requirements of the system into models, where static models describe the data and dynamic models describe the behaviors.

For the static model we will use a UML class diagram that shows objects and associated properties, as well as relationships between them. The relationships are augmented to show such characteristics as role and cardinality.

For the dynamic model we will use a UML state-transition diagram that shows the life cycle states of an object and the events, conditions and actions that cause a transition (or flow of control) to the specified next state.

A complete model of the system takes into account the life cycle of important business objects (a business process model), as well as how a given user can access important system functions (an application flow model).

The business process model can be developed first, followed by an application flow model to provide access to the functions defined. This approach is sometimes called “enterprise out”. Conversely, the application flow model can be developed first with the actions and data defined driven into the business process model. This approach is sometimes called “application in” (or when applied to Web applications: “Web up”).

For purposes of our sample online-buying application, we will use the enterprise out approach and analyze the requirements of the business process first, then focus on those of the application flow.

3.1.1 Business process model for an Order

Probably the hardest part of business process analysis is knowing where to start. There are many approaches, but one that works reasonably well is to identify an object that represents the relationship between user and system roles.

In our example, two major roles are the company that makes products available for sale and the customer that orders them. An order represents the relationship between the two. The life cycle we define for an order will describe the business process that governs the way customers and employees (and possibly agents) of the company interact.

For the purposes of our simple example, we will say that an Order has three states in its business process life cycle:

1. Entry, where a Customer (or a Customer agent) can create an order, add or modify line items, and finally, submit or cancel it.
2. Fulfillment, where a person from the Shipping department can pack one or more of the order's line items and ship them to the customer. Packing and shipping continues until all the items are shipped.
3. Completed, where a representative from Marketing can perform various data mining queries on the orders in the system until they no longer find the data useful, in which case, they purge it from the system.

Figure 4 shows this life cycle in a graphical form known in the Unified Modeling Language (UML) as a state-transition diagram (STD). In a STD, the nodes show the life cycle states of the associated object and the directed edges show transitions (events, actions and conditions) that cause a flow of control from one life cycle state to the next. The transitions describe the units of work that are accessible from a given state by a given role. We have made a minor extension to the STD notation to show the role that owns the order in that state.

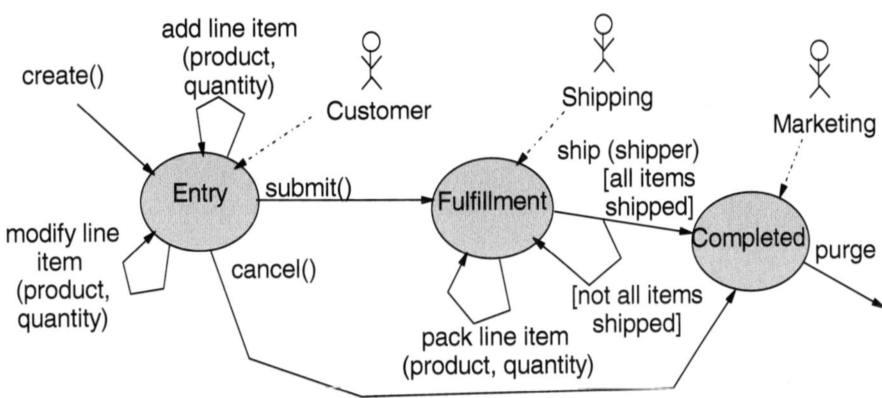

Figure 4. Online buying business process state-transition diagram

After the dynamic model for a given object is completed, the next step is to develop the static model that holds in the context of each life cycle state. A static model shows a given object, its properties, and relationships to other objects.

One way to develop a static model is to infer the objects and specific characteristics of the relationships (typically role and cardinality) from the descriptions of the units of work associated with the transitions in the dynamic model. Another approach is to reverse engineer existing data sources.

Our focus for this example will be the Customer role, so we will only specify the relationships that hold between various objects associated with an order in the Entry state:

- A Customer is associated with all the Orders that they have opened; only one Order may be in the opened status for a Customer at any given time, although a given Customer may have no associated open Order.
- An Order has an ID and a status indicating whether it is open, submitted or cancelled. An Order is also associated with the Customer that created it. Further, an Order is associated with zero or more Line Items.
- A Line Item indicates the ID of the product with which it is associated and the quantity of that Product to be associated with the Order within which it is contained.
- A Product has a number called a "sku" which serves as the ID, and an associated description. Of course, a real order entry system would have price, discounts and other associated attributes that we omit here for simplicity.

Figure 5 on page 21 shows these static relationships between objects in a graphical fashion known in UML as a class diagram. In a class diagram, the boxes represent the objects with associated attributes. Lines connect the object to those with which it is associated, with containment, labels and cardinalities listed to help clarify the relationships. The labels closest to an object describe the role of the object on the far end of the relationship. The numbers closest to an object describe the cardinality of that object with respect to that on the far end of the relationship.

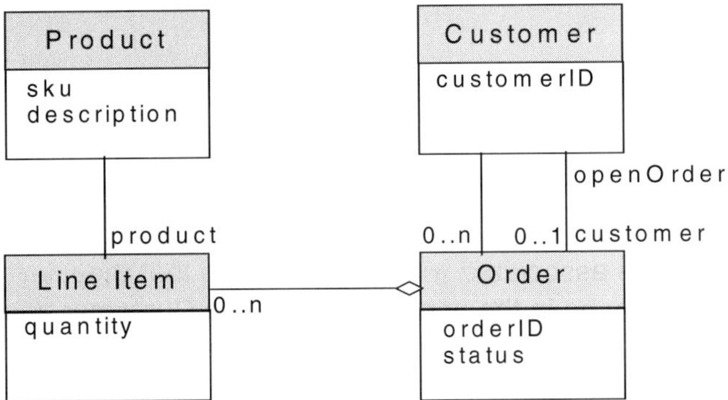

Figure 5. Class diagram of an order in entry state

For example, Figure 5 on page 21 shows that a Customer can have up to one Order, its role being labeled "openOrder".

A complete analysis of the business process requirements would repeat this process for the static models associated with the Fulfillment and Completed states. It would also likely analyze dynamic models for how a Product is moved into and out of inventory, and how Customers are registered and rated (possibly depending on their past behavior and credit history), among other business process models.

However, using object technology makes it easy to develop an application incrementally and iteratively, beginning architecture and design after a set of end-to-end functions (often called use cases) are defined.

The business process model describes the back end of the end-to-end flow, while the application flow model discussed next describes the front end.

3.1.1.1 Application flow model for Customer

An application flow model describes how a given user role invokes functions of the business process model to which they have access.

Like a business process model, an application flow model has static and dynamic aspects. In this case, however, the static model describes the data visible to the user, and the dynamic model describes the events that a user can trigger. For this reason, class and state-transition diagrams are also ideal for capturing the requirements of a given application flow model.

Depending on the client display technology, the states in a STD can represent pages, screens, windows, panels, forms, pop-ups, pull-downs, and dialogs among other possibilities, while the transitions can represent clicking buttons or links, pressing various keys, and selecting menu items using a touch-screen stylus.

This close mapping to display technologies makes it relatively easy to develop the application flow model from prototypes or by examination of existing applications.

It should be noted, however, that a well-designed application flow model is abstract, and can be applied to any number of specific display technologies. For this reason, use-case analysis is another approach to developing an application flow model.

Still another "top down" approach is to take the states associated with various business process models for a given user role and add "usability" states and transitions, such as confirmations, validations, selections, and helps among others.

In any event, we have chosen for our sample system a rather simple application flow to provide a Customer access to the functions associated with an order in the Entry state. It includes the following states:

1. Customer Home, which is basically a menu providing access to the Product Catalog, Order Status and Order Details states.
2. Product Catalog, which shows a list of products available for purchase, allowing the Customer to add a specified quantity of a selected product to the open order associated with the Customer (opening a new one if necessary).
3. Order Status, which shows the orders opened by the Customer, allowing them to view the details (and possibly modify them, if the order is open). From this state, a Customer can also open a new order, if none is already open.
4. Order Details, which shows the line items associated with a given order, defaulting to the open order associated with the Customer if none is specified. From this state the Customer can modify the line item quantities if the order is open. A Customer can also submit or cancel an open order.
5. Already Open, which occurs when a Customer attempts to open an order when one is already open. It provides the ability for the Customer to view the details of the opened order.
6. Action Result, which displays the result of adding or modifying a line item, or submitting or cancelling an order.

7. Confirm Submit or Cancel, which provides the Customer with the ability to verify that he or she really wants to submit or cancel the open order, as the case may be.

Figure 6 shows this application flow graphically, also using a UML state-transition diagram, where the nodes show the states of the application life cycle, and the arcs show application events that trigger flow of control between states.

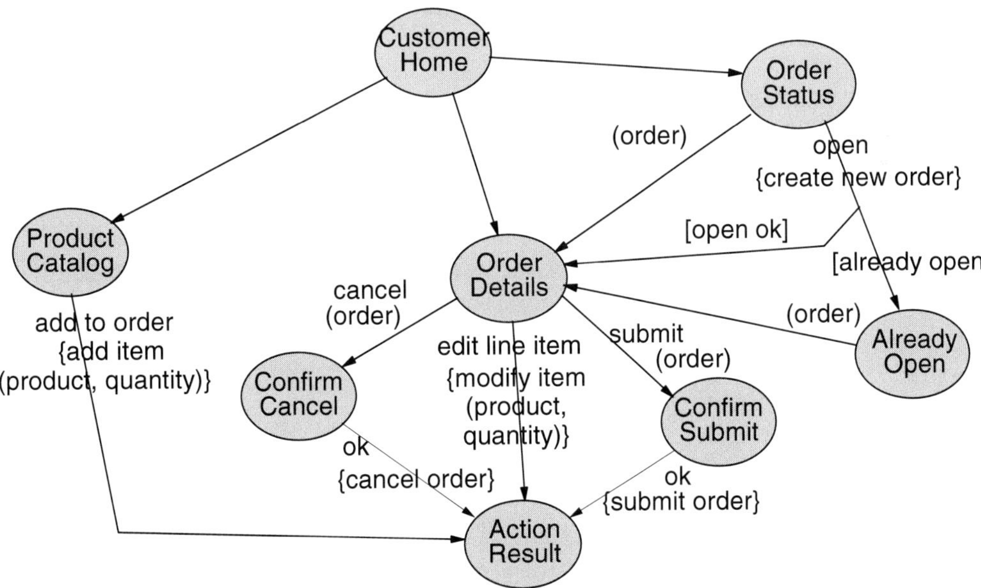

Figure 6. Customer application flow model state-transition diagram

Given the states and transitions described above, we would then do an analysis of the data visible to the Customer role in each state. Figure 7 on page 24 shows a UML class diagram with the results of this analysis.

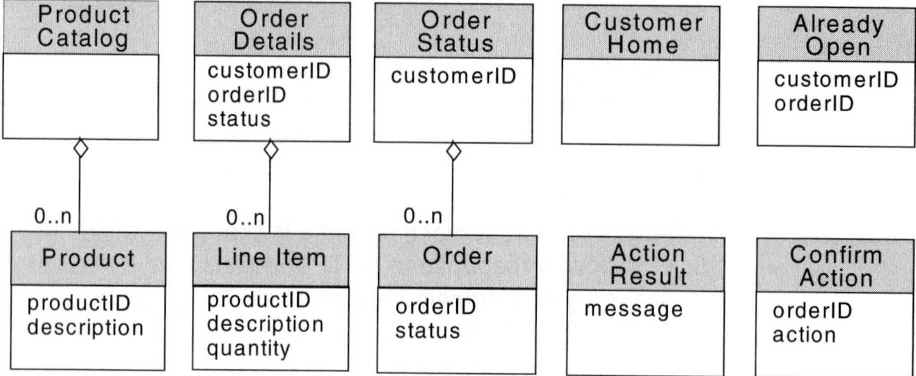

Figure 7. Class diagram showing the object model of states in application flow STD

A complete application flow requirements analysis would repeat this process for the Shipper and Marketing roles. However, as for the business process model, development can proceed in an incremental and iterative fashion rather than a traditional "waterfall" approach.

In any event, the sections to follow will first show how components associated with these models will be distributed across the "tiers" of an application architecture (high-level design). Then we will see how these components are mapped to the features of the WebSphere programming model, depending on the architecture chosen (detailed design).

3.1.2 Architectures supported by WebSphere

Once we have the functional requirements broken into static and dynamic aspects of business process and application flow models, the next step is to determine the application architecture. WebSphere Application Server V3.5 supports three basic application architectures: Web-enabled client/server, distributed object-based, and Web-enabled distributed object-based.

We will discuss each in terms of its features, along with advantages and disadvantages to consider when making a decision about which pattern is most appropriate for your application. Of course, any large system will likely use all of the patterns discussed here, so understanding the trade-offs and when that pattern best applies is key to choosing the application architecture.

3.1.2.1 Web-based client/server applications

Web-based client/server applications have a "thin" client tier where a Web browser executes, a "middle" tier that runs the Web application server (such as WebSphere), and a “back-end” tier that hosts servers accessible to the entire enterprise, such as databases, and global directories.

The primary purpose of the Web browser is to display data generated by the Web application server components and then trigger application events on behalf of the user through HTTP requests. The data roughly corresponds to the static model associated with the application flow model states.

The Web application server’s purpose is likewise twofold: it controls the application flow in response to HTTP requests sent by the client. As noted in the previous section, transitions on the application flow model will trigger transitions on an underlying business process model. The business logic associated with the business process model (BPM) transition may access data and functions from enterprise servers.

An enterprise server’s main purpose is to provide access to the data associated with BPM transitions. In some cases, business process functions may be delegated to enterprise servers (such as CICS transactions). The protocol used will depend on the back end.

Figure 8 on page 26 shows the relationship between these three tiers in a graphical fashion, indicating the system components normally hosted on that tier along with the primary protocol by which it communicates with the other tiers (the ‘???’ label on the connection indicates that there are possibly many different ones depending on the system).

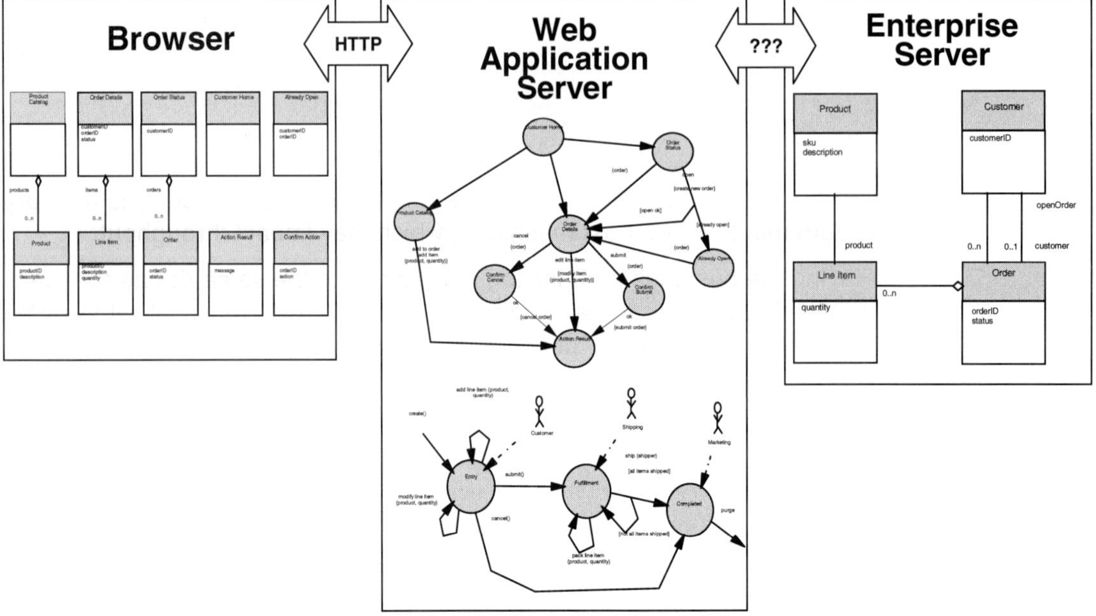

Figure 8. Web--enabled client/server application architecture showing where model components are hosted

Some advantages of a Web-enabled client/server application are as follows:

1. There is no need to install anything specific on the client tier, since the pages are rendered by a Web server or Web application server and passed back as part of a request.
2. The end-to-end path length is relatively short (compared to the other supported architectures), since the Web application server components have direct access to the enterprise servers.
3. HTTP connections are stateless, making it possible to scale to large numbers of clients, especially when load-balancing routers are employed. However, we should note here that a common function provided by Web application servers is to provide "state" for the application. Utilizing this function can reduce the benefits of statelessness (more on this point later).

Some disadvantages include:

1. Controlling the application flow in the Web application server rather than in the client will have an impact on response time, making it crucial to minimize the number of HTTP requests from the browser.

2. Components controlling the business process model must be installed on the Web application server as well as client code to the enterprise servers upon which these components depend, which makes maintenance much more difficult (especially if a number of servers are needed to handle the HTTP traffic).
3. Having both the application flow and business process logic executing in the same Web application server can increase the processor and memory requirements of the host machines, which may impact throughput.
4. Having the business process logic executing in the same tier as the Web application server can be considered a security risk, especially if the Web application is within the “demilitarized zone” (servers outside of the firewall).
5. Also, having both the application flow and business process logic executing in the same Web application server makes it difficult to share the business logic with non-Web-enabled clients.

3.1.2.2 Distributed object-based applications

Distributed object-based applications supported by WebSphere are characterized by:

- An application client tier that controls both the application flow and associated data display.
- One or more servers that host distributed objects encapsulating the logic associated with the business process model.
- One or more back-end enterprise servers that maintain the data associated with the business process model.
- Communication between the client and distributed object server tiers is achieved through the Internet Inter-ORB Protocol (IIOP).

Figure 9 on page 28 shows a graphical view of a distributed object-based application architecture.

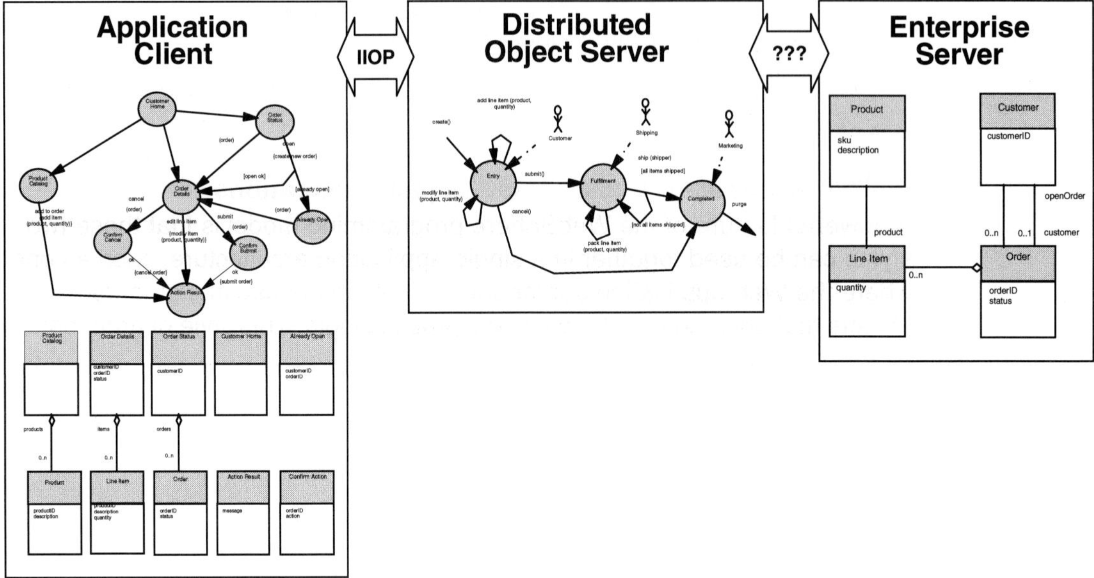

Figure 9. N-tier distributed object-based application architecture showing where model components are hosted

Distributed object-based applications are considered to have "n" logical tiers because distributed objects can actually be clients of other distributed objects. The tiers are logical because the distributed objects can be co-deployed on the same physical tier.

Advantages of a distributed object-based application include:

1. Controlling the application flow on the client tier usually makes for snappier response time, especially where heavily used data is cached locally.
2. The business logic is separated from the application client, providing for better security and maintainability.
3. Having the business logic separated means that it can be shared by multiple clients.
4. It is also possible to load balance across multiple distributed object servers to get higher throughput and system availability.
5. The application clients need not install the client code associated with enterprise servers.

Disadvantages include:

1. Application programs must be explicitly installed on the client tier, making maintenance a consideration. This can also increase the processor and memory requirements of the client machines.
2. There is extra path length incurred by adding a distributed object server between the client, which will have an impact on response time.

3.1.2.3 Web-enabled distributed object applications

A powerful feature of the WebSphere programming model is that these two styles can be used together in a single application architecture, such as one where the Web application server components make use of distributed objects that encapsulate the business process logic. This style of architecture can be considered to be a Web-enabled distributed object-based application, as shown in Figure 10.

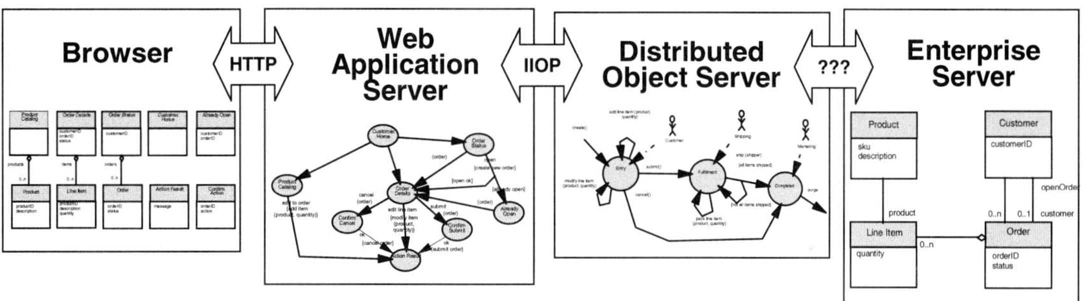

Figure 10. Web-enabled distributed object application architecture showing where model components are hosted

This approach gets the advantages of both, including:

1. There is no need to install anything specific on the client tier, since the pages are rendered by a Web server or Web application server and passed back as part of a request.
2. HTTP connections are stateless, making it possible to scale to large numbers of clients, especially when load balancing routers are employed.
3. The business logic is separated from the application client, providing for better security and maintainability.
4. Having the business logic separated means that it can be shared by multiple clients.
5. It is also possible to load balance across multiple distributed object servers to get higher throughput and system availability.
6. The Web application servers need not install the client code associated with enterprise servers.

A Web-enabled distributed object application has relatively few of the disadvantages of either:

1. Controlling the application flow in the Web application server rather than in the client will have an impact on response time, making it crucial to minimize the number of HTTP requests from the browser.
2. There is extra path length incurred by adding a distributed object server between the client, which will have an additional impact on response time. This impact makes it crucial to minimize the number of distributed object requests from the Web application server.

We will look at our sample application in terms of this hybrid architecture, since it will cover all the features of the programming model by WebSphere Application Server V3.5.

3.1.3 Features of a programming model driven design

Once we have the candidate architecture identified, the next step is design, where we map the requirements specified in the analysis phase to programming model features associated with the architectural tiers.

All programming models, regardless of the architectural tier, have three distinct features that are key to developing an application:

- The components that embody application functions.
- Control flow mechanisms used to invoke one component from another.
- Data flow sources that you can use to pass information from one component to another.

Each of these features will be discussed in a separate section with the following information:

- A basic definition of the component or mechanism
- The role it plays in the architecture, especially with respect to the example application described above
- Some pros and cons as to its usage
- Alternative approaches, if any exist

Together these sections provide an end-to-end overview of how the components and mechanisms (services) can be used together effectively to develop a WebSphere V3.5-based application. Individual chapters that follow will get further into the details of how WebSphere supports the various APIs (which will drive the code phase), and what you can do at deployment time to exploit the WebSphere V3.5 platform.

3.2 Application components

Application components are those that a developer will actually have to program, whether manually or with the aid of tools. The other features of the programming model represent services that the developer can use when coding an application component. The language used to develop a given application component will depend in large part upon the "tier" where the component will be executed at runtime.

For example, browser-based components will tend to use tag and script-oriented languages, while Web application server components will tend towards Java. Enterprise server components may use a variety of languages other than just Java, such as C, C++, COBOL and the like, so we will focus on the distributed object server, which tends towards Java as the language of choice.

Because the language differences tend to divide along tier boundaries, we will divide this section into three separate subsections as we describe the components you develop that are hosted by browsers, Web application servers, and distributed object servers.

We will discuss the components for each tier in turn.

3.2.1 Browser-hosted components

While a browser is not provided by WebSphere V3.5 Advanced Edition, browser-hosted components make up a large part of any Web-enabled application. The reason, of course, is that the browser serves as the runtime engine for the user interface of a Web application.

The browser-hosted components that are most relevant to the WebSphere programming model include:

- HTML
- DHTML and JavaScript
- Framesets and Named Windows
- eXtensible Markup Language (XML), XML Style Language (XSL) and Document Type Definition (DTD)

We will discuss each in turn.

3.2.1.1 HTML

HyperText Markup Language (HTML) is the basic "programming language" of the browser. With HTML, you can direct the browser to display text, lists, tables, forms, images, and just about everything else you can think of.

Role in the architecture

Every state in our example application flow model, from the Product Catalog to the Action Result, will ultimately result in an HTML page or dialog of some sort, However, we need to draw the distinction between static and dynamic content in an HTML page.

In this example, the HTML associated with the Customer Home state is "static". It does not change based on application events, but merely provides access to other states of the application like a menu.

At the other extreme, the HTML associated with the Action Result state is "dynamic" because it needs to display a message specific to the result of the action. For example, the result of adding a line item from the Product Catalog state is to indicate how many of that product are currently ordered.

In the "grey" area are pages associated with states such as Product Catalog. Some companies with small, stable product lines may develop static product catalog pages. Other companies may have large, constantly changing product lines that would require generating the Product Catalog page dynamically from a database.

The reason that this distinction is important is that static HTML pages do not require that the content be generated by programmatic means, such as Web application components hosted within WebSphere (servlets and JSPs). These components will be discussed in the next section.

For our example online buying application, only Customer Home is assumed to be handled by static HTML as shown in Figure 11 on page 33.

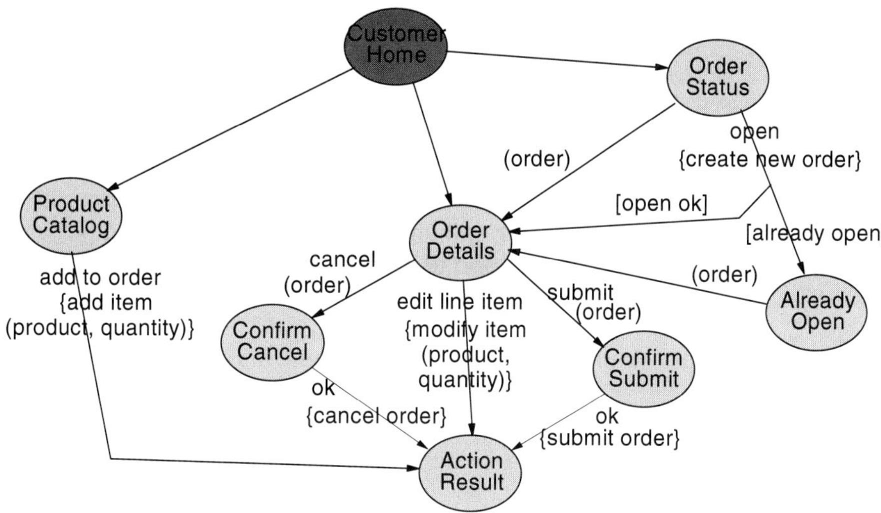

Figure 11. Online buying application flow model showing Customer Home state as static HTML

Pros

The main advantage of using static HTML for Web pages is that they are not generated by Web application components, such as servlets and JSPs. Their static nature means that they can be cached by either the browser or proxy servers.

On the development side, they can be created and maintained with a WYSIWYG (what-you-see-is-what-you-get) editor.

Cons

The downside of using static HTML is that they cannot be customized on the fly based on customer preferences or application events. Even pages that may seem to be “naturally” static, such as the Customer Home, might actually benefit from being generated dynamically. For example, you might limit the functions that a Customer sees based on the class of service for which they are registered.

Alternatives

As mentioned above, the “programming language” of the browser is mainly HTML (with DHTML and JavaScript being the primary exception as described next). However, an XML-enabled browser can be used to generate the HTML on the client side.

Finally, you should consider creating dynamic components for every “top level” (non-dialog state), even if it appears to be static. This approach not only makes it easier to add dynamic content later, but also makes it easier to compose into other pages. Future versions of WebSphere Application Server will provide support for caching dynamic page fragments, which will make composing pages much more efficient. We will discuss this alternative in later sections of this chapter.

3.2.1.2 DHTML and JavaScript

Dynamic HyperText Markup Language (DHTML) is an extension to HTML wherein all the components of the HTML page are considered to be objects. Together these objects make up the Document Object Model (DOM) of the page.

Each object in the DOM has a set of associated attributes and events, depending on the type of object. For example, most objects have attributes describing their background and foreground colors, default font, and whether they are visible or not. Most have an event that is triggered when the object is loaded into the DOM or displayed. An object, such as a button, has attributes that describe the label and events that fire when it has been pressed.

Events are special because they can be associated with a program that executes when the event is triggered. One language that can be used for the program is JavaScript, which is basically a simplified form of Java. JavaScript can be used to change the attributes of objects in the DOM, thereby providing limited control of the application flow by the browser.

Role in the architecture

This ability makes DHTML/JavaScript perfect for handling confirmations, data validations, cascading menus, and certain types of list processing on the browser side without invoking an HTTP request to the Web application server.

Where validations are concerned, it is important to draw the distinction between those that are merely *syntactic* from those that are more semantic in nature.

Syntactic validations include checks on individual fields of an input form. For example, is the entry a minimum length? Is it alpha or numeric? Does it have the right format for a date, phone number or social security number? These simple types of syntactic validations should be done on the client.

Semantic validations are those that ultimately require access to business process logic and data. For example, is an order or product number valid? Will the change in quantity make the resulting line item quantity less than zero? Is the requested price within 10 percent of the current average? Semantic validations belong on the server side.

In the middle ground are more complex syntactic validations that involve multiple fields or begin to incorporate business process policies. For example, is the start date less than the end date? Does the date requested fall on a weekend or holiday? There are arguments both for and against handling complex syntactic validations on the client side. The most forceful arguments against are that it introduces extra complexity and redundancy in the DHTML, and can cause a maintenance problem as policies change.

In our online buying example, we would suggest handling confirmation of the submit or cancel actions in JavaScript rather than bringing up a separate HTML page as shown in Figure 12.

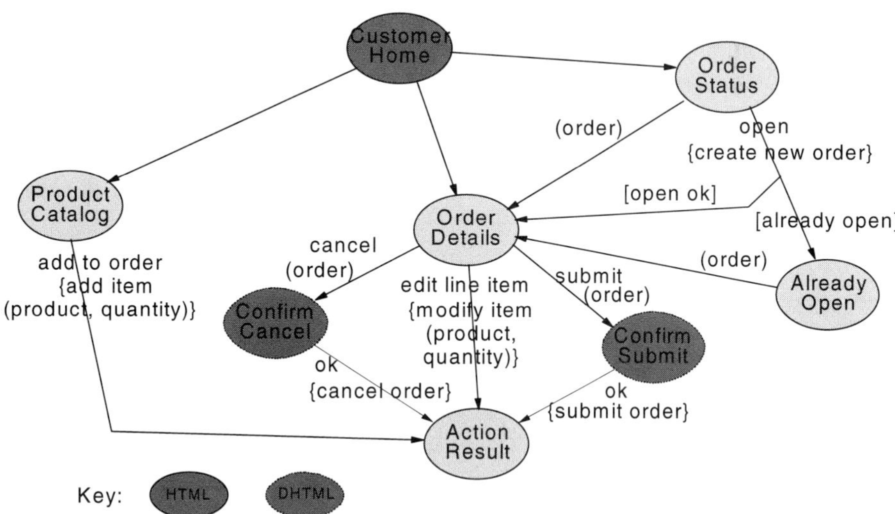

Figure 12. Online buying application flow STD showing states handled by DHTML and JavaScript

This approach effectively “collapses” the two confirmation states into substates of the OrderDetails state.

Although not shown explicitly on the application flow diagram, we also would suggest using JavaScript on the add line item action to validate that the quantity specified is non-zero.

Although it was not required in our example, we have seen cases where developers used sophisticated JavaScript programs to build multiple entry input dialogs where the list of choices appears on one side, with the items chosen on the other. Items can be selected on either side of the list and the appropriate directional arrow button chosen to “move” it to the other side.

Pros

Hopefully, the benefit of using DHTML and JavaScript in these scenarios is obvious: one or more round trips to the Web application server are eliminated, making the application both more efficient and more usable (mainly because the response time is much snappier).

In the case of the Confirm Cancel or Confirm Submit states, it is likely that the associated page would be generated dynamically showing the current state of the Order so that the user knows exactly what they are confirming. With a JavaScript pop-up, the order is still visible in the browser window. The trip to the Web server is eliminated along with a query to get the current state of the order, reducing contention for back-end system resources as well.

Cons

One disadvantage to using DHTML/JavaScript is that developing application control flow, whether it is on the client or server side, requires programming skill. Pages that rely on DHTML and JavaScript are more complicated to develop and test. You cannot use WYSIWYG editors for the code.

Another disadvantage to using DHTML and JavaScript is that there are differences among the browsers in the details of the functions supported. To avoid a browser dependency for the Web application, programmers are forced to either:

- Stay within a common subset of functions supported by all the major browsers.
- Put branching logic that has a case for each browser with code optimized for the version of JavaScript supported by that browser

When syntactic validations (either simple or complex) are handled in DHTML and JavaScript, you will still need to revalidate on the server side for each request just in case the client circumvents the input forms. This leads to redundancy of code on the client and server.

Alternatives

Really, there is no good alternative to DHTML and JavaScript for handling confirmations, validations, menus, and lists. The complexity for the HTML developer can be managed somewhat by having a separate programming group develop a set of common functions that encapsulate the differences between the browsers and have every page designer include this set of functions within their HTML.

3.2.1.3 Framesets and named windows

Framesets and named windows are specialized HTML extensions that break up a page into separate frames (for framesets) or windows (for named windows). Each frame or window can be further subdivided as a frameset as well.

Various browser-initiated control flow actions (described in 3.3.1, "Browser component initiated control flow" on page 80) can be targeted to a given frame or window, leaving the other frames and windows untouched.

The main difference between framesets and named windows is that framesets tile the various frames within a single browser window, while named windows have a separate window for each unique name. Frames in a frameset can have various attributes that define behaviors such as whether they are resizable, scrolling, or have borders. Separate named windows can be cascaded or manually tiled by the user as they see fit.

From a targeting perspective, there is no difference between framesets or named windows. In fact, they can be used together. If no frame or window with a given name is open already, one will be opened by the browser to receive the result of the request. The opened windows can be resized and tiled manually to achieve an effect very similar to framesets.

Role in the architecture

Framesets are an excellent way to group related states in the application flow model. For example, the online buying application Web page could be implemented as a frameset that includes the following three frames (or windows):

- Navigation, an area that is populated with the Customer Home navigation links
- Main, an area that is populated with the Product Catalog, Order Status or Order Details data, depending on the link selected in the Navigation frame. This area would also be the target of an "open new order" action in the Order Status state, so it would possibly be populated with the Already Open page.
- Result, an area that displays the result of an add to order, modify line item, submit, or cancel operation.

Figure 13 on page 38 shows a stylized view of how this page might look using framesets.

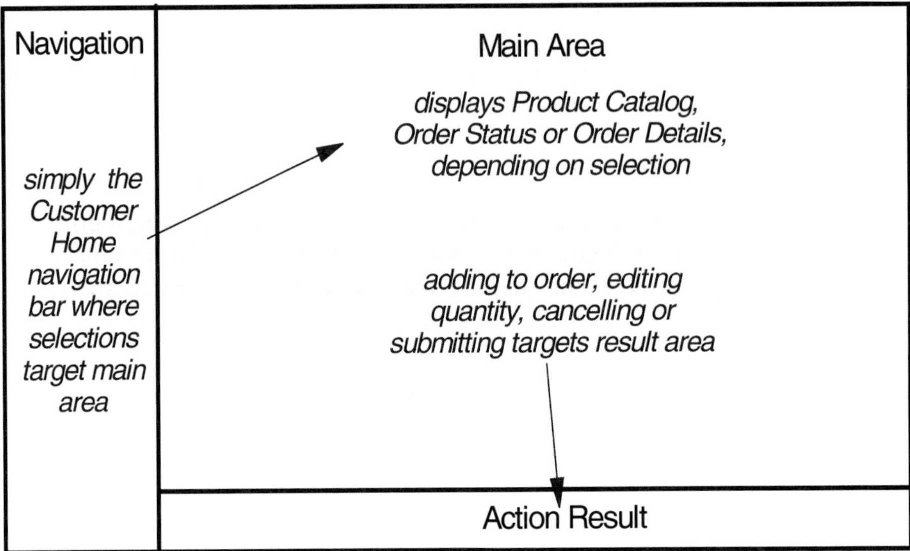

Figure 13. Stylized view of online buying application frameset

Although not explored in any more detail here, a frameset makes it easy to mingle Web publishing and business applications together. In this approach, you provide visual interest such as images, advertisements, news, and such in the “surrounding” frames, and keep the frames associated with the business of the application clean, simple, and most importantly fast (since they can be mostly text based).

Pros

The advantages of a properly defined frameset to the application flow are many:

1. Simplifies navigation. By having the Customer Home state always visible, reliance on the browser “back” button (or explicit navigations coded into each state) is eliminated.
2. Maximizes visibility of the important data and functions. The main displays for the Catalog, Status and Details pages consist of a list of items (products, orders and line items, respectively). This area can be returned as a frameset, with the unchanging data and functions and table headers in the top frame, and the table rows in the bottom area. This approach allows a large list of items to be scrolled without losing access to the action buttons and header information. For example, when viewing an open order on the Order Details page, the Order number, Submit and Cancel buttons will always be visible.

3. Minimizes the size of an individual request. Only the data required for the target area is returned from a given request. For example, when an add, modify, submit or cancel action is invoked, only the result message need be returned to the browser. The main area still has the previous contents and need not be rerendered. The Navigation area need never be rerendered.
4. Improves the application flow and efficiency when errors occur. This advantage is related to #3 above. If an application error occurs, such as trying to submit or cancel an unopened order, or entering an invalid product ID or quantity, the form data is still visible and can be referred to in the result message. It is even possible to use JavaScript to highlight the erroneous fields in the form.
5. Parallelizes requests. When a frameset is rendered, each frame is issued as an individual request, allowing them to be handled and displayed separately. This can have a dramatic effect on usability, as the "static" areas (like the navigation and header areas) will likely come back very quickly, providing cues to the user that the server is processing the request. An example where this is an extremely useful feature is in a "portal" application where user preference data drives individual queries to various back-end services, such as stock quotes, hot news items of interest, etc. The initial request to the user's portal page could return a frameset that has individual frames for the various services selected. Each frame would be a separate request, providing the user with information as it becomes available rather than after the entire page is rendered.
6. Hides "ugly" URLs. The URLs for the individual frames in the frameset do not display in the browser's location line. This is a nice feature especially for some Web applications where the URL has rather lengthy and ugly encoded strings to hold various IDs (see 3.4.1, "Browser-maintained data flow sources" on page 90 for a discussion of browser-maintained data). When using framesets, the URL is usually very "clean".

Cons

There are some disadvantages to using framesets. Improperly designed, the navigation can be confusing. Also, if more than one frame accesses shared system resources, such as HttpSession state or databases, it can cause contention problems that affect performance, and may even cause deadlocks. The design we suggested above does not suffer from these problems.

But beyond this, framesets have some behaviors that are hard to get used to.

For example, when printing within a frameset, only the “active” frame (usually where the cursor is located when the print is requested) is printed. This can be disconcerting when you expect the whole frameset to be printed.

Bookmarking a frameset uses the browser location line, and not the specific content frame URLs. In our example, this means that OnlineBuying.html would be bookmarked, and the “default” page would come up. It wouldn’t matter that we had selected the Order Details for order 12345, or had browsed the Product Catalog down to the raincoats.

Another disadvantage is that the browser back and forward functions work a frame at a time. This can be somewhat disconcerting. Let us examine the situation that occurs when the customer is viewing the Product Catalog, adds an item to the open order, switches to see the Order Details, then modifies the quantity. Pressing back will first redisplay the result area from adding the item to the order. The next back will return to the Product Catalog display.

Probably the most serious disadvantage is that not all browsers support framesets, so a non-frame version must be provided if the application is designed to be browser independent.

Alternatives

Before we abandon framesets because of the disadvantages mentioned above, there are some workarounds to consider:

- Printing. Many developers provide an explicit print function that returns a page suitable for printing. Others like the fact that it prints only the area selected, and consider that a feature (assuming that the user can use the print screen function to get the window contents).
- Bookmarking. Some developers maintain the details of the last page viewed in a customer database, so that those values can be used as defaults. In this manner, the application-level bookmark works nicely and still has an easy-to-read-and-remember URL.
- Back and Forward. Many developers disable the back and forward buttons on the browser, especially when they provide a navigation area like the one we provided in the example.
- Browser support. Many browsers that do not support framesets provide named windows, allowing the basic flow to remain unchanged. The frameset pages take advantage of the “no frameset” tag to open the main windows instead.

If these workarounds cannot be used in your Web application, the only real alternative to framesets is to compose the pages representing the individual states, and pay the cost of rerendering the entire page on every request. In this case we would recommend that each state be handled by dynamic Web application components (HttpServlets and JSPs) in order to take advantage of caching that will be supported in future versions of WebSphere Application Server.

3.2.1.4 XML, DTD and XSL

XML provides a means by which documents can be encoded as a set of tags describing the associated values. The tag language is expressive enough that tags can be nested and can repeat, so that complex data structures can be encoded in a form that is both human and machine readable.

An XML document can be associated with a DTD, which is a special XML file that defines the tags and their structure. A DTD can be used by an XML parser to validate that the XML is not just well formed syntactically, but is also semantically legal with respect to the DTD.

Finally, more and more browsers are becoming XML enabled. XML-enabled browsers can handle XML documents returned from the Web server in response to a request. The XML document can refer to an associated stylesheet coded in XSL. The stylesheet is used by the browser to map the XML tags to the HTML that is ultimately displayed. If no stylesheet is specified, the browser will use a default format that takes advantage of the tag names.

Role in the architecture

As we will see in later sections, XML can play a role in every tier of the application architecture. For a Web-enabled browser tier, the response to a given request can be an XML document containing only the data to be displayed. For example, we could build XML documents representing the data described for each state as shown in Figure 7 on page 24, then provide a default stylesheet in XSL mapping this data to HTML tables and forms.

Pros

One advantage of using XML rather than HTML is that the stylesheet can be modified to change the look and feel without having to change the Web application components (described later) that generate the data.

Another advantage is that the size of the result will be smaller than the resulting HTML in many cases.

Yet another advantage is that the same XML document may be usable in other contexts than a Web browser, making it possible to reuse the Web application components.

Cons
The main disadvantage is that XML-enabled browsers are not yet available every where, although they are rapidly becoming so.

Another disadvantage is that XSL-based stylesheets can be quite complex to code and difficult to debug. WYSIWYG editors for XML/XSL are not yet widely available either.

Alternatives
One alternative is to have the Web application components check the browser type and either generate HTML for non-XML-enabled browsers or return the raw XML for XML-enabled browsers. The next subsection will discuss this idea further.

3.2.2 Web application server hosted components

In the previous section, we discussed how HTML is the ultimate programming language for the browser tier, but drew a sharp distinction between static and dynamic content for Web pages.

We also discussed how a browser is not specifically provided by the WebSphere V3.5 platform. This is not the case for the Web server and Web application server. WebSphere provides the IBM HTTP Server as a Web server that can be used to serve up static pages, but can be configured to use other popular Web servers from Microsoft and Netscape, among others.

Of course, the focus of this section is the WebSphere Application Server V3.5 used to serve up dynamic pages.

By discussing HTML, DHTML, JavaScript, framesets and XML, we have already covered the static components of the programming model. The Web application server components hosted by WebSphere that are most useful in generating dynamic content include:

- Servlets
- JavaServer Pages (JSPs)

While no special support is provided by WebSphere Application Server, there are two other components that are useful for clients (including Web applications) of business logic and data hosted on back-end servers:

- Data Structure Java Beans
- Business Logic Access Beans

Together these components provide the basis for a very effective Model-View-Controller (MVC) architecture, where data structure and access beans represent the business process model (Model), servlets control the application flow (Controller), and JSPs handle the layout (View).

An MVC architecture is effective because of the ability to independently develop, test, deploy and modify the various components.

We will discuss each of these four components in the context of an MVC architecture in the subsections to follow.

3.2.2.1 Servlets

The details of Servlets are discussed in more depth in Chapter 5, "Servlet support" on page 137. For purposes of understanding the programming model, we will say here that you develop HttpServlets to encapsulate Web application flow of control logic on the server side (when it cannot be handled by DHTML on the client side).

An HttpServlet is a subclass of a generic Java servlet. Most people mean HttpServlet when they say servlet, but there is a difference. An HttpServlet is specifically designed to handle HTTP requests from a client.

However, in this redbook, we call it "servlet" unless we need to distinguish them.

The HttpServlet Java class from which you will inherit (extend) has a number of methods that you can implement that are invoked at specific points in the life cycle. The most important ones are:

- init(), executed once when the HttpServlet is loaded
- doGet(), executed in response to an HTTP GET request
- doPost(), executed in response to an HTTP PUT request
- service(), executed in response to a request if a doXXX() method associated with the request type is not implemented
- destroy(), executed once when the HttpServlet is unloaded

The service type methods (for example, doGet() and doPost()) are passed two parameters: an HttpServletRequest and HttpServletResponse, which are Java classes that encapsulate the differences among various Web servers in how they expect you to get parameters and generate the resulting reply back to the client.

Role in the architecture

HttpServlets are designed from the ground up to handle dynamic requests from an HTTP client. In an MVC architecture, HttpServlets represent the Controller component.

However, there is a question of granularity that needs to be addressed. That is, how many servlets are required to control a Web application?

At one extreme, there are those that create only one servlet to control the entire application (or worse, they may only build one servlet, ever). The doGet(), doPost() or service() methods use a parameter from the HttpServletRequest to determine the action to take, given the current state. We do not recommend this extreme because it is:

- Unmaintainable, when implemented as a large case statement (only one programmer can safely work on the code at a given time).
- Redundant with other approaches described next, when implemented by forwarding to an action-specific servlet or JavaServer Pages (you might as well route the request directly to the appropriate servlet).
- Redundant with the servlet APIs themselves, when implemented by loading an action-specific functional class (the class loaded and invoked will need to look just like a servlet, with request and response analogues passed in on the service type methods).
- Security for a given function must be manually coded rather than use per servlet security provided by the WebSphere administration tools.

At the other extreme of the granularity spectrum is one servlet per action. This is a much better approach than a single servlet per application, because you can assign different servlets to different developers without fear that they will step on each other's toes. However, there are some minor issues with this approach as well:

- Servlet names can get really long to insure uniqueness across the application.
- It is more difficult to take advantage of commonality between related actions without creating auxiliary classes or using inheritance schemes.

In the middle is to develop a single servlet per state in the application flow model that has dynamic content or actions. This approach resolves the issues associated with the approaches described above.

For example, it leads to a "natural" naming convention for a servlet: StateServlet. The doGet() method is used to gather and display the data for a given state, while the doPost() method is used to handle the transitions out of the state with update side effects. Ownership can be assigned by state. Further, commonality tends to occur most often within a given state and service method type (doGet() or doPost()).

Using this approach in our example, we would develop the following servlets:

- ProductCatalogServlet, whose init method can read the current list of products into a cache, whose doGet() method reads the cached catalog for display, and whose doPost() handles the add item transition.
- OrderStatusServlet, whose doGet() method reads the list of orders for a given customer to display their current status, and whose doPost() handles the open order transition.
- OrderDetailsServlet, whose doGet() method reads the line items for a given order for display, and whose doPost() handles the modify, submit and cancel transitions.

See Figure 14 for a graphical view, with the STD of the online buying application flow model extended to show where servlets would be used to control transitions, with side effects triggering events on the underlying business process model.

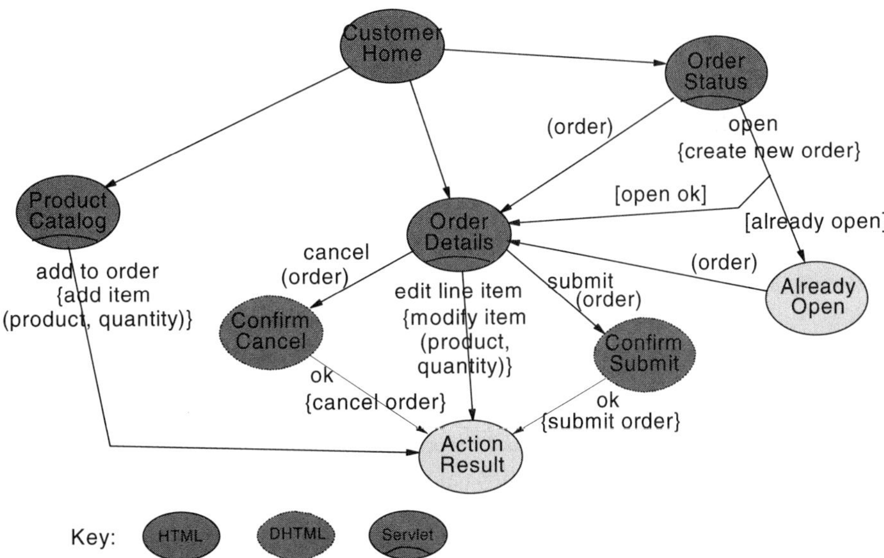

Figure 14. Online buying application flow STD showing states controlled by servlets

Regardless of the approach used, another use for servlets in an application architecture is to develop an inheritance hierarchy to handle the common look and feel of the Web application. For example, we might want to build an

OnlineBuyingServlet that provides common parsing functions, and whose doGet method:

- Checks authentication (routing to a login state if necessary)
- Calls the abstract method doGetOnlineBuying() implemented by the subclass to get the content
- Handles any errors in a common manner

The inherited doPost() method would:

- Attempt to authenticate for login, if shunted there from a previous call (routing back to the original state for display if OK)
- If not authorized, or login failed, reroute to a login state with an appropriate message
- If authorized, call the abstract doPostOnlineBuying() to handle the state-specific action
- Handle errors if any

We will discuss some extensions to this superclass servlet in later sections.

Pros

Before the Servlet API became available, each Web application component (usually a CGI program) had to code to a Web server-specific API (such as Netscape API, otherwise known as NSAPI). By being based on Java, servlets are very portable and can be used with the leading Web servers.

Also, servlets stay resident once they are initialized and can handle multiple requests. CGIs generally start a new process for each request.

Servlets can be multi-threaded, making them very scalable. For example, the Web application server can create new instances or threads as needed to handle the load from the clients.

Since servlets are Java programs, they can be developed with an IDE, such as VisualAge for Java.

Using an inherited servlet to provide a common look and feel and common functions provides all of the benefits of a single servlet approach with none of the disadvantages.

Cons

A minor disadvantage to HttpServlets is that they require explicit compiling and deployment into an application server (see the Chapter 5, “Servlet support” on page 137 for more details on how to deploy servlets into WebSphere).

Alternatives

Although we are strong proponents of using servlets as the controller in an MVC architecture, an alternative is to develop monolithic servlets that handle both the application flow logic and generate HTML (through the PrintWriter accessible from the HttpServletResponse object). Some even go to the extreme of handling business process logic directly within the servlet. The only advantage of this approach is that the end-to-end path length is shorter.

The problem with monolithic servlets is that the layout cannot be developed with a WYSIWYG editor, nor can the business logic be reused in other client types, such as Java applications.

Further, it makes it much more difficult to move the application to alternate output media, such as WAP and WML.

JavaServer Pages, to be discussed next, are considered by some to be a viable alternative to servlets, since they are functionally equivalent.

3.2.2.2 JavaServer Pages

JavaServer Pages (JSPs) are a standard extension to HTML that provide escapes so that values can be dynamically inserted.

There are numerous tags that allow the developer to do such things as import Java classes, and declare common functions and variables. The most important ones used by a JSP developer to generate dynamic content are:

- java code block (<% code %>), usually used to insert logic blocks such as loops for tables, selection lists, options, and so on
- expressions (<%=expression%>), usually used to insert substitute variable values into the HTML.
- bean tag (<jsp:bean>), used to get a reference to a Java Bean scoped to various sources, such as the request, session, or context.
- property tag (<jsp:beanproperty>) is a special-purpose version of the expression tag that substitutes a specified property from a bean (loaded with the bean tag).

There is also a standard tag extension mechanism in JSP that allows the developer to make up new tags and associate them with code that can either convert the tag into HTML or control subsequent parsing (depending on the type of tag created). This feature would allow a developer (or third-party providers) to build tags that eliminate the need to explicitly code expressions and java code blocks, making the JSP code look more HTML-like and less Java like. See Chapter 6, "JSP support" on page 189 for more details. Custom tags can make it very easy for non-programmers to develop JavaServer Pages (those with Java skills can develop specialized tags to generate tables, option lists, and such).

In any event, a JSP is compiled at runtime by WebSphere into a servlet that executes to generate the resulting dynamic HTML. Subsequent calls to the same JSP simply execute the compiled servlet. In Chapter 6, "JSP support" on page 189, we discuss the performance benefits of precompiling JSPs (JSP 1.0 only).

Role in the architecture

JSPs are best used to handle the display of data associated with a given state having dynamic content. This role represents the view in an MVC architecture and contrasts with that of the servlet that represents the controller. The way they work together is that the servlet gathers the data or handles the transition action, and then routes flow of control to the associated JSP to generate the response.

For our example application, this approach would result in the following JSPs being developed, with the naming convention being State.jsp:

- ProductCatalog.jsp, which takes the catalog data provided by the corresponding HttpServlet and primarily formats an HTML table displaying the product IDs and descriptions, along with a form allowing a Customer to specify a quantity to add to the order.
- OrderStatus.jsp, which takes the order data provided by OrderStatusServlet and primarily formats an HTML table displaying the order IDs and current status, along with a button allowing a Customer to view the selected order.
- OrderDetails.jsp, which takes the line items associated with an order provided by the OrderDetailsServlet and formats a table showing the product ID, description, and quantity, along with a form allowing a Customer to specify a modified quantity.
- AlreadyOpen.jsp, which simply formats a page showing the order number that is already open.
- ActionResult.jsp, which simply displays a message describing the result of a given action.

Figure 15 on page 49 shows the online buying application STD extended to show these JSPs.

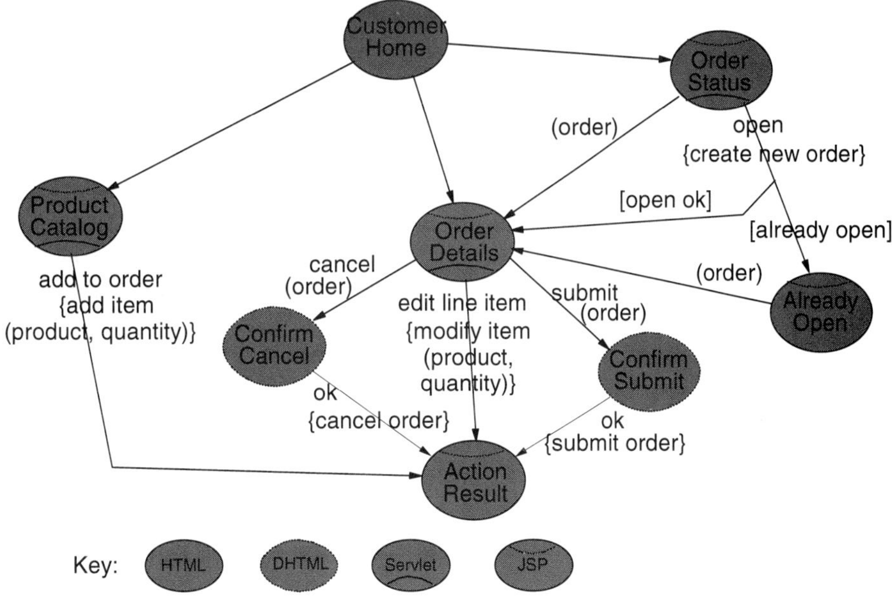

Figure 15. Online buying application STD extended to show display controlled by JSPs

We would likely want to develop specialized tags to handle generating a table by iterating through indexed Java Bean properties. This tag would be used to generate the tables associated with the ProductCatalog, OrderDetails and OrderStatus states. As an example of the differences, here is a fragment of the ProductCatalog JSP with embedded Java:

```
<TABLE BORDER=0 CELLPADDING=2 WIDTH="90%" HEIGHT=25>
<TR BGCOLOR="blue">
   <TH WIDTH="10%" ALIGN=CENTER>
      <FONT SIZE=3 COLOR="white">Product ID</FONT>
   <TH WIDTH="64%" ALIGN=LEFT>
      <FONT SIZE=3 COLOR="white">Description</FONT>
   <TH WIDTH="16%" ALIGN=CENTER>
      <FONT SIZE=3 COLOR="white">Action</FONT>
</TR>
<%
   int sku = 0;
   String description = null;
   online.buying.data.ProductData d[] = v.getCatalog();
   for (int i=0; i < d.length; i++)
   {
      sku = d[i].getSku();
      description = d[i].getDescription();
%>
```

```
<TR>
   <TD WIDTH="10%" ALIGN=CENTER>
      <FONT SIZE=4 COLOR="black"><%=sku%></FONT>
   <TD WIDTH="64%" ALIGN=LEFT>
      <FONT SIZE=4 COLOR="black"><%=description%></FONT>
   <TD WIDTH="16%" ALIGN=CENTER>
      <FORM METHOD=POST
ACTION="/servlet/online.buying.servlets.ProductCatalogServlet">
         <INPUT TYPE=HIDDEN NAME="productID"
VALUE="<jsp:beanproperty name=product property=sku/>">
         <INPUT TYPE=TEXT NAME="quantity" VALUE=1 SIZE=3 MAXLENGTH=3>
         <INPUT TYPE=SUBMIT NAME="action" VALUE="Add to Order">
      </FORM>
   </TD>
</TR>
<%
   }
%>
</TABLE>
```

Here is how the same JSP fragment might look using custom tags:

```
<TABLE BORDER=0 CELLPADDING=2 WIDTH="90%" HEIGHT=25>
<TR BGCOLOR="blue">
   <TH WIDTH="10%" ALIGN=CENTER>
      <FONT SIZE=3 COLOR="white">Product ID</FONT>
   <TH WIDTH="64%" ALIGN=LEFT>
      <FONT SIZE=3 COLOR="white">Description</FONT>
   <TH WIDTH="16%" ALIGN=CENTER>
      <FONT SIZE=3 COLOR="white">Action</FONT>
</TR>
<onlineBuying:indexedProperty
   beanName=v property=catalog
   value=product
   type=online.buying.data.ProductData
>
<TR>
   <TD WIDTH="10%" ALIGN=CENTER>
      <FONT SIZE=4 COLOR="black">
         <jsp:beanproperty name=product property=sku/>
      </FONT>
   <TD WIDTH="64%" ALIGN=LEFT>
      <FONT SIZE=4 COLOR="black">
         <jsp:beanproperty name=product property=description/>
      </FONT>
   <TD WIDTH="16%" ALIGN=CENTER>
```

```
        <FORM METHOD=POST
ACTION="/servlet/online.buying.servlets.ProductCatalogServlet">
            <INPUT TYPE=HIDDEN NAME="productID"
               VALUE="<jsp:beanproperty name=product property=sku/>">
            <INPUT TYPE=TEXT NAME="quantity" VALUE=1 SIZE=3 MAXLENGTH=3>
            <INPUT TYPE=SUBMIT NAME="action" VALUE="Add to Order">
        </FORM>
    </TD>
</TR>
</onlinebuying:indexedProperty>
</TABLE>
```

The example shows that there is no Java required at all when using custom tags.

Whether extended tags are used or not, we recommend developing JSPs such that multiple states can be composed within a single page (see 3.2.1.1, "HTML" on page 32 and 3.2.1.3, "Framesets and named windows" on page 37 for more details on page composition). This approach actually simplifies the individual JSPs since they need not worry about setting headers or the <HTML><BODY> and other enclosing tags. The associated HttpServlet can handle this setup, or can delegate it to an inherited servlet as discussed in the previous section. This approach will also make it easier to exploit dynamic caching that will be supported in later versions of WebSphere Application Server.

Pros

One huge advantage of JSPs is that they are mostly HTML with a few special tags here and there to fill in the blanks from data variables. The standard extension mechanism allows new tags to be developed that eliminate the need to use the Java escape tags at all.

Further, JSPs require none of the "println" syntax required in an equivalent servlet. This tag-oriented focus makes them relatively easy to WYSIWYG edit with tools such as WebSphere Studio Page Designer. This focus also makes it easier to assign the task of building JSPs to developers more skilled in graphic design than programming.

JSPs can be used to provide meaningful error indicators on the same page as the input fields, including specific messages and highlighting. Static HTML does not provide this capability.

Another advantage is that JSPs do not require an explicit compile step, making them easy to develop and test in rapid prototyping cycles. This feature tempts some developers to use JSPs instead of servlets to handle the data gathering and update-transition functions, logic that is traditionally associated with the controller component of an MVC architecture.

Cons

There are some good reasons not to give in to the temptation and use JSPs to control the application flow:

1. Current JSP tools do not provide IDE functions for code blocks. For example, method completion and hierarchy exploration are not available during edit, incremental compile, test and debug facilities are not available in preview mode (usually the logic blocks and escapes show up as strange symbols on the window).
2. While there is no conceptual reason that prevents a JSP tool from providing a "dual mode" capability, combining the two concepts makes it impossible for one developer to handle the control flow of an application and another to handle the layout.
3. Combining application flow and layout logic in a JSP has the same disadvantage as combining them in a servlet: it is much more difficult to migrate the application to use different output media.
4. Finally, JSP 1.0 and beyond have eliminated the ability to override an abstract method defined by a superclass, such as doGetOnlineBuying(). All HTML tags are compiled into the HttpServlet service() method. This makes inheritance of common look-and-feel behaviors in JSPs much more difficult and error prone.

Regardless of whether they are used to control application flow or not, there are some minor issues associated with using JSPs.

1. JSPs compile on the first invocation, which usually causes a noticeable response time delay while the compile, load and init take place. To avoid this delay in production environments, use a batch JSP precompiler if available (see Chapter 6, "JSP support" on page 189 for more details).
2. Communication between the JSP and servlet creates a name, type and data flow source convention issue. In other words, how do you pass data elements between a servlet and the corresponding JSP? The next section discusses using a Java Bean to encapsulate the data needed by a JSP.

Alternatives

If you insist on using JSPs to control the application flow, we recommend building two per state:

1. StateServlet.jsp, playing the role of an HttpServlet with nothing but a script tag implementing doGet() and doPost() type methods, It can safely inherit from a superclass HttpServlet as described in the previous section.

2. State.jsp, playing the role of a JSP as described in this section.

This approach allows you to take advantage of the quick prototyping capability of JSPs early in the development cycle (no compile or deploy step needed). Later on you could convert the "servlet" JSP to a real servlet (to avoid the need to precompile the JSPs as described above).

However, we should say here that such tools as VisualAge for Java Enterprise Edition with its embedded WebSphere Test Environment provide the ability to rapidly develop and test servlets as easily as JSPs, minimizing the development cycle-time advantage described above that might motivate the use of JSPs for application flow control.

Finally, XML actually provides a viable alternative to JSP in some situations. It is possible to have the servlet for a given state return XML directly to an XML-enabled browser, using an XML parser-generator. Even if a user's browser does not support XML, the servlet could use the associated stylesheet to generate the corresponding HTML without using a JSP. We will discuss this possibility further in the next section, where Java Beans can be employed to simplify this process.

3.2.2.3 Data structure Java Beans (data beans)

A Java Bean is a class that follows strictly specified conventions for naming properties, events and methods. An auxiliary class, called a BeanInfo class, contains additional descriptive information that can be used by tools to provide, among other things, extra levels of documentation and runtime support to edit property values.

A data structure Java Bean is usually nothing but a simple set of properties, with no need for events or methods (beyond gets and sets of the associated properties).

Data structure Java Beans are sometimes made "immutable". That is, all properties are private and only get methods are provided to prevent the data from being updated. Also, data structure Java Beans sometimes are associated with a separate key subcomponent that encapsulates those properties that uniquely identify the associated data.

Immutable or not, key or not, a data structure Java Bean should implement the serializable interface that enables it to be passed remotely and stored in various files and databases. An implication of being serializable is that the object properties must be simple types or strings, or that any contained objects must be serializable.

Strictly speaking, WebSphere Application Server V3.5 has no special support for Java Beans. However, data structure Java Beans fill so many useful roles in the end-to-end architecture that we feel required to include them in a discussion about the programming model.

Role in the architecture

In an MVC architecture, data structure Java Beans can be considered to represent the static properties associated with objects in the model. This makes them useful to maintain data reads from back-end systems, or results from executing back-end business functions (more on this in the next section on business logic access beans).

For purposes of the Web application server tier, we also see them used to maintain the data passed between the servlet and other middle-tier components, especially JavaServer Pages (described in the 3.2.2.2, "JavaServer Pages" on page 47) when there is more than one property involved. They may represent data from the model as it is transformed for a specific view associated with a JSP, or as occurs in many cases, it may be that the model object does not need transforming and can be passed to the JSP as is.

Our example online buying application has three servlets that pass complex data to an associated JSP: ProductCatalogServlet, OrderStatusServlet and OrderDetailsServlet. This association leads us to suggest developing three data structure Java Beans, named ProductCatalogData, OrderStatusData and OrderDetailsData, respectively. Figure 16 on page 55 shows the online buying application STD extended to show where data structure Java Beans are being used to model the contract between the servlet and JSP.

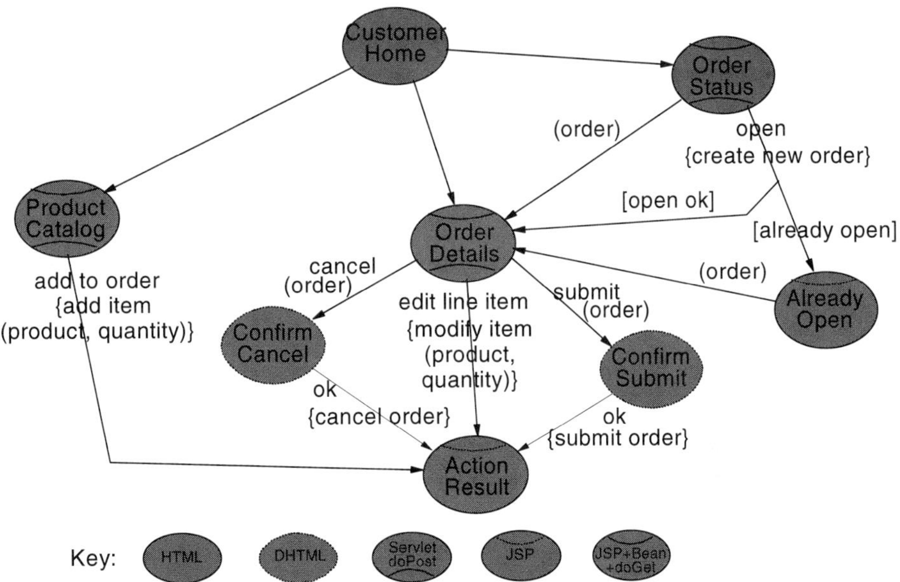

Figure 16. Online buying application STD extended to show data structure Java Beans that encapsulate the dynamic content

Some developers build a data structure Java Bean for every JSP whether it has more than one property or not, and whether or it is associated with a servlet or not. They may also make these data structure Java Beans immutable, as described above, to make them easier to deal with in WYSIWYG editors (only get methods would show in the palette of functions available).

In any event, the properties associated with these data structure Java Beans can be derived directly from the more complex objects in static models associated with the application flow model as shown in Figure 17 on page 56.

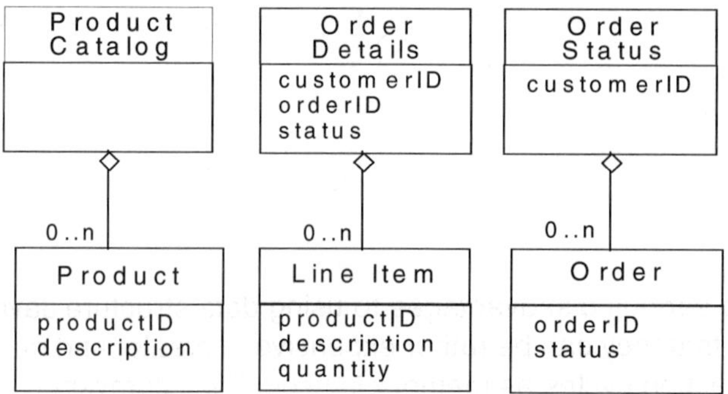

Figure 17. Data structure Java Beans derived from application flow static object model

Pros

Either approach using a data structure Java Bean to contain JSP data has enormous advantages:

1. The data structure Java Bean represents a formal contract between the servlet and JSP developer roles involved.
2. Adding properties to the contract is easy because the servlets already create, populate, and pass the associated Java Bean, while the JSPs already use the bean and property tags. You can independently modify the programs to use the new properties. Also, the new properties can be optional with a default assigned as part of the constructor.
3. Removing a property from the contract without modifying the associated servlets and JSPs that use them will cause errors to be caught at compile rather than runtime.
4. It allows the servlet developer for a given state to focus entirely on Java to control the application control and data flow, while the JSP developer can focus entirely on HTML or XML-like tags that control the layout.
5. Many tools are available that take advantage of Java Bean introspection for such varied functions as providing command completion and selection of properties from a palette at development time, to populating from and generating XML at runtime.
6. Setting properties into a data structure Java Bean, and then setting the whole data structure into a data flow source (such as HttpServletRequest attributes to be discussed in 3.4.2.1, "HttpServletRequest attributes" on page 94) is much more efficient than setting individual properties into that source one at a time.

7. Conversely, getting a single data structure Java Bean from that same source, and then getting its properties locally, is much more efficient than getting multiple properties directly from the source.
8. The same data structure Java Beans are likely to be used as contracts with other components because of their simplicity, providing a high degree of reuse (more on this advantage in the next section).

Cons

There are no serious disadvantages to using data structure Java Beans. The only issue is that they can be rather expensive to create, and may cause extra garbage collection cycles as memory is used. To circumvent this problem, some developers use pooling techniques, where a number of pre-constructed Java Beans wait to be requested, used, and then released back to the pool.

Alternatives

Some XML enthusiasts propose XML as a dynamic substitute for explicitly coded Java Beans (see 3.2.1.4, "XML, DTD and XSL" on page 41). With this approach, a single XML string is passed or stored rather than a data structure Java Bean. The receiving component then uses the XML parser to retrieve the data.

While we are strong proponents of XML, and see its merits as a possible serialized format of a data structure Java Bean, we would not recommend using XML-encoded strings as a substitute, especially in situations where the data structure is known at design time.

The extra overhead of generating and parsing the XML strings, plus the storing, retrieving and transmitting of all the extra tags, makes them very expensive with respect to the equivalent data structure Java Bean. For example, it will take only few bytes to serialize a Java Bean such as LineItemData containing a simple string for the description and couple of integers for the productID and quantity. Using XML could take many, many more bytes, depending on how the tags are specified and how much white space is encoded:

```
<LineItemData>
   <productID>1111</productID>
   <description>Cat food bowl</description>
   <quantity>1</quantity>
</LineItemData>
```

An alternate XML design might be a little more conservative of space, but still is much more expensive than the equivalent serialized data structure Java Bean:

```
<LineItemData productID=1111 description="Cat food bowl" quantity=1/>
```

Don't forget that neither of these fragments include the surrounding tags that make it a well-formed XML document.

In summary, there is honestly no good alternative to using data structure Java Beans as the formal contract between components in the architecture. And, as we will see in the following sections, data structure Java Beans are used just about everywhere, making them well worth the investment.

3.2.2.4 Business logic access beans

We noted in the previous subsection on data structure Java Beans that they represent the static properties of the model. In the same vein, a business logic access bean can be thought of as encapsulating the dynamic behavior of the model.

A business logic access bean is a Java class whose methods encapsulate a unit of work needed by any type of application, be it for the Web or a distributed client/server. In other words, a business logic access bean is intended to be user interface independent.

> **Note**
>
> Access bean as it is used here is intended to be a generic Java wrapper, and not to be confused with the specific kind of access beans generated by VisualAge for Java Enterprise Edition.

The other primary purpose of the business logic access bean is to insulate the client from various technology dependencies that may be required to implement the business logic.

Business logic access beans will almost always make use of data structure Java Beans and associated keys in the input and output parameters. Further, any data cached within an access bean is likely to be in terms of data structure Java Beans and associated keys, so the two concepts go hand in hand.

Like data structure Java Beans, WebSphere Application Server V3.5 has no special support for business logic access beans, However, they are so useful in the end-to-end architecture that we feel required to include them in this discussion as well.

Role in the architecture

We noted in the previous subsection that data structure Java Beans represent the static properties of the model in an MVC architecture. In the same vein, a business logic access bean can be thought of as encapsulating the dynamic behavior of the model.

There are numerous approaches to developing business logic access beans, covering many different aspects that may be useful in a given application. We touch on a few of them here, but it is not within the scope of this book to discuss all the different patterns that may be used (see *Design Patterns: Elements of Reusable Object-Oriented Software*, by Erich Gamma, et al).

The first aspect we consider is whether the business logic is stateless or stateful:

- Stateless access beans have methods whose input parameters include all the data necessary to complete the unit of work and whose return values have the complete result. Stateless access beans retain no memory of what a given client program has done between invocations. However, "statelessness" does not mean that the access bean cannot cache data, just that any data cached must be accessible using parameters passed in a given method signature.
- Stateful access beans have methods that may rely on the result of previous methods, thus having an implied "state" model. Statefulness can be exploited to simplify the method signatures, since parameters or results of previous calls can be cached so that fewer parameters are needed in subsequent method signatures. Stateful access beans must have a one-to-one association with the client so that two different clients in two different "states" do not interfere with each other. This association is often called client/server affinity, and it can make stateful access beans less scalable than an equivalent stateless one by limiting the ability to arbitrarily load balance method calls.
- You can sometimes simulate a stateful access bean with a stateless one by including extra parameters that either identify the client or contain the current state data.

  The identity is used in the first approach to look up state data cached in the access bean. If the second approach is used, the current state data is used in the called method and a new current state is returned to the client (as a data structure Java Bean, as described in the 3.2.2.3, "Data structure Java Beans (data beans)" on page 53) to keep until the next call.

Another aspect to consider is granularity. Like servlets described in 3.2.2.1, “Servlets” on page 43, there is a continuum of granularity that could be considered when developing a business logic access bean:

- On the one extreme, there could be a single business logic access bean per unit of work.
- On the other, all units of work for the business process could be represented by methods on a single business logic access bean.
- In the middle, all the methods needed for the transitions in a given state in the application flow model could be grouped into a single business logic access bean.
- Also in the middle (but coarser grained), all the transitions associated with a state in the business process model could be represented by methods on a single business logic access bean.

Some of you may be familiar with the following types of business logic access beans:

- A command bean is a fine-grained stateful business logic access bean that encapsulates a single unit of work. The programming model for a command bean is to create it (or get one from a pool), set properties (its state) that represent the input parameters, perform the unit of work, and finally get the properties representing the return parameters (also part of the state). See *Design and Implement Servlet, JSPs, and EJBs*, SG24-5754 for more details.
- A business logic access bean that is stateful and holds the data returned from a query result is sometimes called a rowset. A rowset can be considered to be a specialized form of command bean. Its programming model is to set parameters representing a query, perform the query, then iterate through the results in the rowset.

By way of an example, if we decided to use a stateless approach with a business logic access bean per state in the online buying business process model, we might end up with the following:

1. EntryAccess, with the following stateless methods:
   - OrderKey create(CustomerKey), where a new order is created on behalf of the customer and the key is returned
   - void addLineItem(CustomerKey, ProductKey, quantity), where the specified quantity of a product is added to the open order for the specified customer. If no order is open, a new one is opened.

- void modifyLineItem(CustomerKey, ProductKey, quantity), where an existing line item on an order is modified.
- void submit(CustomerKey), where the open order associated with the customer is submitted to the Shipping department for Fulfillment.
- void cancel(CustomerKey), where the open order associated with the customer is cancelled and moved to the Completed state for data mining by the Marketing.

2. FulfillmentAccess, with the following stateless methods:
   - void packLineItem(Shipper, OrderKey, ProductKey, quantity), where the specified quantity of product up to the line item quantity is added to a shipment associated with the order. If no shipment is open, a new one is created.
   - void ship(Shipper, OrderKey), where the shipment associated with an order is shipped. If all line items associated with the order have been shipped, then the order is moved to the Completed state.
3. CompletedAccess, with the following stateless methods:
   - void purge(Marketer, OrderKey), where the order is finally deleted from the system after all data mining activities have been exhausted.

Figure 18 shows the business process model from which these access beans and associated methods were derived.

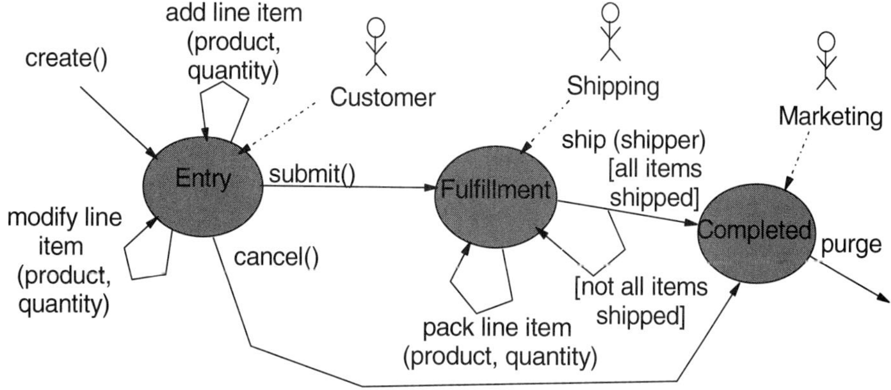

Figure 18. Online buying business process model driving the business logic access beans

These descriptions only show the update methods associated with the business logic access beans. The assumption is that there would be read-only methods that provide access to data associated with the static model underlying the business process state. For the OrderEntry state we might see the following read-only methods:

- ProductData[] getProducts(), which returns the current list of products in the catalog.
- OrderDetails getOpenOrderDetails(CustomerKey), which returns the details of the open order associated with the customer passed in (or null if no order is open).
- OrderDetails getOrderDetails(OrderKey), which returns the details for the order passed in (or null if the order does not exist).
- OrderData[] getOrders(CustomerKey), which returns the list of orders associated with the customer.

The OrderDetails class derived from the application flow static object model is used to pass data for the getOpenOrderDetails() and getOrderDetails() methods, while the ProductData and OrderData classes used to return data from the getProducts() and getOrders() methods are derived from the static object model associated with the business process OrderEntry state as shown in Figure 19.

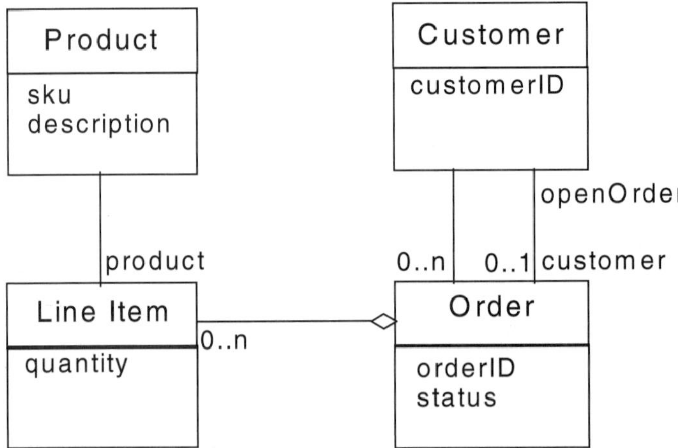

Figure 19. Static object model of Order in Entry state driving read-only calls

It often makes sense to wrap the business objects used by the business logic access beans with access beans as well, to provide the ability for each to be maintained in a separate data store transparent to the business logic. In this case, we would have a business object access bean for Product, Customer, Order, and LineItem respectively (named ProductAccess, CustomerAccess, OrderAccess and LineItemAccess).

Pros
One big advantage of wrapping the business logic associated with the business process model is that wrappers provide an encapsulating layer that hides the details of where and how the business logic gets invoked from the client. This insulation will make it possible to evolve the technology used by the application over time. For example, in early stages, the code may make direct calls to JDBC, and then over time migrate to use Enterprise JavaBeans, all without having to recompile the client applications.

Another big advantage is that once the method signatures are defined, it is possible to build the client applications in parallel with the back-end business logic, and speed the overall development process. Testing becomes simpler too, since the logic controlling the application flow is cleanly separated from the logic controlling the business process, minimizing the number of code segments that need to be tested.

Cons
There is absolutely no downside to wrapping business logic in objects separate from the client, even in cases where there is little or no opportunity to reuse the business logic in other applications.

Alternatives
That said, there is an alternative to wrapping business logic into "vanilla" Java classes, and that is to directly use Enterprise JavaBeans in the client code. In the next section, we discuss the various types and applications in the next section that we feel make this a viable alternative.

3.2.3 Distributed object server-hosted components

The WebSphere programming model provides support for Java-based distributed objects called Enterprise JavaBeans (EJBs). EJBs can be thought of as a standard mechanism to wrapper enterprise business logic and data (usually hosted on some enterprise server) that can take advantage of the following object services:

- Distribution, the ability for the server to be remote from the client
- Persistence, maintenance of the essential data associated with the component
- Transactions, providing ACID characteristics for the units of work
- Security, control of the roles that can access the objects and associated methods
- Trace and monitoring, configurable instrumentation for debugging and performance tuning

There are two main types of EJBs that can be developed as part of the programming model: session and entity. In a nutshell, session EJBs are those that have a very short life cycle that lasts only as long as both the client and server maintain a reference to the session. This reference can be lost if the client explicitly removes the session, or if the server goes down or "times out" the session.

An entity EJB is one that once created (either explictly or implicitly) can be subsequently found with a "key" for use by a client application. It persists until the remove() operation is invoked by a client application or until the data is explicitly removed from the underlying store.

Within a session EJB there are three implementation types to choose from (stateless, stateful, and stateful with session synchronization). Within an entity EJB there are two implementation types depending on how persistence is managed: container-managed persistence (CMP), and bean-managed persistence (BMP).

This section will discuss each implementation choice at a high level with respect to their role in the architecture, what the pros and cons of each type are, and alternatives to each. Details of how to deploy EJBs are found in Chapter 11, "Enterprise Java Services" on page 393.

3.2.3.1 Stateless session EJBs

Stateless session EJBs are those whose method signatures have all the parameters needed to complete the associated unit of work; they return the complete result in the method return value (or exceptions that may be thrown).

The effect of being stateless is that any active instance of a stateless session EJB can service a request from any client in any sequence. This feature makes stateless session EJBs the most scalable.

There is no guarantee that two calls to the same stateless session EJB will be services by the same instance on the server. Because of this feature (good for scalability), there is a common misconception that stateless session EJBs cannot have instance variables and thus maintain "state". They can, as long as the values can be used by any client, and in any sequence. For example, many applications cache connections to back-end resources and frequently used stable read-only data in stateless session EJBs.

Role in the architecture

Stateless session EJBs are ideal for implementing the business logic associated with the business process model, as we described in see 3.2.2.4, “Business logic access beans” on page 58.

You could use the stateless session EJBs directly by the client program, or have the business logic access bean wrapper calls to the stateless session bean. In either case, the method signatures of the stateless session EJBs would look exactly like those described in 3.2.2.4. The method signatures for the Entry stateless session bean derived from the online-buying business process model as shown in Figure 20 are:

- OrderKey createOrder(CustomerKey), where a new order is created on behalf of the customer and the key is returned.
- void addLineItem(CustomerKey, ProductKey, quantity), where the specified quantity of a product is added to the open order for the specified customer. If no order is open, a new one is opened.
- void modifyLineItem(CustomerKey, ProductKey, quantity), where an existing line item on the open order associated with the customer is modified.
- void submitOrder(CustomerKey), where the open order associated with the customer is submitted to the Shipping department for Fulfillment.
- void cancelOrder(CustomerKey), where the open order associated with the customer is cancelled and moved to the Completed state for data mining by the Marketing department.

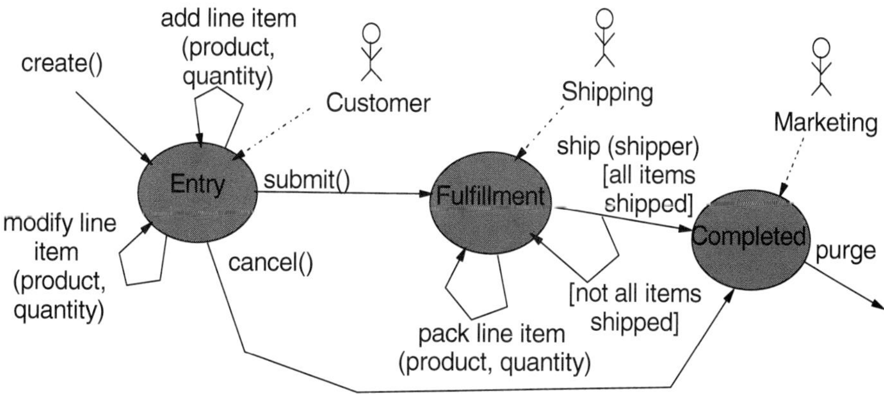

Figure 20. Stateless session EJBs derived from business process model

Note: add a CustomerKey to every transition to derive method signatures.

The implementations of the methods can be exactly the same as those provided for the business logic access beans, or they can take advantage of the features of stateless session EJBs.

For example, if the code manually manages a connection pool for a relatively expensive resource, you can cache the connection in the stateless session EJB (as long as it is not client specific). This approach effectively lets the EJB container act as the pooling mechanism, and makes getting the connection transparent to the business logic, which can simply use the connection.

As another example, if the methods managed standard JTA (Java Transaction API) transactions at the beginning and end of the business logic to provide ACID properties, this code could be removed, since it is provided automatically by the container.

Pros

Besides simplifying the code to handle connection pooling, transactions and security, a key advantage gained when using stateless session EJBs is that the business logic can be moved out of (distributed from) the client tier without having to reprogram the client or server components. This ability can be important for security purposes.

For example, we may be happy to have the Web server and servlets within the DMZ (since the application flow can be inferred by navigating the Web site anyway), but we would probably want to host the business logic behind the inner firewall of the DMZ to protect it from direct access by hackers. In other cases we may want to co-deploy the business logic with the application flow logic, but put both behind the DMZ (using WebSphere's OSE Remote deployment option).

Another advantage of using stateless session EJBs is that it is possible to efficiently load balance them across multiple application servers and achieve a high degree of scalability.

Distributing the business logic out of the client tier can make the client much "thinner" since there is no need to install (possibly very expensive) connectivity options. Only the Enterprise Java Servers would need to maintain the connectivity to the back-end systems. It can communicate with the client, with the client-side ORB providing RMI/IIOP connectivity. In large Web application server farms, or Java applets, having a thin middle tier can be a very attractive advantage.

Finally, distributing the business logic out of the client means that it can be reused in multiple application types, not just Web applications, as we show in the introduction (3.1.2.2, "Distributed object-based applications" on page 27).

Cons

One disadvantage to using EJBs in general is that the overhead (distributed calls, security checks and transaction management) can be quite expensive even when the client and server are co-deployed. For this reason, you must take care to design the EJBs to minimize the number of calls required per unit of work (our design requires only one call per unit of work after the EJB is created).

The second disadvantage to using EJBs is that the need to find a Home in the JNDI context, narrow it to the specific home interface type, and create the remote interface prior to using it adds complexity to the client programming model.

Still a third disadvantage when using EJBs is the increased complexity in testing, debugging, deployment, and administration.

Specific to stateless session EJBs, a disadvantage with respect to other EJB types is the need to pass in extra parameters on the call, and receive all the data on the return value. This requirement can significantly increase the data transmission costs, if the objects are not carefully designed.

Also, expensive computations may be repeated (if the EJB is called more than once in the logical session), because a stateless session EJB retains no memory of previous calls.

Alternatives

If, for example, all the logic is handled by back-end CICS transactions, or all the data is maintained in a single DB2 database using precompiled SQLJ queries, then a simple business logic access bean that directly accesses these back-end systems may be the preferred approach.

Rather than look up the home in the JNDI context, narrow it, and create the session over and over again for each request, you can create the session once and cache it in the client (either the servlet or, preferably, the business logic access bean). This approach should be considered a "best practice" even though the IBM implementation of the JNDI context in WebSphere Application Server V3.5.2 automatically caches homes to provide a high degree of scalability.

Also, it is a common practice to cache stable read-only data in a stateless session EJB (or in an associated singleton object) to minimize repeating expensive computations. For example, we may want to cache the product catalog data within a singleton referenced by the stateless session bean.

3.2.3.2 Stateful session EJBs

Stateful session EJBs have a complex life cycle model that allows methods to maintain state between calls. The effect is that a given task can span multiple invocations.

Unlike stateless session EJBs, stateful session beans can support a custom create that takes parameters useful in initializing the state. This feature can be very useful in simplifying the other method signatures, since they can assume that the state of the session EJB includes those parameters useful for the lifetime of the session.

Role in the architecture

Since the "business logic" of our example application only allows a single order to be open for a customer at a given time, we could have designed a stateful session EJB for the OrderEntry state in the online buying business process model as follows:

- OrderEntry ejbCreate(CustomerKey), where the session is created and the current open order for the customer (if any) is cached. This method would appear on the OrderEntryHome as a custom create.
- void addLineItem(ProductKey, quantity), where the specified quantity of a product is added to the open order for the stored customer. If no order is open, a new one is opened.
- void modifyLineItem(ProductKey, quantity), where an existing line item on the open order associated with the session is modified.
- void submitOrder(), where the open order is submitted to the Shipping department for Fulfillment.
- void cancelOrder(), where the open order is cancelled and moved to the Completed state for data mining by the Marketing department.

Figure 21 on page 69 shows how the OrderEntry stateful session EJB methods were derived more directly from the associated business process model state (customer was added only as a parameter to the create method).

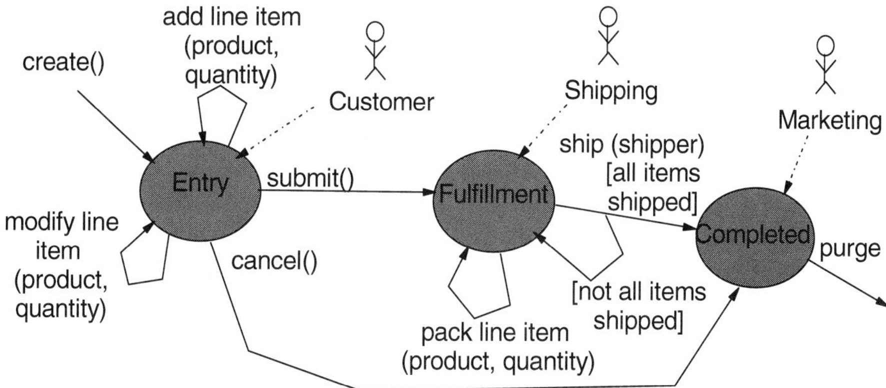

Figure 21. The business process model from which stateful session EJB methods were derived

Pros

One benefit of using stateful session EJBs is that the methods map more closely to the transitions associated with the business process model than those of the stateless session EJB (or business logic access bean) described previously. Also, the fewer number of parameters means that there is less data to marshal and demarshal in a remote method invocation.

Another benefit of a stateful session EJB is that it can reduce the number of calls to the back end by caching frequently used data as part of its state. In our example, caching the open order associated with the customer eliminates the need to keep reading the database to retrieve it, as would be required in just about every method associated with the "equivalent" stateless session EJB.

Taking this idea to an extreme, stateful session EJBs can cache data considered to be work-in-progress, eliminating all calls to the back end until specific "checkpoint" type transitions. This can be especially advantageous in situations where application events may terminate the processing before its logical conclusion.

For example, we could have opted to cache the order line item data in the OrderEntry stateful session EJB until the submit or cancel is invoked. Only on the submit would it access the back-end system to move the cached data to a persistent store.

A middle of the road approach would both cache the state in the EJB, and store it persistently on the back end. Any update methods on the stateful session EJB (such as addLineItem) would write to the persistent store, and if successful, would update the cache to reflect the results. Read-only methods (such as getOrderLineItems) on the EJB would simply use the data in the cache.

Whatever you decide to cache using stateful session EJBs, the “state” is managed automatically by the container rather than by explicit programming. All the programmer need do is specify the instance variables as non transient, and they are considered to be part of the state that gets managed. If memory gets overloaded with sessions, the container will passivate one (probably one that is least recently used, or LRU), reactivating it later if necessary.

Also, a properly designed stateful session EJB makes these caching decisions transparent to the client.

Cons

The primary disadvantage to using stateful session EJBs is that there are very few quality of service guarantees with respect to the ACID properties you might expect when working with components:

1. For example, the container is not obligated by the specification to provide for failover of stateful sessions by backing up the nontransient instance variables in a shared file or database; so in general, if the server hosting the stateless session EJB goes down, the state is lost.
2. Further, even if failover of stateful sessions was provided for by a shared database (which WebSphere does not support), the session may time out due to inactivity. Timeout always causes the state to be lost.

Both of these cases would probably be considered to be disastrous in the example where line item data was only maintained as state within the stateful session EJB, since a significant amount of work by the Customer would be lost. However, a stateful session can be coded to manually back up the data in a persistent store. In this case timeout or failover would only require reinitialization of the session during the ejbCreate() method.

Another disadvantage related to the quality of service guaranteed for stateful session EJBs is that the container does not roll back the state if the overall transaction fails. For example, if the client application made multiple addLineItem() calls to the Entry stateful session in the context of a single transaction that subsequently fails, the state data would be incorrect. The backing store may be in an inconsistent state as well.

Still another disadvantage to using stateful session EJBs is that scalability is affected, since (unlike stateless sessions) a client must be attached to the server hosting the specific stateful session EJB that is referenced. This requirement for client/server affinity limits the ability to balance the workload among multiple servers. If the clients are not able to share the reference to the EJB (either through a serialized handle or some other mechanism), then client/server affinity must "ripple" all the way back to the client. This ripple effect can greatly affect the scalability, performance, and failover characteristics of the application.

Finally, another downside is that the mapping of data from the non-transient variables to the backing store (file or database) during passivation/activation is through the serialization mechanism. In short, the data is stored as a Blob (Binary Large Object). The effect is that you cannot index or retrieve the data using complex queries, as you could if you explicitly mapped the data to specific columns.

Alternatives

There are alternatives to using stateful session EJBs. For example, any of the approaches for converting a stateful to stateless access bean described in 3.2.2.4, "Business logic access beans" on page 58 can be used. These same approaches could be used to convert a stateful session EJB into a stateless one, especially in situations where the data is stable and read only, or if client/server affinity is already being used.

In either of these cases, a singleton memory cache can be shared by all instances of a stateless session EJB within the same JVM to maintain data. It is also possible to cache this data in the client or Web application server (see 3.4, "Data flow sources" on page 90 for details).

Another alternative to stateful session EJBs when failover and ACID properties are required is to use an entity EJB (discussed in detail below). In this case, the "pseudo session" life cycle would be explicitly managed by the application, but its state data would be immune to timeout as well as server and transaction failures.

3.2.3.3 Session EJBs with session synchronization

Session beans can support the session synchronization interface, which lets them participate in the container's transaction processing. The session synchronization interface includes methods that signal when a transaction has been started, when it is being prepared for commit, and when it is finally completed, either with a commit or a rollback.

The effect is that the same session EJB can be called one or more times in the context of a single transaction, and the container (in conjunction with the transaction controller) manages the calls required to close out the transaction without an explicit call from the business logic methods.

Session synchronization requires that the session EJB be stateful, since it adds life cycle states associated with transactional semantics. However, you should think of it as "converting" either a stateless or a stateful session EJB to support synchronization. The reason this is important is that the advantages and disadvantages of the underlying session EJB type tend to dominate. Also, from a programming model perspective, this characterization associates the choice of session synchronization with deployment rather than with the business logic itself.

Role in the architecture

Let's say that in our online buying application, we decided to cache the Entry data in a stateful session bean because going to the database for each update was too expensive. We initially felt comfortable in this decision because it was determined that timeout of stateful sessions was actually desirable, and that client/server affinity and lack of failover support were not issues. However, we realized that many of the business logic methods could fail after partially updating the cached data, and the programming required to restore the data to its previous state was more or less complex depending on the business logic.

One way to reduce the complexity is to support the session synchronization interface on the Entry stateful session. The afterBegin() implementation would simply make a backup copy of the current state, and hold it in an instance variable. The beforeCompletion() implementation could simply return true, since there is no need to do anything. Finally, the afterCompletion() implementation would restore the current state to the previous copy, if the input parameter indicates that a rollback is required.

The business logic methods can throw a system exception or set a flag to cause a rollback; they can throw application exceptions or exit normally to cause a commit.

Another situation where session synchronization may apply is in situations where data is backed up in a resource with a non-JTA-based transaction model. For example, Persistence Builder (PB) is a VisualAge for Java feature that provides advanced object model to relational mappings, such as preload caching of related objects, that are not yet available in our CMP entity EJB implementations. Unfortunately, PB has its own transactional model that must be followed.

Let's say that in our online buying application the Entry stateless session was coded to use a number of "business object" access beans that wrappered individual PB object types for Product, Customer, Order and OrderLineItem (Figure 22 on page 73).

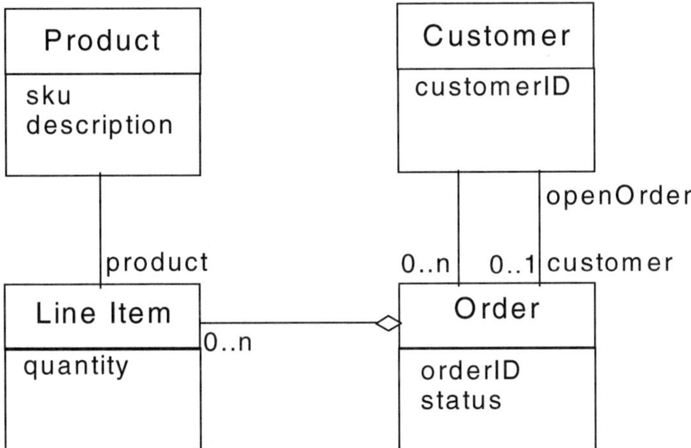

Figure 22. Static object model of Order in Entry state driving business object access beans

The problem is that a given business object access bean is written to be independent of the others. It cannot safely start a PB transaction since it does not know if the client (stateless session EJB) will call another one in the context of the same transaction. We certainly do not want multiple PB transactions to run under a single unit of work, nor do we want to clutter up the business logic with PB specific calls.

In this case, we would consider making the Entry support session synchronization, where the afterBegin() starts the PB transaction, the beforeCompletion() simply returns true (since PB transactions do not support a prepare state - otherwise we would call the appropriate method and return its result), and the afterCompletion() does a commit or a rollback on the PB transaction depending on the input parameter (commit on true or rollback on false, respectively).

Pros

The nice thing about session synchronization is that the business logic of the session no longer needs to be concerned with managing transactions and cached state. Instead, business logic methods need only throw an exception when an error occurs to cause a rollback, or return successfully to cause a commit. In either case, the associated state is properly managed. If the code needs to cause a rollback without throwing an exception (say for read-only methods), it can explicitly invoke a setRollbackOnly() on its EJB transaction retrieved from the context.

In cases where the session EJB was originally stateless and only added session synchronization (and state) to hold a transaction, then failover and timeout is definitely not an issue, since the client (HttpSession or business logic access bean) will create one as needed anyway.

Cons

Except for the simple cases described above, the session synchronization interface can be very difficult code to implement, especially if the underlying resource does not provide support.

Also, the code to manage transactions must apply to all methods on the session that require a transaction. For example, there is no way to process the backup/restore differently based on the method(s) invoked without involving the methods themselves. In this case, it may be best to handle the compensation in the methods themselves.

Implementing the session synchronization interface cannot be considered to support true two-phase commit. The reason is that the transaction coordinator is not obligated to resurrect the session and complete the transaction if there is a failure between phases. The net effect is that there is a window of opportunity where resources can become out of synch.

Finally, session synchronization is relatively expensive to achieve at runtime, because it adds an additional set of methods that must be called to manage a transaction. There should never be more than one or two per unit of work (either of our designs above have only one).

Alternatives

If a stateful session EJB is being converted to use session synchronization simply to provide transactional semantics of the cached data, then consider using a CMP entity EJB. The advantage would be transparent transactional semantics on the persistent properties.

In other cases, the best alternative is to defer session synchronization implementation to the deployer role and have the business logic developer code the session methods to be as independent of transactional semantics as possible. This alternative takes session synchronization out of the "normal" programming model and makes it a deployment responsibility.

3.2.3.4 Container-managed persistence entity EJBs

While a session EJB represents an object with a transient identity lasting only as long as the client and server both maintain a reference to it, an entity EJB represents an object with a persistent identity that lasts until the object is actually removed from the container. Because of this difference, entity EJBs have an associated key, and the home supports methods to find references in various ways:

- Find methods that return a single EJB reference based on the primary key or a set of properties that uniquely identify an entity
- Find methods that return multiple EJB references based on zero or more properties that identify a subset of all entities in the container

An entity has a set of properties, including those that make up the key, which are considered to be part of its persistent state. The associated business logic methods operate upon these properties without regard to how they are loaded and stored.

In a CMP entity EJB, the container manages the persistent properties. When bean-managed persistence (BMP) is specified, the developer explicitly codes well-defined methods invoked by the container to manage the persistent properties.

Role in the architecture

In our online buying application, the business objects associated with the various states in the business process model are the most natural fit for CMP entity EJBs, whether we wrap these business objects with access beans or not (see Figure 23).

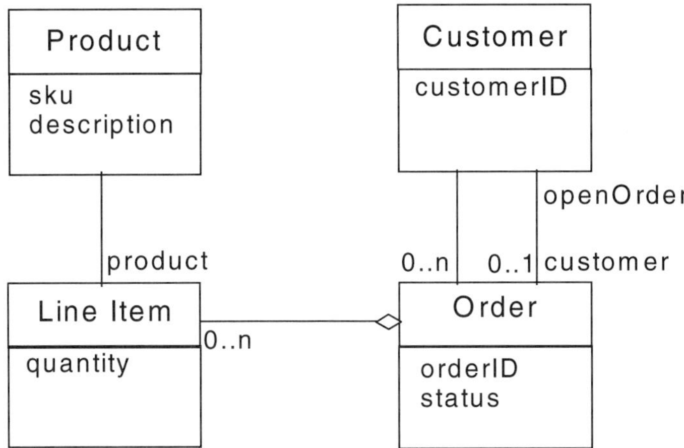

Figure 23. Static object model of Order in Entry state driving CMP entity EJBs

As with all EJBs, care must be taken to minimize the interactions between the client and server, even if the two will be co-deployed (as when the client is a session EJB). For entity EJBs, we recommend the use of the following approaches:

- Custom creates. These are designed to create the object and initialize its properties in a single call, rather than the default create that takes just the key properties followed by individual sets (or a call to a copy helper method as described below). For example, we would likely want a create(sku, description) method on a Product entity EJB to initialize all the data in a single call.

- Custom finders. These are designed to return a subset of the entity EJBs associated with the underlying data store, usually by passing in various properties that are used to form a query. For example, we would want to provide a findItemsForOrder(orderID) on the OrderLineItem entity to return all the OrderLineItems associated with an Order and prevent us from having to iterate through the entire set, looking at those matching the orderID.
- Copy helpers. These are get and set methods that use data structure Java Beans to return or pass a number of properties at once. For example, we would probably want to provide a getOrderData() copy helper on the Order to return the orderID and status in a single call.
- Custom updates. These are designed to do some update function and return a result in a single call. An example is an incrementQuantity(int) method on a LineItem entity EJB that adds an additional quantity to the current value and returns it in a single call instead of having the client do something like the following:

```
OrderLineItem item = lineItemHome.find(orderID, productID);
int currentQty = item.getQuantity();
item.setQuantity(currentQty + additionalQty);
```

As a general rule, you can design entity EJBs such that you do at most a single call to them after a find for a given unit of work. This "single call" includes the create if necessary, as the following example shows:

```
try {
   lineItemHome.find(orderID, productID).setQuantity(quantity);
}
catch (FinderException e) {
   lineItemHome.create(orderID, productID, quantity);
}
```

Of course, exceptions to this rule do exist, such as when the entity is to be deleted based on the method result (an entity EJB doesn't "remove itself" very well):

```
OrderLineItem item = lineItemHome.find(orderID, productID);
int newQuantity = item.incrementQuantity(quantity);
if (newQuantity <= 0) {
   item.remove();
}
```

Following this rule will insure that the application can be distributed as painlessly as possible (although it is usually best to co-deploy client and server, unless the logic executed on the server side is expensive enough to warrant load balancing).

Where entity EJBs are used, you will usually end up with the following:

- <Entity>Key, a data structure Java bean that holds the key properties
- <Entity>Data, a data structure Java bean that holds both key and data properties of the entity. Some go as far as to create a <Entity>DataOnly that holds only the non-key properties to minimize the marshalling overhead for the gets and sets.
- <Entity>Home, the Home interface for finding/creating the EJB, usually with the following methods:
  - <Entity> create(<Entity>Data) creates a new entity and initializes all the properties
  - <Entity> findByPrimaryKey(<Entity>Key) finds based on the key
  - Enumeration find<Entity>sFor<RelEntity>(<RelEntity>Key key) returns those entity EJBs associated with the related entity
- <Entity>, the EJB remote interface with at least the following methods:
  - <Entity>Data get<Entity>Data() returns the data structure Java Bean representing the data
  - void set<Entity>Data(<Entity>Data data) sets the non-key properties from the data
- <Entity>Impl implements the business logic methods specified in the <Entity> interface above

Of course, there are numerous approaches that can be used. For example, many like to include methods that have individual properties passed in rather than forcing the use of a data structure Java Bean.

Also, many will add methods on the entity EJBs to aid in navigation across associations between objects. Of course, the implementations of these navigation methods ultimately use the custom finders described above.

Pros

The primary benefit of CMP entity EJBs is that persistence and transactions are completely transparent to the business logic methods. When we used session EJBs, the only way to get similar functionality was to implement the session synchronization interface and use the methods to load or store the state from a backing store.

This advantage is key from an evolutionary perspective. Let's say our early iterations used PB behind the business object access beans and thus required session synchronization in the stateless session EJB associated with the Entry business logic access bean. Later, we migrate the business object access beans to use entity EJBs. Once all the access beans are converted, we could reimplement the stateless session bean to drop session synchronization without having to touch the business logic. The transaction started by the stateless session bean propagates through to each entity so that any changes are all or nothing.

Cons

As with all EJBs, the downside to CMP entities shows how having a rich set of object services can be a double-edged sword: the overhead associated with managing distribution, security, and transactions can be very expensive. CMP entity EJBs require the developer to trust the container implementation to provide persistence in an efficient manner.

Currently, there are numerous deployment choices available within WebSphere Application Server V3.5 for entity EJBs. While this is not a problem for the programming model, and should be considered to be an advantage, it does complicate the decision whether or not to use entity EJBs in the first place.

At the same time that there are a large number of choices, there are never enough. Some would like CMP containers for CICS VSAM files, or IMS DL/I. Others are fine with relational databases, but would like even more bells and whistles, such as preloading of related objects.

Alternatives

There are at least three alternatives to CMP entities when our current container implementations do not seem to meet your requirements:

1. Client access beans. This option may make sense if you cannot afford the remote method call overhead associated with EJBs, even if they are co-deployed with the client and no-local copies is specified.
2. Session EJBs. This option may make sense if you need a thin client tier or must isolate the business logic from the client for integrity or load-balancing purposes, and otherwise cannot afford the extra object services overhead.
3. BMP entity EJBs. This option may make sense if having a simplified programming model for the business logic is the biggest requirement, but you have database requirements not met by our current container implementations.

The first two options have already been discussed in detail in this section. All three options can be used together effectively: business logic access beans passing through to session EJBs, which use business object access beans passing through to BMP entity EJBs. We will discuss BMP entities next.

3.2.3.5 BMP entity EJBs

A BMP is simply an entity EJB where the developer manually implements the service methods, most notably ejbLoad() to load the persistent state from the backing store and ejbStore() to store it.

Role in the architecture

We recommend that all entity EJBs be implemented as if they were CMP for the business logic programming model. That is, business logic methods should assume that all instance variables are loaded prior to the method executing, and that they will be stored if needed when the method completes. The BMP methods to load and store the persistent instance variables should be implemented as part of the deployment process when the characteristics of the data store are known. This approach is very much the same as what we suggested for session synchronization methods on session EJBs.

In short, the ability to develop BMP methods expands the applicability of entity EJBs to situations where tighter control of the underlying data store is required. This requirement can occur when WebSphere does not support a legacy database. It can also occur when performance considerations preclude using the “vanilla” code generated for CMP entities.

Pros

This approach not only makes the business object logic much simpler to write, but also much easier to migrate to CMPs later, if the required container options eventually become available. Following this approach means that the BMP method implementations can be discarded and the entity EJBs can simply be redeployed, without having to change either the business logic methods or the client code.

Cons

The downside is that the persistence logic can be relatively complicated to implement efficiently. For example, in custom finders, you almost always need to cache the results of the query so that the iterative calls to the ejbLoad() for each instance merely retrieve the data from the cache. In short, it can be very difficult to minimize the number of transactions and back-end accesses.

Alternatives

The alternatives have already been discussed in the previous section: mainly, directly accessing the back end in a business logic access bean or session EJB.

As with CMP entity EJBs, it is almost always a better practice to use a session EJB of some type as a wrapper, hiding the entity from the client. The advantage is that the session EJB can coordinate the transaction across multiple EJBs.

3.3 Control flow mechanisms

If you have designed anything other than a monolithic component architecture (where all the application functions are controlled by a single program component) then you will need to understand the mechanisms by which you will transfer control from one component (the source) to another (the target).

Like the components themselves, the mechanisms vary by the tier upon which the source component executes at runtime. We will likewise divide this section up accordingly and have a subsection devoted to control flow mechanisms that can be initiated from:

- Browser-based components, such as HTML
- Web application server-based components, such as servlets

We deliberately do not include the enterprise tier, not because there are no mechanisms by which control flow is affected, but because they are pure Java method calls.

We will discuss the control flow mechanisms for each of the above in turn.

3.3.1 Browser component initiated control flow

As we discovered in the previous section, all browser-hosted components eventually are converted into HTML (or DHTML and JavaScript). And while there are lots of specific ways to transfer control between Web pages, they boil down to two that we will consider in this section:

- Those that issue HTTP GET requests.
- Those that issue HTTP POST requests.

3.3.1.1 HTTP GETs

An HTTP GET request can be effected in a number of ways:

1. An HREF tag associated with text or an image.

2. Image maps, that allow specific areas of an image to target a given URL when clicked.
3. JavaScript onclick='location=<URL>' associated with a visible and clickable DOM object.
4. A FORM with ACTION=GET and an associated SUBMIT invoked either through an associated INPUT TYPE=SUBMIT button, or a JavaScript submit() action associated with a browser event.

Once the link is established by any of these mechanisms, a user can click the link to transfer control to the next state.

Role in the architecture

HTTP GETs are used when the source state can directly transfer control to another because there are no update side effects, and where a small amount of data needs to be passed to the target. In our online buying application, the following navigations are best handled by HTTP GET requests:

- From the Customer Home to ProductCatalog, OrderDetails and OrderStatus
- From OrderStatus to OrderDetails (a specific order is selected and passed)
- From AlreadyOpen to OrderDetails (also passes the open order)

The online buying application flow STD has been updated to show the HTTP GET transitions graphically. It also shows where the target state is controlled by pure HTML, a JavaServer Pages or a servlet. See Figure 24 on page 82.

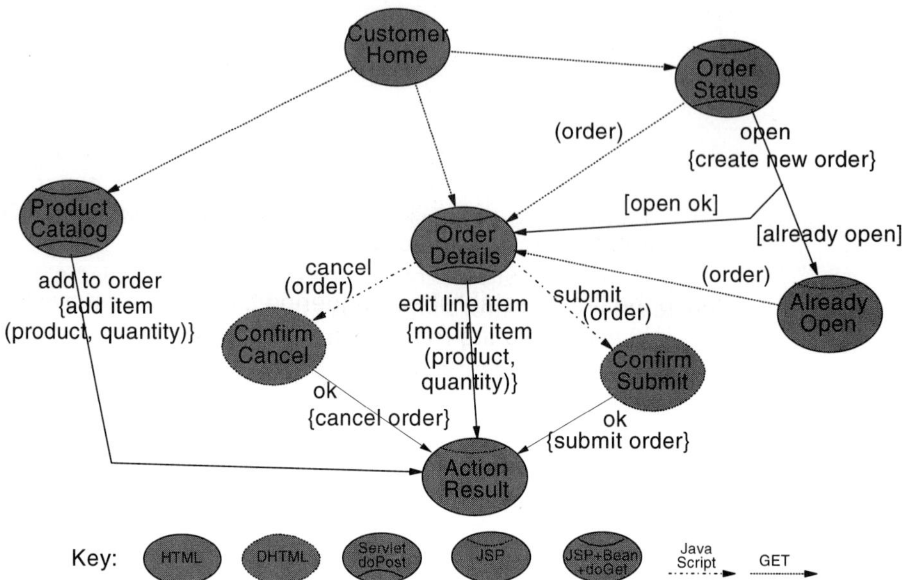

Figure 24. Online buying application STD extended to show transitions controlled by JavaScript and HTTP GET

Pros

Since there is no side effect involved, using HTTP GETs is the most efficient way to transfer control from one state to the next, especially where the next state is pure HTML that may be already cached by the browser.

Pages invoked with an HTTP GET can be easily bookmarked to return to the same page with the same data where dynamic content is involved.

Cons

When using HTTP GETs, the ability to transfer data to the target state is limited to the URL query string (more on this in the next section), which has definite size limitations (often dependent on the Web server handling the request). Also, the location includes the data passed, which can be really distracting.

Alternatives

There is no good substitute for an HTTP GET to transfer control with no side effects, since there is no need to involve an "intermediate" Web application component such as a servlet or JSP. However, you should remember that updating most of the data flow sources can be considered to be a side effect, which may be best handled by some other HTTP request type (such as a POST).

3.3.1.2 HTTP POST (and other method types except for GET)

Unlike HTTP GETs, HTTP POST (and other types) can only be invoked from within a FORM with METHOD=POST. However, once a FORM context has been established, there are two primary mechanisms by which control is actually transferred:

1. Clicking an INPUT TYPE=SUBMIT button associated with the FORM
2. The JavaScript <FORM>.submit() function, usually associated with a button or other clickable type

Once the link is established, triggering the associated event (such as clicking the link) will cause the POST request to be issued to the Web server. Usually, POST requests must be handled by a Web application component, such as a servlet or JSP.

Role in the architecture

HTTP POSTs are best invoked when update side effects are associated with the transition to the next state in the application flow model. In the online buying application flow, the following transitions have update side effects, and thus are best handled by an HTTP POST request:

- Add to order from ProductCatalog to ActionResult
- Cancel from OrderDetails to ActionResult
- Submit from OrderDetails to ActionResult
- Open from OrderStatus to OrderDetails or AlreadyOpen (depends on the result of the open)

The transitions of the online-buying application STD shown in Figure 25 on page 84 have been annotated to show how they are being handled.

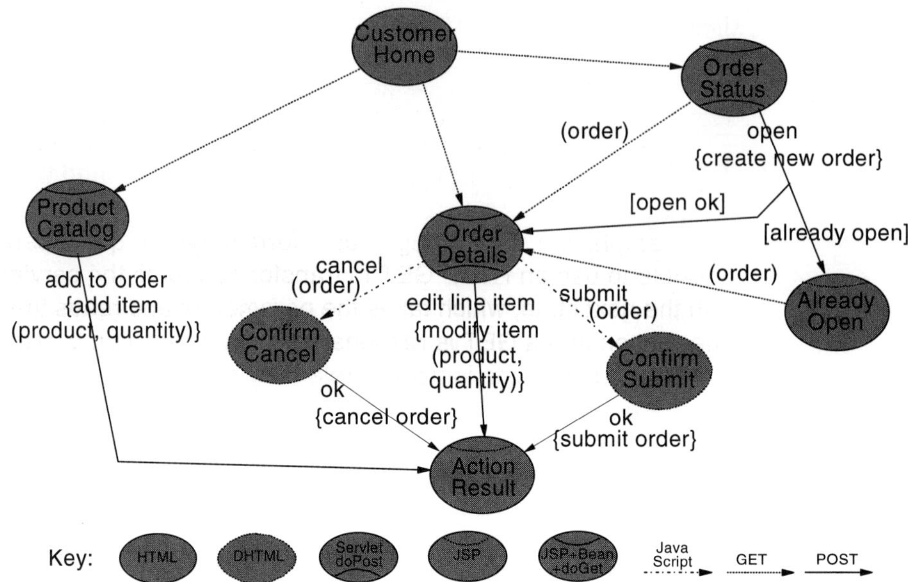

Figure 25. Online buying application STD extended to show transitions controlled by HTTP POST

Pros

One advantage of an HTTP POST is that there are no absolute limits to the amount of data that can be passed to the Web server as part of the request. Also, the data passed does not appear on the location line of the browser.

Another advantage of an HTTP POST is that the browser will warn the user if the request needs to be reinvoked (such as through a resize, back, forward or other browser event that needs the page to be reloaded).

Cons

However, some browsers display a rather ugly message if an HTTP POST request needs to be reinvoked due to a browser event, telling the user to reload the page.

Also, an update side effect is usually expensive, so HTTP POST requests should be minimized by handling as many confirmations and validations as possible on the client side.

Another disadvantage of a POST request is that it cannot be bookmarked because the associated data is not available in the URL query string as mentioned above (more on this in 3.4, "Data flow sources" on page 90). Also, if a servlet receives a POST request, it cannot use the forward mechanism (discussed in the 3.3.2, "Web application server component initiated control flow" on page 85) to transfer control to a static HTML file.

Alternatives

There is really no substitute for an HTTP POST to attempt a transition with an update side effect. However, some transitions that may seem to have a side effect can actually be handled with an HTTP GET.

For example, if a source page has a form to gather query parameters, it is possible to use an HTTP GET to transfer control to the servlet associated with the next state, which takes the parameters and reads the data to display. The reason that a GET is reasonable is that the action is read only and the amount of query data is usually relatively small.

3.3.2 Web application server component initiated control flow

Just as all browser-based components reduce to HTML or DHTML and JavaScript, all Web application server components eventually compile to a servlet and use the Servlet APIs.

We will briefly explore three mechanisms by which servlets can invoke other Web application components:

1. RequestDispatcher forward
2. RequestDispatcher include
3. HttpServletResponse sendRedirect

3.3.2.1 RequestDispatcher forward

The RequestDispatcher is an object that can be obtained from the HttpServlet's context (through the getServletContext() method). The RequestDispatcher allows a target Web application component (HttpServlets and JSPs) to be invoked from a source component in two ways: forward() and include(). We will discuss forward() in this section and include() in the next section.

Role in the architecture

The forward() method is best used when the HttpServlet completely delegates the generation of the response to a JavaServer Page. In our online buying application, the doGet() methods of the ProductCatalog, OrderDetails, and OrderStatus servlets gather the data and forward to the associated JSP to generate the HTML.

Pros
When the forward() call is used, the target has complete freedom to generate the response. For example, it can write headers, or forward() or include() to other Web application components as it sees fit.

This freedom for the target makes programming the source component much simpler: it does not need to generate any headers or set up prior to delegating to the forwarded component.

Cons
A source component that invokes a target cannot generate any response prior to the forward() call. Nor can it generate any response after the call returns. This restriction means you cannot compose pages with forward().

A source component that was itself invoked by an include() call (see 3.3.2.2, "RequestDispatcher include" on page 86) cannot use the forward() call. This restriction means a source component (one that will transfer control to another) has to know how it is being used.

The target component must be a Web application component, requiring that targets of forward() calls must be converted to JSPs, even if they contain purely static HTML.

Alternatives
The most viable alternative to forward() is for a servlet to set up the headers and enclosing HTML tags, then use the include() mechanism (discussed next). This approach provides the ability to compose the response from multiple JSP components with as few changes as possible.

This alternative also simplifies the JSPs involved, since they do not need to generate headers and enclosing HTML tags.

3.3.2.2 RequestDispatcher include
The include() method on the RequestDispatcher neither opens nor closes the response, nor does it write any headers, which means that multiple components can be included in the context of a single request.

Role in the architecture
Rather than use forward() in the ProductCatalog, OrderDetails and OrderStatus servlets doGet() method to transfer control to the associated JSP, it may make sense to include() the associated JSP instead.

Pros

One reason to consider this approach is that the included components are much simpler to code, since they do not need to generate the <HTML>, <HEADER>, and <BODY> tags. For JSPs, the calling servlet can handle the code often required to prevent caching, simplifying them even further.

The included components can often be reused in multiple places. For example, if we were not able to use framesets in our application due to restrictions on the browser, we could convert the CustomerHome.html to a JSP and compose the pages in the servlets:

- The ProductCatalogServlet doGet() would compose CustomerHome.jsp, ActionResult.jsp, and ProductCatalog.jsp
- The OrderDetailsServlet doGet() would compose CustomerHome.jsp, ActionResult.jsp, and OrderDetails.jsp
- The OrderStatusServlet doGet() would compose CustomerHome.jsp, ActionResult.jsp, and OrderStatus.jsp

The components can be included by a superclass HttpServlet to provide a common look and feel across all states in the application. For example, the doGet() method of the OnlineBuyingServlet would include CustomerHome.jsp and ActionResult.jsp, and then call the doGetOnlineBuying() method of the subclass HttpServlet to include the "main area", specifically the JSPs for ProductCatalog, OrderDetails and OrderStatus.

In future versions of WebSphere, included components can be cached, making it much more efficient to compose pages from multiple states. The ability to more easily exploit this feature when it becomes available is another good reason to consider including components.

Cons

Included components cannot write to the header or close out the response. Therefore, these actions must be done by the source component.

Included components cannot be static Web pages (or fragments), requiring that they be converted to JSPs.

Alternatives

When pages need to be composed, there is no really good alternative to include() except to use framesets or named windows (see 3.2.1.3, "Framesets and named windows" on page 37).

3.3.2.3 HttpServletResponse sendRedirect

The sendRedirect() method is implemented on the HttpServletResponse object that is passed in on the service methods associated with an HttpServlet. It generates a special response that is essentially code telling the browser that the requested URL has temporarily moved to another location (the target URL). No other response is generated by the source component.

The browser intercepts the response and invokes an HTTP GET request to the URL returned as part of the response, effectively causing a transition to the next state.

Role in the architecture

The sendRedirect() method is best used in a servlet after actions that cause update side effects to cause transition to the next state. In our online buying application, the following transitions in the application flow model trigger transitions on the Entry state in the underlying business process model:

- The add to order transition out of the ProductCatalog state triggers the add line item transition on the Customer's open order, completing with a sendRedirect to the ActionResult state to display the result.
- The submit and cancel transitions out of the OrderDetails state trigger the corresponding transaction on the Customer's open order, completing with a sendRedirect to the ActionResult state to display the result.
- The edit line item transition out of OrderDetails triggers the modify line item transition on the Customer's open order, completing with a sendRedirect to the ActionResult state to display the result.
- The open transition out of the OrderStatus state triggers the create new order transition, completing with a sendRedirect to the OrderDetails state for the new order to be successfully created, or to the AlreadyOpen state if an open order already exists for the Customer.

These actions are handled by the doPost() method of the associated servlets, as illustrated in Figure 26 on page 89

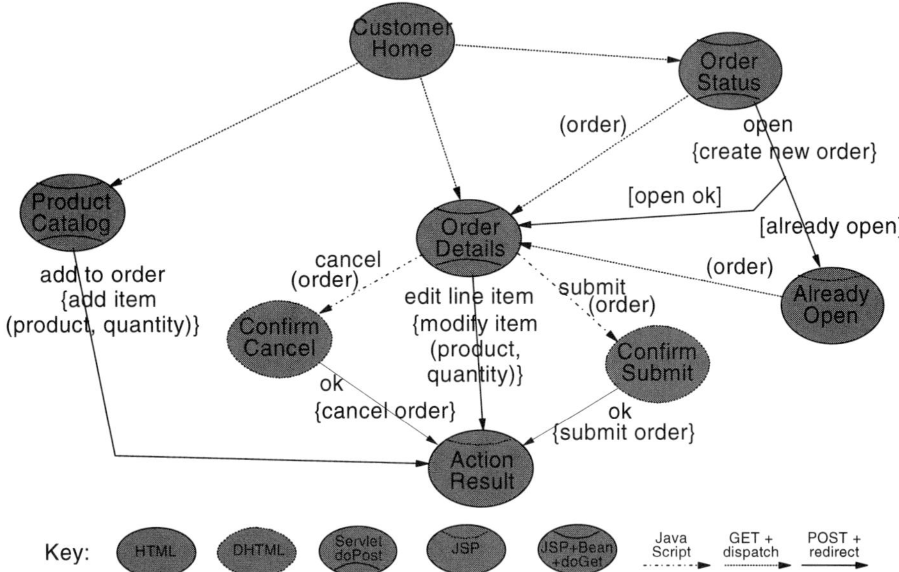

Figure 26. Online buying application STD extended to show dispatches and redirects

Pros

One benefit of using sendRedirect() is that it prevents inadvertent re-execution of the side effects based on such browser events as forward, back, resize, print, view source, or reload among others (this unfortunate effect is sometimes called the reload problem).

The reason sendRedirect() solves this problem is another advantage: the URL for the update never appears in the browser's location line or history. The effect is that only the URLs of the "states" in the application flow model appear in the location and history, which is exactly the behavior desired.

Cons

The one disadvantage of sendRedirect() is that it causes an extra round-trip between the browser and Web application server. Luckily, this extra round-trip only occurs during major transitions in the application flow model, and is well worth it, since sendRedirect() solves a major source of data integrity errors in Web applications.

Alternatives

There are no good alternatives to using a sendRedirect() after processing requests in servlets that require update side effects.

3.4 Data flow sources

Whenever two components must interact, whether they are separately developed components, or whether a single component is iteratively executed over time, it is likely that there will be a need to flow data from one to the other.

Like the first two sections, this section is divided into subsections describing data sources associated with each of the three tiers:

- Browser
- Web application server
- Enterprise servers

And as with control flow mechanisms, we show how the choice of data source can have a huge impact on the overall performance and integrity of the application.

3.4.1 Browser-maintained data flow sources

There are a number of browser-maintained data sources that we will discuss in this section:

- URL query string
- POST data
- Cookies

All of these sources provide the best scalability characteristics (since the data is maintained on the client), but with a trade-off that they may not be completely reliable (since the user has control over the data source).

The discussion in this section will address the details of these and other trade-offs.

3.4.1.1 URL query string

Whenever an HTTP GET is invoked, data can be passed in the *query string* part of the target URL. This includes FORM data (hidden or otherwise) when METHOD=GET.

In any event, the query string syntax is:

```
?<name>=<value>{&<name>=<value>}
```

Neither the names nor values can have embedded spaces; instead spaces and other special characters must be encoded.

The values can be retrieved through various methods associated with the HttpServletRequest object, most notably getParameter(), which returns the value for a given name.

Role in the architecture

The most obvious place to use the query string in the online-buying application flow model is where data is being passed from one state to the next along a transition without side effects. For example an order ID is passed:

- From OrderStatus to OrderDetails when an order is selected
- From AlreadyOpen to OrderDetails, for the button providing navigation

But another place to use the query string is in the various sendRedirect() calls after update side effects:

- To flow the order number from OrderStatus to OrderDetails when open action is successful
- To flow the order number from OrderStatus to AlreadyOpen when the open fails because one is already open
- To flow the result message from ProductCatalog or OrderDetails to ActionResult to show the result of the action

Another use for a URL query string is URL encoding of the session ID for HttpSession on the Web server (see 3.4.2.2, "HttpSession state" on page 96) instead of cookies (discussed later in this section).

Pros

The benefit of using the query string is that it is very simple to retrieve the associated data.

Cons

There are some downsides to using the query string to pass data from the browser to Web application components:

- Encoding the URL query string in sendRedirect() calls and generated HREFs can be quite complicated
- Only a small amount of data can be passed
- The query string is visible on the location line, and can sometimes be very long and confusing to look at
- This visibility in the query string extends to hidden fields in forms (when METHOD=GET)

Alternatives

There is no good substitute for the URL query string to send a few small key values to the target component. However, where the data is common across most states in the application flow, it may be better to use cookies or HTTP sessions (both discussed later) to make the data flow transparent to the programs.

3.4.1.2 POST data

When an HTTP POST is invoked from an HTML FORM with METHOD=POST, the input fields in the form are passed as part of an encoded input stream to the HttpServlet. The HttpServletRequest can be used to access the fields in two ways: directly from the stream, or through the getParameter() methods as if they were part of the URL query string (even though they are not).

Role in the architecture

Where we will use POST data in the online buying application flow model is to pass data to the HttpServlet handling an action. Specifically, we will use POST data to pass:

- ProductID and quantity, for the add to order transition out of ProductCatalog
- Order, to the submit and cancel transitions out of OrderDetails
- Order, product and quantity, to the edit line item transition out of OrderDetails

Pros

As with the URL query string, one benefit to using POST data is that it is easy to retrieve, either by name or iteratively.

However, unlike the URL query string, the main benefit to using POST data is that there is no absolute limit to the amount of data that can be sent.

Finally, the data passed does not clutter up the URL, so hidden fields remain hidden to the casual user, and the encoding of the data is transparent to the source component.

Alternatives

As with the URL query string, there is no good substitute to POST data to provide the input parameters to actions with update side effects. However, where hidden fields are used to provide common data across the entire browser session, it may be wise to consider using cookies or HTTP sessions.

3.4.1.3 Cookies

Cookies are data maintained on the client by the browser on behalf of the server. Cookies can be made to persist within or across browser sessions. Cookies are passed to the Web server in the header of the request. Any updates are passed back on the header in the response.

Within the Servlet API, there are methods that allow you to get and set cookies.

Role in the architecture

Cookies are the preferred way to pass a HttpSession ID, if any, to the Web application server. The same approach can be used for other data that is constant across the Web application. For example, in our online buying application it might make sense to store the customer ID in a cookie to eliminate having to use URL encoding or hidden fields.

Cookies are an excellent way to store a small amount of user preference data. For example, it may be desirable to tailor the ProductCatalog list by Customer based on the past history of visits to the site. In this case, we might maintain a persistent cookie with the last query used to select products.

Pros

Cookies are automatically passed in the header, and thus do not require explicitly coding hidden fields or URL query strings in the HTML and JSPs. This feature of cookies makes the application much simpler to develop, test, and maintain.

The ability to maintain persistent cookies means that the client machines can be enlisted to help share the cost of running the application. In an e-business application with millions of users, not having to maintain often used preference data for each one can be a significant savings in both space needed to store it and time needed to retrieve it.

Cons

Passing cookies back and forth can be relatively expensive. Further, the amount of data that can be maintained per server may be limited by the browser. The effect is that cookies should be used sparingly.

Another problem is that not all browsers or levels of browsers support cookies. Even if they are supported, users can turn cookies off as a security or privacy measure, which means that either:

- Your Web application will need to be coded for the case where cookies are not available, and use alternative techniques (discussed below); or,

- You must make an explicit decision to support only users with browsers having cookies enabled.

Also, other HTTP-based clients, such as applets, may have trouble dealing with cookies, restricting the servlets that they may invoke.

Alternatives

URL encoding techniques can be used to put the equivalent data in the URL query string rather than relying on cookies.

3.4.2 Web application server maintained data flow sources

There are three main sources of data maintained by the WebSphere:

- HttpServletRequest attributes
- HttpSession state
- ServletContext attributes

All these sources share a characteristic not associated with the other ones: only a Web application component (servlet or JSP) can store or retrieve data using them.

We discuss the advantages and disadvantages of each in the context of the role that source should play in the architecture. We also discuss any alternatives.

3.4.2.1 HttpServletRequest attributes

HttpServletRequest attributes (or more simply, request attributes) are maintained by the Web application server for the duration of the request in what amounts to an internal Hashtable.

The HttpServletRequest interface has methods to set and get the attribute values by name. You can also retrieve a list (Enumeration) of all the attribute names currently maintained in the request.

A JSP can use the expression syntax or Java escape tags to get request attributes using the Servlet API, or it can use a bean tag scoped to the request (the default) with introspection to automatically load attributes whose names match the bean properties.

Role in the architecture

The most prevalent purpose of request attributes is for maintaining the data bean passed to a JSP by the servlet doGet() method handling the display of a state. Specifically:

- ProductCatalogServlet loads ProductCatalogData, sets it into the "ProductCatalog" request attribute, and dispatches to the ProductCatalog.jsp, which uses the bean tag to access the ProductCatalogData during generation of the response
- OrderDetailsServlet loads OrderDetailsData, sets it into the "OrderDetails" request attribute, and dispatches to the OrderDetails.jsp, which uses the bean tag to access the OrderDetailsData during generation of the response
- OrderStatusServlet loads OrderStatusData, sets it into the "OrderStatus" request attribute, and dispatches to the OrderStatus.jsp, which uses the bean tag to access the OrderStatusData during generation of the response

The point here is that by having a systematic naming convention, the contract between the servlet and JSP developer roles is very clear.

Pros

Of all the data sources, whether maintained by the browser, Web application server, or enterprise servers, HttpRequestAttributes are the second most efficient (behind passing the data directly in parameters of a method or in a shared variable).

Since its scope is limited to the request, there is no need to write logic to "clean up" the data.

Cons

Setting too many objects into request attributes can cause problems with:

- The contract between the source and target component developers. For example, what do you name the attributes? What is their type? Our sample application servlets never set more than one attribute with a well-defined name and type (based on the state name "root").
- Performance, because each set is a Hashtable put and each get is a Hashtable lookup. Our sample application does only one put and lookup of a Java Bean, after which it employs much more efficient property operators.

The HttpServletRequest object does not persist across calls, so it cannot be used to hold data between states in the application flow model. The net effect is that request attributes can be passed only to targets using forward(0 and include(). Request attributes cannot be passed to targets invoked through sendRedirect().

Alternatives

When using forward() or include() to dispatch to an associated JSP, a controlling servlet can pass data through HttpSession and ServletContext.

When invoking a JSP or servlet through the sendRedirect(), data can be passed using cookies or the URL query string.

3.4.2.2 HttpSession state

An HTTP session is a short term (transient) relationship established between a client browser and a Web application server through which data can be maintained. It "lives" as long as both the client and the server maintain the reference to the relationship.

HttpSession state (in this section simply session state) is maintained by the Web application server for the lifetime of the session in what is basically a Hashtable of Hashtables, the "outer" one keyed by the session ID (the session Hashtable) and the "inner" one keyed by the state variable name (the state Hashtable).

When the session is created, the ID is passed back and forth to the browser through a cookie (the preferred approach) or URL encoding.

The session is effective as long as both:

- The browser stays up to maintain the session ID cookie (or the pages with the ID encoded in the URLs), and
- WebSphere maintains the state Hashtable for the session

The outer session Hashtable can be lost if the Web application server goes down (and the session is not backed up). The inner state Hashtable can be lost on a timeout or through explicit application events (the remove() method, for example).

The HttpServletRequest interface has methods to get the session (optionally causing it to create a new one if none exists), which returns a reference to the HttpSession object. Once you have a reference to the session, you can get and set state values by name. You can also retrieve a list (Enumeration) of all the state names currently maintained in the session.

A JSP can use the expression syntax or Java escape tags to get session state using the Servlet API, or it can use a Bean tag scoped to session with introspection to automatically load states whose names match the bean properties.

Role in the architecture

Many Web applications handle login explicitly as part of the application flow, rather than use the security mechanism provided by the Web Apoplication Server.

In this case it is customary to store some sort of "login" token into the session state. The session state maintained could be as simple as a customerID, or it could be a complex object that includes additional data common to all the states in the application flow, such as open order. This extra data could be used as a default in the following cases to eliminate the need to access the back end:

- In the add to order transition of the ProductCatalog state, the order ID defaults to the open Order (creating a new one if none exists)
- Even though the transitions from OrderStatus and AlreadyOpen to OrderDetails pass the selected order ID to display, the transition from the CustomerHome state does not, defaulting to the open order

The data gathered in each of the three "main" states (ProductCatalog, OrderDetails and OrderStatus) could be stored in session state so that repeated reloads of that page for such browser events as resize do not cause the back-end access to read the data again (see the discussion about the reload problem in 3.3.2.3, "HttpServletResponse sendRedirect" on page 88).

Pros

Session state is rather easy to use in the program (especially if a data structure Java Bean is stored instead of individual values). The Web application server manages it at runtime based on configuration parameters, making it easy to tune non-functional characteristics such as failover and performance. This ease of use makes it tempting to store some application flow data (the current open order for example) in the session state rather than in a database that has to be explicitly administered.

When the data is already being stored in the back end, and when accesses are expensive, the performance gains of using session state to cache the data can be significant.

Cons

Session state suffers from the same problems that request attributes do if you store too many objects in them in the course of a single request: there is a name and type contract problem with the target component, and a performance penalty with every additional Hashtable put and lookup.

Session state has some additional disadvantages:

1. Timeout. A session can time out when you least expect, making it risky to store significant application flow data. How would the user react if the line items in an open order were lost because of a bathroom break during the session? Usually you end up explicitly modeling and programming "save" and "load" type flows to make the problem less acute.
2. Server failure. Even if you have an infinitely long timeout (and expect servlets to programmatically invalidate the session state), the server can fail, causing the data to be lost. Specifying that a session state be backed up in a database gets around this, and provides for failover.
3. Cache consistency. When a session state is used to cache back-end data, how do you make sure the session state is in synch with the data stored in the back-end system, for example when a new order is selected or when there are update transitions that affect the cached data? To provide for cache consistency means adding code to the doGet() methods to check the key of the data in a session state with that in the request, and adding code to the doPost() methods to remove the affected session states.
4. Cluster consistency. It is likely that you will want to scale the Web site by adding a cluster of WebSphere application servers. Even if you add all of the extra logic to manage cache consistency from the previous item, you must either force client/server affinity (see 3.2.3.2, "Stateful session EJBs" on page 68) and lose failover support, or back the session up in a shared database and impact performance.

Of course, the memory resources required for session state should be taken into consideration. Indiscriminate use of HttpSession can use up vast amounts of data. For example, if there were 1000 active user sessions each needing to maintain a megabyte of data, your application would use up a gigabyte of memory for the session state alone.

Alternatives

When a session state is used to cache data stored in back-end servers, a viable alternative is to delegate caching to access beans or even EJBs, keeping the application flow logic in the servlet clean and simple. Another advantage to this approach is that the access beans are best able to keep the cache consistent because of their knowledge of the business logic.

If you use WebSphere security so that the getRemoteUser() method on the HttpServletRequest returns an authenticated user ID, you can avoid the use of HttpSession altogether by keying explicitly modeled business objects with this user ID. The development costs of explicitly modeling session as a business object may be worth it in the ability to use that data by other types of applications (client server or distributed object as the case may be). Of course the primary benefit of eliminating the use of session state is that the application will scale much better, since client-server affinity is not required between the browser and Web application server.

If security is not turned on (maybe the application does not require it), and there is only a small amount of data to be stored, you can use cookies as described above, with the advantage that the client maintains the data.

However, there is no good substitute for HttpSession in scenarios with relatively small amounts of data that are relatively stable and must be maintained on the Web application server for security purposes, such as a login token.

3.4.2.3 Servlet context cache

The Web application server provides a context within which properties can be shared by all servlets and JSPs within that scope. This context is commonly called the "servlet context" and is accessible through the getServletContext() method on the Servlet API.

Servlet context is used to obtain a RequestDispatcher through which forward() and include() can be invoked to flow control from one component to another (see 3.3.2, "Web application server component initiated control flow" on page 85).

Like request attributes and session state, servlet context also maintains an object that is the equivalent of a Hashtable, providing methods to get and set attributes by name as well as list the names stored within.

Unlike request attributes, which are scoped to a request, and session state, which is scoped to a session, servlet context is scoped by a Web application.

And unlike HttpSession, the current specification explicitly states that sharing of servlet context in a cluster is unsupported.

Role in the architecture

One possible use of servlet context in our online-buying application is to store the ProductCatalog data, since it is stable and read-only in this application, and the same data can be used by all Customers.

Another interesting use of servlet context in our application is to cache references to business logic access beans (even if they are singleton wrappers).

If used for either purpose, we would likely set attributes into the servlet context as part of the init() method in the ProductCatalogServlet and

OrderDetailsServlet, which would allow both servlets to use the catalog for validation of product IDs and display without having to access the back end.

Pros
Proper use of servlet context can greatly reduce both the amount of session state data and the number of back-end accesses required to load it. For example, if the product catalog data were stored in a session state, there would be one copy of the catalog per user, with a back-end access required for each user to load the data.

As with session state, servlet context is very easy to deal with, and can eliminate the need to explicitly model extra business objects.

Since servlet context attributes cannot be shared in a cluster, there is no requirement that data stored therein be serializable. This allows servlet context to be used to store very complex objects, such as access beans (preferred) or EJB references.

Also, storing singleton references in a servlet context can prevent them from being garbage collected, since the reference is maintained for the life of the Web application server.

Cons
Also as with session state (and request attributes), you should minimize the number of attributes stored, and make sure that there is a systematic name and type convention in place.

Unlike HttpSession, the specification prohibits sharing of servlet context in a cluster, primarily to force its use as a true cache. This limitation is not really a disadvantage when servlet context is used as a cache for stable read-only data, since each application server will perform better having its own copy of the data in memory.

If for some reason there is a requirement to store common data, yet allow updates to it, then client/server affinity must be used to prevent cluster consistency issues. Of course, this means that the updates have to be associated with a specific user. Also, since the servlet context is shared by the entire Web application, you have to be careful to manage the code carefully, since multiple servlet threads could be accessing the same attributes simultaneously.

Alternatives
Where servlet context is being used to store data from the back end to avoid extraneous accesses (a caching pattern), an alternative is to delegate

caching the data to the business logic access bean. This alternative was also discussed in 3.4.2.2, “HttpSession state” on page 96.

Where the default servlet context is accessed (the parameterless version of the API), then a viable alternative is to use the singleton pattern.

These alternatives do not supersede the advantages of storing business logic access beans or connection objects in a servlet context to hold a reference and prevent garbage collection.

3.4.3 Enterprise server-maintained data sources

Of course, there are many enterprise server-maintained data flow sources provided by and fully supported by IBM, such as CICS, IMS, and MQ. But in a discussion of the WebSphere programming model, we are only concerned with those that use standard Java APIs to provide access to the data or function maintained:

- Java Naming and Directory Interface (JNDI)
- JDBC

What separates these data sources from the others is that they can be used outside the context of a Web application server.

3.4.3.1 Java Naming and Directory Interface (JNDI)

JNDI provides a name value pair oriented interface very much like the Web application server-maintained data flow sources (request attributes, session state and servlet context cache).

The primary difference is that the JNDI name context is managed by a distributed name server, which allows the names and values to be shared across requests, sessions, application servers, and a cluster.

There are three types of objects that can be maintained in JNDI:

- Simple serializable Java Beans.
- Distributed object references, such as EJB homes and remote interfaces.
- Common object services, such as transaction contexts.

The JNDI implementation provided in WebSphere Application Server V3.5 caches home references after lookup, providing for additional scalability in a multi-user distributed environment.

Role in the architecture

One common use of JNDI in an application is to maintain user preference data, including credentials that aid in authentication.

In our Web application, JNDI would be used by business logic and business object access beans to get access to the Home for the OrderEntry session EJB, and the Customer, Order, OrderLineItem and Product entity EJBs.

Pros

The benefit to using JNDI is that is designed for storing small to medium amounts of relatively stable data per name, without requiring the involvement of a database administrator to create and maintain a new table.

The fact that JNDI is distributable, sharable, and persistable makes it applicable in Web application scenarios where the other data flow sources cannot be used.

Cons

JNDI accesses are relatively expensive even with the automated caching support provided by WebSphere Application Server V3.5. Therefore, calls to them should be limited using the techniques discussed in 3.2.3.1, "Stateless session EJBs" on page 64. This approach will make it easier to port to competitive products without having to worry about their implementation.

Updates are even more expensive, so only relatively stable data should be stored in JNDI name contexts. The pattern is write once, read many. For example, User preference data fits into this category, but Customer data, with its reference to the currently open order, does not.

Alternatives

You can always explicitly model the data stored in JNDI as a business object and use either JDBC or EJBs (preferably behind an access bean).

3.4.3.2 JDBC

JDBC provides a Java interface to relational databases, allowing dynamic SQL statements to be created, prepared, and executed against pooled database connections.

Any database that supports relational semantics can be wrapped with the JDBC interfaces and provide a "driver" for use in the client application or creating a data source.

Role in the architecture

In our online buying application, we would use JDBC to implement the business object access beans in cases where performance is crucial. For example, the submit method needs to take the line items associated from the specified order in the entry table and copy them into the fulfillment table (with a zero shipped quantity).

Another example of when we might use JDBC is in loading the product catalog into the cache (distributed object overhead may be considered to be excessive for the benefits achieved).

Pros

JDBC provides all the benefits of relational databases to Java applications in an implementation-independent manner.

Directly using JDBC in a client application will likely provide the most efficient implementation of the application, especially if connection pooling of data sources is used.

Cons

JDBC client code can be rather complicated to develop properly. Minimizing the number of statements executed in the course of a unit of work is key.

Also, explicitly managing the transaction context can be complicated. If auto commit is turned off, care must be taken in the program code to commit or rollback the transaction as appropriate. If auto commit is left on, care must be taken when there are multiple statements in a single unit of work: each statement is a separate transaction, which can cause significant extra overhead and complicate error handling logic.

Directly using JDBC locks your application into relational technology, although wrapping it within a business object access bean can help insulate the client application code, and make it easier to migrate later.

Even if wrappers are used, JDBC requires that a JDBC driver be installed on the application server, potentially making it a “thicker” client that it would be if EJBs were used.

Alternatives

The best standards-based alternative to JDBC is to use EJBs, which makes persistency transparent to the business object programming model, and allows the client to be “thinner”.

Of course, you can use non-standard connector-based technology such as CICS, MQ, and IMS. But whether behind wrappers or not, these connectors make the client even thicker by requiring additional software to be installed.

3.5 Chapter summary

We showed how dividing the programming model into its three fundamental features makes it easier to understand the issues that you will face when developing a WebSphere V3.5-based application. We will summarize these aspects in this section.

Throughout this chapter, we applied the programming model aspects to an online buying application to provide a concrete example. We will briefly summarize the mapping in this section as well, and show how the WebSphere programming model meets the challenges outlined in the chapter introduction.

3.5.1 Summary of programming model aspects

Table 2 shows the various features of the WebSphere programming model at a glance.

Table 2. WebSphere programming model features

	Browser	**Web Application Server**	**Enterprise Server**
Component	HTML, DHTML and JavaScripts, XML, framesets	Servlets, JavaServer Pages, Java Beans	Session and Entity Enterprise JavaBeans
Control flow mechanism	HTTP (GET & POST)	Java (forward, include, sendRedirect)	Java (RMI/IIOP)
Data flow source	URL query string, POST data, cookies	Request attributes, session state, servlet context	JNDI, JDBC

Table 3, Table 4 on page 106, and Table 5 on page 106 summarize the details of the components, control flow mechanisms and data flow sources.

Table 3. Programming model components

Component	Tiers	Role in architecture
HTML	Browser	Specifies page content associated with a given state in the application flow model
DHTML and JavaScript	Browser	Handles client-side validations, confirmations, cascading menus, list processing and so on to minimize requests to Web server
Frameset and Named Windows	Browser	Groups related states on a single page to allow for smaller, more parallel requests and minimize need for explicit navigations
XML, DTD, and XSL	Browser	Allows request results to consist of data only and provide client control of display format
Servlet	Web application	Controls application flow for a given state; Inherits common look and feel from superclass HttpServlet
JavaServer Pages	Web application	Handles generation of HTML/DHTML/XML for a given state in an application flow model
Data structure Java Bean	Java application	Serializable data passed between the other components such as servlets and JSPs/access beans, EJBs and copy helpers, etc.
Business logic access bean	Java application	Wrapper encapsulating units of work (can be equated with transitions in the business process model); can be stateless or stateful
Business object access bean	Java application	Wrapper encapsulating persistent business objects (can be identified by object model associated with states in the business process model)
Stateless session EJB	Enterprise Java server	Distributable implementation of stateless units of work (analogous to business logic access bean)
Stateful session EJB	Enterprise Java server	Distributable implementation of stateful units of work that cache resources or data on behalf of a user for the duration of a session
Session synchronization	Enterprise Java server	Methods added at deployment time to allow session EJBs to support transparent transactional semantics in business methods
CMP entity EJB	Enterprise Java server	Distributable implementation of persistence layer and associated business logic (analogous to business object access bean)
BMP entity EJB	Enterprise Java server	Methods added at deployment time to allow entity EJBs to control quality of persistence service

Table 4. Control flow mechanisms

Mechanism	Source Components	Target Components	Role in architecture
HTTP GET	HTML or DHTML	Any URL	Directly invoke the target URL associated with the next state, invoking a servlet or JSP for dynamic content
HTTP POST	HTML FORM	Servlet	Invokes the target servlet indicated in the ACTION to handle update side effects
Dispatcher forward	Servlet doGet()	JSP	Delegate the generation of the HTTP response to the target JSP
Dispatcher include	Servlet doGet()	JSP	Compose the response from one or more target JSPs that generate response fragments
Response sendRedirect	Servlet doPost()	Any URL	Transfer control to the target URL representing the next state based on the ACTION result

Table 5. Data flow sources

Data flow source	Managed by	Control flow mechanism	Role in architecture
URL query string	Browser	HTTP GET sendRedirect	Pass small amounts of "key" data used to drive queries in doGet of the servlet associated with the target state
POST data	Browser	HTTP POST	Pass input data used to drive updates in the doPost of the servlet associated with the current state
Cookie	Browser	Any	Maintain data common to the user or session used to drive queries or updates in any state
HttpRequest attribute	Web application server (WebSphere)	Dispatcher forward and include	Pass data representing the dynamic content between the controlling servlet and the associated JSP used to generate the response
HttpSession state	Web application server (WebSphere)	Any	Maintain stable data common to the session used to drive queries or updates in any state where cookies are not feasible
ServletContext cache	Web application server (WebSphere)	Any	Maintain a cache of stable read-only data accessible for all requests on a single server to drive queries or updates in any state

Data flow source	Managed by	Control flow mechanism	Role in architecture
JNDI	Name server (WebSphere)	Any	Maintain small amounts stable data accessible to all servers
JDBC	Database server	Any	Maintain any amount of any type of data accessible for any request

3.5.2 Applying the programming model to our sample application

Taking the business process flow model of our online buying application from the introduction, here is a reasonable mapping of the Order Entry state and associated static objects to the programming model components, control flow mechanisms and data sources summarized above.

3.5.2.1 Order Entry

This state has the following components:

1. OrderEntryAccess, a singleton business logic access bean whose methods pass through to an OrderEntry created by an OrderEntryHome cached in the constructor, and removed when the method is complete.
2. OrderEntryHome, an EJB home allowing an OrderEntry session EJB to be created.
3. OrderEntry, a stateless session EJB with the following methods:
   - createOrder(customerID), which uses CustomerAccess to get an orderID, for the customerID, and if not already open, uses OrderAccess to create a new one with status set to "Opened" for the customerID and return the order ID
   - addLineItem(customerID, productID, quantity), which uses CustomerAccess to get the open order for the customerID (creating one if necessary), and LineItemAccess to increment the quantity of the productID specified (creating a new one if necessary)
   - modifyLineItem(customerID, orderID, productID, quantity), which uses OrderAccess to check that the resulting order is "Opened", and LineItemAccess to set the quantity of the productID specified (creating a new one if necessary)
   - submit(customerID, orderID), which uses OrderAccess to set the status of the order specified to "Submitted" if still "Opened"
   - cancel(customerID, orderID), which uses OrderAccess to set the status of the order specified to "Cancelled" if still "Opened"

- getProducts(customerID), which uses ProductAccess to get a ProductData array, the list of products that may be ordered by the customer
- getOrders(customerID), which uses OrderAccess to get OrderData, the list of orders associated with the customer
- getOrderDetails(customerID, orderID), which uses:
  • CustomerAccess, if no order is passed in, to get the open order for the customer
  • OrderAccess to get the status of the resulting order
  • LineItemAccess to get LineItemData, the list of line items associated with the order, returning an OrderDetailsData

Figure 27 shows this description graphically.

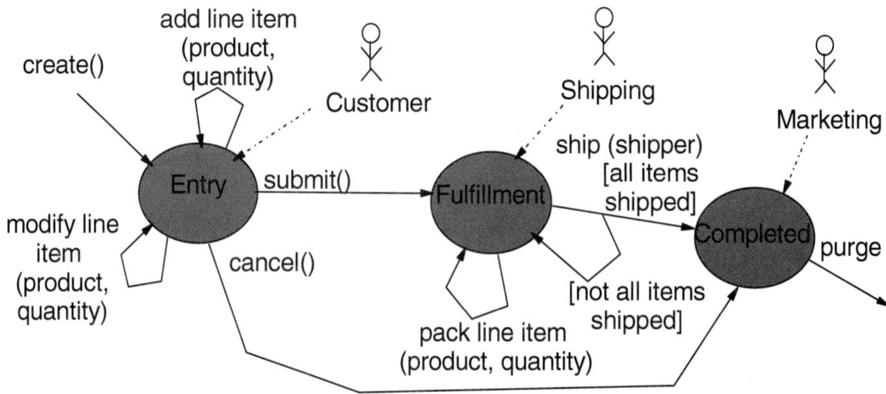

Figure 27. Business logic access beans and stateless session EJBs derived from business process model

Note: add Customer and Order to every transition to derive method signatures.

The details of the read-only methods and business object related components described above are shown graphically in Figure 28 on page 109.

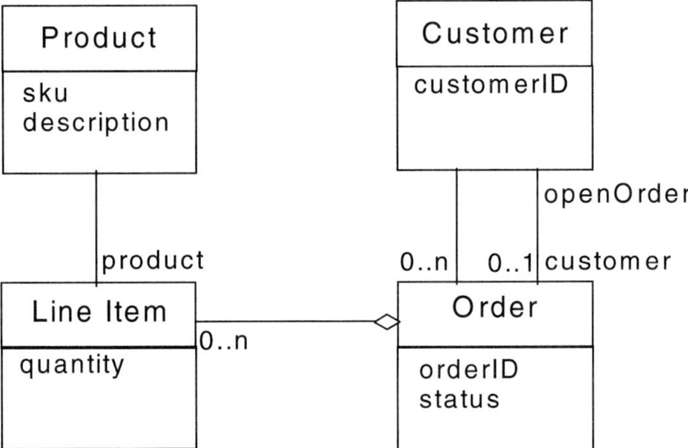

Figure 28. Static object model of Order in Entry state driving read-only calls

Taking the application flow model from the introduction, here is a reasonable mapping of the states to the programming model components, control flow mechanisms and data sources summarized above associated with the browser and Web application server tiers.

3.5.2.2 Customer Home

This state maps to a CustomerHome.html, with buttons linking to ProductCatalogServlet, OrderDetailsServlet and OrderStatusServlet.

3.5.2.3 Product Catalog

This state maps to the following three components:

- ProductCatalogServlet, with the following methods:
  - doGet():
    - Loads ProductCatalogData from OrderEntryAccess
    - Sets it as “ProductCatalog” into the request
    - Includes ProductCatalog.jsp
  - doPost(), with a branch looking for the action add to order that:
    - Gets the productID and quantity parameters from the request,
    - Adds the specified quantity of the product to the open order using OrderEntryAccess, and
    - Does a sendRedirect to the ActionResult.jsp with the result of the add passed in the URL query string

- ProductCatalogData, which has a products property, which is an array of ProductData (with sku and description properties)
- ProductCatalog.jsp, which generates the table of ProductData (and a modifiable quantity input field) from the products property in ProductCatalogData accessed using the bean tags

3.5.2.4 Order Details

This state maps to the following three components:

- OrderDetailsServlet, with methods:
  - doGet():
    - Gets the order from the request (if specified)
    - Loads OrderDetailsData for the order from OrderEntryAccess
    - Sets it as "OrderDetails" into the request
    - Includes OrderDetails.jsp
  - doPost(), with branches looking for the action:
    - modify line item that:
      a. Gets the order, productID and quantity parameters from the request
      b. Modifies the line item in the specified order to have the specified quantity of the product using OrderEntryAccess
      c. Does a sendRedirect to the ActionResult.jsp with the result of the modify passed in the URL query string
    - submit that:
      a. Gets the order parameter from the request
      b. Submits the specified order using OrderEntryAccess
      c. Does a sendRedirect to the ActionResult.jsp with the result of the modify passed in the URL query string
    - cancel that:
      a. Gets the order parameter from the request
      b. Cancels the specified order using OrderEntryAccess
      c. Does a sendRedirect to the ActionResult.jsp with the result of the modify passed in the URL query string
- OrderDetailsData, which has an items property which is an array of LineItemData (with productID, description and quantity properties)

- OrderDetails.jsp, which generates the table of LineItemData from the items property in OrderDetailsData (with quantity as a modifiable field defaulted from the data) accessed using the bean tags

3.5.2.5 *Order Status*

This state maps to the following three components:

- OrderStatusServlet, with methods:
  - doGet():
    - Gets the customer from the request
    - Loads OrderStatusData for the customer from OrderEntryAccess
    - Sets it as "OrderStatus" into the request
    - Includes OrderStatus.jsp
  - doPost(), with a branch looking for the action open that:
    - Gets the customer from the request
    - Opens a new order using OrderEntryAccess
    - Does a sendRedirect to the OrderDetailsServlet with the order returned by the open if successful, or AlreadyOpen.jsp with the order returned by open if already open; in either case, the order is passed in the URL query string
- OrderStatusData, which has an orders property, an array of OrderData (with orderID and status properties)
- OrderStatus.jsp, which generates the table of OrderData from the orders property in OrderStatusData accessed using the bean tags with buttons referencing OrderDetailsServlet with the selected order in the URL query string

3.5.2.6 *Already Open*

This state maps to AlreadyOpen.jsp, which displays a message indicating that the order found in the request parameters is already open, and provides a button referencing OrderDetailsServlet with the selected order in the URL query string.

3.5.2.7 Action Result

This state maps to ActionResult.jsp, which simply displays the result found in the request parameters.

Figure 29 on page 112 shows this mapping graphically:

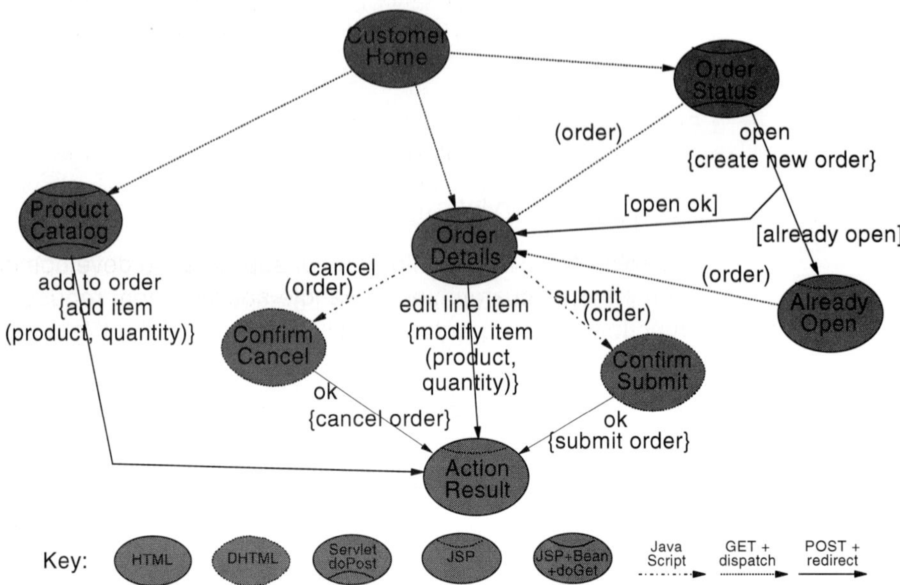

Figure 29. Online buying application STD extended to show programming mode features

The details of the data structure Java Beans described above are shown graphically in Figure 30.

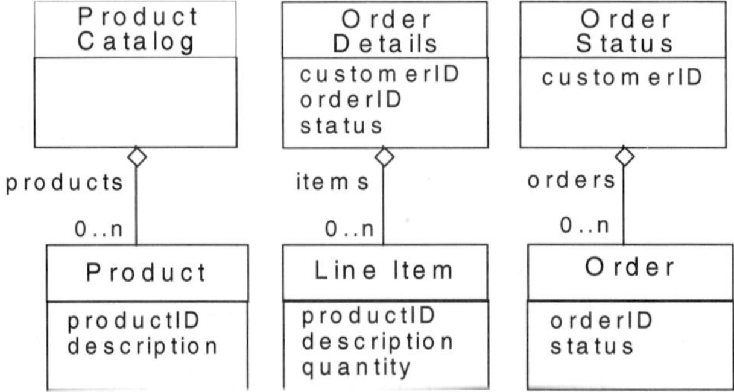

Figure 30. Data structure Java Beans derived from application flow static object model

3.5.3 Meeting the challenges

The WebSphere programming model is compelling because with it you can meet all the challenges associated with developing a quality application that we identified in the chapter introduction:

- Functional - the WebSphere programming model features support everything you need to develop Web-enabled and distributed object applications
- Reliable - by following the approaches discussed in this chapter, you can change the deployment characteristics of WebSphere hosted applications to handle different operational environments without changing the programs
- Usable - the programming model supports the development of components customized to handle specific client requests for application functions that are automatically launched by the WebSphere Application Server
- Efficient - the programming model features have clearly defined trade-offs that govern when they best apply to maximize use of system resources
- Maintainable - the programming model supports a separation of concerns that make it easy to independently develop, test, and modify components
- Portable - the features of the programming model are based on Java standards that make it easy to deploy application components on different platforms without change

Furthermore, the programming model helps you meet the challenges associated with defining an optimal development process:

- Repeatable - analysis, architecture and design, relatively standard steps found in many development processes can be followed to develop quality WebSphere-based applications.
- Measurable - following the analysis, architecture and design steps results in a well defined number of servlets, JSPs, Java Beans and Enterprise JavaBeans.
- Toolable - the systematic mapping from business process models to Java Bean and Enterprise JavaBeans, and from application flow models to servlets, JavaServer Pages and Java Beans has made it possible to use a number of wizards, IDE and WYSIWYG tools.
- Predictable - given specific skill levels and tool choices, a team should be able to make and correct productivity estimates that can be used to drive project plans.
- Scalable - the ability to exploit a separation of concerns with well-defined contract objects not only makes an application easy to maintain, but also enables small or large teams of Java programmers and HTML page designers to work together on projects of any size with minimal amounts of coordination required.

- Flexible - separation of concerns also enables a team to use an iterative and incremental development process driven from the top, bottom, or middle in order to focus attention on high-risk items as early as possible.

If you develop your applications according to these principles, you will have an application that is not only functional, efficient, maintainable and portable, but also is able to exploit the deployment options best suited to your operational environment. Many of these options are discussed in more detail in the remaining chapters of this book.

Chapter 4. WebSphere components

This chapter takes a look at the major components within WebSphere, such as the administrative server, application server, servlet engine, and the EJB container.

We talk about the WebSphere administrative server and all the services that it provides. Then there is a discussion about the application servers. Virtual hosts and enterprise applications are briefly touched upon.

The servlet engine is covered in detail in Chapter 5, "Servlet support" on page 137. The EJB container is discussed in Chapter 11, "Enterprise Java Services" on page 393.

4.1 WebSphere Administrative Server

The administrative server tracks the contents and activities of a WebSphere administrative domain by maintaining the administrative database. The administrative database is the database of information about all WebSphere resources. All administration takes place through the manipulation of objects in the administrative database.

The WebSphere administrative server provides administrators with a single system view of applications and resources, such as servlets and EJBs, that are typically deployed across multiple machines in a distributed environment. An administrator can just as easily administer resources on a remote machine.

In the WebSphere administrative model as depicted in Figure 31 on page 116:

- An administrative domain is a set of one or more nodes and has a shared database.
- A node is a physical machine running an administrative server.
- Each administrative server stores its administrative data in a repository, which is the shared database.
- The WebSphere resources on a node are represented as administrative resources in the administrative domain. An administrative resource, such as a servlet, holds configuration information about the WebSphere resource, such as a servlet file on a node. It provides a way to start, stop, and manage the WebSphere resource.

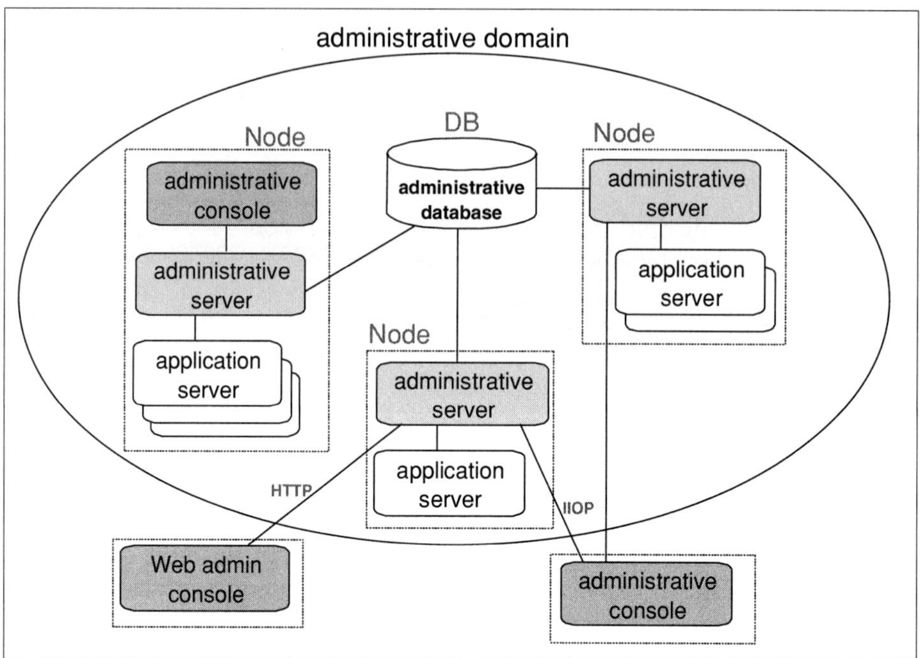

Figure 31. WebSphere administrative model

4.1.1 WebSphere administrative services

The administrative server provides the services that are used to control resources and perform tasks on the administrative database. In addition to the server start/stop/restart functionality and monitoring capabilities, the administrative server also provides shared services for:

- Naming
- Transaction monitoring
- Security

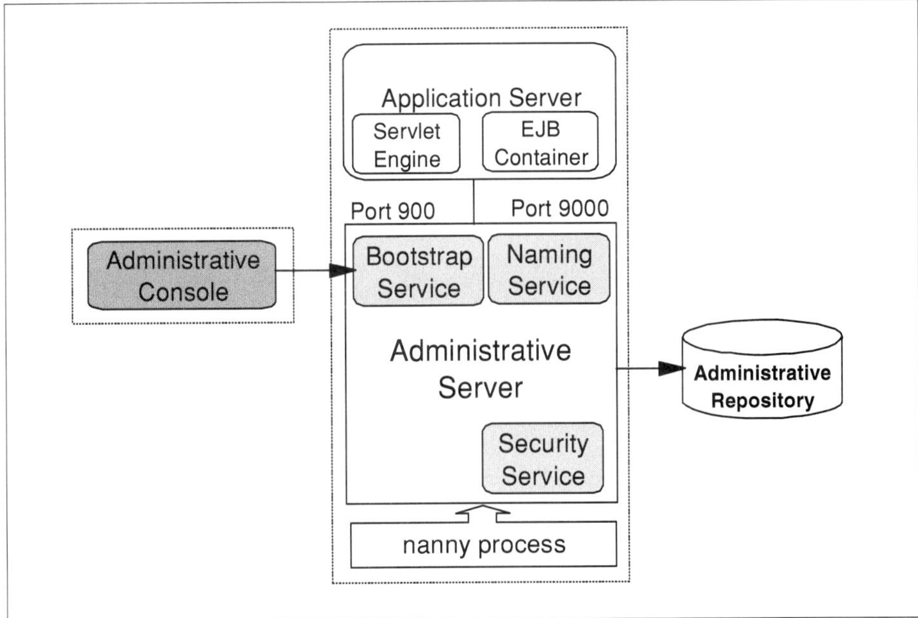

Figure 32. WebSphere V3.5 administrative services

There is a bootstrap service needed by the CosNaming service which listens, by default, on port 900. The WebSphere administrative console connects to the administrative server on port 900.

The JNDI namespace is kept locally by the administrative server. The JNDI naming service is a persistent naming service provided through the CORBA CosNaming API implemented as EJBs. The other Naming Service component, Location Service Daemon (LSD), uses its own Object Request Broker (ORB) and is needed for persistent object references. LSD listens on port 9000.

Every administrative server has a security service that handles authorization and authentication.

Finally, there is a nanny process whose job is to keep the administrative server alive.

4.1.2 Starting the administrative server

On UNIX platforms

a. Go to the bin directory under the WebSphere install directory.

```
cd <WAS_HOME>/bin
```

b. Run the startup server script:

```
./startupServer.sh
```

Where:

- `<WAS_HOME>` is the WebSphere V3.5 installation directory

On Windows platforms

Go to the Windows Services panel, select the service named **IBM WS AdminServer**, and click **Start**.

or at a command prompt, type:

```
net start "IBM WS AdminServer"
```

In WebSphere V3.5 you can also start the administrative server from the Windows Start menu: **Start -> Programs -> IBM WebSphere -> Application Server V3.5 -> Start Admin Server**.

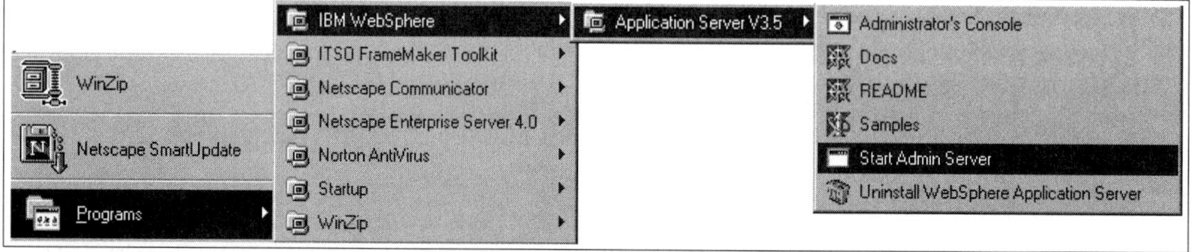

Figure 33. Menu path to start WebSphere V3.5 Administrative Server

4.1.3 Stopping the administrative server

On UNIX platforms

- Find the adminserver via the `ps -aef` UNIX command and get the process ID (pid)
- Issue the UNIX `kill <pid>` command (or `kill -15 <pid>`)

On Windows platforms

Go to the Windows Services panel, select the service named **IBM WS AdminServer**, and click **Stop**.

or at a command prompt, type:

```
net stop "IBM WS AdminServer"
```

4.1.4 Running WebSphere servers as a non-root user

On UNIX platforms, you do not have to be a root user to run the WebSphere Administrative Server, the WebSphere Administrative Console, or any application server.

4.1.4.1 Administrative server as non-root user

WebSphere is installed as "root". To allow the administrative server to be run as a non-root user, there are three things that need to be done:

1. Change the permissions to the installation directories. There are two options for granting non-root user access permissions:
   - Option1
     - Change the owner of all files and directories in the WebSphere install directory to the user/group that you desire to "run-as".
   - Option 2
     - Change the owner of the following specific files and directories to the user/group that you desire to "run-as".
       - <WAS_INSTALL_DIR>/logs/*
       - <WAS_INSTALL_DIR>/properties/*
       - <WAS_INSTALL_DIR>/tranlog/*
       - <WAS_INSTALL_DIR>/temp/*
       - <WAS_INSTALL_DIR>/bin/admin.config
2. Remove any temporary files that might have been created by previous executions of the application server when it was "run-as" a user different from the user that is going to be used. These files will be of the form:

   /tmp/.asXXXXXX

   where, XXXXX is a communications queue name used by WebSphere. For example:

   /tmp/.asibmappserve1

   /tmp/.asibmoselink1
3. To run as a non-root user, the administrative server must use a bootstrap port of 1024 or higher. To override the default value of 900, update the

<WAS_INSTALL_DIR>/bin/admin.config file. Add the following directive to specify a new bootstrap port:

com.ibm.ejs.sm.adminServer.bootstrapPort=NNNN

where NNNN is greater than or equal to 1024

The WebSphere Administrative Server is now ready to be started with the newly configured user/group setting.

4.1.4.2 Administrative console as non-root user

WebSphere is installed as "root". To allow the administrative console to be run as a non-root user there are two things that need to be done:

1. Change the owner permissions to the user/group that you want to allow access to run as in the <WAS_INSTALL_DIR>/bin directory.
2. Change the owner permissions of the following file to the same user/group that you want to allow access to run as:

<WAS_INSTALL_DIR>/properties/sas.client.props

The WebSphere Administrative Console can now be started with the newly configured user/group setting.

Note

If the WebSphere Administrative Server is configured to run on a port other than the default port of 900, remember to invoke the WebSphere administrative client using the “new” port:

```
./adminclient.sh <HOST_NAME> <BOOTSTRAP_PORT>
```

4.1.4.3 An application server as non-root user

To allow an application server to be run as a non-root user there are four things that need to be done:

1. Start the WebSphere Administrative Server as “root”.
2. Bring up the WebSphere Administrative Console. In the Topology tab, select the application server in the navigation pane, and go to the Advanced tab in the workspace pane. Modify the User ID and Group ID fields to the user/group setting that you want to run as.

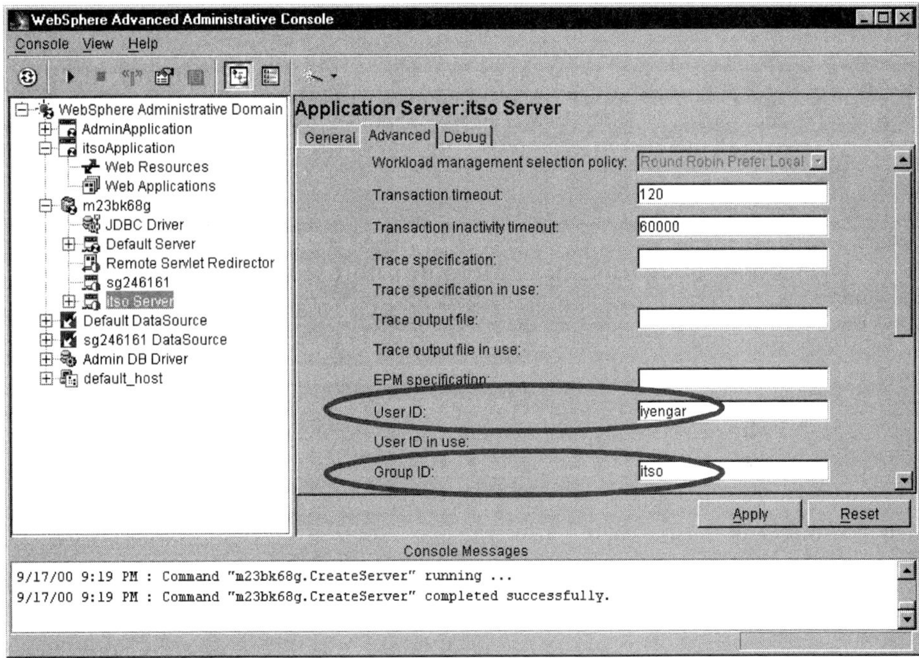

Figure 34. Application Server Advanced tab: User ID and Group ID attributes

3. In the General tab of that same application server, specify the paths for Standard output and Standard error to a directory location that the user/group has permission to write to.
4. Remove any temporary files that might have been created by previous executions of the application server when it was "run-as" a user different from the user that is going to be used. These files will be of the form:

   /tmp/.asXXXXXX

where XXXXX is a communications queue name used by WebSphere. For example:

   /tmp/.asibmappserve1

   /tmp/.asibmoselink1

The application server can now be started with the newly configured user/group setting.

Note

If WebSphere security is to be enabled when running the administrative server as a non-root user, then the local operating system cannot be used as the authentication mechanism. You have to use LTPA in connection with LDAP.

4.2 Application server

In the Standard Edition, the application server contains a servlet engine that is basically a Java program handling servlet and JSP requests. In the Advanced Edition the application server also contains an EJB container.

4.2.1 The application server hierarchy

An application server, EJB server, servlet engine, and its corresponding Web applications are organized in a hierarchy. The application server contains the EJB server and servlet engine, and the servlet engine in turn contains Web applications.

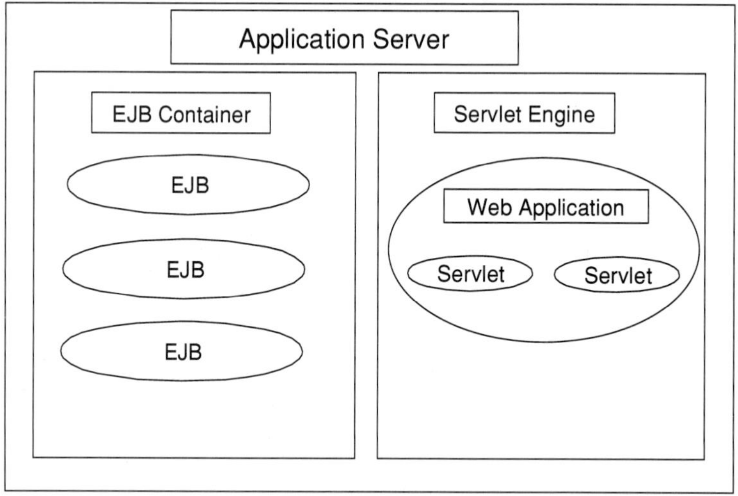

Figure 35. The application server hierarchy

This is true in all cases, including the default application server and its subcomponents as described above, and we can see this hierarchy in a number of ways; here we will examine it using the administrative console.

The administrative console hierarchy is shown in Figure 36 on page 123.

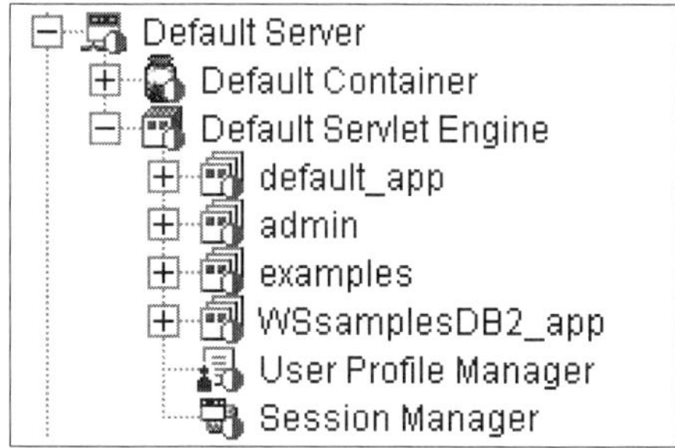

Figure 36. Default application server

The Session Manager components will be covered in Chapter 7, "Session support" on page 245.

It is clear from the figure above that, say, the "default_app" Web application is contained within the "Default Servlet Engine" servlet engine, which in turn is contained within the "Default Server" application server instance.

4.2.2 The Default Server

A default application server, appropriately named "Default Server", can be automatically configured during WebSphere Application Server installation, by choosing the **configure default server and web application** option.

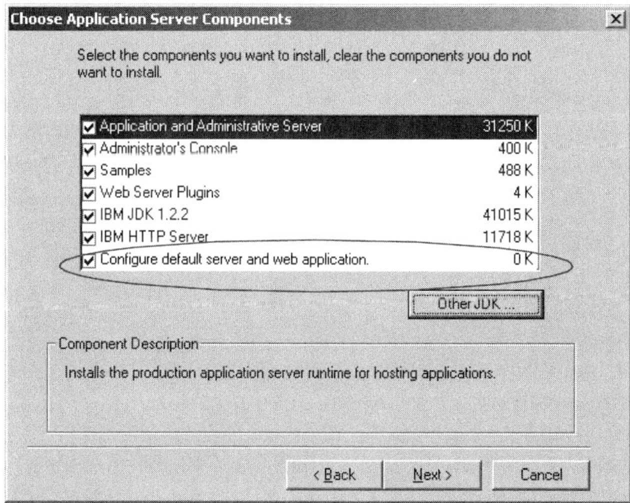

Figure 37. Installation option to configure default server and web application

This will create an application server instance called “Default Server” as shown in Figure 38 on page 124.

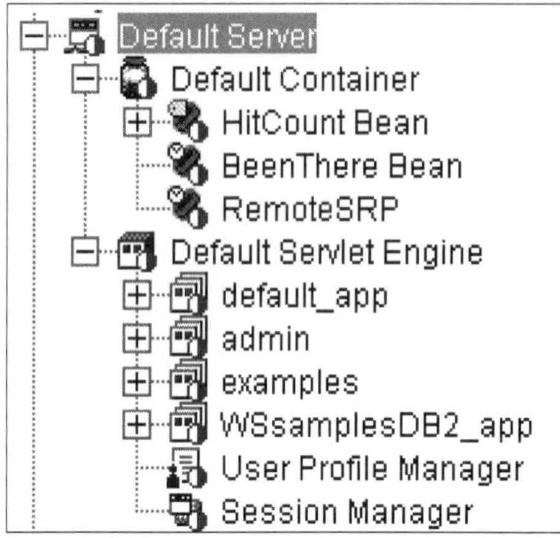

Figure 38. Default Server

4.2.2.1 The Default Container

You get an EJB container called “Default Container” inside Default Server. Note that the “Default Container” entry is for an Enterprise JavaBeans container; WebSphere Application Server uses the term “servlet engine” for the container in which servlets run, to avoid confusion.

4.2.2.2 The Default Servlet Engine

Inside Default Server, there is also a servlet engine, named Default Servlet Engine.

Under the Default Servlet Engine, there will be four Web applications. Each of these Web applications contain some of the internal servlets provided by WebSphere Application Server, as described in 5.6, “Internal servlets” on page 167, as well as some example servlets. Web applications are discussed in more detail in 5.3.2, “Web applications” on page 144.

The default_app Web application

The default_app Web application can be used to deploy simple servlets for testing. It has been designed to ease the migration of servlets and applications from WebSphere Application Server Version 2. You can also use the default_app as a template for your own Web applications. The default_app Web application contains two example servlets, snoop and hello, as shown in Figure 39 on page 125. Both of these have been well documented elsewhere in this redbook. It also contains three internal servlets, ErrorReporter, invoker and jsp10, which are documented in 5.6, “Internal servlets” on page 167.

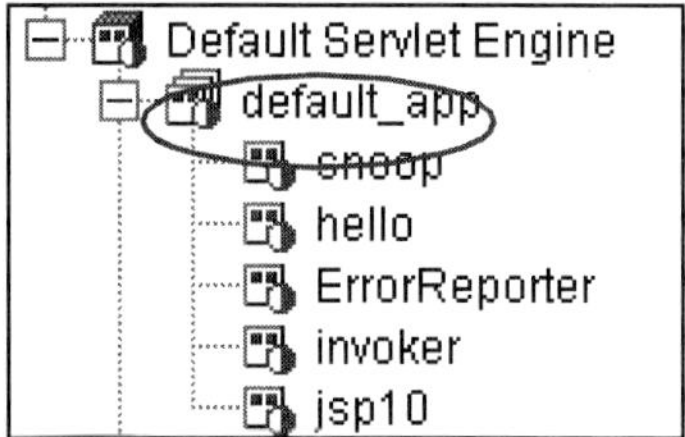

Figure 39. The default_app application

The admin Web application

The admin Web application is used by WebSphere Application Server to install the administrative console and run the Web based administration tool. Note that, as seen in Figure 40, the admin Web application is part of an Enterprise Applications.

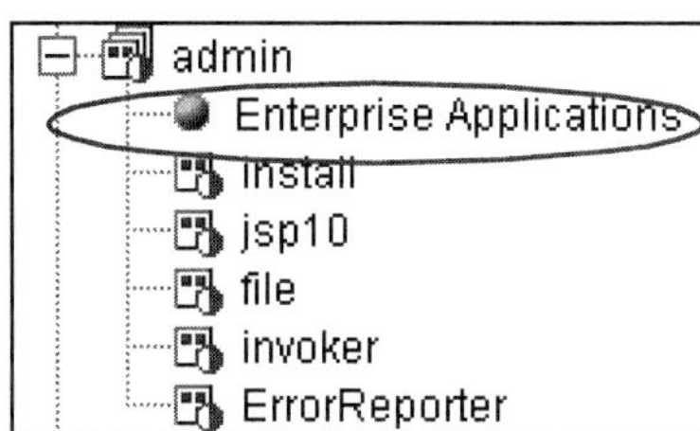

Figure 40. The admin Web application

The examples Web application

The examples Web application, as shown in Figure 41 on page 126, contains a few sample servlets that you can run from day one to test your environment and give you an idea of some basic designs. You can invoke these samples using the URL:

```
http://yourHostName/webapp/examples/
```

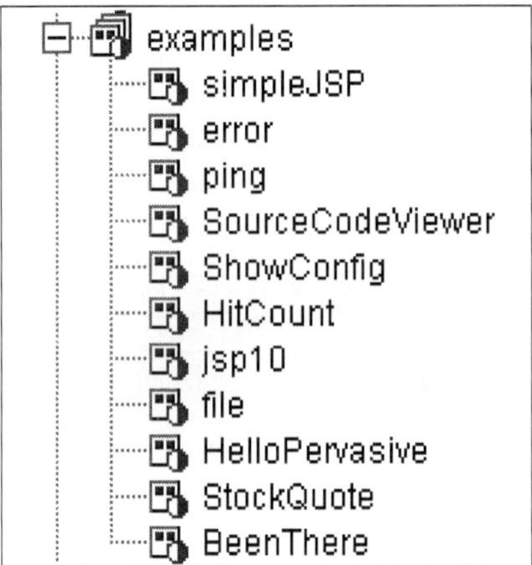

Figure 41. The examples application

The WSsampleDB2_app Web application

The WSsamplesDB2_app application, as shown in Figure 42, contains a sample Web application called YourCo. Take a look at it via the URL:

```
http://yourHostName/WebSphereSamples/YourCo
```

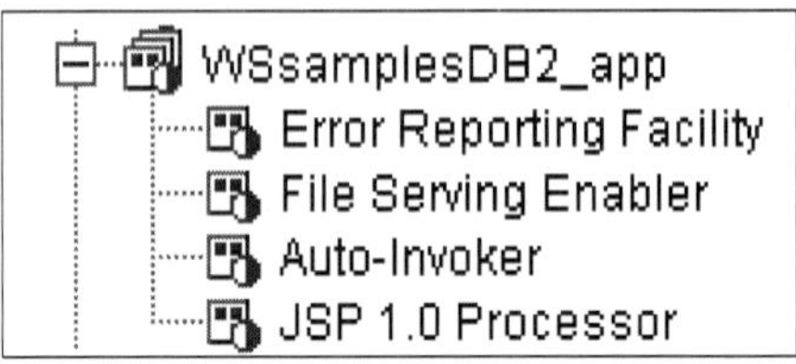

Figure 42. WSsamplesDB2_app application

4.2.3 Create a new application server

Any application server other than the default server has to be created. WebSphere provides more than one way to create a new application server. One way is via the tasks option in the administrative console. Select the node where the application server is to run, click the right mouse button, select **Create**, and highlight **Application Server** as shown in Figure 43 on page 127.

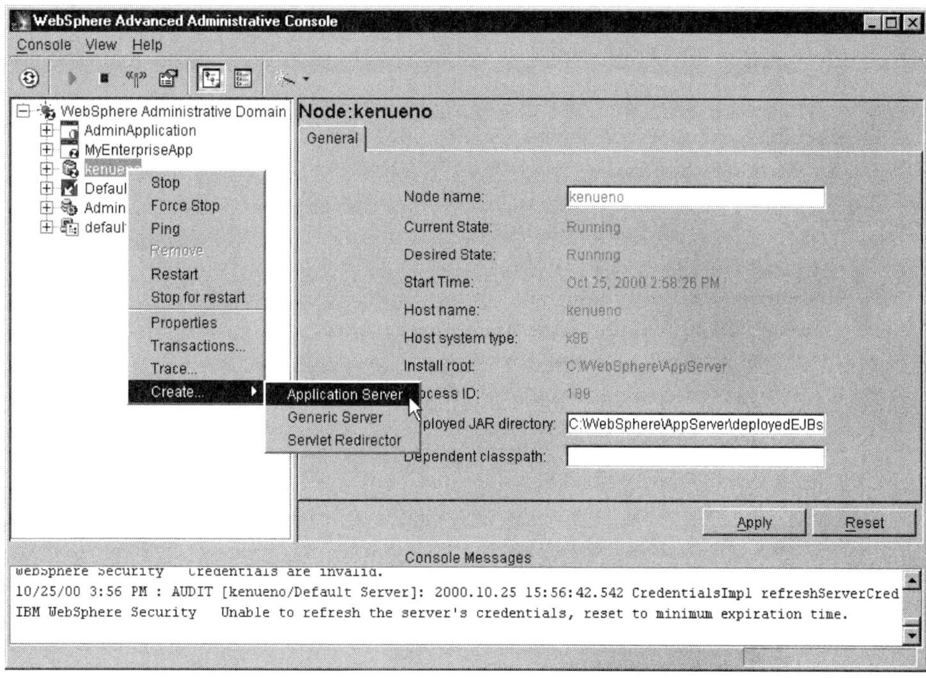

Figure 43. Create an application server

The General properties tab is displayed, as shown in Figure 44 on page 128. The Advanced properties tab is shown in Figure 45 on page 128. And the Debug properties tab is shown in Figure 46 on page 129. There are a lot of options that can be specified, but the application server name is the only required item. Enter the name of the application server and click **OK**.

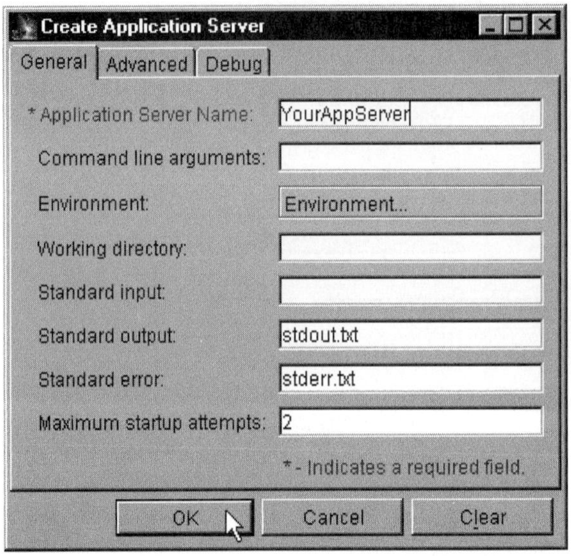

Figure 44. Create Application Server: General tab

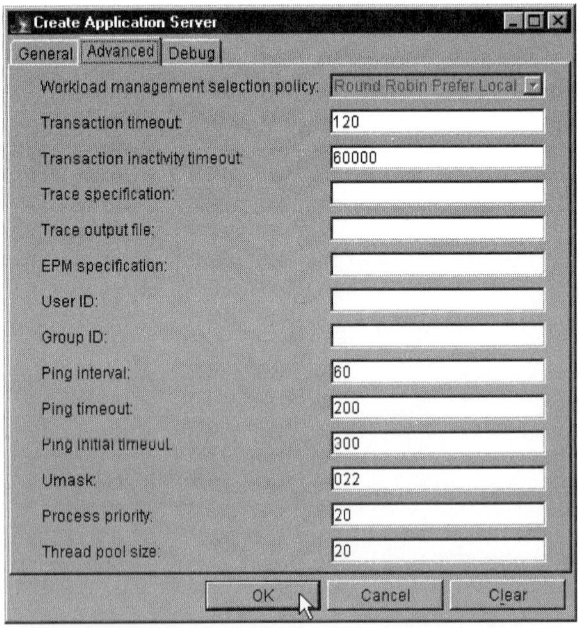

Figure 45. Create Application Server: Advanced tab

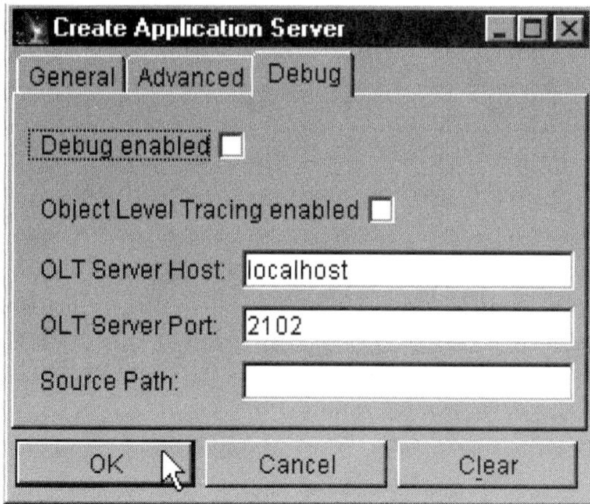

Figure 46. Create Application Server: Debug tab

If everything goes well, a message showing the successful creation of the application server will be displayed.

Upon refreshing the view in the WebSphere Administrative Console, the newly created application server will be seen. See Figure 47 on page 130.

Now you can continue with the creation of a servlet engine, an EJB container, and other resources as needed.

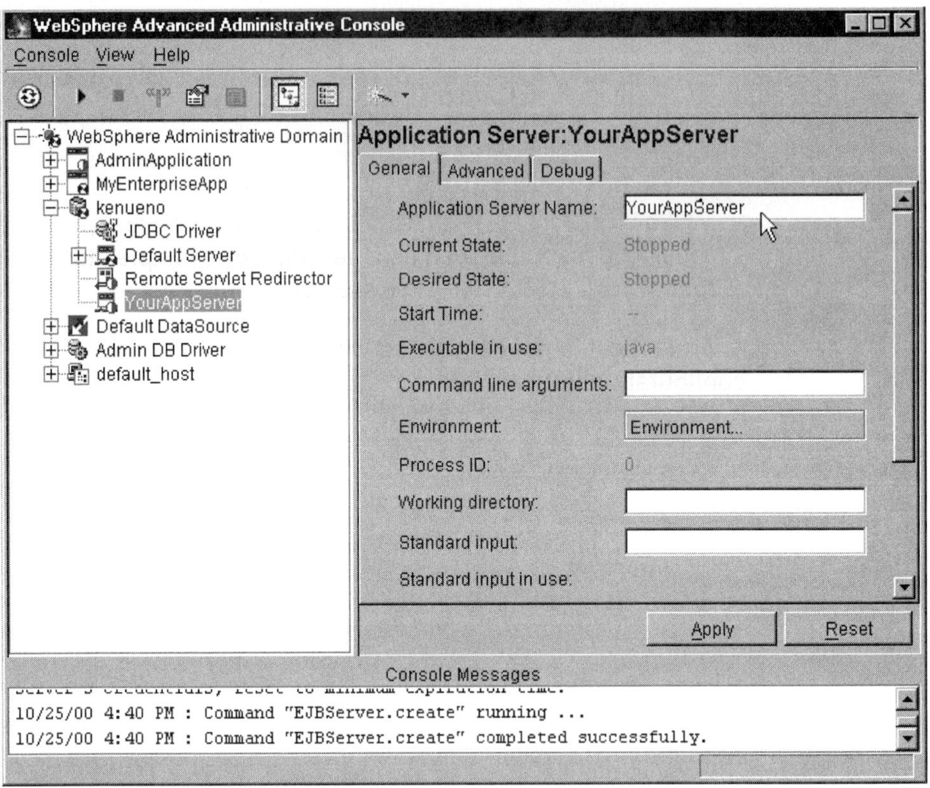

Figure 47. WebSphere Administrative Console displaying the "new" application server

The other way to create an application server is via the Create Application Server menu option in the WebSphere Wizards menu. This wizard asks all the information up front and creates the application server with all the resources in a single step.

4.2.4 Virtual hosts

A virtual host is a configuration enabling a single host machine to resemble multiple host machines. It allows a single physical machine to support several independently configured and administered applications.

Each virtual host has a logical name and a list of one or more DNS aliases by which it is known. A DNS alias is the TCP/IP host name and port number used to request the servlet, for example yourHostName:80. When no port number is specified, 80 is assumed.

When a servlet request is made, the server name and port number entered into the browser are compared to a list of all known aliases in an effort to locate the correct virtual host and serve the servlet. If no match is found, an error is returned to the browser.

The WebSphere Application Server provides a default virtual host with some common aliases, such as the machine's IP address, short host name, and fully qualified host name. The alias comprises the first part of the path for accessing a resource such as a servlet. For example, it is localhost:80 in the request `http://localhost:80/myServlet`.

A virtual host is not associated with a particular node (machine). It is a configuration, rather than a "live object," explaining why it can be created, but not started or stopped. For many users, virtual host creation will be unnecessary because the default_host is provided.

Virtual hosts allow the administrator to isolate, and independently manage, multiple sets of resources on the same physical machine.

Suppose an Internet service provider (ISP) has two customers whose Internet sites it would like to host on the same machine. The ISP would like to keep the two sites isolated from one another, despite their sharing a machine.

The ISP could associate the resources of the first company with VirtualHost1 and the resources of the second company with VirtualHost2. Now suppose both companies' sites offer the same servlet. Each site has its own instances of the servlet, which are unaware of the other site's instances.

If the company whose site is organized on VirtualHost2 is past due in paying its account with the ISP, the ISP can refuse all servlet requests that are routed to VirtualHost2. Even though the same servlet is available on VirtualHost1, the requests directed at VirtualHost2 will not be routed there.

The servlets on one virtual host do not share their context with the servlets on the other virtual host. Requests for the servlet on VirtualHost1 can continue as usual, even though VirtualHost2 is refusing to fill requests for the same servlet.

The administrator can associate the Web paths of resources, such as servlets, Web pages, and JavaServer Pages (JSP) files, with virtual hosts. It is common to say that the resources are "on" the virtual host, even though the virtual host is a configuration, not a physical machine that can hold files.

The Web path of a resource, such as a servlet, is a path by which users can request the resource. For example, an administrator might specify two Web paths for a servlet class named Animals. This allows users to specify either `http://www.companyname.com/Animals` or `http://www.companyname.com/AnimalsToo` to request the servlet.

Because the administrator associates the Web path of a resource, and not the resource itself, with a virtual host, the administrator can associate one Web path of a servlet with one virtual host, and another Web path of the servlet with a different virtual host. WebSphere provides the flexibility to set up virtual hosting in the way that best suits your needs.

4.2.4.1 The default virtual host

The product provides a default virtual host (named default_host). The default uses port 80. The default_host has these aliases:

The IP address of the local machine (yourIPAddress:80)
The "localhost" alias, meaning the local machine (localhost:80)
The DNS name (such as software:80)
The fully qualified host name (such as www.software.ibm.com:80)
The loopback address (127.0.0.1:80)

Once in a while, the fully qualified name cannot be constructed. If several paths containing the fully qualified name do not seem to be working, use the WebSphere Administrative Console to check the virtual host's aliases property to ensure the fully qualified name is registered as an alias.

Unless the administrator specifically wants to isolate resources from one another on the same node (physical machine), he or she probably does not need any virtual hosts in addition to the default host.

When a user requests a resource, WebSphere tries to map the request to an alias of a defined virtual host. The mapping is case insensitive, but the match must be alphabetically exact. Also, different port numbers are treated as different aliases.

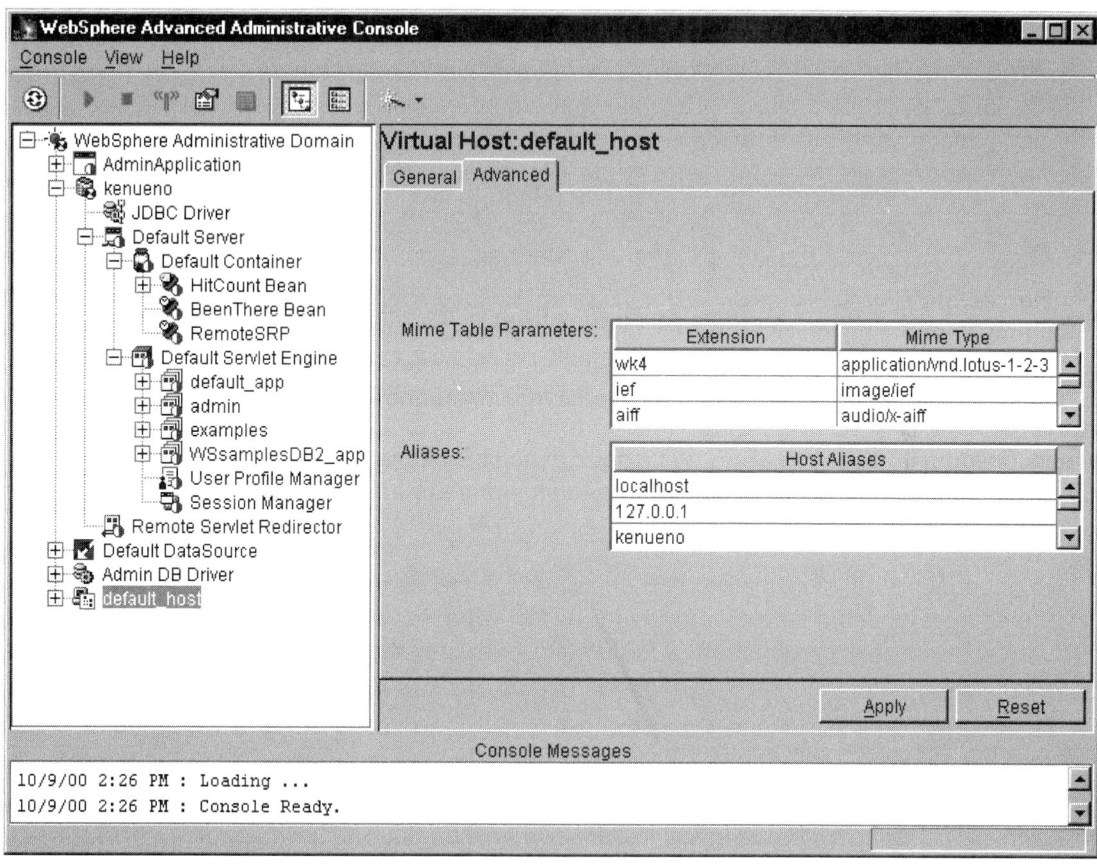

Figure 48. The default_host

For example, the request:

```
http://www.myhost.com/myservlet
```

maps successfully to:

```
http://WWW.MYHOST.COM/MYSERVLET
```

and to:

```
http://Www.Myhost.Com/Myservlet
```

But it does not map successfully to:

```
http://myhost/myservlet
```

or to:

```
http://myhost:9876/myservlet
```

If a user requests a resource using an alias that cannot be mapped to an alias of a defined virtual host, the user will receive a 404 error in the browser used to issue the request. A message will state that the virtual host could not be found.

4.3 What is an enterprise application?

An enterprise application is a combination of resources (building blocks) that work together to perform a business logic function. The resources can include:

- HTML files
- XML files
- JSP files
- Servlets
- Enterprise JavaBeans
- Graphical elements

Although they have the same contents, an enterprise application differs from a Web application in that it involves security and may also contain Enterprise JavaBeans.

An enterprise application, like a Web application, can be managed by the administrator as a single logical unit. A step-by-step configuration is found in Chapter 14, "Application deployment" on page 573.

WebSphere V3.x security is based on the concept of an enterprise application called the AdminApplication. The key to WebSphere security architecture is this central security application running in the WebSphere Administrative Server.

4.4 WebSphere administrative interfaces

The WebSphere Administrative Server provides the services that are used to control resources and perform tasks on the administrative database. The monitoring and configuring of administrative resources are facilitated by four interfaces, as shown in Figure 49 on page 135.

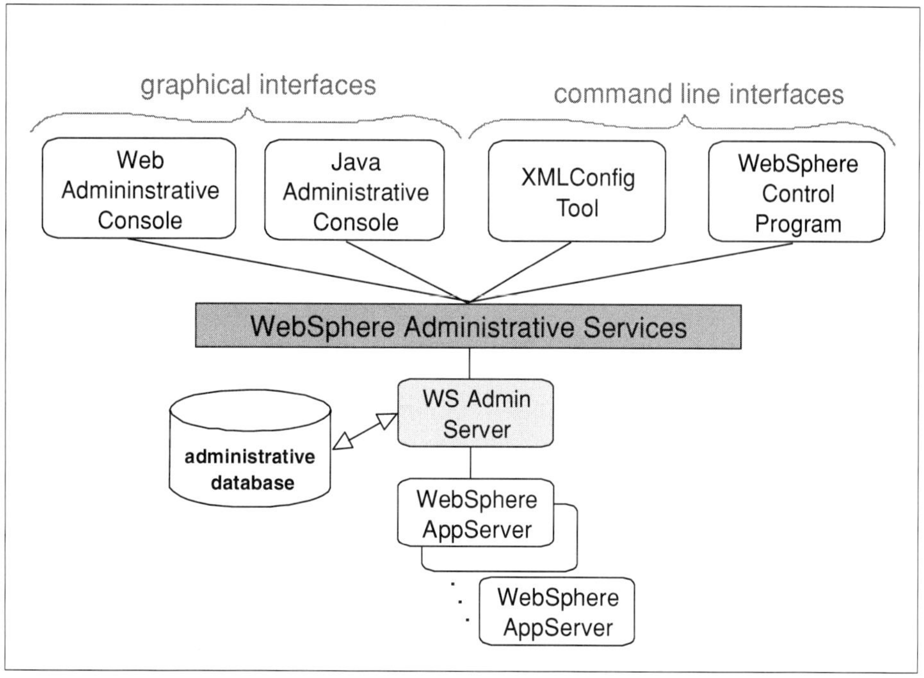

Figure 49. WebSphere V3.5 Administrative Services block diagram

The Java client or the WebSphere Administrative Console, the Web console, the WebSphere Control Program (WSCP), and the XMLConfig program can all be used by administrators to access the administrative server on nodes in the administrative domain, thus enabling the administrator to administer the WebSphere domain resources.

They complement each other, but there are certain scenarios where one is more useful than the other. The graphical clients, for example, provide a view of the domain topology.

Chapter 18, "Administrative console" on page 811 discusses the Java administrative console. Chapter 19, "Web console" on page 843 talks about the HTTP or Web administrative console. Both of the command line interfaces, XMLConfig and WSCP, are covered in detail in this redbook. Chapter 20, "The WebSphere Control Program (WSCP)" on page 855 talks about WSCP and XMLConfig is covered in Chapter 21, "XMLConfig" on page 877.

Chapter 5. Servlet support

The aim of this chapter is to explain how you will use a servlet with the WebSphere Application Server, from an administrative and architectural point of view. We do not try to explain in detail how to write servlets; for that information, please see *Servlet and JSP Programming with IBM WebSphere Studio and VisualAge for Java*, SG24-5755.

We provide an overview of the servlet concept, and a short summary of how servlets work, discussing in brief the process flow, the API, and the life cycle. This has been kept to a minimum; the aforementioned redbook on servlets has a far more in-depth explanation for those readers who are interested.

We discuss how the WebSphere Application Server treats servlets, and where they fit within the application server hierarchy. We then give an example of a very simple servlet for the purpose of demonstrating how you will use the administration environment that comes with WebSphere Application Server to configure your servlet engine and deploy servlets. Finally, we talk about some of the internal servlets that WebSphere Application Server provides, and where and how you would use them.

We recognize that there is an abundance of both online and printed documentation on the topic of servlets, and recommend that you refer to the Sun Java Servlet API Specification, found at `http://java.sun.com/products/servlet/`.

5.1 What is a servlet?

According to the Java Servlet Specification (Version 2.2):

> A servlet is a Web component, managed by a container, that generates dynamic content. Servlets are small, platform-independent Java classes compiled to an architecture-neutral bytecode that can be loaded dynamically into and run by a Web server.

So, a servlet is a server-side software component written in Java, which is loaded and executed within the Java Virtual Machine (JVM) of any Java-enabled application server such as the WebSphere Application Server.

5.2 How servlets work

In order to understand how WebSphere works with servlets, we have to know how servlets themselves work. In the following subsections, we briefly examine the servlet process flow, skim through the Java Servlet API, and discuss the servlet life cycle.

5.2.1 Servlet process flow

Servlets implement a common request/response paradigm for the handling of the messaging between the client and the server. The Java Servlet API defines a standard interface for the handling of these request and response messages between the client and server.

Figure 50 shows a high-level client-to-servlet process flow:

1. The client sends a request to the server.
2. The server sends the request information to the servlet.
3. The servlet builds a response and passes it to the server. That response is dynamically built, and the content of the response usually depends on the client's request. External resources may also be used.
4. The server sends the response back to the client.

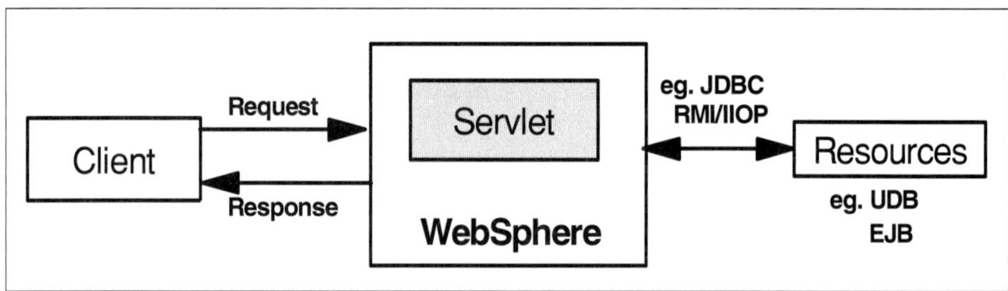

Figure 50. High-level client-to-servlet process flow

Written in Java, servlets have access to the full set of Java APIs, such as JDBC for accessing enterprise databases.

Servlets resemble Common Gateway Interface (CGI) programs in terms of functionality. As in CGI programs, servlets can respond to user events from an HTML request, and then dynamically construct an HTML response that is sent back to the client. Servlets, however, have the following advantages over traditional CGI programs:

- Portability and platform independence

  Servlets are written in Java, making them portable across platforms and across different Web servers, because the Java Servlet API defines a standard interface between a servlet and a Web server. Of course, servlets inherit all of the benefits of the Java language, including a strong-typed system, object orientation, and modularity, to name a few.

- Persistence and performance

  A servlet is loaded once by a Web server/application server, and then invoked for each client request, possibly more than once at the same time using threads. This means that the servlet can maintain system resources, such as a database connection, between requests. Servlets don't incur the overhead of instantiating a new servlet with each request. CGI processes typically must be loaded with each invocation.

5.2.2 The Java Servlet API

The Java Servlet API is a Standard Java Extension API, meaning that it is not part of the core Java framework, but rather is available as an add-on set of packages; it is a set of Java classes that define standard interfaces between a Web client and a Web servlet and between the servlet and the environment in which it runs.

WebSphere V3.5.2 supports Java Servlet API V2.2 (and the related JavaServer Pages API 1.1). Previous versions of WebSphere, V3.5 and V3.5.1, supported earlier versions of those APIs with some extensions. WebSphere V3.5.2 can also be configured to support applications coded to those earlier versions. When you configure a servlet engine you choose which version of the servlet API is to be used. All Web applications deployed in that servlet engine will use the chosen version. We discuss the differences between the two versions in Chapter 8, "Servlet V2.2 in WebSphere V3.5.2" on page 295.

You can choose the version of the Servlet API independently for each servlet engine in the same WebSphere domain. However there is some potential for unexpected behaviors; see 8.3.5, "Session Cookie Names" on page 308.

The API, in both V2.1and V2.2, is composed of two packages:

- javax.servlet
- javax.servlet.http

The javax.servlet package contains classes to support generic protocol-independent servlets. The javax.servlet.http package extends the functionality of the base package to include specific support for the HTTP protocol. In this chapter, for the sake of simplicity, we will concentrate on the classes in the javax.servlet.http package.

The Servlet interface class defines the methods that servlets must implement, including a service() method for the handling of requests. To write an HTTP servlet, we will use a class called HttpServlet, which implements the servlet interface. HttpServlet provides additional methods for the processing of HTTP requests such as GET (doGet() method) and POST (doPost() method). Although our servlets may implement a service() method, in most cases we will implement the HTTP-specific request handling methods.

5.2.3 The servlet life cycle

A Web client does not usually communicate directly with a servlet, but requests the servlet's services through a server, such as the WebSphere Application Server, that invokes the servlet. The server's role is to manage the loading and initialization of the servlet, the servicing of the request, and the unloading or destroying of the servlet.

5.2.3.1 How the life cycle functions

There is one instance of a particular servlet object at a time in the application servers' environment. Each client request to the servlet is handled via a new thread against the original instance object. This is the underlying principle of the persistence of the servlet. The application server is responsible for:

1. Handling the initialization of the servlet when the servlet is first loaded, where it remains active for the life of the servlet
2. Creating the new threads to handle the requests
3. The unloading or reloading of the servlets

WebSphere will unload a servlet when the Web application is brought down, and it will reload all of the classes in the application classpath whenever one of the loaded classes in that class path has been changed. See 5.5.3, "Create a Web application" on page 155 for detailed information about auto reload.

Figure 51 on page 141 shows a basic client-to-servlet interaction:

- Servlet1 is initially loaded by the WebSphere. Instance variables are initialized, and remain active (persistent) for the life of the servlet.
- Two Web clients have requested the services of Servlet1 via the HTTPD. A handler thread is spawned by the application server to handle each request. Each thread has access to the originally loaded instance variables that were initialized when the servlet was loaded.
- Each thread handles its own requests, and responses are sent back to the calling client.

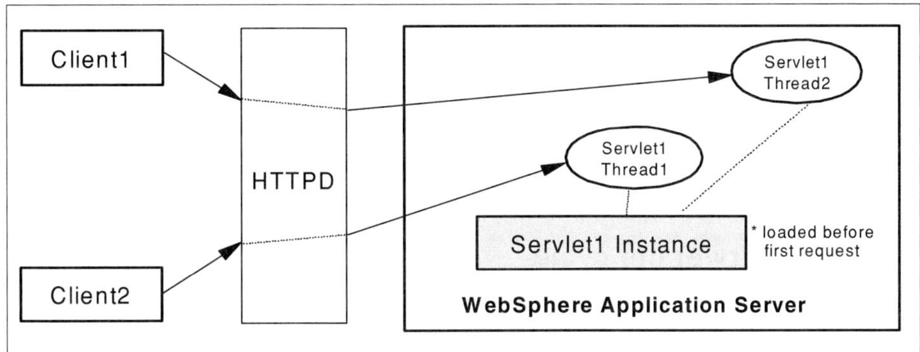

Figure 51. Basic client-to-server interaction

The life cycle of a servlet is expressed in the Java Servlet API in the init(), service() (doGet() or doPost()), and destroy() methods of the Servlet interface. We will discuss the functions of these methods in more detail and the objects that they manipulate. Figure 52 is a visual diagram of the life cycle of an individual servlet.

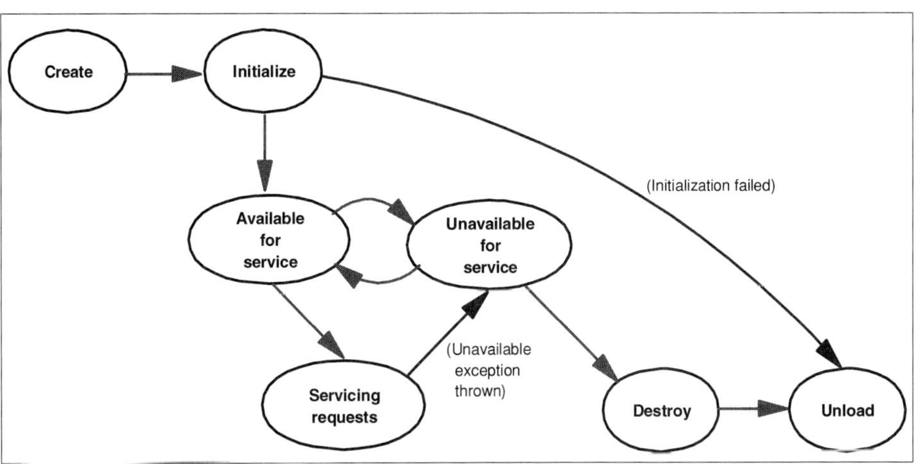

Figure 52. Servlet life cycle

The WebSphere administrator can set an application and its servlets to be unavailable for service (see 5.5.4, "Deploying the servlet" on page 160 for details). In such cases, the application and servlets remain unavailable until the administrator changes them to available.

5.2.3.2 Understanding the life cycle

This section describes in detail some of the important servlet life cycle methods of the Java Servlet API.

Servlet initialization: init() method

Servlets can be dynamically loaded and instantiated when their services are first requested, or WebSphere can be configured so that specific servlets are loaded and instantiated when WebSphere initializes.

In either case, the init() method performs any necessary servlet initialization, and is guaranteed to be called once for each servlet instance, before any requests are handled. An example of a task that may be performed in the init() method is the loading of default data parameters or database connections.

At initialization time, the servlet author can access a ServletConfig object. This interface object allows the servlet to access name/value pairs of initialization parameters that are specific to that servlet. The ServletConfig object also gives us access to the ServletContext object that describes information about our servlet environment.

Servlet request handling

Once the servlet has been initialized, it may handle requests (although it is possible that a loaded servlet may get no requests, for instance if the servlet is set to start when the application server starts, but no requests are made for that servlet). Each request is represented by a ServletRequest object, and the corresponding response by a ServletResponse object. Since we will be dealing with HttpServlets, we will deal exclusively with the more specialized HttpServletRequest and HttpServletResponse objects.

The service() method is declared abstract in the basic GenericServlet class, and so subclasses, such as HttpServlet, must override it. The HttpServlet service() method accepts two parameters, HttpServletRequest and HttpServletResponse. In any subclass of HttpServlet, the service() method must be implemented according to the signature defined in HttpServlet, namely, that it accepts HttpServletRequest and HttpServletResponse arguments.

The HttpServletRequest object encapsulates information about the client request, including information about the client's environment and any data that may have been sent from the client to the servlet. The HttpServletRequest class contains methods for extracting this information from the request object.

The HttpServletResponse is often the dynamically generated response, for instance, an HTML page that is sent back to the client. It is often built with data from the HttpServletRequest object. In addition to an HTML page, a response object may also be an HTTP error response, or a redirection to another URL, servlet, or JavaServer Pages. JavaServer Pages and interactions with servlets will be discussed in Chapter 6, “JSP support” on page 189.

Other servlet methods worth mentioning

- destroy(): The destroy() method is called when WebSphere unloads the servlet. A subclass of HttpServlet only needs to implement this method if it needs to perform cleanup operations, such as releasing database connections or closing files.
- getServletConfig(): The getServletConfig() method returns a ServletConfig instance that can be used to return the initialization parameters and the ServletContext object.
- getServletInfo(): The getServletInfo() method is a method that can provide information about the servlet, such as its author, version, and copyright. This method is generally overwritten to have it return a meaningful value for your application. By default, it returns an empty string.

5.3 WebSphere and servlets

A servlet requires a servlet container, called a *servlet engine* in the WebSphere terminology, in which to run. From the Servlet Specification 2.2:

> A servlet container can either be built into a host Web server or installed as an add-on component to a Web server via that server's native extension API. Servlet containers can also be built into or possibly installed into Web-enabled application servers.

A servlet engine in WebSphere is a Java program that runs inside an application server instance Java Virtual Machine (JVM) configuration.

5.3.1 The servlet engine

A servlet engine is a program that handles the requests for servlets and JavaServer Pages (JSP). The servlet engine is responsible for creating instances of servlets, initializing them, acting as a request dispatcher, and maintaining servlet contexts for use by your Web applications.

WebSphere supports only one servlet engine per application server. For the purposes of the examples in this chapter, we shall create a new application server instance to house our servlet engine; this will be discussed in 5.5, "Deploying the example servlet under WebSphere" on page 147. We could also have used the default servlet engine described above, however for completeness we will demonstrate how to create a new servlet engine and all of its components.

5.3.2 Web applications

A Web application represents a grouping of servlets, JSPs, and their related resources. Managing these elements as a unit allows you to stop and start servlets in a single step. You can also define a separate document root and class path at the Web application level, thus allowing you to keep different Web applications in separate directories in the file system. A Web application definition is contained within a servlet engine definition.

Servlets that are running within a Web application share the same servlet context with others in the same application, allowing them to communicate with each other.

5.3.3 Servlets

The servlets themselves are the innermost level of the hierarchy. They are deployed into the servlet engine and grouped into Web applications.

5.4 Writing a simple servlet example

In this section, we describe a very simple servlet, the HelloWorldServlet. For a detailed discussion of servlets and how they function, please see *Servlet and JSP Programming with IBM WebSphere Studio and VisualAge for Java*, SG24-5755. We are more interested here in how to deploy a servlet under WebSphere V3.5. In 5.5, "Deploying the example servlet under WebSphere" on page 147, we explain how to deploy this servlet in WebSphere.

5.4.1 The HelloWorldServlet

Figure 53 shows the full HelloWorldServlet code:

```
import java.io.*;
import javax.servlet.*;
import javax.servlet.http.*;

public class HelloWorldServlet extends HttpServlet {
   protected void service(HttpServletRequest request,
                 HttpServletResponse response)
                 throws ServletException, IOException {
      response.setContentType("text/html");
      PrintWriter out = response.getWriter();
      out.println("<HTML><TITLE>Hello World</TITLE><BODY>");
      out.println("<H2>Hello, World</H2><HR>");
      out.println("</BODY></HTML>");
      out.close();
   }
}
```

Figure 53. The HelloWorldServlet

HelloWorldServlet is a very simple HTTP servlet that accepts a request and writes a response. Let's break out the components of this servlet so we can discuss them individually.

5.4.2 Basic servlet structure

Figure 54 shows the import statements used to give us access to other Java packages. The import of java.io is so that we have access to some standard IO classes. More importantly, the javax.servlet.* and javax.servlet.http.* import statements give us access to the Java Servlet API set of classes and interfaces.

```
import java.io.*;
import javax.servlet.*;
import javax.servlet.http.*;
```

Figure 54. HelloWorldServlet import statements

Figure 55 on page 146 shows the HelloWorldServlet class declaration. We extend the HttpServlet class (javax.servlet.http.HttpServlet) to make our class an HTTP protocol servlet.

```
public class HelloWorldServlet extends HttpServlet {
```

Figure 55. The HelloWorldServlet class declaration

Figure 56 is the heart of this servlet, the implementation of the service() method for the handling of the request and response objects of the servlet.

```
    protected void service(HttpServletRequest request,
                HttpServletResponse response)
                throws ServletException, IOException {
        response.setContentType("text/html");
        PrintWriter out = response.getWriter();
        out.println("<HTML><TITLE>Hello World</TITLE><BODY>");
        out.println("<H2>Hello, World</H2><HR>");
        out.println("</BODY></HTML>");
        out.close();
    }
```

Figure 56. HelloWorldServlet service() method

5.4.3 Compiling the servlet

In order for our servlet to run in WebSphere, it has to be compiled into bytecode form and stored as a .class file. For the compile to be successful, we need to have access to the classes we are extending (the HttpServlet), which is stored in the servlet.jar file in the WebSphere lib directory. Thus, this jar file must be added to the classpath when compiling. The easiest way to do this is by using the -classpath option of the javac compiler, as shown in Figure 57 on page 147.

Before the compile, we only have the HelloWorldServlet.java file as shown in Figure 53 on page 145. We invoke the javac compiler on the HelloWorldServlet.java file, specifying that it should add the servlet.jar file to its classpath. After the compile is complete, we see that there is also a HelloWorldServlet.class file that can now be deployed to WebSphere.

```
C:\WebSphere\AppServer\Hello>dir
 Volume in drive C is WINDOWS2000
 Volume Serial Number is 0A72-0FE1

 Directory of C:\WebSphere\AppServer\Hello

13/09/2000  09:39       <DIR>          .
13/09/2000  09:39       <DIR>          ..
13/09/2000  09:40                  506 HelloWorldServlet.java
               1 File(s)            506 bytes
               2 Dir(s)   7,084,376,064 bytes free

C:\WebSphere\AppServer\Hello>javac -classpath c:\WebSphere\AppServer\lib\servlet.jar
HelloWorldServlet.java

C:\WebSphere\AppServer\Hello>dir
 Volume in drive C is WINDOWS2000
 Volume Serial Number is 0A72-0FE1

 Directory of C:\WebSphere\AppServer\Hello

13/09/2000  09:39       <DIR>          .
13/09/2000  09:39       <DIR>          ..
13/09/2000  09:40                  506 HelloWorldServlet.java
19/09/2000  18:47                  810 HelloWorldServlet.class
               2 File(s)          1,316 bytes
               2 Dir(s)   7,084,359,680 bytes free

C:\WebSphere\AppServer\Hello>
```

Figure 57. Compiling the HelloWorldServlet

5.5 Deploying the example servlet under WebSphere

For the purposes of this chapter, we will define a new servlet engine and Web application, and deploy our example HelloServlet servlet as part of this Web application.

In order to deploy the example servlet above under WebSphere V3.5, we have to carry out the following tasks:

1. Define a new application server.
2. Define a servlet engine.
3. Create a Web application.
4. Deploy the servlet.

We shall demonstrate how to carry out each of these tasks using two modes: the administrative console and the WSCP command line. Chapter 20, “The

WebSphere Control Program (WSCP)" on page 855 discusses the WSCP command line in detail.

5.5.1 Define a new application server

In this chapter, we are not really interested in the advanced options available when defining a new application server; the creation of an application server is described in detail in Chapter 4, "WebSphere components" on page 115. We will create a new server and accept the defaults for all of the options.

5.5.1.1 Define a new application server via the console

Right click the node on which you want to create the application server, and choose **Create -> Application Server** from the resulting menu, as shown in Figure 58.

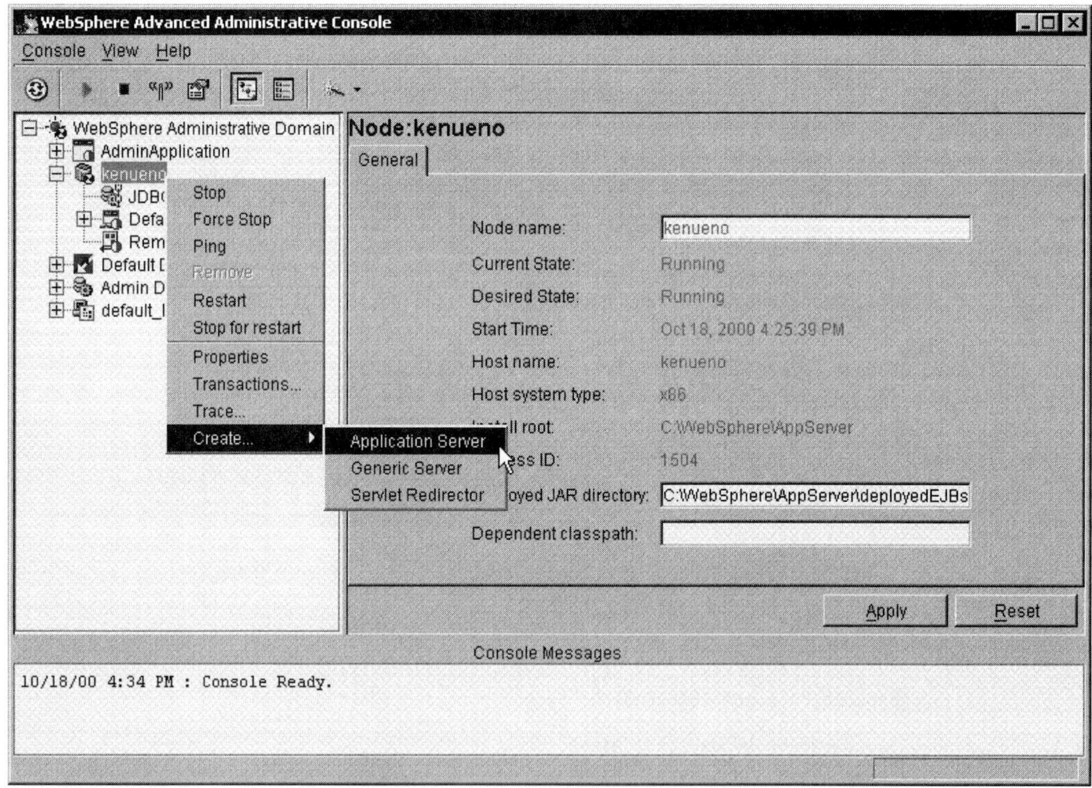

Figure 58. Create a new application server

This will bring up the Create Application Server dialog box, which contains three separate tabs entitled General, Advanced and Debug. For our purposes, the default settings for everything will be fine; see Chapter 4, “WebSphere components” on page 115 for details on the various options available when defining an application server.

Type in the name of your application server and click **OK**. We have used the name HelloAppServer for our application server, as can be seen in Figure 59.

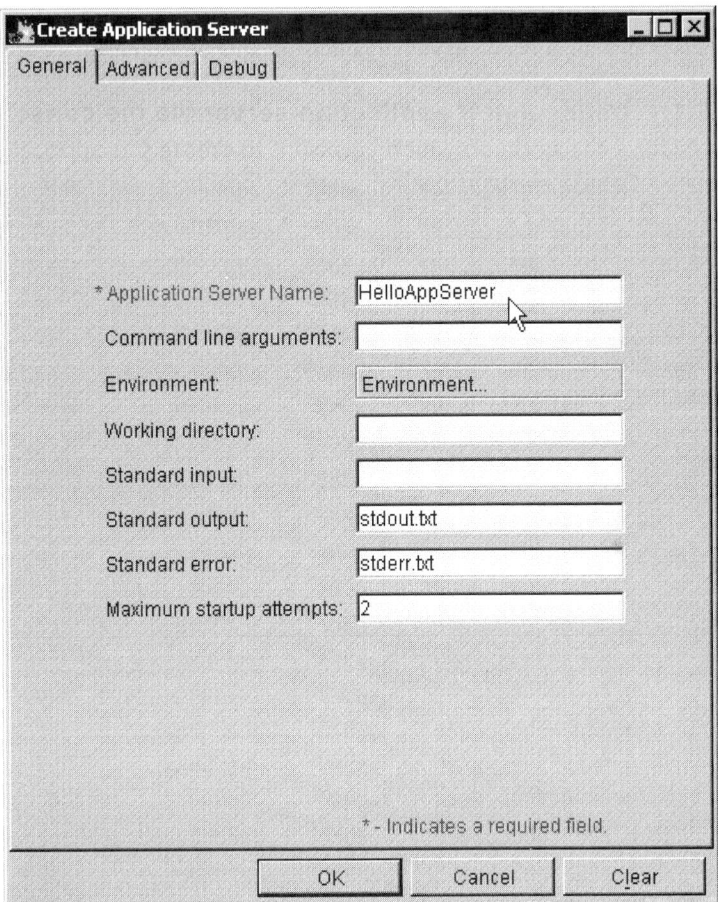

Figure 59. Create Application Server: General tab

Then you will get the Information dialog that says `Command "EJBServer.create" completed successfully` and click **OK**.

Note

After a few seconds, you should see an information dialog box saying that `the EJBServer.create command completed successfully`. This is somewhat misleading, as we have created an application server which we are *not* going to use to serve EJBs - we will only serve servlets (unless we are planning on using the thin Servlet Redirector; more on this later). However, this is WebSphere internal terminology for an application server instance; the messages means simply that the application server has been defined successfully.

5.5.1.2 Define a new application server via the WSCP

Creation of the application server via WSCP is done by calling the create method of the ApplicationServer command object. In the example in Figure 60, we are creating the same application server instance as above, called HelloAppServer, on the node entitled “SZYMON-Laptop”. (The example shows output from Windows 2000, but the syntax is the same on other platforms, such as UNIX).

```
C:\WebSphere\AppServer\bin>wscp
wscp> ApplicationServer create /Node:SZYMON-Laptop/ApplicationServer:HelloAppServer/
wscp> exit

C:\WebSphere\AppServer\bin>
```

Figure 60. Creation of the HelloAppServer application server instance

5.5.2 Define a servlet engine

Creation of the servlet engine is very similar to the creation of an application server. We shall demonstrate using both the administrative console and WSCP.

5.5.2.1 Define a servlet engine via the console

Right-click the application server in which you want to create the servlet engine (in our case, HelloAppServer), and choose **Create -> Servlet Engine** from the resulting menu, as in Figure 61 on page 151.

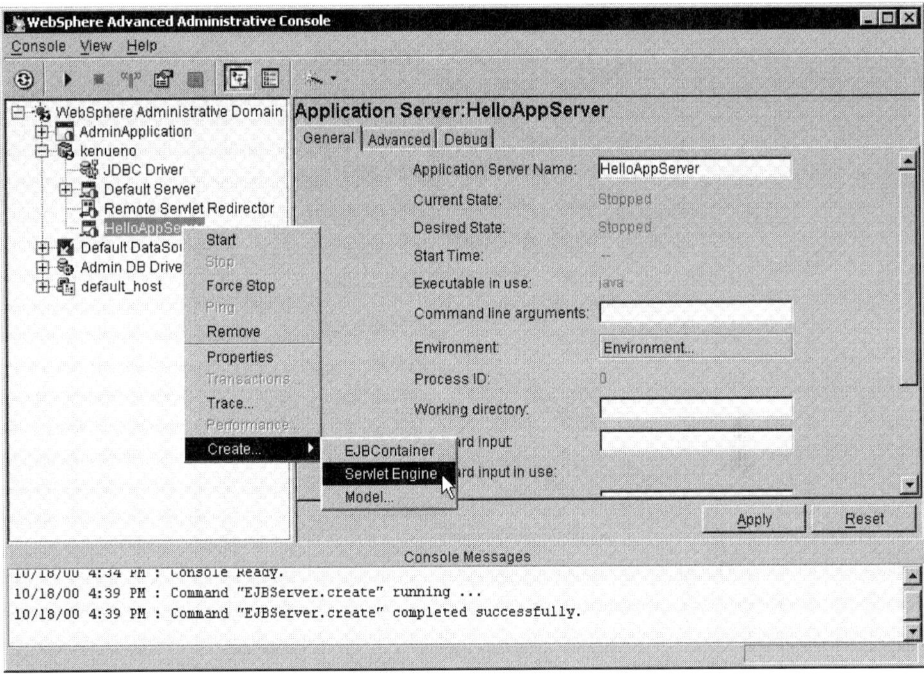

Figure 61. Create a new servlet engine

This will bring up the Create Servlet Engine dialog box, which has two tabs: General and Advanced. In the General tab, fill in the name you would like to use for your servlet engine; in the example we have used the name HelloServletEngine. From the drop-down box, choose the application server where you would like the servlet engine to run; the example depicted in Figure 62 on page 152 shows the HelloAppServer application server defined above being used.

In WebSphere V3.5.2, you can select the Servlet Engine Mode. We describe this in detail in Chapter 8, “Servlet V2.2 in WebSphere V3.5.2” on page 295. For this chapter, we selected the **WebSphere V3.5 Compatibility Mode**.

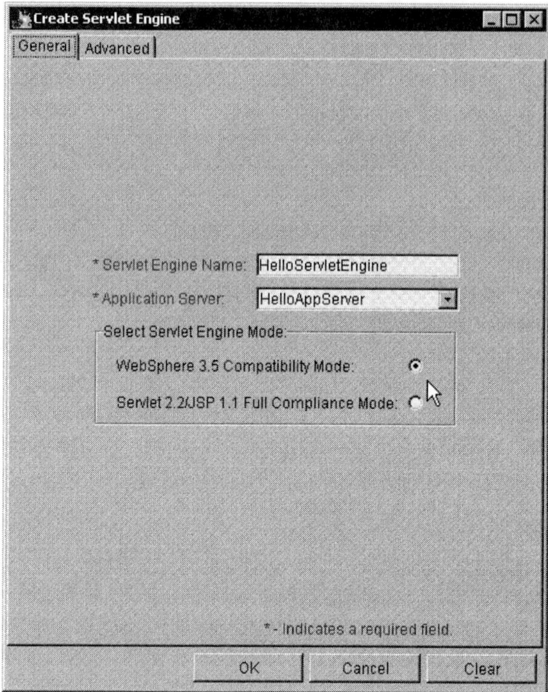

Figure 62. Create Servlet Engine: General tab

Click the **Advanced** tab. Although we will not change any of the settings for our simple example it is useful to know what they all mean. Figure 63 on page 153 shows the Advanced tab of the Create Servlet Engine dialog box, with all of the options. An explanation of the options is given below.

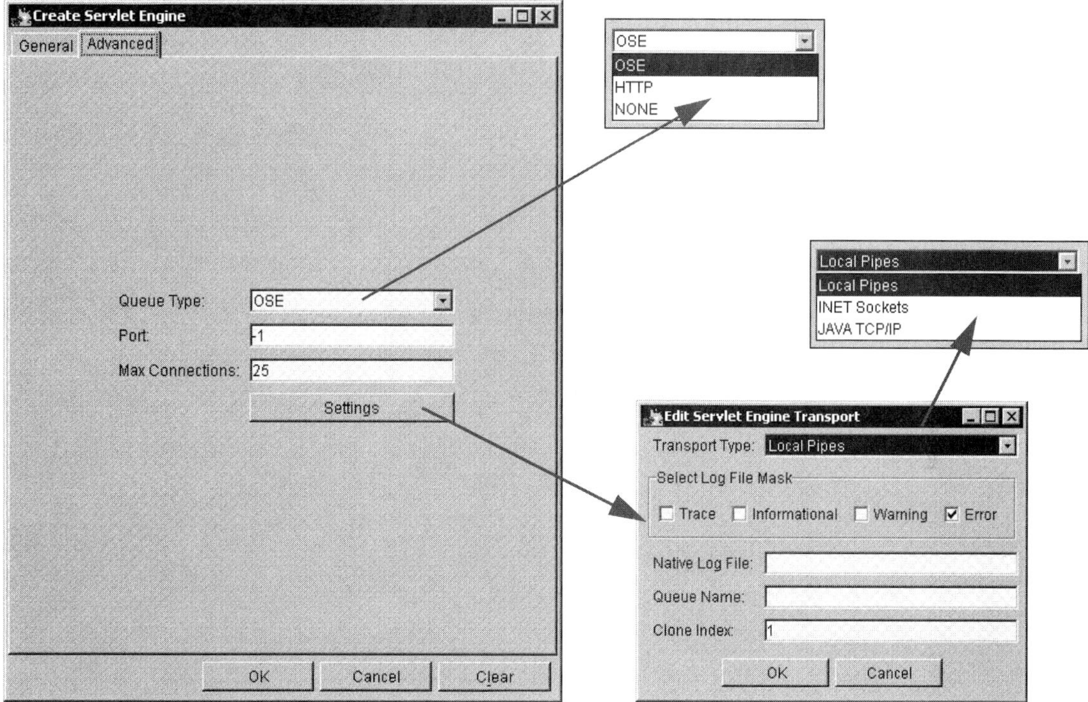

Figure 63. Create Servlet Engine: Advanced tab

Clicking the **Queue Type** drop-down menu brings up three options. The queue type options should be used as follows:

OSE - Used for routing requests locally and for remote OSE
HTTP - Not recommended at this time
None - For use with the Servlet Redirector

Remote OSE and Servlet Redirectors are not within the scope of this redbook; please see *WebSphere Scalability: WLM and Clustering using WebSphere Application Server Advanced*, SG24-6153 for details.

The port option specifies the port that the servlet engine will listen on for servlet requests from the Web server; leave it to the default `-1` to specify an ephemeral port. Max connections defaults to 25 and is the maximum number of concurrent resource requests.

Clicking the **Settings** button brings up another dialog box, which deals with the transport mechanisms used by the servlet engine. Click the **Transport Types** drop-down box to choose between the following using Local Pipes, INET Sockets and JAVA TCP/IP. Local Pipes are generally faster and should be used on Windows and AIX; on Solaris you can only use INET sockets. The JAVA TCP/IP option is a pure Java implementation of INET sockets; this should be used only for debugging.

Then click **OK**.

You will get the Information dialog that says `Command "ServletEngine.create" completed successfully`. Then click **OK**.

After you create a servlet engine successfully, you can see it (in our case, HelloServletEngine) on the administrative console as shown in Figure 64.

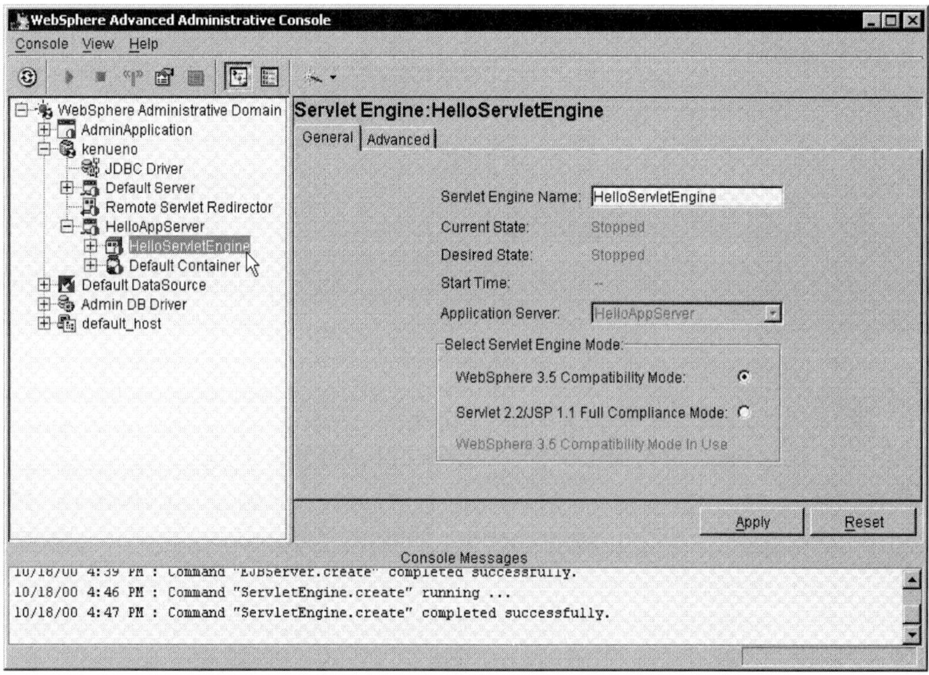

Figure 64. A newly created servlet engine

5.5.2.2 Define a servlet engine via the WSCP

Creation of the servlet engine via WSCP is done by calling the create method of the ServletEngine command object. In the example in Figure 65 on page 155, we are creating the same servlet engine as created above with the administrative console called HelloServletEngine, on the node entitled "SZYMON-Laptop", in the appserver called HelloAppServer. (Again, this example shows output from Windows 2000, but the Tcl syntax is the same on other platforms such as UNIX).

```
C:\WebSphere\AppServer\bin>wscp
wscp> ServletEngine create /Node:SZYMON-Laptop/ApplicationServer:HelloAppServer/
ServletEngine:HelloServletEngine
wscp> exit

C:\WebSphere\AppServer\bin>
```

Figure 65. Creation of the HelloServletEngine servlet engine

5.5.2.3 The RemoteSRP EJB

You will notice that, when you create a servlet engine in an application server instance, an EJB container entitled Default Container will automatically be created and an EJB called RemoteSRP will be deployed inside it.

The RemoteSRP enterprise bean, when using the Servlet Redirector, is used when you want to have WebSphere on a different machine from your Web server (HTTPD). The Servlet Redirector is an EJB client of the RemoteSRP bean. An overview of separating your Servlet Redirector from your application server is given in Chapter 16, “Topologies selection” on page 771, but for detailed information (including instructions on how to do this), see *WebSphere Scalability: WLM and Clustering using WebSphere Application Server Advanced*, SG24-6153.

5.5.3 Create a Web application

We show how to create a Web application via the administrative console, and by using WSCP. XMLConfig and the Web console could also be used for this purpose; for more information on these utilities, please refer to Chapter 21, “XMLConfig” on page 877 and Chapter 19, “Web console” on page 843.

5.5.3.1 Create a Web application via the console

Right-click the servlet engine in which you want to create your Web application (in our case, HelloServletEngine), and choose **Create -> Web Application** from the menu, as shown in Figure 66 on page 156.

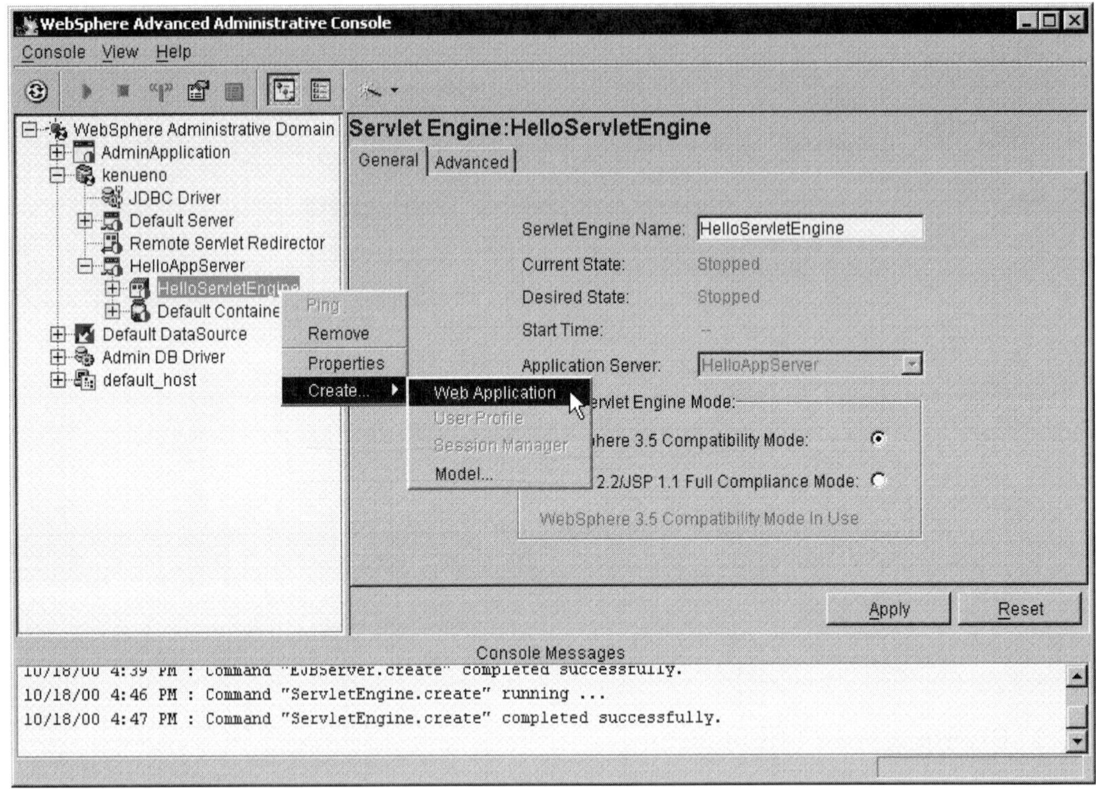

Figure 66. Create a new Web application

This will bring up the Create Web Application dialog box, which contains two tabs - General and Advanced, as shown in Figure 67 on page 157.

On the General tab, fill in the name you want to give to your Web application; in the example, we have used the name HelloWebApp.

From the drop-down dialog box, choose the virtual host on which you would like the Web application to run. We will just choose the default_host for our example; see the 4.2.4, “Virtual hosts” on page 130 for more details of virtual hosts.

Choose a path for your Web application; this will be the first “directory” in the URL. This will default to a prefix of /webapp/ and then whatever you type in as the Web application name (in our case, /webapp/HelloWebApp).

Finally, write a description for the Web application. When you have filled in the compulsory fields, click the **Advanced** tab.

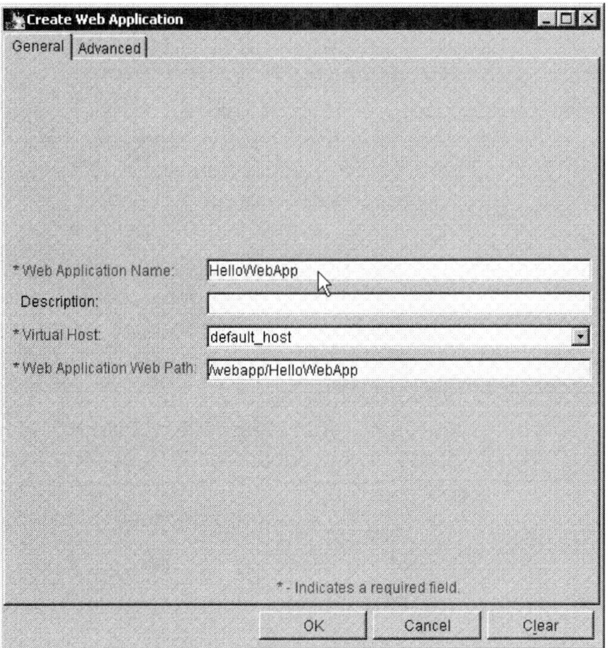

Figure 67. Create Web Application: General tab

Figure 68 on page 159 shows the Advanced tab.

The Document Root is the root directory for HTTP documents in this Web application.

The Classpath defines the application classpath; this should be set to the directory or directories where the class files for your servlets are stored on the local file system.

There are two properties for error page setting: Default Error Page field and Error Pages list.

In the Error Pages list, you may specify a special Web page when a special status code or exceptions occurs. For example, you may specify different Web pages to display when a status 404 and 500 occurs, or you may specify different Web pages to display when exception javax.servlet.ServletException and java.io.IOException are thrown. If a request causes both a status code to be generated and an exception to be thrown, and both these errors have specified error pages, then WebSphere uses the error page configured for the status code. If an error occurs that is not included in the list of error pages, a default error page will be displayed. See Chapter 8, "Servlet V2.2 in WebSphere V3.5.2" on page 295 for detailed information.

The ErrorReporter servlet, described in 5.6.6, "The ErrorReporter servlet" on page 183, may be used here.

The reload settings are at the Web application level. There are two settings for reload: Reload Interval and Auto Reload.

If you set Auto Reload to True, the classpath of the Web application is monitored and all components (JAR or class files) are reloaded whenever it is automatically detected that a component has been updated. It is of great benefit in developing or testing your environment. You may set it to False in a production environment in order to improve performance. A reload Interval is the interval between reloads of the Web application when Auto Reload is set to True. It is set in seconds.

For the MIME table property, specify mappings between extensions and MIME types. The MIME table consists of:

- Extension: Text string describing an extension, such as .txt
- Type: The defined MIME type associated with the extension, such as text/plain

You can also specify MIME table properties at the virtual host level, but the MIME table properties you specify for a Web application take precedence (local scope). In other word, the MIME table of the Web application is searched first. If a match is not found, then the MIME table configured for the virtual host is searched.

Then click **OK**. You will see the Information dialog that says `Command "ServletGroup.create" completed successfully`. Then click **OK**.

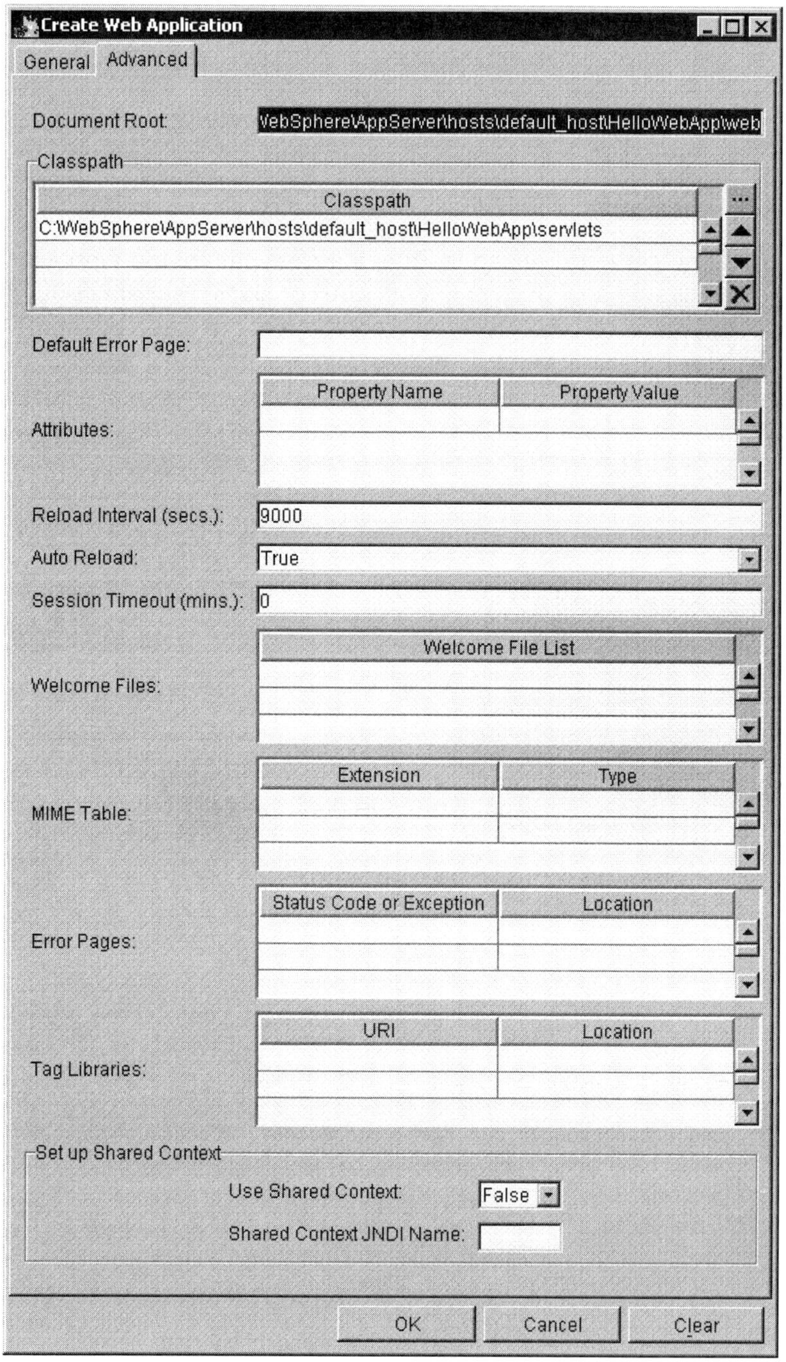

Figure 68. Create Web Application: Advanced tab

5.5.3.2 Create a Web application via the WSCP

The Web application is created in WSCP by calling the create method of the WebApplication command object.

In the example in Figure 69, we are creating the same Web application as created above with the administrative console, called HelloWebApplication, on the node entitled "SZYMON-Laptop", in the servlet engine called HelloServletEngine, within the appserver called HelloAppServer.

Note that this command is more complex than those for creating the application server and servlet engine. This is because for the application server and servlet engine, we simply accepted all of the default options, and the only required option for those objects is the name.

For a Web application, however, it is required to give the classpath for the application, the document root and the Web path; these are the Classpath, DocRoot and URIPath attributes of the WebApplication object in WSCP, and therefore the creation command must specify them using the -attribute option.

Once again, although we show output from Windows 2000, the Tcl syntax is the same on other platforms, such as UNIX.

```
C:\WebSphere\AppServer\bin>wscp
wscp> WebApplication create /Node:SZYMON-Laptop/ApplicationServer:HelloAppServer
/ServletEngine:HelloServletEngine/WebApplication:HelloWebApplication/ -attribute
 {{Classpath C:\WebSphere\AppServer\hosts\default_host\HelloWebApp\servlets} {Do
cRoot C:\WebSphere\AppServer\hosts\default_host\HelloWebApp\web} {URIPath defaul
t_host/webapp/HelloWebApp}}
wscp>exit

C:\WebSphere\AppServer\bin>
```

Figure 69. Creating a Web application via WSCP

Note

Via the administrative console, there is a separate option to specify the virtual host name; however, in WSCP the virtual host is specified as the start of the URIPath attribute, as part of the Web path.

5.5.4 Deploying the servlet

We demonstrate deploying the servlet using the administrative console and WSCP; it is also possible to deploy using XMLConfig.

5.5.4.1 Deploying the servlet via the console

Right-click the Web application in which you want to deploy your servlet, and choose **Create -> Servlet** from the menu, as shown in Figure 70. This will bring up the Create Servlet dialog box, which contains two tabs - General and Advanced.

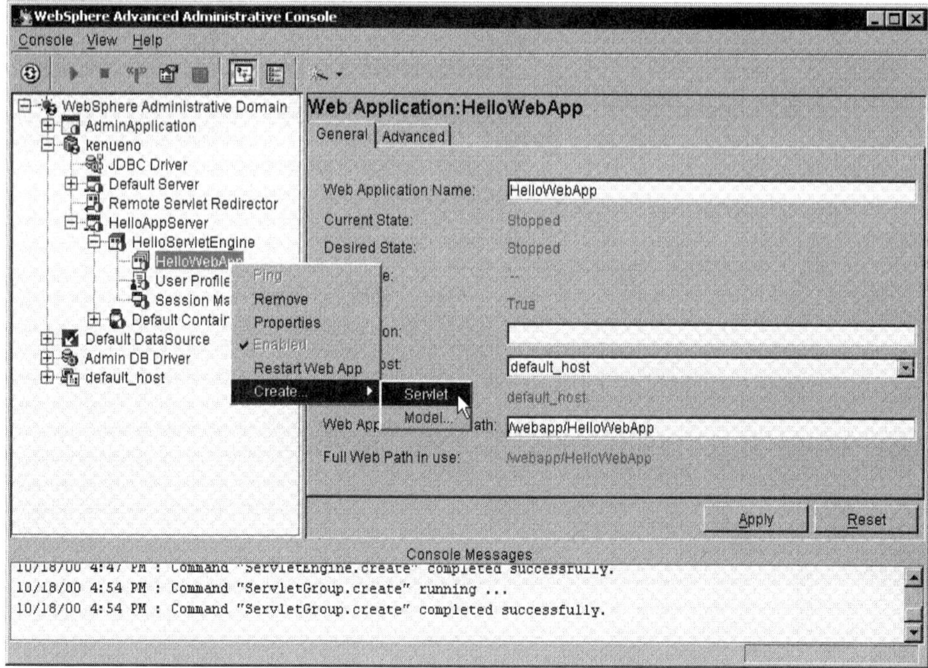

Figure 70. Create Servlet

The General tab of the Create Servlet dialog box is shown in Figure 71 on page 162. There are three mandatory fields: Servlet Name, Web Application and Servlet Class Name.

The Servlet Name field should be used to give your servlet a short descriptive name; this name will be used to refer to this instance of the servlet in the administrative database, so it will show up in the administrative console and WSCP.

The Web Applications drop-down list is by default set to the Web application you are deploying the servlet in, but be warned that the list includes all of the Web applications on the node (even those in other application servers on the same node).

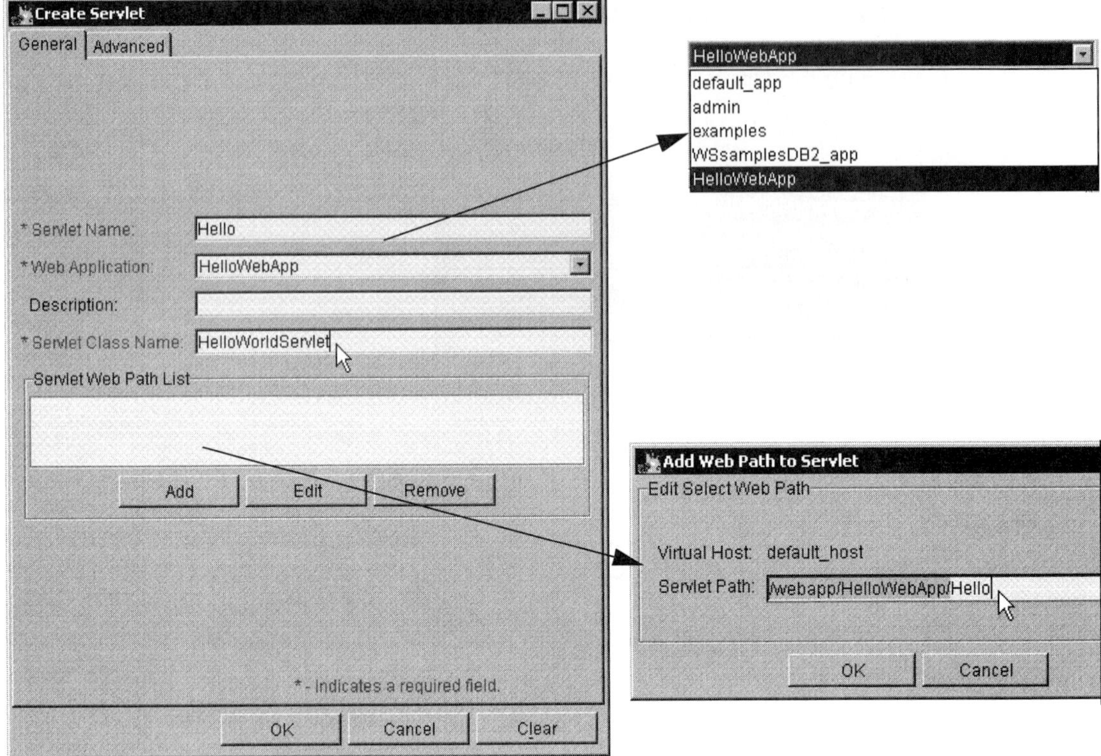

Figure 71. Create Servlet: General tab

The final mandatory field is the Servlet Class Name field; this should contain the full name of the class, such as HelloWorldServlet.

The servlet Web path is the part of the URL after the host, which will be used to access this servlet. It defaults to the Web application Web path (in the example this is /webapp/HelloWebApp), and you should give a name under that path for the servlet to be called. The full URL to access the HelloWorld servlet as shown in the example will be:

```
<hostname>/webapp/HelloWebApp/Hello
```

Then click **OK** on the Add Web Path to Servlet window.

You will see the Servlet Web Path which you specified, as shown in Figure 72 on page 163.

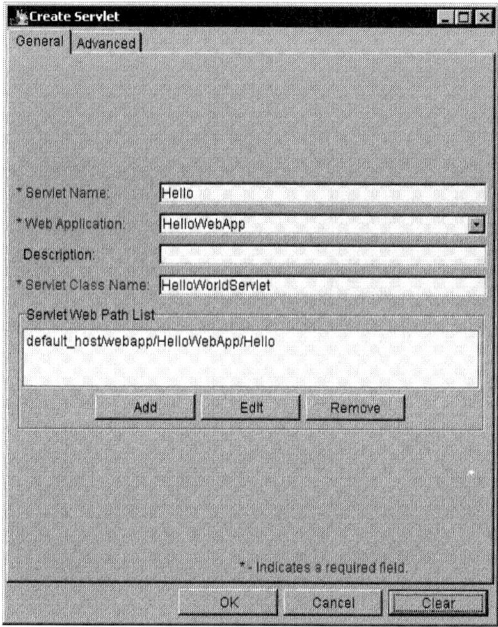

Figure 72. Servlet Web Path List

Click the **Advanced** tab to show the advanced options of the Create Servlet dialog box, as shown in Figure 73 on page 164.

The initial parameters for the servlet can be set here. You can also turn on debug mode, which is discussed in 23.6, "Object level trace (OLT) and the IBM distributed debugger" on page 958.

Finally, you can force the servlet to be loaded at startup (rather than the first time the servlet is accessed).

Then click **OK**.

You will get the Information dialog that says `Command "Servlet.create" completed successfully.` then click **OK**.

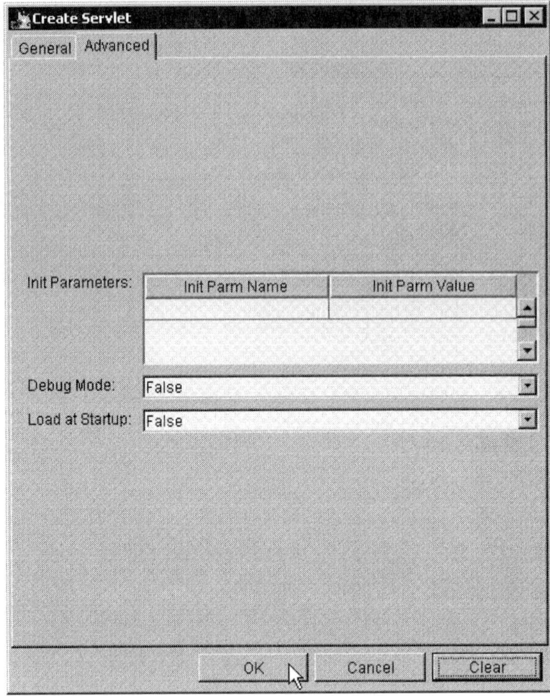

Figure 73. Create Servlet: Advanced tab

After you create a servlet successfully, you will see it (in our case, Hello) on the administrative console as shown in Figure 74 on page 165.

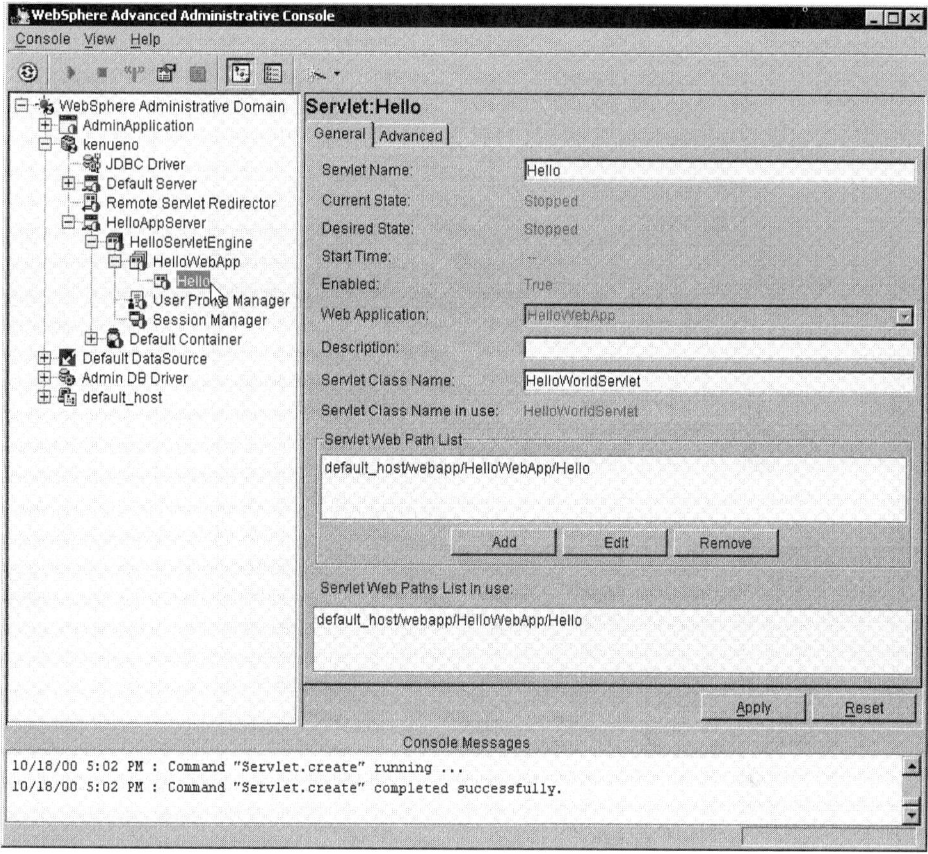

Figure 74. A newly created servlet

5.5.4.2 Deploying the servlet via the WSCP

To deploy the servlet using WSCP, as usual we call the create method of the command object "Servlet".

In the example in Figure 75 on page 166, we are deploying our HelloWorldServlet in the HelloWebApplication Web application, on the SZYMON-Laptop node, in the HelloServletEngine servlet engine, within the HelloAppServer appserver.

Again, this command is slightly more complex than the commands used to create the application server and servlet engine, because instead of accepting all of the default options and only specifying the name, we have a number of required attributes.

We must specify the name of the class and the full Web path of the servlet, as the Code and URIPaths attributes of the servlet object in WSCP.

```
C:\WebSphere\AppServer\bin>wscp
wscp> Servlet create /Node:SZYMON-Laptop/ApplicationServer:HelloAppServer/Servle
tEngine:HelloServletEngine/WebApplication:HelloWebApplication/Servlet:Hello/ -at
tribute {{Code HelloWorldServlet} {URIPaths default_host/webapp/HelloWebApp/Hell
o}}
wscp> exit

C:\WebSphere\AppServer\bin>
```

Figure 75. Deploying a servlet via WSCP

> **Note**
>
> Note that here as well there is no separate option to specify the virtual host name, but rather it is specified as part of the URIPath attribute. Also note that the URIPaths attribute can contain more than one path; if this is desired, they should be presented in braces as a Tcl list.

5.5.5 Invoking the deployed servlet

We could invoke this servlet with either a GET or POST form action method; the service() method will execute for either. Since a URL forces the Web browser to send the request using GET, similar to the way a standard HTML page is requested, the simplest way to invoke the servlet would be by specifying the URL in a Web browser. The example servlet could be invoked from the Web browser with the URL:

```
http://<host>/webapp/HelloWebApp/Hello
```

The output of the servlet is shown in Figure 76 on page 167.

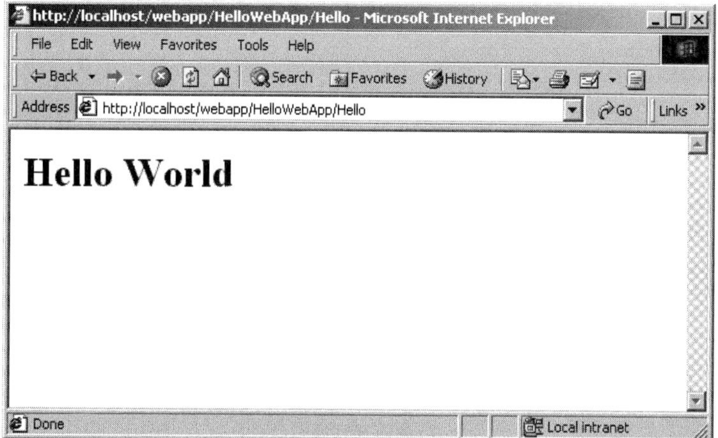

Figure 76. The output of the HelloWorldServlet

5.6 Internal servlets

A number of servlets are supplied by WebSphere in the `default_app` application, and you can also use them as part of your own Web application where appropriate. This includes servlets that allow file serving from WebSphere directories and which add functionality to compile JSPs.

5.6.1 Adding the internal servlets to your Web application

These internal servlets can be added to an existing Web application using the **Console -> Tasks -> Add a Servlet** task, as shown in Figure 77 on page 168.

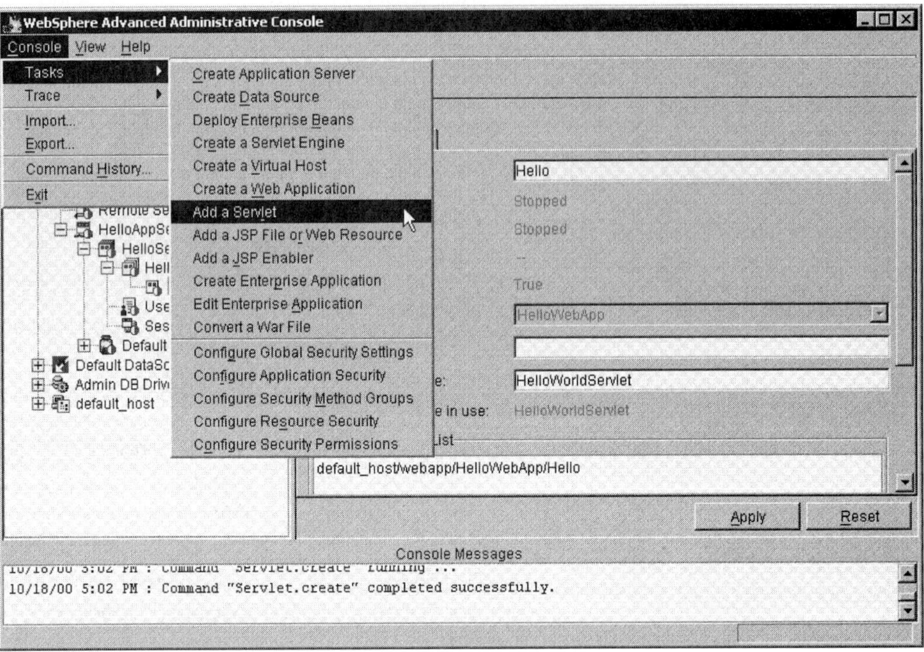

Figure 77. Add a Servlet task

The first dialog box of the Add a Servlet task, shown in Figure 78, asks whether you wish to add servlets from an existing JAR file or directory. Choose **No** to create a new servlet, and click **Next**.

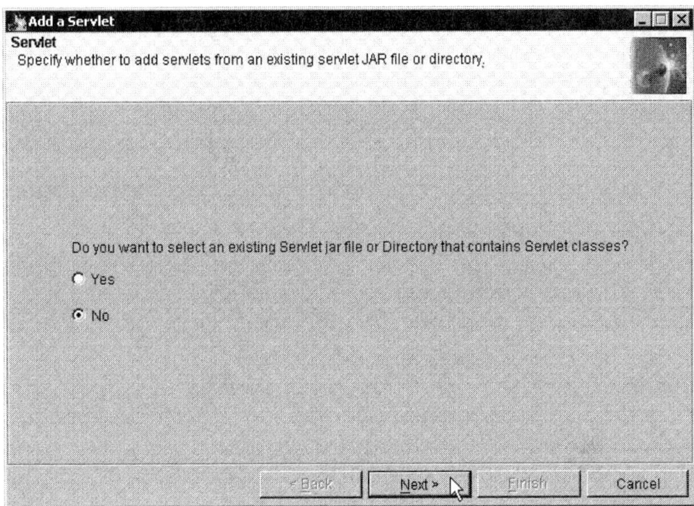

Figure 78. Add a Servlet: Servlet window #1

The next dialog box asks you to choose a Web application in which to add the servlet. Navigate down to the Web application you wish to use (in our case, HelloWebApp), as in Figure 79, and click **Next**.

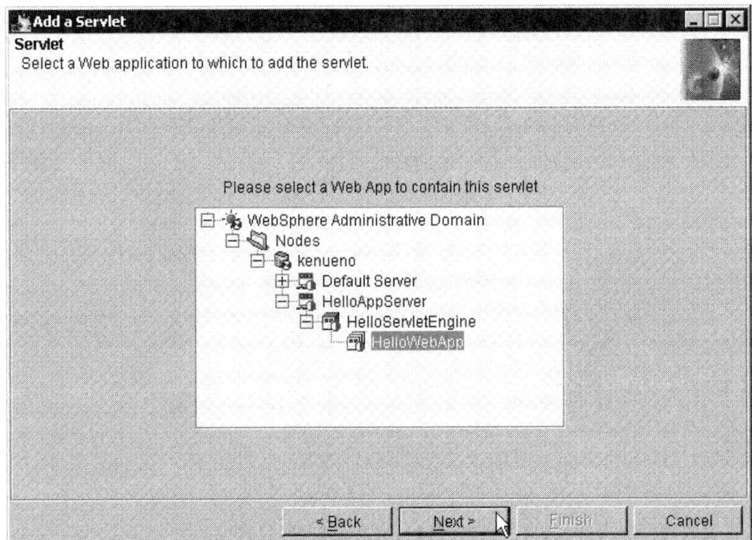

Figure 79. Add a Servlet: Servlet window #2

Finally we come to the dialog box that gives a list of the internal servlets that you can use, as shown in Figure 80.

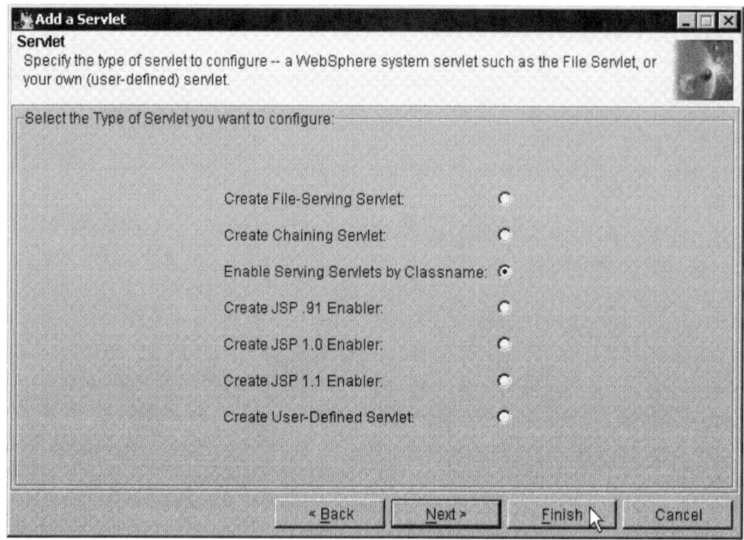

Figure 80. Add a Servlet: Servlet window #3

Choose which servlet you wish to add, and click **Finish**. Note that the chainer servlet creation process has one more dialog box, which will be described in 5.6.5, "The chainer servlet" on page 177.

5.6.2 The invoker servlet

The invoker servlet can be used to invoke servlets by class or code names. Note that it is a security risk to invoke by class in production; this should be seen as more of a development tool.

Follow the instructions in 5.6.1, "Adding the internal servlets to your Web application" on page 167, then select **Enable Serving Servlet by Classname** and click **Finish** as shown in Figure 81.

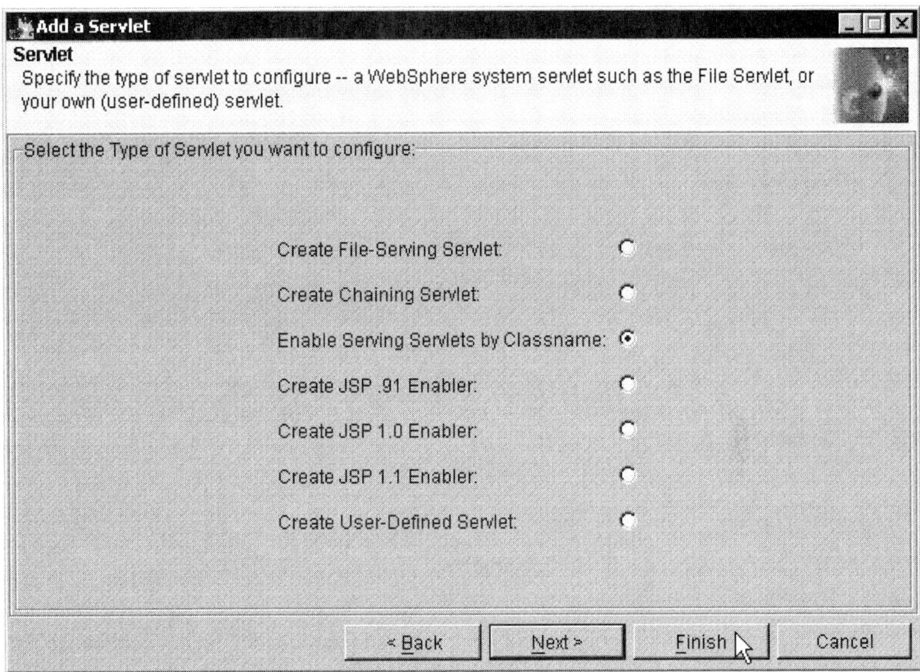

Figure 81. Add the invoker servlet

Then you will see the Information dialog that says `Command "Servlet.create" completed successfully.` and click **OK**.

Now you can use it to invoke other servlets by using the URL of the invoker servlet and adding the name of the class or the short name of the servlet (as held in the administrative database) at the end.

The default setting for the Web path of the invoker servlet is the Web application Web path plus the word "servlet"; this can be seen in Figure 82.

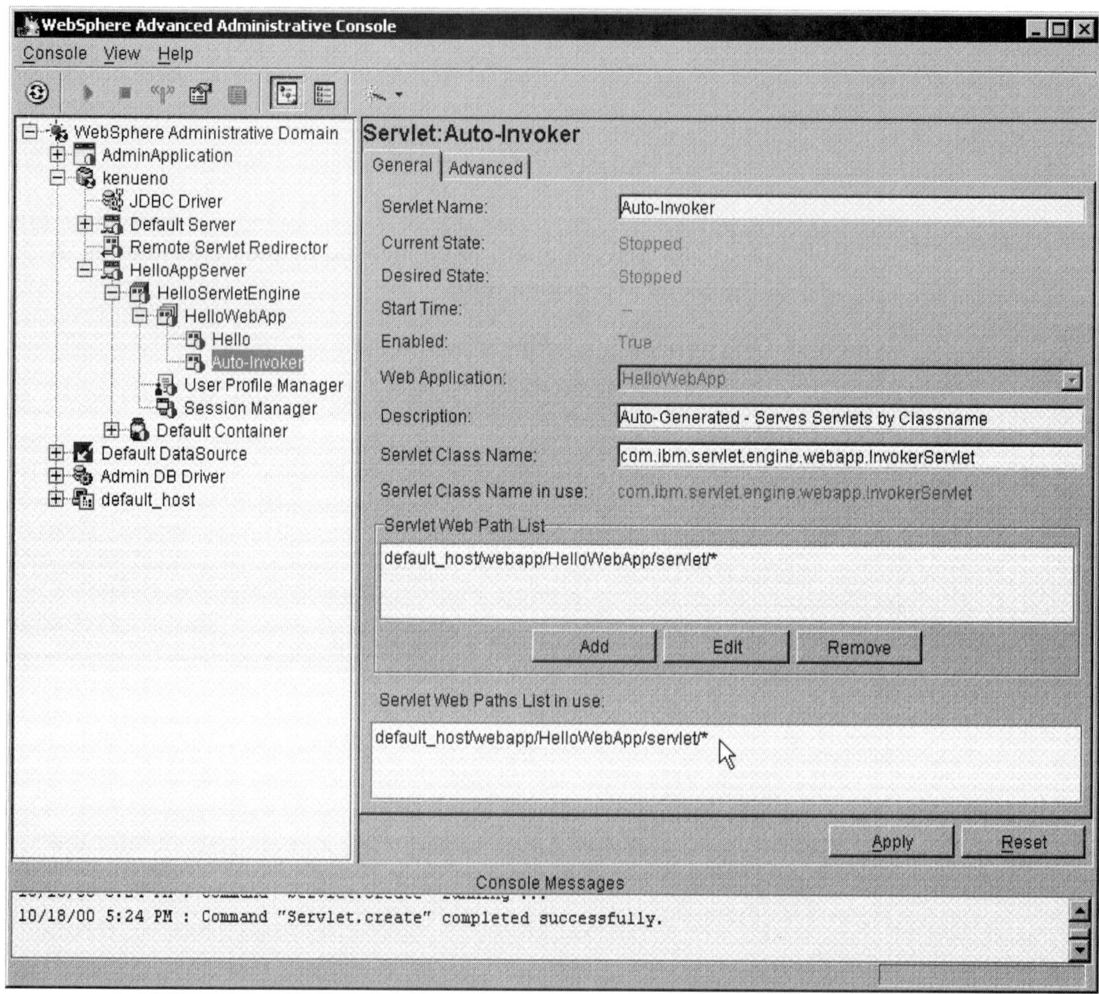

Figure 82. The Web path of the invoker servlet

We can now call our HelloWorldServlet by using two extra URLs:

```
http://localhost/webapp/HelloWorldApp/servlet/Hello
http://localhost/webapp/HelloWorldApp/servlet/HelloWorldServlet
```

The first of these is the short name for the servlet; this is in addition to the normal short name invocation via the Web path. The second URL invokes the servlet using the class name. Note that it is possible to completely delete the actual servlet Web path for the Hello servlet, and still access it via the Invoker servlet.

Using the Invoker servlet is considered a security exposure that can be avoided by performing certain administrative tasks. In addition to invoking the servlet by the servlet Web paths configured via the administrative console, the Invoker servlet enables you to invoke servlets by their class names.

Anyone enabling the Invoker servlet to serve servlets by their class names must take steps to avoid potential security risks. The administrator should remain aware of each and every servlet class placed in the classpath of an application, even if the servlets are to be invoked by their classnames. A summary of the steps is provided here.

To protect each servlet, the administrator needs to:

1. Configure a Web resource based on the servlet class name, such as:

   ```
   /servlet/SnoopServlet
   ```

   for SnoopServlet.class
2. Add the Web resource to the Web Path list of the Invoker servlet in the Web application to which the servlet belongs.
3. Use the Configure Resource Security wizard in the administrative console to secure the Web resource.

Also, the administrator needs to secure the Invoker servlet itself. More details for this procedure can be found in the InfoCenter for WebSphere V3.5.

5.6.3 The file servlet

The file servlet (or file-serving servlet or file serving enabler) can serve HTML or other files in the Web application document root without extra configuration steps. This servlet will simply serve up any file that is placed in the document root of the Web application.

Note

When dealing with static HTML pages, you can choose to have the pages be served by WebSphere or just have them served by the Web Server itself by putting them in the Web Server's document root. In both cases, you can protect the pages using WebSphere security.

For the case were HTML pages are served by the Web Server, as opposed to being served by the WebSphere, there may be an increase in performance since the Web Server is serving the pages directly. Although, when dealing with multiple Web applications, where each has its own document root, using the WebSphere file serving servlet has the advantage of keeping your static pages organized and better encapsulated with the rest of your application.

You follow the instructions as described in 5.6.1, "Adding the internal servlets to your Web application" on page 167, then select **Create File Serving Servlet** and click **Finish** as shown in Figure 83.

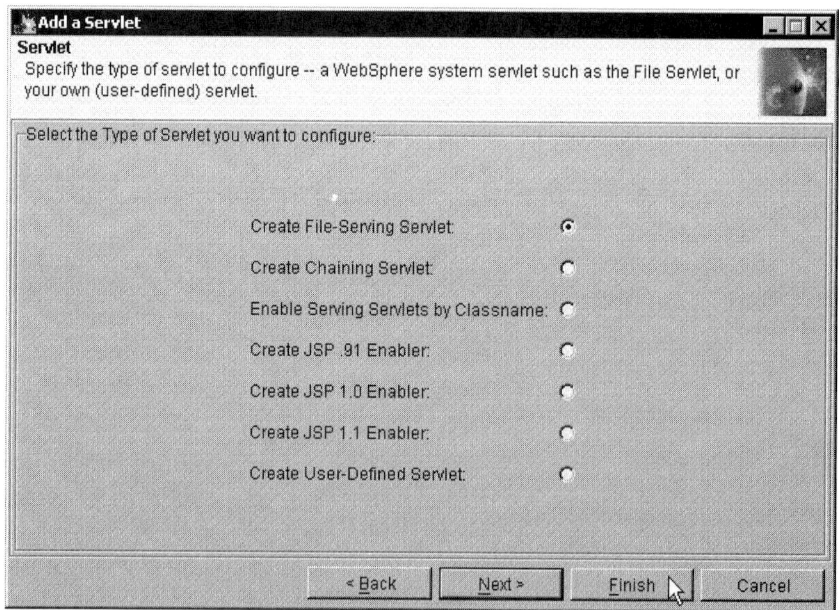

Figure 83. Create File-Serving Servlet

You will see the Information dialog that says `Command "Servlet.create" completed successfully.` and click **OK**.

After you create the file servlet successfully, you will see it on the administrative console as shown in Figure 84.

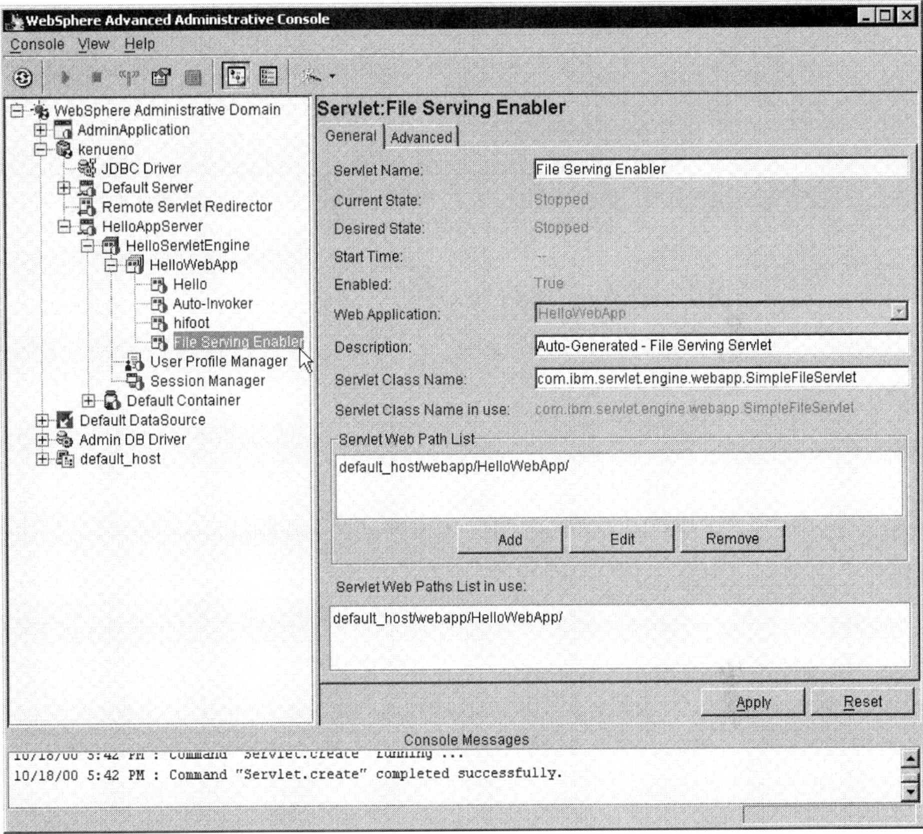

Figure 84. A newly created File-Serving servlet

As an example, after installing the file servlet we placed a file called myzipfile.zip into the document root of our Web application:

```
C:\WebSphere\AppServer\hosts\default_host\HelloWebApp\web
```

We then connected with a Web browser to the following URL:

```
http://localhost/webapp/HelloWebServer/myzipfile.zip
```

The Web browser offered to download the file, as shown in Figure 85 on page 176.

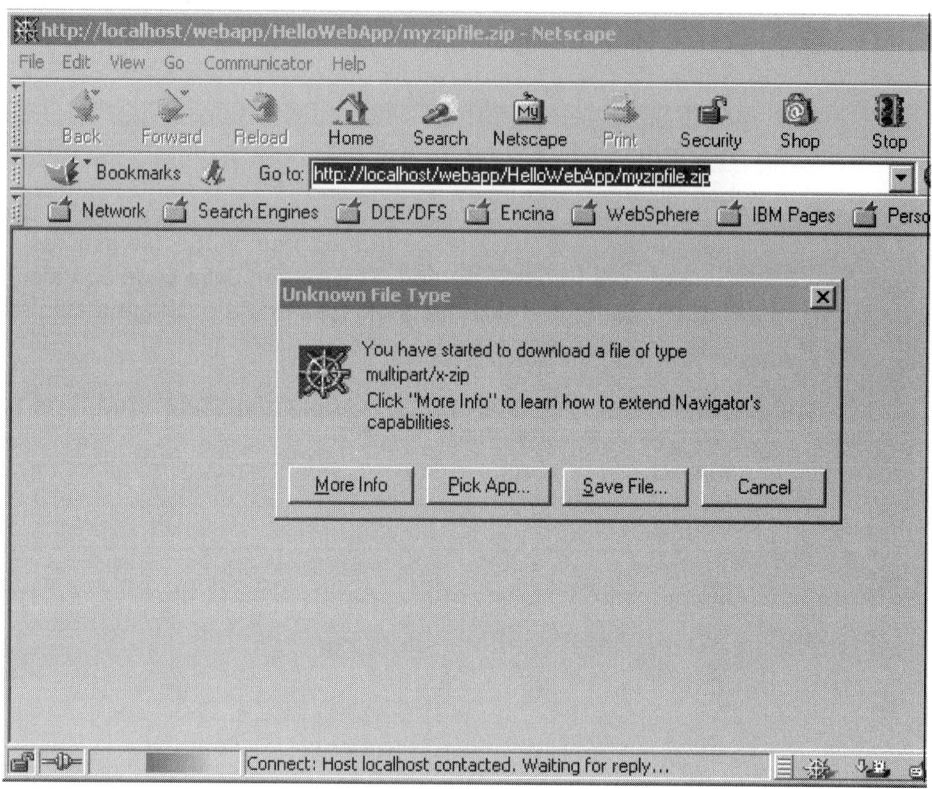

Figure 85. The File-Serving servlet serves a file

5.6.4 JSP compilers

The 1.0 JSP compiler is `com.sun.jsp.runtime.JspServlet`, and the 0.91 JSP compiler is `com.ibm.servlet.jsp.http.pagecompile.PageCompileServlet`. These servlets enable the JSP 0.91 or 1.0 page compiler to allow the Web application to handle JSP files. Adding a JSP processor to an application is required if the Web application contains JSP files.

The JSP processor creates and compiles a servlet from each JSP file. The processor produces two files for each JSP file:

- .java file, which contains the Java language code for the servlet
- .class file, which is the compiled servlet

The JSP processor puts the .java and the .class file in a path specific to the processor, `<app_document_root>\pagecompile` for the JSP 0.91 processor or

`<WAS_install_root>\temp\servlet_host_name\app_name` for the JSP 1.0 processor.

The .java and the .class file have the same filename. The processor uses a naming convention that includes adding underscore characters and a suffix to the JSP filename. For example, if the JSP filename is simple.jsp, the generated files are _simple_xjsp.java and _simple_xjsp.class.

Like all servlets, a servlet generated from a JSP file extends javax.servlet.http.HttpServlet. The servlet Java code contains import statements for the necessary classes and a package statement, if the servlet class is part of a package.

If the JSP file contains JSP syntax (such as directives and scriptlets), the JSP processor converts the JSP syntax to the equivalent Java code. If the JSP file contains HTML tags, the processor adds Java code so that the servlet outputs the HTML character by character.

JSPs will be covered in detail in Chapter 6, "JSP support" on page 189.

5.6.5 The chainer servlet

The chainer servlet enables a servlet chain, in which servlets forward output and responses to other servlets for processing. In servlet chaining, multiple servlets are called for a single client HTTP request, each servlet providing part of the HTML output. Each servlet receives the original client HTTP request as input, and each servlet produces its own output independently. Figure 86 shows the servlet chaining process flow in WebSphere.

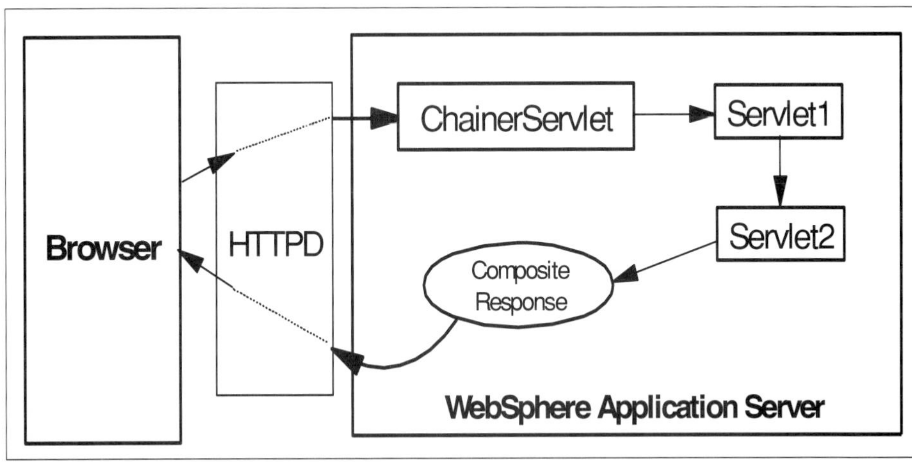

Figure 86. Servlet chaining process flow

The chainer servlet is specified on the original request, and multiple servlets are specified in an initialization parameter as the target. Servlet chaining has the advantage of allowing the Web developer to create modular servlets that can, for example, output standard HTML headers and footers or provide common dynamic content for pages. Each servlet is called in the order specified in the chainer definition, and the output HTML is made up of the output from all of the servlets.

5.6.5.1 Chainer servlet example

The FooterServlet

As an example, let us chain another servlet to our HelloWorldServlet example. This new servlet, called FooterServlet, will add a copyright message to the bottom of the HTML page generated.

```
import java.io.*;
import javax.servlet.*;
import javax.servlet.http.*;

public class FooterServlet extends HttpServlet {
    protected void service(HttpServletRequest request,
                    HttpServletResponse response)
                    throws ServletException, IOException {
        response.setContentType(request.getContentType());
        PrintWriter out = response.getWriter();
        BufferedReader in = request.getReader();
        String line;
        while((line = in.readLine()) != null)
            out.println(line);
        out.println("<P>(c)Copyright IBM Corporation 2000");
        out.println("</BODY></HTML>");
        out.close();
    }
}
```

Figure 87. The FooterServlet adds a copyright message to HTML pages

This servlet also extends HttpServlet. Examining the differences between the FooterServlet and the HelloWorldServlet, we see the following:

1. The `response.setContentType` uses `request.getContentType()` as its argument, to make sure that we set the content type to whatever the content type of the original servlet was.
2. We create a BufferedReader, which gets a reader object from the original servlet, and then do `out.println` for every line that we read from the original servlet output. This replicates exactly the output of the original servlet.
3. Finally, we add our own HTML to the end of the output.

Note

Because we are reading and then printing the output of the original servlet in point 2, it is possible to modify it before printing. This would be *filtering* the output, rather than just *chaining* more HTML to the original output.

For purposes of HTML, we have to remove the line `out.println("</BODY></HTML>");` from the HelloWorldServlet, so that it is only output one time.

Deploying the FooterServlet

Since we already have a node, application server, servlet engine and Web application, we can quickly use WSCP to deploy the FooterServlet servlet, as shown in Figure 88.

```
C:\>wscp
wscp> Servlet create
/Node:SZYMON-Laptop/ApplicationServer:HelloAppServer/ServletEngine:HelloServletEngine/
WebApplication:HelloWebApplication/Servlet:Footer/ -attribute {{Code FooterServlet} {U
RIPaths default_host/webapp/HelloWebApp/Footer}}
wscp>
```

Figure 88. Deploy the FooterServlet using the wscp command

We also need to compile the Java code and copy the resulting FooterServlet.class file into the servlets directory of the Web application:

```
C:\WebSphere\AppServer\Hello>javac -classpath c:\websphere\appserver\lib\servlet.jar
FooterServlet.java
C:\WebSphere\AppServer\Hello>copy FooterServlet.class C:\WebSphere\AppServer\hosts\de
fault_host\HelloWebApp\Servlets
C:\WebSphere\AppServer\Hello>
```

Figure 89. Compile and install the FooterServlet code

The FooterServlet is now ready to go.

Create the chainer servlet

To create the chainer servlet, go to the third dialog box of the Add a Servlet task, as discussed in 5.6.1, “Adding the internal servlets to your Web application” on page 167. Select the **Create Chaining Servlet** option and click **Next** as shown in Figure 90 on page 180. A further dialog box will appear.

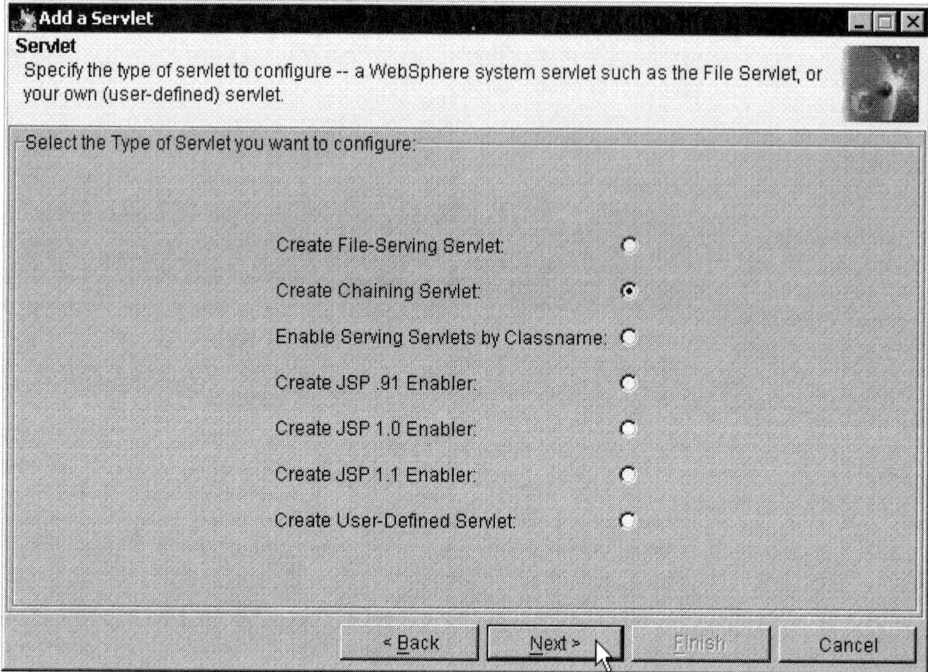

Figure 90. Create the chainer servlet

Fill in the dialog box as in Figure 91 on page 181. The name of the servlet is the short name that WebSphere will store in the administrative database to refer to this servlet; we have called ours hifoot (Hello with a Footer).

The value for the initialization parameter chainer.pathlist should be a list of all of the servlets that this servlet is to chain together, separated by spaces. In our case, we are chaining /Hello and /Footer (both names are relative to the Web path of the Web application), so the value of chainter.pathlist should be set to "/Hello /Footer".

Finally, we need to specify the Web path list, relative to the Web path of the Web application.

Click **Finish**.

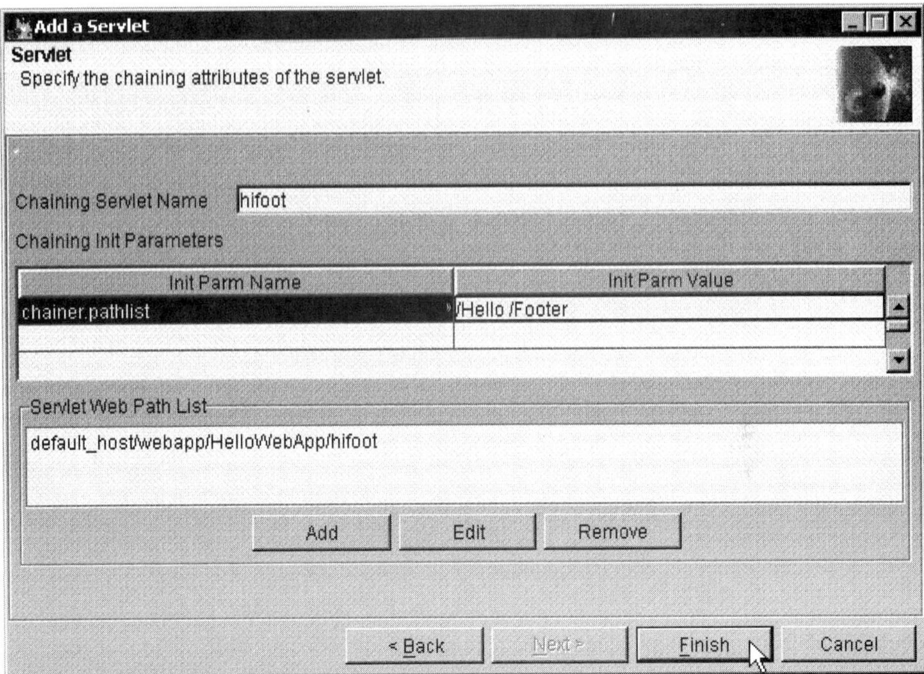

Figure 91. The chaining attributes of the servlet

Then you will get an Information dialog box that says, `Command "Servlet.create" completed successfully.` and click **OK**.

You will see the chaining servlet (in our case, hifoot servlet) on the administrative console as shown in Figure 92 on page 182. The chaining servlet, hifoot, is now ready to go.

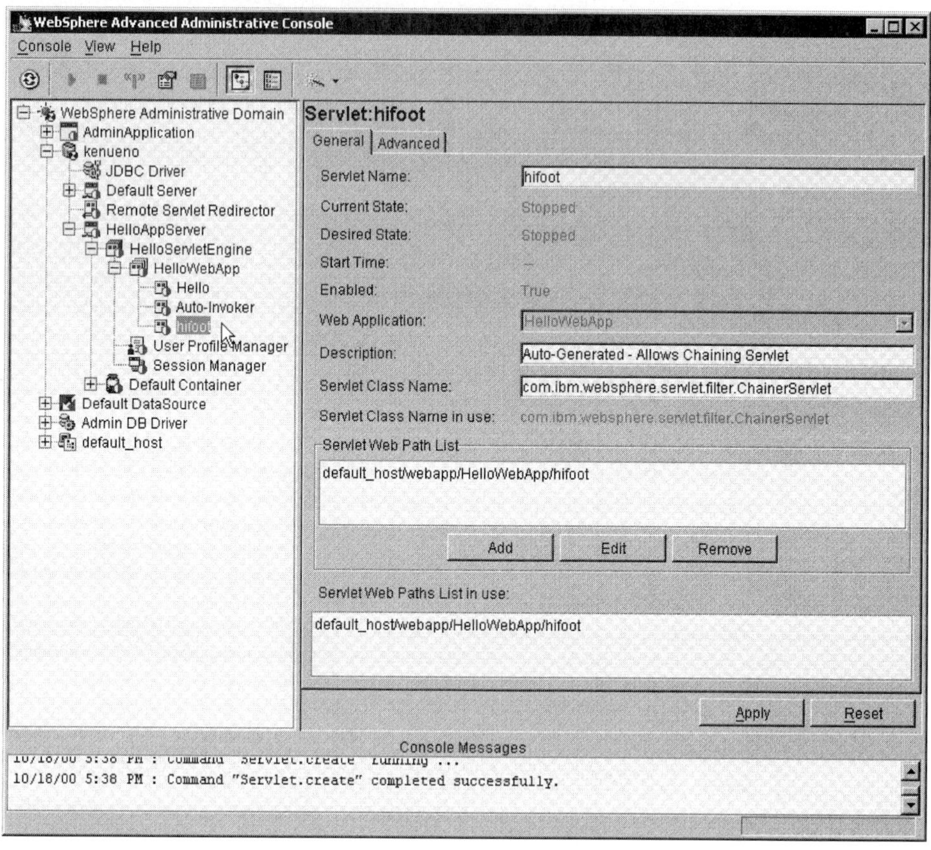

Figure 92. A newly created chaining servlet

Test the chaining servlet

Pointing a Web browser to the URL:

```
http://localhost/webapp/HelloWebApp/hifoot
```

verifies that both servlets are being used, as seen in Figure 93 on page 183.

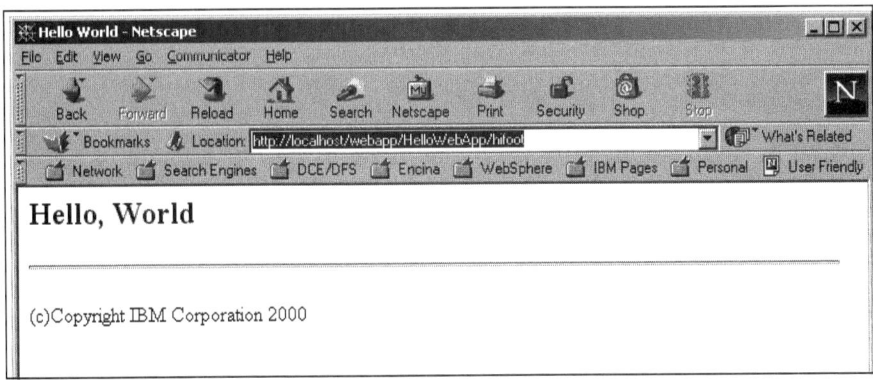

Figure 93. The output of the chaining servlet hifoot

5.6.6 The ErrorReporter servlet

The ErrorReporter servlet enables error reporting through an error page, without having to write your own error page. This servlet is a special case as far as creation of internal servlets is concerned, in that there is no option for it on the Add a Servlet task.

Instead you must choose the **Create User-Defined Servlet** option as shown in Figure 94 and click **Next**.

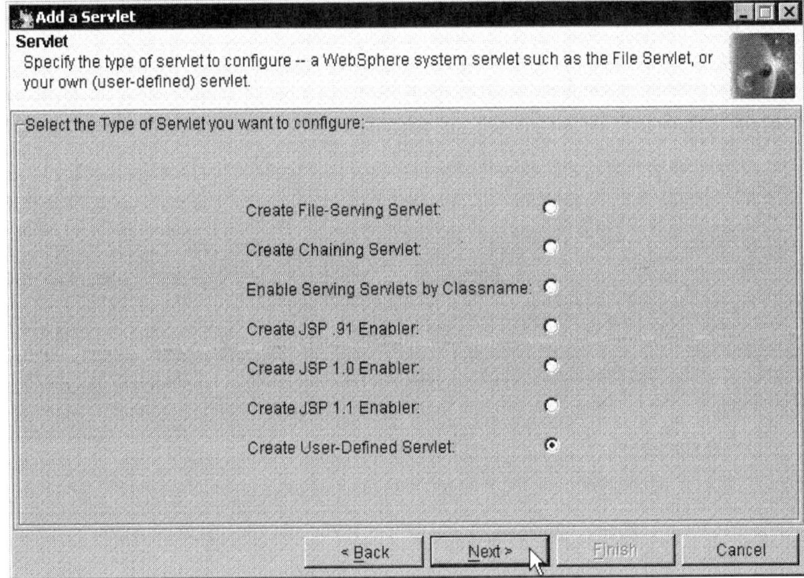

Figure 94. Create the Error Reporter servlet

Then you fill in the fields as in Figure 95.

The class name for the ErrorReporter is com.ibm.servlet.engine.webapp.DefaultErrorReporter.

Add the Servlet Web Path and click **Next**.

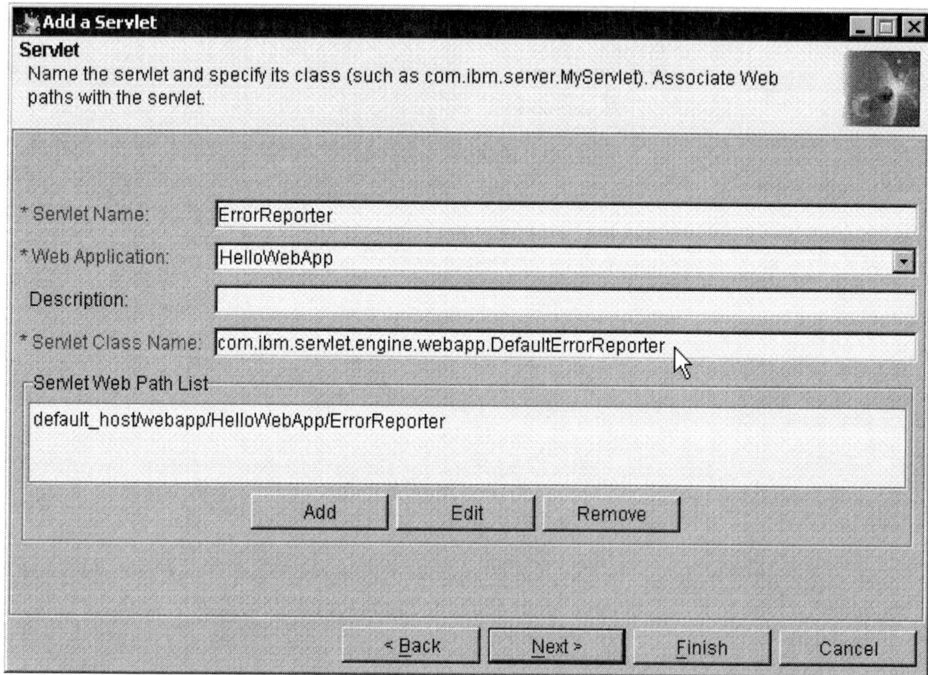

Figure 95. Add the ErrorReporter servlet

Then you will see the Information dialog box that says `Command "Servlet.create" completed successfully.` and click **OK**.

You will see the ErrorReporter servlet on the administrative console as shown in Figure 96 on page 185.

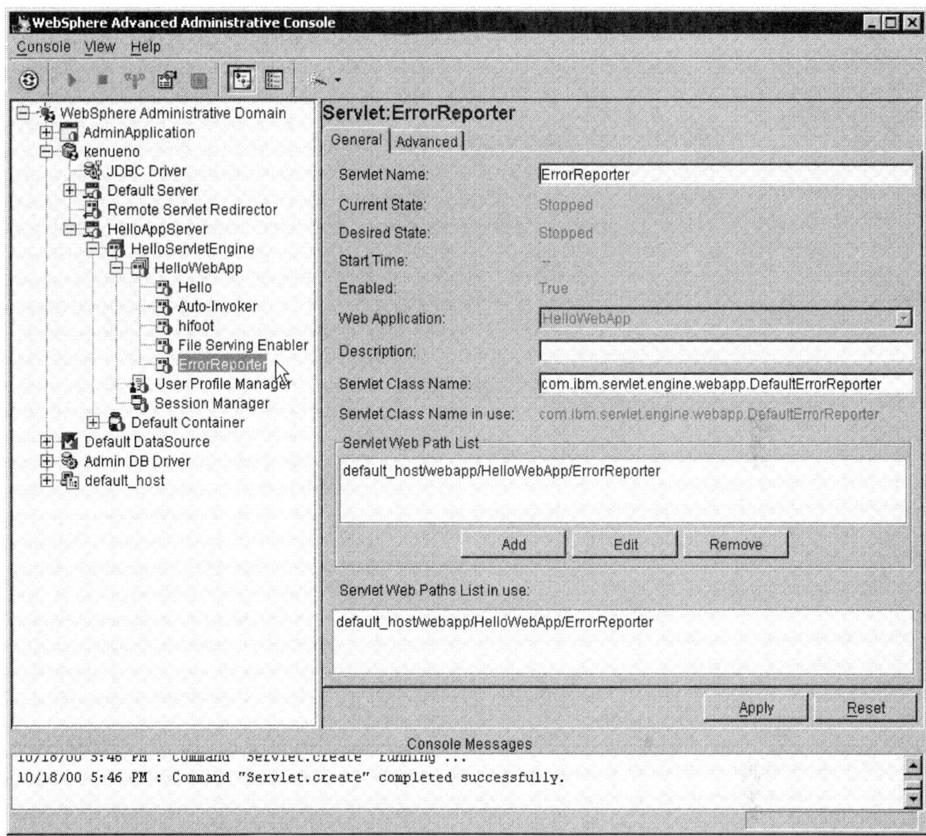

Figure 96. A newly created Error Reporter servlet

You will also need to set the Default Error Page attribute of your Web application to /ErrorReporter on the Advanced tab as shown in Figure 97 on page 186; this will automatically use the version of ErrorReporter in the Web path for the Web application.

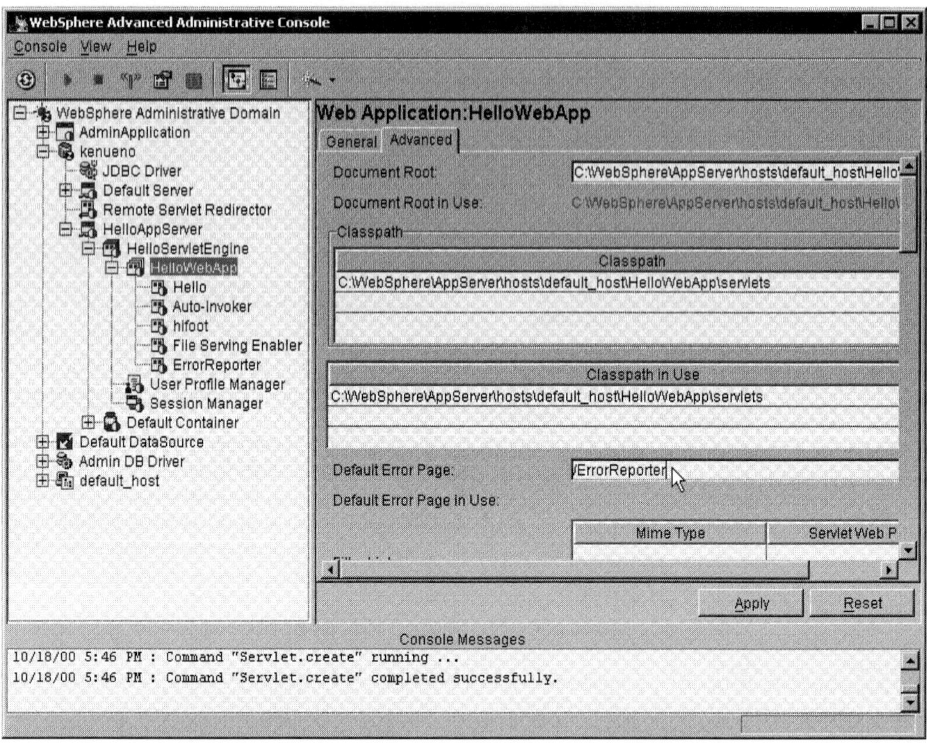

Figure 97. Default Error Page setting

In order to test how the ErrorReporter works, we had to break something.

We therefore deleted the HelloWorldServlet.class file from the hard disk. This broke the Hello servlet in a fairly substantial way.

Without the ErrorReporter servlet, we did not get an error; as you can see in Figure 98 on page 187, we get a message from the Web browser that the document contained no data.

Once the ErrorReporter servlet has been added, however, we do get an error message, as seen in Figure 99 on page 187.

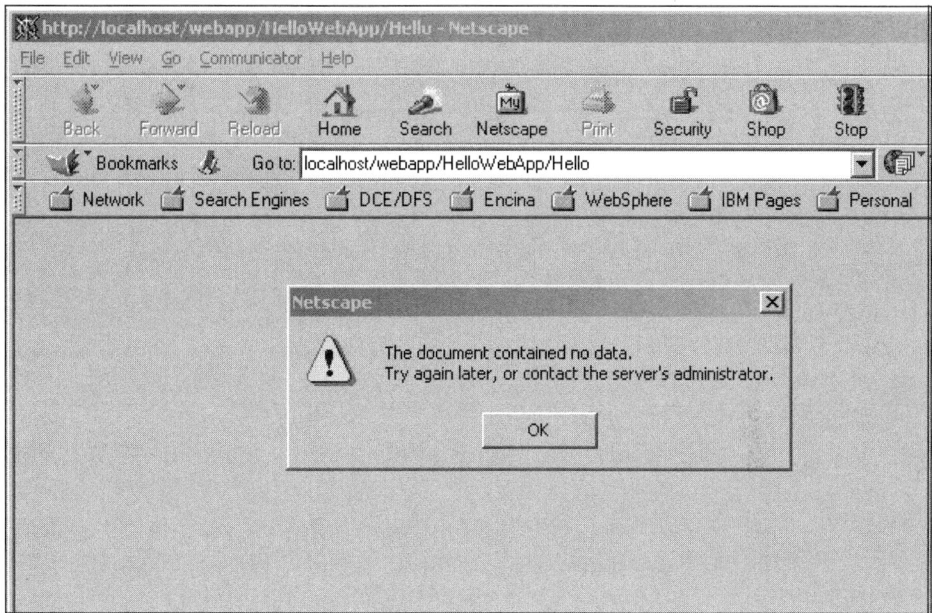

Figure 98. Without the ErrorReporter servlet

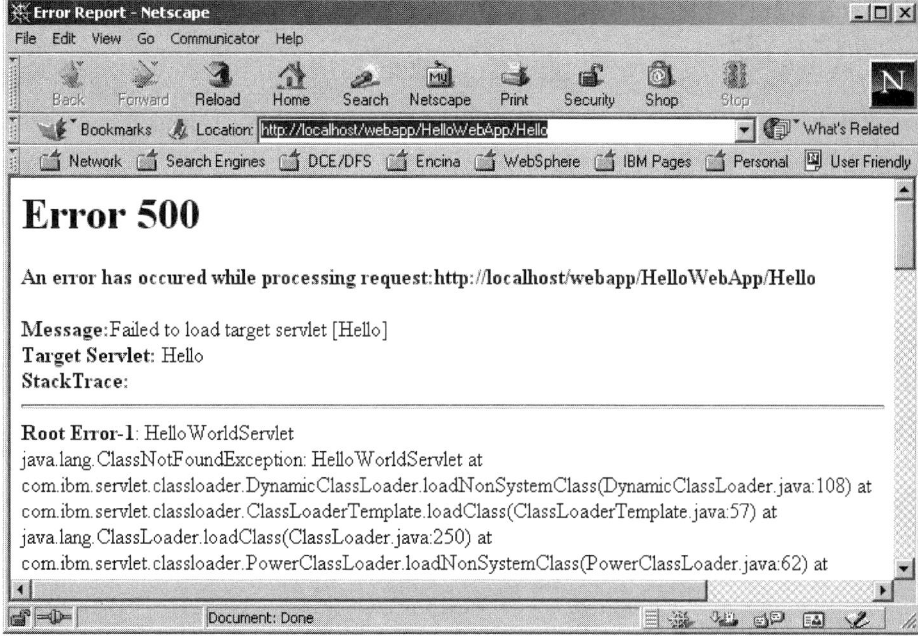

Figure 99. With the ErrorReporter servlet

Chapter 6. JSP support

Chapter 3, "WebSphere programming model" on page 17 discussed how JavaServer Pages (JSPs) fit into a Web application. This chapter shows how to build JSPs within that framework. Several other redbooks show how to use such products as WebSphere Studio to build and test JSPs. This chapter discusses the basic relationship between a JSP and its calling servlet.

This chapter also shows several techniques in which JSPs can be used to develop and debug Web applications. These JSPs would never appear in a production system, but rather would exist temporarily to quickly debug the collaboration between a servlet and JSP or to debug Java code that must run within the servlet runtime environment.

Finally, with the introduction of JSP 1.1 support, JSP authors can make use of libraries of custom tags. The design, development, configuration and use of these custom tags is described in some detail.

6.1 Using JSP to present dynamic content

The JSP syntax is essentially an enhanced template language. In general, a Web developer authors an HTML file containing layout, static HTML and placeholders for dynamic content. These placeholders are JSP tags, or actions, and describe the dynamic content.

These actions can express the Java code (JSP scriptlets or expressions) that produces the dynamic content. They can be directives that set options that in turn affect the generation of the dynamic content. JSP actions can also be in the form of special JSP tags that perform common tasks: specification of an SQL statement, iteration over a database result set, or retrieval of a bean's property.

The JSP syntax and capabilities are so general in nature that it is possible to write the entire Web application within a single JSP. The JSP would describe not only the presentation of dynamic content, but also the business logic that creates the dynamic content, the logic that responds to errors, and the logic that controls overall application flow. Such a monolithic JSP would be harder to develop, debug, and maintain.

Our best practices recommend instead that there be one JSP per Web page seen by the user and that there be a single servlet associated with that JSP. That servlet has the job of processing user input, invoking business logic, and marshalling the results into a small number of beans. These beans are passed to the JSP as attributes on the request object. All the JSP has to do is insert the different bean properties in the appropriate places in the static HTML.

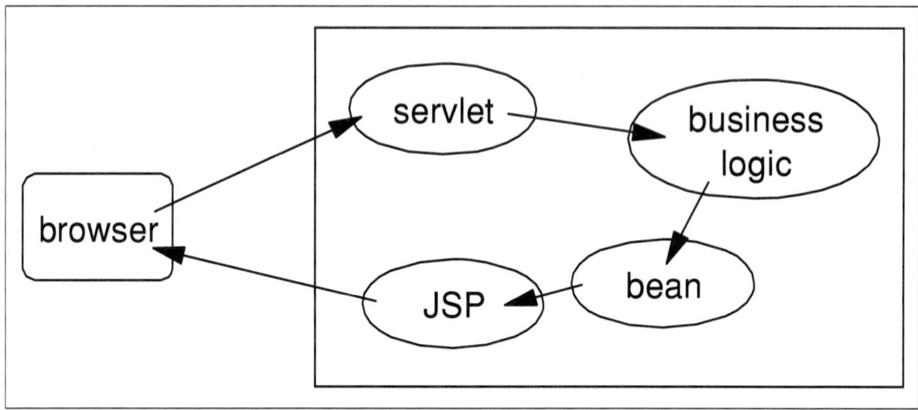

Figure 100. A single servlet associated with that JSP

This recommended use of JSP limits the complexity of individual JSPs and does not exploit the complete set of JSP functionality. It is, however, the most effective use in terms of end-to-end Web application life cycle.

6.2 The collaboration between form, servlet, and JSP

As mentioned above, a servlet processes user input, invokes enterprise business logic and places the results in a single bean. That bean gets passed to a JSP as an attribute of the request object and the JSP inserts the appropriate properties into the appropriate places in the output HTML.

It's quite likely that the HTML being produced contains a form with the expectation that the same sort of servlet and JSP processing will occur again as a result of the form posting its data. Another possible execution path involves the detection of an error in the user-supplied data from the form. In this scenario the servlet will re-invoke the original JSP and will pass to that JSP the data from the posted form. This is an important usability feature: it's very frustrating to spend a lot of time filling in a form, have the form be reset (cleared of what you typed), and be told that there was an error in the information you typed in. A related scenario lets users move back and forth among a series of forms while displaying the information that the user has already typed in.

6.2.1 A bean as contract

So that the data typed in by the user can be easily managed in all of these basic flow scenarios, it is recommended that the application implementation assign a unique bean to each JSP that may be displayed. The bean contains properties for the data retrieved by the preceding servlet as well as properties for each of the fields on each of the forms. This bean can be kept in the HTTP session and retrieved by the JSP at any time.

Once the collaborating servlet and JSP have been identified by the architectural best practices, the next step in the development of the application is the creation of the bean that not only transports data between the servlet and JSP but also holds user-supplied data in case the JSP ever needs to be redisplayed. The beans properties are a union of the set of form fields into which the user enters data and the set of data to be presented by the JSP on behalf of the servlet. The bean can be built with any Java tool once these properties have been identified.

6.2.2 Build the static portion of the JSP

Building the static portion of the JSP is straightforward. It's also outside the scope of this chapter. Any HTML tool (including vi and Notepad) can be used to author the Web page. Dummy text can be used as placeholders for data to be presented by the servlet, while form elements should be set to the desired default values.

6.2.3 Coding the dynamic portion of the JSP

Once the static portion, or template, of the JSP has been developed, the dynamic areas of the JSP can be defined. There are tools, most notably WebSphere Studio, that can assist with the describing of the dynamic content in a JSP. However, to better describe the interactions between servlets, JSPs and beans, this section describes the manual steps necessary to complete the development of a JSP.

Describing a JSP's dynamic content generally requires two steps. The first is the declaration of any beans that are passed from the servlet to the JSP. The second involves specifying which properties of which beans are presented at which location within the Web page.

The bean declaration task requires that a useBean tag be inserted near the top of the JSP source for each bean being accessed by the JSP:

```
<jsp:useBean id="name" scope="request" class="ClassName" />
```

The name of the bean is the attribute name with which the bean was stored in the request or session by the servlet. The scope indicates whether the bean was stored in the request or session and the class is the Java type of the bean.

The task involving the specification of dynamic content involves replacing each dummy text placeholder with a JSP action that writes the dynamic content at that location. There are two approaches. One approach uses the getProperty action and the other uses embedded Java in either expressions or scriptlets.

The getProperty action is straightforward and uses a simple syntax:

```
<jsp:getProperty name="name" property="prop" />
```

The action writes a single property value out at the current location. The name attribute takes the same value as the id attribute of the useBean tag that declared the bean near the beginning of the JSP source. The property attribute is, of course, the name of the property to be written.

The getProperty action is easy to use but is limited to the retrieval of single properties. A more general, albeit more complex, approach uses JSP scriptlets and expressions. A scriptlet is a tag containing a syntactically correctly block of Java code. The expectation is that the execution of that code will result in the output of dynamic content to the Web page at that point. An expression is very much like a scriptlet except that the contained Java code is in the form of a Java expression whose value is to be written out (by the underlying JSP code) to the Web page.

Scriptlets are of the form:

```
<% ... block of Java code goes here ... %>
```

Expressions are of the form:

```
<%= ... Java expression goes here ... %>
```

As soon as developers start embedding Java code into JSPs, the potential for error increases dramatically. Compile errors aren't caught until the JSP is requested and even then it's difficult to match up a compile error with the original line of Java code embedded in the JSP. However, even with the added complexity of using expressions and scriptlets, the added flexibility and capabilities of the Java language make the use of expressions and scriptlets appropriate for the specification of any dynamic content more complex than simple properties.

6.3 Rapid development using JSP

The techniques described in this chapter are not intended to be used in JSPs that run in production-level systems. Rather, these techniques can be used to speed the development of Web applications using JSPs.

Of course, to develop and debug Java code you generally need an industrial-strength Java IDE such as VisualAge for Java which has many useful capabilities including a scrapbook and object inspectors. Most of the time you're better off using VisualAge for Java's functionality to develop and test your Web application. There will be times, however, that JSP can take on the role of inspector, scrapbook and general debugger.

6.3.1 JSP as scrapbook

The scrapbook window in VisualAge for Java is one of the most powerful development tools in that IDE. Code can be entered into a window, selected and executed. The final evaluation can be written to the window at the end of the selected code or the evaluation can be displayed in a separate inspector window.

The ability to type some code, to quickly run the code, to review the results and then to rapidly iterate through that process until the code works as designed makes for very quick experimentation. JSPs can provide the same rapid iteration for code that must run in a servlet runtime environment.

Simply create a JSP whose source consists of the required header followed by a single JSP scriptlet. Enter the code to be run inside the scriptlet and request the JSP. Don't forget to save the JSP. Instrumentation can be added to the code to verify execution results or to display variable data. By writing to a Java variable named "out" (treat it like a Writer), the code can generate HTML text to be displayed in the requesting Web browser.

When you've reviewed the results of the execution, you can modify the Java code in the JSP scriptlet again, save the source, and request the JSP again from your browser. Iterating over these steps will let you quickly develop and test segments of Java code. Once the code works as designed, it can be copied to a Java class in a Java IDE for "proper" deployment to the servlet runtime.

6.3.2 JSP as inspector

The same techniques can be applied to the specific problem of configuring the contents of a bean or other server-side object in the servlet runtime environment.

Simply insert a JSP scriptlet into a JSP and insert Java code to navigate to and to render the properties of interesting server-side objects. Once the contents are understood and the application has been debugged, remove the scriptlet before moving the JSP to production.

6.3.3 JSP as configuration query

A specific use of the inspector technique provides administrators with a view of the WebSphere administration configuration. This includes but is not limited to information about which servlets have been defined under which Web applications and with which attributes, which application servers are running on which nodes (as perceived by the administrative database), and what URLs are recognized by both the application server and the Web server plug-in.

This technique relies on the program interface provided by the XMLConfig class. XMLConfig can return a complete representation of the current WebSphere configuration in a DOM representation. By traversing and relating the information found in different parts of the tree, different JSPs can be built to report on various aspects of the WebSphere configuration.

6.3.4 Testing the servlet/JSP collaboration

The initial design of servlet and its presentation JSP probably involved the specification of named properties that were presented dynamically in the JSP and which were either created or retrieved by the servlet or input originally by the user. There is a contract in the form of a small number of beans and single attributes that are sent from the servlet to the JSP via the request object. It may be hard to believe, but there are times when a typographical or capitalization error in the name of an attribute results in the failure of the JSP to properly present one or more dynamic property values.

Given that the attribute names in both the servlet source and the JSP source must agree, it can be difficult to find the problem. One technique is a modification of the inspection technique using a scriptlet that writes to the out writer the entire contents of the request (or session) object. There would be one row for each attribute and a column each for attribute name, value and value type. An enumeration over the complete set of attribute names can be requested from the request object.

6.4 JSP life cycle

JSP files are compiled into servlets. After a JSP is compiled, its life cycle is similar to the servlet life cycle as shown in Figure 101 on page 195.

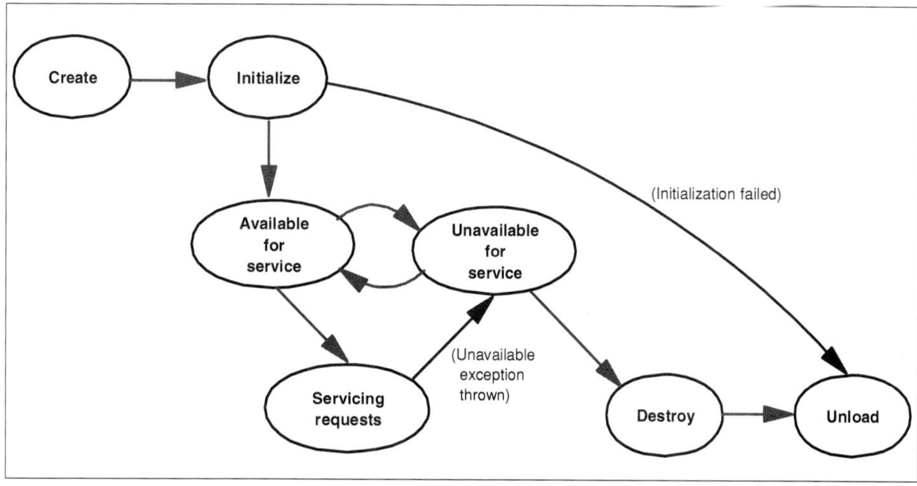

Figure 101. JSP life cycle

6.4.1 Java source generation and compilation

When a servlet engine receives a request for a JSP file, it passes the request to the JSP processor.

If this is the first time the JSP file has been requested or if the compiled copy of the JSP file is not found, the JSP compiler (JSP processor) generates and compiles a Java source file for the JSP file. The JSP processor puts the Java source and class file in the JSP processor directory (see 6.5.2, "JSP processors" on page 197 for detailed information).

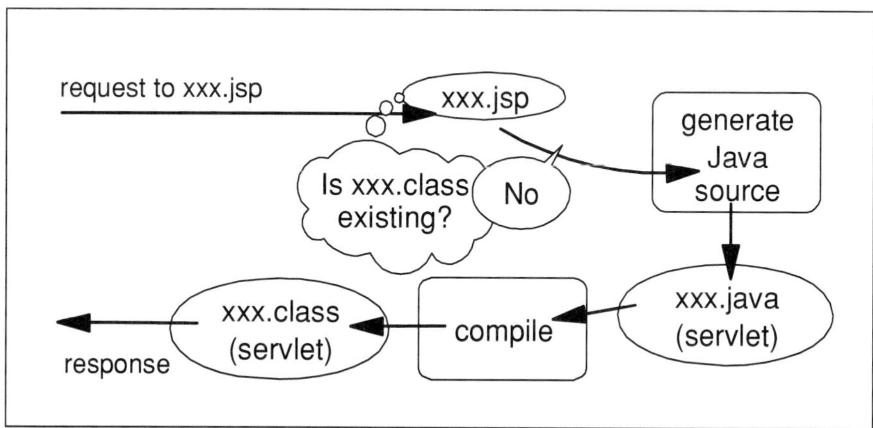

Figure 102. Java source generation and compilation

By default, the JSP syntax in a JSP file is converted to Java code that is added to the service() method of the generated class file. If you need to specify initialization parameters for the servlet or other initialization information, add the method directive set to the value `init`.

6.4.2 Request processing

After the JSP processor places the servlet class file in the JSP processor directory (see 6.5.2, "JSP processors" on page 197), the servlet engine creates an instance of the servlet and calls the servlet service() method in response to the request. All subsequent requests for the JSP are handled by that instance of the servlet.

When the servlet engine receives a request for a JSP file, the engine checks to determine whether the JSP file (.jsp) has changed since it was loaded. If it has changed, the servlet engine reloads the updated JSP file (that is, generates an updated Java source and class file for the JSP). The newly loaded servlet instance receives the client request.

6.4.3 Termination

When the servlet engine no longer needs the servlet or a new instance of the servlet is being reloaded, the servlet engine invokes the servlet's destroy() method. The servlet engine can also call the destroy() method if the engine needs to conserve resources or a pending call to a servlet service() method exceeds the timeout. The JVM performs garbage collection after the destroy.

6.5 Administering JSP files

The WebSphere administrator should know the following about administering JSP files.

6.5.1 Enable JSP handling at the Web application level

- The ability of the product to serve JSP files is controlled at the Web application level. It is quite simple: if a Web application contains a JSP enabler servlet, the Web application can handle requests for JSP files. We also call this servlet JSP Processor (or JSP compiler or JSP container).
- WebSphere provides the JSP enabler servlets. There is one for each supported JSP specification level. See the following section for detailed information.
- The administrator is responsible for permanently adding a JSP processor to Web applications requiring the ability to handle JSP requests:

- A Web application can contain zero or one JSP enablers.
- A Web application cannot contain more than one JSP enabler.
- A Web application that does not need to serve JSP files can contain zero JSP enablers.

6.5.2 JSP processors

WebSphere V3.5.2 provides a JSP processor for each supported level of the JSP specification, .91, 1.0 and 1.1. Each JSP processor is a servlet that you can add to a Web application to handle all JSP requests pertaining to the Web application.

When you install WebSphere on a Web server, the Web server configuration is set to pass HTTP requests for JSP files (files with the extension .jsp) to WebSphere.

By specifying either a .91, 1.0 or 1.1 JSP Enabler (JSP processor) for each Web application containing JSP files, you configure Web applications to pass JSP files in the Web application folder to the JSP processor corresponding to the JSP specification level of the JSP files.

The JSP processor creates and compiles a servlet from each JSP file. The processor produces three files for each JSP file:

- .java file, which contains the Java language code for the servlet
- .class file, which is the compiled servlet
- .dat file, which contains the static content of the JSP

Note: The JSP 1.0 processor deletes the .java file after it is compiled into the .class file. However, you can configure to keep the .java file. To do that, from the administrative console, select **WebSphere node -> application server -> servlet engine -> Web application -> JSP 1.0 Processor -> Advanced tab** then specify keepgenerated in the InitParm Name field and true in the InitParm Value field of the Init Parametrs entry. However, the JSP 0.91 and 1.1 processors have a different behavior: generated code is always kept and a keepgenerated init parameter is not accepted.

The JSP processor puts the .java (if you specify keepgenerated as we described before with JSP 1.0 processor), the .class, and the .dat files in a path specific to the processor. The .java, the .class, and the .dat files have the same file name.

For JSP 1.1 processor:

- Processor servlet name: JspServlet
- Class name and location: org.apache.jasper.runtime.JspServlet in ibmwebas.jar
- Where processor puts output:

  <WAS_HOME>\temp\servlet_host_name\app_name\

  For example, if the JSP file is in:

  c:\WebSphere\AppServer\hosts\default_host\examples\web

  the .java (if you specify keepgenerated as described before), .dat and .class files are put in:

  c:\WebSphere\AppServer\temp\default_host\examples\

Like all servlets, a servlet generated from a JSP file extends the javax.servlet.http.HttpServlet. The servlet Java code contains import statements for the necessary classes and a package statement, if the servlet class is part of a package.

If the JSP file contains JSP syntax (such as directives and scriptlets), the JSP processor converts the JSP syntax to the equivalent Java code. If the JSP file contains HTML tags, the processor adds Java code so that the servlet outputs the HTML character by character.

6.5.3 JSP-enabled Web applications look at all JSP requests

By default, JSP enablers allow a Web application to consider all JSP requests (*.jsp) directed to the particular Web application.

To restrict the attention of the Web application only to particular JSP files (instead of *.jsp), the administrator can remove the Web application Web path specifying *.jsp and replace it with Web paths specifying particular JSP files by name.

6.5.4 Place JSP files and configure Web applications to find them

- For the Web application to fulfill a JSP request, the requested JSP file must be in the document root of the Web application, or in a subdirectory of the document root, allowing the Web application to find it. See 6.8.1, "Configuring WebSphere for JSP 1.1" on page 213 for related information.
- If a JSP file depends on other files, such as servlets, JavaBeans, or the like, the files must reside in directories specified in the classpath setting of the Web application.

Alternatively, the resources can be specified in a more general classpath, such as that of the administrative server pertaining to the domain containing the Web application.

6.5.5 JSP reloading

You can configure how often JSP 1.0 processor will look for revised JSP files that need to be recompiled. By default, the JSP 1.0 processor will check for the presence of a class file every time a JSP is called, and compile the class file if one doesn't already exist. For performance purposes, you may wish to disable this check entirely or only after the JSP is called for the first time. Additionally, you may wish to configure the amount of time between checks. Two init parameters of JSP 1.0 processor (servlet) are used to specify how you want this done for each Web application. Note that these don't work with the JSP 0.91 processor or the JSP 1.1 processor.

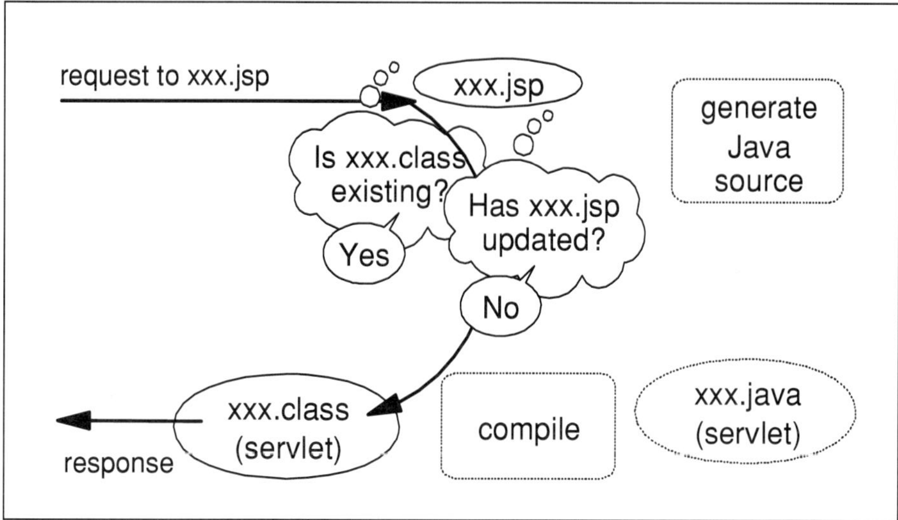

Figure 103. JSP reloading

6.5.5.1 checkjspfiles

This init parameter has three possible values:

- "true" (or "always") - this will cause the application server to check for the presence of a class file each time the JSP is called or each X number of milliseconds specified in the reload interval below.
- "firsttime" - the application server will check for the presence of the class file only once: when it is called for the first time.

- "false" (or "never") - the JSP 1.0 processor will never check for the class file (you must ensure that a class file already exists for the JSP to work properly).

6.5.5.2 reloadinterval

The reloadinterval is the number of milliseconds between each check. This variable only works when you have selected "true" (or "always") as the value for checkjspfiles above.

6.6 Batch compiling JSP files

As an IBM enhancement to JSP support, WebSphere V3.5 provides a batch JSP compiler. Use this function to batch compile your JSP files and thereby enable faster responses to the initial client requests for the JSP files on your production Web server.

It is best to batch compile all of the JSP files associated with an application. Batch compiling saves system resources and provides security on the application server by specifying if and/or when the server is to check for a class file or recompile a JSP file. Unless you have configured the Web application as described the above section, the application server will monitor the compiled JSP file for changes, and will automatically recompile and reload the JSP file whenever the application server detects that the JSP file has changed. By modifying this process, you can eliminate time- and resource-consuming compilations and ensure that you have control over the compilation of your JSP files. It is also useful as a fast way to resynchronize all of the JSP files for an application.

The process of batch compiling JSP files is different for JSP 0.91 files and JSP 1.0 files and does not exist at all for JSP 1.1 files. Consult the page corresponding to the JSP level for your files. See InfoCenter for detailed information.

6.7 JSP 1.1

While the best practice of splitting application logic and data presentation into servlets and JSPs provides a number of benefits to Web application developers, the practice does have one drawback. In practice, JSPs tend to fill up with embedded Java code, which makes that logic harder to edit and debug than if it were entered into a Java IDE. The Java code tends to be simple code for controlling which sections of the JSP source get processed, iterating over a bean's indexed property, or for interacting with system, runtime, or other business objects. While the Java code seems to be common across many JSPs and fits into a small number of simple patterns, it still significantly raises the level of skills required to author a JSP.

JSP 1.1 provides a simple solution to the problems caused by embedded Java code in JSPs. The JSP 1.1 specification describes an interface with which custom tags can be built to perform the same function as the embedded Java code. JSP authors can then use the tags to author JSPs without any embedded Java code.

This section describes how to design, build and debug JSP 1.1 custom tags in WebSphere.

6.7.1 Custom tags

Custom tags, as specified by the JSP 1.1 specification, can perform a number of tasks that fall into several categories:

a. Conditional inclusion or iteration over sections of JSP source

b. Creation of, reference to, and invocation of application objects

c. Invocation of system or application functions such as logging or e-mail

The kinds of tasks performed by a specific custom tag determine the best way to implement that tag. A cookbook approach to implementing custom tags is described below.

6.7.2 The custom tag environment

There are a number of files and objects that get involved in the execution of a JSP with custom tags and it's important to understand how they define and affect the execution of these custom tags.

6.7.2.1 The JSP container

JSP authors and Web application developers working with WebSphere have understood what happens within the JspServlet as the JSP compiler (or JSP processor) responds to a request for a JSP page. The JSP 1.1 specification now defines that system behavior in terms of a JSP container.

The JSP container manages all resources necessary for the interpretation and invocation of the JSPs in a Web application. The container accepts a request for a JSP, invokes the JSP, interacts with any custom tags in that JSP and finally returns the result of that JSP execution to the client.

Custom tags have a life cycle defined in terms of methods that are called before, during and after the custom tag is encountered in a JSP. The JSP container invokes those methods and ensures that references are available to all of the information and objects needed by each custom tag.

6.7.2.2 The JSP source

The source of the JSP is the place where JSP authors use custom tags. The way in which each tag is used varies by tag. The tag designer can allow information to be specified either as attributes of the custom tag, as the content (the section of the JSP source between the begin and end tags) of the custom tag or as a combination of the two. Custom tags can also reference and cooperate with other custom tags and that collaboration is specified in terms of referencing ID's as attribute values or in terms of the way the custom tags are nested.

```
<%@ taglib uri="test.tld" prefix="tst" %>
<%@ page import="com.ibm.itso.*" language="java" %>

<p>This section appears only once in the browser.</p>

<tst:months beanName="mb" >
<p>This section of the JSP will be repeated once for
each month.  The month for this iteration is
<%= mb.getMonthName() %> </p>

</tst:months>

<p>This section appears only once in the browser.</p>
```

Figure 104. months.jsp

In the above example, the <tst:months> tag can be used by a JSP author to repeat a section of the JSP source (including the processing of any nested tags) once for each month in the year.

6.7.2.3 Tag handlers

The primary benefit of custom tags is the ability to define very complex JSPs that do not contain any embedded Java. Of course, the Java is still there. It's just been moved to a place where the JSP author doesn't have to deal with it. That place is in a set of classes called tag handlers. These tag handlers are the application classes (from WebSphere's perspective) that are invoked whenever a custom tag is encountered during JSP processing.

There are a number of interfaces and convenience superclasses that describe exactly what a tag handler should look like and how it should behave. A large percentage of the effort required to implement a set of custom tags is related to the building of these tag handlers.

6.7.2.4 Bean Info classes for the tag handlers

The JSP container expects tag handlers to be Java beans so that inspection can reveal the setter methods to be used by the container. The JSP container uses that information to call the appropriate setter methods for any attributes found in the custom tag's begin tag. While not absolutely necessary, it is recommended that bean info classes be provided for the tag handlers so that the introspection is quick and correct.

6.7.2.5 Tag libraries

A tag library (or taglib) is a collection of tag handlers. Since the only objects that interact with the tag handlers are specified completely by various components of the J2EE specification, a taglib should be portable across different implementations of the J2EE specification (for example Web application servers from different vendors). The portability will also depend on the portability of business and other system objects used by the tag handlers.

6.7.2.6 Tag library definition

In order for the JSP container to find custom tags in a JSP source and to then invoke the corresponding tag handlers correctly, the JSP container has to know what it's looking for. That information is provided as part of the tag library in an XML file called the tag definition library (TLD).

The TLD content provides most, but not all, of the information necessary for the JSP container to interact with the custom tags in that taglib. The rest of the necessary information is provided at runtime on a tag instance by tag instance basis.

Of the tags used in the TLD, some are not completely obvious:

<tag> - describes one custom tag in the taglib.

<name> - provides the name of the tag as it appears in the JSP source.

<tagclass> - the name of the tag handler class.

<teiclass> - the name of a TagExtraInfo class for the custom tag. At runtime this class will provide any necessary information specific to each instance of the custom tag.

<attribute> - provides the name of a single attribute of the custom tag and indicates whether this attribute is required.

<bodycontent> - describes how the JSP container is supposed to process any content provided for an instance of the custom tag.

The sample TLD (Figure 105) contains definitions for three tags. One of those tags, the months tag, is described as having com.ibm.itso.jsp11.MonthsTag as its tag handler. Class com.ibm.itso.jsp11.MonthsTEI will provide additional runtime attribute verification and will describe the objects referenced or created by each instance of the tag. The body of the tag can contain JSP source and there is a single (required) attribute named beanName.

```
<?xml version="1.0" encoding="ISO-8859-1" ?>
<!DOCTYPE taglib
        PUBLIC "-//Sun Microsystems, Inc.//DTD JSP Tag Library 1.1//EN"
        "web-jsptaglib_1_1.dtd">

<!-- This TEI describes an example custom tag library -->

<taglib>
  <!-- after this the default space is
   "http://java.sun.com/j2ee/dtds/web-jsptaglibrary_1_1.dtd"
   -->

  <tlibversion>1.0</tlibversion>
  <jspversion>1.1</jspversion>
  <shortname>simple</shortname>
  <info>
   A simple tab library for the examples
  </info>
<!-- called tag -->
  <tag>
    <name>called</name>
    <tagclass>com.ibm.itso.jsp11.CalledTag</tagclass>
    <teiclass>com.ibm.itso.jsp11.CalledTagTEI</teiclass>
    <bodycontent>empty</bodycontent>
    <info>
   This tag is referred to by the CallerTag.
    </info>

<attribute>
   <name>id</name>
   <required>true</required>
    </attribute>
    <attribute>
   <name>color</name>
   <required>true</required>
    </attribute>
  </tag>
```

Figure 105. Test.tld (1/2)

```
<!-- caller tag -->
 <tag>
   <name>caller</name>
   <tagclass>com.ibm.itso.jsp11.CallerTag</tagclass>
   <teiclass>com.ibm.itso.jsp11.CallerTagTEI</teiclass>
   <bodycontent>empty</bodycontent>
   <info>
  This tag refers to called tags.
   </info>

   <attribute>
  <name>id</name>
  <required>true</required>
   </attribute>
   <attribute>
  <name>shape</name>
  <required>true</required>
   </attribute>
   <attribute>
  <name>refId</name>
  <required>true</required>
   </attribute>
 </tag>

 <tag>
   <name>months</name>
   <tagclass>com.ibm.itso.jsp11.MonthsTag</tagclass>
   <teiclass>com.ibm.itso.jsp11.MonthsTEI</teiclass>
   <bodycontent>JSP</bodycontent>
   <info>
  This tag iterates over the months.
   </info>

   <attribute>
  <name>beanName</name>
  <required>true</required>
   </attribute>
 </tag>

</taglib>
```

Figure 106. Test.tld (2/2)

The XML file containing the TDL is named in the URI attribute of the taglib directive in the JSP source. When the JSP Container encounters this directive, it uses the information in the TLD to update its list of custom tags to look for.

6.7.2.7 The TEI class

There are custom tags that are difficult to describe using only XML. Some of these tags have complex rules about which combinations of attributes are valid. Other custom tags create or refer to objects whose names appear in the tags' attributes. For these tags, it is much easier to implement in Java code both the description of which attribute combinations are valid and the list of objects that are created or referenced by the custom tags. This logic is coded in a class called a TagExtraInfo (TEI) class. The name of the class is provided as part of the tag definition in the TLD.

6.7.2.8 The PageContext

During execution of the tag handler for a given custom tag, the tag handler instance has access to all of the well-known servlet runtime objects (request, response, out, servlet config, servlet context, etc.) as well as access to other lesser page compile objects of interest. All of these objects are accessible through the page context.

When a custom tag is encountered in JSP source, a new instance of the tag handler is constructed. Once constructed, the tag handler is automatically given a reference to the pageContext as well as to attribute values specified on that tag.

6.7.3 Building a custom tag

A single custom tag can perform a number of tasks, including conditionally processing its contents and interacting with other custom tags. This section lists the possible behaviors of a custom tag and describes the implementation specifics for each behavior.

These behaviors are all gathered in a tag handler class. There are several ways to define the class depending on whether or not the tag handler needs to access the contents of the custom tag. If the tag handler does not need to access the contents of the custom tag, the tag handler class should implement the javax.servlet.jsp.tagext.Tag interface. A convenience class, javax.servlet.jsp.tagext.TagSupport, provides default implementations of each method in the Tag interface. If the tag handler needs to access the custom tag's content then the tag handler should implement the javax.servlet.jsp.tagext.TagBody interface instead. A convenience class, javax.servlet.jsp.tagext.TagBodySupport, is also provided.

Although there are a number of methods you could override, there are four methods (appropriately stubbed in the convenience classes) in which you provide the behaviors, described in Table 6, that process the custom tag.

Table 6. Methods for the custom tag

Methods	Description
doStartTag()	Invoked once when the JSP container encounters the begin tag
doInitBody()	Invoked once before the JSP container begins to process the custom tag's content
doAfterBody()	Invoked by the JSP container after each time the custom tag content is processed (could be multiple times)
doEndTag()	Invoked once when the JSP container encounters the end tag

6.7.3.1 Accessing the tag's attribute values

The JSP container assumes that the tag handler is a bean with a property for each possible attribute (as defined in the TLD). When the container encounters a custom tag in the JSP source, an instance of the corresponding tag handler is constructed and the appropriate setter is invoked for each attribute present in that instance of the tag, At any point in the processing, the tag handler instance can access the provided attribute values simply by accessing its properties.

In the months.jsp example, the tst:months tag has a single attribute, beanName. When the processing reaches that specific tag instance, the setter method for the beanName property will be invoked with the value of the attribute ("mb", in this case).

Note that the JSP container will also invoke the setters for parent and pageContext when a custom tag is encountered.

6.7.3.2 Ensuring the tag is empty

There will be custom tags for which nested content (text between begin and end tags) has no meaning. If you want the JSP container to ensure that no content is provided for a custom tag, specify a value of "empty" for the bodycontent tag in the TLD.

In the sample TLD, for example, the bodycontent for both the caller and called custom tags is "empty".

6.7.3.3 Taking some action for a tag

By implementing the logic necessary to take some action in one or more of the appropriate Tag or TagBody methods, you can cause that action to take place at the correct point in the custom tag processing. The method in which you implement your logic is usually dependent on the kind of action.

If you want to take some action that requires only the tag attributes, you could implement your logic in the doStartTag() method. The logic would be invoked whenever the begin tag is encountered during JSP processing, For example, the processing required for the caller tag requires only the values of the caller tag's attributes. That processing is implemented in the doStartTag().

If you want to take some action that requires knowledge of what happened in a single processing pass of a custom tag's content, override the doAfterBody() method. This method has access to the buffer containing the results of processing the tag's content. In the months tag, for example, the tag handler has to increment the current month after each pass through the tag's contents. This behavior goes into the doAfterBody() method since that method will be invoked once after each pass through the tag's content.

If you want to take some action that requires knowledge gained from potentially multiple processing passes of a custom tag's content (for example, for an iterative custom tag), override the doEndTag() method.

6.7.3.4 Accessing the tag contents

In the simplest cases, the contents of a custom tag are processed without the custom tag builder having to do anything. These tags don't reference their content in any way. In the more complex custom tags that do need to refer or in some way act on their content, the custom tag builder needs to write some content processing logic.

In the doAfterBody() method, a call to the getBodyContent() method returns a subclass, BodyContent, of JspWriter. This subclass adds the ability to access (via Reader or String) the results of processing the custom tag's content. See the doAfterBody() method in the MonthsTag class for an example of accessing the tag's content from the current BodyContent.

The custom tag builder must also specify how the custom tag's content should be processed. The <bodycontent> tag for the custom tag's definition in the TDL can contain either "JSP" or "tagdependent".

A value of "JSP" directs the JSP container to invoke tag handlers for any custom and scripting tags found within the custom tag's content. The BodyContent for a pass over the content would then contain the output of those scripting and custom tags. This is a useful technique for scripting tag-dependent content. If a tag were to contain a valid SQL statement, for example, a user could use JSP scriptlets and expressions to fill in data that changes from jsp invocation to JSP invocation.

A value of "tagdependent" suspends any tag processing in the custom tag's content and the source of any scripting or custom tags would appear in the results returned by the BodyContent.

6.7.3.5 Deciding whether to process the tag contents

In addition to whatever behavior you implement as part of the doStartTag() method (the one that's invoked when the begin tag is encountered), the method must return an integer value that tells the JSP container whether or not to process the custom tag's contents.

A return value of SKIP_BODY causes the JSP container to bypass any content in the custom tag. Nothing is processed and if there are custom tags nested in that content, their corresponding tag handlers are not invoked.

A return value of EVAL_BODY_INCLUDE indicates that the content is to be processed and that the results of that processing should be written directly to the output stream. This value is only appropriate for tag handlers that implement the Tag interface or subclass the TagSupport class.

If the doStartTag() returns EVAL_BODY_TAG, the content will be processed with the expectation that the tag handler will request the results in the doAfterBody() method. This return value is appropriate only for implementers of the TagBody interface or for subclasses of TagBodySupport.

6.7.3.6 Deciding whether to process the tag contents again

Just as the return value of the doStartTag() method controls whether a first pass is made over a custom tag's content, the return value of the doAfterBody() method controls subsequent passes over that same content. If logic in the doAfterBody() method determines that no further passes should be made, the method should return SKIP_BODY. On the other hand, a return value of EVAL_BODY_TAG forces another single pass over the content followed by another invocation of the doAfterBody() method. The loop continues until the doAfterBody() method returns SKIP_BODY.

In the months tag example, the doAfterBody() method returns EVAL_BODY_TAG unless the current month number is 13. When the current month number is 13, the iteration is complete and the method returns SKIP_BODY.

6.7.3.7 Deciding whether to process the rest of the page

The return value of the doEndTag() method controls whether the JSP container continues processing or whether the overall page processing should stop (in case of an error). A return value of SKIP_PAGE tells the JSP container that no further processing should be performed on this page for this request while a return value of EVAL_PAGE indicates that processing should continue.

6.7.3.8 Writing something to the response

In earlier versions of JSP, Java code wrote text to local variable out which was always declared to be some form of Writer. In JSP 1.1, tag handlers must get a Writer by sending the getOut() method to the pageContext (a local variable). The Writer returned by the getOut() method is an instance of BodyContent, a subclass of Writer that's able to answer back (as a Reader or String) what was written to it. See the caller tag source to see how text can be written to the current out.

The JSP container manages a stack of BodyContent instances that map to nested BodyTag tag handlers. For BodyTag tag handlers, the JSP container will create a new BodyContent and push it on the stack before continuing to process the tag's contents. Once the contents have been processed, the Bodycontent will be popped off of the stack and discarded. It is up to the tag handler's doAfterBody() method to get what was written to the current BodyContent and write that string to the second BodyContent in the stack.

See the doStartTag() method in the sample class CallerTag for an example of writing a simple string to the JSP output. The doAfterBody() method of the MonthsTag class gives an example of saving the results of a single pass through a BodyTag tag's contents.

6.7.3.9 Accessing another tag handler by name

At runtime, a tag handler for one custom tag can get a reference to the tag handler for another custom tag. This is useful for taglibs in which one tag initializes resources (for example, obtains a database connection) and the other tags refer back to that tag in order to access those resources.

For a tag handler (or any object created by that tag handler) to be accessed by another tag handler, a TagExtraInfo (TEI) class must be built for the referenced tag. The TEI has a getVariableInfo() method that accepts information about the attributes and values specified for an instance of the custom tag and returns an array of VariableInfo objects. For each object that the tag handler will export (make available for access by other tag handlers) there should be an element in the returned VariableInfo array describing the name by which the object will be accessed, whether the object is being created by this tag handler, the type of the object, and the scope of the object.

The scope of an object refers to the portion of the JSP source in which that object can be referenced. There are three possible values.

Table 7. Possible values of the scope of the object

Values	Description
AT_BEGIN	The object can be referenced at any point after the start tag
AT_END	The object can be referenced at any point after the end tag
NESTED	The object can only be referenced between the start and end tags

When the TEI for a custom tag reports that objects will be created, the tag handler for that custom tag must make those objects available by using the setAttribute() method on the pageContext for each object. The called tag demonstrates how a tag handler can put itself into the pageContext so that other tag handlers can access the tag's attribute values. The months tag show how beans other than the tag handler can be put into the pageContext.

As long as another custom tag is within the declared scope of an exported object, that tag can get a reference to the object by calling the getAttribute() method on PageContext.

6.7.3.10 Determining the containing tag

The nesting of custom tags is a special case of one tag handler referring to another. When one custom tag only makes sense when nested within another custom tag, it is likely that the nested tag handler will need to access context information held by the other tag handler.

This is coded in the nested tag handler. A call to the nested tag handler's own findAncestorWithClass() method returns the other tag handler. The arguments to the method are the nested tag handler itself and the class of the nesting tag handler.

6.8 Configuring and running your JSPs

Before you run JSPs with custom tags, you need to configure the WebSphere Application Server for JSP 1.1 and you need to deploy your application components to the correct directories.

6.8.1 Configuring WebSphere for JSP 1.1

Most of the configuration for JSP 1.1 is handled by the administrative console.

In Version 3.5.2 of WebSphere Application Server, the JSP support for a Web application defaults to JSP 1.0. The easiest way to configure JSP 1.1 support is to create a new application server. From the **Wizards** icon on the administrative console, choose the **Create Application Server** item as shown in Figure 107.

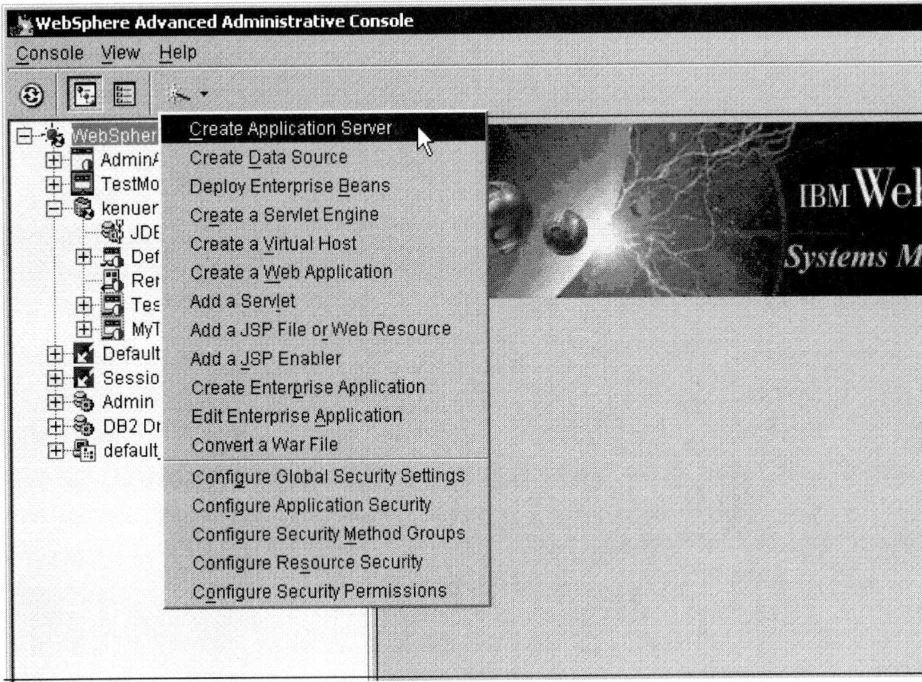

Figure 107. Create a new application server

The first page in the Create Application Wizard is the Types of Resources window as shown in Figure 108 on page 214. Make sure the **Web Applications** box is checked and click the **Next** button.

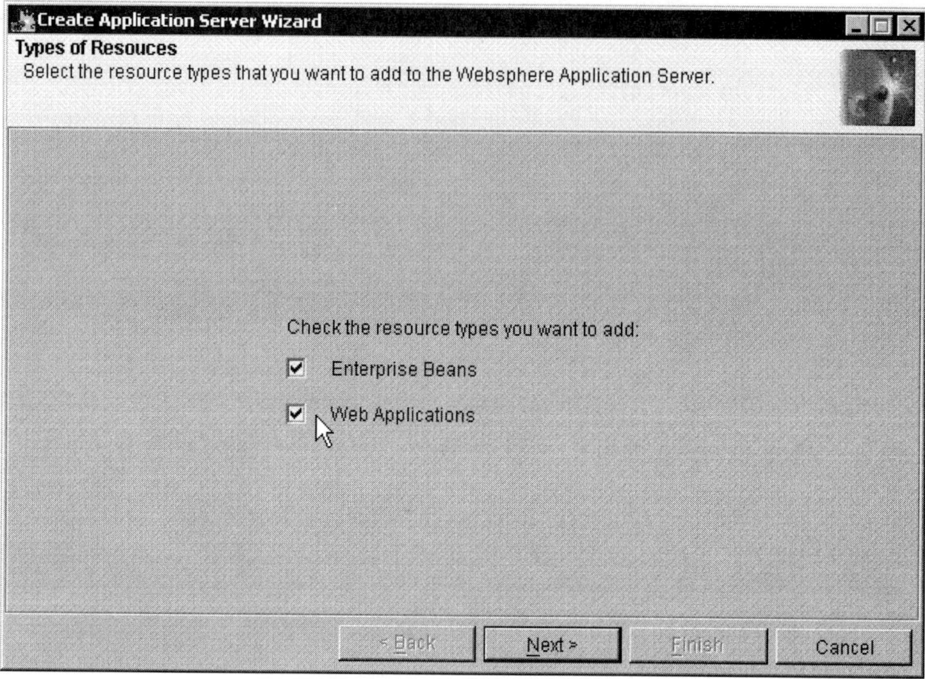

Figure 108. Types of Resources

The next page asks for general information about the application server to be created. Choose a short name for your application server name (in our case, `ITSO` was entered as shown in Figure 109 on page 215) and enter two fully qualified file names for standard out and standard error. These files are very important because many of the errors and debug information you need will be written only there. If the default names are used, you run the risk of different application servers overwriting the same log files; a better choice would be to uniquely identify these using the file names such as “jspout.txt” and “jsperr.txt”. A good directory for these two files is the logs directory in the WebSphere install directory (in our case, C:\WebSphere\AppServer\logs directory). Then click **Next**.

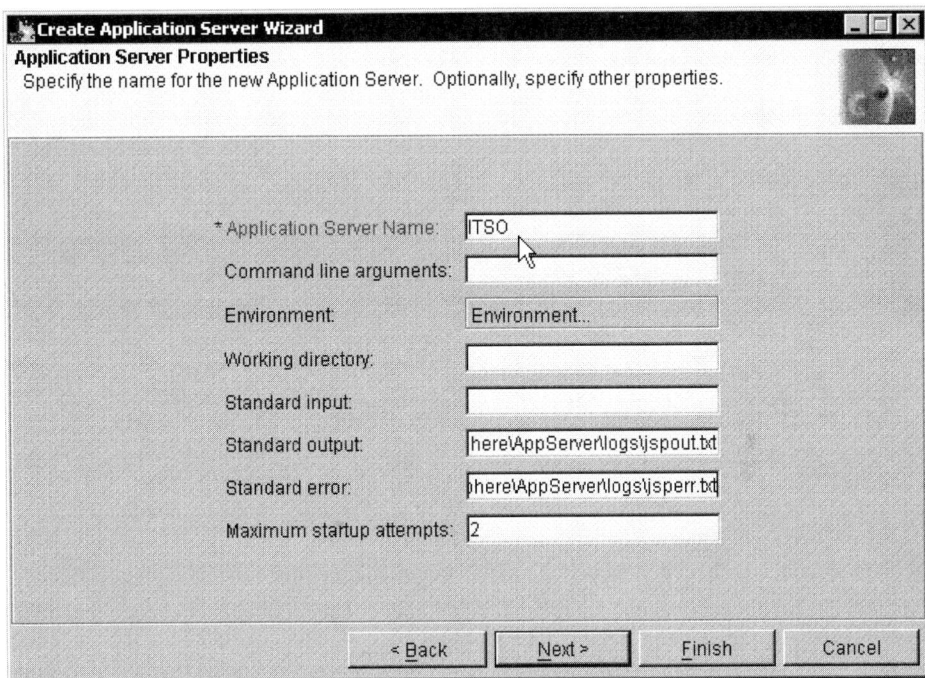

Figure 109. Application Server Properties

The next page (Application Server Start Option) asks you whether you want to start the new Application Server automatically after its creation. For our example, we leave it at the default setting, which means do not start the server. Then click **Next**.

On the next page (Node Selection), you need to select the node on which the new WebSphere Application Server will run. Select the node (in our case, kenueno) then click **Next**.

On the next page (Add Enterprise Beans), if you want to add enterprise beans, do so. For our example, we don't need to do it. Therefore, we click **Next** without adding enterprise beans.

On the next page (EJBContainer Properties), you specify the EJBContainer Name. In our case, we specify ITSOContainer and then click **Next**.

The next page (Select Virtual Host) asks you to specify (or select) a Virtual Host name. In our case, we selected default_host and click **Next**.

The next page (Servlet Engine Properties) we choose to run in **Servlet 2.2 and JSP 1.1 Full Compliance Mode** as shown in Figure 110. You must choose this option if you want to run JSP 1.1. This is also why you have to create a new application server in order to run JSP 1.1; the existing application servers were probably created without this option. Then click **Next**.

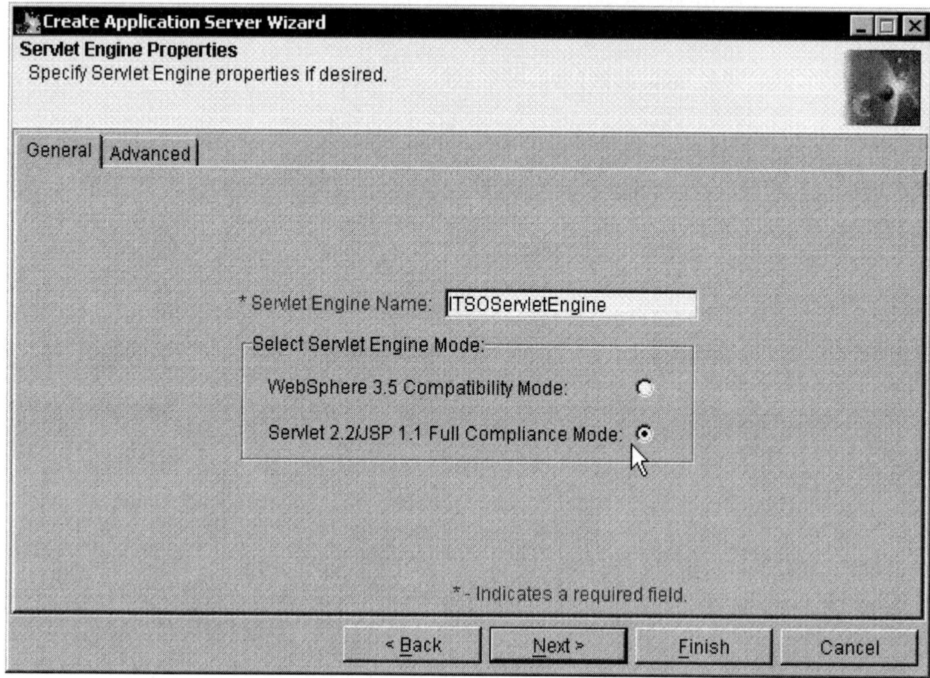

Figure 110. Servlet Engine Properties: General tab

When you create an application server you also create a Web application. The wizard presents you with a default name and Web path, but the default names are generally too long (remember that the Web path becomes part of every URL). Enter names that are long enough to be descriptive yet are not too verbose, as shown in Figure 111 on page 217. Then click **Next**.

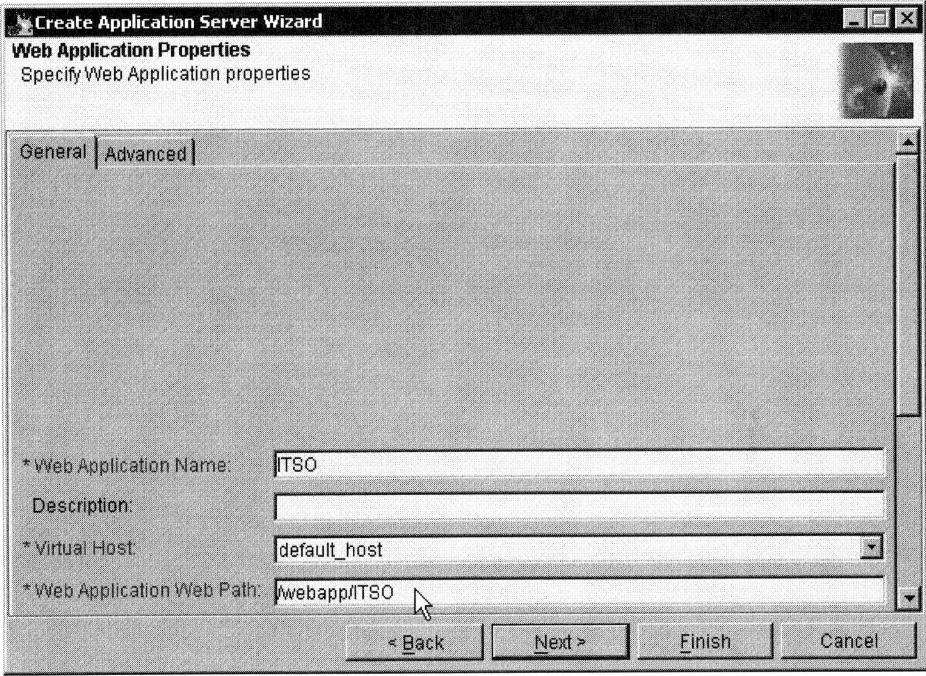

Figure 111. Web Application properties

The final page lets you choose which version of JSP runs in the new Web application. Choose **Enable JSP 1.1** as shown in Figure 112 on page 218.

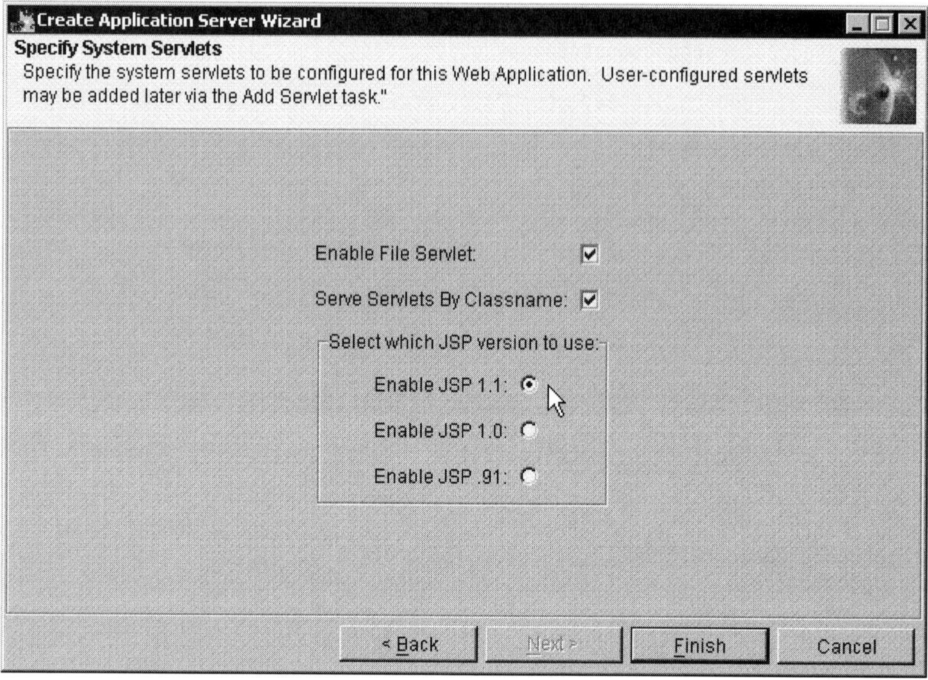

Figure 112. Specify System Servlets

When you click **Finish**, you will get the Information dialog as shown in Figure 113.

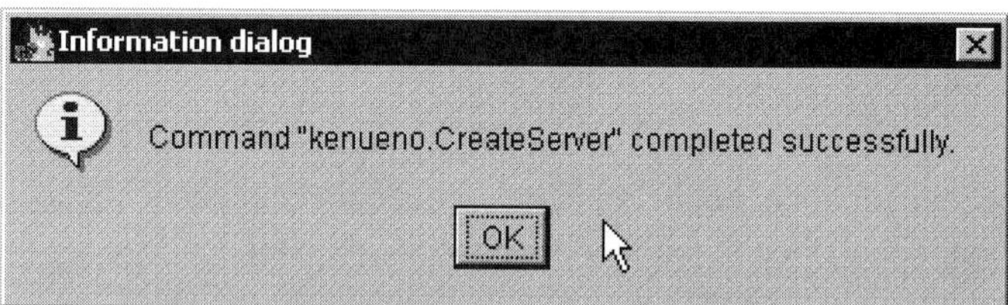

Figure 113. Information dialog

Click **OK**, and the application server and Web application will be created.

It is recommended that you verify the configuration of the WebSphere domain. Fully expand the nodes (see Figure 114 on page 219) for the application server you just created (in our case, ITSO) and select the new Web application (in our case, ITSO) under the servlet engine (in our case, ITSOServletEngine). Click the **Advanced** tab to see the Documentation Root for the Web application. All HTML and JSP files need to go in this directory or one of its subdirectories. You can change the directory to use if you wish.

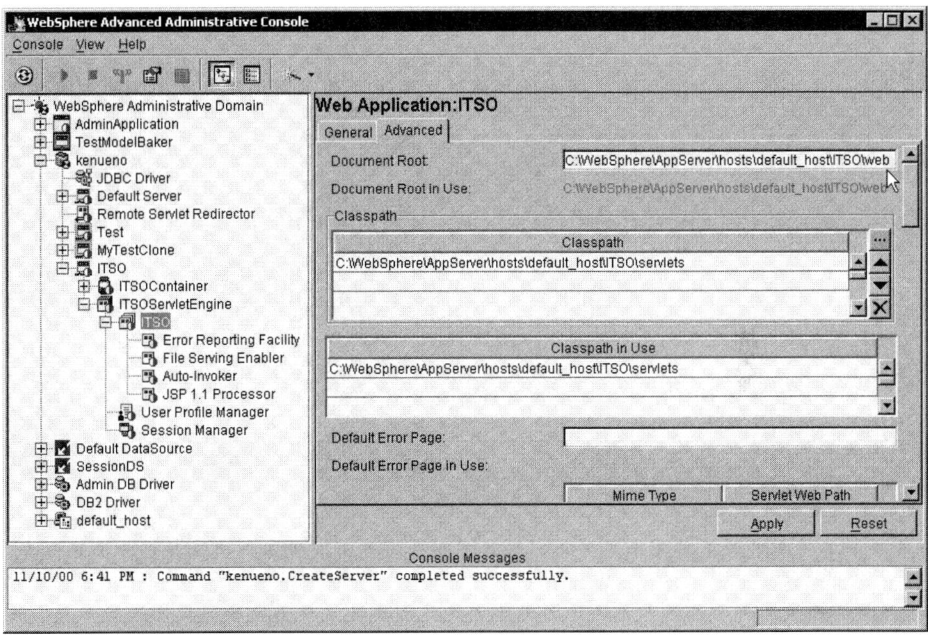

Figure 114. Web Application: Advanced tab

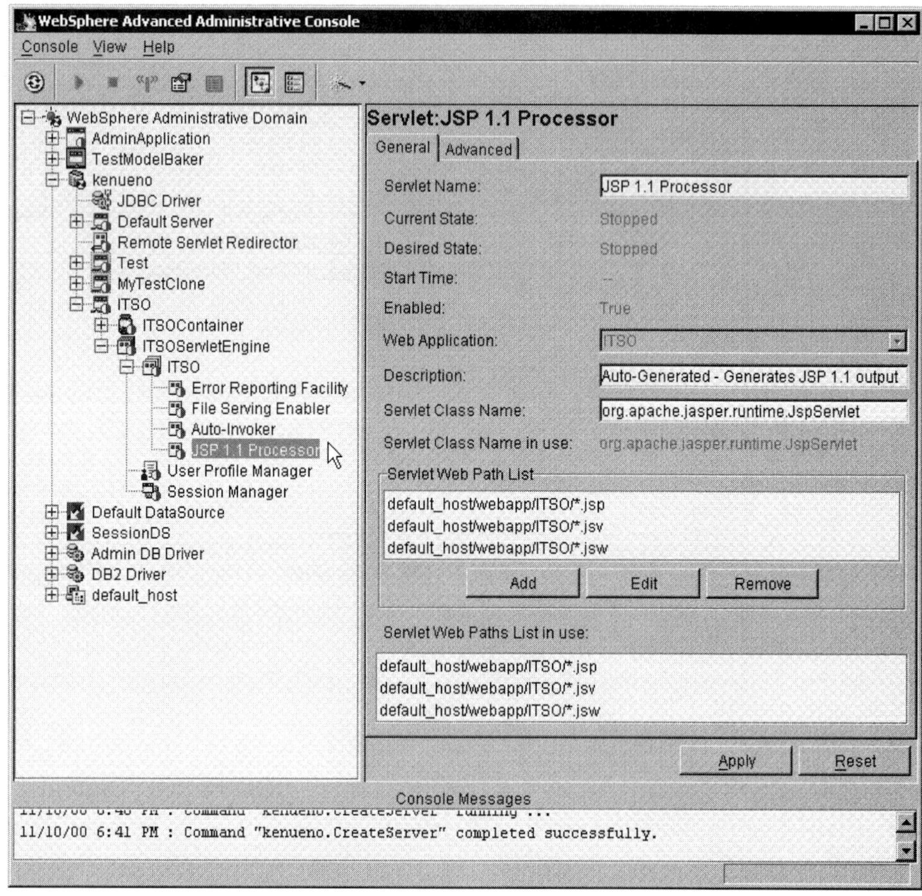

Figure 115. JSP 1.1 Processor: General tab

Note that under the ITSO Web application, there is a servlet called JSP 1.1 Processor. That is the JSP processor (or JSP enabler) that we discussed in 6.5.2, “JSP processors” on page 197. The servlet Java source and class files that are generated by this JSP Processor are stored in the <WAS_HOME>/temp/default_host/ITSO directory in our case as shown in Figure 116 on page 221.

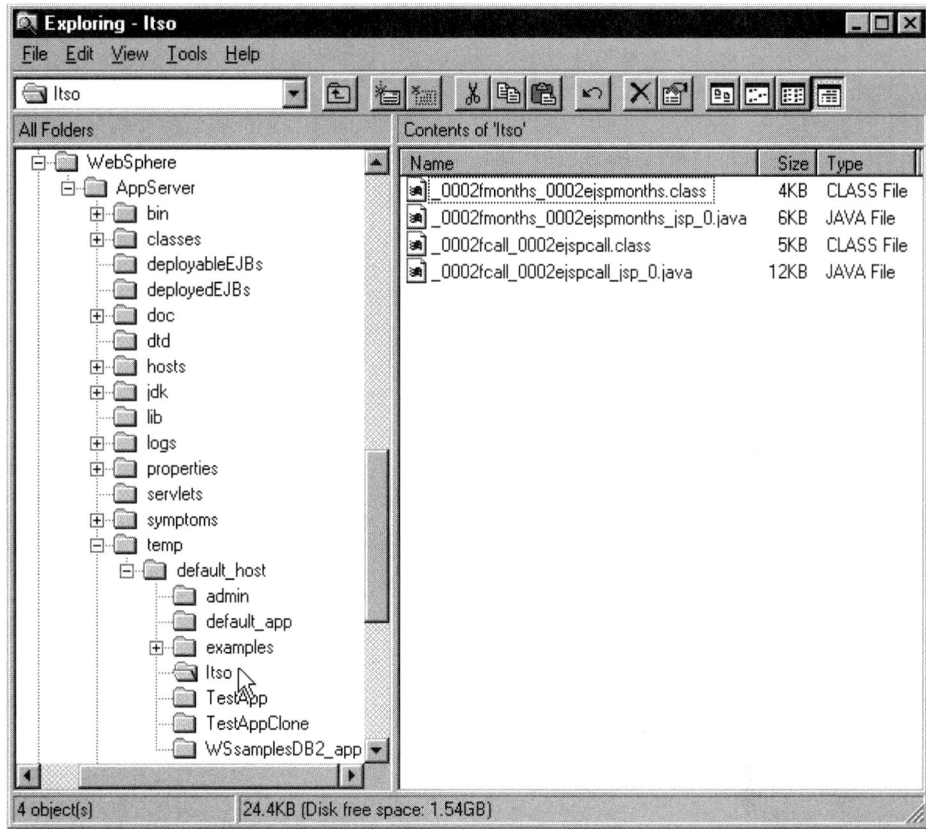

Figure 116. Servlet Java source and class files generated by the JSP container

In WebSphere V3.5.2, the Jasper JSP processor developed by Apache.org is used. You can see it in the Servlet Class Name entry on the General tab of the JSP 1.1 processor, as shown in Figure 115 on page 220.

6.8.2 Deploying application components

The JSP source, taglibs and TLDs all must be deployed to the correct directories before the JSP processor can locate them.

6.8.2.1 JSP source

JSP source, like HTML files, is placed in the web directory for the Web application. This is the directory name displayed in the Document root attribute on the Advanced tab for the Web application (see Figure 114 on page 219).

6.8.2.2 The TLD

The TLD can be placed almost anywhere since its location is specified as a URL in the JSP source. It's a good idea, though, to put the TLD in the same directory as the JSP source and to reference the file using a relative file name. See the sample JSP source files for examples. In our case, we placed the sample JSP source file and TLD the <WAS_HOME>/hosts/default_host/ITSO/web directory, as shown in Figure 117.

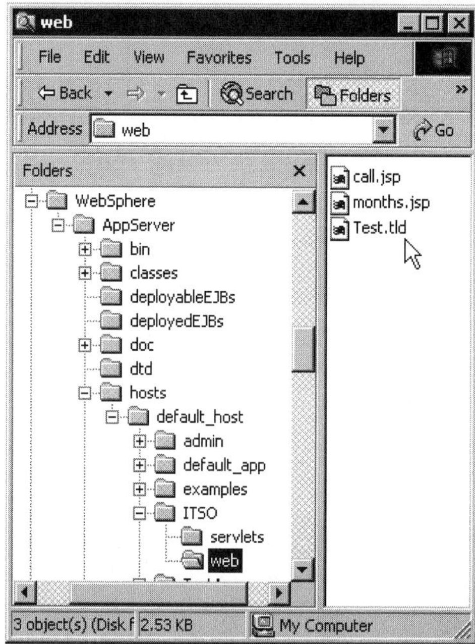

Figure 117. The location of the JSP source files and TLD

6.8.2.3 The custom tag handlers

The custom tag handler classes, their bean info classes and their corresponding TEI classes should be put into a JAR file. The JAR file's fully qualified file name needs to be entered as one of the classpath entries for the Web application (it's on the Advanced tab along with the document root attribute). While the JAR can be placed anywhere, it's a good idea to put the JAR into the Web application's servlets path (see Figure 118 on page 223) or, if the tag library will be shared by several Web applications, into the general servlets directory for WebSphere. In our case, we created jsp11tag.jar as shown in Figure 119 on page 223 and placed it in the <WAS_HOME>/hosts/default_host/ITSO/servlets directory as shown in Figure 120 on page 224.

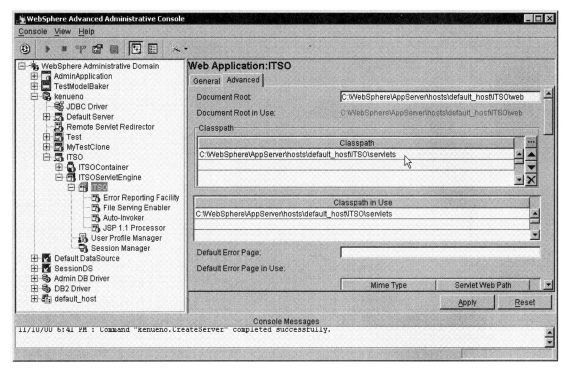

Figure 118. Web application classpath

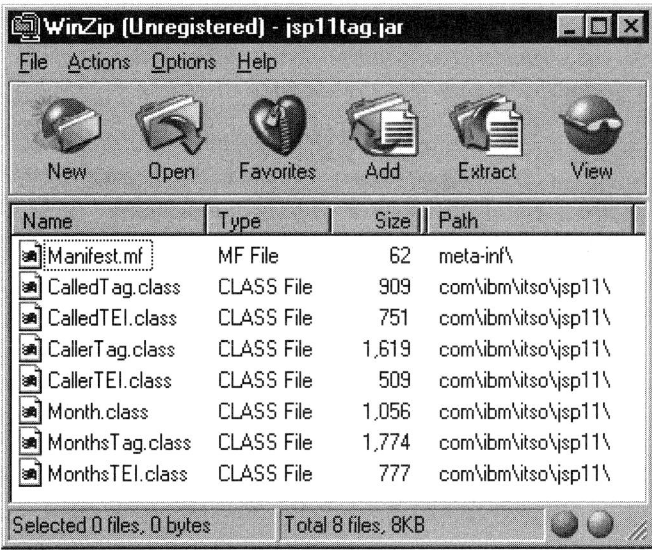

Figure 119. jsp11tag.jar

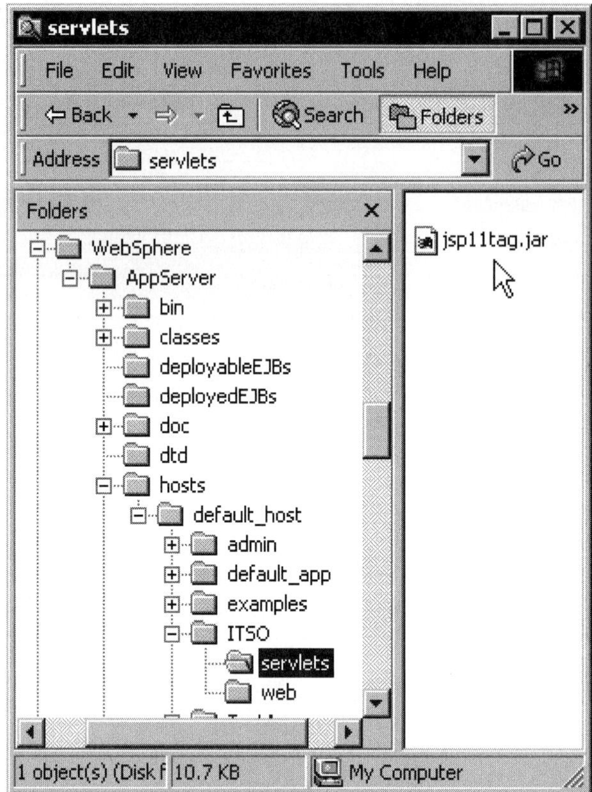

Figure 120. The location of the custom tag handlers

6.8.3 Start the Web application

Once you've made sure that the JSP source, the tag handlers and the TLD are all correctly deployed, you can now start the application server. On the administrative console, right click your application server (in our case, ITSO) and click **Start** as shown in Figure 121 on page 225.

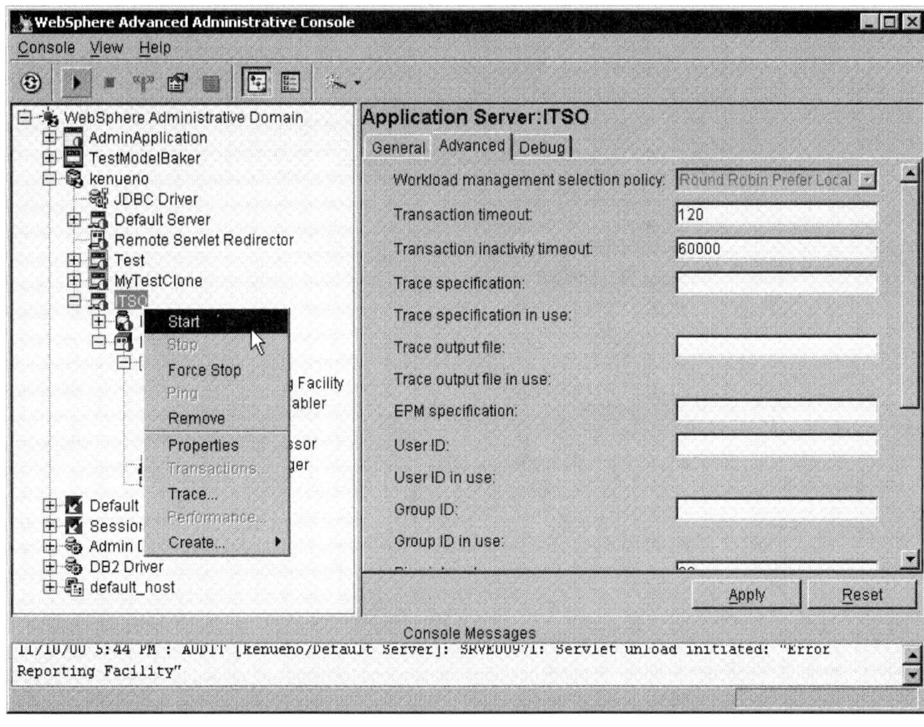

Figure 121. Start the application server

6.8.4 Invoking the JSP

Now, you can determine the URL with which to invoke the JSP.

The JSP's URL is made up of several names. The host name (which must be one of the virtual host names) is optional but is followed by the Web path of the Web application (as shown on the General tab). The Web application's Web path is the relative path of the JSP with respect to the root web directory.

For example, in the examples shown elsewhere in this chapter, the call.jsp would be invoked using the following URI.

```
http://<server_name>/webapp/ITSO/call.jsp
```

Figure 122 on page 226 shows you the result of invoking the call.jsp.

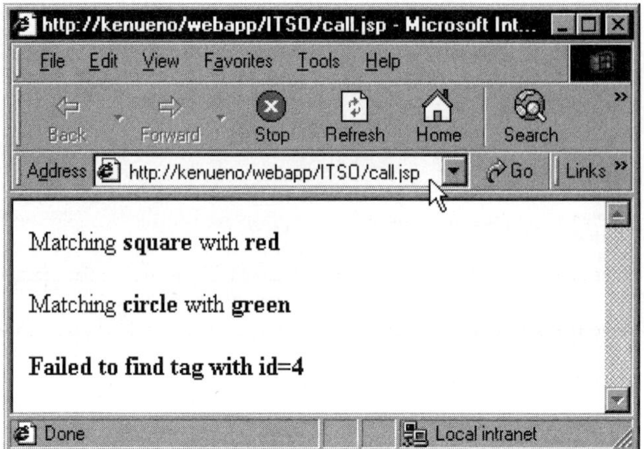

Figure 122. Invoking the call.jsp

The other example, the months.jsp, would be invoked using the following URI:

```
http://<server_name>/webapp/ITSO/months.jsp
```

Figure 123 on page 227 shows you the result of invoking the months.jsp.

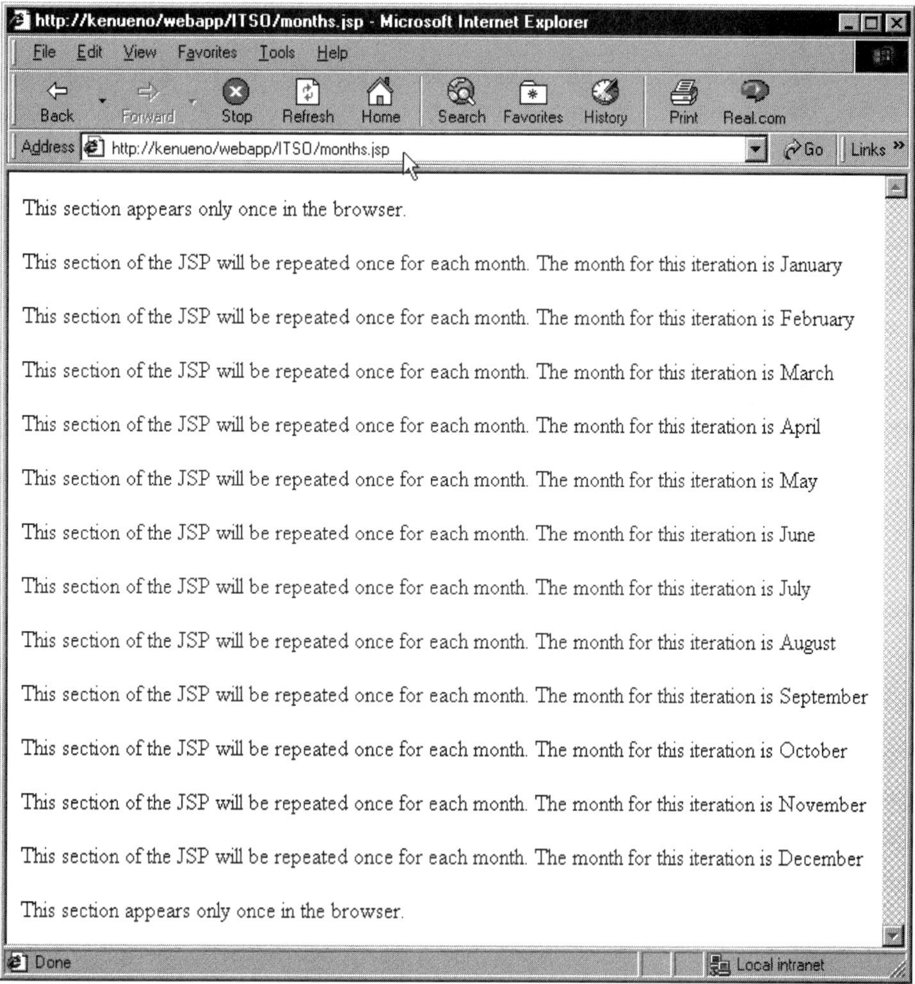

Figure 123. Invoking the months.jsp

Several problems are common when trying to request a JSP for the first time. If you get an Internal Server Error, it's quite possible that the URL was recognized but that the Web application's application server was not yet started. A 404 error indicates that the URL wasn't put together properly. A generic error message usually indicates that a compile error prevented the JSP from processing to completion. Check the standard output and standard error files defined for the application server hosting the JSP 1.1 processor (the names were entered as part of the configuration step) for more informative error messages.

6.9 Custom tag examples

This section describes a set of overly simple custom tags that demonstrate the techniques in the section on building custom tags. The TLD defines the three tags (called, caller and months), and source code is provided for the tag handler and TagExtraInfo class for each of the tags.

The caller and called tags demonstrate how one tag handler can reference the tag handler for another tag. The tag handler for a called tag will put itself into the page context using the specified id attribute value as a key. The tag handler for the caller tag will ask the page context for the object saved with an id equal to the value of the refId attribute. If the object is found, the caller tag handler will write out a message containing attributes from both tags. If no object is found, the tag handler will write out an error message.

The months tag is a simple iteration example. The contents of the months tag is processed once for each month of the year. During any one iteration, the months tag handler will put into the page context a bean representing the month for the iteration. This bean is named with the beanName attribute and can be referenced by that name in embedded Java code in the JSP.

```
<?xml version="1.0" encoding="ISO-8859-1" ?>
<!DOCTYPE taglib
        PUBLIC "-//Sun Microsystems, Inc.//DTD JSP Tag Library 1.1//EN"
        "web-jsptaglib_1_1.dtd">

<!-- This TEI describes an example custom tag library -->

<taglib>
  <!-- after this the default space is
   "http://java.sun.com/j2ee/dtds/web-jsptaglibrary_1_1.dtd"
   -->

  <tlibversion>1.0</tlibversion>
  <jspversion>1.1</jspversion>
  <shortname>simple</shortname>
  <info>
   A simple tab library for the examples
  </info>

  <!-- called tag -->
  <tag>
    <name>called</name>
    <tagclass>com.ibm.itso.jsp11.CalledTag</tagclass>
    <teiclass>com.ibm.itso.jsp11.CalledTagTEI</teiclass>
    <bodycontent>empty</bodycontent>
    <info>
   This tag is referred to by the CallerTag.
    </info>

    <attribute>
   <name>id</name>
   <required>true</required>
    </attribute>
    <attribute>
   <name>color</name>
   <required>true</required>
    </attribute>
  </tag>
```

Figure 124. test.tld (1/2)

```
<!-- caller tag -->
 <tag>
   <name>caller</name>
   <tagclass>com.ibm.itso.jsp11.CallerTag</tagclass>
   <teiclass>com.ibm.itso.jsp11.CallerTagTEI</teiclass>
   <bodycontent>empty</bodycontent>
   <info>
  This tag refers to called tags.
   </info>

   <attribute>
  <name>id</name>
  <required>true</required>
   </attribute>
   <attribute>
  <name>shape</name>
  <required>true</required>
   </attribute>
   <attribute>
  <name>refId</name>
  <required>true</required>
   </attribute>
 </tag>

 <tag>
   <name>months</name>
   <tagclass>com.ibm.itso.jsp11.MonthsTag</tagclass>
   <teiclass>com.ibm.itso.jsp11.MonthsTEI</teiclass>
   <bodycontent>JSP</bodycontent>
   <info>
  This tag iterates over the months.
   </info>

   <attribute>
  <name>beanName</name>
  <required>true</required>
   </attribute>
 </tag>

</taglib>
```

Figure 125. test.tld (2/2)

```
package com.ibm.itso.jsp11;

import javax.servlet.jsp.tagext.*;
import javax.servlet.jsp.*;
import java.io.*;
/**
 * The CalledTag class is the tag handler for the
 * called custom tag.  The id attribute is used by
 * the caller custom tag to refer to a specific
 * instance of the called tag.  The color attribute
 * is simply a value to be accessed by the caller tag.
 * @author: Chris Gerken
 */
public class CalledTag extends TagSupport {
   private String id;
   private String color;
/**
 * CalledTag constructor comment.
 */
public CalledTag() {
   super();
}
public int doStartTag() throws JspException {

// So that this tag handler can be referenced by other
// tag handlers, we need to put this object into the
// page context.  The value of this tag's id attribute
// is used as the key.

   pageContext.setAttribute(getId(),this);

// We're through wih processing for this tag.

   return SKIP_BODY;
}
/**
 * Return this object's color.
 * @return java.lang.String
 */
public java.lang.String getColor() {
   return color;
}
```

Figure 126. CalledTag.java (1/2)

```
/**
 * Return this object's id.
 * @return java.lang.String
 */
public java.lang.String getId() {
   return id;
}
/**
 * Set this object's color.
 * @param newColor java.lang.String
 */
public void setColor(java.lang.String newColor) {
   color = newColor;
}
/**
 * Set this object's id.
 * @param newId java.lang.String
 */
public void setId(java.lang.String newId) {
   id = newId;
}
}
```

Figure 127. CalledTag.java (2/2)

```
package com.ibm.itso.jsp11;

import javax.servlet.jsp.tagext.*;

/**
 * This TagExtraInfo subclass describes
 * the called tag and the object it creates.
 * The tag is expected to have an id
 * attribute which holds the name of the
 * created object.
 * @author: Chris Gerken
 */

public class CalledTEI extends TagExtraInfo {

public CalledTEI() {
   super();
}

public VariableInfo[] getVariableInfo(TagData data) {
   String idValue = data.getId();

   if (idValue == null) {
       return new VariableInfo[0];
   } else {
       VariableInfo idInfo = new VariableInfo(
                        idValue,
                        "gerken.jsp11.tag.CalledTag",
                        true,
                        VariableInfo.AT_BEGIN);
       VariableInfo[] list = { idInfo } ;
       return list;
   }
}

public boolean isValid(TagData data) {
   return true;
}



}
```

Figure 128. CalledTEI.java

```
package com.ibm.itso.jsp11;

import javax.servlet.jsp.tagext.*;
import javax.servlet.jsp.*;
import java.io.*;
/**
 * The CallerTag class is the tag handler
 * for the caller custom tag.  The refId
 * attribute is used by the caller custom
 * tag to refer to a specific instance of
 * the called tag.
 * @author: Chris Gerken
 */
public class CallerTag extends TagSupport {
   private String id;
   private String shape;
   private String refId;
/**
 * Caller constructor comment.
 */
public CallerTag() {
   super();
}
public int doStartTag() throws JspException {

   try {

      // Request the tag handler for the instance of
      // the called tag whose id attribute equals this
      // tag handler's refId value.

      CalledTag called = (CalledTag)
pageContext.getAttribute(getRefId());
      if (called == null) {

         // If no tag handler was found, write a suitable
         // error message to the response object.

         pageContext.getOut().println(
            "<p><b>Failed to find tag with id="+getRefId()+"</b></p>"
            );
      } else {
```

Figure 129. CallerTag.java (1/3)

```
            // If a tag handler was found, write out this
            // tag's shape attribute and that tag's color
            // attribute.

            pageContext.getOut().println(
                "<p>Matching <b>"+getShape()+
                "</b> with <b>"+called.getColor()+
                "</b></p>"
                );
        }
    } catch (Throwable t) {}

    // There's no more tag processing.

    return SKIP_BODY;
}
/**
 * Return the id.
 * @return java.lang.String
 */
public java.lang.String getId() {
    return id;
}
/**
 * Return the referenced id.
 * @return java.lang.String
 */
public java.lang.String getRefId() {
    return refId;
}
/**
 * Return the shape.
 * @return java.lang.String
 */
public java.lang.String getShape() {
    return shape;
}
/**
 * Set the id.
 * @param newId java.lang.String
 */
```

Figure 130. CallerTag.java (2/3)

```
public void setId(java.lang.String newId) {
   id = newId;
}
/**
 * Set the reference id.
 * @param newRefId java.lang.String
 */
public void setRefId(java.lang.String newRefId) {
   refId = newRefId;
}
/**
 * Set the shape.
 * @param newShape java.lang.String
 */
public void setShape(java.lang.String newShape) {
   shape = newShape;
}
}
```

Figure 131. CallerTag.java (3/3)

```
package com.ibm.itso.jsp11;

import javax.servlet.jsp.tagext.*;

/**
 * This TagExtraInfo subclass describes
 * the caller tag.  It doesn't create any
 * objects and performs no additional
 * attribute validation.
 * @author: Chris Gerken
 */
public class CallerTEI extends TagExtraInfo {
public CallerTEI() {
   super();
}

public VariableInfo[] getVariableInfo(TagData data) {
   return new VariableInfo[0];
}

public boolean isValid(TagData data) {
   return true;
}



}
```

Figure 132. CallerTEI.java

```
<%@ taglib uri="test.tld" prefix="ttl" %>

<ttl:called id="1" color="green" />
<ttl:called id="2" color="red" />
<ttl:called id="3" color="white" />

<ttl:caller id="a" shape="square" refId="2" />
<ttl:caller id="b" shape="circle" refId="1" />
<ttl:caller id="c" shape="triangle" refId="4" />
```

Figure 133. call.jsp

```
package com.ibm.itso.jsp11;

import javax.servlet.jsp.tagext.*;
import javax.servlet.jsp.*;
import java.io.*;
/**
 * The MonthsTag is the tag handler for the
 * months tag which processes its contents (the
 * JSP source between the months begin tag and
 * the months end tag) once for each month of
 * the year.  A bean representing the current
 * month of the iteration is made available to
 * tag handlers of nested tags.
*/
public class MonthsTag extends BodyTagSupport {
   private String beanName;
   private intcurrent;
/**
 * MonthsTag constructor comment.
 */
public MonthsTag() {
   super();
}
public int doAfterBody() throws JspException {

   // By default, we plan to stop iterating unless we
   // determine that there are more months.

   int result = SKIP_BODY;

   try {

      // Since the body of the tag was just processed,
      // we need to write the processing results to
      // the output stream.

      BodyContent body = getBodyContent();
      body.writeOut(getPreviousOut());
      body.clearBody();
   } catch (IOException ex) {
      String msg = "Months error: "+ex.getMessage();
      throw new JspTagException(msg);
   }
```

Figure 134. MonthsTag.java (1/3)

```
    // Increment the month counter.If there's another
    // month, store a new bean into the page context
    // to represent the next month and return
    // EVAL_BODY_TAG to indicate to the JSP container
    // that the body of this tag needs to be
    // processed again.

    current = current + 1;
    if (current < 13) {
       setMonth();
       result = EVAL_BODY_TAG;
    }

    return result;
 }
 public int doStartTag() throws JspException {

    // Initialize the iteration.

    current = 1;

    // Store a bean representing the iteration
    // state into the page context.

    setMonth();

    // Return EVAL_BODY_Tag to indicate to the
    // JSP container that the body of this tag
    // needs to be processed.

    return EVAL_BODY_TAG;

 }
 /**
  * Return the name of the bean that holds
  * the state of the iteration.  Tag handlers
  * for nested tags can use this name to
  * request the Month bean that gives the
  * current month for an iteration over
  * this tag's content.
  * @return java.lang.String
  */
```

Figure 135. MonthsTag.java (2/3)

```
public java.lang.String getBeanName() {
   return beanName;
}
/**
 * Sets the name to use when writing the
 * Month bean to the page context.
 * @param newBeanName java.lang.String
 */
public void setBeanName(java.lang.String newBeanName) {
   beanName = newBeanName;
}
/**
 * Write out a Month bean that holds the
 * state of the current tag's iteration.
 */
private void setMonth() {

   // Create a new Month bean.

   Month currentMonth = new Month();

   // Store the current month into the bean.

   currentMonth.setMonthNumber(current);

   // Write the bean to the page context.

   pageContext.setAttribute(getBeanName(),currentMonth);

}
}
```

Figure 136. MonthsTag.java (3/3)

```
package com.ibm.itso.jsp11;

import javax.servlet.jsp.tagext.*;

/**
 * This TagExtraInfo subclass describes the months tag and
 * the bean it creates to describe the state of its iteration..
 * The tag is expected to have an beanName attribute which
 * holds the name of the created object.
 * @author: Chris Gerken
 */
public class MonthsTEI extends TagExtraInfo {

public MonthsTEI() {
   super();
}

public VariableInfo[] getVariableInfo(TagData data) {

   // Get the value of the beanName attribute

   String bname = data.getAttributeString("beanName");

   // Create and return an array indicating that
   // processing this tag will result in the creation
   // of a single object of type Month.  The object
   // will only be available to other tags nested
   // within this Months tag.

   VariableInfo info = new VariableInfo(
                    bname,
                    "com.ibm.itso.jsp11.Month",
                    true,
                    VariableInfo.NESTED);
   VariableInfo[] list = { info } ;
   return list;
}

public boolean isValid(TagData data) {
   return true;
}
}
```

Figure 137. MonthsTEI.java

```
package com.ibm.itso.jsp11;

/**
 * The Month bean represents the state of the
 * iteration provided by the months tag.
 * @author: Chris Gerken
 */
public class Month {
   private intmonthNumber;
   private String monthName;
   private static  String[] months = {
      "January", "February", "March",
      "April", "May", "June", "July",
      "August", "September", "October",
      "November", "December" };
/**
 * Month constructor comment.
 */
public Month() {
   super();
}
/**
 * Return the month's name
 * @return java.lang.String
 */
public String getMonthName() {
   return monthName;
}
/**
 * Return the month's index.
 * @return int
 */
public int getMonthNumber() {
   return monthNumber;
}
/**
 * Set the month's name.
 * @param newMonthName String
 */
public void setMonthName(String newMonthName) {
   monthName = newMonthName;
}
```

Figure 138. Month.java (1/2)

```
/**
 * Set the month's index.
 * @param newMonthNumber int
 */
public void setMonthNumber(int newMonthNumber) {
   monthNumber = newMonthNumber;
   monthName = months[newMonthNumber-1];
}
}
```

Figure 139. Month.java (2/2)

```
<%@ taglib uri="test.tld" prefix="tst" %>
<%@ page import="com.ibm.itso.jsp11.*" language="java" %>

<p>This section appears only once in the browser.</p>

<tst:months beanName="mb" >
<p>This section of the JSP will be repeated once for
each month.  The month for this iteration is
<%= mb.getMonthName() %> </p>

</tst:months>

<p>This section appears only once in the browser.</p>
```

Figure 140. months.jsp

Chapter 7. Session support

This chapter discusses session support in the WebSphere Application Server V3.5. Session support allows a Web application developer to maintain state information regarding a user's visit.

Web applications require more information than their static, "brochure-ware" predecessors. In a true Web application, a user dynamically builds a course through the site based on a series of selections at each page. Where the user goes next, and what the application displays as the user's next page (or next choice, or next advertisement) may depend on what the user has chosen previously from the site. (For example, if the user clicks the **Checkout** button on our site, the next page must contain the user's shopping selections from this visit.)

Therefore, a Web application needs a mechanism to hold the user's state information over a period of time (typically known as a visit). However, HTTP alone doesn't recognize or maintain a user's state. HTTP treats each user request as a discrete, independent entity.

The Java Servlet specification provides a mechanism for servlet applications to maintain a user's state information, and this mechanism addresses some of the problems of more traditional strategies such as a pure cookie solution. This mechanism, known as a session, allows a Web application developer to maintain all user state information at the host, while passing minimal information back to the user via cookies or another technique known as URL encoding.

This chapter discusses the following aspects of the session specification:

- Differences in WebSphere V3.5 and V3.02 session state
- Session state enabling techniques (cookies and URL rewriting)
- Servlet 2.1 Session API
- Storing the HttpSession object (local and persistent session storage)
- IBM Servlet API extensions
- Session clustering
- Session performance considerations

7.1 V3.02.x vs. V3.5 overview

The session support in WebSphere Application Server V3.5.1 remains very consistent with the WebSphere V3.0x implementations, including V3.02x. WebSphere Application Server 3.5.2 allows the Web developer to use the Servlet 2.2 specification.

WebSphere V3.5 (and V3.02x) in combination with e-fix PQ42166 eliminates session locking, and allows concurrent session access. Due to this change, the WebSphere forces the use of the session cache (regardless of the setting in the administrator console) when the e-fix is applied.

7.2 Session feature overview

This section covers the major features of WebSphere Application Server session support. These features include classes for the Web application developer, as well as administrative options for the WebSphere Application Server administrator.

7.2.1 Cookies

WebSphere Application Server supports cookies as one mechanism for transferring a user's session ID between the user's browser and the Web application.

7.2.1.1 Cookie session support overview

WebSphere session support keeps the user session information at the server. The WebSphere passes the user an identifier known as a session ID either in a cookie, or in encoded URL links on the retuned page. The session ID correlates an incoming user with a session object maintained at the server.

Many sites choose cookie support to pass the user's identifier between WebSphere and the visiting user. WebSphere Application Server session support generates a unique session ID for each visitor, and returns this ID to the visitor's browser via a cookie.

(A cookie consists of information embedded as part of the headers in the HTML stream passed between the server and the browser. The browser holds the cookie, and returns it to the server when the user makes a subsequent request. By default, WebSphere defines its cookies so they are destroyed if the browser is closed.)

The cookie passes between WebSphere and the visitor's browser on each subsequent request to the Web site. This cookie holds only an identifier and a timestamp (used by the WebSphere for determining the "freshness" of session objects held in cache). The remainder of the visitor's session information resides at the server.

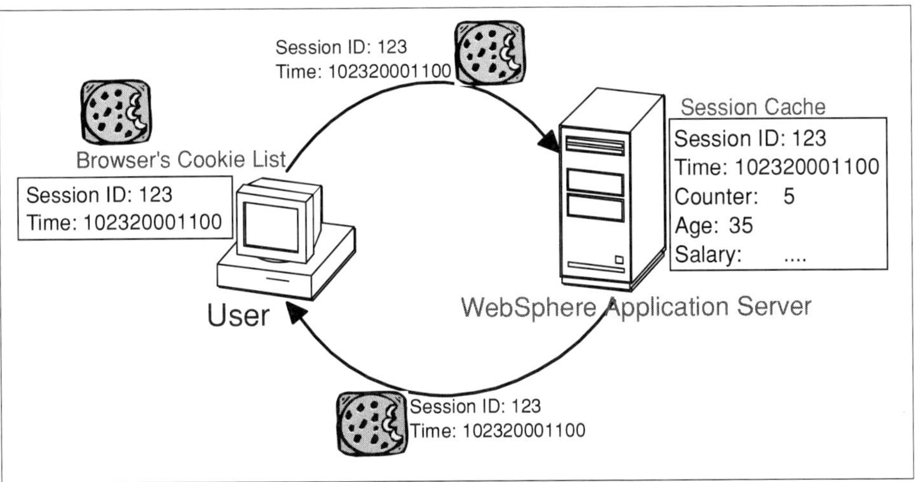

Figure 141. Cookie session support

At the server, WebSphere manages the cookie for the Web application transparently. The Web application developer never manipulates the session identifier or timestamp in the cookie directly. In fact, the Web application never needs to know the identifier assigned to a particular user to obtain their session information.

The Web application developer uses the HTTPRequest object standard interface to obtain the session:

```
HTTPSession session = request.getSession(true);
```

The WebSphere places the visitor's identifier in the outbound cookie whenever the servlet completes its execution, and the HTML response stream returns to the end user. Again, neither the cookie nor the session ID within it require any direct manipulation by the Web application. The Web application only sees the contents of the session.

7.2.1.2 Cookie disadvantages

Cookies provide a transparent means for passing the session identifier between the user and the WebSphere instance. However, not all browsers and user installations support cookies.

Some users, either by choice or mandate, cannot receive cookies from Web sites. Most browsers also allow users to turn off the ability to receive cookies. If a site supports large numbers of users who cannot or will not receive cookies, WebSphere supports an alternative technique known as URL encoding for passing user session IDs between the user and the Web application server instance.

However, URL encoding requires specific actions on the part of the Web developer to function. Also, URL encoding imposes restrictions on site flow not present in cookie-based session management. Because of these limitations, many sites require users to permit cookie passing if they want to use site features requiring WebSphere session support.

7.2.1.3 Enabling cookie support

The WebSphere defaults to session support with cookies (Enable Cookies=Yes) as shown in Figure 142.

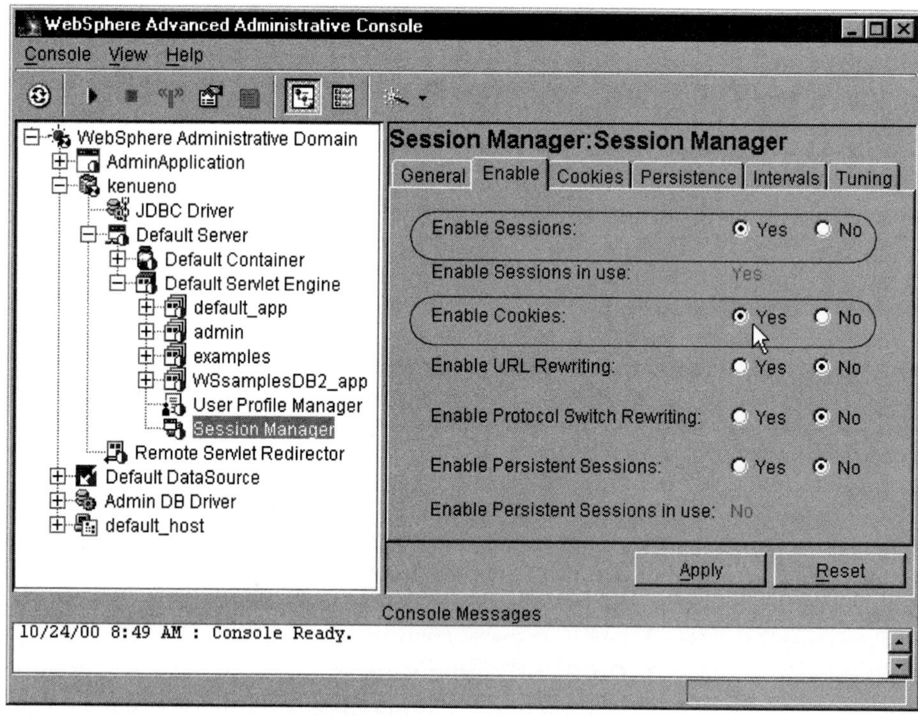

Figure 142. Default session enablement settings

Control for session state management resides at the servlet engine level. All changes for a given servlet engine apply to all Web applications running in that engine.

Note

In WebSphere Application Server V3.5.2, the WebSphere Application Server allows the administrator to override the session timeout value on a per Web application basis. This allows the administrator to tailor session support to better fit the requirements of each Web application. The value entered at the Web application level overrides the values set at the Session Manager in the servlet engine where the Web application resides.

7.2.1.4 Session sample

WebSphere, as stated earlier, handles all of the session state cookie processing required by the Web applications. The Web developer uses Servlet standard interfaces to retrieve the session information for a user. The WebSphere retrieves the user's session ID from the cookie, and finds the corresponding session data associated with the user. The Web application developer never needs to handle the identifier directly.

Here's an example of maintaining a counter in the user's session information using cookie-based session ID passing:

```
/*
 * @(#)MyCount.java
 *
 */
import java.io.*;
import javax.servlet.*;
import javax.servlet.http.*;
import com.sun.server.http.*;
import java.util.*;

public class MyCount extends HttpServlet
{
    public void init(ServletConfig config) throws ServletException
    {
        super.init(config);

    }

    public void service (HttpServletRequest req, HttpServletResponse res)
throws ServletException, IOException
    {
```

```
        ServletOutputStream         out;
        String                      count      = null;
        StringBuffer                outBuff    = new StringBuffer();

        out = res.getOutputStream();

        outBuff.append("<html><head><title>MyCount Session
Example</title></head><body bgcolor='#ffffff'>");
        outBuff.append("<H1>Counter Value: </H1>");
        outBuff.append("<p>");

        // Increment session state, creating if necessary
        HttpSession session = req.getSession(true);
        if ( session == null )
            outBuff.append("Cannot create session as expected!");
        else
        {
            Integer value = (Integer)session.getValue("MyCount.COUNTER");
            if ( value == null )
            {
                value = new Integer(1);
                outBuff.append("1 (from new session)");
            }
            else
            {
                value = new Integer(value.intValue() + 1);
                outBuff.append(value + " (from existing session)");
            }
            session.putValue("MyCount.COUNTER", value);
        }
        outBuff.append("</body></html>");
        out.println(outBuff.toString());
    }
}
```

In this very simple example, the servlet places a counter value in the user's session object, and updates this counter on subsequent requests by the user. This example points out the simplicity of cookie-based session state management for the Web application developer. The application accesses the session information through the HttpRequest object. After the method completes, the WebSphere saves the updated (or new) session information for the application. The WebSphere stores the information without an explicit command from the application. This is known as automatic update mode, and is the default for WebSphere.

7.2.2 URL rewriting

WebSphere also provides URL encoding for session ID passing. While session management is transparent to the Web application, URL encoding requires the developer to use special encoding APIs, and to set up the site page flow to avoid losing the encoded information.

URL encoding works by actually storing the session identifier in the page returned to the user. WebSphere encodes the session identifier as a parameter on any link or form the user may submit from the page. For example:

```
<a href="store/catalog;$sesessionid$DA32242SSGE2">
```

In this example, when the user clicks this link to move to the store/catalog page, the session identifier passes into the request as a parameter.

URL encoding requires explicit action by the Web application developer. If the servlet returns HTML directly to the requester (without using a JavaServer Page (JSP)), the servlet calls the following API to encode the returning content:

```
out.println("<a href=\"");
out.println(response.encodeURL ("/store/catalog"));
out.println("\">catalog</a>");
```

Even pages using redirection (a common practice, particularly with servlet/JSP combinations) must encode the session ID as part of the redirect:

```
response.sendRedirect(response.encodeRedirectURL("http://myhost/store/cata
log"));
```

When JavaServer Pages (JSPs) use URL encoding, the JSP calls a similar interface to encode the session ID:

```
<% response.encodeURL ("/store/catalog"); %>
```

URL encoding limits the flow of site pages exclusively to dynamically generated pages (such as pages generated by servlets or JSPs). WebSphere inserts the session ID into dynamic pages, but cannot insert the user's session ID into static pages (.htm or .html pages).

Therefore, after the application creates the user's session data, the user must visit dynamically generated pages exclusively until they finish with the portion of the site requiring sessions. URL encoding forces the site designer to plan the user's flow in the site to avoid losing their session ID.

7.2.2.1 Enabling URL rewriting

The WebSphere administrator enables URL rewriting from the Session Manager as shown in Figure 143. This change applies to every Web application assoicated with the Session Manager's servlet engine.

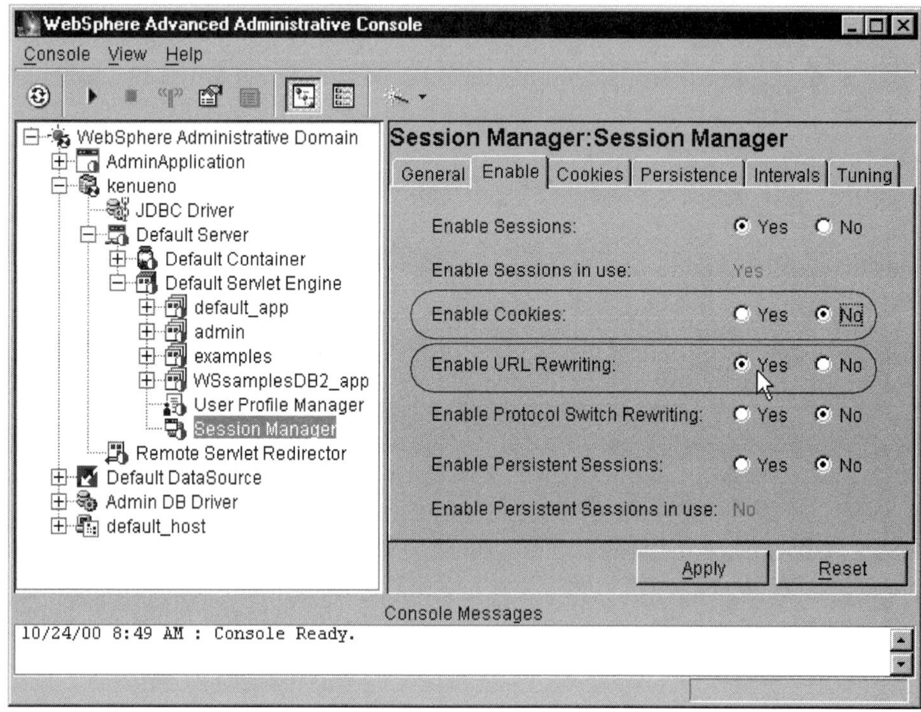

Figure 143. Enabling URL rewriting

7.2.2.2 Using URL rewriting

As mentioned earlier, URL rewriting requires some action from the Web application developer to function properly. Here is a simple example using URL rewriting:

```
import java.io.*;
import javax.servlet.*;
import javax.servlet.http.*;
import com.sun.server.http.*;
import java.util.*;

public class MyLinkCount extends HttpServlet
{
    public void init(ServletConfig config) throws ServletException
    {
```

```
        super.init(config);

    }

    public void service (HttpServletRequest req, HttpServletResponse res)
throws ServletException, IOException
    {
        ServletOutputStream         out;
        String                      count       = null;
        StringBuffer                outBuff     = new StringBuffer();
        String                      nextLink    =
"/webapp/TestApp/MyLinkCount";

        out = res.getOutputStream();

        outBuff.append("<html><head><title>MyCount Session
Example</title></head><body bgcolor='#ffffff'>");
        outBuff.append("<H1>Counter Value: </H1>");
        outBuff.append("<p>");

        // Increment session state, creating if necessary
        HttpSession session = req.getSession(true);
        if ( session == null )
            outBuff.append("Cannot create session as expected!");
        else
        {
Integer value = (Integer)session.getValue("MyLinkCount.COUNTER");
            if ( value == null )
            {
                value = new Integer(1);
                outBuff.append("1 (from new session)");
            }
            else
            {
                value = new Integer(value.intValue() + 1);
                outBuff.append(value + " (from existing session)");
            }
            session.putValue("MyLinkCount.COUNTER", value);
        }

        outBuff.append("<br><br>");
        outBuff.append("<a href=");
        outBuff.append(res.encodeURL(nextLink));
        outBuff.append(">Next!</a>");
        outBuff.append("</body></html>");
        out.println(outBuff.toString());
    }
```

```
}
```

In this example, the servlet provides a convenient link to the counting servlet. The Web developer passes the link (in this case, /webapp/TestApp/MyLinkCount) to the HttpServletResponse object for URL encoding.

The application retrieves the session object in the same manner as a servlet interacting with cookie-based servlet support. However, the application must encode any links on the outbound HTML with the user's session ID. The servlet uses the encodeURL() method for encoding the session ID onto the link.

If this WebSphere uses URL Rewriting to pass session IDs, the result from the encodeURL() method contains the link URL and the session ID (as a parameter). For example:

```
/webapp/TestApp/MyLinkCount;$sessionid$IACYYOYAAAAAACJFGDU31UI
```

If this WebSphere does not use URL rewriting, the call to the encodeURL() method returns the same text it received. It does not add the session ID to the URL.

WebSphere allows the administrator to enable both URL rewriting and cookie support. In this case, the call to encodeURL() returns a URL encoded with the session ID. However, the WebSphere also returns a cookie containing the session ID. Such a configuration may prove useful for applications serving mixed audiences, or if the administrator must support some applications that are using URL rewriting, and others that are not, within the same servlet engine.

7.2.3 Session API

This section covers the Session API defined by the Servlet specification. See 7.2.6, “IBM extensions” on page 265 for more details on IBM extensions to the servlet specification.

7.2.3.1 Obtaining the session

The Servlet specification defines the operation and interfaces for session data. An application obtains the user's session through the request object:

```
javax.servlet.http.HTTPRequest req;
javax.servlet.http.HTTPSession session = req.getSession(true);
```

The API supports getting a session only if one already exists, or providing a new session if this user doesn't have one yet. By passing true to the getSession() method, the application receives the user's existing session, if one exists, or the WebSphere creates a session if the user does not have one. Likewise, by passing false to the getSession() method, the application receives a session only if one was previously created for the user. (getSession() without a parameter defaults to the getSession(true) case.)

(Some applications use the presence or absence of session data to monitor the flow of the user's site visit. A user without a session, for example, may have not completed a logon process. The application may use redirection to force the user to the logon page rather than letting him continue with shopping.)

7.2.3.2 Storing and Retrieving session data

The javax.servlet.http.HTTPSession class functions much like the java.util.Dictionary class. Applications store information associated with a key:

```
session.putValue("mydata","information");
```

Retrieving information works similarly:

```
String myValue = (String)session.getValue("mydata");
```

Note

Persistent session management requires that all objects stored in the session be serializable.

Note

The Session 2.2 API deprecates getValue() and putValue(), and replaces them with getAttribute() and putAttribute().

Session data management requires some planning on the part of the Web developer. On many sites, several servlets (and in some cases, several Web applications) share the same session data for a given user. Applications storing information in the session may overwrite each other's entries. A naming scheme to ensure uniqueness helps.

For example, two shopping applications on the same Web site share a user's session data. Both applications use the value TOTAL, which they store in the user's session. Obviously, these applications need a naming scheme, or the value of TOTAL will be overwritten whenever the user moves between the applications.

So, the sporting goods site application uses the following prefix for its entries in the user's session data:

```
session.putValue("bobs.sports.TOTAL",110);
```

The cooking site application uses this prefix for its session entries:

```
session.putValue("happychef.TOTAL",434);
```

This naming scheme allows both applications to share the user's session data without overwriting each other's data.

Use a naming scheme even if the session data isn't currently shared between applications. A naming scheme, implemented early, allows the site to grow without collisions between new and existing applications.

Note

Multi-row persistent session management eliminates the need for a naming scheme for differentiating values between Web applications. See 7.3.2, "Multirow persistent session management" on page 290 for more details.

7.2.3.3 Sessions and classpath

If multiple Web applications share a session, the objects placed in the session must be in the classpath of all the Web applications. If this is not possible, the administrator may use multi-row persistent session management to avoid loading objects in the session outside the scope of their Web application. See 7.3.2, "Multirow persistent session management" on page 290 for more details.

7.2.3.4 Saving session information

WebSphere saves any new or updated session information after the servlet or JSP call completes. Alternatively, IBM provides an extension to the Servlet specification that allows the application to specify when session contents should be saved. See 7.2.6, "IBM extensions" on page 265 for more details.

7.2.3.5 Invalidating sessions

If the user no longer requires a session object, the application removes the session through the invalidate() method.

```
session.invalidate();
```

The invalidate() method requires great care from the application not to destroy sessions in use by other applications. See 7.3.1.5, "Invalidate unneeded sessions" on page 289 for a more detailed discussion.

> **Note**
>
> In the Servlet 2.1 specification, session context (that is, the scope of sessions visible to a given application) is per virtual host. In Servlet 2.2, the session context is per Web application. See Chapter 8, "Servlet V2.2 in WebSphere V3.5.2" on page 295 for a more detailed discussion of this topic.

7.2.3.6 Changing a session's timeout

The administrator defines the default timeout values for session objects in a particular application server. However, some applications may require longer or shorter timeouts based on the application the user visits, or the class of service for which the user qualifies.

For example, a portal site might give users checking their internet mail accounts 30-minute session intervals. This gives them time to read a message, or compose a lengthy reply without fear of losing their sessions. However, users visiting the weather site might only get a 10-minute timeout, which should be plenty of time for them to quickly check a forecast.

Set the interval using the setMaxInactiveInterval() method. The method expects the interval in seconds. So, to set the interval for 10 minutes, issue the following:

```
session.setMaxInactiveInterval(600);
```

Again, be aware of setting this interval when the other applications may be sharing the user's session object. Also, using this interface limits the administrator's ability to control session timeout intervals. For future site growth and scaling, the Web developer may want to consider placing these timeouts in a resource file where they can be adjusted by the administrator, if necessary. See 7.3, "Session performance considerations" on page 287 for details on how sessions may impact site performance.

7.2.3.7 Session listeners

Before terminating a session, WebSphere notifies session objects implementing this interface:

```
javax.servlet.http.HttpSessionBindingListener
```

Sessions timeout (even persistent sessions) so this interface allows the application to manage session information before the session timeout completes and the session data is destroyed. The object provides this logic; WebSphere only provides the notification via the HttpSessionBindingListener interface.

If multiple Web applications share session objects, the objects referenced defined as listeners must be in the classpath of any Web application in which they may be invoked.

For example, Web application A defines a listener for the terminate event. However, the terminate event actually occurs later while Web application B is processing the session object. In this case, Web application B also needs the listener defined by Web application A in its classpath in order to run the listener properly.

7.2.4 Local sessions

Most Web application developers use the simplest form of session management while developing their applications: the in-memory, local session cache. The local session cache keeps session information in memory and local to the machine and Web application server instance where the session information was first created.

Local session management doesn't share user session information with other clustered machines. Users only obtain their session information if they return to the machine and Web application server instance holding their session information on subsequent accesses to the Web site.

Most importantly, local session management lacks a persistent store for the sessions it manages. A server failure takes down not only the WebSphere instances running on the server, but also destroys any sessions managed by those instances.

WebSphere allows the administrator to define a limit on the number of sessions held in the in-memory cache via the administrative console settings on the Session Manager as shown in Figure 144 on page 259. This prevents the sessions from acquiring too much memory in the Java Virtual Machine associated with the WebSphere instance.

The Session Manager also allows the administrator to permit an unlimited number of sessions in memory. If the administrator enables the Allow Overflow setting on the Session Manager via the administrative console (see Figure 144 on page 259), the Session Manager permits two in-memory caches for session objects. The first cache contains only enough entries to accommodate the session limit defined to the Session Manager (1000 by default). The second cache, known as the overflow cache, holds any sessions the first cache cannot accommodate, and is limited in size only by available memory. The Session Manager builds the first cache for optimized retrieval, while a regular, unoptimized hashtable contains the overflow cache. For best performance, define a primary cache of sufficient size to hold the normal working set of sessions for a given WebSphere instance.

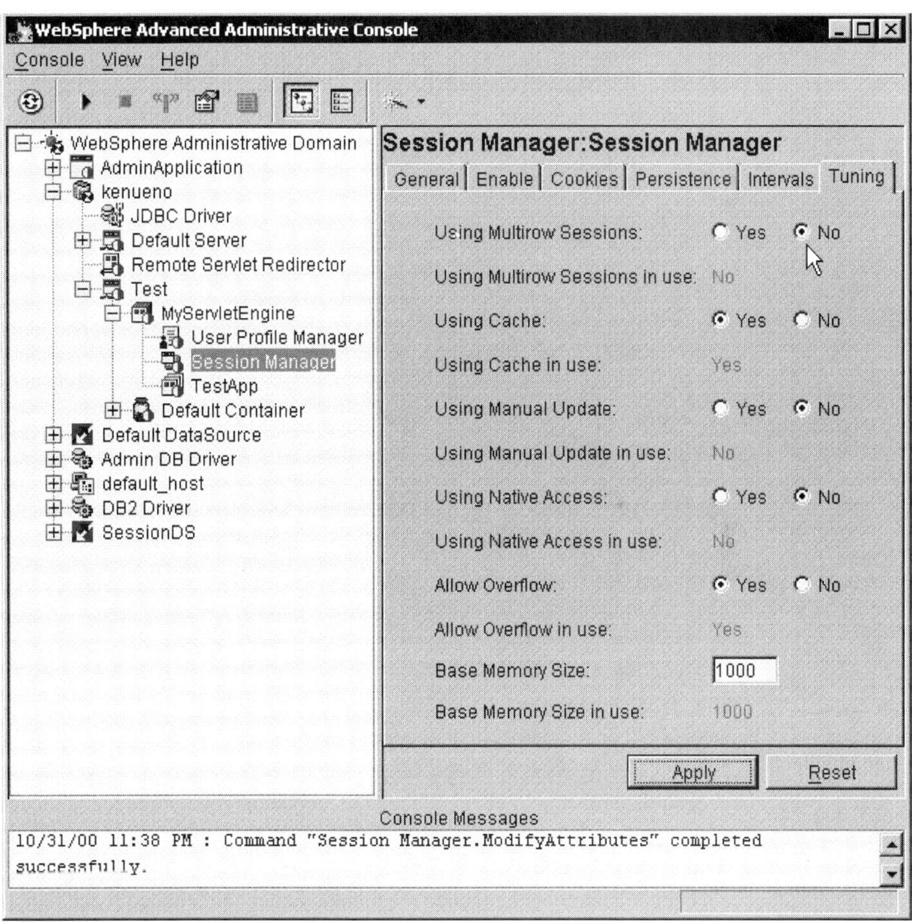

Figure 144. Session Manager: Tuning tab

Also, note that with overflow enabled, the Session Manager permits an unlimited number of sessions in memory. Without limits, the session caches may consume all available memory in the WebSphere instance's heap, leaving no room to execute Web applications. This scenarios arises if:

- The site receives greater traffic than anticipated, generating a large number of sessions held in memory.
- A malicious attack occurs against the site where a user deliberately manipulates their browser so the application creates a new session repeatedly for the same user.

7.2.5 Persistence

By default, WebSphere places session objects in memory. However, the administrator has the option of enabling persistent session management, which instructs the WebSphere to place session objects in a database.

Administrators enable persistent session management when:

- Multiple WebSphere instances need to share session objects (also known as clustering).
- The user's session data becomes too valuable to lose through unexpected failure at the WebSphere node.
- The administrator desires better control of the session cache memory footprint. By sending cache overflow to a persistent session database, the administrator controls the number of sessions allowed in memory at any given time.

All information stored in a persistent session database must be serializable. All of the objects held by a session must implement java.io.Serializable if the session might be stored in a persistent session database.

In general, consider making all objects held by a session serializable, even if immediate plans do not call for the use of persistent session management. If the Web site grows, and persistent session management becomes necessary, the transition between local vs. persistent management occurs transparently to the application if the sessions hold serializable objects. If not, a switch to persistent session management requires coding changes to make the session contents serializable.

Persistent session management does not impact the Session API, and Web applications require no API changes to support persistent session management. However, as mentioned above, applications storing unserializable objects in their sessions require modification before switching to persistent session management.

7.2.5.1 Enabling session persistence

The WebSphere administrator enables session persistence using the administrative console by selecting **WebSphere node (kenueno) ->**

Application Server (Test) -> Servlet Engine (MyServletEngine) -> Session Manager as shown in Figure 145.

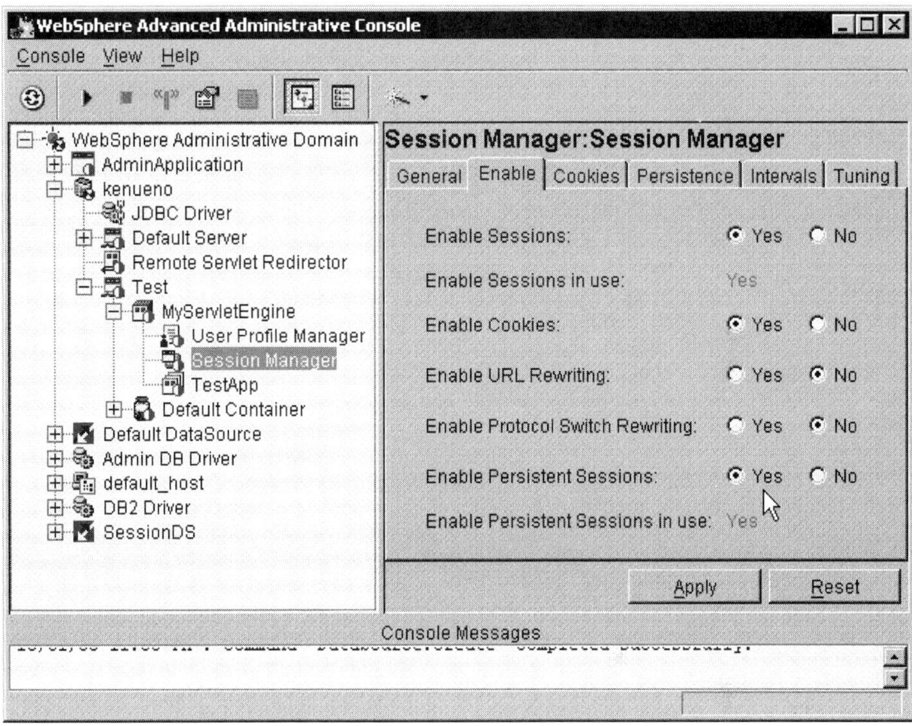

Figure 145. Enable persistent sessions

The administrator indicates a directodb connection by selecting **WebSphere node (kenueno) -> Application Server (Test) -> Servlet Engine (MyServletEngine) -> Session Manager -> Persistence** as shown in Figure 146 on page 262.

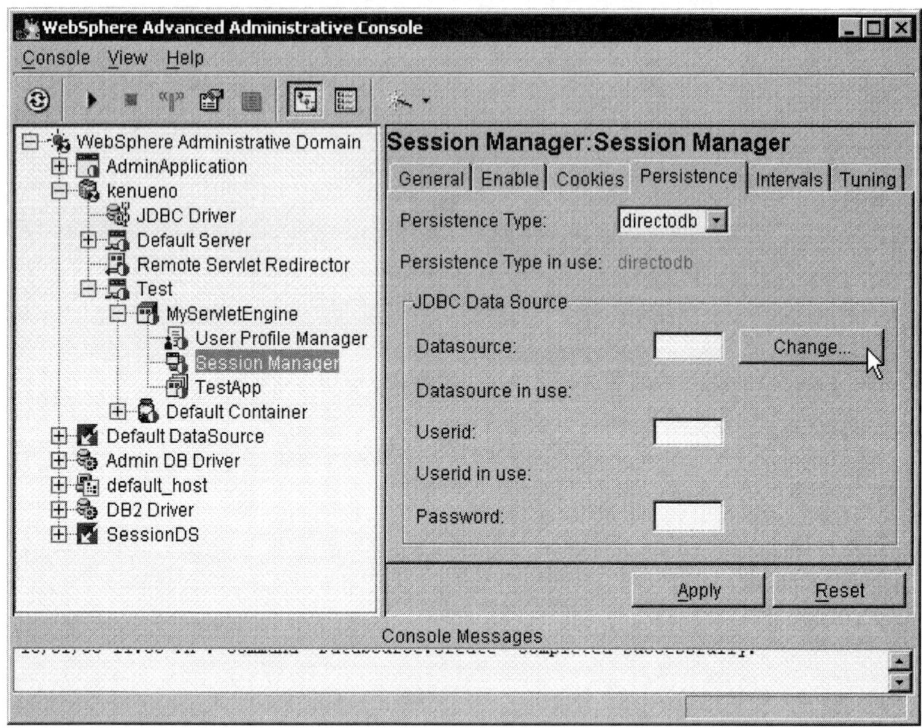

Figure 146. Session Manager: Persistence tab

Select a datasource for the Session Manager to use by clicking **Change - > Datasource (SessionDS) -> Ok** as shown in Figure 147.

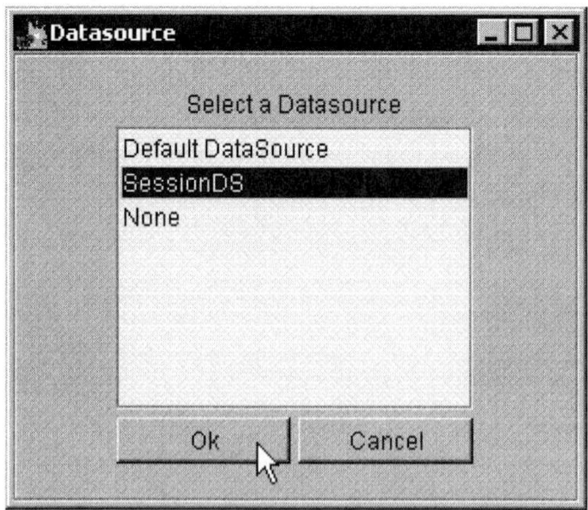

Figure 147. Select a Datasource

The administrator also provides the user ID and password required to access the database associated with the datasource as shown in Figure 148.

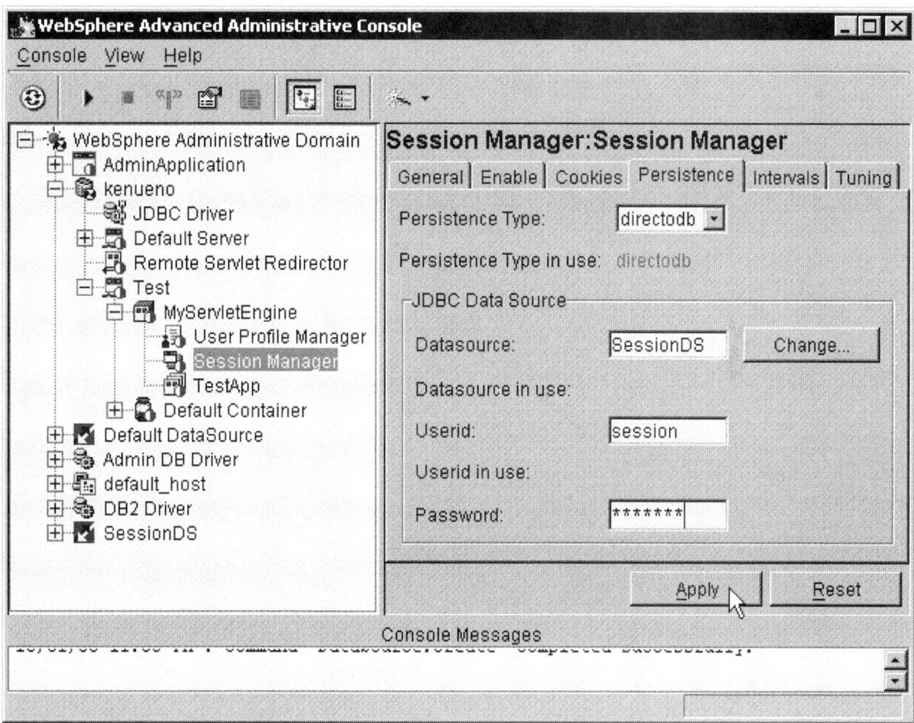

Figure 148. Session Manager: Persistence tab

After defining the persistent datastore, the administrator may choose additional tuning parameters for the persistent sessions, as shown in Figure 149 on page 264.

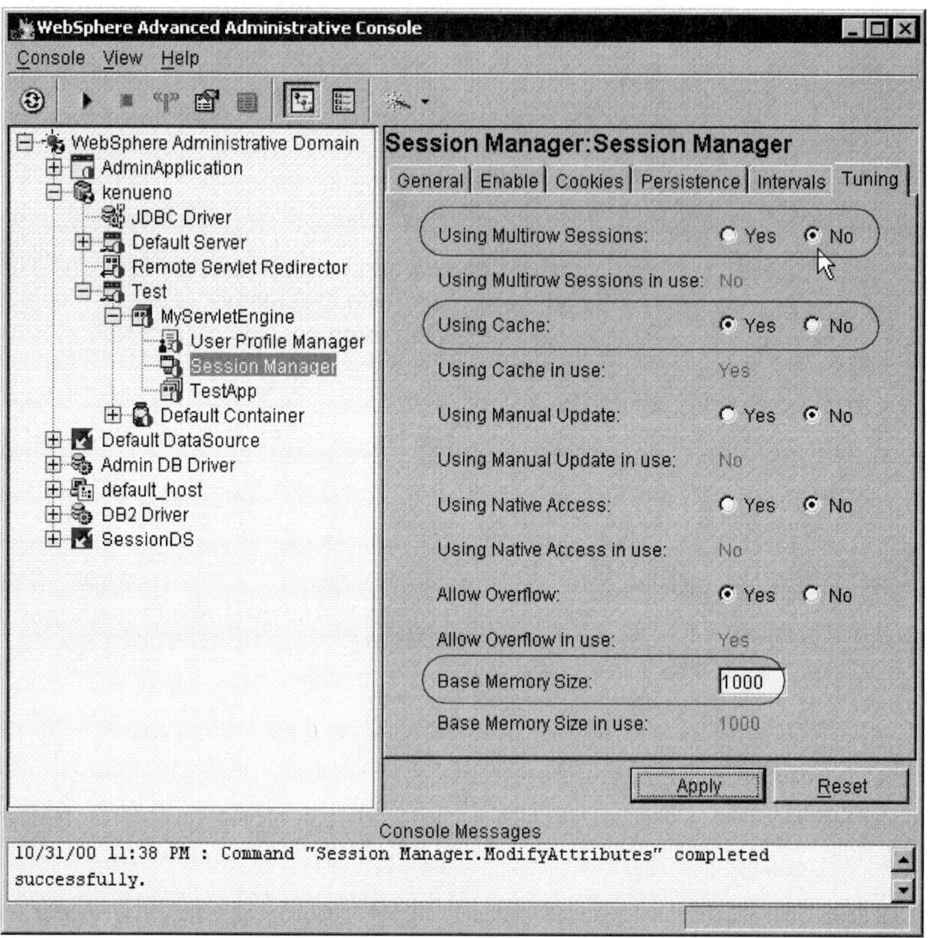

Figure 149. Session Manager: Tuning tab

Using multirow sessions becomes important if the size of the session object exceeds the size for a row, as permitted by the database vendor. If the administrator requests multirow session support, the WebSphere Session Manager breaks the session data across multiple rows as needed. This allows WebSphere to support large session objects. Also, this provides a more efficient mechanism for retrieving session contents under certain circumstances. See 7.3.2, “Multirow persistent session management” on page 290 for information on this feature.

Using cache lets the Session Manager maintain a cache of most recently used sessions in memory. Retrieving a user session from the cache eliminates a more expensive retrieval from the persistent database. The

Session Manager uses a “least recently used” scheme for removing objects from the cache. If the cache overflows, the Session Manager stores the overflow sessions in the persistent session database. (Without persistent session management activated, overflow sessions reside in an overflow cache in memory, if overflow is permitted. See 7.2.4, “Local sessions” on page 258 for more details.)

The Base Memory Size field defines the maximum number of sessions permitted in memory. In essence, base memory size defines the size of the in-memory session cache when using persistent sessions. Notice, this attribute only concerns itself with the number of session objects in the cache. Applications using extremely large session objects can overflow the available memory before they overflow the cache.

> **Note**
>
> Persistent session management sends sessions directly to the persistent data store if the session cache overflows. Therefore, the Use Overflow setting does not apply in persistent session management.

7.2.6 IBM extensions

WebSphere provides extensions to the standard HTTPSession APIs. Using these functions impacts the portability of the Web application to non-IBM environments implementing the Servlet standard. Web application developers must weigh the functional advantages of these APIs against the likelihood of porting the application to a non-IBM servlet runtime environment.

7.2.6.1 Locking and releasing session transactions

WebSphere Application Server 3.5 supports the traditional locking strategy used in Version 3.02. Also, WebSphere Application Server supports a new, open locking strategy through applying e-fix PQ42166, or upgrading the installation to PTF 3. The following sections describe both strategies in more detail.

Traditional session locking strategy

Sometimes, particularly with persistent session management, the Web application developer wants better control of locking and releasing sessions. Normally, WebSphere locks a session as a result of the HTTPRequest.getSession() method. Likewise, the session unlocks when the HTTPSession service() method completes, and (if session persistence is enabled) the Session Manager writes the updated session data to the datastore.

This class:

```
com.ibm.websphere.servlet.session.IBMSession
```

allows the Web application developer to release the session lock before the service() methods completes. The application calls the sync() method to release the lock. (If the application needs the lock again, it calls the HTTPRequest.getSession() method again.)

Locking with e-fix PQ42166 or V3.5 PTF 3

With e-fix PQ42166 or planned WebSphere V3.5 PTF3, the Session Manager no longer locks the session object in the persistent session store for exclusive access by a servlet. Instead, the Session Manager retrieves the desired session, releases the lock, and returns to the calling servlet. The session object resides in the common session cache for a given WebSphere instance.

This change allows WebSphere to better support Servlet standard 2.2. However, the change poses greater risk to Web applications accessing the same session information concurrently. The most likely scenario for contention involves multiple JSPs or servlets called from a frame set. In this case, multiple threads within the Web site may attempt to access the user's session information on behalf of different servlets or JSPs.

Also, because of the concurrency change, WebSphere forces the enablement of the session cache. The WebSphere instance uses a session cache regardless of the setting on the Session Manager in the administrative console.

7.2.6.2 Manual session update

WebSphere also supports a manual mode for session writing. Manual mode allows the application to decide when a session should be stored persistently (normally, WebSphere stores modified data after the servlet's service() method completes). In manual mode, the Session Manager only sends changes to the persistent data store if the application explicitly requests a save of the session information.

Manual mode requires that an application developer use the IBMSession class for managing sessions. When the application invokes the sync() method, the Session Manager writes the session information to the persistent session database. If the servlet or JSP terminates without invoking the sync() method, the Session Manager saves the contents of the session object into the session cache (if caching is enabled), but does not update the session object in the session database.

This interface gives the Web application developer additional control of when (and if) session objects go to the persistent data store. If the application does not invoke the sync() method, and manual update mode is specified, the session updates go only to the local session cache, not the persistent data store. Web developers use this interface to reduce unnecessary writes to the session database, and thereby to improve overall application performance.

All servlets in the application must perform their own session management in manual mode.

7.2.6.3 Manual session update example

The following servlet, MyManualCount, drives the manual session update example:

```
/*
 * @(#)MyManualCount.java
 *
 */
import java.io.*;
import javax.servlet.*;
import javax.servlet.http.*;
import com.sun.server.http.*;
import java.util.*;

public class MyManualCount extends HttpServlet
{
    public void init(ServletConfig config) throws ServletException
    {
        super.init(config);

    }

    public void service (HttpServletRequest req, HttpServletResponse
res) throws ServletException, IOException
    {
        ServletOutputStream         out;
        String                      count       = null;
        StringBuffer                outBuff     = new StringBuffer();
        String                      saveLink    =
"/webapp/TestApp/MyManualCount?MODE=SAVE";
        String                      dropLink    =
"/webapp/TestApp/MyManualCount?MODE=DROP";
```

Figure 150. MyManualCount.java (1/3)

```
        out = res.getOutputStream();

        outBuff.append("<html><head><title>MyManualCount Session
Example</title></head><body bgcolor='#ffffff'>");
        outBuff.append("<H1>Counter Value: </H1>");
        outBuff.append("<p>");

        String mode = req.getParameter("MODE");
// Use the IBM Session to hold the session information
        // We need the IBM Session object because it has the manual
update method sync()
        com.ibm.websphere.servlet.session.IBMSession session =
(com.ibm.websphere.servlet.session.IBMSession)req.getSession(true);

        if ( session == null )
            outBuff.append("Cannot create session as expected!");
        else {

            //Check for existing counter value in the session object
            Integer value =
(Integer)session.getValue("MyManualCount.COUNTER");
            if ( value == null ){
                value = new Integer(1);
                outBuff.append("1 (from new session)");
            }
            else{
                value = new Integer(value.intValue() + 1);
                outBuff.append(value + " (from existing session)");
            }

            //Update the in-memory session stored in the cache
            session.putValue("MyManualCount.COUNTER", value);

            //The servlet saves the session if:
            //  1) It's our first time in the servlet
            //  2) We click the "Increment and Save" link on subsequent
requests
            if ((mode==null) || (mode.equals("SAVE"))) {

                System.out.println("Saving Session!");
                session.sync();
            }
        }
```

Figure 151. MyManualCount.java (2/3)

```
        outBuff.append("<br><br>");
        outBuff.append("<a href=");
        outBuff.append(saveLink);
        outBuff.append(">Increment and Save!</a>");
        outBuff.append("<br><br>");
        outBuff.append("<a href=");
        outBuff.append(dropLink);
        outBuff.append(">Increment Only!</a>");
        outBuff.append("</body></html>");

        out.println(outBuff.toString());
    }
}
```

Figure 152. MyManualCount.java (3/3)

In this example, the servlet MyManualCount updates a counter kept in the user's session object. However, in this case, the user decides when to send the updated count to the session database.

The WebSphere administrator must set up the Web application to use session persistence, as described earlier in this chapter. The administrator must also enable the Manual Update field on the Session Manager as shown in Figure 153 on page 270.

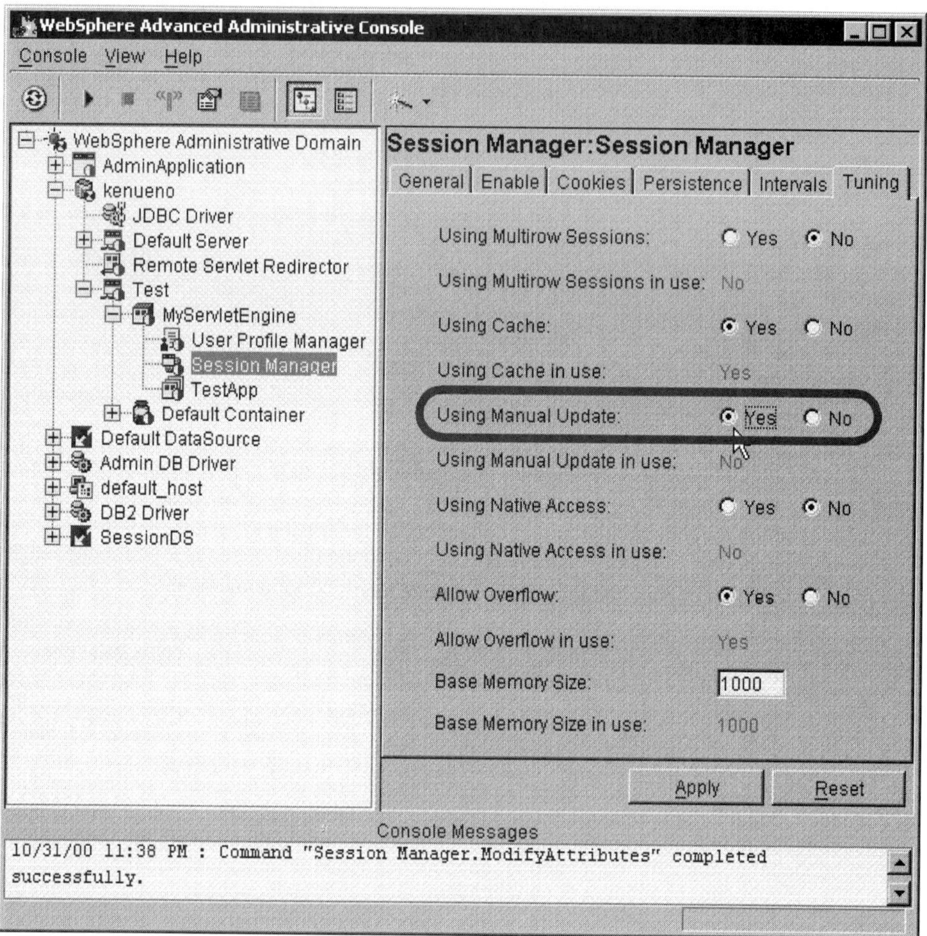

Figure 153. Session Manager: Using Manual Update

Also, for the purposes of this example, the administrator should enable the Using Cache feature (this feature is enabled by default).

In this example, the servlet only writes the user's session information to the persistent store if:

- The counter did not exist previously (the first time this user entered this servlet). The initial value of the counter (1) is always saved to the persistent session database.
- The user explicitly requests the counter to be saved to the persistent session database by clicking the **Increment and Save** link from the HTML page.

The first time the user accesses the servlet by requesting the URL, and the resulting HTML returns to the user:

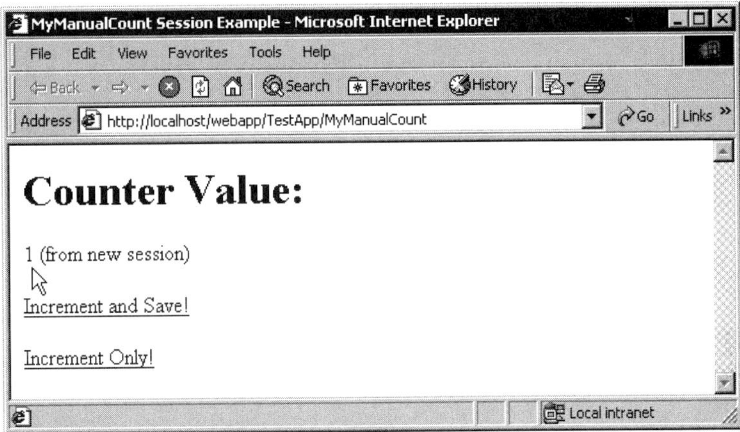

Figure 154. Initial result from MyManualCount

If the user then selects the **Increment Only!** link from this page, the following HTML returns:

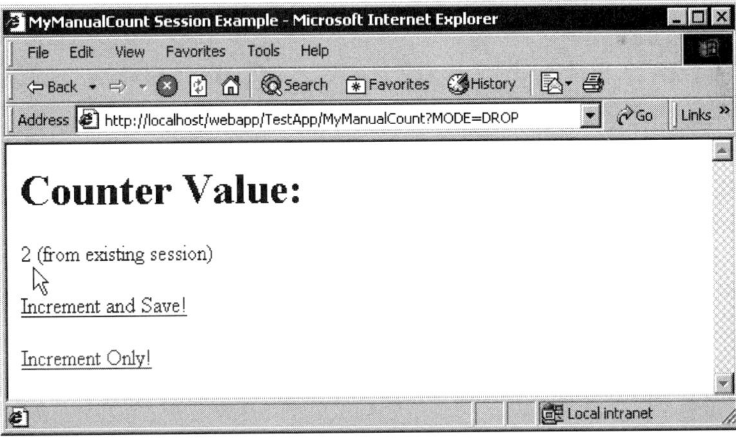

Figure 155. Result of first Increment Only! request

If the user selects the **Increment Only!** link once again, the following HTML returns:

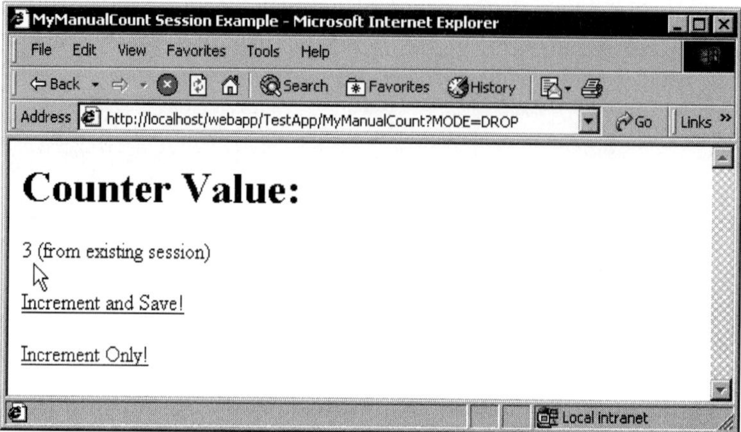

Figure 156. Result of second Increment Only! request

This result seems surprising at first. Even though the user has not requested the session object be saved to the persistent session database, the counter still increments. Keep in mind the session object remains in the session cache (assuming the cache is enabled) even though its current state is not represented in the persistent session database.

So how can the user be certain WebSphere saves the data when the com.ibm.websphere.servlet.session.IBMSession sync() method is invoked? In order to show this function, the user in this scenario makes three additional requests to the servlet:

- **Increment and Save!**, which advances the counter to 4, and saves the resulting session object to the persistent data store.

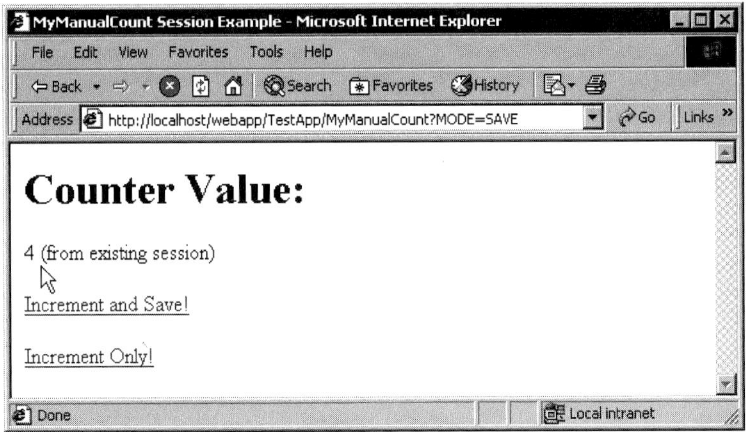

Figure 157. Result of Increment and Save!

- **Increment Only**!, which advances the counter to 5 without saving to the persistent data store.

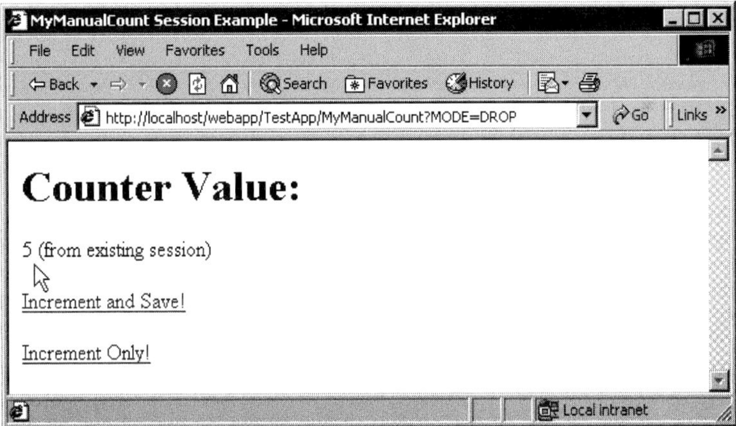

Figure 158. Result of Increment Only! #1

- **Increment Only!**, which advances the counter to 6 without saving to the persistent data store.

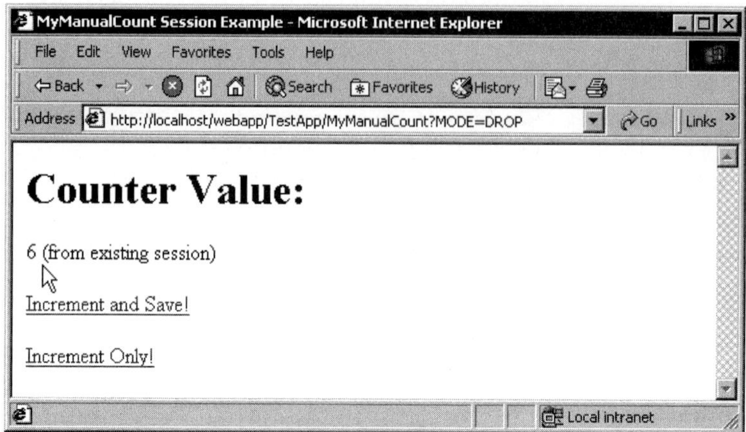

Figure 159. Result of Increment Only! #2

The WebSphere administrator now stops and starts the application server in which the servlet resides, and the user does not stop their browser (this allows the browser to keep the session cookie with the user's session ID intact).

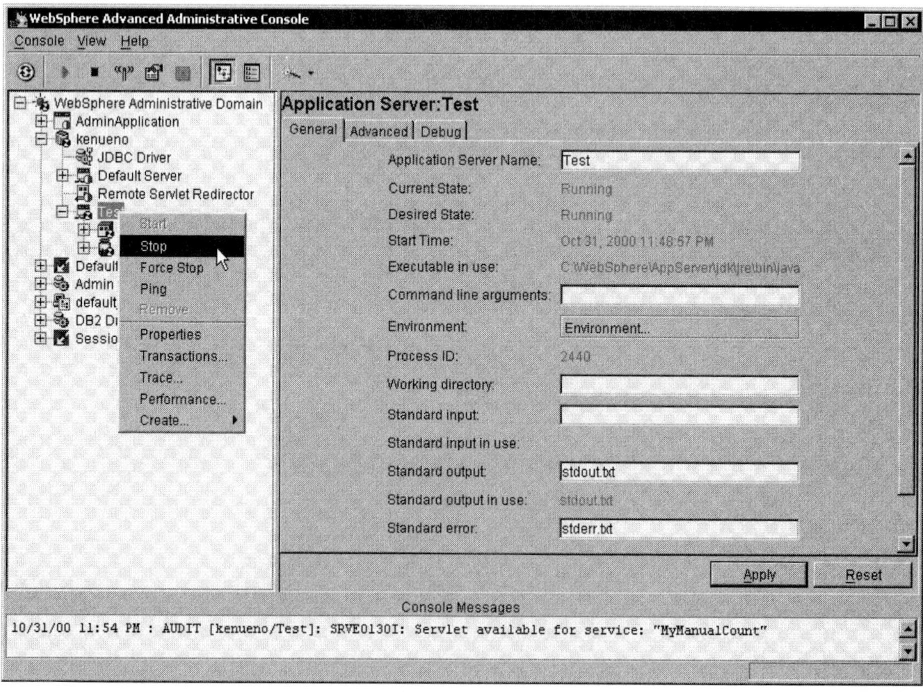

Figure 160. Stopping the application server

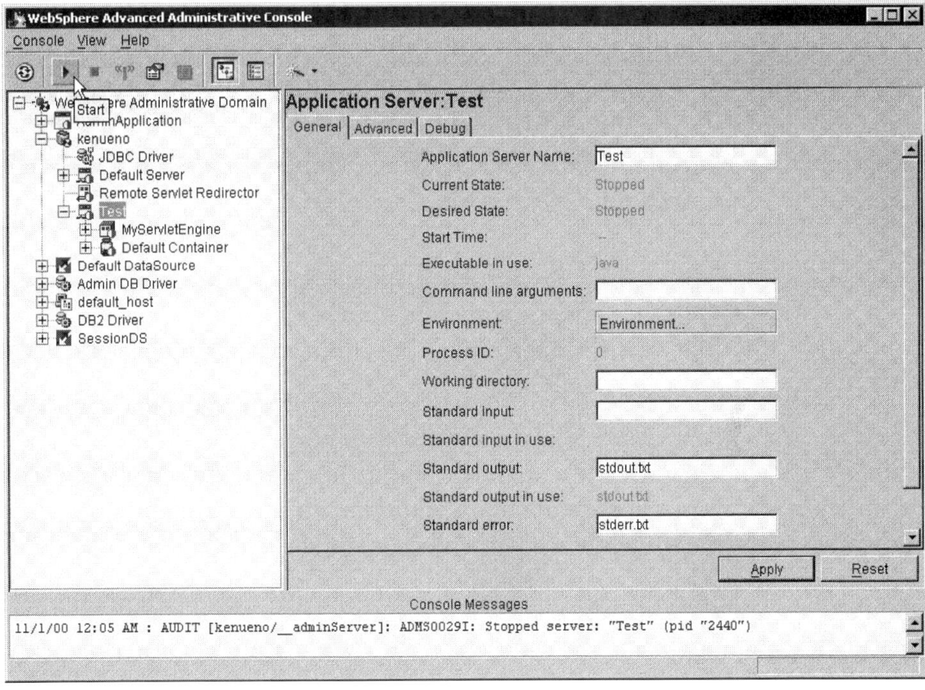

Figure 161. Starting the application server

After stop and starting the application server, if the user does an Increment Only! from their existing browser window, the following HTML returns from the servlet:

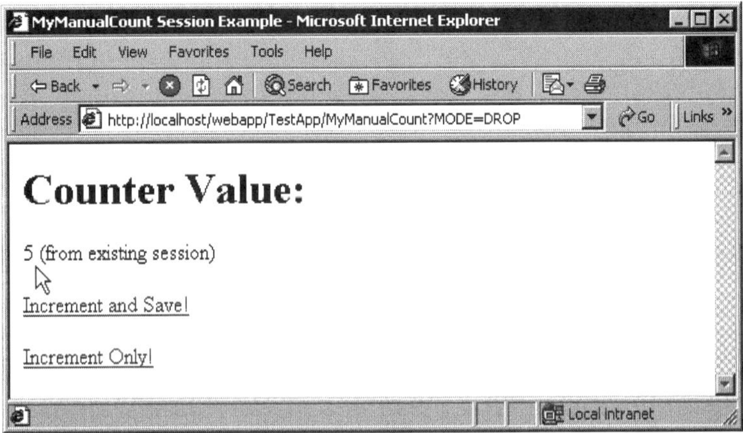

Figure 162. Result of Increment Only! after restarting

The user receives “5” back from the servlet because the last value saved to the datastore was “4”. The subsequent updates the user made resided only in the session cache, and did not survive the recycling of the application server.

7.2.6.4 Troubleshooting this example

Users may experience different results when using this example if:

- Session persistence is incorrectly enabled.
- The cookie timeout is set low (the cookie may timeout before the application server starts, thus losing the session ID), or the example is interrupted for a period of time exceeding the session timeout (the default timeout is 30 minutes).
- The example is used in conjunction with clones.
- The user stopped and restarted the browser after starting the example, and tried to continue. Stopping the browser, by default, destroys the WebSphere cookie. Therefore, the user can no longer retrieve his session information. Start the sample again to build new session data.

The servlet writes a message to the stdout file (if defined) every time the servlet tries to save the session information.

7.2.7 Session clustering

Persistent session management also gives the site the ability to cluster session data. Clustering allows a group of application server instances to share sessions among themselves. So, regardless of which instance handles the user’s request, that instance has access to the previous session update for that user.

These instances share session objects by sharing a common persistent session database. For all application server instances wanting to share sessions, they must:

- Enable persistent session management for each instance.
- Each instance must use the same database table for storing sessions (defined in the datasource object).

Cloning provides an easy way to create a cluster of application server instances. After defining the initial application server to use persistent session management, the administrator defines a model based on the application server. All clones based on this model share the same session database.

7.2.7.1 Affinity routing and session clustering

Although several clustered instances may share a user's session information through a shared session database, many sites achieve better performance by routing a user repeatedly to the same instance for all the user's requests. This technique is known as affinity routing, and, in conjunction with session caching at each instance, may improve site performance (sometimes dramatically).

Caching allows the instance to maintain the most current copy of the user's session object in memory, as well as storing it to the persistent store. If the user returns to the same instance repeatedly, the instance does not need to retrieve the user's information from the database. The data already resides in the in-memory cache. This eliminates unnecessary database interaction.

Of course, if the instance's cache reaches its limit, the user's session object may be bumped from the cache. If the user's session object no longer resides in the cache, affinity routing no longer provides a performance benefit for the user.

WebSphere provides affinity routing through the WebSphere HTTP server plug-in, and uses affinity routing by default.

> **Note**
>
> In WebSphere V3.5.2 and later, applications using the Servlet 2.2 APIs cannot participate in affinity routing with applications using Servlet 2.1 APIs.

7.2.7.2 Failover and clustering

Clustering also provides a solution for instance failure. By definition, clustered WebSphere Application Servers share a common persistent session database. Therefore, instances in the cluster have the ability to see any user's session saved to persistent storage. If one of the instances fails, the user may continue to use their session information with other instances in the cluster. This is known as failover. Failover works regardless of whether the nodes reside on the same machine or several machines.

After a failure, WebSphere redirects the user to another instance, and the user's affinity switches to this replacement instance as well. After the initial read from the database, the replacement instance places the user's session object in the in-memory cache (assuming the cache has available entries).

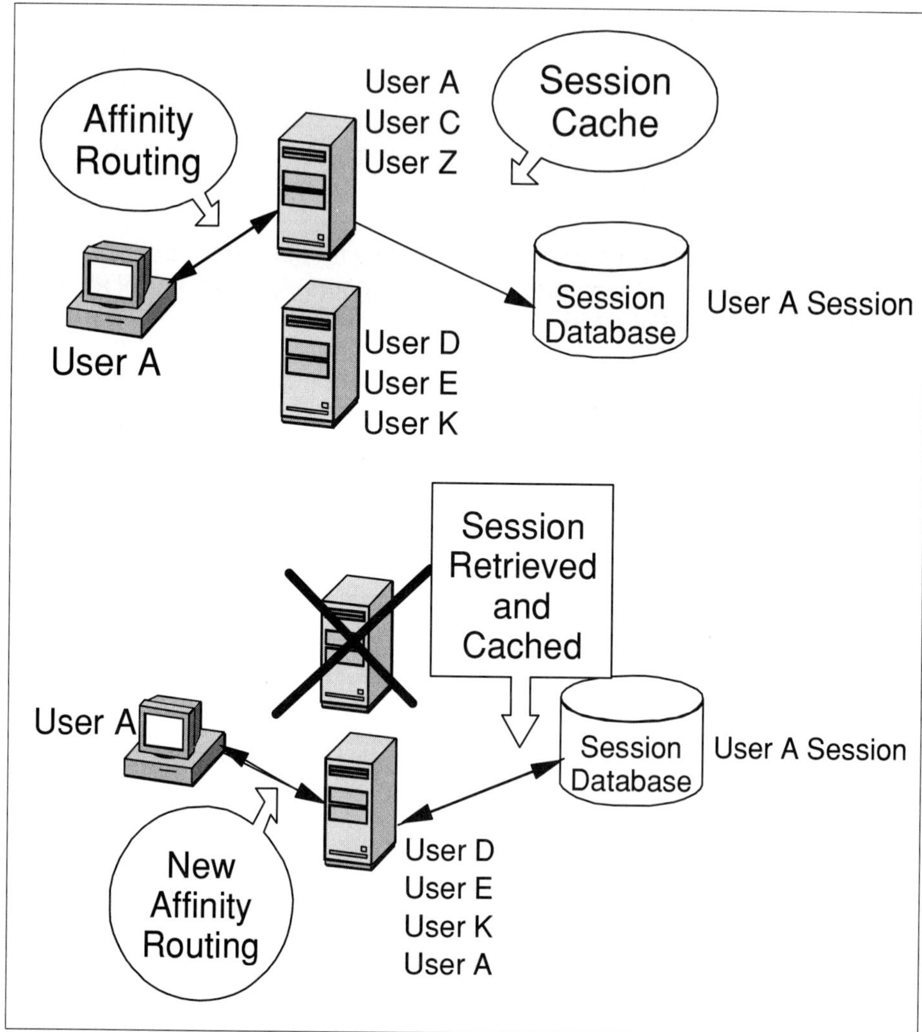

Figure 163. Failover with session affinity routing enabled

7.2.7.3 Clustering and failover example

This example uses the servlet from the previous example on manual servlet update. Note that caching and failover do not require the manual servlet update mode to function, but the example uses manual update as a convenient way to demonstrate clustering and failover.

The example also requires the WebSphere administrator to:

- Create an application server using persistent session management and manual update mode, as described earlier
- Define the MyManualCount servlet to the application server, as in the previous example
- Create a model of this application server (See *WebSphere Scalability: WLM and Clustering using WebSphere Application Server Advanced*, SG24-6153)
- Create a clone based on this model (See *WebSphere Scalability: WLM and Clustering using WebSphere Application Server Advanced*, SG24-6153).

The final result should look something like this:

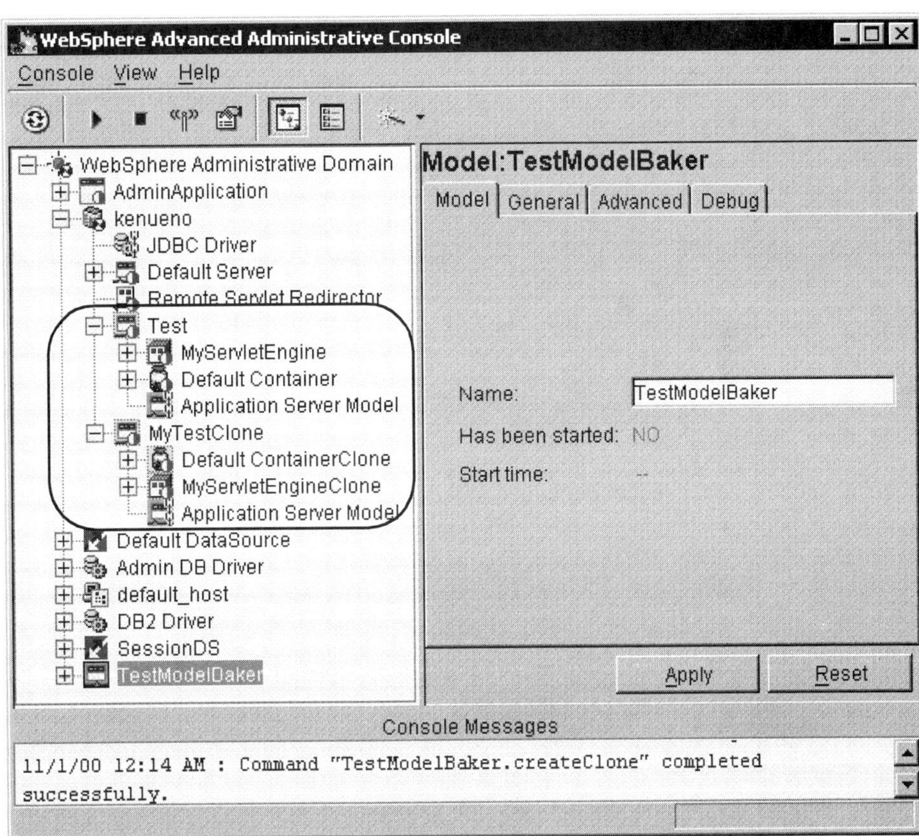

Figure 164. Administrative console with two application servers

Two identical application servers, Test (on which the model for the clone was created), and MyTestClone, an identical clone of the Test Application Server, exist on the same node. Again, both use persistent session management because the administrator defined these settings for the Test application server before creating a model based on it. The clone, created from the model, picks up the attributes of the original Test application server.

Now, start the model. This should cause both Test and MyTestClone to start.

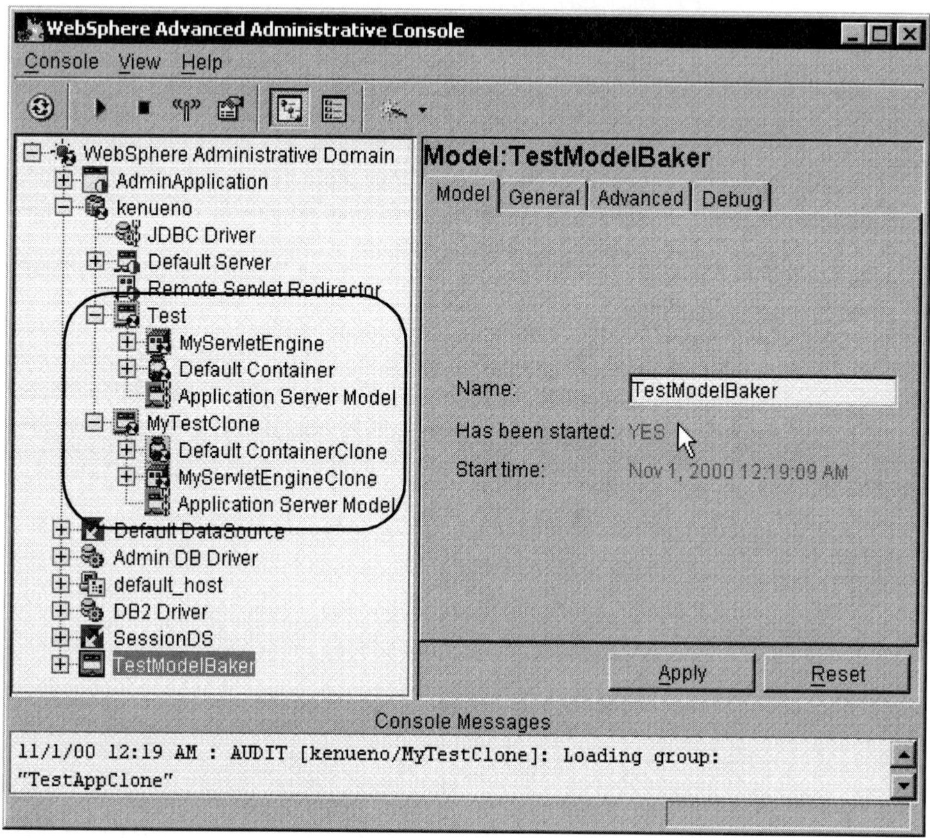

Figure 165. Administrative console after starting the model

Now, stop MyTestClone.

After stopping the clone, the administrative console looks like this:

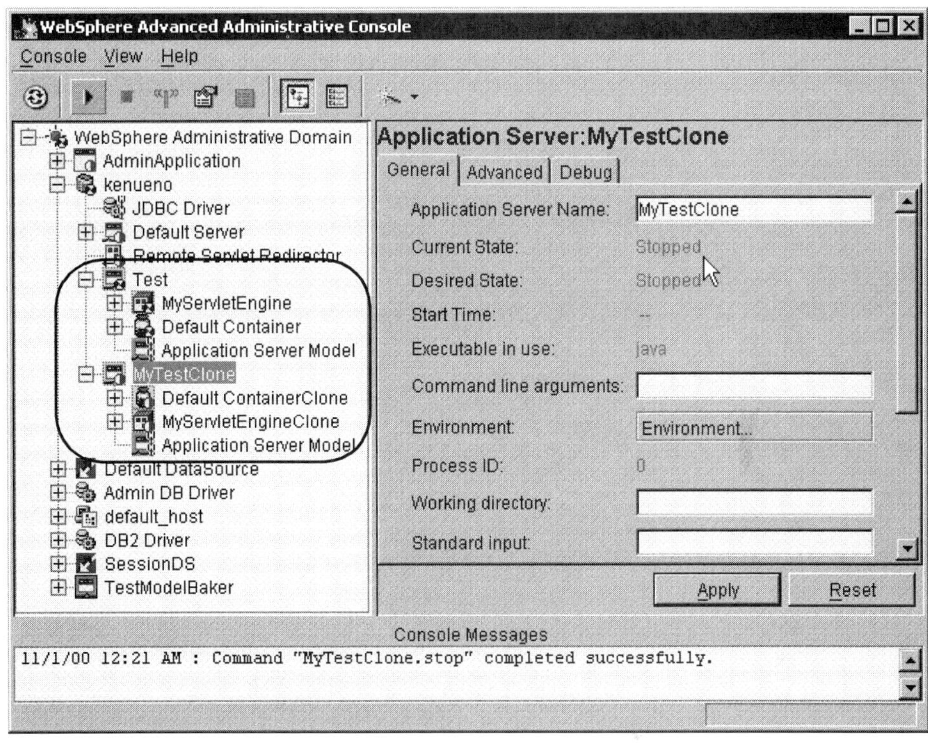

Figure 166. Administrative console after stopping the clone

Now from the browser, request the MyManualCount servlet as in the previous example, which displays this HTML:

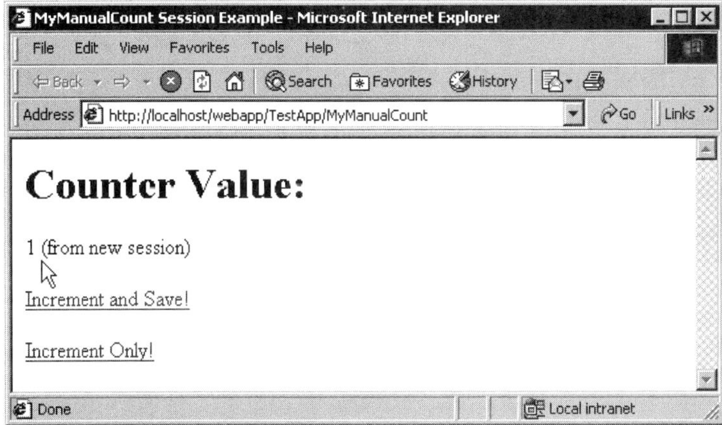

Figure 167. Result of first request to MyManualCount

Now, make the following series of requests to the servlet via the HTML page:

- Increment and Save! which moves the count to "2" and saves it to the persistent session database.

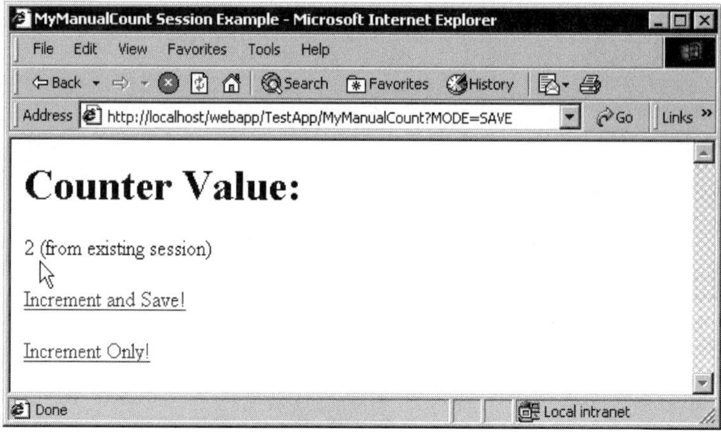

Figure 168. Result of Increment and Save!

- Increment Only! which increments the count to "3", but does not save it to the persistent session database.

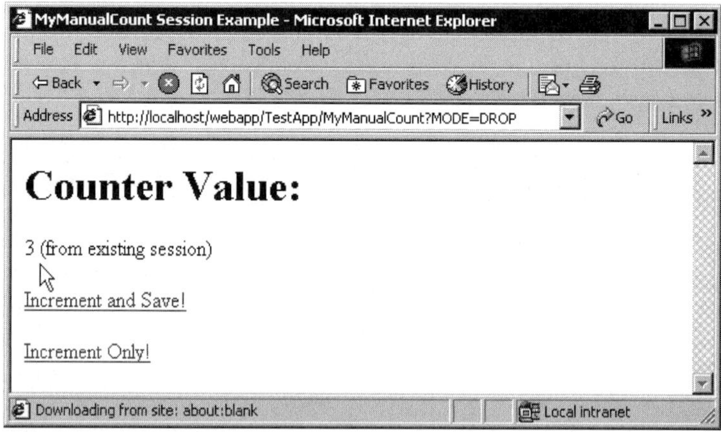

Figure 169. Result of Increment Only!

- Increment Only! which increments the count to "4", but does not save it to the persistent session database.

The HTML returned for the last step should look like this:

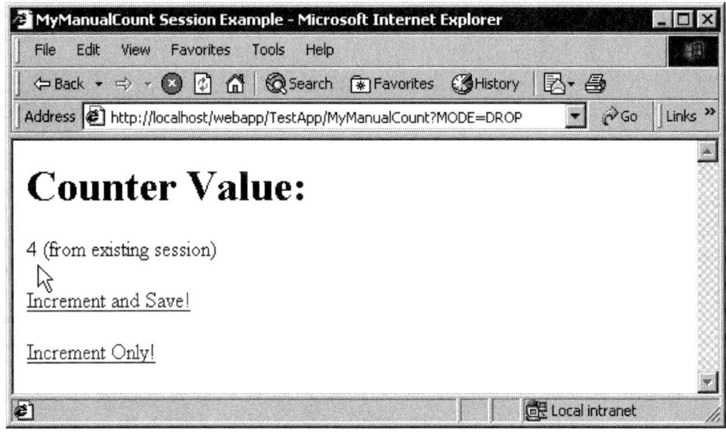

Figure 170. Result after second Increment Only! request

Now, stop the Test application server as shown in Figure 171.

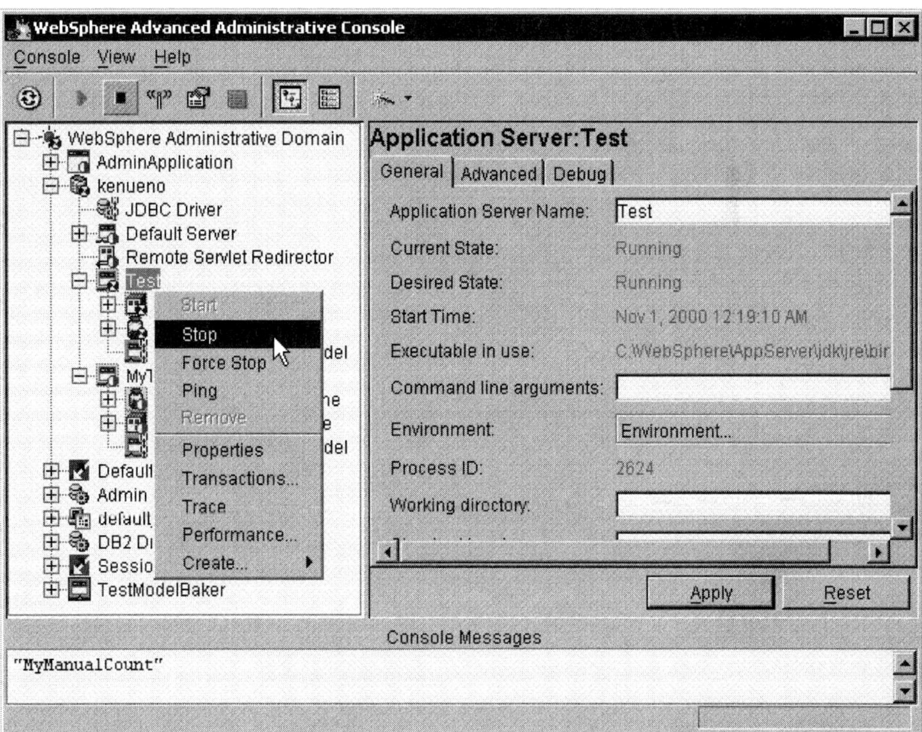

Figure 171. Stopping the Test application server

After the Test application server stops, start the MyTestClone clone as shown in Figure 172.

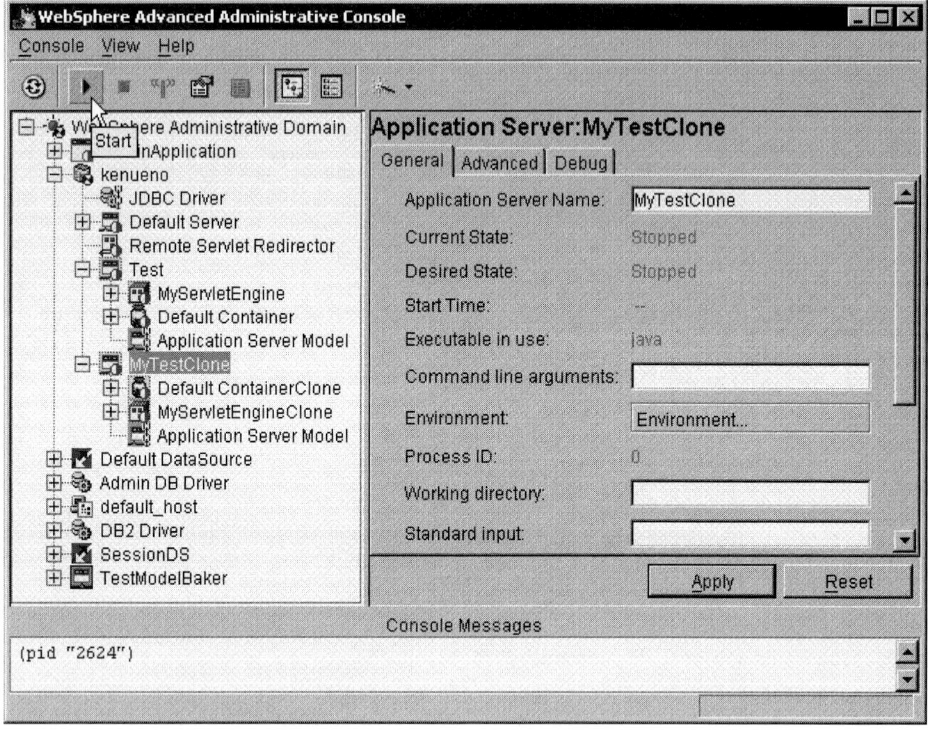

Figure 172. Starting the MyTestClone

The administrative console should look like this after stopping the Test application server, and starting the clone:

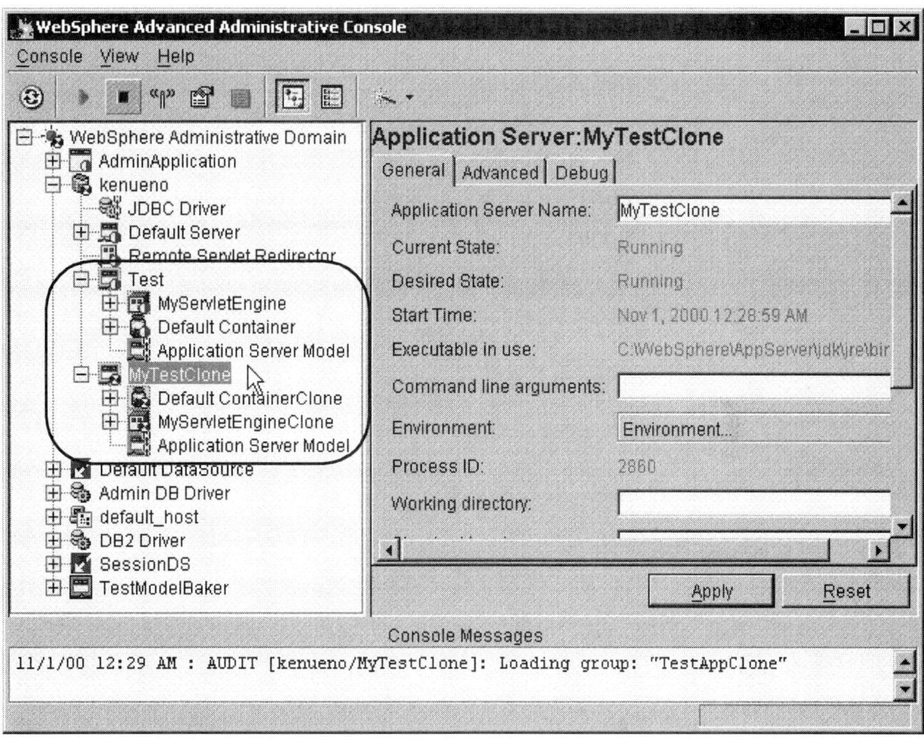

Figure 173. Administrative console after completing stop/start

Now, select **Increment Only!** from the browser. The following HTML returns:

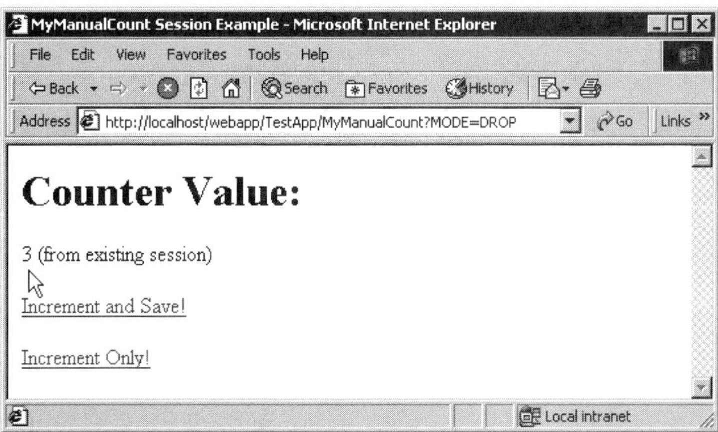

Figure 174. Result of Increment Only! after stop/start procedure

The servlet returns “3”. This indicates the user’s request went to the MyTestClone instance when the Test instance was no longer available. The servlet in the MyTestClone instance requested the user’s session data from the shared persistent store. The session object contained “2” for its counter, and the servlet running in MyTestClone incremented this value and returned it to the user.

If the user selects **Increment Only!** again, the count increases as shown in Figure 175.

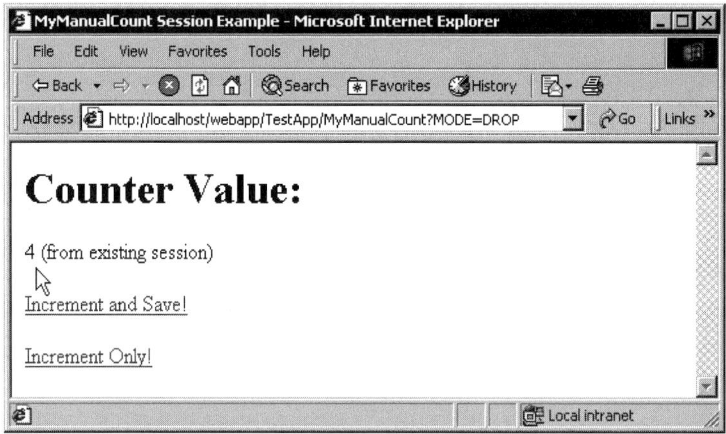

Figure 175. Result of additional Increment Only!

This shows the instance MyTestClone has an entry in the session cache for this user now. Of course, if the user selects **Increment and Save!**, the servlet running in MyTestClone increments the counter, and saves the session object to the persistent session database.

> **Note**
>
> This example requires fix PQ42166 to function properly.

7.2.7.4 Debugging the example

The same debugging tips expressed in the manual update section also apply to this example. Also, double-check the following:

- The administrator must complete the application server setup before creating the model.
- The administrator must stop and start the servers involved in the correct order as specified in the example.

7.3 Session performance considerations

This section includes guidance for developing and administering scalable, high-performance Web applications using WebSphere Application Server Session support.

7.3.1 Session size

Large session objects pose several problems for a Web application. If the site uses session caching, large sessions reduce the memory available in the WebSphere instance for other tasks, such as application execution.

For example, assume a given application stores 1 MB of information per user session object. If 100 users arrive over the course of 30 minutes, and the session timeout remains at 30 minutes, the WebSphere Application Server instance must allocate 100 MB just to accommodate the newly arrived users in the session cache. (Note this number does not include previously allocated sessions not yet timed out. The actual memory required by the session cache could be considerably higher than 100 MB.)

```
1 MB per user Session * 100 users = 100 MB
```

Web developers and administrators have several options for reducing the memory footprint of the session cache:

- Reduce the size of the session object
- Reduce the size of the session cache
- Add additional instances
- Increase the memory available
- Invalidate unneeded sessions
- Reduce the session timeout interval

7.3.1.1 Reduce session object size

To implement the first option, Web developers must carefully consider the information kept by the session object. Removing information easily obtained or easily derived helps keep the session object small. Also, rigorous removal of unnecessary, unneeded, or obsolete data from the session also reduces the size of the memory footprint.

7.3.1.2 Reduce session cache size

As discussed earlier in this chapter, the Session Manager allows administrators to define a smaller session cache to reduce the cache's memory footprint. By default, the session cache holds 1000 session objects.

By lowering the number of session objects in the cache, the administrator reduces the memory required by the cache.

However, if the user's session is not in the cache, the WebSphere must retrieve it from either the overflow (for local caching), or the session database (for persistent sessions). If the Session Manager must retrieve persistent sessions frequently, the retrievals may impact overall application performance.

WebSphere maintains overflowed local sessions in memory, as discussed in 7.2.4, "Local sessions" on page 258. Local session management with cache overflow enabled allows an "unlimited" number of sessions in memory. In order to limit the cache footprint to the number of entries specified in Session Manager, the administrator should use persistent session management, or disable the overflow.

Note

When using local session management without specifying the Allow Overflow property, a full cache will result in the loss of user session objects.

7.3.1.3 Add additional instances

WebSphere also gives the administrator the option of creating additional instances (clones). Creating additional instances spreads the demand for memory across more JVMs, thus reducing the memory burden on any particular instance. Depending on the memory and CPU capacity of the machines involved, the administrator may add additional instances within the same machine. Alternatively, the administrator may add additional machines to form a hardware cluster, and spread the instances across this cluster.

Note

When configuring a session cluster, affinity routing provides the most efficient strategy for user distribution within the cluster, even with session persistence enabled. With clones, the WebSphere plug-in provides affinity routing among clone instances.

7.3.1.4 Increase available memory

The WebSphere allows the administrator to increase an instance's heap size. By default, WebSphere allocates 128 MB as the maximum heap size. Increasing this value allows the instance to obtain more memory from the system, and thus hold a larger session cache.

A practical limit exists, however, for an instance's heap size. The machine memory containing the instance needs to support the heap size requested. Also, if the heap size grows too large, the length of the garbage collection cycle with the JVM may impact overall application performance (sometimes quite dramatically).

7.3.1.5 Invalidate unneeded sessions

If the user no longer needs the session object (if they went through the logoff process for the site, for example), the session becomes an excellent candidate for invalidation. Invalidating a session removes it from the session cache, as well as from the session database.

If multiple applications share the same session context, and the opportunity exists for multiple applications to share the same users, invalidating a session object may impact other applications still using data contained in the session object.

A safer strategy calls for applications to remove their data from the session object and leave the object to time out. This minimizes the session object footprint, and leaves the session object in case other applications are actively using it.

7.3.1.6 Reduce the session timeout interval

By default, each user receives a 30-minute interval between requests before the Session Manager invalidates the user's session. Not every site requires a session timeout interval this generous. By reducing this interval to match the requirements of the average site user, the Session Manager purges the session from the cache (and the persistent store, if enabled) more quickly.

Avoid setting this parameter too low and frustrating users. The administrator must take into account a reasonable time for an average user to interact with the site (read returned data, fill out forms, etc.) when setting the interval. Also, the interval must represent any increased response time during peak times on the site (such as heavy trading days on a brokerage site, for example).

Finally, in some cases where the persistent session database table contains a large number of entries, frequent execution of the timeout scanner reduces overall performance. In cases where the database contains many session entries, avoid setting the session timeout so low it triggers frequent, expensive scans of the persistent session database for timed-out sessions.

7.3.2 Multirow persistent session management

When multiple Web applications share sessions, or when a session contains multiple objects accessed by different servlets/JSPs in the same Web application, multirow session support provides a mechanism for improving performance. Multirow session support stores session data in the persistent session database by Web application and value. Table 8 shows a simplified representation of a multi-row database table.

Table 8. Simplified multirow session representation

Session ID	Web application	Property	Small value	Large value
DA32242SSGE2	ShoeStore	ShoeStore.First.Name	“Alice”	
DA32242SSGE2	ShoeStore	ShoeStore.Last.Name	“Smith”	
DA32242SSGE2	ShoeStore	ShoeStore.Big.String		“A big string....”
DA32242SSGE2	AirTravel	AirTravel.Frequent.Flyer .ID	“1234”	
DA32242SSGE2	AirTravel	AirTravel.Big.String		“Another big string....”

In this example, if the user visits the ShoeStore application, and the servlet involved needs her first name, the servlet retrieves this information through the Session API. The Session Manager brings into the session cache only the value requested. Thus the ShoeStore.Big.String item remains in the persistent session database until the servlet requests it. Likewise, the entries for the AirTravel Web application remain in the persistent session data store if the user confines her visit to the ShoeStore application. This saves time both in reducing the serialization overhead for data the application does not use, as well as retrieving unnecessary information.

After the Session Manager retrieves the items from the persistent session database, these items remain in the in-memory session cache. The cache accumulates the values from the persistent session database over time as the various servlets and Web applications request them. With session affinity routing enabled, the user returns to this same cached session instance repeatedly. This reduces the number of reads against the persistent session database, and gives the Web application better performance.

Likewise, if a servlet or JSP modifies values in a session, the Session Manager only writes out the individual values changed rather than the entire session (this is true for both manual and automatic update modes). The servlet or JSP must use putValue() to save the modified value in the session. Otherwise the Session Manager does not save modifications made after a getValue() without a corresponding putValue().

Even with multirow session support, Web applications perform best if the overall contents of the session objects remain small. Large values in session objects require more time to retrieve from the persistent session database, generate more network traffic in transit, and occupy more space in the session cache after retrieval.

Multirow session support provides a good compromise for Web applications requiring larger sessions, or shared sessions. However, single-row persistent session management remains the best choice for Web applications with small session objects. Single-row persistent session management requires less storage in the database, and requires fewer database interactions to retrieve a session's contents (all of the values in the session are written or read in one operation). This keeps the session object's memory footprint small, as well as reducing the frequency of network traffic between the WebSphere and the persistent session database.

Note

Avoid circular references within sessions if using multirow session support. The multirow session support does not preserve circular references in retrieved sessions.

7.3.3 Managing your session connection pool

When using persistent session management, the Session Manager interacts with the defined database through a WebSphere Application Server datasource. As described in a previous example, the administrator defines the datasource to the Session Manager for use in storing sessions persistently.

Each datasource controls a set of database connections known as a connection pool. By default, the datastore opens a pool of no more than 10 connections. The maximum pool size represents the number of simultaneous accesses to the persistent session database available to the Session Manager.

For high-volume Web sites, the default settings for the persistent session datasource may not be sufficient. If the number of concurrent session database accesses exceeds the connection pool size, the datasource queues the excess requests until a connection becomes available. Datasource queueing can impact the overall performance of the Web application (sometimes dramatically).

For best performance, match the connection pool size with the maximum need of the Session Manager. If at peak times the Session Manager handles 40 simultaneous database requests for session objects, set the connection pool maximum to support this.

However, large connection pools do not necessarily improve application performance. Each connection represents memory overhead. A large pool decreases the memory available for WebSphere to execute applications. Also, if database connections are limited because of database licensing issues, the administrator must share a limited number of connections among other Web applications requiring database access as well.

As discussed above, affinity routing combined with session caching reduces database read activity for session persistence. Likewise, manual session update and multi-row persistent session management reduce unnecessary writes to the persistent database. Incorporating these techniques may also reduce the size of the connection pool required to support session persistence for a given Web application.

> **Note**
>
> The persistent session database performs best if it is not shared with other databases, such as the WebSphere administrative database. This eliminates contention for resources, such as connections, which impacts performance.

7.4 Alternatives to session support: cookies

A cookie, as discussed earlier, is a piece of data passed between a Web server and a Web browser. The Web server sends a cookie that contains data it requires the next time the browser accesses the server. This is one way to maintain state between a browser and a server.

Sites sometimes use cookies when mixed applications reside at the site (for instance, servlets and CGI scripts). However, storing all of a user's state information in a cookie raises concerns about securing the cookie (if sensitive information is stored inside), and the size of the data returned (since the data travels roundtrip between the browser and server, the size of the cookie can impact the user's perceived response time. Large cookies can also cause network congestion). Also, this solution presents problems if the user does not, for whatever reason, accept cookies.

WebSphere best practices recommend the use of sessions as defined by the session standard. (For further information on cookie management, refer to *Servlet and JSP Programming with IBM WebSphere Studio and VisualAge for Java*, SG24-5755.)

Chapter 8. Servlet V2.2 in WebSphere V3.5.2

WebSphere V3.5.2 introduced support for Servlet API V2.2. In this chapter we describe the new features and behaviors introduced in that version. In summary these new features are:

1. You can now configure a servlet engine to offer either compliance with the Servlet API V2.2 standard or compatibility with the API as offered in WebSphere V3.5.
2. WebSphere V3.5.2 introduces additional configuration options that arise from support for the Servlet API V2.2.
3. The Servlet API V2.2 defines a Web Application Archive (WAR) file format. WAR files contain the set of artifacts (for example HTML files, Java classes and libraries) that comprise an application along with a deployment descriptor that defines how the application is to be configured. WebSphere will configure a Web application from the contents of a WAR files.

In the following sections we describe these new features and their implications.

8.1 WebSphere support for Servlet API V2.2

From the coder's perspective the Servlet API V2.2 may seem to be a relatively minor extension of the API offered by WebSphere V3.5. (In contrast the JavaServer Pages API V1.1 also enabled by WebSphere V3.5.2 has very significant new functionality.) The V2.2 API does have some useful additional functionality and overall the V2.2 specification is more complete than the V2.1 specification, and V2.2 provides many important clarifications of behavior.

WebSphere V3.5.2 allows you to configure servlet engines to operate in either of two modes: WebSphere V3.5 Compatibility Mode and Servlet 2.2/JSP 1.1 Full Compliance Mode. For brevity we will refer to these modes as *Compliance Mode* and *Compatibility Mode* respectively.

The interface of the Compliance Mode API is as defined by the Servlet API V2.2, with some exceptions discussed later. It is a super-set of that offered in WebSphere V3.5 and 3.5.1; it has additional methods, but all V3.5 methods are still available.

At first sight you might then expect that a V3.5 application would function correctly in Compliance Mode. However, there are some differences in semantics between the V3.5 and Compliance Mode APIs. These differences are explained in 8.3.3, “Semantic differences” on page 301.

These semantic differences explain the need for Compatibility Mode. In this mode the existing V3.5 behavior is provided and hence applications coded in a WebSphere V3.5 environment will be deployable in V3.5.2 provided that you use a servlet engine running in Compatibility Mode.

You should also note that although the configuration options of Compliance Mode and Compatibility Mode are the same there are some differences between the meaning between the two modes. All Compatibility Mode options that were available in V3.5 will behave as V3.5 did.

A servlet engine running in Compatibility Mode will behave like V3.5 for all existing API calls. However, the additional methods offered in Compliance Mode are also available. Hence programs coded to the new API will deploy successfully in a servlet engine in either mode.

Table 9 and Table 10 give examples of these differences. More detailed explanations of the meanings of the specific differences are given in the following sections.

Table 9. API differences

Method	Compatibility Mode	Compliance Mode
getCharacterEncoding()	If the client request did not send any character encoding data, the default encoding of the server JVM is returned.	If the client request did not send any character encoding data, null is returned.
getMimeType()	If the file extension does not map to a valid MIME type, the MIME type “www/unknown” is returned.	If the file extension does not map to a valid MIME type, null is returned.

Table 10. Behaivior differences

Function	Compatibility Mode	Compliance Mode
Default content type on response buffer reset	On response buffer reset, the content type of the request is reset to “text/html”.	On response buffer reset, the content type is cleared and not set to a default value.

Function	Compatibility Mode	Compliance Mode
HTTP session scoping	Values placed in the HTTP session object have global scope across all Web applications.	Values placed in the HTTP session object have a scope limited to the Web application that created the value.

8.2 Selecting Servlet V2.2 support

When you create a servlet engine you select either Compatibility or Compliance Mode. See 5.5.2, “Define a servlet engine” on page 150 for more details. You can determine the mode of a particular servlet engine by selecting it in the Topology tab, and then clicking the **General** tab as shown in Figure 176. The default is Compatibility Mode.

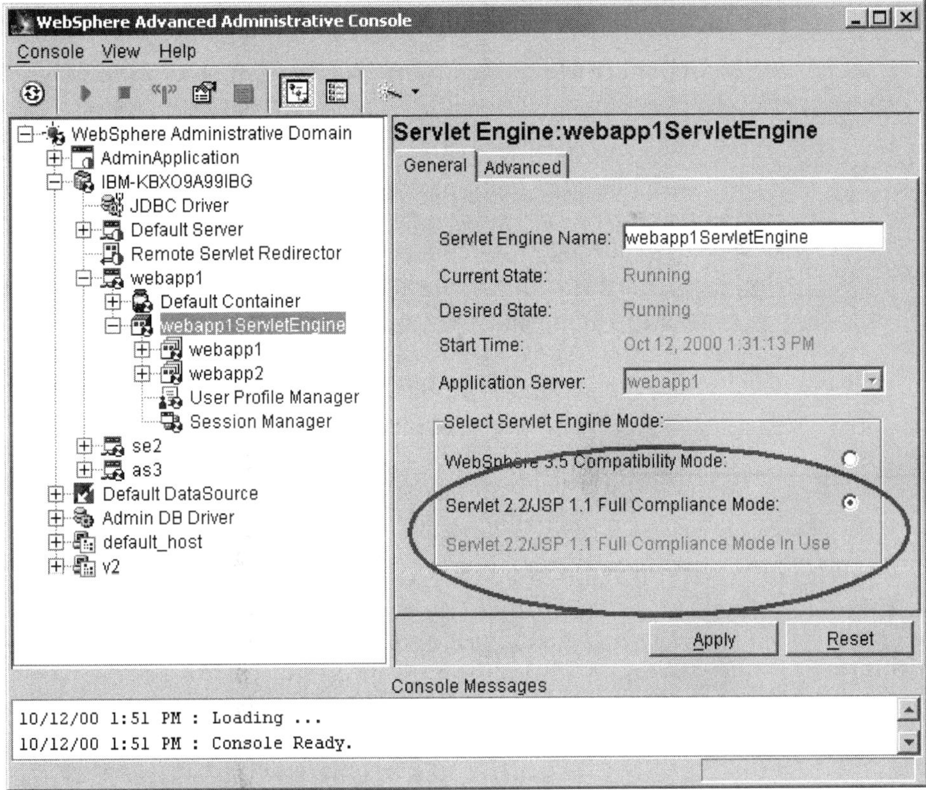

Figure 176. Servlet engine modes

You can change the configuration of an existing servlet engine by selecting the appropriate mode, clicking **Apply** and then restarting the application server. However you should note that there are significant differences between the two modes. In general you will need to adjust the configuration of an application that runs correctly in Compliance Mode before it will run correctly in Compatibility Mode, and vice versa. Depending upon which portions of the Servlet API your application uses, you may also need to make code changes.

The configuration changes required in moving between the two modes are described in 8.3.3, "Semantic differences" on page 301. The servlet V2.2 API changes are discussed in 8.3, "Comparison of the Servlet API versions" on page 298 and this section also describes those APIs whose behaviors change between the two modes.

8.3 Comparison of the Servlet API versions

The following sections describe the new interfaces available in Compliance Mode and the semantic differences between the two modes.

8.3.1 New interfaces in Servlet API V2.2

We describe new API features in the following sections. You should notice that in a few cases new interfaces specified in the Servlet API V2.2 are intended to replace existing interfaces. In those cases existing methods are marked as deprecated in the specification and you should plan to migrate to the new methods specified in the standard.

8.3.1.1 Response buffering

The ServletReponse interface now includes the methods getBufferSize(), setBufferSize(), flushBuffer(), isCommitted() and reset(). These allow control of the buffering of responses from servlets and you may be able to exploit these facilities to improve the efficiency of your application.

In WebSphere V3.5.x, WebSphere provided response buffering control, through a very similar interface in the WebAppDispatcherResponse class. You should plan to migrate any application code that uses this class to the new, standard interface.

8.3.1.2 Getting a RequestDispatcher

Compliance Mode offers two new methods for obtaining a RequestDispatcher in addition to the getRequestDispatcher() method of the ServletContext. That method required an absolute URL as the argument.

The RequestDispatcher can be specified as URL relative to the servlet by calling the new getRequestDispatcher() method offered by the ServletRequest.

A RequestDispatcher can also be obtained by name by using the new getNamedDispatcher() method of the ServletContext.

8.3.1.3 Application level initialization parameters

Compliance Mode permits servlet initialization parameters to be specified at the Web application level. You will therefore no longer need to duplicate the specification of commonly used parameters.

Servlets access these parameters by using the new ServletContext methods getInitParameter() and getInitParameterNames().

In WebSphere, the ServletContext Init parameters are handled as Web Application Group Attributes. Therefore, in the administrative console, Web Application Init Parameters are set in the Group Attributes table. The Servlet 2.2 API specification refers to these initialization parameters as a <context.param> in the WAR DTD.

8.3.1.4 Attribute access naming change

The getValue() family of methods for accessing attributes in an HttpSession are now replaced by the more consistent getAttribute() family. The old methods are still present in the API but are deprecated. Applications should plan to migrate from getValue(), getValueNames() and setValue() to getAttribute(), getAttributeNames() and setAttribute() respectively. The new method removeAttribute() is also now available.

8.3.1.5 Additional Request functionality

Additional methods are provided for requests in the HttpServletRequest interface or its parent the ServletRequest.

HttpServletRequest now offers the method getRequestHeaders() that returns an enumeration of all headers matching a specified name. The Servlet API V2.2 specification gives Cache-Control as a plausible example of a header element that might be duplicated.

HttpServletRequest also offers two additional convenience methods, getIntHeader() and getDateHeader() for accessing commonly used non-string header types.

You can use the getContextPath() method of the HttpServletRequest interface offers to obtain the Web application Web path for a servlet. For example, a Web application might have a Web path of:

```
/webapp/itso
```

and a servlet configured in that Web application might be associated with the servlet Web path:

```
/webapp/itso/request/resign
```

The HttpServletRequest API allows you to extract the various portions of the request as shown in Table 11.

Table 11. HttpServletRequest request APIs

Method	Result	New in Servlet V2.2?
getRequestURI()	/webapp/itso/request/resign	No
getServletPath()	/request/resign	No
getContextPath()	/webapp/itso	Yes

ServletRequest now offers the getLocale() method allowing the retrieval of the client, locale and the isSecure() method to indicate whether or not the request was transmitted via a secure transport such as HTTPS.

8.3.1.6 Response Headers

The HttpSerlvetResponse interface offers the new method addHeader() allowing you to create of multiple headers with the same name. Also you can use convenience methods addIntHeader(), and addDateHeader() for non-String headers.

8.3.1.7 Servlet Name

The ServletConfig interface now offers the method getServletName() interface to allow a servlet to obtain the name by which it is known to the system.

8.3.2 Optional Servlet APIs not supported

Some optional Java Servlet API V2.2 features are not supported. The unsupported features are:

- Role-based security, including the HttpServletRequest methods isUserInRole() and getUserPrinciple().
- JNDI-based access to configuration information in the servlet environment.

8.3.3 Semantic differences

There is one major difference in operation between the two modes. This concerns the scope of an HttpSession. There are also some minor differences that you can accommodate by correctly configuring WebSphere. We mention these configuration changes here, in a section that is largely considering the specifics of coding APIs, because faulty configuration will probably result in symptoms that appear similar to those caused by coding defects.

8.3.4 HTTP session scope

HttpSessions are described in detail in Chapter 7, "Session support" on page 245. For the purposes of the current discussion we can simply note that if a user browses a Web site and visits the URLs of the following two servlets:

```
http://ahost/webapp/myapp/servlet1
```

and

```
http://ahost/webapp/myapp/servlet2
```

then servlet1 can place a value in the HttpSession using the setAttribute() API method and servlet 2 will be able to retrieve that value using the getAttribute(). A contrived example of this would be servlet1 responding to a request to puchase an item by adding a value to a Shopping Cart object stored in the HttpSession and servlet2 computing the value of the purchases found in that object.

You should note that the user might well have visited many other servlet pages between the calls to servlet2 and servlet2. The differences we are discussing here concern the scope of the session; which of those other servlets can access the data prepared by servlet1?

We are thinking about only requests directed to the same WebSphere domain. To demonstrate some of the issues we constructed a single WebSphere domain with one node. We created two virtual hosts and three application servers, each with a servlet engine. We ran two servlet engines in Compatibility Mode and one in Compliance Mode. We created two Web applications in each servlet engine and deployed a servlet into each Web application. This configuration is summarized in Table 12.

Table 12. Test configuration

Host	Servlet Engine Mode	Web Application Name	Servlet Name
HostOne	Compatibility	HostOneAppOne	servlet1

Host	Servlet Engine Mode	Web Application Name	Servlet Name
		HostOneAppTwo	servlet2
HostTwo	Compatibility	HostTwoAppOne	sevlet3
		hostTwoAppTwo	servlet4
HostTwo	Compliance	hostTwoAppThree	servlet5
		hostTwoAppFour	servlet6

We then could invoke the servlets using URLs such as:

```
http://HostOne/webapp/hostOneAppOne/servlet1
http://HostTwo/webapp/hostTwoAppFour/servlet6
```

to invoke servlet1 and servlet6 respectively.

We put code to display and update some session state in the body of all the servlets. The code we used is shown in Figure 177 on page 303.

```
public void doGet(HttpServletRequest req, HttpServletResponse res)
throws ServletException, IOException {
   res.setContentType("text/html");
   PrintWriter os = res.getWriter();
   os.println("<html>");
   os.println("<head><title>Session Tester</title></head>");
   os.println("<body>");

   HttpSession session = req.getSession(true);
   Integer value = (Integer)session.getAttribute("Value");

   String time = DateFormat.getTimeInstance().format(new Date());

   if (value == null ) {

      session.setAttribute("Value", new Integer(0) );
      os.println("Time = " + time + ", Created new session value<BR>");

   } else {
      os.println("Time = " + time  + ",  Value was " + value + "<BR>");

      value = new Integer( value.intValue() + 1 );

      session.setAttribute("Value", value);
   }
      os.println("</body></html>");
}
```

Figure 177. Code for HttpSession data update and display

The code shown in Figure 177 attempts to retrieve a value from the session. If no value exists then it prints a message and creates a new value in the session. If a value does exist, the servlet displays it and updates the session with a modified value.

8.3.4.1 Compatibility Mode behavior

Using this code we could see that in Compatibility Mode servlets in different Web applications on the same host could access each other's session data. That is, servlet1 would see servlet2's updates, and vice versa. You can see this in effect in Figure 178 on page 304. The value stored by serlvet1 is seen and updated by serlvet2; the result is then visible in serlvet1.

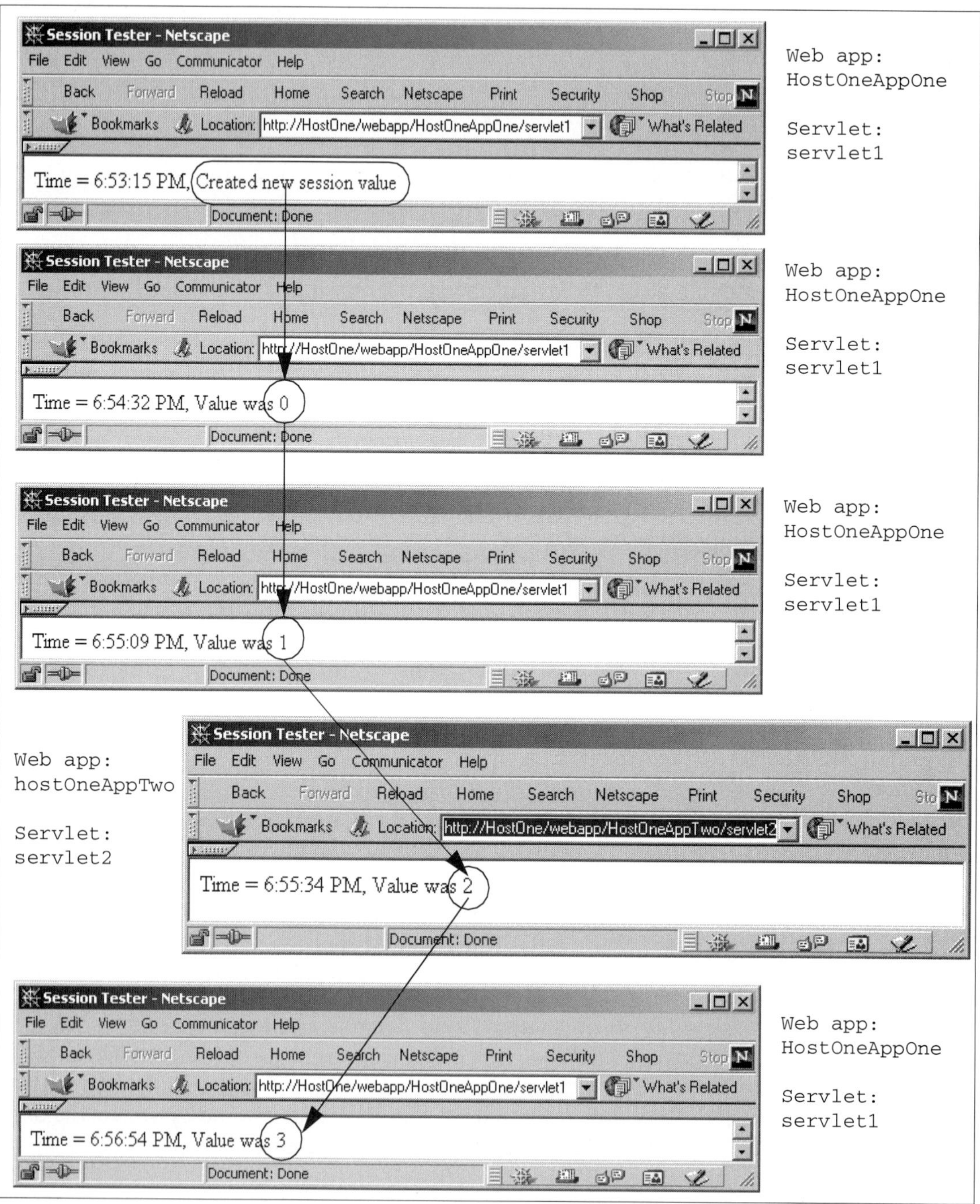

Figure 178. Compatibility Mode - session maintained across Web applications

We see the same behavior for our other pair of Compatibility Mode Web applications; that is, servlet3 and servlet4 also shared a common state.

However, servlets on different virtual hosts did not share session state, so, the servlet1/servlet2 pairing and the servlet3/servlet4 pairing were independent. We show this in Figure 178 on page 304.

In Figure 179 on page 306 you can see the sessions used by serlvet1 and servlet4 updating independently.

To summarize: in Compatibility Mode the scope of session data is not confined to a single Web application, but rather to a virtual host.

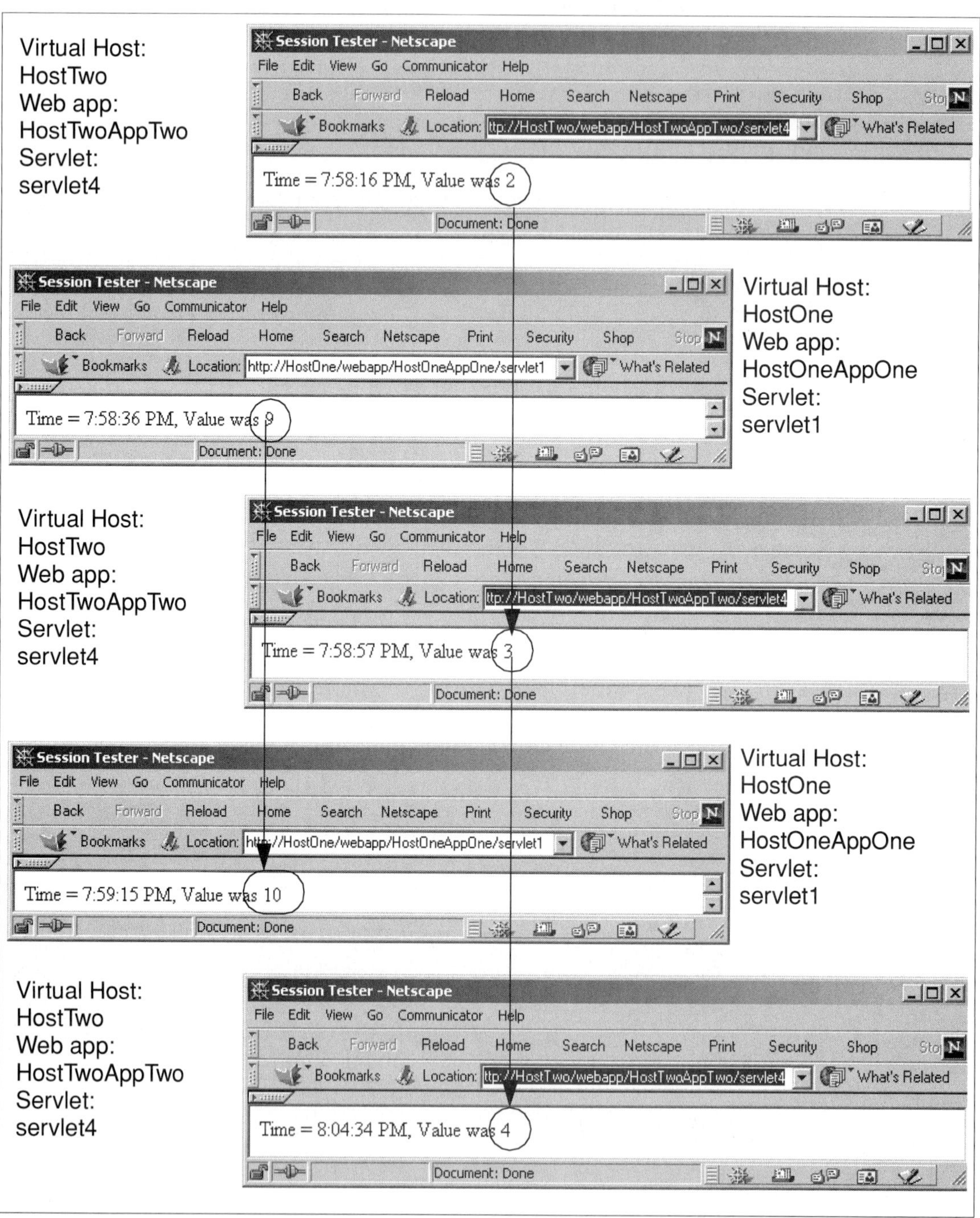

Figure 179. Compatibility Mode - sessions are not shared across virtual hosts

8.3.4.2 Compliance Mode behavior

The Servlet API V2.2 specifically requires that session scope should be limited to the Web application. WebSphere complies with that requirement and so servlet5 and servlet6 did not access each other's state, as shown in Figure 180.

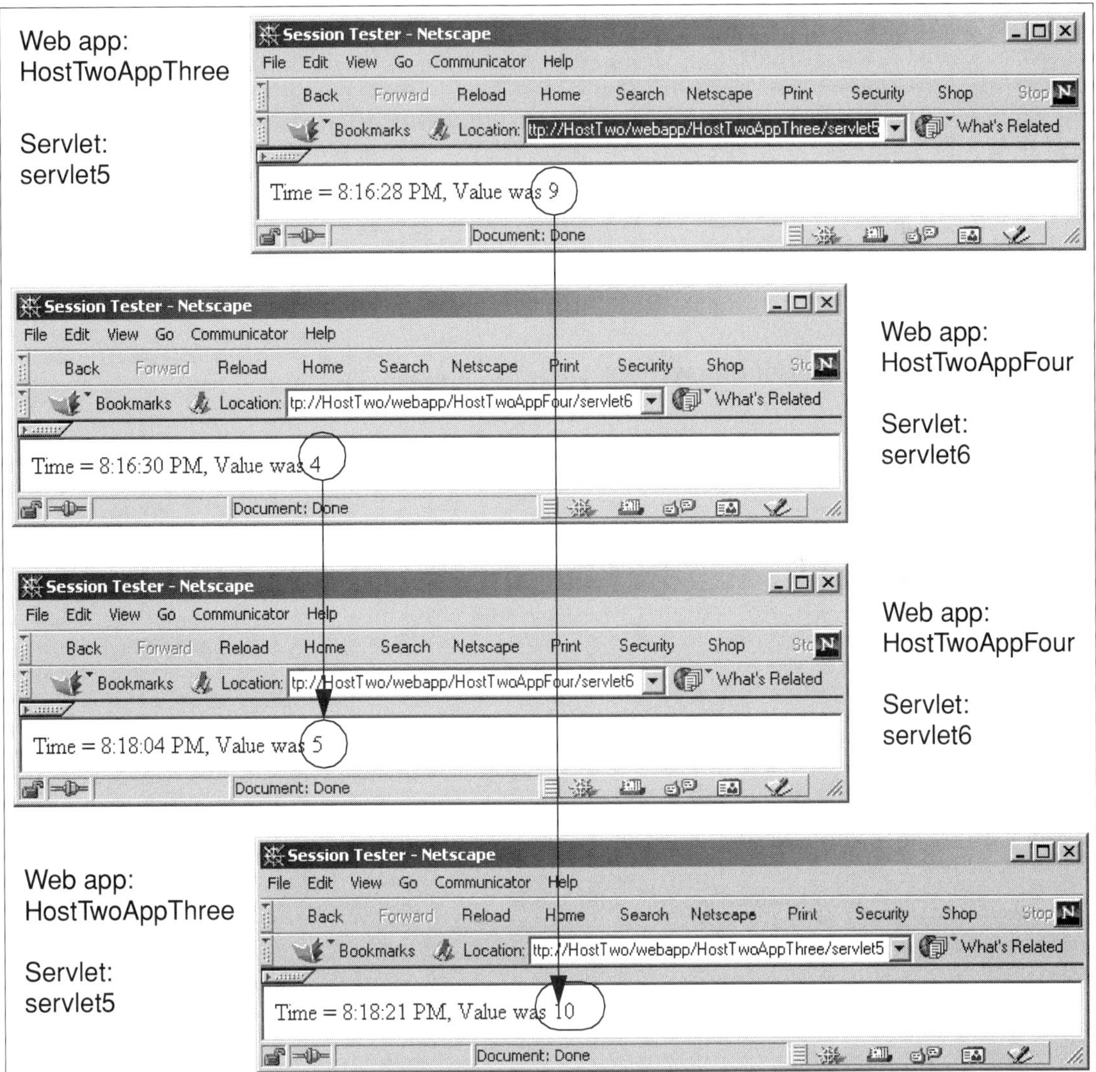

Figure 180. Compliance Mode - sessions are not shared between Web applications

We speculate that users of WebSphere in versions prior to V3.5.2 may have taken a fine-grained approach to deploying their systems and used HttpSession state to communicate between code running in different Web applications. In such a situation significant changes in deployment practice or in code would be required due to the Servlet API 2.2 specification.

8.3.5 Session Cookie Names

We discovered an unexpected interaction between servlet engines running in Compliance Mode and servlet engines running in Compatibility Mode on the same virtual host, for example between servlet4 and servlet5 in Table 12.

Servlet 5 is running in a Compliance Mode servlet engine and so its session scope is limited to its Web application. So as expected servlet4, running in a different Web application, cannot see servlet5's session data, and vice versa.

Figure 181 on page 309 shows the unexpected effect. You see servlet5 displaying an already established session value. The figure then goes on to show how the two servlets' sessions interact.

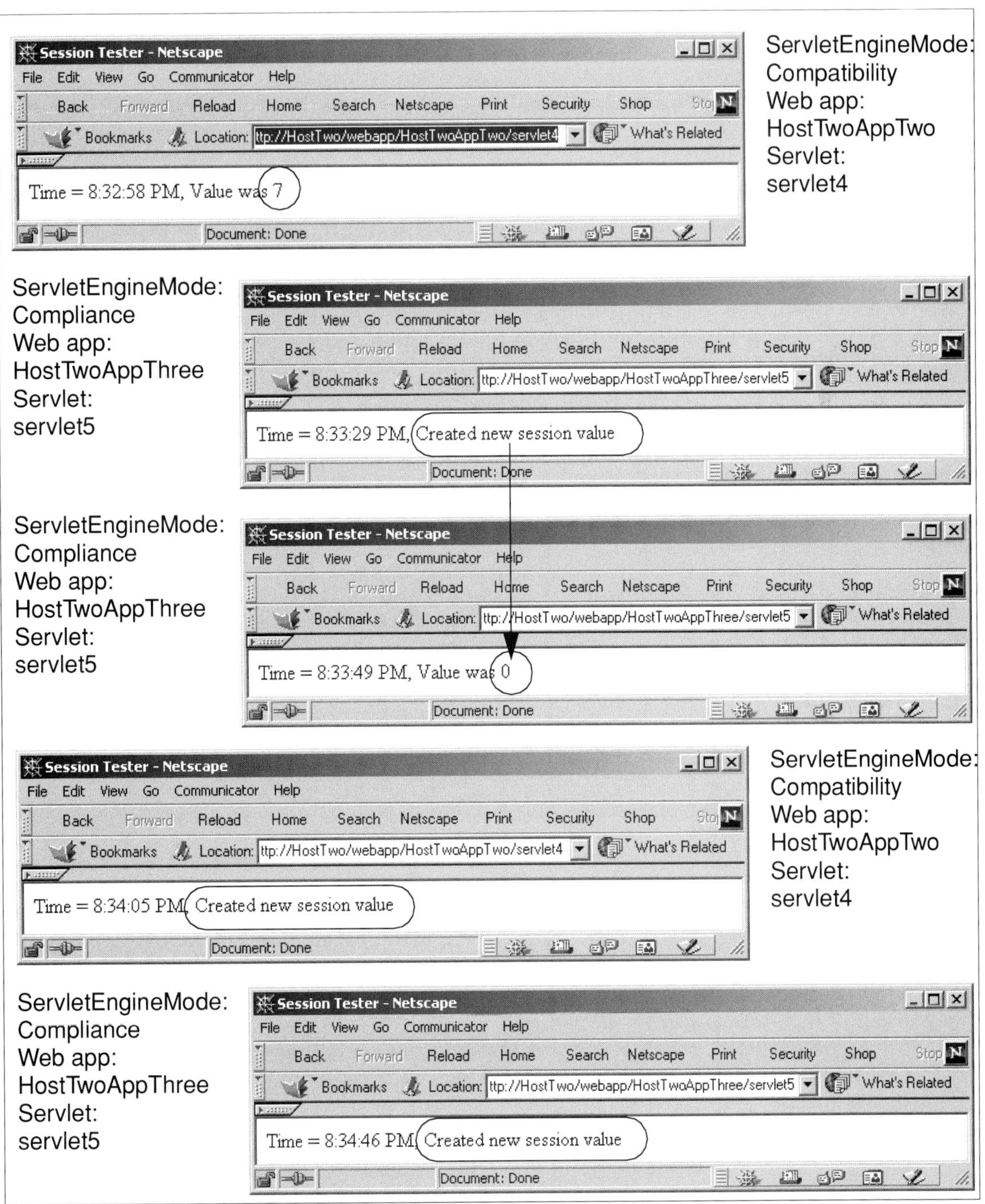

Figure 181. Session interference between Compatibility Mode and Compliance Mode

The unexpected effect was that when serlvet4 created its session data servlet5s session data was destroyed. The same effect occurred when servlet5 created its session data, servlet4's data was destroyed.

We avoided this problem by changing the value of the cookie name used by the Session Manager for the servlet engine: **Session Manager->Cookies ->Cookie Name** as shown in Figure 182.

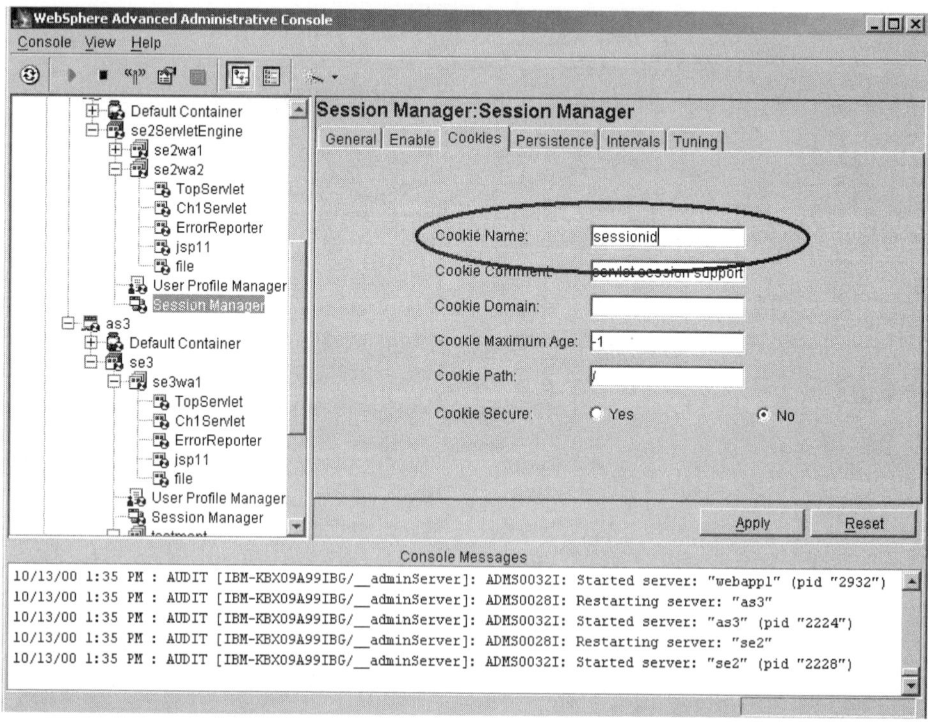

Figure 182. Session Manager: Cookie Name

Now when the session is established different cookie names are used by the two servlet engines for session management. We can verify this enabling the browser capability to display cookie values.

Figure 183 on page 311, shows the browser receiving two different cookie IDs, *sessionid* from one and *se3sessionid* from the other.

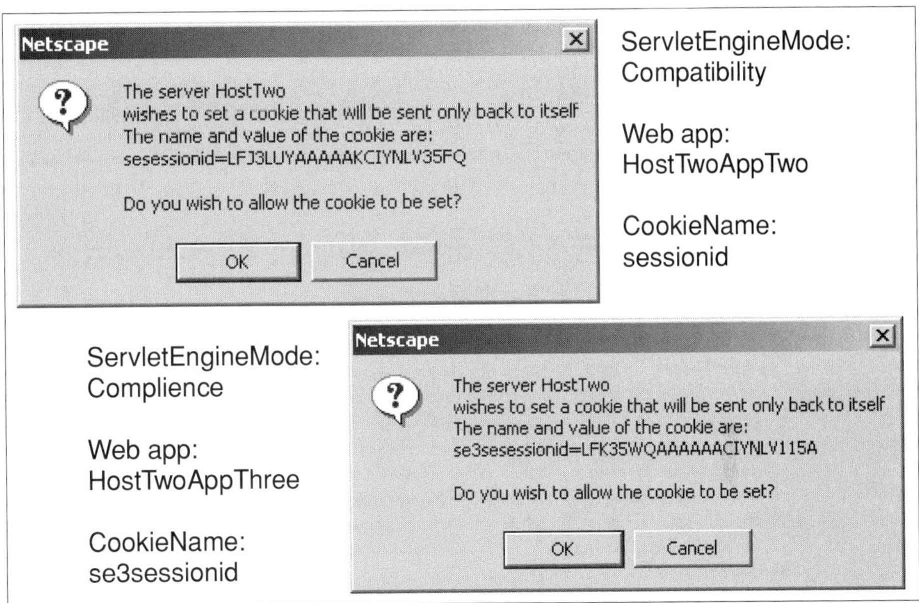

Figure 183. Different cookie names from different servlet engines

Once we had ensured that the cookie names were unique our servlets ran as expected. You can see the effect in Figure 184 on page 312. You can see the two sets of session data being modified independently.

This interaction of the sessions is troublesome because you can trigger it simply by creating servlet engines with default values. All servlet engines will use the same default value, *sessionid*, unless you explicitly change it in the Session Manager configuration.

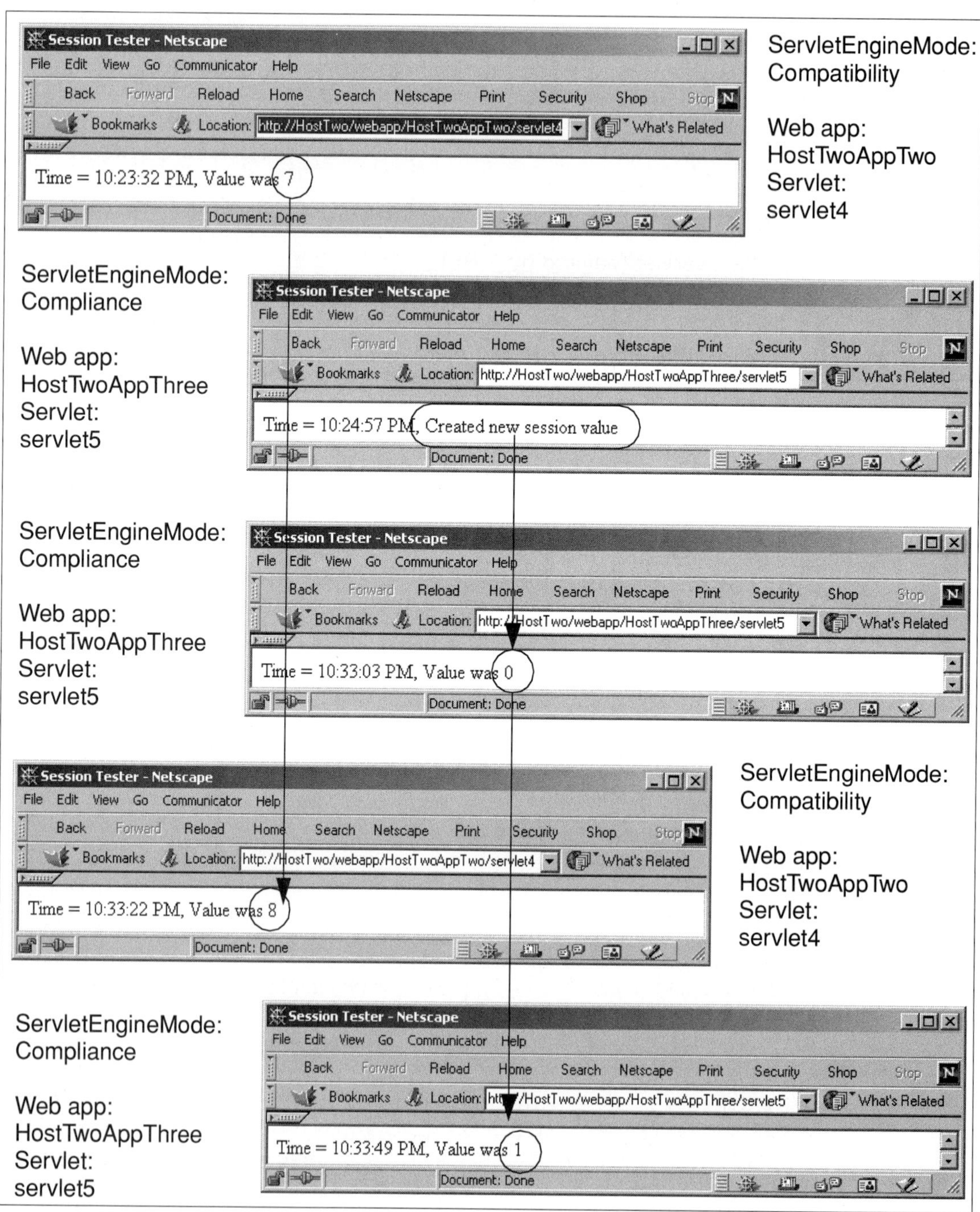

Figure 184. After setting cookie names, Compliance and Compatibility Modes operate independently

8.3.6 Web Path mapping (request mapping)

Servlet 2.2 clarifies exactly how requests for resources are to be mapped to the appropriate resource. Request mapping is to proceed in the following manner:

1. Exact match
2. Longest wildcard match
3. Matching extension
4. Default servlet (defined by /URL)

To specify the URL, the Servlet 2.2 specification allows the following syntax:

1. A string beginning with '/' and ending with '/*' specifies a wild card match.
2. A string beginning with '*.' specifies an extension mapping.
3. All other strings are used as exact matches.
4. A string containing only the '/' character indicates the default servlet for the Web application.

When you define a servlet in a servlet engine you specify one or more Web paths by which it will be invoked. For example we used

```
http://HostOne/webapp/hostOneAppOne/servlet1
```

to invoke servlet1 in the example 8.3.4, "HTTP session scope" on page 301. We are aware of a common idiom of setting up a dispatcher servlet. Such a servlet might be configured to respond to all requests of the form:

```
http://HostOne/webapp/hostOneAppOne/dispatcher/aRequest
```

where the last portion of the URL is used by the dispatcher to determine the required processing.

When you specify such a mapping of a set of requests to a single servlet you use a different specification format in Compliance Mode from the one you use in Compatibility Mode. The difference is minor and obvious but we labor the point in the hope of sparing some teams a little grief.

In Compliance Mode you must specify an explicit wildcard character at the end of the mapping string, whereas in Compatibility Mode the wildcard is implicit. So in **your Servlet -> General -> Servlet Web Path List,** you specify the path in Compliance Mode as `webapp/hostOneAppOne/dispatcher/*` as shown in Figure 185 on page 314.

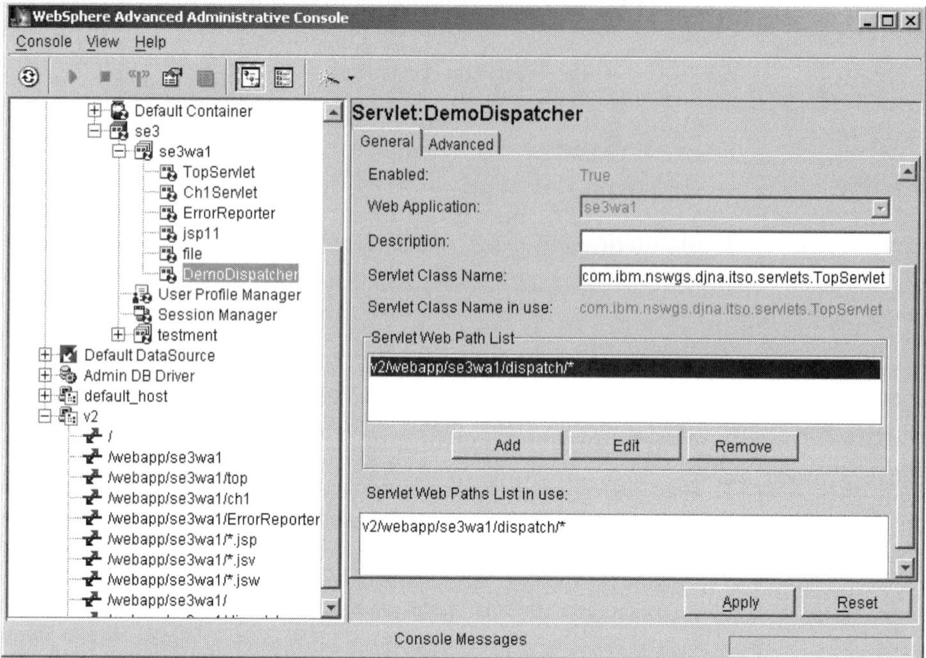

Figure 185. Web path mapping

Whereas in Compatibility Mode (and existing V3.5 installations), it will be simply be `webapp/hostOneAppOne/dispatcher/` with no explicit * wildcard specification.

8.3.7 Other API differences

There are three other minor differences between Compatibility Mode and Compliance Mode:

1. The HttpResponse method getCharacterEncoding() will return a default value in Compatibility Mode and a null in Compliance Mode.
2. In Compliance Mode a reset() of the response buffer clears the content type. In Compatibility Mode it sets it to a default of text/null.
3. The MimeFilterInfo method getMimeType() returns a default of “www/unknown” in Compatibility Mode and a null in Compliance Mode.

8.4 Multiple error pages

The Servlet API V2.2 defines facilities to let you specify error handling for each Web application. You can specify:

1. A default error page, and
2. Specific error pages for error conditions, for example an error page to be displayed when a particular status code is produced, or a particular Java exception is thrown.

8.4.1 Properties introduction

You may configure the error pages in the WebSphere Administrative Console on the Advanced tab of the Web Application properties panel. Default Error Page is a field and Error Pages is a list.

Both properties should specify the fully qualified URL of the Web page to display when in the following cases:

- sendError()
- sendRedirect()
- Uncaught exception thrown by servlet

The Web page should be a servlet or JSP file. It is possible that your error page has only static content and so you might expect to create a file of type HTML, with extension .html. It will be preferable to give your file an extension of .jsp. There are two reasons for this:

1. Often, production sites will have all HTML files served by the Web Server, they do not enable the File Serving servlet in the application server and so WebSphere cannot serve .html files. For clarity it may be preferable to maintain this separation of concerns.
2. The file serving servlet does not handle all types of HTTP requests.

In the error pages properties list, you may specify special Web pages when a special status code or exception occurs. For example, you may specify different Web pages to display when statuses 404 and 500 occur, or you may specify different Web pages to display when exceptions such as javax.servlet.ServletException and java.io.IOException are thrown.

If a request causes both a status code to be generated and an exception to be thrown, and both these errors have specified error pages, then WebSphere uses the error page configured for the status code.

If an error occurs that is not included in the list of error pages, the default error page will be displayed.

8.4.2 Test case for error pages

In this section we describe the test case we produced to explore the error page facilities.

8.4.2.1 Scenario of the test case

In this test case, we will use the Web application default_app, which is included in the default configuration of WebSphere. We will configure default_app to handle different errors with different error pages as shown in Table 13.

Table 13. Error pages setting

Error(Status Code or Exception)	Error Page
404	/error/err404.jsp
java.io.IOException	/error/errIOException.jsp
javax.servlet.ServletException	/error/errServletException.jsp
other	/ErrorReporter

We have a servlet named TestServlet to produce the different error conditions. We select the error code by specifying a value for a parameter "e", as shown in Figure 186 on page 317. We need three JSP files to handle the different errors we specified. Any other errors are handled by ErrorReporter. This is an internal servlet that is added to default_app by default.

```
import java.io.*;
import javax.servlet.*;
import javax.servlet.http.*;

public class TestServlet extends HttpServlet {
public void service(ServletRequest req, ServletResponse res) throws
ServletException,IOException
{
   String eType = req.getParameter("e");
   if (eType == null) {
      PrintWriter out=res.getWriter();
      res.setContentType("text/html");
      out.println("<html><head></head><body><h2>This the TestServlet
for Error Pages.<br> Please specify the Exception
Type.<br></h2></body></html>");
      out.close();return;
   }

   if (eType.equals("ioe")) {
      System.out.println("Exception Type == IOException");
      IOException ioe = new IOException();
      throw ioe;
   } else if (eType.equals("se")) {
      System.out.println("Exception Type == ServletException");
      ServletException se = new ServletException();
      throw se;
   } else {
      System.out.println("Other Exception");
      EOFException e = new EOFException();
      throw e;
   }
}
}
```

Figure 186. Source code of servlet TestServlet

8.4.2.2 Configuration for the test case

On the Advanced tab of properties panel of default_app, verify the setting of Default Error Page. It should be /ErrorReporter as shown in Figure 187 on page 318.

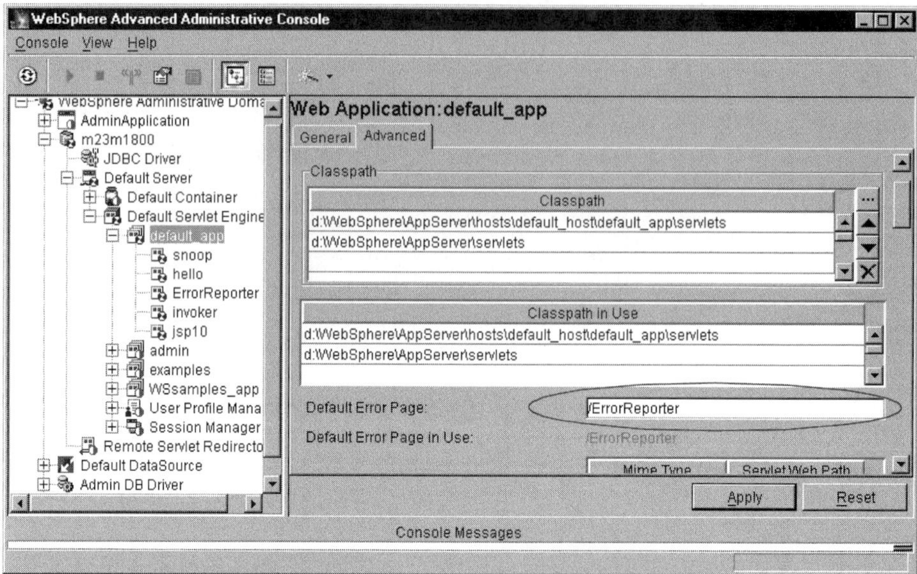

Figure 187. Default Error Page setting

Also on the Advanced tab, we configured the error pages list containing three rows as shown in Figure 188.

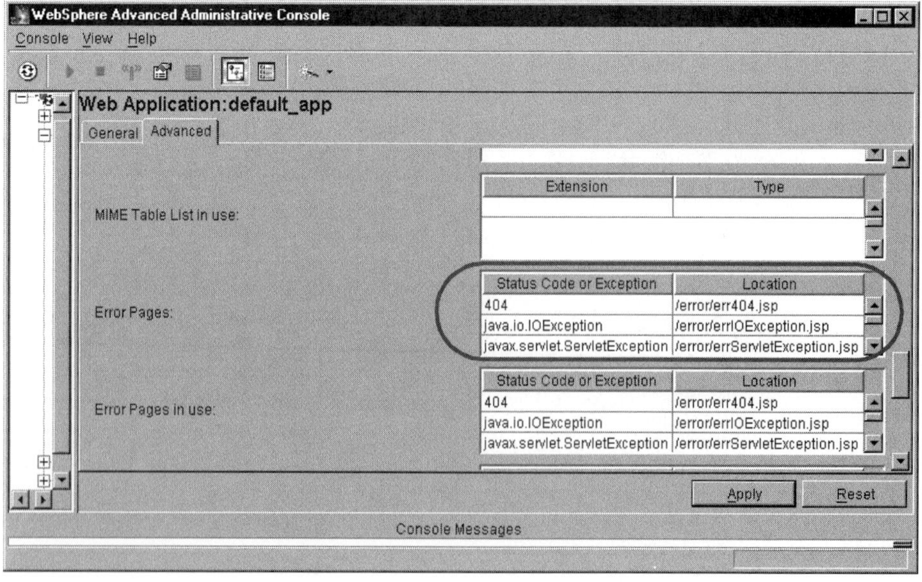

Figure 188. Error Pages setting

We entered the values shown in the previous figure and clicked **Apply**. Then we right-clicked **default_app** in the Topology tree and selected **Restart Web App** to make the setting active.

We then installed the servlet code and the Error Page JSPs. We copied the TestServlet.class to the classpath of default_app. In our installation this was:

```
C:\WebSphere\Appserver\hosts\default_host\default_app\servlets
```

We then created a directory named error in the document root of default_app:

```
C:\WebSphere\Appserver\hosts\default_host\default_app\web
```

and copied the three JSP files into the error directory.

8.4.2.3 Testing

We verified the error page configuration by using a browser to request specific URLs intended to produce the different error conditions.

Handle 404 error with /error/err404.jsp

We requested a URL for a file that does not exist.

```
http://<hostname>/x.jsp
```

A missing file should generate a 404 status code and WebSphere should then use /error/err404.jsp according to the configuration of property error pages.

We saw the result of err404.jsp displayed in a browser, as shown in Figure 189.

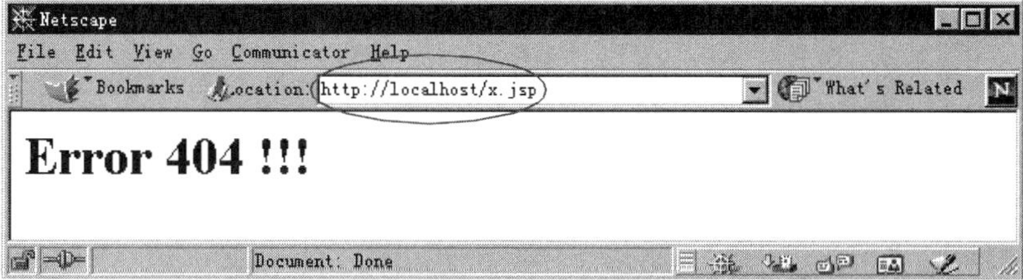

Figure 189. Handling 404 error with /error/err404.jsp

Handle IOException with /error/errIOException.jsp

We used our test servlet to generate an IOException. We requested the URL:

```
http://<hostname>/servlet/TestServlet?e=ioe
```

The TestServlet code interprets the `e=ioe` parameter and throws a java.io.IOException. WebSphere is configured to handle IOException with the error page /error/errIOException.jsp.

We saw the expected output from errIOException.jsp displayed in the browser as shown in Figure 190.

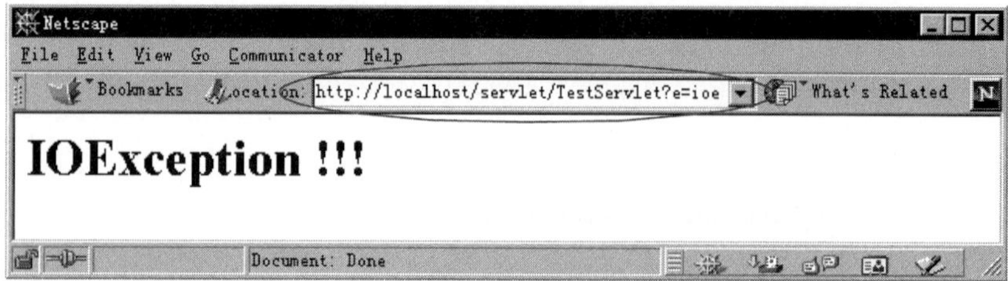

Figure 190. Handling java.io.IOException with /error/errIOException.jsp

Handle ServletException with /error/errServletException.jsp

We again used the test servlet to generate the exception we needed. We requested the URL:

```
http://<hostname>/servlet/TestServlet?e=se
```

The TestServlet throws javax.servlet.ServletException in response to the parameter `e=se`.

WebSphere then uses the configured error page, /error/errServletException.jsp, The result of errServletException.jsp was displayed in the browser as shown in Figure 191.

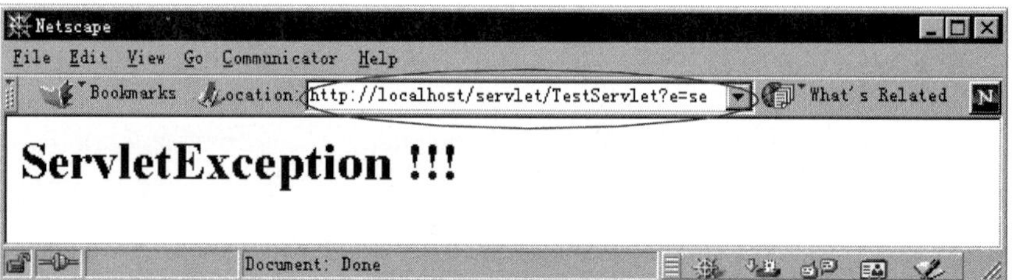

Figure 191. Handling javax.servlet.ServletException with /error/errServletException.jsp

Handle other errors with /ErrorReporter

We used the test servlet to generate an exception for which no error page was configured. We requested the URL

```
http://<hostname>/servlet/TestServlet?e=e
```

The TestServlet throws a java.io.EOFException in response to parameter `e=e`. No specific error page is configured for that exception so WebSphere uses the default error page and invokes the /ErrorReporter servlet. We saw the result of /ErrorReporter in a browser as shown in Figure 192 on page 321.

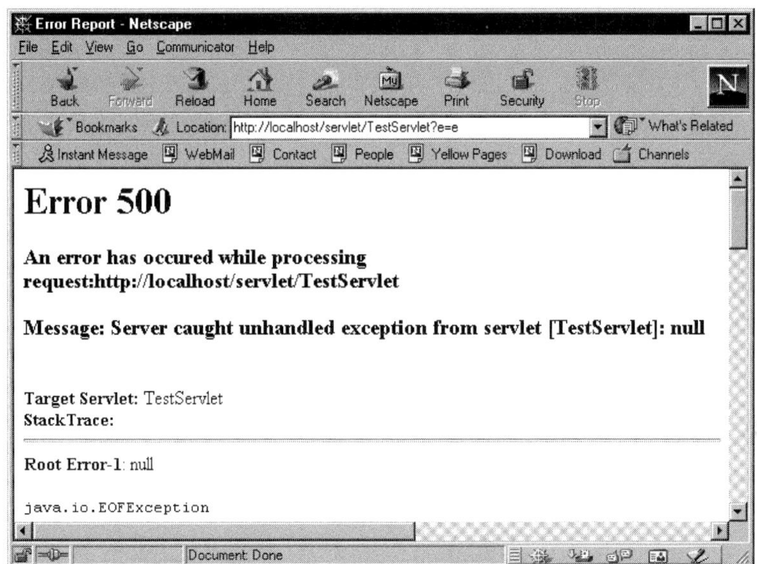

Figure 192. Handing other errors with /ErrorReporter

Custom error handling

A Web application may specify that when errors occur, other resources in the application are used. These resources are specified in the deployment descriptor. If the location of the error handler is a servlet or a JSP, the following request attributes can be set:

- javax.servlet.error.status_code
- javax.servlet.error.exception_type
- javax.servlet.error.message

These attributes allow the servlet to generate specialized content depending on the status code, exception type and message of the error.

8.5 Welcome file lists

The Servlet API V2.2 defines facilities for specifying a list of welcome files for Web applications. Welcome files define the response to requests without a specific file name. For example a request URL such as

```
http://myHost/webapp/myApp
```

which simply gives the Web path of the Web application.

In WebSphere the welcome fIle list is specified on Advanced tab of the Web Application properties panel. Welcome files are only effective when the Web application enables the file serving enabler as described in 5.6.3, “The file servlet” on page 173.

WebSphere will search the list of welcome files and return the first file in the list that is actually present on disk. If none of the specified welcome files can be found, then WebSphere looks for the default, index.html.

You also can set the init parameter for the file serving servlet of default.page to configure the default page desired.

The following sections show one sequence of tests demonstrating the feature of welcome file lists.

We create a Web application with a file serving enabler and whose Web path is `/webapp/test`. We configure its welcome files as index1.html and index2.jsp as shown in Figure 193.

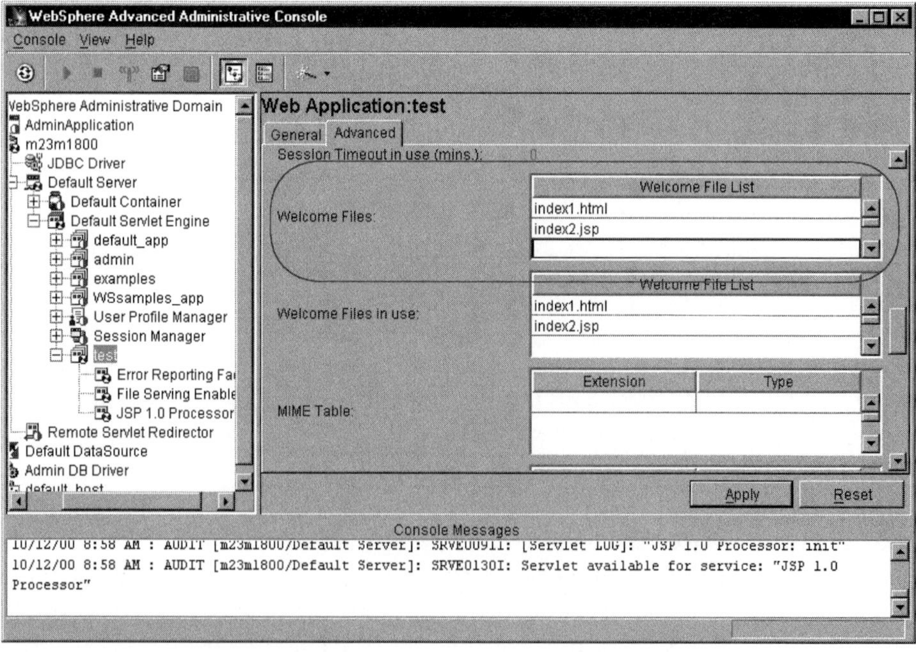

Figure 193. Configuring welcome files

We clicked **Apply** then right-clicked Web application in the topology tree and selected **Restart Web App** to activate the setting.

We put files named index1.html and index2.jsp into the document root of this Web application.

We then used a browser to request the URL:

```
http://myHost/webapp/test
```

Both welcome files exist, and WebSphere returned index1.html, as shown in Figure 194, because it is ahead of index2.jsp in the list of welcome files.

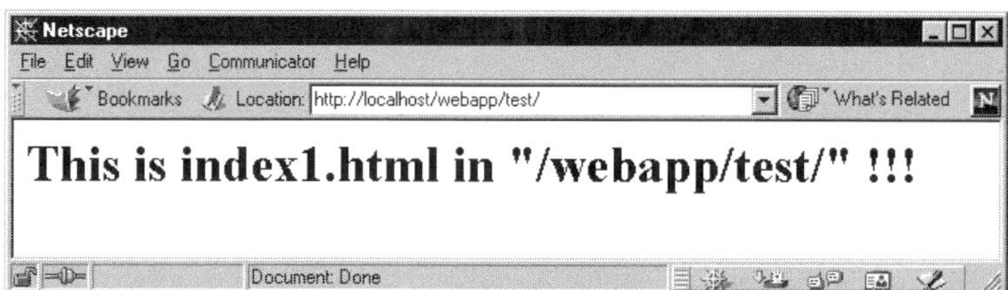

Figure 194. The first welcome file returned

We then deleted the file named index1.html and kept the file named index2.jsp in the document root. The we resubmitted the same request. Because the first welcome file now did not exist, WebSphere returned the second file in the list, index2.jsp as shown in Figure 195.

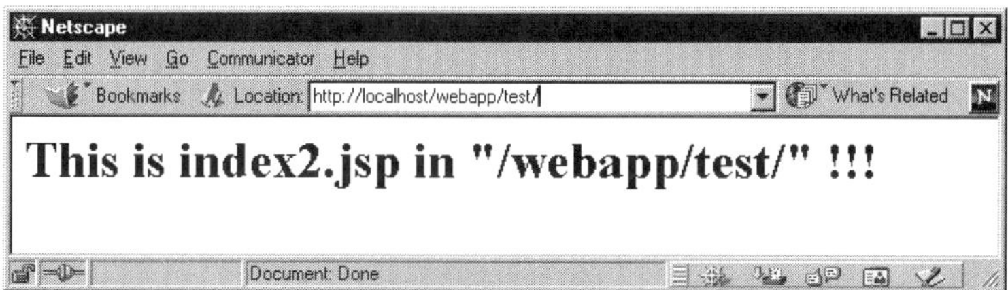

Figure 195. The welcome file returned when the first welcome file doesn't exist

8.6 The Web Application Archive (WAR)

The Servlet API V2.2 specification introduced a valuable new facility to aid deployment of applications. This is the Web Application Archive (WAR). A WAR file contains both the deployable components of a Web application (servlet code, HTML pages and JavaServer Pages) along with a deployment descriptor that specifies how these elements are to be installed.

In this section we discuss the contents of a WAR file and in the following section we explain how to use one.

A WAR files holds three categories of content:

- Static data that should be installed in the document root of the Web application. These are items such as HTML files, JSP files and images.
- Executable code such as Java class files for servlets and JAR files containing Java libraries.
- A deployment descriptor that determines how the Web application is to be configured.

A WAR file is simply a standard JAR file that contains the above elements. There is no requirement that you produce the file in the way we describe in the following sections. However, some structured process is clearly desirable.

8.6.1 Create a directory structure

Choose or create an empty directory. In the following sections we term this directory the WAR-ROOT. Create a directory called WEB-INF in WAR-ROOT.

8.6.2 Place any static content in the main hierarchy

Copy your hierarchy of static content to WAR-ROOT. The exact hierarchy you create will be deployed in the document root of your Web application. You may have previously prepared your content in some structure under a “web” directory (for example in the VisualAge for Java WebSphere Test Environment). Ensure that when you copy such a structure you copy the contents of “web” and not “web” itself.

8.6.3 Place any Java class files in the WEB-INF/ classes directory

If you have any Java classes, for example servlet files, create a classes subdirectory of WAR-ROOT/WEB-INF and copy all your class files into that directory. You must use the correct package hierarchy. So for a class MyServlet in package com.mycompany you need to create com and mycompany directories giving a class file in a directory structure of

```
WAR-ROOT/WEB-INF/classes/com/myCompany/MySerlvet.class
```

If you are using VisualAge for Java, then a directory export to WAR-ROOT/WEB-INF/classes will give the effect you need.

8.6.4 Place any JAR files in WEB-INF/ lib

If you have any JAR files to deploy, create a lib subdirectory of WAR-ROOT/WEB-INF (that is, create WAR-ROOT/WEB-INF/lib) and copy all your JAR files directly to that directory.

You should note that when the WAR file is deployed both your classes and your JAR files will be added to the Web application classpath. There is some cost to placing large numbers of classes in this classpath. Depending upon your application structure and its relationship with other Web applications you may prefer to add dependent JAR files to the application server classpath.

8.6.5 Create the deployment descriptor in the WEB-INF directory

The deployment descriptor is in the form of an XML file. The DTD for descriptor is specified in the Servlet API V2.2. You should note that the portions of the DTD relating to J2EE specific constructs such as roles are not used by WebSphere V3.5.2.

We will show a minimal descriptor sufficient to deploy one servlet.

Our sample consisted of a few HTML and JSP files in a conventional directory structure and one servlet class MyServlet in package com.myCompany. We copied those files into our WAR-ROOT as shown in Figure 196.

```
index.html
Tournament/Player.html
Tournament/Player.jsp
Tournament/PlayerDetails.html
Tournament/PlayerDetails.jsp
WEB-INF/classes/com/myCompany/MyServlet.class
WEB-INF/web.xml
```

Figure 196. Contents of WAR-ROOT

We constructed the deployment descriptor as shown in Figure 197 on page 326.

```
<!DOCTYPE web-app PUBLIC "-//Sun Microsystems, Inc.//DTD Web
Application 2.2//EN" "http://java.sun.com/j2ee/dtds/web-app_2_2.dtd">

<web-app>
   <display-name>ITSO</display-name>
   <servlet>
      <servlet-name>MyServlet</servlet-name>
      <servlet-class>com.myCompany.MyServlet</servlet-class>
   </servlet>
   <servlet-mapping>
      <servlet-name>MyServlet</servlet-name>
      <url-pattern>/runMyServlet</url-pattern>
   </servlet-mapping>
</web-app>
```

Figure 197. WAR descriptor example

The entries in the descriptor define the Web application that will be created. In our case we simply need a definition for the one servlet that is to be created. The static content is installed in the document root implicitly.

The `<servlet>` entry defines the name and class for the servlet. Note that the name is entirely arbitrary and that the classname is fully qualified.

Our `<servlet-mapping>` specifies a name that must correspond to the `<servlet-name>` in the previous entry, and a URL pattern. At deployment time WebSphere combines the URL pattern with the Web application Web path to produce the URL by which you can invoke the servlet.

8.6.6 Create the WAR file

You can create WAR files using the standard JDK JAR file utility. We created the directory C:\BuildWar for our WAR-ROOT and created an empty directory c:\TargetWar. Figure 198 on page 327 shows these two directories.

```
C:\>dir /s TargetWar
Directory of C:\TargetWar

10/13/2000  02:31p      <DIR>          .
10/13/2000  02:31p      <DIR>          ..
               0 File(s)              0 bytes

     Total Files Listed:
               0 File(s)              0 bytes
               2 Dir(s)  10,764,271,616 bytes free

C:\>dir /s BuildWar /A -d /B
C:\BuildWar\Tournament
C:\BuildWar\WEB-INF
C:\BuildWar\asimple.jsp
C:\BuildWar\index.html
C:\BuildWar\Tournament\PlayerDetails.jsp
C:\BuildWar\Tournament\Player.jsp
C:\BuildWar\Tournament\PlayerDetails.html
C:\BuildWar\Tournament\Player.html
C:\BuildWar\WEB-INF\web.xml
C:\BuildWar\WEB-INF\classes
C:\BuildWar\WEB-INF\classes\com
C:\BuildWar\WEB-INF\classes\com\myCompany
C:\BuildWar\WEB-INF\classes\com\myCompany\MyServlet.class
```

Figure 198. Directory structure for WAR file creation

We used the following command. It must be issued from the build directory.

```
jar -cvf C:\TargetDir\myApp.war .
```

The f option for `jar` specifies the name and directory for the output file and we simply specified the current directory, using **.**, the location of WAR-ROOT as the source of the JAR contents.

We did not create the WAR file in WAR-ROOT because, unless we remember to remove an old version of the WAR when creating a new one, there is a danger of accidently attempting to include the old file inside the new one. Such an attempt fails with a generic error message that may be diffcult to interpret.

Figure 199 on page 328 shows the execution of the `jar` command and the creation of the WAR file.

```
C:\>cd BuildWar
C:\BuildWar>
:\BuildWar> c:/websphere/appserver/jdk/bin/jar -cvf c:/TargetWar/myapp.war .
added manifest
adding: Tournament/(in = 0) (out= 0)(stored 0%)
adding: Tournament/PlayerDetails.jsp(in = 1230) (out= 540)(deflated 56%)
adding: Tournament/Player.jsp(in = 211) (out= 153)(deflated 27%)
adding: Tournament/PlayerDetails.html(in = 994) (out= 439)(deflated 55%)
adding: Tournament/Player.html(in = 612) (out= 351)(deflated 42%)
adding: WEB-INF/(in = 0) (out= 0)(stored 0%)
adding: WEB-INF/web.xml(in = 1092) (out= 306)(deflated 71%)
adding: WEB-INF/classes/(in = 0) (out= 0)(stored 0%)
adding: WEB-INF/classes/com/(in = 0) (out= 0)(stored 0%)
adding: WEB-INF/classes/com/myCompany/(in = 0) (out= 0)(stored 0%)
adding: WEB-INF/classes/com/myCompany/MyServlet.class(in = 5822) (out= 2638)(de
flated 54%)
adding: asimple.jsp(in = 107) (out= 69)(deflated 35%)
adding: index.html(in = 237) (out= 168)(deflated 29%)

C:\>dir /s C:\TargetWar
 Volume in drive C is WINDOWS2000
 Volume Serial Number is 0A72-0FE1

 Directory of C:\TargetWar

10/13/2000  02:31p      <DIR>          .
10/13/2000  02:31p      <DIR>          ..
10/13/2000  02:46p               6,916 myapp.war
               1 File(s)          6,916 bytes

     Total Files Listed:
               1 File(s)          6,916 bytes
```

Figure 199. WAR file creation

Once you have created a WAR file you have a portable image of your Web application that you can deploy into any WebSphere V3.5.2 instance. We describe how to do that in the next section.

8.7 Deploying an application from a WAR file

As part of our exploration of the Servlet V2.2 facilities we obtained some example WAR files from the JavaSoft Web site. These files deployed successfully and we will describe the deployment procedure and its effects by referring to one of these example files.

8.7.1 Obtaining the example WAR file

We chose to use the WAR file template.war. This file is in the archive referenced by the URL:

```
http://java.sun.com/products/jsp/tutorial/examples/examples.zip
```

The WAR file contains the expected combination of static content and Java classes as shown in Figure 200:

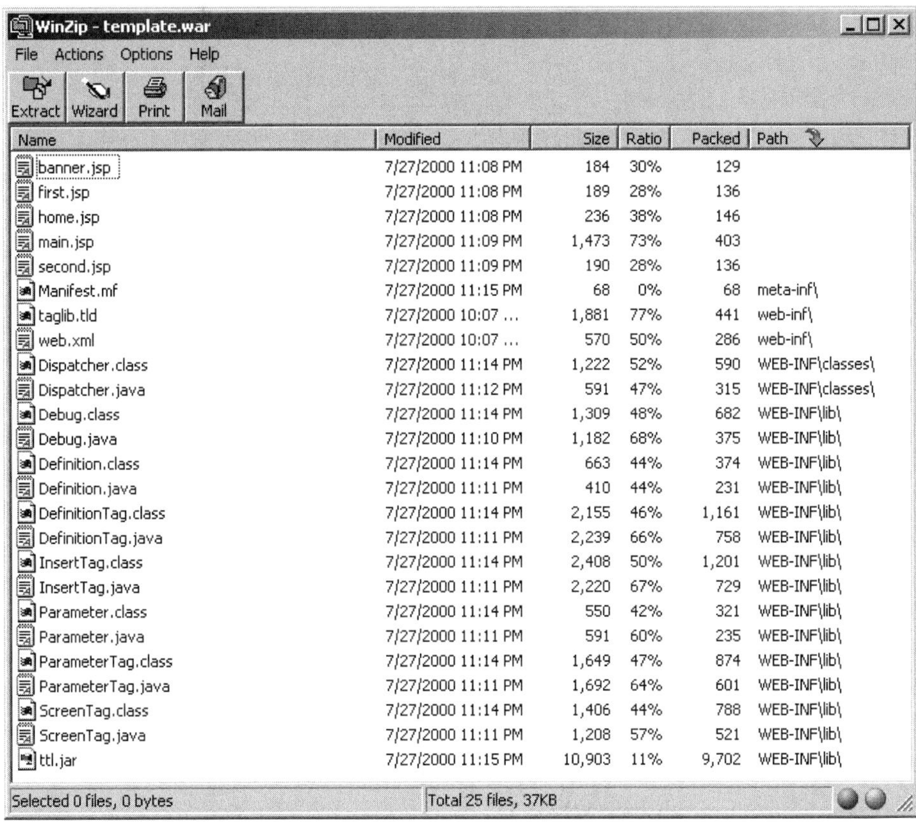

Name	Modified	Size	Ratio	Packed	Path
banner.jsp	7/27/2000 11:08 PM	184	30%	129	
first.jsp	7/27/2000 11:08 PM	189	28%	136	
home.jsp	7/27/2000 11:08 PM	236	38%	146	
main.jsp	7/27/2000 11:09 PM	1,473	73%	403	
second.jsp	7/27/2000 11:09 PM	190	28%	136	
Manifest.mf	7/27/2000 11:15 PM	68	0%	68	meta-inf\
taglib.tld	7/27/2000 10:07 ...	1,881	77%	441	web-inf\
web.xml	7/27/2000 10:07 ...	570	50%	286	web-inf\
Dispatcher.class	7/27/2000 11:14 PM	1,222	52%	590	WEB-INF\classes\
Dispatcher.java	7/27/2000 11:12 PM	591	47%	315	WEB-INF\classes\
Debug.class	7/27/2000 11:14 PM	1,309	48%	682	WEB-INF\lib\
Debug.java	7/27/2000 11:10 PM	1,182	68%	375	WEB-INF\lib\
Definition.class	7/27/2000 11:14 PM	663	44%	374	WEB-INF\lib\
Definition.java	7/27/2000 11:11 PM	410	44%	231	WEB-INF\lib\
DefinitionTag.class	7/27/2000 11:14 PM	2,155	46%	1,161	WEB-INF\lib\
DefinitionTag.java	7/27/2000 11:11 PM	2,239	66%	758	WEB-INF\lib\
InsertTag.class	7/27/2000 11:14 PM	2,408	50%	1,201	WEB-INF\lib\
InsertTag.java	7/27/2000 11:11 PM	2,220	67%	729	WEB-INF\lib\
Parameter.class	7/27/2000 11:14 PM	550	42%	321	WEB-INF\lib\
Parameter.java	7/27/2000 11:11 PM	591	60%	235	WEB-INF\lib\
ParameterTag.class	7/27/2000 11:14 PM	1,649	47%	874	WEB-INF\lib\
ParameterTag.java	7/27/2000 11:11 PM	1,692	64%	601	WEB-INF\lib\
ScreenTag.class	7/27/2000 11:14 PM	1,406	44%	788	WEB-INF\lib\
ScreenTag.java	7/27/2000 11:11 PM	1,208	57%	521	WEB-INF\lib\
ttl.jar	7/27/2000 11:15 PM	10,903	11%	9,702	WEB-INF\lib\

Figure 200. Contents of template.war file

Figure 201 on page 330 shows the deployment descriptor for the application. It is very similar to our example in the previous section.

```
<!DOCTYPE web-app PUBLIC "-//Sun Microsystems, Inc.//DTD Web
Application 2.2//EN" "http://java.sun.com/j2ee/dtds/web-app_2_2.dtd">

<web-app>
   <display-name>template</display-name>
    <servlet>
      <servlet-name>dispatcher</servlet-name>
      <servlet-class>Dispatcher</servlet-class>
    </servlet>
   <servlet-mapping>
      <servlet-name>dispatcher</servlet-name>
      <url-pattern>/example/*</url-pattern>
   </servlet-mapping>
   <taglib>
     <taglib-uri>/tlt</taglib-uri>
     <taglib-location>/WEB-INF/taglib.tld</taglib-location>
   </taglib>
</web-app>
```

Figure 201. The template example deployment descriptor

The one additional section defines the tag library, a JSP 1.1 feature, used by some of the JSPs in the application. This section is giving instructions to install the tag library descriptor file taglib.tld and to associate it with the URI `/tlt`. You may wish to observe in 8.7.4, "Resulting configuration" on page 338 how the resulting Web application fulfills these requirements.

8.7.2 Preparation

WebSphere uses a WAR file to define a Web application. It extracts the contents of the WAR file and uses information from the deployment descriptor to create and configure a Web application, copying the static content to the document root and the executable code to the classpath.

So, in order to deploy the WAR file we need to determine the following pieces of information.

8.7.2.1 The servlet engine

We selected one of our existing engines, `se3` running in application server `as3`. Alternatively we could have chosen to create a new engine.

In general WAR files can be deployed into servlet engines running in either mode, but it is possible the application may require one mode or the other.

8.7.2.2 Virtual host

We selected our existing virtual host v2. It would have been possible to set up a new virtual host dedicated to the new application.

8.7.2.3 Web application details

When you deploy a WAR file you need to specify a Web application name and its Web path.

With some care, you can deploy two compatible WAR files into the same Web application. However this would be both contrary to the meaning of WAR files and dangerously error prone.

So we selected a new name, `newTemplate`, and a new Web path `/webapp/newTemplate` for our Web application.

8.7.2.4 Directory location

The deployment process will create a document root and Web application classpath for the Web application. When you request WebSphere to deploy a WAR file it requires that you supply a directory. WebSphere will create a directory whose name matches the name of the WAR file in the location you specify, and then creates web and servlet directories in that directory.

So, if you are deploying template.war and supply C:\deployHere, then WebSphere creates the following three directories:

- C:\deployHere\template
- C:\deployHere\template\web for document root
- C:\deployHere\template\servlets for classpath

There are two considerations here:

1. If you deploy the same WAR file twice, into two separate Web applications and select the same directory location, then your two Web applications will share the same document root and classpath. This may well not be what you intend, in which case you need to plan a different directory structure.
2. In understanding how WAR files are deployed, you can make the best choice of directory for compliance with your current standards and practices.

8.7.2.5 Summary

Our deployment decisions are summarized in Table 14:

Table 14. Administrative console deployment data

Item	Chosen Value
Servlet Engine	se3 in as3
Virtual Host	vh2
Web Path	/webapp/newTemplate
Web Application	newTemplate
Deployment Directory	c:\deployedWar\as3\se3

8.7.3 Deployment

You can deploy a WAR file either through the administrative console or by using command line scripts. We anticipate that the script approach will be widely used when repetitive deployments are needed.

We first describe the use of the administrative console. This allows us to both explain the data to be input in detail and also gives a convenient mechanism for seeing the effects of deployment. We describe deployment using the command line in 8.7.5, “Command line deployment” on page 342.

Before deploying the template.war, our initial situation was as follows. We had placed all our WAR files in directory c:\TargetWar and we had created a plausible directory structure for the deployment directory. We intended to deploy into the directory c:\DeployedWar\as3\se3.

Figure 202 on page 333 shows the initial situation.

```
C:\>dir /s TargetWar /A -d /B
C:\TargetWar\myapp.war
C:\TargetWar\iteration.war
C:\TargetWar\template.war

C:\>dir /s DeployedWar\as3\se3
Directory of C:\DeployedWar\as3\se3

10/13/2000  09:31p      <DIR>          .
10/13/2000  09:31p      <DIR>          ..
               0 File(s)              0 bytes

     Total Files Listed:
               0 File(s)              0 bytes
               2 Dir(s)  10,759,094,272 bytes free
```

Figure 202. The initial situation before deploying a WAR file

Our application server and servlet engine were configured and started. You will see from Figure 203 that the servlet engine had an existing Web application already installed and running. Deploying the WAR file did not interfere with the existing Web application provided that we chose distinct values for the deployment directory and Web path values.

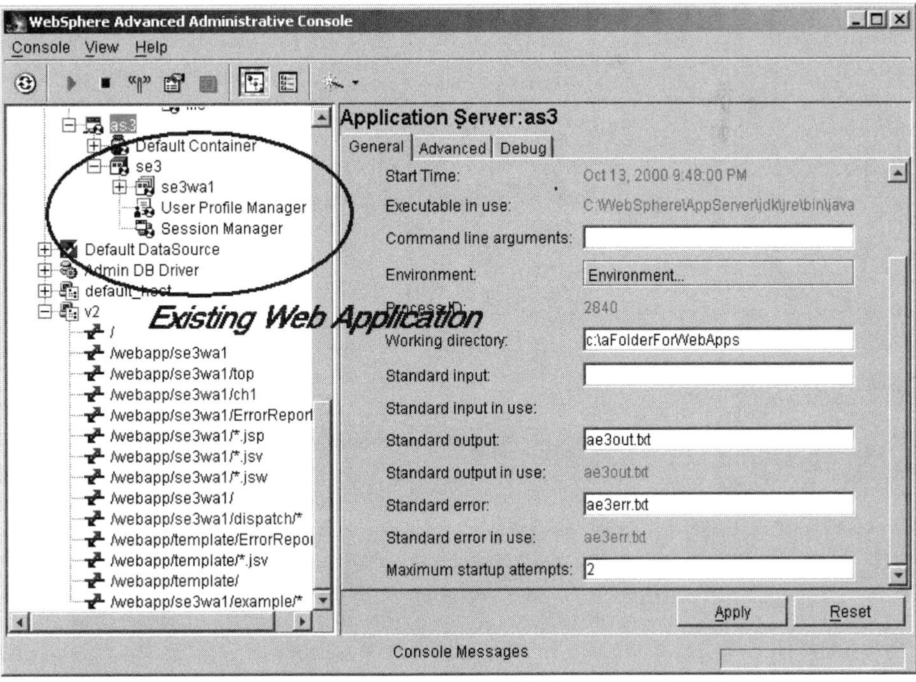

Figure 203. Configuration before WAR deployment

8.7.3.1 Initiating the deployment

We clicked **Wizard -> Convert a War File** as shown in Figure 204.

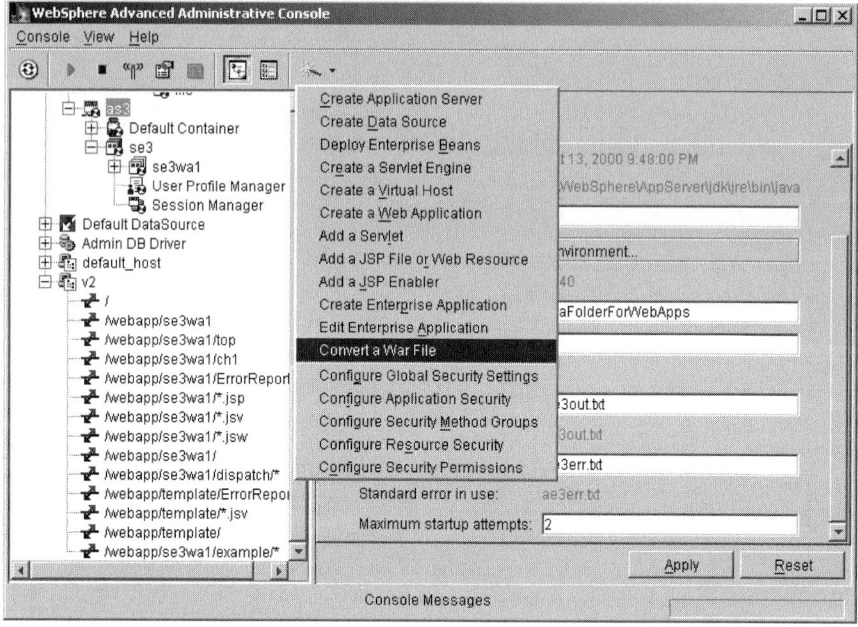

Figure 204. Convert War File

This brings up the WAR deployment task as shown in Figure 205.

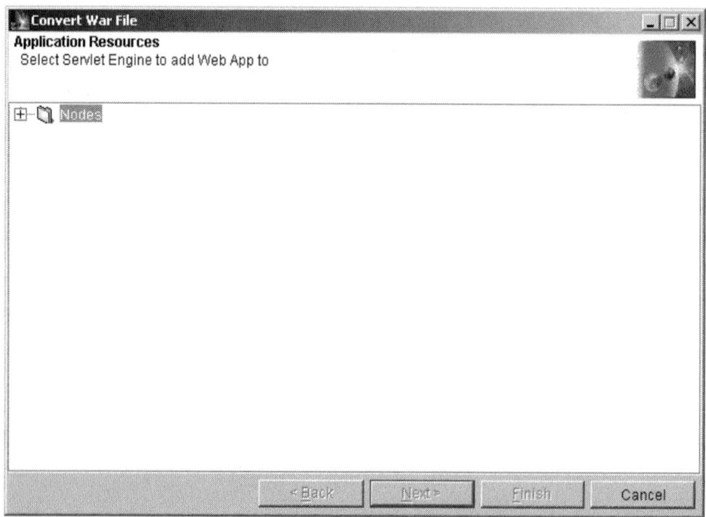

Figure 205. Convert War File window: Select Servlet Engine #1

We then moved through the steps described in the following sections.

8.7.3.2 Selecting servlet engine and virtual host

We expanded the tree to find our servlet engine se3, selected it and clicked **Next** as shown in Figure 206.

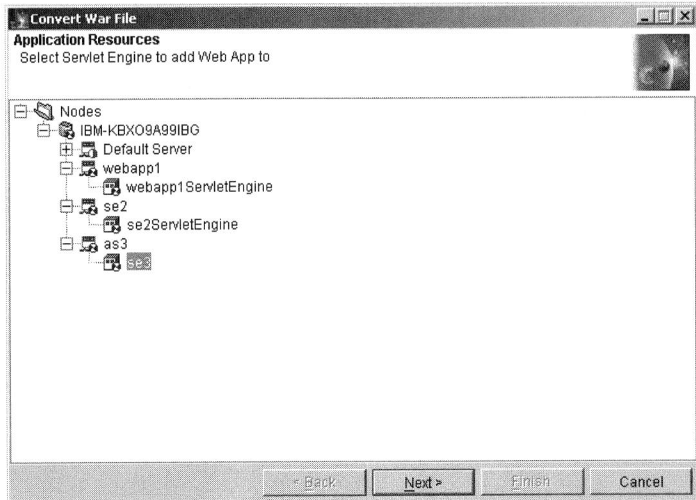

Figure 206. Convert War File window: Select Servlet Engine #2

This brought up the virtual host selection step as shown in Figure 207. We selected our chosen host v2 and again clicked **Next**.

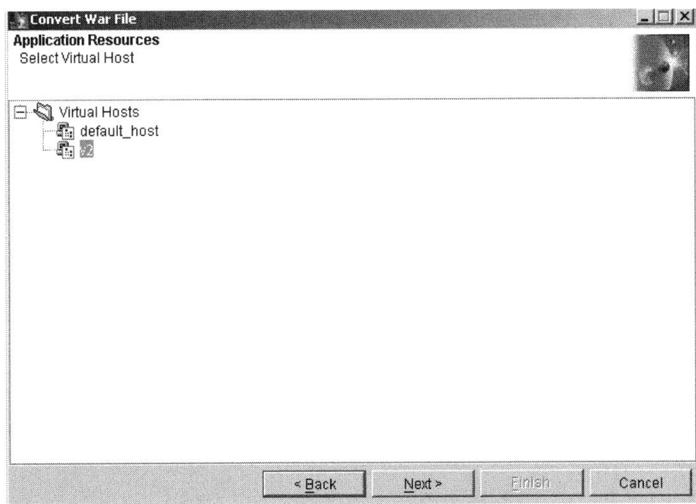

Figure 207. Convert War File window: Select Virtual Host

8.7.3.3 Selecting the WAR file

We selected the WAR file by clicking **Browse** as shown in Figure 208.

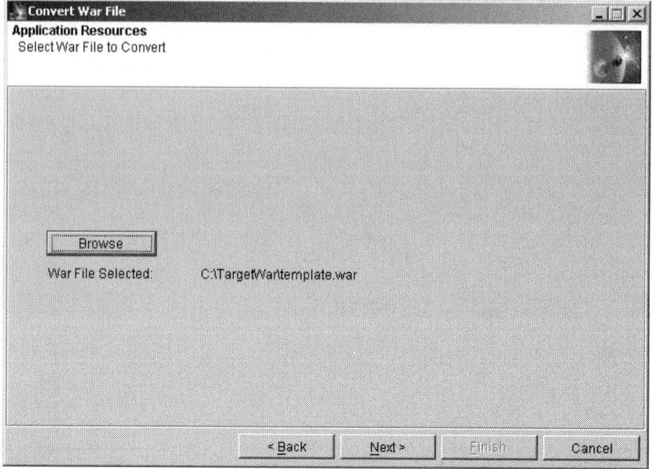

Figure 208. Convert War File window: Select War File to Convert

We navigated to c:\TargetWar. We selected `template.war` as shown in Figure 209, clicked **Open** and then **Next**.

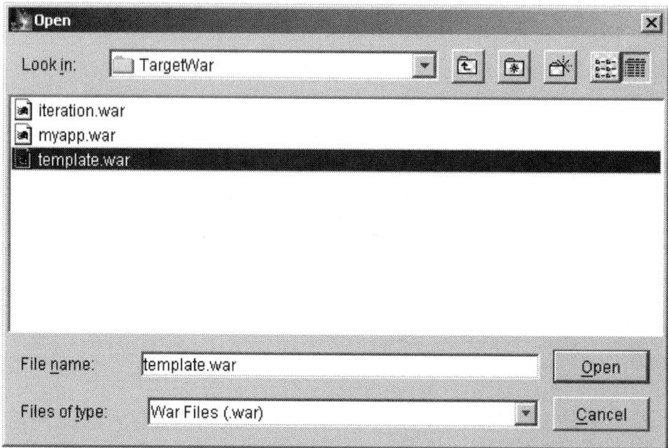

Figure 209. Convert War File window: Select template.war file

8.7.3.4 Selecting the deployment directory

We now specified the directory for the document root and classpath. We clicked **Browse** as shown in Figure 210 on page 337.

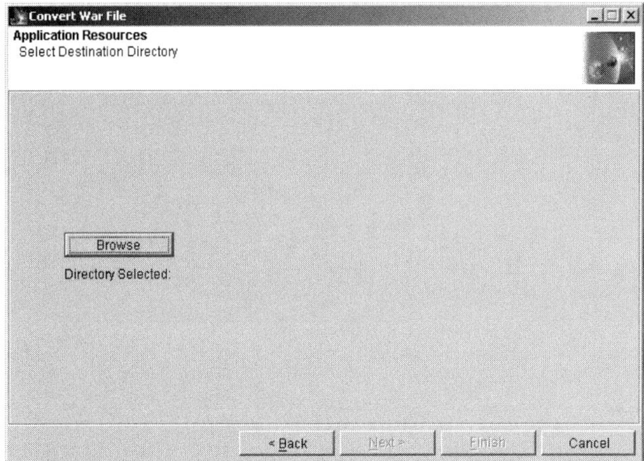

Figure 210. Convert War File window: Select Destination Directory

Then we navigated to c:\DeployedWar\as3\se3 and clicked **Open** followed by **Next** as shown in Figure 211.

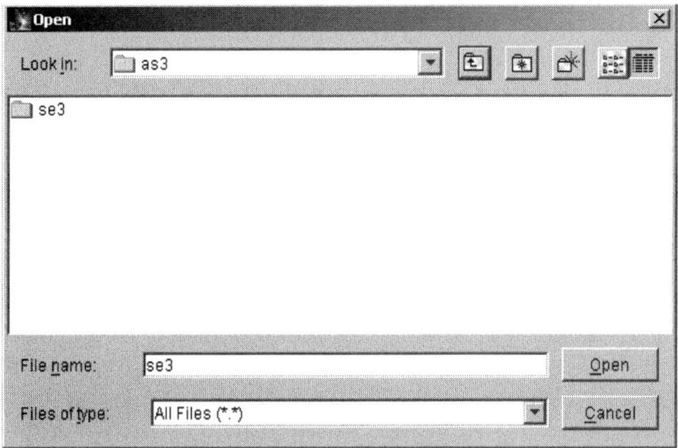

Figure 211. Select a directory

8.7.3.5 Specifying the Web path and application aame

FInally we entered the Web application path, /webapp/newTemplate and the Web application name, `newTemplate` as shown in Figure 212 on page 338. We then clicked **Finish**.

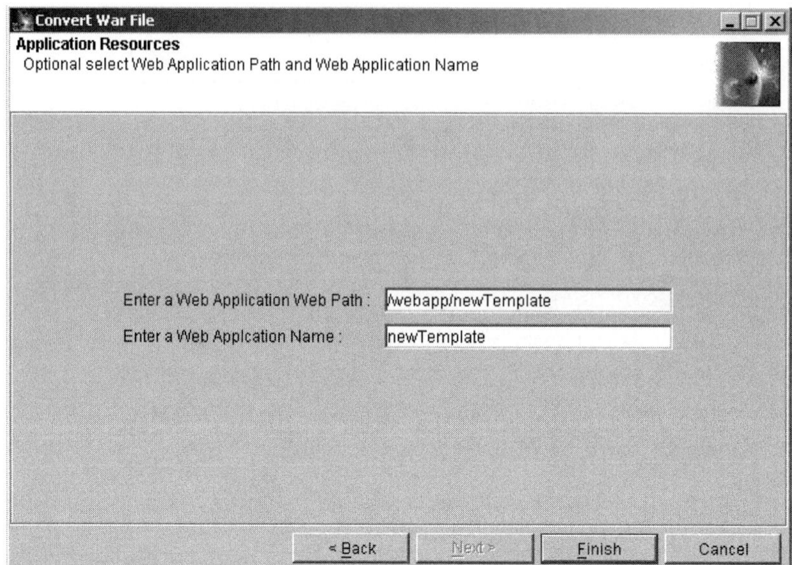

Figure 212. Specifying the Web path and application name

Deployment took a little time but eventually a confirmation dialog box appeared. The following section describes the results of the deployment.

8.7.4 Resulting configuration

You can see the effects of deploying the WAR file in two places: the physical files and directories created, and in changes to the WebSphere configuration.

8.7.4.1 Files and directories

We specified the directory `c:\deployedWar\as3\se3` for the deployment of our WAR file. As expected, the deployment process created a directory called template corresponding to our WAR file name in the deployment directory, and subdirectories for the document root and classpath.

The document root

The document root directory for our Web application is the directory:

```
c:\deployedWar\as3\se3\template\web
```

Figure 213 on page 339 shows the contents of this directory.

```
C:\>dir /s DeployedWar\as3\se3\template\web

Directory of C:\DeployedWar\as3\se3\template\web

10/13/2000  10:59p      <DIR>          .
10/13/2000  10:59p      <DIR>          ..
10/13/2000  10:59p      <DIR>          WEB-INF
10/13/2000  10:59p                 189 first.jsp
10/13/2000  10:59p                 236 home.jsp
10/13/2000  10:59p                 190 second.jsp
10/13/2000  10:59p               1,473 main.jsp
10/13/2000  10:59p                 184 banner.jsp
               5 File(s)          2,272 bytes

 Directory of C:\DeployedWar\as3\se3\template\web\WEB-INF

10/13/2000  10:59p      <DIR>          .
10/13/2000  10:59p      <DIR>          ..
10/13/2000  10:59p               1,881 taglib.tld
10/13/2000  10:59p                 570 web.xml
               2 File(s)          2,451 bytes

     Total Files Listed:
               7 File(s)          4,723 bytes
               5 Dir(s)  10,753,966,080 bytes free
```

Figure 213. Files deployed into document root of Web application

In the document root we see the JSP files for the application. There happen to be no HTML files or images in this particular WAR file. In the WEB-INF directory we see the WAR file deployment descriptor and also the tag library descriptor. The location of the latter is important. You will see it referenced in the next section.

8.7.4.2 WebSphere configuration

Figure 214 on page 340 shows that the WebSphere configuration now contains the Web application whose name we specified, newTemplate.

In Figure 214 on page 340 we can see the Web application name, virtual host and Web path that we specified when deploying the WAR file.

We can also see that three servlets were created:

1. The default ErrorReporting servlet.
2. The servlet to enable JSP V1.1.
3. The dispatcher servlet; this was the only servlet defined in the WAR file.

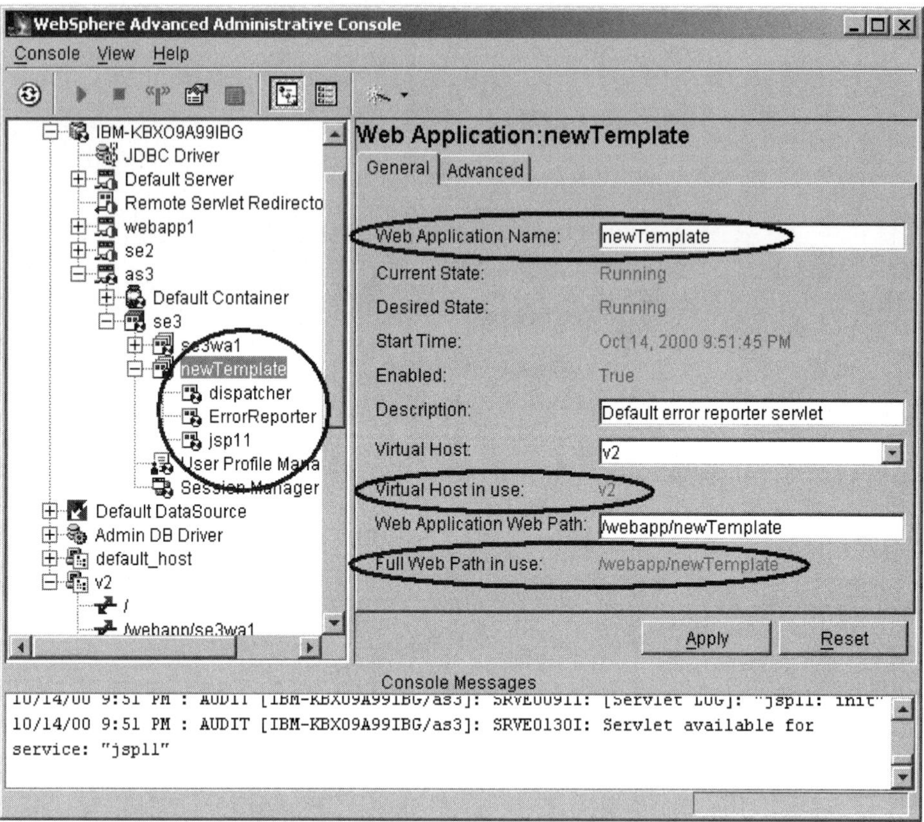

Figure 214. New Web application

When we move to the Advanced tab, as shown in Figure 215 on page 341 we can see the configuration of document root and classpath. You will notice that these match the physical directories described in 8.7.4.1, “Files and directories” on page 338.

If we had been deploying this application by hand, without using a WAR file, then we would have been responsible for ensuring this consistency. The WAR file approach is less error prone and can save much effort when repeatedly deploying applications. If you are repeatedly deploying WAR files then you may find the command line deployment facilities useful. We describe those in 8.7.5, “Command line deployment” on page 342.

Another configuration item inserted when deploying the WAR file was the default error page. Figure 215 on page 341 also shows that the ErrorReporter servlet has been configured for that purpose.

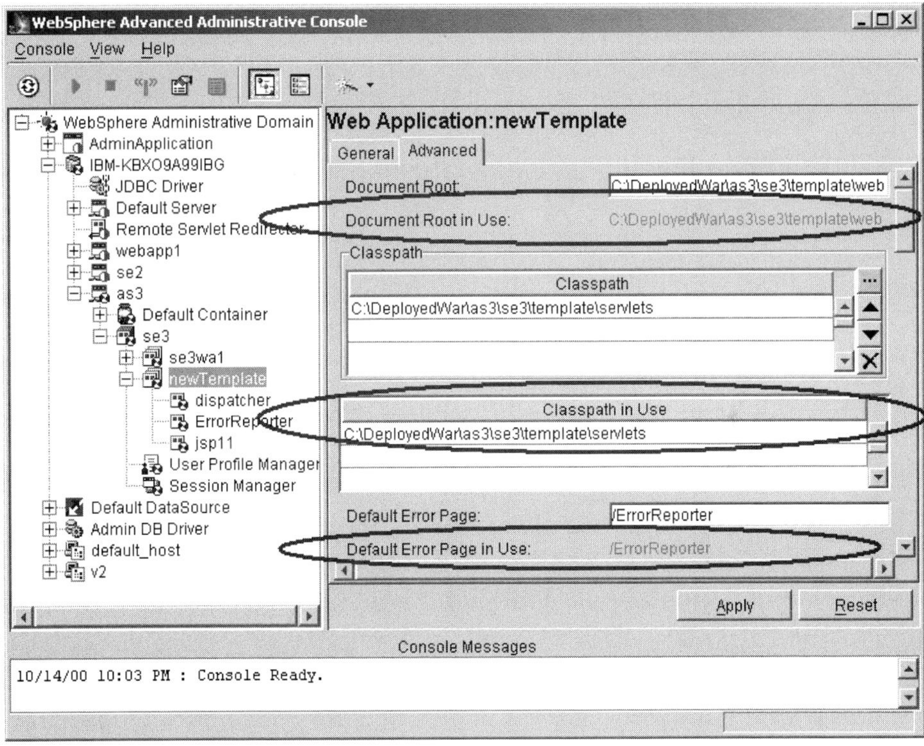

Figure 215. Web Application - Advanced tab

The Advanced tab displays two other features worth noting. First, the reload interval controls how frequently the servlet engine checks to determine whether any servlet files should be reloaded. In WebSphere V3.5.2, the default value for this is 9000 seconds. You should adjust this value to appropriate values for your development and production systems. You are able to change the <WAS_HOME>/properties/xmlconfig.xsl file to control this default value.

Figure 216 on page 342 shows the configuration of the JSP 1.1 Tag Library we mentioned in 8.7.1, “Obtaining the example WAR file” on page 328.

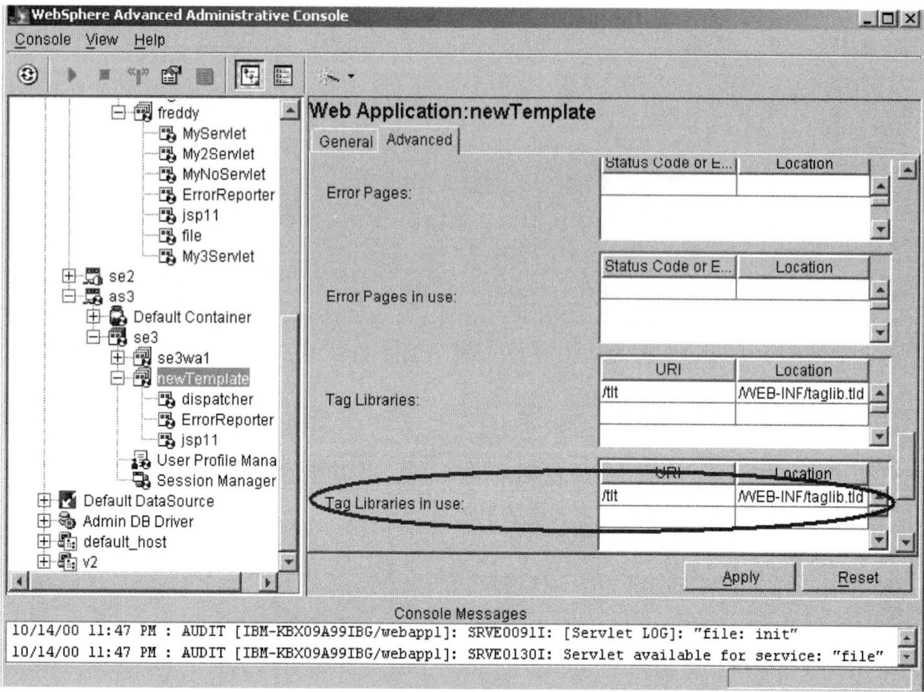

Figure 216. Web Application Advanced tab: Tag Libraries

Having examined these configuration features we started the resulting Web application by right-clicking it in the Topology tab, and clicking **Restart Web App**.

8.7.5 Command line deployment

You can deploy a WAR file from the command line using the procedure we describe below. You still need to prepare for deployment in the way we described in 8.7.2, "Preparation" on page 330. In addition you also need to ensure that you have the WebSphere bin directory on your path.

```
C:\work>path
PATH=C:\WINNT\system32;C:\WINNT;C:\WINNT\System32\Wbem;
C:\Lotus\Notes;c:\websphere\appserver\bin
```

Figure 217. Example path including WebSphere bin directory

The bin directory location will depend on your choice of installation directory for WebSphere. You will be executing the command `wartoxmlconfig` and you may wish to check that this is in the bin directory you added to your path.

The command requires parameters whose meaning is equivalent to the values we entered in the administrative console in the previous sections. However, they are specified in a slightly different way. The following table lists the parameters, all of which are compulsory, their meaning, and the value we entered. You may wish to compare these with the table of values we used for the administrative console deployment in Table 14 on page 332.

Table 15. Command line deployment parameters

	Parameter Meaning	Our Value
1	Path of WAR file to be deployed	c:\TargetWar\template.war
2	Deployment directory	c:\DeployedWar\as3\se3
3	Administrative server node, explained later	myhost
4	Node for Servlet Engine	myhost
5	Application server in that node	as3
6	Servlet engine	se3
7	Virtual host	v2
8	Web application path	/webapp/newTemplate
9	Web application name	newTemplate

Parameter 3 determines the location of the administrative Server that will perform the required configuration. We did not experiment with specifying different values for parameters 3 and 4.

We issued the command:

```
wartoxmlconfig c:\TargetWar\template.war c:\DeployedWar\as3\se3 myHost
myhost as3 se3 v2 /webapp/newTemplate newTemplate
```

and the deployment ran successfully producing identical effects to those produced by the administrative console deployment. Figure 218 on page 344 shows the output produced by the command.

```
C:\work>wartoxmlconfig c:\TargetWar\template.war c:\DeployedWar\as3\se3
myhost myhost as3 se3 v2 /webapp/newTemplate newTemplate
Buildfile: C:\WebSphere\AppServer\properties\convertwar.xml

init:

unpack.war:
    [unzip] Expanding: C:\TargetWar\template.war into C:\WebSphere\AppServer\bin
\template

copyto.webapp:
    [mkdir] Created dir: C:\DeployedWar\as3\se3\template
    [mkdir] Created dir: C:\DeployedWar\as3\se3\template\web
    [mkdir] Created dir: C:\DeployedWar\as3\se3\template\web\WEB-INF
    [mkdir] Created dir: C:\DeployedWar\as3\se3\template\servlets
  [copydir] Copying 5 files to C:\DeployedWar\as3\se3\template\web
  [copydir] Copying 2 files to C:\DeployedWar\as3\se3\template\web\WEB-INF

copy.war.classes:
  [copydir] Copying 2 files to C:\DeployedWar\as3\se3\template\servlets

copy.war.lib:
  [copydir] Copying 15 files to C:\DeployedWar\as3\se3\template\servlets

transform.to.xmlconfig:
  [deltree] Deleting: C:\WebSphere\AppServer\bin\template

run.xmlconfig:
  [wasjava] [00.10.16 15:27:13:189 GMT+01:00] 5375f61d NodeConfig    A Importing
 Node : IBM-KBXO9A99IBG
  [wasjava] [00.10.16 15:27:13:439 GMT+01:00] 5375f61d ApplicationSe A Importing
 ApplicationServer : as3
  [wasjava] [00.10.16 15:27:13:689 GMT+01:00] 5375f61d ServletEngine A Importing
 ServletEngine : se3
  [wasjava] [00.10.16 15:27:13:920 GMT+01:00] 5375f61d WebApplicatio A Importing
 WebApplication : newTemplate
  [wasjava] [00.10.16 15:27:14:911 GMT+01:00] 5375f61d ServletConfig A Importing
 Servlet : dispatcher
  [wasjava] [00.10.16 15:27:15:612 GMT+01:00] 5375f61d ServletConfig A Importing
 Servlet : ErrorReporter
  [wasjava] [00.10.16 15:27:16:123 GMT+01:00] 5375f61d ServletConfig A Importing
 Servlet : jsp11
  [wasjava] [00.10.16 15:27:16:714 GMT+01:00] 5375f61d ServletConfig A Importing
 Servlet : file
   [delete] Deleting: C:\WebSphere\AppServer\bin\template.xml

BUILD SUCCESSFUL

Total time: 15 seconds
```

Figure 218. Command line WAR deployment

8.7.6 Execution

The servlet for the template is called dispatcher. You can see the configuration for dispatcher in the administrative console in Figure 219.

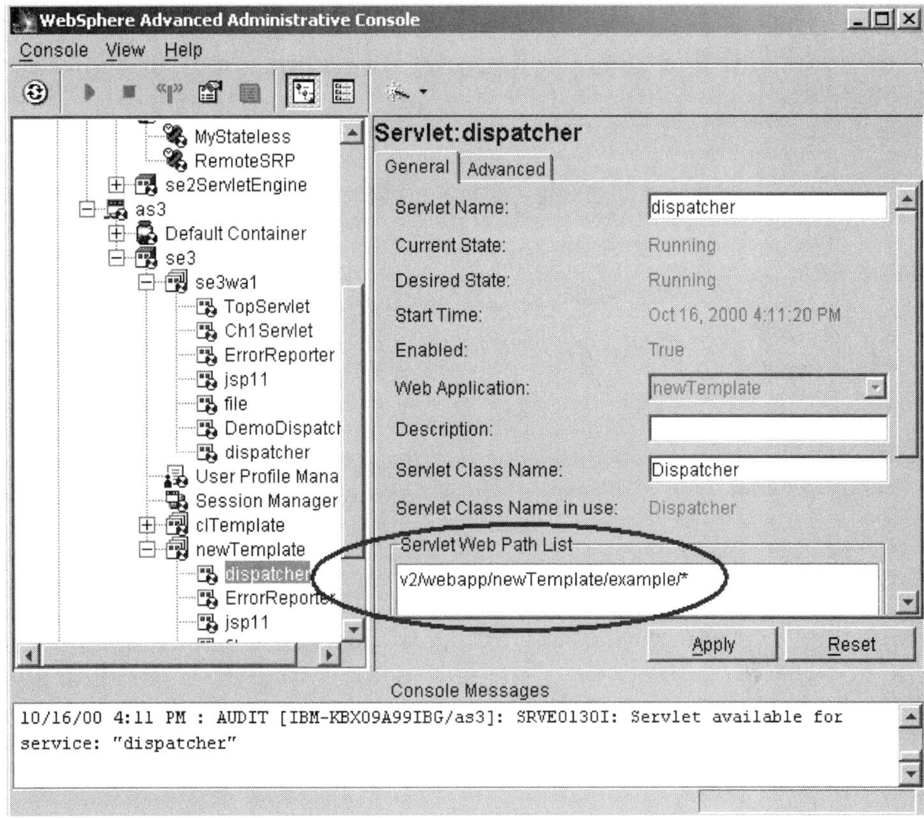

Figure 219. Web path for the servlet

We note that the servlet is invoked by any URL beginning:

```
http://v2/webapp/newTemplate/example
```

We note that the path is specified correctly for Servlet API V2.2 with a trailing wildcard character. The documentation for this sample application explains that the initial URL we should use is:

```
http://v2/webapp/newTemplate/example/home
```

We invoked the application from our browser using the Web path specified during deployment. Figure 220 on page 346 shows the results of requesting that URL in our browser, and then clicking the “first” link.

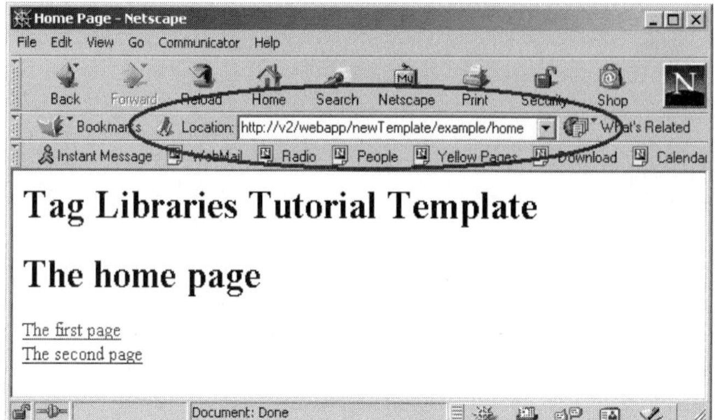

Figure 220. Executing the deployed application #1

The displayed data was produced by JSPs using the tag library that we mentioned earlier.

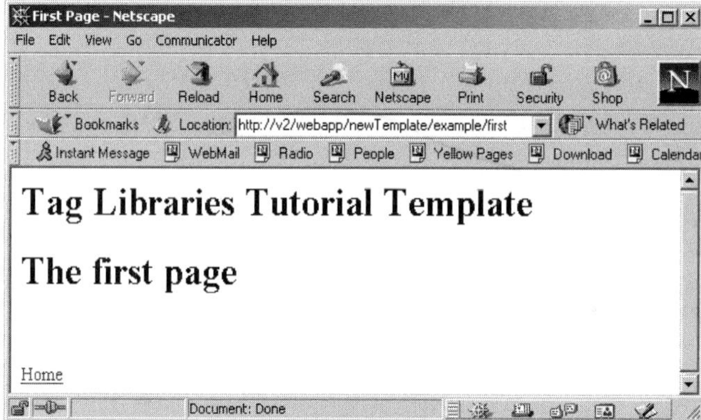

Figure 221. Executing the deployed application #2

Java compilation problem

The application ran correctly in most of our test environments. However, on a small number of machines we saw a failure to compile Java code. The code that was failing to compile was the Java sources of the tag library.

This code was supplied in the WAR file for educational purposes and does not constitute part of the application proper; the compiled code is delivered in a JAR file. On the machines where we saw the problem we simply removed the .java files and our application ran successfully.

Chapter 9. Using JNDI to access LDAP

In an object-oriented distributed computing environment, clients must have a mechanism to locate objects providing the services they require. A naming service is such a mechanism. It allows object to register their locations under chosen names and clients to access the objects by those names. Client code is expressed in terms of names of objects rather than in terms of the physical hosts or network addresses where the objects are located.

The naming service allows clients to access distributed objects in a location-transparent manner; the client code does not change if you decide to re-locate the objects providing certain services. This flexibility is essential if you intend to build scalable, resilient systems.

The Java Naming and Directory Interface (JNDI) sits in the middle, between someone using a naming or directory service and the actual naming or directory service. It provides a common interface, but some aspects of the underlying naming or directory service show through the JNDI interface. So it doesn't totally isolate the user from knowing about the underlying system. Also, the interface for naming is a subset of directory. WebSphere provides an implementation of JNDI that uses the JNDI naming support (Context interface) and it is layered over a CosNaming Name Server. The names that a user of this JNDI use look like this:

"hosts/xyz.austin.ibm.com/resources/homes/PolicyHome".

WebSphere implements this implementation of the JNDI Context interface. Also WebSphere ships an implementation of JNDI that uses the JNDI directory support (DirContext interface) and it is layered over an LDAP server. The names that a user of this JNDI use look like this:

"cn=russ newcombe, ou=websphere, ou=austin development, o=ibm, c=us".

There are three major usage of the JNDI with WebSphere:

- WebSphere uses the JNDI Naming framework to provide JNDI support that satisfies the Naming needs for EJBs and applications using EJBs.
- WebSphere security used LDAP for some aspects of security, and for this they use the JNDI directory framework.
- You can write your own Java application programs or servlets which access LDAP server.

We discuss the JNDI overview and specifications. Also we provide sample programs which use the JNDI directory support over LDAP. However, we don't address neither JNDI as used by the EJBs nor administering security with LDAP in a WebSphere environment.

9.1 What is JNDI?

JNDI, as defined by Sun Microsystems, provides naming and directory functions to Java programs. JNDI is an API independent of any specific directory service implementation.

The definition prevents, by design, the appearance of any implementation-specific artifacts in the API. The API is designed to cover the common case. JNDI was developed as part of the Java Enterprise API set that also includes Enterprise JavaBeans (EJB) and JDBC. The EJB specification has a special relationship with JNDI, because EJB clients use this mechanism to find entity beans or Session beans.

JNDI provides a generalized naming and directory service interface. For example, JNDI could be used to retrieve files from a file system. The file system acts as a naming service. JNDI could also be used to retrieve an X509 public key certificate from an LDAP directory service, or to get the IP address of a host name using the DNS as a naming service.

The JDNI API has several classes that can be used by developers to retrieve entries or attributes of a Naming Service. JNDI provides a Service Provider Interface (SPI) that enables access to the particular underlying directory service. The SPI is usually written by the vendor of the underlying naming and directory service and is supplied as a Java class library.

Figure 222 on page 349 shows the JNDI architecture from Sun's JNDI specifications (found at `http://java.sun.com/products/jndi/`).

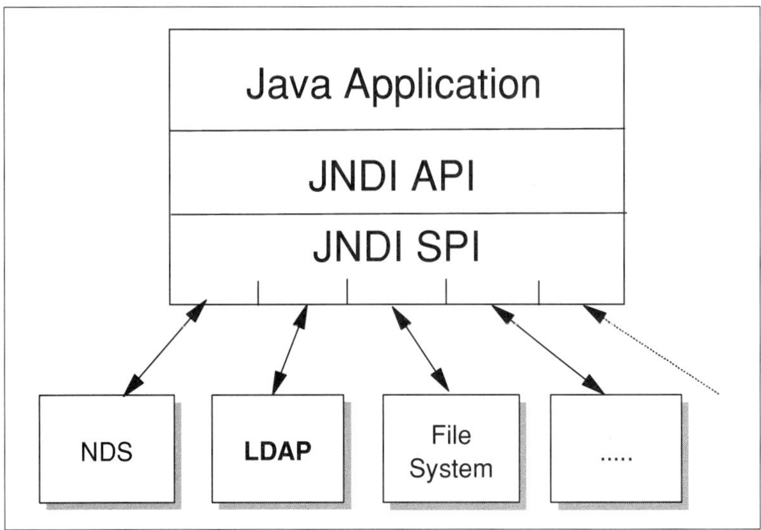

Figure 222. JNDI API and SPI interfaces

Java clients use JNDI to communicate with different types of naming services.

9.2 Naming concepts

A naming service is an entity that associates names with objects. In the following we describe some of the basic concepts used in JNDI.

Atomic: An atomic name is a simple, basic, indivisible component of a name. For example in the string C:\Winnt\Profiles, Winnt and Profiles are atomic names.

Compound: A compound name is a sequence of zero or more atomic names composed according to naming conventions. For example, the entire string C:\Winnt\Profiles is a compound name.

Binding: A binding is the association of a name with an object. For example, the file name config.sys on the Windows operating system has a binding to a file on the hard disk. Note that a compound name such as C:\Winnt\Profiles consists of multiple bindings, one to Winnt and one to Profiles.

Context: A context is an object that contains zero or more bindings. For example, a folder named /MyFolder that contains two files, file1 and file2 on a file system, is a Context that contains two bindings, one for file1 and another for file2 as shown in Figure 223 on page 350.

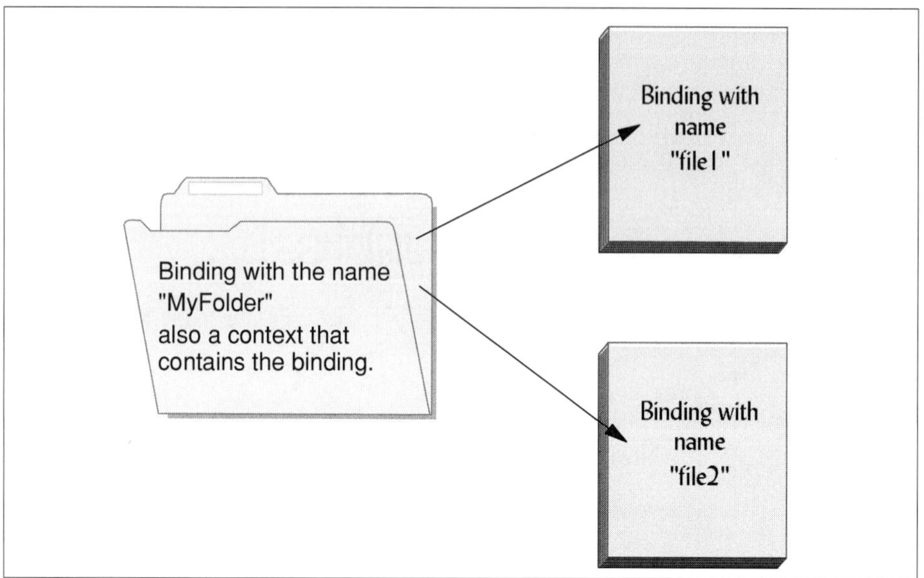

Figure 223. MyFolder is a context containing two binding

SubContext: Let's consider a folder C:\Winnt with subfolders C:\Winnt\Profiles and C:\Winnt\system32. Here, C:\Winnt is a context that contains the atomic names Profiles and system32. Subfolders are called subcontexts, each with its own name-object binding similar files or subfolders. A subcontext is a context within a context.

Naming system: A naming system is a connected set of contexts, for example, a folder tree in a file system.

Name space: A name space is all the names contained within a naming system.

InitialContext factory: JNDI performs all naming operations relative to a context. To assist in finding a place to start, the JNDI specification defines an InitialContext class. This class is instantiated with properties that define the type of naming service in use. This class also provides the ID and password to use when connecting for the naming services that provide security.

Directory objects: A directory object is a particular type of object that is used to represent the variety of information in a computing environment. Directory objects are usually associated with attributes. An attribute has an identifier and a set of values.

Figure 224 illustrates some of the concepts described above.

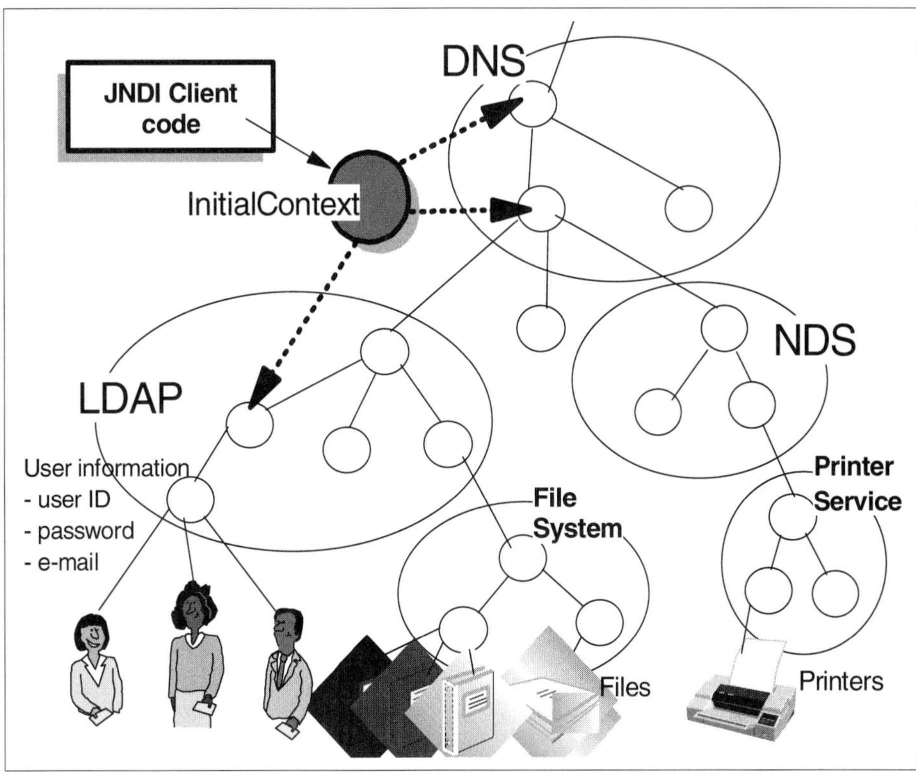

Figure 224. A Composite name space

9.3 JNDI specifications

This section discusses some important JNDI specifications.

9.3.1 JNDI packages

The JNDI packages that are provided are:

- javax.naming: Contains classes and interfaces for accessing naming services.
- javax.naming.directory: Extends the core javax.naming package to provide access to directories.
- javax.naming.event: Contains classes and interfaces for supporting event notification in naming and directory services.

- javax.naming.ldap: Contains classes and interfaces for supporting LDAP V3 extensions and controls.
- javax.naming.spi: Contains classes and interfaces that allow various naming and directory service providers to be dynamically plugged in beneath the JNDI API.

9.3.2 JNDI standard environment properties

The JNDI standard environment properties are described in Table 16.

Table 16. JNDI properties and their definitions

Environment property	Use
java.naming.factory.initial	Specifies the SPI
java.naming.provider.url	LDAP URL that specifies the LDAP server
java.naming.ldap.version	Specifies the LDAP version to use
java.naming.ldap.noBind	Specifies whether the client should bind to the server
java.naming.referall	Specifies if referral should be followed, ignored, or thrown an exception
java.naming.security.principal	Identity of user to authenticate
java.naming.security.credentials	Password or other security credential
java.naming.security.sasl	Class name of the SASL plug-in used to bind
java.naming.factory.url.pkgs	Colon-separated list of package prefixes to use when loading URL context factories
java.naming.dns.url	Specifies the DNS host and domain names
java.naming.batchsize	Specifies the preferred batch size to use when returning data via the services protocol

To use the LDAP V3 classes, one of the these two properties must be passed to the InitialDirContext constructor:

1. java.naming.factor.initial: This must be set to "com.ibm.jndi.LDAPCtxFactory" if you are going to use the context factory non-URL syntax.
2. java.naming.factor.url.pkgs: This property must be set to "com.ibm.jndi" if you are going to use the LDAP URL syntax.

9.4 JNDI sample application

LDAP servers are widely used in enterprise systems to store data such as users, profiles, and permissions.

Java programs can use JNDI to communicate with LDAP servers in the same way that they do to communicate with other naming systems such as WebSphere name server. There are some LDAP specific APIs provided by LDAP vendors, but the mechanism used to communicate between a Java program and an LDAP server is almost the same whether this program is communicating with an LDAP server or another naming server (such as WebSphere naming server). First we have to create an Initial Context, and then use it to connect and interact with the name server.

The JNDI code used by WebSphere to talk to LDAP servers is in a file called ibmjndi.jar. This JNDI implementation will work with the IBM SecureWay LDAP server and also works with other LDAP servers, such as Netscape Directory Server. Therefore, you don't need to install any LDAP server on the WebSphere node.

The following sample application describes how we can use JNDI to retrieve LDAP information in a WebSphere environment. This application allows a user to create a new entry in the LDAP server from an HTML page and also allows him to retrieve information from the LDAP server in a browser. Users must also authenticate before using the application. Figure 225 shows our test environment and Figure 226 on page 354 shows the architecture of our application.

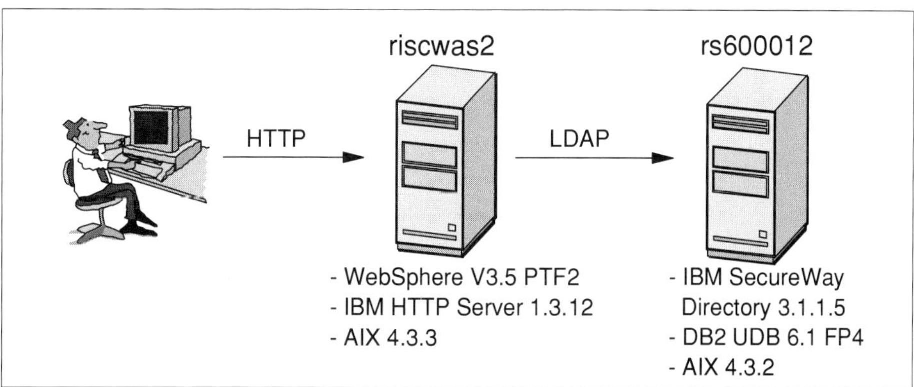

Figure 225. LdapSample test configuration

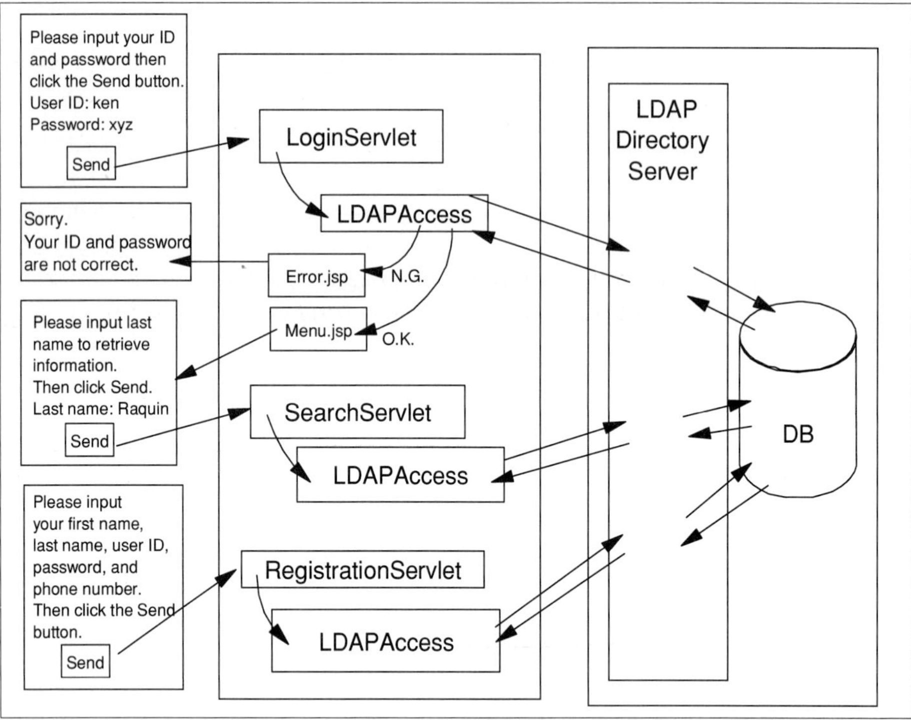

Figure 226. LdapSample architecture

9.4.1 Sample application design

In this sample application, all LDAP access is delegated to the class LDAPACCESS.

This class provides all the methods for authenticating users, retrieving information and adding new entries to the LDAP server.

Below is a description of this class's methods:

- authenticateUser(userId, password):

  Authenticates a user by trying to access the LDAP server using userId and password. Throws authenticationException if user is not allowed.

- addAttribute(userId,password,mail,firstName,LastName):

  Adds a new entry to the LDAP server. Parameters are passed as arguments to the method.

- retreiveAttribute(userID):

Retrieves information from the LDAP server by submitting a search on the userId supplied.

This class also stores information about LdapServer name, LdapRootName, ldapRootPassword and InitialContextFactory to use as instance variables. They are initialized from a properties file.

The application contains the following servlets:

- LoginServlet:

  Servlet for authenticating users. Invokes LdapAccess.authenticateUser(userId,password) for authentication.

- RegisrationServlet:

  Servlet for registering a user, that is adding a new entry to the LDAP server. Invokes LDAPAccess.addAttribute(userId, password,..).

- SearchServlet:

  Servlet for searching an entry in the LDAP server. Invokes LDAPAccess.searchAttribute(String userId).

9.4.2 Running the JNDI sample application

In the following, we demonstrate our sample JNDI application.

9.4.2.1 Adding a new entry

Before we register a new user using our sample program, there is only one entry under ou=ITSO, c=us in the LDAP server. Figure 227 on page 356 shows entries in the LDAP server before registration.

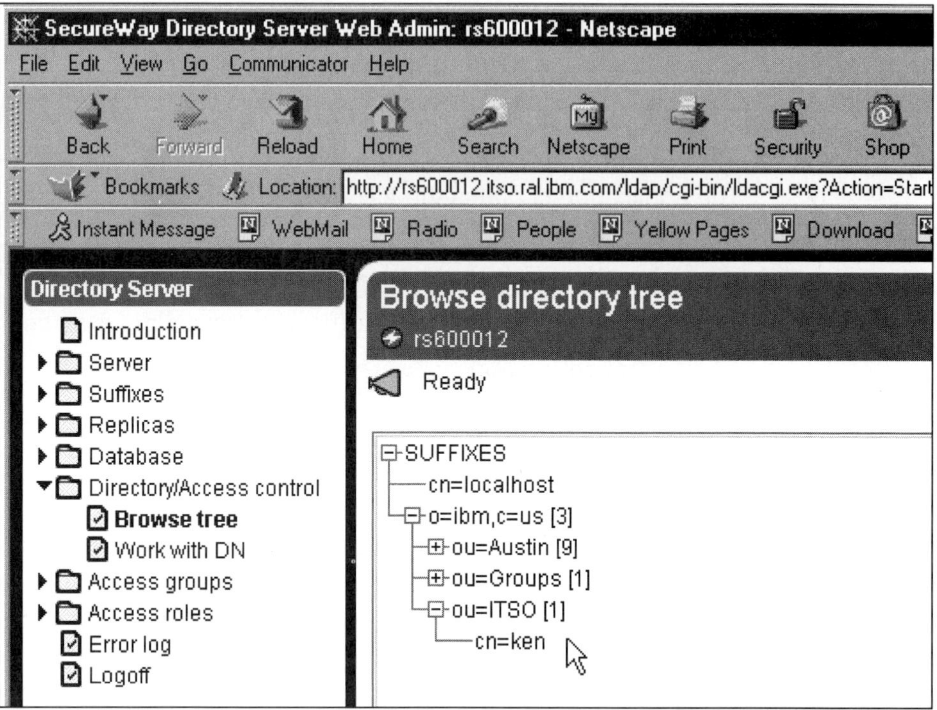

Figure 227. Entries in LDAP before registering a new user

We will add a new entry to the LDAP server using the HTML form (LdapLogin.html) as shown in Figure 228 on page 357. When the user clicks the **Submit** button, the Registration servlet is called with the parameters specified in the form. In our test case, we specified mohamed for the user ID and Ramdani for the last name. Note the last name Ramdani will be used later to retrieve detailed information about this user.

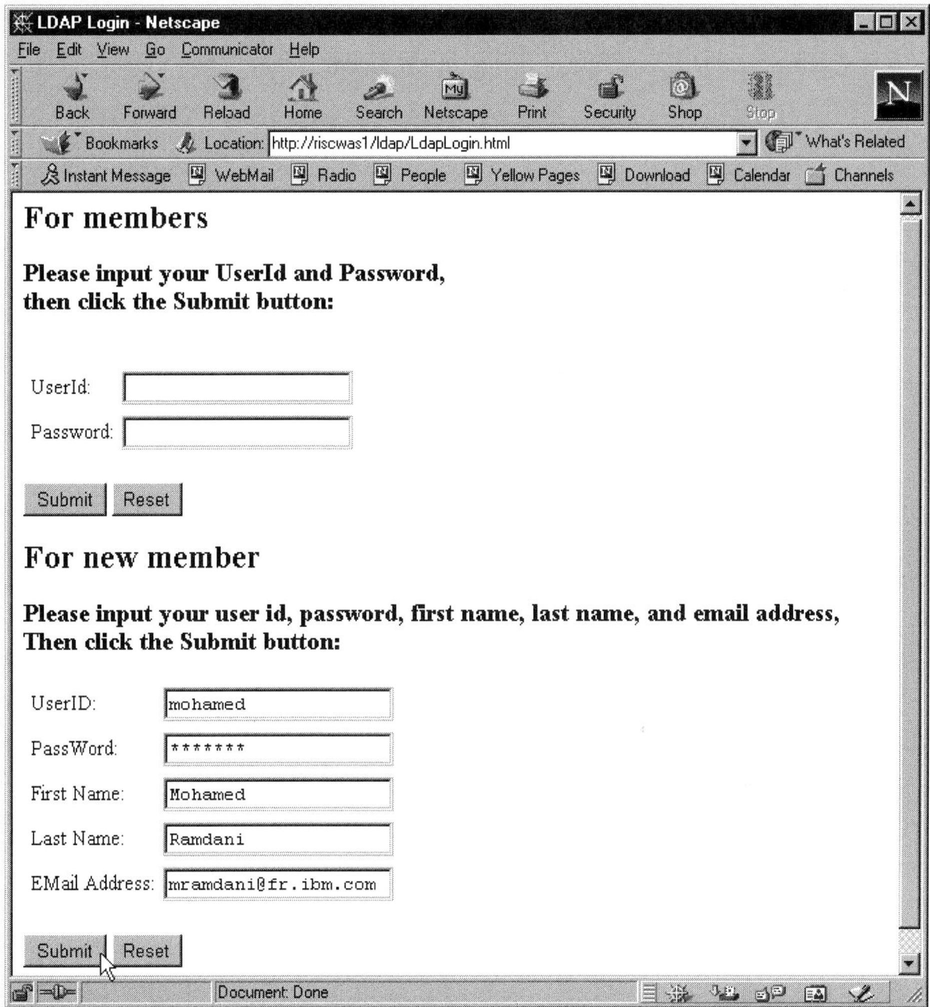

Figure 228. Welcome page for our sample

A new entry will be added to the LDAP server using the LDAPAccess class.

If the RegistrationServlet executes successfully (without any exception), a confirmation page will be sent to the browser as shown in Figure 229 on page 358.

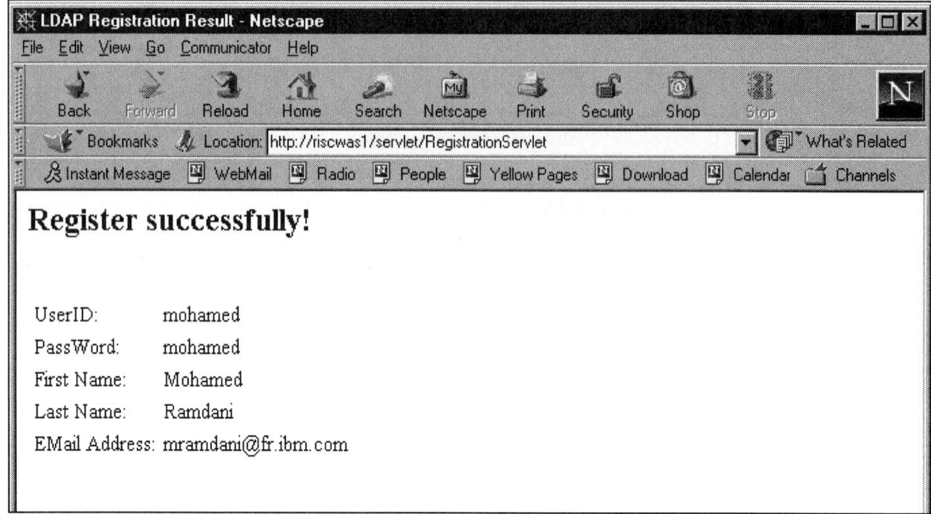

Figure 229. Successful registration

A new entry (in our case, cn=mohamed) was added to the LDAP server as shown in Figure 230.

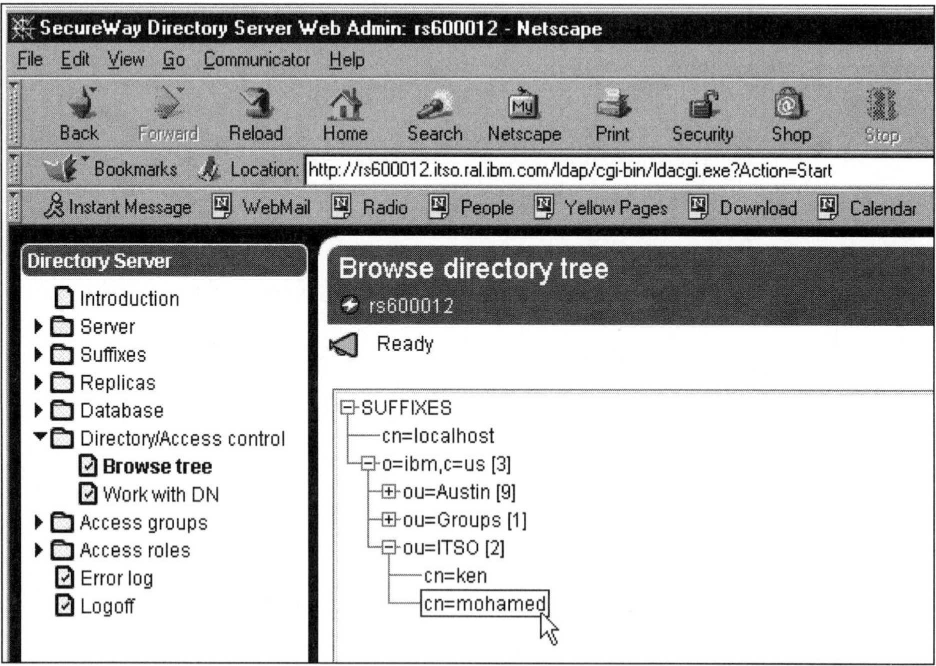

Figure 230. New entry added to LDAP server

Figure 231 shows you detailed information about the new registered user.

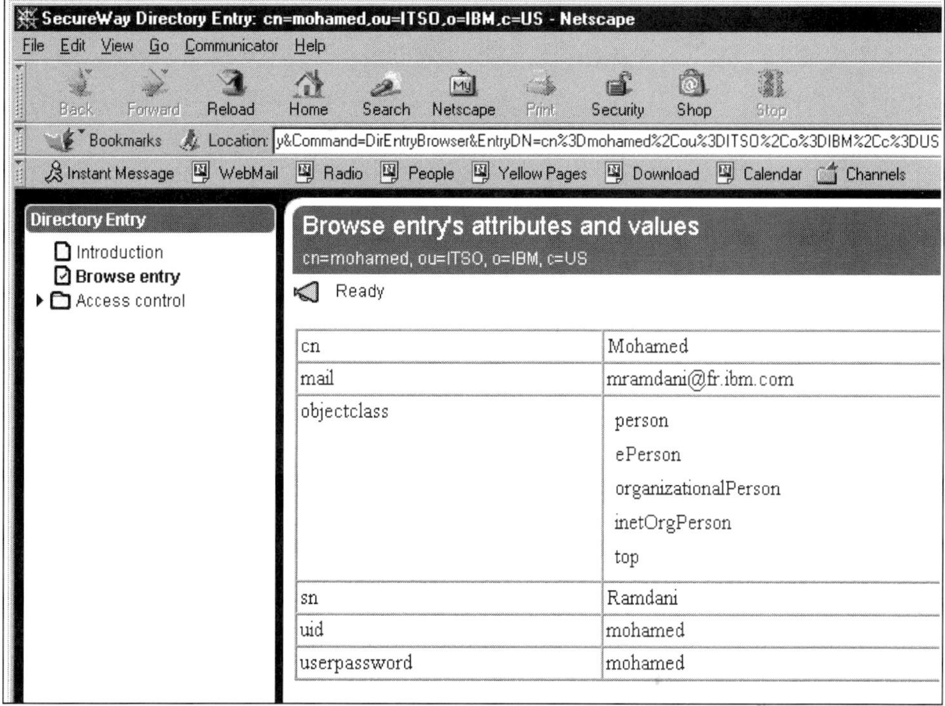

Figure 231. New registered user

9.4.2.2 Authenticating a user

The user has to authenticate first to access the search functionality of our application. The user ID and password provided in the HTML form (LdapLogin.html) as shown in Figure 232 on page 360 will be used to check if this user is declared and allowed to access the LDAP server.

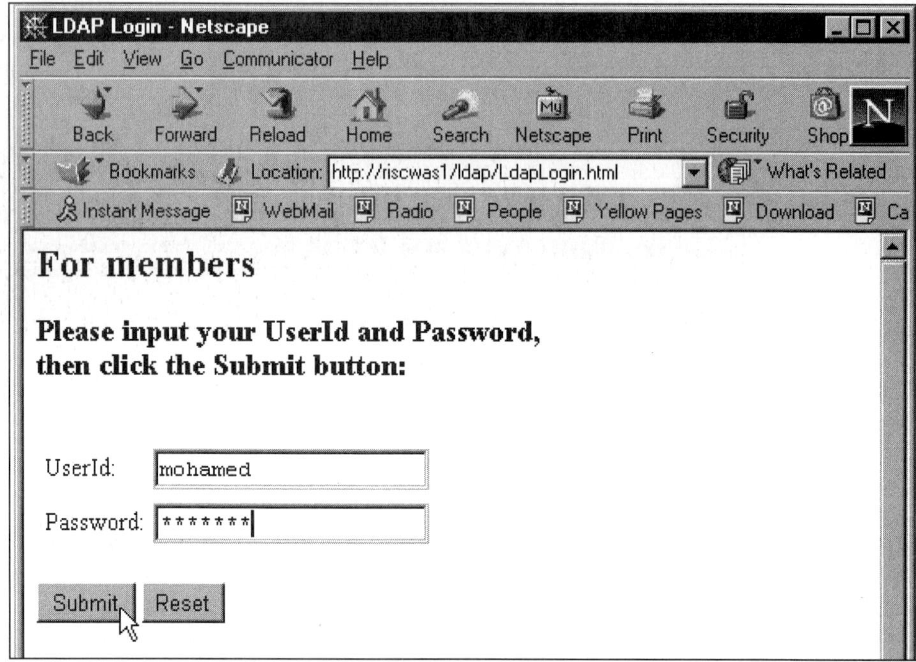

Figure 232. Authenticating a user

After clicking the **Submit** button, the LoginServlet servlet is called with the parameters UserId and password. The method authenticateUser(UserId,password) of the LDAPAccess class is called to check if this user is allowed to access LDAP.

9.4.2.3 Searching an entry

If the user authenticates successfully, the search information page is sent to the browser as shown in Figure 233 on page 361.

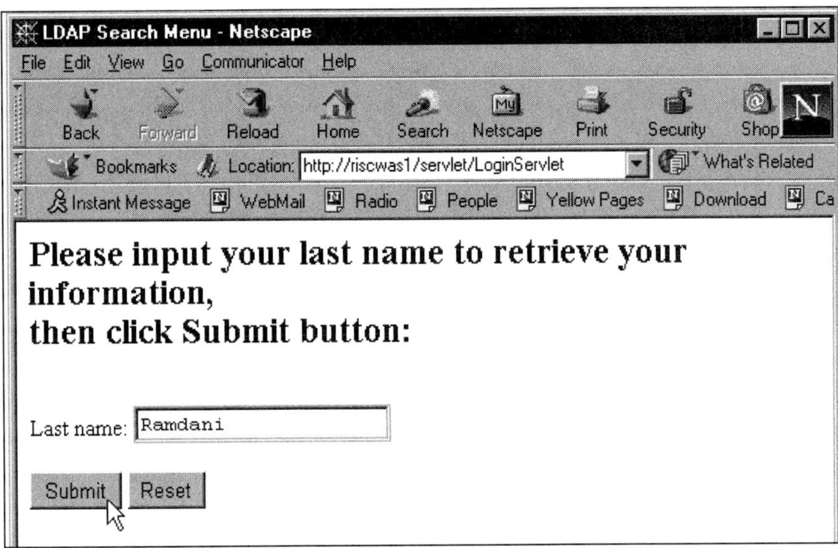

Figure 233. Searching an entry in LDAP

The last name provided in the HTML form will be used by the SearchServlet servlet to search LDAP for detailed information about the entry corresponding to sn=xxx (in our case, sn=Ramdani).

If an entry is found, all information is sent back to the browser as shown in Figure 234 on page 362.

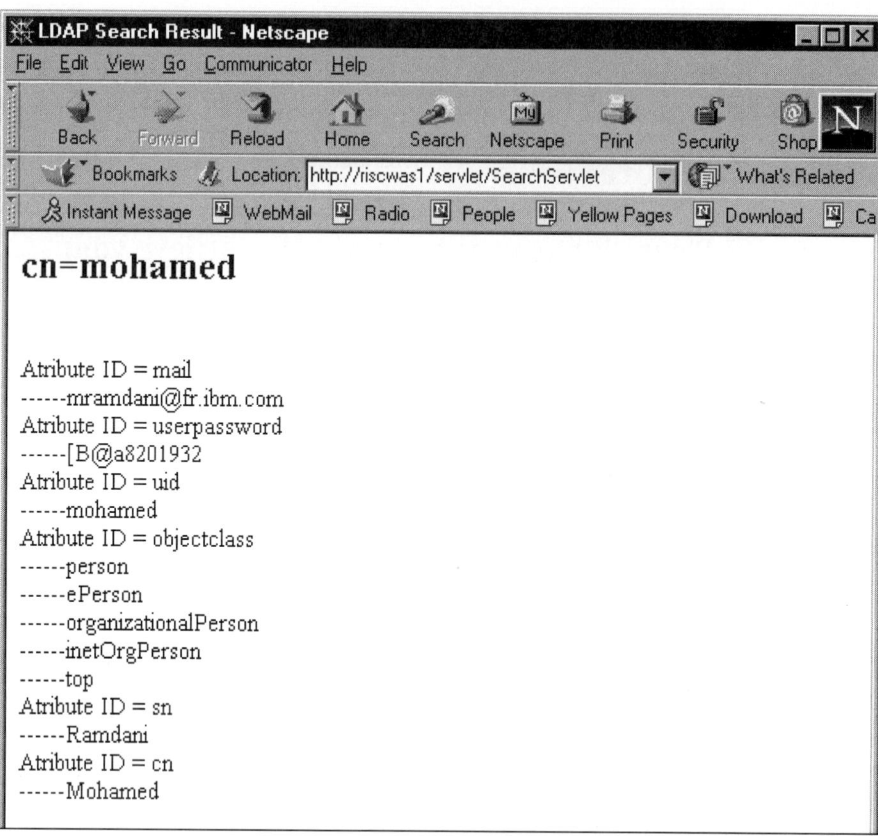

Figure 234. Retrieving information from LDAP

Information returned to the browser corresponds to the entry in the LDAP server illustrated in Figure 231 on page 359.

9.4.2.4 Authenticating with wrong user ID/password

If the user ID and password provided in the HTML form (LdapLogin.html) doesn't match an existing entry in the LDAP server (in our case, the correct password of mohamed has 8 characters but we specified 3 characters only, as shown in Figure 235) an error page will be sent to the browser as shown in Figure 236 on page 363.

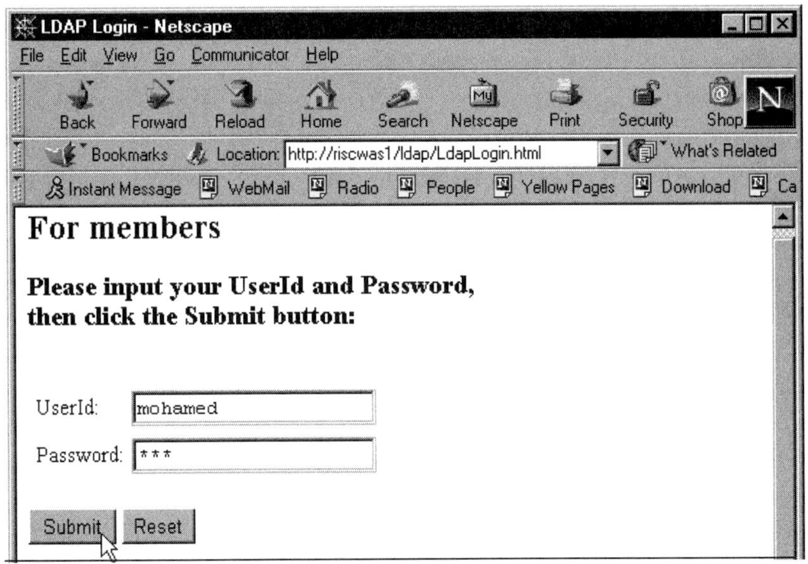

Figure 235. Log in with a wrong password

Figure 236. Error page

9.4.2.5 Searching a non-existing entry

If the last name provided in the HTML form does not exist in the LDAP server (in our case, user Kapadia is not registered), an error page will be sent to the browser as shown in Figure 238 on page 364.

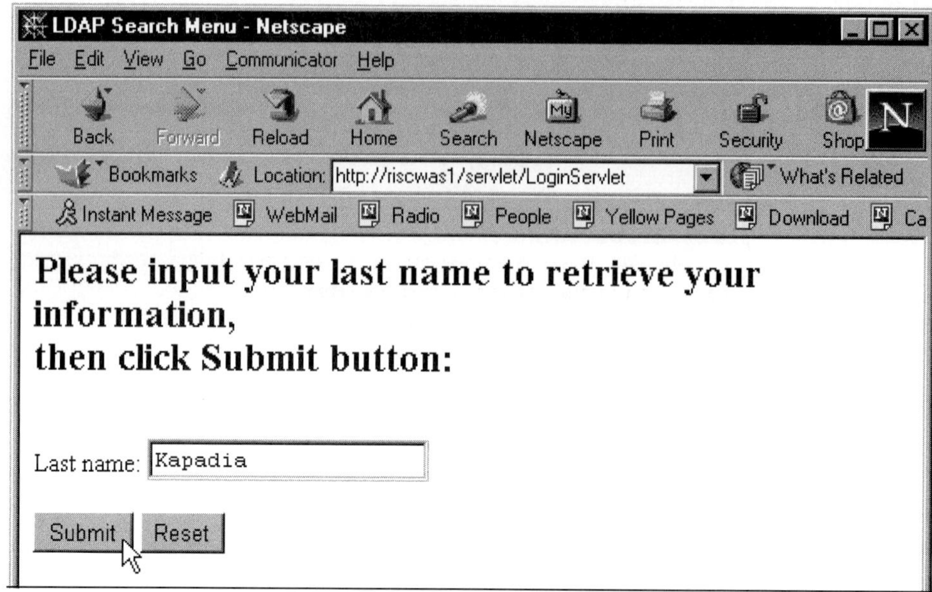

Figure 237. Searching a non-existing entry

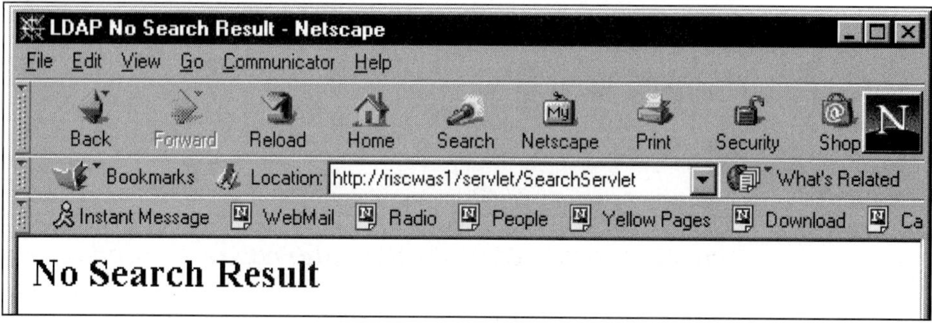

Figure 238. Error page

9.4.3 Sample LDAP access implementation

The following is the sample code for the class LDAPAccess. We describe the methods for authenticating, adding, and searching an entry from our LDAP server.

9.4.3.1 Authenticating to LDAP using user ID and password

```
public  void authenticateUser(String userID, String password) throws
NamingException {
   // initialize environment variables
   Properties env = new Properties() ;
   env.put("java.naming.factory.initial",initialContextFactory);
   env.put("java.naming.provider.url","ldap://"+LDAPServerName);
   // The following parameters are used for authentication
env.put("java.naming.security.principal","cn="+userID+",ou=itso,o=IBM,c
=us") ;
   env.put("java.naming.security.credentials",password) ;
   // connect to LDAP server using parameters specified above
   DirContext ctx = new InitialDirContext(env) ;
   return;
   }
```

Figure 239. Authenticating a user

In the environment properties we specify the Initial Context Factory and provider url as shown in Figure 240. These are general parameters that has to be specified.

```
   env.put("java.naming.factory.initial",initialContextFactory);
   env.put("java.naming.provider.url","ldap://"+LDAPServerName);
```

Figure 240. initialContextFactory and provider url

The java.naming.security.principal specifies the distinguished name to bind with, and the java.naming.security.credentials specifies the password for the distinguished name used for authentication as shown in Figure 241.

```
env.put("java.naming.security.principal","cn="+userID+",ou=itso,o=IBM,c
=us") ;
   env.put("java.naming.security.credentials",password) ;
```

Figure 241. Security principal and credentials

We authenticate by creating a new InitialDirContext using the properties specified before as shown in Figure 242 on page 366.

```
DirContext ctx = new InitialDirContext(env) ;
```

Figure 242. Creating a DirContext

If the user is not declared on the LDAP server, a naming exception is thrown. It is caught by the LoginServlet servlet as shown in Figure 243.

```
public  void authenticateUser(String userID, String password) throws
NamingException {
```

Figure 243. Naming exception

9.4.3.2 Adding an entry to the LDAP server

```
public void addAttribute(
   String firstName,
   String lastName,
   String mail,
   String uid,
   String password) {
   // set up properties to connet to ldap server
   Properties env = new Properties();
   env.put("java.naming.factory.initial",
"com.ibm.jndi.LDAPCtxFactory");
   env.put("java.naming.provider.url", "ldap://"+LDAPServerName);
   env.put("java.naming.security.principal", "cn="+LDAPRoot);
   env.put("java.naming.security.credentials", LDAPRootpassword);
   try {
      DirContext ctx = new InitialDirContext(env);
      String dn = "cn=" + uid + ",ou=ITSO,o=IBM,c=US";
      Attributes atrs = new BasicAttributes();
      Attribute objclasses = new BasicAttribute("objectclass");
      objclasses.add("top");
      objclasses.add("person");
      objclasses.add("organizationalPerson");
      objclasses.add("inetOrgPerson");
      objclasses.add("ePerson");
      atrs.put(objclasses);
      Attribute cn = new BasicAttribute("cn", firstName);
      Attribute sn = new BasicAttribute("sn", lastName);
      Attribute pwd = new BasicAttribute("userPassword", password);
      Attribute mail1 = new BasicAttribute("mail", mail);
      Attribute uid1 = new BasicAttribute("uid", uid);
      atrs.put(cn);
      atrs.put(sn);
      atrs.put(pwd);
      atrs.put(mail1);
      atrs.put(uid1);
      ctx.createSubcontext(dn, atrs);
   }
   catch (Exception e) { // we catch all exceptions here
      System.out.println("Error add attribute ");
      e.printStackTrace();
   }
}
```

Figure 244. Adding an entry to LDAP server

Before adding an entry to the LDAP server, we need to authenticate using a distinguished name and a password. This user must have write access to add an entry. In our example we used Root for authentication as shown in Figure 245.

```
    Properties env = new Properties();
    env.put("java.naming.factory.initial",
"com.ibm.jndi.LDAPCtxFactory");
    env.put("java.naming.provider.url", "ldap://"+LDAPServerName);
    env.put("java.naming.security.principal", "cn="+LDAPRoot);
    env.put("java.naming.security.credentials", LDAPRootpassword);
```

Figure 245. Setting properties to connect to the LDAP server

We create all the attributes using BasicAttribute and BasicAttributes classes as shown in Figure 246.

```
        Attributes atrs = new BasicAttributes();
        Attribute objclasses = new BasicAttribute("objectclass");
        objclasses.add("top");
        objclasses.add("person");
        objclasses.add("organizationalPerson");
        objclasses.add("inetOrgPerson");
        objclasses.add("ePerson");
        atrs.put(objclasses);
        Attribute cn = new BasicAttribute("cn", firstName);
        Attribute sn = new BasicAttribute("sn", lastName);
        Attribute pwd = new BasicAttribute("userPassword", password);
        Attribute mail1 = new BasicAttribute("mail", mail);
        Attribute uid1 = new BasicAttribute("uid", uid);
        atrs.put(cn);
        atrs.put(sn);
        atrs.put(pwd);
        atrs.put(mail1);
        atrs.put(uid1);
```

Figure 246. Creating attributes

We finally add the entry by calling the createSubContext on the DirContext object as shown in Figure 247 on page 369.

```
      ctx.createSubcontext(dn, atrs);
```

Figure 247. Adding an entry

9.4.3.3 Searching information

```
public NamingEnumeration searchAttribute(String uid) {
   Properties env = new Properties() ;
   env.put("java.naming.factory.initial",initialContextFactory) ;
   // we use root and root password for authentication. The user has
already authenticated
   env.put("java.naming.provider.url","ldap://"+LDAPServerName);
   env.put("java.naming.security.principal","cn="+LDAPRoot) ;
   env.put("java.naming.security.credentials",LDAPRootpassword) ;
   // we explicitly specify the base and the filter for the search
   String base = "ou=ITSO,o=IBM,c=US";
   String filter ="sn="+uid;
   NamingEnumeration results=null;
   SearchControls constraints = new SearchControls();
   constraints.setSearchScope(SearchControls.SUBTREE_SCOPE);
try
   {
      DirContext ctx = new InitialDirContext(env) ;
      results = ctx.search(base,filter,constraints) ;
   } catch (Exception e) {
      System.out.println("Error accessing LDAP Server");
      e.printStackTrace();
   }
   return results;
}
```

Figure 248. Searching for an entry in LDAP server

For searching information, we need to set up the JNDI properties as shown in Figure 249 on page 370.

```
    Properties env = new Properties() ;
    env.put("java.naming.factory.initial",initialContextFactory) ;
    // we use root and root password for authentication. The user has
already authenticated
    env.put("java.naming.provider.url","ldap://"+LDAPServerName);
    env.put("java.naming.security.principal","cn="+LDAPRoot) ;
    env.put("java.naming.security.credentials",LDAPRootpassword) ;
```

Figure 249. JNDI properties

Then we need to authenticate. We explicitly specify a base and a filter for the search as shown in Figure 250.

```
    String base = "ou=ITSO,o=IBM,c=US";
    String filter ="sn="+uid;
    NamingEnumeration results=null;
    SearchControls constraints = new SearchControls();
    constraints.setSearchScope(SearchControls.SUBTREE_SCOPE);
```

Figure 250. Specifying the base, the filter and the search scope

We then call the search method with those parameters on the DirContext object as shown in Figure 251.

```
        DirContext ctx = new InitialDirContext(env) ;
        results = ctx.search(base,filter,constraints) ;
```

Figure 251. Connecting to the LDAP server and executing the search

The return result is a NamingEnumeration object that we need to parse to get each attribute as shown in Figure 252.

```
    NamingEnumeration results=null;
```

Figure 252. Returning a NamingEnumeration

See *LDAP V3 Client for Java Programing Guide* that comes with IBM SecureWay for detailed information.

Chapter 10. JDBC 2.0 support

The JDBC API was designed to provide a Java application programming interface to data access of relational databases. JDBC 1.0 provided the basic functionality for this access. JDBC 2.0 API extends the JDBC 1.0 API to provide additional functionality, simplify coding, and increase performance.

WebSphere V3.5 supports the JDBC 2.0 API.

This section discusses the explicit coding to the JDBC API. The following topics are covered:

- The JDBC 2.0 Core API
- The JDBC 2.0 Extension API
- Administration of data sources
- Best practices for JDBC data access

In this chapter, we describe explicit coding to the JDBC API for data access. The JDBC API can be used for data access using Java beans, servlets, or bean-managed persistence (BMP) EJBs. Container-managed persistence (CMP) EJBs can also be used for data access, but they do not require explicit coding to the JDBC API. EJBs are discussed in Chapter 11, "Enterprise Java Services" on page 393. JSPs can also access data using special tags that are provided in WebSphere's JSP support.

10.1 JDBC 2.0 Core API

The JDBC API provides data access through three basic steps:

- Establish a connection with a data source
- Send queries or update (SQL) statements to the DBMS
- Process the results

The code fragment in Figure 253 on page 372 shows a simple example of accessing the table sample in the data source employees. The code creates a connection using the DriverManager interface (JDBC 1.0), creates an SQL query statement to obtain three fields (the employee number, the employee first name, and the employee last name), and then iterates through the ResultSet.

```
try {
Connection conn =
DriverManager.getConnection(dbDriver,userid,password);
Statement stmt = conn.createStatement();
ResultSet rs = stmt.executeQuery("SELECT EMPNO, FIRSTNME, LASTNAME FROM SAMPLE");
while (rs.next()) {
String empno = rs.getString("EMPNO");
String firstnme = rs.getString("FIRSTNME");
String lastname = rs.getString("LASTNAME");
}
}
catch (Exception theException) {
// Handle Exception
}
```

Figure 253. Sample program using the DriverManager interface

The JDBC 2.0 API includes new features to simplify application design and development, and to improve performance. JDBC 2.0 is divided into JDBC 2.0 Core API and JDBC 2.0 Optional Extension API. The JDBC 2.0 Core API is a superset of JDBC 1.0. New features supported include scrollable result sets, batch updates, programmatic insert, delete, and update, and SQL 3 data type support. These are discussed in this section.

The JDBC 2.0 Core API is defined by the classes and interfaces in the java.sql.* package. Table 17 and Table 18 on page 373 show the javadoc for the classes and interfaces of the java.sql.* package.

Table 17. java.sql. class summary*

Class name	Description
Date	A thin wrapper around a millisecond value that allows JDBC to identify this as a SQL DATE.
DriverManager	The basic service for managing a set of JBDC drivers.
DriverPropertyInfo	Driver properties for making a connection.
Time	A thin wrapper around java.util.Date that allows JDBC to identify this as a SQL TIMESTAMP value.
Timestamp	This class is a thin wrapper around java.util.Date that allows JDBC to identify this as a SQL TIMESTAMP value.
Types	The class that defines constants that are used to identify generic SQL types, called JDBC types.

Table 18. java.sql. Interface summary*

Interface name	Description
Array	Array.
Blob	Binary Large Object.
CallableStatement	The interface used to execute SQL stored procedures.
Clob	Character Large Object.
Connection	A connection (session) with a specific database.
DatabaseMetaData	Comprehensive information about the database as a whole.
Driver	The interface that every driver class must implement.
PreparedStatement	An object that represents a precompiled SQL statement.
Ref	A reference to an SQL structured type value in the database.
ResultSet	A ResultSet provides access to a table of data.
ResultSetMetaData	An object that can be used to find out about the types and properties of the columns in a ResultSet.
SQLData	The interface used for the custom mapping of SQL user-defined types.
SQLInput	An input stream that contains a stream of values representing an instance of an SQL structured or distinct type.
SQLOutput	The output stream for writing the attributes of a user-defined type back to the database.
Statement	The object used for executing a static SQL statement and obtaining the results produced by it.
Struct	Structure.

10.1.1 Scrollable ResultSets

A ResultSet is an enumeration of rows of information that are returned from SQL queries. JDBC 1.0 supported forward-only ResultSets. This provided the ability to scroll forward through a ResultSet processing each row.

JDBC 2.0 supports forward-only, scroll-insensitive, or scroll-sensitive ResultSets. A scroll-insensitive or scroll-sensitive ReultSet allows rows to be examined by scrolling forward (first to last), backward (last to first) or positioning at an absolute row position.

A scroll-insensitive ResultSet is unaware of changes made to the underlying database while it is open. A scroll-sensitive ResultSet is aware of the underlying database updates.

10.1.2 Batch update

Batch update allows multiple update SQL requests to be specified with a single Statement object and submitted at one time to the DBMS. JDBC 1.0 required that each SQL Statement would request one action. Multiple actions required multiple requests issued to the DBMS.

Batch update allows multiple requests (for updates, not queries) to be issued to the DBMS at one time. Batch Update can be requested using a Statement object, a PreparedStatement object, or a CallableStatement object. (A Statement is a fully specified SQL statement without variables. A PreparedStatement is an SQL statement that contains parameters that are specified prior to executing the statement. A CallableStatement is a macro that requests a pre-specified set of SQL statements that are known to the DBMS.)

10.1.3 Fetch size

The fetch size is the number of rows retrieved from a database query. JDBC 2.0 allows the fetch size to be specified, thus allowing performance tuning of the size of the results obtained from the DBMS.

10.1.4 Advanced datatypes

Advanced datatypes defined as part of SQL3 are supported in JDBC 2.0. These include two new built-in types called Binary Large Objects (BLOB) and Character Large Objects (CLOB), SQL3 structured types (structures of built-in types and other structures), constructed types (including arrays), and locator types (which are logical pointers to DBMS data).

10.2 JDBC 2.0 Optional Extension API

The JDBC 2.0 Optional Extension API is an extension of the Core API. The optional extension supports integration with new Java standards including JNDI (Java Naming and Directory Interface), Java Beans, JTA (Java Transaction API), and EJBs (Enterprise JavaBeans).

The Optional Extension API is specified in the javax.sql.* package. Table 19 and Table 20 show the classes and interfaces of the javax.sql.* package.

Table 19. javax.sql. Class summary*

Class name	Description
ConnectionEvent	The ConnectionEvent class provides information about the source of a connection-related event.
RowSetEvent	A RowSetEvent is generated when something important happens in the life of a RowSet, such as when a column value changes.

Table 20. javax.sql. Interface summary*

Interface name	Description
ConnectionEventListener	A ConnectionEventListener is an object that registers to receive events generated by a PooledConnection.
ConnectionPoolDataSource	A ConnectionPoolDataSource object is a factory for PooledConnection objects.
DataSource	A DataSource object is a factory for Connection objects.
PooledConnection	A PooledConnection object is a Connection object that provides hooks for the connection pool manager.
RowSet	The RowSet interface adds support to the JDBC API for the JavaBeans component model.
RowSetInternal	A rowset object presents itself to a reader or writer as an instance of RowSetInternal.
RowSetListener	The RowSetListener interface is implemented by a component that wants to be notified when a significant event happens in the life of a RowSet.
RowSetMetaData	The RowSetMetaData interface extends ResultSetMetaData with methods that allow a metadata object to be initialized.
RowSetReader	An object implementing the RowSetReader interface may be registered with a RowSet object that supports the reader/writer paradigm.
RowSetWriter	An object that implements the RowSetWriter interface may be registered with a RowSet object that supports the reader/writer paradigm.

Interface name	Description
XAConnection	An XAConnection object provides support for distributed transactions.
XADataSource	A factory for XAConnection objects.

10.2.1 JNDI for naming databases

In JDBC 1.0, the DriverManager interface was used exclusively to obtain a connection to a data source. The database driver, user ID, and password for the data source were specified explicitly in the getConnection request. A single connection (not a connection in the connection pool, see 10.2.2, "Connection pooling" on page 376) would be provided using the following method:

Connection conn = DriverManager.getConnection(dbDriver,userid,password);

In JDBC 2.0, a Naming Service locates the data source. An initial naming context is obtained, and then the data source is located by doing a lookup. The data source "name" provided on the ctx.lookup(name) is not the physical name of the data source, but is the logical name for the data source that has been defined administratively. This allows change to the JDBC driver to be updated administratively rather than by code compilation.

```
try {
   java.util.Hashtable env= new java.util.Hashtable();
   env.put(Context.INITIAL_CONTEXT_FACTORY,
   "com.ibm.ejs.ns.jndi.CNInitialContextFactory");

   // Create the Initial Naming Context.
   ctx = new InitialContext(env);

   // Perform a naming service lookup to get a DataSource object.
   ds = (javax.sql.DataSource) ctx.lookup(dbJndi);
}
catch (Throwable theException) {
   // Handle Exception
   theException.printStackTrace();
}
```

10.2.2 Connection pooling

Each Web request that requires access to a database must connect to that database (generally via a TCP/IP connection). The overhead to acquire a new connection, maintain it, and release it often far surpasses the time to perform the actual database query. There is significant performance gain from pooling connections so that connections are only acquired and released when necessary.

The Optional Extension API allows (optionally) connection pooling using the javax.sql.DataSource object as a factory for these connections. The DataSource object acquires a pool of connections and manages those connections. Applications then acquire a connection and release a connection to/from the pool of connections respectively.

In the code fragment in Figure 254, a connection is obtained from the connection pool using the DataSource factory using getConnection(). The connection is returned to the connection pool using close().

```
try
      {
//          Get a Connection from DataSource Factory
//          Get a Connection object conn using the DataSource factory.
            conn = ds.getConnection(dbAttr.userid, dbAttr.pwd);
      // execute query
      // process results
       }

      catch (Exception theException)
      {
   // Handle Exception
      }

   finally {
      if(conn!=null) conn.close();
   // other cleanup
}
```

Figure 254. Sample program using the connection pool

In Version 2.0x of WebSphere, the JDBC 2.0 API was not available. There was no standard means of providing connection pooling. WebSphere V2.0x provided a proprietary means for applications to achieve connection pooling through the IBM Connection Manager API. The IBM Connection Manager APIs are still supported in WebSphere V3.5x; however, this support is deprecated. It is strongly recommended that applications migrate to the new JDBC 2.0 connection pooling standard; it is the JDBC 2.0 connection pooling that is discussed in this chapter.

10.2.3 Distributed transaction support (JTA support)

Distributed transactions are transactions where commands are sent to multiple databases (on single node or multiple nodes). The Java Transaction API (JTA) specifies the Java interfaces between a transaction manager and the parties involved in a distributed transaction system. These parties include the application, the resource manager, and the application server.

The key object in JTA is the javax.transaction.UserTransaction. Developers can use a UserTransaction to begin, commit, or roll back transactions. The UserTransaction interface can be used in WebSphere for Java clients including servlets, JSPs, and stand-alone programs. JTA is described in detail in Chapter 12, "Transactions" on page 503.

10.2.4 RowSets

A RowSet object is a JavaBean component that can be used to represent tabular data on top of JDBC. Such objects can be transmitted across the network, and thus simplify distributed applications.

10.2.5 IBM JDBC 2.0 extensions

In addition to the JDBC 2.0 extensions provided in javax.sql.* package as described above, IBM also provides some extensions to JDBC 2.0. Further information on these is contained in the WebSphere InfoCenter but in brief:

- Access DataSourceFactory.createJDBCDataSource(.....) and createJTADataSource(......), bindDataSource , rebindDataSource etc, is provided from the package:

  ```
  import com.ibm.websphere.appserver.cm.factory.*;
  ```

- To Access ConnectionWaitTimeoutException and IllegalIsolationLevelChangeException the following package is required:

  ```
  import com.ibm.ejs.cm.pool.*;
  ```

- Support for StaleConnectionException (discussed futher in 10.5, "Recovery from DB failures" on page 389) is provided by:

  ```
  import com.ibm.ejs.cm.portability.*;
  ```

WebSphere data sources

In WebSphere V3.02, data sources are indexed by database URL, user name and password in use. Therefore, a pool is created for every unique combination of URL, user, password. In V3.5 the data source implementation was rewritten to index the data source by the DataSource name, which corresponds to the database URL. Hence, a single connection pool is created with one DataSource, and the pool can have connections for different database users/passwords.

Consider the following example:

Two servlets use the same data source with different user IDs and each servlet is only invoked once. Assuming that the maximum connection pool size for the data source is at least two (or greater), then you will observe two connections for the data source in the WebSphere Resource Analyzer.

This is because it is not possible to change the user ID/password on an existing connection. You'll not observe reuse of a connection until a user needs a connection and finds one already in the pool for his user ID. If there is not one in the pool for his user ID, then the connection manager will create a new one. If the connection pool maximum is hit, and the connection manager cannot find a connection in the free pool for a given user, but there are connections in the freepool, the connection manager will destroy one of the free connections and allocate a new one on behalf of the requesting user ID.

10.3 Administration of data sources

Administration of a data source requires creating a DataSource via the WebSphere Administrative Console or via XMLConfig. Creation of a data source requires specification of a DataSource name (the logical JNDI name), the name of the underlying datasource (DBMS name) as well as the database driver to be utilized.

From the administrative console, select **Topology view -> WebSphere Administrative Domain**, then right click and select **Create -> DataSource** as shown in Figure 255 on page 380.

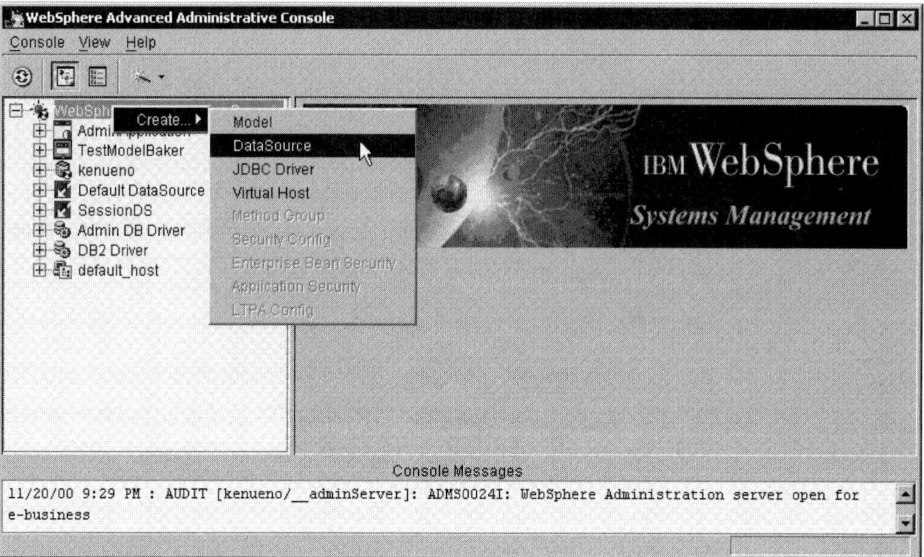

Figure 255. Create DataSource from Topology view

Then you will get the Create a DataSource window as shown in Figure 256 on page 381.

On the General tab, you need to specify data source name, database name and driver name. In this example, we use the sample database that is provided with DB2, and the administrative database driver.

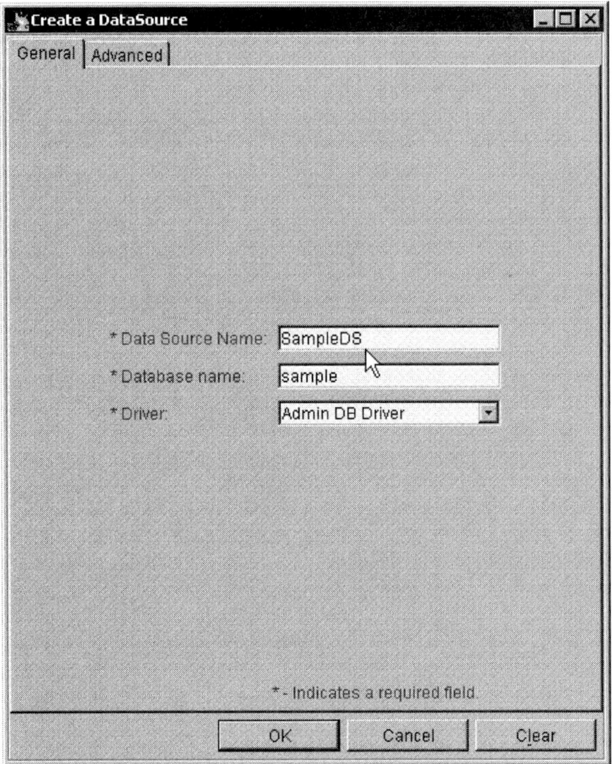

Figure 256. Create a DataSource: General tab

On the Advanced tab, there are several parameters that can be configured for a data source as shown in Figure 257 on page 382.

The minimum connection pool size is the initial number of connections established (even without requests).

The maximum connection pool size is the maximum number of connections that can be established.

There are three timeouts that are specified:

1. The connection timeout is the maximum amount of time in seconds that a request for a connection will wait if all connections in the pool are in use.
2. The idle timeout is the maximum amount of time in seconds that an idle (not utilized) connection remains in the connection pool before being freed.

3. The orphan timeout is the maximum amount of time in seconds that an allocated connection remains before being returned to the pool (taken away from the object to which it was allocated).

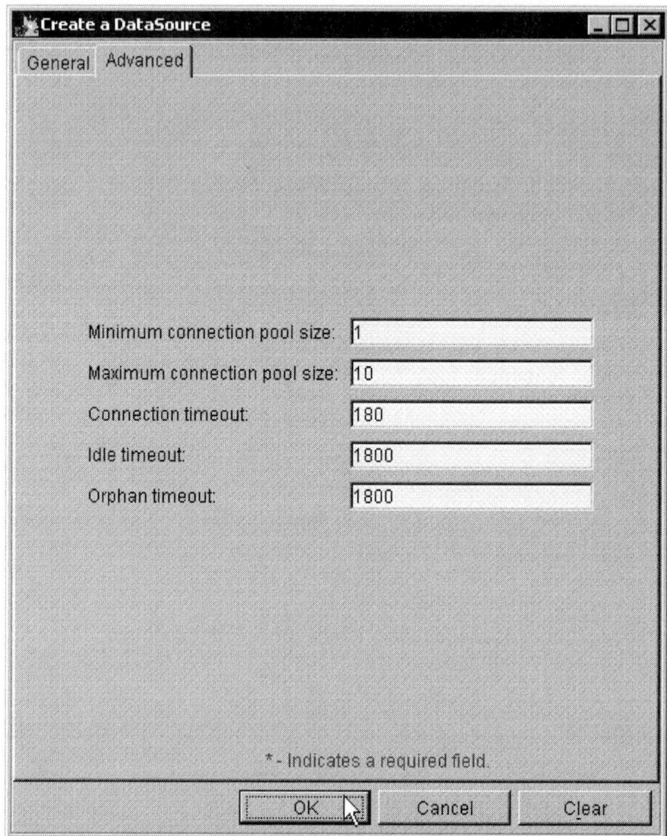

Figure 257. Create a DataSource: Advanced tab

Then click **OK**.

You will get the confirmation dialog and click **OK** as shown in Figure 258.

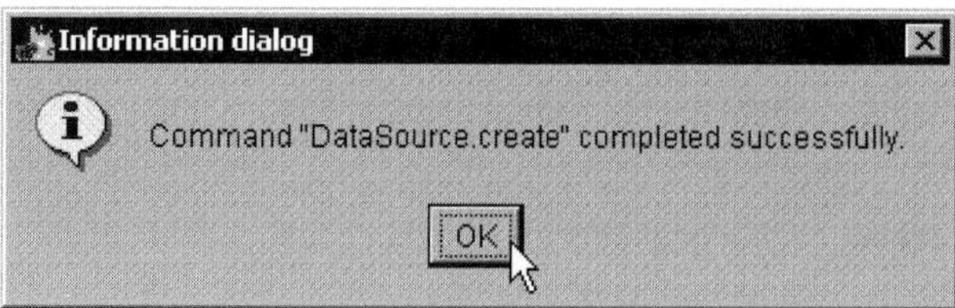

Figure 258. DataSource creation confirmation dialog

10.3.1 datasources.xml property file

The datasources.xml property file can be used to further configure DataSources. The datasources.xml property file can be created in <WAS_HOME>/properties directory (c:\WebSphere\AppServer\properties by default on Windows) to reflect the additional configuration settings.

The only property in the datasources.xml file that WebSphere supports for all databases is the PreparedStatementCache size. This is the number of precompiled PreparedStatement objects held in an in-memory WebSphere cache. The default value for this cache size (in the absence of datasources.xml information) is 100. Guidelines for sizing of the cache are discussed in *WebSphere V3 Performance Tuning Guide*, SG24-5657.

In addition to the PreparedStatementCache size, other database properties, such as a defaultRowPrefetch, can be specified. If the database supports further properties on a connection, then WebSphere passes those properties to the database when a connection is obtained; it is solely the responsibility of the database/JDBC driver as to which additional properties can be specified. Review the online manual (InfoCenter) for their database/JDBC drivers to determine which properties may be set.

Figure 259 is a sample datasources.xml property file that specifies the PreparedStatement cache size (a property used by WebSphere) and the default row prefetch size (a property passed to the database driver for processing).

```
<data-sources>
   <data-source name="sample">
      <attribute name="statementCacheSize" value="150" />
      <attribute name="defaultRowPrefetch" value="25" />
   </data-source>
</data-sources>
```

Figure 259. datasources.xml property file

10.4 Best practices for JDBC 2.0 data access with WebSphere

There are a variety of best practices for application coding and configuration of data access using JDBC 2.0 with WebSphere. These are described below.

10.4.1 Select database manager/driver capabilities

WebSphere V3.5x provides generic support for both the JDBC 2.0 Core API and Optional Extensions API. However, some advanced features (specifically of the Optional Extensions API) are supported only by some database drivers.

Several database drivers have been tested with WebSphere. The database drivers that have been tested are those that can be chosen for the WebSphere administrative database. All of the database drivers tested (which are suitable for the WebSphere administrative database) support connection pooling. The support for two-phase commit (and JTA) are detailed in the tables below. Table 21 shows the DB2 support, Table 22 shows the Oracle support, and Table 23 shows the Sybase support. New drivers are added to the supported list periodically. Please refer to the IBM WebSphere Web site to obtain the latest information.

Table 21. DB2 support

DB 2 Support 2PC/JTA	DB2 6.1 [FP 4/5]	DB2 7.1 [FP 1]
AIX	Yes	Yes
Solaris	Yes	Yes
HP-UX	No	No
Windows NT/x86 and 2000	Yes	Yes

Table 22. Oracle support

Oracle Support 2PC/JTA	Oracle 8.1.6 (Thin and Thick) and Oracle 1241123
AIX	No (Oracle Limitation*)
Solaris	No (Oracle Limitation*)
HP-UX	No (Oracle Limitation*)
Windows NT/x86 and 2000	No (Oracle Limitation*)

*Oracle does not support xa_recover and xa_forget. See `http://technet.oracle.com`.

Table 23. Sybase support

Sybase Support	Sybase ASE 12.0	Sybase 11.9/11.5 WebSphere V3.5.1 Required
AIX	Yes	Yes (with jConnect 5.2)
Solaris	Yes	Yes (with jConnect 5.2)

Sybase Support	Sybase ASE 12.0	Sybase 11.9/11.5 WebSphere V3.5.1 Required
Windows NT/x86 (WebSphereV3.5.1)	Yes	Yes (with jConnect 5.2)

10.4.2 Use connection pooling for JDBC access

Connection pooling makes a significant impact on application performance. If a JDBC driver is selected that supports connection pooling, and a DataSource object is used to acquire connections, then connection pooling is used without requiring significant application coding.

Initializing the data source via JNDI rather than using the DriverManager interface allows for the database driver to be specified administratively, rather than hard-coded.

10.4.3 Configure connection pool sizes

There are five parameters configured via the WebSphere Administrative Console for connection pools: minimum (or starting) connection pool size, maximum connection pool size, connection timeout, idle timeout, and orphan timeout.

The maximum connection pool size should be large enough to provide a high probability that a new request has access to an open connection. The size of the pool needs to be balanced against the performance impact of creating too large a pool and the delay incurred when a request has to wait for an open connection. The specifics for any environment should be made through performance experiments prior to production deployment, and confirmed using the Resource Analyzer during production. The maximum connection pool size should also ensure that the maximum number of connections does not exceed the available database licenses or network infrastructure capability.

The minimum connection pool size should be sufficiently large to address the startup performance penalty that can occur when the connection pool grows in response to an increase in load.

10.4.4 Configure connection pool timeouts

The connection timeout is the maximum amount of time in seconds that a request for a connection (a getConnection() request) will wait if all connections in the pool are in use. In general, the connection timeout should be less than the expected browser timeout value. This allows the connection timeout to occur, the exception to be caught by the application, and user-friendly error page (such as server busy, please retry) to be displayed to the user, rather than a browser timeout error page. In addition, in a system whose database or database connections are overloaded, a sufficiently small connection timeout value would prevent the database query from being performed when the results would (of necessity) be discarded by the application due to a browser timeout. The connection timeout should be large enough to allow for reasonable queueing delays to the database server.

The idle timeout is the maximum amount of time in seconds that an idle (not utilized) connection remains in the connection pool before being freed. The idle timeout should be configured to allow reasonable sharing of connection resources between the WebSphere processes and any other processes using the same database.

The orphan timeout is the maximum amount of time in seconds that an allocated connection remains before it is deemed orphaned, and returned to the pool (taken away from the object to which it was allocated). The orphan timeout is a provision to handle an application's failure to release connections or other similar failures. The orphan timeout should be large enough to ensure that all database requests made upon obtaining the connection can be completed (including queueing delays) in non-failure situations. The orphan timeout should be small enough so that it permits reasonable recovery time in the event of failures.

10.4.5 Specify database attributes at deployment time

The database attributes such as the user ID, password, JNDI name, etc. should be modifiable administratively without requiring code changes. This simplies the process of migrating from a staging environment to a production environment. This can be accomplished by including these parameters as InitParameters for a servlet or by reading these parameters from a properties file or resource bundle.

10.4.6 Perform expensive JNDI lookups once per data source

JNDI lookups are expensive from a performance perspective. The JNDI lookup should be performed once. It can be performed in an init method or by initializing the class variable to null, and then performing the lookup only if it is still null. The data source when obtained can be stored as a private variable. Once it is obtained, it is used during each request without requiring an additional JNDI lookup.

The following code sample illustrates the initialization of a DataSource using JNDI:

```
// Initializes the DataSource via JNDI.
public void initDataSource(String dbJndi) {

   Context ctx = null;

   try {
      java.util.Hashtable env= new java.util.Hashtable();
      env.put(Context.INITIAL_CONTEXT_FACTORY,
         "com.ibm.ejs.ns.jndi.CNInitialContextFactory");

      // Create the Initial Naming Context.
      ctx = new InitialContext(env);

      // Perform a naming service lookup to get a DataSource object.
// The DataSource object is a factory used to request
// individual connections.
// The dbJndi is the JNDI name or logical name of the database.

ds = (javax.sql.DataSource) ctx.lookup(dbJndi);
   }
   catch (Throwable theException) {
      // Handle Exception
      theException.printStackTrace();
   }
   finally {
      try {
         if(ctx!=null)
            ctx.close();
      }
      catch (Exception e) {
         // Handle Exception
      }
   }

}
```

WebSphere V3.5.2 includes an enhancement to provide support for caching the JNDI results within the WebSphere Application Server. This substantially reduces the performance penalty associated with failure to cache JNDI lookups; it is still a good programming practice to cache JNDI lookups.

10.4.7 Use proper try/catch/finally logic to release JDBC resources

The process of performing a data access task (such as a database query or update) should be structured using judicious try/catch/finally logic. The process of obtaining a connection, creating a statement, executing the query and processing the results of the query should be within a try block. A catch block handles exceptions that occur within the try block. The finally block is the appropriate place to ensure that all JDBC resources are released. The JDBC resources to release include the Connection (released back to the connection pool), the Statement (or CallableStatement or PreparedStatement), and the ResultSet.

Structuring the application using a try/catch/finally block substantially reduces the possibility of leaking JDBC resources. Failure to release these resources can result in out-of-resource conditions for long-running applications.

```
// Perform a Data Access Task
public void performTask()
{
    Connection conn  = null;
    PreparedStatement pStmt = null;
    ResultSet rs = null;

    try
    {
//          Get a Connection from DataSource Factory
//          Get a Connection object conn using the DataSource factory.
            conn = ds.getConnection(dbAttr.userid, dbAttr.pwd);

// Execute SQL Statement, e.g, query
   String employeeInfo = null;
   conn = ds.getConnection(dbuser,dbpwd);
   pStmt = conn.prepareStatement("SELECT EMPNO, FIRSTNME, LASTNAME FROM
EMPLOYEE",
         ResultSet.TYPE_SCROLL_SENSITIVE,ResultSet.CONCUR_READ_ONLY);
   rs = pStmt.executeQuery();
// Generate a View
   if(rs!=null) {
      while(rs.next()) {
         // obtain results from ResultSet
      }
   }
    }

    catch (Exception theException)
    {
   // Handle Exception
```

```
      }
// Release JDBC Resources
      finally
      {
      // Clean up all resources, regardless of failure/success
      // of JDBC request

      try {
         // release ResultSet
         if(rs!=null)
            rs.close();
      }
      catch (Exception theException) {
         // Handle Exception
}

      try {
         // release PreparedStatement
         if(pStmt!=null)
            pStmt.close();
      }
      catch (Exception theException) {
         // Handle Exception
}

      try {
         // release Connection
         if(conn!=null)
            conn.close();
      }
      catch (Exception theException) {
         // Handle Exception
}
```

10.4.8 Configure PreparedStatement cache size

WebSphere maintains a cache of precompiled PreparedStatement objects. The default cache size for PreparedStatement objects is 100. If the application uses more than 100 different PreparedStatements, the cache size can be modified using the datasource.xml file (as discussed in 10.3.1, “datasources.xml property file” on page 383).

10.5 Recovery from DB failures

A connection pool is a cache of database connections. This cache could be rendered stale/invalid in the following cases:

- Scheduled database shutdowns
- Database administrative actions such as issuing the command `force applications all` has been issued with DB2 or `shutdown` with Oracle
- Network problems

WebSphere provides a solution to this problem that functions in the following manner:

1. Catch SQLException on database operations
2. Examine the exception for SQLSTATE string, error codes
3. Compare with list of known state strings and error codes
4. Destroy the connection

In your application program, you will need to write a catch block which can catch SQLException called "StaleConnectionException" as shown in Figure 260.

```
try {
   boolean retry = true;
   while( retry) {
      try {
         Connection conn1 = ds1.getConnection();
         Statement stmt1 = conn1.createStatement();

         // assume that the connection becomes stale here somehow.
         // eg. force application all.

         // the following call will fail.
         ResultSet res = stmt1.executeQuery(stmtString);
         .......
         // if all the database work was successful.
         retry = false;
         ............
      }  catch (StaleConnectionException ex) {
         conn1.close();
           retry = true;
      }
   }
} catch( Exception ex) {
}
```

Figure 260. StaleConnectionException

Table 24 is the list of the state strings and error codes that WebSphere can handle.

Table 24. List of state strings and error codes

	SQLSTATE	Error code	Messages
DB2	55032, 08001, 08003, 40003, S1000	-1015, -1034, -1035, -6036, -3008, -1224, -1229, -30081	
Oracle	55032, 08001, 08003, 40003, S1000	17002, 1089, 1034, 1033, 3113, 3114, 1012	Connection reset by peer
Sybase	55032, 08001, 08003, 40003, S1000		

10.6 Reference information

- *JDBC API Tutorial and Reference*, Second Edition, by White, Fisher, Cattell, Hamilton, and Hapner.
- *"JDBC 2.0 API"*, by Seth White and Mark Hapner. Version 1.0. June 4, 1998, available at `http://www.javasoft.com`.
- *Servlet and JSP Programming with IBM WebSphere Studio and VisualAge for Java*, SG24-5755
- *WebSphere V3 Performance Tuning Guide*, SG24-5657

Chapter 11. Enterprise Java Services

Enterprise JavaBeans (EJB) allow developers to focus on writing the business logic necessary to support their applications without having to deal with the intricacies of the underlying middleware.

EJB containers insulate the enterprise beans from the underlying EJB server and provide a standard application programming interface (API) between the beans and the container. The EJB Specification defines this API. The EJB container provide crucial services such as transactions, security, naming, and persistence.

Enterprise Java Services (EJS) is the WebSphere component that allows the deployment and management of Enterprise JavaBeans in EJB containers.

In this chapter we discuss:

- How to prepare WebSphere so that you can deploy your EJBs.
- How to deploy your EJBs into a WebSphere container.
- Some example EJBs that explore key behaviors you will see when your EJBs execute in WebSphere.
- EJB security.

We will not discuss how to develop EJBs or EJB clients. This is beyond the scope of this redbook. For detailed information, refer to *Developing Enterprise JavaBeans with VisualAge for Java*, SG24-5429 and *Design and Implement Servlets, JSPs, and EJBs for IBM WebSphere Application Server*, SG24-5754.

11.1 Configuring Enterprise Java Services

In order to run EJBs in WebSphere V3.5. you need to create an EJB container. Any application server can hold an EJB container. When you create the application server called “Default Server”, an EJB container is automatically created. See 14.5, “Create an application server and other basic resources” on page 587 for details on how to set up an application server.

In this chapter we will cover the specific of creating an EJB container in more detail.

If you are creating EJBs that access databases, for example a container-managed entity bean, then you will also need to create one or more

JDBC drivers and data sources. You can find details on how to do this in 14.4, "Create a JDBC driver and data source" on page 579.

11.1.1 Creating a container

In order to create a container, from the administrative console, select the application server you want to create the container in.

Right click and select **Create -> EJBContainer** as depicted in Figure 261.

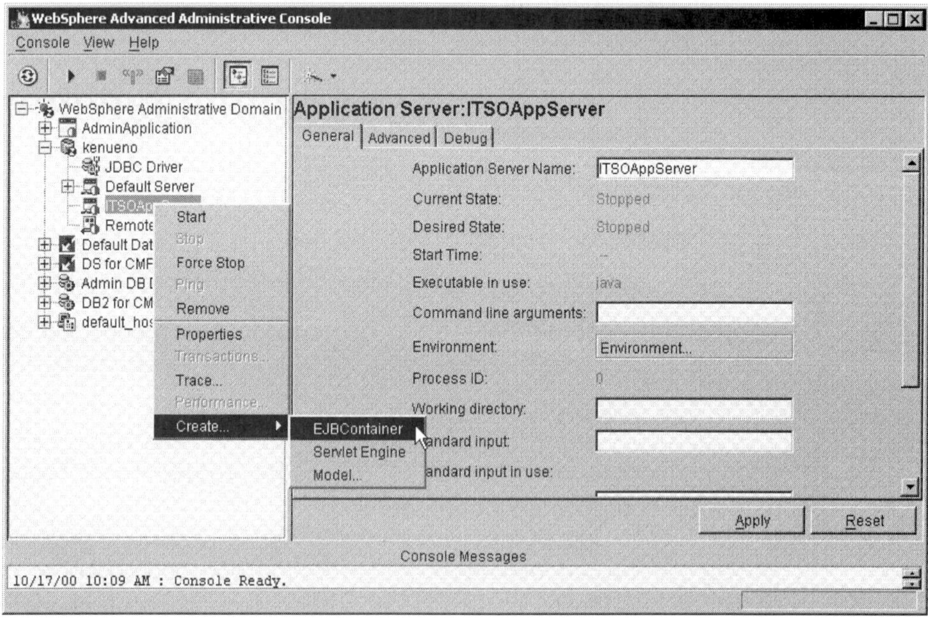

Figure 261. Creating a container

A new window, Create EJBContainer, will pop up. This window contains three tabs. The General tab is shown in Figure 262 on page 395.

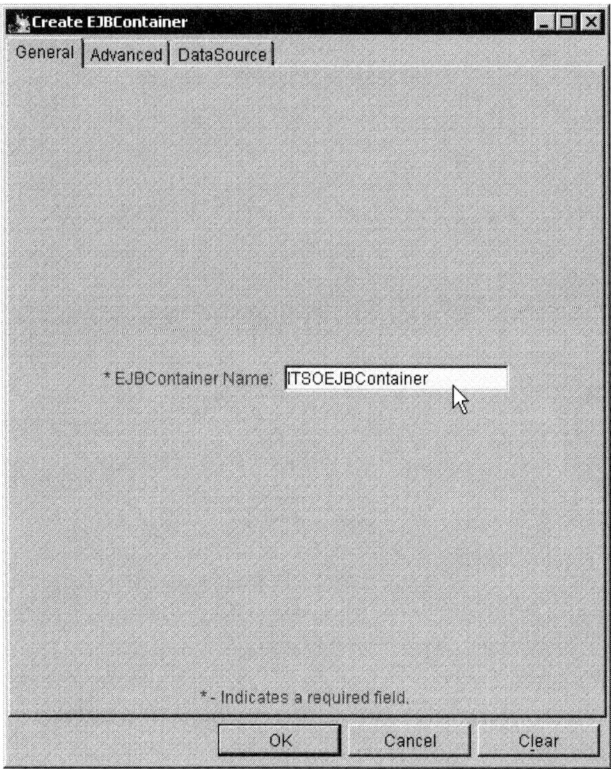

Figure 262. Create EJBContainer: General tab

You need to enter a name for your EJB container on the General tab. The default value offered will normally be acceptable. Click the **Advanced** tab. This is shown in Figure 263 on page 396.

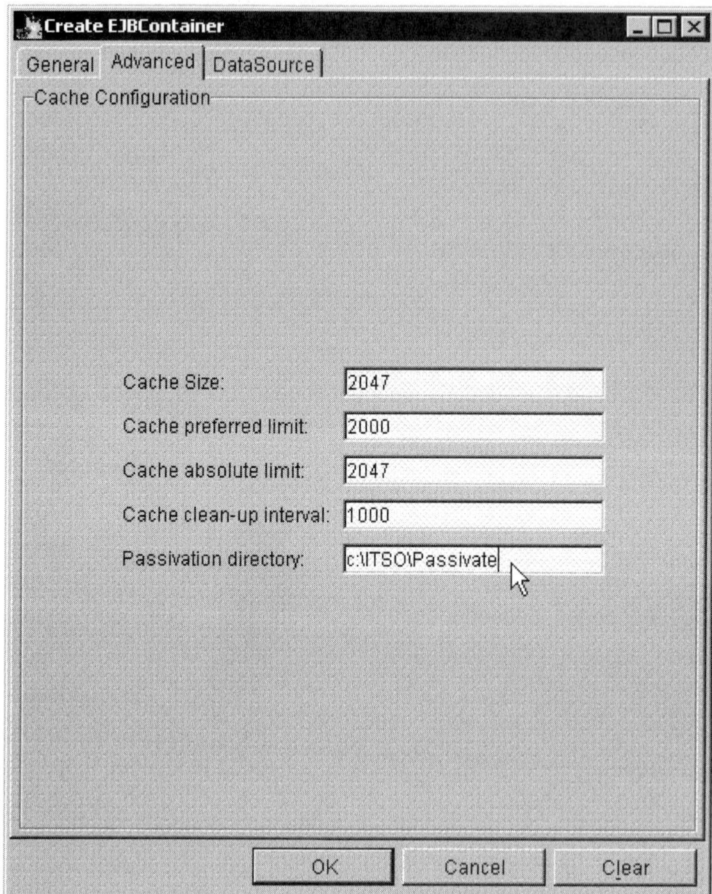

Figure 263. Create EJBContainer: Advanced tab

The fields on the Advanced tab fall into two categories. First there are four fields that define EJB cache management. These are used in performance tuning. It is unlikely that you will need to adjust these fields in a development situation. Refer to the *WebSphere V3 Performance Tuning Guide*, SG24-5657 for information related to tuning these parameters in a production environment.

In addition to the four cache management parameters, there is one parameter that allows you to specify the passivation directory. This directory is used for passivation of stateful session EJBs. The EJB container may choose to remove an EJB from the cache in order to utilize the cache for other requests. This is known as passivation and involves the serialization of state information as a means of temporarily saving the EJBs, when the cache is full.

If you are using stateful session EJBs you will probably find it easier to manage your system if you create a suitable directory and specify its location in this field.

If you click the **DataSource** tab you will see that you can specify a default data source for your EJBs. This is shown in Figure 264. You do not have to specify values here. You can instead specify them separately on each EJB as you create it.

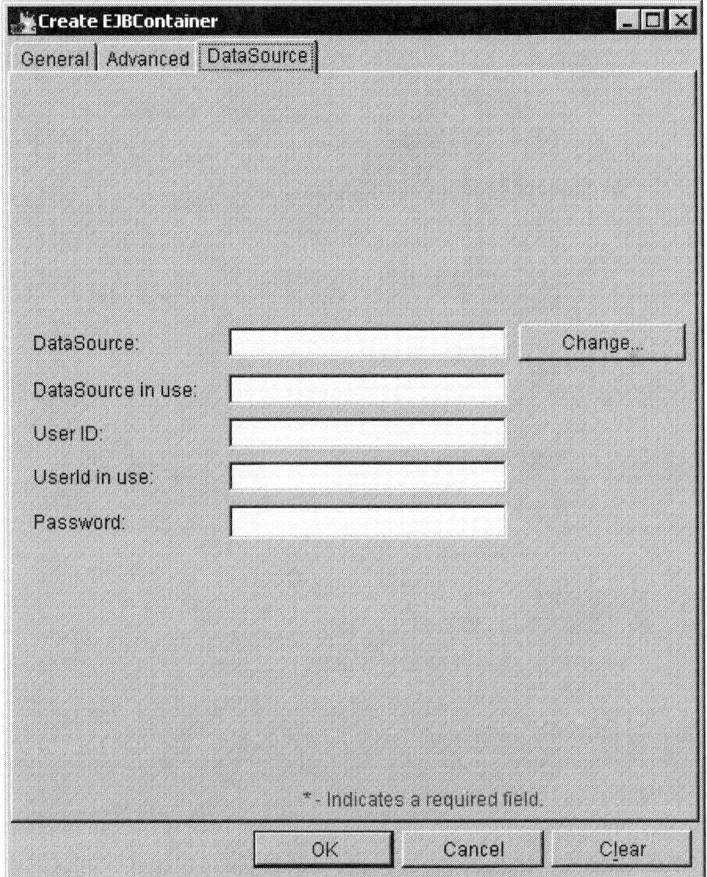

Figure 264. Create EJBContainer: DataSource

If you do want to specify the data source, click **Change** to bring up the Data Source selection tab shown in Figure 265 on page 398.

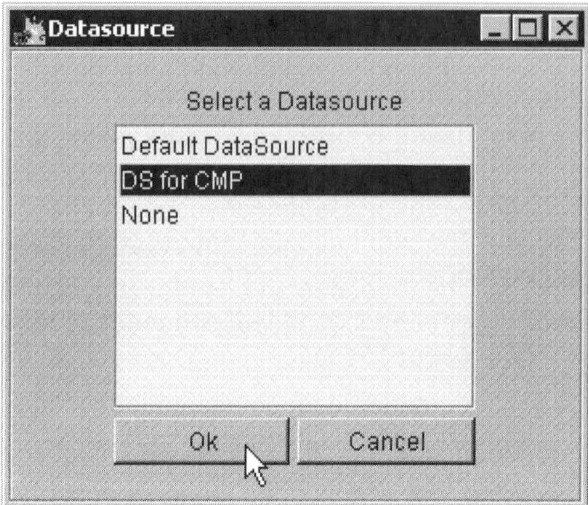

Figure 265. Select a DataSource

You can then select a data source and click **OK.** Then fill in the appropriate user name and password as shown in Figure 266

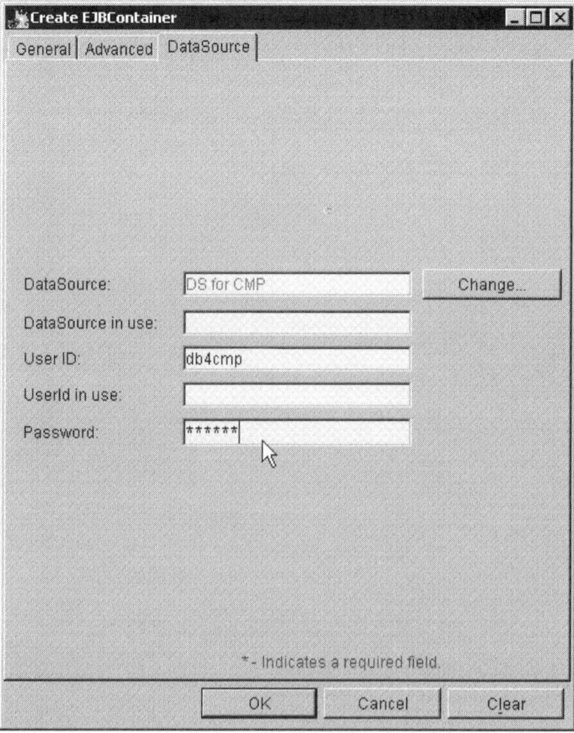

Figure 266. EJB data source selected

When you click **OK** the EJB container will be created and you will see a confirmation dialog. Your administrative console will now show your new EJB container as shown in Figure 267.

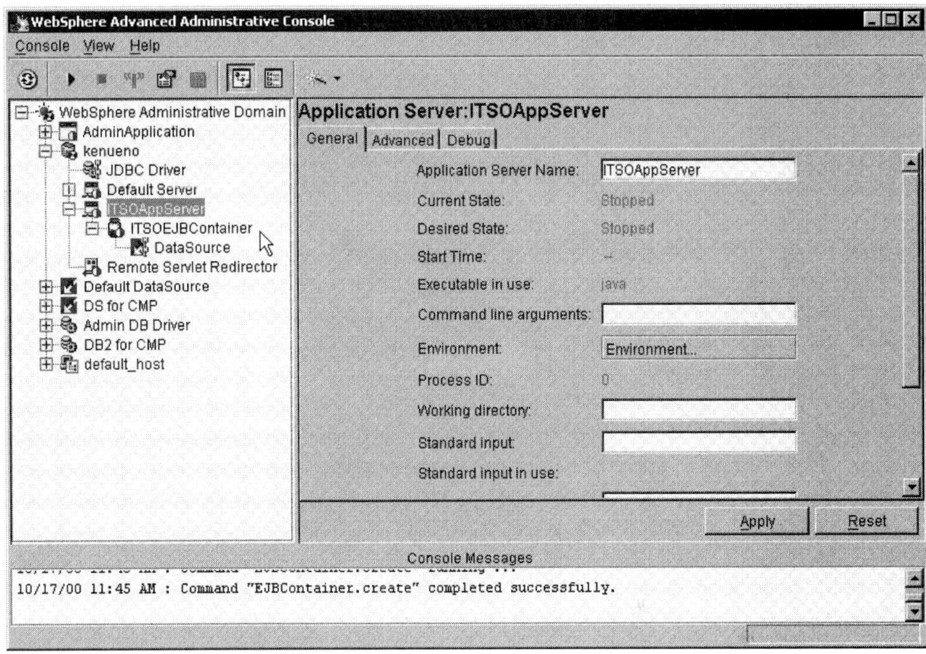

Figure 267. New EJB container

11.1.2 Removing a container

If you should wish to remove a container, you have to stop it first. Then right click and select **Remove** as depicted in Figure 268 on page 400.

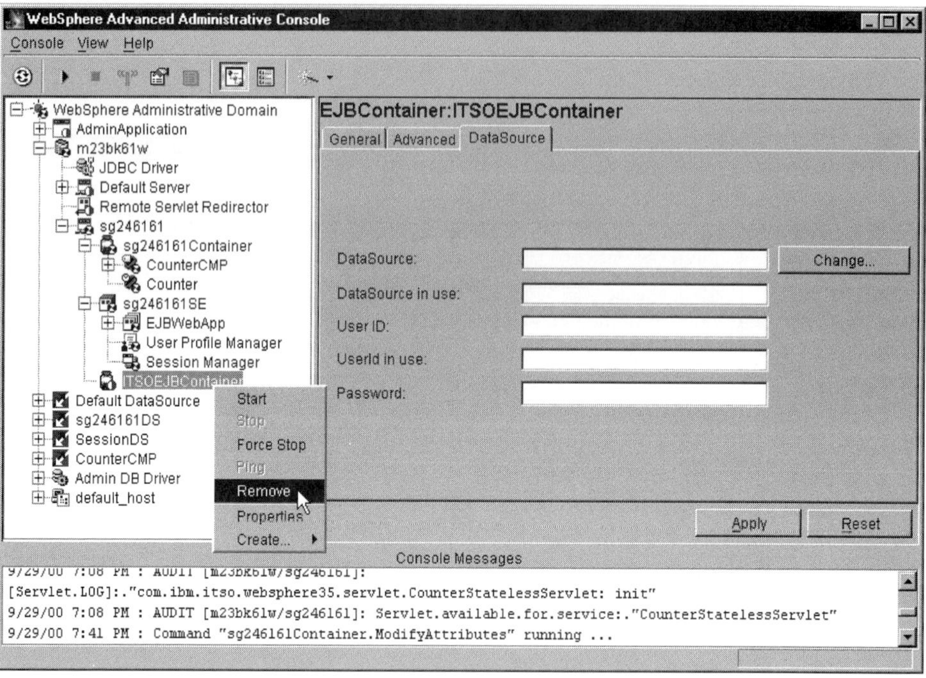

Figure 268. Removing a container

11.2 Installing an EJB into a container

After you have developed your Enterprise JavaBeans, they need to be installed into an EJB container so that you can run them. Words such as "install" and "deploy" have very similar connotations in everyday speech. In the context of EJBs in WebSphere, "deploy" has a specific meaning that we will explain as we examine the installation process.

We assume that we are starting with an EJB JAR file, which contains only the EJB home and remote interfaces and the EJB implementation class.

Figure 269 on page 401 shows the three steps in the installation process.

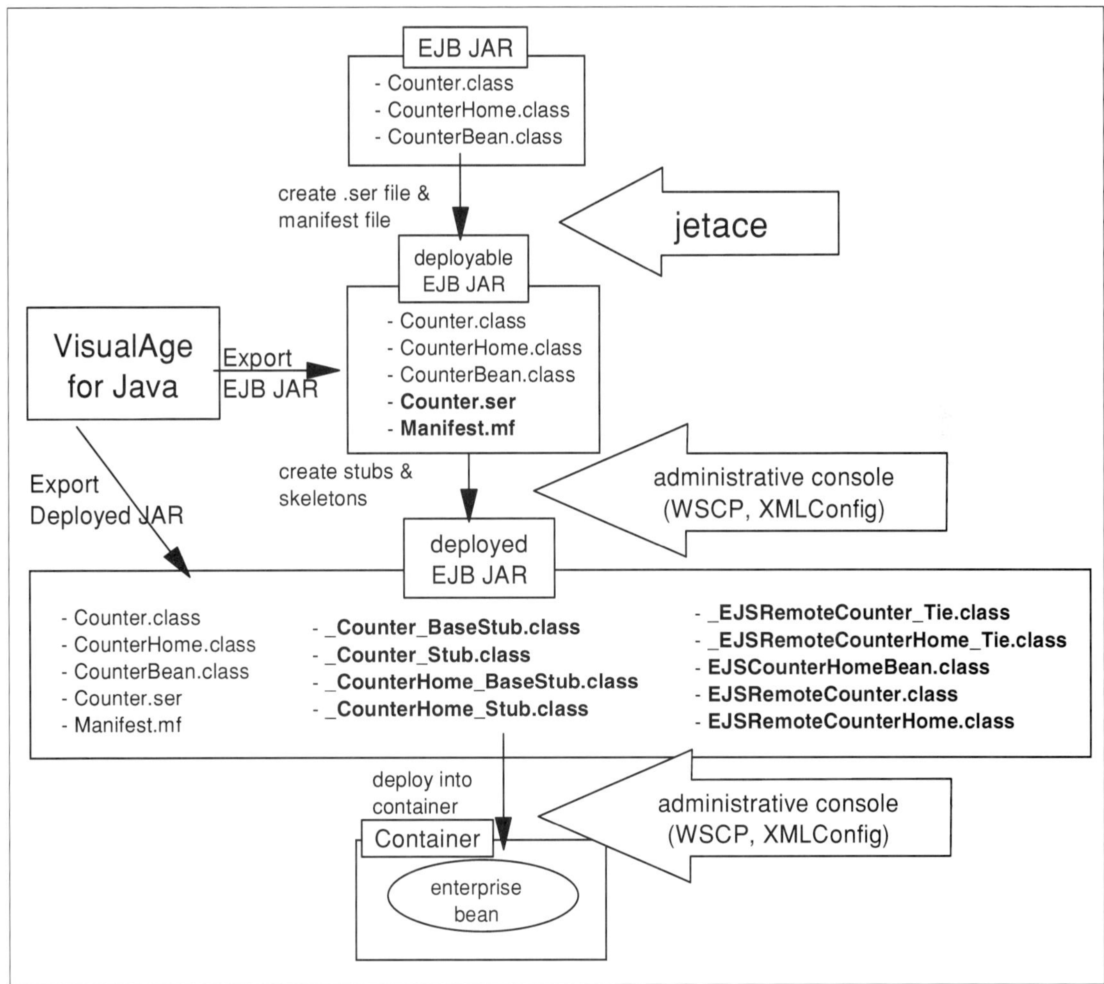

Figure 269. EJB deployment process

The figure also shows that it is possible both to install an EJB using only WebSphere tools and also to use VisualAge for Java to perform some of the tasks.

We will first briefly describe the three steps and then give detailed explanations of how to use the WebSphere tools and how to use the alternative of the VisualAge for Java facilities.

11.2.1 Creating the deployment descriptor

The deployment descriptor defines the EJBs run-time configuration. You can specify items such as the transactional requirements of the EJB and whether individual methods of an entity bean are read-only.

The deployment descriptor is added to the EJB JAR in the form of a serializable object on a file with extension .ser.

An EJB JAR with deployment descriptor is sometimes referred to as "deployable".

11.2.2 Generating stubs and skeletons

An EJBs clients access the EJB using RMI/IIOP. We therefore need code to manage the RMI interactions for each EJB. This code is in a set of stub and skeleton classes generated by WebSphere and added to the EJB JAR.

This code is WebSphere specific. If you took your deployable EJB JAR to a different vendor's EJB container you might see a similar set of classes generated, but there is no expectation that the generated code would be the same.

An EJB JAR containing the stub and skeleton code is termed *Deployed.* As we will show later, VisualAge for Java can deliver a JAR file that contains both deployment descriptor and generated code; it can deliver a deployed JAR file.

11.2.3 Create EJB in a container

WebSphere will add an EJB to an EJB container. This is an administrative process and the result is that your EJB becomes visible in the administrative console and can be stopped and started.

You normally create an EJB from a deployed JAR file. However, the administration process will accept a deployable JAR file and will perform the code generation before adding the EJB to the container.

This section will describe two different ways to perform this installation.

You can deploy an EJB in WebSphere V3.5 using VisualAge for Java or the JETACE tool, which is a component of WebSphere V3.5.

11.2.4 Creating the deployment descriptor using jetace

Jetace is a tool used to create a deployable EJB JAR file, one that contains a deployment descriptor.

The input is a JAR, zip, or directory containing the classes for one or more EJBs.

Output is a deployable EJB JAR file that contains:

- EJB class files
- Deployment descriptor file
- EJB-compliant manifest file

Jetace is in your standard WebSphere installation at:

<WAS_install_dir>/bin/jetace

11.2.4.1 Running the JETACE tool

We will show you how to deploy a sample bean (Counter CMP EJBs) using the JETACE tool.

To deploy this EJB we need to perform the following steps:

1. Create a JAR file
2. Launch jetace
3. Load the JAR file
4. Set up the properties for the EJB
5. Save it as the deployable JAR file (this JAR file now contains the deployment descriptor)

> **Note**
>
> If you are using associations or inheritance between your EJBs with VisualAge for Java, before launching jetace, you need to add a JAR file to the system's classpath. For our tests, we exported the Project IBM EJB Tools to a JAR file (we called ejbruntime35.jar) and we added this JAR to the system's classpath by issuing the following command:
>
> ```
> set classpath=%classpath%;D:/Mohamed/EJBs/ejbruntime35.jar
> ```

From the <WebSphere_install_dir>/bin directory, issue the command `jetace`.

```
C:\WebSphere\AppServer\bin>jetace
```

Figure 270. Invoking jetace

You will have a jetace GUI as shown in Figure 271.

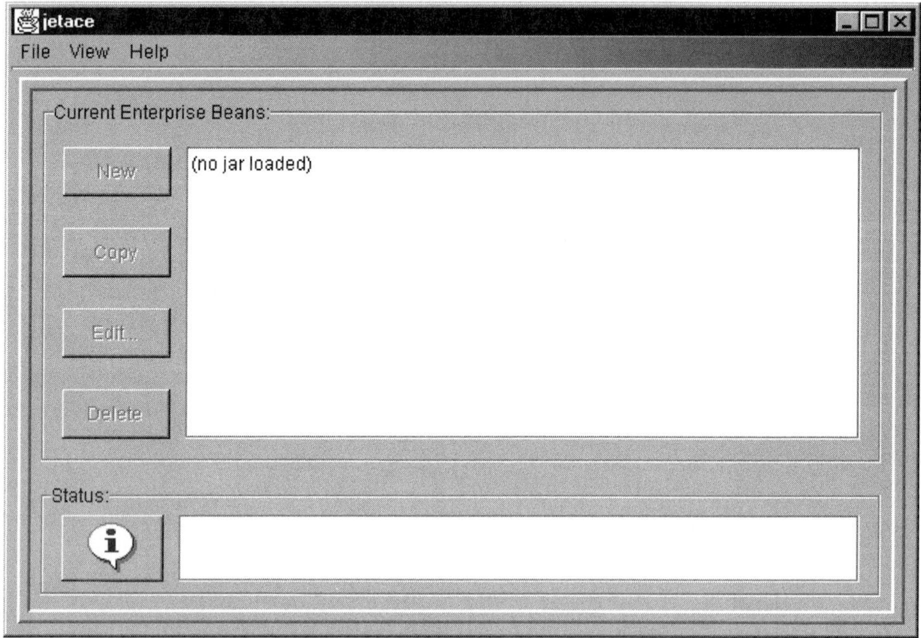

Figure 271. jetace initial window

Select **File -> Load** as depicted in Figure 272 on page 405.

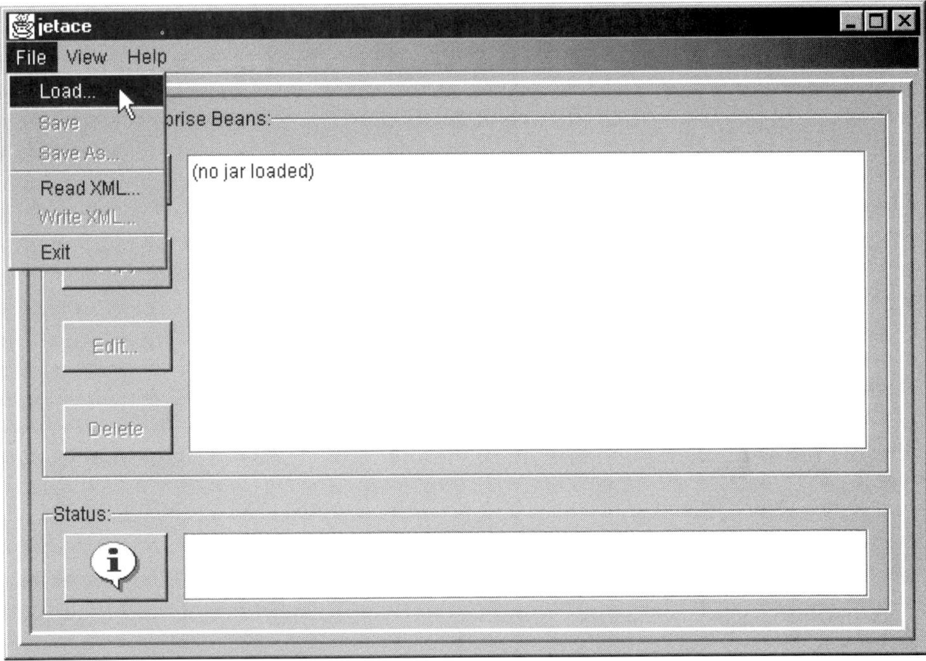

Figure 272. Loading the EJB JAR file

Browse to the directory where you created your EJB JAR file and select your EJB JAR file (in our case, CounterCMPNonDeployed.jar) and click **Open** as shown in Figure 273.

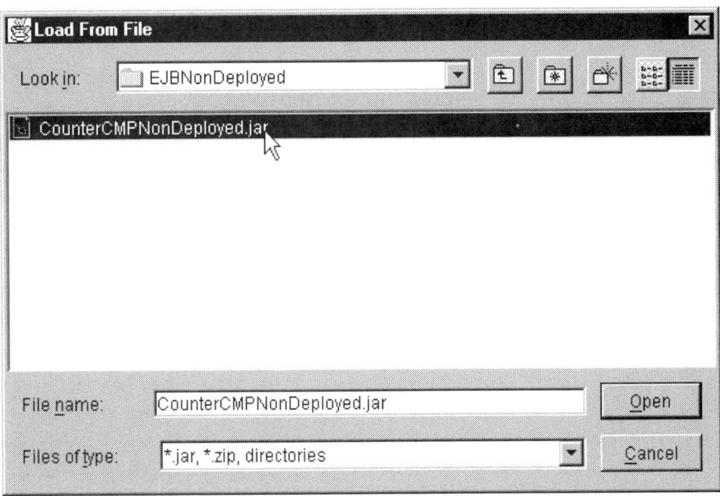

Figure 273. Select your EJB JAR file

Now we need to create the deployment descriptor.

Click **New** in the jetace window as shown in Figure 274.

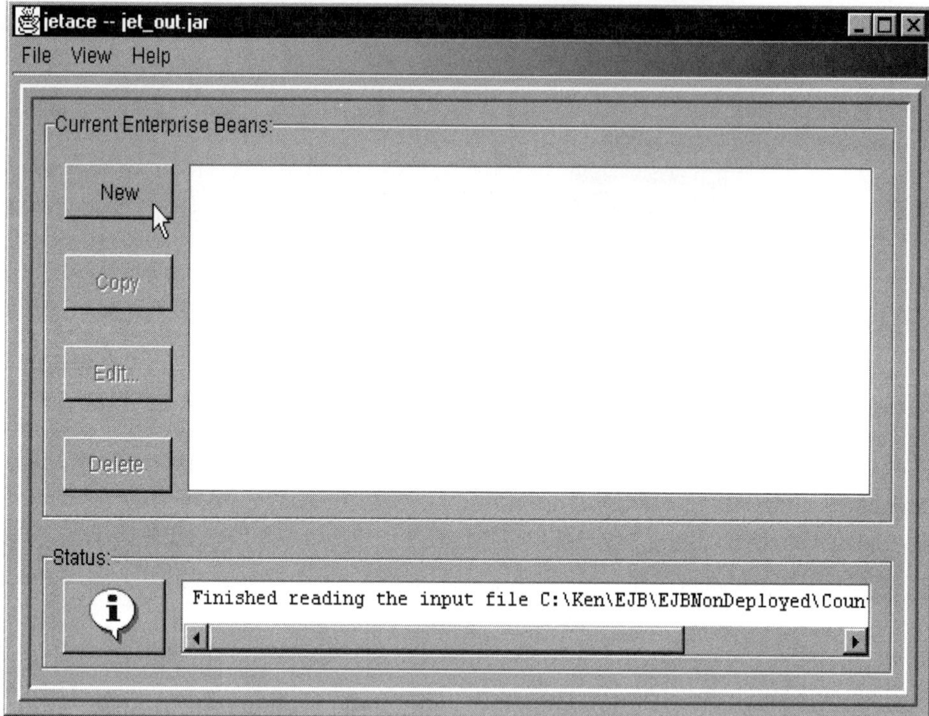

Figure 274. Finished reading the input file

You will be ready to start editing a deployment descriptor.

In the Basic tab, we need to specify:

- Deployed name (name of the deployment descriptor)
- EJB class name
- Home interface name
- Remote interface name
- JNDI name

In our case, we specified:

- Deployed Name: Counter.ser
- Enterprise Bean Class: com.ibm.itso.websphere35.ejb.cmp.CounterCMPBean

- Home Interface: com.ibm.itso.websphere35.ejb.cmp.CounterCMPHome
- Remote Interface: com.ibm.itso.websphere35.ejb.cmp.CounterCMP
- JNDI Home Name: Counter

These are shown in Figure 275.

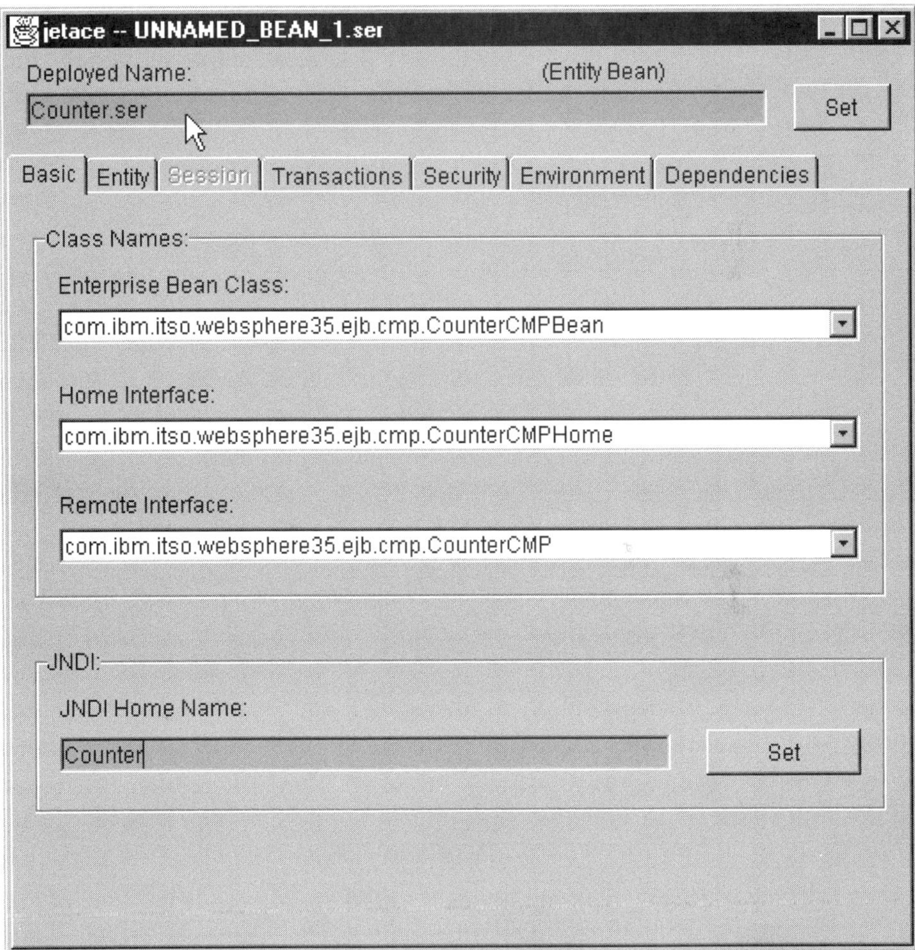

Figure 275. jetace: Basic tab

In the Entity tab, we specify:

- Primary key class: com.ibm.itso.websphere35.ejb.cmp.CounterCMPKey
- Container managed fields: select both cunterKey_ and theCount_ as shown in Figure 276 on page 408.

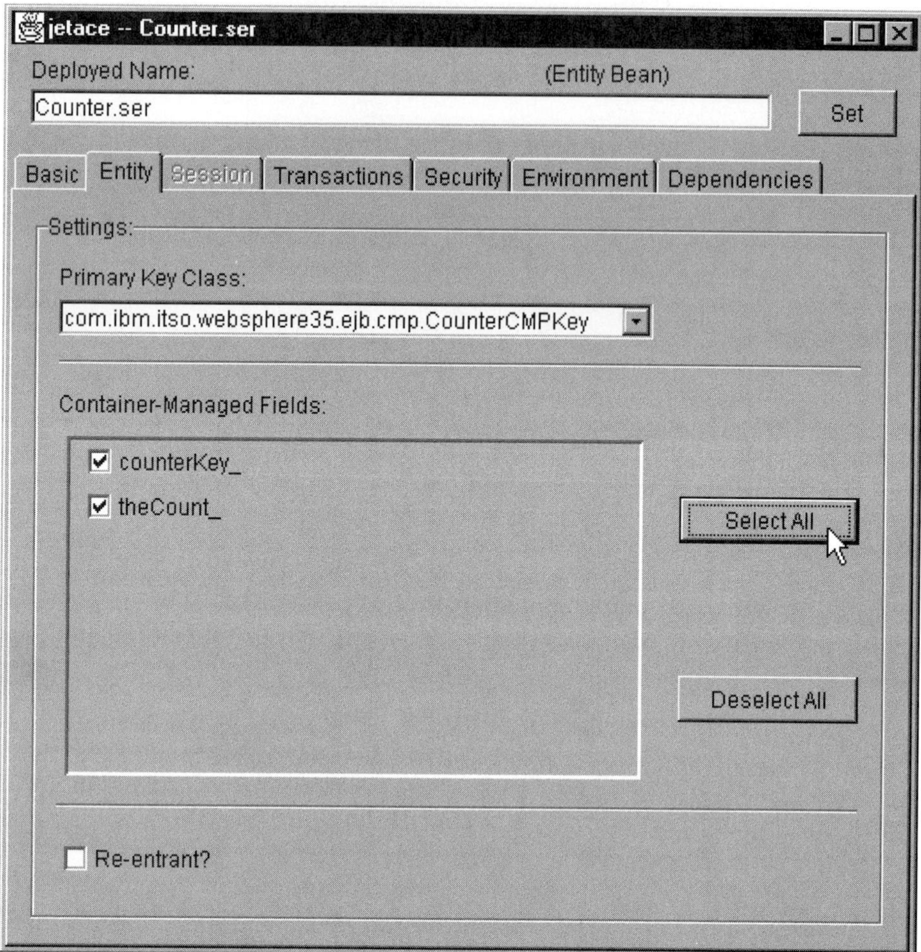

Figure 276. Entity attributes

In the Transactions tab, we must specify the following attributes:

- Transaction attribute. We specify TX_REQUIRED. This means that the counter bean either must be invoked with the context of an existing transaction or the container will create a new transaction when invoking this EJB.
- Isolation level: we keep the default value (READ_COMMITTED)

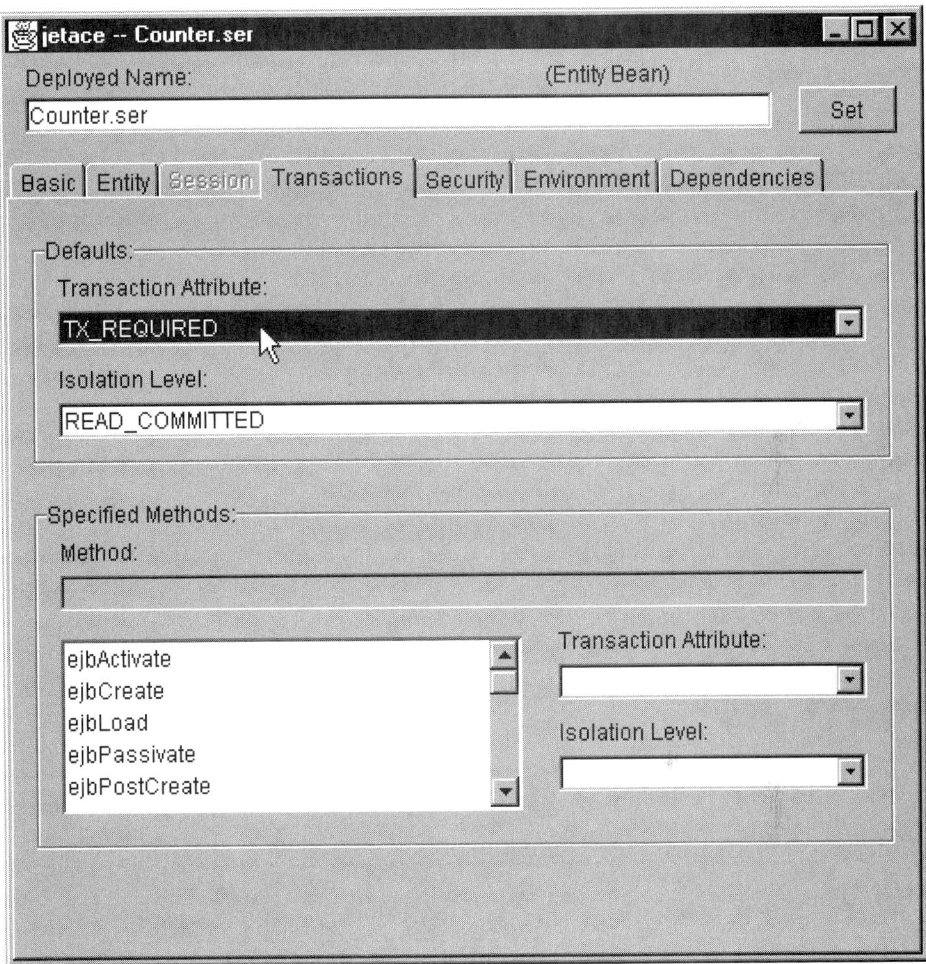

Figure 277. jetace: Transactions tab

To save the current configuration to an EJB JAR file:

1. Click **File--> Save As...**

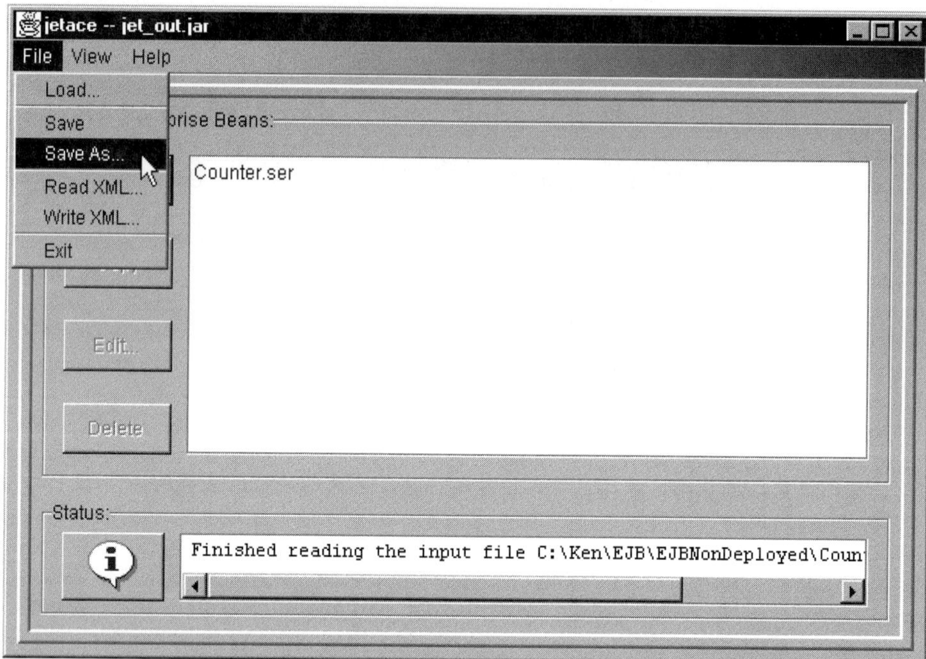

Figure 278. Saving a configuration of an EJB JAR file

2. In the Save To File window, specify the directory (or folder) and the JAR file name (in our case, C:\WebSphere\AppServer\deployableEJBs\CounterCMPNonDeployed.jar) and then click **Save**.

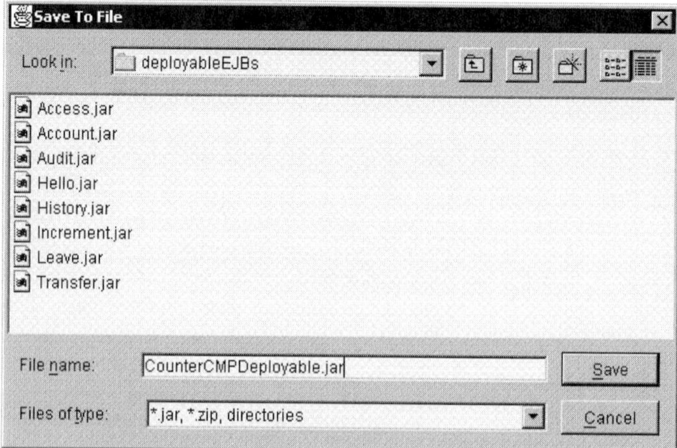

Figure 279. Save deployable EJBs

Then you will see `Finished saving the output file` message in the Status line as shown in Figure 280.

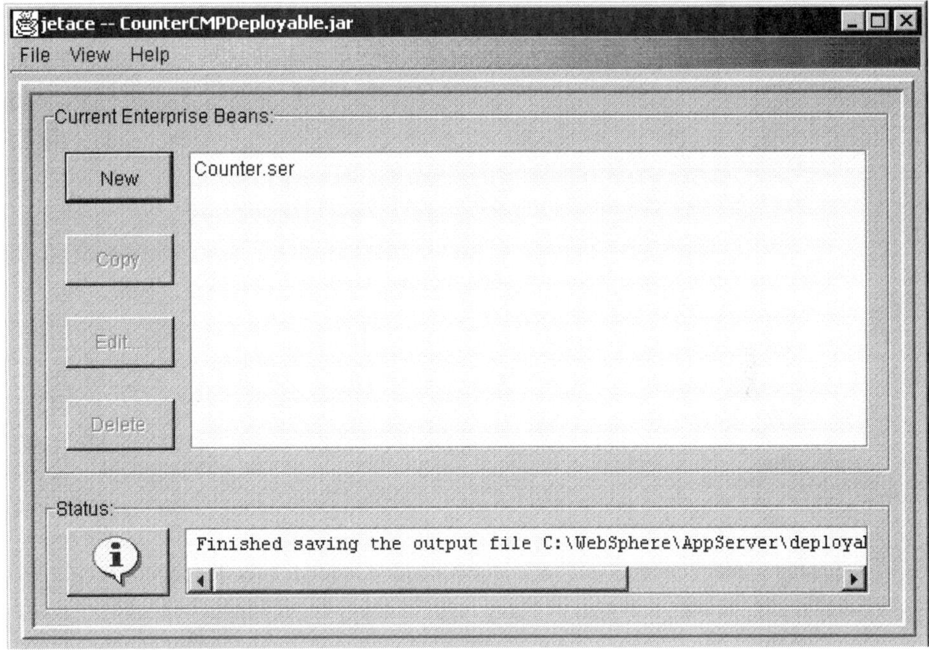

Figure 280. Finished saving the output file

Now, we exit from jetace by clicking **File -> Exit**.

Now that we have created the deployment descriptor (Counter.ser) and our EJB JAR file (we specified CounterCMPDeployable.jar), we are ready to deploy our EJB in WebSphere.

11.2.5 Create an enterprise bean

You can create an enterprise bean with the administrative console as described in the following:

1. With the administrative console, select a container, right click and select **Create-> EnterpriseBean** as depicted in Figure 294 on page 423.

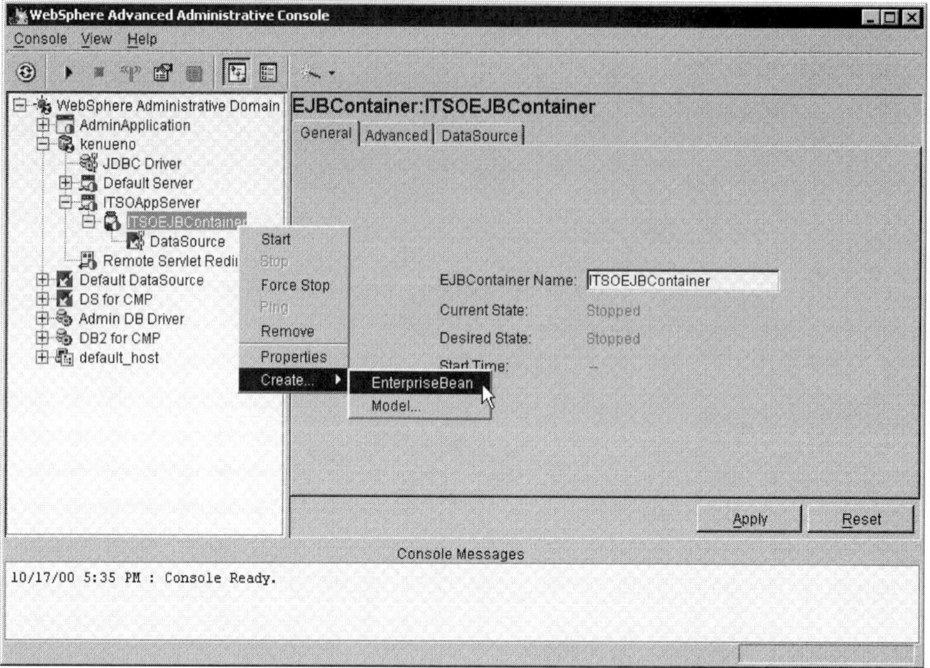

Figure 281. Create an enterprise bean

Then you will get the Create EnterpriseBean window as shown in Figure 282 on page 413.

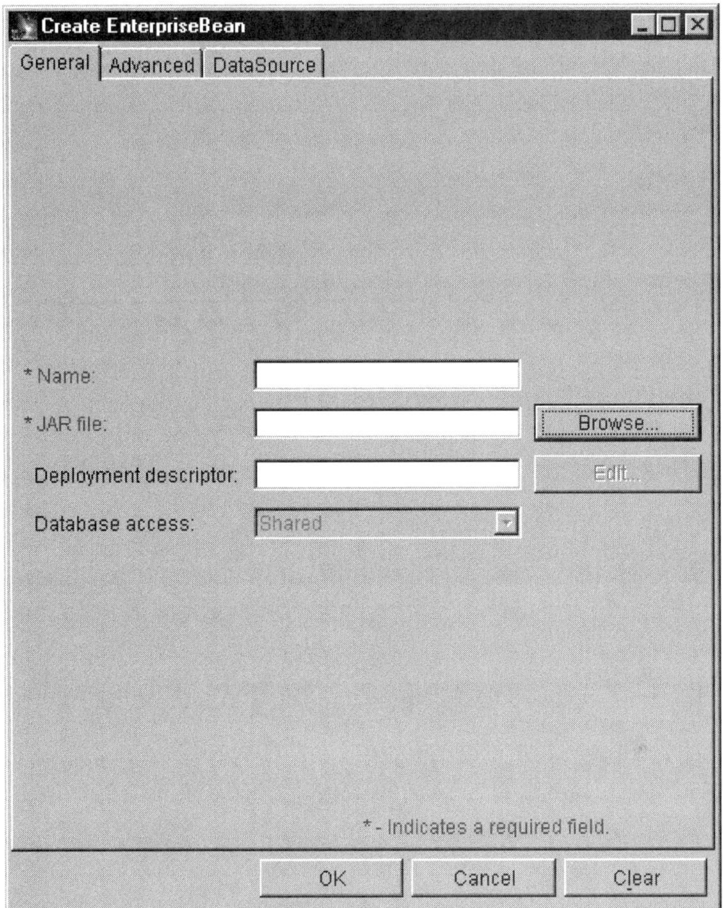

Figure 282. Creating an enterprise bean using the administrative console

If you know the JNDI name, you can specify it in the Name field (this is the Bean properties for those using VisualAge for Java). If you don't know it, click **Browse**...

In the Open window, locate the respective JAR file as depicted in Figure 283 on page 414. Then double click the JAR file (in our case, CounterCMPDeployable.jar).

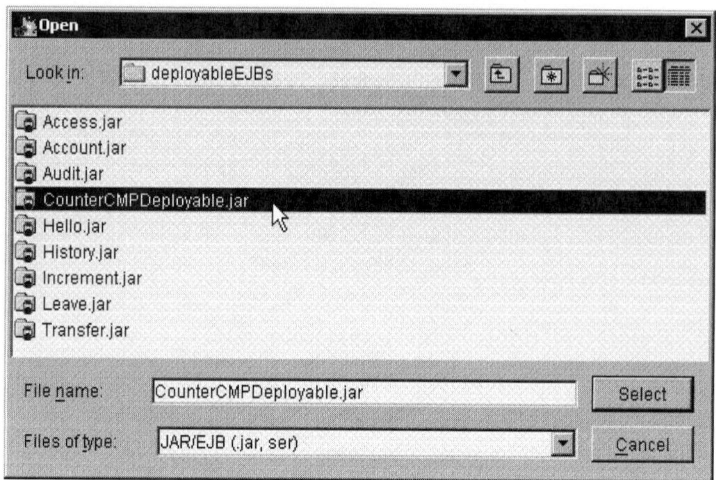

Figure 283. Select CounterCMPDeployable.JAR

Then you will see the .ser file that you created before. Choose it (in our case, Counter.ser) and click **Select** as shown in Figure 284

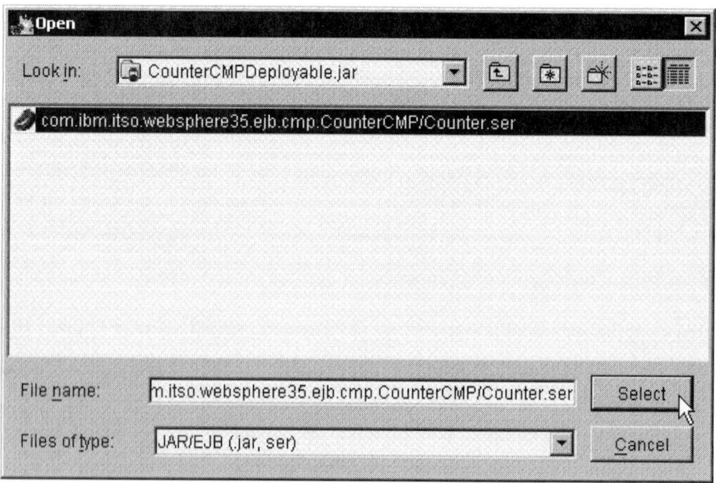

Figure 284. Select Counter.ser

You will get the Confirm dialog window. Click **Yes** and WebSphere will bring up a new confirm dialog window asking if you want to enable WLM on this bean as depicted in Figure 285 on page 415. Choose **Yes** or **No**, depending on whether you are planning to use WebSphere WLM. In our case, we clicked **Deploy Only**.

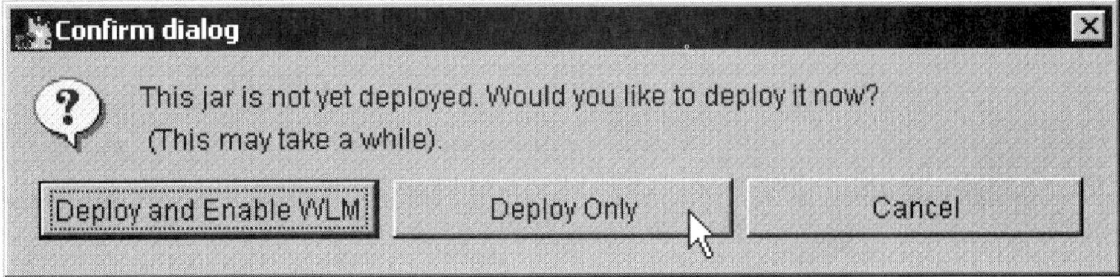

Figure 285. Confirm dialog

WebSphere will deploy your enterprise bean.

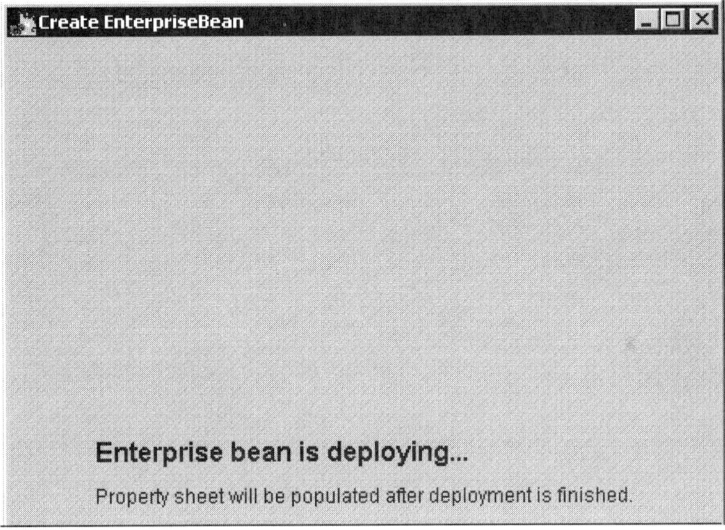

Figure 286. Deploying enterprise bean

When deployment is finished, you will see the Information dialog saying `Command "Deply JarFile" completed successfully`. Then click **OK**.

Then we come back to the Create EnterpriseBean window. Every field is now filled in as shown in Figure 287 on page 416.

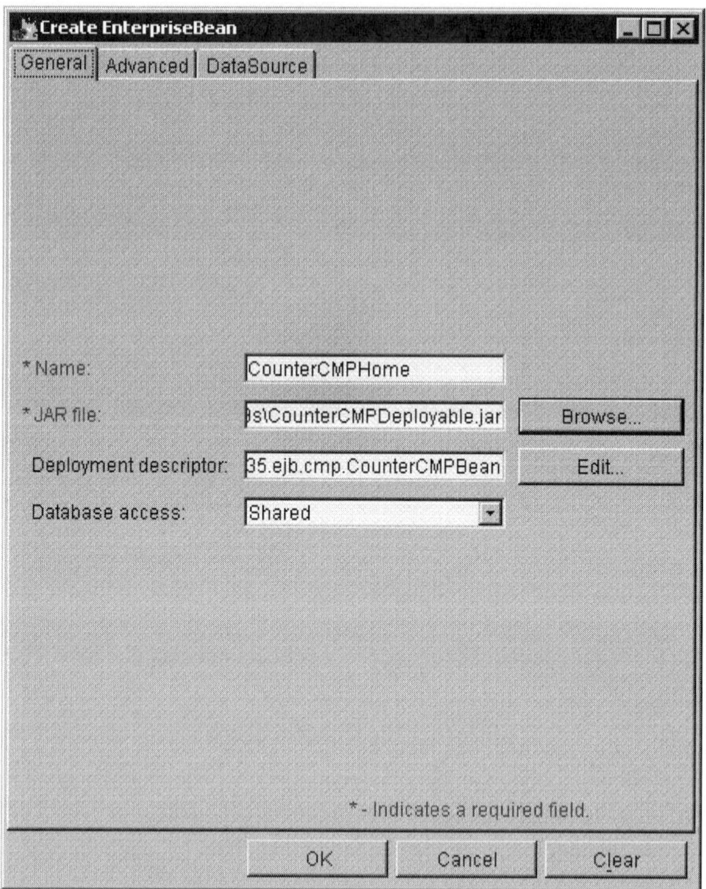

Figure 287. Create EnterpriseBean: General tab

In the Advanced tab, you can specify the instance pool size.

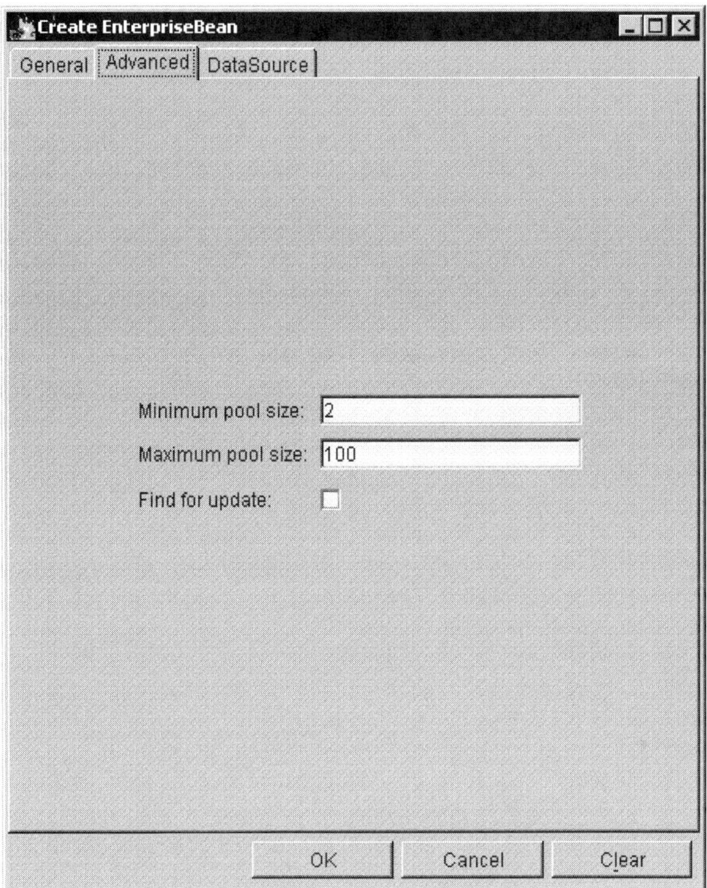

Figure 288. Create EnterpriseBean: Advanced tab

You can change these value after you create an EnterpriseBean from the administrative console. Therefore, it's not necessary to update these values now. We will describe these parameters later in this chapter.

In the DataSource tab, you can specify DataSource for the EnterpriseBean that you are creating. Note that the data source does not need to be specified for session beans.

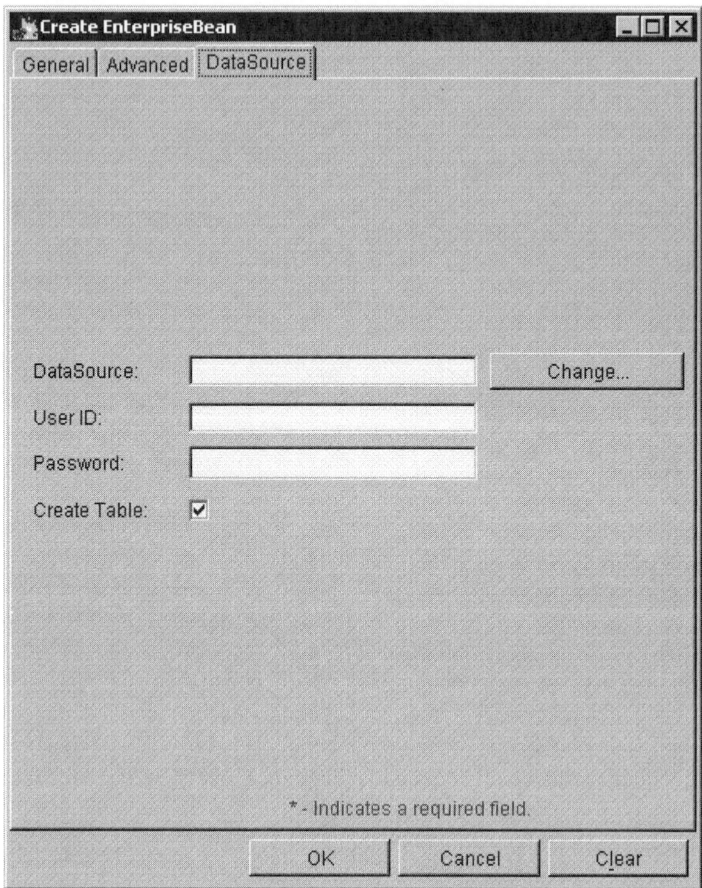

Figure 289. Create EnterpriseBean: DataSource tab

By clicking the **Change** button, you will get the Datasource window. Select an appropriate data source as shown in Figure 290 on page 419. In our case, we selected DS for CMP.

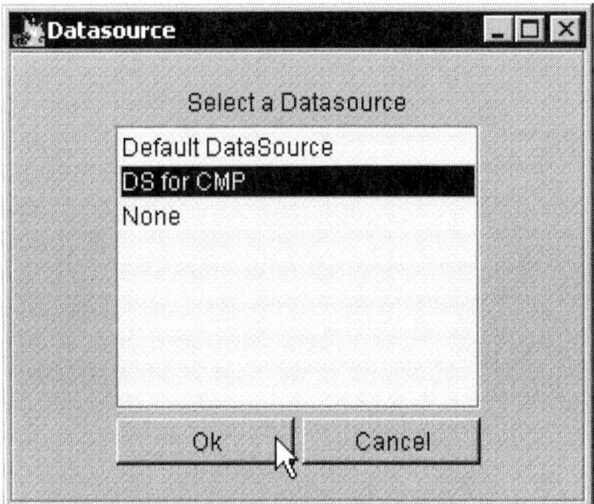

Figure 290. Select a Datasource window

Returning to the DataSource tab, you then specify the user ID and password for the database (or table), which is defined by the DataSource that you selected. Also, if you need to create a table now, check the **Create Table** check box as shown in Figure 291 on page 420. Note that even if the box is checked, the table will not be created immediately, but on the first start of the bean.

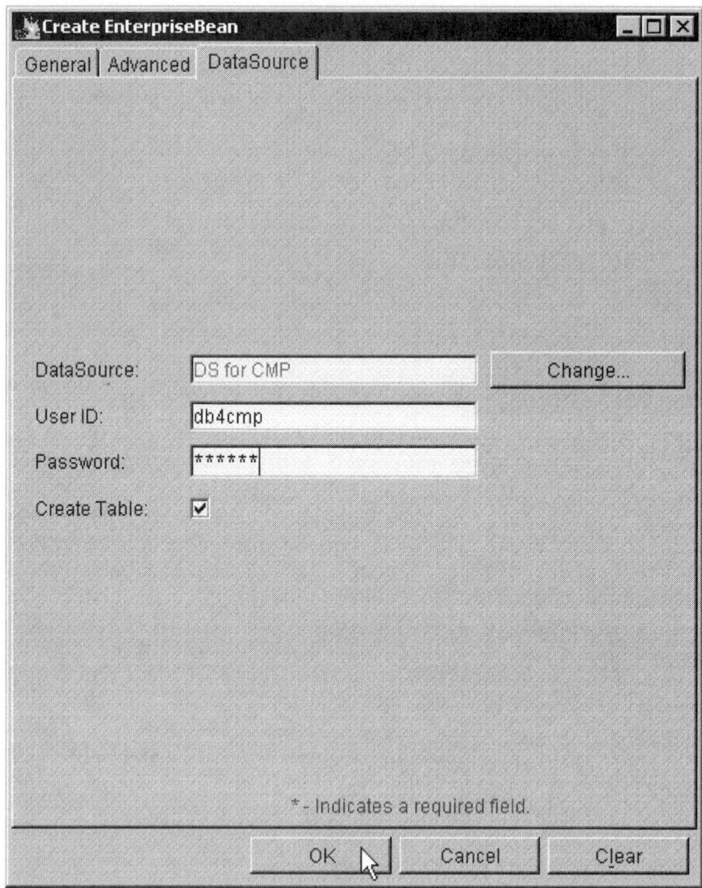

Figure 291. Create EnterpriseBean: DataSource, user ID, and password

Click **OK** to finish creating your EJB.

WebSphere brings up a new information dialog saying that the creation of the EJB has completed successfully. Click **OK** to finish the creation of the EJB.

Now we go back to the administrative console, and make sure our EJB (CounterCMPHome) has been created successfully, as depicted in Figure 292 on page 421.

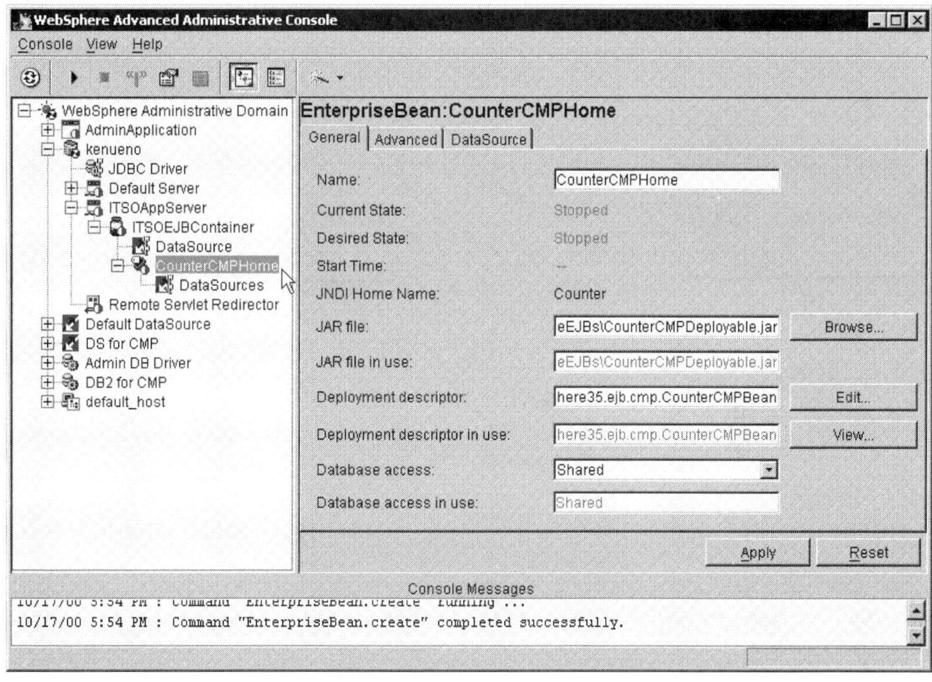

Figure 292. Newly created enterprise bean

You can check the bean properties and modify them if you wish by editing the deployment descriptor.

11.2.6 Creating a deployed JAR using VisualAge for Java

You can also create a deployed EJB JAR directly from VisualAge for Java.

1. Select the bean you want to deploy and right click.
2. Select **Export-> Deployed JAR** as shown in Figure 293 on page 422.
3. Export the deployed code to a directory.
4. Now that the JAR file is exported from VisualAge for Java. You need to copy the JAR file to the WebSphere server.

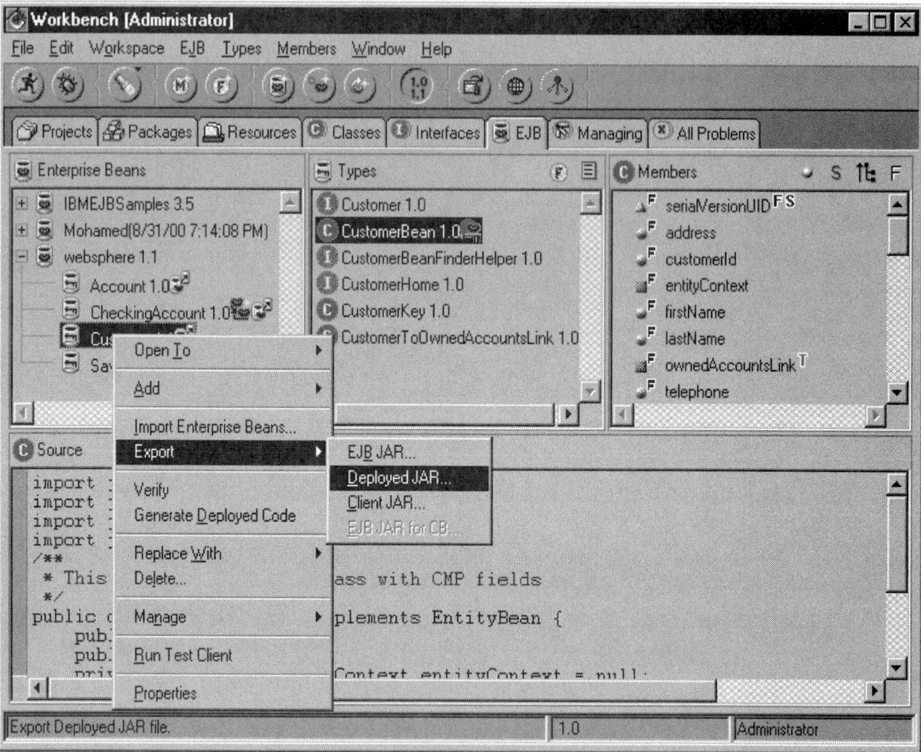

Figure 293. Deploying from VisualAge for Java

You can create the EJB with the administrative console as described in the following:

1. With the administrative console, select a container, right click and select **Create-> Enterprise Bean**. You will get the Create EnterpriseBean window as depicted in Figure 294 on page 423.

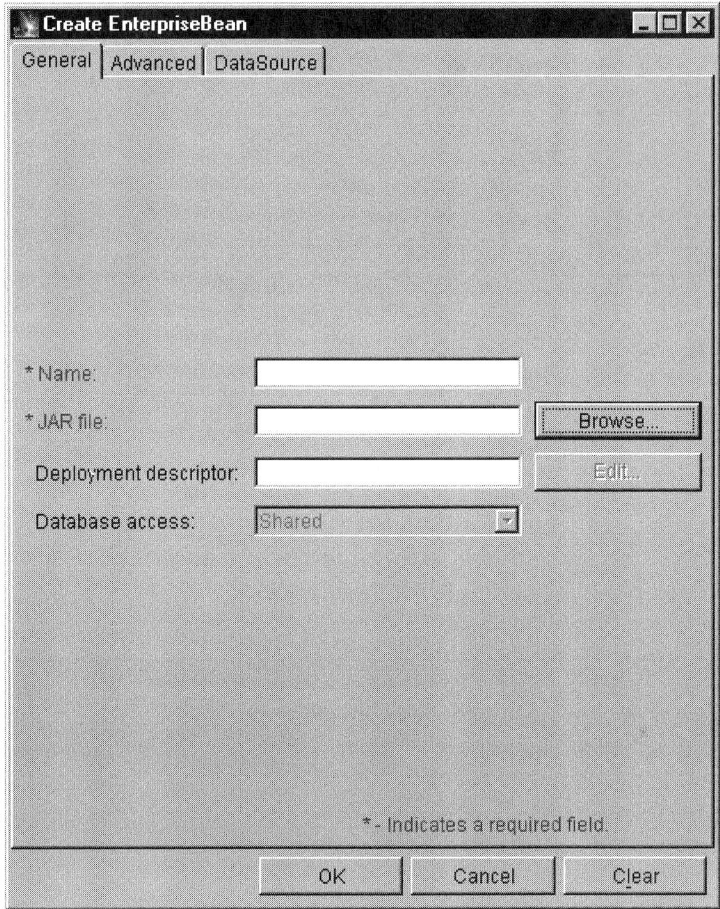

Figure 294. Creating an enterprise bean using the administrative console

2. If the JNDI name is known it can be specified in the Name field, which corresponds to the Bean Properties in VisualAge for Java. Alternatively, click **Browse** and locate the respective JAR file as depicted in Figure 295 on page 424.

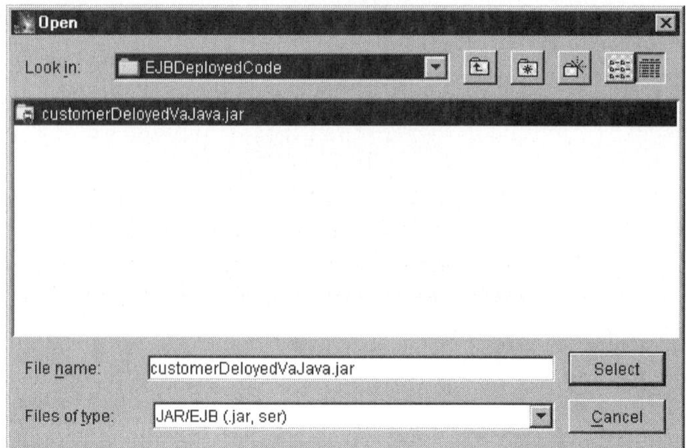

Figure 295. Selecting the exported EJB deployed JAR file

3. Choose the exported JAR file and click **Select**. WebSphere detects the deployed bean in the JAR file and brings up a confirm dialog window as depicted in Figure 296. Then click **Yes**.

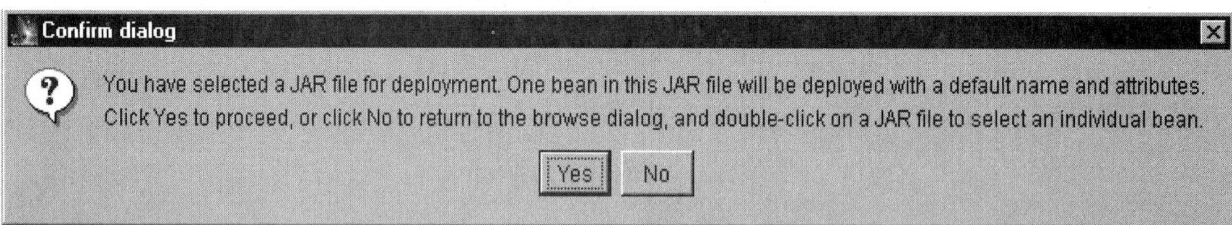

Figure 296. Deploying the customer EJB

Note that in WebSphere V3.5.2, you will get a new confirm dialog window asking if you want to enable WLM on this bean as depicted in Figure 297. Choose **Yes** or **No**, depending on whether you are planning to use WebSphere WLM. If you are using VisualAge for Java, you will not get this dialog window in WebSphere V3.5.3.

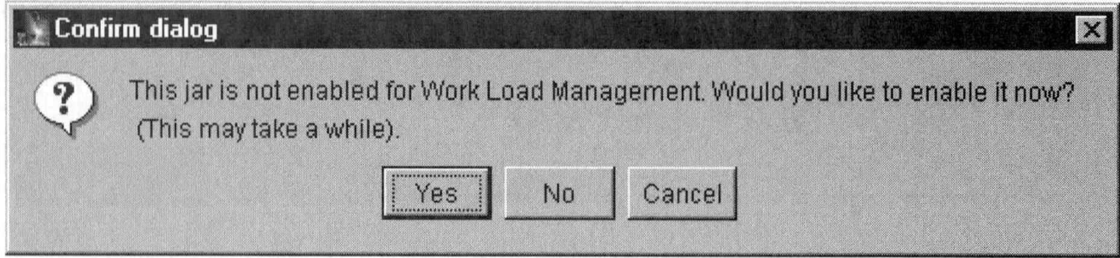

Figure 297. Click Yes if you are planning to use WLM

If the deployment succeeds, an Information dialog window appears as depicted in Figure 298. Click **OK** to finish deploying your EJB.

Figure 298. Deployment succeeds

Then we come back to the Create EnterpriseBean window. The fields Name and JAR file are now filled in.

It's not necessary to configure several parameters in the Advanced and DataSource tabs. Therefore, we don't specify them now. Click **OK** to finish creating your EJB as depicted in Figure 299 on page 426.

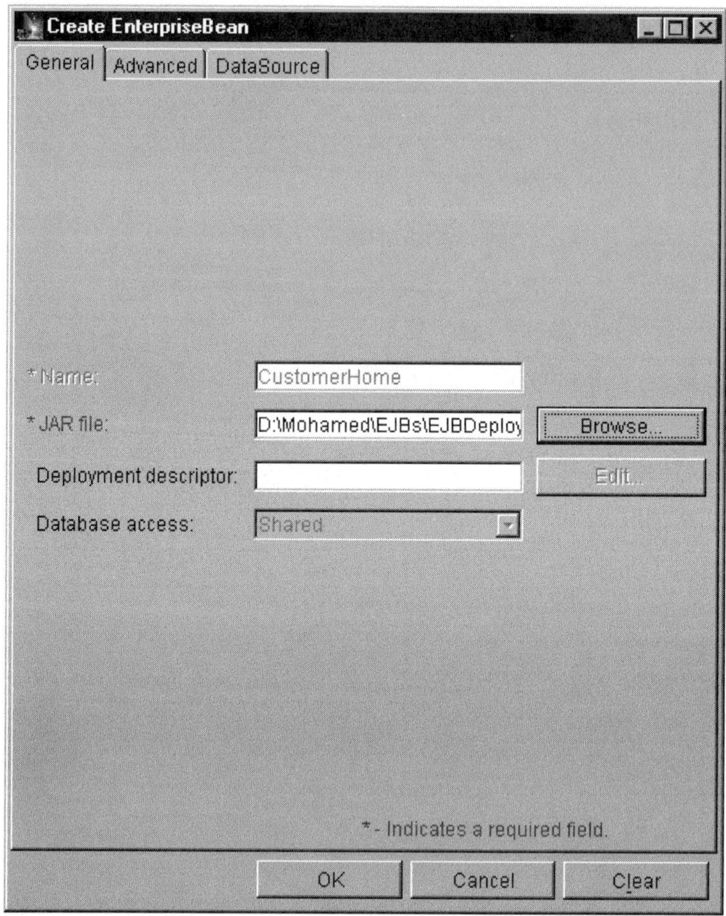

Figure 299. Click OK to create your EJB

WebSphere brings up a new information dialog saying that the creation of the EJB has completed successfully. Click **OK** to finish the creation of the EJB.

Now we go back to the administrative console, and make sure our EJB (CustomerHome) has been created successfully as depicted in Figure 300.

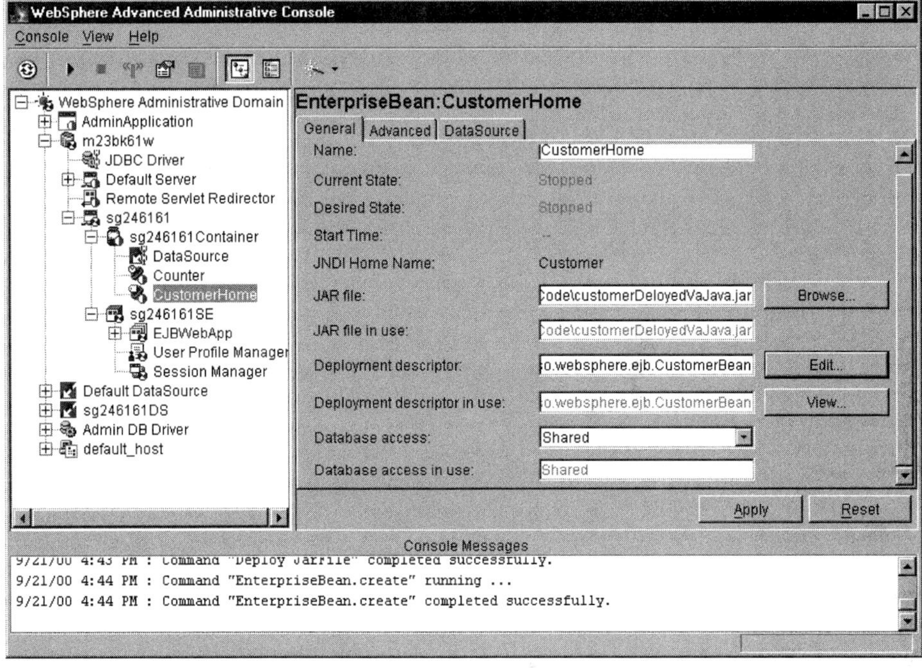

Figure 300. Newly created enterprise bean

You can check the bean properties and modify them if you wish by editing the deployment descriptor.

11.3 Stateless session beans

Now that we have been able to install our EJBs into WebSphere we can explore how they behave at run time.

In this section we show you the behavior of EJB stateless session beans in WebSphere V3.5. In the following sections we examine stateful session beans and entity beans.

Our tests emphasize the fact that we cannot use stateless session beans to maintain client state across calls to multiple business methods.

11.3.1 The life cycle of a stateless session bean

The stateless session bean's life cycle has two states:

- The does-not-exist state.
- The method-ready pool state.

When a bean instance is in the does-not-exist state, this means that it has not yet been instantiated.

When a bean instance is instantiated by the container and is ready to serve client requests, it is in the method-ready pool state. The container moves a stateless session beans from the does-not-exist state to the method-ready pool state by performing the following three operations:

- Invoke the Class.newInstance() method on the stateless bean class.
- Invoke the SessionBean.setSessionContext(SessionContext context) method on the bean instance.
- ejbCreate() method is invoked on the bean instance.

Note

A stateless session bean only has one ejbCreate() method, which takes no arguments.

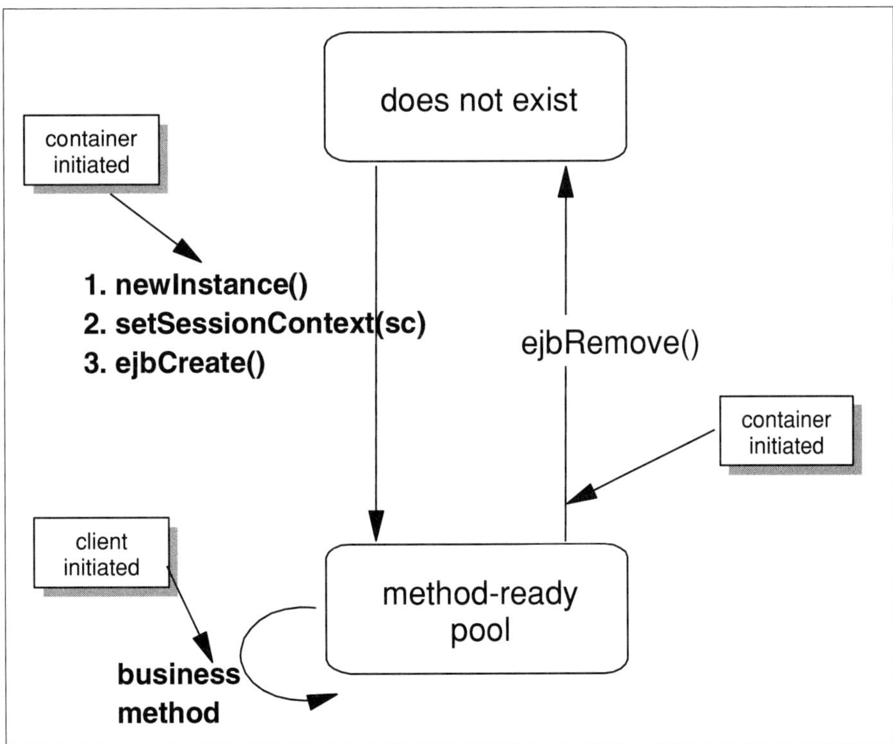

Figure 301. Stateless session bean life cycle

11.3.1.1 Sample stateless session bean application

We developed a sample application to illustrate the stateless session beans life cycle and the instance pool associated with these beans.

The application is composed of a servlet (CounterStatelessServlet) and a stateless session bean CounterBean.

The CounterBean class contains only one instance variable (theCount_) that represents the number of times the bean is being accessed.

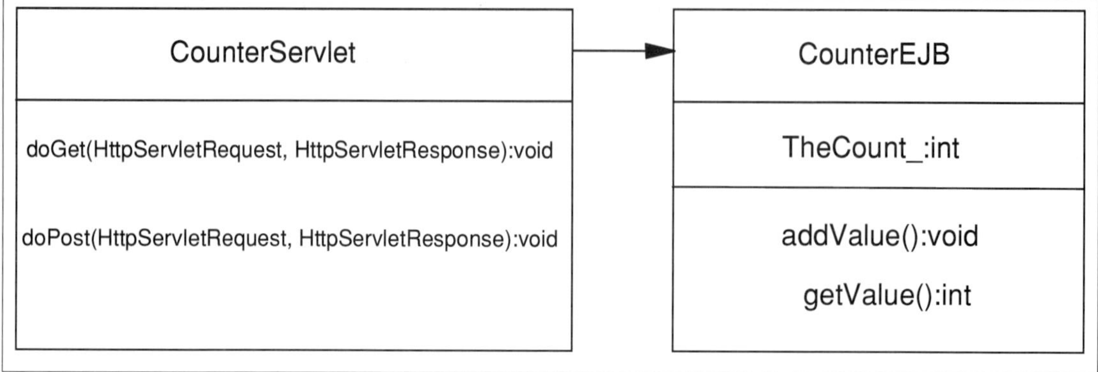

Figure 302. Sample application for stateless session bean

11.3.1.2 The Counter stateless session bean

The remote interface contains only one business method addValue() that increments the the_Count variable. Clients never call this method directly. They call it through the EJBObject implemented by the container. We added trace facilities to track the methods called in the CounterBean. We created and used the class from the com.ibm.itso.trace packages. Note that we will not describe this class.

The CounterBean class is defined as shown in Figure 303.

```
import java.util.Properties;
import javax.ejb.*;
import com.ibm.itso.trace.*;
/**
 * This is a Session Bean Class
 */
public class CounterBean implements SessionBean {
   private javax.ejb.SessionContext mySessionCtx = null;
   private int theCount_;
   // we use a TraceComponent for tracing
   private static final TraceComponent tc =
Tr.register(CounterBean.class);

   final static long serialVersionUID = 3206093459760846163L;
}
```

Figure 303. CounterBean class

In order to trace all the methods called by the container during the life cycle of the CounterBean, a trace method was added to EJB implementation.

Other important methods are defined as follows:

- setSessionContext(SessionContext ctx):

  This method is called by the EJBContainer to associate a new CounterBean instance with a session context.

```
/**
 * setSessionContext method comment
 * @param ctx javax.ejb.SessionContext
 * @exception java.rmi.RemoteException The exception description.
 */
public void setSessionContext(javax.ejb.SessionContext ctx) throws
java.rmi.RemoteException {
   mySessionCtx = ctx;
   if (tc.isEntryEnabled()) Tr.event(tc,"called setEntityContext()
method with ctx="+ctx.toString());
}
```

Figure 304. setSessionContext() method

- ejbCreate():

  The EJB client never calls this method directly. It is called via the create() method defined in the home interface. In our example, we set the theCount_ variable to 0 each time a new instance of a CounterBean is created.

```
/**
 * ejbCreate method comment
 * @exception javax.ejb.CreateException The exception description.
 * @exception java.rmi.RemoteException The exception description.
 */
public void ejbCreate() throws javax.ejb.CreateException,
java.rmi.RemoteException {
   this.theCount_=0;
    if (tc.isEntryEnabled()) Tr.event(tc,"called ejbCreate() method
with ctx="+mySessionCtx.toString());

   }
```

Figure 305. ejbCreate() method

- ejbActivate():

  This method is called when the container activates a passivated EJB. It does not apply to stateless session beans but applies to stateful and entity EJBs. We defined this method and added tracing to it in order to validate that it is never called by the container because our Counter EJB is stateless.

```
/**
 * ejbActivate method comment
 * @exception java.rmi.RemoteException The exception description.
 */
public void ejbActivate() throws java.rmi.RemoteException {
   if (tc.isEntryEnabled()) Tr.event(tc,"called ejbActivate() method
with ctx="+mySessionCtx.toString());
   }
```

Figure 306. ejbActivate() method

- ejbPassivate():

  This method is called when there are too many instances of stateful session beans or entity beans. To passivate an EJB, the container writes the instance to the file system using the serialization mechanism. This method does not apply for a stateless session bean. We defined this method and added tracing to it in order to validate that it is never called by the container because our Counter EJB is stateless.

```
/**
 * ejbPassivate method comment
 * @exception java.rmi.RemoteException The exception description.
 */
public void ejbPassivate() throws java.rmi.RemoteException {

   if (tc.isEntryEnabled()) Tr.event(tc,"called ejbPassivate() method
with ctx="+mySessionCtx.toString());
   }
```

Figure 307. ejbPassivate() method

- ejbRemove():

  When the EJBContainer removes an EJB instance, it invokes the ejbRemove() method. We added code to this method to insure that resources such as sockets or JDBC connections are freed.

```
/**
 * ejbRemove method comment
 * @exception java.rmi.RemoteException The exception description.
 */
public void ejbRemove() throws java.rmi.RemoteException {
   if (tc.isEntryEnabled()) Tr.event(tc,"called ejbRemove() method with
ctx="+mySessionCtx.toString());
   }
```

Figure 308. ejbRemove() method

- addValue():

  This is the only business method exposed in the remote interface of our stateless session bean.

```
public int addValue() throws java.rmi.RemoteException {
   theCount_++;
   return theCount_;
}
```

Figure 309. addValue() method

11.3.1.3 CounterStatelessServlet servlet

We developed a CounterServlet servlet to access our CounterBean EJB. The WebSphere programming model suggests accessing EJBs always through servlets. See Chapter 3, "WebSphere programming model" on page 17 for more information.

The home interface of a Counter EJB is stored as an instance variable of CounterServlet servlet. It is initialized at the init of the servlet. In this way, we guarantee that the lookup() on the home interface of the Counter EJB is done only once, since the servlet is a new instance. Lookup() calls can be very expensive in terms of performance. In our case, if we configure the CounterServlet servlet to be loaded at the startup of our server, the lookup on the home interface is done at the startup of the server, and our application is much more performable.

The init(ServletConfig) method of the CounterServlet is defined as Figure 310 on page 434.

```
/**
 * Initializes the servlet.
 */
public void init(ServletConfig config) throws ServletException {
   //
   super.init(config);
   try {
      // create initial naming context
      Hashtable params = new Hashtable();

params.put(Context.INITIAL_CONTEXT_FACTORY,"com.ibm.ejs.ns.jndi.CNIniti
alContextFactory");
      Context ctx = new InitialContext(params);
      home_ = (CounterHome)
javax.rmi.PortableRemoteObject.narrow(ctx.lookup("Counter"),CounterHome
.class);

   } catch(Exception e) {
      System.out.println("Servlet Init() exception: " +
e.getMessage());
         e.printStackTrace();
   }

      }
```

Figure 310. init(ServletConfig) of CounterServlet servlet

Note

For deploying our sample application, we must configure the classpath of the server running the servlet to contain the deployed EJB-JAR. This is because the CounterServlet servlet, which is the EJB client in this case, needs the stub classes included in the deployed EJB-JAR. When the client (the servlet in our example) is in the same JVM (WebSphere Application Server) as the EJB, then no explicit actions are required, since all required classes are in scope for the application server classloader. When the client and the EJB are *not* in the same JVM, then the deployed EJB client classes (JAR file) will need to be added to the classpath for the application server running the servlet.

11.3.1.4 Verification of stateless session bean state

In our tests, we access the CounterStatelessServlet servlet from different clients. We see that each time we access it, we have a different count result. A stateless session is an instance that contains a conversation state and which spans a single method invocation. Our CounterBean is stateless, so it does not maintain the state (theCount_) spanning multiple method calls. Therefore, a client will get an irregular increment value per method call when the EJBContainer dispatches requests to another CounterBean instance in a pool.

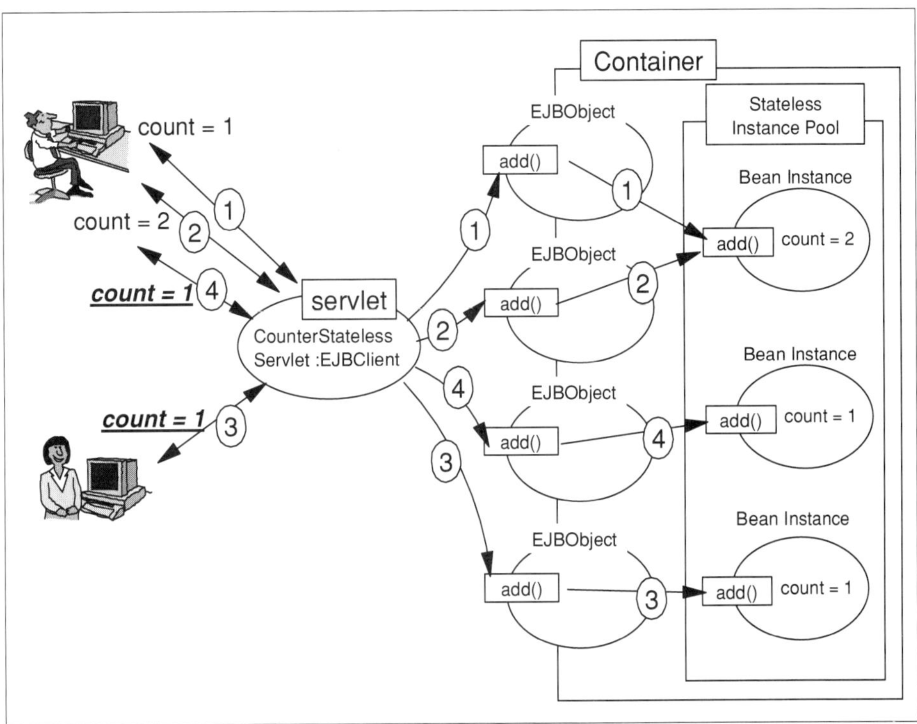

Figure 311. The EJBObject does not always use the same instance

Accessing from browser A

The first time we access the CounterStatelessServlet, we see the output shown in Figure 312 on page 436.

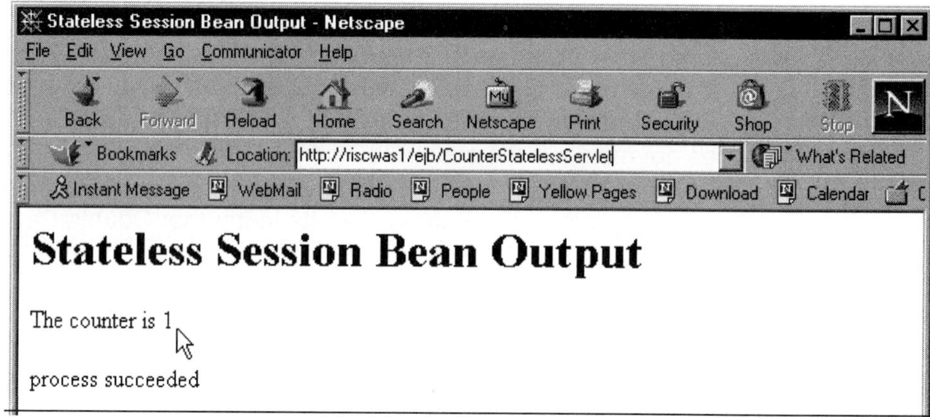

Figure 312. First access to the CounterStatelessServlet servlet

When access the CounterServlet several times from the same browser, the count increments correctly. When we access the CounterStatelessServlet from different browsers, we never get a regular count. The CounterBean does not maintain state between different method calls as shown in Figure 313.

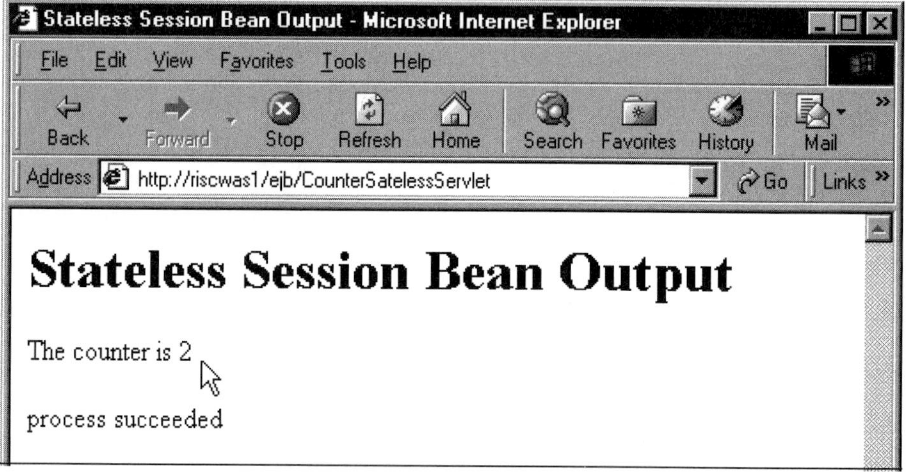

Figure 313. Accessing the CounterServlet from a different browser

When accessing the CounterStatelessServlet from multiple clients, we always get an irregular value as shown in Figure 314 on page 437.

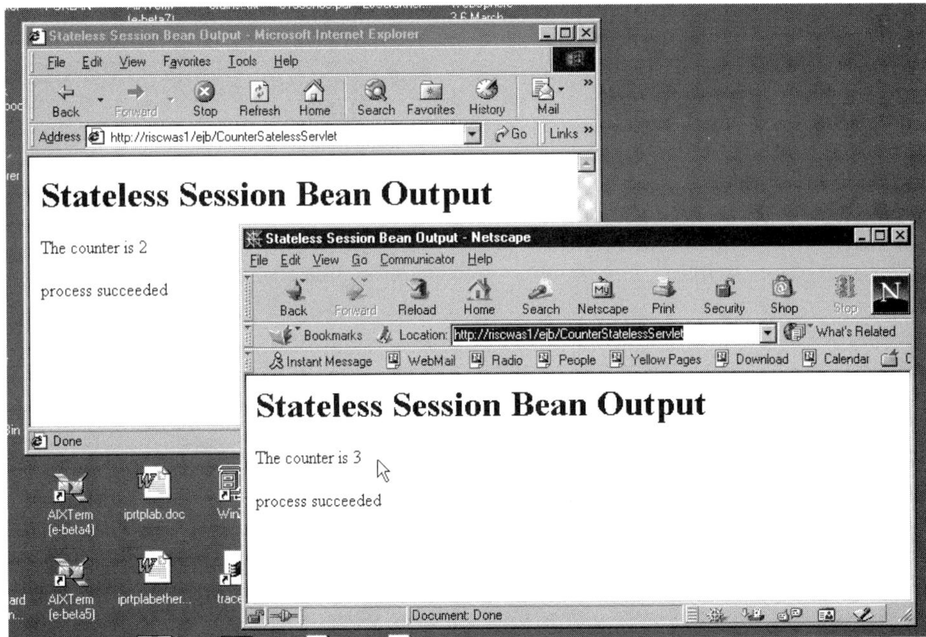

Figure 314. Output after accessing the CounterServlet from multiple clients

11.3.2 Stateless session beans instance pool

In this section we show how stateless session beans can be reused or shared by many clients without destroying or creating an instance per client unlike stateful session beans. We do this by checking that the number of stateless session beans in the container is smaller than the number of clients using our application simultaneously. We also show that stateless session beans are pooled by tracking the ejbCreate() and ejbRemove() methods.

Figure 315 on page 438 shows how stateless session beans are reused among multiple clients.

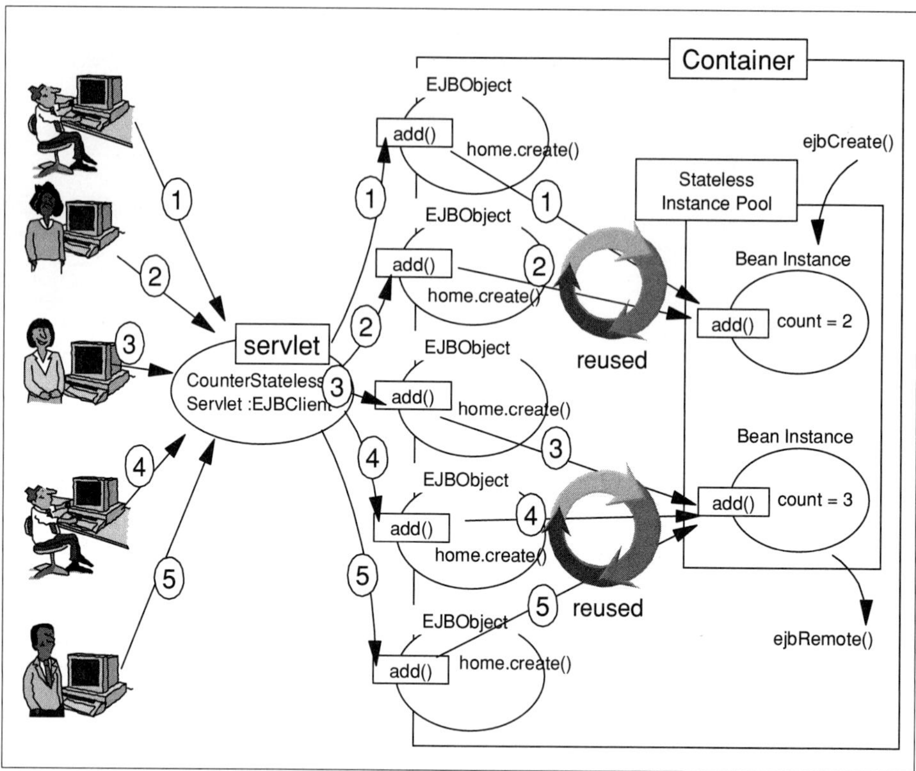

Figure 315. Stateless session beans instances pool

11.3.2.1 Test results

We want to verify that the number of instances in the pool is less than the number of concurrent clients accessing our CounterStatelessServlet servlet.

Simulating multiple concurrent accesses

We used a Web client's load simulation tool to generate multiple concurrent requests on our sample application. We then collected the trace to check the number of instantiated CounterBeans, the number of ejbRemove() methods and the number of the business method addValue() invoked.

Our load simulation tool was configured to generate 20 concurrent clients, executing each 10 requests, so that we have 200 requests overall.

Test results

Our test results are summarized in Table 25.

Table 25. Life cycle of CounterBean

method	Times called by the container
CounterBean()	31
setSessionContext(Context)	15
ejbCreate()	15
add()	200
ejbRemove()	13

Reusing instances

The business method add() has been called 200 times. The number of ejbCreate() instances is smaller that the number of concurrent access clients. We can see that the same bean can service different client requests, and that bean instances are reused.

The ejbRemove() was called 13 times. Therefore, there were two instances in the instance pool. This number is specified as the Minimum pool size on the Advanced tab of the EnterpriseBean. The container will automatically remove unused instances response to changes in container workload.

11.4 Stateful session beans

In this section we will illustrate the basics of stateful session beans. The stateful session bean life cycle is explained together with a sample application that shows that stateful session beans retain the state across the calls spanning multiple business methods.

Unlike stateless session beans, stateful session beans are not shared among multiple clients. Furthermore, stateful beans are not pooled. A stateful session bean is dedicated to one client for the life cycle of the bean instance. Once a stateful session bean is instantiated, it is dedicated to an EJBObject for its whole life cycle. This allowd us to retain state in instance variables of stateful session beans for the life of the instance.

11.4.1 The life cycle of the stateful session beans

Stateful session beans are neither shared nor reused among multiple clients. Unlike stateless session beans and entity beans, they are not pooled.

The life cycle of a stateful session bean has three states. Figure 316 shows the different states for a stateful session bean.

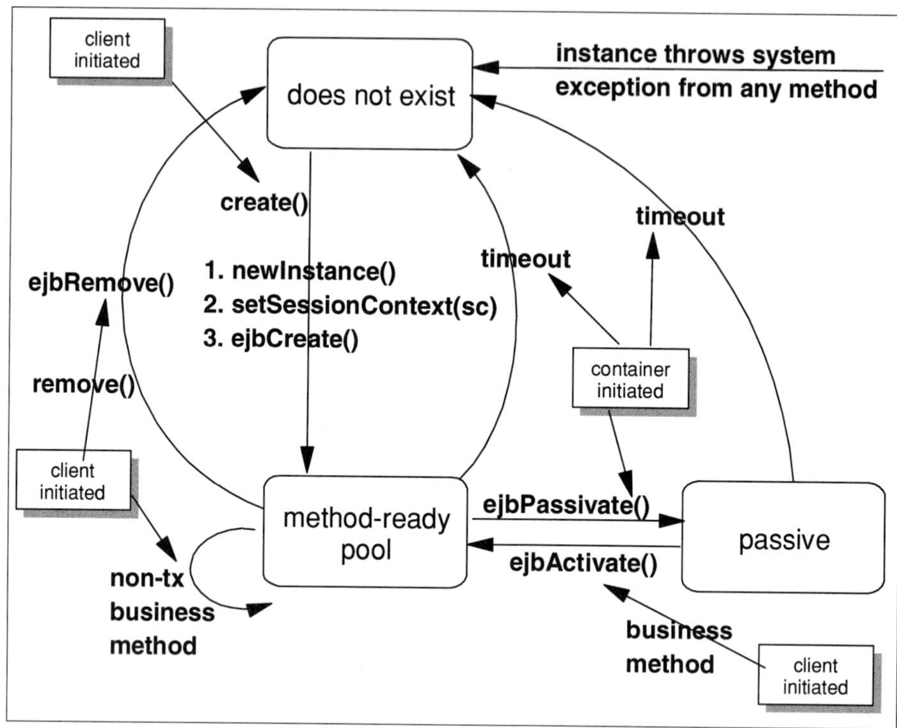

Figure 316. Stateful session beans life cycle

- Does-not-exist state

  This is the same for stateless session beans and entity beans. In this state, the bean has not been instantiated yet and it does not exist in memory.

- Method-Ready state

  When a client needs to work with a stateful session bean instance, it invokes the create() method on the EJBHome object provided by the container. To achieve this, the container instantiates a new bean and assigns it to the EJBObject. The instance bean is then ready to service client requests. Since each instance is assigned to an EJBObject, stateful session beans consume much more resources than stateless session beans.

- Passivated state

When a stateful session bean is not actively used (not servicing client requests) the container may decide to passivate it. The container saves its state to the passivation directory specified at the container level properties.

11.4.1.1 Verifying stateful session beans life cycle

In order to verify how the WebSphere EJS runtime manages the life cycle of stateful session beans, we will run our previous sample application (for stateless session beans).

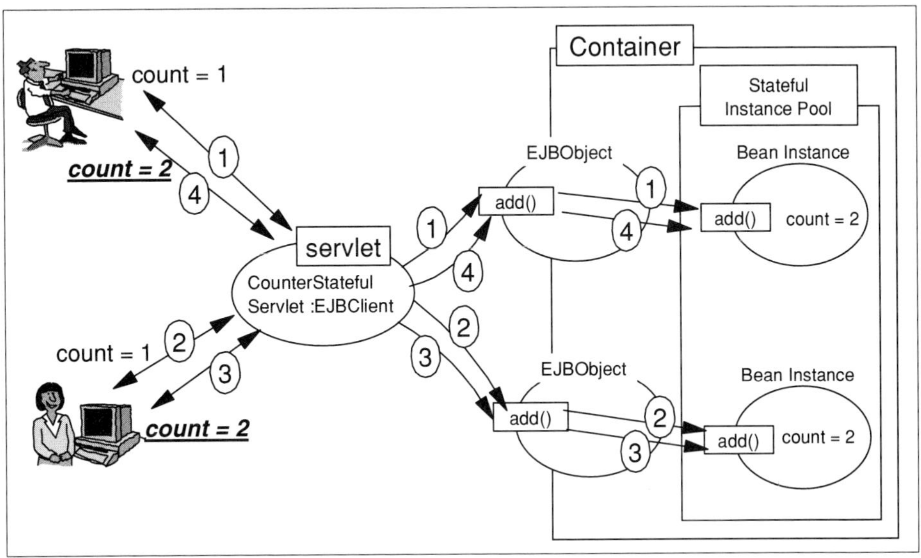

Figure 317. Stateful session beans sample application

However, in this case, we redeploy the CounterBean and declare it as a stateful session bean as depicted in Figure 318 on page 442.

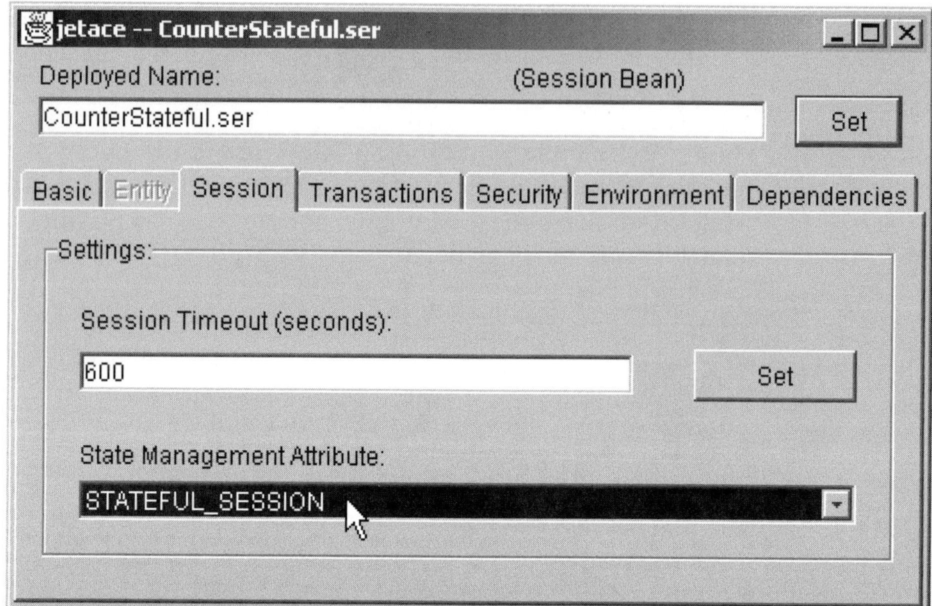

Figure 318. Redeploying CounterBean as stateful session bean with jetace

The CounterStatefulServlet servlet, the EJB Client in this case, now accesses a stateful session bean.

The first time the servlet has a reference to the EJBObject, this reference is stored in the HttpSession Object. The next time the servlet wants to invoke the Counter EJB, it gets the EJBObject from the HttpSession object, and then invokes methods on it. However, since the Counter EJB is now stateful, the EJBObject will always talk to the same CounterBean instance. The state (theCount_ value) is now maintained across multiple method calls.

Figure 319 on page 443 shows the flow of our sample stateful session bean application.

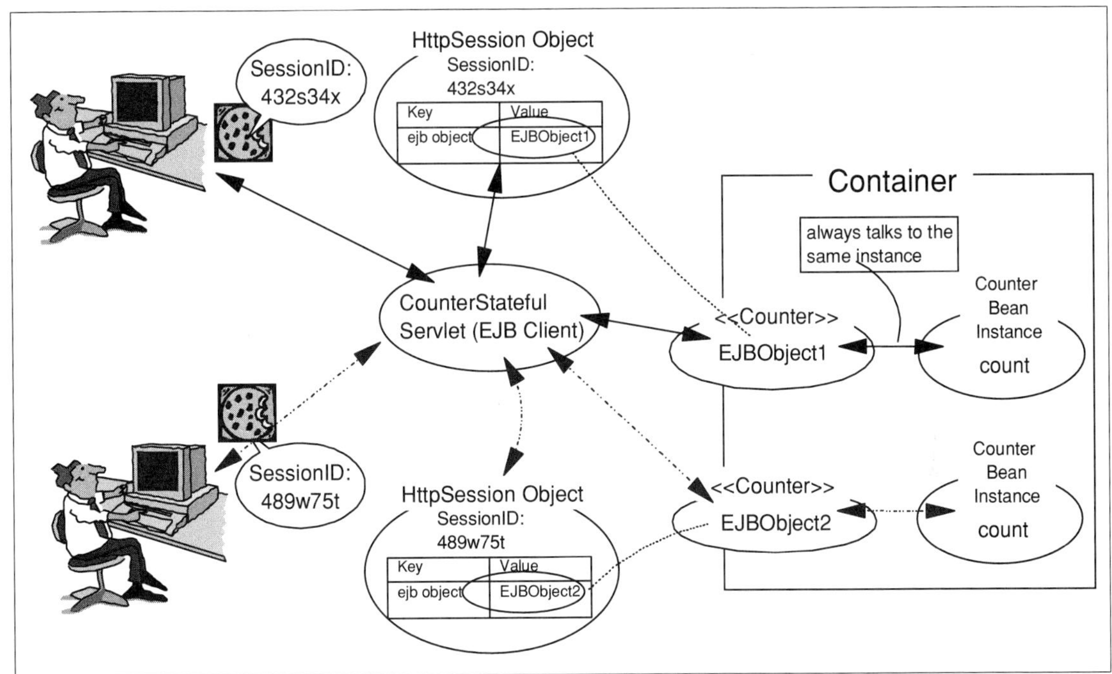

Figure 319. Stateful session beans with HttpSession

The doGet() method of CounterStatefulServlet as depicted in Figure 320 on page 444.

```
public void doGet(HttpServletRequest request, HttpServletResponse
response) {
long time = System.currentTimeMillis();
      PrintWriter out=null;
      String title = "Stateful Session Bean Output";
      String msg = " process succeeded";
      int result;
      Counter counter;
      try {
         // get the session and the EJB Object
         HttpSession session = request.getSession(false);
         if (session== null) {
            session = request.getSession(true);
            counter = (Counter)home_.create();
            session.putValue("ejbObject",counter);
         }
         else {
            counter = (Counter) session.getValue("ejbObject");
         }
      result = counter.addValue();
      response.setContentType("text/html");
      out = response.getWriter();
      out.println("<HTML><HEAD><TITLE>");
      out.println(title);
      out.println("</TITLE></HEAD><BODY>");
      out.println("<H1>"+title + "</H1>");
      out.println("<P>"+"The counter is " + result+"</P>");
      out.println("<P>"+"Current time is  " + time+"</P>");
      }
   catch(Throwable e)
   {
      e.printStackTrace(System.err);
      msg = "error" + e.getMessage();
      response.sendError(500,msg);
   }
   out.println("</p>"+msg+"</P>");
   out.println("</B></P>");
   out.println("</BODY></HTML>");
   out.close();
```

Figure 320. doGet() method of our CounterStatefulServlet

We also use a timestamp to track each time that the servlet is called.

When accessing our CounterStatefulServlet servlet for the first time we observed the result shown in Figure 321.

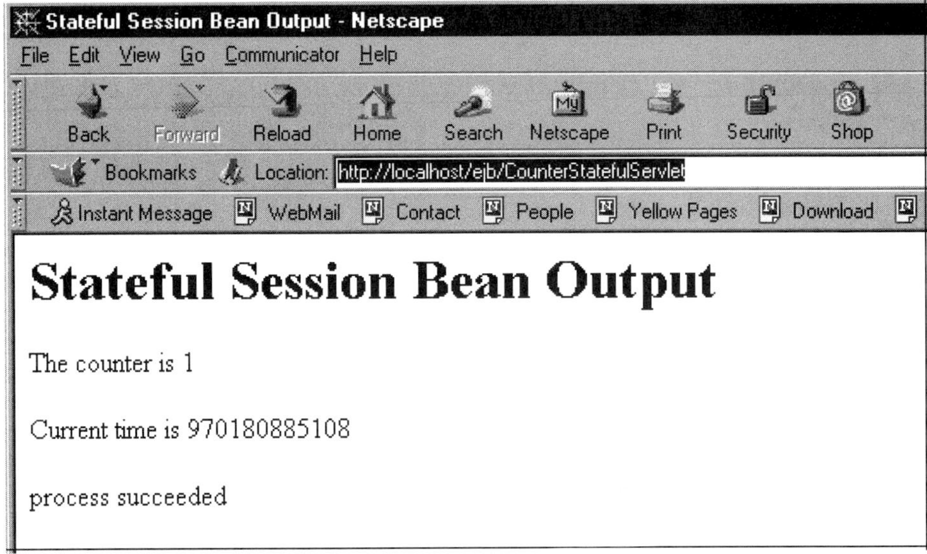

Figure 321. Accessing the CounterStatefulServlet servlet the first time

We have a regular count value when accessing the CounterStatefulServlet a second (and subsequent) time(s). Our Counter EJB is stateful as shown in Figure 322 on page 446.

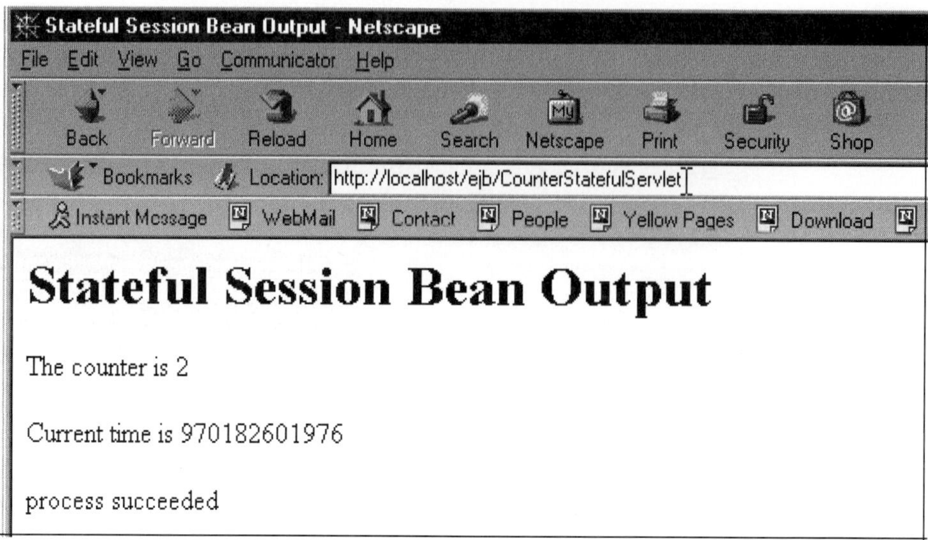

Figure 322. Accessing the CounterStatefulServlet

We always have a regular count value since our Counter EJB is now stateful. The second browser (Internet Explorer) gets 1 as count value since it's accessing the CounterStatefulServlet for the first time, which in turn will result in an new EJB instance be associated with this request. This is shown in Figure 323 on page 447.

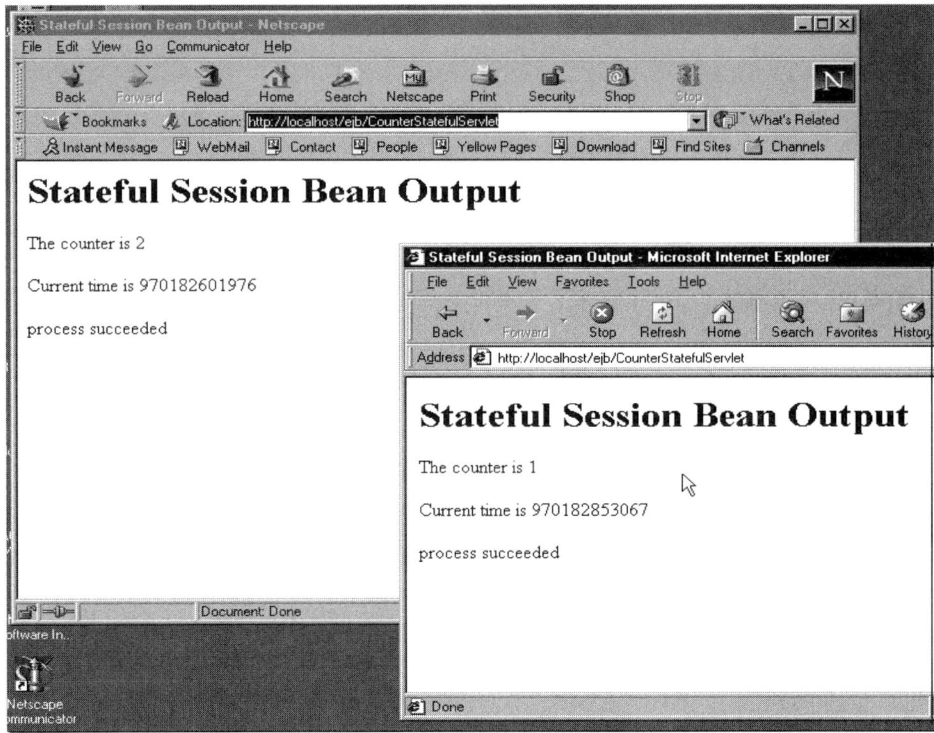

Figure 323. Accessing the CounterStatefulServlet from a different browser

11.4.2 Stateful session beans instance pool

When a stateful session bean is created, it is dedicated to an EJBObject for its whole life cycle. So the number of instances in the container at a certain time should be equal to the number of client, unless the container has passivated the bean instance in response to a long period of inactivity or in response to container workload.

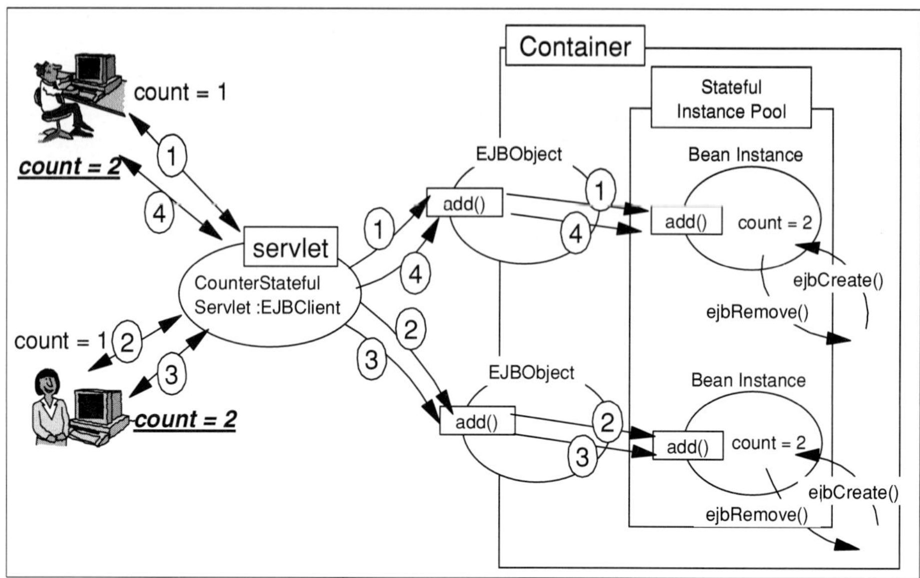

Figure 324. Stateful session beans instance pool

11.4.2.1 Verifying stateful session beans instance pooling

To verify that the number of EJBObjects and stateful session beans are always the same (so that each instance is dedicated to an EJBObject for its whole life cycle), we run a Web client's load simulation tool.

We configured 30 concurrent clients each accessing 10 times our CounterStatefulServlet so that we have a total of 300 requests.

The results are depicted in Table 26.

Table 26. Stateful session bean instance pooling

method	Times called by the container
CounterBean()	30
setSessionContext(SessionContext ctx)	30
ejbCreate()	30
add()	300
ejbRemove()	0

We can see that the methods CounterBean() and ejbCreate() were called 30 times by the container, which is equal to the number of clients simulated by a tool. The number of ejbCreate() instances is equivalent to the number of concurrent access clients. This means that requests for a stateful session bean require more system resources (depending on the number of maximum concurrent access clients) than a corresponding number of requests for a stateless session bean.

The business method add() is called 300 times, which is equal to the number of page requests.

The ejbRemove() method is never called. Therefore, 30 instances are in the stateful session bean pool.

When we access our CounterServlet with a browser after having run the Web client load generation tool, we always have a regular count.

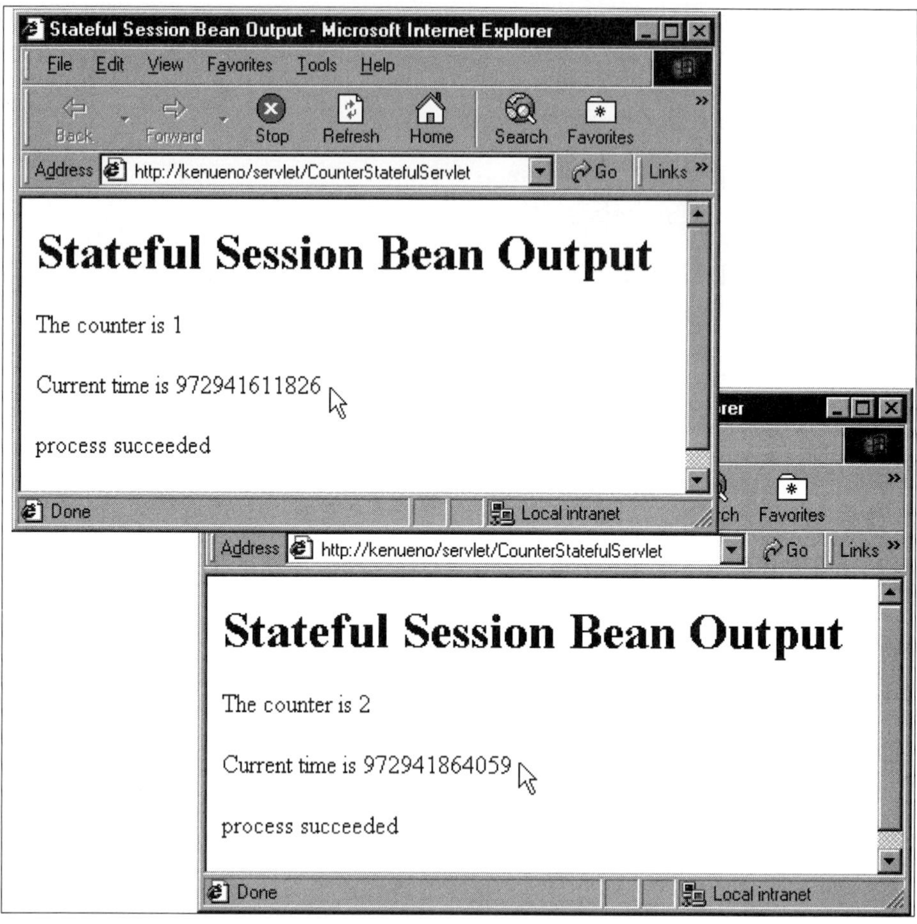

Figure 325. Stateful session beans maintain the state

11.4.3 Stateful session beans passivation/activation

If an instance of a stateful session bean is not used for a long period of time, or when the EJBContainer has reached the limit of instantiated EJBs (the Cache preferred limit), the bean will serialize the conversational state and write the state out to the file system directory that we specified as a passivation directory. The passivation directory can be specified from the container properties as shown in Figure 326 on page 451.

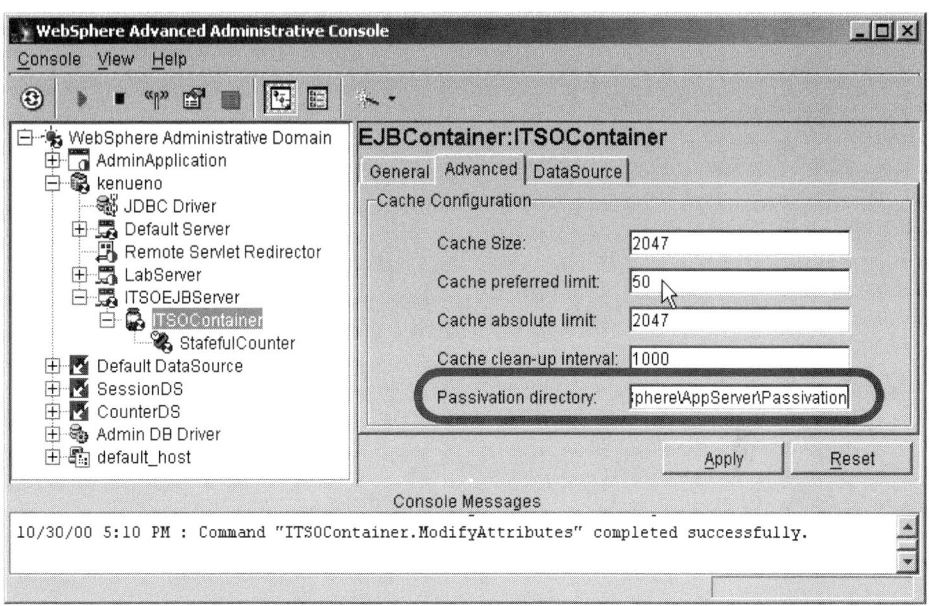

Figure 326. Passivation directory location

When the stateful session bean has been successfully passivated, the instance is removed from memory, allowing the container to preserve resources. When an instance bean is passivated, its ejbPassivate() method is called. At this time the bean has to free all the resources, such as JDBC connections and sockets, and set all nontransient, nonserializable fields to null.

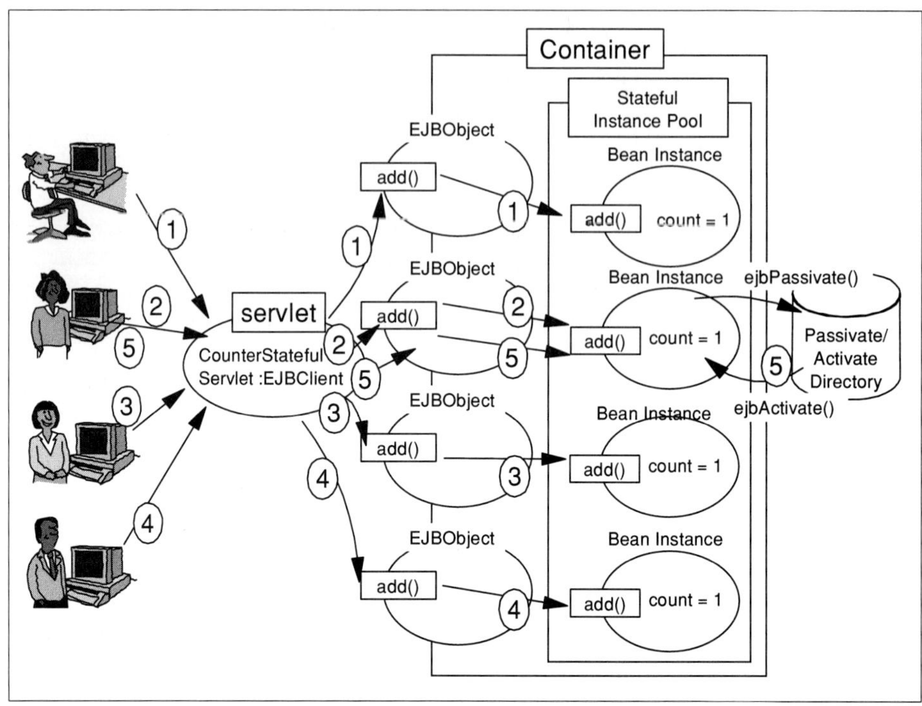

Figure 327. EJB passivation/activation

To verify this mechanism in WebSphere V3.5:

1. We decreased the property "Cache preferred limit" to be equal to 50 as shown in Figure 326 on page 451.
2. We ran a Web client load generation tool with 70 concurrent clients each accessing the CounterStatefulServlet 10 times.

Test results

Our test results are summarized in Table 27.

Table 27. Stateful session bean passivation/activation

method	Times called by the container
ejbCreate()	70
add()	700
ejbRemove()	0
ejbPassivate()	94

method	Times called by the container
ejbActivate()	73

After collecting the trace, the number of ejbCreate() instances is equivalent to the number of concurrent access requests.

The number of calling a business method (in our case, the add() method) is the same as the number of total page requests.

The ejbPassivate() method has been called 94 times by the container.

The number of calling ejbPassivate() (in our case, 94) minus the number of ejbActivate() (in our case, 73) equals 21. There are 21 instances in the passivate state, which can be verified by looking at the passivation directory as shown in Figure 328.

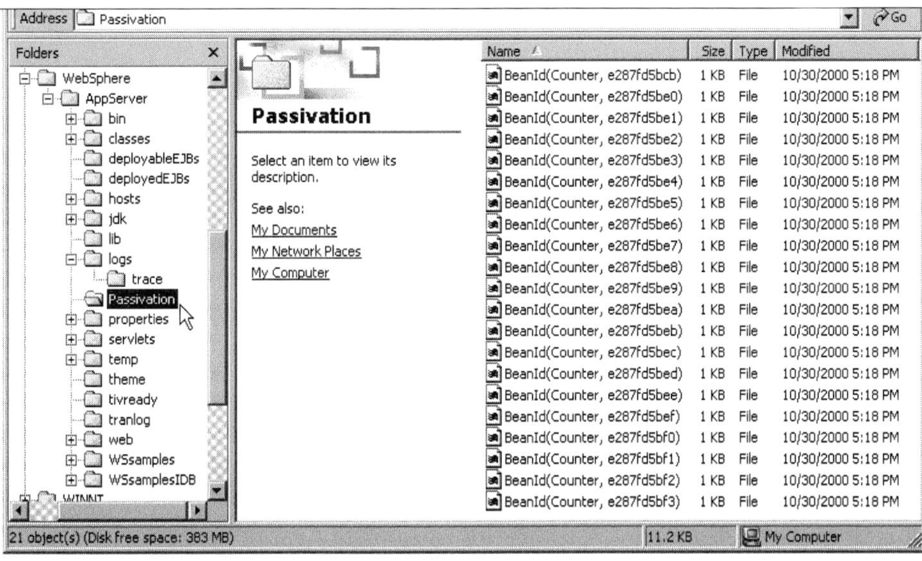

Figure 328. Passivate objects in the passivation directory

11.4.4 Understanding EJBObject handles

EJBObject handles are mainly persistent references to EJBObjects. If for some reason a client needs to disconnect from an EJBObject but needs to use it later without losing the state, it can use a handle to store the EJBObject in permanent storage and read it later to resume execution.

We show you a sample application that stores a stateful session bean EJBObject handle into an HttpSession persistence database, and then reestablishes access to the original stateful session bean instance using that EJBObject handle.

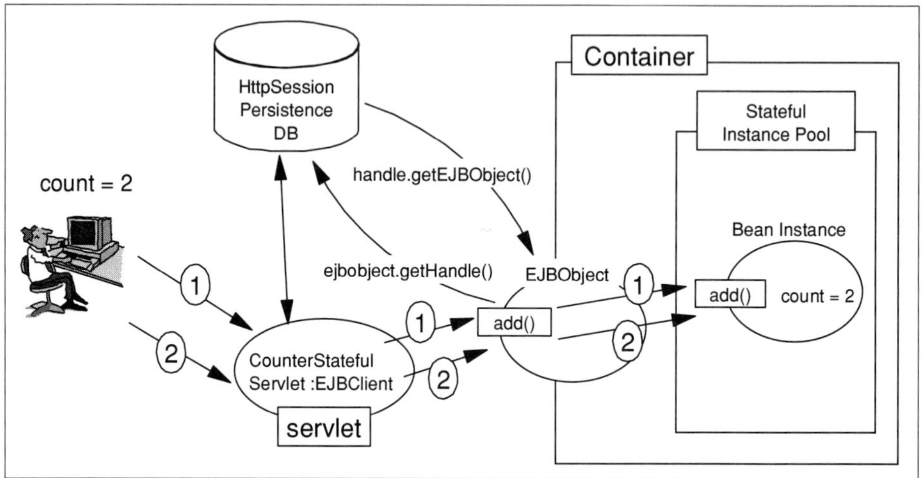

Figure 329. Using handles

11.4.4.1 Sample application for EJBObject handles

We modify the CounterServlet servlet described earlier to store an EJBObject handle in a persistent database session.

For configuring persistent sessions in WebSphere V3.5, see Chapter 7, “Session support” on page 245.

The doGet(HttpServletRequest,HttpServletResponse) method of our new CounterStatulServlet is described in Figure 330 on page 455.

```
public void doGet(HttpServletRequest request, HttpServletResponse
response) throws ServletException, IOException {
PrintWriter out=null;
      String title = "Statelful Session Bean EJBObject Handle Output";
      String msg = " process succeeded";
      int result;
      Counter counter;
      Handle counterHandle;
      try {
         // get the session and the EJB Object
         HttpSession session = request.getSession(false);
         if (session== null) {
            session = request.getSession(true);
            counter = (Counter)home_.create();
             counterHandle = counter.getHandle();
            session.putValue("handle",counterHandle);
            }
         else {
            counterHandle = (Handle) session.getValue("handle");
            counter = (Counter)counterHandle.getEJBObject();
         }
            result = counter.addValue();
      response.setContentType("text/html");
      out = response.getWriter();
      out.println("<HTML><HEAD><TITLE>");
      out.println(title);
      out.println("</TITLE></HEAD><BODY>");
      out.println("<H1>"+title + "</H1>");
      out.println("<P>"+"The counter is " + result+"</P>");
      }
   catch(Throwable e)
   {
      e.printStackTrace(System.err);
      msg = "error" + e.getMessage();
      response.sendError(500,msg);
   }
   out.println("</p>"+msg+"</P>");
   out.println("</B></P>");
   out.println("</BODY></HTML>");
   out.close();
```

Figure 330. CounterServlet using handles

The doGet(HttpServletRequest, HttpServletResponse) method initially obtains a stateful session bean serializable handle and puts into a HttpSession Object as described in Figure 331. The HttpSession Manager stores it in a persistent database (DB2) in our case.

```
counterHandle = counter.getHandle();
session.putValue("handle",counterHandle);
```

Figure 331. Getting an EJBObject handle

To recreate the EJBObject, we obtain the handle from the HttpSession Object and we re-create the reference to the original stateful session object instance as described in Figure 332.

```
counterHandle = (Handle) session.getValue("handle");
counter = (Counter)counterHandle.getEJBObject();
```

Figure 332. Recreating the EJBObject from the handle

Test procedure and result

The following procedures demonstrate re-connection of the original stateful session bean instance after re-starting a servlet engine.

1. Access the CounterStatefulServlet.

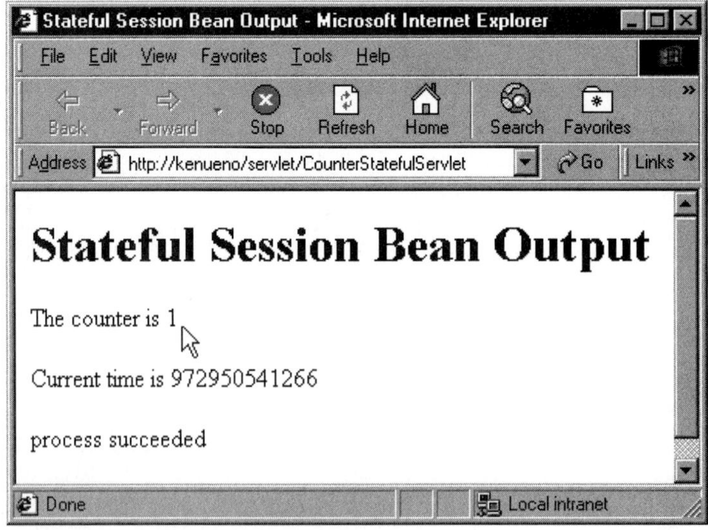

Figure 333. Access the CounterStatefulServlet

The counter number is “1”.

2. Stop the application server that contains the CounterStatefulServlet.

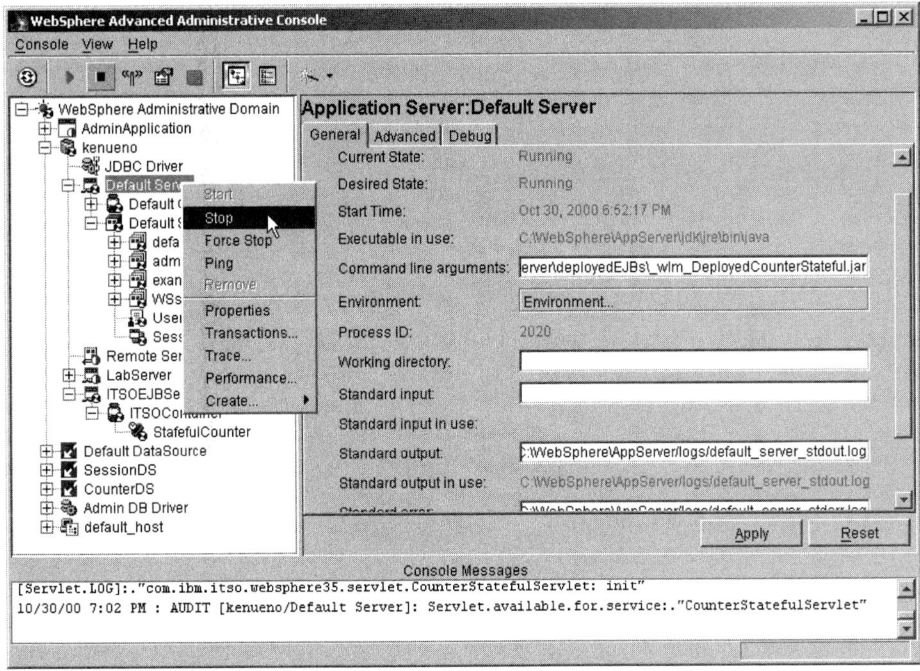

Figure 334. Stop the application server

The CounterStatefulServlet and HttpSession instance are destroyed by stopping the application server.

3. Restart the application server that contains the CounterStatefulServlet.

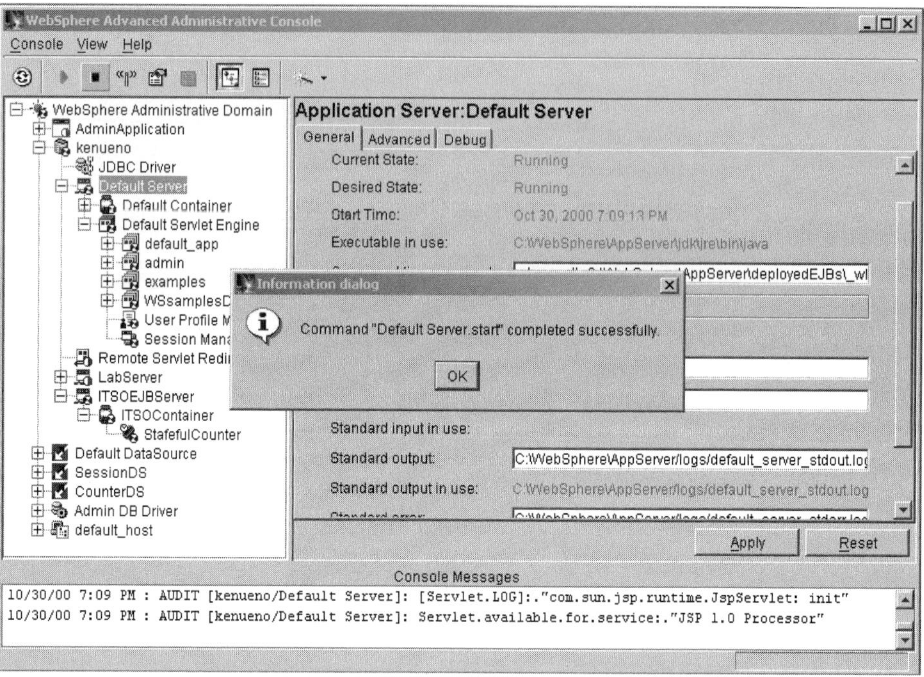

Figure 335. Restart the application server

4. Re-access the CounterStatefulServlet from the same browser.

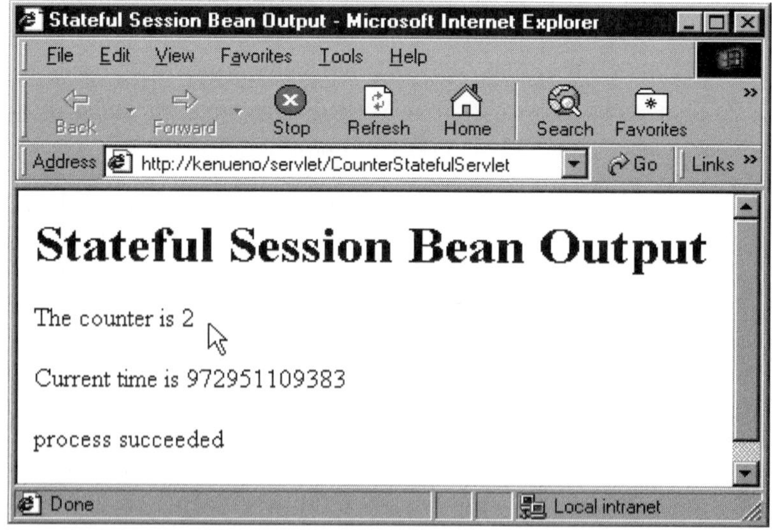

Figure 336. Re-access the CounterStatefulServlet

The counter number is “2”.

You connected the original stateful session bean instance after restarting the application server.

11.5 Container managed persistence (CMP) entity beans

A container-managed persistence (CMP) bean is an entity bean for which the container handles the interactions between the enterprise bean and the data source. The container is responsible for synchronization of instance fields with the persistent store. When you develop a container-managed persistence bean, the application is insulated from the details of the persistence mechanism.

11.5.1 Entity beans life cycle

Once an enterprise bean is deployed into a container, clients can create and use instances of that bean as required. Within the container, instances of an enterprise bean go through a defined life cycle. The events in an enterprise bean’s life cycle are derived from actions initiated by either the client or the container.

The life cycle of entity beans has three states:

- Does-not-exist state

  At this stage, no instances of the bean exist.

  An entity bean instance’s life cycle begins when the container creates that instance. After creating a new entity bean instance, the container invokes the instance’s setEntityContext() method. This method passes to the bean instance a reference to an entity context interface that can be used by the instance to obtain container services and to retrieve information about the caller of the client-invoked method.

- Pooled state

  Once an entity bean instance is created, it is placed in a pool of available instances of the specified entity bean class. While the instance is in this pool, it is not associated with a specific EJBObject. Every instance of the same enterprise bean class in this pool is identical. While an instance is in this pooled state, the container can use it to invoke any of the bean’s finder methods.

- Ready state

  When a client needs to work with a specific entity bean instance, the container picks an instance from the pool and associates it with the EJBObject initialized by the client. An entity bean instance is moved from the pooled to the ready state if there are no available instances in the ready state.

There are two events that cause an entity bean instance to be moved from the pooled state to the ready state:

- When a client invokes the create() method in the bean's home interface to create a new and unique entity of the entity bean class (and a new record in the data source). As a result of this method invocation, the container calls the bean instance's ejbCreate() and ejbPostCreate() methods and the new EJBObject is associated with the bean instance.
- When a client invokes a finder method to manipulate an existing instance of the entity bean class (associated with an existing record in the data source). In this case, the container calls the bean instance's ejbActivate() method to associate the bean instance with the existing EJBObject.

When an enterprise bean instance is in the ready state, the container can invoke the instance's ejbLoad() and ejbStore() methods to synchronize the data in the instance with the corresponding data in the data source. In addition, the client can invoke the bean instance's business methods when the instance is in this state. All interactions required to handle an entity bean instance's business methods in the appropriate transactional (or non-transactional) manner are handled by the container, unless the EJB developer has decided to handle these interactions.

When a container determines that an entity bean instance in the ready state is no longer required, it moves the instance to the pooled state. This transition to the pooled state results from either of the following events:

- When the container invokes the ejbPassivate() method.
- When the client invokes a remove() method on the EJBObject associated with the bean instance or on the EJB home object. When the remove() method is called, the underlying entity is removed permanently from the data source.

The diagram in Figure 337 on page 461 illustrates the entity bean life cycle.

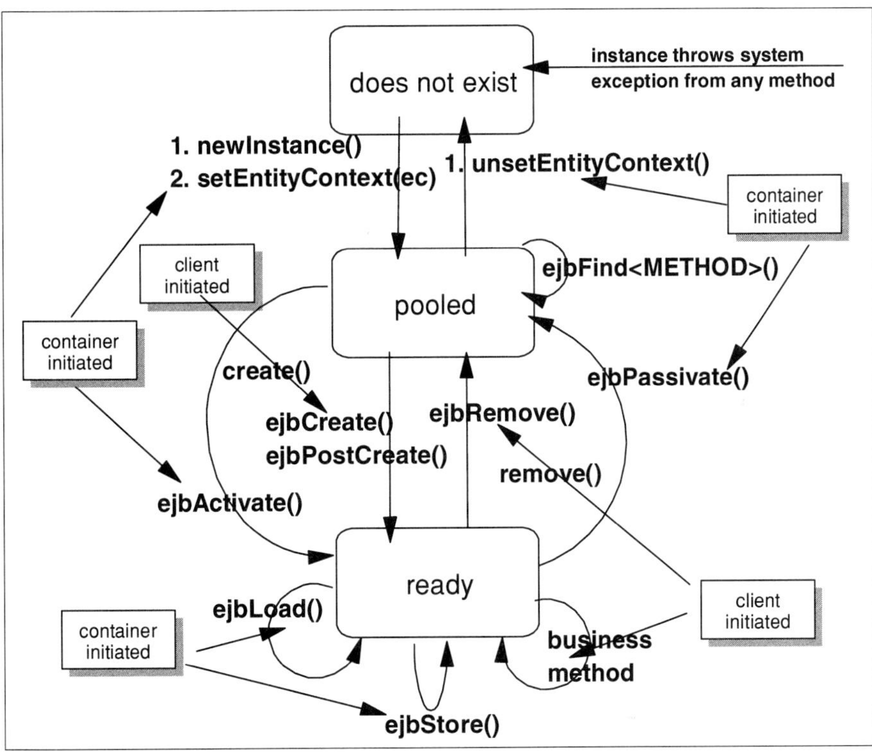

Figure 337. Entity beans life cycle

11.5.1.1 Sample application for entity beans

We use a sample application to understand how WebSphere V3.5 manages multiple EJBClients accessing the same container-managed persistence EJB (Counter EJB). We also use a trace facility which we created to track when the container calls the ejbActivate(), ejbLoad(), ejbStore() and ejbPassivate() method.

We developed a sample container-managed persistence EJB Counter having only one CMP field, theCount_, and two business methods, addValue() and getValue().

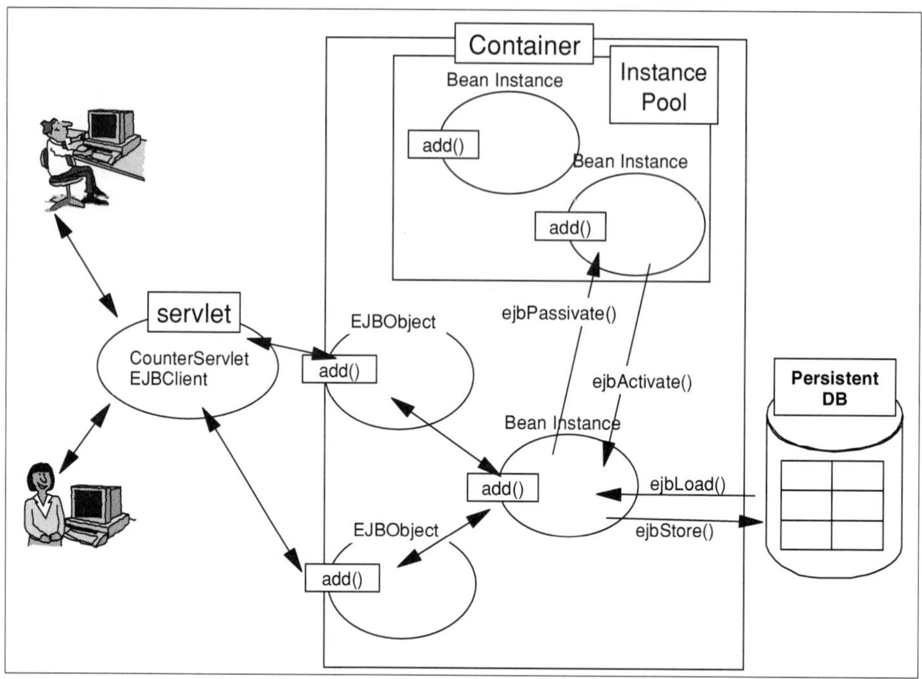

Figure 338. Counter CMP

We also developed a servlet that uses this EJB. The doGet() method of this servlet is described in Figure 339 on page 463.

```
public void doGet(HttpServletRequest request, HttpServletResponse response)
{
PrintWriter out=null;
      String title = "Container Managed Persistence Bean Output";
      String msg = " process succeeded";
      int result;
      CounterCMP counter;
      Handle counterHandle;
      try {
         // get the session and the EJB Object
         HttpSession session = request.getSession(false);
         if (session== null) {
            session = request.getSession(true);
            CounterCMPKey cmpkey = new CounterCMPKey();
            try {
               counter = (CounterCMP)home_.findByPrimaryKey(cmpkey);
            } catch (ObjectNotFoundException e) {
               counter = home_.create(cmpkey.counterKey_);
            }
            counterHandle = counter.getHandle();
            session.putValue("handle",counterHandle);
         }
         else {
            counterHandle = (Handle) session.getValue("handle");
            counter = (CounterCMP)counterHandle.getEJBObject();
         }
      result = counter.incrementTheCount();
      response.setContentType("text/html");
      out = response.getWriter();
      out.println("<HTML><HEAD><TITLE>");
      out.println(title);
      out.println("</TITLE></HEAD><BODY>");
      out.println("<H1>"+title + "</H1>");
      out.println("<P>"+"The counter is " + result+"</P>");
      }
   catch(Throwable e)
   {
      e.printStackTrace(System.err);
      msg = "error" + e.getMessage();
      response.sendError(500,msg);
   }
   out.println("</p>"+msg+"</P>");
   out.println("</B></P>");
   out.println("</BODY></HTML>");
   out.close();
}
```

Figure 339. doGet() method of the CounterCMPServlet

The servlet does the lookup on the home interface of the CounterCMP EJB in its init, and it stores it as an instance variable.

To access an instance of the CounterCMP EJB, we first construct a CounterCMPKey object, and we call the findByPrimaryKey() method on the home interface to get a reference on the remote interface as depicted in Figure 340.

```
CounterCMPKey cmpkey = new CounterCMPKey();
try {
      counter = (CounterCMP)home_.findByPrimaryKey(cmpkey);
      } catch (ObjectNotFoundException e) {
      counter = home_.create(cmpkey.counterKey_);
      }
```

Figure 340. Finding an instance of CounterCMP

The findByPrimaryKey() method can throw an ObjectNotFound Exception, if an instance of the corresponding entity bean is not found. In this case, we create a new instance, by calling the create() method on the home interface.

When we have a reference to an entity bean, we store a handle to it in the HttpSession object associated with servlet request. This is similar to what we did for the stateful session bean.

11.5.2 Understanding the entity beans persistence

Entity beans are persisted to a database. Each bean instance represents a row in a table from the database. In this test scenario we will show that data of bean instances is synchronized with corresponding rows in the database.

Before accessing our CounterCMPServlet servlet, the CounterCMP table is empty as depicted in Figure 341.

```
db2 => select * from countercmp

THECOUNT_   COUNTERKEY_
----------- ------------------------------

  0 record(s) selected.

db2 =>
```

Figure 341. CounterCMP table before accessing CounterCMPServlet

We access our CounterCMPServlet servlet for the first time. The result is depicted in Figure 342.

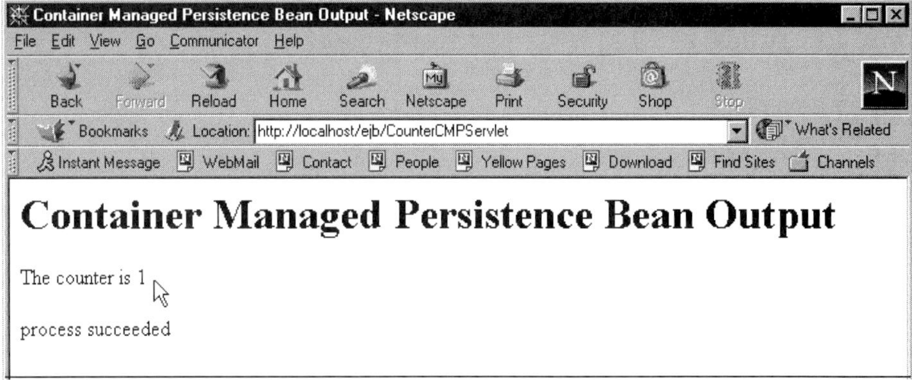

Figure 342. Accessing CounterCMPServlet servlet

The CounterCMP table in the counter database now has one row as depicted in Figure 343.

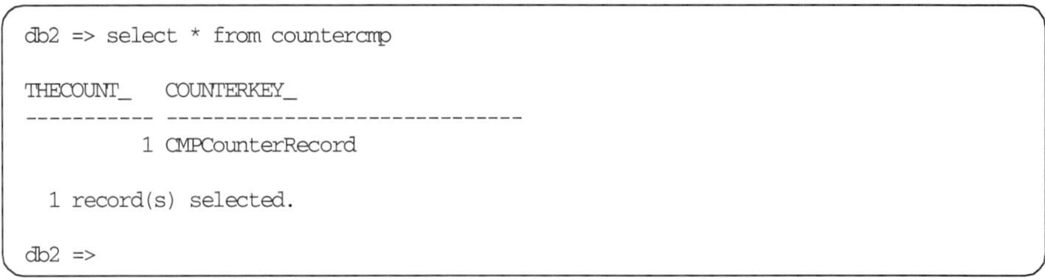

```
db2 => select * from countercmp

THECOUNT_   COUNTERKEY_
----------- ------------------------------
          1 CMPCounterRecord

  1 record(s) selected.

db2 =>
```

Figure 343. CounterCMP table contents after first accessing

We connect our CounterCMPServlet servlet a second time. The result is depicted in Figure 344 on page 466.

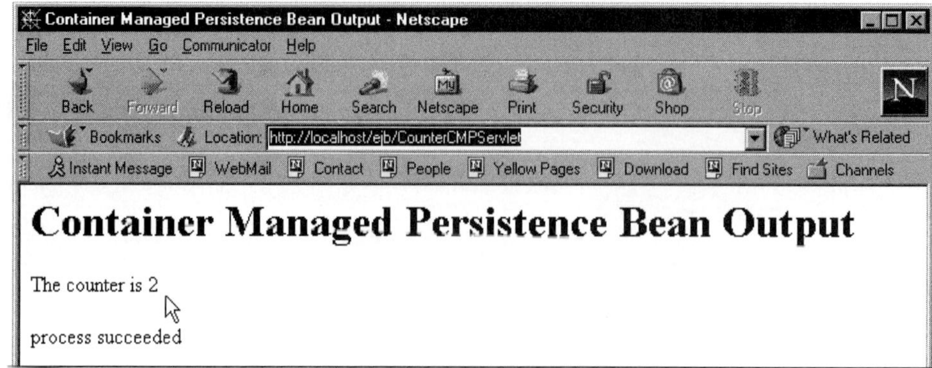

Figure 344. Accessing CounterCMPServlet for the second time

The counter has been incremented and the primary key is always CMPCounterRecord as depicted in Figure 345.

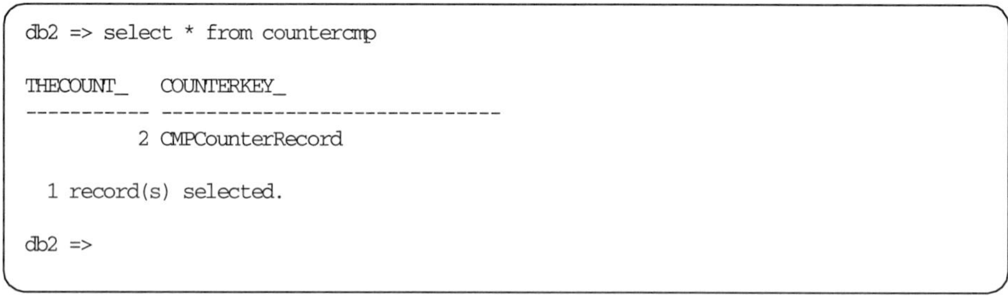

```
db2 => select * from countercmp

THECOUNT_   COUNTERKEY_
----------- ------------------------------
          2 CMPCounterRecord

  1 record(s) selected.

db2 =>
```

Figure 345. CounterCMP table contents after second accessing

11.5.3 Understanding the entity beans life cycle

In order to verify an entity bean's life cycle under EJS runtime, we executed a Web client generation tool with 20 clients, each executing 10 requests, resulting in a total of 200 requests.

The results in the trace file obtained are depicted in Table 28.

Table 28. Entity beans life cycle

method	times called
setEntityContext()	20
unsetEntityContext()	0
ejbCreate()	0
business method: IncrementCounter()	200

method	times called
ejbRemove()	0
ejbPassivate()	240
ejbActivate()	240
ejbLoad()	240
ejbStore()	200

The ejbCreate() is never called. The servlet never calls the home.create() method.

We had 200 requests each calling a business method, thus we have 200 method calls.

The ejbStore() method is called 200 times, with each client updating the counter, so we can validate that there is an access to the database corresponding to each ejbStore() method.

11.5.4 Understanding CMP commit option A, C caching

In this section we examine the difference between commit (caching) options A and C as described in section 9.1.10 of the EJB Specification.

When specifying **option A caching**, WebSphere imposes a significant restriction in that the bean instance must be the *only* updater of data in an underlying persistent store. WebSphere does not enforce this restriction, so it is the bean deployer's responsibility to ensure that this restriction is satisfied. This means that the beans utilizing this option will only be used within a single container, and it is thus the responsibility of all clients of that bean to always direct their requests to the one bean instance within that specific container. This means you cannot use option A caching with WLM-enabled servers or with a database that is shared among multiple applications that are trying to modify the data.

With **option C caching**, on the other hand, the bean is always reloaded from the database at the beginning of each transaction. To understand this, consider two sequential transactions that touch bean A. The first transaction loads the bean into the cache, does its work, commits, and removes the bean. The second transaction then has to reload the bean and repeat. Therefore, it is acceptable for a client to attempt to access the bean and start a new transaction on any container that has been configured to host that bean. The shared state is maintained in a shared database, and can be accessed from any server when required.

We will use our entity bean sample application to examine the behavior of the WebSphere EJS runtime with commit options A and C.

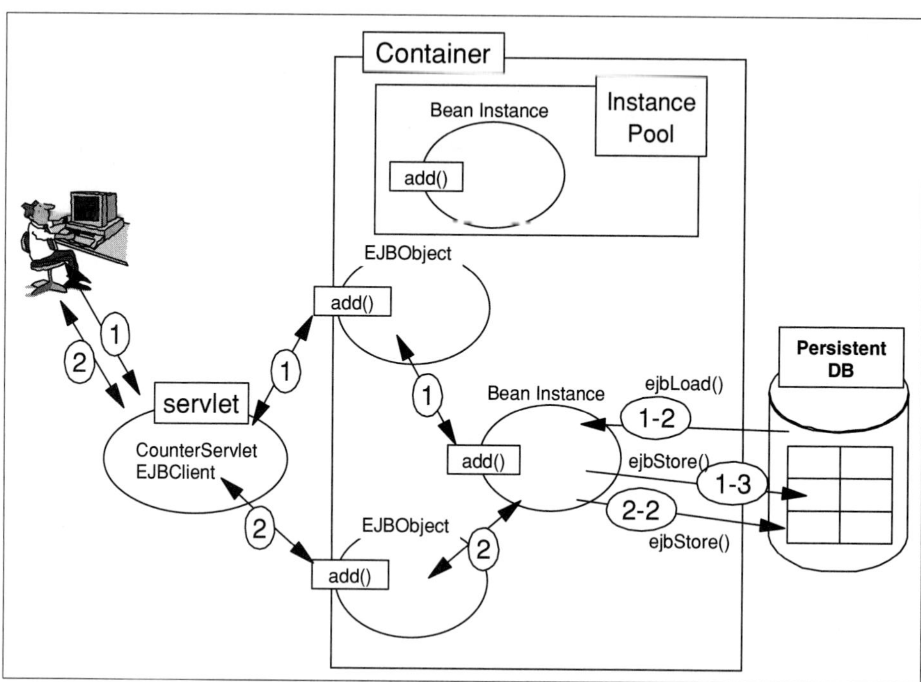

Figure 346. Commit option A caching

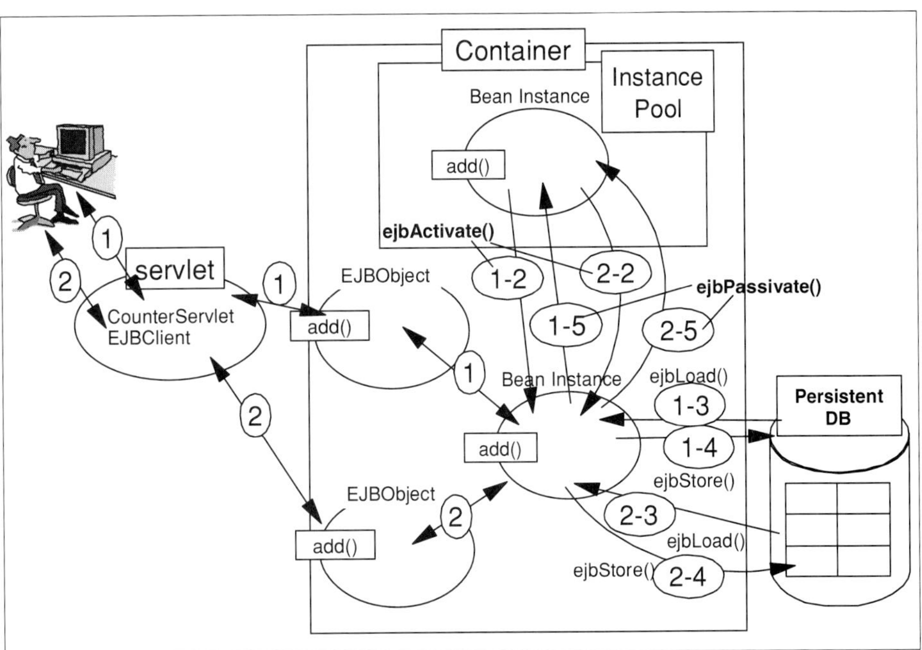

Figure 347. Commit option C caching

11.5.4.1 Commit option A

To configure commit option A on CounterCMP, select it and on the General tab select **Exclusive** in the Database access field as depicted in Figure 348 on page 470.

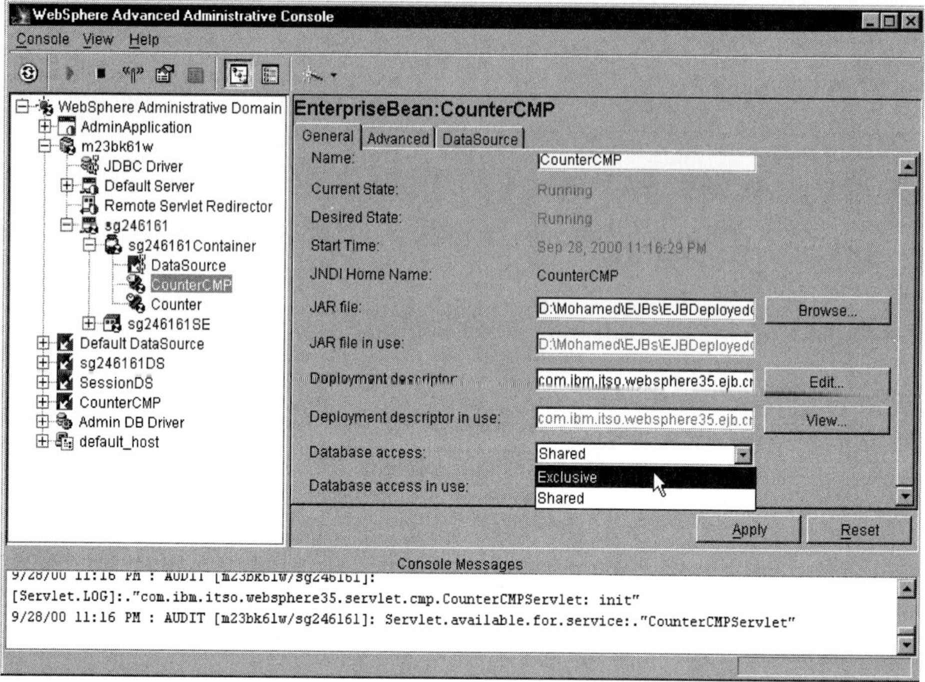

Figure 348. Configuring commit option A (Exclusive)

We restart our application server (we call it sg246161) to invalidate HttpSession, then we called the CounterCMPServlet twice.

Figure 349 shows the trace file when we configured the commit option A.

```
1c9585f1 CounterCMPBea E called setEntityContext() method
1c9585f1 CounterCMPBea E called ejbActivate() method
1c9585f1 CounterCMPBea E called ejbLoad() method
1c9585f1 CounterCMPBea E called incrementTheCount() method
1c9585f1 CounterCMPBea E called ejbStore() method
284485f1 CounterCMPBea E called incrementTheCount() method
284485f1 CounterCMPBea E called ejbStore() method
```

Figure 349. Trace with commit option A

We can see that the EJB container doesn't call the ejbPassivate() method after committing a transaction.

We also see that the EJB container doesn't invoke the ejbActivate() and ejbLoad() methods before calling a business method, because it keeps cached the latest EJB instance data.

11.5.4.2 Commit option C

To configure commit option C on CounterCMP, select it and on the General tab select **Shared** in the Database access field.

We restart our application server (sg246161) to invalidate HttpSession, then we called the CounterCMPServlet twice.

Figure 350 shows the trace file when we configured the commit option C.

```
19360073 CounterCMPBea E called setEntityContext() method
19360073 CounterCMPBea E called ejbActivate() method
19360073 CounterCMPBea E called ejbLoad() method
19360073 CounterCMPBea E called ejbPassivate() method
19360073 CounterCMPBea E called ejbActivate() method
19360073 CounterCMPBea E called ejbLoad() method
19360073 CounterCMPBea E called incrementTheCount() method
19360073 CounterCMPBea E called ejbStore() method
19360073 CounterCMPBea E called ejbPassivate() method
19560073 CounterCMPBea E called ejbActivate() method
19560073 CounterCMPBea E called ejbLoad() method
19560073 CounterCMPBea E called ejbPassivate() method
19560073 CounterCMPBea E called ejbActivate() method
19560073 CounterCMPBea E called ejbLoad() method
19560073 CounterCMPBea E called incrementTheCount() method
19560073 CounterCMPBea E called ejbStore() method
19560073 CounterCMPBea E called ejbPassivate() method
```

Figure 350. Trace with commit option C

With commit option C, the EJB container always calls the ejbPassivate() method after each business method called.

Table 29 is the comparison of the commit protocols.

Table 29. Commit option A vs. option C

	Option A	Option C
First access		
	setEntityContext()	setEntityContext()
findByPrimaryKey()	ejbActivate()	ejbActivate()

	Option A	Option C
	ejbLoad()	ejbLoad()
		ejbPassivate()
		ejbActivate()
		ejbLoad()
incrementTheCount()	incrementTheCount()	incrementTheCount()
	ejbStore()	ejbStore()
		ejbPassivate()
Second access		
		ejbActivate()
		ejbLoad()
		ejbPassivate()
		ejbActivate()
		ejbLoad()
incrementTheCount()	incrementTheCount()	incrementTheCount()
	ejbStore()	ejbStore()
		ejbPassivate()

11.6 WebSphere EJB security

The EJB server and container components provide or give access to many services for the enterprise beans that are deployed into it. The security service is a part of them.

Here, we will describe the WebSphere EJS security service and EJB delegation. Also we will describe how to configure EJB security and demonstrate the delegation situations with our sample program Big3, which you may find in more detail in Appendix E, “Big3 application” on page 1111.

11.6.1 WebSphere EJS security service

EJBs can only be used by EJB clients. There are two general types of EJB clients:

- HTTP-based clients that interact with the EJB server by using either Java servlets or JavaServer Pages (JSP) by way of the Hypertext Transfer Protocol (HTTP).
- Java applications that interact directly with the EJB server by using Java remote method invocation over the Internet Inter-ORB Protocol (RMI/IIOP).

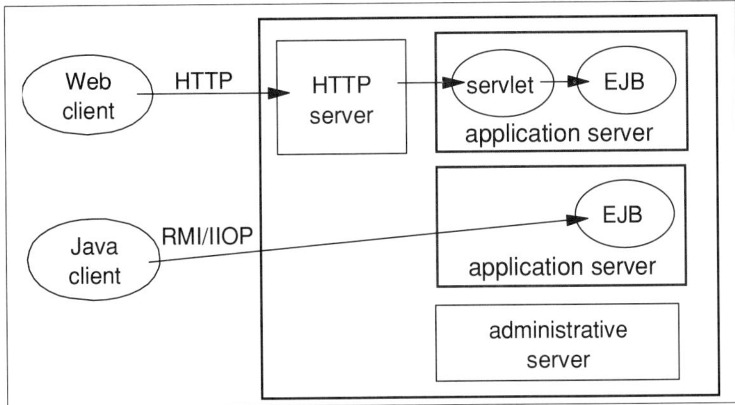

Figure 351. EJB clients

EJB clients that access an EJB server over HTTP encounter the following two layers of security:

1. Universal Resource Locator (URL) security enforced by the WebSphere Application Server Security Plug-in attached to the Web server in collaboration with the security service.
2. Enterprise bean security enforced at the server working with the security service.

When the user of an HTTP-based EJB client attempts to access an enterprise bean, the user may be authenticated as description in 15.2, "WebSphere security model" on page 652.

All EJB clients that access an EJB server by using IIOP encounter the second security layer only. Like HTTP-based EJB clients, these EJB clients must authenticate with the security service.

Once an EJB client is authenticated, it can attempt to invoke methods on the enterprise beans that it manipulates. A method is successfully invoked if the principal associated with the method invocation has the required permissions to invoke the method. These permissions can be set at the application level and at the method group level. An application can contain multiple method groups.

EJBs are protected by default when security is enabled, contrary to that servlets, JSPs and other Web resources are not protected by default. So when security is enabled, we must configure the EJBs' security to give some users or groups permission to access them, and we should configure other resources' security to make them be protected.

11.6.2 Delegation in WebSphere

Delegation comes into play when a client uses an intermediary (such as an EJB) to invoke a method on a target resource. It allows an enterprise bean method to execute under another identity.

Depending on the active delegation policy, the intermediary invokes a method under a certain identity:

- The client identity

  The bean method will run with the identity of the client requesting the method invocation as shown in Figure 352.

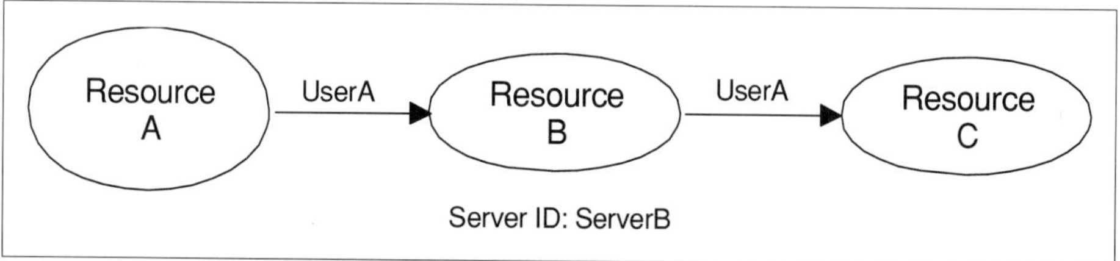

Figure 352. Client identity

- The system identity

  The bean method will run with the identity of the server hosting the intermediary resource that will invoke the method on the target object as shown in Figure 353 on page 475.

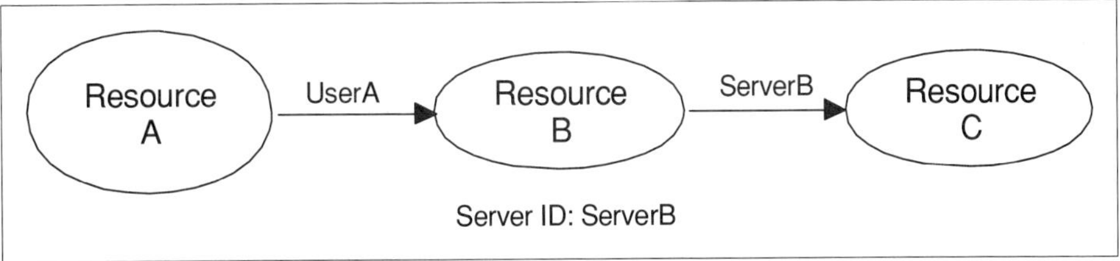

Figure 353. System identity

- The specified identity

  The bean method will run with the Run As Identity, as specified explicitly in the delegation policy as shown in Figure 354.

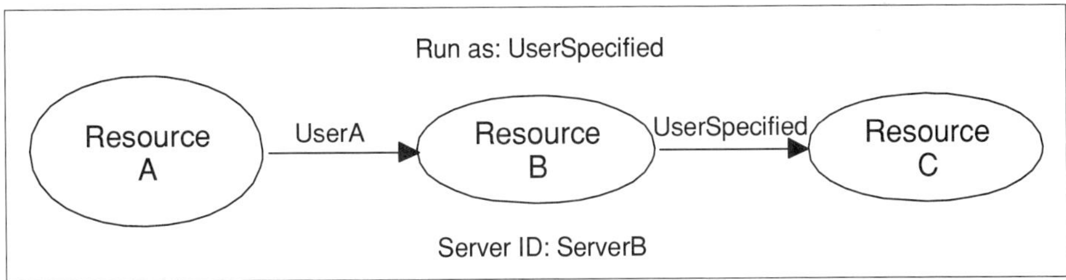

Figure 354. Specified identity

The application environment determines whether a client, system or specified identity is most appropriate. To summarize, delegation is the process of forwarding a principal's credentials along with the requests that occur within the context of work that the principal either originated or is having performed on its behalf.

You may configure the Run-As Mode for each enterprise bean in "Configure Resource Security Wizard" as shown in Figure 355 on page 476. The detailed configuration steps may refer to 11.6.3.4, "Configure Resource Security wizard" on page 485.

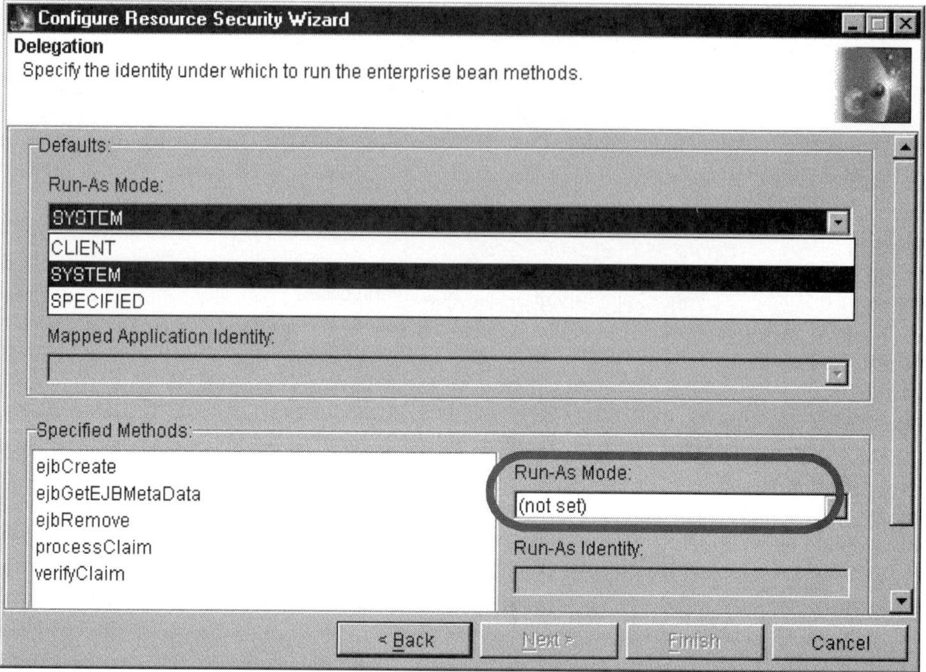

Figure 355. Delegation configuration

The delegation settings you specify here will override any run-as information in the deployment descriptor of the enterprise bean.

11.6.3 Configure EJB security

We will use sample program Big3 to describe how to configure EJB security and demonstrate the delegation situation.

The Big3 program is shown in Figure 356 on page 477.

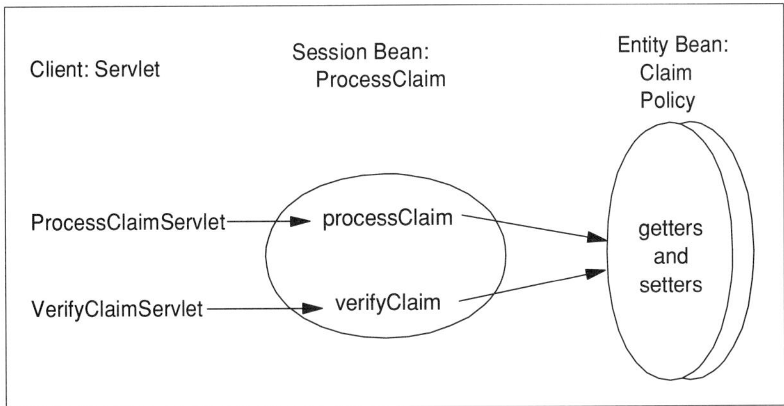

Figure 356. Big3 scenario

We configured an enterprise application named Big3App to comprise the two servlets and three EJBs, as shown in Figure 357.

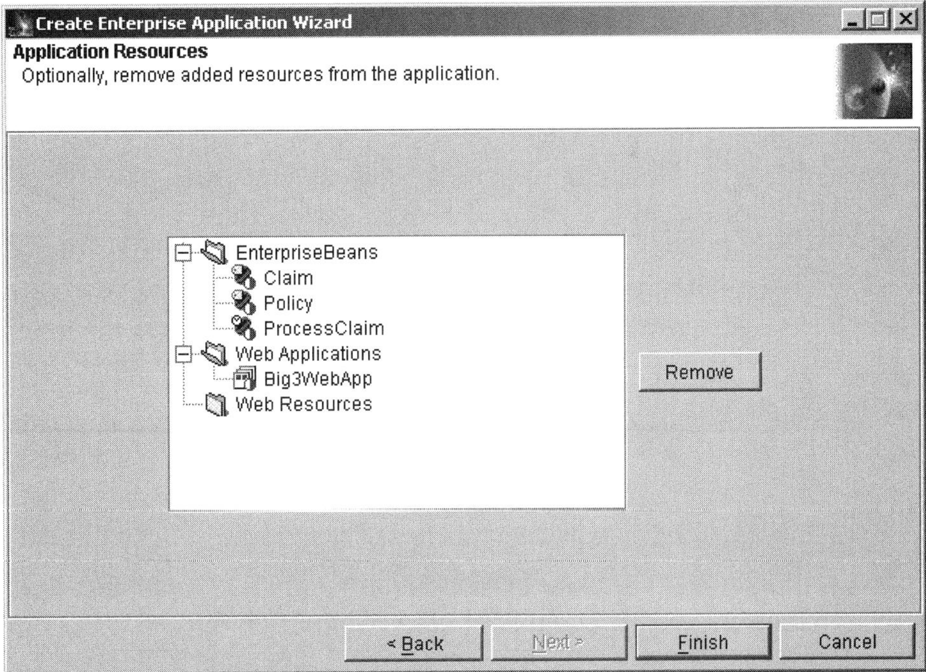

Figure 357. Enterprise application Big3App

In this test case, we registered three users in the local operating system, which are wassecurity, wasadmin and wasuser. We will configure the security server ID as wassecurity, and the enterprise application Big3App identity as wasadmin. We will only allow wasadmin to access the getters and setters of the entity beans. The user wasuser represents all other registered user on this machine.

In order to demonstrate the EJB security delegation, we will configure the security as shown in Figure 358.

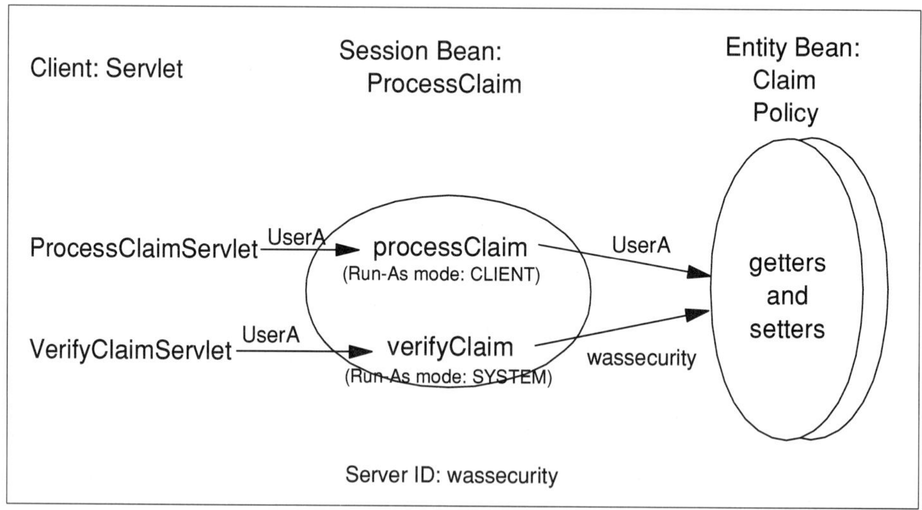

Figure 358. Big3 security configuration

In order to verify the delegation configuration, we will create a new Method Group named myMG to protect the getters and setters of the entity beans, and we will only grant its permission to user wasadmin.

Because most of the configuration steps are the same as configuring a servlet, we will only pay attention to the fields and steps related to EJB security. Now, we begin to configure. There are five steps:

1. Configure global security settings
2. Configure application security
3. Configure security method groups
4. Configure resource security
5. Configure security permissions

11.6.3.1 Configure Global Security Settings wizard

In the administrative console, by clicking the **Wizards** button and selecting **Configure Global Security Setting**.

On the **General** tab, we need to check **Enable Security** as shown in Figure 359. Then click **Next** (or click **Application Defaults** tab).

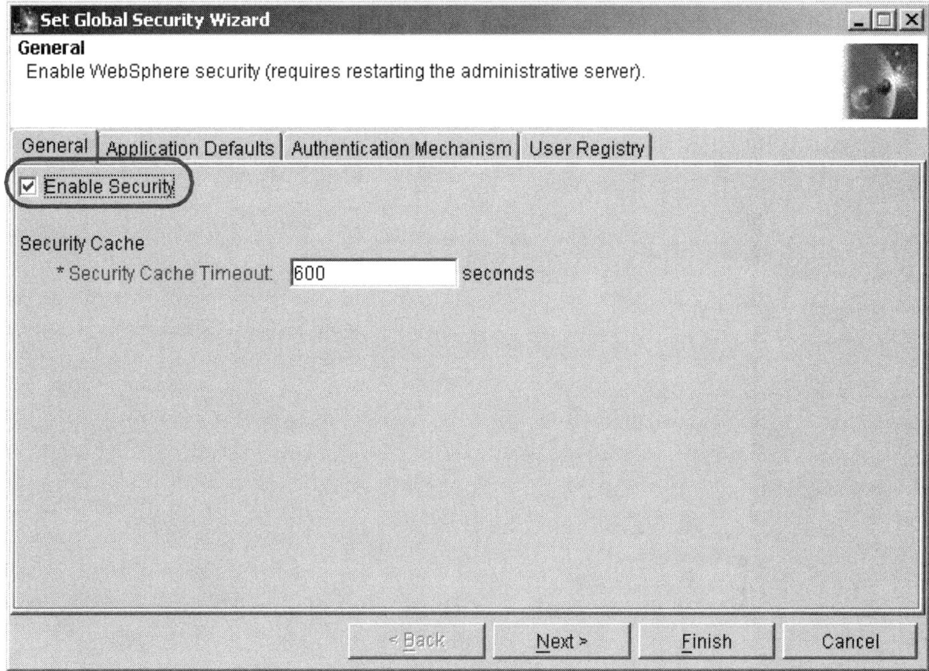

Figure 359. Set Global Security Wizard: General tab

On the Application Defaults tab, we keep the default setting. We choose the **Basic (User ID and Password)** challenge type as shown in Figure 360 on page 480.

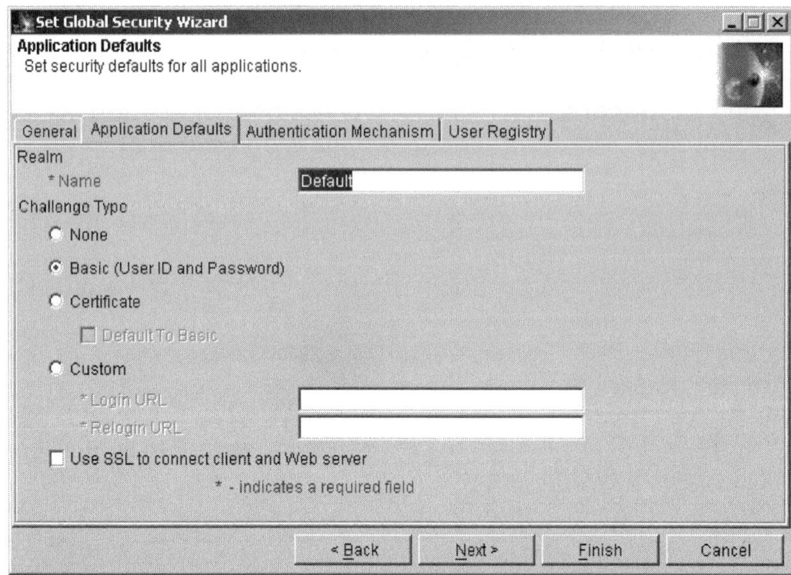

Figure 360. Set Global Security Wizard: Application Defaults tab

On the Authentication Mechanism tab, we keep the default setting too. We choose **Local Operating System** as the authentication mechanism as shown in Figure 361. Then click **Next** (or User Registry tab).

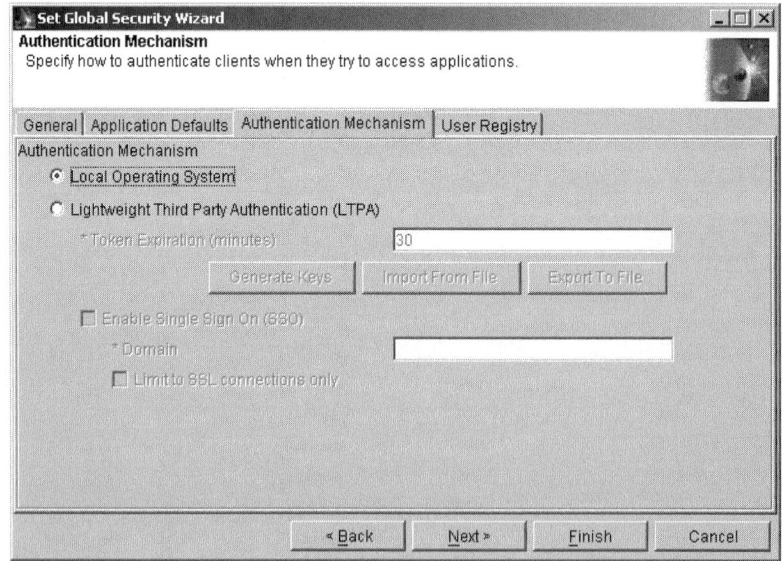

Figure 361. Set Global Security Wizard: Authentication Mechanism tab

On the User Registry tab, we specify wassecurity as the security server ID as shown in Figure 362. This ID is the identity that the bean methods will run with when the Run-As Mode is specified as SYSTEM.

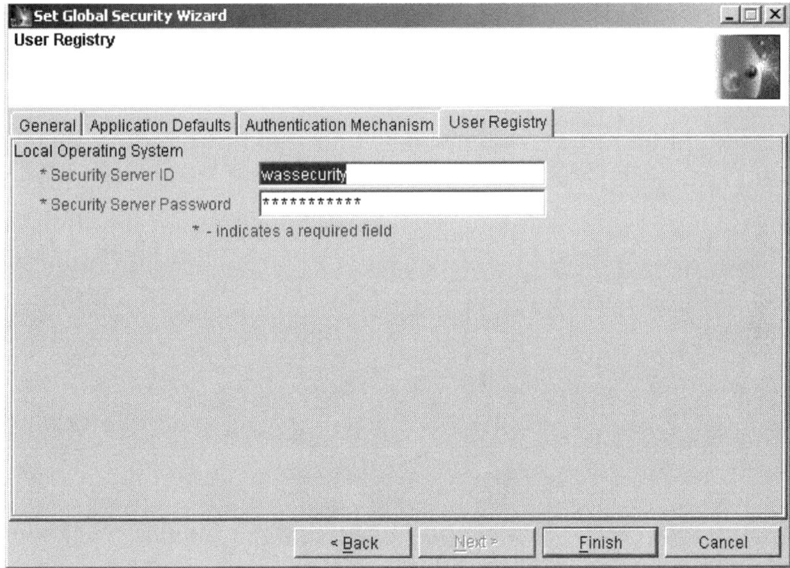

Figure 362. Set Global Security Wizard: User Registry tab

Click the **Finish** button to complete the global security configuration. Restart WebSphere Administrative Server to activate the change.

11.6.3.2 Configure Application Security wizard

Start the Configure Application Security wizard by clicking the **Wizards** button and selecting **Configure Application Security**.

Expand the Enterprise Applications folder and put the cursor on Big3App as shown in Figure 363 on page 482. Click the **Next** button to continue.

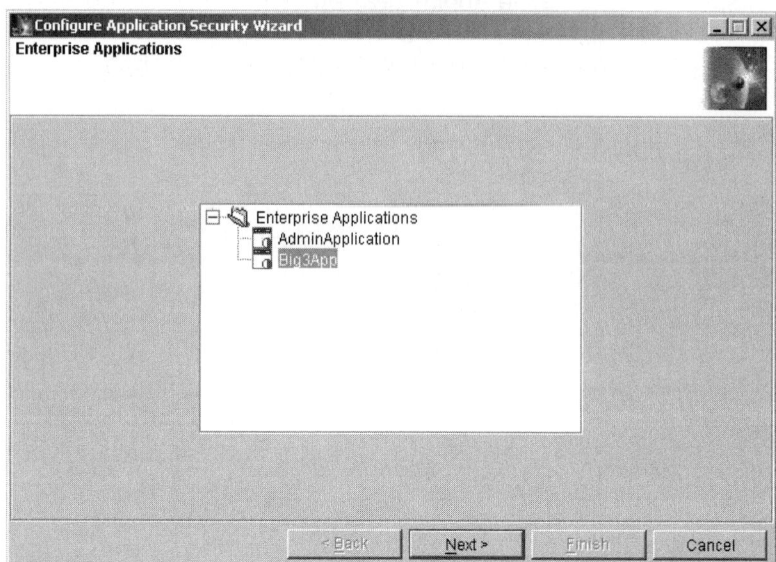

Figure 363. Configure Application Security wizard: Enterprise Applications

You will get the Realm and Challenge Type window. You keep default setting of Realm and Challenge Type as shown in Figure 364, then click **Next** to continue.

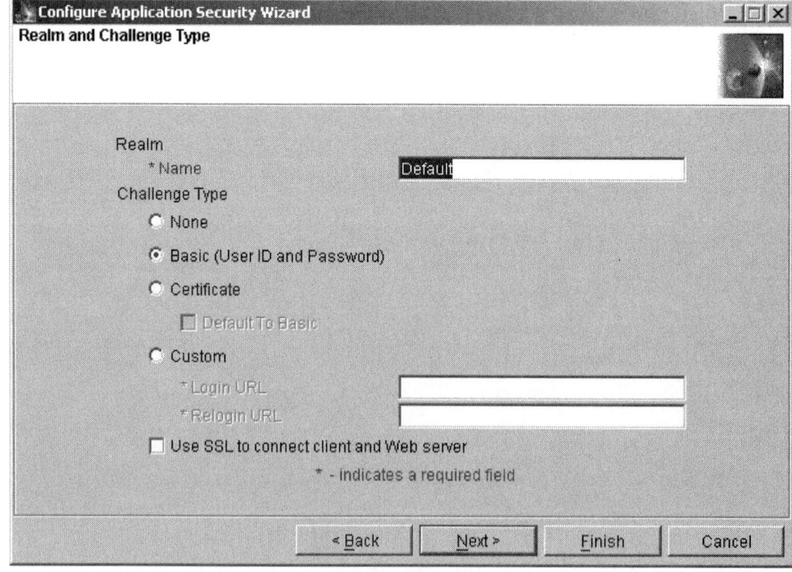

Figure 364. Configure Application Security wizard: Realm and Challenge Type

Then you will get the Application Identity window as shown in Figure 365. The application identity is the possible delegation identity for enterprise beans in this application when the Run-As Mode is selected as SPECIFIED.

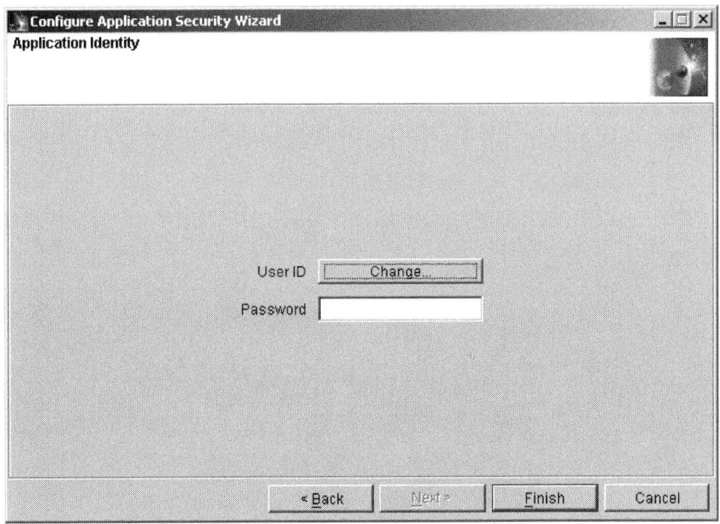

Figure 365. Configure Application Security wizard: Application Identity

Click the **Change** button for User ID. A Search window will display.

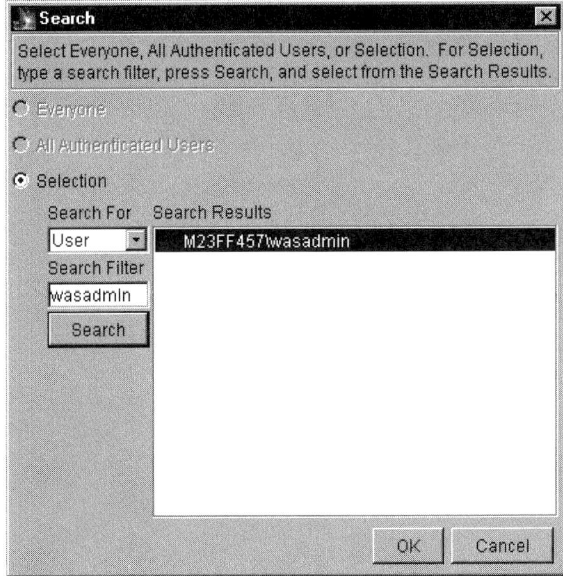

Figure 366. Search window

Input the user name into the Search Filter field and click the **Search** button. The user following the host name will be listed in the Search Results pane as shown in Figure 366 on page 483. Put the cursor on it and click **OK** to return to the Configure Application Security Wizard. We use wasadmin (M23FF457 is the host name) as the user here.

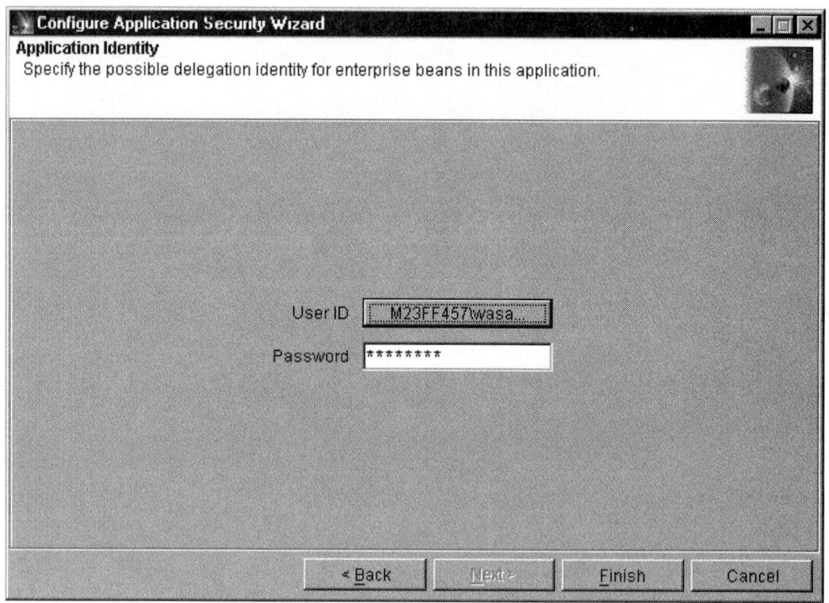

Figure 367. Configure Application Security wizard: Application Identity with password

Input the password as shown in Figure 367 and click the **Finish** button to complete the application security setting.

11.6.3.3 Configure Security Method Groups wizard

Start the Configure Security Method Groups wizard by clicking the **Wizards** button.

We only need to add a new method group named myMG as depicted in Figure 368 on page 485.

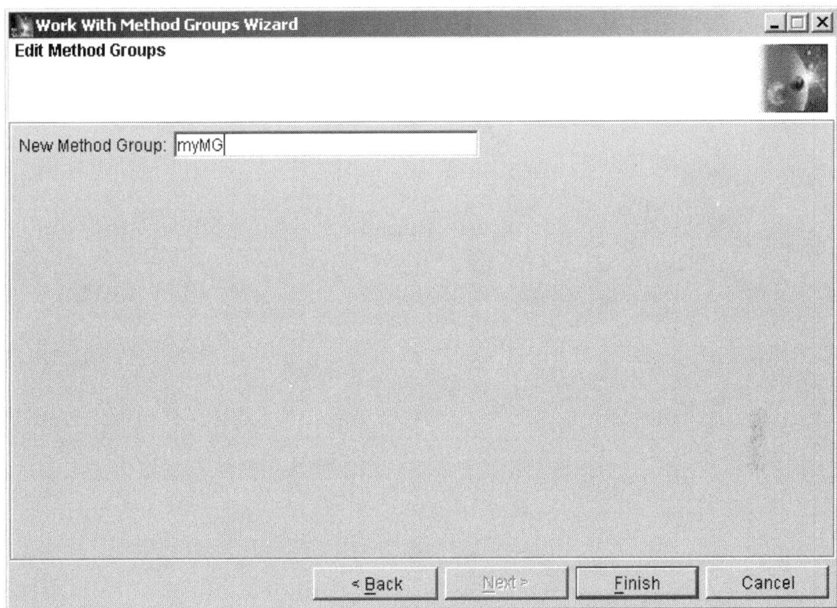

Figure 368. Work With Method Groups wizard: Edit Method Groups

11.6.3.4 Configure Resource Security wizard

Start the Configure Resource Security wizard by clicking **Wizards** button. We will configure session bean (ProcessClaim), entity beans (Claim and Policy) and servlets (ProcessClaimServlet and VerifyClaimServlet) in turn.

Configure session bean (ProcessClaim)

Expand the EnterpriseBeans folder and put the cursor on ProcessClaim as shown in Figure 369 on page 486.

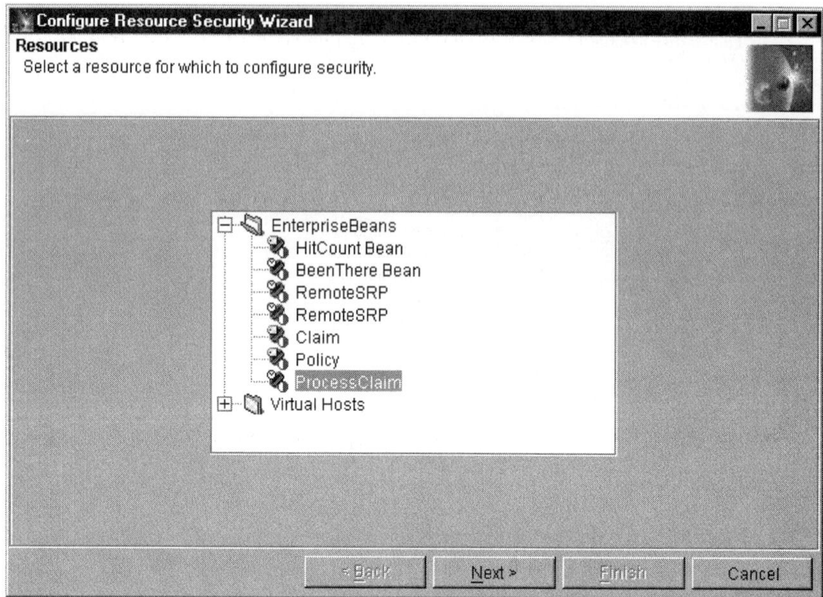

Figure 369. Configuring Resource Security wizard: Resources

Click **Next** to proceed. A prompt asks whether you want to use the default method groups. Click **Yes** as shown in Figure 370.

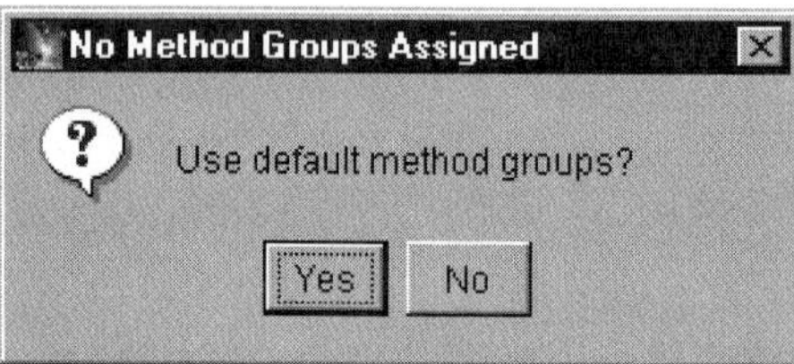

Figure 370. Use default method groups

The next panel (in Figure 371 on page 487) shows how WebSphere Application Server has grouped the methods of the ProcessClaim bean into method groups for protection.

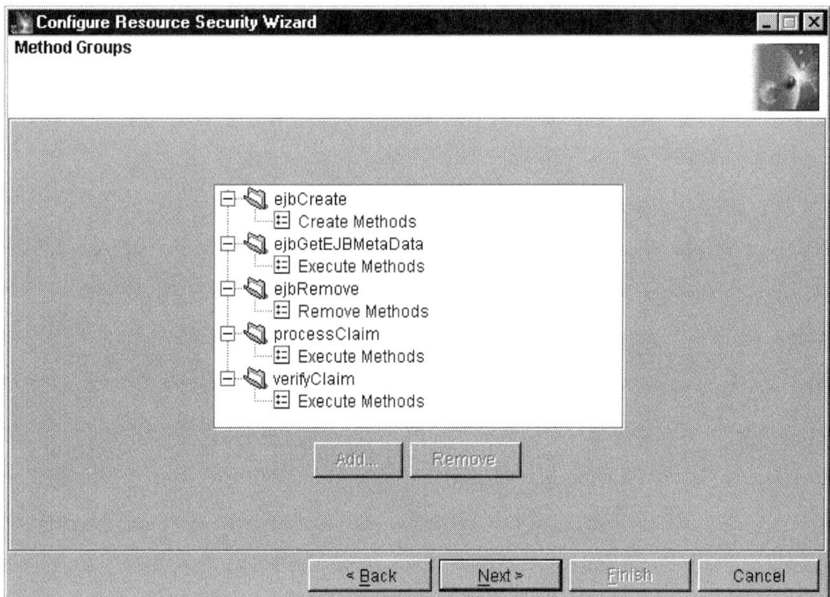

Figure 371. Configuring Resource Security Wizard: Methods Groups

You keep the default setting and click **Next** to continue. The panel of the delegation setting displays.

To configure the delegation of this bean, first we will set the default Run-As Mode for all methods, then override it for the method processClaim, and we will verify the inheritance setting of another method, verifyClaim.

1. Configuring the default Run-As Mode to SYSTEM for EJB methods

   The top half of the task panel (Defalults pane) is for specifying the default identity under which bean methods will execute. If you select **SPECIFIED**, you must map the delegation ID to an application identity established using the Configure Application Security wizard. We keep the default Run-AS Mode as SYSTEM here.

   The bottom half of the task panel (Specified Methods: field) is used to select a particular method for which you want to override the default Run-AS Mode. Click the method, then select **SYSTEM**, **CLIENT**, or **SPECIFIED** in the Run-As Mode field. If you select SPECIFIED, map the application identity. The default setting is (not set), as shown in Figure 372 on page 488.

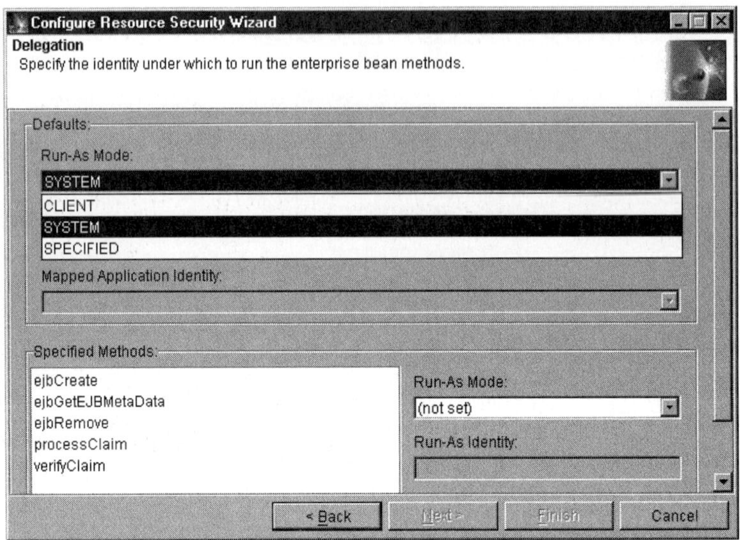

Figure 372. The default Run-AS Mode

2. Overriding Run-As Mode to CLIENT for method processClaim

   In the Specified Methods pane, select the method **processClaim** and select **CLIENT** as the Run-As Mode, as shown in Figure 373 on page 488. The Run-As Mode of method processClaim will override the default setting and be set to CLIENT.

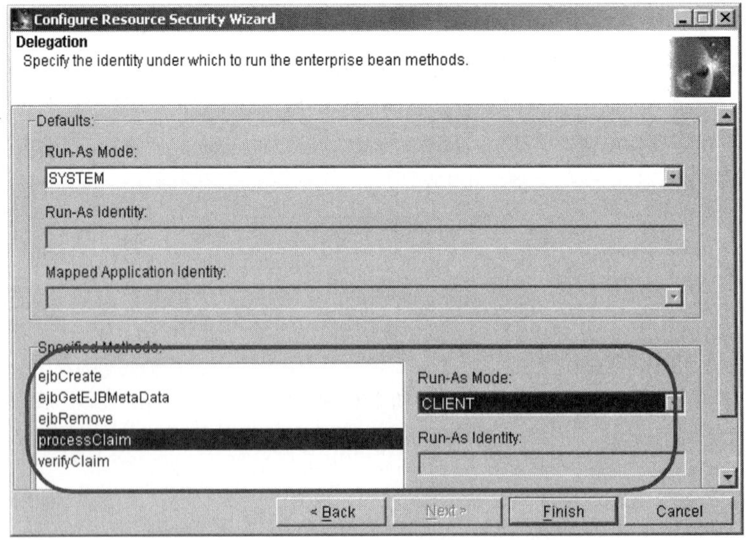

Figure 373. Configure the delegation of method processClaim

3. Inheriting Run-As Mode as SYSTEM for method verifyClaim

   In the Specified Methods pane, select the method **verifyClaim** and verify the Run-As Mode is (not set) as deputized in Figure 374 on page 489. The Run-As Mode of method verifyClaim will inherit the default setting in the Defaults pane, where the value is SYSTEM.

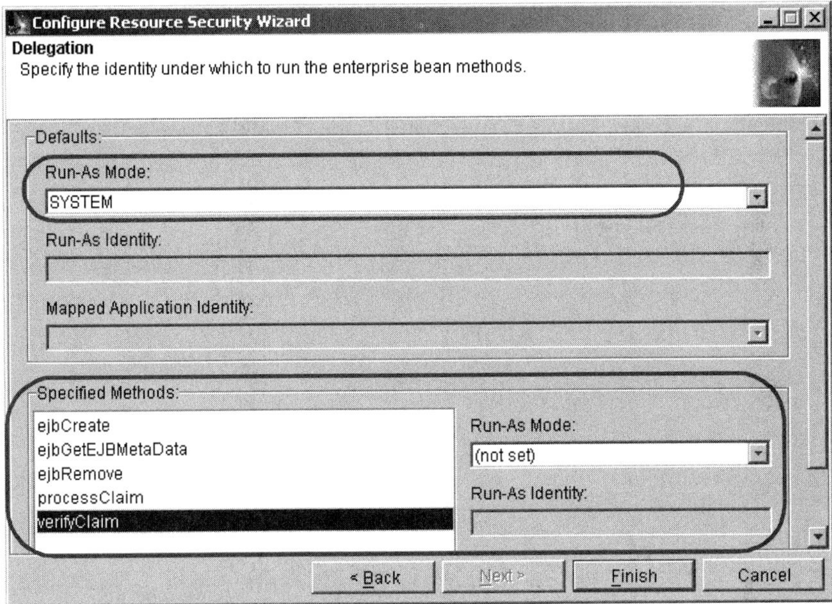

Figure 374. Configure the delegation of method verifyClaim

Click **Finish** to complete the security setting of EJB ProcessClaim.

Configure entity beans (Claim and Policy)

To configure the two entity beans, the steps are similar to the above, except we need to change the method groups that protected the getters and setters for them.

The default method group for getters is named Read Methods and it for setters is Write Methods as shown in Figure 375 on page 490.

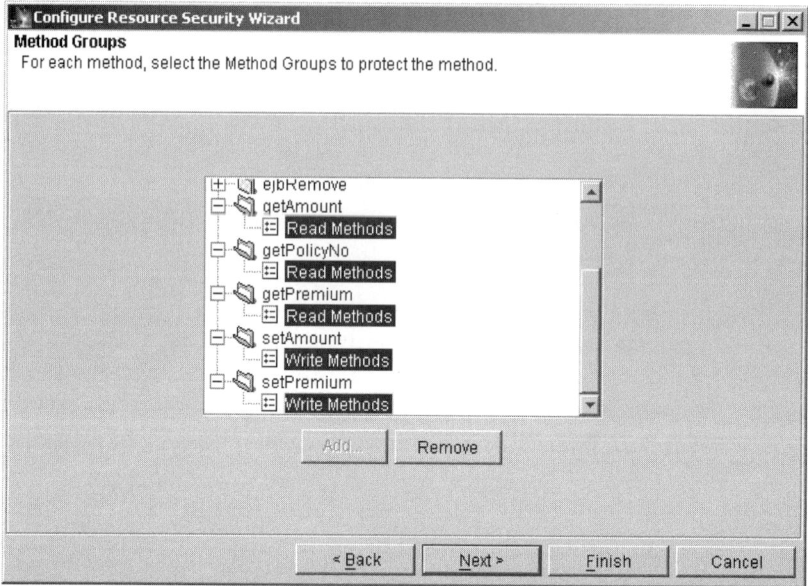

Figure 375. Default method groups of getters and setters

We may remove the default method groups and add myMG to protect the getters and setters, showing as Figure 376.

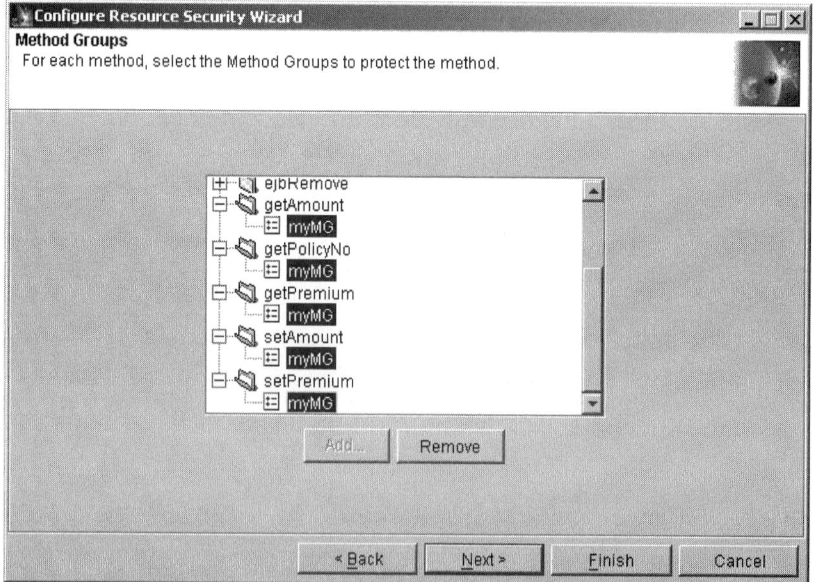

Figure 376. Using method group myMG to protect getters and setters

On the delegation setting panel, keep the setting of defaults and all methods that were configured in the deployment descriptor because we don't want them for both entity beans in this test case.

Configure servlets (ProcessClaimServlet and VerifyClaimServlet)
To configure the servlets security, expand the Virtual Hosts folder then default_host folder, select Web resources /Big3/servlet/big3.servlet.ProcessClaim and /Big3/servlet/big3.servlet.VerifyClaim in turn and configure their security. There is no delegation concept for servlets, so there is no configuration step for delegation when you configure security for the servlets. You may accept the default method groups to protect the servlets.

11.6.3.5 Configure Security Permissions wizard

Start Configure Security Permissions wizard by clicking **Wizards** button. We will grant myMG's permission only to user wasadmin, and give other permissions to All Authenticated Users, as depicted in Figure 377.

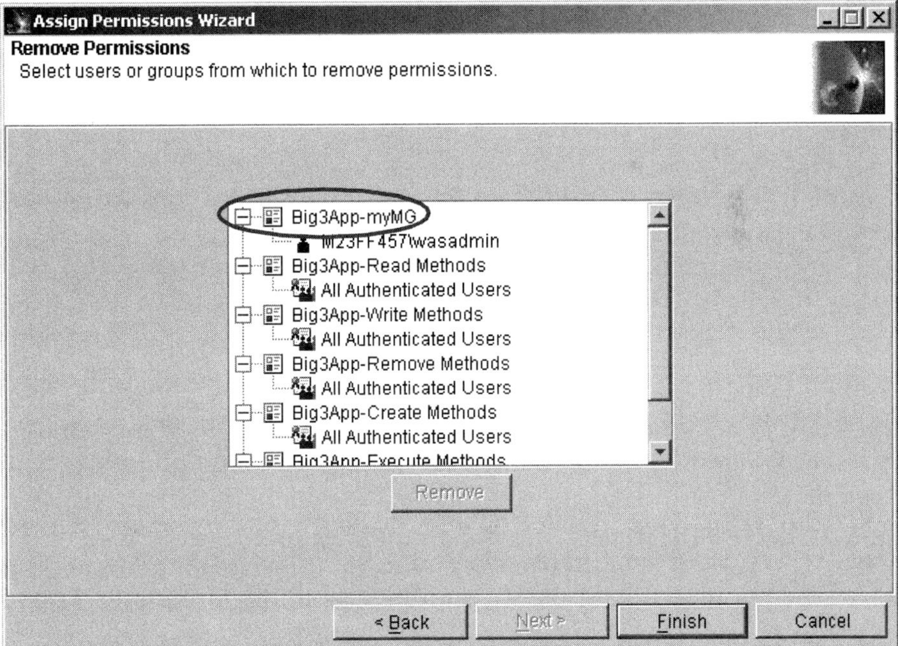

Figure 377. Permissions in enterprise application Big3App

Click the **Finish** button. Now, the EJB security configuration is finished. We need to restart the application server hosting Big3 to enable the security setting. Then we may begin to verify the security setting.

11.6.4 Verify EJB security

We will verify the delegation types respectively.

Access the Big3 Home Page (`http://hostname/big3/`) as depicted in Figure 378. If you click the link **Process a claim** in the left frame and click the **Submit** button, the servlet ProcessClaimServlet will be invoked. If you click the link **Verify a claim** then **submit**, the servlet VerifyClaimServlet will be invoked.

Remember, only user wasadmin can access the getters and setters of the two entity beans (Claim and Policy) in the above configuration.

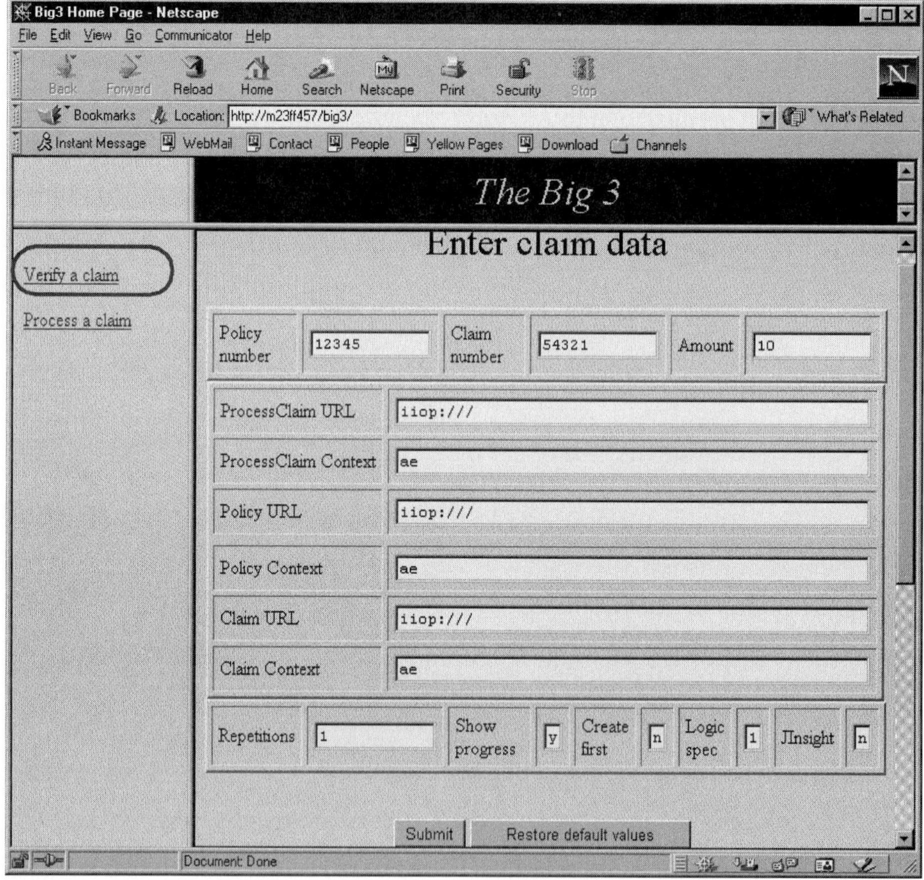

Figure 378. Big3 Home Page

11.6.4.1 Verify delegation type CLIENT

We configured the Run-As Mode of method processClaim of session bean ProcessClaim to CLIENT previously. In this verification, we need to invoke servlet ProcessClaimServlet by clicking the link **Process a claim** in the left frame.

After clicking the **Submit** button, a challenge window will appear to require a user name and password. This is the result of the "Basic" challenge type configured in enterprise application Big3App as shown in Figure 379.

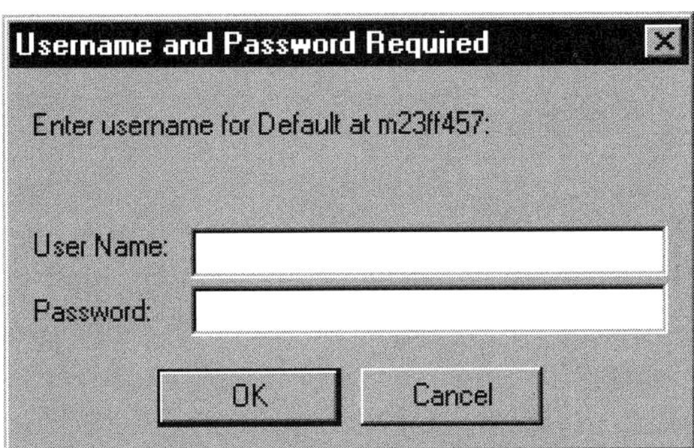

Figure 379. Challenge window

Accessing with valid user and password

Input user wasadmin with its password. Then click **OK** to proceed. You will see the successfully running result in the browser as shown in Figure 380 on page 494 and there is no error message in the WebSphere Administrative Console.

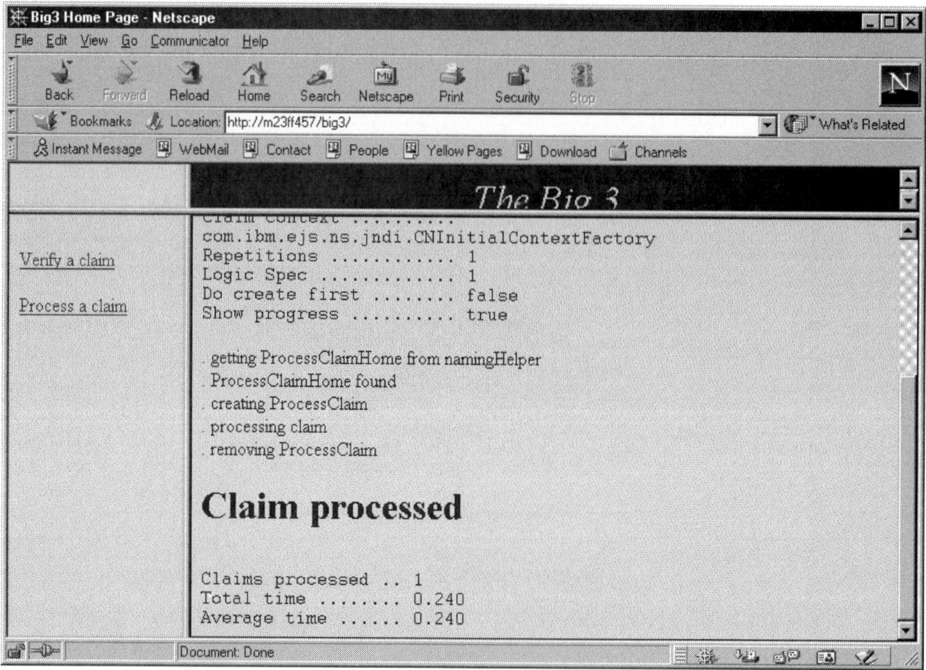

Figure 380. Successfully running result in browser

Accessing with invalid user and password

Close all browser windows then restart them, repeating the last steps. Input user wasuser with its password this time. You will see the unsuccessfully running result in the browser as depicted in Figure 381 on page 495.

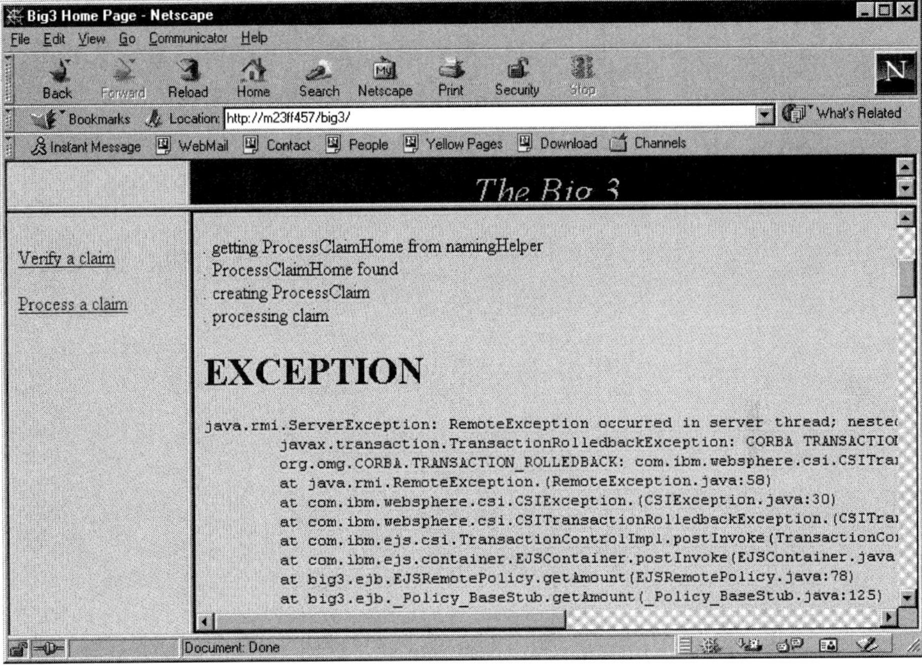

Figure 381. Unsuccessfully running result in browser

You will also see the message `Authorization failed for M23FF457/wasuser while invoking (Bean)big3/ejb/Policy getAmount` in the administrative console as shown in Figure 382 on page 496.

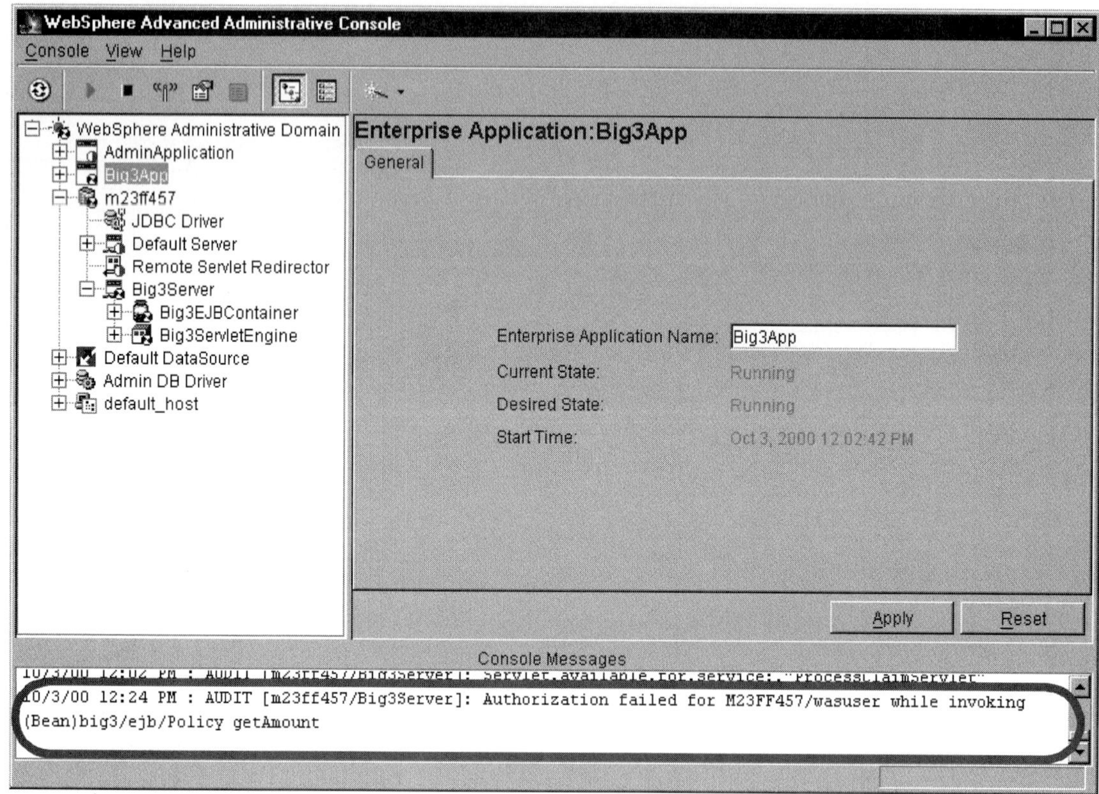

Figure 382. Auhorization failed message in the administrative console

In fact, if you are repeating the steps and inputting different registered users, only user wasadmin can run successfully. All other users will fail with an `Authorization failed` message in the administrative console, and the failed user is consistent with what you input. This result can prove that the method processClaim runs with the client identity, that is to say, its Run-As Mode is CLIENT as depicted in Figure 383 on page 497.

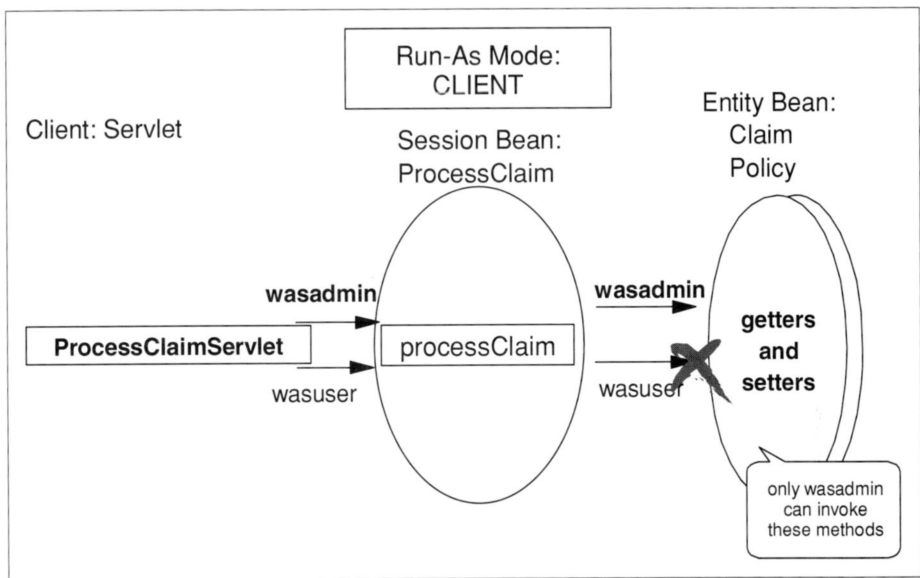

Figure 383. Run-As Mode: CLIENT

11.6.4.2 Verify delegation type SYSTEM

We configured the Run-As Mode of method verifyClaim of session bean ProcessClaim to SYSTEM previously. In this verification, we need to invoke servlet VerifyClaimServlet by clicking the link **Verify a claim** in the left frame in the Big3 Home Page.

You will get a challenge window. No matter who the registered user which you input into the challenge window is, you always will see the message of `Authorization failed` for the user "M23FF457/wassecurity" in the administrative console as shown in Figure 385 on page 499. Remember, we configure the Security Server ID as wassecurity in the Set Global Security wizard (see Figure 362 on page 481). This result can prove that the method verifyClaim runs with the server identity, that is to say, its Run-As Mode is SYSTEM as shown in Figure 384 on page 498.

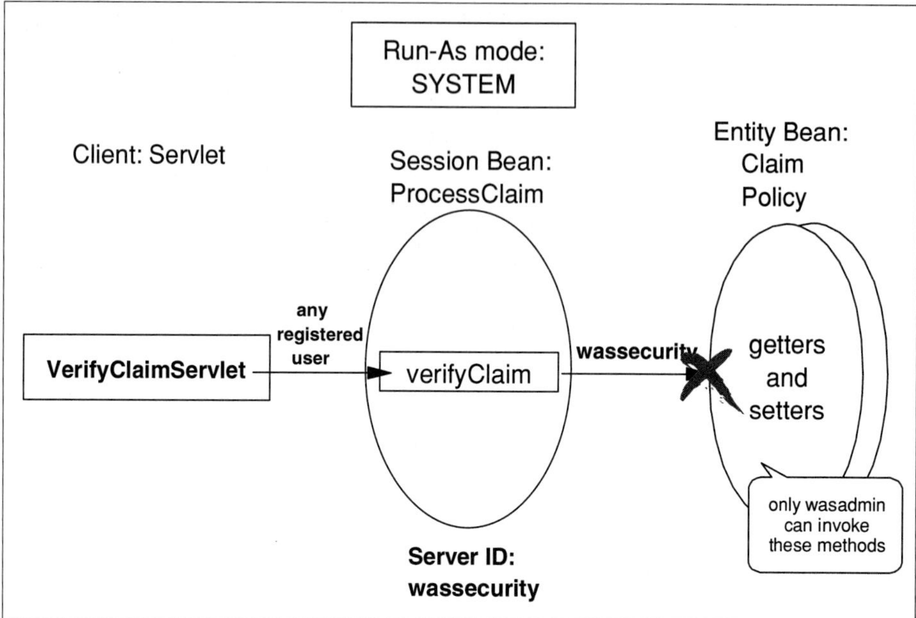

Figure 384. Run-As Mode: SYSTEM

For configuration in a production environment, you must configure according to the real requirements. The objective of the configuration here is only to help you understand the delegation clearly.

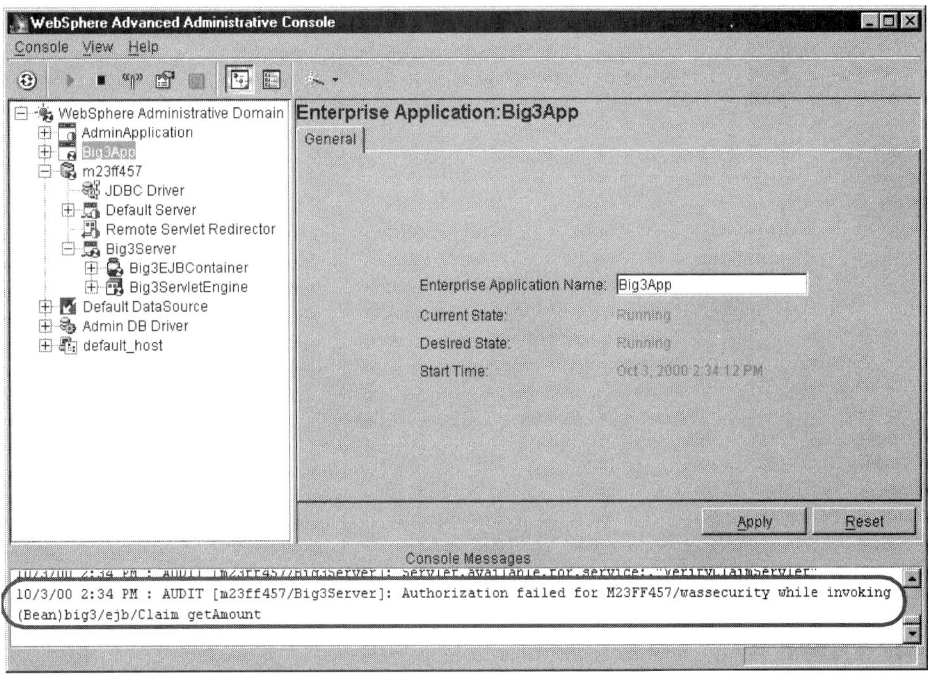

Figure 385. Authorization failed message in the administrative console

11.6.4.3 Verify delegation type SPECIFIED

We did not configure the Run-As Mode of any methods to SPECIFIED previously, so we need to change the Run-As Mode of method processClaim to SPECIFIED.

On the delegation setting panel of the Configure Resource Security wizard for session bean ProcessClaim, specify the method processClaim, change the Run-As Mode to SPECIFIED, and map the Application Identity by selecting **M23FF457/wasadmin**, which is established on the Application Identity panel of the Configure Application Security wizard as shown in Figure 386 on page 500. Click the **Finish** button to complete the setting. Restart the application server hosting the Big3 to activate the change.

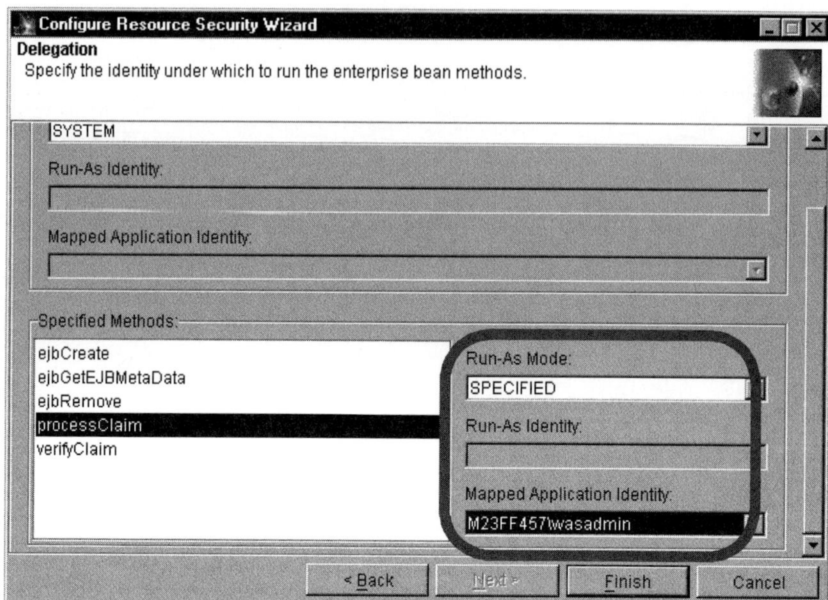

Figure 386. Change Run-As Mode to SPECIFIED

In this verification, we need to invoke servlet ProcessClaimServlet by click the link "Process a claim" in the left frame on the Big3 Home Page.

You will get the challenge window. No matter the registered user which you input into the challenge window is the invocation will success. Remember, only wasadmin can access the getters and setters of the two entity beans (see Figure 377 on page 491). This result can prove that the method processClaim runs with the wasadmin identity, that is to say, its Run-As Mode is SPECIFIED to wasadmin as shown in Figure 387 on page 501.

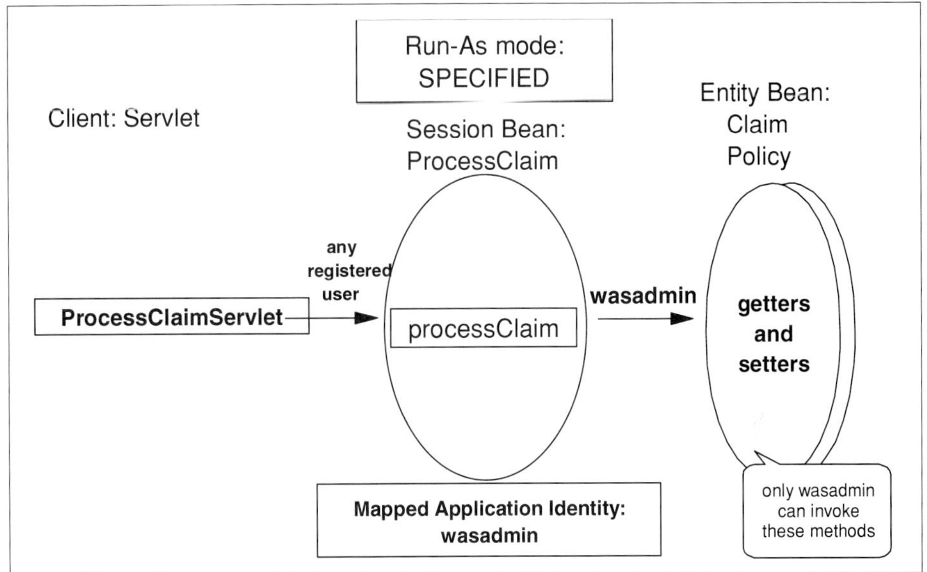

Figure 387. Run-As Mode: SPECIFIED

Chapter 12. Transactions

This chapter provides an overview of transaction support in Java 2 Enterprise Edition (J2EE) and describes some of the best practices for leveraging that support in WebSphere. One of the key components of the J2EE architecture is the Enterprise JavaBeans (EJB). A prominent feature of EJBs is support for distributed transactions. EJBs execute within WebSphere's EJB container. WebSphere also supports servlets and JSPs that run in a Web container often referred to as the servlet engine. Both containers provide a standard set of services to the application components. Services that are relevant to this chapter include the Java Transaction API (JTA), which provides declarative transaction management, and JDBC, which provides connectivity with database systems.

In this chapter we discuss the following topics:

- Transaction basics
- The Java support for transactions and WebSphere implementation details
- The transaction support provided by EJBs
- Some additional EJB concurrency control mechanisms provided by WebSphere
- Guidelines for selecting EJB and WebSphere settings based on the intended read/update usage of an EJB
- The necessary settings to enable transaction propagation between WebSphere Advanced and Enterprise Editions

12.1 Transaction basics

Transactions are used to assure that data or the objects that encapsulate data remain in a coherent state after undergoing a set of changes known as the unit of work. A transaction has the following characteristics:

- Atomic: all changes are done (committed) unless interrupted by failure, in which case all changes are undone (rolled back).
- Consistent: effects of a transaction preserve the invariant properties of the data. The data won't be in a partially invalid state.
- Isolated: intermediate states are transparent to other transactions; transactions appear to execute serially.
- Durable: effects of a completed transaction are persistent and never lost.

These properties are commonly referred to by their acronym as the ACID properties.

The Object Management Group, Inc. (OMG) developed a specification for Object Transaction Service (OTS) that established common definitions for participants in a transaction in a distributed object environment.

A transactional client is an arbitrary program that can invoke operations on many transactional objects in a single transaction.

A transaction manager takes care of manages transactions behind the scenes.

A resource manager manages the transaction for a single resource.

A transactional object is an object whose behavior is affected by being invoked within the scope of a transaction. EJBs are a examples of an object that can be transactional.

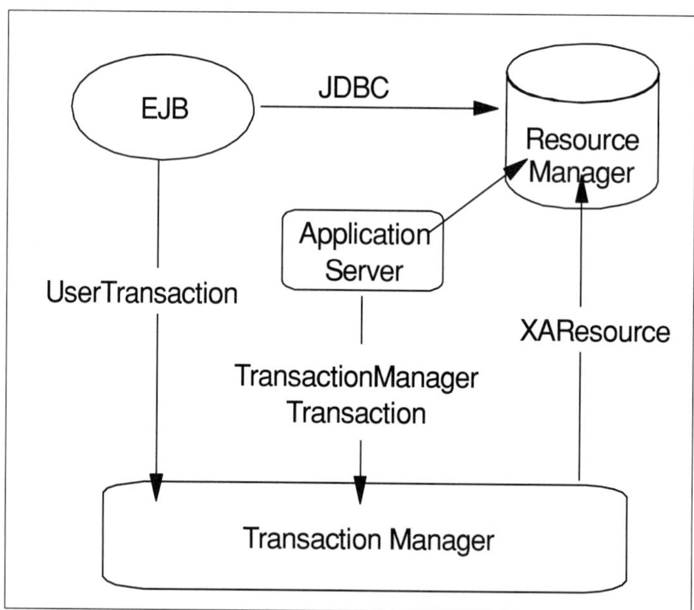

Figure 388. Transaction service

A transaction context represents the transaction shared by participating transactional objects. The context is automatically propagated (usually) to transactional objects as they are used. This allows synchronization of affected transaction objects when changes are committed or rolled back.

A transaction that involves a single resource manager is commonly referred to as a local transaction. Transactions involving multiple resource managers are called distributed transactions. Distributed transactions are more complex than local ones. In a distributed transaction, you must not only ensure the ACID properties for a single process, but you must ensure them across a set of processes on a network. In a local transaction, the only component that can fail is the process itself. In a distributed transaction, any one of the processes or the network connecting them can fail.

Distributed transactions use a two-phase commit protocol to determine the transactions outcome among the multiple resources as shown in Figure 389.

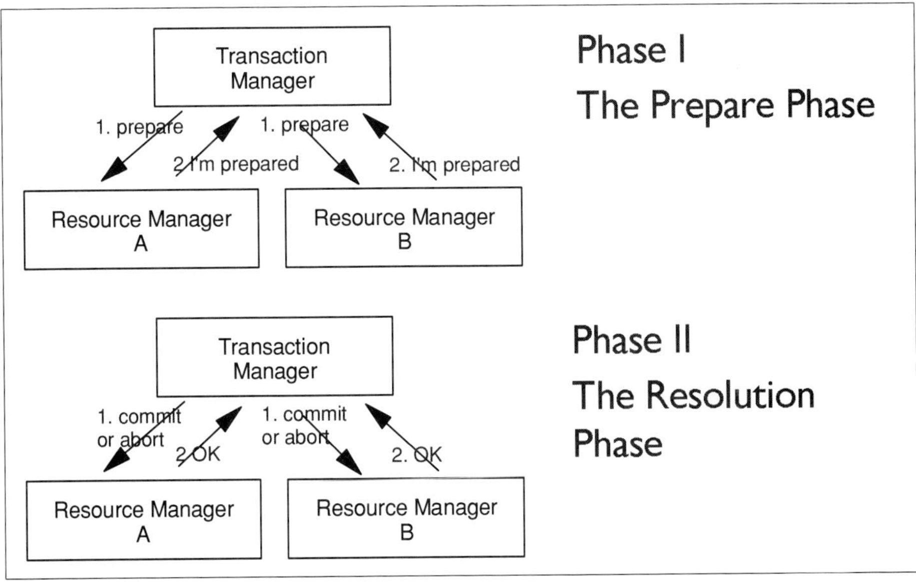

Figure 389. Distributed transaction - two-phase commit

In Phase I, the coordinator (transaction manager) sends a message to each participant (resource manager) to prepare to commit. In Phase II, the coordinator tallies the responses. If all participants and the coordinator are prepared to commit, the transaction commits; otherwise, the transaction is rolled back. The WebSphere EJB container provides the infrastructure for EJBs to participate in a distributed transaction.

12.2 Java and transactions

There are two Java APIs related to transactions. The Java Transaction API (JTA) specifies local Java interfaces between a transaction manager and the parties involved in a distributed transaction system (application, resource manager and application server). It is the high-level interface that your applications use to control transactions.

The key object in JTA is the javax.transaction.UserTransaction. Developers can use a UserTransaction to begin, commit, or roll back transactions.

The EJB 1.1 specification requires that the javax.transaction.UserTransaction interface be made available by the EJB container for session EJBs with bean-managed transaction demarcation.

WebSphere also makes the UserTransaction interface available to Java clients including servlets, JSPs, and standalone programs.

Another API related to transactions is the Java Transaction Service (JTS). JTS implements the Java mapping of OMG's Transaction Service. JTS is a lower-level interface that can be used by the EJB container to facilitate interoperability. It is not required by EJB specification and is typically not used by application developers.

12.2.1 JDBC

Data that is updated during transactions is usually stored in a relational database. JDBC is an API that lets you access virtually any relational data source from the Java programming language. It provides cross-database management system connectivity to a wide range of SQL databases. The JDBC API allows developers to take advantage of the Java platform's "Write Once, Run Anywhere" capabilities for industrial strength, cross-platform applications that require access to enterprise data. With a JDBC technology-enabled driver, a developer can connect all corporate data even in a heterogeneous environment. JDBC API makes it possible to do three things:

- Establish a connection with a database or access any relational data source
- Send SQL statements
- Process the results

JDBC Version 2.0 provides a standard two-phase commit API for multiple databases and a mechanism to look up data sources via the Java Naming and Directory Interface (JNDI). The javax.sql.DataSource interface that is defined in the JDBC 2.0 extension specification is a factory for JDBC connections. WebSphere's implementation of the data source object also provides connection pooling to boost performance. A data source is configured via the WebSphere Administrative Console (see 10.3, "Administration of data sources" on page 379 for more information). The application accesses the data source by looking it up using JNDI.

The following code fragment shows a servlet updating records from two different JTA-enabled data sources and bracketing the work with a user transaction. Some of the code details are removed ("...") to keep the sample small.

```
public class UserTranServlet extends javax.servlet.http.HttpServlet
{
   private static javax.sql.DataSource policyDS = null;
   private static String policyDSUser = null;
   private static String policyDSPassword = null;
   Context policyCtx = null;

   private static javax.sql.DataSource claimDS = null;
   private static String claimDSUser = null;
   private static String claimDSPassword = null;
   Context claimCtx = null;

...

public void doGet(
                   javax.servlet.http.HttpServletRequest request,
                   javax.servlet.http.HttpServletResponse response)
   throws javax.servlet.ServletException, java.io.IOException
   {

...

   // Local Variables
      Connection policyConn = null;
      Connection claimConn = null;
      ResultSet rs = null;
      UserTransaction ut = null;
      try
      {
...
// Lookup the UserTransaction - could use either ctx
         ut = (UserTransaction) policyCtx.lookup("jta/usertransaction");
```

```
          // Begin Transaction
          ut.begin();

          // Begin SQLs
          psSelectPolicy =
policyConn.prepareStatement(selectPolicySqlString);
          psSelectPolicy.setInt(1, policyNumber);
          rs = psSelectPolicy.executeQuery();

...
          {
             psUpdatePolicy =
policyConn.prepareStatement(updatePolicySqlString);
             psUpdatePolicy.setDouble(1, amount);
             psUpdatePolicy.setDouble(2, premium);
             psUpdatePolicy.setInt(3, policyNumber);
             psUpdatePolicy.executeUpdate();
             out.println("<br>UPDATE Policy SET amount = " + amount +
                         ", premium = " + premium + " WHERE policyNo = " +
policyNumber);
}

          psSelectClaim = claimConn.prepareStatement(selectClaimSqlString);
          psSelectClaim.setInt(1, claimNumber);
          rs = psSelectClaim.executeQuery();
...
{
             psUpdateClaim =
claimConn.prepareStatement(updateClaimSqlString);
             psUpdateClaim.setDouble(1, amount);
             psUpdateClaim.setInt(2, state);
             psUpdateClaim.setInt(3, claimNumber);
             psUpdateClaim.executeUpdate();
             out.println("<br>UPDATE Claim SET amount = " + amount +
                         ", state = " + state + " WHERE claimNo = " +
claimNumber);
}

ut.commit();
...
}
      catch (Exception e)
      {
...}
}
}
```

Using the UserTransaction assures that updates to both data sources complete (commit case) or none of the updates complete (rollback case).

Although this example showed the relational database updates could be orchestrated within a servlet, it is not considered best practice. 12.3, "Enterprise JavaBeans distributed transaction support" on page 511 outlines a simpler approach using Enterprise JavaBeans with container-managed persistence (CMP) and container-managed transactions (CMT).

12.2.2 WebSphere JDBC support

Table 30 shows the class names of the JDBC drivers that are supported by WebSphere:

Table 30. Database driver class

DB	Class	URL Prefix	JTA	2PC
DB2 6.1/7.1	COM.ibm.db2.jdbc.app.DB2Driver	jdbc:jta:db2	true	yes
Oracle 8i (8.1.6)	oracle.jdbc.driver.OracleDriver	jdbc:oracle:thin:@<db_hostname>:<port_number>	false	no
Sybase 12	com.sybase.jdbc2.jdbc.SybDriver	jdbc:sybase:Tds:<db_hostname>:<port_number>	true	yes

Data sources that use these drivers can be accessed and used within Java programs. For example, a developer can use a data source to control the persistence of an EJB with bean-managed persistence (BMP) or access data directly from a servlet as shown in the previous example. These drivers are considered fully supported because they can be used as repositories for the WebSphere configuration information and as the backing store for entity EJBs with CMP. The developer does not have to write the JDBC code for those cases. Other databases with JDBC drivers can be used by servlets and for EJB BMP but not for EJB CMP or as an administrative database. New drivers can be added to the supported list periodically. You should refer to the online product documentation to see the most up-to-date list.

Distributed database transactions are supported across homogeneous DB2 servers or Oracle servers. Table 31 on page 510, Table 32 on page 510, and

Table 33 on page 510 show the database capabilities on each platform that WebSphere supports:

Table 31. DB2 6.1 support

DB2 6.1	JTA/2PC	Persistence (CMP/BMP)	Administrative database support
AIX	Yes	Yes	Yes
Solaris	Yes	Yes	Yes
HP-UX	No	Yes	Yes
Windows NT/2000	Yes	Yes	Yes
OS/390	Yes (DB2 Connect)	BMP only	No
OS/400	Yes	Yes	Yes

Please note that OS/390 and AS/400 have product-specific release structuring for DB2.

Table 32. Oracle support

Oracle 8.1.6	JTA/2PC	Persistence (CMP/BMP	Administrative database support
AIX	No (Oracle limitation)	Yes	Yes
Solaris	No (Oracle limitation)	Yes	Yes
HP-UX	No (Oracle limitation)	Yes	Yes
Windows NT/2000	No (Oracle limitation)	Yes	Yes
OS/390	No (Oracle limitation)	No	No

Table 33. Sybase 11 support

Sybase ASE11	JTA/2PC	Persistence (CMP/BMP	Administrative database support
AIX	Yes	Yes	Yes
Solaris	Yes	Yes	Yes
HP-UX	No	No	No
Windows NT/2000	No	No	No

Refer to the online WebSphere documentation to learn the database Fix Pack level recommended for WebSphere.

12.3 Enterprise JavaBeans distributed transaction support

A key feature of Enterprise JavaBeans (EJBs) is support for distributed transactions. EJBs are transactional objects.

12.3.1 Update databases with EJBs

One of the distributed transaction capabilities of the Enterprise JavaBeans is updating multiple database in a single transaction. This section describes two scenarios.

12.3.1.1 Update of multiple databases

Enterprise JavaBeans makes it possible for an application program to update data in multiple databases in a single transaction.

Figure 390 on page 512 depicts multiple databases being updated within the same transaction by two enterprise beans. A request from a client results in two enterprise beans being invoked within the same transaction. Enterprise bean X updates data in two databases, A and B. Then enterprise Bean X calls enterprise bean Y, which updates data in database C. The Enterprise JavaBeans perform the database updates through the JDBC API, and the EJB server manages the database connections. When the transaction completes, the EJB server and the underlying DBMS(s) perform a two-phase commit to ensure atomic update across all databases involved in the transaction. The EJB developer does not have to be concerned about the transactional (ACID) properties of the transaction.

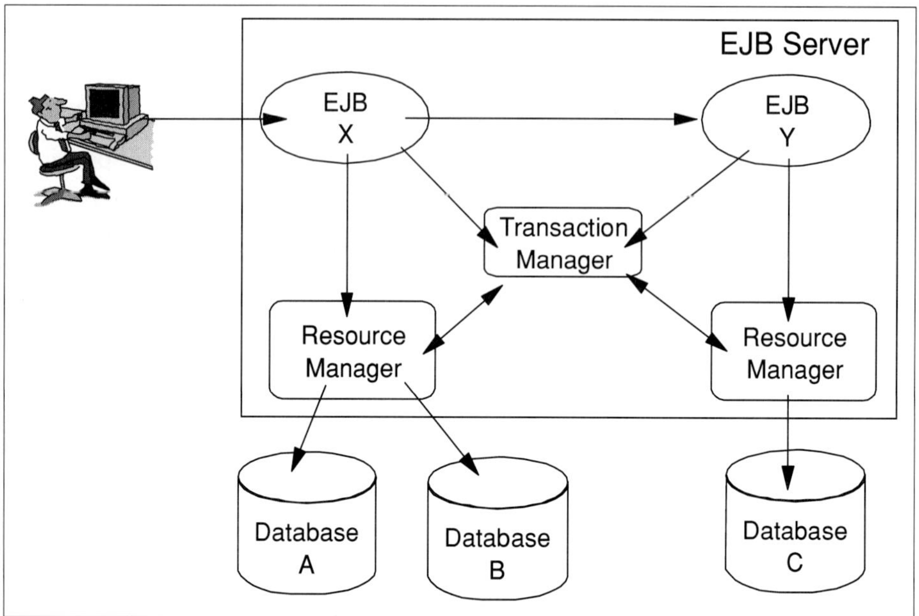

Figure 390. Update multiple databases in a single transaction

12.3.1.2 Update of databases via multiple EJB servers

Enterprise JavaBeans makes it possible for enterprise Beans to update databases across multiple EJB servers within the same transaction. The EJB servers can be network connected and located at different sites. This capability is illustrated in Figure 391.

A client invokes the enterprise bean X. X updates data in database A, and then calls another enterprise bean Y, which updates data in database C on another EJB server. The EJB servers are located on different systems that are connected through a network.

The two EJB servers propagate the transaction context from enterprise bean X to enterprise bean Y. When the transaction completes, the two servers use a distributed two-phase commit protocol to ensure the atomic property of the transaction. The propagation of transaction context, as well as other ACID properties of the transaction, are transparent to the EJB developer.

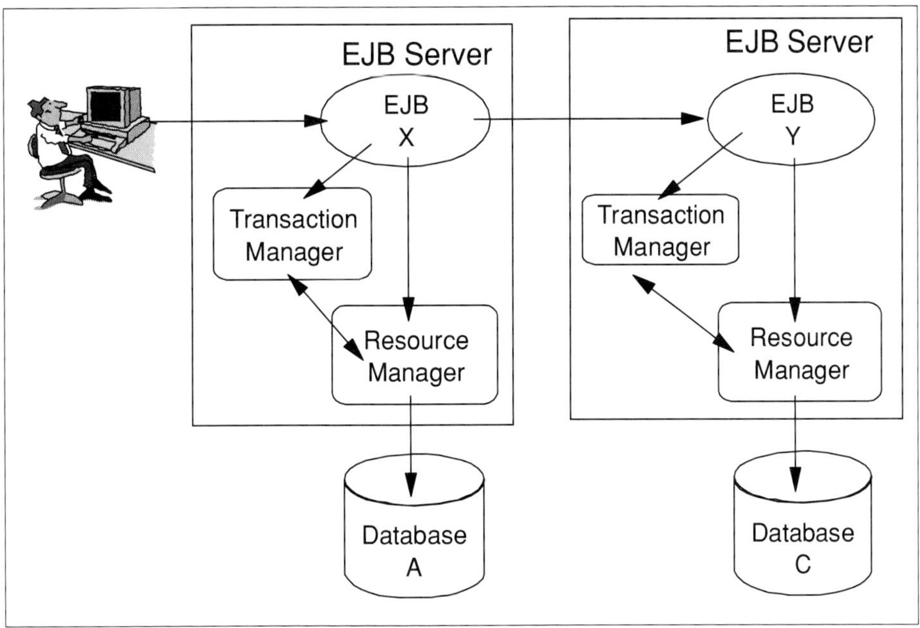

Figure 391. Update multiple databases via multiple EJB servers

12.3.2 Transaction demarcation

The EJB model offers a variety of ways to make use of transactional services. Transaction demarcation determines who is responsible for starting and completing a transaction. Developers have two choices:

- Using programmatic transaction demarcation, where they write the code to begin and commit transactions using the javax.transaction.UserTransaction interface.
- Using a declarative transaction demarcation where they specify a transaction attribute during deployment and the container handles the transaction demarcation automatically.

The declarative approach is recommended because it reduces the code that must be maintained and offers more flexibility, since attributes can be changed at deployment time without changing the code.

Container demarcation is available for entity beans and session beans. The application assembler or deployer uses the deployment descriptor to specify (declare) the required transaction semantics. The container provides the necessary support code.

Client demarcation is explicit transaction management. Developers use the JTA UserTransaction API directly in the code.

Bean demarcation is similar to client demarcation with the explicit transaction management occurring with a session bean method. The following figures show the different options available.

12.3.2.1 Container demarcation

The declarative approach as shown in Figure 392 is recommended because of flexibility and lower code maintenance.

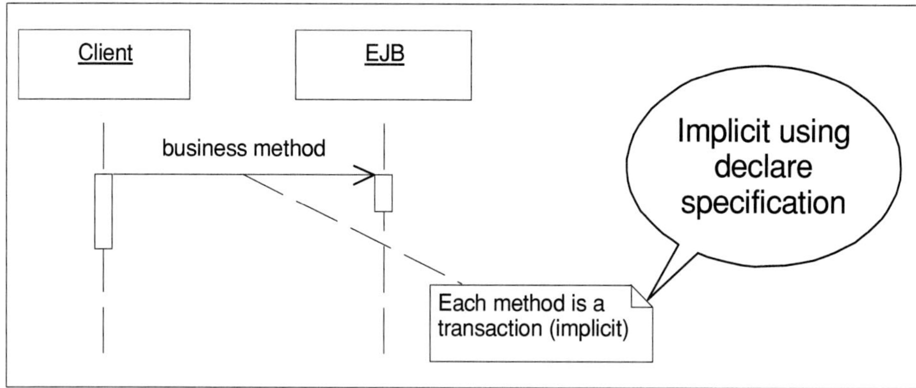

Figure 392. The declarative scenario for container-managed transactions

12.3.2.2 Bean demarcation

The bean-managed demarcation is possible with session EJBs that are deployed with a transaction attribute set to TX_BEAN_MANAGED as shown in Figure 393 on page 515.

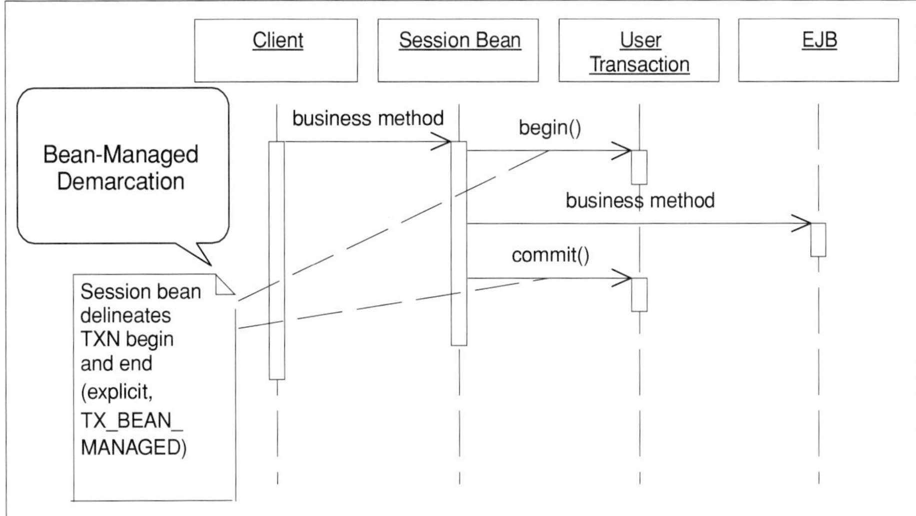

Figure 393. Bean-managed scenario

For this case, the UserTransaction is acquired from the SessionContext.

```
javax.transaction.UserTransaction = sessionCtx.getUserTransaction();
```

For stateless session beans, a method that starts a transaction is not allowed to return if the transaction is still active. This is good because it favors short-lived transactions.

For stateful session beans, a method can start a transaction and return, leaving the transaction active. This capability can lead to long-running transactions that hold critical system resources like database locks.

Stateful session beans can implement the javax.ejb.SessionSynchronization interface to receive callbacks for transaction life cycle events afterBegin, beforeCompletion, and afterCompletion.

12.3.2.3 Client demarcation

In the client demarcation scenario, as shown in Figure 394 on page 516, the client acquires a UserTransaction through a JNDI lookup:

```
InitialContext ic = new InitialContext(properties);
javax.transaction.UserTransaction = ic.lookup(jta/usertransaction");
```

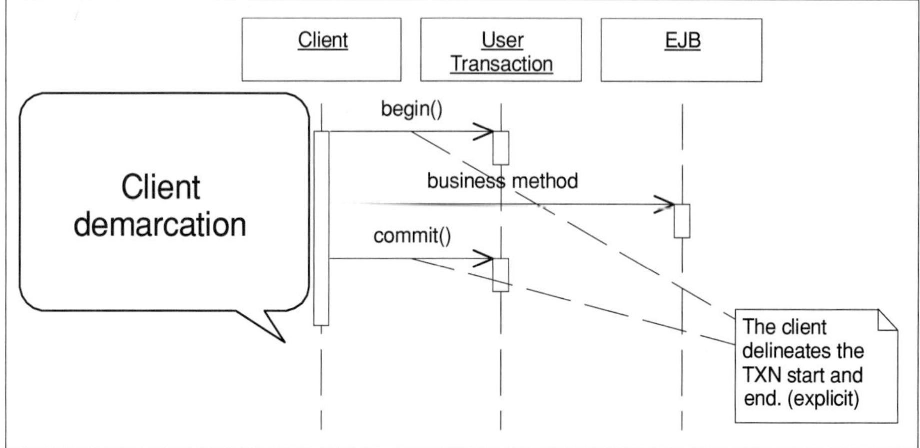

Figure 394. Client demarcation scenario

The client begins a transaction that results in a new transaction context being associated with a client's thread of execution. The client calls methods on EJBs and EJBs become implicitly associated with a client's transaction. When the client issues a commit, the EJBs changes are committed. Use of client-demarcated transactions are not recommended for several reasons. They require more code to be written and maintained. They move the management of transactions from the robust system layer that has traditionally been responsible for this function. They create the possibility of long-running transactions.

12.3.3 Transactional specifiers

For container-managed transactions, a bean indicates its requirements through two attributes: the transaction attribute and the isolation attribute.

The transaction attribute defines the transactional requirements and can be set for the bean or for individual methods.

The transaction-isolation attribute determines how transactional reads are isolated and can be set for the bean or for individual methods.

These two transactional specifiers are set in the deployment descriptor. When the bean is deployed, the container generates the necessary transaction-support code. The values chosen for these specifiers give the container the information it needs to provide that support code. The transaction attribute indicates the transactional requirements for beans. The isolation attribute simply affects how database locks are held for reads that occur within transactions. This provides the ability to sacrifice accuracy of reads in favor of greater concurrency at the database. It does not affect updates.

12.3.4 Transaction attributes

This section describes in simple terms what is meant by each of the EJB transactional attributes (WebSphere V3.5 follows the EJB 1.0 specification) that can be assigned to an EJB or EJB method. It also indicates what transactional context (if any) is passed to downstream beans.

This attribute determines if and how transactions are needed. The values can be:

- TX_MANDATORY
- TX_REQUIRED
- TX_REQUIRES_NEW
- TX_SUPPORTS
- TX_NOT_SUPPORTED
- TX_BEAN_MANAGED

The first five possible values indicate container-managed transactions, and these can be applied to an entire bean or to individual methods within a bean.

TX_MANDATORY: The container must call methods from the transactional context established by the client. If the client has a transaction context, it is propagated to the bean. If the client does not have a transaction context, the container throws a TransactionRequiredException. Consider using TX_MANDATORY with entities to assure a transaction is active before the entity is called.

TX_REQUIRED: The container must invoke methods within a transactional context. If the client has a transaction context, it is propagated to the bean. If not, the container starts a transaction. Consider using TX_REQUIRED with session beans.

TX_REQUIRES_NEW: The container must start a new transaction for the method. If the client has a transaction context, it is suspended for the duration, and a new one is started. If not, the container starts a transaction.

TX_SUPPORTS: The container must use a client's context for the transaction. If the client has a transaction context, it is propagated to the bean. If not, the method is run under what the EJB specification calls the unspecified transaction context.

TX_NOT_SUPPORTED: The container must not invoke methods transactionally. If the client has a transaction context, it is suspended for the duration. If not, the method is run under what the EJB specification calls the unspecified transaction context.

The TX_BEAN_MANAGED value indicates that the bean itself, rather than the container, assumes responsibility for starting and ending transactions. Only session beans can request bean-managed transactions. This value applies to the entire bean, and cannot be specified for individual bean methods. Using bean-managed transactions will require you to write and maintain more code and will limit your options at deployment time. However, it does provide you with an opportunity to develop sophisticated exception recovery that your bean users would have difficulty duplicating.

The following section indicates what is passed to any downstream beans.

Some terminology used in this section:

- The term called bean refers to the application EJB bean that has the transactional attribute being discussed.
- Downstream bean refers to the application EJB bean that is called from the called bean.
- Upstream bean refers to an application EJB bean or client application that invokes the called bean.

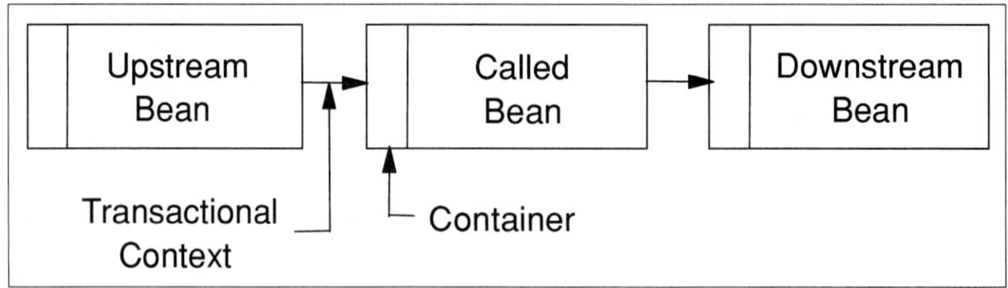

Figure 395. Relation between the upstream bean, called bean and downstream bean

An Upstream bean's transactional context (if one exists) is always passed to the calling bean by the container. It is up to the called bean's container to do one of the following with the transactional context. The called bean's container can:

- Retain the context in the case where the bean's transaction attribute is TX_REQUIRED, TX_SUPPORTS, or TX_MANDATORY
- Suspend the callers transactional context in the case where the bean's transaction attribute is TX_REQUIRES_NEW, or TX_NOT_SUPPORTED. The callers transactional context is resumed when the call returns.
- Create a new transactional context in the case where the bean's transaction attribute is TX_REQUIRES_NEW – the callers transactional context is suspended until the bean returns.

In the situation where the upstream bean has no transaction context, the called beans container will:

- Create a new transactional context in the case where the bean's transaction attribute is TX_REQUIRED or TX_REQUIRES_NEW
- Continue without a transaction context where the bean's transaction attribute is TX_NOT_SUPPORTED, or TX_SUPPORTS
- Reject the transactional context in the case where the bean's transaction attribute is TX_MANDATORY

Table 34 summarizes the transaction context used by a bean based on the transaction attribute setting and whether the client has a transaction context established.

Table 34. Transaction attribute summary

Transaction attribute	Client transaction context	Bean transaction context
TX_MANDATORY	No transaction	Not allowed
	Client transaction	Client transaction
TX_NOT_SUPPORTED	No transaction	No transaction
	Client transaction	No transaction
TX_REQUIRES_NEW	No transaction	New transaction
	Client transaction	New transaction
TX_REQUIRED	No transaction	New transaction
	Client transaction	Client transaction
TX_SUPPORTS	No transaction	No transaction
	Client transaction	Client transaction

12.3.4.1 Transactional attribute considerations

You need to consider a number of things when developing transaction-aware beans. For example, what will happen when your transaction context is passed and used by a downstream EJB. Do you want another bean to be part of your transaction? Are you prepared for it to potentially cause a rollback? If the bean you are calling will suspend your transaction, will that cause a deadlock? Consider the following:

- If the downstream bean uses your transaction context and throws a non-application exception, it may cause the transaction you are in to be marked for rollback by the downstream container and there will be nothing you can do about it.
- If the downstream bean marks the transaction for RollbackOnly, there is nothing you can do about it either. There is no unsetRollbackOnly() method. The transaction (that you may have started) will be rolled back.

Even if your transaction may have been marked for rollback, it is still possible for your bean to perform some processing under the following conditions:

- You can continue to execute code within your bean so long as you do not attempt to call any other bean.
- If you attempt to call another bean, it will fail with a RollbackException indicating that it was improperly started.
- If you attempt to call JNDI, it will fail with an org.omg.CORBA.ROLLEDBACK_EXCEPTION as well.

In WebSphere V3.0.2, you were allowed to make a call to a bean marked as TX_NOT_SUPPORTED. In WebSphere V3.5, this is no longer the case. The calling bean's container simply refuses to pass a rolled-back transaction context to a downstream bean, in anticipation that it will be of no use and the call will eventually fail. The EJB specification does not make it clear how these situations should be handled. So expect that other EJB implementations may handle these situations differently (even between releases).

If you do not wish the transaction you are in (or that you started) to be affected by a downstream call, you have the following options:

- Ensure that any downstream bean you call directly has a transaction attribute of TX_REQUIRES_NEW, or TX_NOT_SUPPORTED. By doing this your transaction will be suspended and not be affected directly by the downstream call.
- Start an explicit transaction from your EJB (your bean must be TX_BEAN_MANAGED to do this) and call the downstream bean in with a

transaction context you explicitly created. This way the transaction context is associated with the bean that started it, and not with the calling thread, and it will not be managed by the (downstream, or any) container.

- Use a non-EJB class to perform explicit client-demarcated transactions. Note that the client here means a non-EJB caller of an Enterprise JavaBean, not user or client application.

The bottom line: if you are marked for rollback you have little choice except to clean up and let the rollback occur. Only the calling client (that is, a non-EJB client or bean in a different transaction scope) can do something about the situation.

We discourage the use of TX_SUPPORTS and TX_NOT_SUPPORTED because if your application accesses multiple entities with container-managed persistence in a single high-level operation, such as a servlet invocation, you may see unexpected results. The bean methods for these cases are run under "an unspecified transaction context" where the container determines the semantics. In the absence of a transaction, the current implementation of the container executes the database accesses in a local transaction. If those local transactions use different connections to the same database, deadlocks can occur. This is true regardless of whether there is a single or multiple application servers, and whether JTA is enabled.

You can reduce project risk by selecting the options where the semantics are clearly defined. Use TX_REQUIRED or TX_REQUIRES_NEW in you session beans to assure a transaction is started. Use TX_MANDATORY in your CMP entity beans to assure the changes are part of a bigger transaction being coordinated by the session bean.

12.3.5 Transaction isolation attribute

The transaction isolation attribute tells the container how to limit concurrent reads in a database. The EJB 1.1 specification removed the guidelines for managing transaction isolation levels for beans with container-managed transaction demarcation. But since bean deployers still require mechanisms to govern EJB concurrency, WebSphere continues to support it along with other mechanisms discussed in the next section.

12.3.5.1 Transaction isolation levels

Transaction isolation levels provides a trade-off between accuracy of reads versus concurrent readers. The levels can best be described by the types of read anomalies they permit and forbid. Consider the read anomalies that can occur with two concurrent transactions, T1 and T2:

- Dirty read: T1 reads data that has been modified by T2, before T2 commits.
- Non-repeatable read: this is caused by fine-grained locks.
  - T1 reads a record and drops its lock.
  - T2 updates; T1 rereads different data.
- Phantom read: A non-repeatable read involving a range of data and inserts or deletes on the range.
  - T1 reads a set of records that match some criterion.
  - T2 inserts a record that matches the criterion.
  - T1 continues processing the set, which now includes records that were not part of the original matching set.

There are four possible values for the transaction isolation attribute.

TRANSACTION_READ_UNCOMMITTED: Permits all the read anomalies including dirty reads, non-repeatable reads, and phantom reads.

TRANSACTION_READ_COMMITTED: Permits non-repeatable and phantom reads and forbids dirty reads.

TRANSACTION_REPEATABLE_READ: Permits phantom reads and forbids both dirty and unrepeatable reads.

TRANSACTION_SERIALIZABLE: Forbids all the read anomalies.

The container applies isolation attribute as follows:

- For entity beans with CMP: The container generates code that assures the desired level of isolation for each database access.
- For session beans and BMP entity beans: The container sets the isolation level at the start of each transaction, for each database connection.

The transaction isolation level is tied to a database connection, and the connection will use the isolation level specified in the first bean that uses the connection. If the connection is used by another bean method that has a different isolation level, the container will throw an IsolationLevelChangeException.

A database may not support all isolation levels, as Table 35 shows.

Table 35. Database support for various transaction isolation attributes

	Read Uncommitted	**Read Committed**	**Repeatable Read**	**Serializable**
DB2	✓	✓	✓	✓
Oracle		✓		✓
Sybase	✓	✓		✓

For the current set of database drivers being used, Oracle does not support read uncommitted or repeatable read isolation, and Sybase does not support repeatable reads. To learn more, refer to the documentation provided by the database product.

The DB2 definitions for isolation levels follow the naming conventions used in Jim Gray's classic book on transaction processing, *Transaction Processing: Concepts and Techniques*. Table 36 shows a map between EJB and DB2 isolation levels.

Table 36. EJB to DB2 isolation level names

EJB Isolation Level	**DB2 Isolation Level**
TRANSACTION_SERIALIZABLE	Repeatable Read
TRANSACTION_REPEATABLE_READ	Read Stability
TRANSACTION_READ_COMMITTED	Cursor Stability
TRANSACTION_READ_UNCOMMITTED	Uncommitted Read

The bean behavior for a given isolation level can vary with databases. For example, the behaviors of DB2 and Oracle are considerably different with TRANSACTION_READ_COMMITTED isolation. Oracle holds a read lock until the transaction commits. DB2 holds the lock as long as a cursor is positioned on the row.

The current implementation of the container closes the result set used to load the bean prior to invoking the business method. As a result, this causes the DB2 cursor to close and release the row read lock. Therefore we recommend you specify TRANSACTION_REPEATABLE_READ or greater for cases where container-managed EJBs are mapped to DB2 and those EJBs can experience concurrent client updates. This will provide DB2's read stability isolation level. The level works best when there is an index defined over the field being scanned. That is the normal case when the field is the primary key.

12.3.5.2 Setting the isolation level with VisualAge for Java

If developing your EJBs in VisualAge for Java (VAJ), you can set the isolation level in the bean's property sheet. To open the property window, right-click the EJB in the Enterprise Bean pane and select **Properties**. The Properties window like that shown in Figure 396 on page 524 will appear.

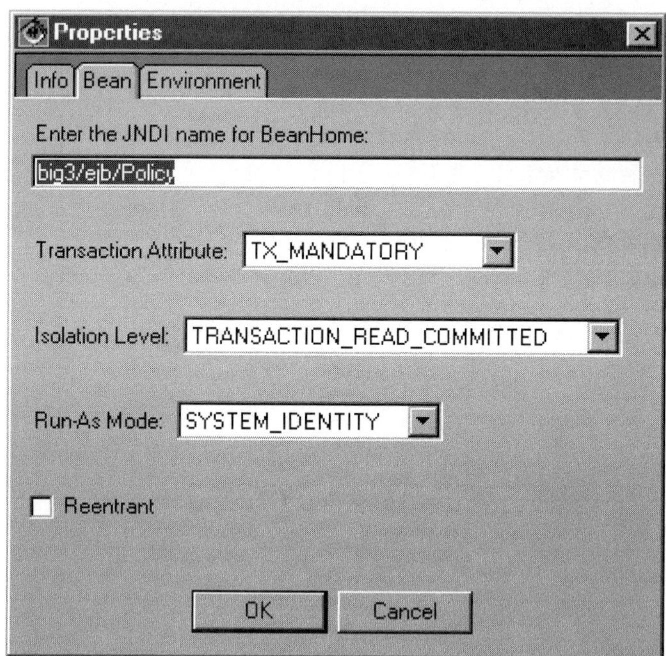

Figure 396. Entity property sheet from VisualAge for Java

12.3.5.3 Setting the isolation level with JETACE tool

You can also change the isolation level using the stand-alone JETACE tool. Start jetace on Windows in a command window, for example, by typing `jetace` in the <WAS_HOME>\bin directory, where <WAS_HOME> is the WebSphere installation directory such as c:\WebSphere\AppServer.

Load the EJB JAR of interest by using the **File -> Load...** menu option. Highlight the EJB you want to edit and click the **Edit** button.

Select the **Transactions** tab to change the transaction attribute or isolation level as shown in Figure 397 on page 525.

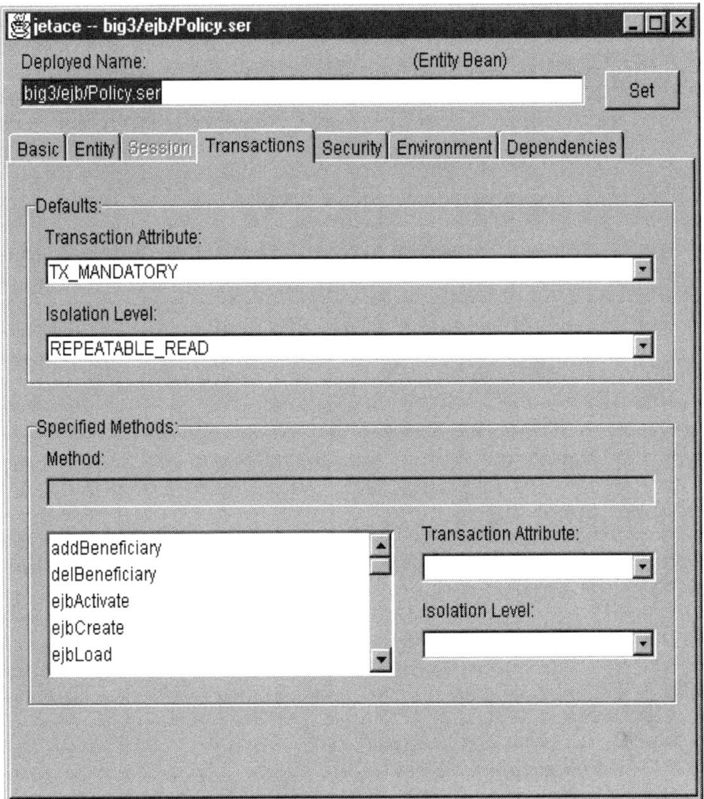

Figure 397. Jetace transaction panel

Note

VisualAge for Java offers more capabilities for deployment, including the ability to specify read-only methods on an entity bean. That information can be lost if you use JETACE tool to update the deployment JAR exported from VisualAge for Java.

12.4 EJB concurrency control

In addition to the transaction isolation level, WebSphere supports the ability to specify which entity methods are read-only and should not result in changes to persistent data. Bean deployers can also specify whether an entity retrieved via its primary key is likely to be updated. Both mechanism can affect the database locking behavior.

12.4.1 Setting read-only method with VisualAge for Java

Use VisualAge for Java to indicate which entity methods are read-only.

The container can use this information to optimize database operations. For example, if all methods executed on an entity during a transaction are marked as read-only, the container can skip the ejbStore() operation at the end of the transaction.

This avoid possible read to write lock promotions and improving performance by omitting the database write that can result in exceptions caused by conflicts.

To indicate an entity method is read-only, right-click the method within the member pane of the bean, then select **EJB Method Attributes -> Read-only Method** as shown in Figure 398.

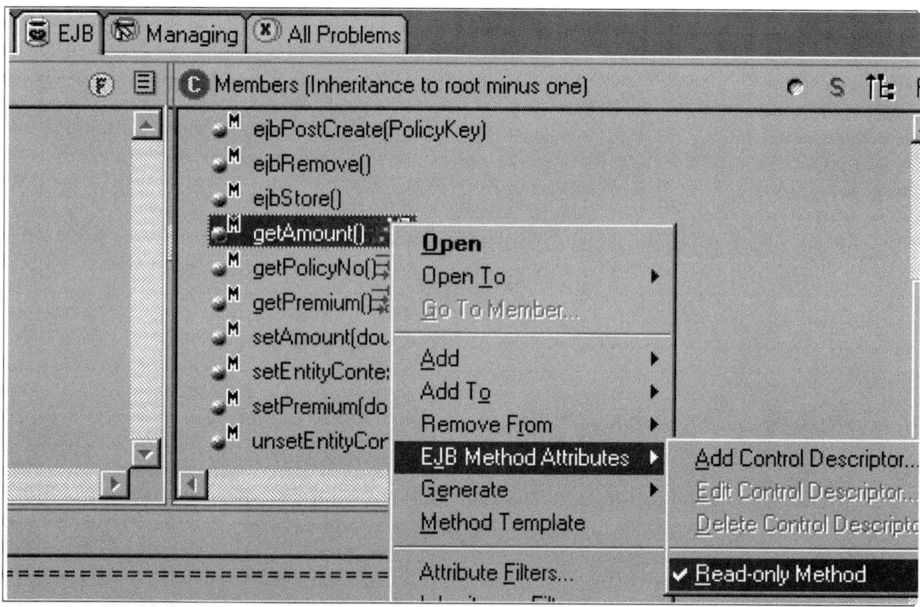

Figure 398. Setting an entity bean method to be read-only within VisualAge for Java

12.4.2 Setting read-only method with administrative console

Another way to set the read-only method indications is to use the WebSphere Administrative Console.

To do that, stop the application server and select the enterprise bean node on domain tree.

Click the **Edit** button associated with the deployment descriptor on the General tab.

That brings up the Deployment Properties wizard shown in Figure 399.

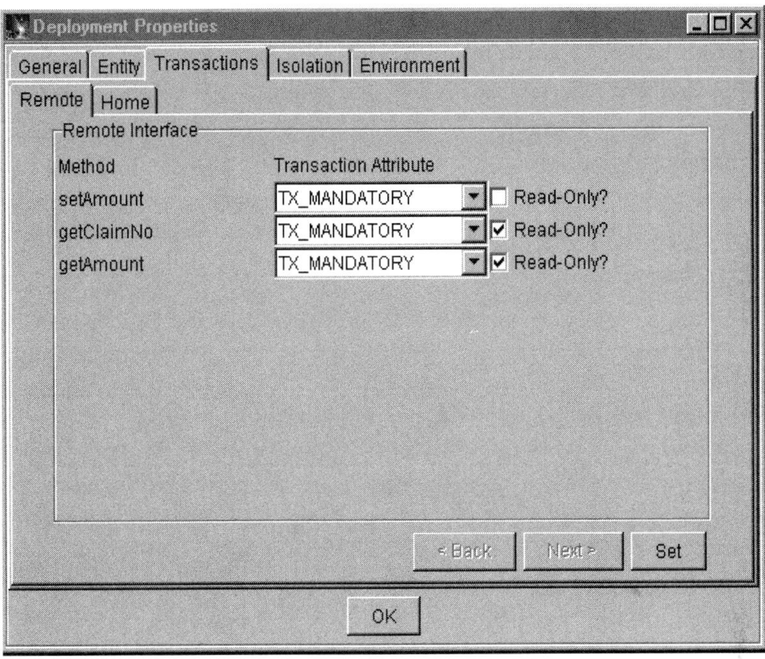

Figure 399. Deployment Properties: Transaction Attribute Read-Only

After checking the **Read-Only** boxes click the **Set** and **OK** buttons followed by the **Apply** button at the bottom of the bean's General tab.

Note

The Deployment Properties wizard also shows the transaction attribute and isolation levels (on the Isolation tab). At the time of this writing the property wizard allowed the transaction attributes and isolation levels to be changed on the remote business methods but not the methods defined on the Home such as create and findByPrimaryKey. Changing only some of the method properties could cause isolation level mismatch problems. A WebSphere V3.5 fix is being developed that will allow the Home methods to be updated from the Deployment Properties wizard. That fix will make the wizard the most convenient way to update the transaction attributes and isolation levels.

12.4.3 Database locking with EJB

Deadlocks occur when two concurrent transactions place a shared lock on the same resource (table or row) when they read it then attempt to update the information at commit time. This can happen when the same EJB is accessed and updated by two or more clients at the same time. When using DB2, a deadlock like this would result in one of the clients getting a rollback exception.

You can verify when this is happening by activating an application server trace on the com.ibm.ejs.cm.portability component.

Figure 400 is a sample of trace data that shows the DB2 exception details:

```
[00.10.09 11:15:35:959 CDT] 50b052fd PortabilityLa > translateException
                              COM.ibm.db2.jdbc.DB2Exception: [IBM][CLI Driver][DB2/NT]
SQL0911N The current transaction has been rolled back because of a deadlock or
timeout.
Reason code "2". SQLSTATE=40001
    at java.sql.SQLException.<init>(SQLException.java:45)
    at COM.ibm.db2.jdbc.DB2Exception.<init>(DB2Exception.java:71)
```

Figure 400. WebSphere Trace output showing a deadlock condition

Unfortunately, the recovery from exceptions due to conflicts can be non-trivial. What is needed is a way to indicate that the bean is being accessed with the intent to update it so the deadlock conditions can be avoided. That is exactly what the Find for update option does. This option can be found on an entity bean's Advanced tab on the WebSphere Administrative Console as shown in Figure 401 on page 529.

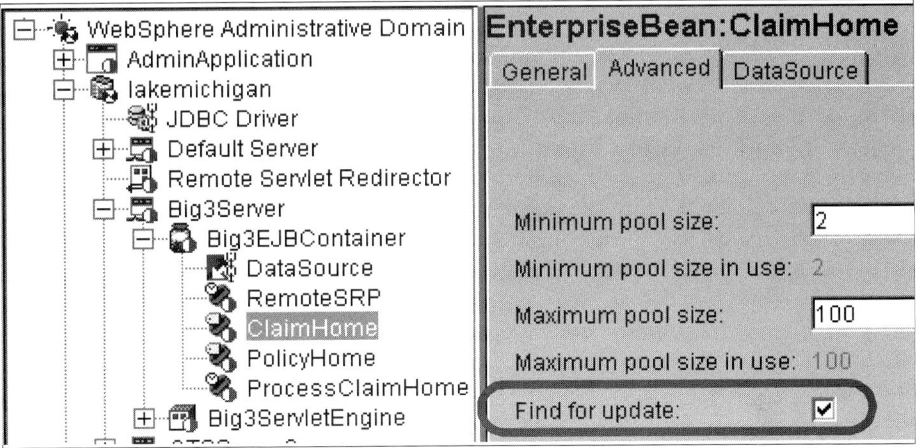

Figure 401. Find for update check box for entity beans in the administrative console

When this option is enabled, an entity found via the findByPrimaryKey() method is accessed with a write intent or write lock, resulting in multiple concurrent client requests being serialized. The result is deadlock avoidance.

12.5 Settings based on EJB usage

Now that you understand what choices you can make for the EJB deployment settings we are going to do testing to determine which choices work the best for various EJB usage patterns. The patterns include:

- Read only - multiple clients get data from an entity bean but do not update that bean. The rows in the database associated with the bean have populated before running the application.
- Read mostly - multiple clients get data from an entity and occasionally update that bean.
- Update often - multiple clients often update an entity bean.

In order to test these patterns we developed a Java client for the big3 application where the percentage of read-only operations is an input parameter of the application. We then executed two clients accessing the same EJBs with the same usage pattern (read-only, read-mostly, and update often). See the \floppy.35\big3\client\MainRetry.java code for details. The batch file used to start the test is called RunClientWithRetry.bat. Here is an example of the command:

```
RunClientWithRetry 100 1113 2224 10 95 lakemichigan
```

Here is the associated output for that command:

```
---------------- Run Big3 java Client ------------------
-     Repetitions          = 100
-     Policy number        = 1113
-     Claim number         = 2224
-     Amount               = 10.0
-     Create first         = false
-     ProcessClaim Context = com.ibm.ejs.ns.jndi.CNInitialContextFactory
-     ProcessClaim URL     = iiop://lakemichigan/
-     Policy Context       = com.ibm.ejs.ns.jndi.CNInitialContextFactory
-     Policy URL           = iiop://lakemichigan/
-     Claim Context        = com.ibm.ejs.ns.jndi.CNInitialContextFactory
-     Claim URL            = iiop://lakemichigan/
-     PercentReads         = 95
-
-     Geting initial context...
-     Lookup ProcessClaimHome...
<< create ProcessClaim object >>
<< calling the ProcessClaim object
rrrrrrrrrrrrrrrrrrwrrrrrrrrrrrrrrrrrrrrwrrrrr
rrrrrrrrrrrrrrrrrrrrrrrrrrrrrrrrrrrrrrrrrrrrrrrrrr >>
<< remove ProcessClaim object >>
---------------- Execution Results ---------------------
-     Reps         = 100
-     Total time   = 1703 milliSeconds
-     Average time = 17
-     Reads        = 98
-     Writes       = 2
-     Retries      = 0
---------------------------------------------------------
```

For our testing, the error recovery performed in the client test is simple. Exceptions resulting from commit failures are retried forever. We expect a production application would require more sophisticated recovery.

The DB2 database was used for these tests and the EJB database access set to shared mode. This is consistent with option C caching defined in the EJB specification. This is the required setting when multiple WebSphere processes or processes outside WebSphere's control are accessing the same bean data. The isolation level was set to REPEATABLE_READ.

The test results are shown in Table 37 on page 531 and Table 38 on page 532. The first table is the baseline results for a single client. The second table shows the result when two clients are running.

Both tables have the same format, where the first column indicates whether the getter methods on entity beans were marked as read-only.

The second column indicates the state of the Find for update check box for the entity beans.

The third column indicates which percentage of the operations were read-only versus update.

The fourth column shows the number of retries for the client(s) required to execute 1000 successful operations.

The fifth column shows the average time for each operation for the client(s).

Table 37. EJB read/write single client test results

Read-only methods set	**Find For Update check box**	**% Reads**	**Retries**	**Avg Time (ms)**
yes	false	100	0	14
yes	false	95	0	15
yes	false	10	0	19
no	false	100	0	16
no	false	95	0	16
no	false	10	0	20
yes	true	100	0	17
yes	true	95	0	18
yes	true	10	0	19
no	true	100	0	17
no	true	95	0/0	18
no	true	10	0/0	19

The single client test showed the average response time for the 100% read case was about 10-35% better then the mostly write case.

The Resource Analyzer for WebSphere was used to verify that the ejbLoad() and ejbStore() were happening when expected.

A read test loop count of 1000 resulted in 3000 bean method calls, 2000 entity activations, 2000 entity loads, and 2000 entity passivations.

The write test calls an additional bean method so a 100% write test resulted in 4000 bean method calls, 2000 entity activations, 2000 entity loads, 2000 entity stores, and 2000 entity passivations.

Table 38. EJB read/write multi client test results

Read-only methods set	Find For Update check box	% Reads	Retries	Avg TIme (ms)
yes	false	100	0/0	31/29
yes	false	95	7/4	156/156
yes	false	10	72/54	361/355
no	false	100	50/57	296/299
no	false	95	67/68	349/357
no	false	10	81/83	415/412
yes	true	100	0/0	33/30
yes	true	95	0/0	34/32
yes	true	10	0/0	40/38
no	true	100	0/0	34/36
no	true	95	0/0	34/35
no	true	10	0	39/38

The best response times for the multi-client case were recorded when both clients were calling read-only methods that had been marked as read-only within VisualAge for Java. Lock conflicts were avoided because the container did not have to call ejbStore() for the entities. The Find for update check box was not checked (false). These are good settings for entities used in a read-only fashion.

The worst response times were observed when the clients had to recover from exceptions. Those occur when the Find for update check box was not checked (false) and write operations are involved. That included the cases where the clients only called read methods but those methods were not flagged as read-only using VisualAge for Java.

Even the read-mostly case (95% reads) showed a dramatic increase in response time. It was five times worse then the case with 100% reads. We also observed varying and erratic recovery times for failed operations. Sometimes an operation had to be retried as much as ten times to recover.

The best all-around times were observed when the Find for update check box was set to true. No exceptions were observed in this mode and the execution of request appeared fair. This was the best setting for the read-mostly and update-often cases.

For cases where finer grained locking is needed, for example, you want to read a EJB in one transaction and update in another, you can develop EJB finders to return the lock you need. For example, the read case would use a findByPrimaryKey() method while the write case could use a findForUpdate ByPrimaryKey().

See Vesselin Ivanov's article titled *EJBs and Transaction Management in WebSphere Advanced Edition* on the VisualAge Developer Domain Web site (http://www.software.ibm.com/vadd) for details of this design pattern.

12.6 Transaction exception handling

In this section, we describe how exceptions are handled with transactions.

12.6.1 The preliminaries

What are the types of exceptions available?

An exception is unchecked if it extends RuntimeException or Error. Unchecked exceptions do not need to be specified in the throws clause of a method.

An exception is checked if it is specified in the throws clause of a method.

An application level exception is an exception that is checked and extends Exception. It cannot extend RuntimeException, Error, or RemoteException. CreateException, RemoveException and FinderException are application exceptions.

A system level exception is any exception other than an application level exception; it includes all unchecked exceptions.

The application exception handling has been changed in WebSphere V3.5 to match the EJB 1.1 specification. More on this will be given in the next sections.

12.6.2 What you can assume

If you catch an exception (any exception) and do not pass it to the container (by throwing it again and returning from the bean), it is up to you to handle the situation correctly. Note that an EJB cannot catch all exceptions, since exceptions may be thrown by the infrastructure that is between the EJB and its caller, and which is invoked before and after the EJB method.

The EJB developer can assume that the container will pass all application level exceptions to the caller unchanged (this is an EJB 1.1 specification that has been implemented in WebSphere V3.5). If the container is the initiator of the transaction, the transaction will be committed first before the exception is thrown. The EJB developer must call the setRollBackOnly() method explicitly if he or she wants the transaction to be marked for rollback. In previous releases all application exceptions would cause a transaction to be marked for rollback.

Only the container that initiated the transaction will initiate a rollback. Intermediate containers that catch system exceptions only mark the transaction for rollback. The container that initiated the transaction after rolling back will throw a RemoteException to the upstream caller.

12.6.3 What an application can do

An EJB can instruct the container to roll back by calling the method EJBContext.setRollbackOnly(). A downstream bean which inherits/assumes/continues with the transaction from the upstream bean can cause that transaction to roll back using that same mechanism.

An application can detect if the current transaction (the transaction it is a part of) is or will be rolled back by calling the method EJBContext.getRollbackOnly().

If an application receives a RemoteException it cannot automatically know that the call was successful or not.

- A RemoteException can be thrown if there was a communication error
- A RemoteException can be thrown if the called beans container detected an unchecked exception
- A RemoteException can be thrown if the called beans container detected a System Exception or another RemoteException
- A RemoteException can be thrown if the called bean started its own transaction, failed and was rolled back

If an application receives a TransactionRolledbackException it can assume that the transaction it is a member of will be rolled back and it is fruitless to continue processing. A bean can continue limited processing in this state.

12.6.4 What a container will do

If a container receives an unchecked (runtime) exception and is participating in a transaction (not necessarily the initiator of the transaction), it will mark it for rollback. The caller will be thrown a TransactionRolledbackException. If the container is the initiator, a RemoteException will be thrown. In both cases the rollback will occur.

If the container receives a RemoteException it will rethrow the RemoteException or a subclass of it. If the container initiated the transaction, it will cause a rollback and throw a RemoteException.

If an application wants to throw a serious non-application exception and cause a rollback, it should continue to throw subclasses of RemoteException. The EJB 1.1 specification provides another exception (EJBException) specifically for this situation. However, the EJBException defined in WebSphere V3.5 is not compliant with the EJB 1.1 specification and should not be used. Continue to use RemoteException in WebSphere V3.5 to throw non-application level exceptions.

12.6.5 TransactionRolledbackException

The EJB specification (1.0 and 1.1) prescribes that a container must throw a javax.transaction.TransactionRolledBackException when it has marked a transaction for rollback that it did not start. However, in WebSphere V3.5 you can receive different exceptions under different circumstances.

- org.omg.CORBA.ROLLEDBACK_Exception (extends RuntimeException)
- javax.transaction.TransactionRolledbackException (extends RemoteException)

You can count on the fact that the getEJBContext().getRollbackOnly() will return true if the transaction has been marked for rollback in either case.

For now, applications should catch both exceptions and treat them the same.

12.6.6 Dos and don'ts (EJB 1.0, WebSphere V3.5 specific)

Here are some guidelines to follow.

- Application beans should explicitly make the decision to cause a rollback and not leave it to the container.

They can do this by calling the EJBContext.setRollbackOnly() method. Remember, application exceptions result in a commit unless you explicitly call the setRollbackOnly() method.

- When calls are returned from downstream EJBs, application beans should check if their transaction has been marked for rollback using the EJBContext.getRollbackOnly() method call, and act accordingly. They should not just rely on getting this notification as a result of a rollback exception.
- An application can setRollbackonly() without necessarily throwing an exception, although this should be avoided.
- Application exceptions should follow the EJB 1.1 specification and no longer extend RuntimeException or RemoteException or any of its subclasses.
- Application beans should throw an exception that extends RuntimeException if it wants to cause a rollback and indicate a system level error. In the EJB 1.1 specification, the application would have been required to throw an EJBException, but this has not yet been implemented in WebSphere V3.5.
- When a call to a bean results in a thrown RemoteException, you cannot know that the target bean rolled back, or was even called. In this case (unless you really know what you are doing) you should call EJBContext.setRollbackOnly() and throw an appropriate application or RemoteException and cause the entire transaction to roll back. Leave it to the next level up to retry the transaction if desired.
- If an application bean wants to report a system type problem and cause a rollback, it should continue to throw a RemoteException until WebSphere fully supports EJB 1.1.
- If an Application bean wants to ensure that its work is committed regardless of the outcome of calls to other downstream beans, the downstream bean's transaction attribute should be marked as TX_REQUIRES_NEW or TX_NOT_SUPPORTED, or the calling bean should manage its own transaction (TX_BEAN_MANAGED). This will cause the caller's transaction to be suspended when the downstream bean is called.
- Note that a transactional attribute of TX_REQUIRES_NEW can set the stage for a deadlock, if the new and the suspended transactions try to use the same resources, depending on their transaction isolation levels.

It is generally stated in EJB books and articles that bean-demarcated transaction management should be avoided. While this is true in most cases, it should not be dismissed as a bad thing. In the case where a session bean is coordinating a complex process or set of activities, it may be more practical to use bean-demarcated transactions. This will allow you to split the processing into multiple transactions, recover from downstream beans that cause rollback, and explicitly ensure that a downstream bean will not affect your processing. If you find yourself fighting transaction problems, consider using bean-demarcated transactions in your main session bean. Alternatively, instead of a session bean, you can resort to a non-EJB caller that will demarcate transactions explicitly, but that requires writing even more code.

12.7 WebSphere family interoperability

The next generation of the EJB specification includes focus on interoperability between Web application servers. Interoperability can be achieved using the RMI over IIOP support and its capabilities to propagate transaction and security contextes. WebSphere is well on its way to providing this function by supporting distributed transactions involving EJBs running in both the Enterprise Edition/Component Broker (EE/CB) server and the Advanced Edition (AE) server. To enable the interoperability, set the following flags in an AE server's command line arguments:

"-Dcom.ibm.ejs.jts.jts.ControlSet.nativeOnly=false"

"-Dcom.ibm.ejs.jts.jts.ControlSet.interoperabilityOnly=true"

To set the arguments with the administrative console, select the application server node in the administrative domain tree, then add them to the Command line arguments field in the General tab.

12.8 Conclusion

The J2EE and EJB specifications have eased the development of portable, n-tier, enterprise applications. More than ever, developers can focus on developing the application's business logic and leverage the common plumbing provided by J2EE application servers. One area the specifications can improve on is standardization of concurrency control mechanisms like isolation levels, read-only methods, and the update intent associated with an entity access. The requirement for these types of mechanism will grow as application throughput demands grow.

Chapter 13. XML and WebSphere

The eXtensible Markup Language (XML) is a specification for creating markup languages that are used to represent information in the form of documents. XML allows documents to be easily exchanged between organizations and allows programs to intelligently process documents without human intervention.

WebSphere V3.5 includes support for generating, parsing, and manipulating XML documents. A discussion of the details and nuances of XML and XML support in WebSphere could fill an entire book. This chapter provides a brief but in-depth overview of the commonly used features of XML. Much of the discussion is illustrated by examples rather than formal syntax diagrams. This chapter shows how data in XML format can be used at various points in a WebSphere application.

13.1 XML overview

XML is a simplified subset of SGML (Standard Generalized Markup Language). SGML has been in use successfully for many years at large corporations and government agencies, but it was too complex and resource intensive to become widespread. XML eliminates some of the less used but complicating features and is becoming very widespread, especially as more documents are being interchanged via the Internet and World Wide Web.

XML is a markup language. Markup languages add tags to the content of a document to describe the document. For example, in HTML a <p> tag indicates a paragraph, but the <p> is not part of the document itself. Markup languages such as HTML or word processors specify how to format or display information (bold, 14 point) but not what it is (a chapter heading, the title of a song). This makes it difficult for a computer program to understand what the document means. A document, when understood, can have real-world effects. For example a purchase order might cause a factory to produce and ship goods.

XML, in addition to being a markup language, is a metalanguage. A metalanguage can be used to define other languages. What this essentially means is that new tags can be created to describe the contents of a document. In HTML one is limited to a predefined set of tags such as <p> or <table>. In XML one can create an <artist> tag to describe the artist that performed a song.

With the freedom to create tags XML markup can structure a document in a semantically significant way. For example, it might describe a purchase order as having a list of items purchased, a shipping address, and so on. Although an artificial intelligence program could use character recognition to scan a printed purchase order and understand what to do with it, such programs in reality are not practical. XML markup makes it easier for a program to understand how to process a document.

XML by itself does not specify how to display a document. Extensible Stylesheet Language (XSL) and Cascading Style Sheet (CSS) stylesheets (see 13.5, "XML and Web browsers: XSL and CSS" on page 552) can be associated with an XML document to specify how it should be displayed. XML itself only specifies the content of the document. The receiver of a document can do anything they want with the document such as:

- Automatically process the document and based on the contents cause other actions to take place, such as shipping goods.
- Transform the document into HTML for display in a browser or into speech for audio display.
- Intelligently search the document for songs containing "stone" so that the song "Like a Rolling Stone" is found while the artist "Rolling Stones" is not found.

13.2 Using XML in WebSphere

Depending on the application and the capabilities of the different software components involved, XML can be used at various points in the application data flow as shown in Figure 402 on page 541.

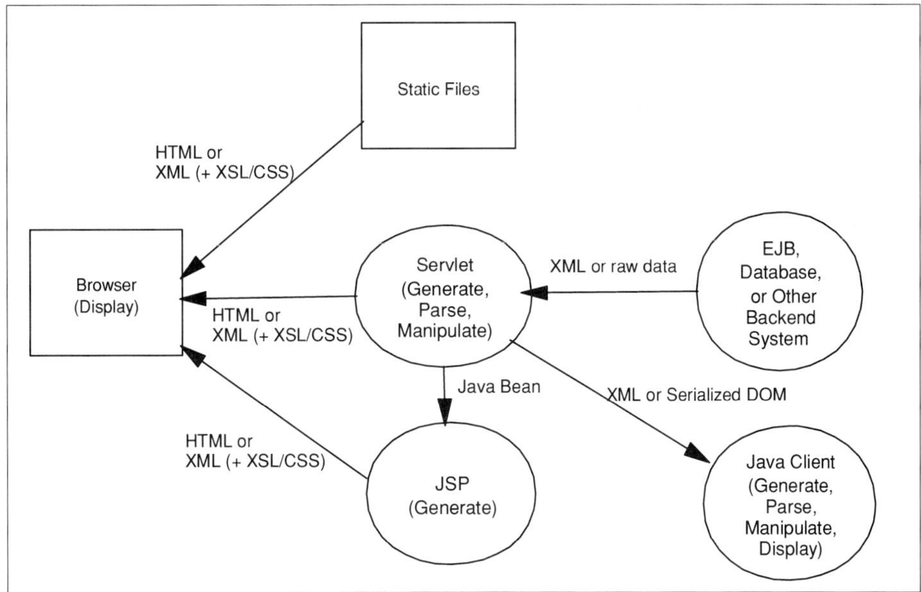

Figure 402. Possible flows of XML data in a WebSphere application

A browser can browse static files. These files can be HTML as usual, or XML. XSL and CSS stylesheets can be associated with the XML document to instruct the browser how to display the document.

A servlet can dynamically generate XML documents in various ways. The servlet might communicate with EJBs, a database, or some other back-end system such as CICS or MQ to obtain some data. This data could be in any non-XML format, or it could be returned as XML. Depending on how the data is returned the servlet could then parse it, manipulate it, and/or generate an XML document. The XML could be sent to a browser. Since some browsers do not support XML the servlet might need to first convert the XML into HTML. Alternatively, the servlet could package the data in a Java Bean and forward the request to a JSP, which could generate the XML or HTML.

In addition, a Java client can interact with the servlet. The servlet could return XML (as characters) or as a serialized object representation of the XML called a DOM (Document Object Model) (see 13.4.4, "An overview of XML parsing" on page 550). The client could then parse, manipulate, generate, or display the XML data as it wished.

These concepts will be discussed in detail in the sections that follow. It is clear that XML can be used and manipulated at almost any point in the application data flow. The best way to use XML in any particular situation depends on the specific application requirements.

13.2.1 XML versions supported

XML is a rapidly evolving area so it is difficult to keep up with the latest versions of the various specifications and APIs. For example XSL is relatively new, and the only browser that currently supports it is Microsoft Internet Explorer 5.5.

There are two groups of programming APIs: parsing APIs and XSL Transformation APIs. IBM originally implemented the parsing APIs in the XML for Java (XML4J) toolkit available on the alphaWorks Web site. The early versions of XML4J that were used in WebSphere V2.x contained a version of the parser API called the TX parser. WebSphere V3.5 still supports the TX compatibility classes, but any new code should not use them. The TX compatibility classes will not be discussed further.

WebSphere V3.5 includes XML4J 2.0.15. This supports parsing APIs known as SAX level 1 and DOM level 1. IBM has donated XML4J to Apache where it is known as Xerces. IBM continues to develop XML4J to keep up with and to contribute to Xerces. The newer Xerces and XML4J 3.0.1 now support SAX 2 and DOM 2 APIs, but the specifications for these APIs is not completely finalized. Code developed today with the SAX 1 and DOM 1 APIs will soon be deprecated. However, migrating to the newer APIs should be fairly straightforward; some object and method names have changed, but the basic flows and concepts are the same.

The XSL Transformation APIs allow an XSL stylesheet to be applied to an XML document to convert the XML into another format, such as HTML. XSL Transformations are discussed in detail in 13.6.4, “Dynamic XML formatted on the server with LotusXSL” on page 563. Lotus created the LotusXSL Processor and associated APIs to perform these transformations. LotusXSL is also available on the IBM alphaWorks Web site. LotusXSL was also donated to Apache, where it is known as Xalan.

Newer versions of LotusXSL and Xalan will also become available. However, the basic API for LotusXSL is very simple. The LotusXSL processor relies on an XML parser to help it apply the XSL transformation. The LotusXSL processor shipped with WebSphere V3.5 defaults to a newer version of a parser than is shipped with WebSphere V3.5. But the LotusXSL processor can be configured to use an older version of the parser.

Although newer versions of the XML parsing and XSL Transformation APIs are available, they are not supported by WebSphere. Only the versions shipped with WebSphere should be used. Trying to replace the versions of the XML APIs shipped with WebSphere with other versions can cause problems with WebSphere startup and administration, which use the XML APIs shipped with WebSphere. Future WebSphere releases and fixpacks will upgrade to support newer XML versions.

13.3 An XML example

Throughout this chapter, a document describing a list or catalog of music CDs will be used to illustrate XML concepts. Several XML and XML-related files will be discussed and a servlet and Java client that process XML data will be developed. The instructions needed to run the example can be found in Appendix C, "XML sample programs" on page 1087 and the source code and files are also available on the CD-ROM along with the class files.

Each CD in the list has information such as the CD title, the artist, and so on. A CD can also have multiple tracks or songs. The tracks have titles, running times, and so on.

The behavior of various browsers is discussed below. However, browsers are constantly changing so the results observed with different releases of browsers might be different. The examples to be discussed are reached from the HTML form shown in Figure 403 on page 544.

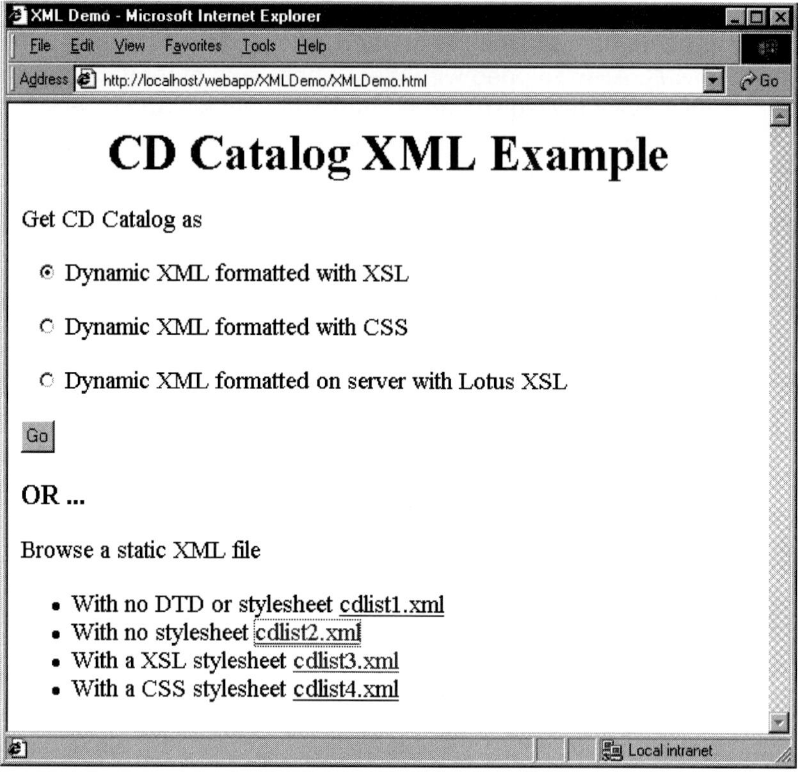

Figure 403. HTML form for the CD Catalog example

The second part of the form links to static files that are discussed below. The radio buttons and Go button send requests to the servlet, which returns the CD Catalog in various formats. In addition a Java client is developed that communicates with the servlet to retrieve the catalog.

13.4 XML basics

To begin, examine the file cdlist1.xml shown in Figure 404 on page 545. This is a simple XML file that contains a list of CDs. The entire XML document forms a tree structure. There is always one root element in an XML document, in this case <cdlist>. The children of cdlist are CDs. Each CD is a node that has children, such as title and artist. These nodes have leaf nodes with text values such as "Steely Dan". XML parsers read through an XML file transforming it into a tree structure called a Document Object Model (DOM) that can be manipulated in different ways. For example, the CD nodes could be reordered (conceptually from left to right under their cdlist parent) to sort them by title or by artist.

```
<?xml version='1.0' encoding='UTF-8' standalone="yes"?>
<!-- A list of CDs -->
<cdlist>
  <!-- The 1st CD. -->
  <cd>
    <id>1</id>
    <title>Pretzel Logic</title>
    <artist>Steely Dan</artist>
    <category>Rock</category>
    <label>MCA</label>
    <producer>Gary Katz</producer>
    <date>1974</date>
    <track cd-id="1">
       <track-number>1</track-number>
       <track-title>Riki Don't Lose That Number</track-title>
      <running-time>4:30</running-time>
    </track>
    <track>
       <track-number>2</track-number>
       <track-title>Night By Night</track-title>
      <running-time>3:36</running-time>
    </track>
    <track>
       <track-number>3</track-number>
       <track-title>Any Major Dude Will Tell You</track-title>
      <running-time>3:05</running-time>
    </track>
  </cd>
```

Figure 404. cdlist1.xml (partial)

A node in the DOM tree corresponds to an element in the XML document. Each element is defined by a tag and its associated end tag: <tag>text</tag>. Elements with no text still need to be closed like this <tag/> or this <tag></tag>. The tag structure defines an element or node in the tree. Elements can contain other elements properly nested (<a><b></b></a>, not <a><b></a></b>) thus forming a parent-child relationship in the document tree. Elements can also have attributes defined within their start tag (<tag myattr="text">) to further describe the element. Documents that follow rules such as this are syntactically correct and are said to be well-formed. However, nonsensical tags that says, for example, that a CD has a hat size could still be added to the document. To define what tags are allowed in a document, a Document Type Definition (DTD) is used. Documents that are well-formed and follow a DTD are said to be valid.

13.4.1 Document Type Definitions (DTDs)

Notice that cdlist1.xml does not specify a Document Type Definition (DTD). That means any elements or attributes can be put into the XML file as long as they are well-formed. For simple XML files used within a small application, this is probably sufficient and makes XML very simple and flexible. But if documents are exchanged with other organizations or applications the formality of a DTD is useful. A DTD defines what is and is not allowed in the document. There are DTDs that describe HTML, electronic components, Mathematical Markup Language, Vcards, etc.

Cdlist.dtd, a DTD for CD catalog documents, is shown in Figure 405 on page 547. The DTD defines what attributes and other elements an element must or can contain. (#PCDATA) means an element contains parsed character data, which is essentially any text. The special characters following element names indicate how many times the element can occur.

none The element must occur exactly once.

+ The element can occur one or more times.

***** The element can occur zero or more times.

? The element can occur zero or one times.

```
<!-- cdlist.dtd -->

<!-- A cdlist consists of 0 or more cds. -->
<!ELEMENT cdlist (cd*)>

<!-- A cd has an id, a tittle, ... Label and producer are optional (0 or
1). There can be 0 or more tracks. -->
<!ELEMENT cd (id, title, artist, category, label?, producer?, date,
track*)>

<!-- The elements of a cd are parsed character data. -->
<!ELEMENT id (#PCDATA)>
<!ELEMENT title (#PCDATA)>
<!ELEMENT artist (#PCDATA)>
<!ELEMENT category (#PCDATA)>
<!ELEMENT label (#PCDATA)>
<!ELEMENT producer (#PCDATA)>
<!ELEMENT date (#PCDATA)>

<!-- Description of a track. -->
<!ELEMENT track (track-number, track-title, running-time)>

<!-- Just to show an attribute as opposed to an element, a track can
have an optional CD_id.  It is a matter of choice to make data an
element or an attribute.  We could have make track-number, track-title,
and running-time attributes instead of elements if we wanted. -->
<!ATTLIST track cd-id CDATA #IMPLIED>

<!ELEMENT track-number (#PCDATA)>
<!ELEMENT track-title (#PCDATA)>
<!ELEMENT running-time (#PCDATA)>
```

Figure 405. cdlist.dtd

The next example file, cdlist2.xml, is the same as cdlist1.xml except for the first two lines, which specify that this document must adhere to the cdlist DTD.

```
<?xml version='1.0' encoding='UTF-8' standalone="no"?>
<!DOCTYPE cdlist SYSTEM "cdlist.dtd">
```

Figure 406 on page 548 shows a part of cdlist2.xml.

```
<?xml version='1.0' encoding='UTF-8' standalone="no"?>
<!DOCTYPE cdlist SYSTEM "cdlist.dtd">

<!-- A list of CDs -->
<cdlist>
  <!-- The 1st CD. -->
  <cd>
    <id>1</id>
    <title>Pretzel Logic</title>
    <artist>Steely Dan</artist>
    <category>Rock</category>
......
......
```

Figure 406. cdlist2.xml (partial)

The DOCTYPE tag indicates that the DTD is on the local system and is in the same directory as the XML document. The DTD could be specified as a URL and retrieved across the network and/or could be registered as a publicly available DTD:

```
<!DOCTYPE cdlist PUBLIC "-//Society of CDCollectors//DTD"
      "http://www.cdcollectors.org/cdlist.dtd">
```

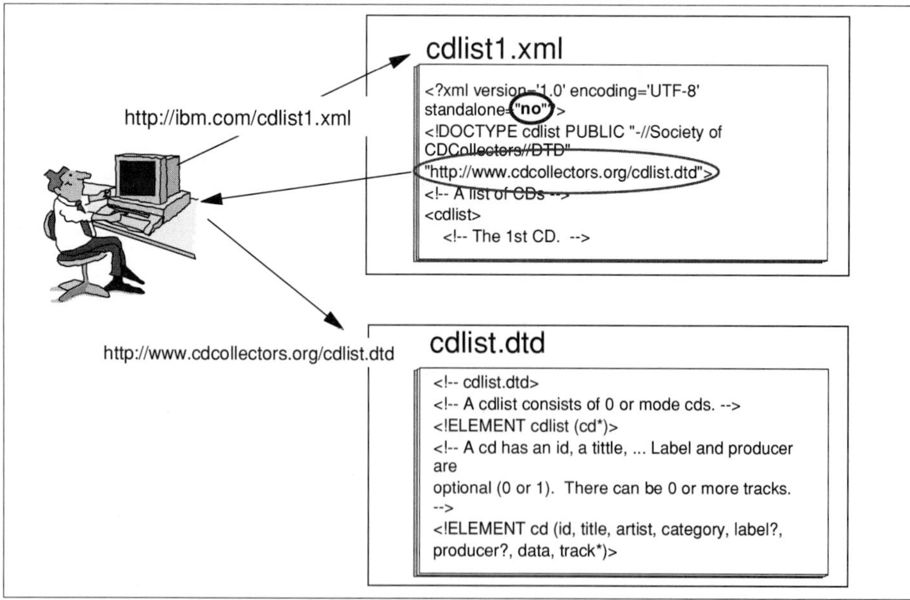

Figure 407. The DTD could be specified as a URL

Any software could now check the validity of the document. So in addition to the need to be well-formed, a CD cannot have a hat size.

13.4.2 DTD catalogs

When an industry group develops a DTD, they register a public identifier to identify the DTD. For example the Mathematical Markup Language is defined by a DTD with the public identifier "-//W3C//DTD MathML 1.0//EN". Instead of going to an organization's Web site to retrieve the DTD every time it is needed, local copies of the DTD can exist. A DTD catalog associates public identifiers with URLs for the DTDs themselves. The DTDs can be local or remote. A parser can be told to use a particular DTD catalog to look up any DTDs it needs when validating documents.

Copies of some standard DTDs are supplied with WebSphere in the directory *installation_root*/web/xml/grammar/dtd. The catalog standard itself is undergoing change. The catalog dtd.cat is supplied with WebSphere. This style of catalog is for an older version of parser APIs. The newer parser APIs support the XML catalog standard, which is still not finalized. The DTD for this new style of catalog is provided in the xmlcatalog subdirectory.

13.4.3 XML namespaces

Sometimes an XML document needs to use tags that were developed by different organizations. For example an XML document might need to use tags describing both electronic components and mathematical equations. The element tags and attribute names from these different sources could potentially have the same names and conflict with each other.

Name conflicts do not always arise when using tags from different organizations. In the CD catalog we could have used a title tag for both a CD title and a track title. In this case we could create a namespace for the CD title and a different namespace for the track title.

XML namespaces solve name conflicts by qualifying element and attribute names by associating them with namespaces identified by URI references.

The XSL stylesheet discussed in 13.5.3, "An XSL stylesheet example" on page 556 uses tags from the XSL namespace. The XSL stylesheet specifies that it uses the XSL namespace (xmlns:xsl) as follows.

```
<xsl:stylesheet xmlns:xsl="http://www.w3.org/TR/WD-xsl" version="1.0">
```

The XSL tags are qualified with "xsl:". If the document already used the stylesheet tag for some other purpose, it would not be confused with the xsl:stylesheet tag.

13.4.4 An overview of XML parsing

An XML parser reads an XML document and extracts the elements and structures in the document. For example parsing a CD catalog XML document would identify a CD element, its associated tittle, tracks, and so on. An XML document must be well-formed to be parsed. Otherwise, a parsing error similar to a syntax error in a programming language will be generated. Parsers can also check the XML document against a DTD and report errors if the XML document is not valid. Such parsers are called validating parsers. Parsers that do not validate a document even if a DTD is available are called non-validating parsers.

There are two standard APIs for XML parsing. The SAX API (Simple API for XML) and the DOM API (Document Object Model). A SAX parser is used with the SAX APIs and a DOM parser is used with the DOM APIs. Either type of parser can be validating or non-validating. Validation against a DTD requires more time and resources from the parser. If one is confident that the document to be parsed is valid (it is from a trusted source or was generated dynamically by a trusted program) a non-validating parser is appropriate. Otherwise, a validating parser is appropriate.

SAX is an event-driven API. A program instantiates a SAX parser, gives it a document, and instructs the parser to parse the document. As the document is parsed and tags, attributes, text, and comments are encountered, the parser generates events or callbacks to the program. These callbacks indicate events such as "beginning of document encountered", "beginning of element <cd> encountered, "text 'Steely Dan' encountered", "error encountered", and so on. The program handles these callbacks by implementing the interfaces DocumentHandler, DTDHandler, and/or ErrorHandler, depending on which events are of interest. Or as a simplification the program can extend the (subclass) HandlerBase which provides null implementations of all these interfaces. Then the program can override the methods for the events of interest.

The DOM represents a complete document in its tree structure. For the CD catalog the cdlist element is the root, CDs are its children, the children of a CD are its title, artist, and so on. To use a DOM parser the program instantiates a DOM parser, gives it a document, and instructs the parser to parse the document. The parser returns a DOM object of type Document. Using the DOM APIs the program can traverse this document, reorder the nodes in the document, delete nodes from the document, add new nodes, etc. For example, some of the APIs are getNodeValue(), setNodeValue(), getFirstChild(), getNextSibling(), getParentNode(), and so on.

The SAX and DOM APIs each have advantages and disadvantages.

The SAX API does not keep the entire document in memory, so very large documents can be processed with fewer resources. For tasks that require the serial processing of a document the SAX API is a good choice. Examples include printing a document, searching for songs with the word “stone” in their title, or rewriting a document and omitting all home phone numbers.

The DOM represents the entire document as an object that is held in memory. For large documents this can be costly. On the other hand, DOM allows documents to be manipulated based on their surrounding structure (for example, sorting the CDs alphabetically by artist). Another advantage of DOM is that the DOM structure can be shared with other programs in memory or serialized and transferred across a network. Instead of passing the XML document itself and requiring another program to again parse the document, the already parsed DOM object is passed to the other program.

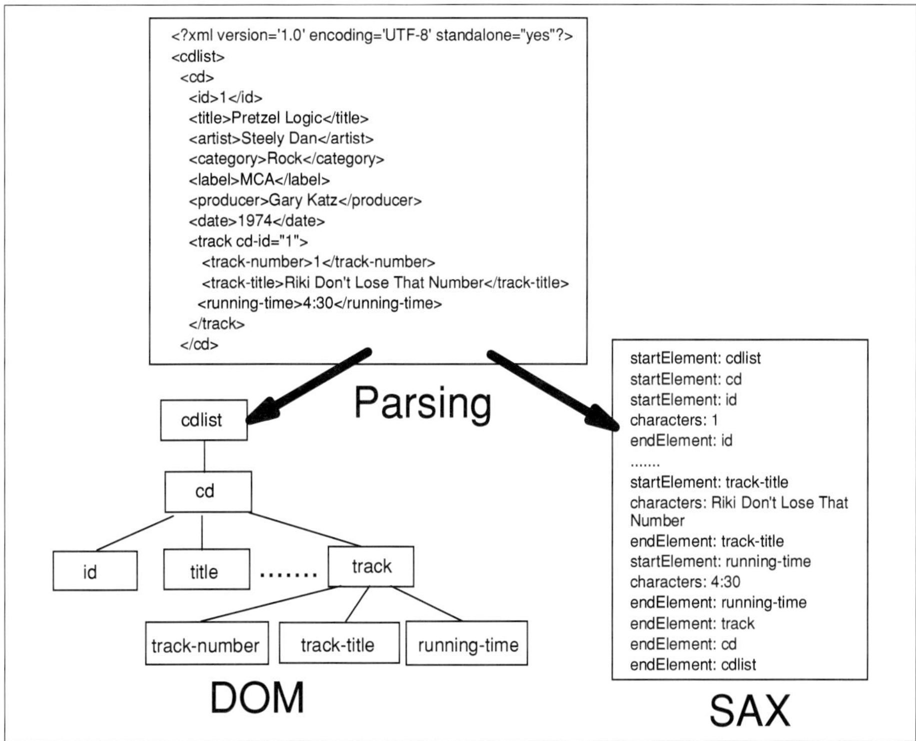

Figure 408. The SAX and DOM APIs

13.5 XML and Web browsers: XSL and CSS

One common use of XML documents is displaying them in a Web browser. XML does not specify how the document should be displayed. Some browsers just display whatever PCDATA they find between tags. Try browsing cdlist2.xml. There is no difference between browsing cdlist1.xml and cdlist2.xml since the only difference is that one includes a DTD. If the Web browser does not understand XML it might offer to save the file to disk (Navigator 4.7). Opera 4.01 and Netscape 6 (preview release 2) will just display all the PCDATA in the elements as shown in Figure 409 on page 552.

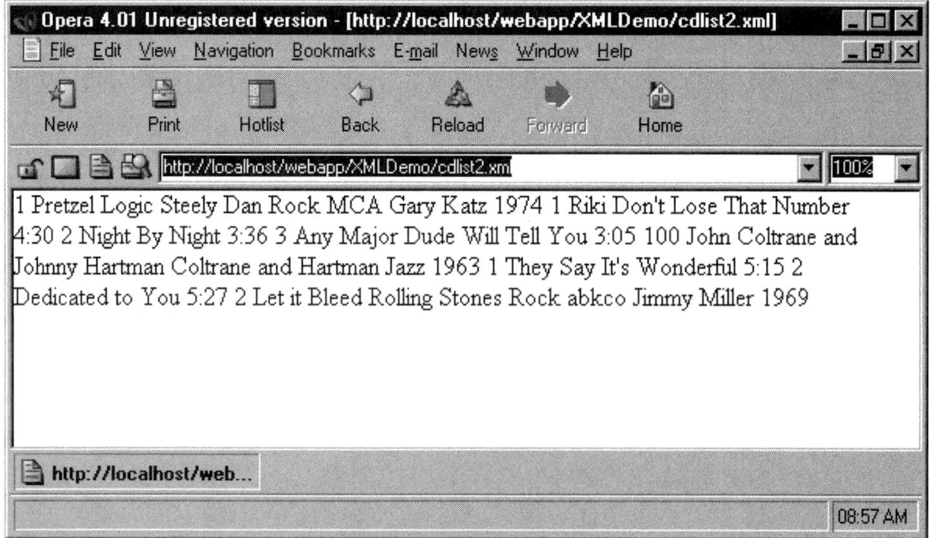

Figure 409. cdlist2.xml displayed in the Opera browser

Display of an XML document is a common operation, and standards are evolving to control it. Stylesheets contain display formatting instructions that can be associated with an XML document. There are two types of stylesheets: CSS (Cascading Style Sheet) and XSL (eXtensible Stylesheet Language) stylesheets. Cdlist2.xml does not use a stylesheet. However, as shown in Figure 410 on page 553, when cdlist2.xml is displayed in Microsoft Internet Explorer 5.5 (IE) it looks quite different.

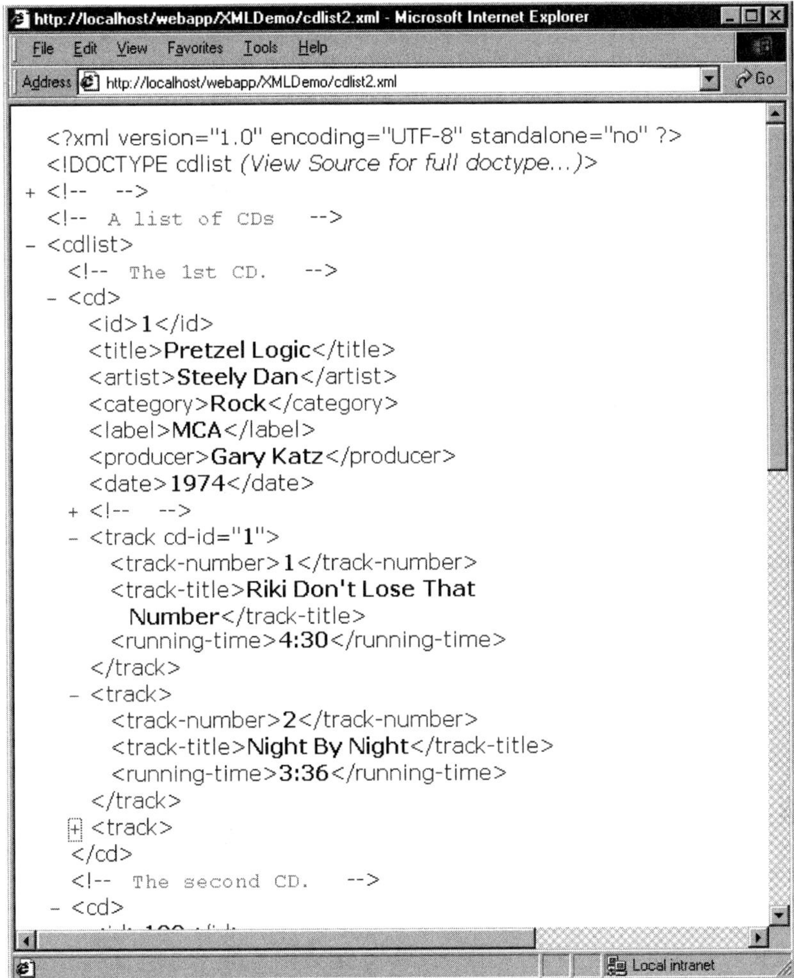

Figure 410. cdlist2.xml displayed in IE 5.5

In IE the tree structure of the elements is displayed through indentation. Nodes can be collapsed or expanded by clicking the +/- symbols. Several nodes in the figure have been collapsed. The reason IE displays the XML differently from the other browsers is because as of this writing IE is the only browser that supports XSL stylesheets. When IE displays an XML document that does not have a stylesheet, it uses a default XSL stylesheet that gives the expanding/collapsing node view shown above. This default XSL stylesheet transforms the XML document into HTML that includes JavaScript to enable the expanding of nodes.

13.5.1 Stylesheet processing instruction

A processing instruction (PI) can be placed in the XML (cdlist2.xml does not contain a PI) instructing a display engine to use a stylesheet written in CSS or XSL to format the document for display.

Cdlist3.xml (shown in Figure 411) contains one more line than cdlist2.xml. This is the PI that specifies what stylesheet to use:

```
<?xml-stylesheet href="cdlist.xsl" type="text/xsl"?>
```

The PI must appear before the first tag. The `href` is the location of the stylesheet relative to the document being displayed and can be a URL.

```
<?xml version='1.0' encoding='UTF-8' standalone="no"?>
<!DOCTYPE cdlist SYSTEM "cdlist.dtd">
<?xml-stylesheet href="cdlist.xsl" type="text/xsl"?>

<!-- A list of CDs -->
<cdlist>
  <!-- The 1st CD. -->
  <cd>
    <id>1</id>
    <title>Pretzel Logic</title>
......
```

Figure 411. cdlist3.xml (partial)

When cdlist3.xml is displayed in IE, the stylesheet cdlist.xsl is used to format the document as shown in Figure 412 on page 555.

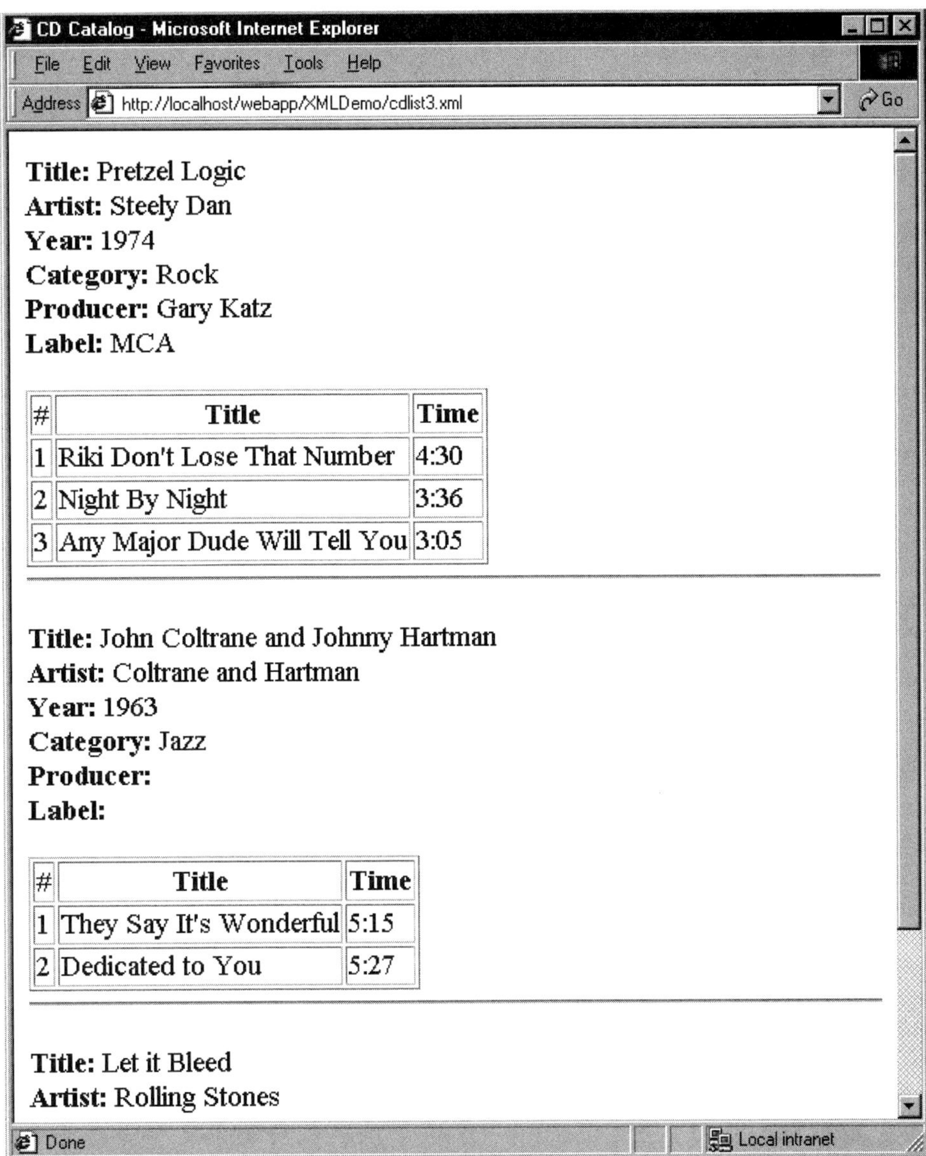

Figure 412. cdlist3.xml displayed in IE with an XSL stylesheet

13.5.2 XSL overview

XSL consists of two parts. Formatting objects (FOs) specify how to display an object. Formatting objects can specify very complex layouts and are not implemented by any XSL processors yet. But the second part of XSL, XSL Transformations (XSLT), is implemented by IE 5.5 and the LotusXSL/Xalan processor. XSLT is a transformation language based on the idea of matching nodes in a document tree structure against a template and transforming the nodes that match. For example a transformation could specify that when a CD element is encountered, output the HTML to draw a horizontal rule, then output the CD information. Thus, the input document or source tree is transformed into an output document or result tree.

Converting XML to HTML for display on a browser is a common transformation that is well suited to XSLT. XSLT could also be used to convert an XML document containing a personnel list to an XML document containing the same personnel list with home phone numbers omitted or with the names sorted by postal code. A Java program using parsing and DOM APIs could accomplish the same task. But in some cases it might be simpler to use XSLT, just as in some cases it makes more sense to use a high-level scripting language rather than to write a program in Java or C.

The IE support for XSL is not completely up-to-date, but it is pretty complete. There are also some Microsoft extensions that are not yet standardized, such as XML schema and XML data islands. There are some small differences between XSL stylesheets used by IE and LotusXSL/Xalan.

13.5.3 An XSL stylesheet example

The cdlist.xsl stylesheet used to format cdlist3.xml in Figure 412 on page 555 is shown in Figure 413 on page 557. Processing begins at the document root ("/") and the HTML for the title is output. The statement `<xsl:apply-templates/>` looks through the document trying to find nodes that match other templates defined in the stylesheet. The template for CD, `<xsl:template match="cd">`, matches each CD and causes the HTML to be output that displays the CD information.

```
<?xml version="1.0"?>
<!-- The cdlist XSL stylesheet is an XML document itself. -->

<xsl:stylesheet xmlns:xsl="http://www.w3.org/TR/WD-xsl" version="1.0">

<!-- Start at the document root "/", the cdlist element.  Output the
HTML title and the body. -->
<xsl:template select=".">
   <html>
      <head>
         <title>CD Catalog</title>
      </head>
      <body>
         <!-- Apply templates will recursively process the children of
cdlist. Any templates that are applicable will be applied as they are
encountered. -->
         <xsl:apply-templates/>
      </body>
   </html>
</xsl:template>
.....
.....
```

Figure 413. The XSL stylesheet cdlist.xsl (partial)

A for-each loop is used to output the tracks in the order they occur in the document, which happens to be by track number. There is a sort specification that can be placed in the for-each loop:

```
<xsl:sort select="track-number" data-type="number" order="ascending"/>
```

but IE does not support it yet. Instead IE uses a non-standard order-by="track-number" clause, because the sort specification was not finalized when IE 5.5 was being developed.

Note that the HTML tags in the stylesheet must be well-formed since they are part of an XML document (the stylesheet is an XML document). In HTML it is not required to include end tags such as </p>. Such tags as <hr> have no end tags. But in an XSL stylesheet <hr> must be written <hr/> or <hr></hr> or the browser will generate an error when parsing the stylesheet.

The stylesheet shows that XSL transforms XML (into HTML in this case). Template matching is used to find nodes within the document and then output them in whole or in part, decorated with extra HTML as desired to create tables and so on. The looping and conditional constructs can be used to process the XML in a very general way.

The for-each loop in the example could be replaced by another `<xsl:apply-templates/>` statement and a template for a track. Then a recursive application of template matching would be used rather than iterating through a loop. It could be argued that such a template matching approach is more desirable than the for-each approach and is a more typical way to write a stylesheet. The for-each approach was used only to illustrate more of the language constructs available in XSL.

13.5.4 A CSS stylesheet example

Many newer browsers support XML formatted with CSS. Cdlist4.xml includes the PI `<?xml-stylesheet href="cdlist.css" type="text/css"?>` to reference a CSS stylesheet as shown in Figure 414.

```
<?xml version='1.0' encoding='UTF-8' standalone="no"?>
<!DOCTYPE cdlist SYSTEM "cdlist.dtd">
<?xml-stylesheet href="cdlist.css" type="text/css"?>

<!-- A list of CDs -->
<cdlist>
  <!-- The 1st CD. -->
  <cd>
    <id>1</id>
    <title>Pretzel Logic</title>
    <artist>Steely Dan</artist>
    <category>Rock</category>
.......
```

Figure 414. cdlist4.xml (partial)

Figure 415 on page 559 shows cdlist4.xml viewed with Netscape Navigator 6.

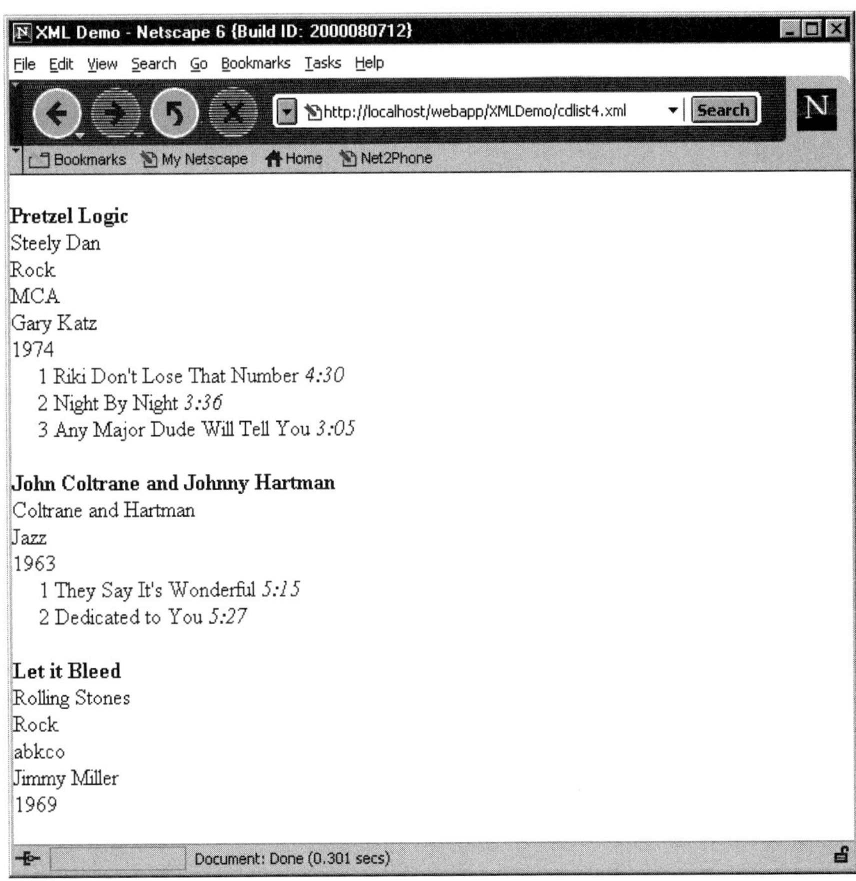

Figure 415. dlist4.xml displayed in Netscape with a CSS stylesheet

The CSS stylesheet cdlist1.css is shown in Figure 416 on page 560. The stylesheet controls the format used to display each element type.

```
/* A CSS stylesheet to display a catalog of CDs */

cdlist { display: block; }

/* Display CD info each on its own line. */
cd { display: block; }
id { display: none; }       /* id is not displayed */
title { display: block;
        font-weight: bold;
        margin-top: .5cm; }
artist { display: block; }
date { display: block; }
label { display: block; }
producer { display: block; }
category { display: block; }

/* Display each track on a single line. */
track { display: block;
        text-indent: .5cm; }
track-title { display: inline; }
running-time { display: inline;
               font-style: italic; }
```

Figure 416. The CSS stylesheet cdlist.css

13.5.5 XSL and CSS comparison

Perhaps a more sophisticated CSS stylesheet could be written, but CSS and XSL do have different capabilities. CSS is HTML technology that has been extended to XML. It is used to decorate HTML/XML. CSS can indicate that paragraphs should be blue, Gothic, and 10 point; that list items should be indented 3cm; or that CD titles should be bold. But CSS can only decorate what is there in the order in which it appears. It cannot add extra text (such as labels like “Title:”). It cannot add tags (for example to create a table). HTML tags such as <table> can be added to the XML document itself using the HTML namespace qualifier, but this requires modification of the XML with display instructions. Elements cannot be reordered or displayed multiple times (the date is at the end of the CD information). Information stored in attributes cannot be accessed (though not used here, this would be the CD-ID of the track). In some documents a large amount of information is stored in attributes).

XSL on the other hand is a general transformation language. The document can be processed in any order, and arbitrary text and tags can be added to change the XML into HTML or any other format. However, XSL is more expensive and is not currently widely supported by browsers. CSS decorates documents and XSL transforms them. XML/XSL can either be sent to a browser that supports it, or it can be transformed on the server into HTML and then sent to the browser. XSL and CSS can be used together by transforming XML into HTML that includes (or references) a CSS stylesheet. This is especially useful since formatting objects (FOs) are not yet supported in XSL.

13.6 Programming with XML

To illustrate how a Web application can generate, parse, and manipulate XML data, a servlet, the CDOXMLServlet, was developed for the CD Organizer example. The complete source code is included on the CD-ROM provided with this book. The CDOXMLServlet generates and returns XML data in various ways depending on the value of the catalog type (cattype) parameter in the HTTP request. The general coding of the servlet will not be discussed. Only the code specific to XML will be discussed.

The CDOXMLServlet builds the CD catalog and then based on the value of the HTTP request parameter cattype (catalog type) calls a method to return the catalog in some XML-related form. The following sections discuss the processing preformed by these methods.

13.6.1 Obtaining the CD catalog data

The servlet must first obtain the CD catalog data. A real application could construct catalogs containing only CDs in a certain category (Rock, Jazz, ...) or by a certain artist. This data could be retrieved from EJBs directly from a database using JDBC or from any number of back-end systems. The data could even be returned in XML format from these sources. Or if the data is returned in a non-XML format it could be stored in a JavaBean so other parts of the program could process it easily.

In this example the CDListJBean JavaBean is used to store the list of CDs. Each CD in the list is represented by a CDJBean, and each track of a CD is represented by a TrackJBean. To keep this example simple the data used to populate the CDListJBean is not retrieved from a back-end system but is hard coded. The CDListJBean constructor assigns constant data to the CD Catalog. This allows the example to be set up without configuring a database or EJB to retrieve the data, although the CD Catalog is always the same.

13.6.2 Dynamic XML formatted with XSL

The servlet's catalogXSL() method returns XML that includes a PI referencing an XSL stylesheet. It does this by passing the CDListJBean representing the catalog to the XMLCatalog JSP. The JSP does all the work. It loops through the CDs and tracks and instead of printing HTML tags it prints XML tags describing the CD. The result is XML that looks like the static file cdlist3.xml.

Notice that the JSP begins with

```
<?xml version='1.0' encoding='UTF-8' standalone="no"?>
<?xml-stylesheet href="cdlist.xsl" type="text/xsl"?>
```

The first line specifies that this is an XML document and the second line is the PI that specifies the stylesheet. Then in addition to disabling caching for the page, the content type is set to text/xml rather than text/html.

```
response.setHeader("Content-Type", "text/xml");
```

The JSP then prints the tag to define the root element <cdlist>. Notice at the end of the JSP this tag is closed with </cdlist>. The JSP loops through the CDs printing information about each CD enclosed in the appropriate tags. For example, the line to print information about the title of the CD is:

```
<title><%= catalog.getCd(i).getTitle() %></title>
```

An inner loop then prints information about the tracks of the CD using statements like:

```
<running-time>
<%= catalog.getCd(i).getTrackList().getTrack(j).getRunningTime() %>
</running-time>
```

Producing XML from a JSP is exactly like producing HTML. Remember that XML is a metalanguage that describes other languages. Here we have a language that describes CD Catalogs. HTML is a language that also has an XML definition. The JSP is just writing characters to an output stream. It does not matter what the characters mean.

13.6.3 Dynamic XML formatted with CSS

The servlet's catalogCSS() method produces XML that refers to a CSS stylesheet. Except for the PI referring to the stylesheet, this is no different from producing XML that refers to an XSL stylesheet. A JSP could be used just as in the catalogXSL() method in 13.6.2, "Dynamic XML formatted with XSL" on page 562. However, in order to illustrate a different programming technique catalogCSS() writes its own output directly to the response stream.

```
   // Set the headers for no caching and content type XML.
```

```
res.setHeader("Pragma", "No-Cache");
res.setDateHeader("Expires", 0);
res.setHeader("Cache-Control", "no-Cache");
res.setHeader("Content-Type", "text/xml");
PrintWriter out = res.getWriter();
out.println(
   "<?xml version='1.0' encoding='UTF-8' standalone=\"yes\"?>" +
   "<?xml-stylesheet href=\"cdlist.css\" type=\"text/css\"?>" +
   catalog.getXMLString());
```

After disabling caching of the page, the content type is set to text/xml. The XML document header and PI for the CSS stylesheet are then printed. Then the CD catalog is printed as an XML string. The work of converting the catalog to an XML string is done by the CDListJBean, which returns a representation of itself as a string of XML.

The logic of the CDListJBean's getXMLString() method is just like the logic of the XMLCatalog JSP. The getXMLString() method puts all the text it is producing into a StringBuffer using statements like:

```
sb.append("<title>" + getCd(i).getTitle() + "</title>");
```

and:

```
sb.append("<running-time>" +
   getCd(i).getTrackList().getTrack(j).getRunningTime() +
   "</running-time>");
```

The StringBuffer is then converted to a String and returned.

IE 5.5 was able to display the dynamically generated XML formatted with CSS correctly. The other browsers did not display this page correctly even though they did display the CSS formatted static page cdlist4.xml correctly.

13.6.4 Dynamic XML formatted on the server with LotusXSL

As discussed in 13.5, “XML and Web browsers: XSL and CSS” on page 552 not all browsers are capable of displaying XML formatted with XSL. The servlet could determine what type of browser is being used. If the browser does not support XML/XSL the servlet can convert the XML/XSL to HTML and send the HTML to the browser. The CDOXMLServlet's catalogLotusXSL() method converts XML with an XSL stylesheet to HTML. However, to keep the example simple it does not first check what type of browser is being used.

The LotusXSL processor which is included with WebSphere V3.5 accepts an XML document and an XSL stylesheet and produces a transformed document. In this case the document is transformed into HTML. If the XML document already has a PI that refers to a stylesheet, the LotusXSL processor will use that stylesheet.

```
// Set the headers for no caching and content type HTML.
   res.setHeader("Pragma", "No-Cache");
   res.setDateHeader("Expires", 0);
   res.setHeader("Cache-Control", "no-Cache");
   res.setHeader("Content-Type", "text/html");
   PrintWriter out = res.getWriter();
   String doc =
      "<?xml version='1.0' encoding='UTF-8' standalone=\"yes\"?>"
         + catalog.getXMLString();

   // Have the XSLTProcessorFactory obtain a interface to a new
   // XSLTProcessor object.  Set up a liaison so the XSLTProcessor
   // interfaces to an older parser instead of the default parser.
   try {
      XSLTProcessor processor =
         XSLTProcessorFactory.getProcessorUsingLiaisonName(
            "com.lotus.xml.xml4j2dom.XML4JLiaison4dom");

      // Have the XSLTProcessor processor object transform the XML doc
      // using the cdlist1.xsl stylesheet.
      // The transformed document (which is HTML) is sent to out.
      String path =
         getServletConfig().getServletContext().getRealPath("/");
      processor.process(
         new XSLTInputSource(new StringReader(doc)),
         new XSLTInputSource(path + "/cdlist1.xsl"),
         new XSLTResultTarget(out));
   } catch (org.xml.sax.SAXException e) {
      throw new java.rmi.RemoteException(
         "SAXException in catalogLotusXSL: " + e.getMessage());
   }
```

The XSL processor defaults to a new version of the parser. The XSL processor can be told to use an intermediate liaison object to interface with older parsers. In the code above the XSLTProcessor object is created by the XSLTProcessorFactory using a liaison to the version of the parser used by WebSphere V3.5.

Notice that the content type of the response is text/html since the servlet returns HTML. The XSLTProcessor.process() method performs the conversion. The XML document and stylesheet are input as XSLTInputSource objects. These input sources can be strings, files, or DOM nodes (an internal object representation of a document). The output of the XSLTProcessor is sent to the response output stream.

Notice that the cdlist1.xsl stylesheet is slightly different from the cdlist.xsl stylesheet used when browsing static pages with IE. LotusXSL and IE support slightly different levels of XSL. The namespace declaration is different, and the selection of the root node is different. See comments in cdlist1.xsl for details as shown in Figure 417.

```
<?xml version="1.0"?>
<!-- The cdlist XSL stylesheet is an XML document itself. -->
<!-- The LotusXSL processor supports a slightly different version of
XSL. The next statement and the first xsl:template below are changed.
The statements that work with IE 5.5 are commented out for reference.
-->
<!--xsl:stylesheet xmlns:xsl="http://www.w3.org/TR/WD-xsl" -->
<xsl:stylesheet xmlns:xsl="http://www.w3.org/1999/XSL/Transform"
version="1.0">
<!-- Start at the document root "/", the cdlist element.  Output the
HTML title and the body. -->
<xsl:template match="cdlist">
<!--xsl:template select="."-->
<style type="text/css">
   th {background-color : blue;
       color : YELLOW;}
   td {background-color : silver;
       color : black;}
</style>

<html>
      <head>
         <title>CD Catalog</title>
      </head>
      <body>
         <!-- Apply templates will recursively process the children of
cdlist. Any templates that are applicable will be applied as they are
encountered. -->
         <xsl:apply-templates/>
      </body>
   </html>
</xsl:template>
```

Figure 417. cdlist1.xsl used with LotusXSL

Hopefully, as the standards and implementations mature, such differences will disappear. IE5.5 has been updated to use the actual 1.0 version of the XSL Transform specification, rather than the version based on the working draft which was released with IE4.

Also notice that a CSS style tag was added in cdlist1.xsl to add color to the table of tracks. This has nothing to do with XSL versions or implementation compatibility. It is simply meant to illustrate how CSS styles can be included in an XSL transformation.

13.6.5 Supporting a Java client

There are two more methods in the servlet to discuss: catalogPlainText() and catalogDOM(). These methods were written to support a Java client named CDOXMLClient. The CDOXMLClient communicates with the servlet over HTTP. The communication is handled by a URLConnection object. See the client code (as shown in Appendix C, "XML sample programs" on page 1087) for details of this standard communication method.

The client illustrates SAX parsing of an XML document and traversal of a DOM tree. The client presents a menu that allows the user to choose one of two actions. The client can retrieve the CD Catalog from the servlet as a string of XML and then use a SAX parser to parse and print the catalog. Or the client can retrieve the CD Catalog as a serialized DOM object and then traverse the DOM object and print the catalog. Since the DOM object is already parsed a DOM parser is not used. The output of both options looks the same, a print out of the CD Catalog.

A sample run of the client is shown below. An optional command line parameter that defaults to localhost specifies where the servlet is running.

```
C:\WebSphere\AppServer\hosts\default_host\XMLDemo\client>CDOXMLClientSetup
C:\WebSphere\AppServer\hosts\default_host\XMLDemo\client>runCDOXMLClient
Retrieve and display CD Catalog using
  S - SAX
  D - DOM
===>s

**********
CD Catalog
**********

CD
===========================
id: 1
title: Pretzel Logic
```

```
artist: Steely Dan
category: Rock
label: MCA
producer: Gary Katz
date: 1974
track-number: 1
track-title: Riki Don't Lose That Number
running-time: 4:30
track-number: 2
track-title: Night By Night
running-time: 3:36
track-number: 3
track-title: Any Major Dude Will Tell You
running-time: 3:05

CD
===========================
id: 100
title: John Coltrane and Johnny Hartman
artist: Coltrane and Hartman
...
... remaining output not shown
...
***** End of CD Catalog *****
```

13.6.5.1 XML text string/SAX parsing

When option S is chosen, the servlet returns a string containing the CD Catalog as an XML document. The client then uses the SAXCatalogPrint class to parse and print the catalog:

```
SAXCatalogPrint cp = new SAXCatalogPrint(catalog);
```

Often the CDOXMLClient class itself would extend HandlerBase to allow it to handle SAX events as the document is parsed. However, to illustrate a slightly different approach, a separate class, SAXCatalogPrint, was created. This is also more modular in the case of the CDOXML client that uses both SAX and DOM.

```
public class SAXCatalogPrint extends HandlerBase {
```

All the work of parsing and printing the catalog is done in the SAXCatalogPrint constructor, which sets up the SAX parser and starts parsing the document.

```
public SAXCatalogPrint(String catalog) {
   try {
      // Create a non-validating SAX parser and use this class
```

```
        // to handle document parsing and error events.  We do not
        // override any error event handlers though.
        SAXParser parser = new SAXParser();
        parser.setDocumentHandler(this);
        parser.setErrorHandler(this);

        // Parse the document.
        parser.parse(new InputSource(new StringReader(catalog)));
    } catch (Exception e) {
        // If there was a problem, print a stacktrace and exit.
        e.printStackTrace();
        System.exit(1);
    }
}
```

A number of event handlers are implemented by SAXCatalogPrint to handle events generated by the SAX parser. These event handlers print out the various parts of the document. For example at the beginning of the document a header is printed:

```
public void startDocument() {
    System.out.println("\n**********\nCD Catalog\n**********");
}
```

When an element tag such as <cd> or <artist> is encountered it is either ignored, a heading is printed, or its name is printed as a label.

```
/**
 * Called when a new element is being parsed.
 * Based on the name of the element we either ignore it,
 * print a heading, or just print it's name as a label.
 * You could get as fancy as you want, but this illustrates
 * the basics of what you can do.
 * @param name java.lang.String
 * @param attrs org.xml.sax.AttributeList
 */
public void startElement(String name, AttributeList attrs) {
    if ("cdlist".equals(name) || "track".equals(name)) {
        return;
    } else if ("cd".equals(name)) {
        System.out.println("\nCD\n===========================");
    } else {
        System.out.print(name + ": ");
    }
}
```

When character data is encountered, it is printed. This prints the text inside elements, such as “Steely Dan”.

```
public void characters(char[] ch, int start, int length) {
   System.out.println(new String(ch, start, length));
   }
```

By the time the document is parsed these event handlers have been called for all the elements in the CD Catalog and the formatted document is printed. When the SAXCatalogPrint constructor returns the catalog has been printed, and there is nothing else for the SAXCatalogPrint object to do.

13.6.5.2 DOM object creation and traversal

When option D is chosen from the CDOXMLClient's menu the servlet returns a serialized DOM object which represents the already parsed document as a tree structure. The client then traverses and prints the DOM tree.

The servlet could generate the DOM object by first generating the XML representation of the CD Catalog, instantiating a DOM parser, and then parsing the XML. The DOM parser would return the DOM object. This would be very simple to program since a method to turn the CD Catalog into XML already exists. However, it might make more sense, and it is probably more efficient, to build the DOM tree directly, perhaps as data is collected from back-end systems.

The work of turning the CD catalog into a DOM tree occurs in the CDListJBean's getDOM() method. First getDOM() creates an empty DOM document object:

```
Document doc =
   (Document)Class.forName("com.ibm.xml.dom.DocumentImpl").newInstance();
```

Then it creates an element to represent the root of the document, which is a <cdlist> element:

```
Element root = doc.createElement("cdlist");
```

At this point the cdlist element is empty. Also, it is not part of the DOM tree. It is attached to the document as follows:

```
doc.appendChild(root);
```

Then a loop works through the CD list creating CD elements.

```
Element cd = doc.createElement("cd");
```

The CD element then has the various fields and tracks appended to it as children. For example the artist element is added as follows:

```
Element artist = doc.createElement("artist");
artist.appendChild(doc.createTextNode(getCd(i).getArtist()));
```

```
cd.appendChild(artist);
```

Then the cd is attached to the cdlist:

```
root.appendChild(cd);
```

In this way the DOM tree is built up by creating nodes and attaching them to the tree as each piece of data in the CDListJBean is processed.

After the DOM is returned the client uses the printDOM() method to traverse and print the tree. PrintDOM() is a recursive function which takes a node as a parameter. It prints the node and then recursively prints all the children of the node. A node can be a document (the top level node that represents the whole DOM), an element such as <cd> or <artist>, or text such as “Steely Dan”. Based on the type of node printDOM() prints out headings or the value of the node. The children of each element node are processed using a for loop to loop through all the children. When the top level call to printDOM() returns, the entire catalog has been printed.

```
/**
 * Print the DOM node.  Called initially with the top level document node.
 * Calls itself recursively to handle all the nodes. We assume the document
 * is of the structure we expect.
 */
public void printDOM(Node node) {
   // Determine the node type and handle it accordingly.
   switch (node.getNodeType()) {
      case node.DOCUMENT_NODE :
         // The top level document.  Print a heading and process the
         // root node (the cdlist).
         System.out.println("\n**********\nCD Catalog\n**********");
         printDOM(((Document) node).getDocumentElement());
         break;
      case node.ELEMENT_NODE :
         // For an element, see what element it is and handle
         // accordingly.
         String name = node.getNodeName();
         if ("cd".equals(name)) {
            // Print a heading for a CD.
            System.out.println(
                  "\nCD\n===========================");
         } else if ("track".equals(name) || "cdlist".equals(name)) {
            // Print nothing for a track or cdlist.
         } else {
            // Print the element name.  This will give us labels
            // like "artist: ", "running-time: ", etc.
            System.out.print(name + ": ");
```

```
            }
            // For any kind of Element loop through all children.
            for (Node child = node.getFirstChild();
               child != null;
               child = child.getNextSibling()) {
               printDOM(child);
            }
            break;
         case Node.TEXT_NODE :
            // Print text of a node.  This will print text like
            // "Steely Dan" under an artist element.
            System.out.println(node.getNodeValue());
            break;
      }
   }
```

13.7 Summary

This chapter illustrated the basic features of XML and concentrated on how XML can be used in a WebSphere application. XSL, a powerful transformation language, can be used to convert XML into HTML for display by a browser. Data can be gathered from EJBs, a database, or any back-end system and then converted into XML. The XML can be parsed and manipulated at various points in the application data flow by servlets, JSPs, and clients.

XML-related standards are rapidly evolving, and it is difficult to keep up with the latest versions. Many products such as browsers only support XML partially. As XML matures the specifications should become more stable and more products will implement XML-related technologies at compatible levels. Even so, XML is ready for production use today.

Chapter 14. Application deployment

As an administrator, you have to consider how to organize and administer the files in the WebSphere administrative domain. There are two important factors to consider when creating an application: availability and security. In this chapter, we focus on availability, not security.

We describe how to deploy your application using the administrative console step by step. We will relate how to create virtual hosts, JDBC drivers, data sources,application servers, EJBContainer, servlet engines, Web applications, servlets, enterprise beans and enterprise applications. We do not refer to security because information relating to the subject can be found in Chapter 15, "WebSphere security" on page 651.

You may find information about the administrative console in Chapter 18, "Administrative console" on page 811, such as how to start and stop the administrative console, and the features of the administrative console.

Many configurations could be set according to your real requirements, although we accept most default settings in this chapter. You could get context-sensitive help for "What is it?", "How do I?" and "Property Help" from the help menu of the administrative console.

For the newest update, please visit the Web site:

`http://www.ibm.com/software/webservers/appserv/infocenter.html`

Finally in this chapter, we discuss the various WebSphere classpaths and how to use them when deploying larger applications, for example where to locate classes that are used in the interface to several different EJBs in several different deployable JAR files.

14.1 Samples we used

Shipped with WebSphere is a classic servlet sample named HelloWorldServlet, together with a simple entity bean sample named Increment. In this chapter, we use the two samples to describe how to deploy these resources.

- HelloWorldServlet servlet sample

  This sample will return one line: "Hello World"

  Resource:

  ```
  <WebSphere install_root>\servlets\HelloWorldServlet.class
  ```

```
<WebSphere install_root>\servlets\HelloWorldServlet.java
```

- Increment EJB samples

  This is the next-to-simplest sample enterprise bean. The sample has:

  - An input form to invoke the servlet

    ```
    <WebSphere
    install_root>\hosts\default_host\WSsamples_app\web\Increment\increme
    nt.html
    ```

  - A Java servlet, VisitIncrementSite, that accesses the Increment enterprise bean and returns the formatted HTML

    ```
    <WebSphere
    install_root>\hosts\default_host\WSsamples_app\servlets\WebSphereSam
    ples\Increment\
    ```

  - An enterprise bean, Increment, that adds 1 to a counter and returns the value of the counter.

    ```
    <WebSphere install_root>\deployableEJBs\Increment.jar
    ```

  For this sample, we will use a sample database of DB2 called "sample" as its persistent database.

14.2 Before configuration

If the Configure Default Server and Web application option is chosen when installing WebSphere Application Server, an application server named "Default Server" and some resources will be configured automatically when WebSphere is started for the first time, as shown in Figure 418 on page 575. Refer to 4.2.2, "The Default Server" on page 123 to get detailed information about the Default Server and its resources.

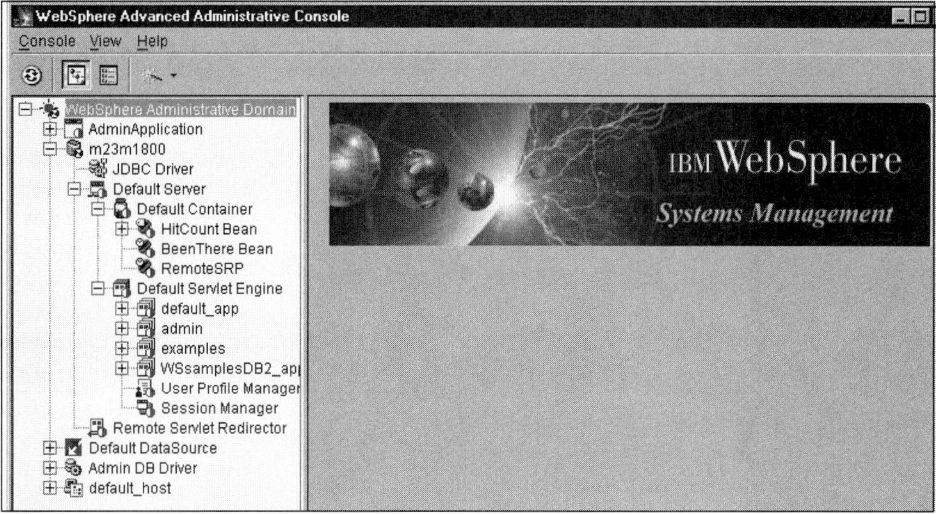

Figure 418. Default Server on the administrative console

We use an empty configuration (see Figure 419 on page 576) for our application deployment in this chapter. We will follow the steps:

1. Creating a virtual host
2. Creating a JDBC driver and data source
3. Creating an application server together with EJBcontainer, servlet engine and Web application
4. Placing source files
5. Adding a servlet
6. Creating enterprise beans
7. Creating enterprise applications

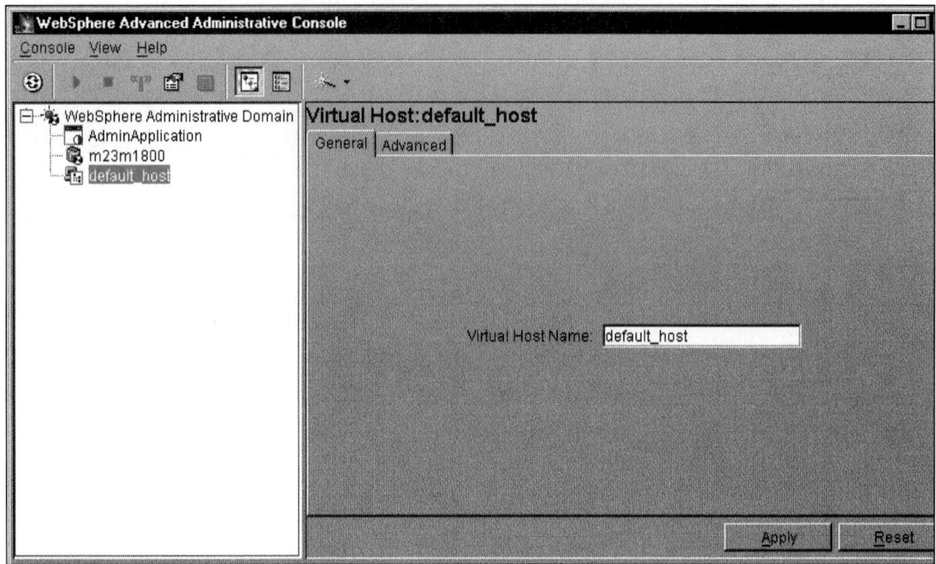

Figure 419. The empty configuration

14.3 Create a virtual host

For a description of a virtual host, please refer to 4.2.4, “Virtual hosts” on page 130.

Even if we do not create the Default Server, a virtual host named default_host will be created automatically. If you need more than one virtual host, you may start creating it by clicking **Wizards-->Create a Virtual Host** as shown in Figure 420 on page 577.

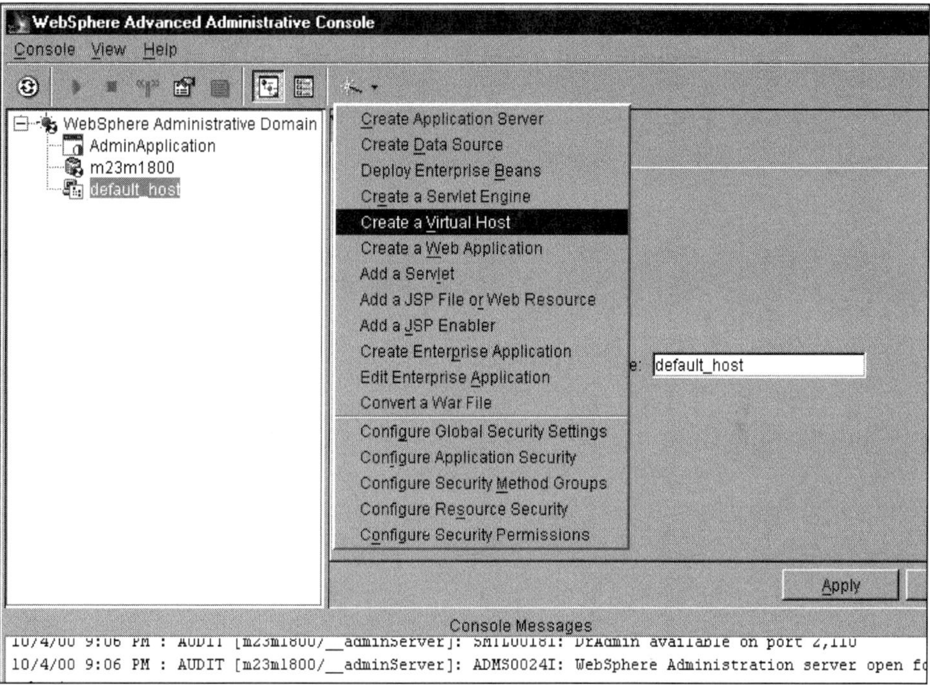

Figure 420. Creating a virtual host

You will get the Create Virtual Host window. Indicate the name of the virtual host for the Virtual Host Name entry, then click **Next**. In our case, we specified ITSO Virtual Host.

In the next window (Virtual Host), specify the MIME types to recognize and DNS host aliases for the virtual host to be known by, then click **Finish** as shown in Figure 421 on page 578. Because we only need one virtual host, we will skip this step and use default_host. Let us check the configuration of default_host.

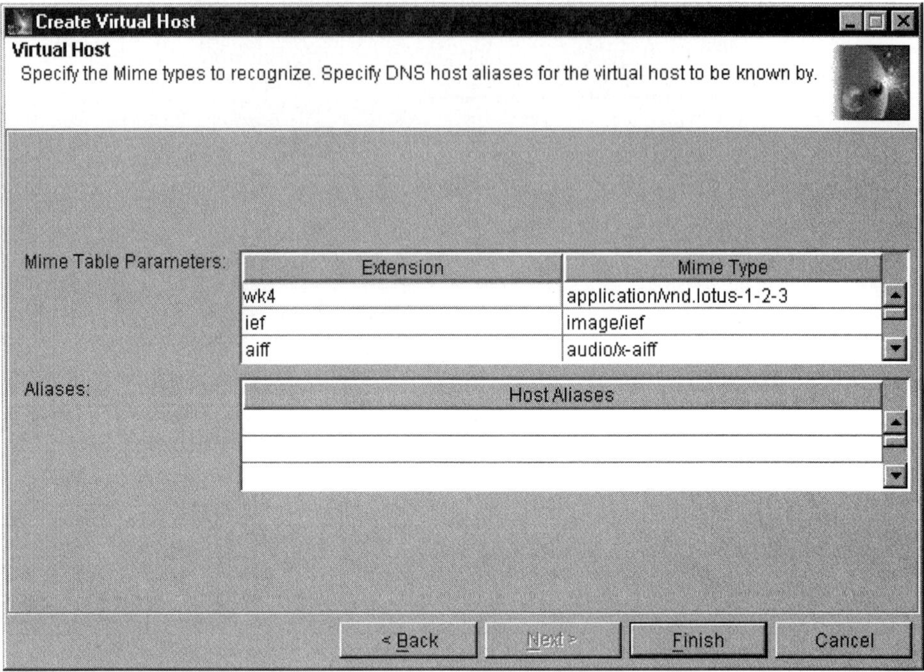

Figure 421. Creating a virtual host: Virtual Host

Click **default_host** in the topology tree as shown in Figure 422 on page 579. The properties will be displayed on the right side of the administrative console. Pay attention to the Aliases on the Advanced tag. The default includes "localhost" and the loopback address "127.0.0.1", because it represents the local machine, and also includes the host name and IP address of the machine (for example, "m23m1800" and "9.24.106.250"). It should include the fully qualified name of the machine but it may not be constructed sometimes. All aliases should be added by which the virtual host will be known to the list. For example, add the fully qualified name, "m23m1800.itso.ral.ibm.com". Then click **Apply**. The virtual host will be known as listening on port 80 by default. If you want it to listen on other ports, for example, if you enable the HTTPS protocol whose default port is 443, you need to add the aliases followed by the port to the list.

If you change the configuration of the virtual host after creating application servers, you will need to restart all application servers working on this virtual host to activate the change.

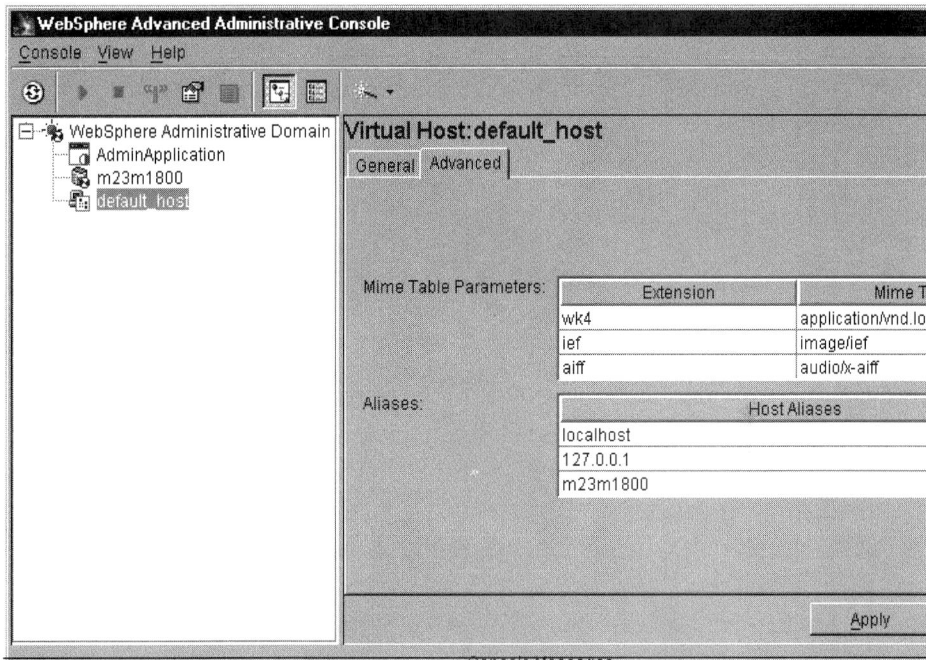

Figure 422. The default setting of default_host

14.4 Create a JDBC driver and data source

We will now configure the resources for database support. This is necessary for any resource that needs to access the database. For example, entity beans and other servlets need such access. (In this test environment, we use DB2 as the application database, so we will principally describe the configuration steps related to DB2.)

We will follow the steps:

1. Create a JDBC driver
2. Install a JDBC diver
3. Create a data source

14.4.1 Create a JDBC driver

To create a JDBC driver, switch to Type View. Right-click **JDBC Drivers** and select **Create...** option as shown in Figure 423 on page 580.

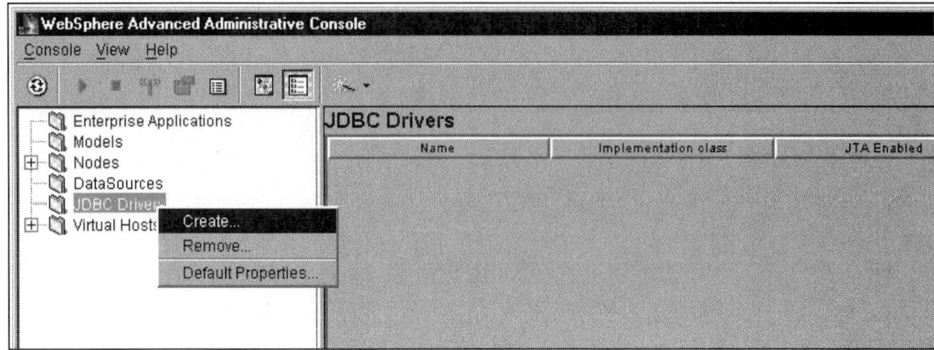

Figure 423. Creating a JDBC driver

The JDBC driver properties dialog box will appear as shown in Figure 424 on page 581. Specify the properties for the JDBC driver:

- Name

  This is the name by which to administer the driver. Any value can be used.

  Specify DB2 JDBC Driver as the name.

- Class Name

  This is the implementation class of the driver code.

  Specify the DB2 driver choice as com.ibm.db2.jdbc.app.DB2Driver.

- URL prefix

  This is the URL prefix with which this driver is associated. The URL prefix is comprised of the protocol and subprotocol, separated by a colon (":"). It is followed by the database name of the data source to compose the full JDBC URL of the database.

  Accept the default jdbc:db2.

- JTA Enable

  JTA is a transaction API for Java applications. This property specifies whether the driver can handle Java-based two-phase commit transactions. If not performing distributed transactions, set this value to False.

  For WebSphere Application Server V3.0x, if JTA Enabled is selected as True, the URL prefix has to be set to jdbc:jta:db2. But for WebSphere V3.5, selecting JTA Enabled is sufficient, since the URL Prefix value is independent of whether JTA is enabled.

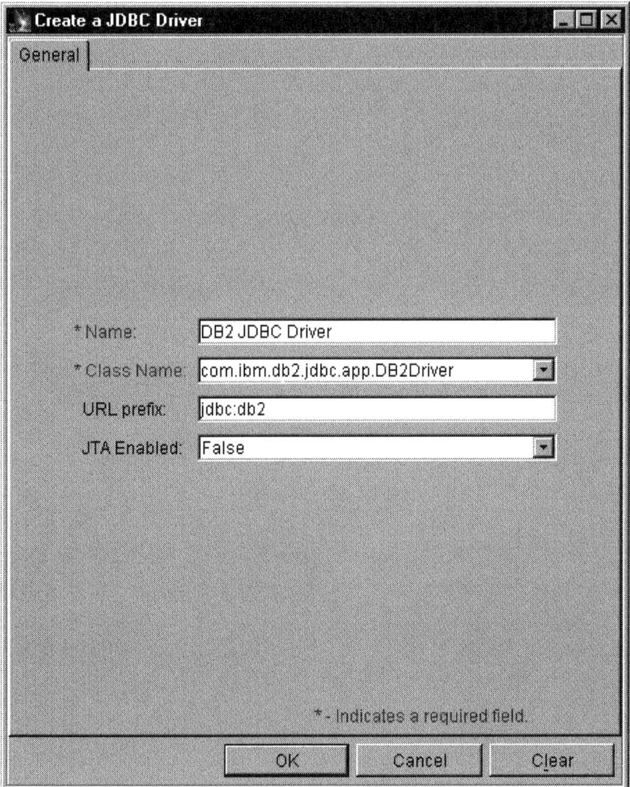

Figure 424. Create a JDBC Driver: General tab

If you want to create a JDBC driver for other databases, you will need to specify the proper implementation class name and the URL prefix.

WebSphere provides four more choices for Class Name. When you select one, the URL prefix will be changed automatically as shown in Figure 425 on page 582. For example, if you choose **oracle.jdbc.driver.OracleDriver**, the URL prefix will be set as jdbc:oracle:thin:@hostname:1521 at the same time, you will need to change “hostname” to the real host name (Oracle Server).

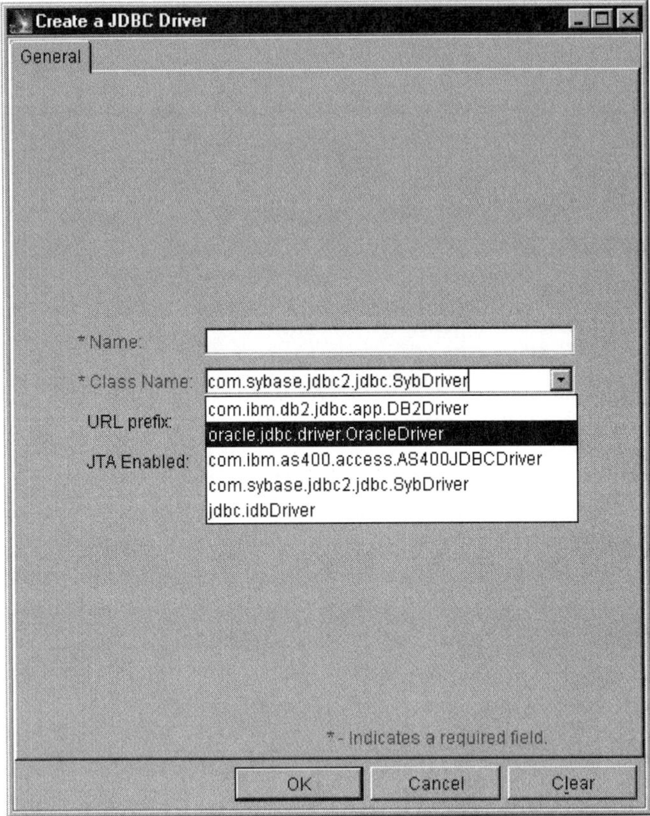

Figure 425. Create a JDBC Driver: the choices for class name

After you specify all information, click **OK** to create JDBC Driver. An information dialog box will show that the command was completed successfully.

14.4.2 Install a JDBC driver

To install a JDBC driver means specifying the location of the Java code for the driver. To perform the function, switch to the Topology view. Put the cursor on the DB2 JDBC driver previously created under the WebSphere administrative domain. The properties are displayed on the right side of the administrative console. Right-click **DB2 JDBC Driver** then click **Install...** as shown in Figure 426 on page 583.

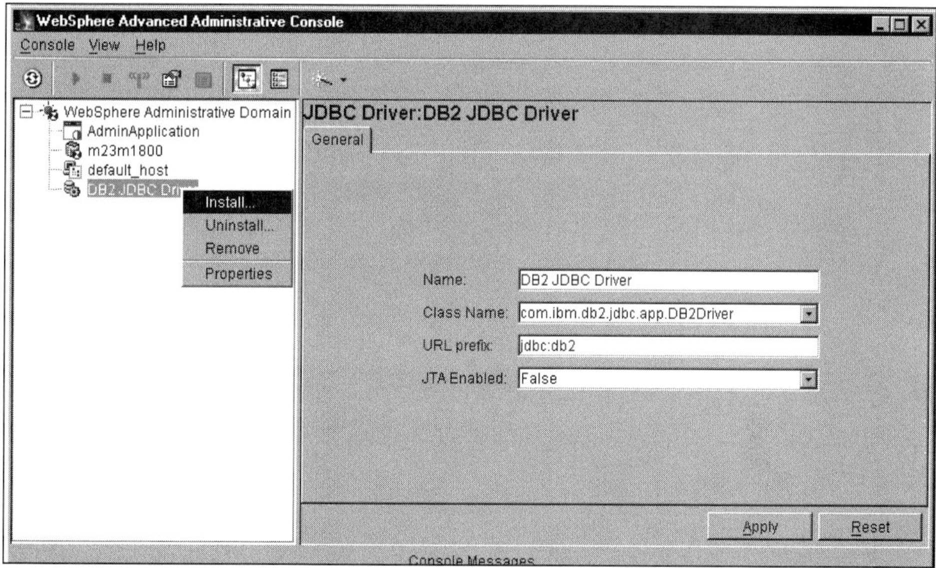

Figure 426. Installing a JDBC driver

The Install Driver dialog box is displayed as shown in Figure 427. Select the node on which you want to install the driver. The Browser button will then become active. In our environment, it is m23m1800.

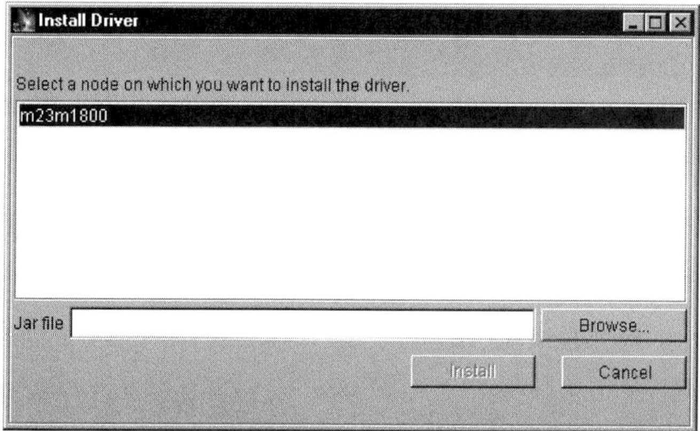

Figure 427. Installing driver #1

Click the **Browse** button for the DB2 JDBC driver code. On the Windows platform, it should be <db2 install directory>\java\db2java.zip, On AIX, it should be <DB2 instance home>\sqllib\java12\db2java.zip.

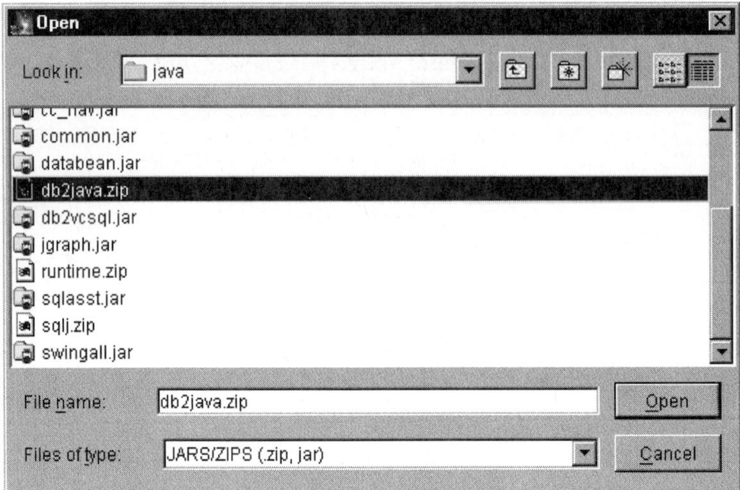

Figure 428. Installing a JDBC driver: Open window

When you locate the db2java.zip file, select it and click the **Open** button to return to the driver installation dialog. It will be displayed in the JAR file field as shown in Figure 428.

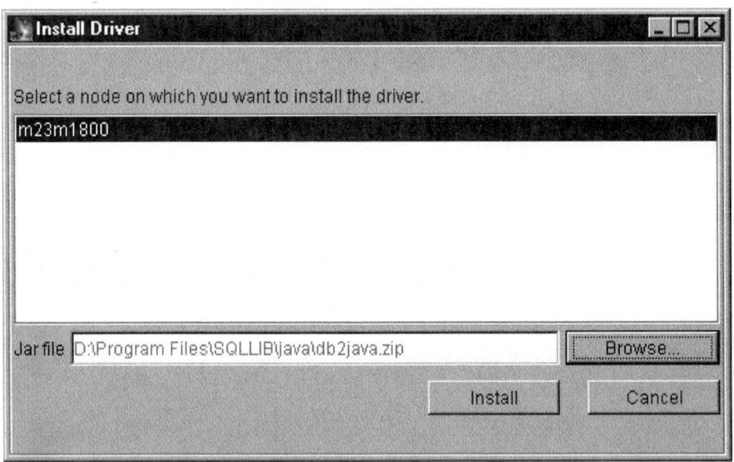

Figure 429. Installing driver #2

Click the **Install** button as shown in Figure 429. An information dialog box informs you that the command completed successfully.

Note: This operation does not change the location of the db2java.zip file. It simply specifies the location of the file to the WebSphere Administrative

Server. Indeed we could install the JDBC driver on any node when it is running in the administrative domain.

14.4.3 Create a data source

Click **Wizards-->Create a Data Source** to start as shown in Figure 430.

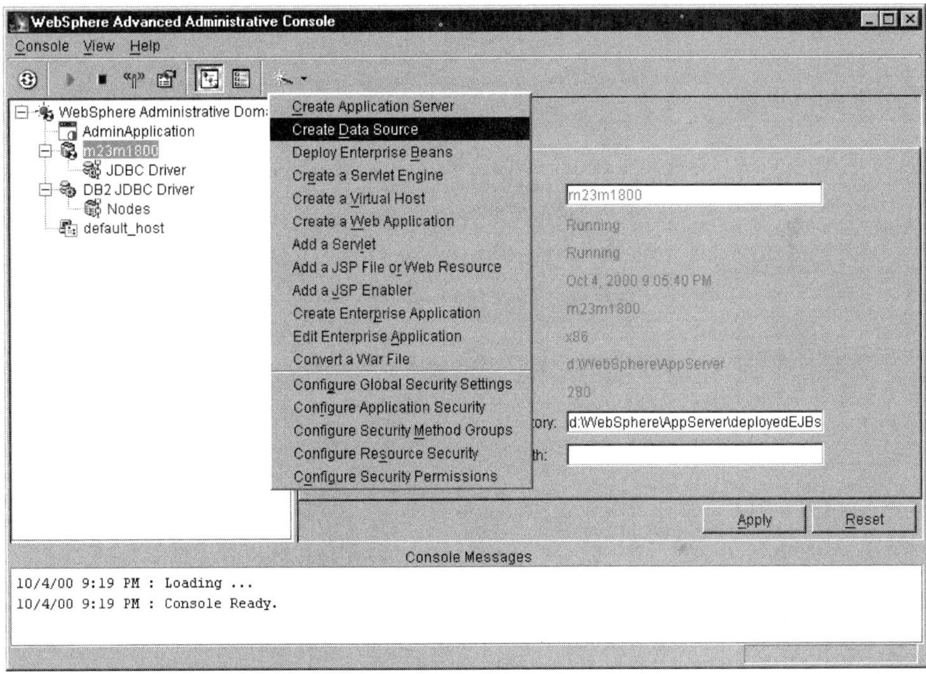

Figure 430. Creating a data source

The Create Data Source Wizard window will be displayed as depicted in Figure 431 on page 586. Select **Use an already installed JDBC Driver**. If you didn't do the steps in 14.4.1, "Create a JDBC driver" on page 579 and 14.4.2 to create and install a JDBC driver before, you could select option **Create and install a new JDBC Driver** to do it now.

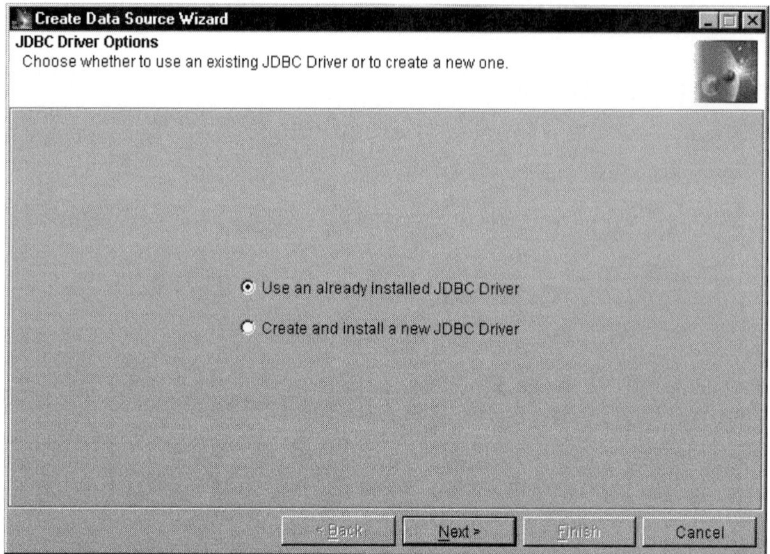

Figure 431. Creating a data source: JDBC driver options

Click **Next** and the panel shown in Figure 432 on page 587 displays. Specify the properties for data source. For an Increment entity bean, we will use a database called sample as be persistent database.

- Data Source Name

  This is the name by which you will administer the data source. You can make up any value you like for this property.

  It is recommended that you enter a name that is suggestive of the database you will use.

  Specify "sample" as the name. The JNDI lookup for such a data source would be "jdbc/sample".

- Database name

  This specifies the name of the database used.

  Enter "sample". This would make the data source point to jdbc:db2:sample.

- Driver

  This specifies the name of the JDBC driver that this data source is using.

  Select **DB2 JDBC Driver** configured recently.

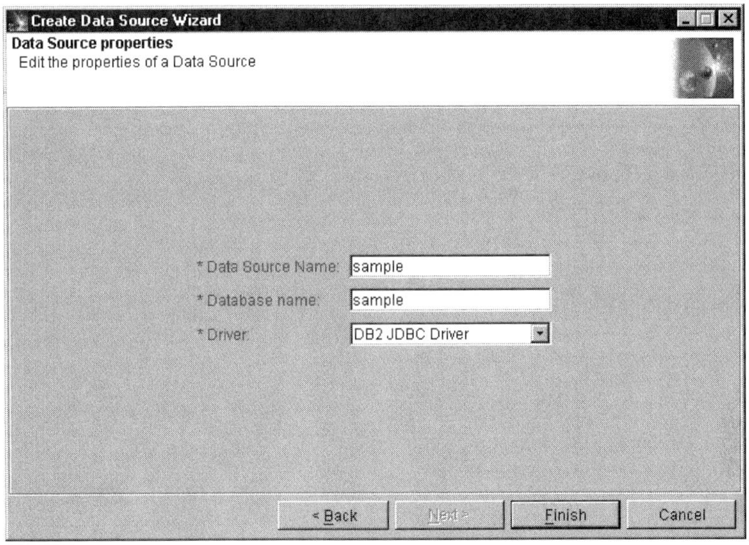

Figure 432. Creating Data Source: Data Source properties

After inputting values in the fields, the **Finish** button will become active. Click it and an information dialog will inform you that the command completed successfully.

Next, we complete the configuration for database access.

14.5 Create an application server and other basic resources

In this step, we will use the Create Application Server wizard to create an application server, together with an EJBcontainer, a servlet engine and a Web application at the same time. You may create them individually. For example, you may create Web applications using the Create a Web Application wizard.

An application server is the basic resource in WebSphere. It provides a JVM. In one application server, there could be one or more EJBContainers. Together, the container and server provide the EJB runtime environment. In one application server, there could be only one servlet engine, which handles requests for servlets, JSP files, and other types of server-side coding. Servlets and other files can belong to a Web application (servlet group). Indeed, every servlet in the administrative domain must belong to a Web application whose classpath specifies where to find the servlet class file.

Click **Wizards-->Create Application Server** as shown in Figure 433 on page 588, and the wizard will then display.

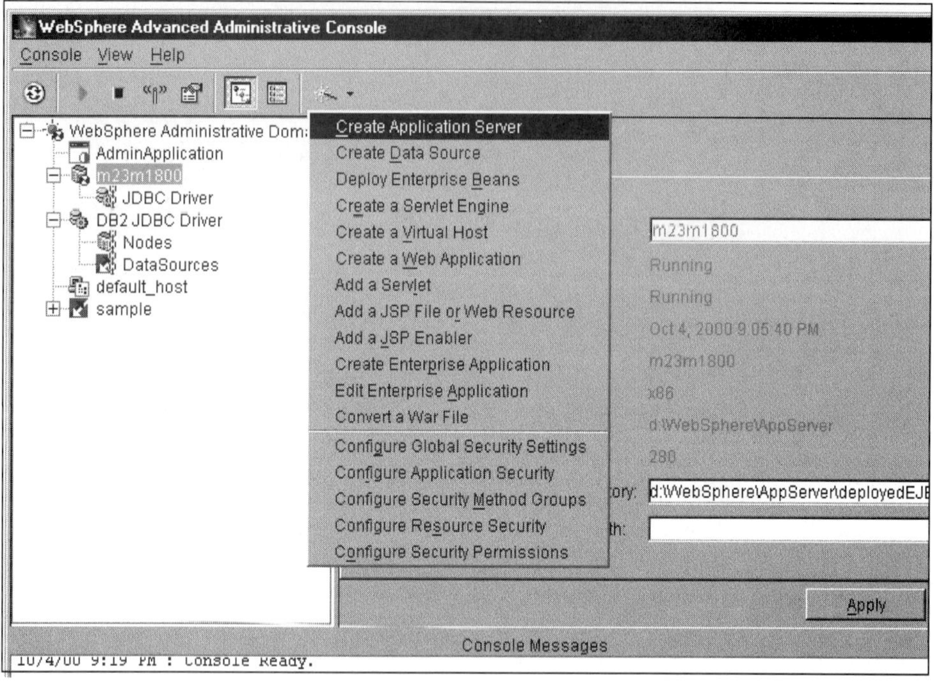

Figure 433. Creating an application server

14.5.1 Types of resources

In the Advanced Edition, there are two check boxes: Enterprise Beans and Web Applications, as shown in Figure 434 on page 589. In the Standard Edition, there is only one check box - Web Applications.

Check the resource types you want to add to the Application Server. There are various choices:

- Check Enterprise Beans to configure the application server, a container, and enterprise beans.
- Check Web Applications to configure the application server, a servlet engine, Web applications, and servlets.
- Check both options to configure all of the above.
- Check neither option to configure just the application server.

Both check boxes are checked by default. Accept it and click **Next**.

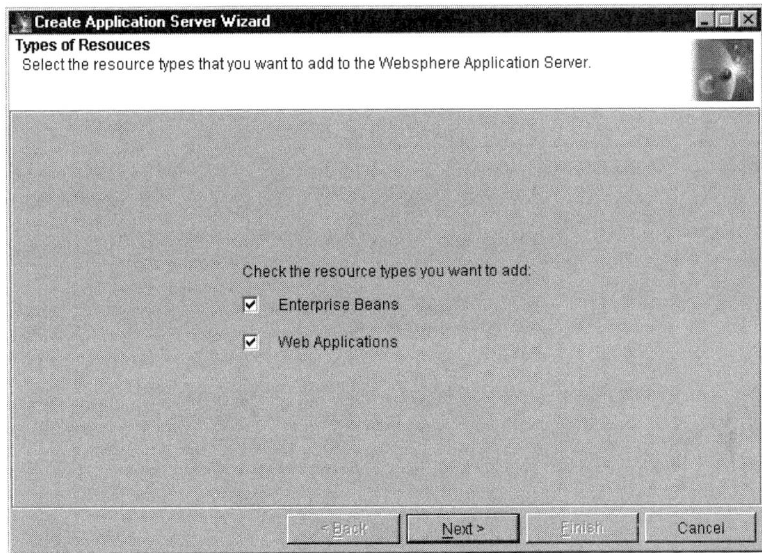

Figure 434. Creating an application server: types of resources

14.5.2 Application server properties

We need to specify some properties of the application server, as shown in Figure 435 on page 590.

Required is the Application Server Name. This is the name by which to administer the application server. Any value you like may be used for this property. We specify the name as "ITSOAppServer".

You may keep the default values of other properties, which are optional. Here, we will change the standard output and standard error as follows:

Standard output: <WAS_HOME>\logs\itsoappserv_stdout.txt

Standard err: <WAS_HOME>\logs\itsoappserv_stderr.txt

Click **Next** to continue.

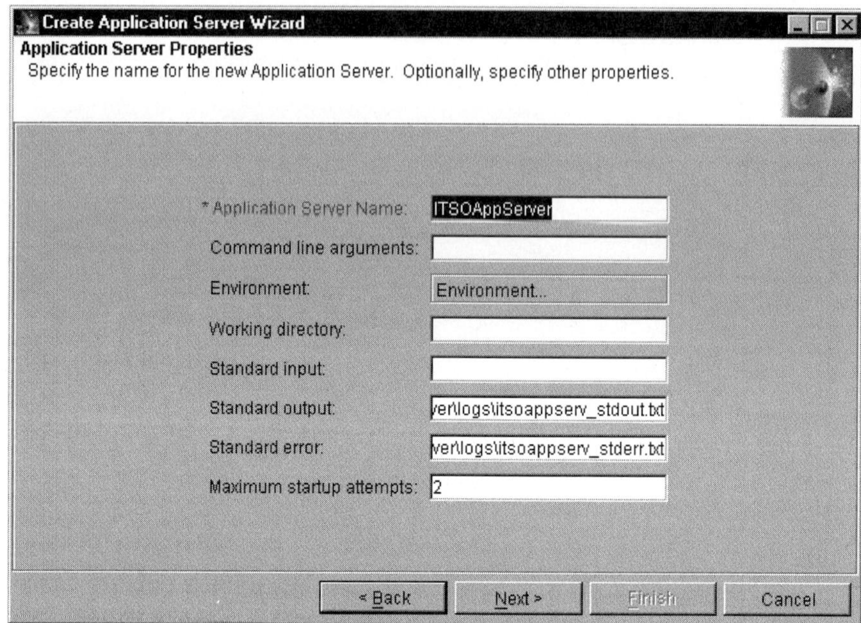

Figure 435. Creating an application server: application server properties

14.5.3 Application Server Start Option

Choose the default **Do not start the server automatically after creating it**, as shown in Figure 436 on page 591. Click **Next**. We could start it in the Topology view manually after completing the configuration.

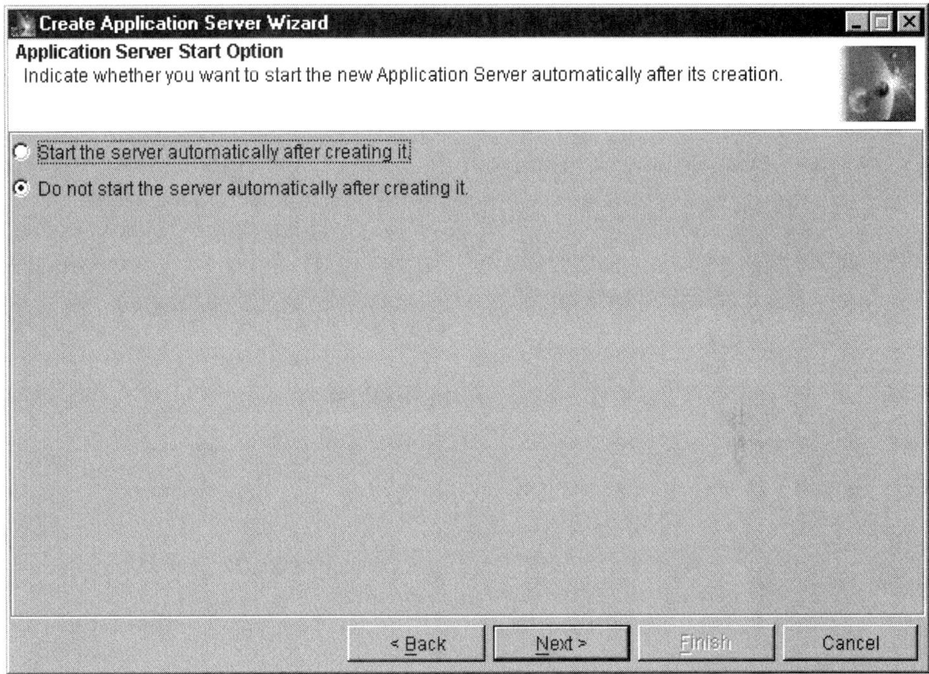

Figure 436. Creating an application server: application server start option

14.5.4 Node selection

Select the node on which the application server will run on. We select **m23m1800** as shown in Figure 437 on page 592, and the Next button will now become active. Click **Next** to continue.

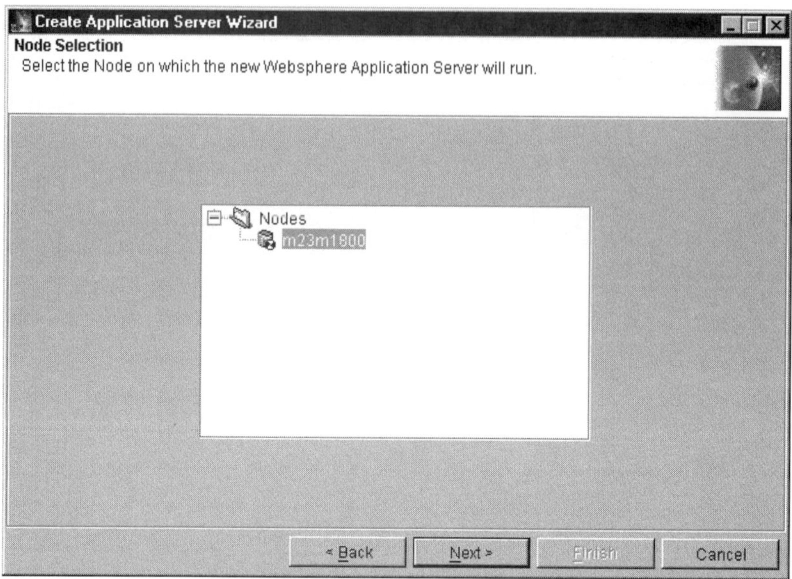

Figure 437. Creating an application server: node selection

14.5.5 Add enterprise beans

You could click the Browse button to start adding EJBs. However we will skip this step now and describe it in 14.8, "Create enterprise beans" on page 606. On the Add Enterprise Beans window, we clicked **Next** to continue.

14.5.6 EJBContainer properties

The EJBContainer Name is required. This is the name by which the EJBContainer is administered. You may keep the default name or make up any value you like for this property. We will accept the default name, ITSOAppServerContainer as shown in Figure 438 on page 593.

You could switch to the DataSource tag to configure the data source used by this EJBContainer, including data source, user ID and password. We will skip this step and configure the data source for the EJB when we create it.

Click **Next** to continue.

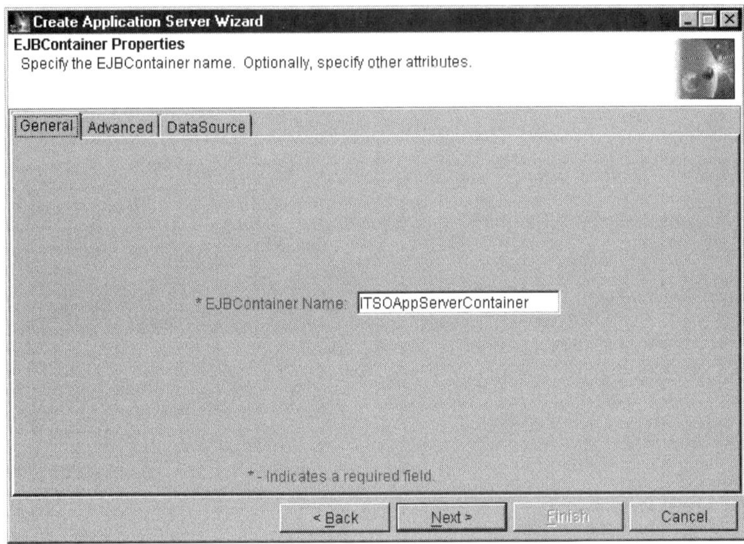

Figure 438. Creating an application server: EJBContainer properties

14.5.7 Select a virtual host

Select a virtual host, and the Next button will become active. Click it to continue. We use default_host as shown in Figure 439.

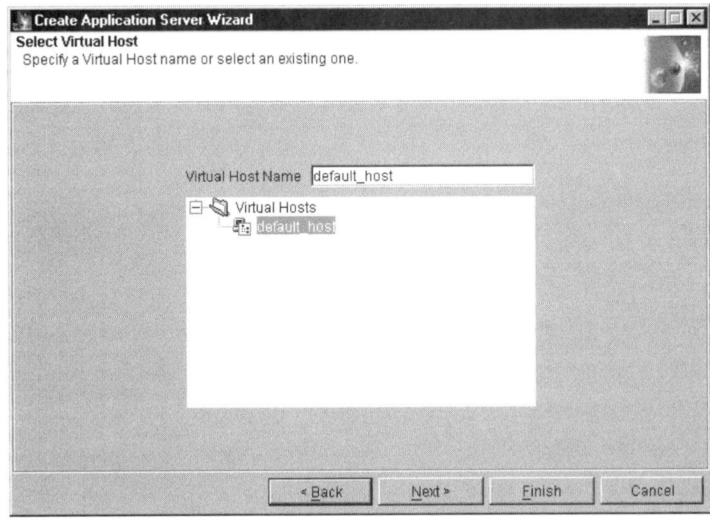

Figure 439. Creating an application server: select virtual host

14.5.8 Servlet Engine properties

The servlet engine name is required. This is the name by which the servlet engine is administered. You may keep the default name or use any value you like for this property. We will accept the default name, ITSOAppServerServletEngine, as shown in Figure 440. We will keep the default servlet engine mode, which is WebSphere 3.5 Compatibility Mode.

Click the **Next** button. We will begin to create a Web application.

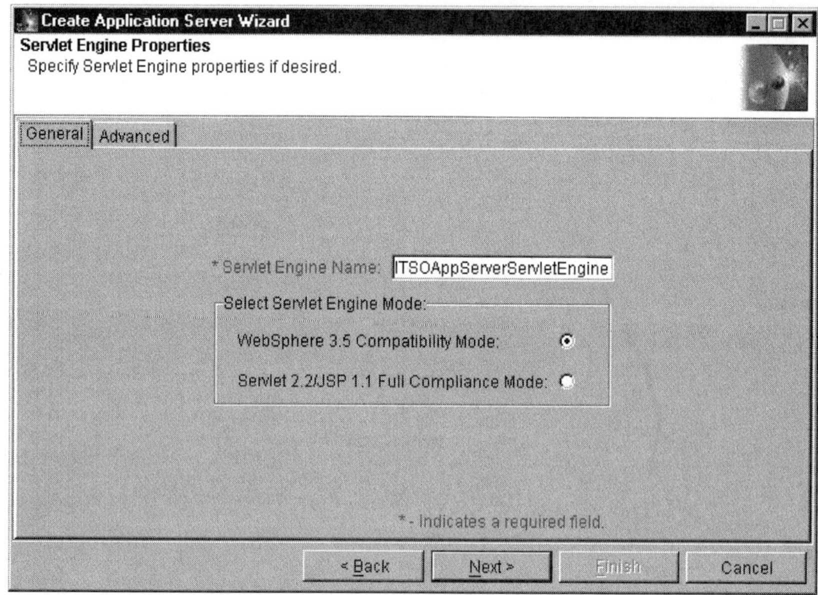

Figure 440. Creating an application server: servlet engine properties

14.5.9 Web application properties

We need to specify the properties of the Web application, as shown in Figure 441 on page 595.

- Web Application Name

  This is the name by which to administer the Web application, and part of the default value of the Web application Web path.

  Keep the default, ITSOAppServerWebApp.

- Virtual Host

  Select default_host from the list.

- Web Application Web Path

The default value is "/webapp/ITSOAppServerWebApp". We change it to "/".

The virtual host and the Web path indicate a path for accessing the Web application from a browser.

If we keep the default value of the Web path, it should be:

```
http://Valid_host_Alias/webapp/ITSOAppServerWebApp
```

After we change the Web path to "/", it should be:

```
http://Valid_host_Alias/
```

where `Valid_host_Alias` is any valid alias for the virtual host which we specified.

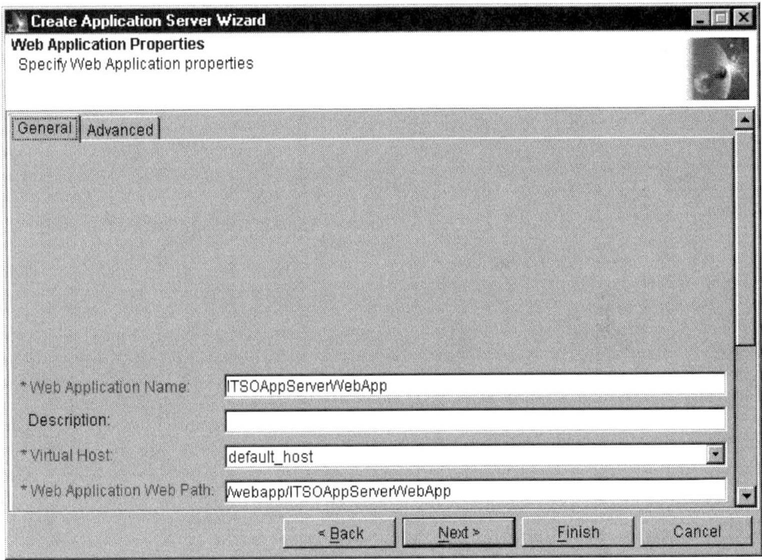

Figure 441. Creating an application server: Web application properties General tab

Switch to the Advanced tag in order to see more properties of the Web application, as shown in Figure 442 on page 596. These properties are very notable, especially for placing files when deploying the application.

The default values are:

Document Root: `<WAS_HOME>\hosts\default_host\ITSOAppServerWebApp\web`

Classpath: `<WAS_HOME>\hosts\default_host\ITSOAppServerWebApp\servlets`

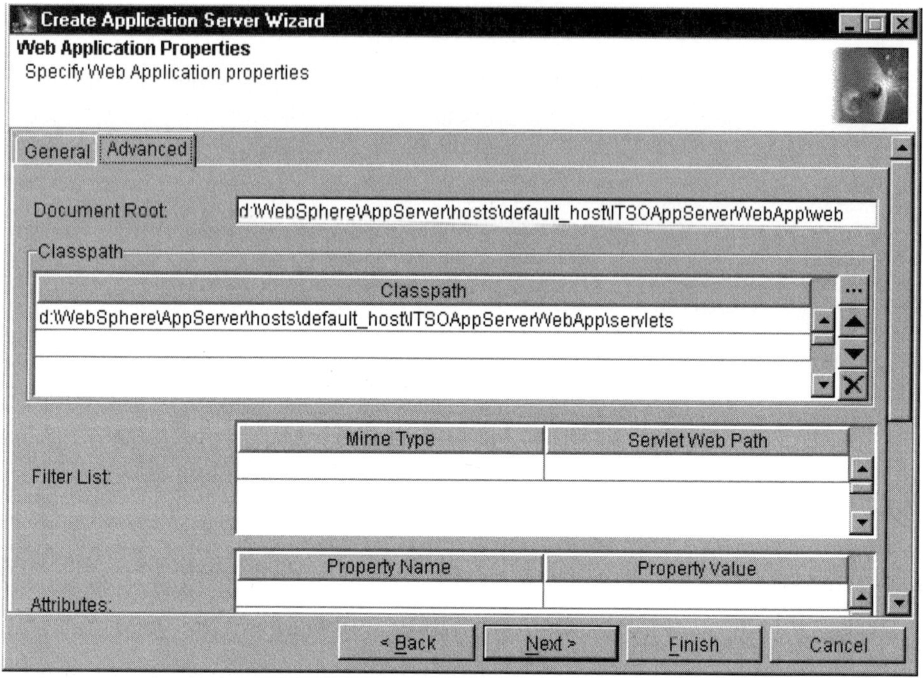

Figure 442. Creating an application server: Web application properties Advanced tab

Accept the default values and click **Next** to continue.

14.5.10 Specify system servlets

WebSphere V3.5 provides internal (built-in) WebSphere servlets that we can add to Web applications to enable optional functions. In this panel, we may add some to the Web application, as shown in Figure 443 on page 597.

- Enable File Servlet

  Check this servlet.

  This enables Web pages to be served from the Web application document root just specified.

  It will add a servlet named "File Serving Enabler" to the Web application whose implementation class is com.ibm.servlet.engine.webapp.SimpleFileServlet.

  In addition to selecting this check box, make sure the Web server configuration file does not contain any pass rules that will override the Web application document root.

- Serve Servlets By Classname

Check this servlet.

This enables servlets to be invoked by class or code names in the servlets directory specified in the Web application classpath.

It will add a servlet named “Auto-Invoker“ to the Web application whose implementation class is com.ibm.servlet.engine.webapp.InvokerServlet.

- Select JSP version to be used

  Select **Enable JSP 1.0**.

  This specifies that the JSP enabler servlet supporting the 1.0 level of the JavaServer Pages (JSP) specification will be included.

  It will add a servlet named “JSP 1.0 Processor“ to the Web application whose implementation class is com.sun.jsp.runtime.JspServlet.

You could remove any of them from the Topology tree, or add them by clicking **Wizards-->Create a Servlet** again.

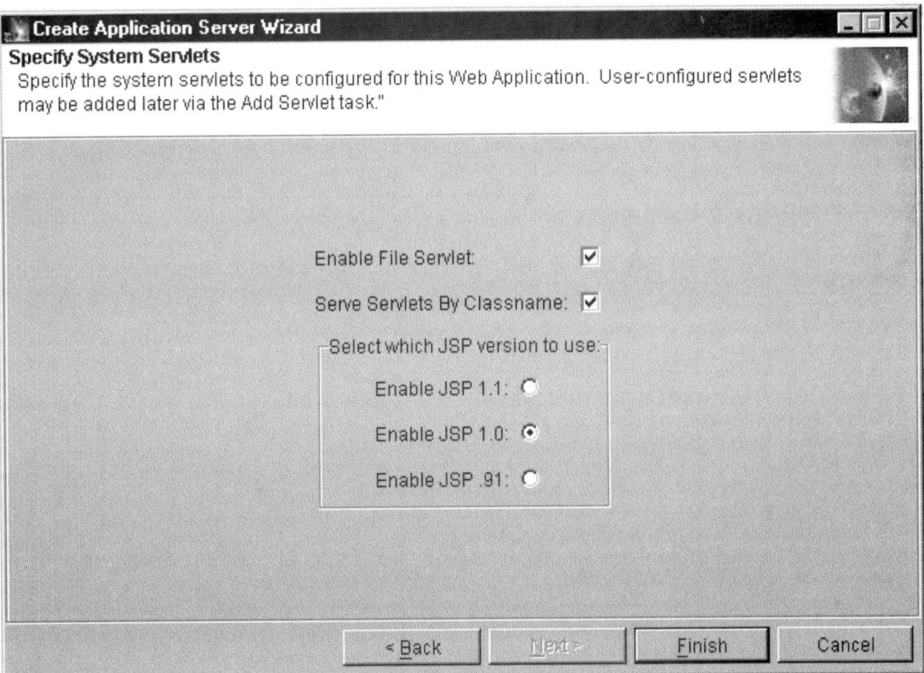

Figure 443. Creating an application server: specify system servlets

Click the **Finish** button to complete creating the Application Server Wizard.

The administrative console will then show the application server that you created, as shown in Figure 444 on page 598.

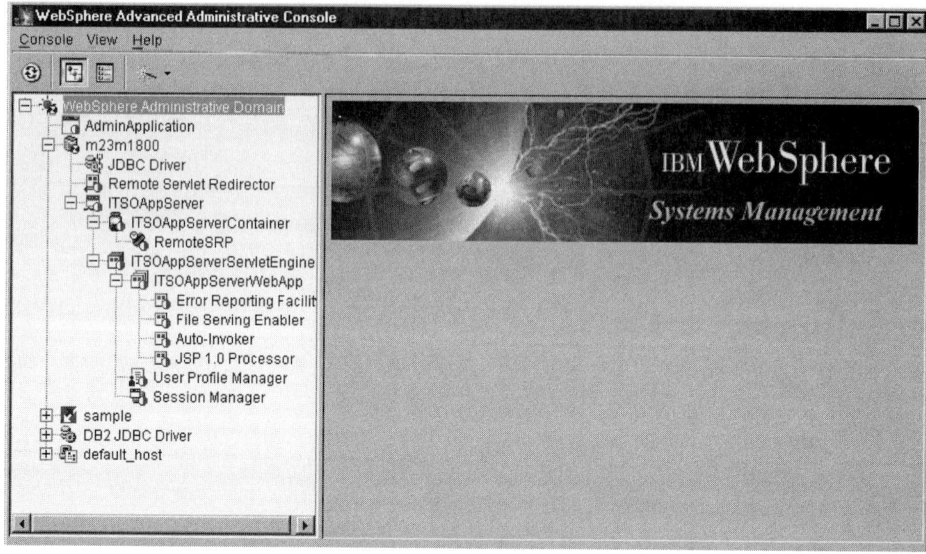

Figure 444. A newly created application server

14.6 Placing source files

When deploying servlets, Web applications, and Enterprise JavaBean applications, ensure that the component files are in the correct directories. WebSphere Application Server does not provide any tools for managing files and directories. This means that you must plan how your applications will be structured and copy the files and directories to the correct locations on each node.

Table 39 is a quick reference for this task:

Table 39. Placing files reference

File description	File extension	Directory path
HTML documents and related static files	.html, .shtml, .jhtml, .gif, .au, and so on	These can be either served by the Web server, or placed in the Web application document root with the WebSphere file servlet enabled.

File description	File extension	Directory path
JavaServer Pages files	.jsp	Web application document root
Servlets that are to be reloaded	.class or .jar	Web application classpath. If the servlets are in a package and using class files instead of JAR files, mirror the package structure as subdirectories under the Web application classpath.
Servlet that are not to be reloaded	.class or .jar	Application server classpath
Servlet configuration file	.servlet	Directory that contains the servlet
Enterprise bean	.jar	Application server deployable EJBs directory
JavaBean (not an enterprise bean) or other object to be reloaded	.ser or .jar	Web application classpath
JavaBean (not an enterprise bean) or other object not to be reloaded, such as serialized objects and servlets that use Java Native Interface methods	.ser or .jar	Application server classpath

File description	File extension	Directory path
Java objects added to a session	.class, .jar, or .ser	Application server classpath This requirement applies to non-EJB objects in either of the following conditions: 1)Session persistence is enabled (the default setting). 2)The application server is part of a session cluster. In a session cluster, be sure to place the objects in the application server classpath on each cluster host and cluster client. An object in the application server classpath is not reloaded when its source file changes.
Objects passed as arguments for remote calls		Application server classpath

For the Web application ITSOAppServerWebApp, the document root is "<WAS_HOME>\hosts\default_host\ITSOAppServerWebApp\web", and the classpath is "<WAS_HOME>\hosts\default_host\ITSOAppServerWebApp\servlets".

First, we need to create the corresponding directory under <WAS_HOME>\hosts\default_host\.

Then, we need to copy files to the correct directory:

- For servlet sample HelloWorldServlet

  Copy HelloWorldServlet.class to directory "servlets"

- For EJB sample Increment

  (**Note**: Because we change the URL of this sample, we need to modify the source code to enable it to run correctly.)

  - Copy increment.html to directory "web".

    We need to modify this file to let it invoke the servlet correctly.

Open it with a text editor, and find "/WebSphereSamples/servlet/WebSphereSamples.Increment.VisitIncrementSite". Change it to "/servlet/WebSphereSamples.Increment.VisitIncrementSite"

- Make directory WebSphereSamples\Increment under directory "servlets", then copy all files in directory <WAS_HOME>\hosts\default_host\WSsamples_app\servlets\WebSphereSamples\Increment\ to it.

  We need to modify the VisitIncrementSite.java and compile it in order to let the servlet return the correct HTML.

  Open it with a text editor, find "/WebSphereSamples/servlet/WebSphereSamples.Increment.VisitIncrementSite" and change it to "/servlet/WebSphereSamples.Increment.VisitIncrementSite"

  Then compile it in the command line with:

```
<WAS_HOME>\jdk\bin\javac -classpath <WebSphere
install_root>\hosts\default_host\ITSOAppServerWebApp\servlets;<WebSp
here install_root>\lib\servlet.jar;<WebSphere
install_root>\lib\ujc.jar <WebSphere
install_root>\hosts\default_host\ITSOAppServerWebApp\servlets\WebSph
ereSamples\Increment\VisitIncrementSite.java
```

- We do not have to move the Increment.jar. It has been configured "in place."

14.7 Add Servlet

Now we begin to configure the servlet HelloWorldServlet.

Click **Wizards-->Add a Servlet**. The wizard will then display as shown in Figure 445 on page 602.

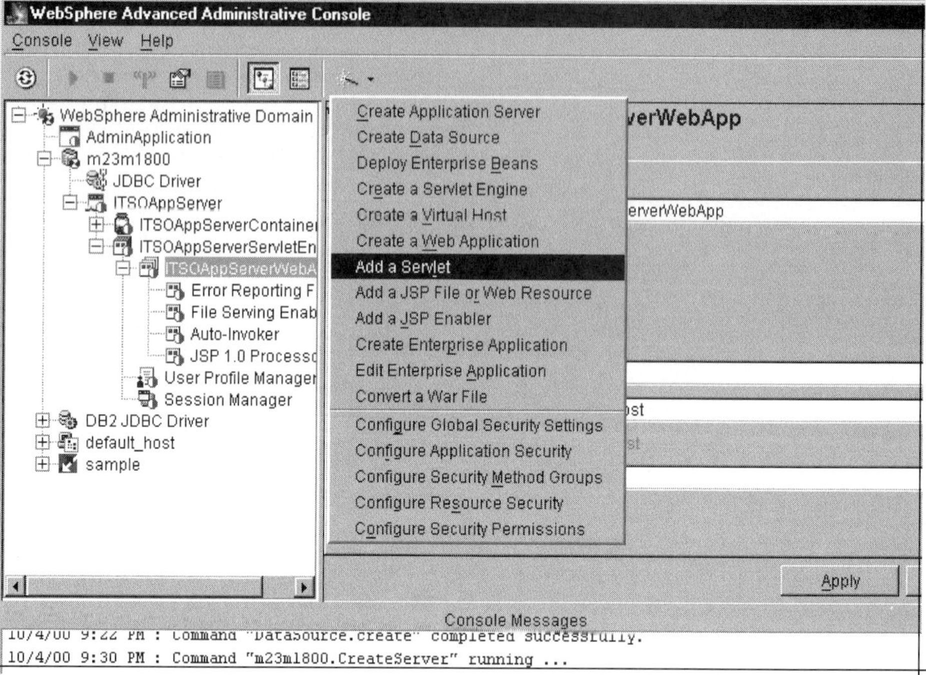

Figure 445. Adding a servlet #1

On the next window, specify whether to add servlets from an existing servlet JAR file or directory. Keep the default “No“, then click **Next** to continue.

We need to specify a Web application to contain this servlet. Select **ITSOAppServerWebApp** as shown in Figure 446 on page 603. The **Next** button will then become active. Click it to proceed.

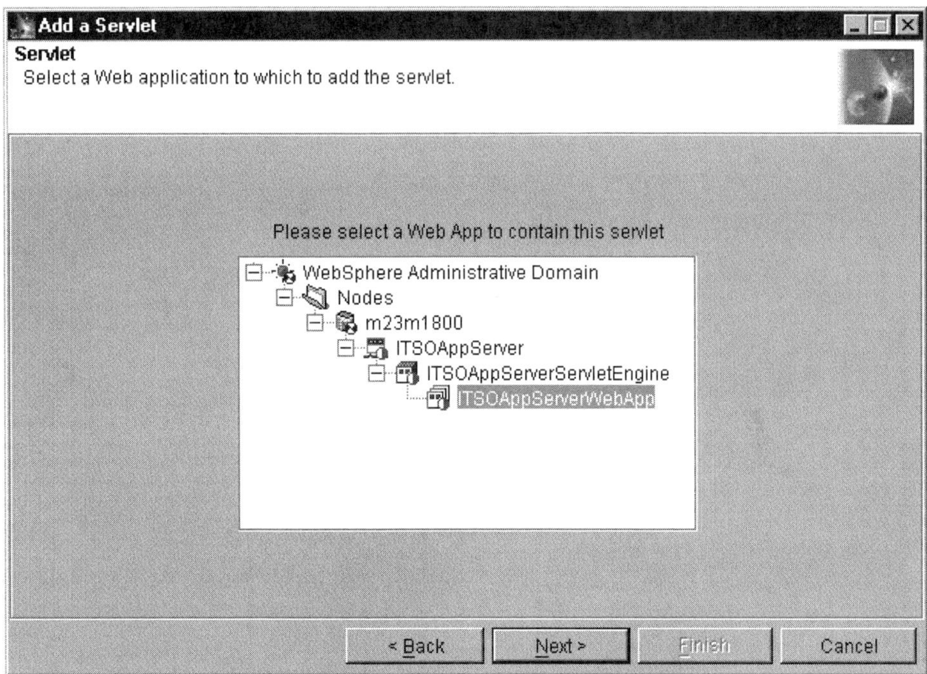

Figure 446. Adding a servlet #2

We can now select the type of servlet we want to configure, including a system servlet and user-defined servlet. If the system servlet was not configured correctly at the time of the Web application creation, there is now another entry to modify the configuration. We will configure our own servlet, so select **Create User-Defined Servlet** as shown in Figure 447, then click **Next** to continue.

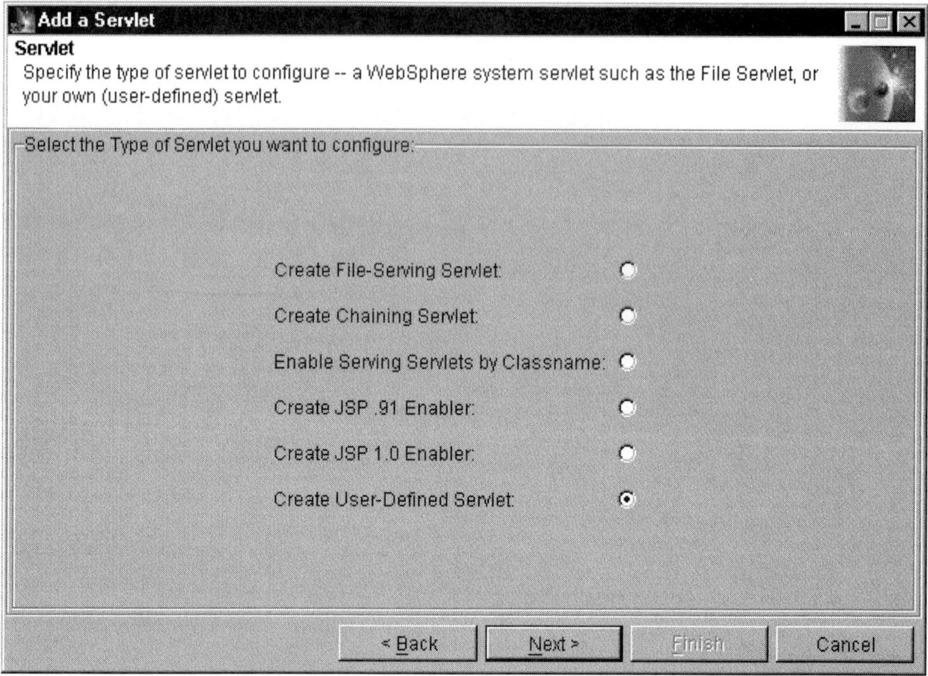

Figure 447. Adding a servlet #3

We need to specify part properties of this servlet, as shown in Figure 448 on page 605.

- Servlet Name

  This is the name of the servlet. You may use any value you like.

  Specify "hello".

- Web Application

  This is the Web application with which the servlet is associated.

  Keep the default value "ITSOAppServerWebApp".

- Servlet Class Name

  This is the servlet implementation class name. Specify the package, but do not include the .class extension.

  Specify "HelloWorldServlet"

- Servlet Web Path List

  We could specify one or more Uniform Resource Identifiers (URIs) by which this servlet can be located and invoked.

Click the **Add** button and a dialog displays. Specify "servlet/hello" following the Web Application Web Path "/", then click **OK** to return to the wizard.

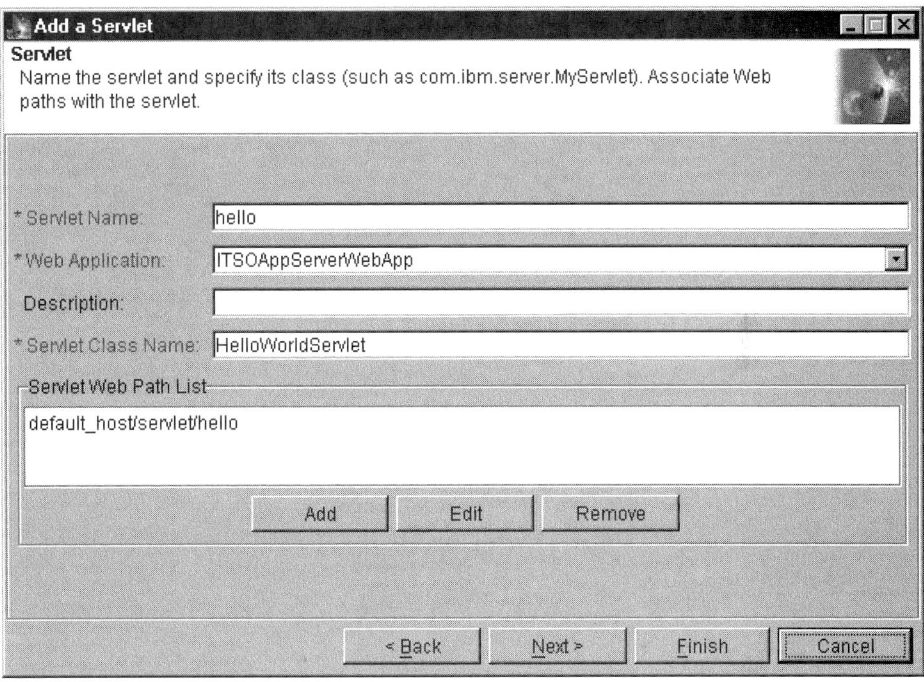

Figure 448. Adding a servlet #4

Click **Next** to continue. You may see other properties as shown in Figure 449 on page 606. However keep the default and click the **Finish** button. An information dialog will inform you that the command completed successfully.

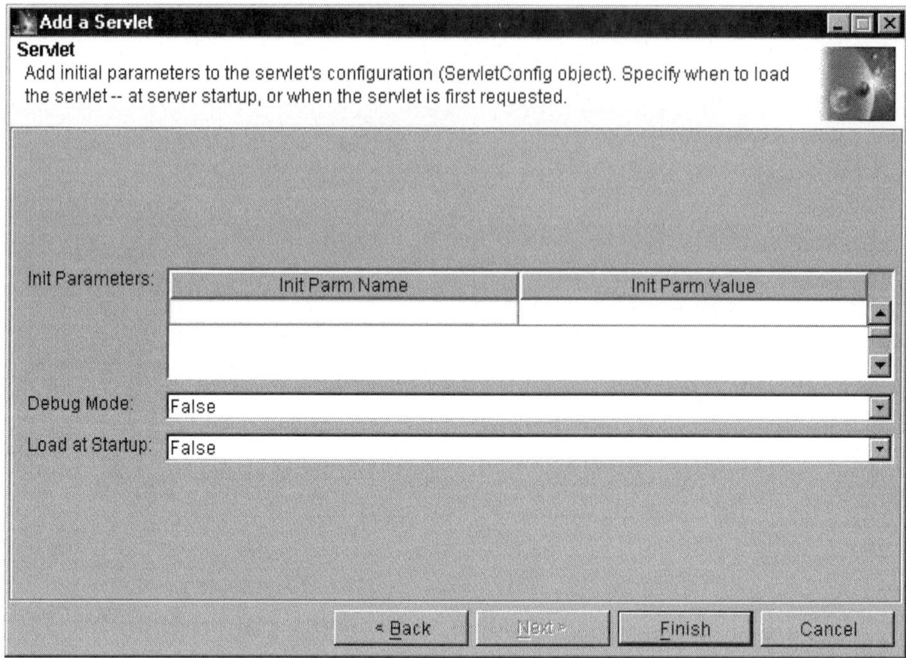

Figure 449. Adding a servlet #5

14.8 Create enterprise beans

Now we begin to create the EJB Increment. To use EJBs with an EJB server, they must be deployed. Increment.jar is a deployable file. WebSphere will automatically deploy it when creating the EJB in the administrative console.

Right-click the **ITSOAppServerContainer** then select **Create-->EnterpriseBean** to begin as shown in Figure 450 on page 607.

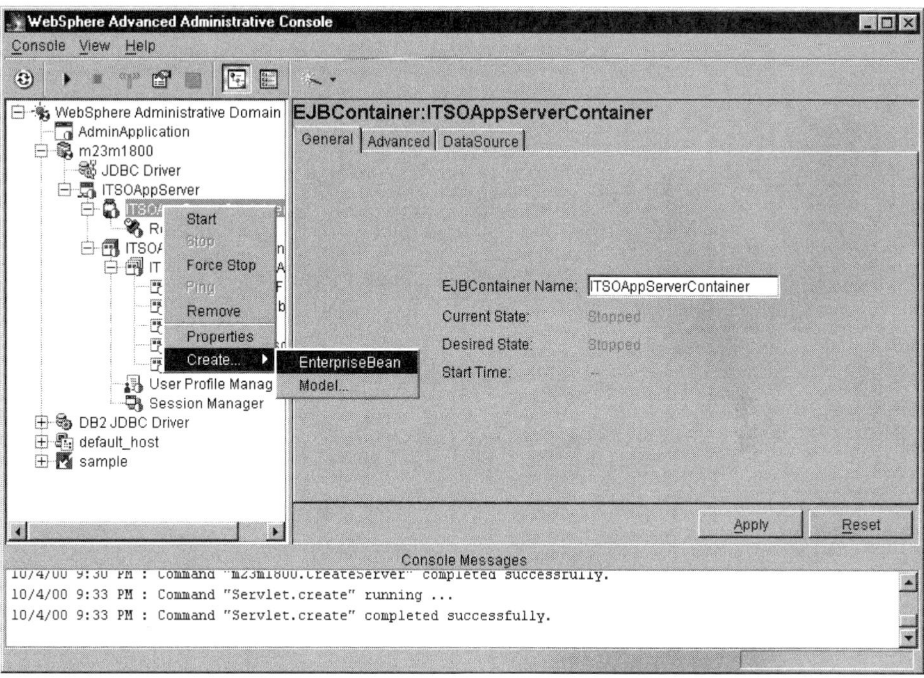

Figure 450. Creating EnterpriseBean

On the General tag, specify the name and JAR file. Click the **Browse** button to select the JAR file as shown in Figure 451 on page 608.

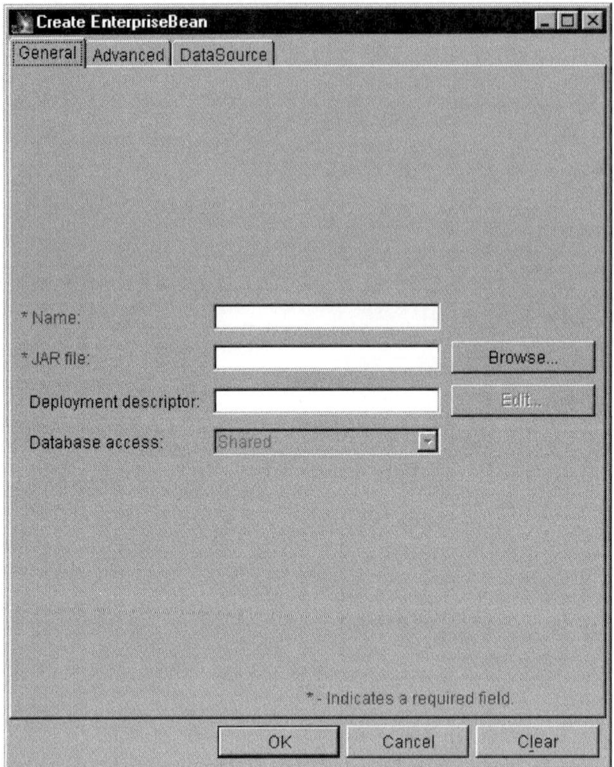

Figure 451. Creating EnterpriseBean: General tab #1

Switch to the directory deployableEJBs, and put the cursor on the Increment.jar file as shown in Figure 452 on page 609.

Note

Don't select the JAR file and click the Select button because all beans in the JAR file will be deployed with default values. This may not be appropriate in all cases.

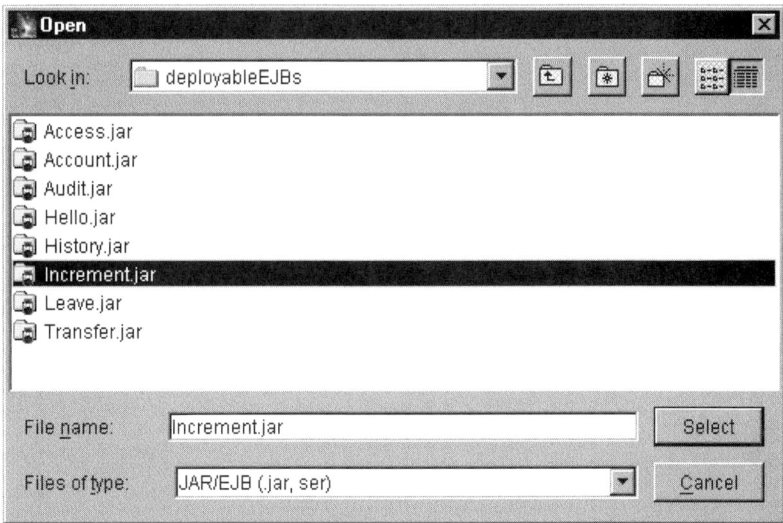

Figure 452. Creating EnterpriseBean: Opening a file

Double-click the JAR file. It will be opened and the deployment descriptors (.ser file) will be listed as shown in Figure 453. You may select a single one to deploy it.

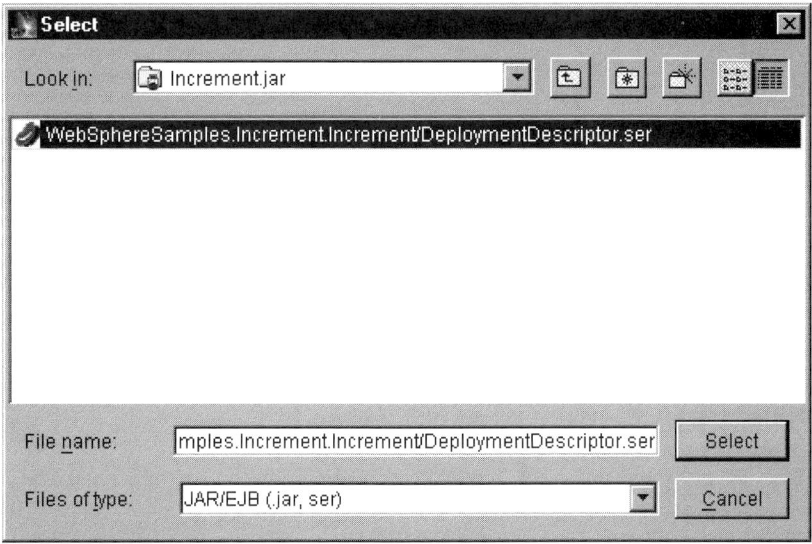

Figure 453. Creating EnterpriseBean: Selecting a file

Select the DeploymentDescriptor.ser file you need, then click the **Select** button. A confirm dialog box will display. Click **Deploy and Enable WLM** or **Deploy Only** to continue according to your actual environment, as shown in Figure 454.

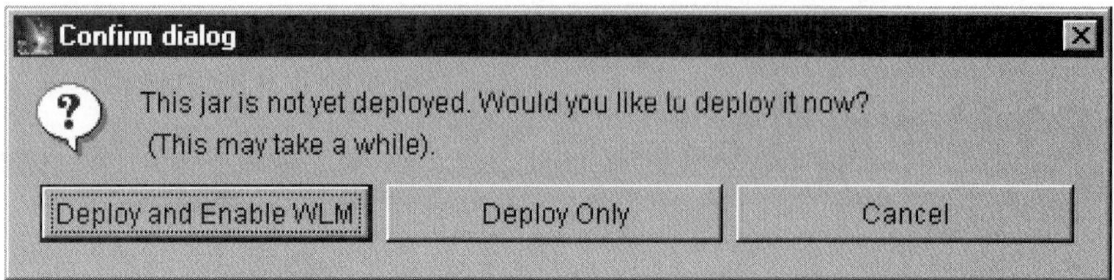

Figure 454. Creating EnterpriseBean: confirmation dialog #1

If the confirmation dialog box displays instead as shown in Figure 455, the deployment descriptor must not be selected. Click **No** to return to the browse dialog. Make sure you click the .ser file before clicking the **Select** button.

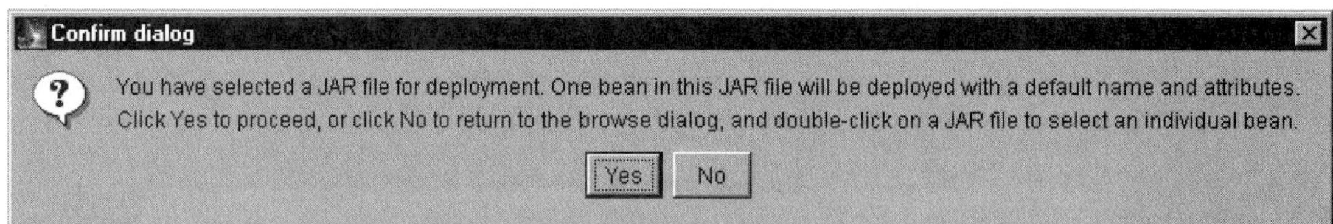

Figure 455. Creating EnterpriseBean: confirmation dialog #2

The deployment may take a while. Wait for the message `Command completed successfully`. Click **OK** to return to the Create EnterpriseBean window. The properties in the General tag will be filled in, as shown in Figure 456 on page 611. In the directory <WAS_HOME>\deployedEJBs, a new JAR file should have been created. If you click **Deploy and Enable WLM** to continue to the last step, it will be the _wlm_DeployedIncrement.jar file, and if you click **Deploy Only**, it will be DeployedIncrement.jar.

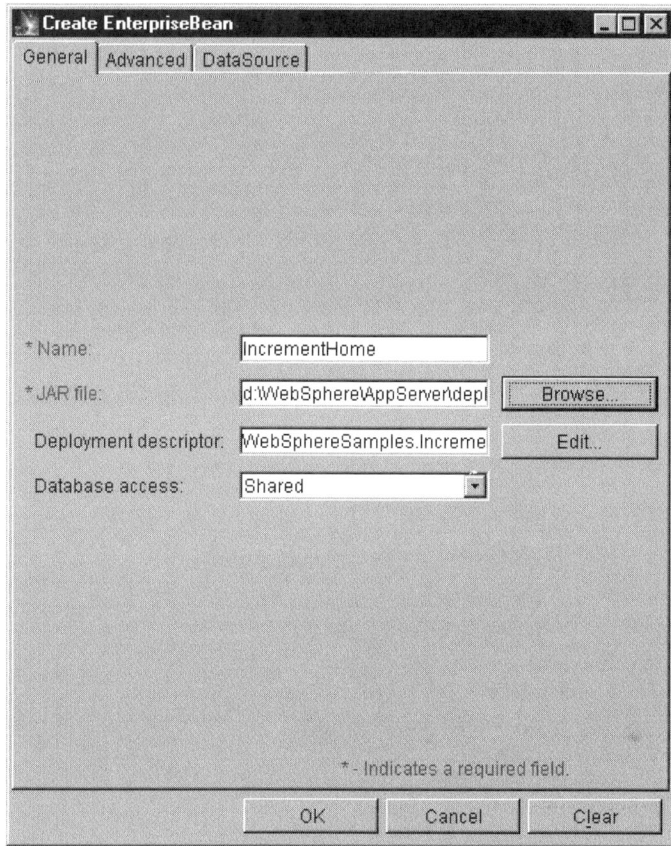

Figure 456. Creating EnterpriseBean: General tab #2

You may click **Edit** to change the deployment properties. In that case, you will get the Deployment Properties window as shown in Figure 457 on page 612. Keep the original values here.

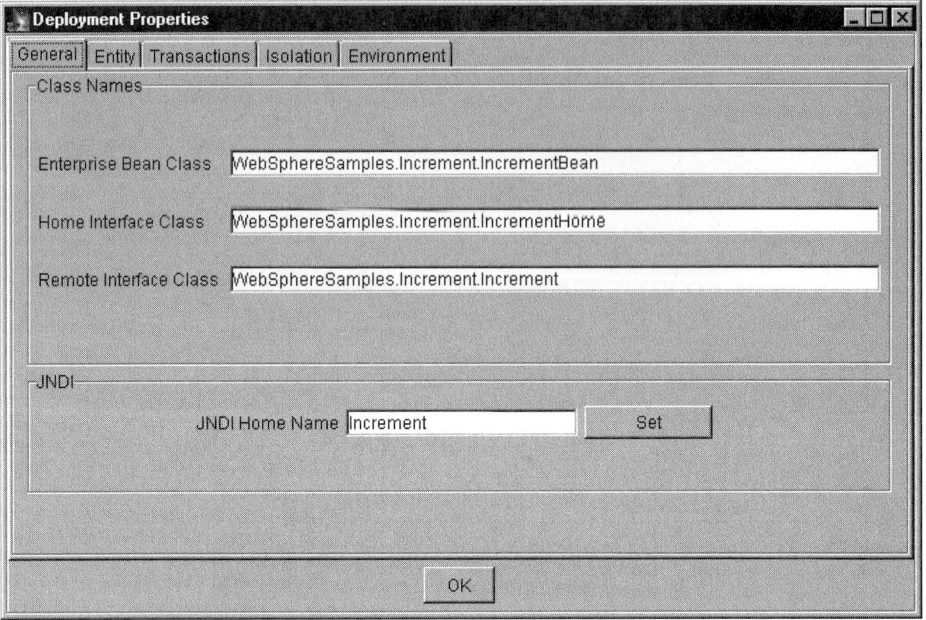

Figure 457. Deployment Properties window

Switch to the DataSource tag, specify the DataSource information that the EJB will use as shown in Figure 458 on page 613. Note that, if the EJB is a session bean, this tag will be inactive.

- DataSource

  Click **Change** to select the DataSource that has been created. We will use the sample DataSource.

- User ID and Password

  Specify the user ID and password to access the database that is represented by the data source.

- Create Table

  Make sure the check box is checked. This means the table for this entity bean will be created when it starts, and the property will be changed to unchecked after it starts successfully.

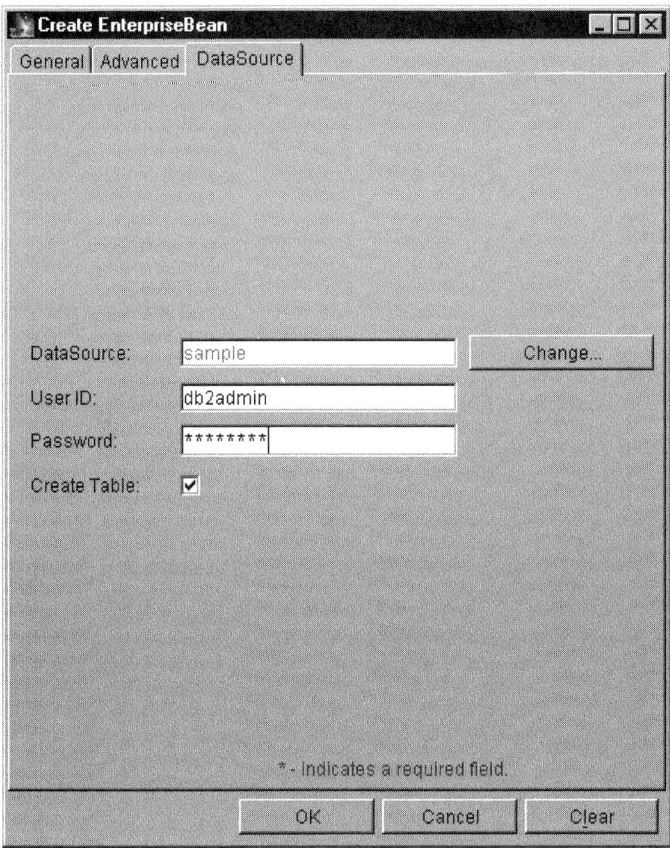

Figure 458. Creating EnterpriseBean: DataSource tab

Click **OK** to complete creating the EJB. You will see a message that `Command completed successfully`.

14.9 Verification of the servlet and EJB

These resources could now in fact already run separately.

In the Topology view, we could right-click the IncrementHome then select **Start** to start this EJB, and right-click **ITSOAppServerWebApp**, then select **Restart Web App** to start Web application.

To make sure of the running status of resources, you may need click the **ITSOAppServer** in the Topology viewer, then click the **Refresh selected subtree** button.

Start the HTTP Server if it is not running. You may input URLs into the browser to verify that the resources are working.

- For servlet HelloWorldServlet

  `http://Valid_host_Alias/servlet/hello`

  (This URL can verify that the configuration of the user-defined servlet “hello“ is working.)

  `http://Valid_host_Alias/servlet/HelloWorldServlet`

  (This URL can verify that the configuration of system servlet “Auto-Invoker“ is working.)

- For EJB Increment

  `http://Valid_host_Alias/increment.html`

  (This URL can verify that the configuration of system servlet “File Serving Enabler“ is working.)

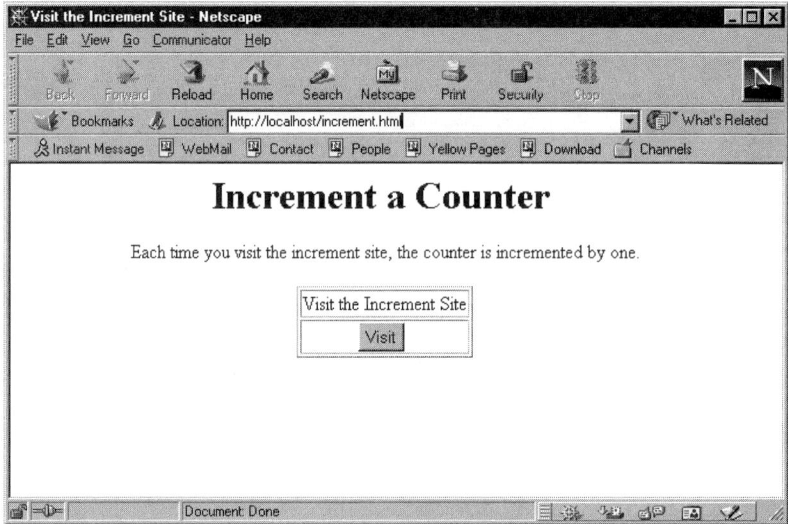

Figure 459. Increment EJB #1

Then click **Visit** and you will get the number of visits to the Increment site as shown in Figure 460 on page 615. This can verify the EJB Increment is working.

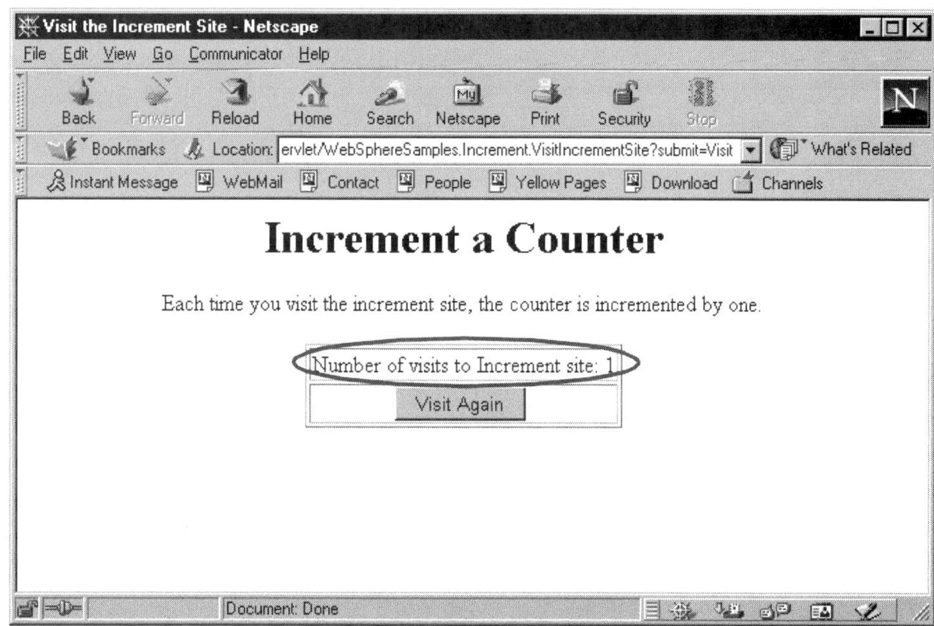

Figure 460. Increment EJB #2

14.10 Create an enterprise application

An enterprise application (often referred to as just an application) combines many kinds of resources into one named entity that can be managed as a unit.

In this section, we will in essence "wrap" the Web application with an application and add the Increment Bean to the application. This is necessary because security is applied to enterprise applications, not to Web applications.

After using the administrative console to configure an enterprise application, we can start and stop the resources in the application together by starting and stopping the application.

(Stop ITSOAppServer by clicking **ITSOAppServer** then selecting **Stop** before the next steps.)

Start the Configure a new Application task by clicking **Wizards-->Create Enterprise Application** as shown in Figure 461 on page 616.

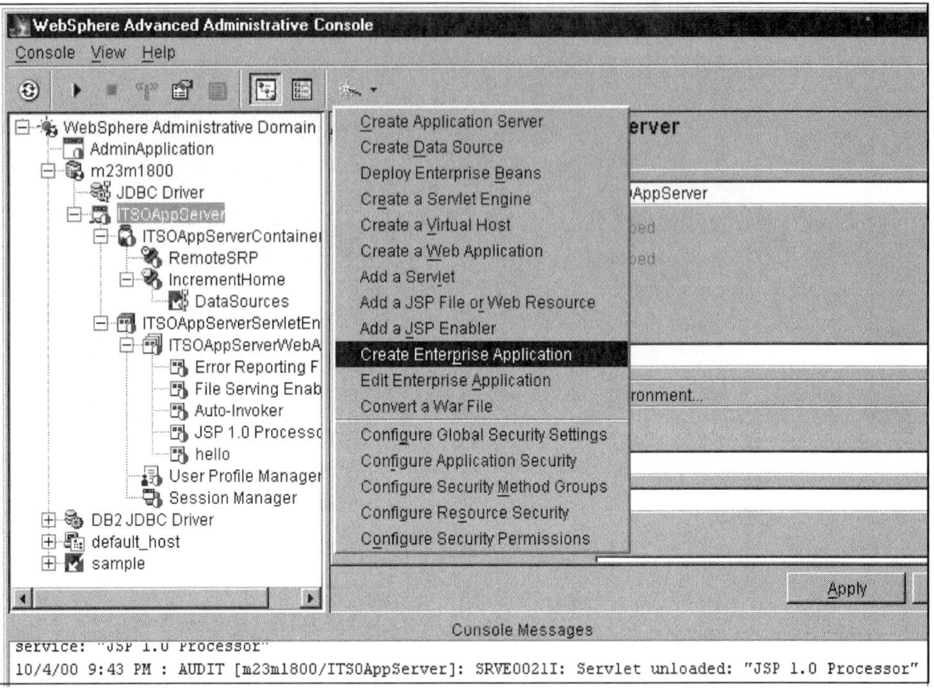

Figure 461. Creating an enterprise application

Specify ITSOApplication as the Enterprise Application Name as shown in Figure 462. Click **Next** to continue.

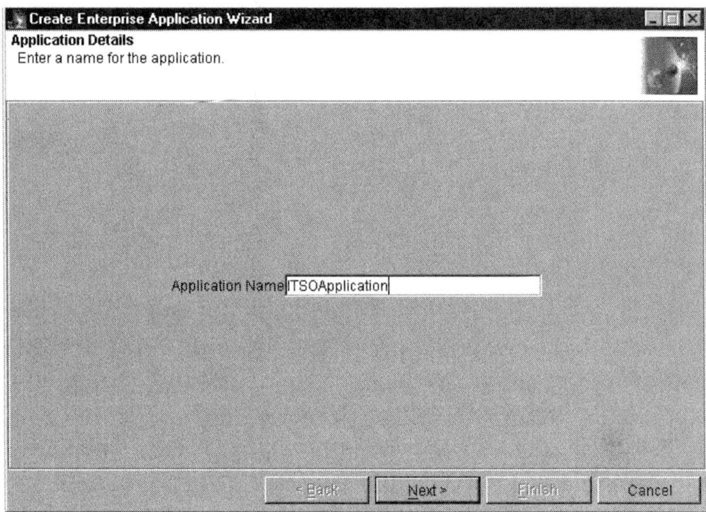

Figure 462. Creating an enterprise application: application details

Then we need to add one or more resources to the application in the next window, shown in Figure 463.

- Expand the EnterpriseBeans tree, put the cursor on the IncrementHome then click **Add** button.
- Expand the Web Applications tree, put the cursor on the ITSOAppServerWebApp then click **Add** button.

You may see the message `command "Application.addResource" completed successfully` in the administrative console.

After adding all the needed resources to the application, click **Next** to proceed.

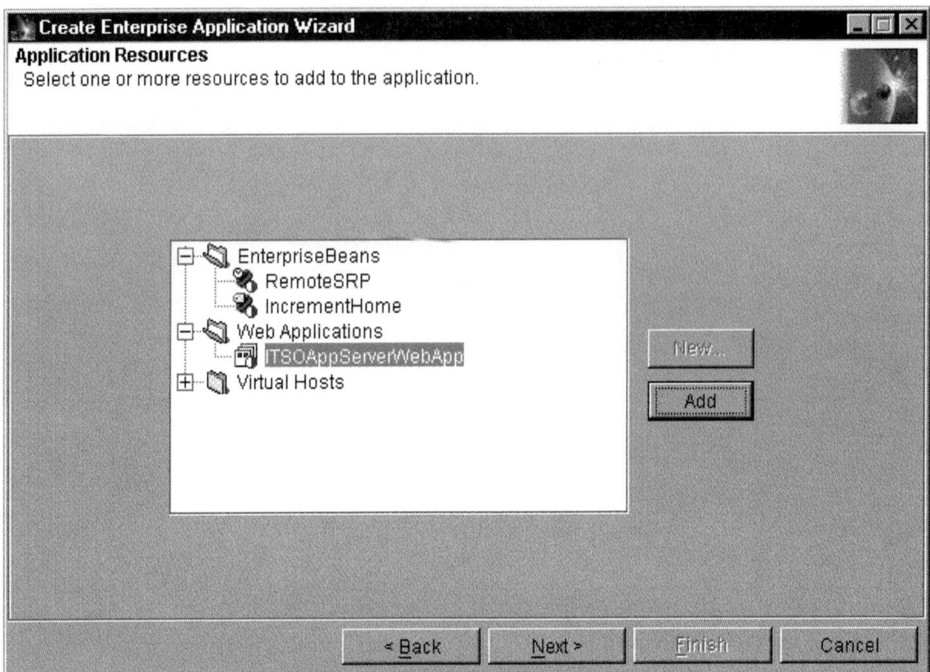

Figure 463. Creating an enterprise application: application resources #1

It is now possible to review those resources added to the application as shown in Figure 464 on page 619. If any resources are missing, click the **Back** button to return to the last panel. Equally, if any resources are not wanted, it is possible to remove them on this panel.

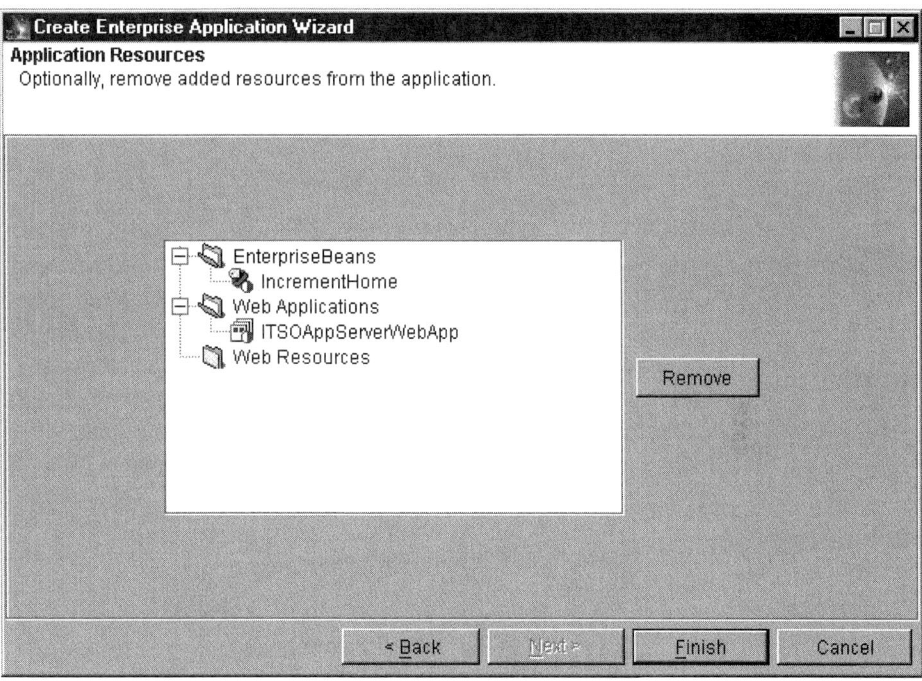

Figure 464. Creating an enterprise application: application resources #2

Click the **Finish** button to complete creating an enterprise application. After the message `command completed successfully`, you will see Enterprise Application "ITSOApplication" on the administrative console as shown in Figure 465 on page 620.

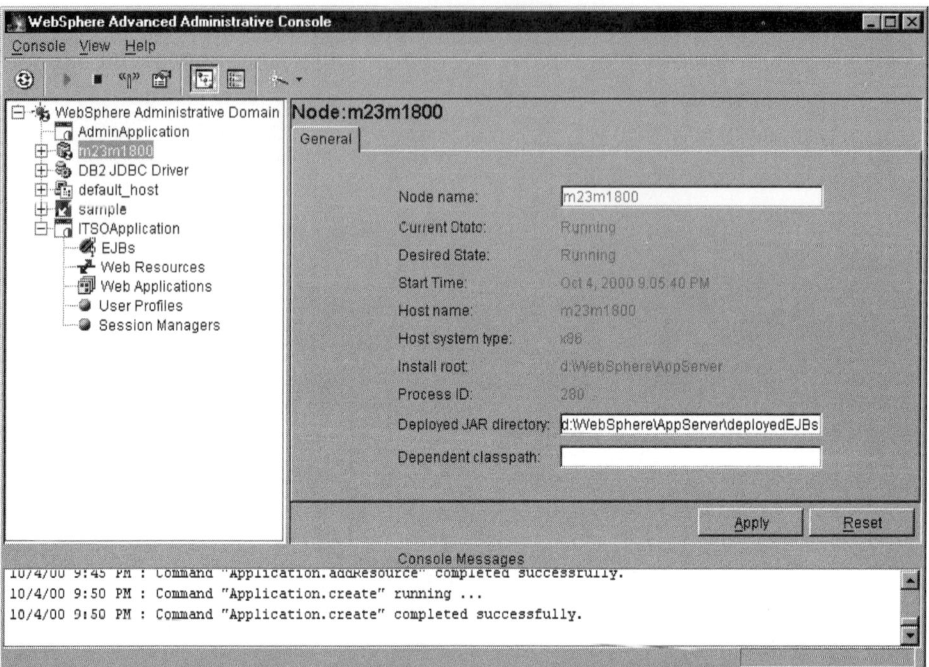

Figure 465. A newly created enterprise application

In the same administrative domain, we can add multiple resources into one application regardless if they are on different application servers or different nodes. However, it should be configured with the resources that must be available together and be used by a common set of users. In terms of security, there are security settings that apply to the whole application. All resources in the same application must use the same security settings, such as the challenge type. The administrator, therefore, must pay attention to how to organize the resources.

14.11 Verification of an enterprise application

To verify that an enterprise application works, right-click the **ITSOApplication** in the Topology viewer, then select **Start** as shown in Figure 466 on page 621. An information dialog box will inform you that the command completed successfully.

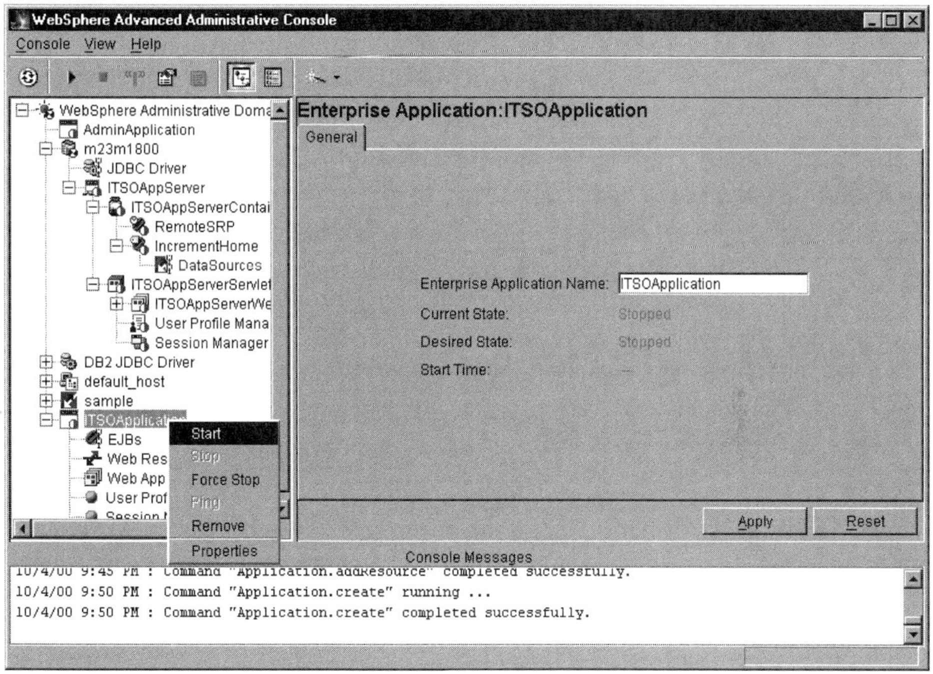

Figure 466. Starting an enterprise application

You may need to refresh the ITSOAppServer subtree to check if the resources in this enterprise application are running.

You could use the URLs in Verification 1 to check if the resources are working.

14.12 Deployment and classpaths

Now that we have seen how to deploy combinations of servlets and EJBs, we can consider a more complex deployment. Our intention is to explore the WebSphere classpaths using some concrete examples. We want to consider some special cases, each of which demonstrates a feature of the classpaths. The cases we will consider are:

1. Suppose that a servlet wishes to access an EJB running in the same application server. What classpath specifications are needed?
2. Suppose a servlet running in a different application server wants to access that same EJB. How does it access the classes it needs?

3. Suppose two EJBs, produced by two different development groups wish, as part of their implementation, to reference a common class. Where should that code be placed?
4. Suppose the same EJBs wish to reference the same class in their interface. What additional problems arise?

14.12.1 Classpaths and classloaders

Before considering our examples, here is a brief overview of the classpaths and classloaders we will encounter. You can find a more detailed explanation in the WebSphere InfoCenter.

14.12.1.1 The classpath test code

In order to illustrate the situation, we developed one interface and three classes.

The Messenger interface defines one interface method, doMessage(). The intent is that implementors of this interface should write out the supplied argument. This interface is shown in Figure 467.

```
package com.myCompany;

public interface Messenger {

   void doMessage(String message);

}
```

Figure 467. The Messenger interface

The first class, SimpleMessage implements an interface, Messenger. The doMessage() method is implemented to print a message using our own message logging class.

We use the logging class because it displays messages with date and time stamps and also gives an easy way to display the name of the class that is requesting the log to be written. The reason why we want to see this last piece of information will become apparent later.

The code for SimpleMessage is shown in Figure 468 on page 623. We will not go into detailed about how the logging classes work, it is sufficient to note that the call `log.Info("a string")` will display a suitably labelled string to standard out.

```
package com.myCompany;

import com.ibm.swservices.log.*;
public class SimpleMessage implements Messenger {
   private ILoggerFactory m_logFactory =
               Log.getLoggerFactory(getClass());

public void doMessage(String label)
{
   LocalLogger log = m_logFactory.getLocalLogger( "doMessage");

      log.info("Message is " + label);

}
}
```

Figure 468. The SimpleMessage class

The second class is the DynamicCaller. This class has one method that loads a specified class by name, creates an object of that class, casting it to type Messenger. It then calls the doMessage() method of the resulting object reference.

The purpose of the class is allow us to execute an application and verify the presence or absence of the desired class at run time. This allows us to demonstrate more clearly the classpaths and classloaders used by WebSphere.

The code for the DynamicCaller class is shown in Figure 469 on page 624. Note that the DynamicCaller traps any exception thrown by the attempt to create the requested class, so if the class cannot be found on the classpath we get a clear error message.

```
package com.myCompany;

import com.ibm.swservices.log.*;
public class DynamicCaller {
   private ILoggerFactory m_logFactory =
Log.getLoggerFactory(getClass());

public void doCall(String className)
{
   LocalLogger log = m_logFactory.getLocalLogger("doCall");


   log.entry("className = " + className);

   try {
      Class messengerClass = Class.forName(className);
      Messenger messenger = (Messenger)messengerClass.newInstance();
      messenger.doMessage("From dynamic caller");
   } catch (Exception problem ) {
      log.exception("Problem calling messenger", problem );
   }
}
}
```

Figure 469. The DynamicCaller class

Finally we developed a servlet whose doGet() method makes an instance of SimpleMessage and calls its doMessage() method, and then makes an instance of DynamicCaller and requests that DynamicCaller make an instance of SimpleMessage and also invoke the doMessage() method.

Figure 470 on page 625 shows the code for the servlet doGet() method.

```
public void doGet(HttpServletRequest req, HttpServletResponse res)
throws ServletException, IOException {
   res.setContentType("text/html");

   PrintWriter os = res.getWriter();
   os.println("<html>");
   os.println("<head><title>Demonstrating classpath</title></head>");
   os.println("<body>");


   os.println("In MyServlet");

   SimpleMessage theMessage = new SimpleMessage();
   theMessage.doMessage("From Servlet");

   DynamicCaller theCaller = new com.myCompany.DynamicCaller();
   theCaller.doCall("com.myCompany.SimpleMessage");


   os.println("</body></html>");
}
```

Figure 470. The servlet doGet() method

14.12.1.2 The Web application classpath

We created a Web application whose classpath was

```
C:\aFolderForWebApps\as4\se6\servlets
```

We enabled the Auto-Invoker servlet so that servlets classes would be loaded by name. We copied just the servlet code to the classpath, creating the necessary package subdirectories.

```
C:\aFolderForWebApps\as4\se6\servlets>dir /s /a-d

 Directory of C:\aFolderForWebApps\as4\se6\servlets\com\myCompany\servlet

10/17/2000  11:05p             1,299 MyServlet.class
               1 File(s)        1,299 bytes
```

Figure 471. Servlet class installed

We attempted to run this servlet by using a browser to request the URL:

```
http://localhost/webapp/wa8/servlet/com.myCompany.servlet.MyServlet
```

As expected this failed. We had not installed the other two classes or the logging library. The standard out log for the servlet engine showed the following error message:

```
 "com.myCompany.servlet.MyServlet"
      "Failed to load servlet"
      javax.servlet.ServletException: Servlet
[com.myCompany.servlet.MyServlet]: com.myCompany.servlet.MyServlet
was found, but is missing another required class.
This error typically implies that the servlet was originally compiled
with a classes which cannot be located by the server.
Check your classpath to ensure that all classes required by the servlet
are present.
```

Figure 472. Error message for missing class

You will notice that the error message does not indicate which class cannot be found. In the current situation we actually know the missing classes but usually we need to diagnose the problem.

To determine the missing class you can turn on verbose tracing for the JVM. To do this select the application server in the Topology tab and add the value `-verbose` to the command line arguments as shown in Figure 473 on page 627. Then click **Apply** and restart the application server to make the change effective.

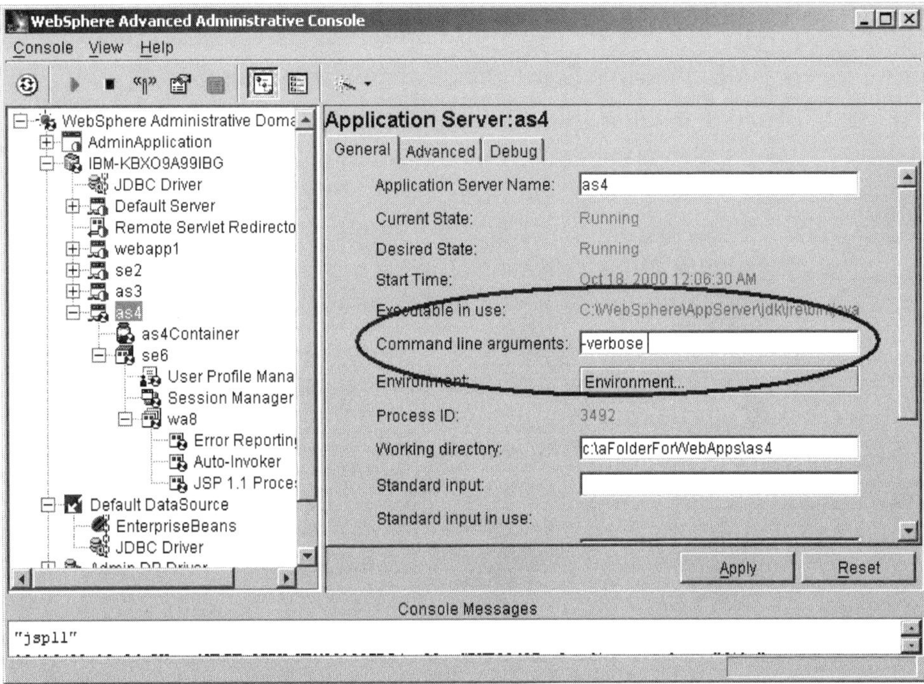

Figure 473. Setting verbose flag for an application server

After restarting the application server and resubmitting our request from the browser we now see additional information in the standard error file of the application server.

The verbose flag is well named. A great deal of output is produced. However, searching for the string *NoClassDefFoundError* quickly yielded the diagnostic we needed. Figure 474 shows the information that the missing class is

```
com.myCompany.SimpleMessage
```

```
[Signaling in VM: java/lang/NoClassDefFoundError, message:
com/myCompany/SimpleMessage]
    at com.myCompany.servlet.MyServlet.doGet(MyServlet.java)
    at javax.servlet.http.HttpServlet.service(HttpServlet.java:740)
    at javax.servlet.http.HttpServlet.service(HttpServlet.java:853)
```

Figure 474. Missing class identification in standard error

We now needed to add the missing classes to the classpath. As a first step we created two JAR files, one containing our own classes, the other containing the logging library. We simply copied these two JAR files to the servlets directory of the Web application.

You should note two things about this procedure:

1. It is not necessary to adjust the classpath for the Web application. All JAR files placed in any directory in the Web application classpath are automatically added to the classpath.

   Furthermore, as Auto-loading is enabled, we do not even need to restart the Web application. The Web application classpath is special in these respects. Other classpaths we will discuss later do not have these special facilities.

2. This dynamic approach to deployment is very useful in development situations. However, we do not recommend this approach as a production deployment technique.

   First, because classes such as the logging library will probably be used by many Web applications, they should be placed in some shared classpath, rather than in a classpath specific to one Web application.

   Secondly, auto-loading is probably inappropriate for a controlled production environment where it should be unusual to deploy new classes in a gradual manner.

Having deployed all the required classes, we resubmitted the request from the browser and got the expected response in the browser as shown in Figure 475.

Figure 475. Response to servlet request

More interesting is the output that appears in the Application Server standard out. This is shown in Figure 476 on page 629.

```
Tue Oct 17 22:56:32 GMT+01:00 2000
com.myCompany.SimpleMessage doMessage()
Message is From Servlet

Tue Oct 17 22:56:32 GMT+01:00 2000
com.myCompany.DynamicCaller doCall()
className = com.myCompany.SimpleMessage

Tue Oct 17 22:56:32 GMT+01:00 2000
com.myCompany.SimpleMessage doMessage()
Message is From dynamic caller
```

Figure 476. Application server standard out

Each entry in the output has three parts: the timestamp, the class and method producing the entry, and the text of the entry itself. In the figure each of these three elements appears on a separate line.

As expected we see three messages:

1. The SimpleMessage class producing text in response to the Servlet's request.
2. The DynamicCaller stating which class is to be instantiated by name, in this case another instance of SimpleMessage.
3. The second SimpleMessage object producing the message at the request of the dynamic caller.

So far the behavior is unsurprising but we will now begin to show how minor adjustments to the classpath will produce less obvious results.

14.12.2 The application server classpath

We noted earlier that we do not recommend that you should place all classes on the Web application classpath. Instead we want to put them on the classpath for the application server. We do this by adding a classpath command line argument to the application server.

First we created a suitable directory for these non-servlet "helper" classes, and then removed the logging library and our application JARs from the Web application servlets directory and placed them in the new directory. Figure 477 on page 630 shows the directory contents.

```
C:\aFolderForWebApps\as4>dir /s /-a d lib

 Directory of C:\aFolderForWebApps\as4\lib

10/17/2000  11:33p      <DIR>          .
10/17/2000  11:33p      <DIR>          ..
10/15/2000  10:23p              99,302 SwServices.jar
10/17/2000  11:44p               1,848 myCompany.jar
               2 File(s)        101,150 bytes

     Total Files Listed:
               2 File(s)        101,150 bytes
               2 Dir(s)  10,501,046,272 bytes free
```

Figure 477. Application server helper class JARs

We then used to the administrative console to set the classpath by selecting the application server and entering the classpath as shown in Figure 478.

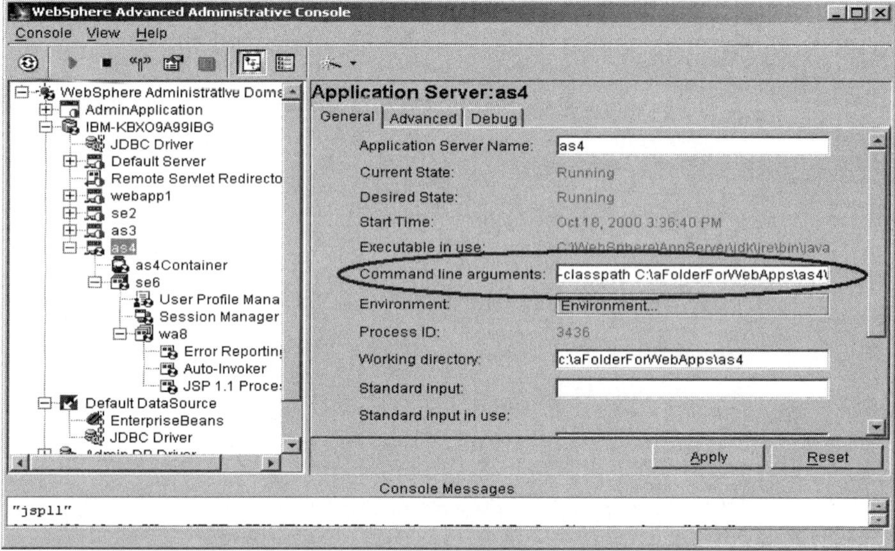

Figure 478. Setting the application server classpath

Unlike when adding JARs to the Web application classpath, we need to explicitly reference the two JARs we want to add. The string that we need to type is long and the area available is small, so editing is troublesome. We find it easier to assemble long command line arguments in a text editor and then cut and paste into the entry field.

The value we entered is shown in Figure 479 on page 631.

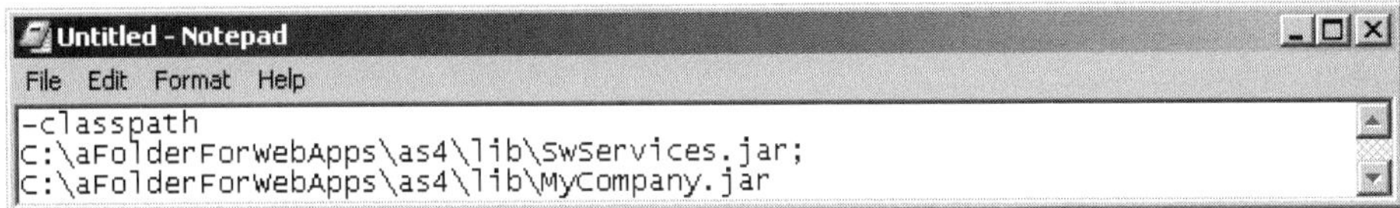

Figure 479. Creating the command line arguments in Notepad

You should note that we split actual command line into three separate lines so that it could be seen completely in the figure. Before cutting and pasting we reassembled it into one long line.

Also notice that when assembling the classpaths we did not leave any spaces between the semi-colon (;) separator and the surrounding paths. If you do leave such a space you will see the error symptom shown in Figure 480.

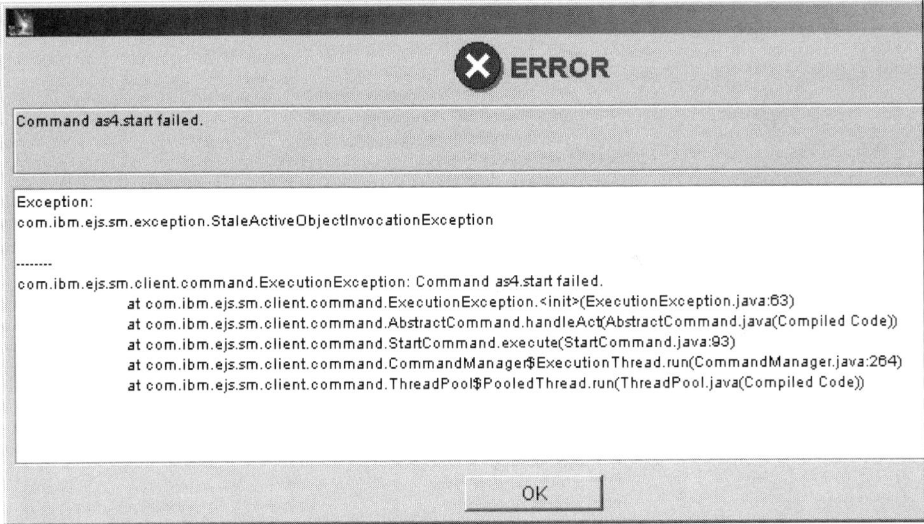

Figure 480. Symptom of syntactic error in classpath

The exception StaleActiveObjectInvocationException may not be immediately suggestive of your having left a space in your command line options.

Having updated the text field we then clicked **Apply** and restarted the application server. We then resubmitted our request and, as expected our application ran as before producing the same successful output we saw in Figure 475 on page 628 and Figure 476 on page 629.

14.12.3 The classloader effect

Now we made one small change and our application ceased to function.

Suppose that your application were more substantial than our cut-down example. It is quite possible that one development team might deliver the interface definition Messenger and the class DynamicCaller that can operate on any class implementing the interface. A completely different team might deliver the SimpleMessage implementation of Messenger.

We simulated such a scenario by creating a version of our MyCompany.jar that contained only the Messenger and DynamicCaller classes. We replaced our previously installed, complete JAR with this reduced version.

Now when we attempt to execute our servlet we get the expected error due to the missing SimpleMessage class.

So now we want to deploy the SimpleMessage class. We copied the class file to the correct package structure in the Web Application classpath.

```
C:\aFolderForWebApps\as4\se6\servlets>dir /s /-a d
.
D
 Directory of C:\aFolderForWebApps\as4\se6\servlets\com\myCompany

10/17/2000  11:05p      <DIR>          .
10/17/2000  11:05p      <DIR>          ..
10/17/2000  11:05p      <DIR>          servlet
10/18/2000  03:02p                 915 SimpleMessage.class
               1 File(s)            915 bytes

 Directory of C:\aFolderForWebApps\as4\se6\servlets\com\myCompany\servlet

10/17/2000  11:05p      <DIR>          .
10/17/2000  11:05p      <DIR>          ..
10/17/2000  11:05p               1,299 MyServlet.class
               1 File(s)          1,299 bytes

     Total Files Listed:
               2 File(s)          2,214 bytes
              11 Dir(s)  10,481,795,072 bytes free
```

Figure 481. Helper class in the Web application classpath

You can seen the two class files in the Web application classpath in Figure 481.

Now when we attempt to run the servlet it does appear to work, the browser shows a successful execution as in Figure 475 on page 628. However when we examine the standard out file we see a problem. Compare the result we got from a successful execution as shown in Figure 476 on page 629 with the output shown in Figure 482.

```
Tue Oct 17 23:45:53 GMT+01:00 2000
com.myCompany.SimpleMessage doMessage
Message is From Servlet

Tue Oct 17 23:45:53 GMT+01:00 2000
com.myCompany.DynamicCaller doCall
className = com.myCompany.SimpleMessage

Tue Oct 17 23:45:53 GMT+01:00 2000
com.myCompany.DynamicCaller doCall
Exception: Problem calling messenger java.lang.ClassNotFoundException:
com.myCompany.SimpleMessage
```

Figure 482. Unexpected ClassNotFound Exception

In the new figure we see, as expected, the servlet create an instance of SimpleMessage and the instance generates the required output. However, we then see the DynamicCaller, running in the same JVM, fail to instantiate a second instance of the same class, with a ClassNotFoundException.

14.12.3.1 The classloader hierarchy

To understand this seemingly inconsistent behavior we need consider not only the classpaths we have configured but also the class loaders used by WebSphere.

We have already mentioned that the classpaths for the application server and Web application behave differently. The former is static, and we specify JAR files explicitly. The latter can auto-reload changed classes and will use any JAR file in the specified directory. Behind the scenes WebSphere achieves this effect by using different classloaders.

Before we discuss the WebSphere classloader, we describe the J2SE classloader. When the JVM needs to load a new class for an application, it searches for and loads the class in the following locations, in order:

1. Bootstrap classes: Classes that comprise the Java platform, including the classes in <JAVA_HOME>/jre/lib/rt.jar and i18n.jar.
2. Extension classes: Classes that use the Java Extension mechanism. These are bundled as .jar files located in the extensions directory.

3. User classes: Classes defined by developers and third parties such as WebSphere that do not take advantage of the extension mechanism.

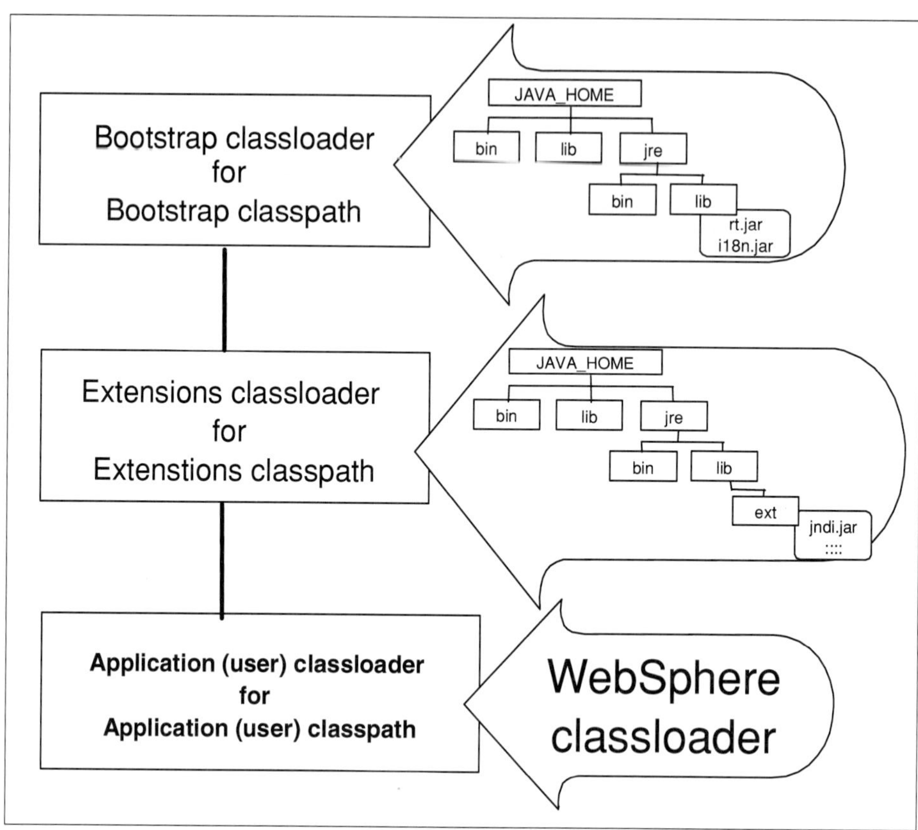

Figure 483. Hierarchy of J2SE classloaders

There are three types of WebSphere classloader:

1. The primordial classloader uses the application server classpath. (Note that this classpath contains both the directories and JAR files you specify as command line arguments and some more that we will discuss later.)
2. The EJB JAR classloader. We have yet to bring EJBs into this discussion, but it might be expected that the EJB JARs would need special treatment because you are able to add an EJB without restarting the application server.
3. The Web application classloader, this is sometimes called the Power classloader. This classloader uses the Web application classpath. So if your application server has more than one Web application you have more one Power classloader for each Web application.

These classloaders are arranged in a hierarchy, as shown in Figure 484.

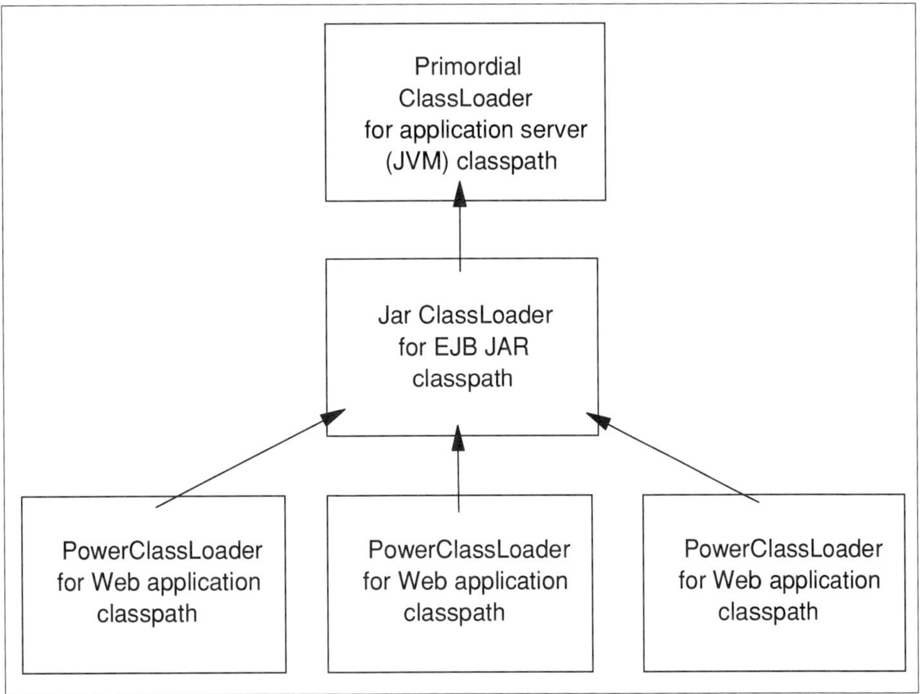

Figure 484. Hierarchy of WebSphere classloaders

14.12.3.2 The problem explained

This hierarchy has several important effects:

1. Each class we load is loaded by one classloader. Any class can use only classes loaded by its own classloader or its classloader's parents. For example, a class loaded by an EJB classloader cannot see classes loaded by the Web application classloaders.
2. Each classloader will always ask its parent for classes that should be loaded, and they in turn will ask their parents. Only if a class is not available to a parent classloader will the classloader itself load the class.

   This treatment ensures that system classes loaded by the JVM classloader cannot be replaced or hidden by newer versions introduced higher up the hierarchy.
3. Each Web application is insulated from the others. Classes loaded by the classloader in one Web application are not available to other Web applications.

We can now understand why our application failed.

- The servlet is in the Web application classpath and so was loaded by a Powerloader.
- The servlet needed the SimpleMessage class and so the Powerloader asked its parents for it. No parent had SimpleMessage available, so the Powerloader found it in its classpath and loaded it.
- The servlet needed the DynamicCaller class and so the Powerloader asked its parents. The JVM loader had DynamicCaller available and so loaded this class, making it available to all its children.
- The DynamicCaller needed the SimpleMessage class and asked the JVM loader for it. The JVM loader does not have SimpleMessage in its classpath and cannot ask its children. So we get the ClassNotFound message.

14.12.3.3 Conclusions

It is important to understand that this simple example represents the kinds of problems that occur in realistic situations. The crucial element of the problem is the dependencies between the classes. The problem was caused by installing classes in classloaders in a way that did not reflect the class dependencies.

The loading of classes by name was introduced only to make the problem occur at run time; it is not the cause of the problem.

The conclusion is that we need to take considerable care in deciding which classes are deployed in which JAR files. As a rule of thumb we prefer to keep our servlet and EJB JARs small and move helper classes to separate JARs that we deploy on the application server classpath using the JVM loader.

We will see how this general approach applies to our deployment scenarios in the following sections.

14.12.4 Servlet accessing a local EJB

We constructed a simple stateless session EJB and a servlet to act as a client of the EJB.

14.12.4.1 The test code

The EJB was named *MyFirst*. It has a single method in its remote interface: getMessage(). We show the interface and implementation in Figure 485 on page 637 and Figure 486 on page 637 respectively.

```
package com.myCompany.ejb;

public interface MyFirst extends javax.ejb.EJBObject {

   java.lang.String getMessage() throws java.rmi.RemoteException;

}
```

Figure 485. EJB remote interface

```
public String getMessage() {
   return "A string from the EJB";
}
```

Figure 486. EJB method implementation

The MyEjbInvoker servlet accesses the EJB using a VisualAge for Java-generated Access Bean. Although the use of Access Beans is not mandatory we believe that they save unnecessary work, and since they are used widely we want to describe the classpath issues that arise when you use them.

Figure 487 on page 638 shows the code for the servlet's doGet() method.

```
public void doGet(HttpServletRequest req, HttpServletResponse res)
throws ServletException, IOException {
   res.setContentType("text/html");

   PrintWriter os = res.getWriter();
   os.println("<html>");
   os.println("<head><title>Demonstrating nothing</title></head>");
   os.println("<body>");

   try {

   com.myCompany.ejb.MyFirstAccessBean ab
         = new com.myCompany.ejb.MyFirstAccessBean();

      String theMessage = ab.getMessage();

   os.println("The invoker got this message: "
                    + theMessage + "<BR>");

   } catch ( Exception e ) {
      os.println("Exception <BR>" + e + "<BR>");
   }

   os.println("</body></html>");
}
```

Figure 487. The doGet() method for the MyEjbInvoker servlet

We created a JAR file for the EJB and add it to the EJB container as described earlier in this chapter. Then we copied the servlet class file to the Web application classpath.

14.12.4.2 Classpath adjustment

Our servlet needs three things on its classpath in order to execute.

The EJB clients stubs

The stubs are generated when the EJB is deployed. If you examine the JAR file you will find class files such as _MyFirst_Stub.class. These classes are immediately available to our servlet because the EJB classloader has loaded the EJB JAR when we added the EJB to the container. You will recall from Figure 484 on page 635 that the Web application classloader will request classes from its parent the EJB loader.

The MyFirstAccessBean code

The Access Bean class is generated by VisualAge for Java. It seems clear that, because any Web application might wish to use the Access Bean, then code should not be placed in any one Web application classpath.

We also note that if the EJB interface were to change, then the Access Bean will also need to be regenerated and re-released. We therefore decided to put the Access Bean into the EJB JAR. By default, when exporting an EJB deployable JAR, VisualAge for Java does not include the Access Bean. It is a trivial matter to add this extra class when exporting the EJB.

Figure 488 shows the contents of our JAR file.

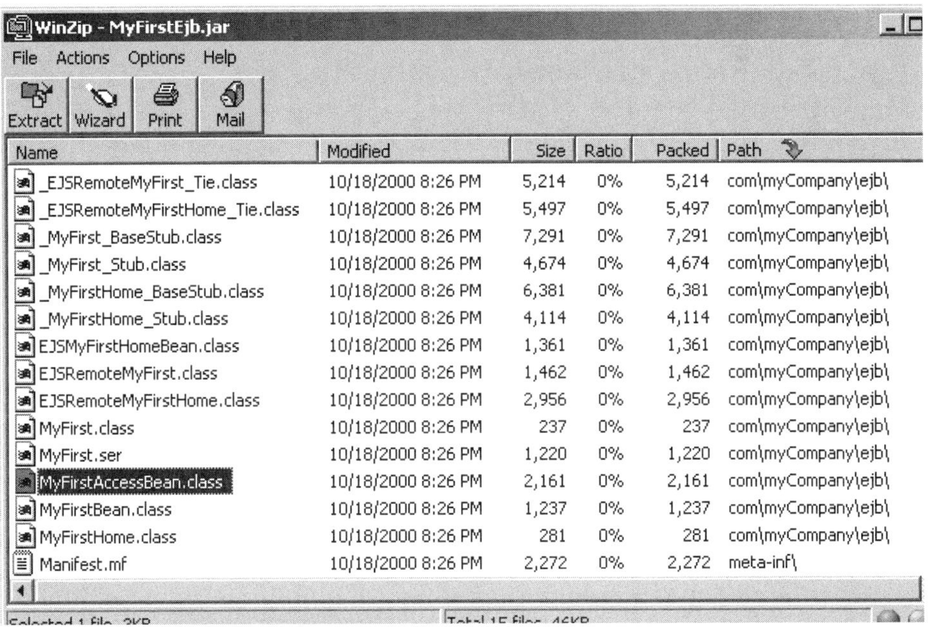

Figure 488. EJB JAR contents, with Access Bean

The generic Access Bean classes

Our EJB-specific Access Bean, MyFirstAccessBean, uses some generic code provided by VisualAge for Java. The WebSphere installation includes this code in the JAR file:

```
C:\WebSphereAppServer\lib\ivjejb35.jar
```

We need to add this JAR to a suitable class path.

It should be clear that this needs to be added to a classpath whose classloader is accessible to the EJB loader. So we choose to add the JAR to the application server classpath. We do this by adjusting the command line arguments for the application server JVM in the way we described in 14.12.2, "The application server classpath" on page 629.

For this example we are using only this one new JAR file and so we set the command line argument to

```
-classpath C:\WebSphereAppServer\lib\ivjejb35.jar
```

14.12.4.3 Execution

We used a browser to request the URL:

```
http://localhost/webapp/wa8/servlet/com.myCompany.servlet.MyEjbInvoker
```

The result is shown in Figure 489.

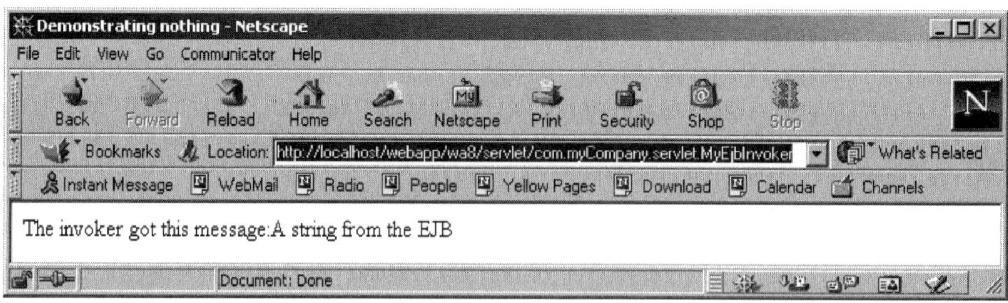

Figure 489. Invoking the EJB

14.12.5 Servlet access to a remote EJB

WebSphere has optimizations to improve performance when EJBs and their client servlets are co-located in the same application server. However, it is likely that there will be situations where the EJBs and servlets must be in separate locations.

For example responsibility for developing and deploying some EJBs may be partitioned on departmental lines. It could still be entirely reasonable for servlets running in one department's environment to use an EJB provided by another. We consider that kind of situation in this section.

14.12.5.1 Test scenario

We created a second application server similar to the first. It differed in two respects:

1. We set the Web application Web path to /webapp/client.

2. We did not deploy our EJB into this application server.

We copied the MyEjbInvoker servlet to the Web application classpath. Then, immediately, before making any class path adjustments, we attempted to run the servlet.

As expected this failed, because the Access Bean class could not be loaded.

14.12.5.2 The client JAR

We have already established that the deployed EJB JAR file, when enriched with the Access Bean, would provide everything the client needs. However, it does not seem desirable that the client of the EJB should have access to implementation details.

For this reason we suggest using an EJBClient JAR. If you are using VisualAge for Java then there are facilities to export a client JAR, and by default the client JAR does include the Access Bean. If you are not using VisualAge for Java, these are the classes we need in a client JAR:

- MyFirstAccessBean.class
- MyFirst.class
- MyFirstHome.class
- _MyFIrst_BaseStub.class
- _MyFIrst_Stub.class
- _MyFIrstHome_BaseStub.class
- _MyFIrstHome_Stub.class

In addition to the AccessBean, we see the interfaces for the bean and its home and the local stubs for the bean and home.

14.12.5.3 Classpath

We set the classpath for the application server to include the client JAR and the generic access bean JAR that we used earlier. We did this by setting the application server command line arguments to include the string

```
-classpath C:\WebSphereAppServer\lib\ivjejb35.jar;
C:\mylib\MyEjbClient.jar
```

Note that this string is entered unbroken, with no spaces around the semi-colon (;) as described in 14.12.1.2, “The Web application classpath” on page 625.

14.12.5.4 Execution

We used a browser to request the URL:

```
http://localhost/webapp/client/servlet/com.myCompany.servlet.MyEjbInvoker
```

The result was exactly as before, as shown in Figure 489 on page 640.

14.12.6 EJBs with shared implementation helper classes

It is very likely that you will factor out implementation code for your EJBs into separate classes. We will refer to these classes as *"helper classes".*

In small-scale development, where a single team produces a single JAR containing all EJBs, it may seem natural to include the helper classes in the EJB JAR. This will work, and makes for very simple deployment.

However, when the same helper classes are needed in more than one EJB JAR then a different approach is needed. It seems unwise to create dependencies between EJB JAR files, so that EJBs in one JAR file require implementation classes from another. Such an approach does not lend itself to flexible deployment; it is difficult to deploy chosen sub-sets of EJBs to different servers. It also creates configuration management problems if different teams are producing different JAR files.

Our approach is to factor out the helper classes into one or more JAR files and add these JARs to the application server classpath. The EJB JAR contains only the EJBs themselves and the classes created when deploying the EJB; the same set of classes are shown in Figure 488 on page 639.

14.12.7 EJBs with shared interface classes

Finally, we consider the case of classes that appear in the interface of your EJBs. For example, it is quite common for a remote method of an EJB to take as an argument an instance of a JavaBean.

14.12.7.1 The test scenario

Suppose that we define a JavaBean that represents the state of a Person. As a simplified example, consider the Bean shown in Figure 490 on page 643.

```
package com.myCompany;

public class MyPersonBean implements java.io.Serializable{
   private java.lang.String fieldName = new String();
   private int fieldGrade = 0;

public MyPersonBean() {
   super();
}

public int getGrade() {
   return fieldGrade;
}

public java.lang.String getName() {
   return fieldName;
}

public void setGrade(int grade) {
   fieldGrade = grade;
}

public void setName(java.lang.String name) {
   fieldName = name;
}

}
```

Figure 490. Example JavaBean

It may be reasonable to express the interface to an EJB in terms of such a bean. Arguably, it is preferable to have a coarse-grained method operating on a bean then fine-grain methods operating on individual data items. This is because each EJB method call is potentially a remote call, and for good performance we should aim to reduce the number of remote method calls.

So we add a method operating on a MyPersonBean object to our EJB. This method is shown in Figure 491 on page 644.

```
public String tellPerson(MyPersonBean who) {
   return who.getName();
}
```

Figure 491. EJB Method with JavaBean as parameter

We adjusted our servlet to use this method, as shown in Figure 492.

```
public void doGet(HttpServletRequest req, HttpServletResponse res)
throws ServletException, IOException {
   res.setContentType("text/html");

   PrintWriter os = res.getWriter();
   os.println("<html>");
   os.println("<head><title>Demonstrating nothing</title></head>");
   os.println("<body>");

   try {
   com.myCompany.ejb.MyFirstAccessBean ab
         = new com.myCompany.ejb.MyFirstAccessBean();

   MyPersonBean person = new MyPersonBean();
   person.setName("Shusaku");
   person.setGrade(9);

   String theMessage = ab.tellPerson(person);

   os.println("The invoker got this message: "
                        + theMessage + "<BR>");

   } catch ( Exception e ) {
      os.println("Exception <BR>" + e + "<BR>");
   }

      os.println("</body></html>");
}
```

Figure 492. Servlet invoking EJB with JavaBean parameter

In order to prove that the EJB and servlet work correctly we redeployed them to our application server. We created a new deployed EJB JAR containing the EJB classes and, as before, the Access Bean class. We also included the JavaBean class for MyPersonBean.

It should be clear that this “all-in-one” approach to deploying the EJB is not our recommended approach for realistic applications. Figure 493 shows the contents of the JAR. The JavaBean is the first entry.

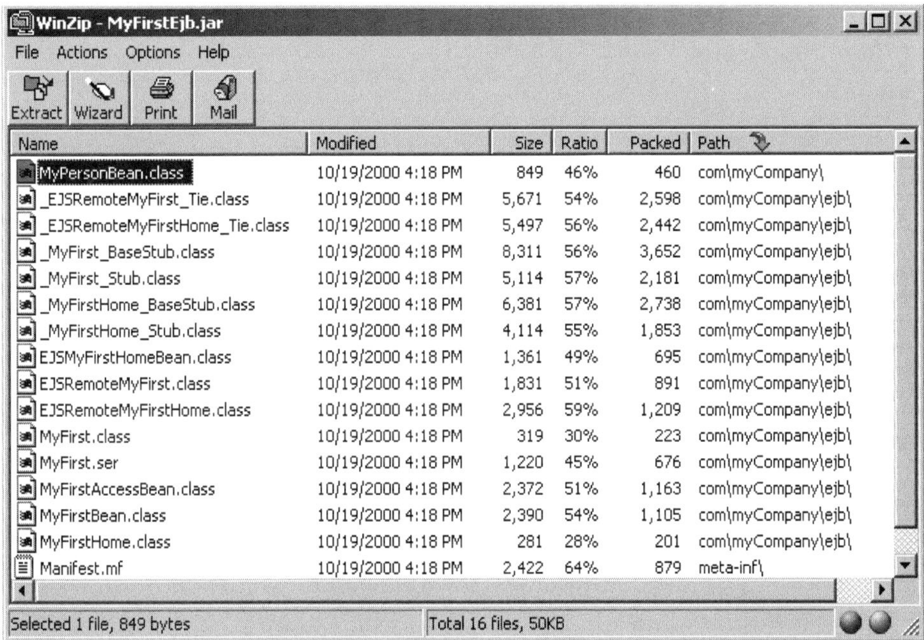

Figure 493. EJB JAR including interface class

We deployed the JAR and servlet class as before and then used a browser to invoke the servlet. The servlet ran successfully, obtaining the MyPersonBean class from the EJB JAR, and produced the output shown in Figure 494.

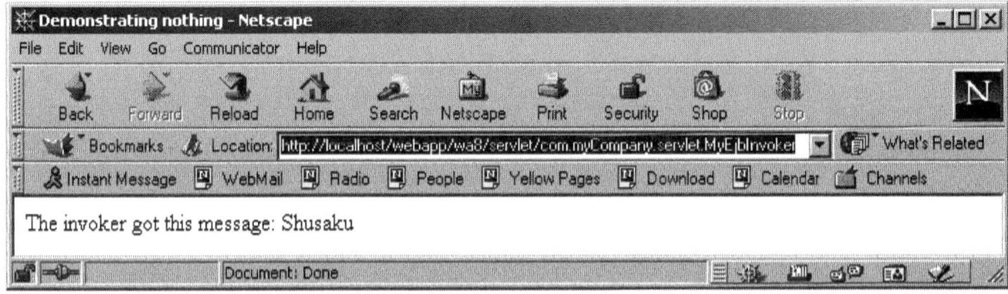

Figure 494. Invoking the EJB using a JavaBean

14.12.7.2 Separating the interface classes

Now we can consider a preferred location for the MyPersonBean class. It seems likely that a JavaBean such as this would be used by more than one

EJB. By the same argument that we used in 14.12.6, “EJBs with shared implementation helper classes” on page 642, it seems best to move the implementation class to a separate JAR file. It will then be available to any EJBs that need it and can be deployed independently of any specific EJB.

So, we create a new JAR file. We will call it MyInterface.jar, and in this JAR we have just the MyPersonBean.class. You can see the contents in Figure 495.

WinZip - MyInterface.jar

File Actions Options Help

Extract Wizard Print Mail

Name	Modified	Size	Ratio	Packed	Path
MyPersonBean.class	10/19/2000 4:57 PM	567	0%	567	com\myCompany\
Manifest.mf	10/19/2000 4:57 PM	25	0%	25	meta-inf\

Selected 0 files, 0 bytes   Total 2 files, 592 bytes

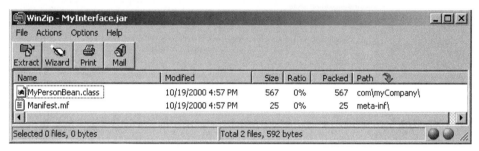

Figure 495. Interface JAR containing MyPersonBean.class

We also recreate the EJB JAR file so that it no longer contained the MyPersonBean class; so it now is reverted to the state shown in Figure 488 on page 639.

We add the interface JAR to the application server classpath. You can see the classpath option we needed in Figure 496. Again, we have broken the line of text for clarity in the figure; when pasting into the administrative console we reassemble the line.

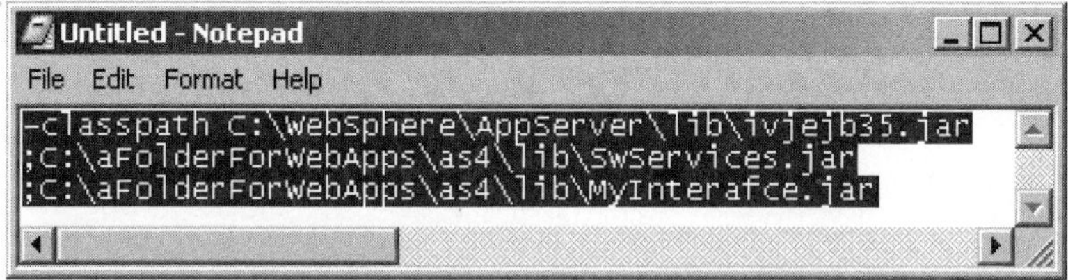

Figure 496. Application server classpath with EJB interface JAR

14.12.7.3 Creating the EJB

We remove the EJB from our EJB container because we want to explore the various steps in deploying the EJB.

So we use the administrative console to take the EJB JAR and create the EJB in our container. We select our EJB container and right-click **Create EJB** then we click **Browse** and select our JAR.

This gives an error as shown in Figure 497.

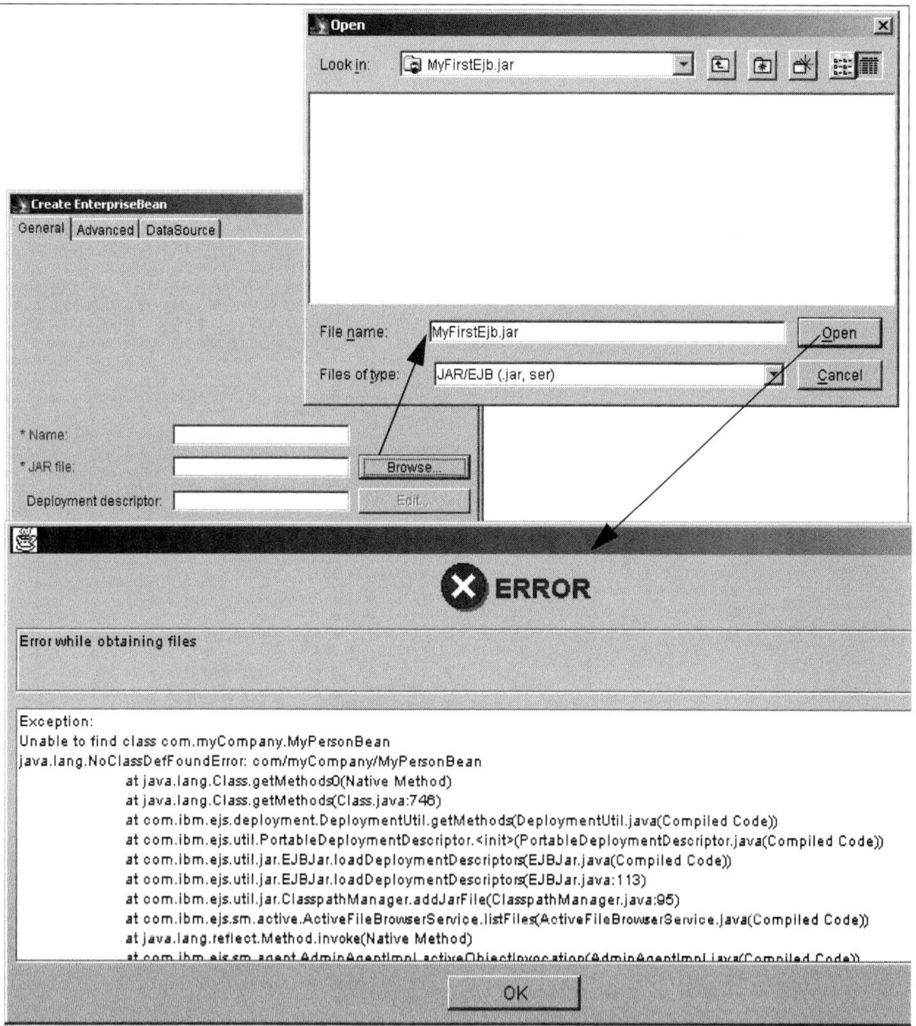

Figure 497. Failure to create EJB with dependent class in interface

The error message indicates that the MyPersonBean is not found. And yet we have already added it to the application server classpath.

14.12.7.4 The node dependent class path

The reason for this error is that it is not the application server that is actually performing the EJB creation we are requesting. It is, in fact, the administrative server. Remember that the administrative console is a client of the administrative server. At EJB creation time the administrative server needs to see all classes in the EJB interface. So we need to make MyInterface.jar available to the administrative server. We do this by setting the *dependent classpath*.

This classpath is set, through the administrative console, by selecting the node on which you intend to create the EJB. You will then see the data entry field for the classpath as shown in Figure 498.

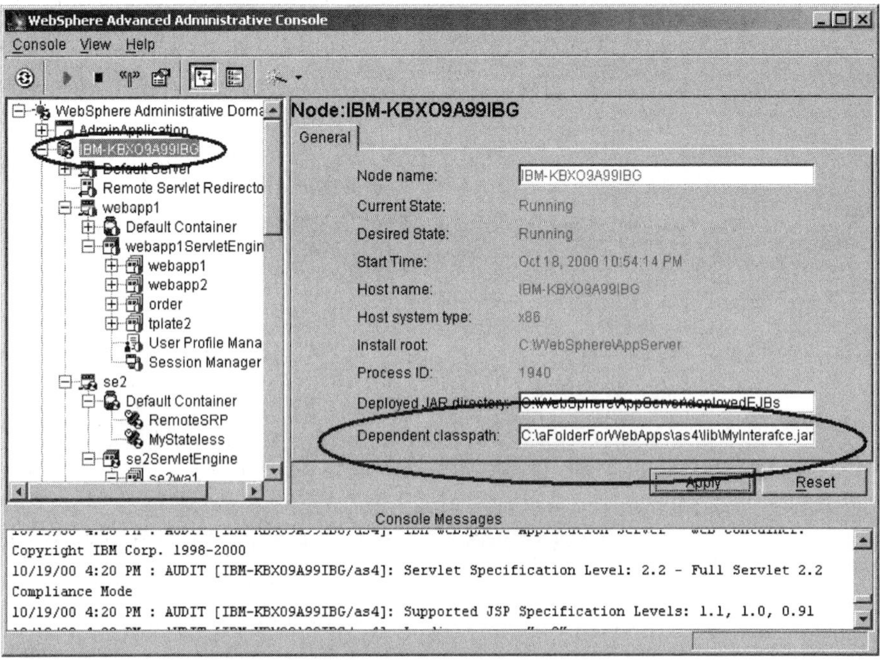

Figure 498. Setting the dependent classpath

We enter the full path of the MyInterface.jar JAR file and clicked **Apply**. It is not necessary to restart the node.

We can now create the EJB and our application executed correctly as before.

14.12.7.5 Dependent classpath or application server classpath

We now have found that we can put the MyInterface.jar file onto two different classpaths: the dependent classpath and the application server classpath.

This begs the question: under what conditions should we use these classpaths?

It turns out that there is no entirely satisfactory answer to the question. We find:

- Classes on the dependent classpath are visible to all Web applications. So our EJBs can use MyInterface.jar, but so can all other EJBs in all other application servers.
- The dependent classes are loaded into the application server by the EJB loader. So only classes loaded by the EJB loader (for example the EJB) and the Powerloader (for example servlets) can use them.

These two facts present problems if we attempt to use interface classes from the dependent classpath. Table 40 shows three application servers, all running in one WebSphere administrative domain in the same node.

Table 40. Class loader problem

Loaded by	App Server 1	App Server 2	App Server 3
Power loader	Servlet	Servlet	Servlet
EJB loader	EJB		EJB V2
	Interface JAR	Interface JAR	**Interface JAR V2 problem: cannot co-exist with other version**
JVM loader	Helper JAR	**EJB Client JAR Problem: cannot access interface**	

The two problems are:

1. The EJB client JARs loaded by the JVM loader cannot access the interface classes loaded by the EJB loader.
2. The third application server attempts to load a different version of the same EJB, or an EJB that needs a different version of the same interface. As the dependent classpath is common to all application servers, there is a clash because we cannot load two different versions of the same class.

We therefore have adopted the practice of temporarily placing the interface classes on the dependent classpath just while we create the EJB. Then we remove the interface class from the dependent class path and add it to each application server classpath as needed.

14.12.8 Summary of JARs and classpaths

We can now summarize the various JAR files that might be produced by a large-scale development, and the classpaths to which they should be added.

Table 41. JAR files and deployment

JAR Type	Contents	Deployment
EJB JAR	EJB implementation, deployment generated code, Access Beans	Added by EJB creation process
Servlet JAR	Servlet code only	Copy to Web application classpath
EJB Client JAR	EJB interface and stubs, Access Bean	Add to application server classpath if EJB not to be run in Server
Helper JAR	Shared implementation classes	Add to application server classpath
Interface JAR	Shared EJB interface classes	Temporarily added to dependent classpath at EJB creation time, then application server classpaths

We then have three common deployment patterns shown in Table 42.

Table 42. Deployable combinations

	EJB and client servlet	EJB Server	Client
EJB JAR	Yes	Yes	
Servlet JAR	Yes		Yes
EJB Client JAR			Yes
Helper JAR	Yes	Yes	
Interface JAR	Yes	Yes	Yes

From this we can deduce possible deliverable packages from different development teams.

Chapter 15. WebSphere security

Security is a very important, complex and broad subject. This statement is true not only in the general sense, but also as it applies to WebSphere Application Server. Due to space, time and resource considerations, it is impossible to provide a complete discussion of WebSphere security in this redbook. Instead, we present some introductory topics needed to establish a baseline for understanding WebSphere security, followed by a detailed discussion of a single specific topic selected due to its importance relative to WebSphere V3.5.

This chapter begins with a short overview of the WebSphere security architecture and implementation. The overview is followed by a discussion of what is new in WebSphere Version 3.5. One of the items that is essentially new with WebSphere V3.5 is certificate-based authentication. This is the item that is discussed in detail. The discussion includes the use of the IBM SecureWay Directory as the LDAP server, includes a section on certificate management and, finally, includes a detailed description of how to specify the use of certificates to WebSphere.

15.1 Application security

For the purposes of the discussion in this section, the term application means a collection of Web resources (HTML, images, JSPs, servlets, EJBs, etc.) that provides some function for a client request. Application security refers to the policies that support access to those resources by potential users. Application security does not include such topics as network security (firewalls), intrusion detection and computer viruses; hence those topics will not be addressed in this document.

15.1.1 Authentication

Authentication is a component of an application security policy. It is the process of determining that a user (or process) really is who they say they are. This is usually done with some sort of user ID/password lookup scheme or a certificate.

15.1.2 Authorization

Authorization is also a component of an application security policy. It is the process of determining if a user has rights to use a secured resource in some way. For example, the right to invoke a method on an EJB or access a particular HTML page, servlet or JSP.

15.1.3 Delegation

Delegation is another component of an application security policy. It is the process of forwarding a user's credentials along with the cascaded downstream requests that occur within the context of work that the user either originated or is having performed on his/her behalf.

15.1.4 Trust

Decisions on who or what to trust also help make up an application security policy. Ultimately, in a security policy, something must be judged to be trustworthy, be it a user registry that contains user names and passwords or a Certificate Authority that issues certificates.

15.2 WebSphere security model

The WebSphere security model incorporates all the components of application security discussed in 15.1, "Application security" on page 651. Our overview discussion of WebSphere security in this redbook will concentrate on the authentication and authorization components. For additional information on these and the other components of the WebSphere Security Model, see the white paper titled *IBM WebSphere Standard and Advanced Edition, V3.5 Security Overview* available on the WebSphere public Web site:

`http://www-4.ibm.com/software/webservers/appserv/whitepapers.html`.

15.2.1 WebSphere security architecture

Let us start with the basics. The goal of WebSphere security to is make sure that only desired users have access to the resources that make up an application. If we look at Figure 499 on page 653, the bubbles on the right identify the application resources. The bubble on the top identifies resources under the control of and served by the Web server. The bubble on the bottom identifies resources under the control of and served by WebSphere.

15.2.1.1 WebSphere security administration

Before getting into security architecture, it will be good to understand how security is specified for the application resources. WebSphere supports two means to define security, the administrative console, and the XMLConfig tool. Both means support the full range of security specifications. The majority of the security specifications are kept in the administrative database, with a few kept in property files.

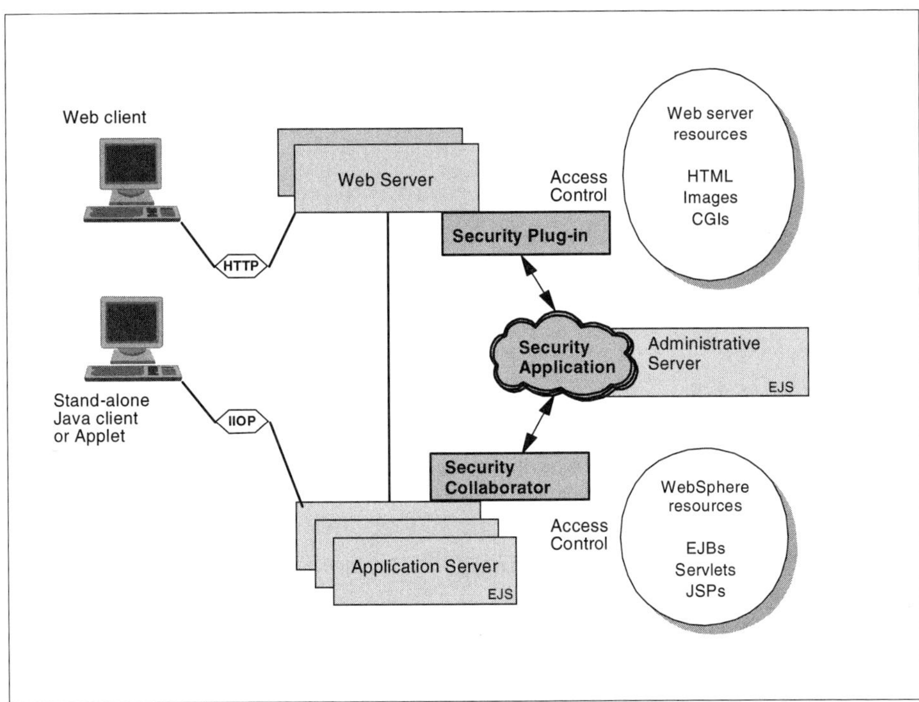

Figure 499. WebSphere security architecture

Security Administration was unified starting with WebSphere V3.0. By unified, we mean that all the application resources, be they controlled by the Web server or by WebSphere, can be administered by the same tool using the same techniques.

The first task when implementing WebSphere security is to define an enterprise application. An enterprise application is comprised of Web applications and Enterprise JavaBeans. A Web application is a WebSphere administrative construct that allows servlets within the same context to be grouped. Authentication and authorization policies are defined relative to an Enterprise Application, and apply to the Web applications and EJBs that make it up.

Even though security policies are specified at the enterprise application level, user permissions to access a resource are specified at the method level. Security administration provides for the specification of method groups to make method level specification easier. The administrator groups methods based on which methods a user or group of users is allowed to have access. For instance, a bank has an Account resource that has several query type methods and several update type methods. It also has a user group called Customers and a user group called Bank Account Executives. An Account Query method group has been defined that contains all the query type methods. Similarly, an Account Update method group exists that contains all the update type methods. Now, a security policy can be defined to allow the user group Customers access only to the methods contained in the Account Query method group and allow the user group Bank Account Executives access to the methods contained in both the Account Query and Account Update method groups.

15.2.1.2 Security application

As can be seen in Figure 499 on page 653, the security application resides within the WebSphere Administrative Server. It supports both the administrative aspects of WebSphere security discussed in 15.2.1.1, “WebSphere security administration” on page 652 and the runtime aspects. At runtime, the security application has access to the authentication and authorization policy information. By providing APIs, it collaborates with the WebSphere security runtime components to make authentication and authorization decisions.

15.2.1.3 Security plug-in

The security plug-in, along with the security collaborator, make up the WebSphere security runtime componentry. As can be seen in Figure 499 on page 653, the security plug-in is attached to the Web server. Essentially, the plug-in provides the interface between the Web server and the security application that has access to the authentication and authorization information.

15.2.1.4 Security collaborator

The security collaborator, along with the security plug-in, make up the WebSphere security runtime componentry. As can be seen in Figure 499 on page 653, the security collaborator is attached to the application servers. Essentially, the collaborator provides the interface between the application server and the security application that has access to the authentication and authorization information.

15.2.1.5 Client types

As can be seen in Figure 499 on page 653, WebSphere supports two types of clients, the Web (browser) type client and the stand-alone Java application or applet. The stand-alone Java client can go directly to an EJB under the control of an application server using the IIOP protocol. Both client types can take advantage of WebSphere security.

15.2.1.6 Security scenario

Now we will examine a more detailed security flow for a request coming from a browser (Web client) user. In our scenario, the request is for a servlet. The flow is as follows:

- The request for a servlet comes from the browser user to the Web server.
- The Web server determines that it does not control the servlet, so passes the request on the application server.
- The application server determines that it controls the servlet and, through the security collaborator, determines that the servlet is secure.
- The application server flows back a challenge to the browser user. In this scenario, the challenge is for the user to enter a user ID and password.
- The user enters a valid user ID and password and flows the information back through the Web server to the application server.
- Using the security collaborator, which in turn works with the security application, the application server authenticates the user ID and password.
- Using the security collaborator, the application server determines that the user is authorized to access the servlet being requested.
- The application server invokes the servlet for the user.

15.2.2 WebSphere security authentication

Authentication is the process of determining if a user is who the user claims to be. WebSphere security authenticates a user in two steps. First, authentication data in the form of a user ID and password or a certificate are obtained for the user. Second, the authentication data is validated against information contained in a user registry.

15.2.2.1 Authentication types

WebSphere supports four types of authentication:

- None

  The user is not challenged. If the resource being requested is secure, then it is not served for the user.

- Basic

  The user is challenged to enter a user ID and password.

- Certificate (X.509 certificate)

  A challenge is made for the client to supply a certificate.

- Custom

  Custom is used when there is a desire to supply an HTML form for a challenge instead of the normal basic challenge.

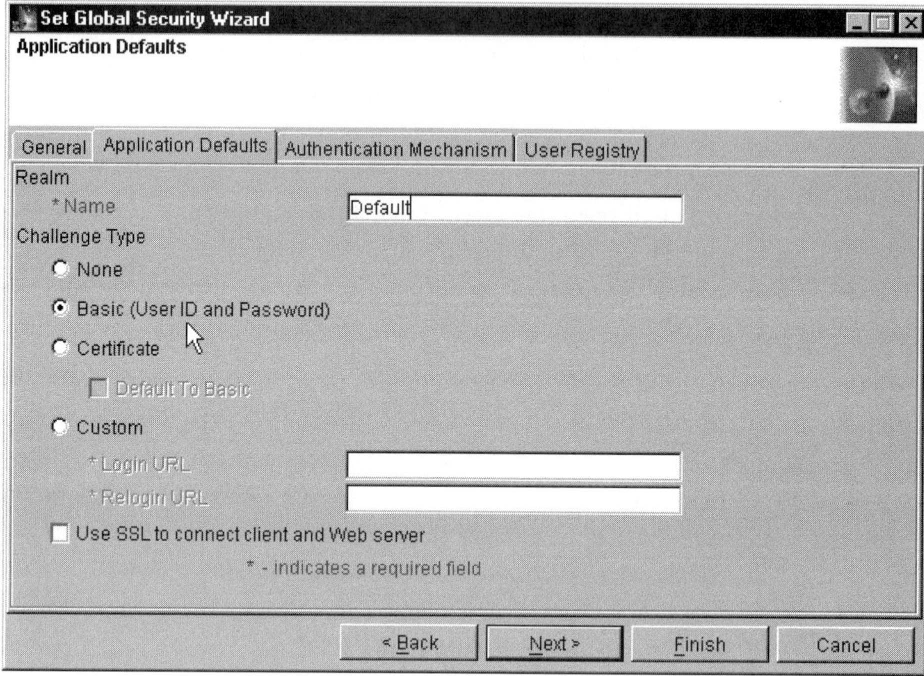

Figure 500. Authentication types

15.2.2.2 Authentication mechanisms

An authentication mechanism validates the authentication information against a user registry. WebSphere supports two mechanisms for authentication:

- Local operating system

  Authentication is based on the user registry of the underlying operating system calling native routines to authenticate the given data. Local operating system supports the basic challenge type.

- Lightweight Third Party Authentication (LTPA)

  Authentication is done using a trusted third-party Lightweight Directory Access Protocol (LDAP) server. LTPA causes a search to be performed against the LDAP directory. LTPA supports both the basic and certificate challenge type.

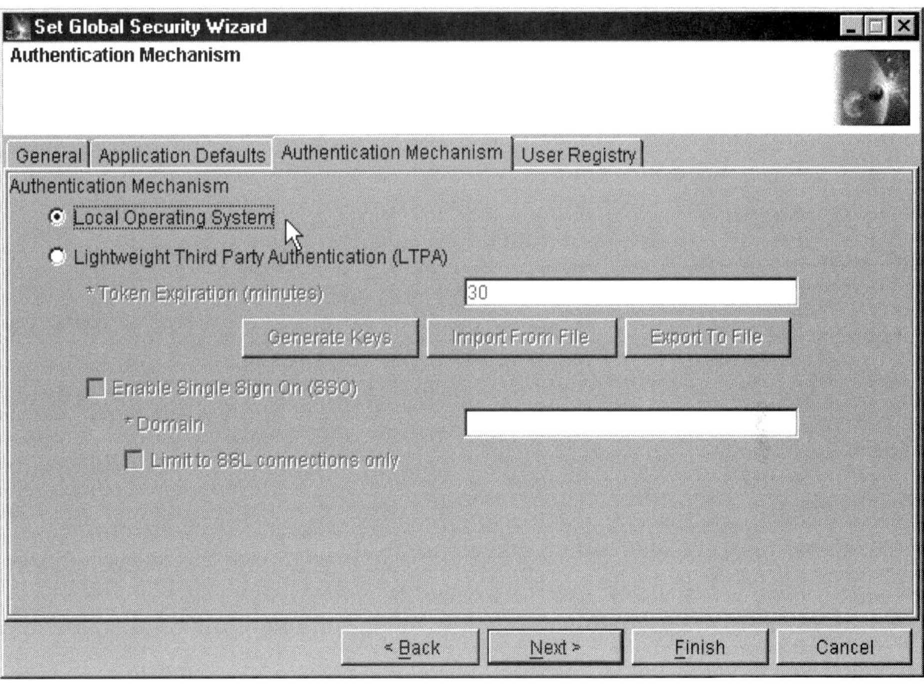

Figure 501. Authentication mechanisms

Note

If WebSphere security is to be enabled when running the administrative server as a non-root user, then the local operating system cannot be used as the authentication mechanism. You have to use LTPA in connection with LDAP.

15.2.3 WebSphere security authorization

Authorization was discussed previously in 15.2.1.1, "WebSphere security administration" on page 652. A user is authorized to access a resource by having permissions granted. User permissions to access a resource are specified at the method level. Security administration provides for the specification of method groups to make method level specification easier. The administrator groups methods based on which methods a user or group of users is allowed to have access.

15.3 What's new in WebSphere V3.5 security

The underlying WebSphere security architecture and model are virtually unchanged from V3.02. However, there have been some enhancements in V3.5 that are of interest:

- Performance has been improved from the previous version. In a development benchmark, application performance was degraded only 10%-12% with security enabled. While this is only a single data point and results will certainly vary depending on application characteristics and security specifications, it does give evidence that security overhead has been reduced. Two performance enhancements worth mentioning are:
  - LTPA/LDAP authentication information is now cached by WebSphere.
  - An unnecessary security check was eliminated. The check was being made by the Web server when the resource was controlled by the application server.
- Stability has been improved.
- Security specifications are now fully supported by the XMLConfig tool. See Chapter 21, "XMLConfig" on page 877 for detailed information.
- Certificate-based authentication is now supported.
- To go along with certificate based authentication, a GUI-based key generation/management tool is provided.
- The Custom login authentication type now supports redirection to the originally requested resource.
- The "SSOToken" has been deprecated. Now, only the "LTPA Token" is used to support Single Sign On (SSO).

15.4 Using client certificate based authentication with WebSphere

One of the important improvements in WebSphere V3.5 is the ability to do certificate-based authentication. In this section we discuss certificates, technologies related to certificates and provide an example of using certificates with WebSphere.

Certificate-based authentication requires the specification of LTPA as the WebSphere authentication mechanism. LTPA provides the means for the WebSphere Application Server to access an LDAP directory that contains the authentication information. For our certificate-based authentication example, we will be using the IBM SecureWay Directory, which is an LDAP conforming registry.

In our example, the following products are used:

- WebSphere V3.5.2 on Windows NT
- IBM HTTP Server V1.3.12 on Windows NT
- IBM SecureWay Directory V3.1.1.5 on AIX
- DB2 Enterprise Edition V6.1 Fix Pak 4 on Windows NT for WebSphere
- DB2 Enterprise Edition V6.1 Fix Pak 4 on AIX for IBM SecureWay Directory
- Microsoft Internet Explorer V5

Our example assumes that WebSphere, IBM HTTP Server, DB2 (on both Windows NT and AIX) and Internet Explorer have all been previously installed. It also assumes that the default server and Web application are available in WebSphere (that is, **Configure default server and Web application** was selected during WebSphere installation).

15.4.1 Web client security flow with certificates

We start our discussion with a scenario that describes the flow of certificate-based authentication in a WebSphere environment. The basic flow is shown graphically in Figure 502 on page 660 and is as follows:

1. The request for the IncServlet servlet comes from the browser user to the Web server.
2. The Web server determines that it does not control the servlet, so passes the request on to the application server.
3. The application server determines that it controls the servlet and, through the security collaborator, determines that the servlet is secure.
4. The application server, through the security collaborator, determines that certificates are to be used for the challenge type.
5. The application server flows back a challenge to the browser. In this scenario, the challenge is for the browser to return a certificate.
6. The browser recognizes the request and returns the certificate. The certificate flows back through the Web server to the application server.
7. Using the security collaborator, which in turn works with the security application, the application server authenticates the certificate. The LTPA server component of the security application works with the LDAP server to perform a credential mapping of the certificate to the contents of the LDAP directory.

8. Using the security collaborator, the application server determines that the user is authorized to access the servlet being requested.
9. The application server invokes the servlet for the user.

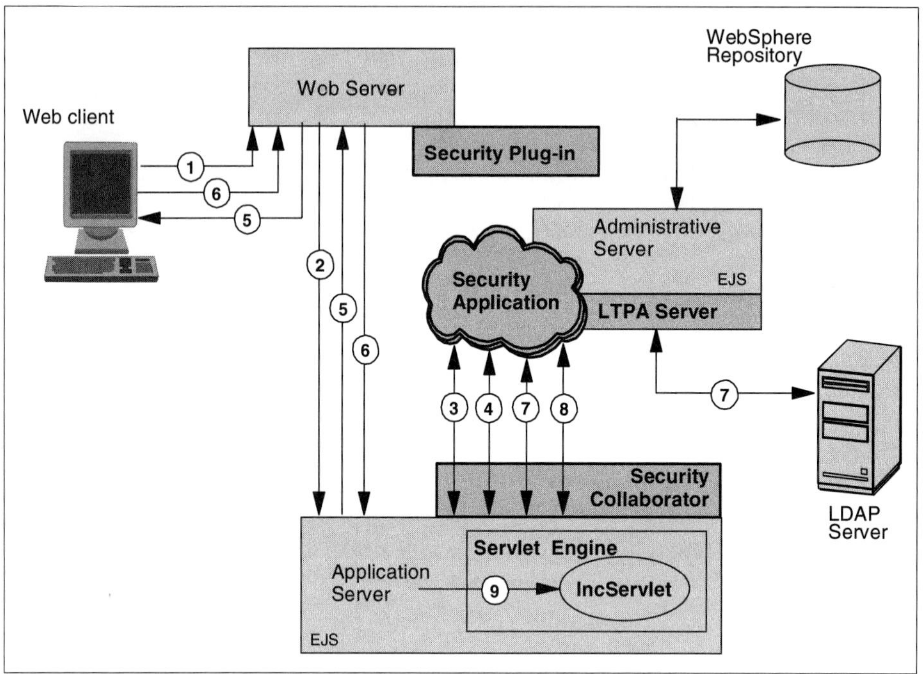

Figure 502. WebSphere security flow using client certificates

15.4.2 Using IBM SecureWay Directory

IBM SecureWay Directory is an LDAP conforming directory and will be used to support WebSphere authentication in our example.

15.4.2.1 Installing IBM SecureWay Directory

This section will guide you through the steps required to install the IBM SecureWay Directory Server V3.1.1.5 for AIX. Installation will be done from a downloaded TAR file using SMIT.

1. Log in to AIX as user root and start an AIX terminal session.
2. Make the directory containing the SecureWay Directory TAR file current. In our example, `cd /downloads/IBMDirectory`.
3. Untar the file. In our example, `tar -xvf ldap3115aix.tar`.
4. Invoke SMIT by entering `smit install_all`.

5. In the INPUT device/directory for software entry field, type the directory containing the SecureWay Directory filesets and click **OK**. In our example the directory entered would be /downloads/IBMDirectory.
6. Click the **List** button associated with the SOFTWARE to install entry field.
7. In the resulting list, select (click) the following:
   - gskrf301
   - gskru301
   - ldap.client
   - ldap.html.en_US
   - ldap.max_crypto_client
   - ldap.max_crypto_server
   - ldap.msg.en_US
   - ldap.server
8. When selection from the list is complete, click **OK**.
9. Now, back in the Install and Update from ALL Available Software window, click **OK**. Then, click **OK** in response to ARE YOU SURE?
10. Check the installation summary at the end of the output to verify successful installation.

Note

If the installation of the ldap.server.xxx filesets fails and the installation of the ldap.max_crypto_server.xxx filesets is cancelled with a series of messages similar to:

- sysck: 3001-037 The name ldap is not a known user for file ....
- sysck: 3001-003 A value must be specified for owner for entry ...

Just try re-installing the ldap.server.xxx and ldap.max_crypto_server.xxx filesets.

15.4.2.2 Configuring IBM SecureWay Directory

This section provides instructions for configuring IBM SecureWay Directory. We will start by running a configuration utility.

1. Log in to AIX as user root and start an AIX terminal session.
2. To start the configuration utility, type `ldapxcfg` and press Enter.

3. The IBM SecureWay Directory Configuration window appears. Select all three configuration choices listed below and click **Next**.
   - Set the directory administrator name and password.
   - Create the directory DB2 database.
   - Configure a Web server for directory administration.
4. To set the directory administrator name and password, type the administrator Distinguished Name (DN) or accept the default (cn=root). Then, type the password and re-type to confirm. Click **Next**. In our case, we will accept the default DN as cn=root.
5. To create the directory DB2 database:
   - Select to either create the default LDAPDB2 database or to use your own. Click **Next**. In our case, we choose to create the default LDAPDB2 database.
   - If prompted for the default DB2 database code page, select either **Create the default DB2 database** or **Create the default UCS-2 DB2 database (UTF-8)**. Click **Next**. In our case, we selected **Create the default DB2 database**.
   - To specify the location for the directory, type the directory path or accept the default(/home/ldapdb2). Click **Next**. On our case, we accepted the default.
6. To configure the Web server for directory administration:
   - Select the Web server you want to use for directory administration. Click **Next**. In our case, we selected the IBM HTTP Web server. All subsequent steps for Web server configuration are those for the IBM HTTP Web server.
   - Enter the full path name of the Web server configuration file. For IBM HTTP Server V1.3.12, type `/usr/HTTPServer/conf/httpd.conf`. Click **Next**.
7. The Configuration Summary is displayed. Review the summary, then click **Configure**.
8. On the Directory configuration complete window, check for successful completion, then click **OK**.
9. Restart the configured Web server. For the IBM HTTP Server, type the following:

```
# cd /usr/HTTPServer/bin
# ./apachectl restart
```

15.4.2.3 Populating IBM SecureWay Directory

This section provides instructions for starting the SecureWay Directory administration server, creating an initial suffix and adding entries into the directory.

To start the administration server:

1. Start the SecureWay Directory Administration GUI by going to a Web browser and entering URL: `http://<hostname>/ldap`, where `hostname` is the host name of the machine where the directory is installed.
2. The SecureWay Directory Administration logon window appears. Enter the administrator name as the user ID and the administrator password. Click **Logon**. In our case, enter cn=root along with the password.
3. In the left navigation frame, expand the Server folder and select **Startup/Shutdown**. Then, click the **Startup** button.
4. Wait until the `The directory server is starting...` message changes to `The directory server is running....` This may take several minutes.

A suffix specifies the Distinguished Name (DN) for the root of a directory in the local database and must be defined before adding user entries. To define a suffix:

1. Make sure the administration server is running.
2. In the left navigation frame, expand the Suffixes folder and click **Add a suffix**.
3. Type the DN to be used as the suffix. Click the **Add a new suffix** button. In our case, type `o=ibm, c=us` as the DN as shown in Figure 503 on page 664.
4. Once the suffix has been successfully added, the administrative server must be restarted. From the left navigation frame, select **Server->Startup/Shutdown->Shutdown**.
5. After the `server was successfully shut down` message appears, click the **Startup** button to restart the server. Then, wait for the `directory server is running...` message.

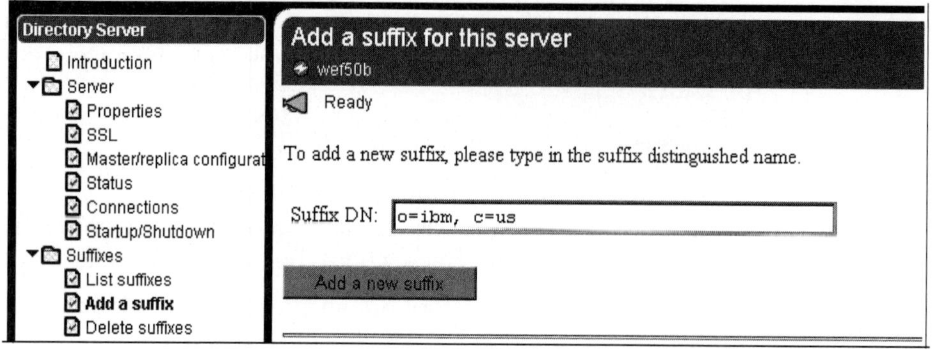

Figure 503. IBM SecureWay Directory Administration GUI - adding a new suffix

There are two methods of adding entries to the directory database:

- An LDIF (LDAP Data Interchange Format) data file using the administrator GUI.
- The Directory Management Tool (DMT).

LDIF is a standard format for representing LDAP entries in text form and is used to import entries into the database. The DMT provides a GUI to add entries to the database. In our case, we will be using the LDIF method.

To make testing of WebSphere certificate-based authentication a little easier, we will create two users in our directory database. One user will eventually be granted permission to access secure resources, the other will not (see 15.4.5.6, "Configuring security permissions" on page 743). The LDIF file that will be used to create the two users is named itsocert.ldif with contents as shown in Figure 505 on page 666. To import the file do the following:

1. Make sure the administrative server is running.
2. In the left navigation frame, select **Database->Add entries**.
3. Type the path and file name of the LDIF file and click **Add entries** to database. In our case, the file name is /usr/ldap/examples/itsocert.ldif.

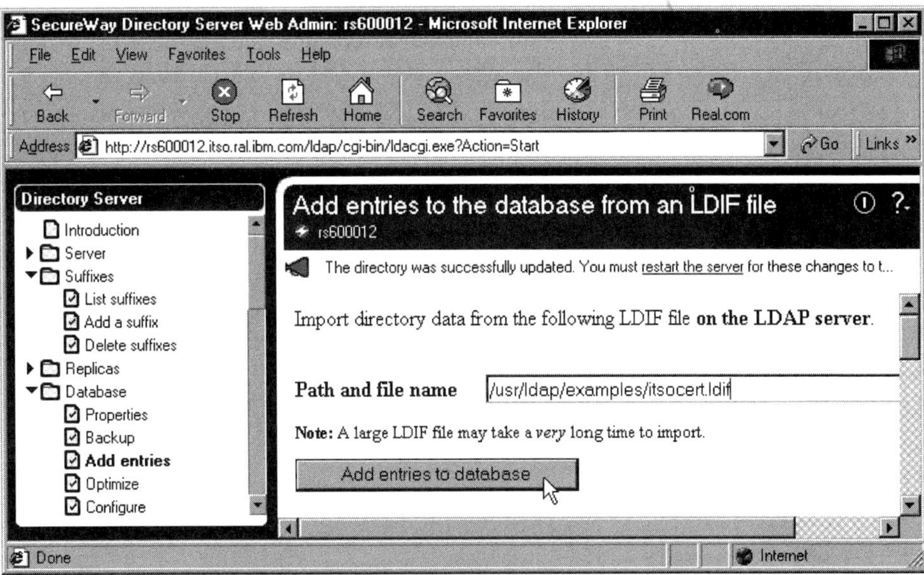

Figure 504. IBM SecureWay Directory Administration GUI - adding new entries via LDIF

4. Wait for a message to appear in Progress Messages that indicates four entries have been successfully added out of four attempts.

```
# SecureWay Directory itsocert LDIF file
#
# The suffix "o=IBM, c=US" should be defined before attempting to
# load this data.

version: 1

dn: o=IBM, c=US
objectclass: top
objectclass: organization
o: IBM

dn: ou=Raleigh, o=IBM, c=US
ou: Raleigh
objectclass: organizationalUnit

dn: cn=Mary Burnnet, ou=Raleigh, o=IBM, c=US
objectclass: inetOrgPerson
objectclass: organizationalPerson
objectclass: person
objectclass: ePerson
cn: Mary Burnnet
sn: Burnnet
uid: MBurnnet

dn: cn=Bob Garcia, ou=Raleigh, o=IBM, c=US
objectclass: inetOrgPerson
objectclass: organizationalPerson
objectclass: person
objectclass: ePerson
cn: Bob Garcia
sn: Garcia
uid: BGarcia
```

Figure 505. IBM SecureWay Directory - sample itsocert.ldif file

A sample LDIF file named sample.ldif is shipped with the SecureWay Directory product. If you choose to use the sample file, note the following:

- The contents of the sample file as shipped will not work with WebSphere V3.5. WebSphere requires the LDAP attribute uid, which is not used in the sample entries.
- The sample file expects the o=ibm, c=us suffix to be already defined.

The DMT tool can be used to verify that the contents of the itsocert.ldif file were imported successfully. To use the DMT tool, do the following:

1. From the AIX terminal command line, type the following and press Enter:

```
# dmt
```

2. When the introductory DMT panel appears, from the left navigation frame select **Tree->Browse tree**.
3. In the Browse directory tree frame, expand o=ibm,c=us.
4. In the Browse directory tree frame, expand ou=Raleigh. The result of the expanded tree is shown in Figure 506.
5. At this point, DMT can be used to view, edit, add and delete entries.

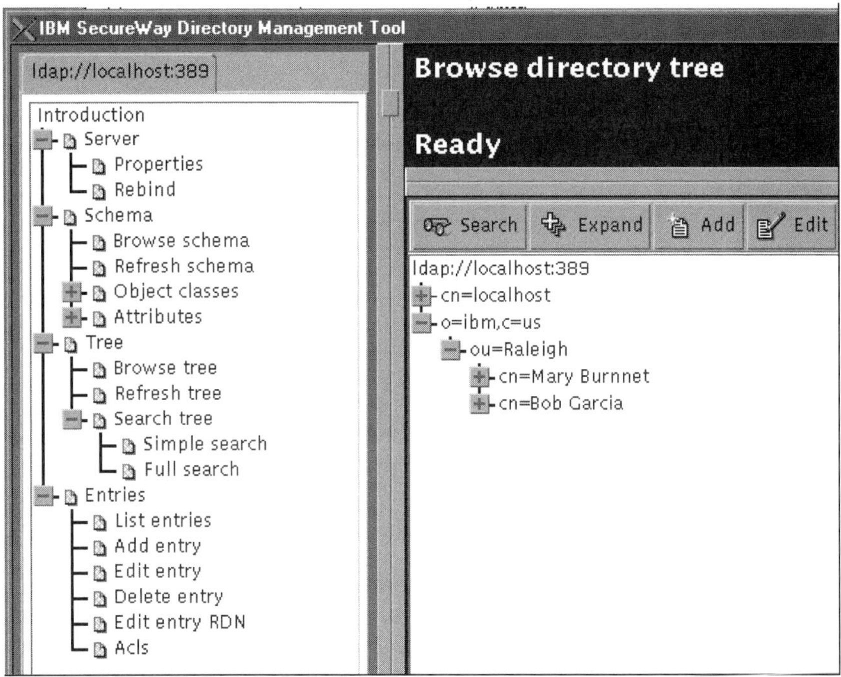

Figure 506. IBM SecureWay Directory Management Tool (DMT) - Browse directory tree

15.4.3 Managing certificates

In our example, we are going to be using certificates for two purposes: first, to allow an SSL connection to be established between the browser client and the Web server and second to support WebSphere authentication of the browser client. We are going to be dealing with a signer certificate from a trusted Certificate Authority (CA), a personal certificate that identifies the server, and a personal certificate that identifies the client.

A key database file located on the WebSphere server machine is created and holds the certificates needed by the server. The server needs:

- The signer certificate of the trusted CA.
- A server certificate signed by the trusted CA.
- A client certificate signed by the trusted CA.

The browser security specifications will also need to be updated to contain the signer certificate of the trusted CA and the client certificate.

WebSphere provides two means to manage certificates:

- A graphical tool called iKeyman, the IBM Key Management tool.
- A package of Java command-line tools, com.ibm.cfwk.tools (CFWK tools).

The CFWK tools support scripting of certificate management, which is useful for administrators who do a lot of this work or who want to automate the work. The iKeyman tool is much easier to use for small tasks, so that is what we will be using for our example.

In our example, we will be using a Windows NT machine for both WebSphere and the IBM HTTP Server.

15.4.3.1 Create a key database for the server

We will create the key database file using the iKeyman tool. To use the iKeyman tool, you must put the necessary files at the front of your classpath. Three of the files, gsk4cls.jar, cfwk.zip and cfwk.sec, are included as part of WebSphere (in the AppServer/lib directory). The fourth, swingall.jar, is part of Java itself. For example, on Windows NT, set the CLASSPATH variable as shown:

```
set classpath=<WS-install>\AppServer\lib\cfwk.zip;
<WS-install>\AppServer\lib\gsk4cls.jar;
<JdkDir>\lib\swingall.jar;
<WS-install>\AppServer\lib;%CLASSPATH%
```

To start the iKeyman tool, use this command:

```
java -Dkeyman.javaOnly=true com.ibm.gsk.ikeyman.Ikeyman
```

A sample Windows NT .bat file used for invoking iKeyman is shown in Figure 507.

```
@echo off

SET WAS_HOME=F:\WebSphere\AppServer
SET JAVA_HOME=F:\WebSphere\AppServer\jdk

set
PATH=%JAVA_HOME%\bin;%JAVA_HOME%\jre\bin;%JAVA_HOME%\jre\bin\classic;%P
ATH%
set CLASSPATH=%WAS_HOME%\lib\swingall.jar;%CLASSPATH%
set
CLASSPATH=%WAS_HOME%\lib\cfwk.zip;%WAS_HOME%\lib\gsk4cls.jar;%CLASSPATH
%

%JAVA_HOME%\bin\java -Dkeyman.javaOnly=true com.ibm.gsk.ikeyman.Ikeyman
```

Figure 507. Sample .bat file for invoking the iKeyman tool

To create the key database file, do the following:

1. Create a working directory in the Windows NT machine to be used during certificate creation and management (in our example F:\ServerCerts). If you choose to use a .bat file to invoke iKeyman, copy it into the newly created directory.
2. Invoke iKeyman.

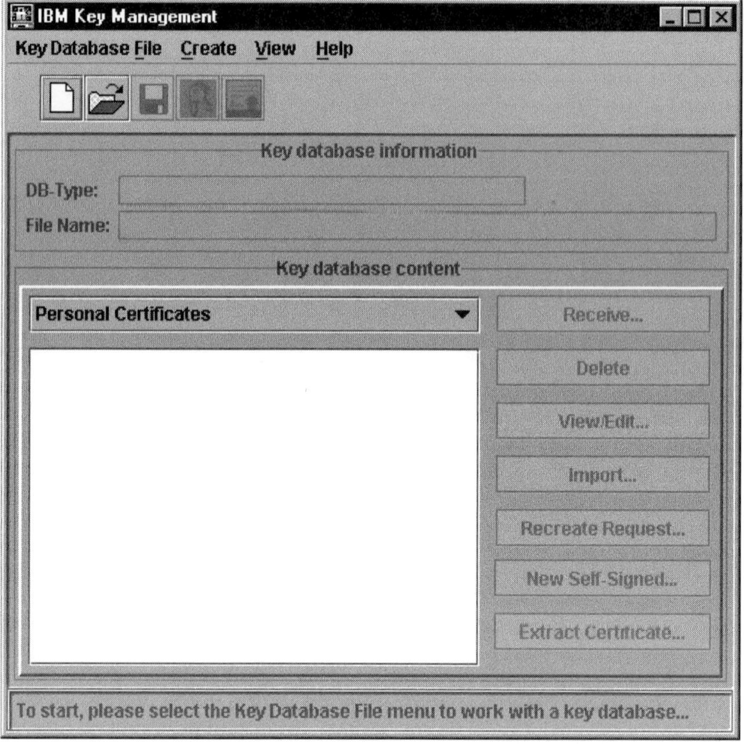

Figure 508. iKeyman initial panel

From the menu bar, select **Key Database File->New...**.

Figure 509. Creating a new key database #1

In the New window:

- Keep the Key database type as CMS key database file.
- Type a file name for the key database (in our case, Serverkey.kdb).
- Make the Location the working directory (in our case, F:\ServerCerts\).
- Click **OK**.

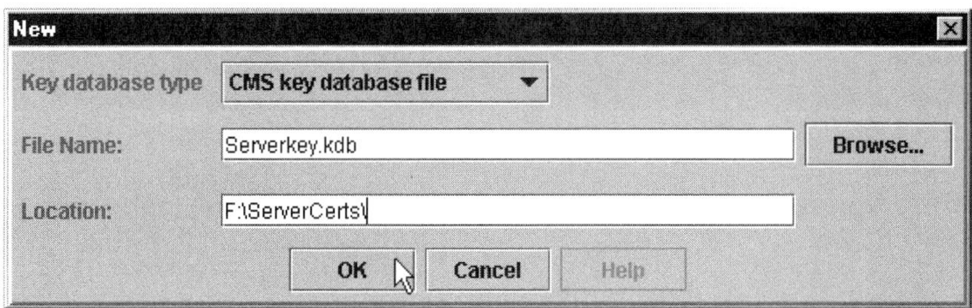

Figure 510. Creating a new key database #2

3. In the Password Prompt window:

   - Type a password and confirm the password used to access the key database. In our case, the password used was WebAS.
   - Check the **Stash the password to a file?** box.
   - Click **OK**.

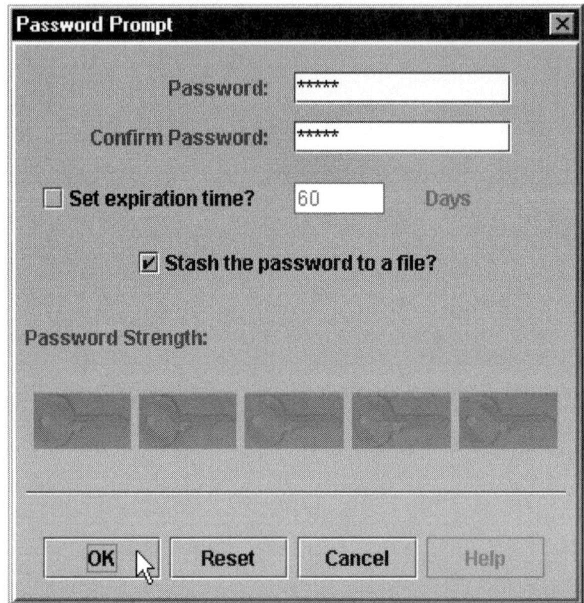

Figure 511. Password Prompt window

   - In the Information window, click **OK**.

Figure 512. Information window

The key database has now been created.

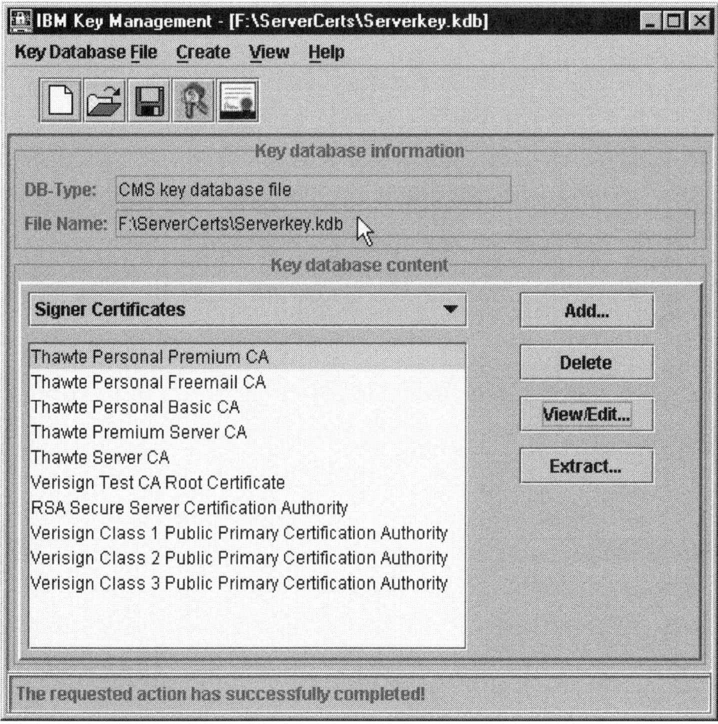

Figure 513. The key database has been created

15.4.3.2 Obtain a signer certificate of a trusted CA

When iKeyman creates a key database, it automatically includes signer certificates from some well-known CAs. You can view the list of CAs by selecting signer certificates from the drop-down list in the Key database content area of the main iKeyman window.

Since we were unable to find a free and easy way to obtain test client and server certificates from these CAs, we choose to use another CA. So, the first thing to do is obtain a new signer certificate.

Certificates will be obtained using a set of Web-based services provided by MicroSoft. To obtain a new CA signer certificate do the following:

1. From a browser, go to URL `http://marting.develop.com/certsrv/`. In our case, we are using Microsoft Internet Explorer.
2. From the Welcome page, select **Retrieve the CA certificate or certificate revocation list** and click **Next**.

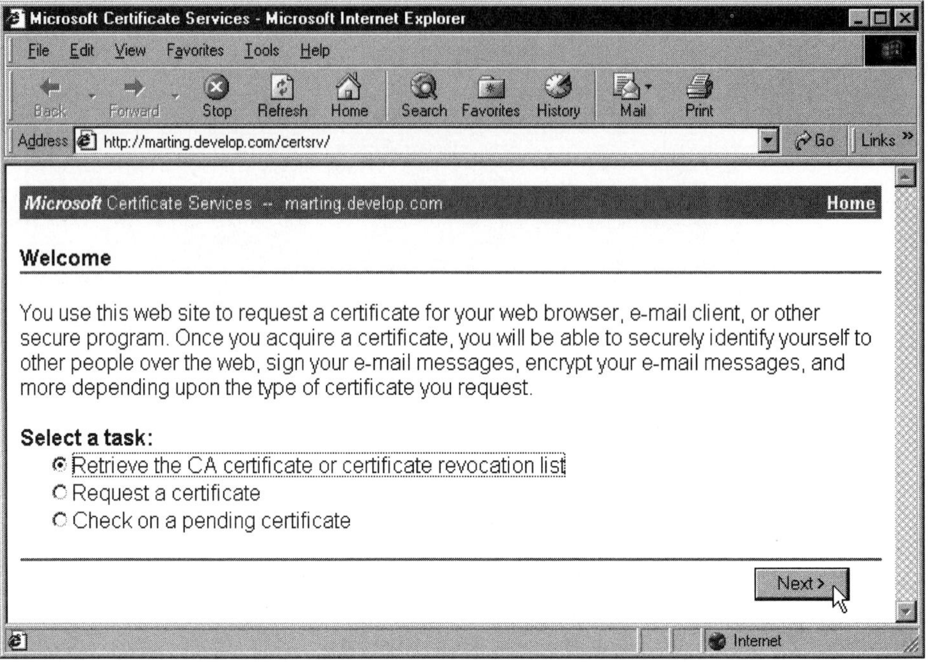

Figure 514. Retrieve the CA certificate

3. Select **Base 64 encoded**.
4. Click **Download CA certificate**.

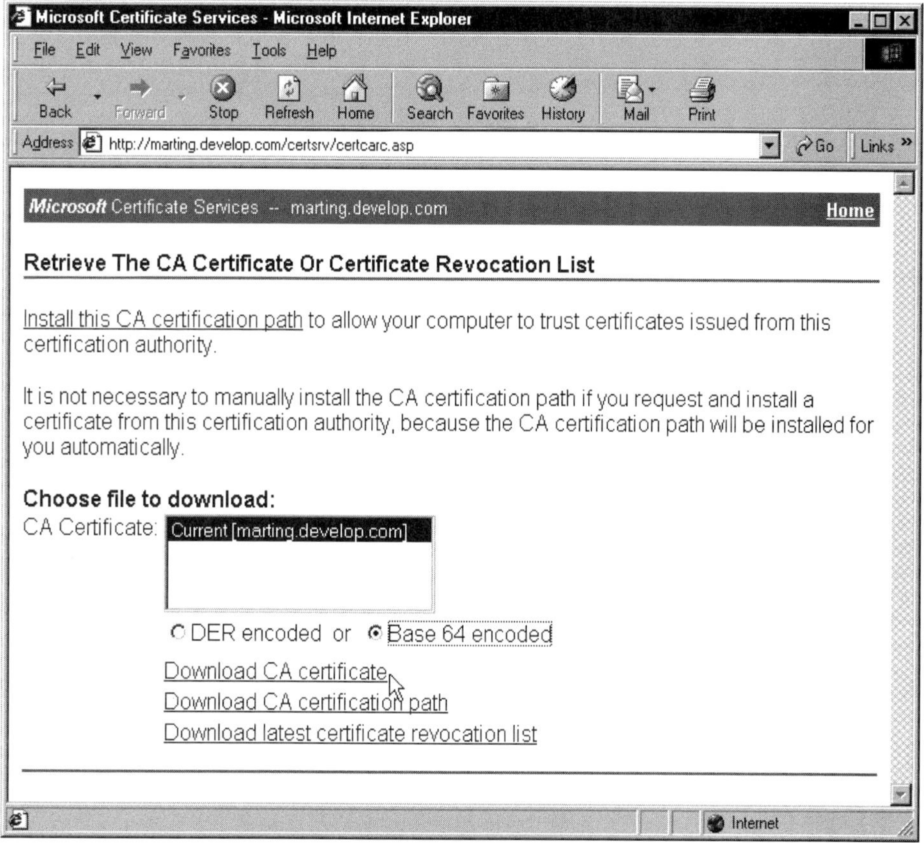

Figure 515. Download CA certificate

5. In the File Download window, make sure that **Save this file to disk** is selected, then click **OK**.
6. Specify a directory to save in and a file name. Then click **Save**. In our case the directory is ServerCerts and file name is CAcertnew.cer.

Figure 516. Save CA certificate

Now, add the CA certificate to the key database. Using iKeyman, do the following:

1. From the main iKeyman window, select signer certificates from the drop-down list in the Key database content area.
2. Click the **Add...** button.

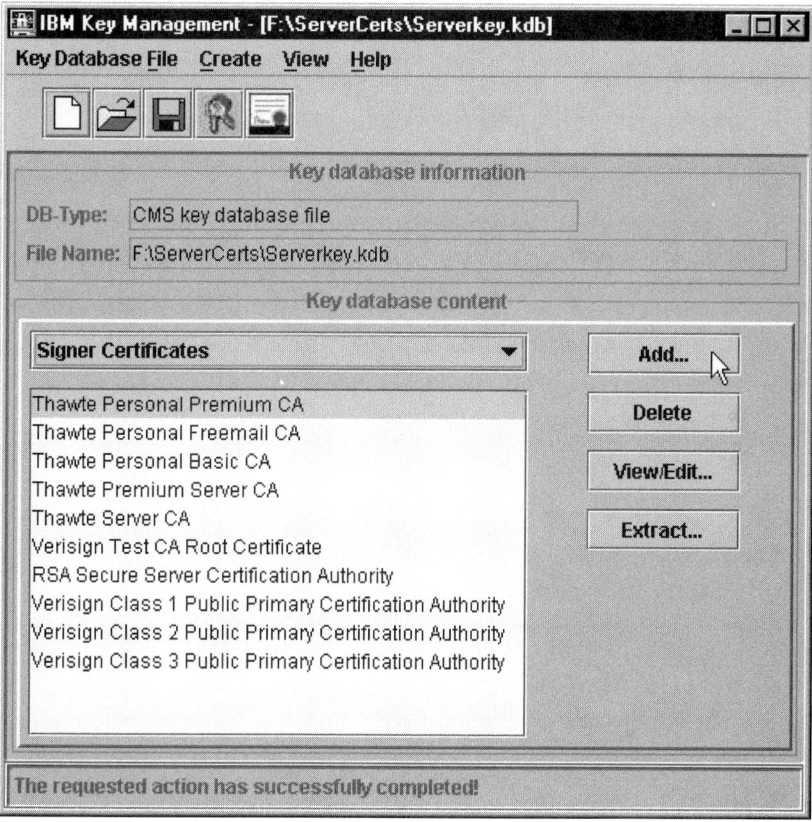

Figure 517. Add a signer certificate

3. In the Add CA's Certificate from a File window:
   - Leave the Data type as Base64-encoded ASCII data.
   - Type the Certificate file name. In our case, the name is CAcertnew.cer.
   - Type the Location. In our case, it is f:\ServerCerts\.
   - Click **OK**.

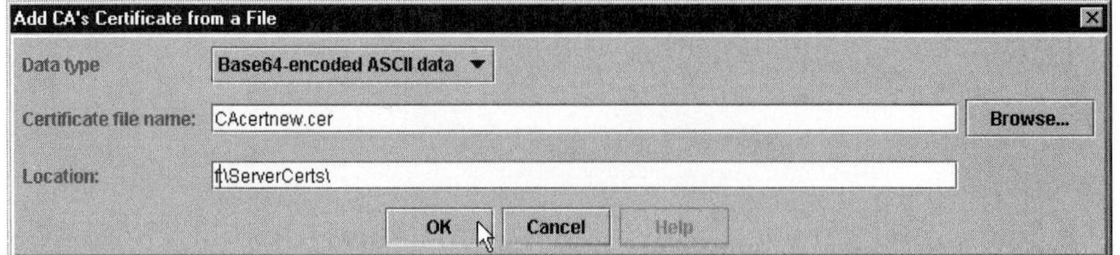

Figure 518. Add CA's Certificate from a File

4. In the Enter a Label window, type the name to be used to identify the certificate as it is listed in iKeyman. In our case, the label is MS Test CA.

Figure 519. Enter a label for the certificate

The iKeyman main window with signer certificates selected should now include the MS Test CA in the certificate list as shown in Figure 520 on page 679.

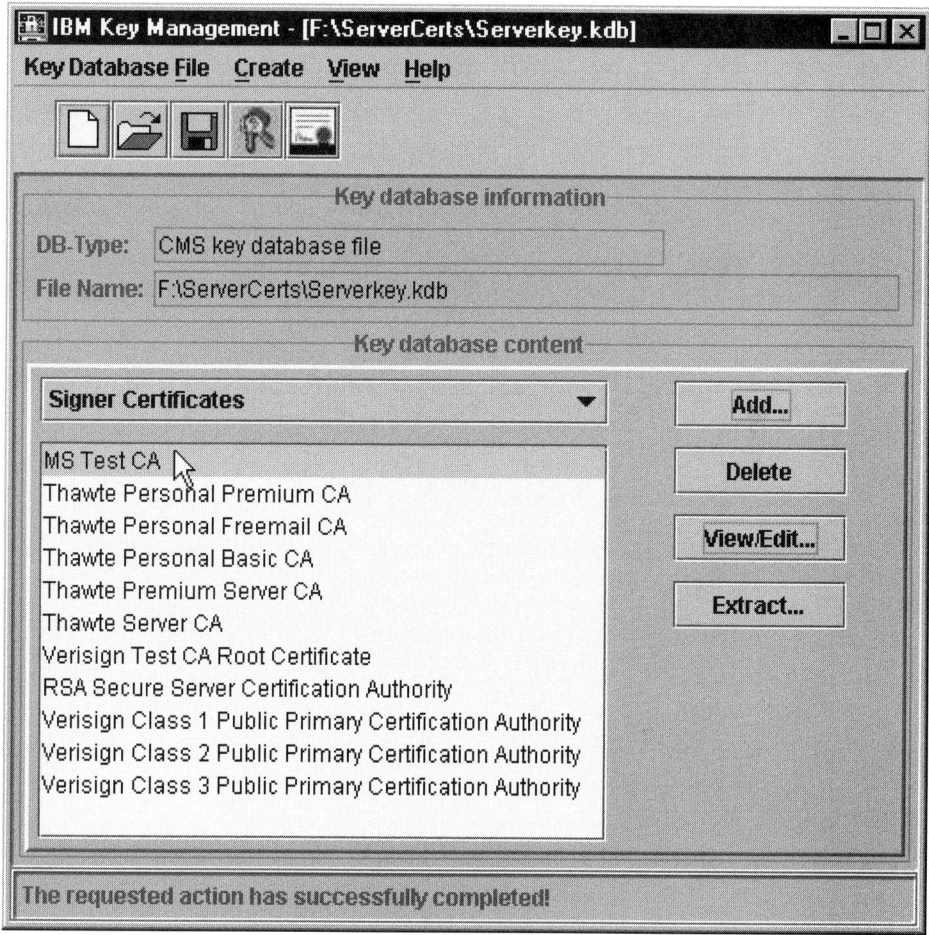

Figure 520. iKeyman - signer certificates list

15.4.3.3 Obtain a server certificate

The first step to obtaining a server certificate is to create a certificate request using iKeyman. That request will then be sent on to the Web-based certificate services, which will return a server certificate signed by our new CA. To create the certificate request, do the following:

1. From the main iKeyman window, select personal certificate requests from the drop-down list in the Key database content area.

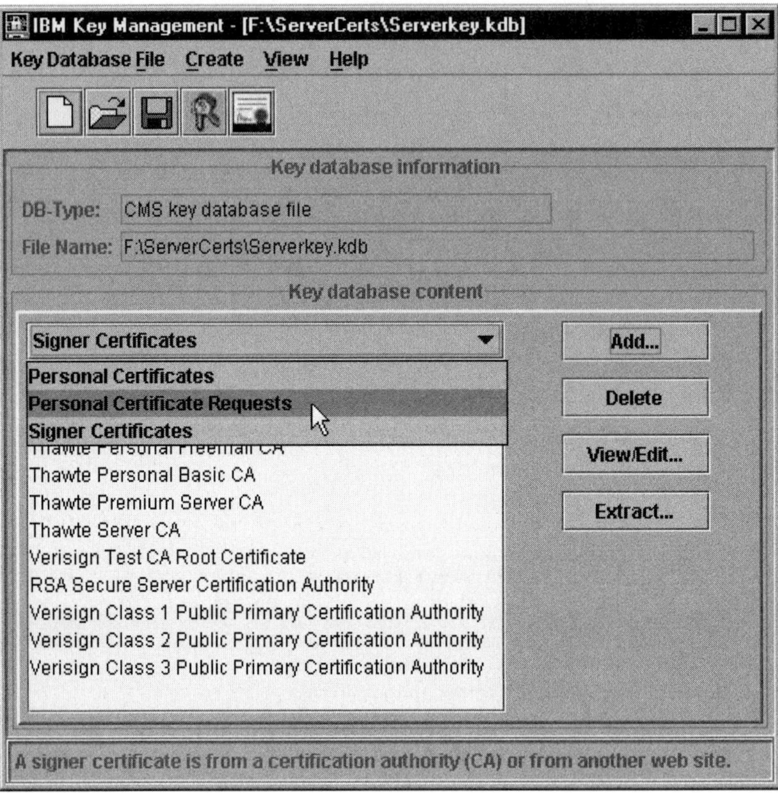

Figure 521. Select personal certificate requests

2. Click **New...**.

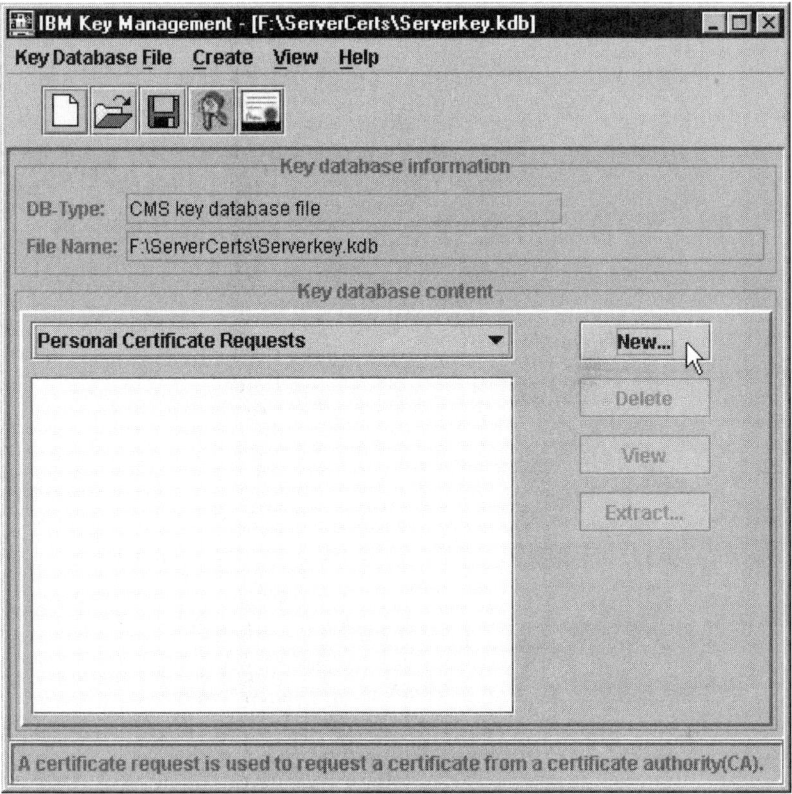

Figure 522. Create new personal certificate requests

3. In the Create New Key and Certificate Request window, enter the appropriate values and click **OK**. In our case, we are using the following values:
   - For Key Label - Server. The Key Label is used to identify the certificate in an iKeyman list.
   - For Key Size - 1024.
   - For Common Name - kenueno.itso.ral.ibm.com. The common name is the host name of the server.
   - For Organization - ibm.
   - For Organization Unit - Raleigh.
   - For Country - US.
   - For the name of a file in which to store the certificate request - F:\ServerCerts\certreq.arm.

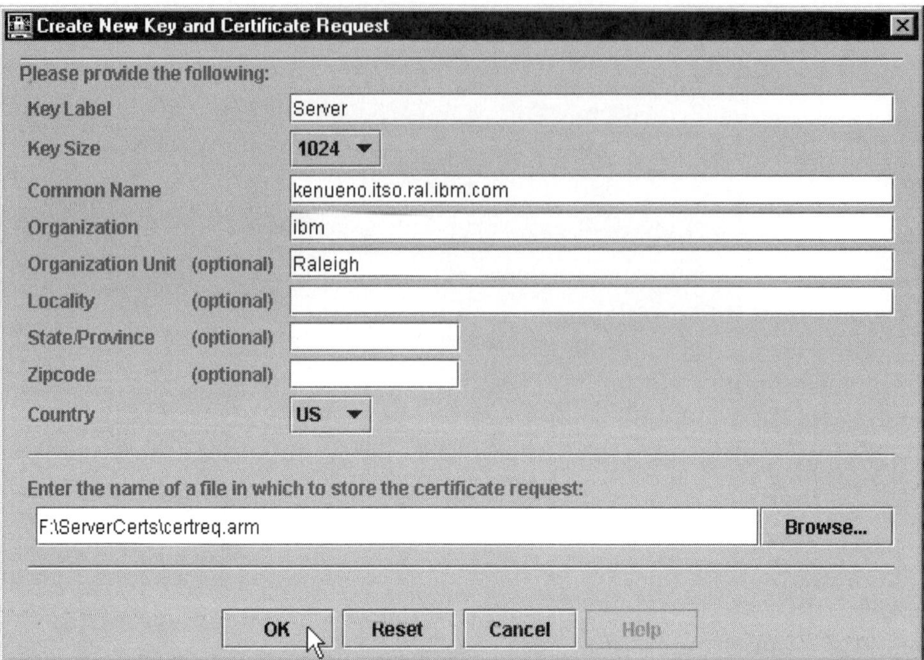

Figure 523. iKeyman - create a request for a new certificate

4. Click **OK** in the Information window.

The Web-based services will now be used to obtain the server certificate. To obtain a new server certificate do the following:

1. From a browser, go to URL `http://marting.develop.com/certsrv/`. In our case, we are using Microsoft Internet Explorer.
2. From the Welcome page, select **Request a certificate** and click **Next**.

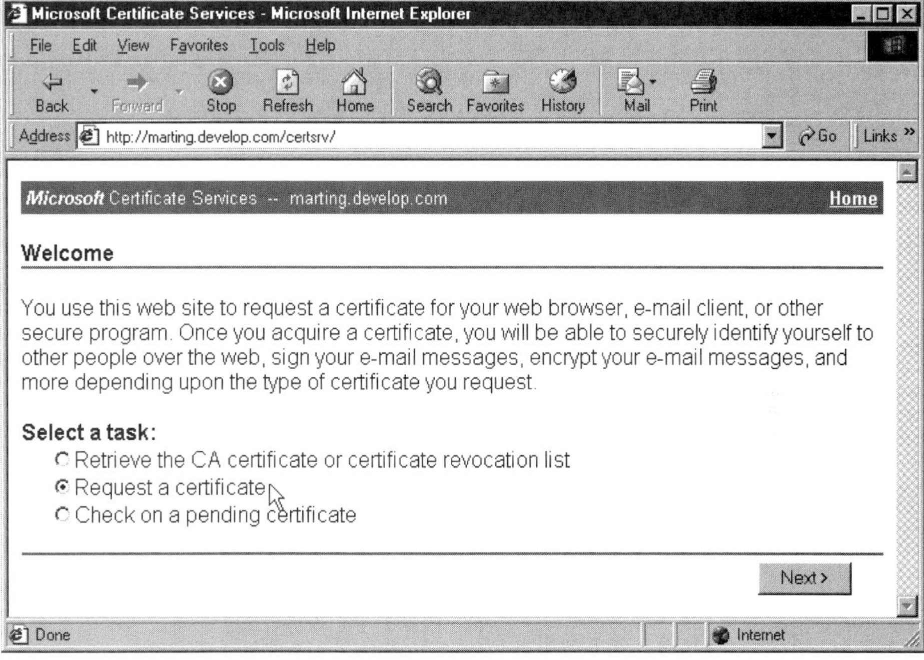

Figure 524. Request a certificate

3. Select **Advanced request** and click **Next**.

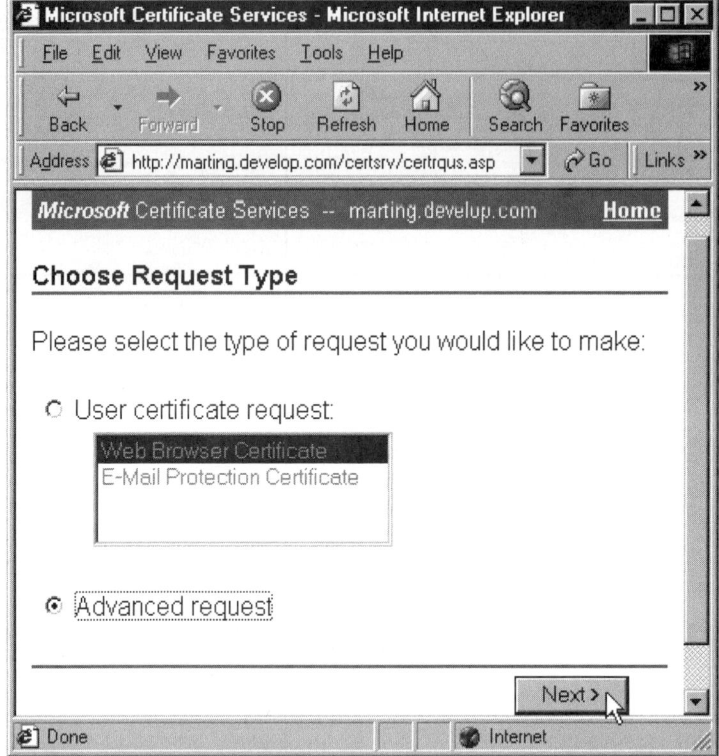

Figure 525. Advanced request

4. Select **Submit a certificate request using a base64 encoded PKCS #10 file...** and click **Next**.

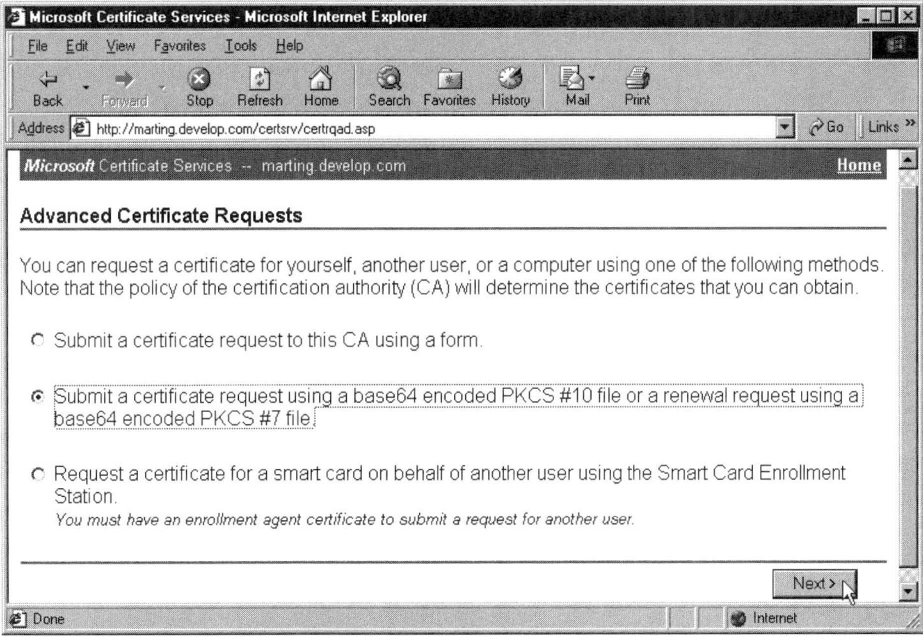

Figure 526. Submit a certificate request using a base 64 encoded PCKS #10 file

5. From a Windows NT DOS prompt window, use Notepad to edit the newly created certificate request file (certreq.arm). Use the Notepad edit functions to copy the entire contents of the file to the clipboard.

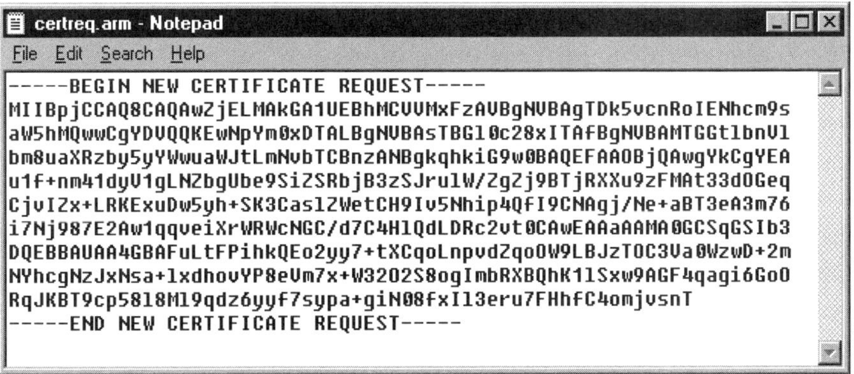


```
-----BEGIN NEW CERTIFICATE REQUEST-----
MIIBpjCCAQ8CAQAwZjELMAkGA1UEBhMCVVMxFzAVBgNVBAgTDk5vcnRoIENhcm9s
aW5hMQwwCgYDVQQKEwNpYm0xDTALBgNVBAsTBGl0c28xITAfBgNVBAMTGGtlbnVl
bm8uaXRzby5yYWwuaWJtLmNvbTCBnzANBgkqhkiG9w0BAQEFAAOBjQAwgYkCgYEA
u1f+nm41dyV1gLNZbgUbe9SiZSRbjB3zSJrulW/ZgZj9BTjRXXu9zFMAt33dOGeq
CjvIZx+LRKExuDw5yh+SK3CaslZWetCH9Iv5Nhip4QfI9CNAgj/Ne+aBT3eA3m76
i7Nj987E2Aw1qqveiXrWRWcNGC/d7C4HlQdLDRc2vt0CAwEAAaAAMA0GCSqGSIb3
DQEBBAUAA4GBAFuLtFPihkQEo2yy7+tXCqoLnpvdZqoOW9LBJzTOC3Va0WzwD+2m
NYhcgNzJxNsa+lxdhovYP8eVm7x+W32O2S8ogImbRXBQhK1lSxw9AGF4qagi6GoO
RqJKBT9cp58l8Ml9qdz6yyf7sypa+giN08fxIl3eru7FHhfC4omjvsnT
-----END NEW CERTIFICATE REQUEST-----
```


Figure 527. Copy the entire contents of the cretificate request file

6. Back in the certificate services page, paste the clipboard contents into the Saved Request edit box. The results should look something like those shown in Figure 528.

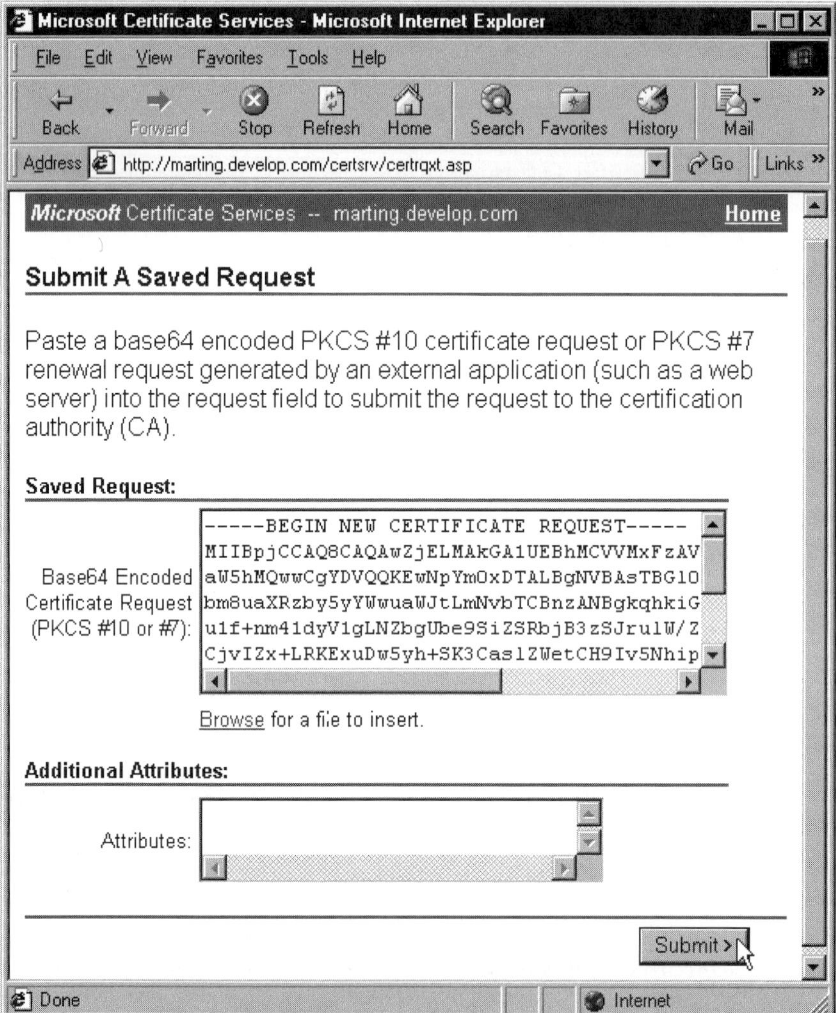

Figure 528. Microsoft Certificate Services - submit a request for a new certificate

7. Click the **Submit** button.
8. In the Certificate Issued page, select **Base 64 encoded** then click **Download CA certificate**.

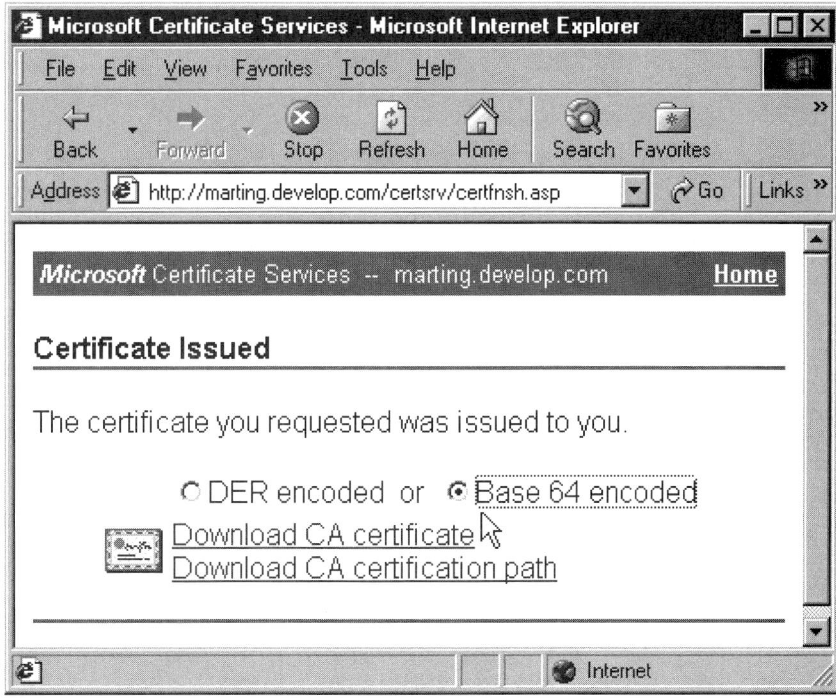

Figure 529. Download CA cerftificate

9. In the File Download window, make sure that **Save this file to disk** is selected, then click **OK**.

10. Specify a directory to save in and a file name, then click **Save**. In our case the directory is ServerCerts and file name is Srvcertnew.cer.

Now, iKeyman will be used to receive the newly obtained server certificate into the server key database. To receive the certificate, do the following:

1. From the main iKeyman window, select personal certificates from the drop-down list in the Key database content area.

2. Click **Receive...**.

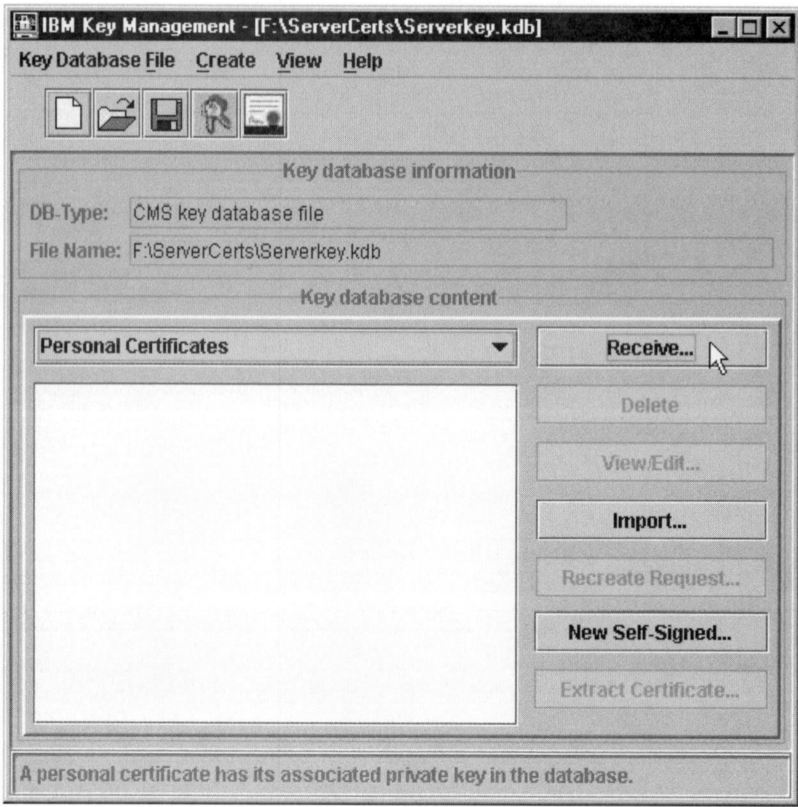

Figure 530. Receive a new personal certificate

3. In the Receive Certificate from File window:
   - Leave the data type as Base64-encoded ASCII data.
   - Type the Certificate file name. In our case, the name is Srvcertnew.cer.
   - Type the Location. In our case, it is f:\ServerCerts\.
   - Click **OK**.

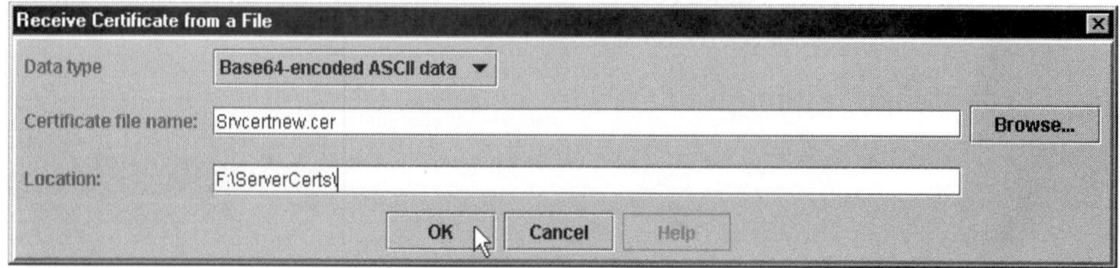

Figure 531. Receive Certificate from a File window

4. You should now see a single entry in the Personal Certificates list called Server.

Figure 532. The server's certificate in the Personal Certificates list

15.4.3.4 Obtain a client certificate

The client certificate will be obtained using the same basic process that was used to obtain the server certificate. To obtain the client certificate, do the following:

1. From the main iKeyman window, select personal certificate requests from the drop-down list in the Key database content area.
2. Click **New...**.

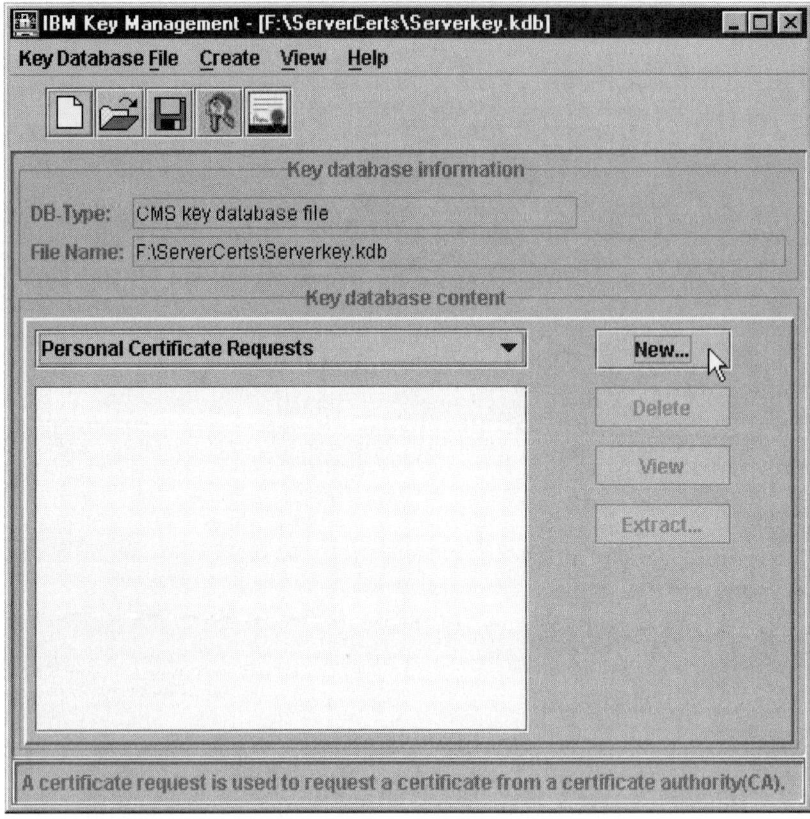

Figure 533. Create a new personal certificate request

3. In the Create New Key and Certificate Request window, enter the appropriate values and click **OK**. In our case, we are using the following values:

- For Key Label - Bob Garcia. The Key Label is used to identify the certificate in an iKeyman list.
- For Key Size - 1024.
- For Common Name - Bob Garcia. The common name must match that of the LDAP user entry. See "Using Certificate Mapping Filters" on page 734 for detailed information.
- For Organization - ibm.
- For Organization Unit - Raleigh.
- For Country - US.

- For the name of a file in which to store the certificate request - F:\ServerCerts\certreq.arm.

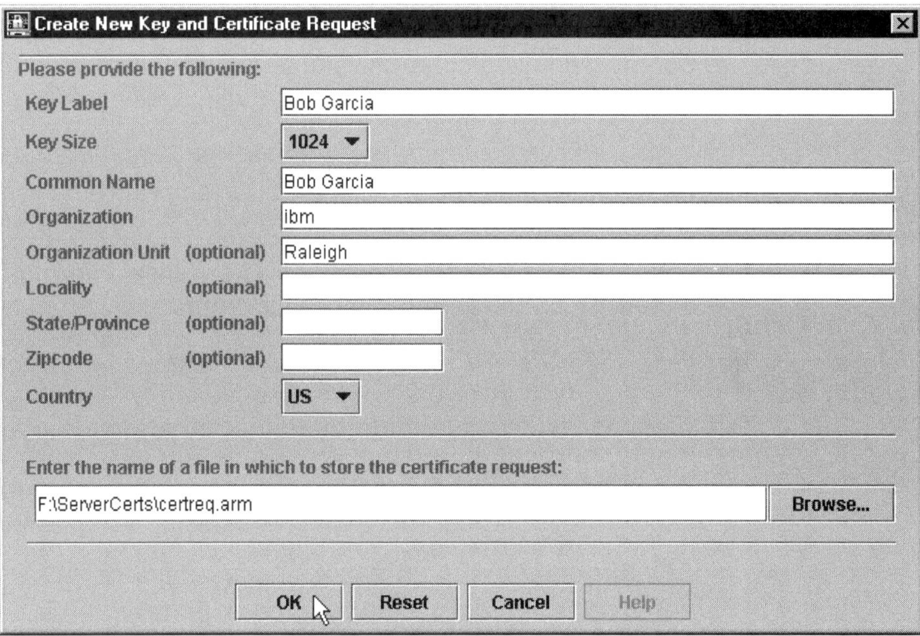

Figure 534. Create New Key and Certificate Request

4. Click **OK** on the Information window.

The Web-based services will now be used to obtain the client certificate. To obtain a new client certificate do the following:

1. From a browser, go to URL `http://marting.develop.com/certsrv/`. In our case, we are using Microsoft Internet Explorer.
2. From the Welcome page, select **Request a certificate** and click **Next**.
3. Select **Advanced request** and click **Next**.
4. Select **Submit a certificate request using a base64 encoded PKCS #10 file...** and click **Next**.
5. From a Windows NT DOS prompt window, use Notepad to edit the newly created certificate request file (certreq.arm). Use the Notepad edit functions to copy the entire contents of the file to the clipboard.
6. Back in the certificate services page, paste the clipboard contents into the Saved Request edit box.
7. Click the **Submit** button.

8. In the Certificate Issued page, select **Base 64 encoded** then click **Download CA certificate**.
9. In the File Download window, make sure that **Save this file to disk** is selected, then click **OK**.
10. Specify a directory to save in and a file name, then click **Save**. In our case the directory is ServerCerts and file name is BGcertnew.cer.

Now, iKeyman will be used to receive the newly obtained Bob Garcia client certificate into the server key database. To receive the certificate, do the following:

1. From the main iKeyman window, select personal certificates from the drop-down list in the Key database content area.
2. Click **Receive...**.

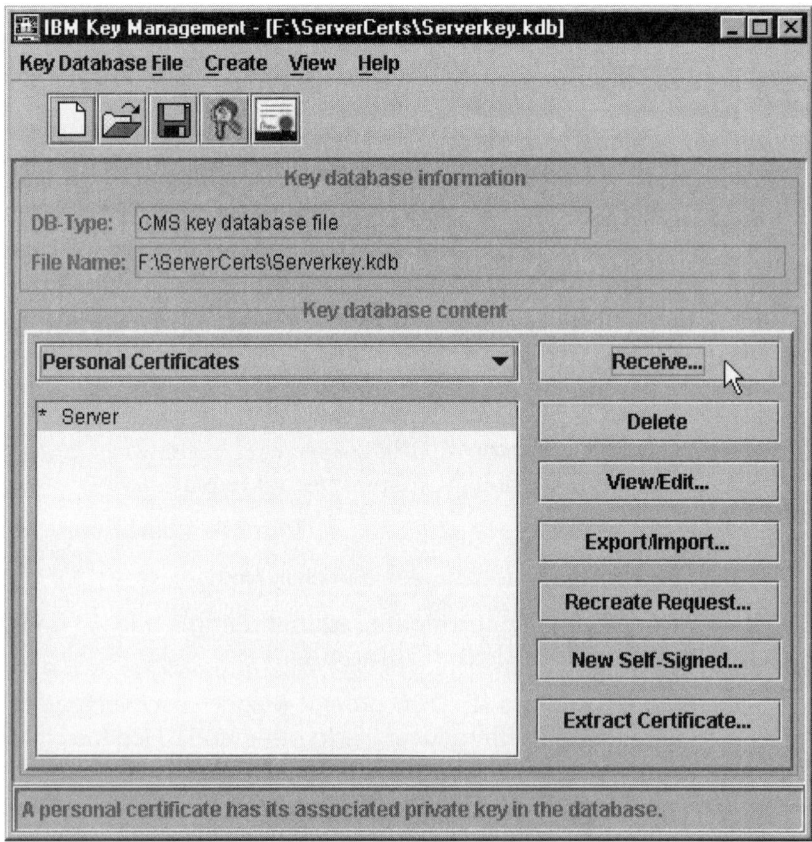

Figure 535. Receive a new Personal Certificate

3. In the Receive Certificate from File window:
   - Leave the data type as Base64-encoded ASCII data.
   - Type the Certificate file name. In our case, the name is BGcertnew.cer.
   - Type the Location. In our case, it is f:\ServerCerts\.
   - Click **OK**.

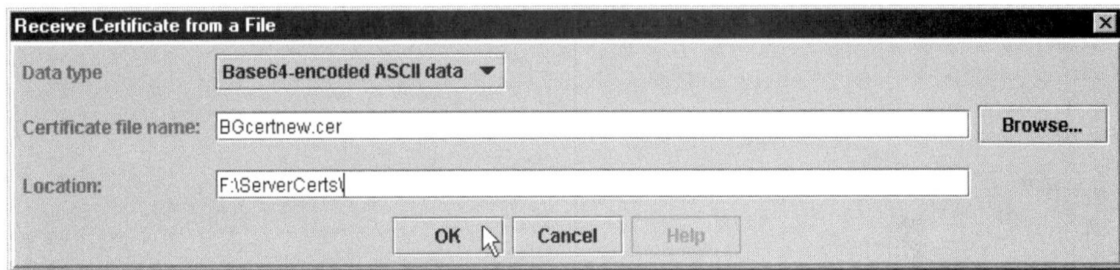

Figure 536. Receive Certificate from a File

   - Click **No** in the Confirm window. Do not set this as the default type for the key database.

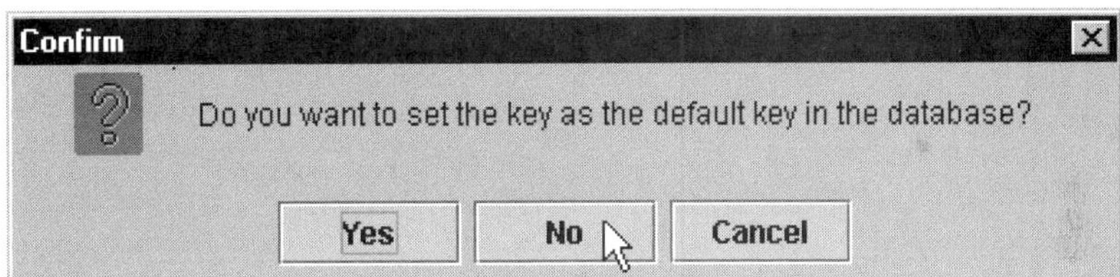

Figure 537. Confirm window

4. You should now see two entries in the Personal Certificates list, one for the server and one for Bob Garcia.

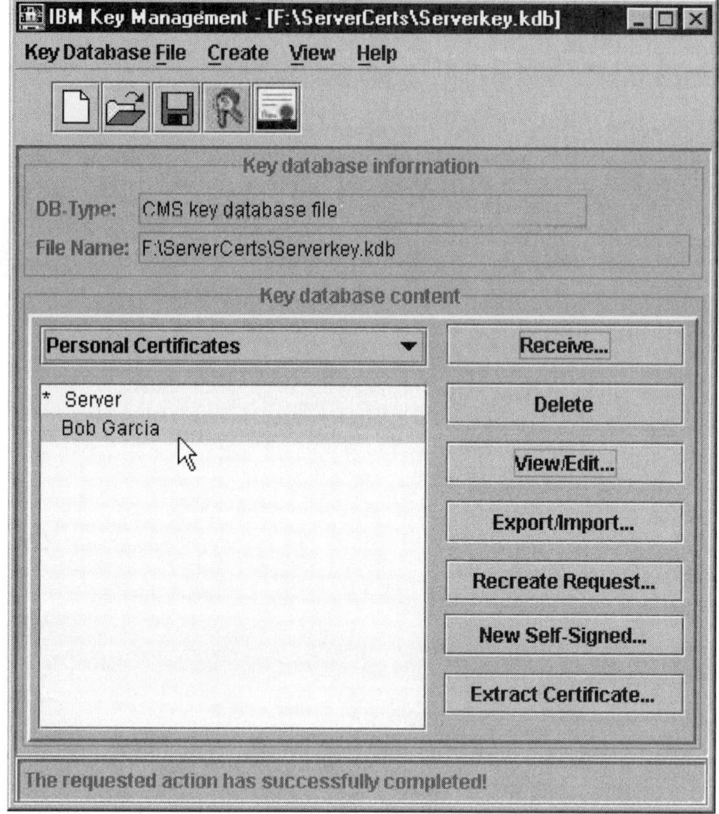

Figure 538. The new client certificate in the Personal Certificates list

15.4.3.5 Update the browser for certificate authentication

The CA signer certificate and the Bob Garcia client certificate need to be imported into the Web browser. In our case, the browser will be located on the same machine as WebSphere, so the certificate files we need to import are already local. We will be using Internet Explorer (IE) V5 in our example.

To import the CA signer certificate into the browser, do the following:

1. From the IE menu bar, select **Tools ->Internet Options...**.
2. Click the **Content** tab.
3. Click the **Certificates** button.

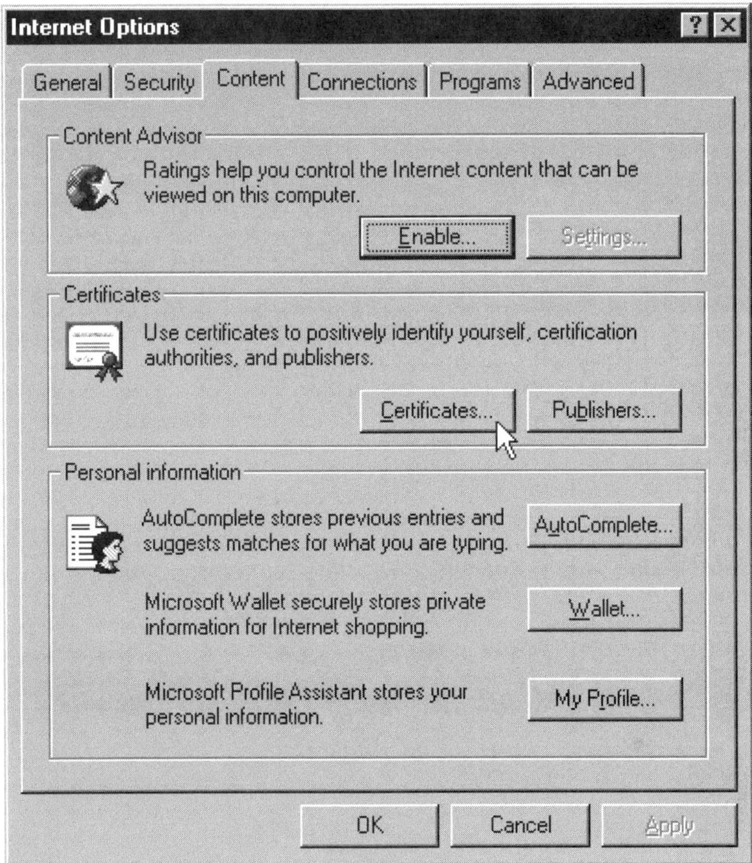

Figure 539. Internet Options in Internet Explorer

4. Click the **Import...** button.

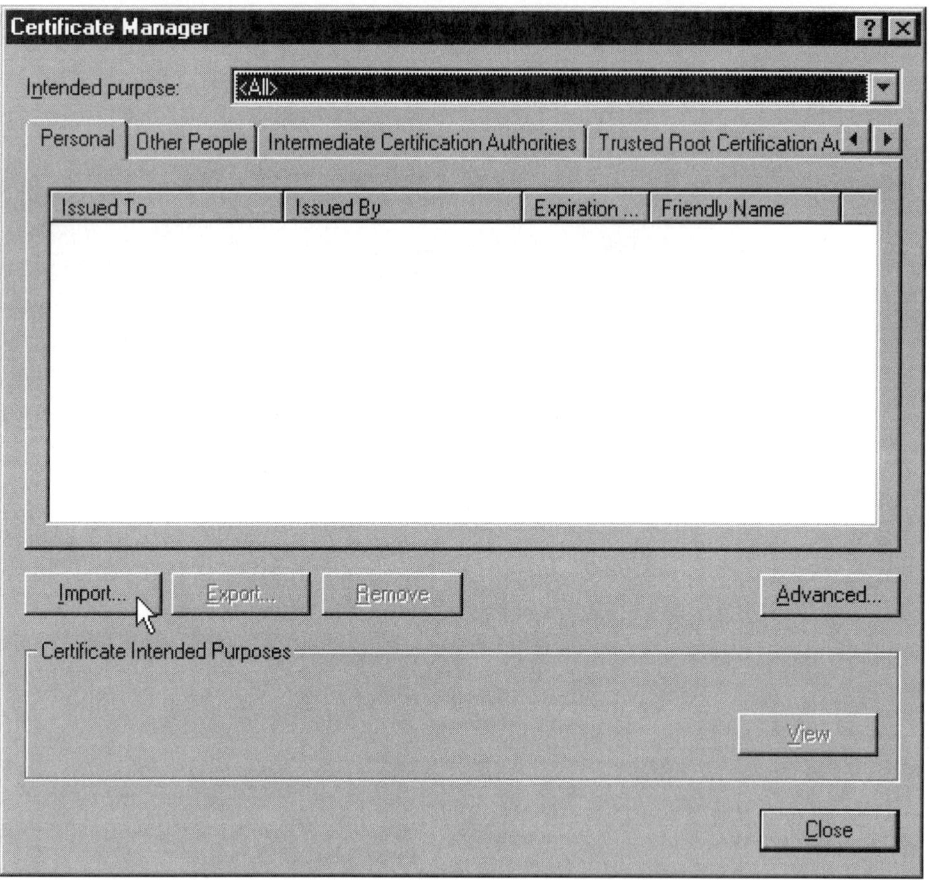

Figure 540. Import the CA signer certificate

5. In the Certificate Manager Import Wizard, click **Next**.
6. Type or browse for the file to import and click **Next**. The file to import is the CA signer certificate. In our case the file name is F:\ServerCerts\CAcertnew.cer.

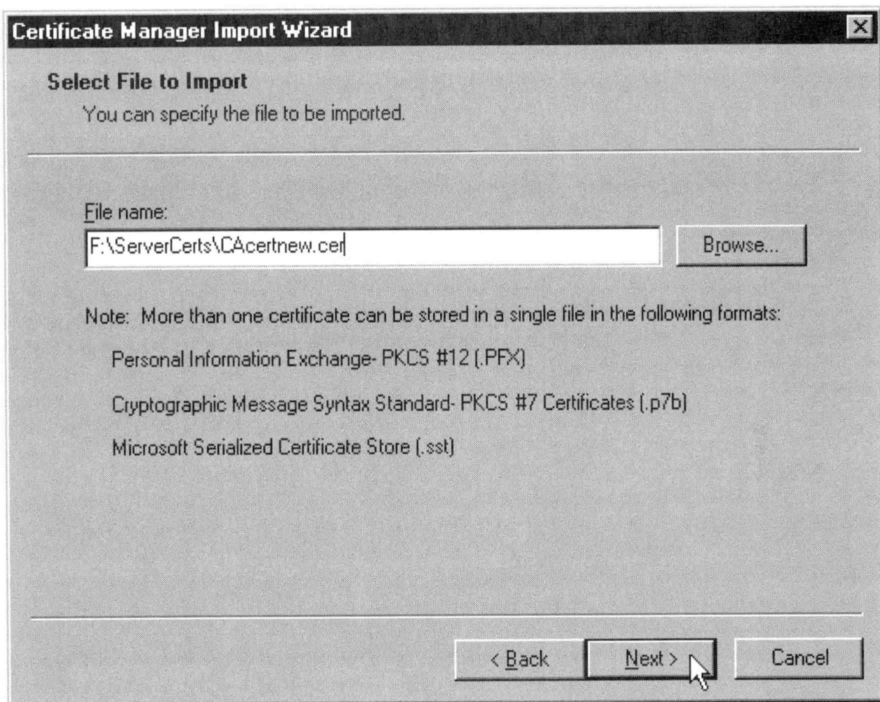

Figure 541. Select File to Import

7. In the Select a Certificate Store window, select **Place all certificates into the following store**.

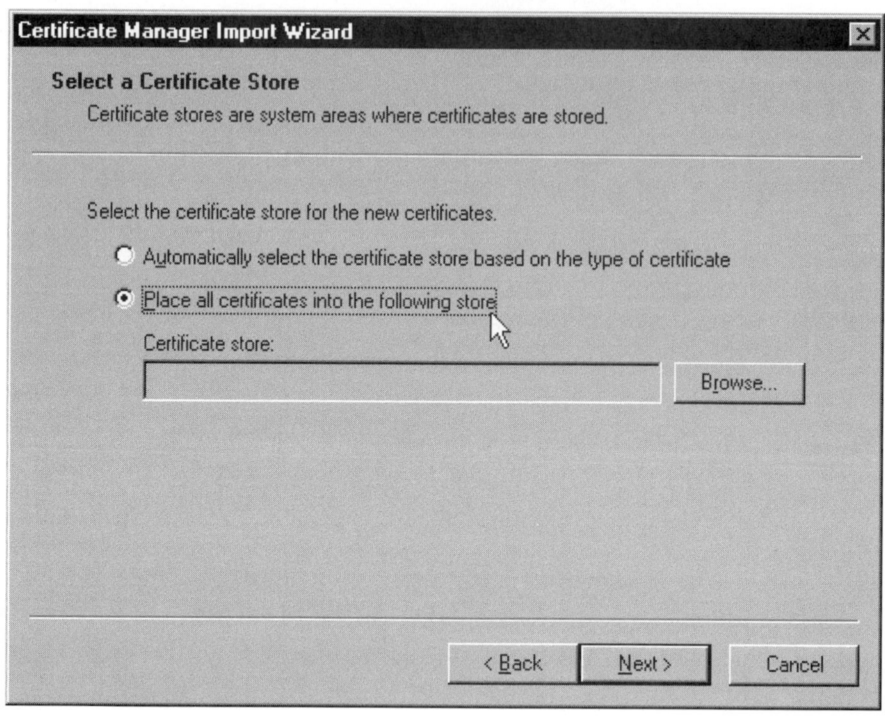

Figure 542. Select a Certificate Store

Then, click the **Browse...** button, select **Trusted Root Certificate Authorities** and click **OK**.

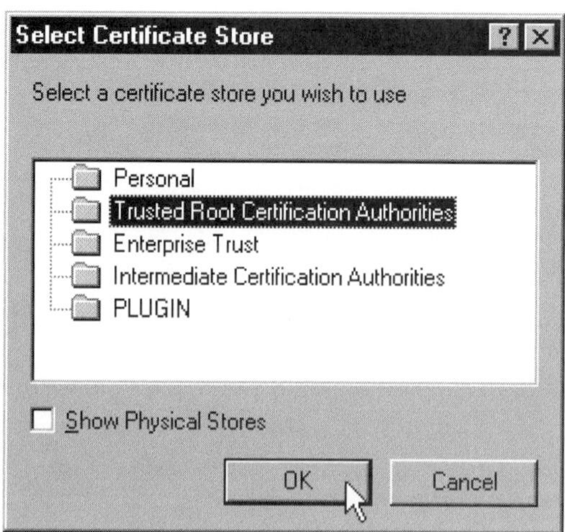

Figure 543. Select a Certificate Store for the Trusted Root Certification Authorities

Back in the Select a Certificate Store window, you will see that the certificate which you will store will be considered one from a trusted root Certification Authority. Then click **Next**.

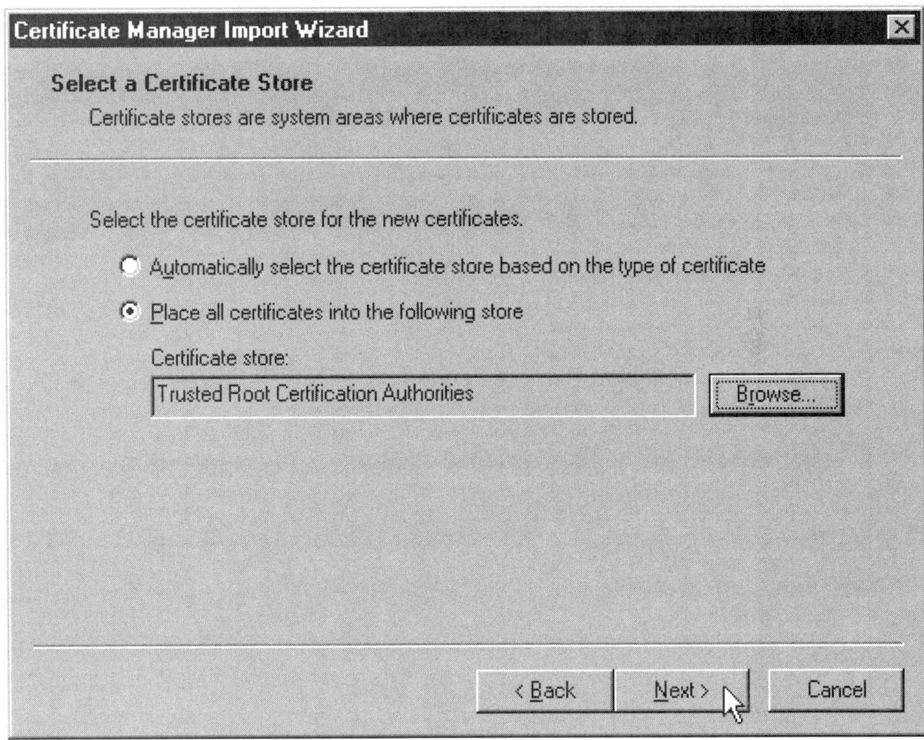

Figure 544. Select a Certificate Store

8. On the Completing the Certificate Manager Import Wizard window, click **Finish**.

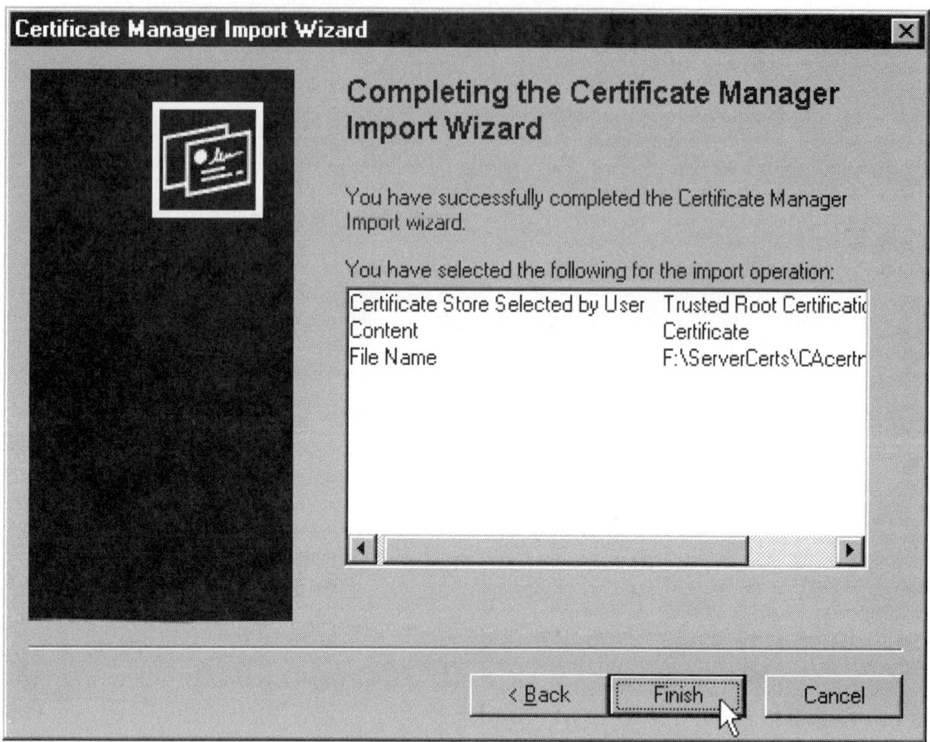

Figure 545. Completing the Certificate Manager Import Wizard

9. Click **Yes** to the Do you want to ADD the following certificate to the Root Store question.

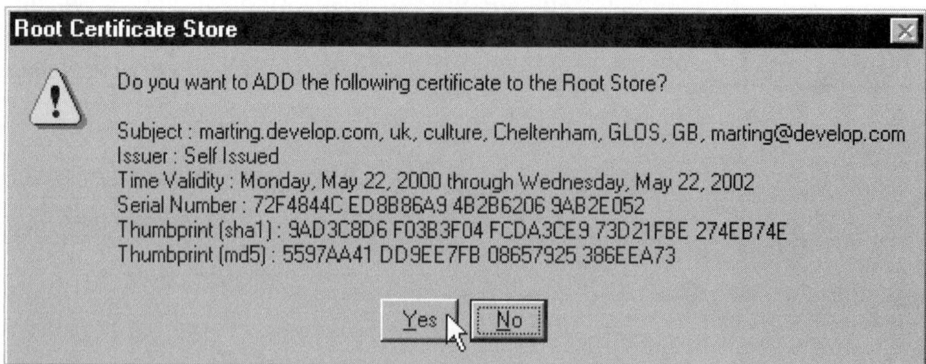

Figure 546. Adding the certificate to the Root Store

10.Click **OK** to `The import was successful` message.

11.Back in the Certificate Manager main window, make sure the Trusted Root Certification Authorities tab is active, then scroll down to the marting.develop.com entry. That is the newly imported certificate. You should see something similar to what is shown in Figure 547.

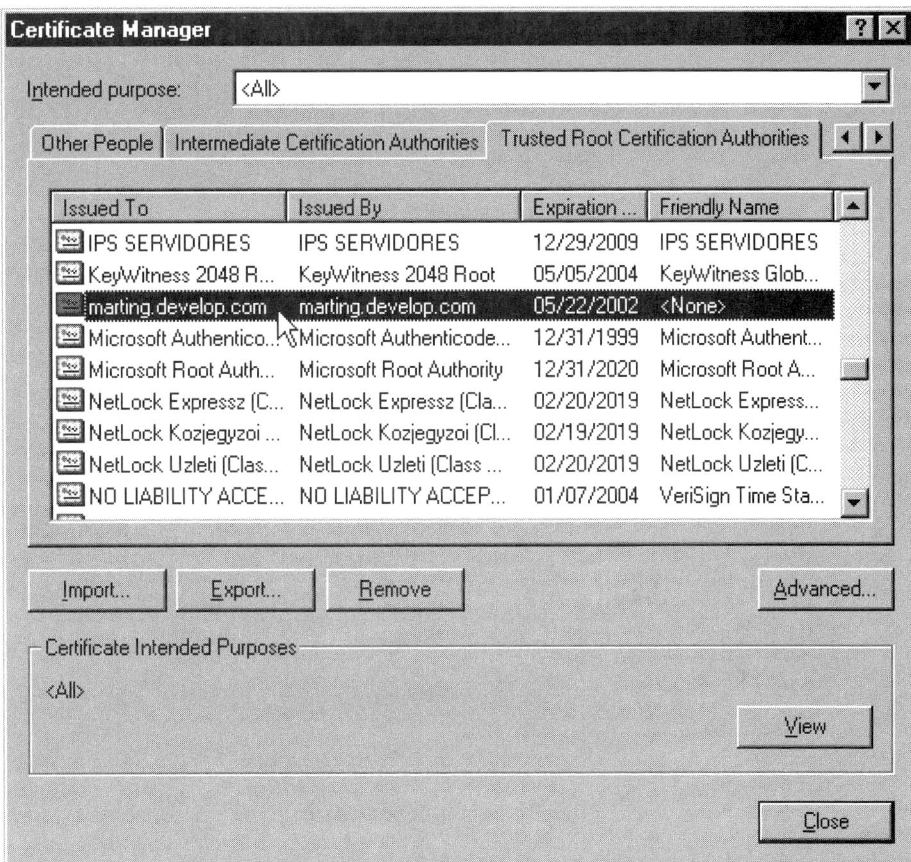

Figure 547. Microsoft IE Certificate Manager - Trusted Root CA list

To import the Bob Garcia client certificate into the browser, we first need to export it from iKeyman into a form that is acceptable to IE. IE does not directly accept the BGcertnew.cer created from the Web-based certificate services. To export the certificate in an acceptable form, do the following:

1. From the main iKeyman window, select personal certificates from the drop-down list in the Key database content area.
2. Select **Bob Garcia** from the certificate list and click **Export/Import...**.

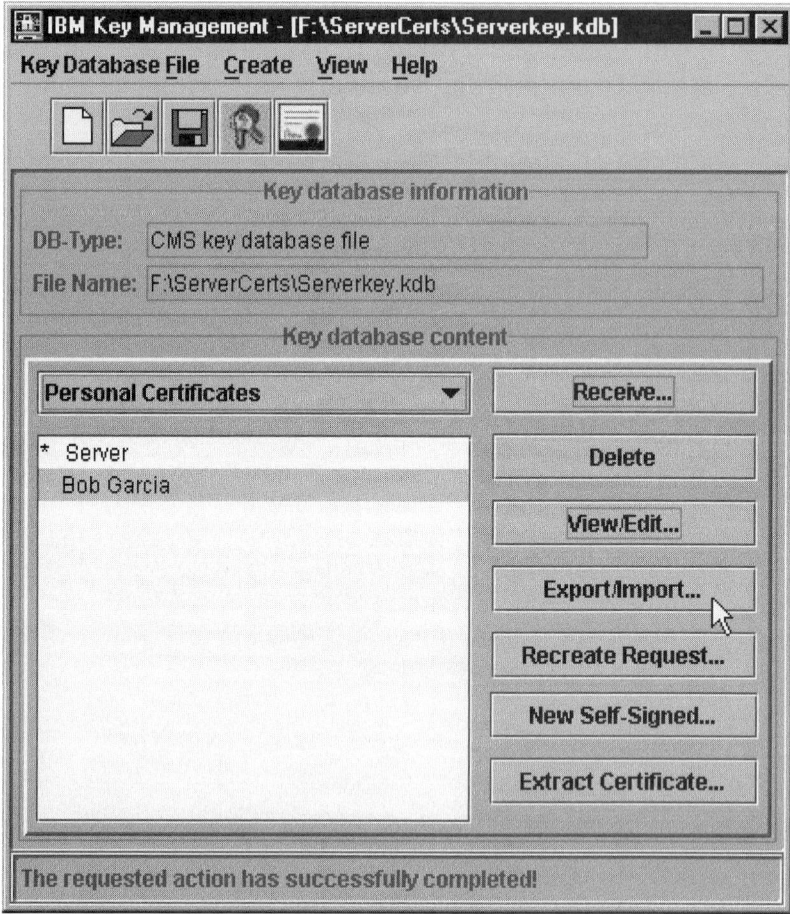

Figure 548. Select the client certificate to export

3. In the Export/Import Key window, do the following:

- Leave the Action Type as Export Key.
- Leave the Key file type as PKCS12 file.
- Type the file name of the resulting exported file, keeping the file type of p12. In our case, the name is BGcertnew.p12.
- Type the Location. In our case, it is f:\ServerCerts\.
- Click **OK**.

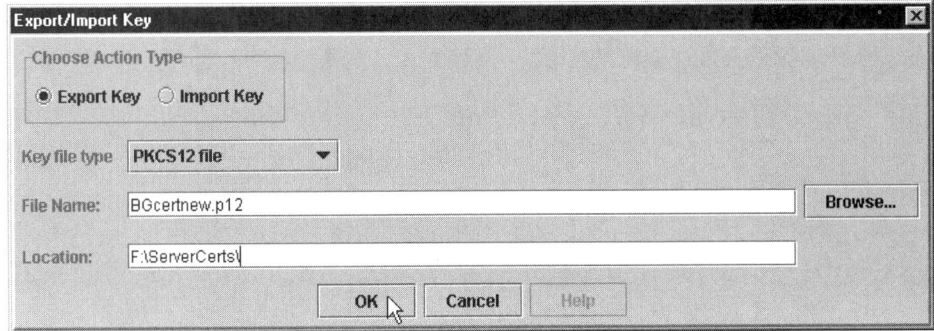

Figure 549. Export/Import Key

4. In the Password Prompt window, type and confirm a password for the exported file and click **OK**.

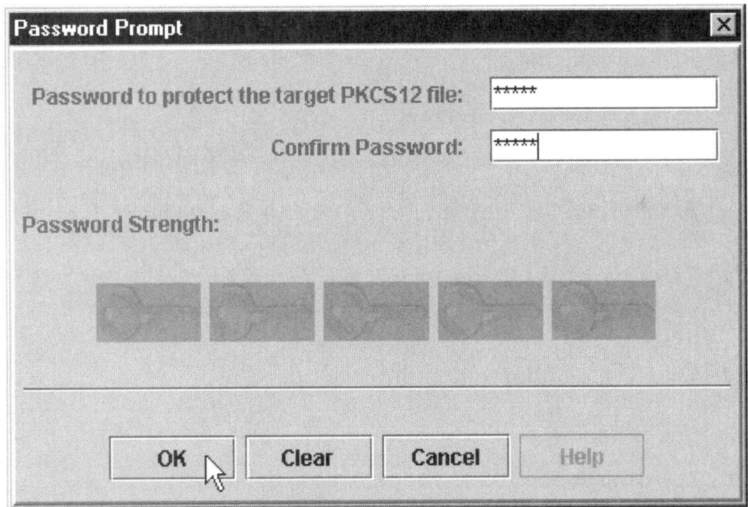

Figure 550. Password Prompt window

5. In the Select Encryption Type window, leave the selection as Strong and click **OK**.

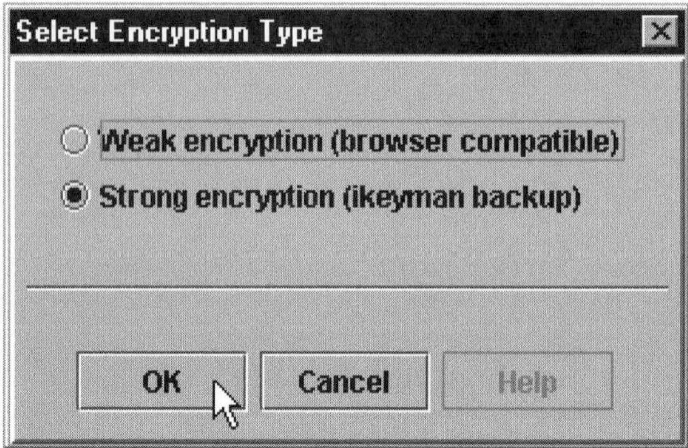

Figure 551. Select Encryption Type

To import the Bob Garcia client certificate into the browser, do the following:

1. From the IE menu bar, select **Tools -> Internet Options...**.
2. Click the **Content** tab.
3. Click the **Certificates** button.
4. Click the **Import...** button.
5. In the Certificate Manger Import Wizard, click **Next**.
6. Type or browse for the file to import and click **Next**. The file to import is the file just exported from iKeyman. In our case the File name is F:\ServerCerts\BGcertnew.p12.

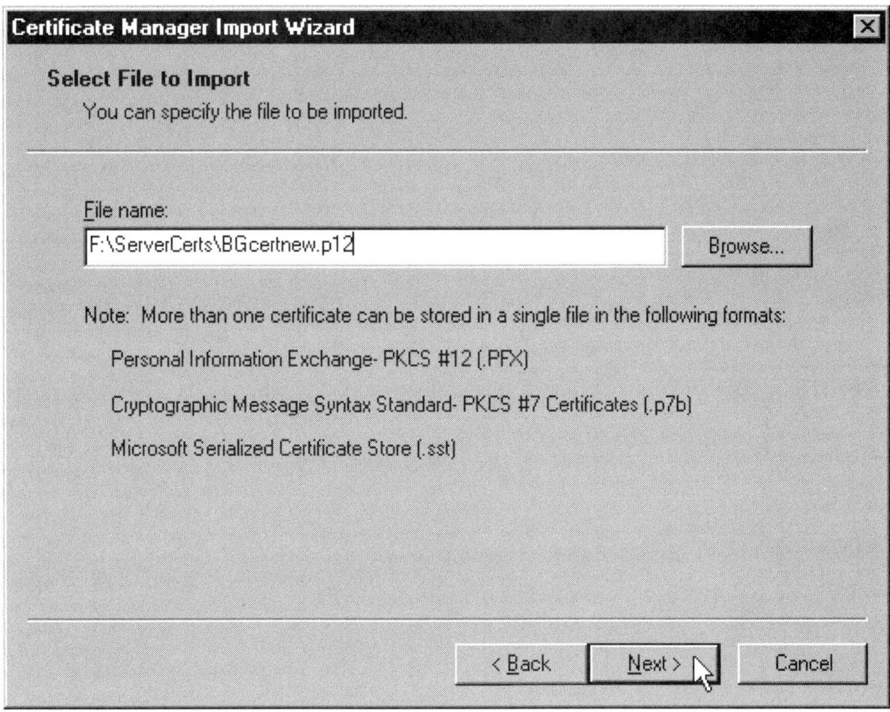

Figure 552. Select File to Import

7. In the Password Protection for Private Keys window, enter the password for the file to import and click **Next**.

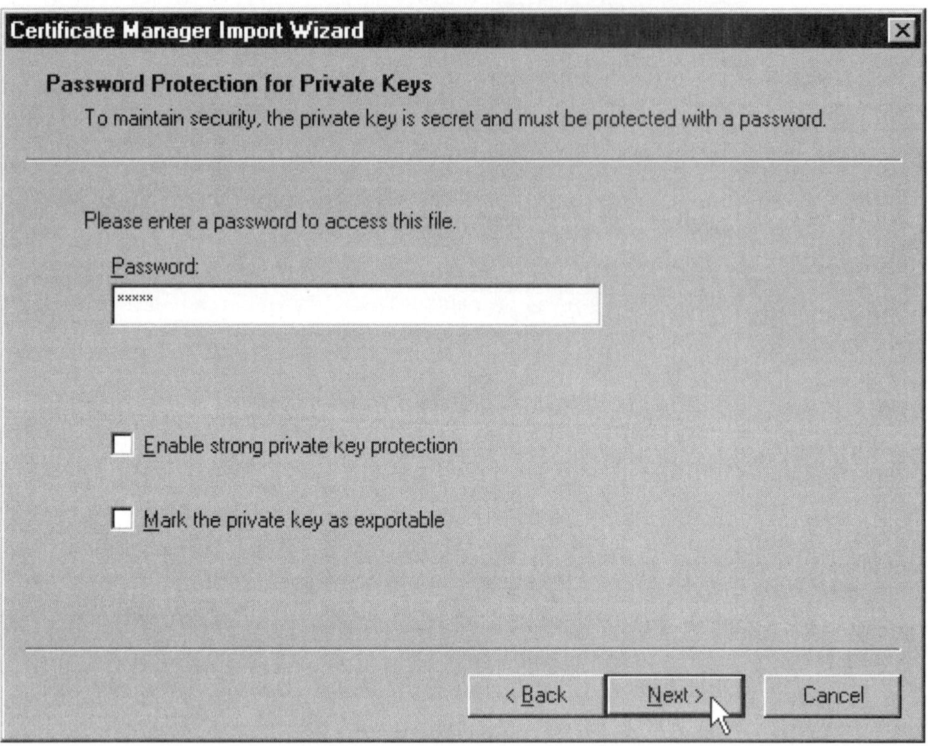

Figure 553. Password Protection for Private Keys

8. In the Select a Certificate Store window, select **Place all certificates into the following store**.

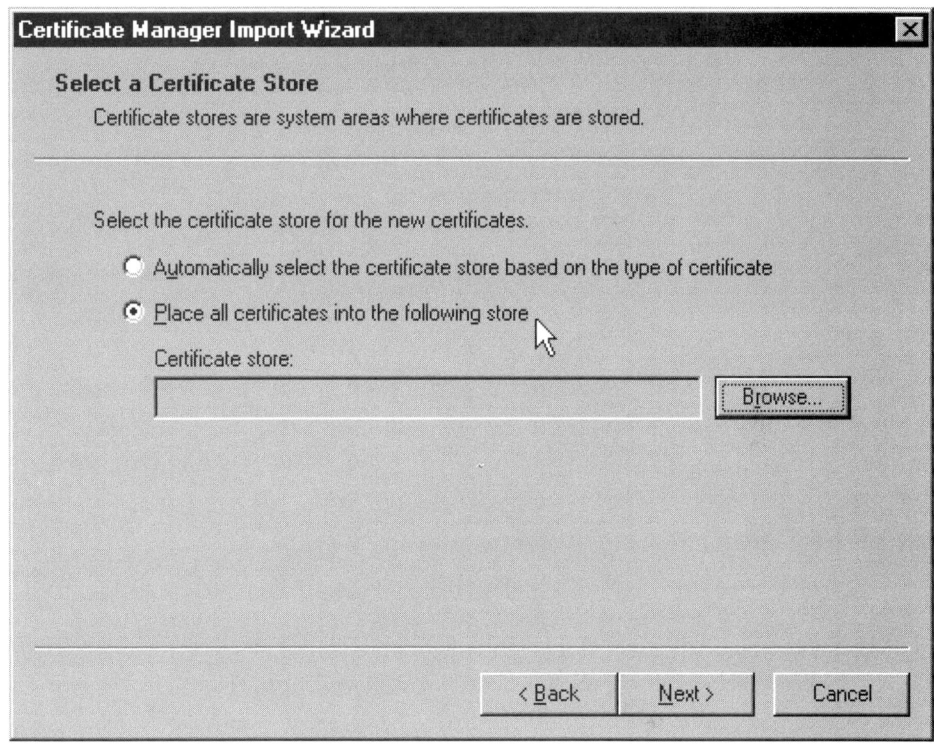

Figure 554. Select a Certificate Store

Then click the **Browse...** button, select **Personal** and click **OK**.

Figure 555. Select a certificate store for the Personal certificate

Then back in the Select a Certificate Store window, click **Next**.

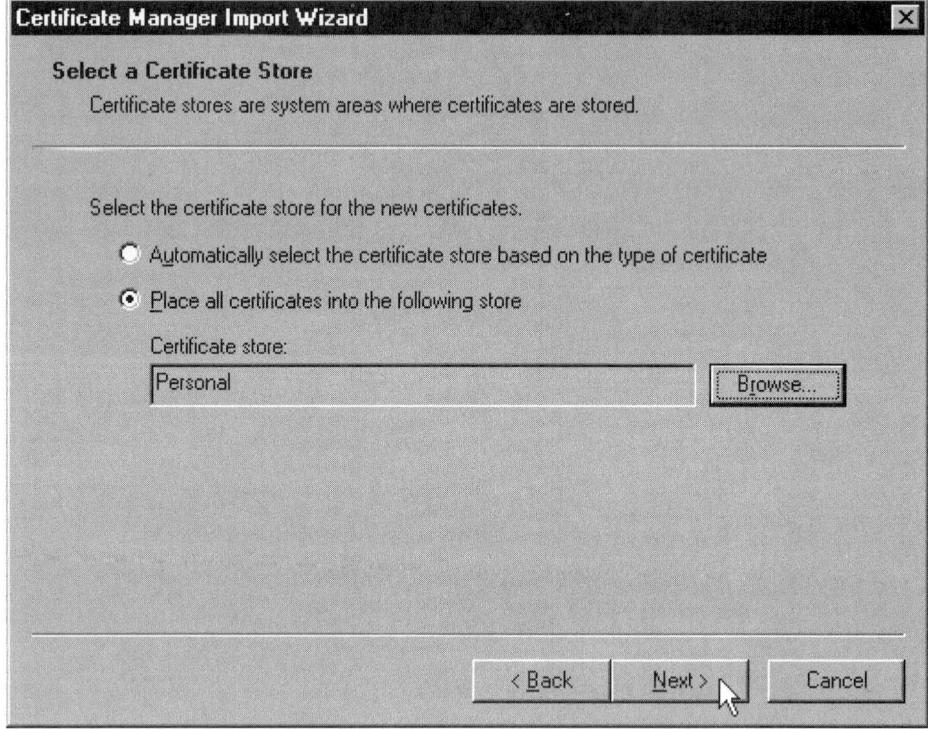

Figure 556. Select a Certificate Store

9. In the Certificate Manager Import Wizard window, click **Finish**.
10. Click **OK** to `The import was successful` message.

Back in the Certificate Manager main window, make sure the Personal tab is active. There should be an entry in the list for Bob Garcia. We have now completed the process for creation of our user Bob Garcia certificate.

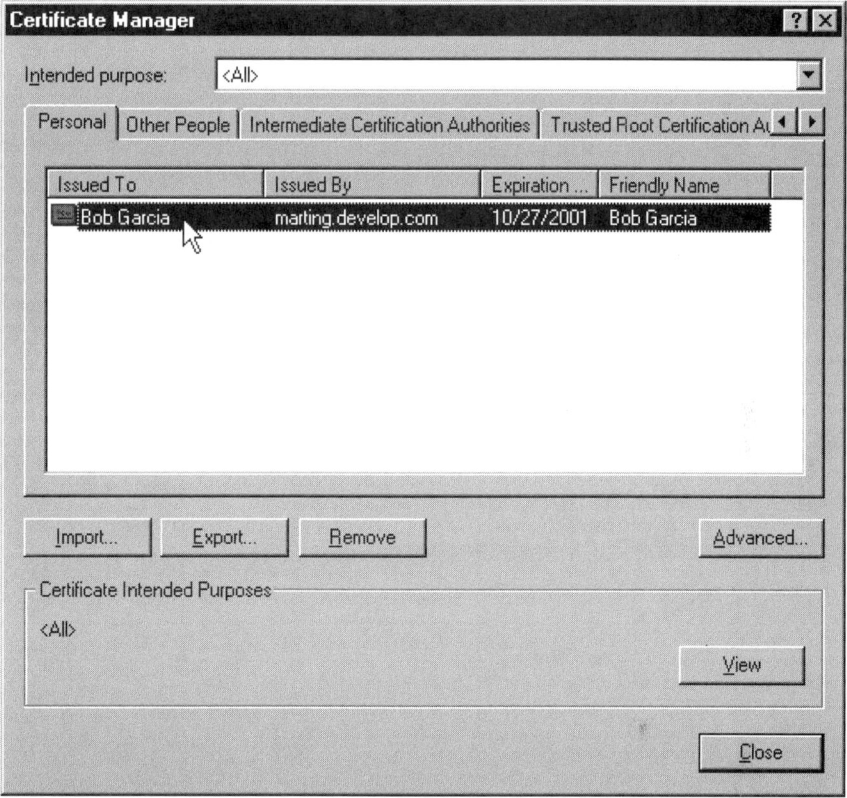

Figure 557. The client certificate in the IE

For testing purposes you may want to create a second client certificate to match the user Mary Burnnet entry in our LDAP directory. Follow the same process used to create and deploy the user Bob Garcia certificate.

15.4.4 Configuring the IBM HTTP Server to support HTTPS

An SSL link must be established in order for the browser and server to exchange certificates. The IBM HTTP server must be configured to allow SSL communications.

To enable SSL for the IBM HTTP Server (IHS), do the following:

1. Make sure that the IBM HTTP Server and the IBM HTTP Administration Server are running.
2. Also make sure that the IHS Administration user ID and password have been set. If not, use the HTPASSWD utility shipped with the product to set the ID and password.

3. Using a browser, access the IHS welcome page by specifying http://hostname as the URL and substitute the host name of your machine. In our case, the URL is `http://localhost`.

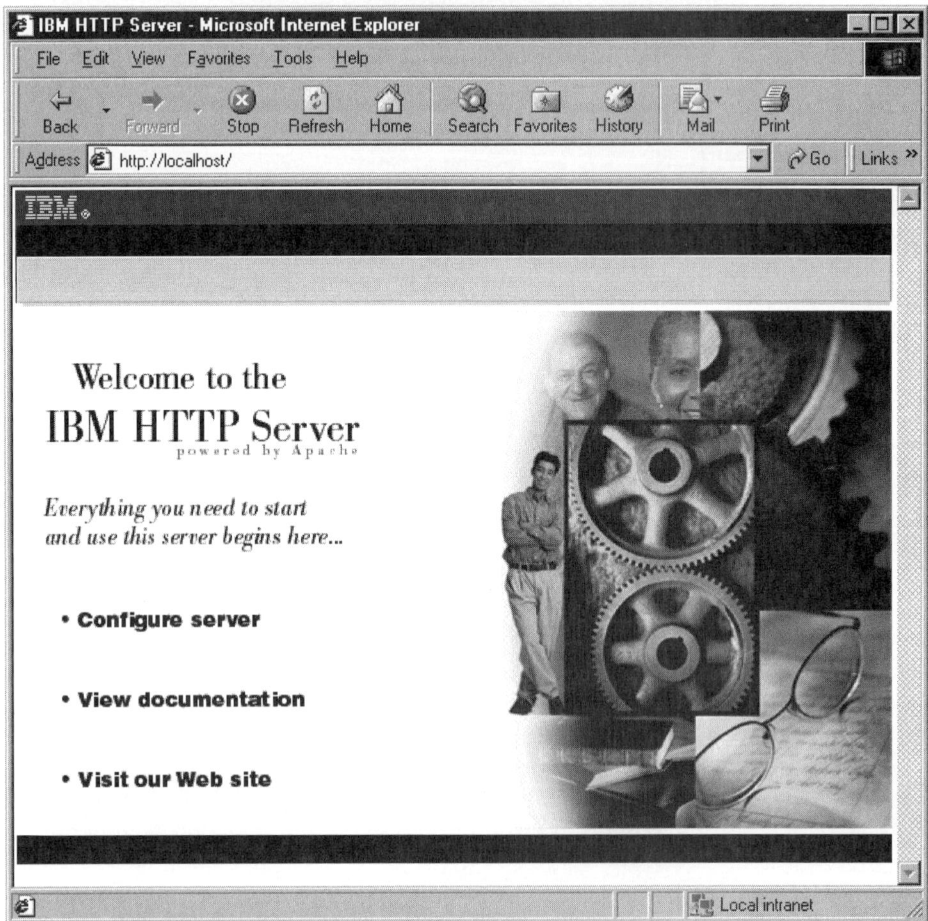

Figure 558. IBM HTTP Server (IHS) welcome page

4. Click **Configure server**. Then, type the IHS Administration user name (user ID) and password and click **OK**. You should come up in the IHS Administration GUI. Be patient. It may take several seconds for the left navigation frame to appear.

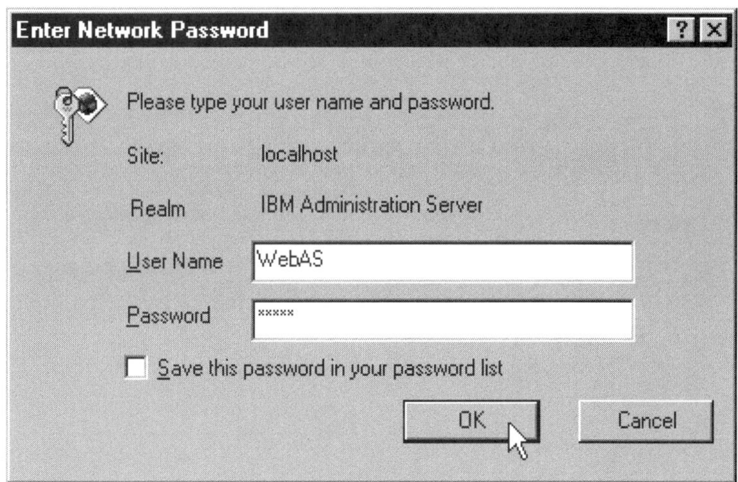

Figure 559. IHS - authorization for server configuration

5. To configure the security module:
   - In the left navigation frame, expand **Basic Settings**.

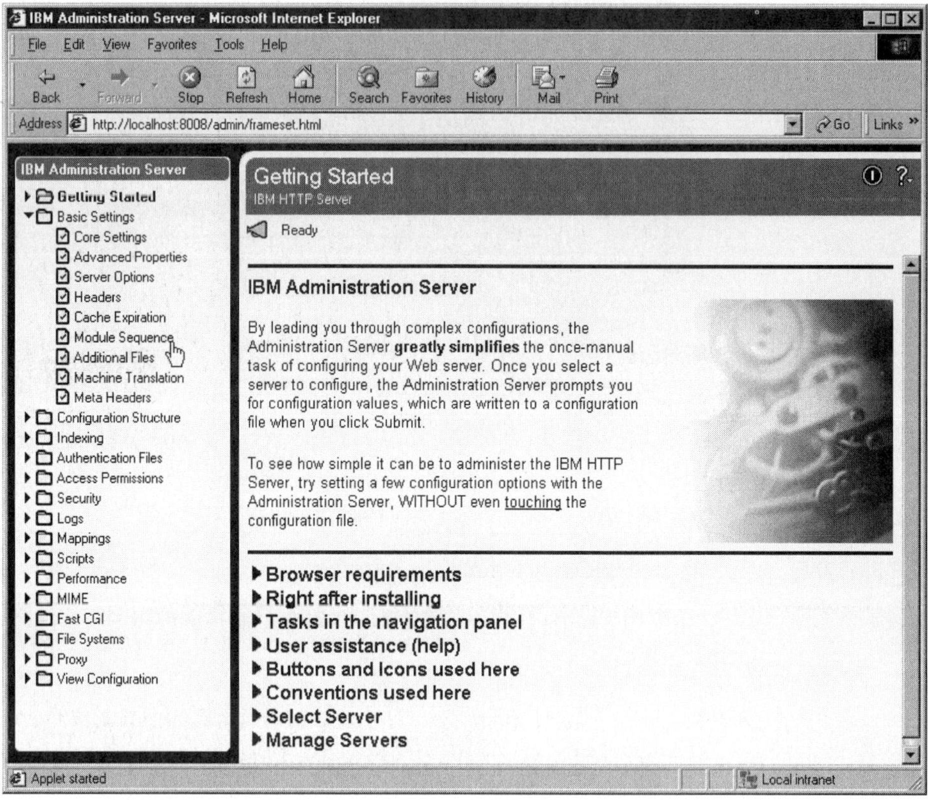

Figure 560. IHS - selecting the Module Sequence function

- Select **Module Sequence**.

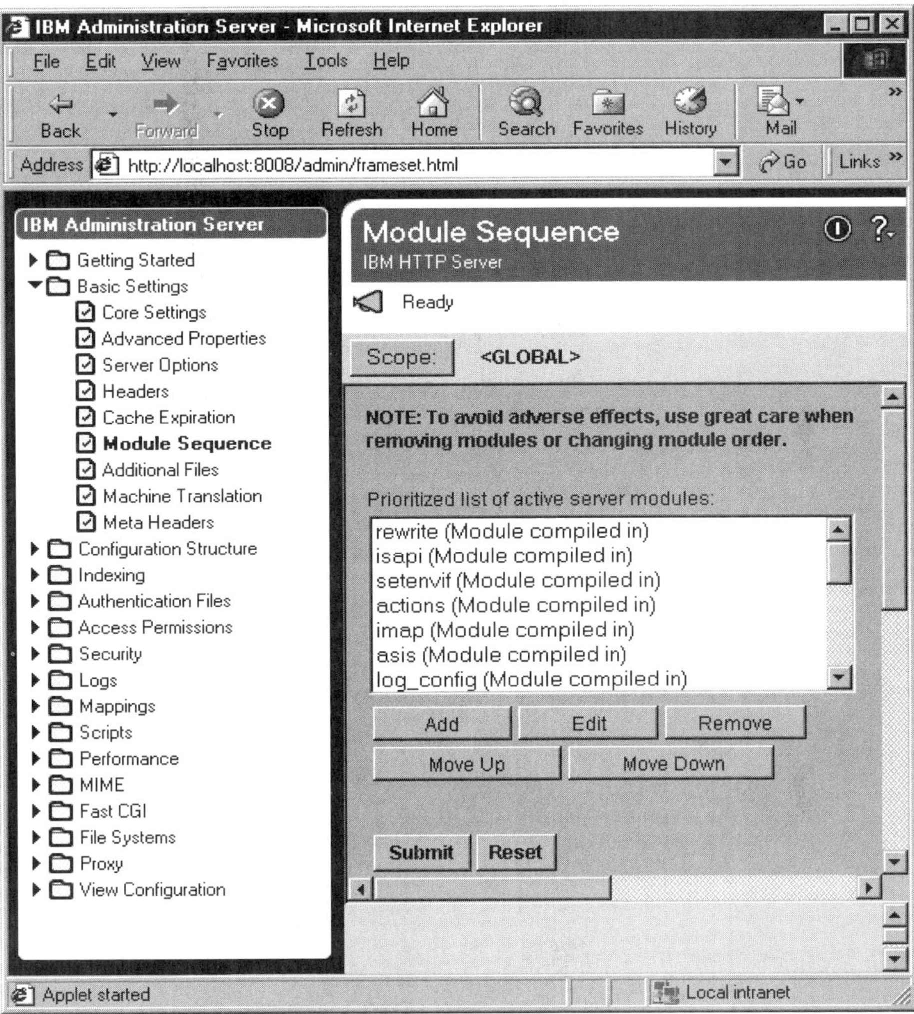

Figure 561. IHS - adding a module to the module sequence

- Make sure the Scope is GLOBAL. If the value to the right of the Scope: button is not <GLOBAL>, click the button and select <GLOBAL>.
- In the Module Sequence frame, click the **Add** button.
- Select **Select a module to add:** and open the drop-down list. Scroll to near the bottom of the list and select **ibm_ssl (IBMModuleSSL128.ddl)**. The Module DLL will be placed to the right.

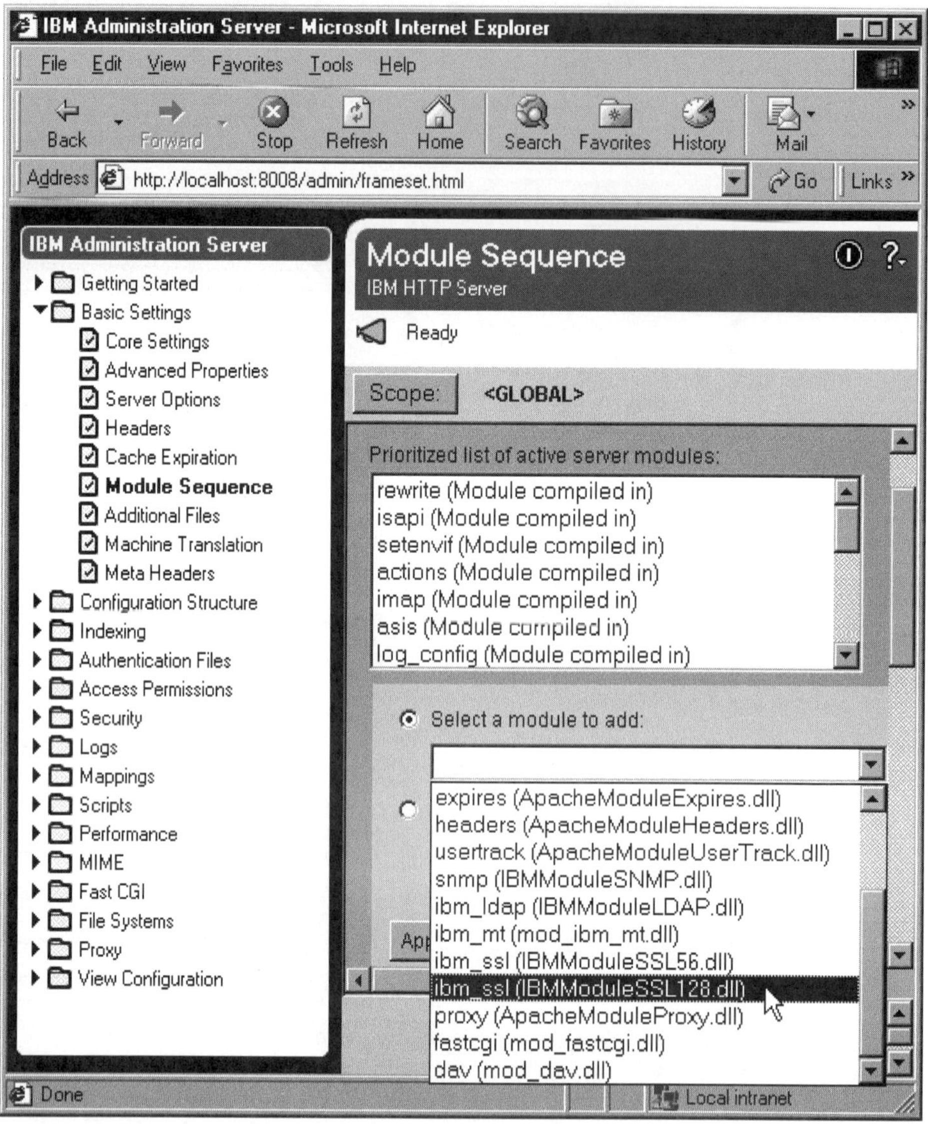

Figure 562. IHS - selecting a module to add to the module sequence

- Click the **Apply** button.

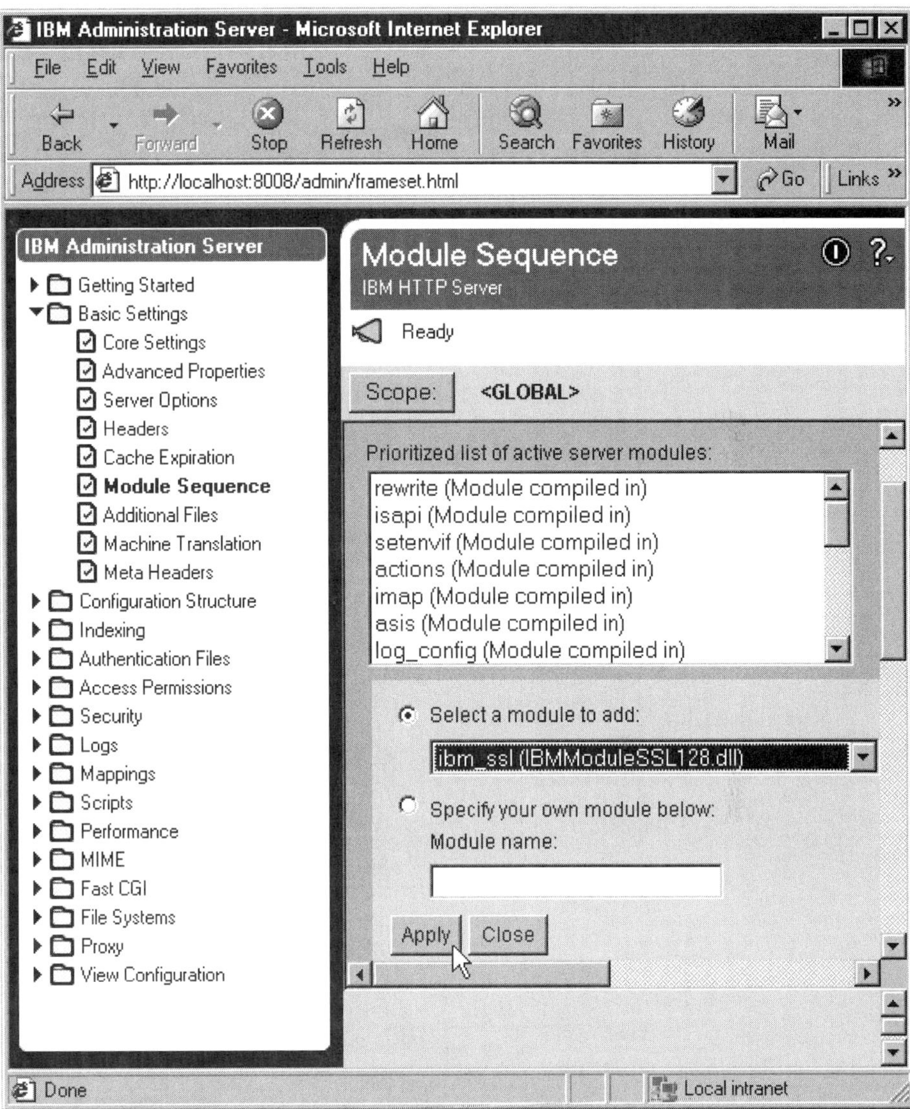

Figure 563. IHS - Apply button for adding to the module sequence

- Click the **Close** button.

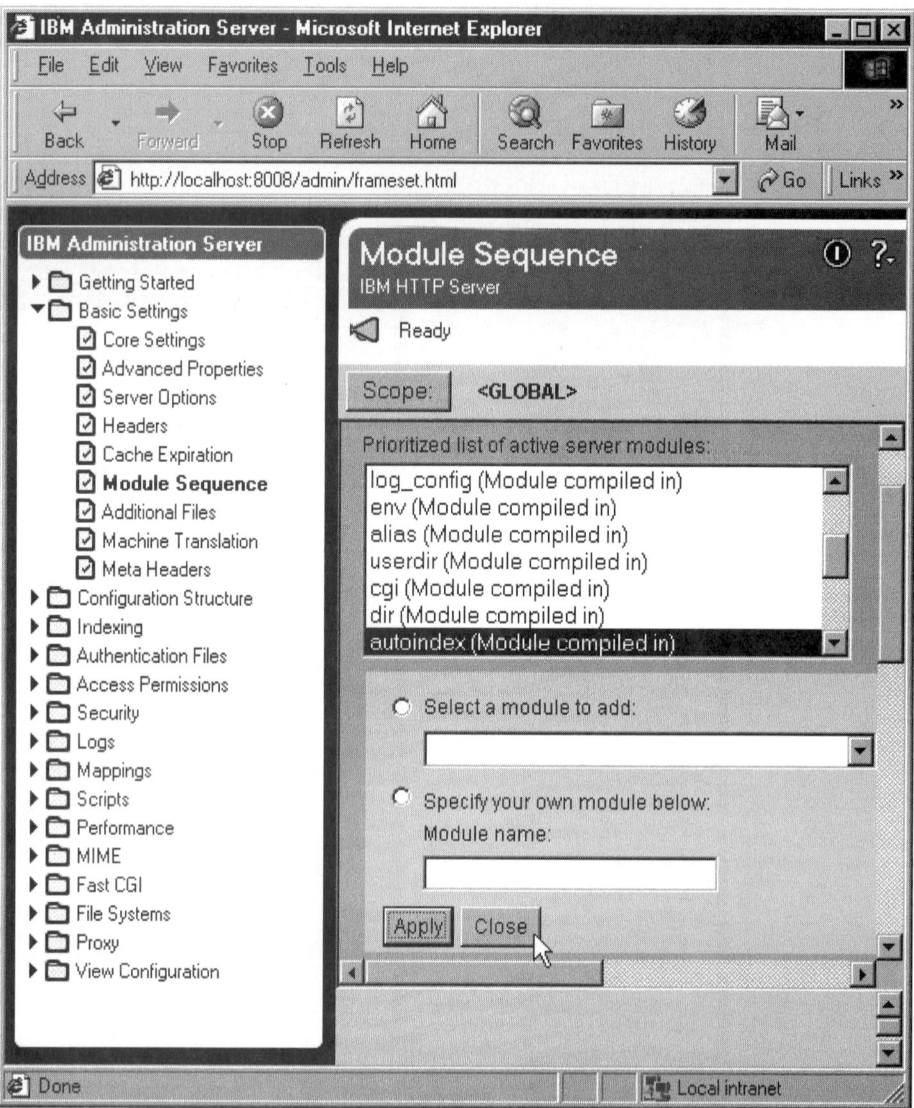

Figure 564. IHS - Close button for adding to the module sequence

- Click the **Submit** button.

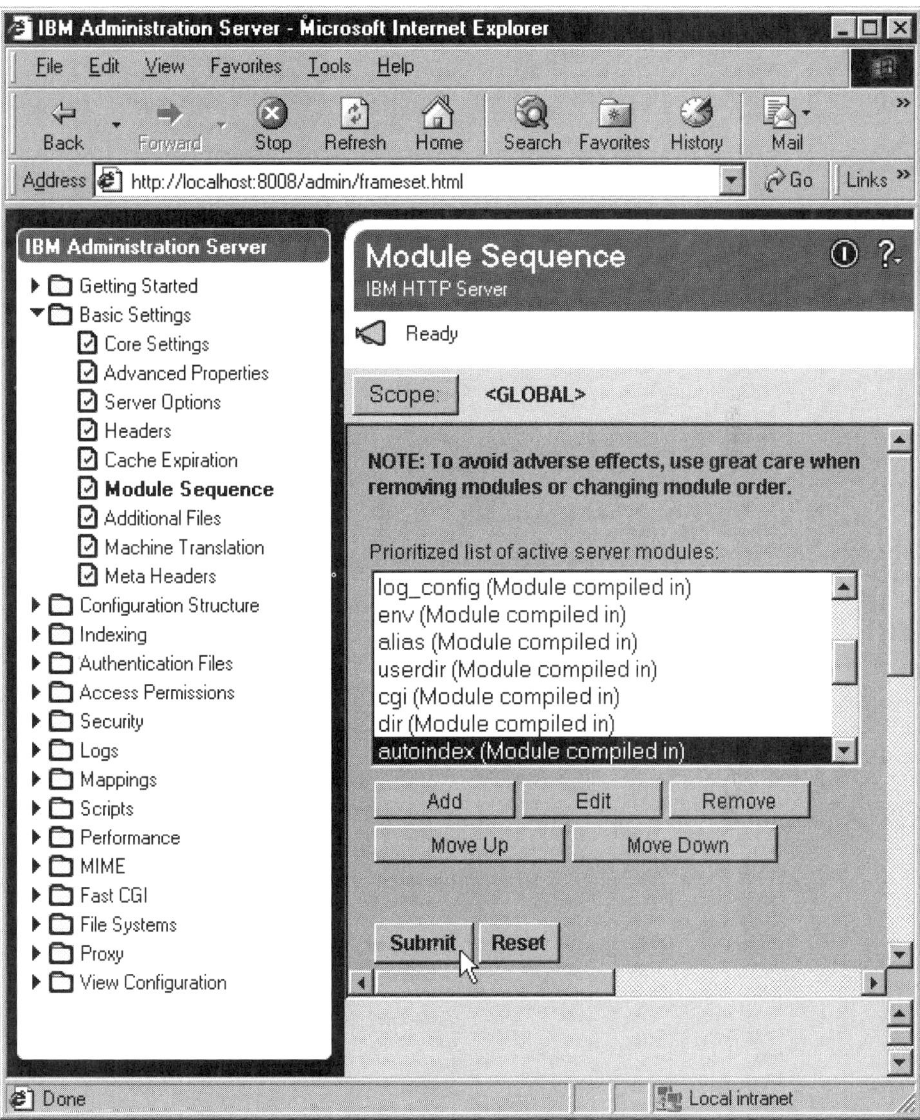

Figure 565. IHS - Submit button for adding to the module sequence

6. To set up the secure host IP and an additional port for the secure server, do the following:
   - In the left navigation frame, under Basic Settings, select **Advanced Properties**. Then, make sure the Scope is GLOBAL.
   - Click the **Add** button for the Specify additional ports and IP addresses field. Leave the IP address field empty and enter 443 in the port field.

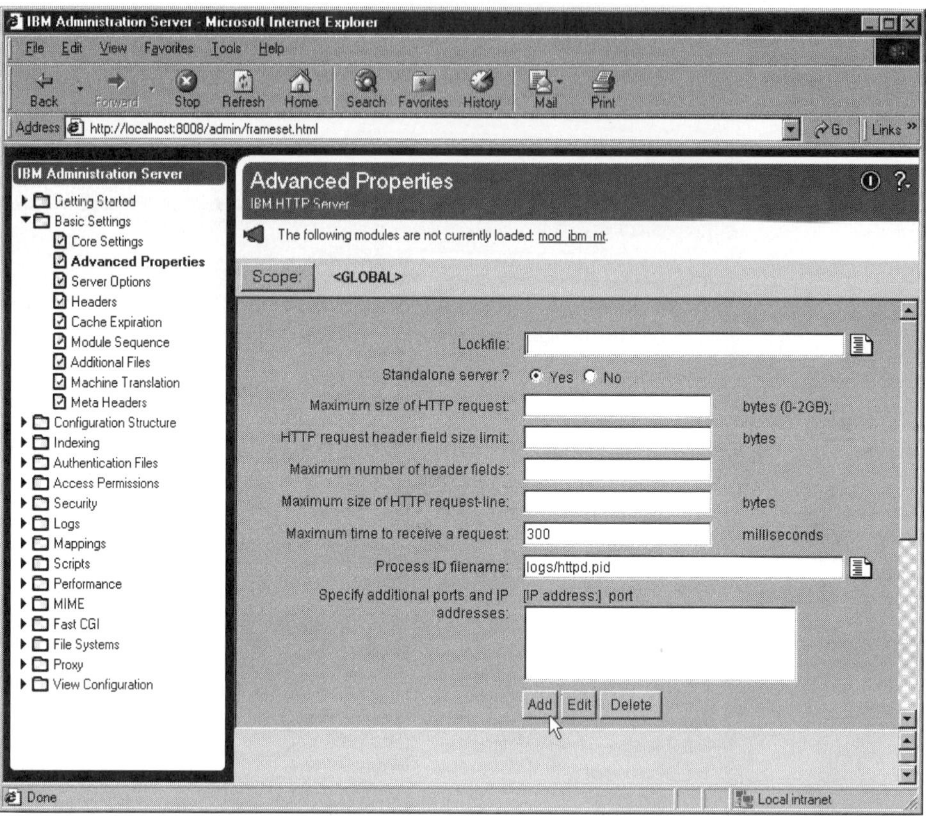

Figure 566. IHS - adding the SSL port

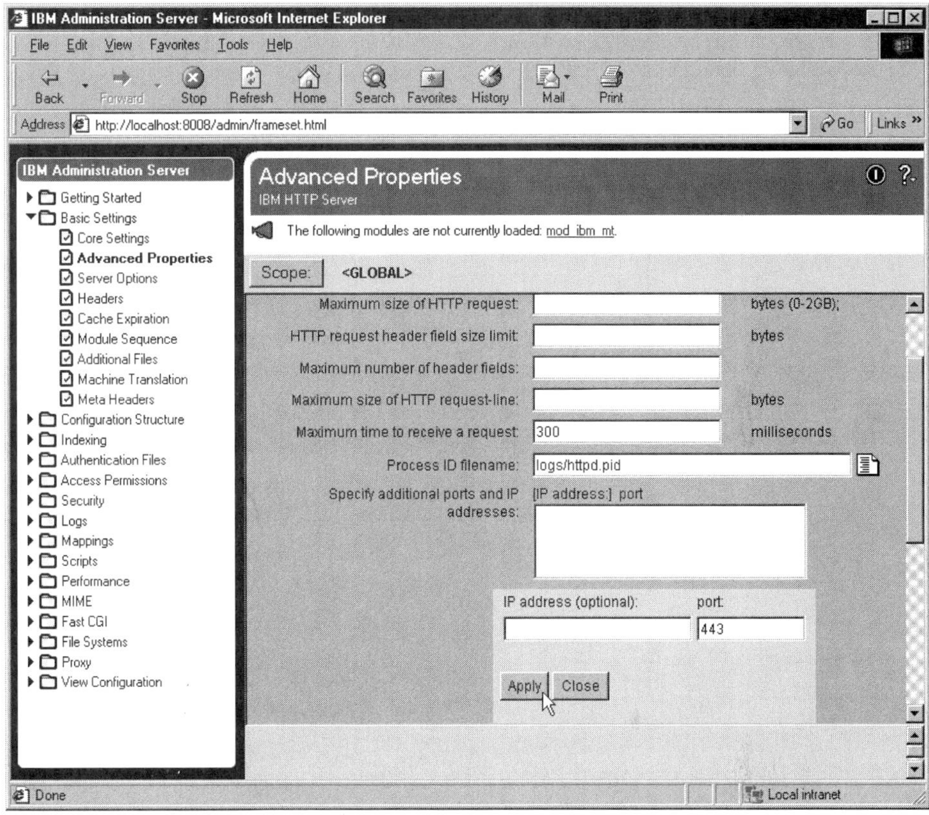

Figure 567. IHS - Apply button for adding the SSL port

- Click the **Apply** button. Click the **Close** button. Click the **Submit** button.

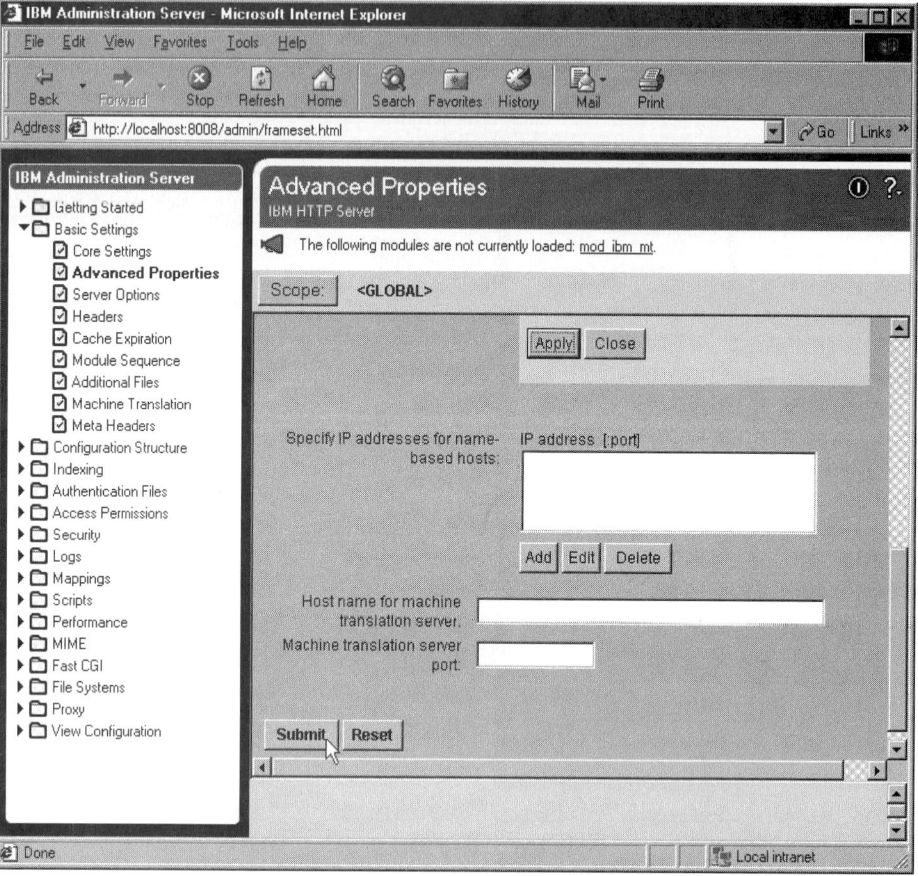

Figure 568. IHS - Submit button for adding the SSL port

7. To set up the virtual host structure for the secure server, do the following:
   - In the left navigation frame, expand **Configuration Structure**.
   - Select **Create Scope**. Then, make sure the Scope is GLOBAL. In this case, <Global> in the tree structure in the right panel should be highlighted.
   - Select **VirtualHost** in the Select a valid scope to insert within the scope selected in the right panel field.

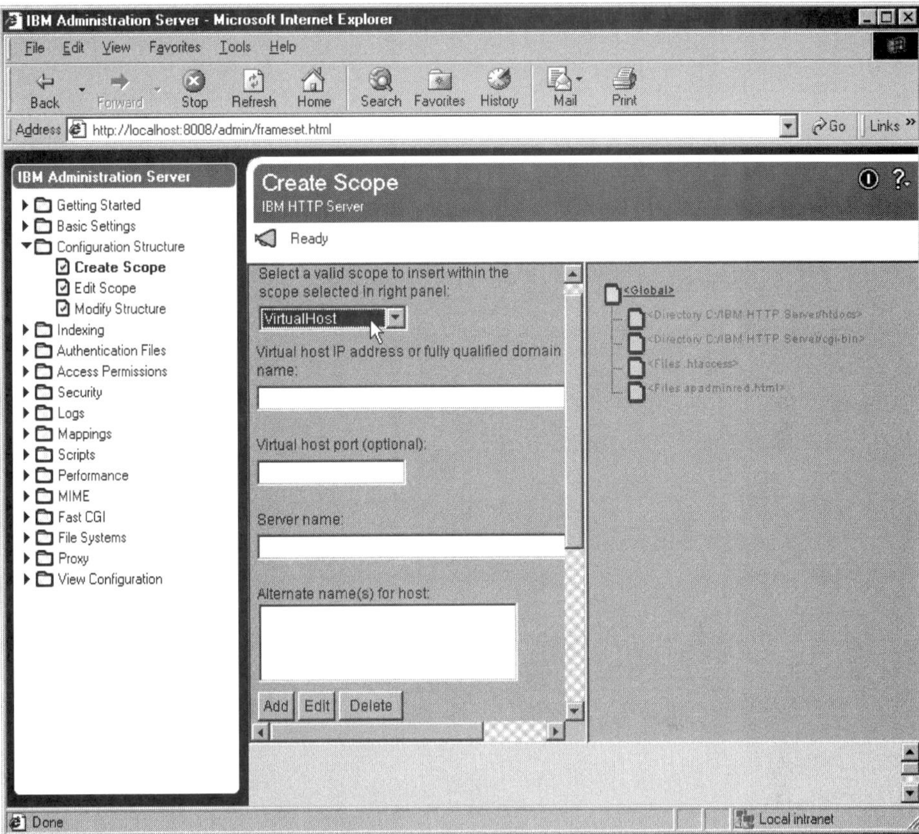

Figure 569. IHS - creating a virtual host

- Type the virtual host IP address or fully qualified domain name. In our case, the value is kenueno.itso.ral.ibm.com.
- Type the virtual host port value as 443.
- Type the server name. In our case, the name is kenueno.itso.ral.ibm.com.
- Leave the alternate name(s) for host blank.
- Click the **Submit** button.

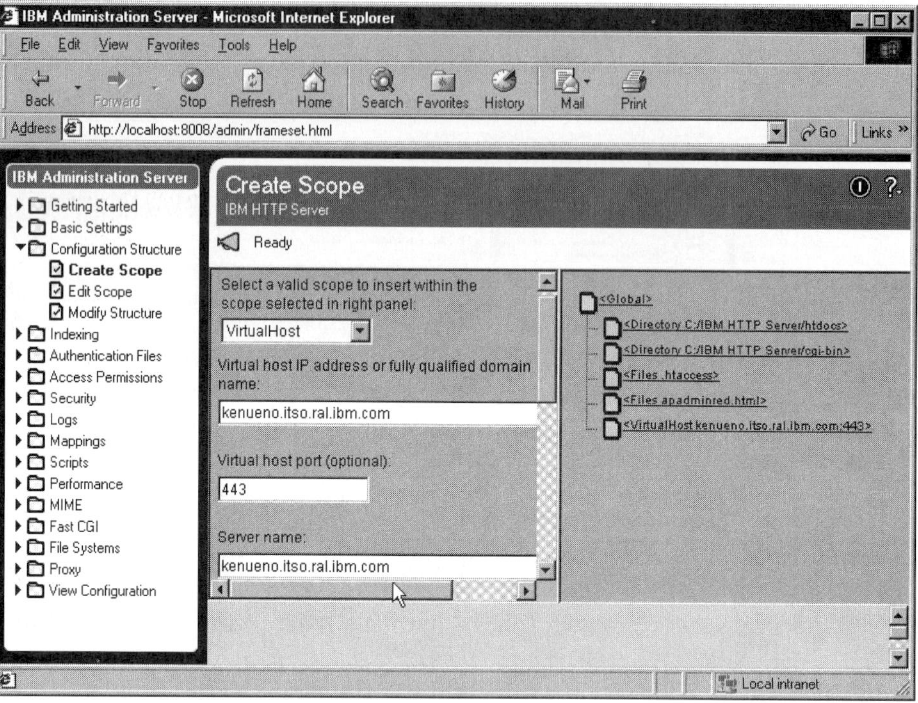

Figure 570. IHS - virtual host specification values

8. To set up the virtual host document root for the secure server, do the following:

- In the left navigation frame, under Basic Settings, select **Core Settings**.
- Make sure the Scope is set to the virtualhost you are now working with. In our case, click the **Scope** button, then select **<VirtualHost kenueno.itso.ral.ibm.com:443>**.
- Type the Server name as a fully qualified domain name. In our case, the name is kenueno.itso.ral.ibm.com.
- Type the Document root directory name. In our case, the name is f:\IBM HTTP Server\htdocs.
- Click the **Submit** button.

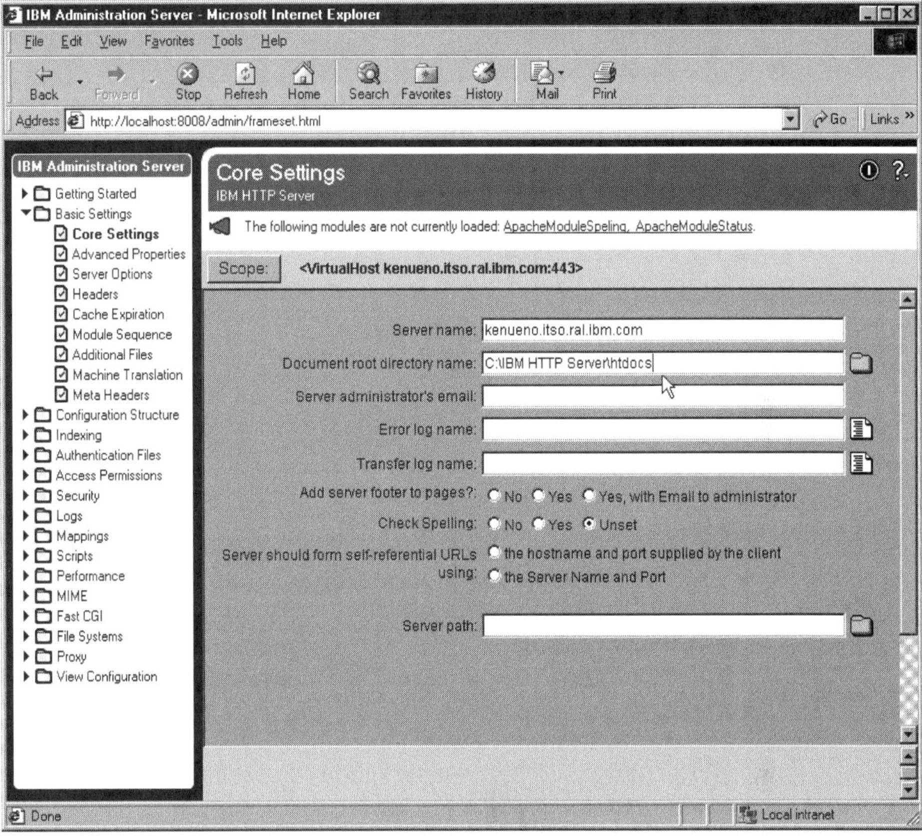

Figure 571. IHS - setting the virtual host document root

9. To set the keyfile and the SSL timeout values for the secure server, do the following:

- In the left navigation frame, expand **Security**.
- Select **Server Security**. Make sure the Scope is GLOBAL.
- Select **No** for Enable SSL. This will disable SSL globally, but we will soon enable SSL for the virtual host we are working with.
- Type the path and file name for the keyfile. In our case, the value is f:\ServerCerts\Serverkey.kdb.
- Type a Timeout value for SSL Version 2 session IDs (100 secs).
- Type a Timeout value for SSL Version 3 session IDs (1000 secs).
- Click the **Submit** button.

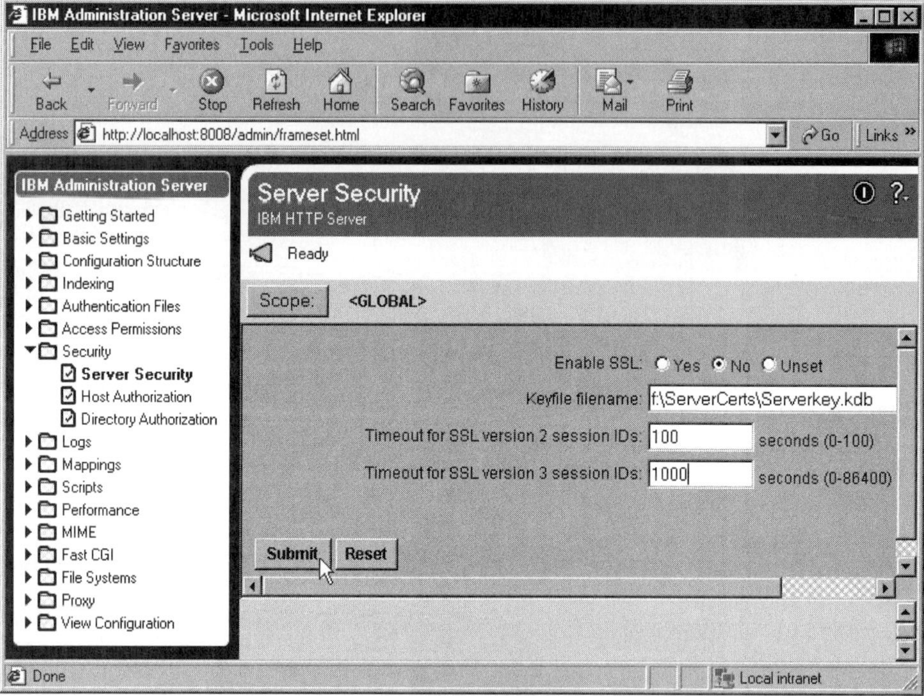

Figure 572. IHS - setting Global security values

10. To enable SSL and set the mode of operation of client authorization for the virtual host, do the following:

- In the left navigation frame, under Security, select Host Authorization.
- Make sure the Scope is set to the virtual host you are working with. To do this, click the **Scope** button and select the virtual host. In our case, the Scope is <VirtualHost kenueno.itso.ral.ibm.com:443>.
- Select **Yes** for Enable SSL.
- Select **Required** for the mode of client authentication to be used. This will require a certificate exchange to be made between the browser and the Web server.
- Click the **Submit** button.

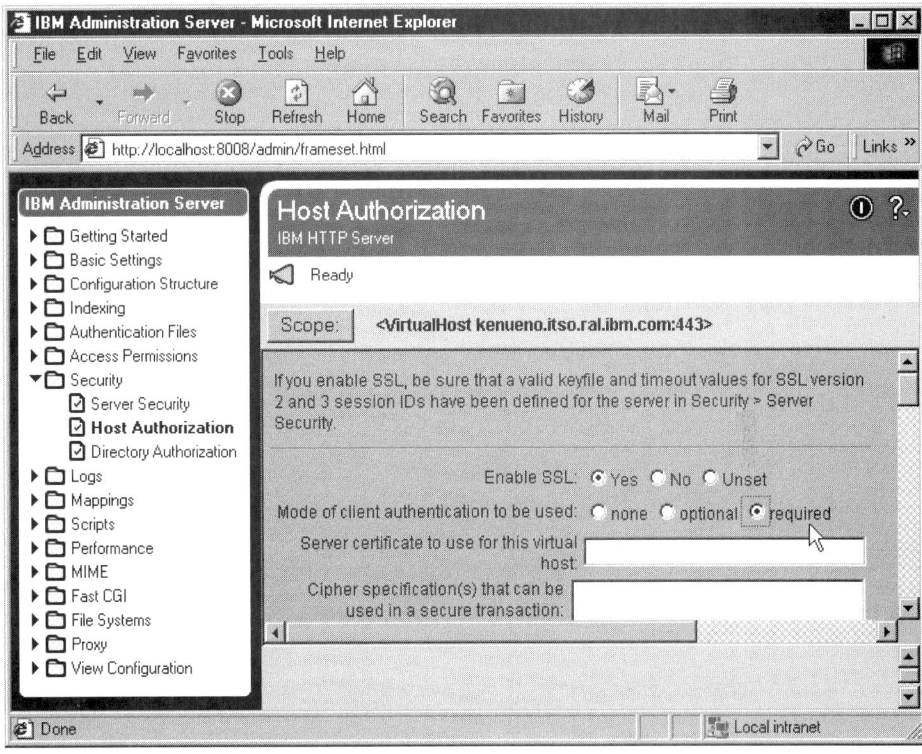

Figure 573. IHS - setting security values for the virtual host

11.Restart the server.

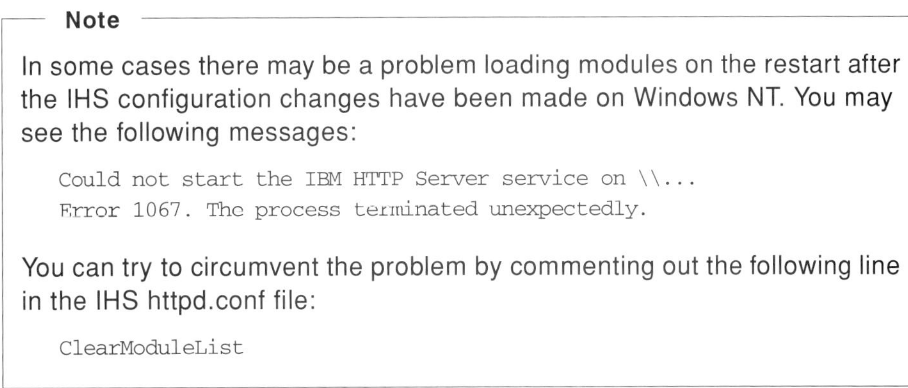

Note

In some cases there may be a problem loading modules on the restart after the IHS configuration changes have been made on Windows NT. You may see the following messages:

```
Could not start the IBM HTTP Server service on \\...
Error 1067. The process terminated unexpectedly.
```

You can try to circumvent the problem by commenting out the following line in the IHS httpd.conf file:

```
ClearModuleList
```

15.4.5 Securing a WebSphere application using certificates

The final step in our installation/configuration process is to specify security for the WebSphere application. We will do this by using the WebSphere Administrative Console. A brief overview of security administration concepts can be found in 15.2.1.1, “WebSphere security administration” on page 652.

In 15.4.3, “Managing certificates” on page 667, we created certificates for users Bob Garcia and, optionally, Mary Burnnet. In this chapter we will secure the showCfg servlet and allow it to be accessed by user Bob Garcia, but not by user Mary Burnnet.

15.4.5.1 Defining an enterprise application

The enterprise application will be defined to contain only the Web application that contains the showCfg servlet. To define the enterprise application, do the following:

1. Make sure that the WebSphere Administrative Server and Administrative Console are up and running.
2. Using the administrative console, on the main menu bar, select **Wizards -> Create Enterprise Application**.

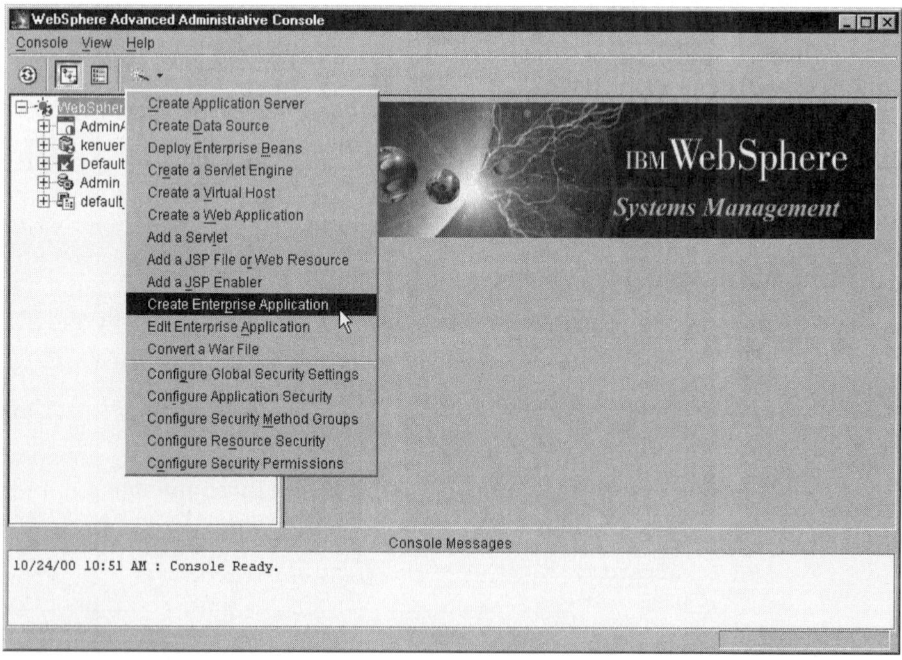

Figure 574. WebSphere Administrative Console - creating an enterprise application

3. On the Application Details window, enter the application name as MyEnterpriseApp and click **Next**.

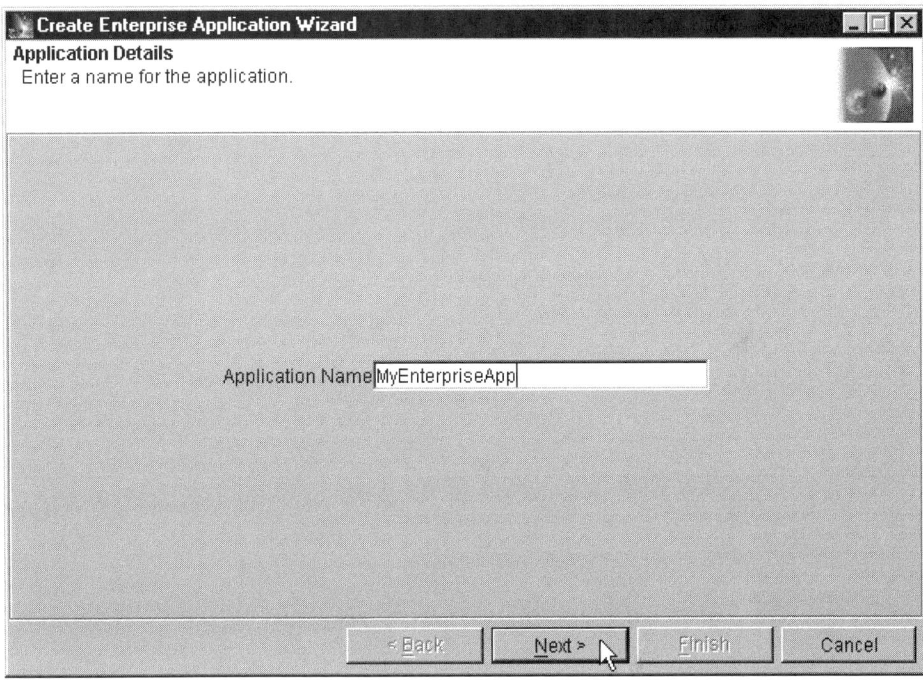

Figure 575. WebSphere Administrative Console - entering the enterprise application name

4. On the Application Resources window, expand the Web Applications folder, select examples (the showCfg servlet is in the examples Web application) and click **Add**.

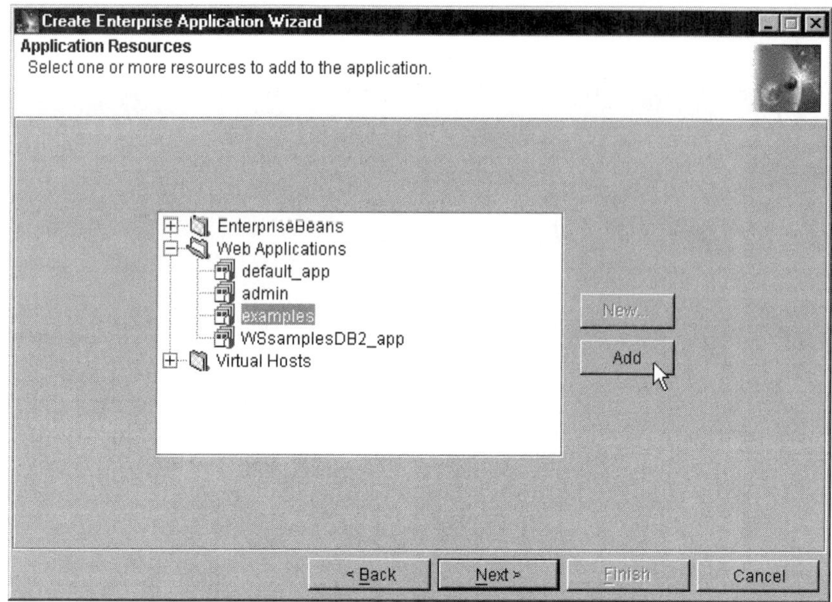

Figure 576. WebSphere Administrative Console - adding resources to an enterprise application

5. After this completes successfully, click **Next**. Click **Finish**.

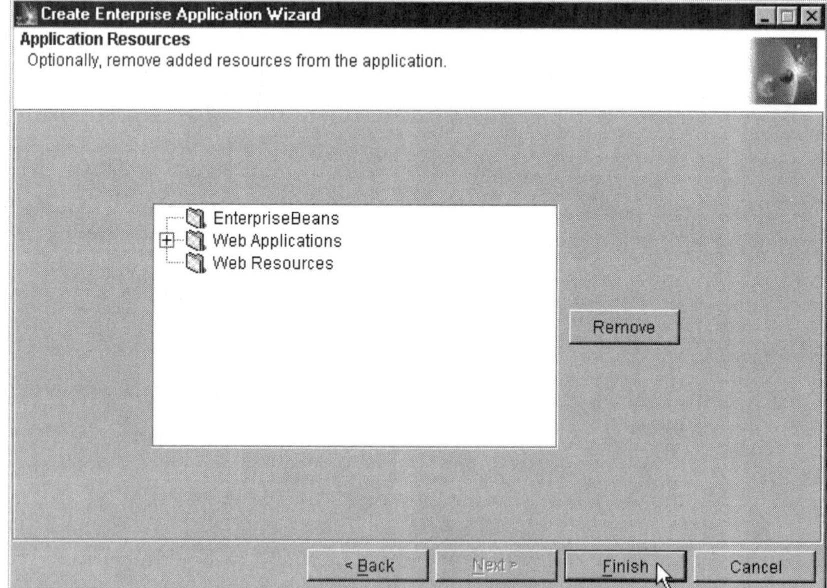

Figure 577. WebSphere Administrative Console - Finish button for adding a resource

6. Click **OK** when you get the `Command "Application create" completed successfully` message.

15.4.5.2 Configuring Global Settings

The Global Setting will be set to use certificate-based authentication. To specify the Global Settings, do the following:

1. Using the administrative console, on the main menu bar, select **Wizards -> Configure Global Settings**.

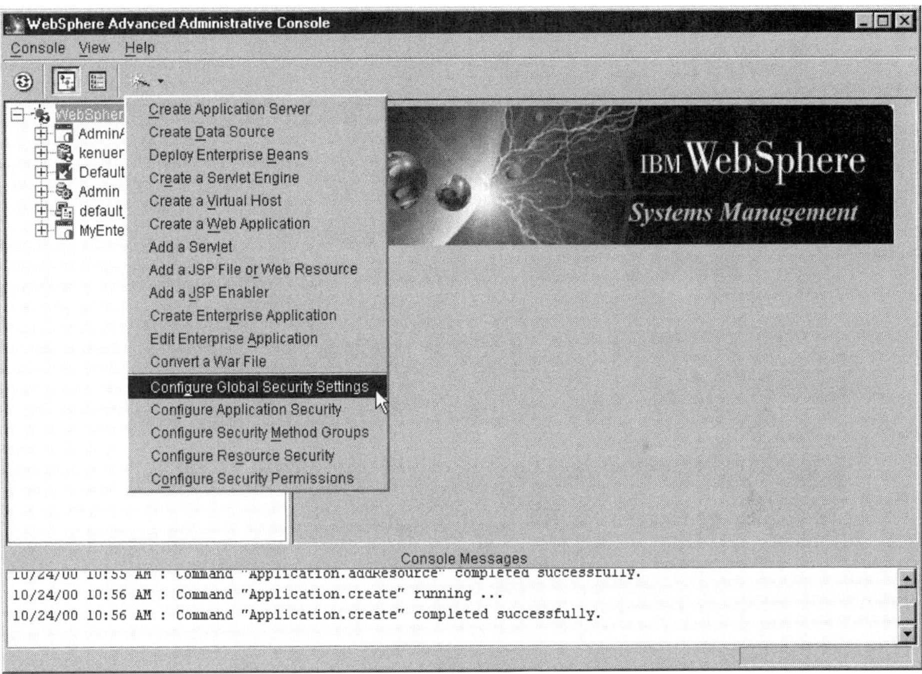

Figure 578. WebSphere security - configuring global settings

2. Make sure the General tab page is active and check the **Enable Security** box.

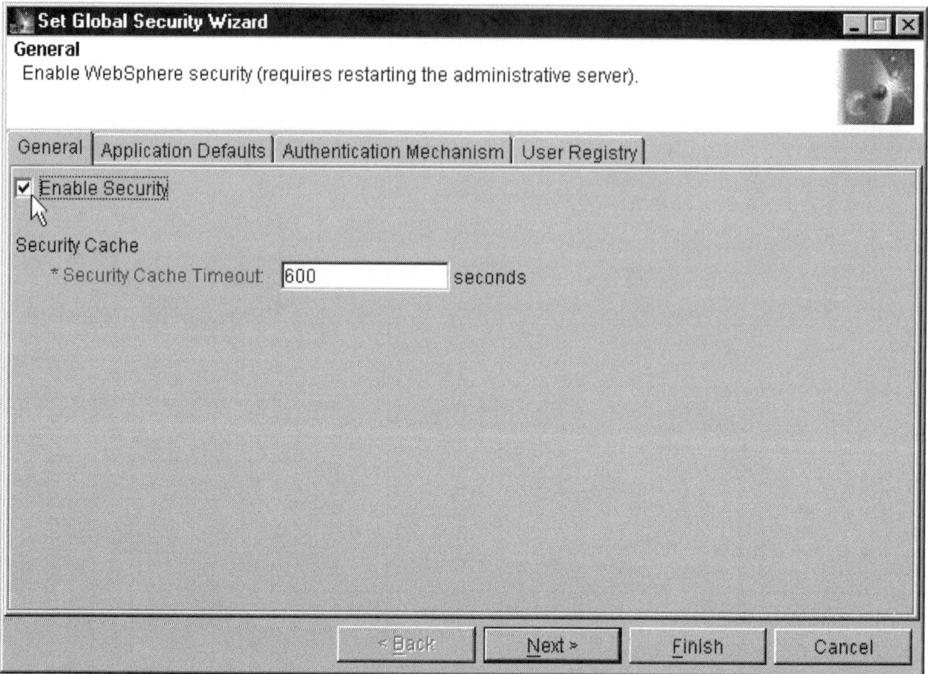

Figure 579. WebSphere security - global settings General page

3. Click the **Application Defaults** tab and specify the following:

- Leave the Realm Name as Default.
- Select **Certificate** as the Challenge Type.
- Check the **Use SSL to connect client and Web server** box.

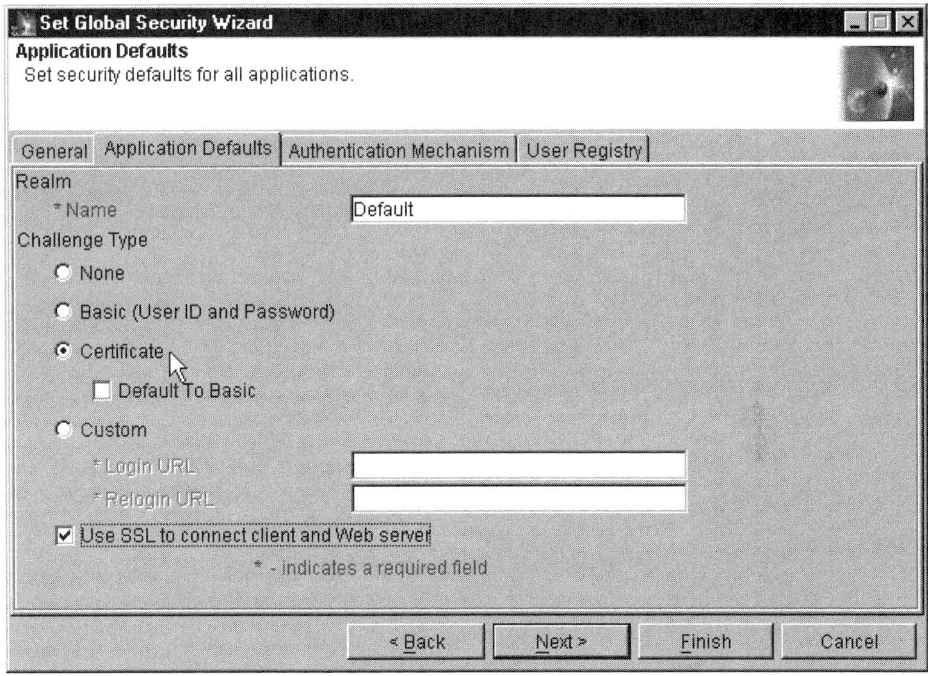

Figure 580. WebSphere security - global settings Application Defaults page

4. Click the **Authentication Mechanism** tab and specify the following:

 - Select **Lightweight Third Party Authentication (LTPA)** as the authentication mechanism.

   Note that when Lightweight Third Party Authentication (LTPA) is selected, the Generate Keys button becomes active. You can use the Generate Keys button to cause new LTPA keys to be generated. These keys are used to encrypt data passed between the client and server. Due to the possibility of offline attacks where the data may fall into the hands of the attacker, it is recommended that new key generation be performed periodically. When the **Generate Keys** button is clicked, you will be prompted to enter an LTPA password. The password you supply will be used by the underlying key generation mechanism.

 - Check the **Enable Single Sign On (SSO)** box.

   SSO is limited to a single domain. In the Domain field, type in the name of the domain in which SSO will be enabled. In our case, the name is itso.ral.ibm.com.

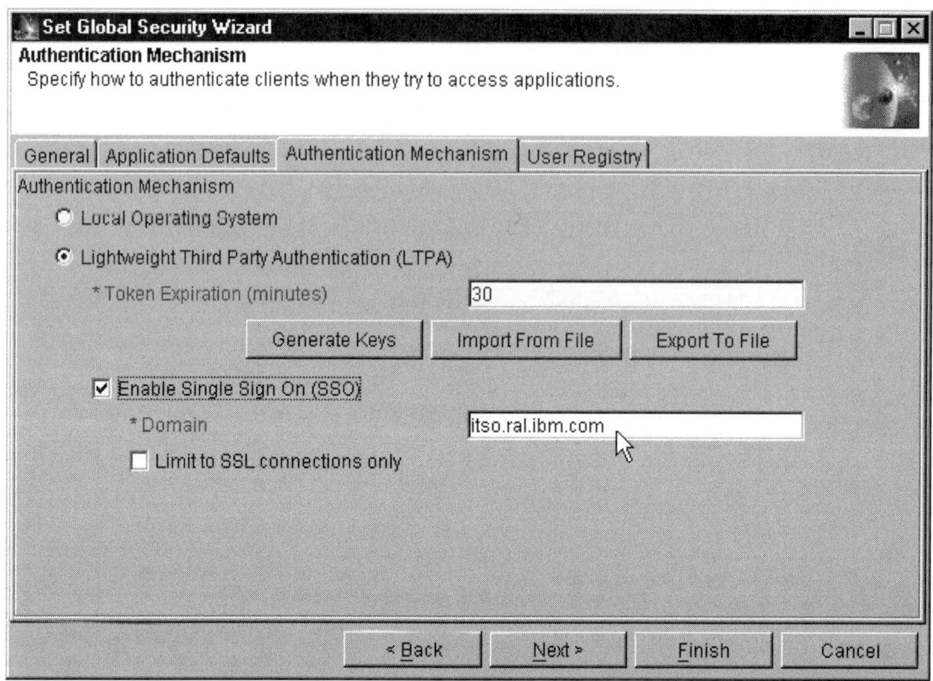

Figure 581. WebSphere security - global settings Authentication Mechanism page

5. Click the **User Registry** tab and specify the following:

- For the security server ID, specify the directory administrator name used when configuring the LDAP directory in 15.4.2.2, "Configuring IBM SecureWay Directory" on page 661. In our case, the ID is cn=root. After enabling WebSphere security, you will need to use this ID and its associated password the next time you start up the administrative console.
- For the security server password, type the password for the security server ID.
- For the directory type, specify SecureWay. Note that during subsequent security operations or specifications, WebSphere may automatically change this value to Custom. This change does not appear to affect the function of WebSphere security at runtime.
- For the host, specify the machine name where the IBM SecureWay Directory is installed. In our case, the name is rs600012.
- For the port, specify 389.
- For the base distinguished name, specify o=ibm, c=US.

  The example User Registry specifications are shown in Figure 582.

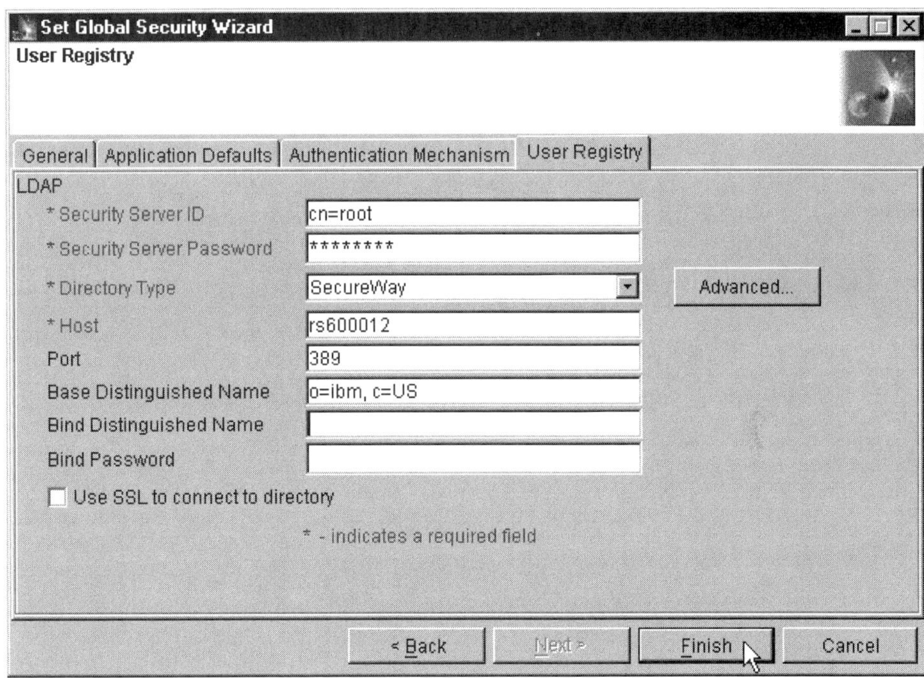

Figure 582. WebSphere security - User Registry specification

6. Click **Finish**.

   Note that the first time you configure WebSphere security to use LTPA as the authentication mechanism, after you click **Finish**, you will be prompted to enter an LTPA password. The value you enter here will be used by WebSphere to automatically generate encryption keys. The value used in our example was WebAS.

7. Then click **OK**.

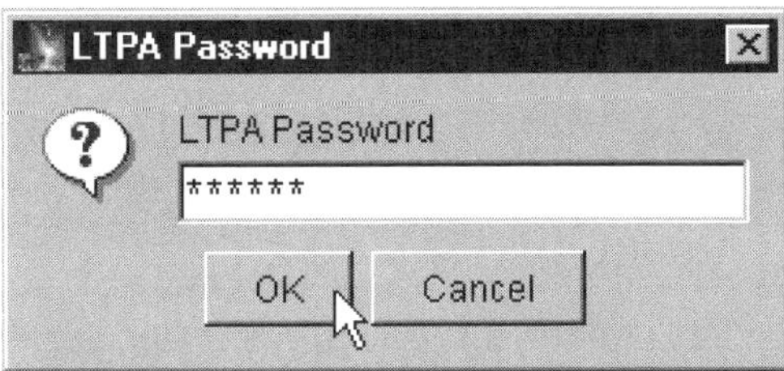

Figure 583. WebSphere security - LTPA password for encryption key generation

8. Click **OK** when you get the `Changes will not take effect until the server is restarted` message.

9. Exit the administrative console. Stop, then restart the administrative server.
10. Restart the administrative console. In the Login at the Target Server window, type the security server ID and password. Click **OK**. In our case the ID is cn=root.

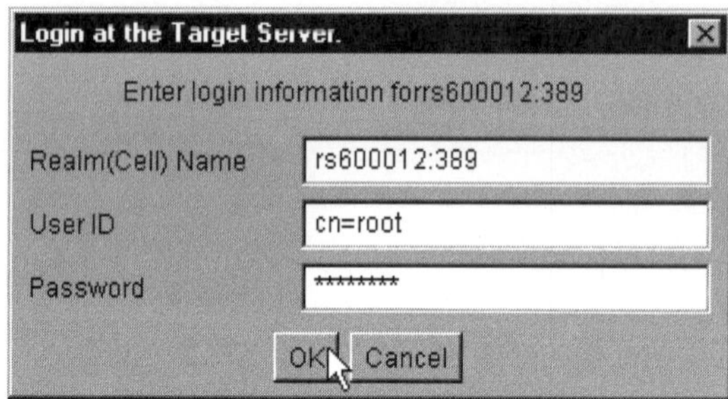

Figure 584. WebSphere Administrative Console - login after security enabled

Using Certificate Mapping Filters

In our example, we want authentication to succeed if the Distinguished Name value in the client certificate exactly matches a Distinguished Name in the LDAP registry. This is the default Certificate Mapping technique used by WebSphere. However, there may be some cases where you want authentication to succeed based on other comparisons. You can do this by specification of a Certificate Filter.

Suppose you want authentication to succeed if the value of the Common Name (CN) in the certificate matches (maps to) the value of the uid attribute in the LDAP registry. To define the certificate filter to make this happen, do the following:

1. From the User Registry page of the Set Global Security Wizard, click the **Advanced**... button.
2. In the Certificate Mapping field, select **Certificate Filter** from the drop-down menu (the default value is Exact Distinguished Name).
3. In the Certificate Filter field, type in the filter value. In our case, the filter value is uid=$(SubjectCN). This specification will cause WebSphere authentication to "map" the uid attribute in the LDAP directory to the CN value in the certificate. Figure 585 on page 735 shows the specification values. For other properties that can be used as filter values, see User Registry settings of the Configure Global Settings task in the WebSphere InfoCenter. Note that the syntax described in the InfoCenter (...$(Subject:cn)) did not work for our case when the syntax shown above (...$(SubjectCN)) did work.

4. Click the **OK** button.
5. Then, back in the User Registry panel, click the **Finish** button.

If you choose to try out using filters, do so after you have completed the specifications for our main example that uses Exact Distinguished Name mapping and have completed the example testing as described in 15.4.6, "Testing the secured application" on page 749.

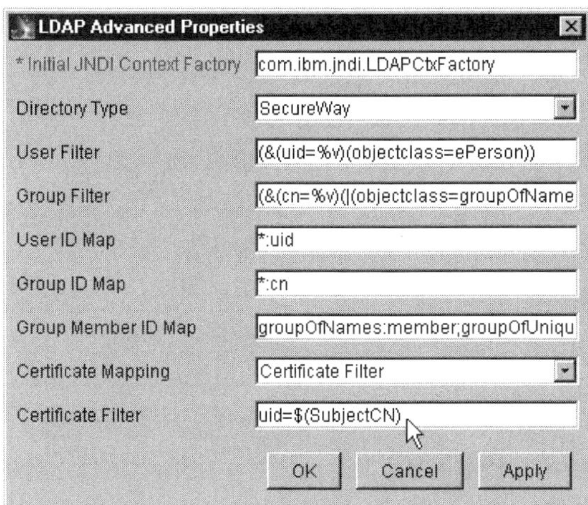

Figure 585. LDAP Advanced Properties window

To test the filter specification described above, create a new entry in the LDAP directory with a uid value of Bob Garcia. To accomplish this, do the following:

1. From the AIX terminal command line, type the following and press Enter:

   ```
   # dmt
   ```

2. We want to make sure that we have proper authority to make additions to the directory, so first we need to rebind to the LDAP server with our directory administrator ID. When the introductory DMT panel appears, from the left navigation frame select **Rebind**.
3. In the Rebind to server frame, select **Authenticated**, type in the User DN value as `cn=root` and type in the administrator password. Click **OK**.
4. In the Browse directory tree frame, expand o=ibm,c=us.
5. In the Browse directory tree frame, expand **ou=Raleigh**. The result of the expanded tree is shown in Figure 506 on page 667.
6. Select **ou=Raleigh**, then click the **Add** button.

7. In the Create an LDAP Entry window, type in `cn=Robert Garcia` as the value for the Entry RDN field as shown in Figure 586. Click **Next**.

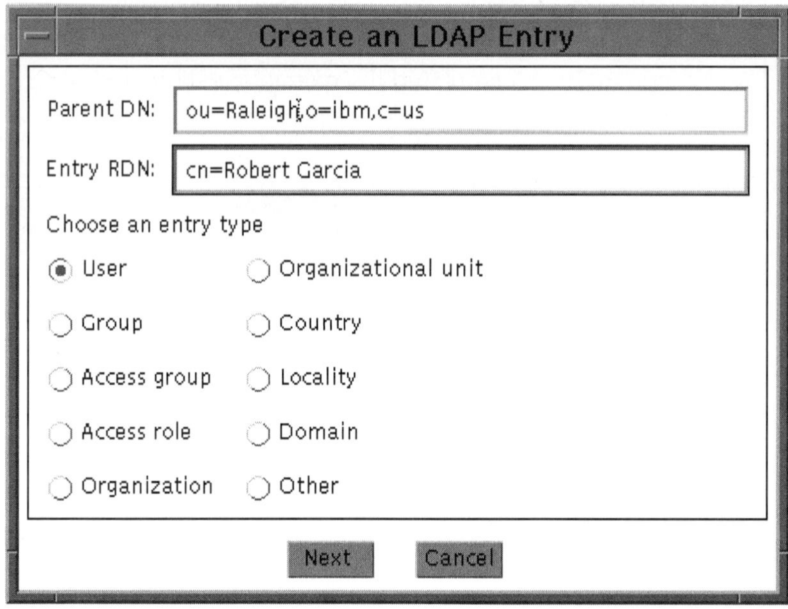

Figure 586. Adding an LDAP entry

8. In the Create an LDAP User window, type in `Robert Garcia` as the Common Name and `Garcia` as the Last Name.
9. Click the **Other** tab and scroll down until you get to the uid attribute. Type in `Bob Garcia` as the value for uid. The contents of the Create an LDAP User window can be seen in Figure 587 on page 737.
10. Click the **Create** button.

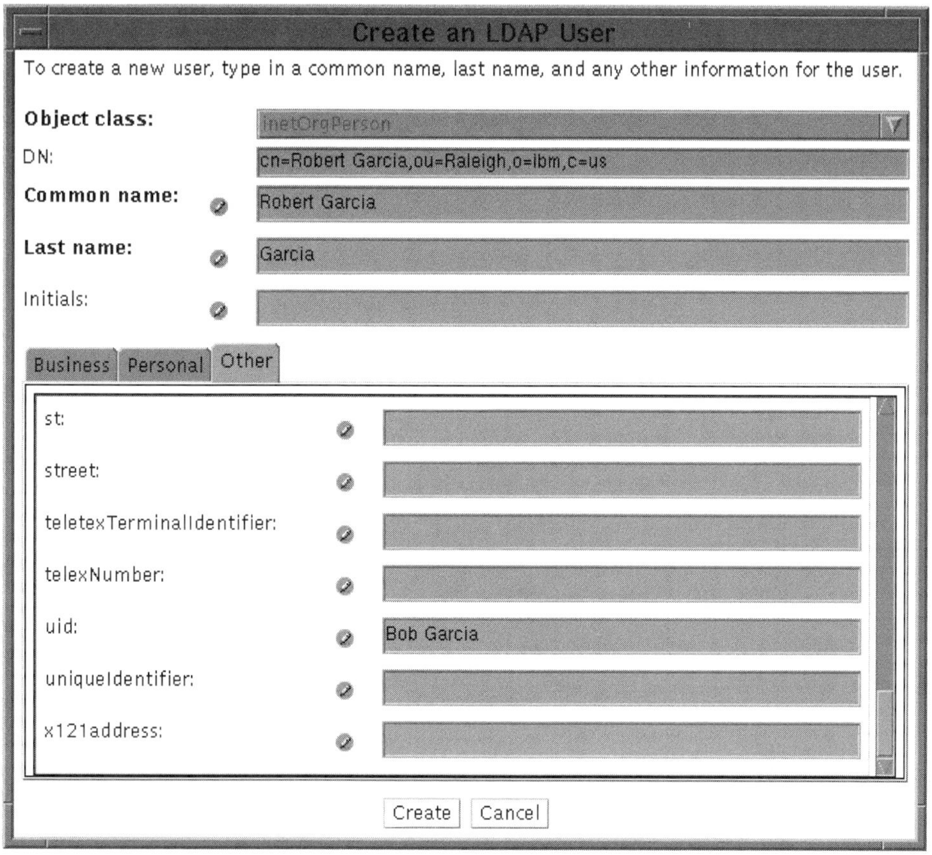

Figure 587. Adding an LDAP user

The new user has now been created in the LDAP directory.

Next, using the WebSphere Administrative Console, run the Configure Security Permissions task as described in 15.4.5.6, “Configuring security permissions” on page 743, only this time select **All Authenticated Users** instead of Selection. Then, complete the task as described.

Now, run the test as described in 15.4.6, “Testing the secured application” on page 749 using the same “Bob Garcia” client certificate. This time, WebSphere will do a mapping between the certificate CN value (Bob Garcia) and the uid attribute value of the entries in the LDAP directory. A match will be found for LDAP user Robert Garcia and he will pass authentication. Because we have now specified that all authenticated users have permission to access our secured resource, the resource will be served to the browser.

15.4.5.3 Configuring Application Security

Click **Configure Application Security** to specify security settings for a specific enterprise application that differ from the global security settings. To configure application security, from the administrative console main menu, select **Wizards -> Configure Application Security**. In our example, we will be using the same values for our enterprise application as those specified for global security. Therefore, there is no need to perform this task.

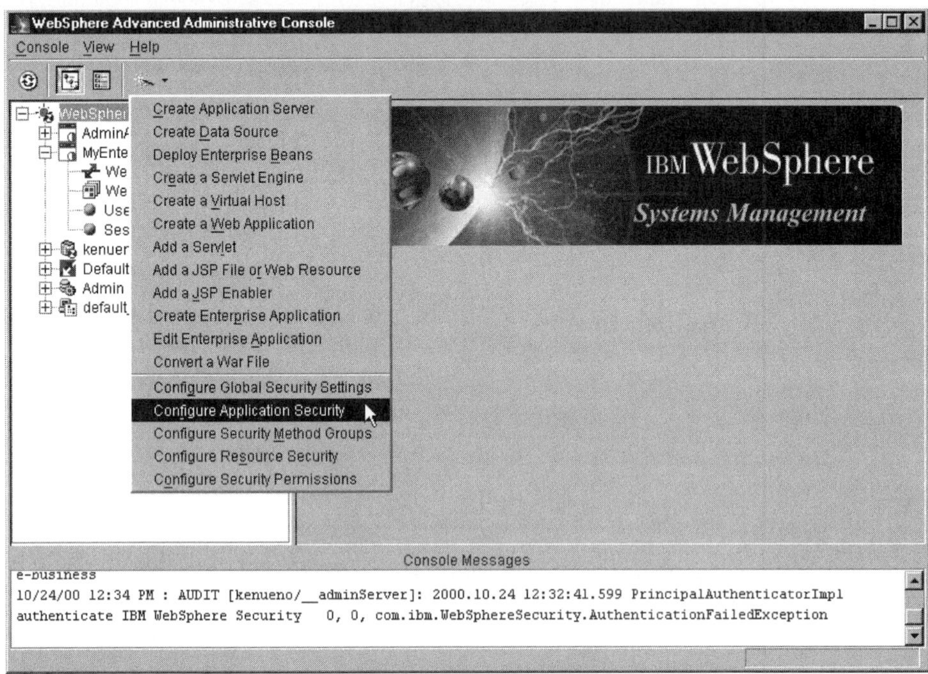

Figure 588. WebSphere security - configuring application security

15.4.5.4 Configuring Security Method Groups

Click Configure Security Method Groups to add new or remove existing method groups. To configure security method groups, from the administrative console main menu, select **Wizards -> Configure Security Method Groups**. In our example, we will be using the default method groups. Therefore, there is no need to perform this task.

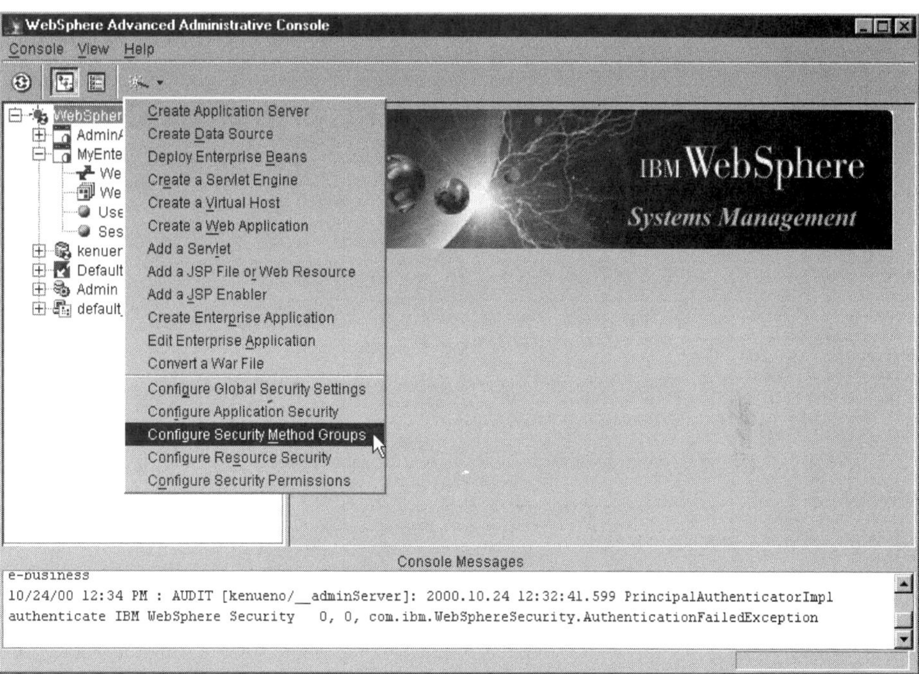

Figure 589. WebSphere security - configuring method groups

15.4.5.5 Configuring Resource Security

Click Configure Resource Security to identify the application resources that are to be secure. In our example, we want to secure only the showCfg servlet resource. To secure showCfg, do the following:

1. Using the administrative console, on the main menu bar, select **Wizards -> Configure Resource Security**.

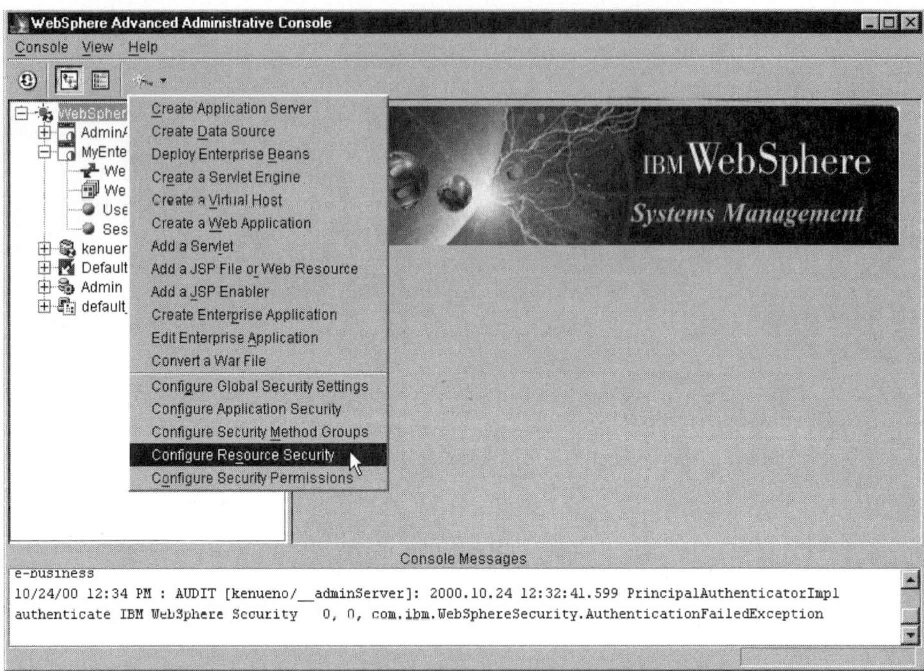

Figure 590. WebSphere security - configuring resource security

2. On the Resources window, expand the Virtual Hosts folder. Then, expand default_host.

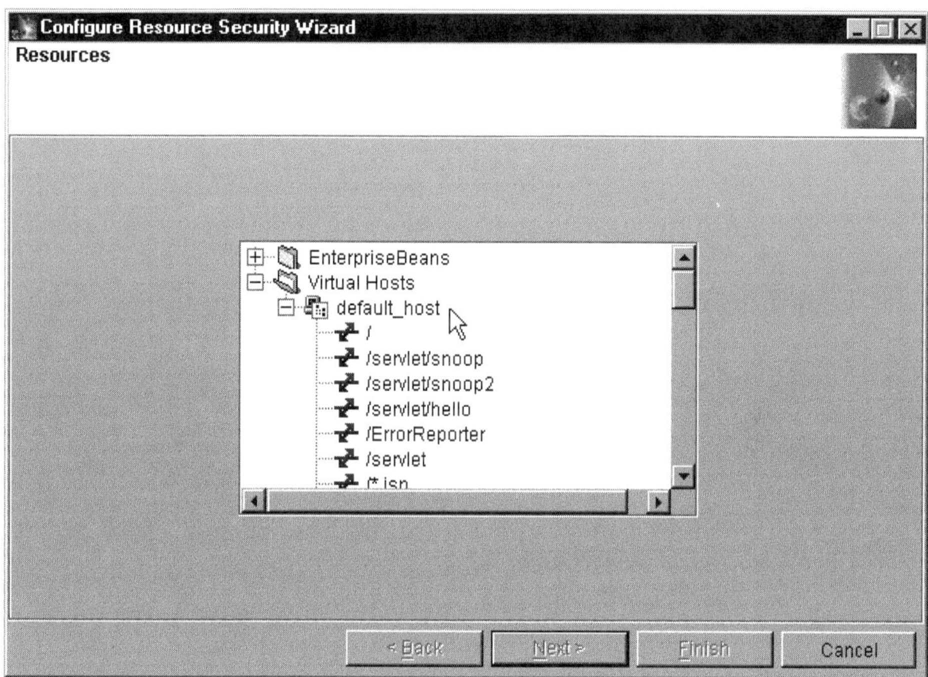

Figure 591. WebSphere security - resources list

3. Scroll down until you see /webapp/examples/showCfg in the list.
4. Select **/webapp/examples/showCfg** and click **Next**.

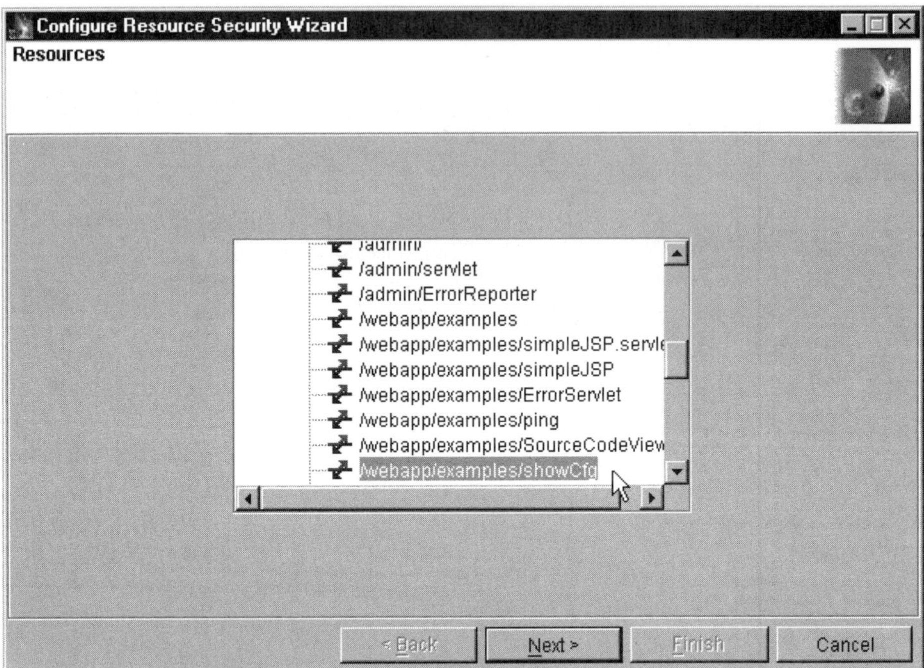

Figure 592. WebSphere security - selecting a resource to secure

5. Click **Yes** in response to `Use default method groups?`.

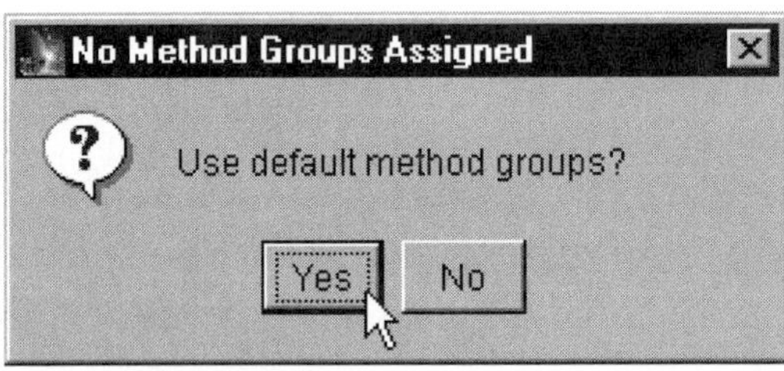

Figure 593. WebSphere security - assigning the default method groups

6. On the Method Groups window, select all the top level (unexpanded) entries in the list then click **Finish**. Note that multiple selections are made Ctrl + left mouse button.

   WebSphere uses a capability-based model for security. In WebSphere, individual resources are collected into applications and methods are collected into method groups. Each user has a set of (application, method-group) pairs, which indicates the methods within an application on which the user has rights. Each (application, method-group) pair is called a permission. For additional information on method groups see the WebSphere InfoCenter.

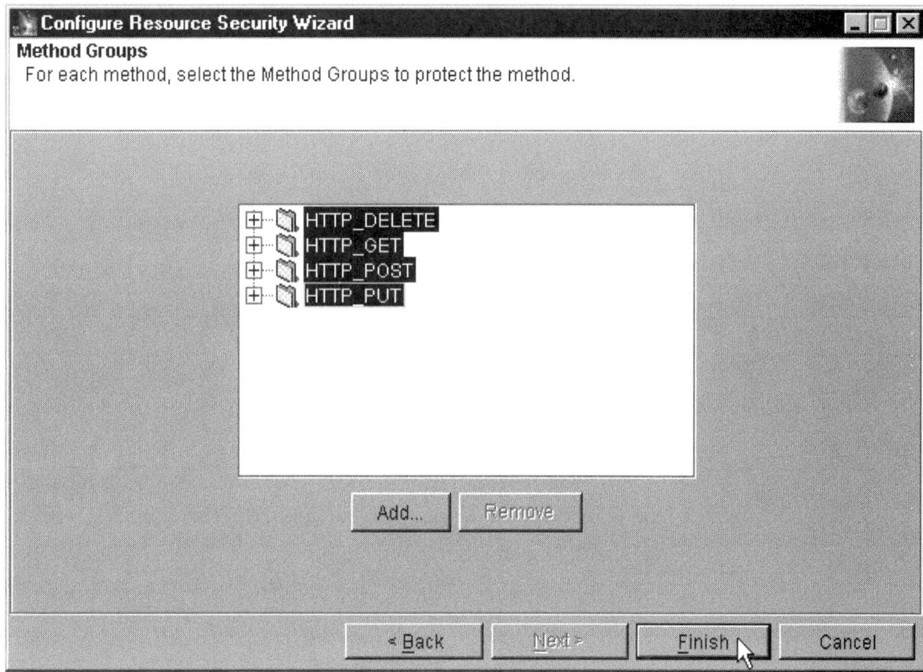

Figure 594. WebSphere security - selecting method groups

15.4.5.6 Configuring security permissions

Choose Configure Security Permissions to identify which users are allowed to access a secure resource. In our case, we are only going to allow access by user Bob Garcia. To configure permissions, do the following:

1. Using the administrative console, on the main menu bar, select **Wizards -> Configure Security Permissions**.

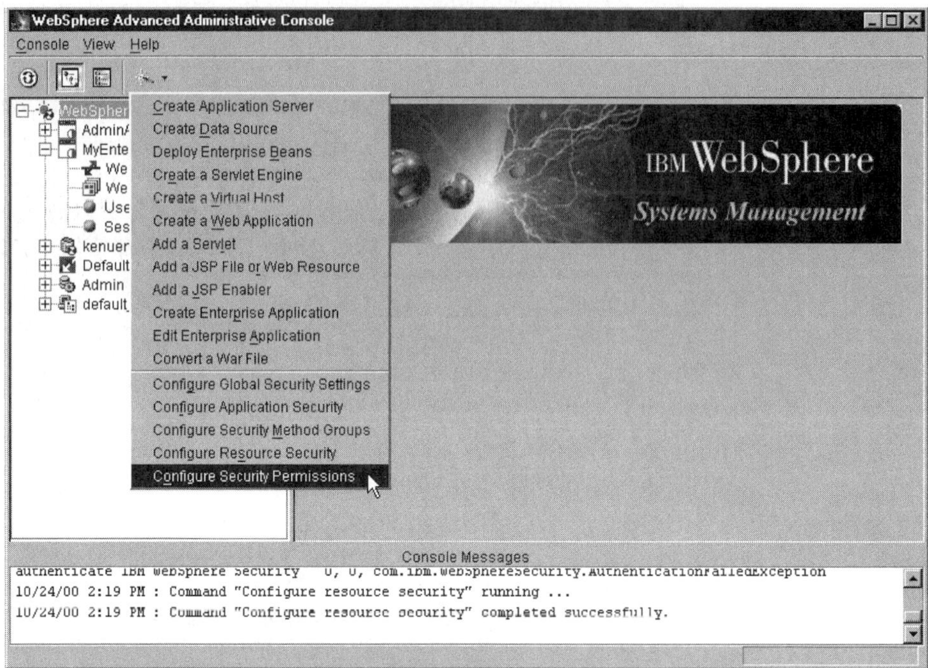

Figure 595. WebSphere security - assigning permissions

2. On the Enterprise Applications window, expand the Enterprise Applications folder. Select **MyEnterpriseApp** then click **Next**.

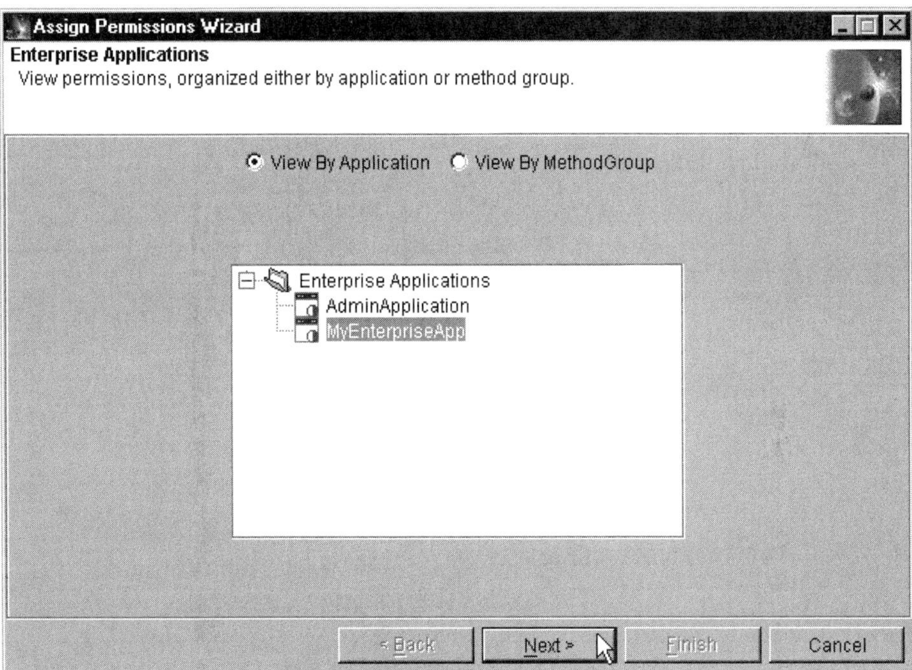

Figure 596. WebSphere security - selecting the enterprise application

3. On the Permissions window, select all the entries in the list, then click **Next**.

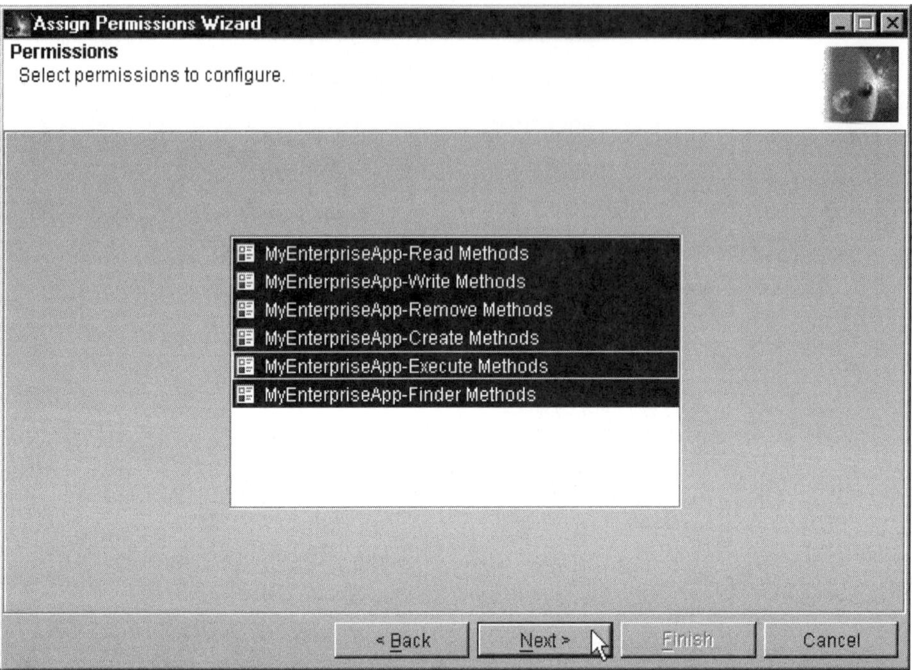

Figure 597. WebSphere security - selecting permissions to configure

4. In the Grant Permissions window, select **Selection**.
5. In the Search For dropdown, select **User**.
6. In the Search Filter entry field, type an * then click the **Search** button. This should return a list of all users defined in our LDAP directory. In our example, the results of the search are shown in Figure 598 on page 747. Note that the name used in the list is the value of the uid attribute as specified for the user in the LDAP directory.

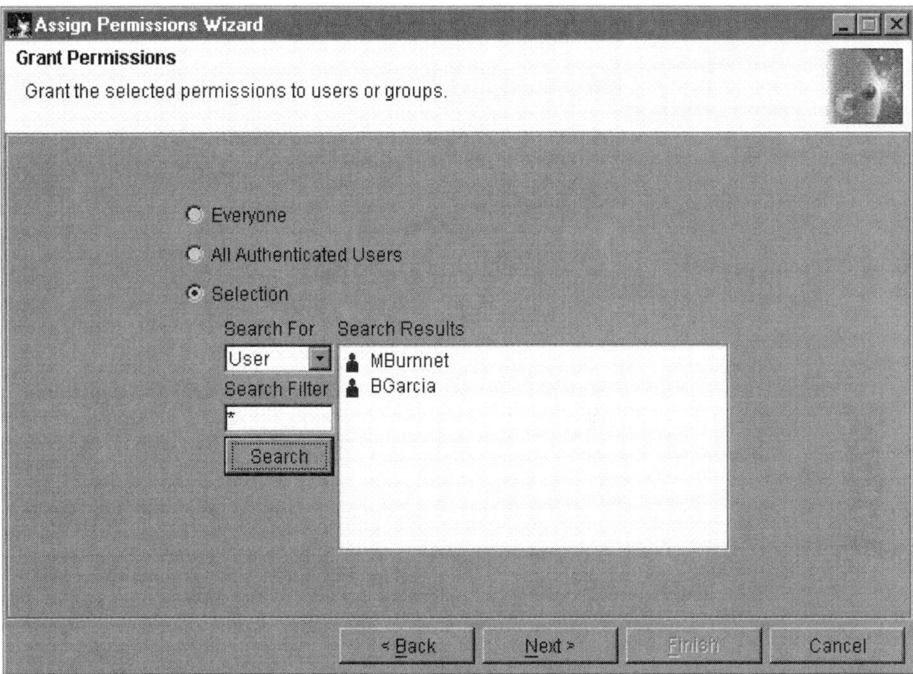

Figure 598. WebSphere security - granting permissions

7. Select the users to be granted access to the secure resource(s) and click **Next**. In our case, select **BGarcia**.
8. On the Remove Permissions window, click **Finish**.

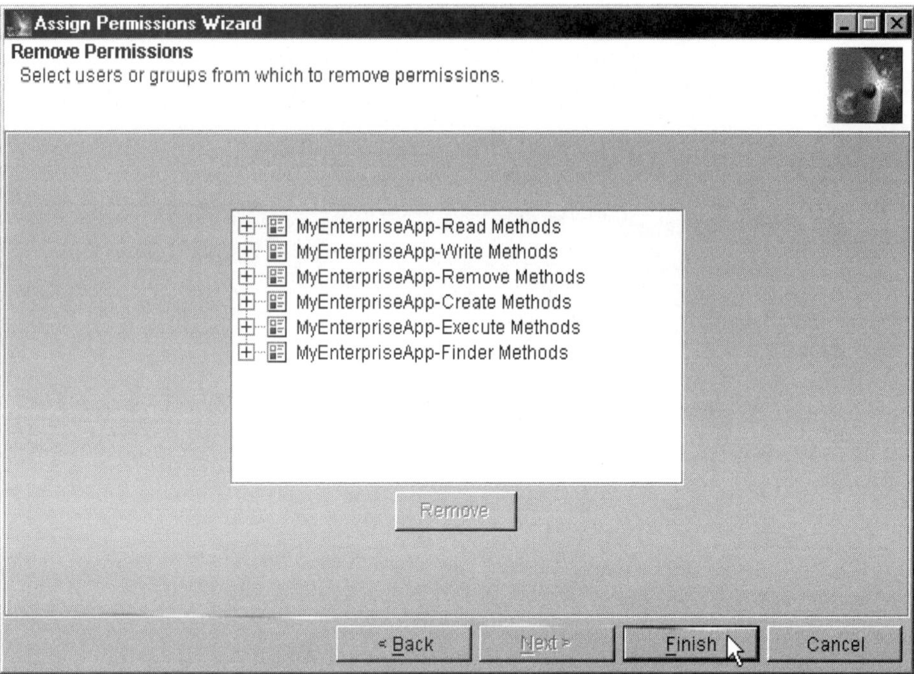

Figure 599. WebSphere security - removing permissions

WebSphere security configuration work is now complete.

15.4.5.7 Defining a virtual host alias for the SSL connection

We need to define a virtual host alias for our SSL connection. To do this, do the following:

1. Make sure that the WebSphere Administrative Server and Administrative Console are up and running.
2. Using the administrative console, in the topology view, select **default_host**. Default_host is the virtual host defined for our example Web application.
3. Click the **Advanced** tab.
4. Type in the alias name in the Host Aliases list, being sure to append the SSL port number. In our case, the alias name is kenueno.itso.ral.ibm.com:443.
5. Click the **Apply** button.

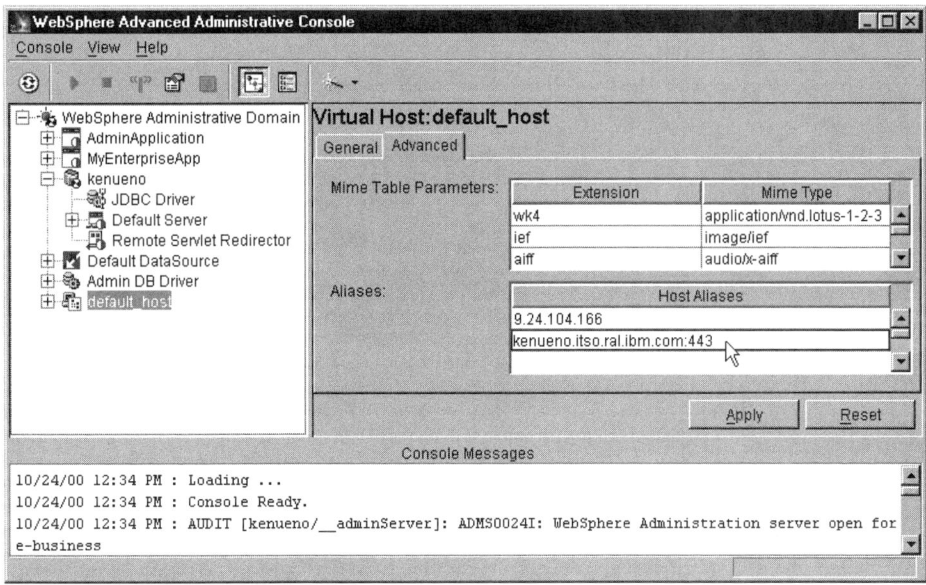

Figure 600. Add virtual host aliases

15.4.6 Testing the secured application

We will now be using our Internet Explorer browser to try to access the secure resource(s). To test our security specifications, do the following:

1. Make sure that the following are all up and running:
   - DB2 on the AIX machine that has our IBM SecureWay Directory
   - IBM SecureWay Directory on the AIX machine
   - DB2 on the Windows NT machine that has our IBM HTTP Server and WebSphere
   - IBM HTTP Server on the Windows NT machine
   - WebSphere Administrative Server on the Windows NT machine
   - WebSphere Administrative Console on the Windows NT machine
2. Using the administrative console, expand WebSphere administrative domain.
3. Expand the node. In our case, the node name is kenueno.
4. Start the application server named Default Server. Do this by selecting Default Server and clicking the Start icon (▸) in the tool bar. Wait until you receive the `Command "Default Server start" completed successfully` message and click **OK**.

5. Start the enterprise application. Do this by selecting the name of the enterprise application (it is an entry in topology under WebSphere administrative domain) and clicking the Start icon in the toolbar. Wait until you receive the `start completed` message and click **OK**. In our case the message will read `Command "MyEnterpriseApp start" completed successfully`.

Figure 601. Enterprise application started successfully

6. Start up the Internet Explorer browser and specify the URL to access the showCfg servlet. Don't forget to specify https as the protocol. In our case the URL is `https://kenueno.itso.ral.ibm.com/webapp/examples/showCfg`.
7. If you receive a Security Alert message from the browser, click **OK**.
8. On the Client Authentication window, select the Bob Garcia certificate and click **OK**. The output of the showCfg servlet should now appear in the browser. The output of showCfg can be seen in Figure 602.

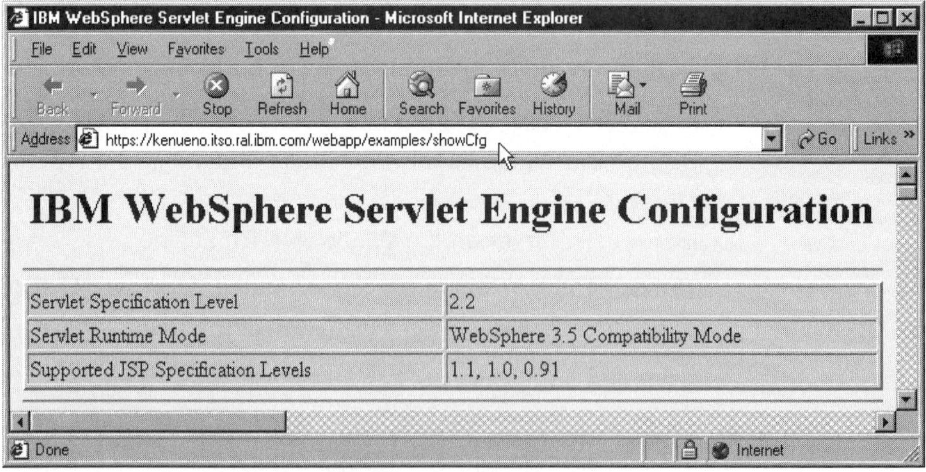

Figure 602. Output from successful showCfg servlet access

User Bob Garcia is now authenticated for the browser session and is authorized to access all secure resources that belong to the enterprise application without any additional browser prompts for security (certificate) information.

Suppose a second enterprise application has been defined that does not grant access permissions to user Bob Garcia. If, after being authenticated and authorized to access a secure resource belonging to the first enterprise application, an attempt is made to access a secure resource belonging to the second enterprise application, user Bob Garcia will be denied access and will receive a message as shown in Figure 603.

If you chose to create a certificate for user Mary Burnnet, now is a good time to see what happens if access is attempted with that certificate. Start up another IE browser instance, enter the showCfg URL and on the Client Authentication window, select the Mary Burnnet certificate. You should receive a message indicating that user Mary Burnnet is not authorized to access that resource as shown in Figure 603.

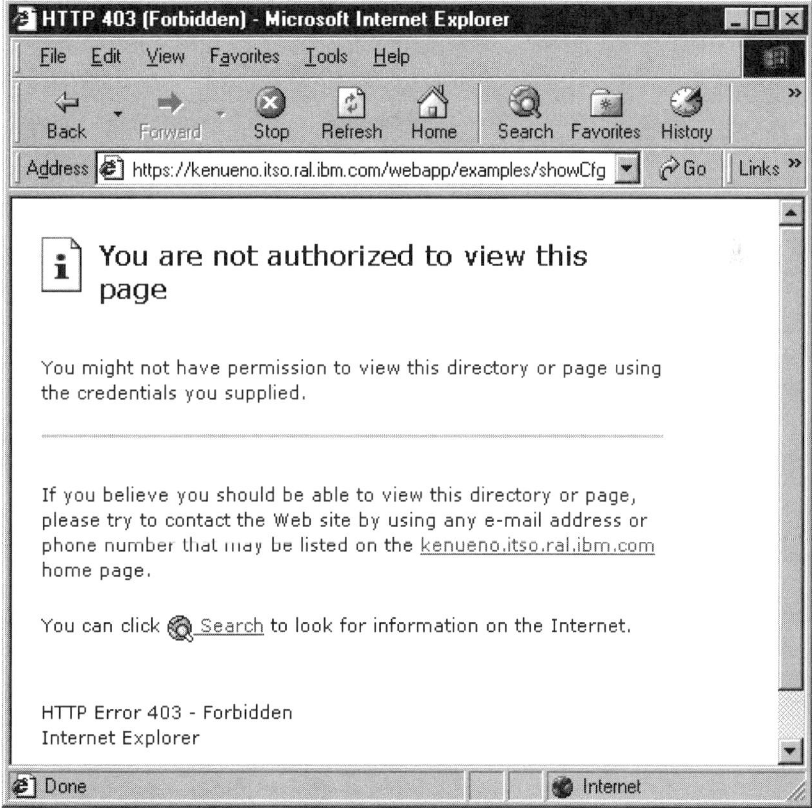

Figure 603. Result of certificate authorization failure

15.5 WebSphere and LDAP servers

WebSphere V3.5 Security Server supports the following LDAP servers for LTPA:

- IBM Secure Way Directory
- Netscape Directory Server
- Lotus Domino 4.6 and 5.0
- Microsoft Active Directory
- Novell Directory Services (NDS)
- Custom

Installation of these LDAP servers is better explained in the respective product installation guides. We only highlight some setup issues. The discussion primarily centers on getting WebSphere security working with the above-mentioned LDAP servers for authentication purposes.

Any changes to the advanced properties of LDAP servers (which can be accessible using the Advanced.. button) gets termed as Custom, and WebSphere automatically changes the Directory type to Custom whenever changes are made.

15.5.1 Netscape Directory Server

After installing Netscape Directory Server 4.1 on a UNIX system, bring up the directory server console. This is found in the installation root directory.

Go to that <NETSCAPE_HOME> directory and execute `startconsole`.

```
# cd /usr/netscape/server4
# ./startconsole
```

Before the console is displayed you will be challenged. Enter the password for the top level administrator (cn=root), and click **OK** as shown in Figure 604 on page 753. This top level user and password is set up during installation.

Figure 604. Netscape Console login window

The Netscape Console is then displayed as shown in Figure 605. Note the User Directory Subtree, (o=ibm.com), because that will be used in the WebSphere global security setting.

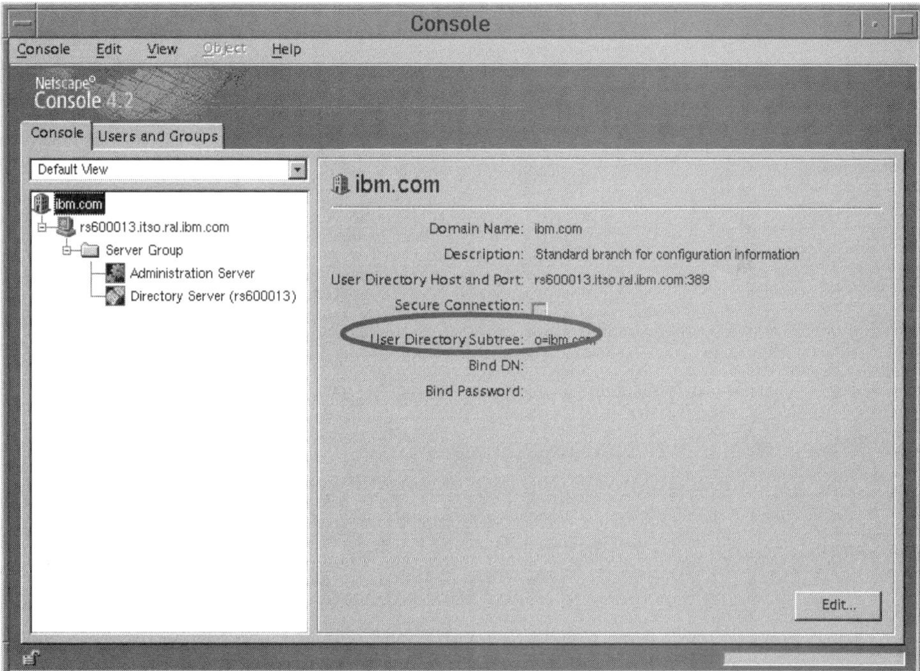

Figure 605. Console tab of the Netscape Console

Users and groups are added, edited, and deleted from the Users and Groups tab. To create a new organizational unit named itso, click the **Users and Groups** tab. See Figure 606 on page 754. From the drop-down list in the bottom right hand corner select **New Organizational Unit**. Then click the **Create...** button.

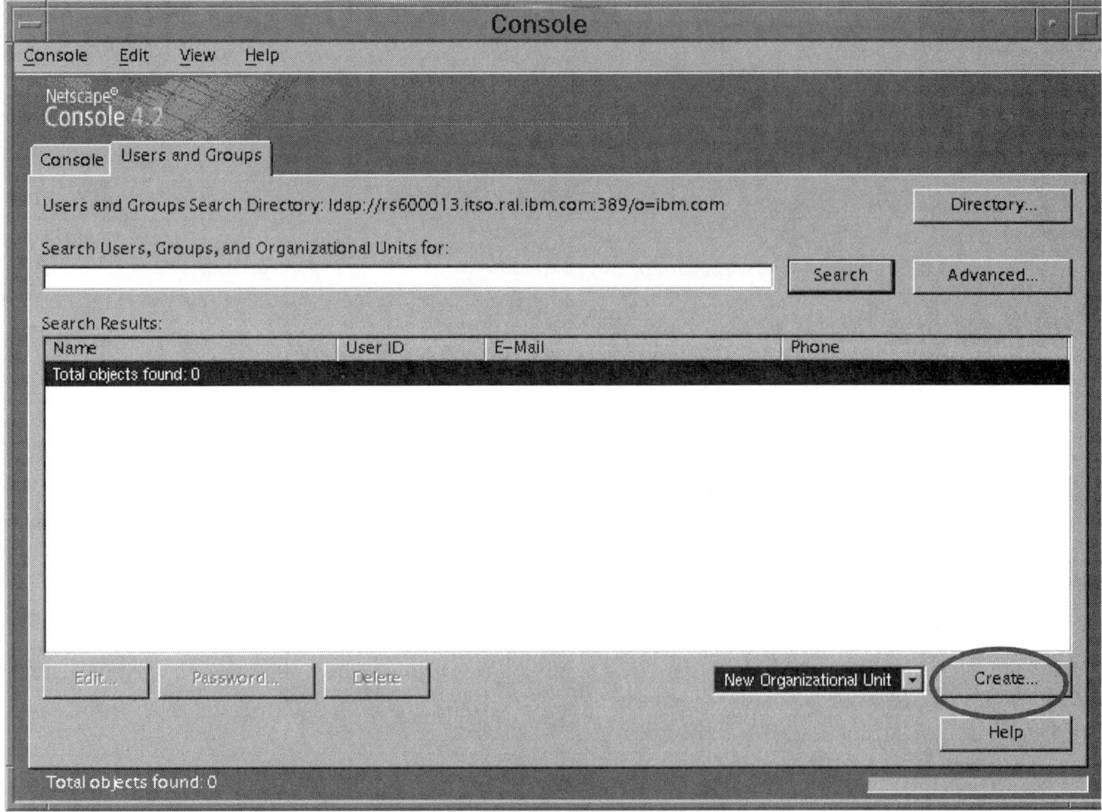

Figure 606. Netscape Console window to create users and groups

In the ensuing window select **Base DN** as the directory in which to create the new organizational unit (OU) and click **OK**.

In the OU properties window, enter the name `itso`, and click **OK**. Other properties are optional.

Follow a similar procedure to create a new user wherein you select **New User** from the drop-down list shown in Figure 606 and click the **Create...** button. The difference is on the ensuing window. Since we want to add users to the itso OU, select **itso** as the directory subtree as shown in Figure 607 on page 755 and click the **OK** button.

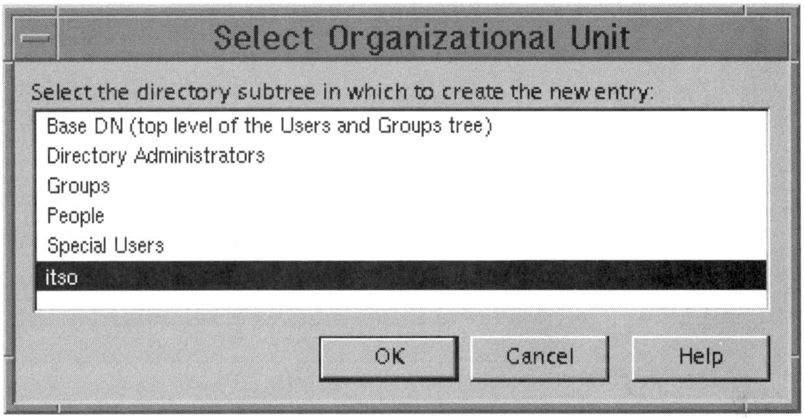

Figure 607. OU selection list

Fill in all the fields in the Create User properties page (See Figure 608 on page 756) especially the ones marked with an asterisk. Note the User ID field, (mohamed), because that will be used in the WebSphere security settings. For the purposes of this redbook, the system-generated common name(s) and user ID values were not used.

Then click **OK**.

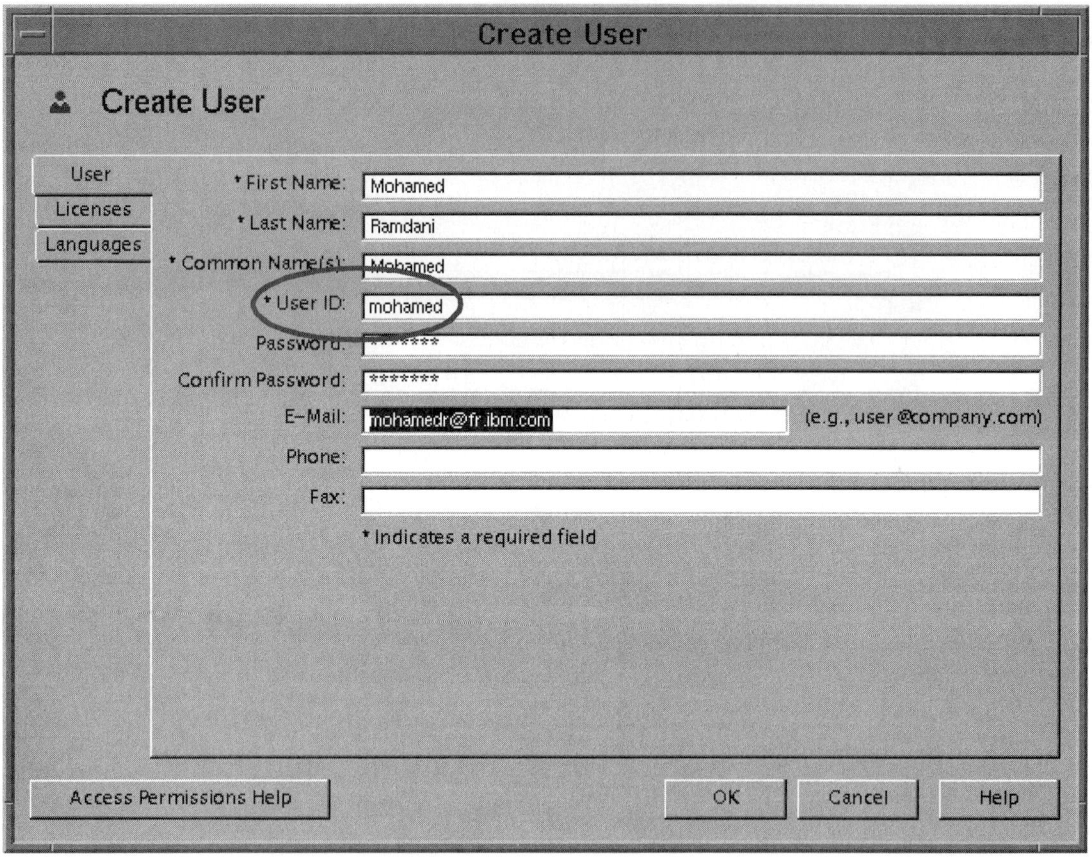

Figure 608. New user creation window within Netscape Console

You can also view the contents of the LDAP directory. On the Netscape Console, click the **Console** tab. In the left pane highlight the Directory Server (rs600013), then click **Open** in the right pane as shown in Figure 609 on page 757.

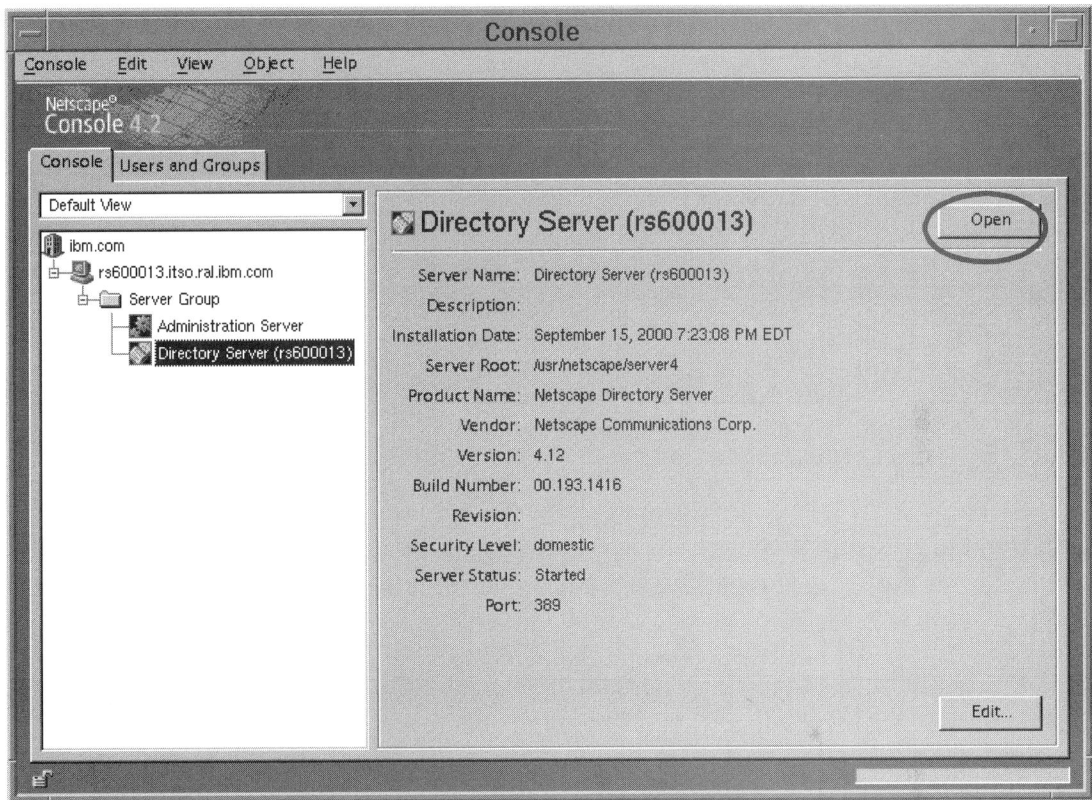

Figure 609. Netscape Console showing the details of a selected directory server

The Netscape Directory Server 4.1 Console will pop up in a new window. Go to the **Directory** tab. Expand the ibm.com folder to see its contents as shown in Figure 610 on page 758. If you highlight the itso organization unit in the Directory tab, you will see the users belonging to that organizational unit. Notice the user Mohamed that we just created.

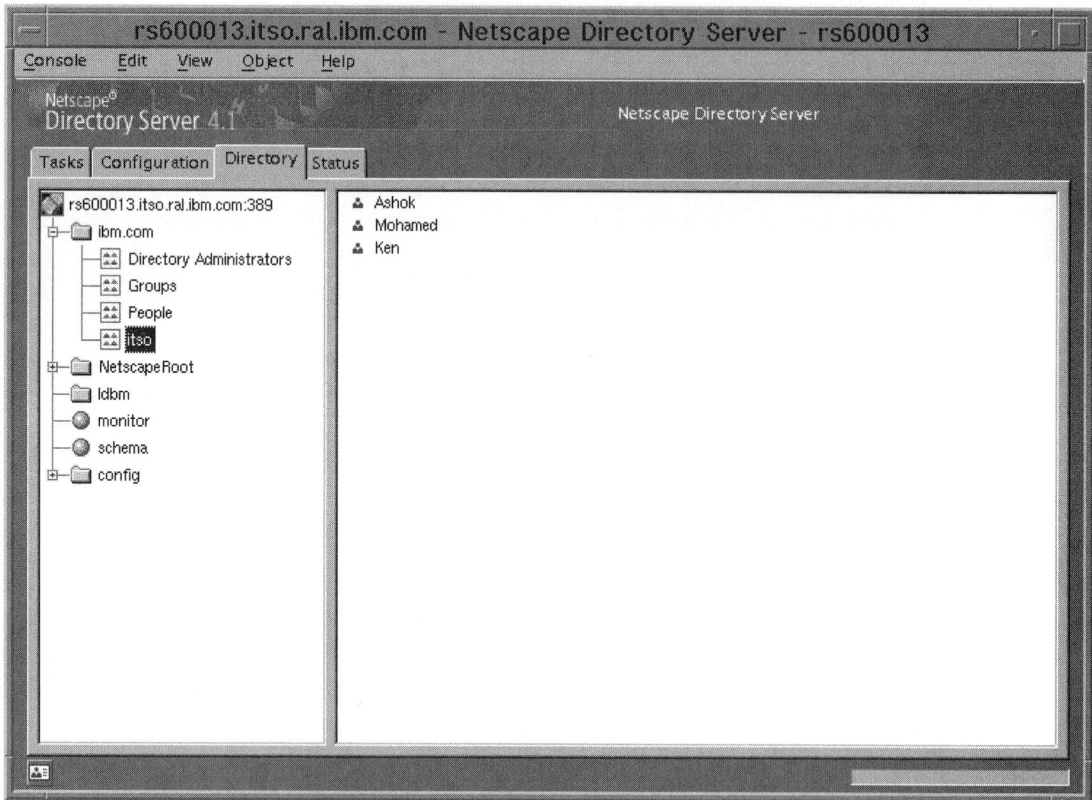

Figure 610. Netscape directory tree showing the contents of the itso organization unit

Now that we have set things up on the Netscape Directory Server, we are ready to enable WebSphere global security.

Bring up the Configure Global Security Settings wizard in the WebSphere Administrative Console. In the User Registry tab, enter details for user Mohamed as shown in Figure 611 on page 759. Note the addition of ou=itso,o=ibm.com for Base Distinguished Name. Port number 389 is optional because it is the default port that is used by LDAP.

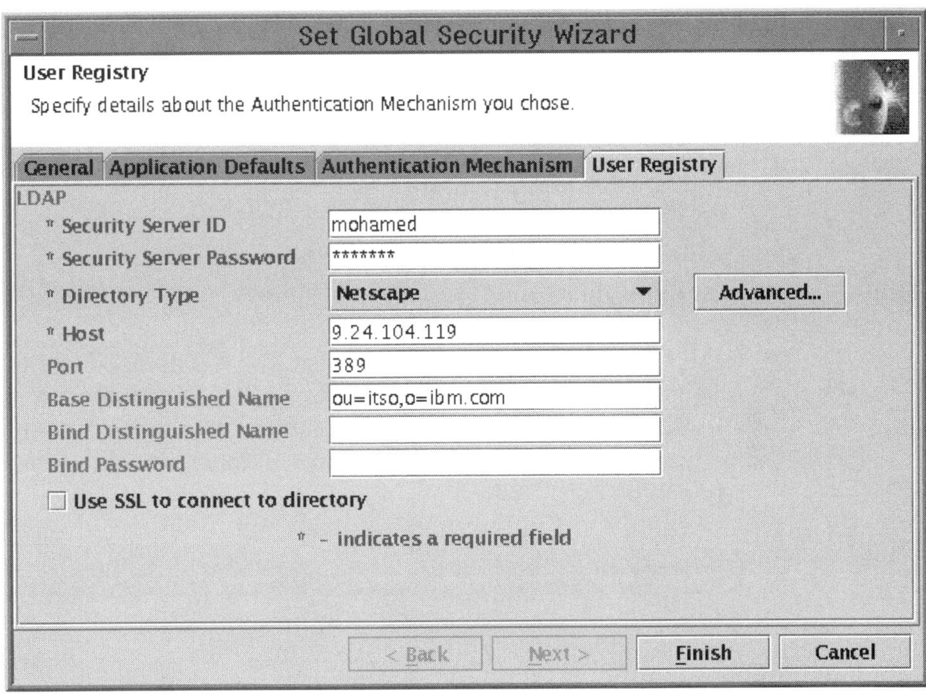

Figure 611. Global security user registry window with Netscape Server details

After you click **Finish**, close the console and restart the WebSphere Administrative Server. When you bring up the administrative console, you will be challenged. At this point enter the user name Mohamed and the given password as shown in Figure 612.

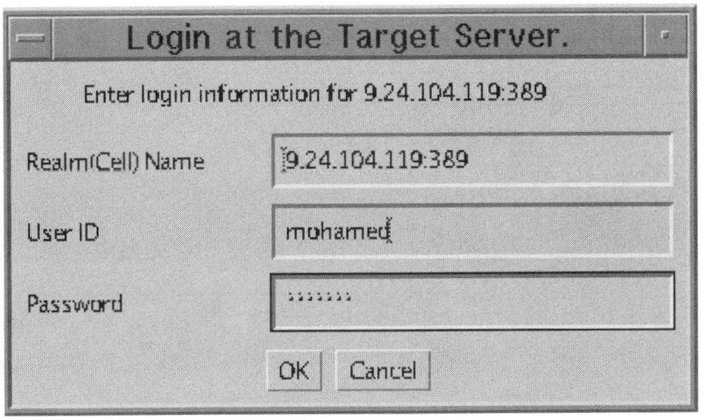

Figure 612. WebSphere Administrative Console login window

Click **OK** to enable the WebSphere Administrative Console.

15.5.2 Domino 5.0

Refer to *Domino and WebSphere Together*, SG24-5955, for detailed instructions on setup and configuration of the Domino Server.

Bring up the Lotus Domino Administration client program. Ensure that you are logged in as a user with administrative privileges.

- Select the server where Domino is installed.
- Go to the **People and Groups** tab.
- Add a new user as shown in Figure 613.

Note the User name attribute because that will be used in the WebSphere Administrative Console. This User name field is a multi-value field, but WebSphere uses only the first name (for example, the first entered name in the User name field). For the purposes of this redbook, we modified the User name to be ken.

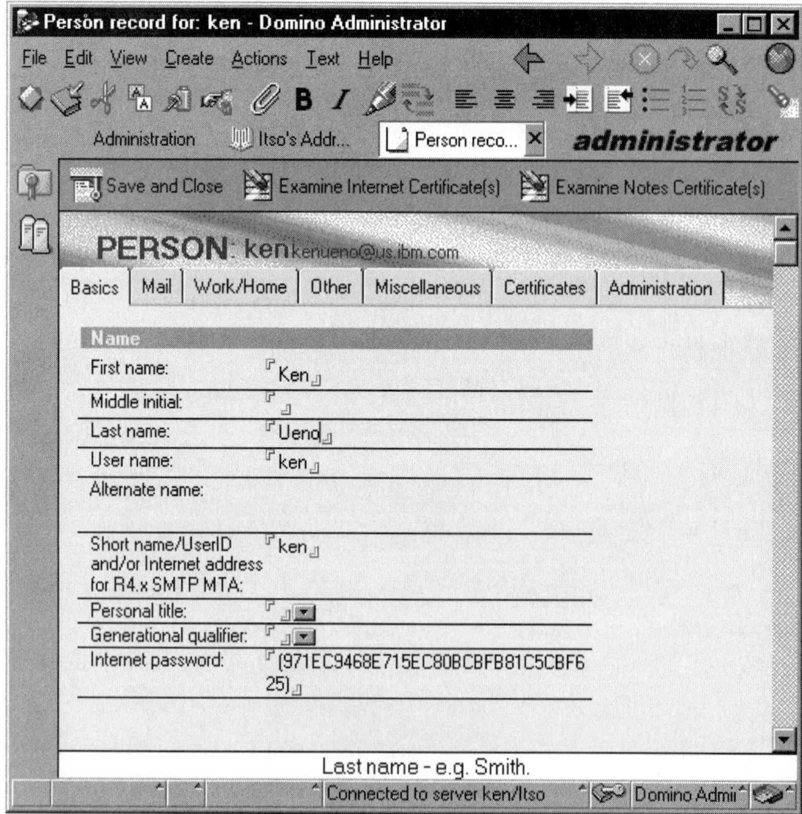

Figure 613. Domino administrator window showing the creation of a new user

Properties on the other tabs are optional. Save and close the new user window.

Now that we have set things up on the Domino Server, we are ready to enable WebSphere global security.

Bring up the Configure Global Security Settings wizard in the WebSphere Administrative Console. In the User Registry tab, enter details for user ken as shown in Figure 614. Note the Base Distinguished Name field is left blank. Port number 389 is optional because it is the default port that is used by LDAP.

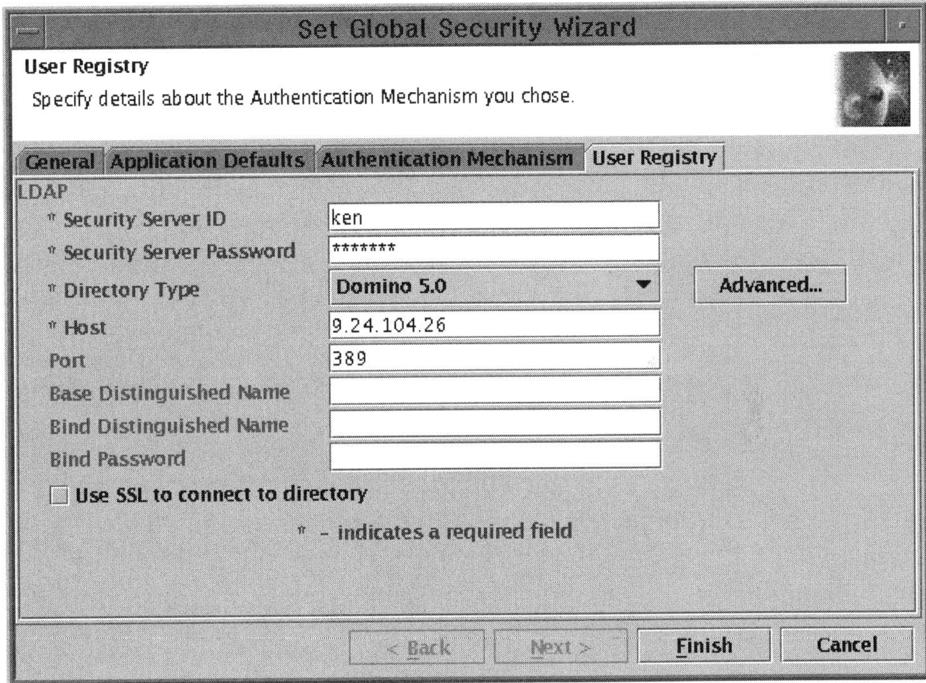

Figure 614. Global security user registry window with Domino Server details

After you click **Finish**, close the console and restart the WebSphere Administrative Server. When you bring up the administrative console, you will be challenged. At this point enter the user name ken and the given password, as shown in Figure 612 on page 759.

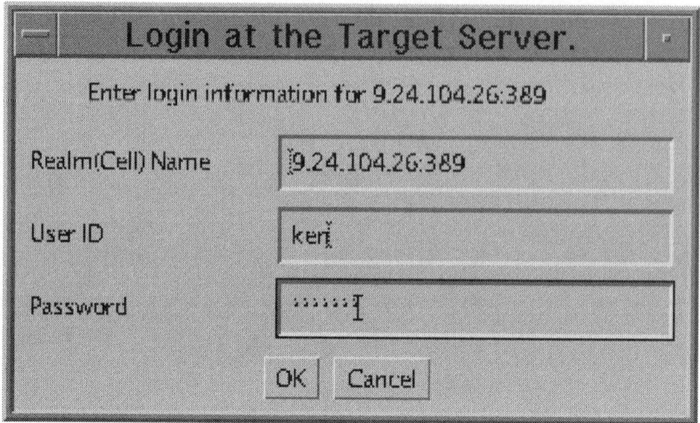

Figure 615. WebSphere Administrative Console login window

Click **OK** to enable the WebSphere Administrative Console.

15.5.3 Microsoft Active Directory

Active Directory is the new directory service that has been integrated into the operating system of the Windows 2000 Server platform. It has a lot of features, one of which is synchronization support through LDAP-based interfaces. LDAP Version 3 is the primary access protocol for Active Directory.

The tools for working with Active Directory remotely come with the Windows 2000 Resource Kit that is contained in the support tools on the Windows 2000 installation CD.

Bring up one of the Active Directory Administrator programs from the Windows program menu, clicking **Start -> Programs -> Administrative Tools -> Active Directory Users and Computers.**

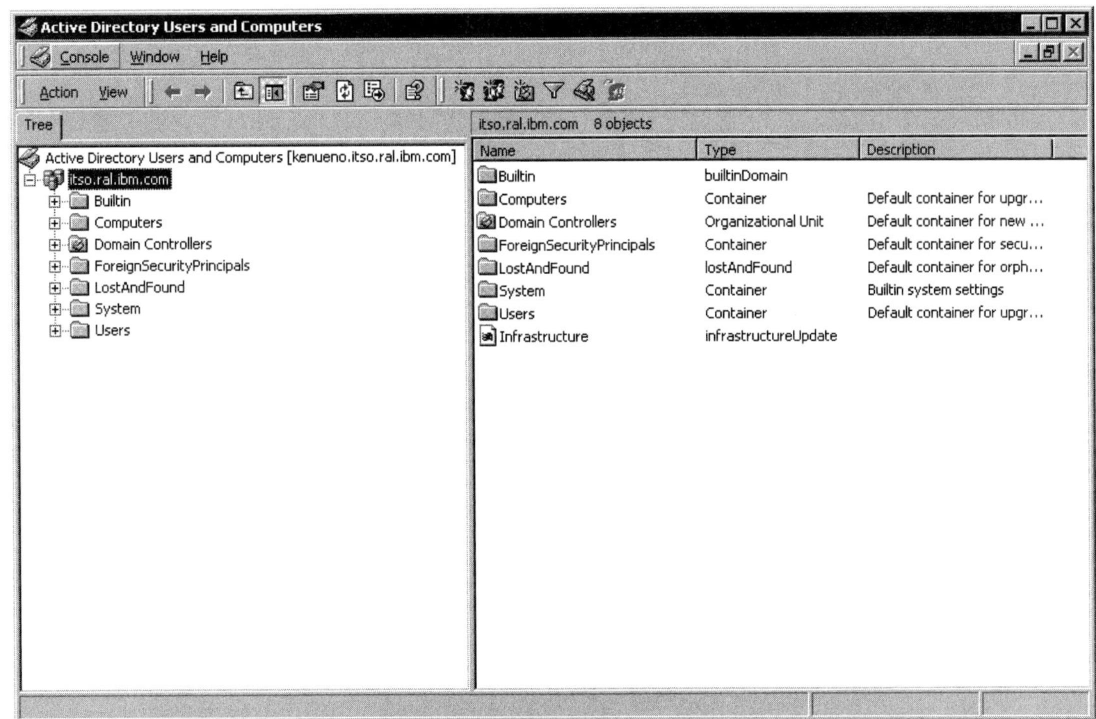

Figure 616. Active Directory Users and Computers window

Create a new organizational unit (OU) named itso in the top level directory. Highlight the top level directory, click the right mouse button, select **New -> Organizational Unit** as shown in Figure 617 on page 764.

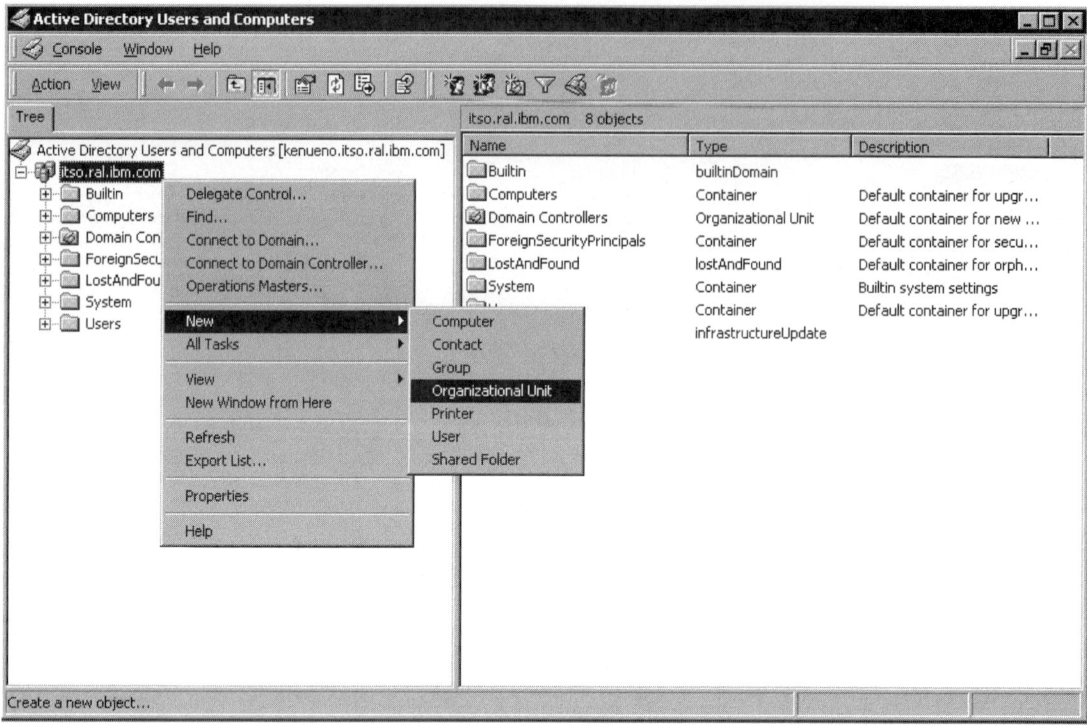

Figure 617. Menu path to create a new organization unit in Active Directory

When the organizational unit property window is displayed, enter the name itso, and click **OK**.

Although this is similar to the procedure to create a new user, but we want to create users in the newly created organizational unit. Highlight **itso**, click the right mouse button, select **New -> User**. Create a new user, simon, with the details shown in Figure 618 on page 765.

Notice the Full Name field. For the purposes of this redbook, the system-generated full name was not used. Enter a user logon name and remember it because that should be used in the WebSphere security settings.

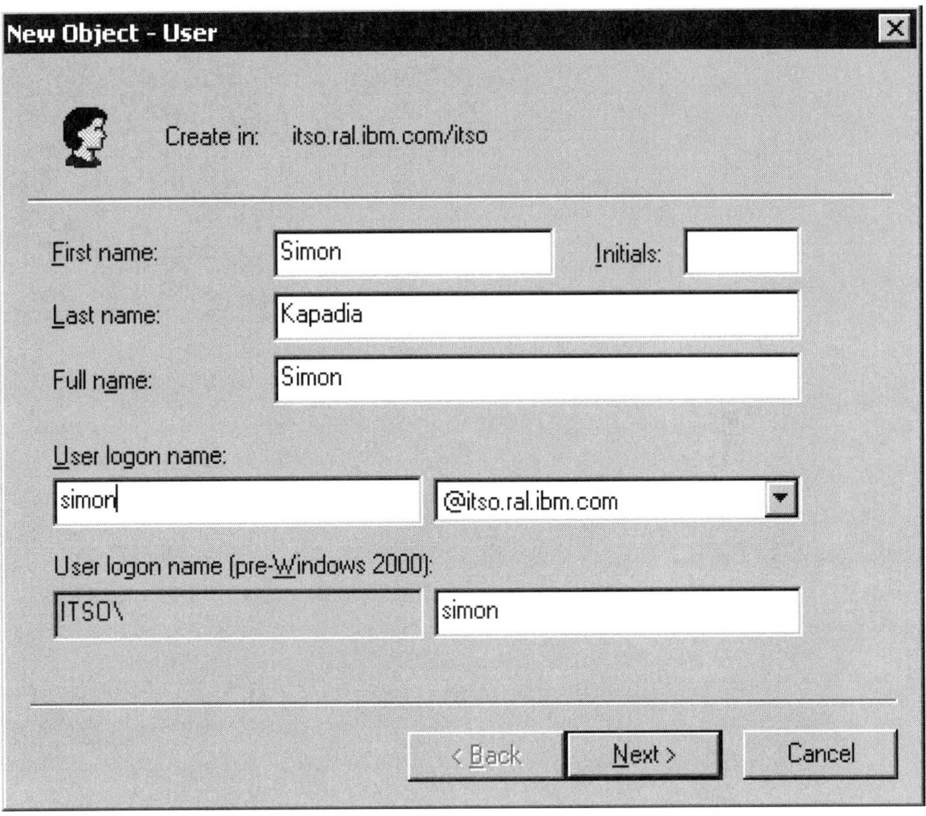

Figure 618. New user property window #1

When you click **Next**, a password entry window is displayed. Enter the password and click **Next** as shown in Figure 619 on page 766.

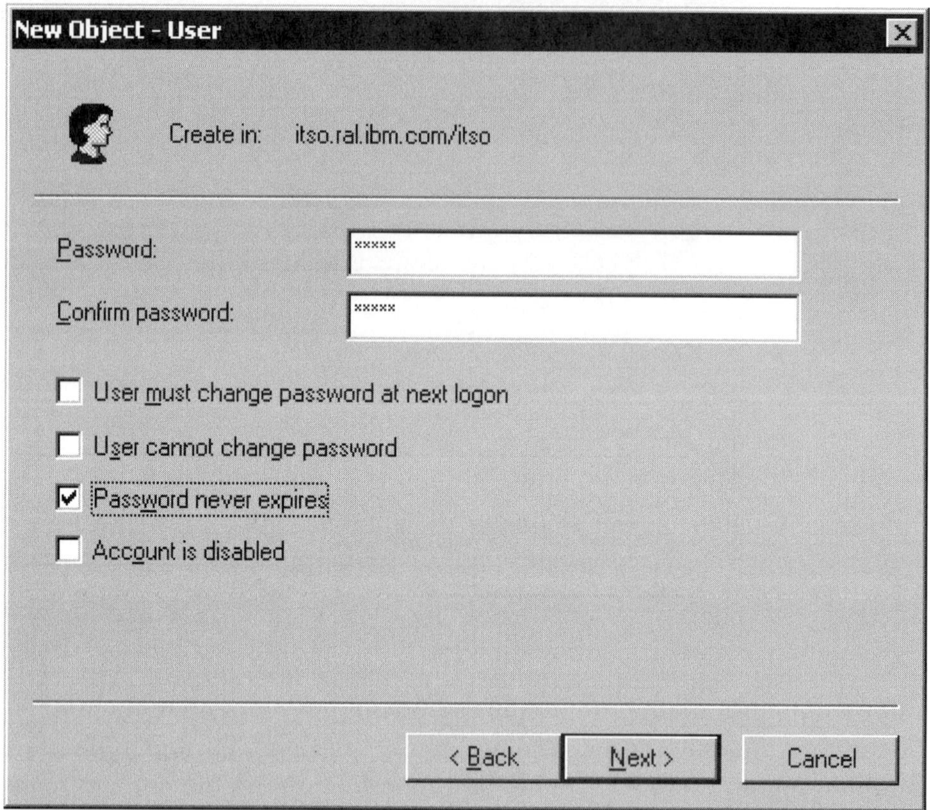

Figure 619. New user property window #2

In the ensuing confirmation window, click **Finish**.

To view the newly added user, refresh the administrative interface and highlight itso. The newly created user, Simon, will be displayed along with any other users in that container as shown in Figure 620 on page 767.

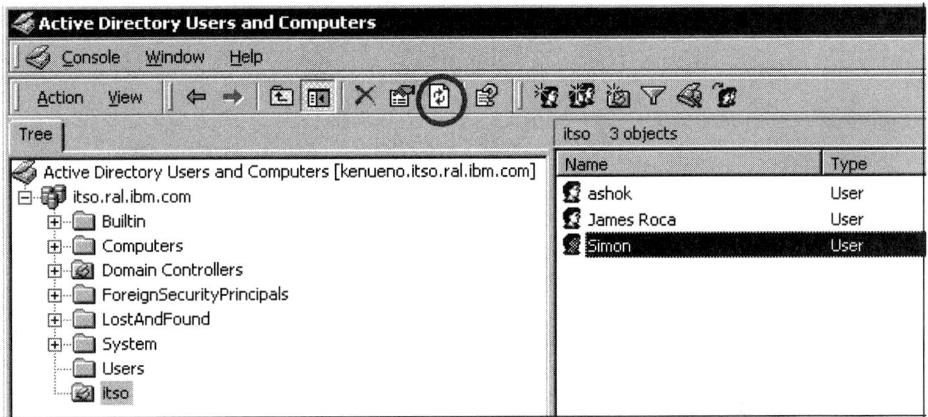

Figure 620. Active Directory Users and Computers window

Now that we have set things up in Active Directory, we are ready to enable WebSphere global security.

Bring up the Configure Global Security Settings wizard in the WebSphere Administrative Console. In the User Registry tab, enter details for user simon as shown in Figure 621 on page 768. Note the Base Distinguished Name field is left blank. Port number 389 is optional because it is the default port that is used by LDAP.

Note

In our test, we could not connect to the Active Directory Server with a short name or uid. The full common name along with the domain name was used instead.

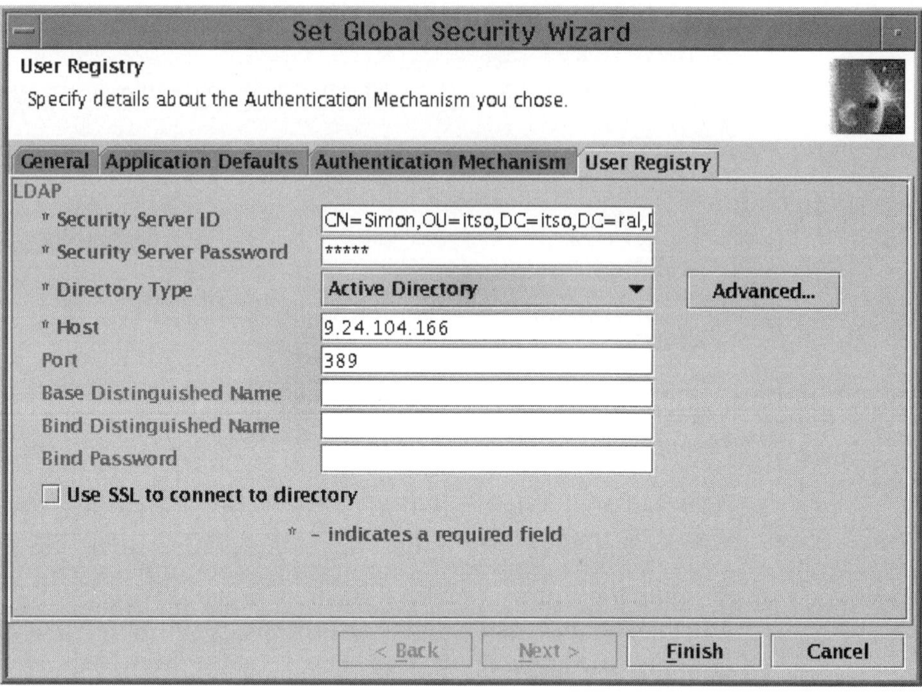

Figure 621. Global security user registry window with Active Directory details

After you click **Finish**, close the console and restart the WebSphere Administrative Server. When you bring up the administrative console, you will be challenged. At this point, type in the fully qualified common name for user simon (CN=Simon,OU=itso,DC=itso,DC=ral,DC=ibm,DC=com) and the given password, as shown in Figure 622.

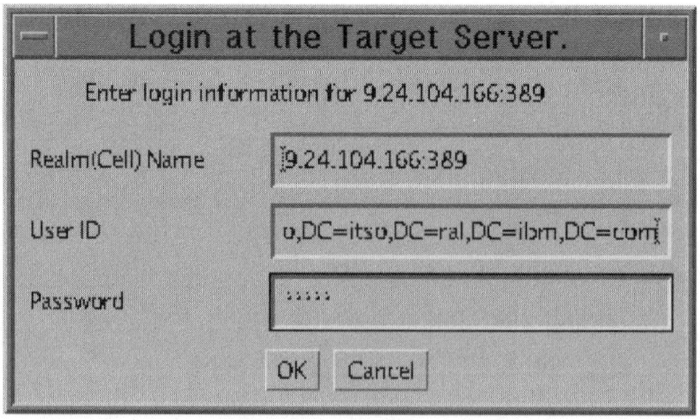

Figure 622. WebSphere Administrative Console login window

15.6 Custom challenge

Challenge types range from no challenge, a user ID and password, a digital certificate, or a custom challenge using Web pages. One of the new features in WebSphere V3.5 security is the custom challenge feature. This feature specifies that clients will log in using servlet-generated Web pages specified by the administrator in the Login URL and Relogin URL fields. These fields are visible when enabling WebSphere global security as shown in Figure 623.

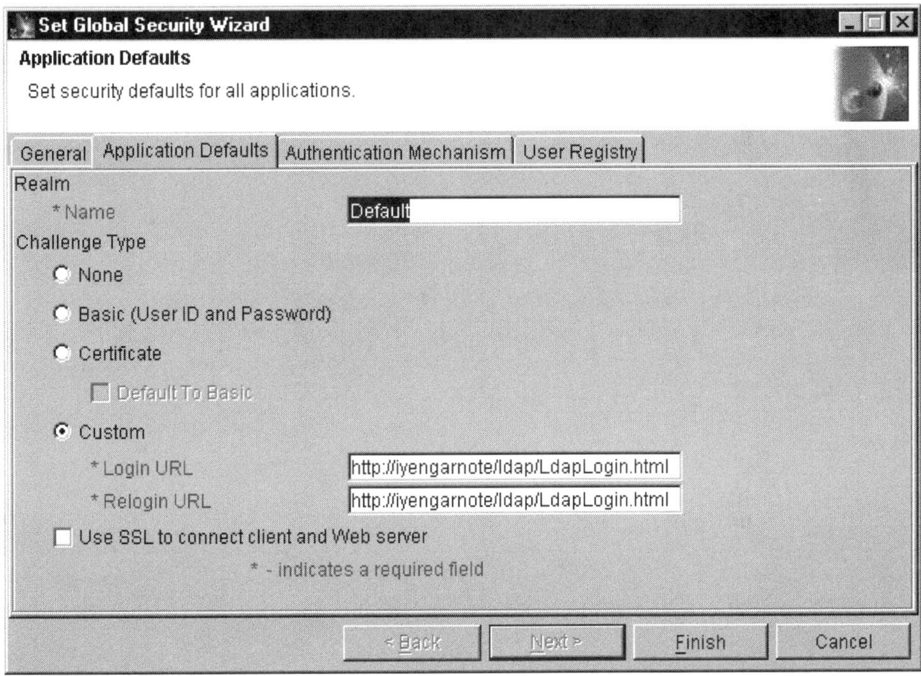

Figure 623. Global security settings wizard window showing Custom Login feature

Currently, the administrator needs to enter the same URL in each of the two fields. The URL is intended to reference a Web page containing an HTML-based login form, but the administrator can enter the URL of any Web page, whether or not it offers a login form. For example, the field could contain the URL `http://host.name.com/login/deny.html` for a Web page created to deny access to users without allowing the users an opportunity to log in.

The Login URL field specifies the fullyqualified path to the Web page to be presented for users to log on to. The administrator should complete this field if he or she specified the custom challenge type. Currently, this field must match the Relogin URL. The product does not validate this field or the Relogin URL.

The Relogin URL filed specifies the fully-qualified path to the Web page to be presented when the connection is released and a user must log on again. Complete this field if you specified the custom challenge type. Currently, this field must match the Login URL.

Furthermore, SSL can be chosen. If SSL is also turned on, then requests that do not arrive over SSL will be refused.

Chapter 16. Topologies selection

This chapter describes various topologies which WebSphere V3.5 supports. In addition, options regarding the use of multiple clones, multiple WebSphere domains, vertical and horizontal scaling as well as multiple tiers (separating the servlet and EJB servers) will be covered. For detailed information including step-by-step configuration, see *WebSphere Scalability: WLM and Clustering using WebSphere Application Server Advanced*, SG24-6153.

16.1 Topology selection criteria

While a variety of factors come into play when considering the appropriate topology for a WebSphere deployment, the primary factors to plan for typically include:

- Security
- Performance
- Throughput
- Availability
- Maintainability
- Session state

16.1.1 Security

Security concerns usually require physical separation of the HTTP (Web) server from the application server processes, typically across one or more firewalls.

EJB security reminder

Enterprise beans and their clones have separate identities. Therefore, you must explicitly protect each and every bean by configuring resource security for the bean and including it in a secured enterprise application.

16.1.2 Performance

Performance involves minimizing the response time for a given transaction load. While a number of factors relating to the application design can affect this, adding additional resources in the following two manners, or a combination of both, can be used to good effect:

- Vertical scaling, which involves creating additional application server processes on a single physical machine in order to provide multiple thread pools, each corresponding to the JVM associated with each application server process.
- Horizontal scaling, which involves creating additional application server processes across multiple physical machines.

16.1.3 Throughput

Throughput while related to performance, more precisely involves the creation of some number of application server instances (clones) in order to increase the number of concurrent transactions that can be accommodated. As with performance the application server instances can be added through vertical and/or horizontal scaling.

16.1.4 Availability

Availability requires that the topology provide some degree of process redundancy in order to eliminate single points of failure. While vertical scalability can provide this by creating multiple processes, the physical machine then becomes a single point of failure. For this reason a high availability topology typically involves horizontal scaling across multiple machines.

16.1.4.1 Hardware-based high availability

By providing both vertical and horizontal scalability, the WebSphere Application Server runtime architecture eliminates a given application server process as a single point of failure. In WebSphere V3.5, the capability to manage the workload of the administrative server process further reduces the potential that a single process failure can disrupt processing on a given node. In fact the only single point of failure in a WebSphere domain/cluster is the database server where the WebSphere administrative database resides. It is on the database server that any hardware-based high availability (HA) solutions such as HACMP, Sun Cluster, or MC/ServiceGuard should be configured. There is very little to be gained from trying to configure WebSphere Advanced to work in conjunction with a hardware-based HA product; moreover it is not a supported configuration as of this writing. The only case where a hardware-based HA solution would provide value is where WebSphere Advanced was serving as the coordinator of a distributed (two-phase commit) transaction. If a WebSphere node were to go down, then any in-doubt transaction (after prepare, before commit) could not be resolved automatically until the node was restored to service. Again, this is not a supported configuration at this time.

16.1.5 Maintainability

While maintainability is somewhat related to availability, there are specific issues that need to be considered when deploying a topology that is maintainable. In fact some maintainability factors are at cross purposes to availability. For instance, ease of maintainability would dictate that one minimize the number of application server instances in order to facilitate online software upgrades. Taken to the extreme, this would result in a single application server instance, which of course would not provide a high availability solution. In many cases it is also possible that a single application server instance would not provide the required throughput or performance. In deciding on the degree of vertical and horizontal scaling that one needs to incorporate in a topology, you should also consider the matter of hardware upgrades (for example, adding CPUs, memory, or upgrading to faster CPUs). As we will see below, one alternative topology for maintainability involves creating more than one WebSphere domain.

16.1.6 Session state

Unless you have only a single application server or your application is completely stateless, then maintaining session state between HTTP client requests will also play a factor in determining your topology. In WebSphere V3.5 the only way to share sessions between multiple application server processes (clones) is to persist the session to a database. Additionally, the configuration of an HTTP splayer such as the Network Dispatcher component of WebSphere Edge Server needs to be considered when session state is important.

16.1.7 Topology selection summary

Table 43 is a summary of topology selection.

Table 43. Topology selection summary

	Security	**Perfor-mance**	**Through-put**	**Maintain-ability**	**Availability**	**Session**
Vertical Clones		Improved throughput on large SMP servers	Limited to resources on a single machine	Easiest to maintain	Process isolation	Required
Horizontal Clones		Best in general	Best in general	Code migration to multiple nodes	Process and hardware redundancy	Required

	Security	Perfor-mance	Through-put	Maintain-ability	Availability	Session
HTTP Separate	Allow for firewalls/ DMZs	Usually better than local	Usually better than local			
Three Tiers	Most options for firewalls	Typically slower than single JVM	Additional clones may improve throughput			
One Domain				Ease of maintenance		
Multiple Domains				Harder to maintain than single domain	Process, hardware and software redundancy	

16.2 Vertical scaling with WebSphere workload management

In the simplest case, one can configure many application server clones on a single machine, and this single machine also runs the HTTP server process. This configuration is depicted in Figure 624.

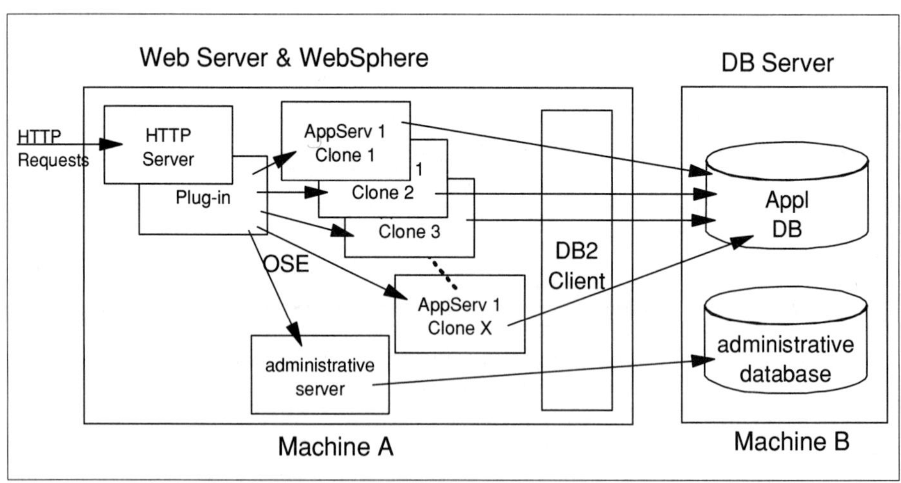

Figure 624. Vertical scaling with clones

At first glance this would appear to be the simplest to configure. However, as we'll see later on, separating the HTTP server(s) from the application server processes on separate physical machines is not significantly harder with WebSphere than the simple case depicted here. Though one is limited to the resources available on a single machine as well as the availability risk when using a single machine, this configuration does provide for process isolation and improved throughput over a configuration where only a single application server process is running. This assumes of course that sufficient CPU and memory are available on the machine.

You will notice that even in the simple "single machine" configuration depicted above, the WebSphere configuration repository resides on a remote database server. There are several reasons why this represents a good practice.

First, most enterprises have already invested in a high availability solution for their database server, and the configuration repository represents a single point of failure in WebSphere, so it pays to make this highly available.

Secondly, the database that houses the configuration repository should be backed up on a regular basis, just as application data is. Housing the repository on the same server as the application data, usually simplifies this task, since appropriate DBA procedures such as database backup processes are already defined for this machine.

Additionally, the database server is typically sized and tuned for database performance, which may differ from the optimal configuration for the application server (in fact on many UNIX servers, installing the database involves modification of the OS kernel).

Lastly, if both the database and application server are placed on the same machine, then under high-load you have two processes: the application server and the database server, competing for increasingly scarce resources (CPU and memory), so in general you can expect significantly better performance by separating the application server from the database server.

16.3 HTTP server separation from the application server

WebSphere provides four different alternatives for physically separating the HTTP server from the application server:

- OSE Remote
- Thick Servlet Redirector
- Thick Servlet Redirector administrative server agent
- Thin Servlet Redirector
- Reverse Proxy / IP Forwarding

When compared to a configuration where the application server and the HTTP server are co-located on a single physical server, each of these alternatives can be utilized to provide varying degrees of improvement in:

- Performance
- Process isolation
- Security

16.3.1 OSE Remote

OSE Remote extends the OSE protocol “off box” to allow for physical separation of the HTTP server and the servlet engine(s). OSE supports clustering and workload management of application servers. This means that the HTTP server can send requests that require intensive processing to multiple application server machines, freeing up the HTTP server machine to process more requests. This option provides for both vertical (as depicted in Figure 625) and horizontal scaling of the WebSphere environment.

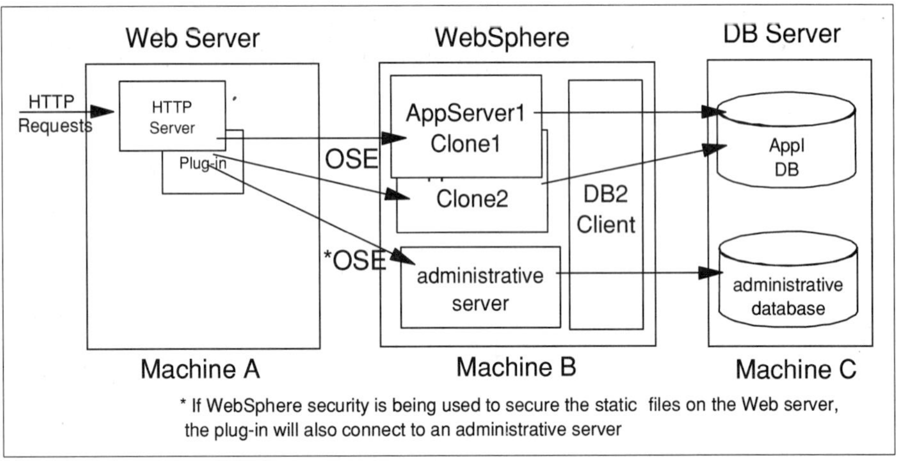

Figure 625. OSE Remote

The OSE link does not, however, support data encryption between the HTTP server and the application server, though it does not preclude use of HTTPS between the browser and the HTTP server. Thus where all data traffic, even that in a DMZ, must be encrypted, OSE Remote is not sufficient, even when WebSphere security is enabled. Recall that all WebSphere Application Server internal IIOP traffic implicitly uses SSL when security enabled. This is not true for OSE. In environments that require that all network communication be encrypted, the Servlet Redirector should be used instead of OSE Remote.

OSE Remote also provides better performance than the Servlet Redirector. Throughput with the Servlet Redirector is typically 15-30% slower than OSE running local. OSE Remote on the other hand performs nearly as well (within a few percent) as OSE local and in some configurations may perform better than OSE local by virtue of separation of the HTTP and application server processes.

In summary the benefits of OSE Remote are:

- Better performance than the Redirector
- Supports WebSphere security
- Does not need database access through a firewall
- Support for NAT firewalls

While the disadvantages to OSE Remote are:

- Manual configuration and administration of the HTTP server plug-in files when changes are made to the application server.
- OSE communication is not SSL encrypted, although one might wish to use a virtual private network (VPN) solution such as IPSec (IP Security) for communication security.

16.3.2 Thick Servlet Redirector

The Servlet Redirector runs as a process on the same server as the HTTP server, intercepts the OSE protocol messages, and forwards each servlet request over IIOP (or IIOP/SSL) to an appropriate servlet engine. The first of the Servlet Redirector configuration options is the thick configuration. In this configuration a WebSphere Administrative Server runs in the same box as the Redirector and takes care of process configuration management. In addition, this topology requires configuration of the appropriate database server client software on the HTTP server machine, which may not be prudent in a secure environment as discussed below.

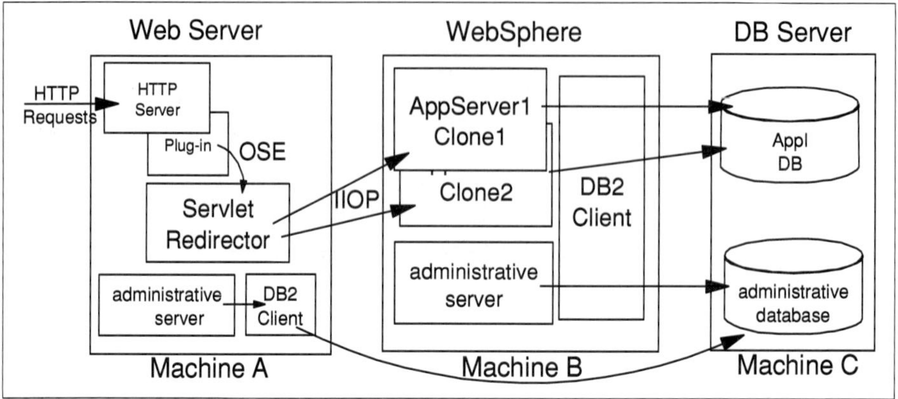

Figure 626. Thick Servlet Redirector

With the thick Servlet Redirector each WebSphere Administrative Server connects directly to the WebSphere administrative database. This requires that either the database be installed locally or that the appropriate database drivers be installed and configured on the machine. More importantly from a security standpoint, a database user ID and password must be stored on the machine for use by the database processes. And also the administrative server on the HTTP server machine requires a TCP connection to the remote database. Therefore you must open a port in the firewall to pass DB traffic. In topologies where security is a concern, such as a server running outside a firewall, this may not be acceptable.

In summary the benefits of a thick Servlet Redirector are:

- Ease of configuration and administration.
  - Automated update of HTTP server plug-in files when changes are made to the application server.
  - Ability to start and stop the Servlet Redirector from the administrative console.
- Supports WebSphere security for servlets/EJBs.
- Encryption of the communications protocol between the Servlet Redirector and the application server.

While the disadvantages to the thick Redirector are:

- Requires access to the database through the firewall.
- Requirement for database principal identity and password to exist outside the firewall.

- Does not support NAT firewalls.
- When used in conjunction with a firewall, the firewall must support IIOP traffic.

16.3.3 Thick Servlet Redirector administrative server agent

An alternative to configuring the database client software on the same machine as the HTTP server is the administrative server agent. In this alternative the administrative server on the HTTP server is configured to run as an agent to an administrative server running on another server. As such the administrative server agent is the recipient of configuration and administration information from the administrative server running on the other node. The administrative server on the other node is responsible for communication with the WebSphere administrative database.

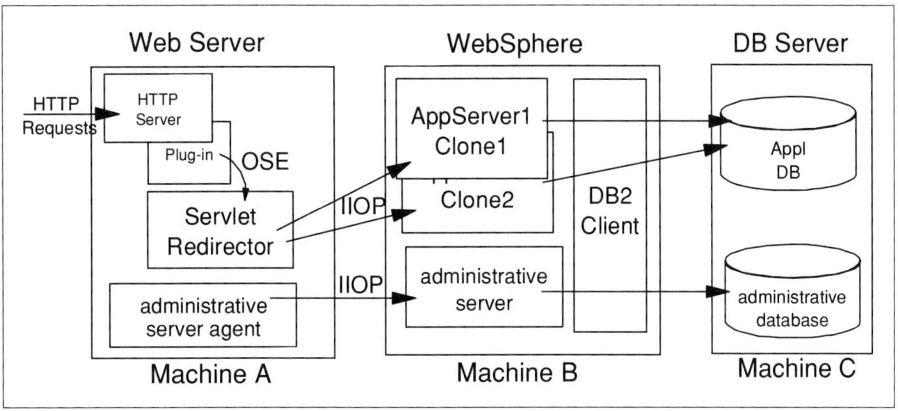

Figure 627. Thick Servlet Redirector administrative server agent

An alternative to the normal administrative server is to configure an administrative server to run in agent mode. In agent mode the administrative server processes on one machine attach to the administrative server process on another machine, and use the remote administrative server to connect to the WebSphere administrative database. Doing so obviates the need to configure the required database components on a machine and also reduces the number of ports that must be opened through a firewall by eliminating the need to open a port or ports for database connections. This also reduces the number of processes running on a machine (for example, DB2 UDB Server or a DB2 client) and helps to improve performance.

In summary the benefits of a thick Redirector in conjunction with an administrative server agent are:

- Supports WebSphere security.
- Encryption of the communications protocol between the Servlet Redirector and the application server.
- Automated update of HTTP server plug-in files when changes are made to the application server.
- Does not need database access through a firewall.
- Database clients and passwords need not be present outside a firewall.
- Ability to start and stop the Servlet Redirector from the administrative console.

While the disadvantages to the thick Redirector administrative server agent are:

- Does not support NAT firewalls.
- When used in conjunction with a firewall, the firewall must support IIOP traffic.

16.3.4 Thin Servlet Redirector

The thin Servlet Redirector provides an alternative to running a WebSphere Administrative Server on the same machine as the HTTP server. Since an Administrative Server is not running on the HTTP server, one must run a script to configure the HTTP server plug-in files as well as a script to start and stop the Redirector. These functions are normally provided by the Administrative Server.

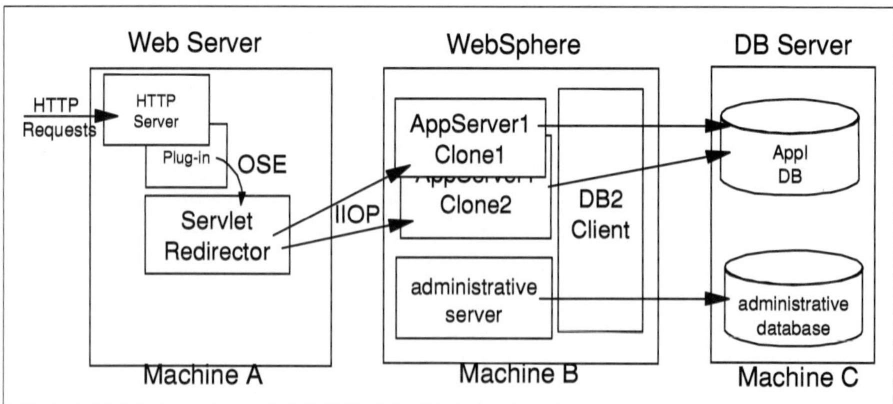

Figure 628. Thin Servlet Redirector

The thin Servlet Redirector provides SSL encryption of the IIOP protocol, but it requires that the HTTP server plug-in files be manually generated and that the Servlet Redirector be started and stopped via a script and not from the administrative console. Additionally by virtue of not running an administrative server process on the HTTP server, more of the processing power available on the box may be used to service HTTP requests.

In summary the benefits of a thin Servlet Redirector are:

- Encryption of the communications protocol between the Servlet Redirector and the application server.
- Minimum process overhead on the HTTP server by virtue of eliminating the need for an administrative server process.
- Does not need database access through a firewall.

While the disadvantages to the thin Redirector are:

- Manual configuration and administration.
  - Manual update of HTTP server plug-in files when changes are made to the application server.
  - Start and stop of the Servlet Redirector by scripts.
- Does not support NAT firewalls.
- When used in conjunction with a firewall, the firewall must support IIOP traffic.

16.3.5 Reverse proxy / IP forwarding

No additional WebSphere administration is required when setting up a reverse proxy configuration; the implementation specifics are determined by the reverse proxy server being used. In this configuration a reverse proxy that resides in the DMZ listens for incoming HTTP(s) requests and then forwards those requests to an HTTP server that resides on the same machine as WebSphere. The requests are then fulfilled and passed back through the reverse proxy to the client, hiding the originating Web server.

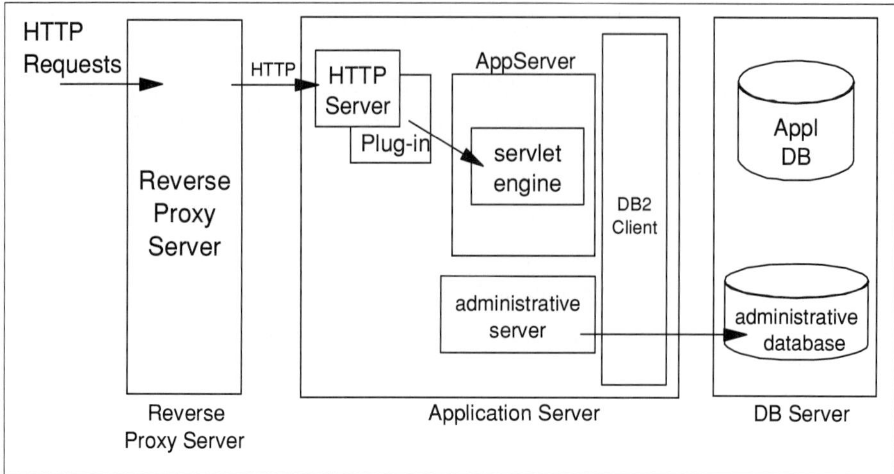

Figure 629. Reverse proxy/IP forwarding

In summary the benefits of the reverse proxy are:

- Does not require database access through firewall.
- Supports WebSphere security.
- Works with NAT.
- The basic reverse proxy configuration is well known and tested in the industry, resulting in less customer confusion.
- Uses HTTP.
- Well-known, dependable format.
- Uses only one HTTP port for requests and responses.

  Note: This is also a disadvantage in some environments where policies prohibit the same port or protocol being used for inbound and outbound traffic across a firewall.

While the disadvantages to the reverse proxy are:

- No WebSphere WLM “awareness”.
- Requires more hardware and software.
- Customers may not want a reverse proxy in the DMZ.

16.3.6 HTTP server separation selection criteria

The following table is a summary of HTTP server separation selection criteria.

Table 44. HTTP server separation selection criteria

Alternative	SSL	DB Password Required	WLM	NAT	Performance	Administration
OSE Remote	No	No	Yes	Yes	High	Manual
Thick Servlet Redirector	Yes	Yes	Yes	No	Medium	Automated
Thick Servlet Redirector - Admin Agent	Yes	No	Yes	No	Medium	Automated
Thin Servlet Redirector	Yes	No	Yes	No	Medium	Manual
Reverse Proxy	Yes	No	No	Yes	High	Manual

16.4 Scaling WebSphere in a three-tier environment

Partitoning your application server processes into servlet application servers and EJB application servers as depicted below can provide some advantages from a security perspective as well as some possible advantages from a performance perspective.

In this topology the EJB layer is closer to the application data, which an entity EJB provides a representation for. When running in an environment where two firewalls are employed, this allows one to provide the same level of security for entity EJBs as is provided for application data.

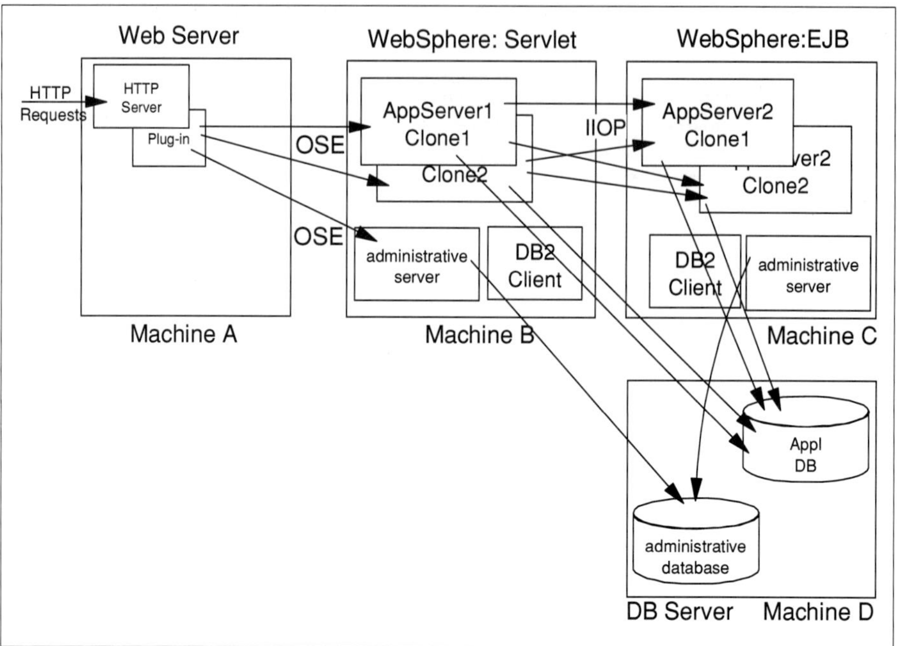

Figure 630. 3-tier environment

In terms of performance this topology allows one to replicate different numbers of application servers (for example, two servlet engines and file EJB servers or vice versa), which may provide better performance. In general, however, elimination of the local JVM optimizations that occur when both the servlet (client) and the EJB (server) are resident in the same application server (JVM) as well as the network latency introduced with the topology will tend to negate any possible performance improvement brought about by virtue of the separate thread pools in each JVM and the additional processing power afforded by a separate physical server.

While providing more redundancy for application server processes, this topology also introduces more possible points of failure. In addition to more application server processes, this means that you'll have more to manage as well.

16.5 Horizontally scaling Web servers with WebSphere

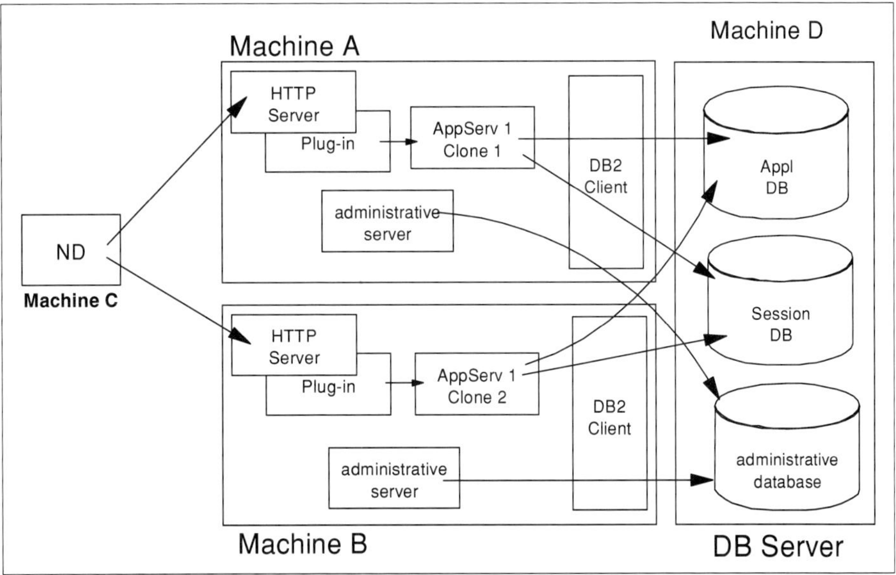

Figure 631. WebSphere with Network Dispatcher

Adding a mechanism for distributing HTTP requests, such as the Network Dispatcher component of WebSphere Edge Server as depicted above, provides the following advantages:

- Network Dispatcher allows for increased number of connected users.
- Network Dispatcher eliminates the HTTP Server as a single point of failure and can be used in combination with WebSphere WLM to eliminate the application server as a single point of failure.
- Increased throughput by virtue of adding multiple servers and CPUs to servicing the workload.

16.6 One WebSphere domain vs. many

While there are no “hard” limits on the number of nodes that can be clustered in a WebSphere domain, one may want to consider creating multiple WebSphere domains for a variety of reasons:

- Two (or more) domains can be employed to provide not only hardware failure isolation, but software isolation as well. This can come into play in a variety of situations:

  - Deployment of a new version of WebSphere. Note that nodes running WebSphere V3.02.x and V3.5 in the same domain is not supported.
  - Application of an e-fix or patch.
  - Roll out of a new application of revision to an existing application.
- In cases where an unforeseen problem occurs with the new software, multiple domains prevent a catastrophic total outage to an entire site. A roll-back to the previous software version can also be accomplished more quickly. Of course, multiple domains imply the software has to be deployed more than once, as would be the case with a single domain.
- Multiple smaller domains may provide better performance than a single large domain, since there will be less interprocess communication in a smaller domain.

Of course, multiple domains will require more effort for day-to-day operations, since administration must be performed on each domain, although this can be mitigated through the use of scripts employing WSCP and XMLConfig. Multiple domains also mean multiple administrative databases, which means multiple backups here as well.

In order to distribute requests across multiple domains as depicted in Figure 633 on page 787, you'll need a mechanism, such as Network Dispatcher for spraying your HTTP requests across the HTTP servers associated with each domain.

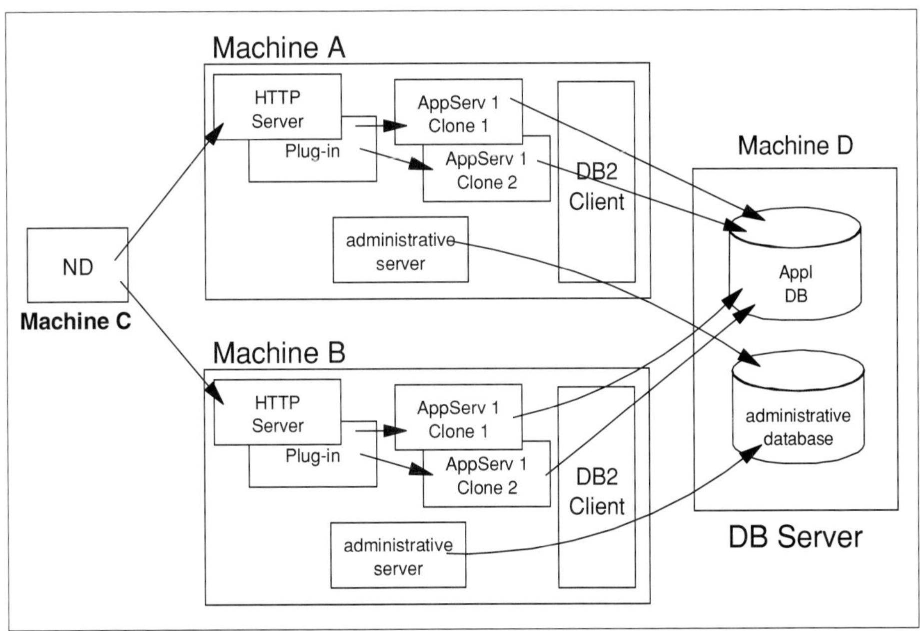

Figure 632. One WebSphere domain

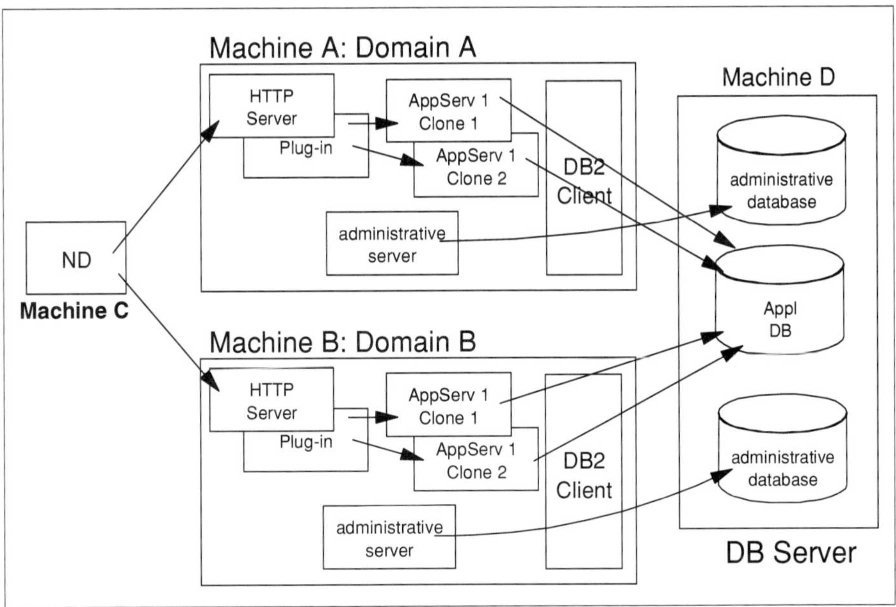

Figure 633. Multiple WebSphere domains

16.7 Multiple applications within one node vs. one application per node

When deciding how to deploy your application, one decision point is whether to deploy clones of an application server across all nodes in a cluster as depicted in Figure 634, or to place all clones of a given application server on a single node as depicted in Figure 635 on page 789.

As discussed previously, horizontal cloning, as depicted in Figure 634 provides:

- Process isolation
- Application software failover
- Hardware failover

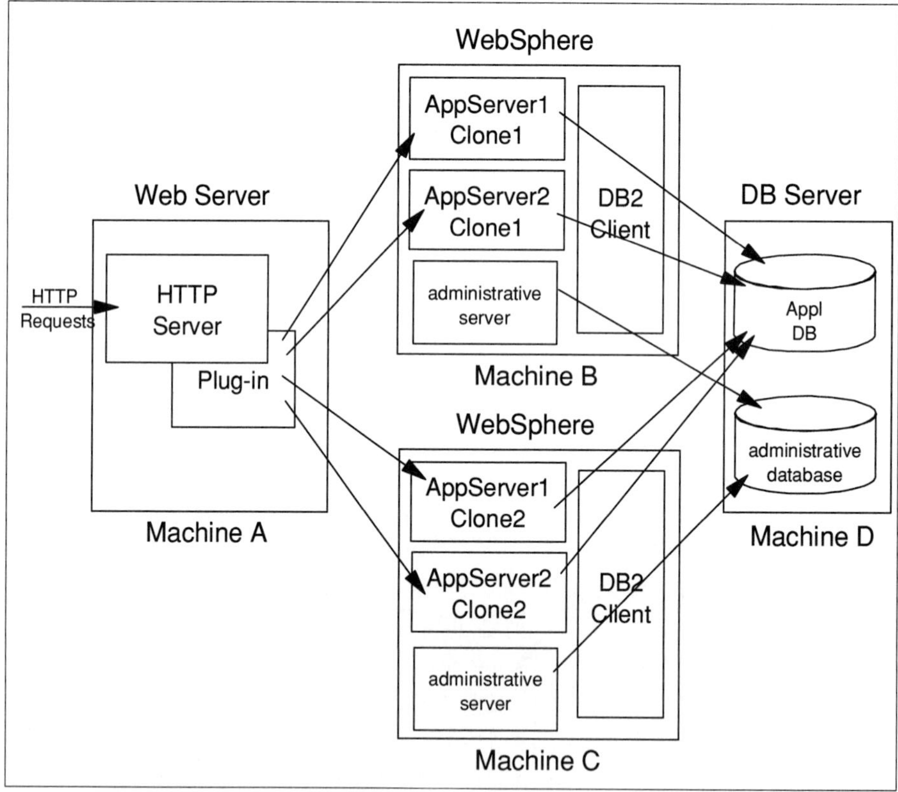

Figure 634. Multiple application servers within one server

As with horizontal cloning, vertical cloning as depicted in Figure 635 on page 789 provides for process isolation and application software failover, but obviously does not provide for any sort of hardware high availability. The primary advantage to vertical cloning is that the executables for a given application have to be distributed to only a single machine. Horizontal cloning on the other hand requires that your application executables be distributed across multiple machines in a cluster. Use of a file system, such as NFS or AFS, that provides a common file mount point for all nodes can ease the distribution of code across multiple nodes.

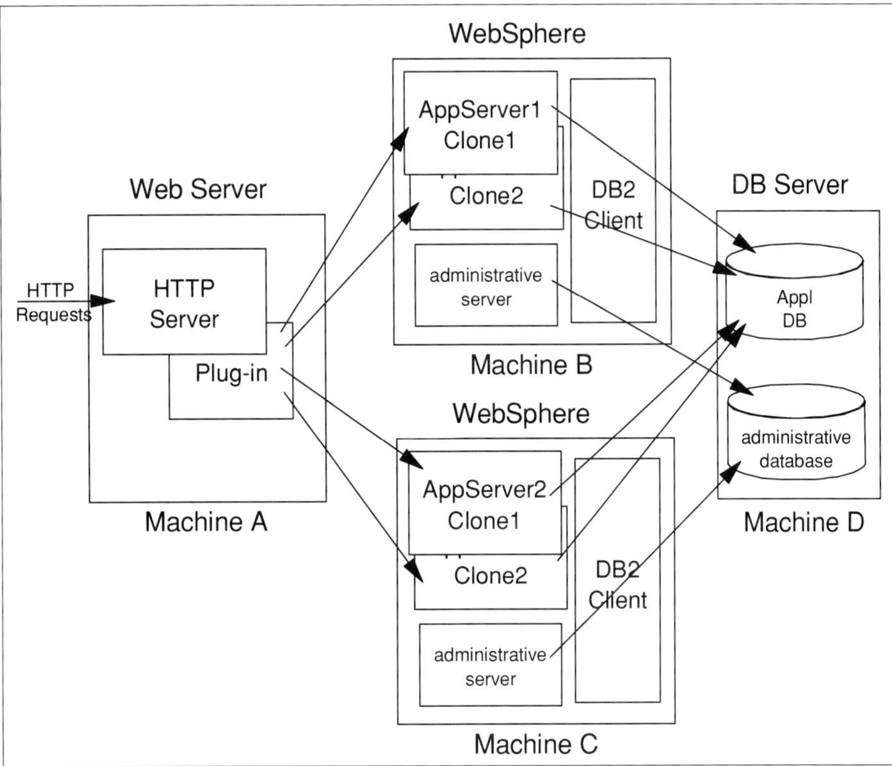

Figure 635. One application server per node

16.8 Closing thoughts on topologies

Whatever topology you decide on, a best practice is to partition your production acceptance environment exactly the same as your production environment. This avoids surprises when deploying your application into production.

Another consideration, when practical for your application architecture, is to create a number of smaller application servers, rather than a single large one.

This has at least two advantages:

- The plug-in config files can be smaller (less complexity of URIs), which leads to better startup performance and possibly better execution performance.
- At least during the development phase, it takes less time to cycle a smaller application server to pickup various configuration changes.

Of course, creation of multiple application servers in this manner should be carefully balanced against the increased complexity of doing so and the potential increase in response time due to inter-process RMI/IIOP calls and network latency.

Chapter 17. Workload management

WebSphere provides a number of tools and techniques that come into play when implementing configurations that provide scalability, load-balancing and failover. We summarize each of them in turn here, then provide in-depth descriptions in subsequent chapters, and finally show how these tools and techniques are combined to create real-life system configurations. For detailed information, including step-by-step configuration, see *WebSphere Scalability: WLM and Clustering using WebSphere Application Server Advanced*, SG24-6153.

17.1 Cloning

Cloning is a mechanism provided by the WebSphere administration system that allows for the creation of multiple copies of an object such as an application server. Cloning is the process of taking a server that you've set up and creating a model based upon that setup. Once you have a model made, you can then create clones of that server. With extra clones running you can improve the performance of your server. There is a point of diminishing returns, a point where the more clones that you add will actually slow you down with the extra maintenance and traffic generated by the clones and the management of them. Since cloning is part of the core of workload management, this is demonstrated in detail throughout this book.

In brief, the system administrator creates a *model* for an application server, and from this model may create any number of copies or *clones*. The model is a logical representation of the application server that exists only as information managed by the WebSphere administration system. It has the same structure and attributes as a real application server: it may contain servlet engines, EJB containers, servlets, EJBs, etc. and allows the administrator to view and modify any properties of these logical objects. But it is not associated with any node, and does not correspond to any real server process running on any node. The clones created from this model, on the other hand, represent real application server processes running on real nodes. They are identical in every way to the model from which they were created except for some clone-specific attributes which must be set on a per-clone basis. Furthermore, if the system administrator makes changes to the model, these changes will be automatically reflected to all the clones. Several clones from the same model may be instantiated on multiple nodes, and it is also possible to instantiate multiple clones on the same node.

In a typical scenario, a system administrator might create a model of an application server, populate it with all the objects necessary for the implementation of his target application, fine-tune the properties of these objects, and finally, when he is ready to deploy the application, create and start a number of clones that will begin to execute the application.

Figure 636 shows an example of a possible configuration that includes clones. Model 1 has two clones on node A, and three clones on node B. Model 2, which is completely independent of model 1, has two clones on node B only. Finally, node A also contains a free-standing application server that is not a clone of any model.

Note

In the example and the discussion above, we only considered the creation of models and clones for entire application servers, which in turn contain servlet engines, EJB containers, etc. In truth, the WebSphere administration system supports the creation of models and clones for objects at any level of the containment hierarchy. For example, it is possible to model and clone an individual EJB, without cloning either the application server or the EJB container in which it has been deployed. Although this capability is very important internally for the implementation of the overall model/clone facility in WebSphere, for the purposes of scalability, we will only consider the cloning of entire application servers. Moreover in terms of a best (or recommended) practice, you should only clone entire application servers, which facilitates the administration of models/clones.

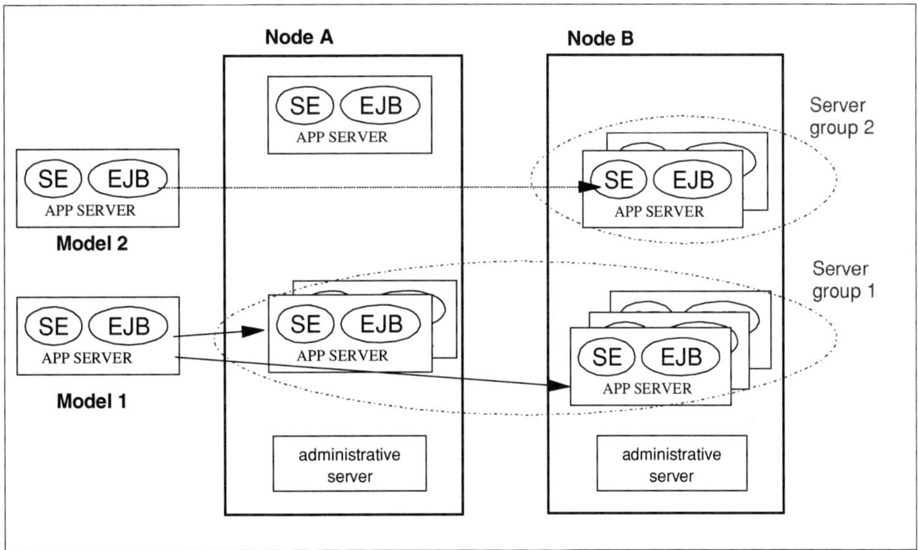

Figure 636. Models and clones

In practice, cloning provides two important benefits:

- It is a way to simplify system administration: clones can be used to quickly create and maintain identical copies of a server configuration.
- It is a way to organize workload distribution for several mechanisms (such as OSE Remote, WLM, and Servlet Redirector) provided with WebSphere. The set of all the clones of one model of an application server constitutes a logical group called a *server group* or *cluster*. The various workload distribution mechanisms use this abstraction of a server group to define the set of application servers among which they are to distribute the client requests. Since by definition all the clones are identical, the workload distribution mechanisms can safely assume that any one of the clones is equally capable of servicing any request.

In subsequent sections, we will see how this notion of clones and server groups is used to control workload distribution with the OSE transport, with the WLM tool for EJBs, and with the Servlet Redirector.

17.1.1 Vertical and horizontal cloning

In practice, we will see scalability used in two distinct contexts within the WebSphere Application Server runtime:

Vertical cloning refers to the practice of defining multiple clones of an application server on the same physical machine. Experience has shown that a single application server, which is implemented by a single JVM process, cannot always fully utilize the CPU power of a large machine and drive the load up to 100%. This is particularly true on large multiprocessor machines, because of inherent concurrency limitations within a single JVM. Vertical cloning provides a straightforward mechanism to create multiple JVM processes, which together can fully utilize all the processing power available.

Horizontal cloning refers to the more traditional practice of defining clones of an application server on multiple physical machines, thereby allowing a single WebSphere application to span several machines while presenting a single system image. Horizontal cloning can provide both increased throughput and failover.

17.1.2 Secure cloned resources

WebSphere V3.5 can be applied with security to cloned resources. WebSphere V3.5 has different steps for protecting cloned enterprise beans and cloned servlets.

17.1.2.1 Protecting cloned enterprise beans

Enterprise beans and their clones have separate identities. Therefore, you must explicitly protect each and every bean by configuring resource security for the bean and including it in a secured enterprise application.

For example, the “BeanThere” and “BeanThereClone” are considered to be two different enterprise beans, although they might be treated as clones in a WLM environment. To protect the beans, the administrator must configure resource security for each bean. Each bean must be explicitly included in a secured enterprise application, such as “BeanThereApplication.”

17.1.2.2 Protecting cloned servlets

In contrast to its approach to enterprise bean clones, WebSphere security does not treat a servlet and its clones as separate resources -- if the original servlet is protected, its clones are too, with no additional steps required by the administrator.

To secure a servlet, add its “Web resource” configuration (URI) to a secured enterprise application.

17.2 WLM

Workload Management (WLM) is the primary mechanism for load-distribution of requests directed at EJBs. In a simple, non-load-balanced EJB in WebSphere, each client of the bean holds a stub that contains a CORBA reference to the corresponding bean on the server. Whenever the client invokes an operation on that bean, the request is simply forwarded to the server object associated with that CORBA reference. Note that the client can be a stand-alone Java program using RMI/IIOP, a servlet operating within a WebSphere servlet engine, or another EJB.

When using the WLM facility, the simple client stub is augmented by a smart stub that contains a collection of CORBA references to multiple instances of the same bean in different servers. Whenever the client invokes an operation on the bean, the smart stub automatically and transparently forwards the request to any one of the available server objects, thereby achieving both load-balancing and failover when appropriate. The smart stubs transparently communicate with the WebSphere EJS runtime to keep track of which servers and EJB instances are available at any given time.

The WLM facility is enabled through one of three alternatives:

1. EJBs developed and deployed from VisualAge for Java are automatically WLM-enabled.
2. EJBs developed and deployed outside of Visual Age for Java must first be deployed inside the WebSphere runtime, then the WLMjar processor (a .bat file on NT, a .sh file on UNIX) must be executed against the deployed EJB with WebSphere V3.02x.
3. With WebSphere V3.5, when you deploy a bean inside the WebSphere runtime, you can specify that the bean is to be WLM-enabled.

All three options generate the smart stubs and other classes required for WLM. These smart stubs behave as outlined above and look exactly the same as simple stubs as far as the client is concerned; there is no need for any change in the client code to take advantage of the WLM facility.

As with other load-distribution facilities in WebSphere, the set of EJB instances that are available for load-distribution through WLM is defined by the set of available clones of any given object. Currently, the WLM facility provides load-distribution among:

- All clones of the home of a session (stateful or stateless) or entity bean (thereby allowing bean instances to be created in different servers)

- All the clones of an instance of a given stateless session bean or the instance of a given entity bean

In fact, the only type of EJB reference not subject to load-distribution through WLM are the instances of a given stateful session bean. This is because stateful session beans cannot be replicated or are not shared between multiple servers.

17.2.1 WLM runtime

The preceding discussion has provided an outline of the WebSphere WLM runtime. The following will provide a more detailed explanation of how the WLM runtime actually works.

The first two steps are depicted in Figure 637.

- During the initial call from an EJB client the underlying WLM client runtime (the “smart stubs” discussed previously) contacts the WebSphere Administrative Server to obtain information about the server group. Note that since the clones that comprise a server group can be distributed across multiple nodes, some of this information may be obtained from the administrative database for all nodes in the cluster.
- In turn the administrative server returns the requested information to the EJB client.

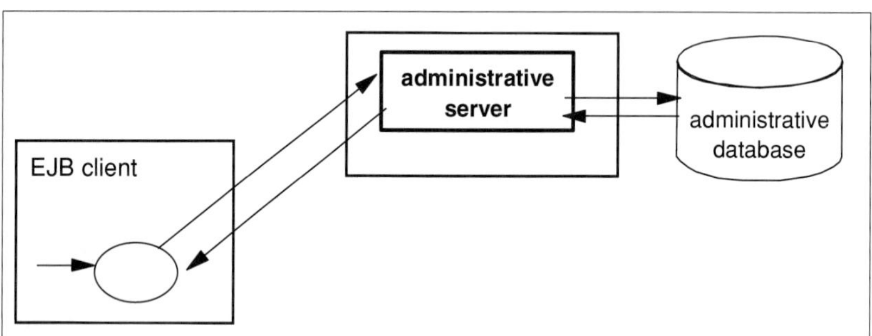

Figure 637. WLM client initial access: steps 1 and 2

The information returned regarding the server group and the currently active clones is in turn used to populate an array of proxy stubs, each one representing an active clone. In the simple case depicted in Figure 638 on page 797, there are two active clones, so two corresponding proxy stubs (labeled Proxy1 and Proxy2) are created.

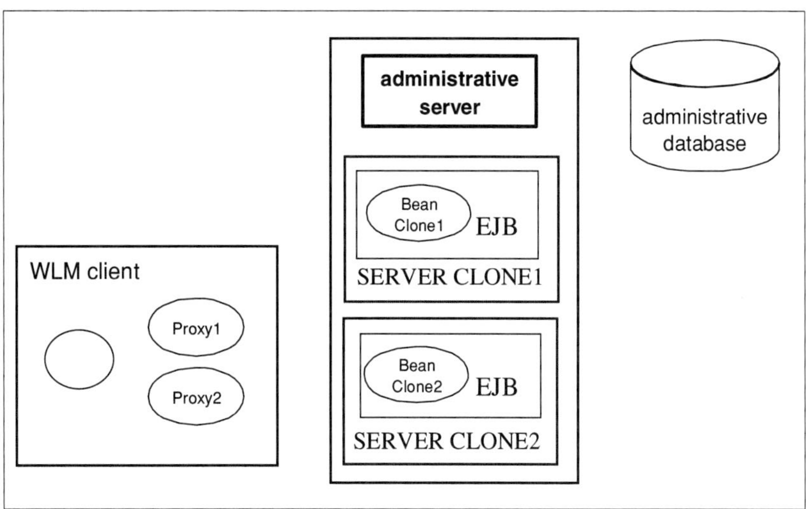

Figure 638. WLM client initial access: step 3

Lastly, as depicted in Figure 639, the WLM runtime proxy manager directs the request to a clone based on the WLM policy in effect at the time.

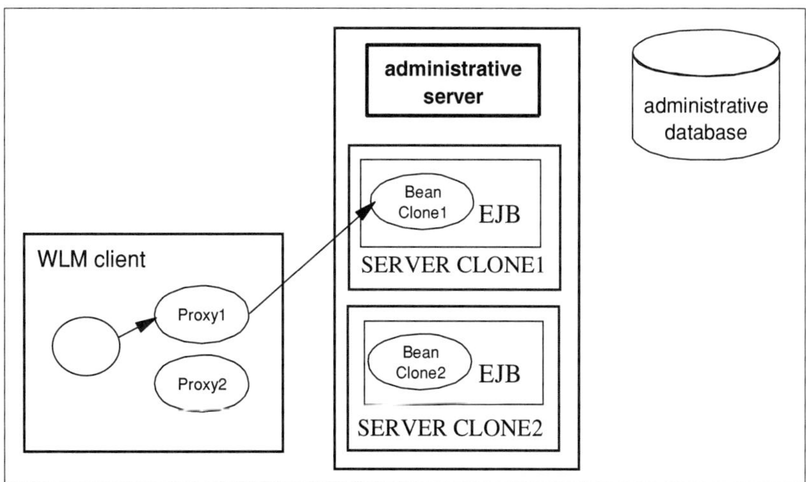

Figure 639. WLM client initial access: step 4

Unless a refresh of the WLM runtime client cache is required, subsequent requests utilize the existing proxies for each active server (we will discuss the refresh mechanisms in detail below). Assuming that there has not been a change in the state of the model server group, the second request is either dispatched to the same clone, if the call is in context of a transaction, or to another clone in the server group as depicted below in Figure 640.

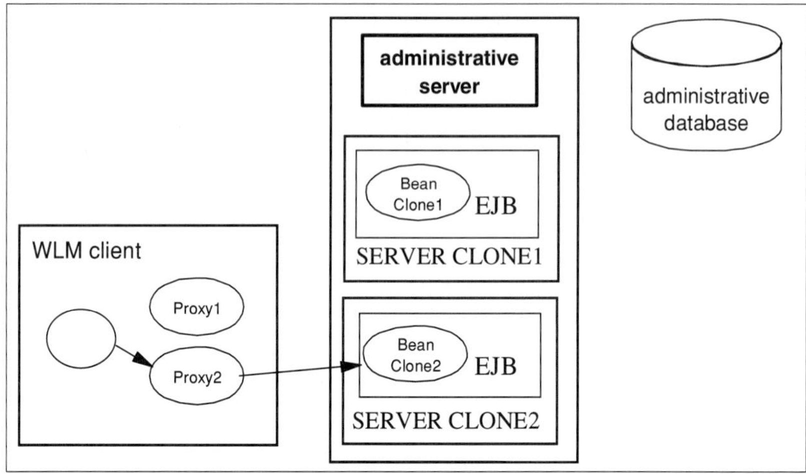

Figure 640. WLM client, subsequent requests

Of course the above would be fine if changes never occurred in the state of the EJB servers. As we all know it is necessary to stop and start servers for maintenance. The runtime also has to be capable of reacting to hardware and software failures.

Let's assume that instead of succeeding that the second client request failed. In this case the WLM client runtime will attempt to determine if more recent information exists for the server model group. If more recent information is not available and it is safe to retry (as discussed below in 17.2.3, "WLM runtime exception handling" on page 806), then a retry is attempted to the same clone, if the clone is still unavailable then the clone is marked as unusable as depicted below in Figure 641 on page 799 and it will remain in that state for a prescribed time interval (UnusableInterval) after which the WLM client runtime will attempt to use the clone again. In the interim the WLM client runtime will direct requests to surviving servers in the server model group as depicted in Figure 641 on page 799.

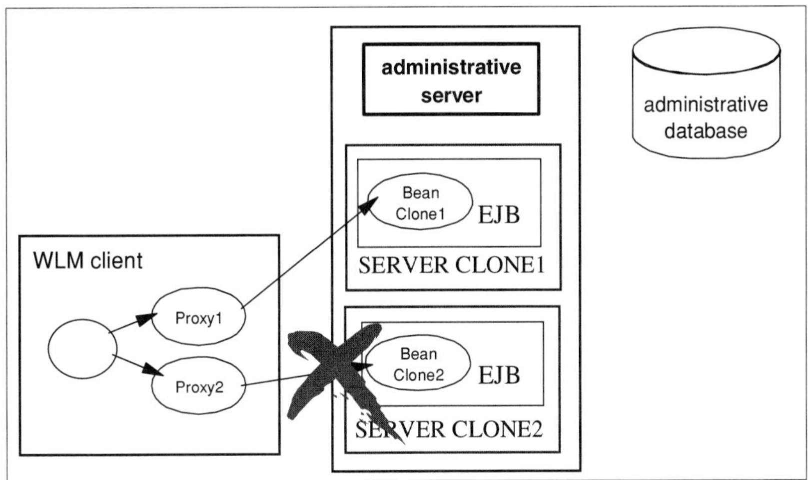

Figure 641. WLM client request to a failed server

If requests to subsequent servers in the model server group are unsuccessful, these exceptions will be handled as described above for all the servers in model server group until a request succeeds or all servers are marked as unusable. In this case the WLM client runtime will contact the administrative server for new model server group information as depicted in Figure 642 on page 799.

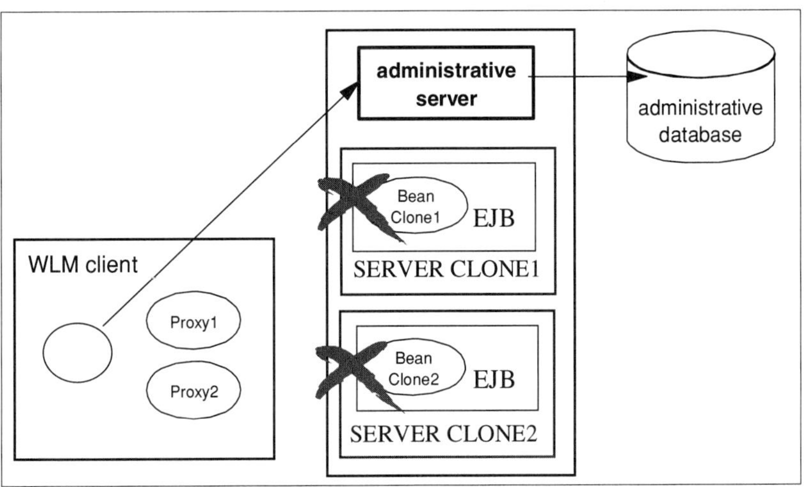

Figure 642. WLM client request failed to all servers

17.2.1.1 WLM runtime refresh mechanisms

As noted above, it is necessary to propagate changes in WLM runtime state to other nodes within a WebSphere domain as well as to clients that may be making requests of servers running on those nodes. There are two components to this: one for the servers and one for the clients.

First let's consider the WLM server refresh that occurs when a change is made to a model server group. As an example, consider the case where a new clone is added to a model. In our example a third clone (Server Clone 3) has been added to the model, and a start for the third clone has been issued from the administrative console as depicted in Figure 643 on page 800 (note that alternatively the server start could be issued from the command line with XMLConfig or WSCP). After the start has been issued from the administrative console, the change in runtime state is sent to the administrative database from the administrative server.

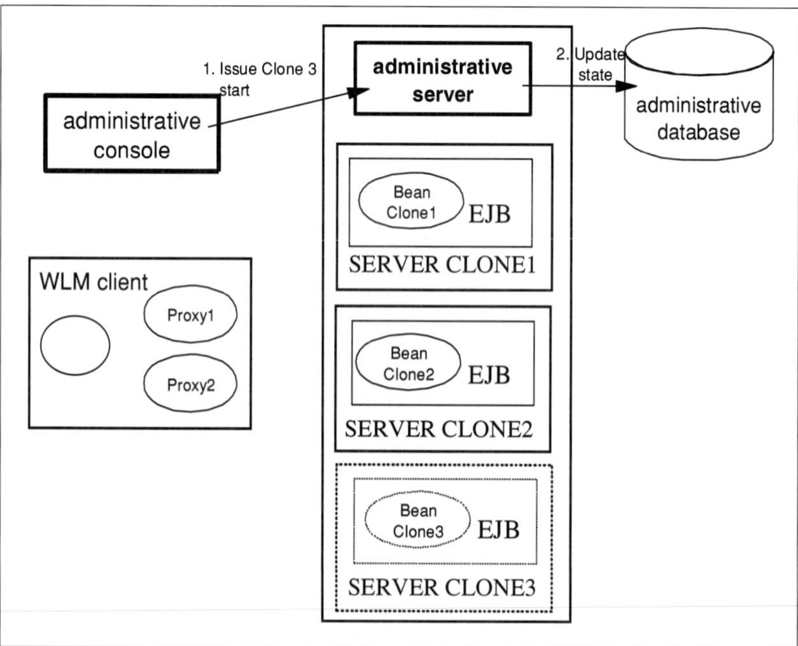

Figure 643. WLM server refresh, the administrative database update

Once the change in runtime state has been issued to the administrative database, the actual start command is issued to the server clone (Server Clone 3 in our example) as depicted in Figure 644 on page 801.

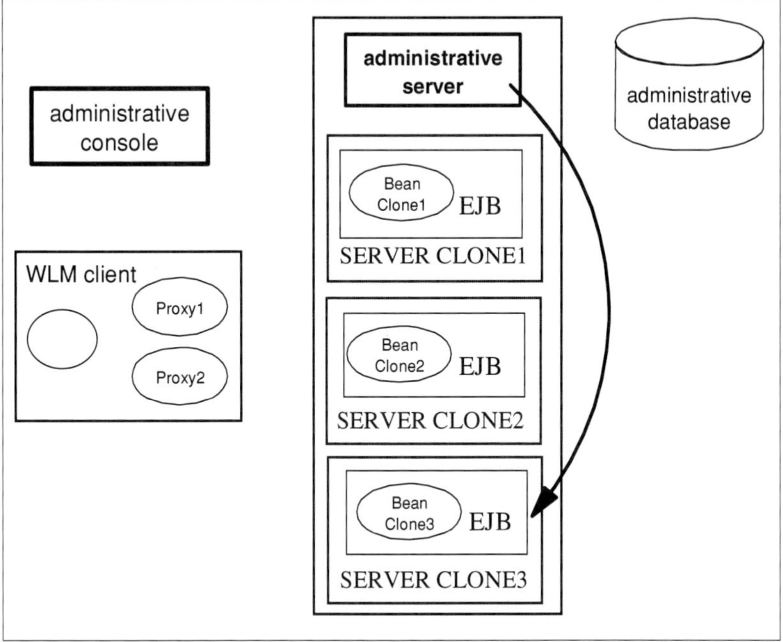

Figure 644. WLM server refresh, server start

The final steps in the process are to propagate the change in the state of the model server group to other clones running on the same machine and then to the administrative servers for other nodes in the WebSphere domain. This is depicted in Figure 645 on page 802. The remote administrative servers will in turn propagate the change in state to any clones for the model server group running on remote nodes.

Note

The propagation of runtime state changes to clones by the administrative server is not instantaneous; it can take up to one minute. Changes in state from the server down are in turn propagated as prescribed by the refresh interval property (-Dcom.ibm.ejs.wlm.RefreshInterval=xxx) which by default is 300 seconds.

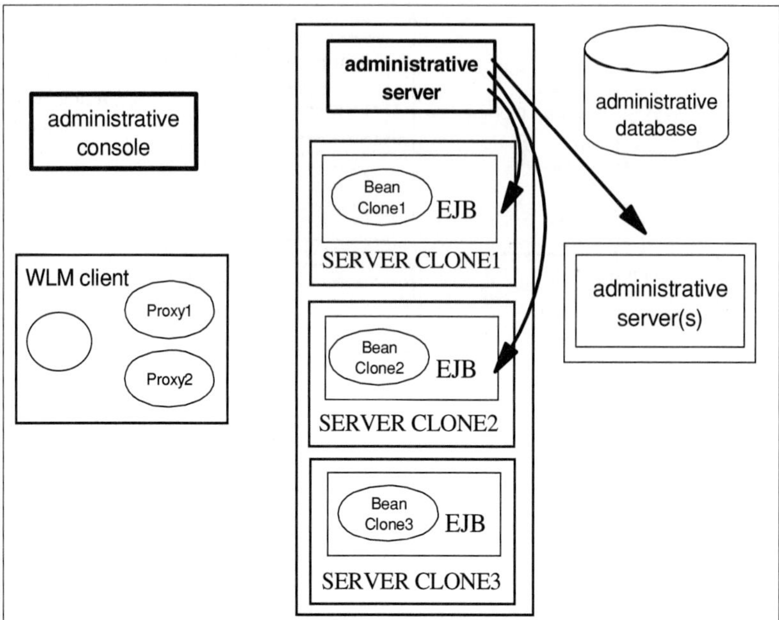

Figure 645. WLM server refresh, servers and nodes

As far as changes propagating to the WLM client, this occurs as part of normal request processing. As depicted in Figure 646 on page 803 a WLM client makes a request, and the request is directed to a known clone based on affinity or WLM selection policy (as appropriate). In this example the request is directed to Server Clone 2.

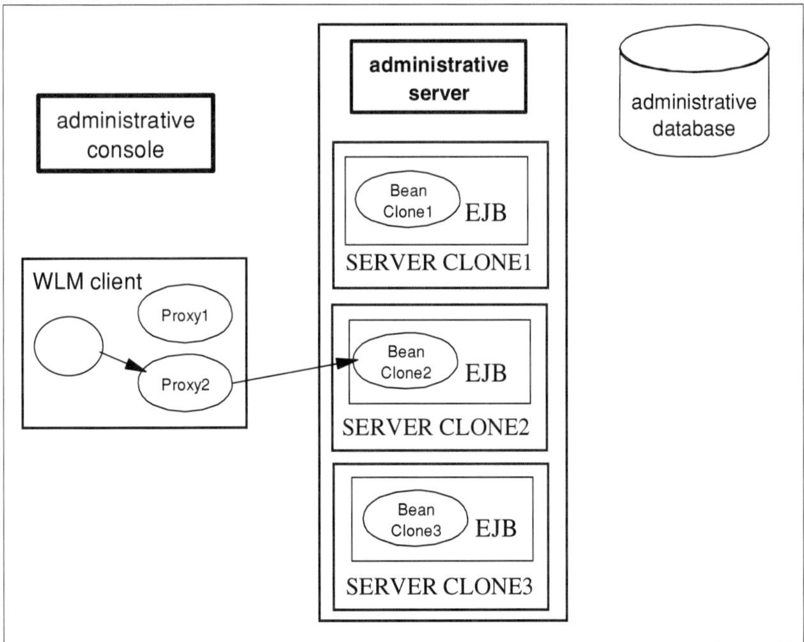

Figure 646. WLM client refresh, client request

Upon receiving the request, the WLM server runtime makes use of an epoch number that is changed each time there is a change to the state of the model server group. A comparison is made between the epoch number received with the client request with that on the server. In this example, the server detects that the client cache is stale (old) since the epoch numbers do not match. As part of the request reply packet to the client, the new WLM state is sent as depicted in Figure 647 on page 804.

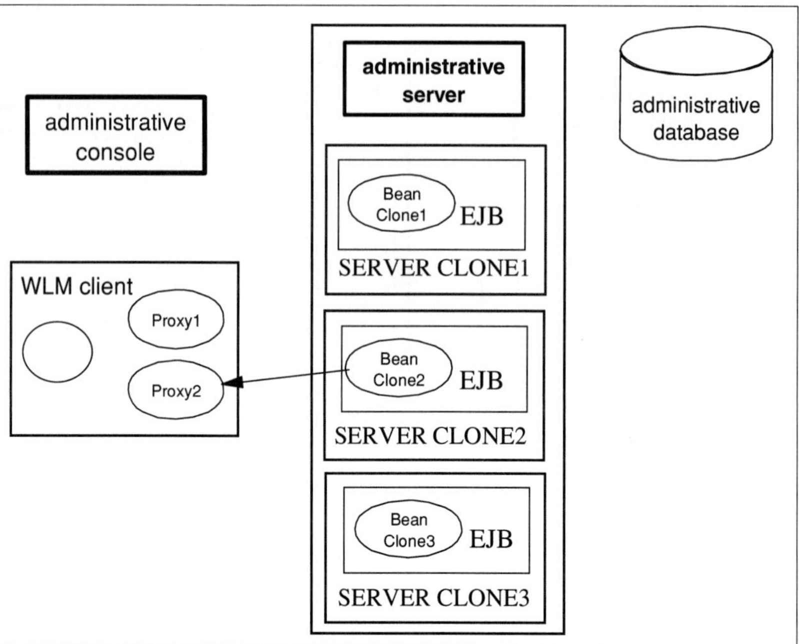

Figure 647. WLM client refresh, client reply

The last step in the process is depicted in Figure 648 on page 805. Once the client receives the request reply, the WLM runtime client is updated to reflect the changes in the model server group. In this case a third proxy is added, corresponding to Server Clone 3.

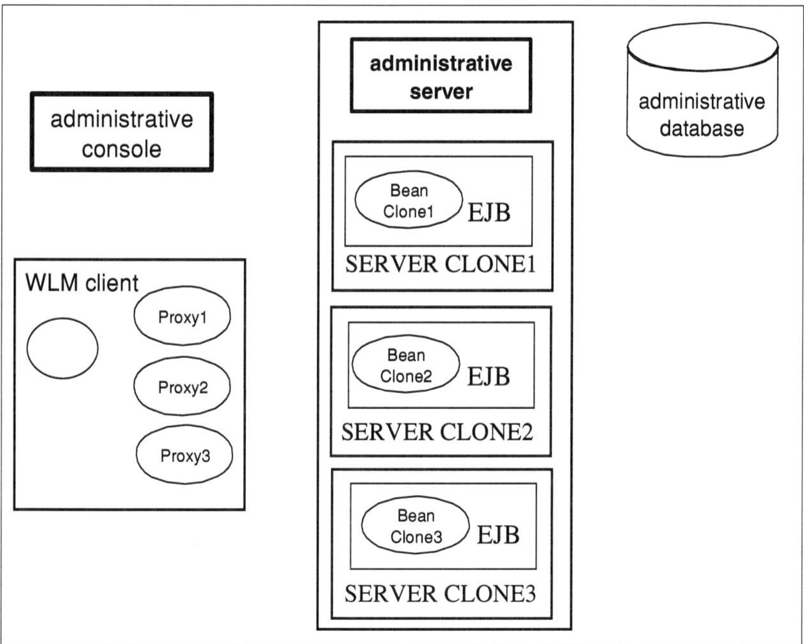

Figure 648. WLM client refresh, updated client runtime

17.2.2 WLM load balancing options

The actual selection of a particular object instance among all available clones of that object is controlled by a load-balancing policy (workload management selection policy) attribute associated with the application server group that contains this object, according to the following rules:

1. If the client that is issuing a request is located within the same JVM (typically an application server) that also contains an available instance of the target object, the WLM facility is bypassed, and the request is always dispatched to that local object instance.
2. If the request is associated with a transaction, and a previous request within the same transaction has already been dispatched to a given instance of a given object, then the new request is also dispatched to that same instance. This implements the transaction affinity property described earlier.
3. If the server group's load-balancing policy (workload management selection policy) is set to random-prefer-local, and there exists one or more available instances of the target object inside an application server that is executing on the same machine as the client (but not in the same

application server, or else rule 1 would apply), the request is dispatched to one of those application servers on the same machine, selected at random. If there are no available instances on the same machine, the request is dispatched to any available instance at random, regardless of which machine the application server is running on.

4. If the server group's load-balancing policy (workload management selection policy) is set to round-robin-prefer-local, and there exists one or more available instances of the target object inside an application server that is executing on the same machine as the client (but not in the same application server, or else rule 1 would apply), the request is dispatched to one of those application servers on the same machine, selected in round-robin fashion. If there are no available instances on the same machine, the request is dispatched to any available instance in round-robin fashion, regardless of which machine the application server is running on.
5. If the server group's load-balancing policy (workload management selection policy) is set to random, the request is dispatched to any available instance at random, regardless of which machine the application server is running on.
6. If the server group's load-balancing policy (workload management selection policy) is set to round-robin, the request is dispatched to any available instance in round-robin fashion, regardless of which machine the application server is running on.

17.2.3 WLM runtime exception handling

In general, if an object instance is found to be unavailable due to a crash or for other reasons, the request will be retried with another available instance, thereby providing automatic failover. Automatic failover does *not* take place when a CORBA COMM_FAILURE exception or a CORBA NO_RESPONSE exception is thrown with "MAYBE" COMPLETION_STATUS, which maps to a java.rmi.RemoteException. This is because WLM cannot know if the operation partially completed or not. In these cases, the application has to expect possible failures and initiate a retry, if appropriate. WLM will then try to find a surviving server and dispatch the request. WLM also does not retry in the case of an application exception, again because WLM cannot know if it is appropriate to do so. Automatic failover will take place when a "COMPLETED_NO" COMPLETION_STATUS is received, since it is safe to do so. Of course, no retry is required with COMPLETED_YES.

A simple example of the application code is depicted in Figure 649 on page 807 for instances of a “MAYBE” COMPLETION_STATUS minor code. In practice, additional code would be required to determine the outcome of the attempted operation. As a matter of course, this type of failure is extremely rare, usually corresponding to network outages (most typically the result of pulling a network cable during a test of WebSphere WLM).

```
success = false;
noRetries = 2; // or some small positive number.
for (i = 0; i < noRetries; i++) {
// We may get back exceptions from the WLM runtime.
// Catch these and retry.
   try {
   serverName = tester.invoke(); //tester represents the remote object
   success = true;
   } catch (RemoteException e) {
   Tr.warning(tc, "tester.invoke() threw Exception", e);
   //Or, do whatever cleanup you want
   }
   if (success) break;//no need to retry.
}
```

Figure 649. Example application retry code

Figure 650 on page 808 shows an example of a WLM-enabled EJB client dispatching requests to two cloned application servers.

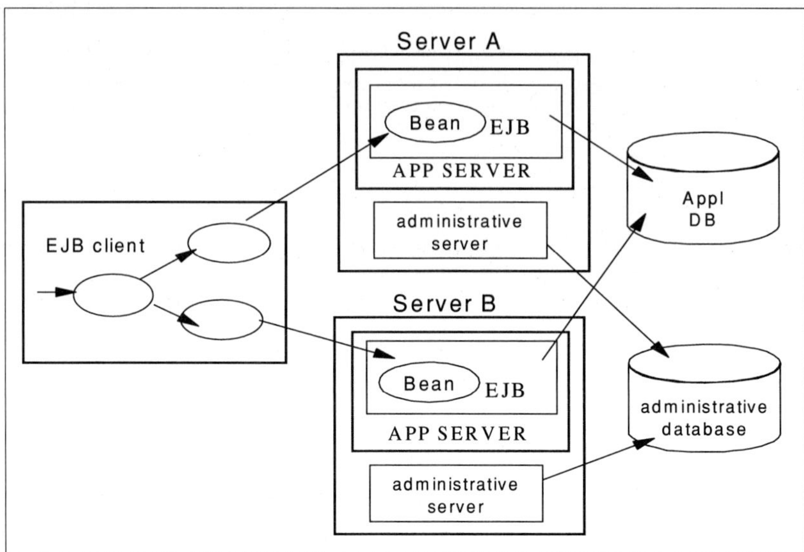

Figure 650. WLM-enabled client

It should be noted that the round-robin selection policy implemented by the smart stubs is in effect independent for each client and each corresponding instance of a smart stub. So, strictly speaking, one should not expect this mechanism to provide a strict round-robin distribution of all incoming requests from all clients, as perceived from the point of view of the servers. However, the main goal, to provide a statistically fair distribution of the load across all servers, is achieved by this implementation. With a large number of independent clients, this approach further approximates a random distribution, without resorting to an explicit randomizing function.

It should also be noted that, for both the random and round-robin policies, each server instance is considered equal to all other instances, and there is no way to cause the system to favor some servers over others (for example servers on different machines, or subject to different background loads). Future versions of WebSphere may provide extensions such a weights associated with each server, or various schemes to use dynamic measures of the load on each server to influence the selection policy.

With the current available selection policies, one way to ensure that one machine receives a larger proportion of the requests than another machine is to use vertical cloning to define a greater number of application servers on the larger machine.

17.2.4 WLM for administrative servers

Administrative servers can participate in workload management. Currently, the primary benefit is that it provides failover capability for administrative servers, improving the availability of administrative and naming services (since the administrative server process also provides naming services).

Workload Management must be enabled (or disabled) for all administrative servers in a domain.

When an administrative server participates in Workload Management, an exception is thrown if the server fails during an administrative task. Subsequent requests are redirected to the other servers in the domain, minimizing the disruption to administrative operations.

For example, a command issued through the WebSphere Administrative Console can fail if a server becomes unavailable while the command is being executed. However, if workload management is enabled, any subsequent attempts to execute the command are redirected to another administrative server. This allows the command to be successfully reissued, with only a slight delay for the initial redirection. (The original administrative server will pick up its share of administrative requests when it comes back online.)

To enabling Workload Management, start all administrative servers in the domain with Workload Management enabled. WebSphere Administrative Server provides two ways to enable Workload Management for administrative servers:

- By setting the following property in the admin.config file:

  ```
  com.ibm.ejs.sm.AdminServer.wlm
  ```

  This enables Workload Management for all administrative servers that are started using this configuration file.

- By specifying the -wlm argument when starting an administrative server from the command line. For instance:

  ```
  java com.ibm.ejs.sm.server.AdminServer -wlm ...
  ```

  where . . . represents any other arguments that are specified when starting the server.

Enabling Workload Management through the admin.config file is recommended because it is easier to administer than enabling it through the command line.

Chapter 18. Administrative console

Some of the most noticeable changes in WebSphere V3.5 have been made to the administrative console. A lot of the changes are in the look and feel of the GUI but there are also functional improvements, changes in the administrative console toolbar, and improved context-sensitive help. There is a new tasks wizard, menu options to import/export configuration in XML, and a commands history feature.

Enterprise beans can now be redeployed from the administrative console without having to restart the administrative server. Remote JAR file browsing works across heterogeneous platforms. That means, if you have a JAR file containing the beans on a Windows machine and you want to deploy the beans on a UNIX box, this can be done from within WebSphere.

This chapter highlights those new and improved features of the WebSphere Administrative Console. The features that existed in WebSphere V3.02.x, such as deploying enterprise beans, creating an application server, creating a servlet engine, etc., are discussed in detail in their respective chapters in this redbook.

The Resource Analyzer is now a separate tool and is covered in Chapter 25, "Resource Analyzer" on page 1009.

18.1 About WebSphere Administrative Console

The WebSphere Administrative Console is a graphical, Java-based client that connects to the WebSphere Administrative Server using Internet Inter-ORB Protocol (IIOP) which is a standard communication protocol. The console supports the full range of administrative activities via a console menu and a set of icons. But first, how do we start and stop the administrative console?

18.1.1 Starting the administrative console

The WebSphere Administrative Server must be running before you start the WebSphere Administrative Console.

1. Start the administrative server (or ensure that it is already running)
2. Start the administrative console:
   - On UNIX platforms

     a. Go to the bin directory under the WebSphere install directory

     ```
     cd <WAS_HOME>/bin
     ```

Make sure the DISPLAY environment variable is set correctly before invoking the WebSphere Administrative Console.

b. Run the administrative console script:

```
./adminclient.sh [<host> [<port>]]
```

- On Windows platforms

  From the Windows Start menu click **Programs -> IBM WebSphere -> Application Server 3.5 -> Administrator's Console**

  or type

```
<WAS_HOME>\bin\adminclient.bat [<host> [<port>]]
```

  Where:

  - `<WAS_HOME>` is the WebSphere V3.5 installation directory
  - `<host>` is the host name or IP address of the WebSphere Administrative Server
  - `<port>` is the port number on which the WebSphere Administrative Server is listening

  By default, the WebSphere Administrative Server running on port 900 on the local node is used.

Note

A WebSphere V3.0.2.x Administrative Console cannot connect to a WebSphere V3.5 Administrative Server.

18.1.2 Stopping the administrative console

To stop the console, on all platforms, click **Console -> Exit** in the main menu as shown in Figure 651 on page 813.

Figure 651. The Console menu option

> **Note**
>
> Exiting the WebSphere Administrative Console does not stop the WebSphere Administrative Server.

18.1.3 WebSphere Administrative Console features

The administrative console looks the same on both the Standard and Advanced Editions. There is more functionality available via the Advanced Edition Console because of EJBs and WLM support within the Advanced Edition.

First, we introduce the items in the main menu - Console, View, and Help. We then talk about the new icons in the toolbar. The functionality within menu items Console and View are discussed. And finally we cover the functionality available in the Wizards icon.

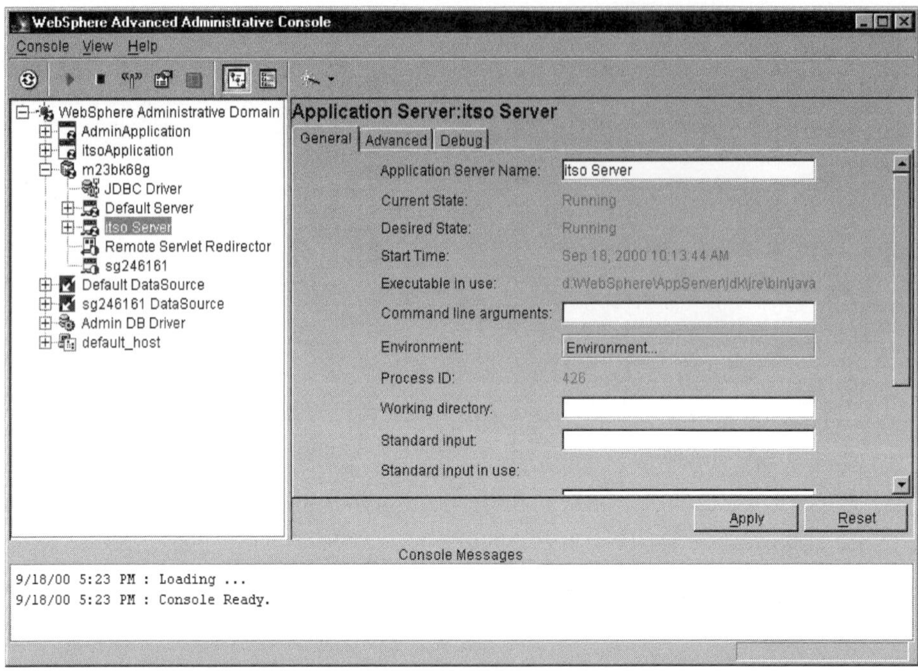

Figure 652. The WebSphere Administrative Console

Console

The console menu allows you to choose administrative tasks, turn on tracing for problem determination, import and export files, view command history, and exit the console.

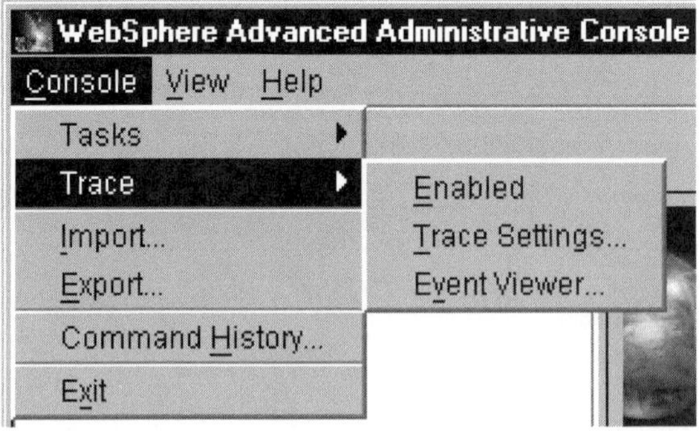

Figure 653. Console menu

The sub-menu under the Tasks option is the same as the sub-menu under the Wizards icon. It is shown in the Wizards section in Figure 661 on page 820.

View

The administrative console offers the administrator two views. The Topology and Type tree views are meant for surveying and manipulating resources in the WebSphere domain. The corresponding view icons are visible on the icon bar.

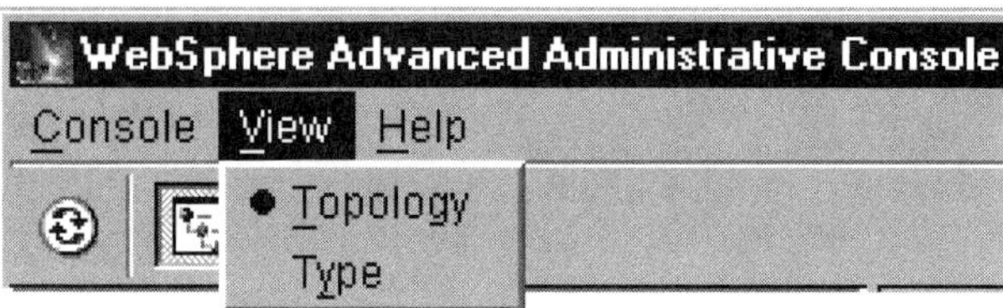

Figure 654. View menu

In the Topology view, which is the default, all resource instances within the administrative domain are displayed. It includes Nodes, Data Sources, Virtual Hosts, Models, and Enterprise Applications.

The administrative server is represented by the node that is shown as the machine name. For each node, the hierarchy of existing resources associated with that node, such as application servers and JDBC drivers, are displayed.

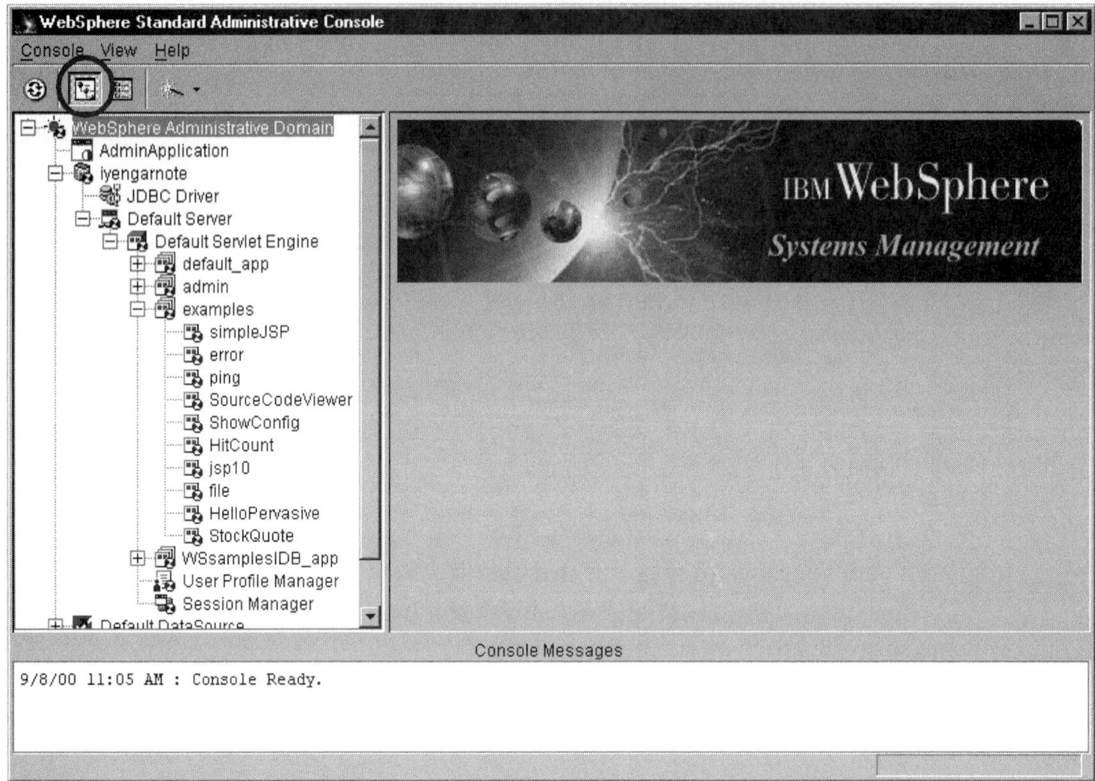

Figure 655. WebSphere V3.5 Standard Edition Administrative Console

The Type view on the other hand shows:

- Items that can be configured in the administrative domain and how many of each exist
- The default properties for each type of resource and the option to edit them
- The relationships among objects in the administrative domain
  - The object types are displayed according to their containment hierarchy which shows the order in which you must configure instances. For example, an EJB container must exist before you can configure an EJB that will reside in that container.

The Type view is shown in Figure 656 on page 817.

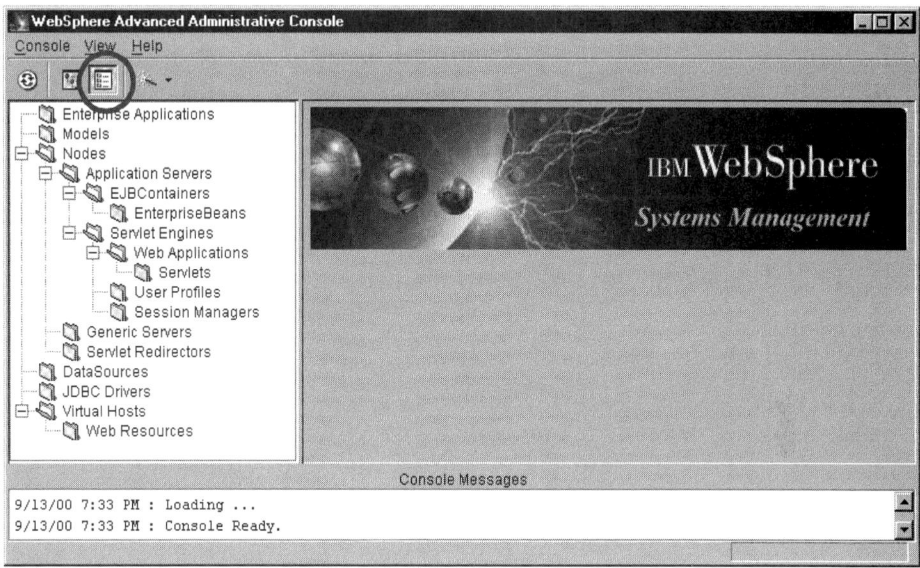

Figure 656. WebSphere V3.5 Advanced Edition Administrative Console

Help

The Help menu has links to the online help.

Figure 657. The Help menu

WebSphere V3.5 features a very robust context-sensitive help. Context-sensitive menus are available by clicking the right-mouse button over an object in the Topology or Type view.

In the Topology view, the context-sensitive menus depend on the object selected but mainly include creating, removing, starting, stopping, and pinging resources.

Whereas in the Type view, you can create, remove, and display the default properties of an instance.

WebSphere V3.5 installation contains a "starter" InfoCenter, which is a set of detailed help files. The full InfoCenter can be downloaded from the WebSphere Web site library page:

```
http://www.ibm.com/software/webservers/appserv/library.html
```

18.1.4 WebSphere Administrative Console functionality

The icons on the WebSphere V3.5 Administrative Console toolbar have a new more compact look. The icons shown in Figure 658 pop up when clicked on a resource, such as an application server, is clicked in the Navigation pane.

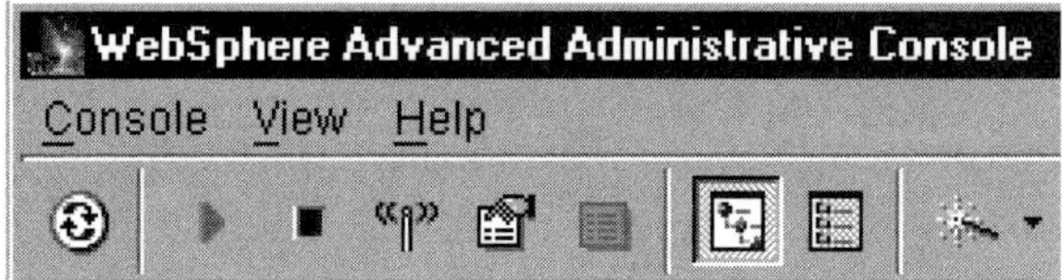

Figure 658. The icons in the WebSphere Administrative Console toolbar

The two most often used icons are the green-colored sideways triangle, which is the Start icon, and the red square, which is the Stop icon.

There are icons for Topology and Type views. There is a Refresh icon at the far left and the new Wizards icon on the far right, which sports a drop-down menu.

18.1.4.1 Refresh

In some instances the changes to the administrative domain are not promptly reflected in the console, specially in the Topology view. When that happens, click the Refresh icon.

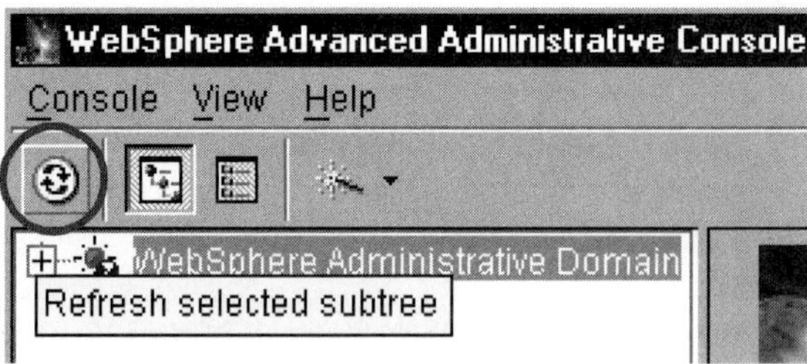

Figure 659. The refresh icon

A refresh can be done at any time and at any level of the tree. The selected subtree is typically refreshed. Watch for the refresh completion message in the console messages area.

18.1.4.2 Wizards

One of the new features in WebSphere V3.5 is the Wizards icon. Task wizards are provided to lead administrators through the configuration and protection of new resources, such as servlets, applications and application servers. This wizards option basically replaces the old Tasks tab and is always visible on the console.

Figure 660. The Wizards menu option

Wizards make common tasks, such as creating and configuring resources, a lot easier. These tasks, as shown in Figure 661 on page 820, are discussed in 18.1.5, "The common tasks" on page 829. These tasks, as mentioned earlier are also available from the main menu by clicking **Console-->Tasks**. Notice the demarcation of the security tasks.

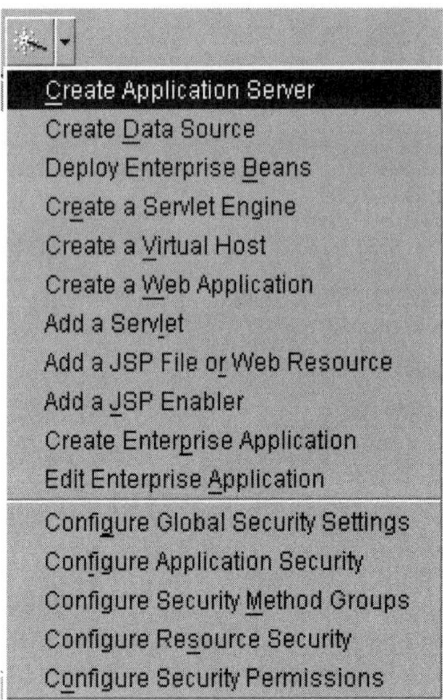

Figure 661. The Wizards menu

Let us defer the common tasks to later and talk about the other functions in the Console menu.

18.1.4.3 Trace

The Trace menu item reflects the command-line trace option for “Enabled” followed by the trace string.

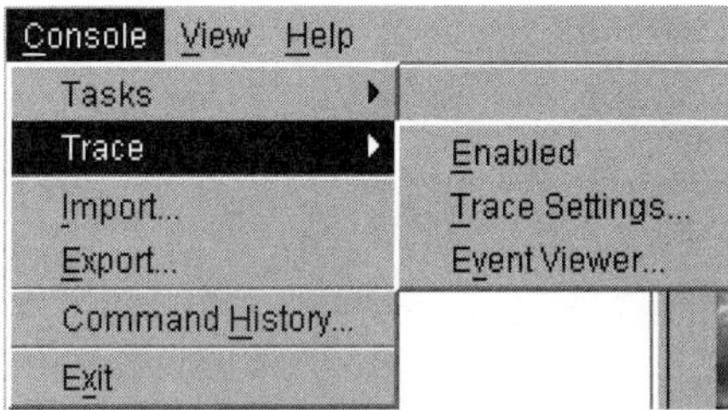

Figure 662. The Trace menu item highlighted in the Console menu list

The Trace -> Enabled item is a toggle. When set, a check mark appears next to the Enabled menu item as shown in Figure 663 on page 821. Re-selecting the Enabled option disables Trace.

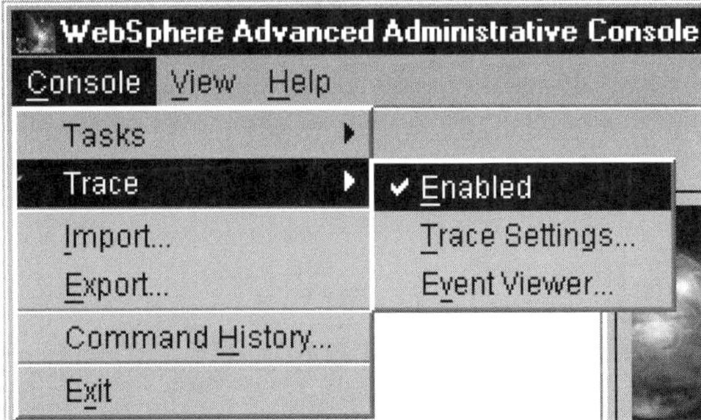

Figure 663. Trace enabled within WebSphere

Trace Settings

Clicking the **Trace Settings...** menu item brings up a window displaying the trace string shown in Figure 664. Click **Apply** to collect trace information for the specified class.

Trace string supports the same format as -traceString, while also preserving backward compatibility.

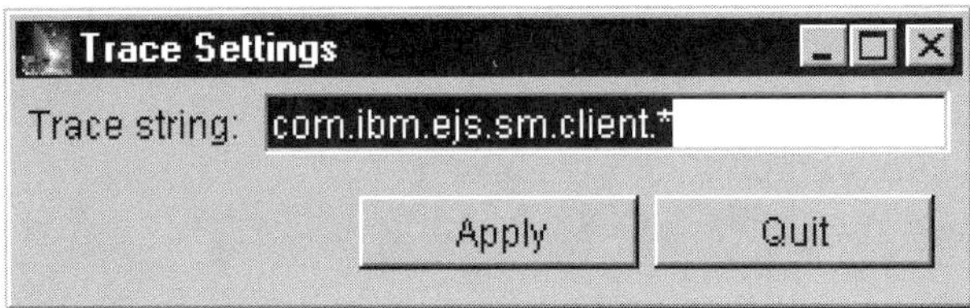

Figure 664. Trace settings window

Event Viewer

Event Viewer used to be named Serious Events. There is now the capability to clear old messages from the event viewer under the Preferences tab.

To bring up the Event Viewer click **Console -> Trace -> Event Viewer...**

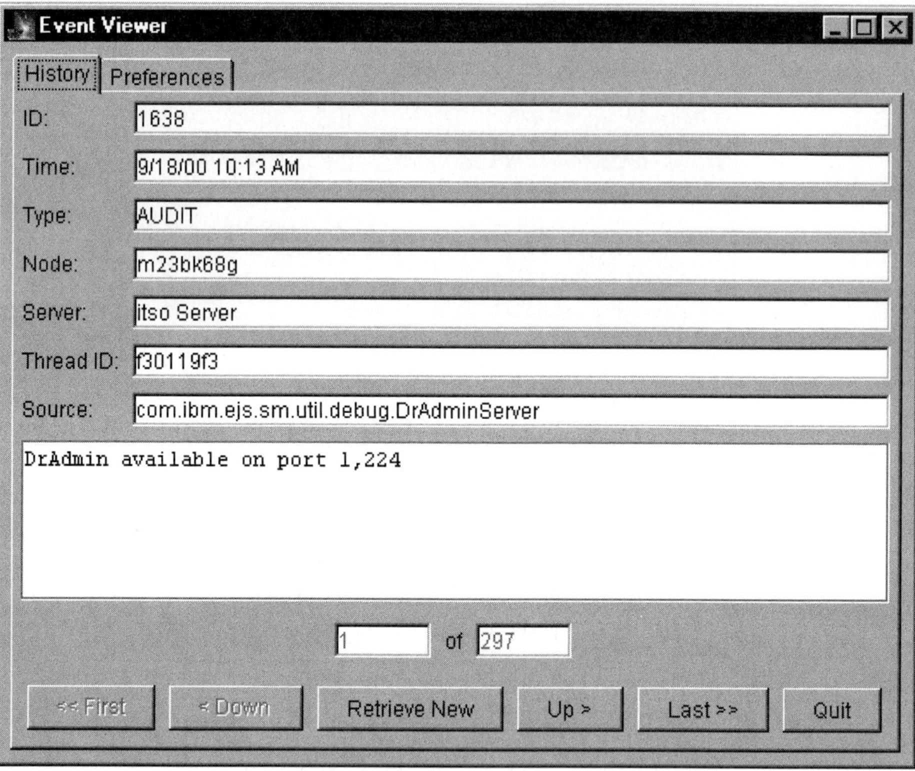

Figure 665. The History tab in the Event Viewer

Under the Preferences tab you can set the tracing interval for serious events, the general level of tracing, and the size of the log file. There are three levels of tracing available: FATALS, WARNINGS, and AUDIT as shown in Figure 666 on page 823.

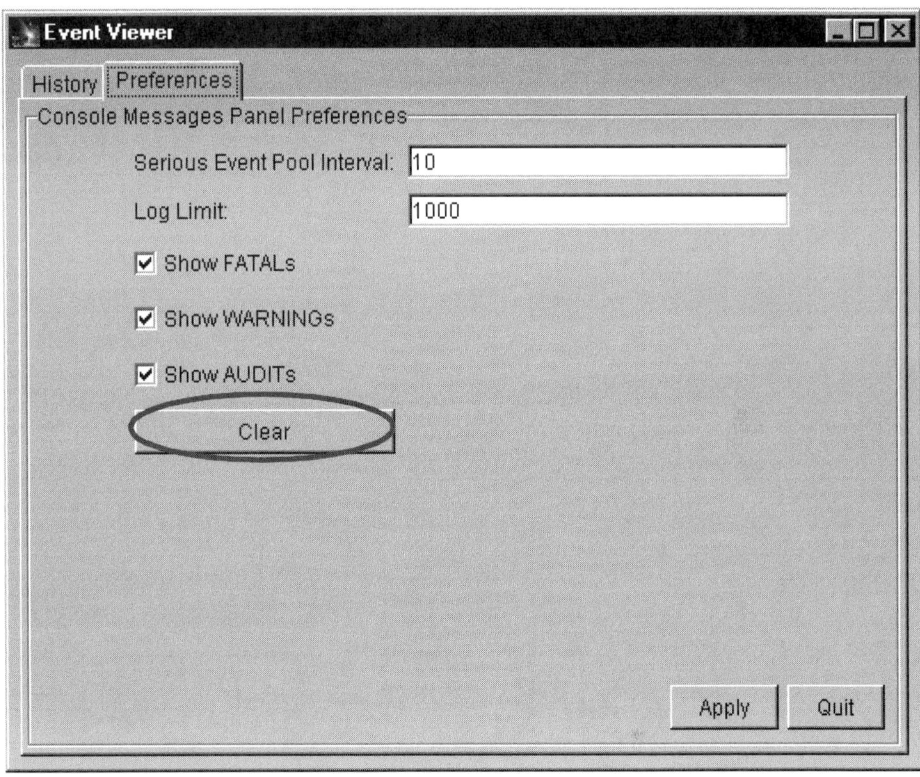

Figure 666. The preferences tab in the Event Viewer

If you want to discard all old trace messages, click the **Clear** button.

18.1.4.4 Exporting a configuration

WebSphere V3.5 offers the option to Import and Export a configuration using XML files. Administrators can use this as a backup feature to save production configurations.

To export, from the main menu, click **Console -> Export...**

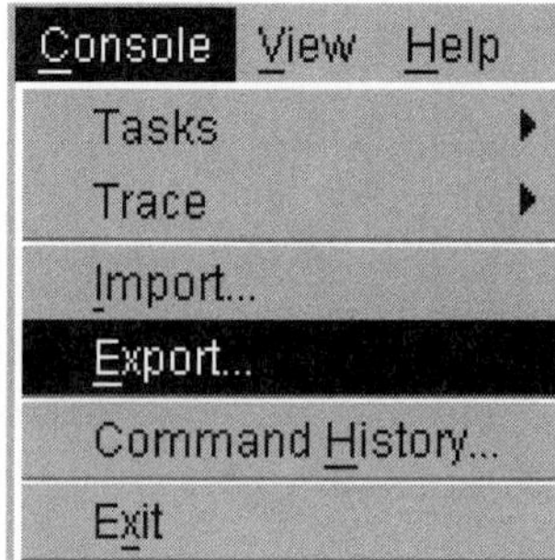

Figure 667. Export option highlighted in the Console menu

Choose the directory or folder where you want the file saved. Type in the file name. By default there is no extension given to the file name. The recommendation is to give a .xml extension as shown in Figure 668.

When you click **Save** the file will be saved on the local machine.

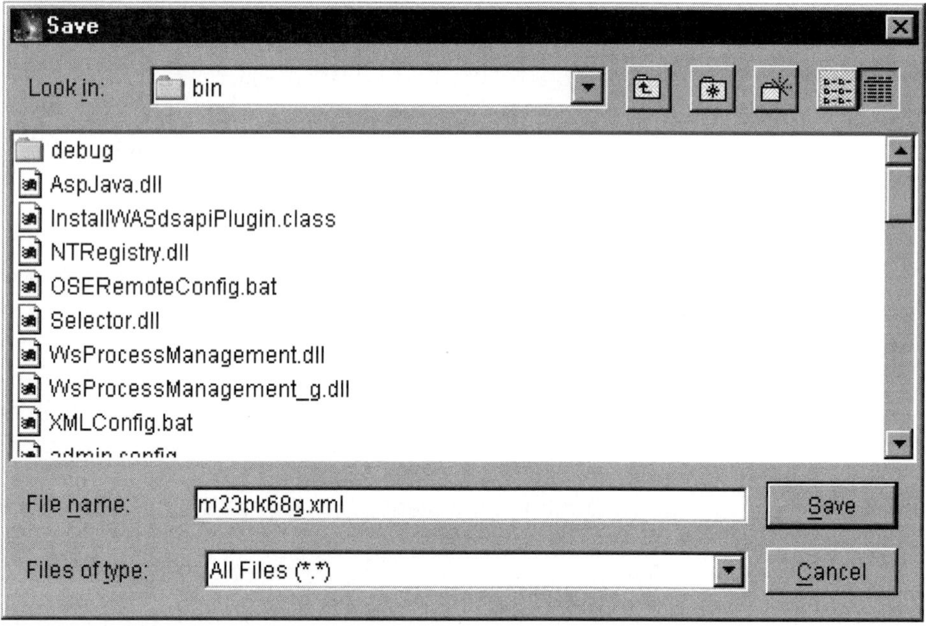

Figure 668. Name and location of XML file to be exported

18.1.4.5 Importing a configuration

Administrators can use this either to restore or replicate a WebSphere configuration.

To export, from the main menu, click **Console -> Import...** as shown in Figure 669.

Figure 669. Import option highlighted in the Console menu

In the Open window, select the directory or folder and choose the XML file containing a WebSphere configuration that you want to import. Choose the file that was just exported, as shown in Figure 670. Then click **Open**.

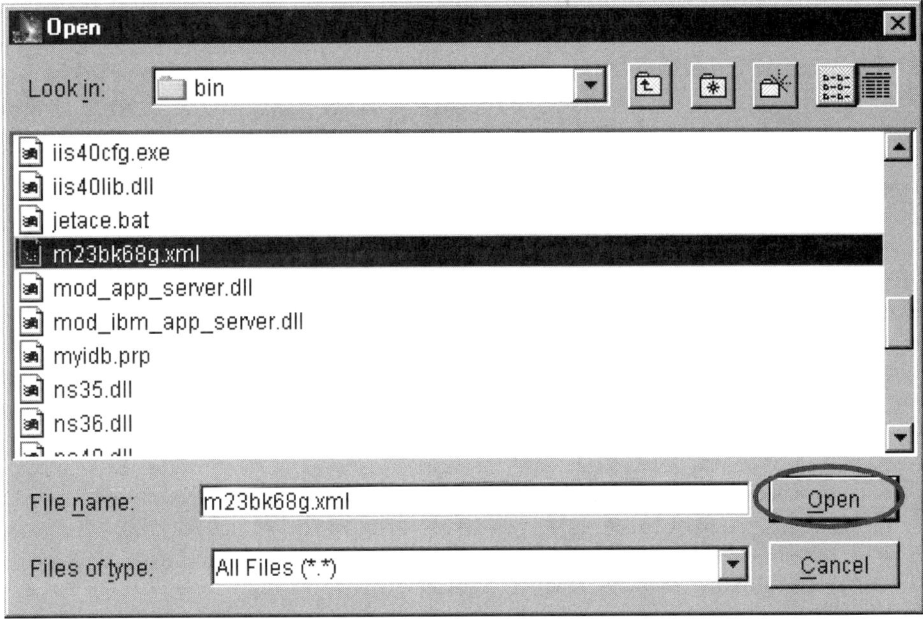

Figure 670. The import XML window

Note

Depending on the complexity of the configuration, this step can take a long time.

The Console messages screen shows the status of the import. Some of the warnings, like those shown below, can be benign.

```
9/15/00 9:58 AM : Command "m23bk68g.import" running ...
9/15/00 10:00 AM : WARNING [m23bk68g/__adminServer]: Encountered an exception:
com.ibm.ejs.sm.exception.DuplicateRelationInstanceException


/15/00 10:00 AM : WARNING [m23bk68g/__adminServer]: Encountered an exception:
com.ibm.ejs.sm.exception.DuplicateRelationInstanceException


/15/00 10:00 AM : WARNING [m23bk68g/__adminServer]: Encountered an exception:
com.ibm.ejs.sm.exception.DuplicateRelationInstanceException


/15/00 10:00 AM : WARNING [m23bk68g/__adminServer]: Encountered an exception:
com.ibm.ejs.sm.exception.DuplicateRelationInstanceException


/15/00 10:00 AM : Command "m23bk68g.import" completed successfully.
```

After the import is complete, refresh the administrative console to view the configuration.

18.1.4.6 Command History

The Command History lists all the previous commands used via the WebSphere V3.5 Administrative Console. Clicking **Console -> Command History...** brings up a separate window listing all the commands for the current session as shown in Figure 671 on page 827.

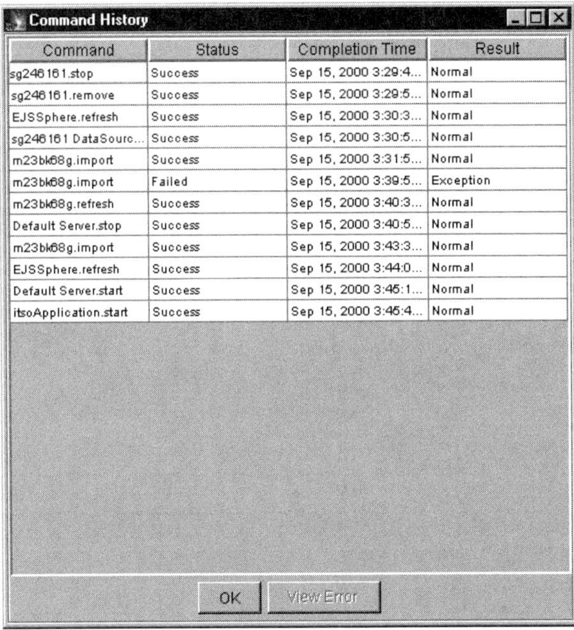

Command History
Command
Status
Completion Time
Result
sg246161.stop Success Sep 15, 2000 3:29:4... Normal
sg246161.remove Success Sep 15, 2000 3:29:5... Normal
EJSSphere.refresh Success Sep 15, 2000 3:30:3... Normal
sg246161 DataSourc... Success Sep 15, 2000 3:30:5... Normal
m23bk68g.import Success Sep 15, 2000 3:31:5... Normal
m23bk68g.import Failed Sep 15, 2000 3:39:5... Exception
m23bk68g.refresh Success Sep 15, 2000 3:40:3... Normal
Default Server.stop Success Sep 15, 2000 3:40:5... Normal
m23bk68g.import Success Sep 15, 2000 3:43:3... Normal
EJSSphere.refresh Success Sep 15, 2000 3:44:0... Normal
Default Server.start Success Sep 15, 2000 3:45:1... Normal
itsoApplication.start Success Sep 15, 2000 3:45:4... Normal
OK
View Error

Figure 671. Command History

Note

The Command History stores all the commands for that console session. If you exit the administrative console, the commands are cleared.

There is a View Error button on the Commands History window that is inactive. If you highlight a command that does not have a Success Status or a Normal Return code, then the View Error button becomes active as evidenced in Figure 672 on page 828.

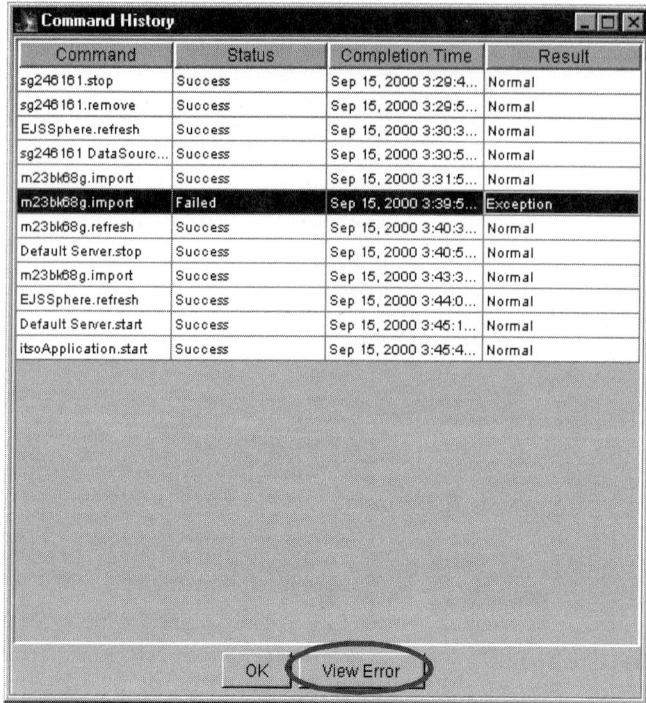

Figure 672. View Error button in Command History window

Clicking on that **View Error** button pops up a separate stack trace window for that error condition as shown in Figure 673.

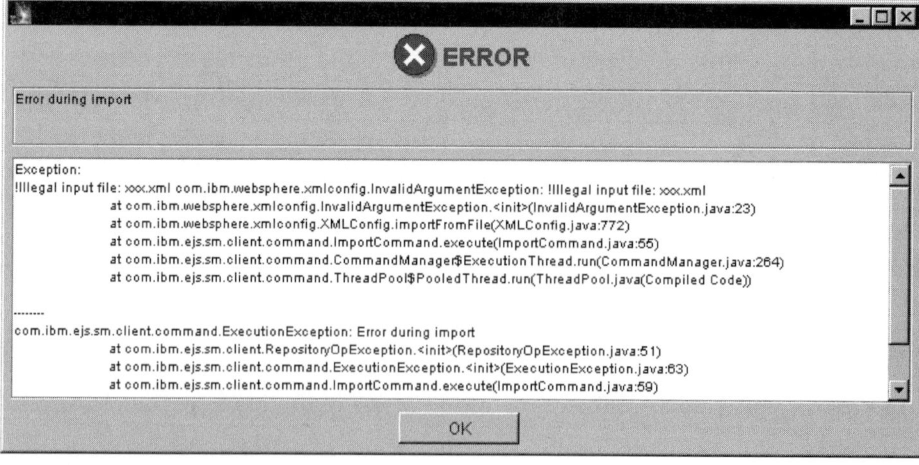

Figure 673. The stack trace for the failed command

18.1.5 The common tasks

The new functions within WebSphere 3.5 tasks wizard are covered in this section. The other common tasks are explained in detail in the relevant chapters in this redbook. For example, the security-related tasks can be found in Chapter 15, “WebSphere security” on page 651.

The common tasks are:

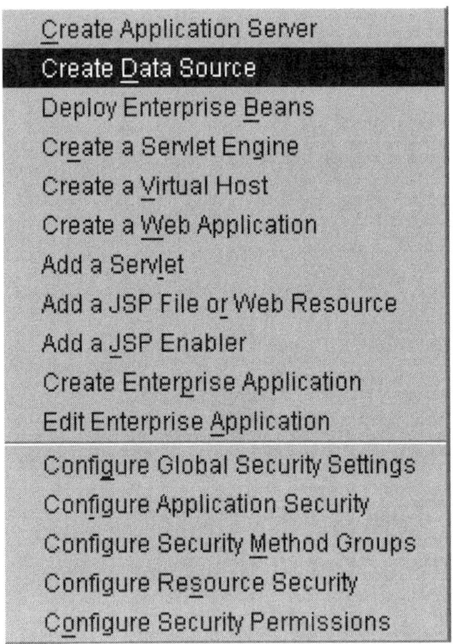

Figure 674. List of common tasks

18.1.5.1 Creating a Data Source

Bring up the Tasks menu and click **Create Data Source**. The initial window has two options: to use an existing JDBC driver and to create a new JDBC driver. That is shown in Figure 675 on page 830.

By creating a new JDBC driver

Select **Create and install a new JDBC driver** and click the **Next** button.

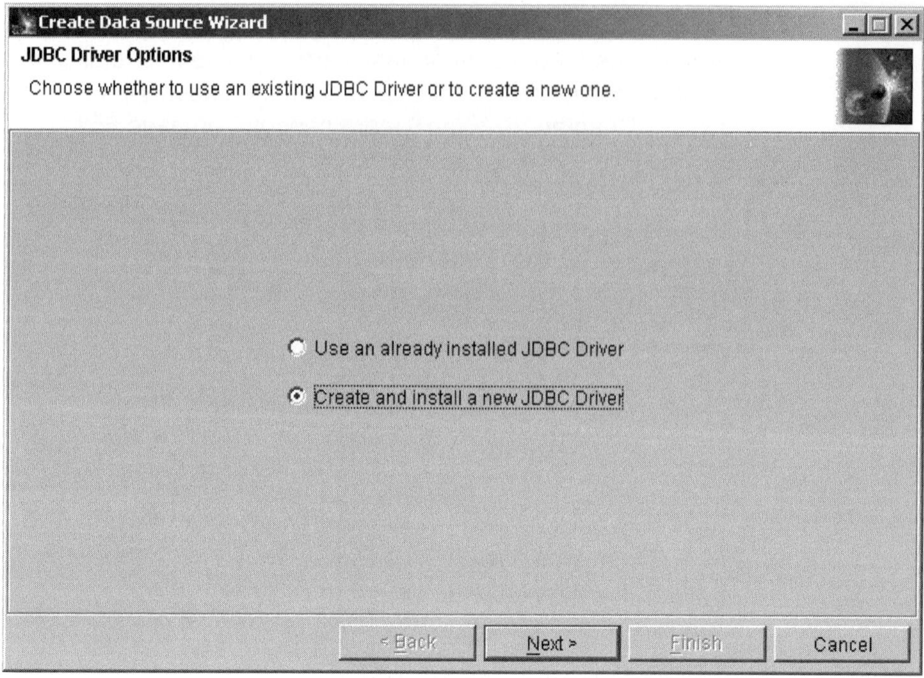

Figure 675. Initial window for creating a data source

On the JDBC properties window shown in Figure 676 on page 831, enter a name for the driver, and from the drop-down list choose the class corresponding to the database to be used. Then enter the driver URL, which usually takes the form:

```
jdbc:<database>:<driver_type>:@<node_name>:<port_number>
```

If the driver supports the Java Transaction API (JTA), select **True** from the drop-down list. Otherwise, leave it as False, which is the default condition.

Click **Next**.

Note

In addition to DB2 and Oracle, WebSphere V3.5 supports the Sybase JDBC driver.

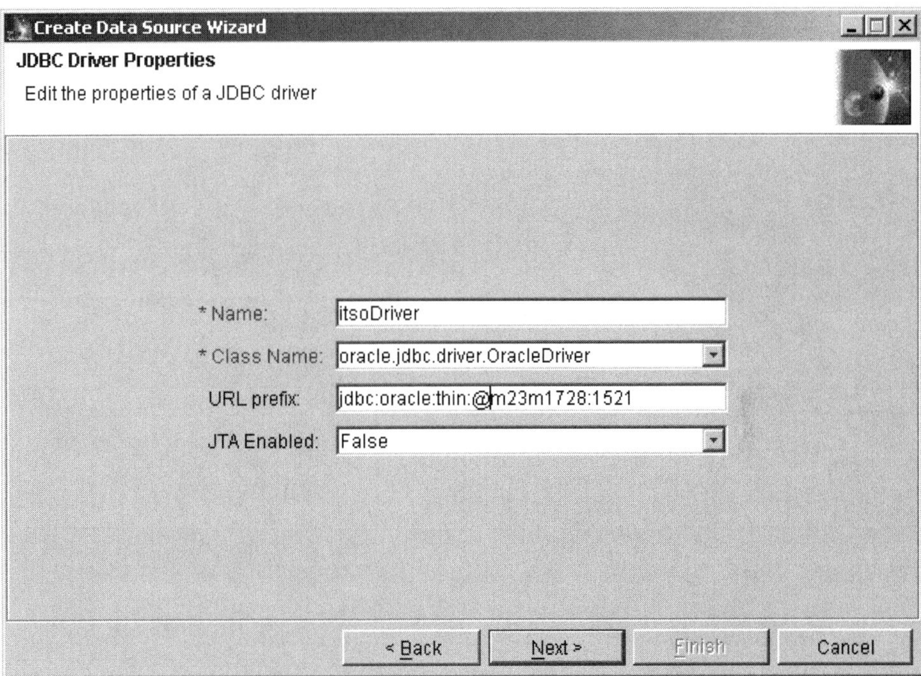

Figure 676. JDBC driver properties window

In the next node selection window as depicted in Figure 677 on page 832, select the node to install the JDBC driver on. More importantly, click the JAR file **Browse** button and select the appropriate JAR or ZIP file containing the classes for the database.

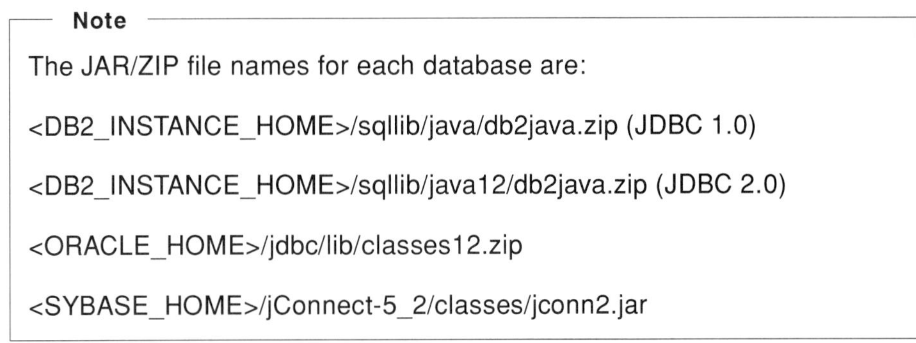

Note

The JAR/ZIP file names for each database are:

<DB2_INSTANCE_HOME>/sqllib/java/db2java.zip (JDBC 1.0)

<DB2_INSTANCE_HOME>/sqllib/java12/db2java.zip (JDBC 2.0)

<ORACLE_HOME>/jdbc/lib/classes12.zip

<SYBASE_HOME>/jConnect-5_2/classes/jconn2.jar

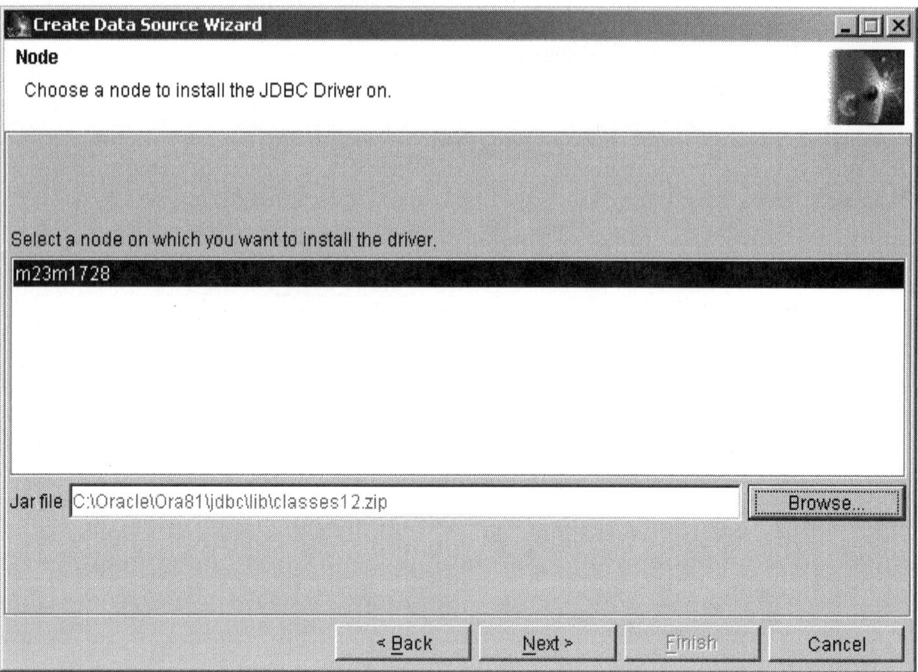

Figure 677. Choose a node to install the JDBC direver on

Specify the appropriate JAR/ZIP file that comes with the database installation and click **Finish**.

By using an existing JDBC driver

In the second option, in the JDBC Driver Options window select **Use an already installed JDBC driver** and click the **Next** button as shown in Figure 678 on page 833.

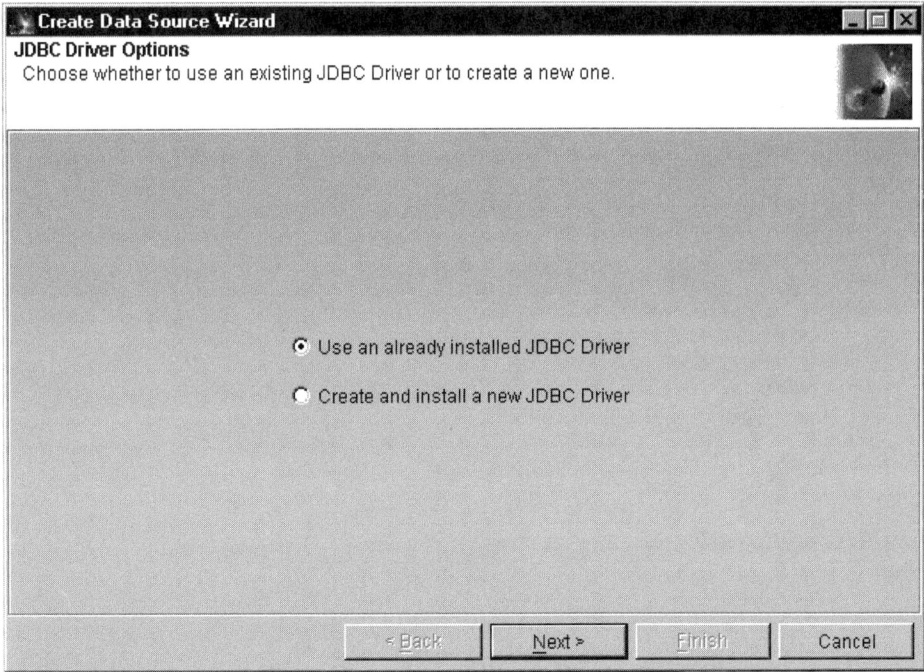

Figure 678. JDBC driver options

Enter a data source name; select the database you want to use; select the JDBC driver from the drop-down list; click **Finish** as shown in Figure 679 on page 834.

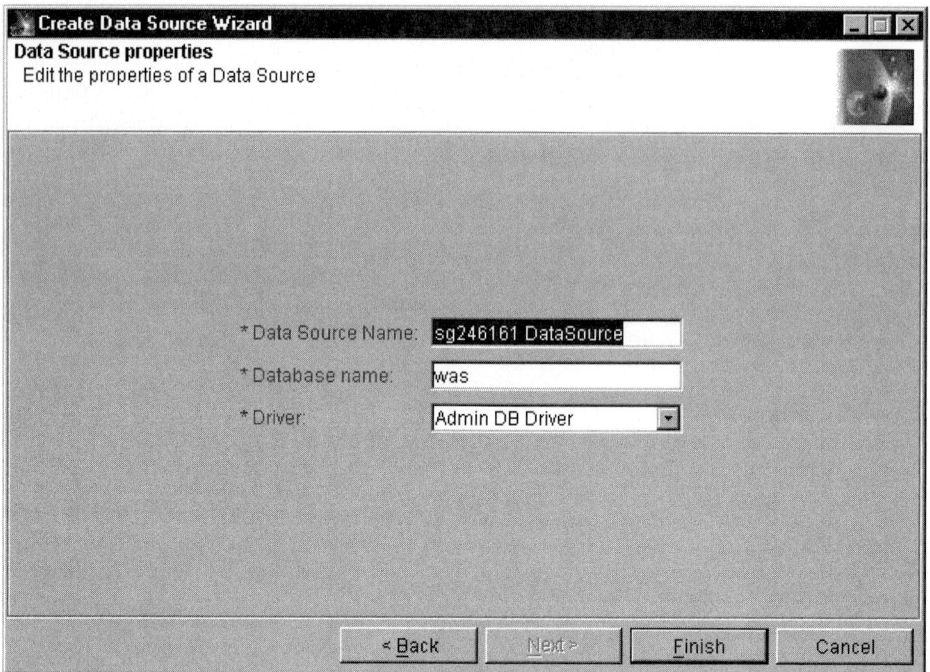

Figure 679. The data source properties window for an existing JDBC driver

When the data source is successfully created, the status window will pop up. The newly created data source should show up in the administrative console as shown in Figure 680 on page 835.

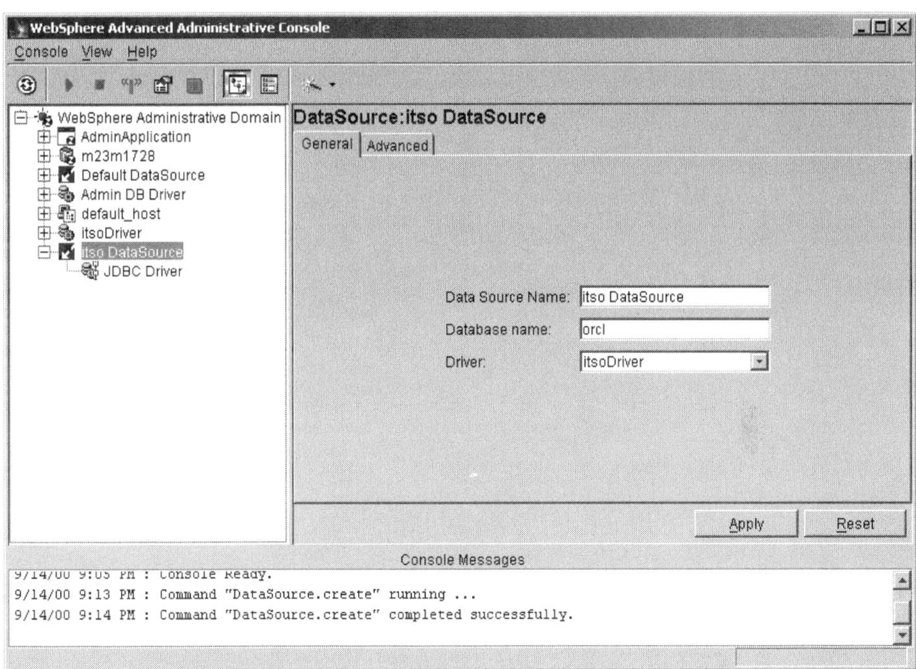

Figure 680. The newly created driver

18.1.5.2 Creating an enterprise application

Bring up the tasks menu and click **Create Enterprise Application**.

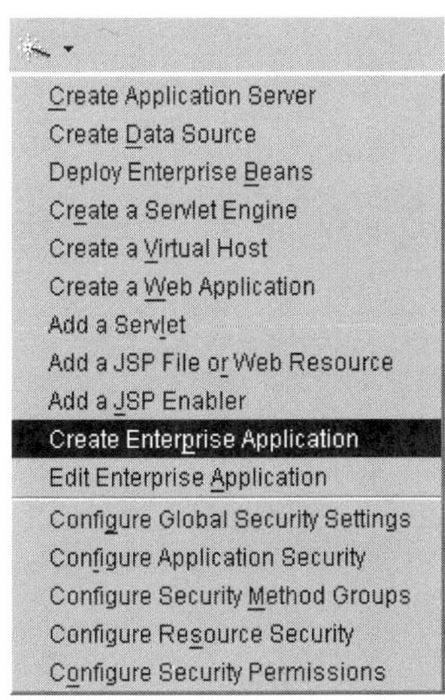

Figure 681. Common tasks menu with Create Enterprise Application highlighted

Enter a name for the application and click **Next**.

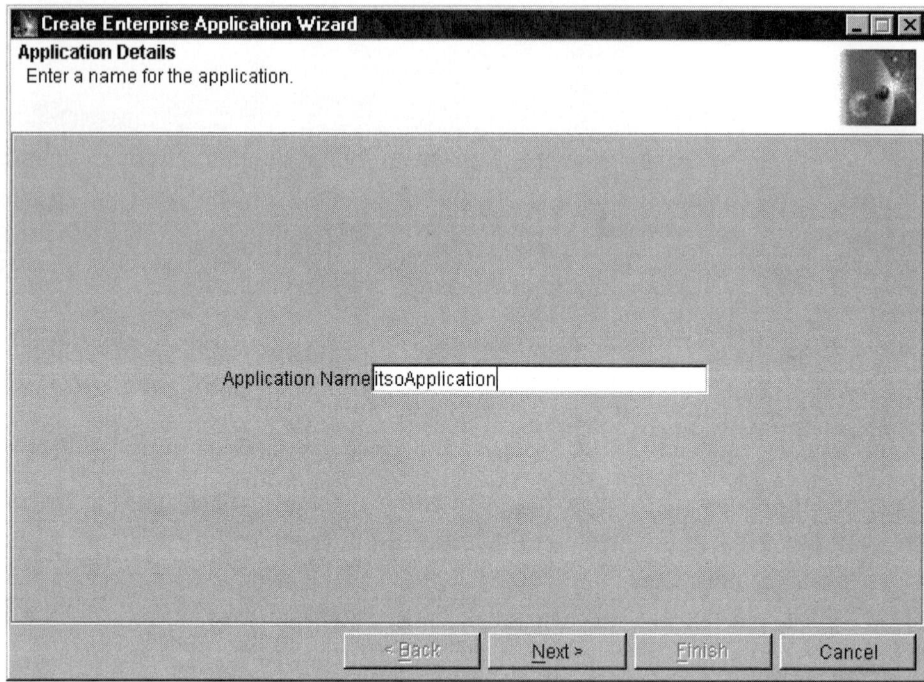

Figure 682. Create enterprise application window

In the following window as depicted in Figure 683 on page 837, you can add one or more resources to the application. Select an existing resource and click **Add** or select a folder and create a new resource by clicking the **New** button.

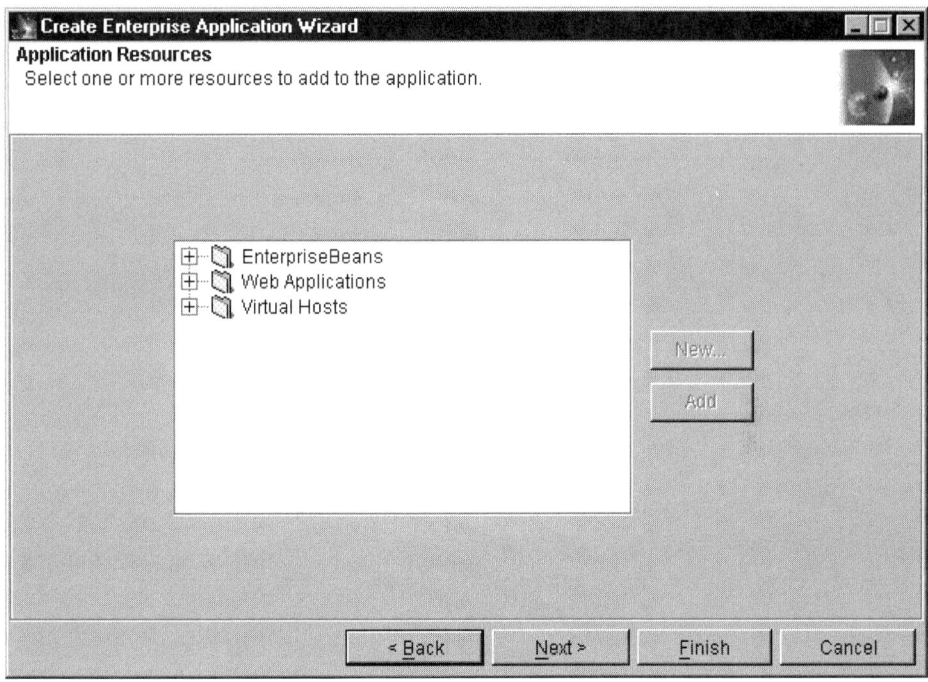

Figure 683. Add resources to enterprise application

Difference in Standard Edition

There are no Enterprise Beans in WebSphere Standard Edition.

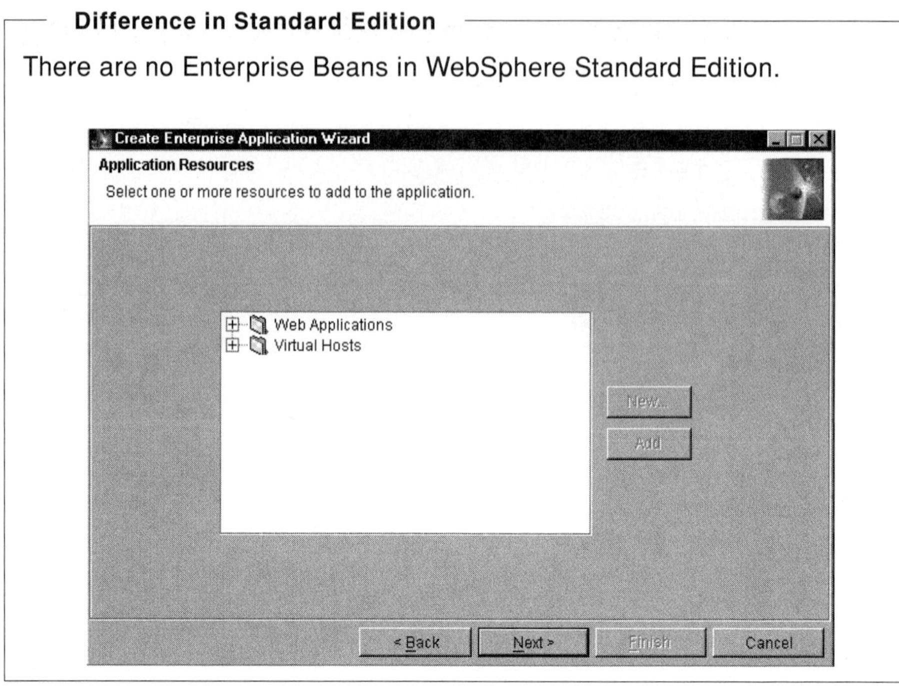

The next window gives you an opportunity to remove any of the added resources. Highlight the resource and click the **Remove** button.

Otherwise, click **Finish** to create the application as seen in Figure 684 on page 839.

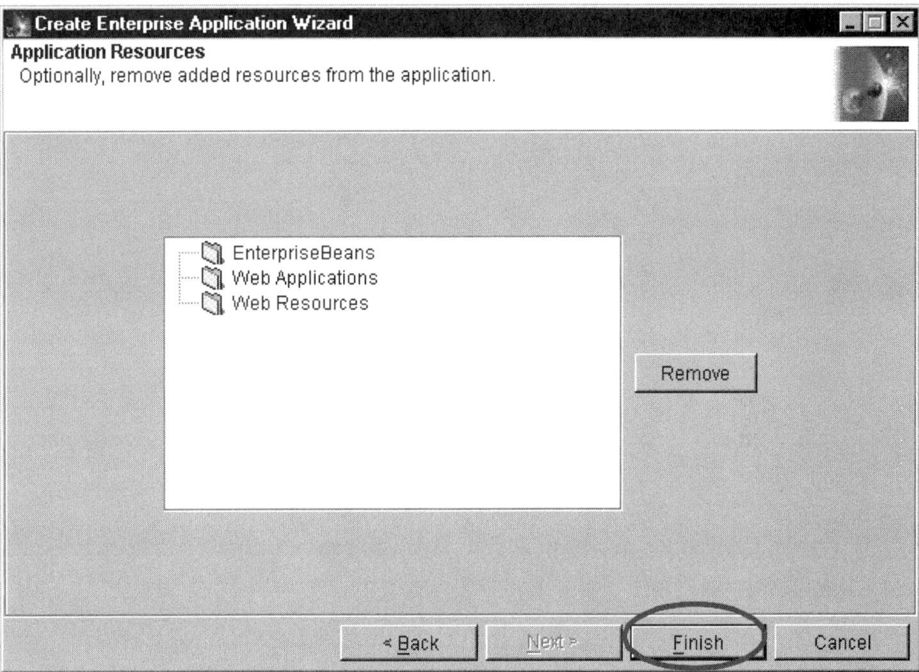

Figure 684. Remove resources from enterprise application

By default, the newly created application is not running as seen in the WebSphere Administrative Console in Figure 685 on page 840.

To start the enterprise application, highlight it, and click the Start icon or press the right-mouse button and select **Start**.

In this sequence no resources were added. But normally, an enterprise application will contain more than one resource.

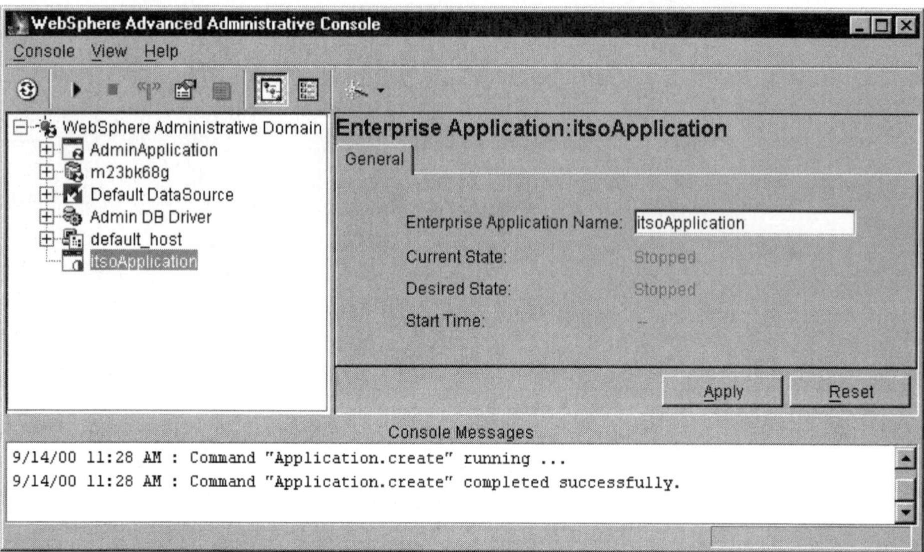

Figure 685. The newly added enterprise application

18.1.5.3 Editing an enterprise application

Bring up the Tasks menu and click **Edit Enterprise Application**.

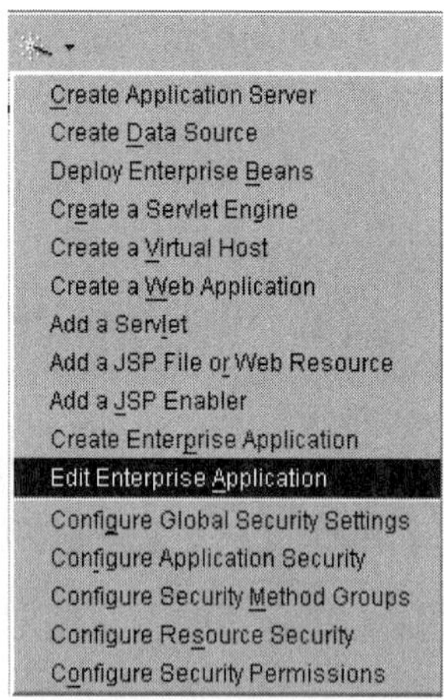

Figure 686. Common tasks menu with Edit Enterprise Application highlighted

In the initial window expand the Enterprise Applications folder, select an application and click **Next** as shown in Figure 687 on page 841.

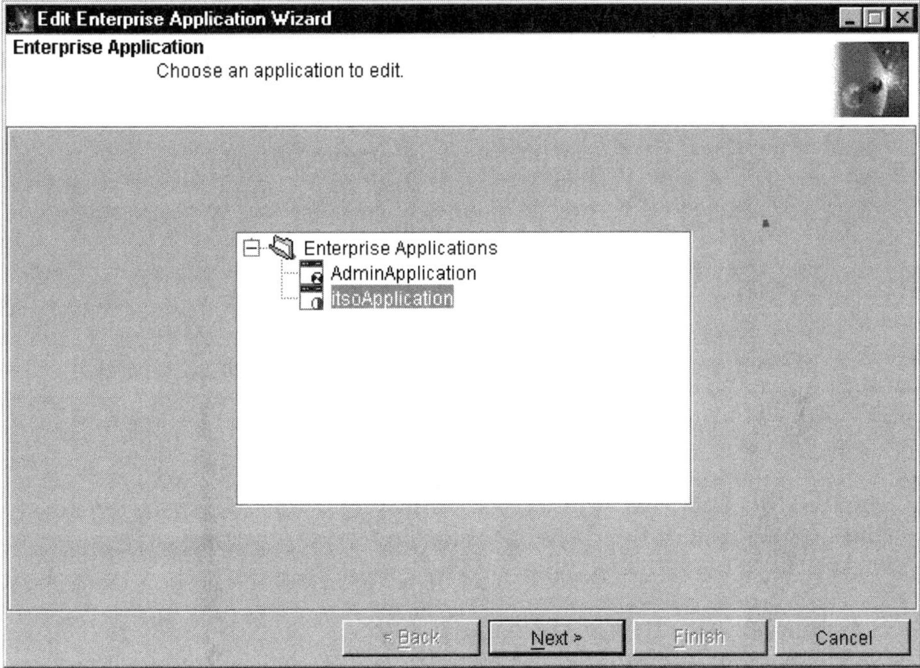

Figure 687. Edit enterprise application

Then the window to add resources and remove resources will come up as we talked about in Chapter 18.1.5.2, "Creating an enterprise application" on page 835.

When you have finished editing the properties of the enterprise application you should see the status window.

Figure 688. Asuccessful edit of an enterprise application

18.2 In conclusion

The WebSphere Administrative Console is the interface that most administrators will use to easily manage and administer their WebSphere configuration. This console works well in heterogeneous platforms.

Chapter 19. Web console

The Web administrative console (Web console) is a lightweight client that runs in a Web browser. You can use it to work with a subset of the resources in the WebSphere administrative domain. It provides the opportunity to work with property files encoded in eXtensible Markup Language (XML). This chapter describes the functionality available by using that graphical interface.

19.1 About Web console

The Web console can be run from any browser while communicating with the WebSphere Administrative Server locally or on a remote machine. It is useful in situations where there is a need to view the WebSphere topology through a firewall.

Two main kinds of tasks can be performed using the Web administrative console:

- Creating objects and configuring them
- Exporting the workspace to XML

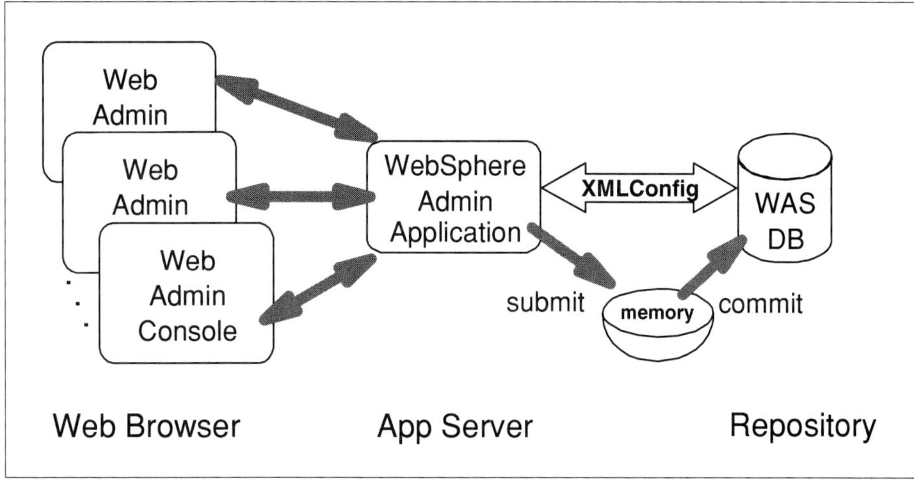

Figure 689. Web administrative console flow diagram

19.1.1 Starting the Web administrative console

The Web administrative console is available on machines where the WebSphere Administrative Server is running via a Web browser. You can even access remote machines.

Before starting the Web administrative console, ensure that the following processes have been started:

- WebSphere Administrative Server
- Default Server
- AdminApplication within the WebSphere administrative domain
- Web server

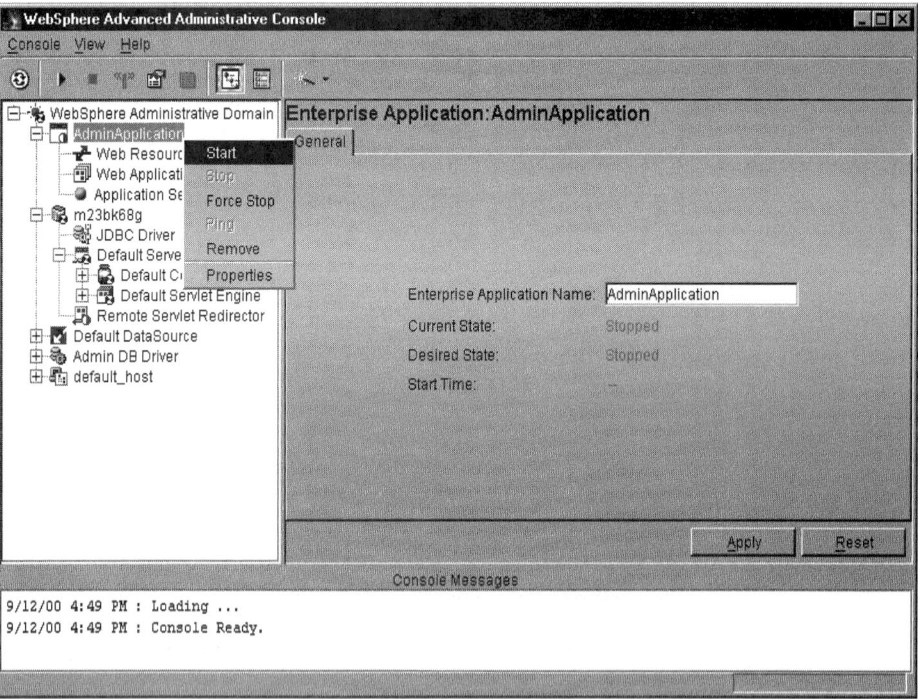

Figure 690. Start the AdminApplication

To bring up the console of the Web console:

1. In a Web browser type the following URL:

```
http://<HOST_NAME>/admin
```

where <HOST_NAME> is the local host if you are starting the Web console on the same machine that is running the WebSphere Administrative Server.

If the Web console is being started on a remote machine, enter the short or fully qualified host name of the machine running the administrative server.

Figure 691. WebSphere V3.5 Web Administration Home Page

2. In the WebSphere Administration Home Page, select **XML Web Administration Tool**.

Then wait for the console to load all the information into the browser.

Note

If you use Microsoft's Internet Explorer you will be prompted to load the Microsoft Virtual Machine.

When the loading is complete, the familiar looking two-paned WebSphere console is displayed. There is the navigation area in the left pane and the work area on the right.

If you click the arrow adjoining the Tasks menu item, the two tasks - Create Objects and Export Workspace to XML - will be displayed. And clicking the arrow next to the Resources shows, among other things, the node that it is connected to.

Figure 692 on page 846 shows the Web console on a Windows 2000 machine while connected to a WebSphere Administrative Server running on an AIX node named riscwas2 (9.24.104.233).

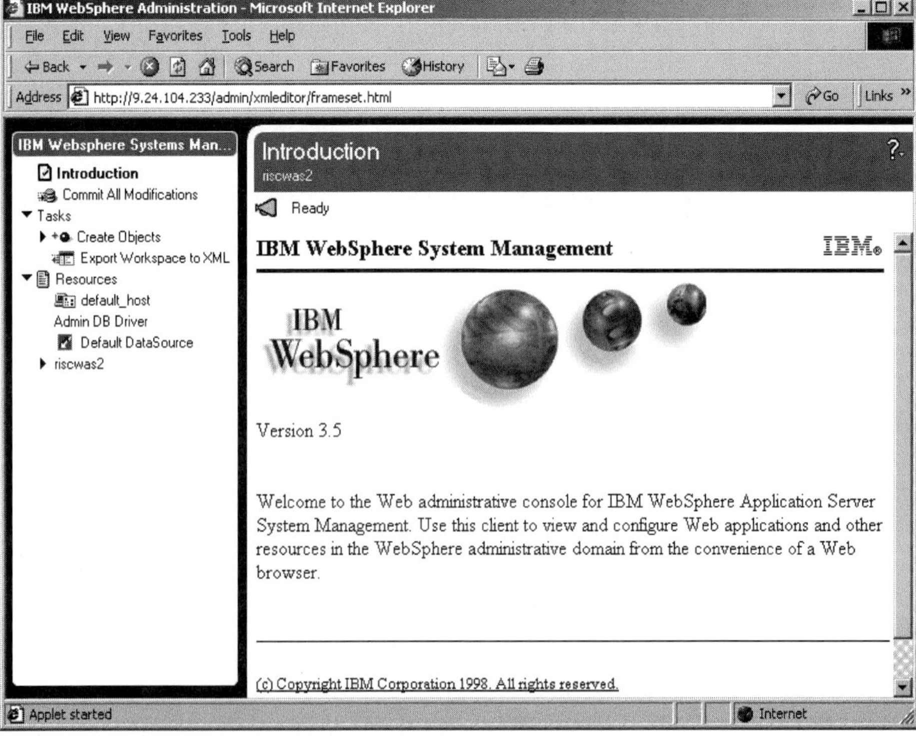

Figure 692. Initial window of the Web administrative console

19.1.2 Stopping the Web console

To stop the Web console simply close the Web browser.

Before you close your console, make sure you have submitted your changes, if any, and either exported them to XML or committed them. Otherwise, the changes will be lost.

19.2 Web console functionality

As mentioned before you can use the Web console to work with a subset of the resources in the WebSphere administrative domain such as create, view, and configure the most common resources.

Additions or changes to the property sheet are made and then submitted. This saves everything in local memory. When ready, you can commit the changes accumulated in the local workspace. Committing the changes to the administrative database makes the administrative domain aware of the changes. If changes are not committed, the changes will be discarded when the browser is closed.

Instead of, or in addition to, committing the modifications, you can save them to an XML file. Later, any other WebSphere Administrative Console can be used to import the file into the WebSphere administrative domain.

Note

You cannot start or stop application servers or restart Web applications from the Web console.

19.2.1 Creating an object

There are basically six steps to create any object via the Web console:

1. Expand Tasks
2. Expand Create Objects
3. Select a "Create" task to display the property form
4. Specify properties in the form
5. Submit the form to save the information on local machine
6. Commit all modifications to apply the changes to administrative domain

While most of the properties are similar to what you see in the WebSphere Administrative Console, there are some that are not available or differ in their names.

19.2.1.1 Steps to create an application server

1. Expand Tasks by clicking the arrow adjoining it
2. Expand the Create Objects option
3. Click **Create Server** to view the property sheet in the work area
4. Enter name of server; specify where the stdout and stderr log files should go and the number of restart attempts.
5. Click **Submit Modifications**

A snapshot of the steps enumerated above is shown in Figure 693.

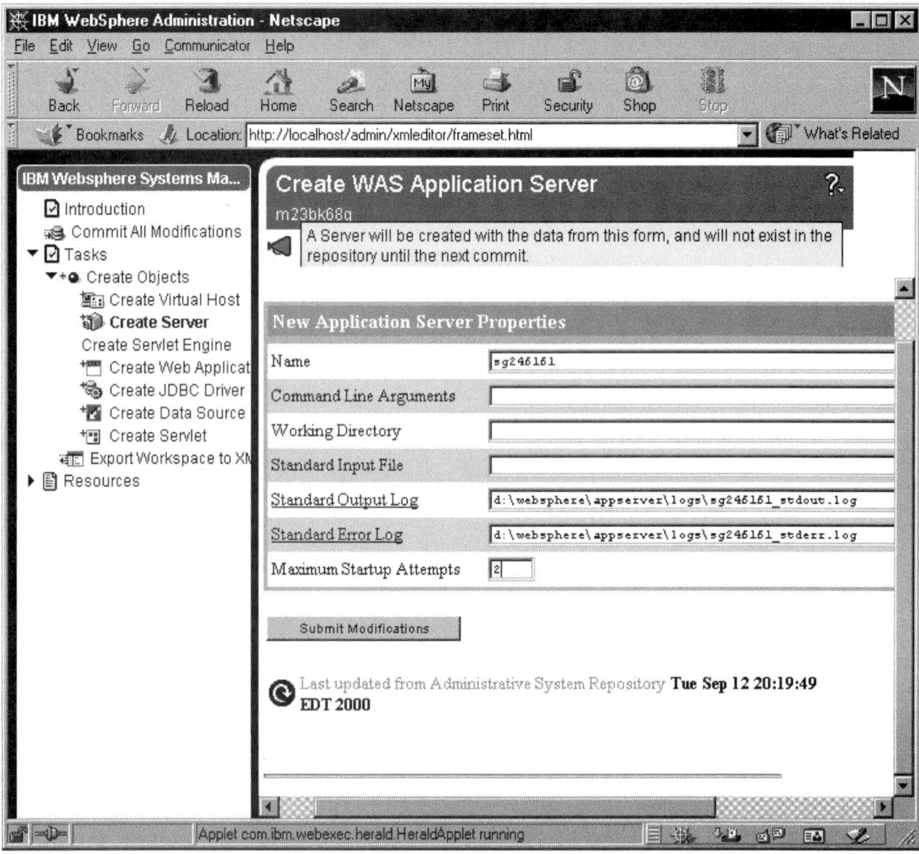

Figure 693. Property sheet for new application server

When the modifications are submitted, they are stored locally in memory and a window displays the said information.

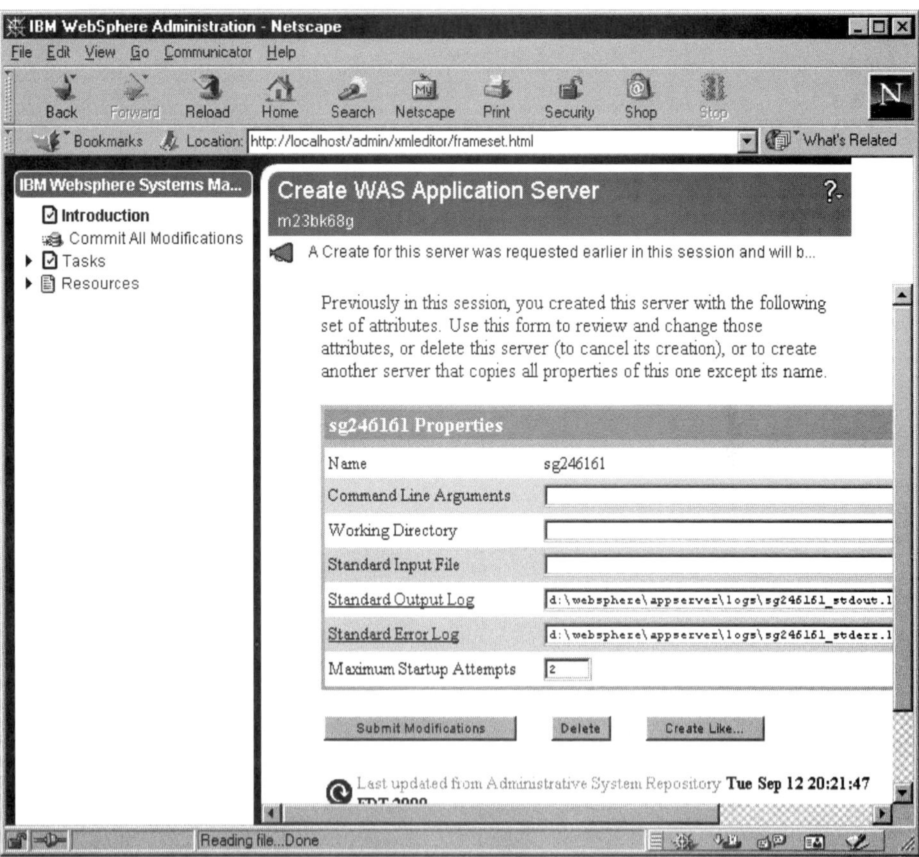

Figure 694. The create application server window after submitting the modifications

You can create or modify another resource at this point or click **Commit All Modifications** in the Navigation pane. The commit choice is displayed in the right pane. When you click **Commit** the console transfers all the information to the WebSphere administrative database and returns with a status.

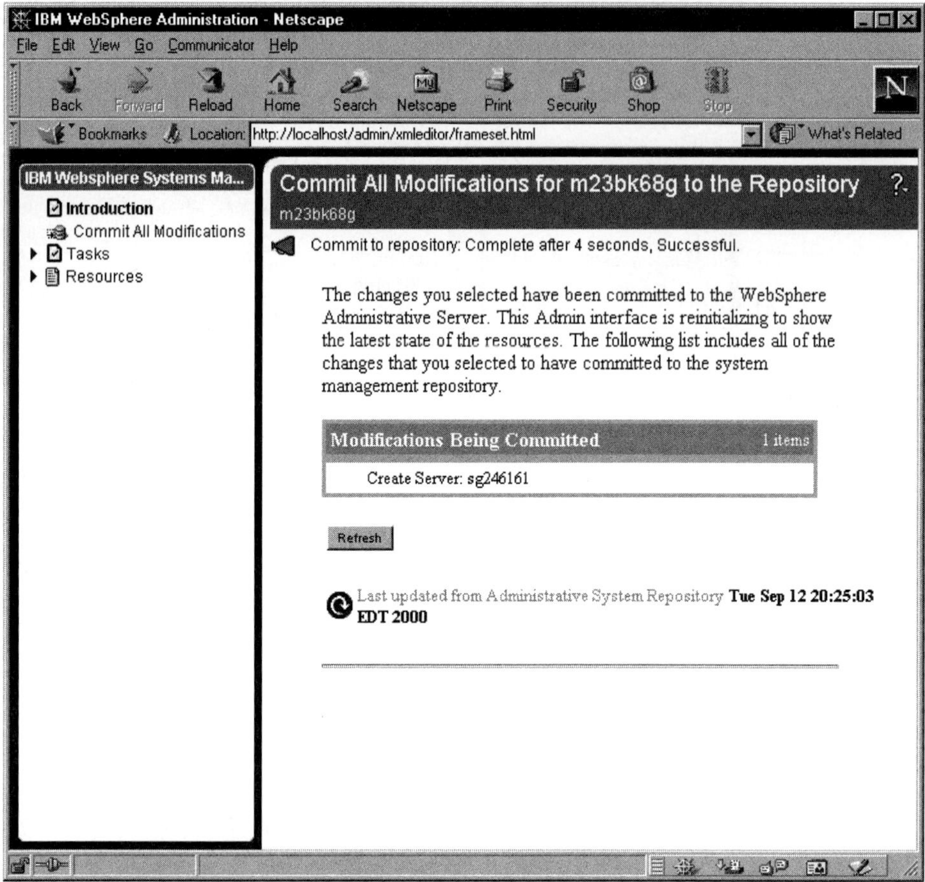

Figure 695. Window showing a successful commit of the modifications

All changes should be viewable in the WebSphere Administrative Console.

> **Note**
>
> Some modifications, such as the addition of an application server, were not displayed in the WebSphere Administrative Console even after a view refresh. The resource showed up only after the WebSphere Administrative Console was exited and restarted.

Verify the same by bringing up the WebSphere Administrative Console and viewing the topology as seen in Figure 696 on page 851.

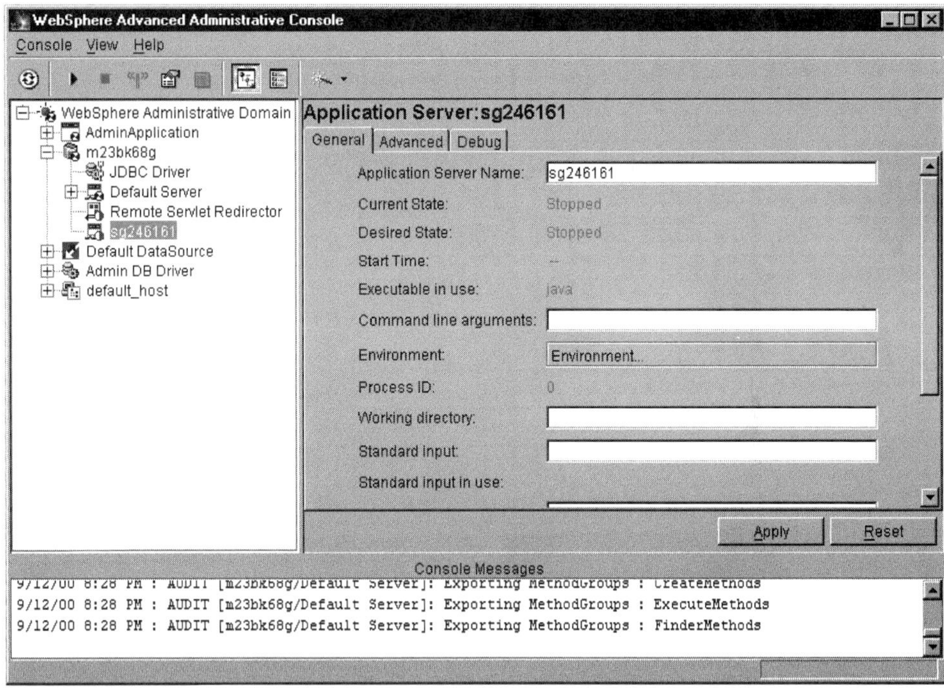

Figure 696. The newly added application server

19.2.1.2 Steps to export workspace in XML

Starting in the navigation pane:

- Expand Tasks by clicking the arrow adjoining it.
- Select **Export Workspace to XML**.
- In the resulting form on the right side of the console, specify the name of the file to store the generated XML.

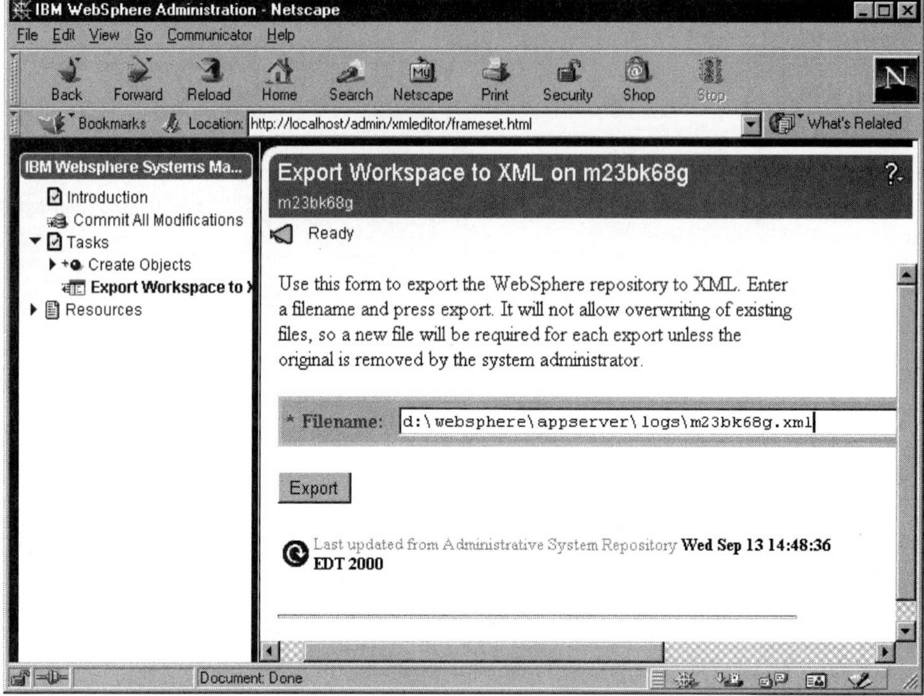

Figure 697. Export workspace to XML property page

A fully qualified file name with a .xml extension is recommended.

Note

If you simply type a file name:

- On Windows NT and Windows 2000, the file is saved in the \winnt\system32 directory.
- On AIX, the file is saved in <WAS_HOME>/bin.

When the XML file is successfully exported, the window displays the said message and the generated XML is also displayed as shown in Figure 698 on page 853.

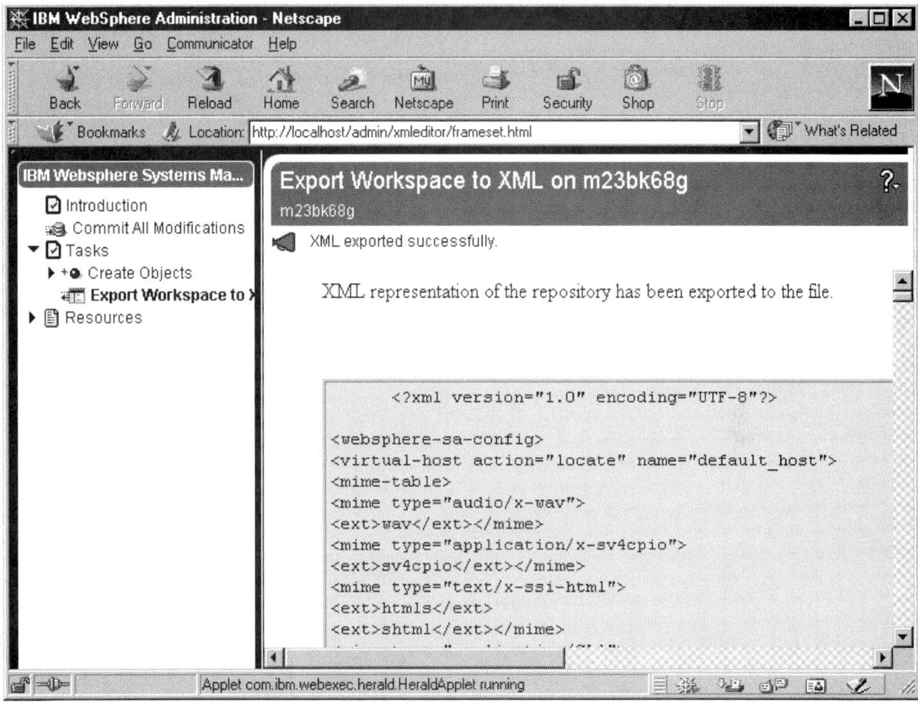

Figure 698. A successful XML export window

19.3 In conclusion

XMLConfig is the underlying tool used by the Web console. The Web application named “admin” supports the Web console and runs under the application server named “Default Server”. Hence, both the Default Server and the enterprise application named “AdminApplication” have to be running before you can bring up the Web console.

Chapter 20. The WebSphere Control Program (WSCP)

This chapter describes WSCP, the WebSphere Control Program. We will introduce Tcl and WSCP, and describe the syntax and usage of both. We go on to present some sample commands and procedures, and explain how WSCP can be used to administer the WebSphere Application Server. Finally, we discuss troubleshooting with WSCP, and the limitations of the tool as it currently stands.

Note

Currently only available for WebSphere Advanced Edition, a version of WSCP is planned for release with WebSphere Standard, but at the time of writing there was no further information available on this. The wscp.bat script from the Advanced edition will work with the Standard Edition, but you must put the property:

```
wscp.qualifyHomeName=false
```

in your properties file. Here is the wscp.bat file, for those who do not have access to the Advanced Edition:

```
@echo off
call setupCmdLine.bat
set WAS_CP=%WAS_HOME%\lib\jacl.jar
set WAS_CP=%WAS_CP%;%WAS_HOME%\lib\tcljava.jar
set WAS_CP=%WAS_CP%;%WAS_HOME%\lib\ibmwebas.jar
set WAS_CP=%WAS_CP%;%WAS_HOME%\lib\ejscp.jar
set WAS_CP=%WAS_CP%;%WAS_HOME%\lib\xml4j.jar
set WAS_CP=%WAS_CP%;%WAS_HOME%\lib\ujc.jar
set WAS_CP=%WAS_CP%;%WAS_HOME%\lib\ejs.jar
set WAS_CP=%WAS_CP%;%WAS_HOME%\lib\console.jar
set WAS_CP=%WAS_CP%;%WAS_HOME%\lib\admin.jar
set WAS_CP=%WAS_CP%;%WAS_HOME%\lib\repository.jar
set WAS_CP=%WAS_CP%;%WAS_HOME%\lib\tasks.jar
set WAS_CP=%WAS_CP%;%WAS_HOME%\lib\servlet.jar
set WAS_CP=%WAS_CP%;%WAS_HOME%\lib\sslight.jar
set WAS_CP=%WAS_CP%;%WAS_HOME%\properties
set WAS_CP=%WAS_CP%;%JAVA_HOME%\lib\classes.zip
set WAS_CP=%WAS_CP%;%JAVA_HOME%\lib\tools.jar
set EXT=-x com.ibm.ejs.sm.ejscp.RemoteExtension
set EXT=%EXT% -x com.ibm.ejs.sm.ejscp.ContextExtension
set EXT=%EXT% -x com.ibm.ejs.sm.ejscp.DrAdminExtension
set EXT=%EXT% -x com.ibm.ejs.sm.ejscp.EjscpExtension
%JAVA_HOME%\bin\java -classpath %WAS_CP% -Dserver.root=%WAS_HOME%
        com.ibm.ejs.sm.ejscp.WscpShell %EXT% %*
```

20.1 Command line administration

In WebSphere Application Server, the administrative server tracks the contents and activities of a domain by maintaining an administrative database - a database of information about all resources in a domain. The administrative database allows the administration of a domain from any machine, and all information is stored in a central location. The administrative database contains descriptive information about the applications that are configured to run in the domain. For example, it contains the names of all application servers, EJB containers, servlet engines, servlets and enterprise beans, and their current state (running, defined, or stopped).

All administration takes place through the manipulation of objects in the administrative database. Each resource in a domain corresponds to an object in the administrative database. For example, when you create an application server, a corresponding application server object is created in the administrative database.

The command line WSCP interface and the administrative console are compatible. The results of actions performed with WSCP are reflected in the console interface, and vice versa, although an explicit refresh is required to display the changes. Both the administrative console and WSCP can be used to do the following:

- Define, configure, and manage application servers, servlets, and other WebSphere Advanced resources from any node in the network.
- Build applications (by using wizards in the administrative console and scripts in WSCP).
- Perform daily administrative operations, such as starting and stopping enterprise beans and making changes to their configuration.
- Replicate objects to improve performance or availability or to simplify administration tasks (by defining and managing models and clones).
- Track the occurrence of specific events by setting and enabling tracing.

20.1.1 What is WSCP?

The WebSphere Control Program is a command line administrative tool for WebSphere. Using WSCP, one can define, configure, and manage administrative database objects from any node, import or export configuration data, and perform diagnostic operations such as enabling a trace.

The command-line program WSCP has an interactive mode, and is particularly useful for scripting. It is based on a standard scripting language,

Tcl (tool command language). You can use WSCP to administer the resources in a domain. It modifies the administrative database in response to user commands, and reflects any changes to the configuration and status of the domain. An administrator will manipulate objects in the administrative database by executing `wscp` commands or scripts.

20.1.2 What is Tcl?

Tcl stands for Tool Command Language. It was originally developed by John Ousterhout, and is now distributed by Ajuba Solutions, formerly named Scriptics. Tcl is open source and therefore free of any licensing fees. There is also a pure-Java implementation of Tcl called JACL, Version 1.2.5; it is this version of Tcl on which WSCP is actually based. In addition to the benefits of using Java rather than platform-specific code, this enables easy invoking of Java methods in scripts using the java:: package.

The Tcl language has a simple and programmable syntax, and it can be used standalone or embedded in other applications. It is extensible, and indeed hundreds of extensions already exist; WSCP extends Tcl by providing a set of commands for manipulating WebSphere objects.

20.2 Tcl language fundamentals

Before learning about WSCP, the user has to have at least a basic idea about Tcl scripting. In this section, we give a very basic summary of the fundamentals of the language. This should be enough for those who know other programming or scripting languages, but have not used Tcl before, to understand the example `wscp` commands presented in this chapter.

Note that this really is just a brief introduction to Tcl syntax. There are many good books available for those who wish to learn Tcl; this introduction is included for those who want a "quick start" to understanding the examples in this book.

20.2.1 Basic Tcl syntax

Tcl is a scripting language. Commands are separated by new lines or semicolons; words are separated by spaces. The following example uses the `expr` command, a simple command that treats the concatenation of its arguments as an arithmetic expression and returns the result as a string.

```
expr 1 + 2
```

The above command consists of four words. It will return the result of the arithmetic expression. All Tcl commands will return a result, even just an empty string.

20.2.2 Variables

Variables in Tcl do not need to be declared; they are created as necessary. The `set` command is used to read and write variables. The syntax is:

```
set <variablename> <value>
```

and the command will return the value that the variable has been set to. For instance:

```
set x 123
```

will set the value of the variable x to "123", and the command will return the value "123". You can use:

```
set <variablename>
```

or

```
$<variablename>
```

to just return the value of the variable. For instance, assume that the variable x is set to "abc". Both of the following:

```
set y $x

set y [ set x ]
```

will set the variable y to "abc", the value of variable x.

Variable substitution can be used as part of a word; if the name of the variable should be enclosed in braces to establish a single interpretation, as follows:

```
set x abc

set y ${x}def
```

This will set the variable y to "abcdef".

20.2.3 Command substitution

Tcl command substitution enables the use of the result of one command as an argument for another. For example:

```
set x [expr 1 + 2]
```

This results in the variable x being set to the value "3" - the return value of the `expr 1 + 2` command. Everything between [and the matching] is evaluated as a nested Tcl command, with the result substituted into the outer command.

20.2.4 Quoting

Words in Tcl are separated by spaces unless quoting is used.

Double-quote characters can be used to surround a word. When this is done, command and variable substitutions are performed inside the quotes, and the quotes themselves are not passed to the command. For instance:

```
set a 1

set b 2

set x "$a + $b == [expr $a + $b]"
```

This results in the variable x being set to the value "1 + 2 == 3". The variables a and b are evaluated throughout the quoted section, and the command substitution inside the square brackets is evaluated. This kind of quoting is called *deferred substitution* because the unevaluated string is often evaluated later in another context (such as in a procedure).

Braces (the { } characters) can also be used to surround a word. However, no substitution is performed (the braces themselves are still not passed to the command).

```
set x {$a + $b == [expr $a + $b]}
```

This results in the variable x being set to "$a + $b == [expr $a + $b]".

20.2.5 Procedures

The Tcl `proc` command is used to create a Tcl procedure. The syntax is:

```
proc name {argument list} {script}
```

Here is an example procedure, called "sum". It takes two arguments, and returns their sum:

```
proc sum {a b} {
   set return [expr $a + $b]
}
```

20.3 Invoking WSCP

The WebSphere Control Program is started from the command line, by running the `wscp.bat` batch file (Windows NT and 2000) or the `wscp.sh` shell script (UNIX), which is in the bin subdirectory of the application server home directory.

20.3.1 Command-line options

The following command-line options are accepted by WSCP, explained below:

```
Usage: wscp [ -h  ]  [ -c command ] [ -f  Tcl_file_name]
[ -p  properties_file_name] [ -x  extension_class]
[ [ -- ] options ]
```

The `-h` option displays the above usage information
The `-c` option specifies a Tcl command to be executed
The `-f` option specifies a file containing Tcl commands to be executed
The `-p` option specifies a Java properties file to be loaded
(.wscprc file in the user's home directory is loaded by default)
The `-x` option specifies a Tcl extension to be loaded

The `[--]` options are used to set the Tcl argc/argv variables.

The `-c`, `-f` `-p` and `-x` options may be repeated on the command line.

If no `-c` or `-f` options are specified, an interactive shell is invoked, which is terminated by the `exit` command. Most of the examples in this chapter are shown using the interactive shell.

20.3.2 The properties file

On startup, WSCP reads a Java properties file as specified by the -p option on the command line. If no properties file is specified, the .wscprc file in the user's home directory is loaded.

At a minimum, the wscp.hostName property should be specified in the properties file to point to the administrative server host. The default is set to localhost, which should work. However, it is generally preferable to explicitly specify this value. Any WebSphere property values can be added to this file, such as tracing, CORBA properties, and so on.

20.3.2.1 Connecting to local and remote nodes

By default, WSCP connects to the administrative server running on the local machine.

Use the wscp.hostName property to specify a different host, and the wscp.hostPort property to specify a port other than the default port 900. For example if your administrative server is running on machine riscwas1.itso.ral.ibm.com and on port 1350, add the following to your properties file:

```
wscp.hostName=riscwas1.itso.ral.ibm.com
wscp.hostPort=1350
```

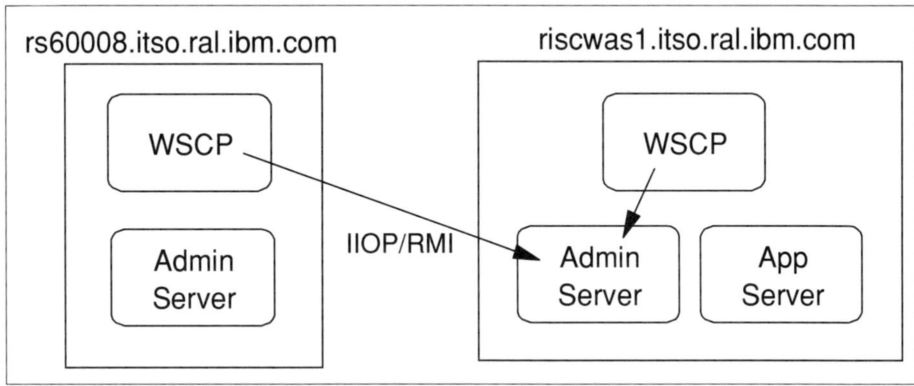

Figure 699. Connecting to local and remote node

20.3.2.2 Authenticating to the administrative server

If security is enabled on the administrative server (as should always be the case in a production system), you have to authenticate in order to use WSCP with that server.

In order to authenticate to the administrative server, you will need to create a properties file with the following properties:

```
com.ibm.CORBA.loginSource=properties
com.ibm.CORBA.loginUserid=<user_id>
com.ibm.CORBA.principalName=<identifier>
com.ibm.CORBA.loginPassword=<password>
com.ibm.CORBA.securityEnabled=true
```

For digital certificates, also include these properties:

```
com.ibm.CORBA.SSLKeyRing=<key_ring>
com.ibm.CORBA.SSLKeyRingPassword=<password>
```

You then need to add the following property to the properties file that you use: either the .wscprc properties file, or another file which you specify with the -p command line option:

```
com.ibm.CORBA.ConfigURL=<URL of properties file>
```

Note that local operating security should be used to protect the security properties file.

20.4 Command syntax of WSCP

In WSCP, each object in the administrative database, such as an application server, EJB container, servlet engine, Web application and so on, is controlled by a Tcl command with the same name as the corresponding administrative database object. Actions are defined to perform operations on them, such as create, show, modify, list, start, stop and so on.

The basic `wscp` command syntax for operating on objects is as follows:

```
<command> <operation> [<object_name>] -<option> <[value]>
```

Where:

`command` is the name of an object type (for example, ApplicationServer)
`operation` is the action to be performed (for example, show)
`object_name` is the name of the object instance
`option` varies by operation
`value` applies to some options that may require values

One important option that is often used is `-attribute`. This is an option that takes a list of attributes or attribute-value pairs as its option value, for example

```
-attribute {{ConnTimeout 300} {DatabaseName WAS} {IdleTimeout 1800}
{JDBCDriver /JDBCDriver:DB2Driver/} {MaxPoolSize 30} {MinPoolSize 1}
{OrphanTimeout 1800}}
```

Each object has a number of attributes; these are the same attributes that are visible via the properties dialog box of the administrative console. Figure 700 on page 863 shows the properties of the SZYMON-Laptop node as seen via the administrative console.

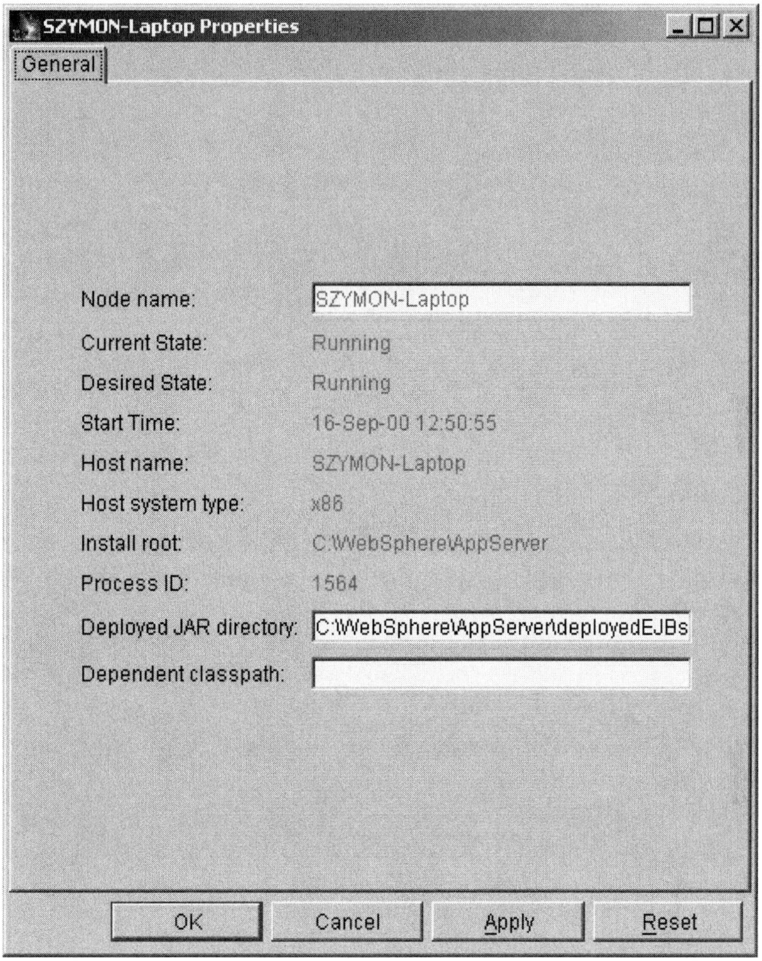

Figure 700. The properties of the WebSphere node via the administrative console

Figure 701 shows the attributes of the same node via WSCP.

```
wscp> Node show /Node:SZYMON-Laptop/
{FullName /Node:SZYMON-Laptop/} {Name SZYMON-Laptop} {CurrentState Running} {Des
iredState Running} {StartTime 969123055710} {DependentClasspath {}} {DeployedJar
Directory {C:\WebSphere\AppServer\deployedEJBs}} {HostName SZYMON-Laptop} {HostS
ystemType x86} {InstallRoot {C:\WebSphere\AppServer}} {ProcessId 1564}
wscp>
```

Figure 701. The attributes of the SZYMON-Laptop node using WSCP

It is possible to list all of the valid attributes of a command object by using the attributes operation. It is also possible to list only the required attributes, which are required in order to create the object, and the read-only attributes, which cannot be changed.

Figure 702 on page 864 shows the attributes, required attributes and read-only attributes of the ApplicationServer object.

```
wscp> ApplicationServer attributes
FullName Name CurrentState DesiredState StartTime CommandLineArgs CommandLineArg
sActive Environment EnvironmentActive Executable ExecutableActive GroupId GroupI
dActive MaxStartupAttempts PingInitialTimeout PingInterval PingTimeout ProcessId
 ProcessPriority ProcessPriorityActive SelectionPolicy ServerId ServerInstance S
tderr StderrActive Stdin StdinActive Stdout StdoutActive Umask UmaskActive UserI
d UserIdActive WorkingDirectory WorkingDirectoryActive AdminAgentIOR DebugEnable
d DebugEnabledActive EpmSpec LogFileSpec LogFileSpecActive OLTEnabled OLTEnabled
Active OLTServerHost OLTServerHostActive OLTServerPort OLTServerPortActive Secur
ityEnabled SecurityEnabledActive SourcePath SourcePathActive SystemProperties Sy
stemPropertiesActive ThreadPoolSize TraceOutput TraceOutputActive TraceSpec Trac
eSpecActive TranInactivityTimeout TranTimeout
wscp> ApplicationServer attributes -required
Name
wscp> ApplicationServer attributes -readOnly
FullName CurrentState DesiredState StartTime CommandLineArgsActive EnvironmentAc
tive Executable ExecutableActive GroupIdActive ProcessId ProcessPriorityActive S
erverId ServerInstance StderrActive StdinActive StdoutActive UmaskActive UserIdA
ctive WorkingDirectoryActive AdminAgentIOR DebugEnabledActive LogFileSpecActive
OLTEnabledActive OLTServerHostActive OLTServerPortActive SecurityEnabledActive S
ourcePathActive SystemPropertiesActive TraceOutputActive TraceSpecActive
wscp>
```

Figure 702. The attributes of the ApplicationServer command object

It is important to note that *everything* in WSCP is case-sensitive; for instance, ITSOApplicationServer is a different object from ItsoApplicationServer.

Objects are referred to using the syntax:

```
/<type>:<object_name>/
```

So to refer to a node called BasilBrush, we would write:

```
/Node:BasilBrush/
```

The above example deliberately portrays a node, the highest level in the administrative database hierarchy. Instances must always be named using their fully qualified names; that is, to name an object, one must name it in relation to all of the objects above it in the hierarchy.

So the application server called ITSOApplicationServer must be named

```
/Node:BasilBrush/ApplicationServer:ITSOApplicationServer/
```

In WSCP, we call this hierarchy the containment hierarchy. You can use the WSCP containment operation if you are unsure of the containment hierarchy of a given object. For instance, to see the containment hierarchy of a servlet, issue the `Servlet containment` command as shown in Figure 703.

```
wscp> Servlet containment
Node ApplicationServer ServletEngine WebApplication Servlet
wscp>
```

Figure 703. The containment hierarchy of a servlet

Spaces may be embedded in an object name, but the name must then be quoted using either quotes or braces:

```
{/Node:BasilBrush/ApplicationServer:Another ITSO AppServer/}
```

The naming syntax precludes the use of colons in object names. Objects with a colon in the name cannot be accessed via WSCP, even though it is possible to create an object containing a colon via the administrative console, and this object will show up in a list via WSCP.

20.4.1 Online help

A `Help` command is built into WSCP. It provides general help on the objects available within the tool. Each object also supports a help operation, which can also give verbose operation information with the `-verbose` option.

20.4.1.1 The Help command

Note

Because the `Help` command in WSCP is implemented as a Tcl object, and because WSCP is case sensitive, it must always be referred to as `Help`, not `help`. This can be confusing at first, when typing `help` returns the phrase `invalid command name "help"`. It is possible to change the name of the `Help` command to `help` by using the Tcl `rename` command:

```
rename Help help
```

or by defining a procedure so that either form can be used:

```
proc help { args } { Help $args }
```

Figure 704 shows the `Help` command.

```
wscp> Help

The general format of all wscp actions is:
        <object-type> <action> [name] [options]

The following is a list of the supported objects:

        ApplicationServer
        Context
        DataSource
        DrAdmin
        EJBContainer
        EnterpriseApplication
        EnterpriseBean
        GenericServer
        Help
        JDBCDriver
        Model
        Node
        Remote
        Servlet
        ServletEngine
        ServletRedirector
        SessionManager
        UserProfile
        VirtualHost
        WebApplication
        WebResource
        XMLConfig

To list all actions an object supports: <object> help
To list all the options for an action:  <object> help <action>
For verbose information on an action:   <object> help <action> -verbose

wscp>
```

Figure 704. The Help object in WSCP

20.4.1.2 Command help

Each command supports a help operation, which gives information about the operations available for that command. A short description is also given of each operation.

Also, more detailed information on any of the operations possible on a given command object can be gained by specifying the name of the operation after the help operation.

Finally, there is a `-verbose` option that will give the highest level of detail available for any given operation; this will also list all of the options available for that operation.

Figure 705 shows the output of the help operation of the ApplicationServer command object, as well as the more detailed description of the show operation and the output with the `-verbose` flag.

```
wscp> ApplicationServer help
The following actions are available for ApplicationServer

attributes          Display the attributes of the object
containment         Display the containment hierarchy for the object
create              Create the specified object
defaults            Display or set attribute defaults
help                Display this help message
list                Display all the instances of this type
modify              Modify the attributes of the specified object
operations          List all the actions available on the object type
remove              Remove the specified object
show                Display the attributes of specified object
start               Start the specified object
stop                Stop the specified object

wscp> ApplicationServer help show

ApplicationServer show <name> [-all] [-attribute <attribute list>]

wscp> ApplicationServer help show -verbose

ApplicationServer show <name>

The following options are available for show

[-all]                          Also display unset attributes
[-attribute <attribute list>]   Display only the specified attributes

wscp>
```

Figure 705. The help operation of the ApplicationServer command object

20.4.2 Status and error information

If a `wscp` command returns success, a result string of the command is returned. This result string may contain a single value, a list of values, or be empty. The interactive `wscp` shell will display non-empty results.

If a `wscp` command fails, three things happen.

1. A TclException is raised. This may be caught using the Tcl `catch` command. If the exception is not caught, execution of the current procedure or command substitution is terminated.
2. The Tcl variable errorCode is set. This will contain status values and statusToString provided by the WscpStatus class. This variable is reset prior to each WSCP-specific command.

3. The Tcl variable errorInfo is set if WSCP caught an exception. This will contain one or more stack traces of the exception(s). The variable contents persist until explicitly set by the next exception. They can be displayed in the same way as variables that you set yourself; `set errorInfo` will display the contents of the errorInfo variable, for instance.

20.4.3 Sample commands

Here are three sample commands; to create, modify and remove an application server. Table 45 shows the syntax for the create, modify and remove operations:

Table 45. The syntax for the create, modify and remove operations

Command	Syntax
create	<objectType> create <name> -attribute <attrList>
modify	<objectType> modify <name> -attribute <attrList>
remove	<objectType> remove <name>

Figure 706 shows the commands to create, modify and remove an application server. The server is to be called NoddyAppServer, and it will be created on the SZYMON-Laptop node.

- The first command creates the server and sets the PingTimeout attribute to 400 and the ThreadPoolSize to 40.
- The second command modifies the application server to increase the size of the PingTimeout to 600 and the ThreadPoolSize to 60.
- Finally, the third command removes the application server.

```
wscp> ApplicationServer create /Node:SZYMON-Laptop/ApplicationServer:NoddyAppSer
ver/ -attribute {{PingTimeout 400} {ThreadPoolSize 40}}
wscp> ApplicationServer modify /Node:SZYMON-Laptop/ApplicationServer:NoddyAppSer
ver/ -attribute {{PingTimeout 600} {ThreadPoolSize 60}}
wscp> ApplicationServer remove /Node:SZYMON-Laptop/ApplicationServer:NoddyAppSer
ver/
wscp>
```

Figure 706. Creation, modification and removal of an application server

20.5 Example WSCP procedures

This section contains a number of sample procedures, which you should feel free to use and modify for your own purposes.

20.5.1 Sample procedures: statusToString, checkStatus

Figure 707 shows two example procedures that may be useful when working with WebSphere.

The first one, statusToString, will convert a WscpStatus to its corresponding string translation. It uses a `java::call` command, part of the Tcl and Java integration, to call an Java method, also called statusToString, of the WscpStatus class. This redbook does not go into detail on the Tcl Java integration; see the resources at the end of this chapter for more information. The default value of -1 in the statusToString procedure makes the argument optional. If no argument is specified, the procedure will translate the current value of the global variable, errorCode.

The second procedure, checkStatus, tests whether the errorCode matches the expected status value. It simply compares the value of the errorCode variable with the parameter passed to it.

```
#
# Converts a WscpStatus to its corresponding string translation
#
proc statusToString {{status -1}} {
    global errorCode
    if {$status == -1 && $errorCode != "NONE"} {
       set status $errorCode
       }
    java::call com.ibm.ejs.sm.ejscp.WscpStatus statusToString $status
}

#
# Tests whether errorCode matches the expected status value
#
proc checkStatus {expectedStatus} {
    global STATUS errorCode
    if {$errorCode == $STATUS($expectedStatus)} {return 1} {return 0}
}
```

Figure 707. Two example procedures

20.5.2 Advanced sample procedures: getAttrs, setAttrs

These example procedures, shown in Figure 708 on page 871, allow for the manipulation of an array of attributes from the named object. The explanation given here may be difficult to understand for those who do not have a knowledge of Tcl.

The getAttrs procedure takes three parameters: name, array and args. The name parameter should be given as a fully qualified object name, such as

```
/Node:SZYMON-Laptop/ApplicationServer:HelloAppServer/
```

The array is the name of the array variable used to store the attribute names and their values; this can be any name, and the array keys will be the attribute names with the corresponding value being the attribute value. Finally, the args option specifies one or more attributes to be stored into the array from the specified object.

> **Note**
>
> The name args is special to Tcl, and means that a call to the procedure may contain more actual arguments than the procedure has formals. All of the actual arguments starting at the one that would be assigned to args are combined into a list (as if the list command had been used); this combined value is assigned to the local variable args.

The first line of the procedure uses an `upvar` command to create a local variable, a, which is a link to the array variable passed in as the second parameter. The procedure then uses a regular expression to extract the type of object from the name passed in as the first parameter. It then puts that type into a variable type, and then runs the show operation on the name, with the args variable, the final parameter, being passed as the list of attributes. This is inside a foreach loop, used to set the entries in the array to the attribute-value pairs returned.

The setAttrs procedure takes just two parameters: a name that has to be a fully qualified object name, and an array that contains a set of attributes. It uses a similar mechanism to the getAttrs procedure described above to create a local string in the format acceptable to the -attribute option of the modify operation; that is, it surrounds the attribute-value pairs with the correct number of braces for the command. Finally, it runs the `modify` command.

```
#
# Get/Set an array of attributes for the specified object
#
proc getAttrs {name array args} {
    upvar $array a
    regexp {.*/([^:]*):} $name unused type
    foreach attr [$type show $name -attribute $args] {array set a $attr}
}

proc setAttrs {name array} {
    upvar $array a
    regexp {.*/([^:]*):} $name unused type
    foreach key [array names a] {append attrs "{$key {$a($key)}}"}
    $type modify $name -attribute $attrs
}
```

Figure 708. The getAttrs and setAttrs procedures

20.5.3 Advanced sample procedure: modEnv

The modEnv procedure makes use of both getAttrs and setAttrs in order to modify the Environment attribute of a server, to either add or change an environment variable. It should be called with the fully qualified name of the server as the first parameter, the name of the environment variable as the second, and the value to which the variable should be set as the final parameter. Figure 709 shows the modEnv procedure.

```
#
# modEnv - procedure for modifying the Environment attribute of a server.
# The specified environment variable is modified (or added if it is not present),
# and the values of other environment variables are retained.
#
# Arguments:
#
# server - the fully qualified name of the server to be modified.
#
# variable - the name of the environment variable to modify.
#
# value - the new value of the environment variable.
#
# To modify the Environment attribute of multiple servers, use the Tcl foreach command,
# for example:
#
# wscp> foreach server [ApplicationServer list] {modEnv $server TEST_VARIABLE 3.5}
#
proc modEnv {server variable value} {
   getAttrs $server attr Environment
   if {[info exists attr(Environment)]} {
         set oldEnv $attr(Environment)
   } else {
       set oldEnv {}
   }

   # append to environment if variable not found; replace it if found
   set i [lsearch -regexp $oldEnv ^$variable=]
   if {$i == -1} {
        set newEnv [lappend oldEnv "$variable=$value"]
   } else {
        set newEnv [lreplace $oldEnv $i $i "$variable=$value"]
   }

   set attr(Environment) $newEnv
   setAttrs $server attr
}
```

Figure 709. The modEnv sample procedure

20.6 Interactive administration with WSCP

The WebSphere Control Program was principally designed for writing scripts to control the WebSphere Application Server. However, it can be used for interactive administration, and indeed may in some situations be the preferred tool - for instance, if you are separated from your application server machines via a firewall which only allows Telnet traffic through. In this situation, when you cannot connect using a remote administrative console, and you cannot set the GUI to display on your local X server (UNIX), WSCP on the remote server would be the choice.

The following hints are provided to make interactive work with WSCP faster and more efficient from the user's point of view.

20.6.1 Keeping track of the container

One of the least user friendly features of WSCP is the fact that in order to work with any object, a fully qualified reference to that object has to be given. Having to refer to, say, a servlet called HelloWorldServlet, as

```
/Node:SZYMON-Laptop/ApplicationServer:Default
Server/ServletEngine:Default Servlet Engine/WebApplication:default_app/
```

in every command can make for a lot of typing or cutting and pasting! The solution is to use Tcl variables, as shown in Figure 710.

```
wscp> set container {/Node:SZYMON-Laptop/ApplicationServer:Default Server/Servle
tEngine:Default Servlet Engine/WebApplication:default_app/}
/Node:SZYMON-Laptop/ApplicationServer:Default Server/ServletEngine:Default Servl
et Engine/WebApplication:default_app/
wscp> Servlet show ${container}Servlet:snoop/
{FullName {/Node:SZYMON-Laptop/ApplicationServer:Default Server/ServletEngine:De
fault Servlet Engine/WebApplication:default_app/Servlet:snoop/}} {Name snoop} {C
urrentState Running} {DesiredState Running} {StartTime 969123086715} {Code Snoop
Servlet} {CodeActive SnoopServlet} {DebugMode 0} {Description {Snoop servlet}} {
DescriptionActive {Snoop servlet}} {Enabled True} {EnabledActive True} {InitPara
ms {{param1 test-value1}}} {InitParamsActive {{param1 test-value1}}} {LoadAtStar
tup False} {LoadAtStartupActive False} {URIPaths {default_host/servlet/snoop def
ault_host/servlet/snoop2}} {URIPathsActive {default_host/servlet/snoop default_h
ost/servlet/snoop2}} {UserServlet True} {UserServletActive True}
wscp>
```

Figure 710. Use of the container variable with a servlet object

Clearly, `${container}Servlet:snoop/` is far easier to type than the fully qualified name of the servlet object. Note that, because there are spaces in the container definition, we have enclosed the whole definition in braces. However, the actual command cannot be in braces because variables are not expanded inside braces. If you do need to quote in the command (because say, your servlet name contains a space), you have to use quotes rather than braces. This can be seen in Figure 711, where we set our container to the Default Server application server, in order to work with the Default Servlet Engine; the name of the servlet engine has to be quoted, because it contains spaces.

```
wscp> set container {/Node:SZYMON-Laptop/ApplicationServer:Default Server/}
/Node:SZYMON-Laptop/ApplicationServer:Default Server/
wscp> ServletEngine show "${container}ServletEngine:Default Servlet Engine/"
{FullName {/Node:SZYMON-Laptop/ApplicationServer:Default Server/ServletEngine:De
fault Servlet Engine/}} {Name {Default Servlet Engine}} {CurrentState Running} {
DesiredState Running} {StartTime 969123090029} {MaxCon 25} {MaxConActive 25} {Tr
ansportAttributes {{linkType 0}{logFile native.log}{cloneIndex 1}{logFileMask 8}
{queueName ibmoselink}}} {TransportAttributesActive {{linkType 0}{cloneIndex 1}{
logFile native.log}{logFileMask 8}{queueName ibmoselink}}} {TransportPort 8993}
{TransportPortActive 8993} {TransportType 0} {TransportTypeActive 0}
wscp>
```

Figure 711. Use of the container variable with the Default Servlet Engine

It may also be useful to create variables for the separate parts of the container, for instance

```
set node {/Node:SZYMON-Laptop/}
set server "${node}ApplicationServer:Default Server/"
set engine "${server}ServletEngine:Default Servlet Engine/"
set webapp "${engine}WebApplication:default_app/"
```

20.6.2 Command line editing

The Tcl interactive mode provides support for scrolling back and editing previous commands. Simply use the arrow keys, Insert, Delete, Home, End and Backspace keys as you would expect.

20.7 Troubleshooting with WSCP

The WSCP tool can be used to manipulate trace for troubleshooting purposes.

20.7.1 Enabling trace

The WebSphere Control Program can be used to manipulate trace in two primary ways - statically, by modifying the TraceSpec attribute of a server and restarting the server, or dynamically, by using the `DrAdmin` command.

20.7.1.1 Modifying trace specifications

Servers contain a TraceSpec attribute. You can use WSCP to modify this attribute to set a certain trace specification, as follows:

```
wcsp> ApplicationServer modify
/Node:SZYMON-Laptop/ApplicationServer:HelloAppServer/ -attribute
{{TraceSpec com.ibm.ejs.container.*=all=enabled}}
```

This examples sets trace specification of the HelloAppServer application server to com.ibm.ejs.container.*=all=enabled. Notice that the application server is referred to by the fully qualified name. Setting the trace specification of a server via WSCP is equivalent to setting the trace specification of a server via the administrative console.

The `wscp` command itself can also be debugged by setting a trace specification, except that this time the initial WSCP trace specification is set via a WSCP property, as follows:

```
wscp.traceString=com.ibm.ejs.sm.ejscp.*=all=enabled
```

20.7.1.2 The DrAdmin command

The DrAdmin command can be used can be used to affect the local WSCP instance or to affect a remote server instance.

Tracing can be enabled dynamically on the local WSCP by using the `DrAdmin local` command as follows:

```
DrAdmin local -setTrace com.ibm.ejs.sm.ejscp.*=all=enabled
```

In order to connect to a remote DrAdmin server, we need to know what port that server is listening on. The output from the server at startup will contain something like:

```
DrAdminServer A DrAdmin available on port 1,086
```

The command would then be:

```
DrAdmin remote 1086 -setTrace com.ibm.ejs.container.*=all=enabled
```

Figure 712 shows the options for the `DrAdmin remote` command:

```
wscp> DrAdmin help remote -verbose
DrAdmin remote <server port>
The following options are available for remote
[-serverHost <string>]          Server host name
[-setTrace <string>]            Process the trace specification
[-setRingBufferSize <string>]   Set number of ringbuffer entries in K
[-dumpRingBuffer <string>]      Dump ring buffer to the specified file
[-dumpState <string>]           Process the dump specification
[-stopServer]                   Stop the server
[-stopNode]                     Stop the node
[-dumpThreads]                  Dump the server threads
```

Figure 712. The syntax of the DrAdmin remote command

20.8 Limitations and additional information

The `wscp` command as it currently stands has a number of limitations. These are described below.

20.8.1 Security objects are not supported

Security objects are not supported by WSCP at this time. These objects must be manipulated outside of WSCP, such as by using the administrative console. Note that XMLConfig import/export does include these objects.

20.8.2 Aggregate tasks are not provided

There is no WSCP equivalent for the administrative console wizards. The reader is encouraged to create Tcl procedures to implement higher-level tasks.

20.8.3 Concurrent use of clients may require coordination

Changes to the administrative database made by WSCP will require a console refresh in the administrative console in order to be visible.

In the same way, a `wscp list` command may be necessary to update the WSCP cache in order to reflect changes made via the administrative console. The only identified area of concern in WSCP is when the administrative console is used to delete an object for which WSCP has a cached reference. That cached reference could lead to an exception if you then try to manipulate the (now non-existent) object via WSCP, but no real harm is done and most commands are unaffected.

The point is just to recognize that concurrent updates have implications for other instances. There is certainly absolutely no reason to not use any combination of consoles and/or WSCP instances for read-only operations. Even insertions and updates are completely benign from the WSCP perspective (and in the console just implies the need to manually refresh instances).

20.9 Additional resources

- *Tcl and the Tk Toolkit* by John K. Ousterhout, published by Addison-Wesley
- Developer Web site: `dev.scriptics.com`
- JACL Web site: `dev.scriptics.com/software/java/`

Chapter 21. XMLConfig

This chapter describes the XMLConfig command-line utility that ships with WebSphere V3.5. We specifically look at the options available and focus on several scenarios where XMLConfig can be used as an alternative to the administrative console. The tool is also a convenient method for extracting administrative database configuration data, both in backup and problem determination situations.

In this chapter, we will discuss:

- Introduction to XML and XMLConfig
- XMLConfig components
- XMLConfig - new feature in WebSphere V3.5
- XML: a suitable markup language for WebSphere
- Customizing XML for the WebSphere XMLConfig tool
- XML elements and actions for XMLConfig
- XMLConfig examples and uses
  - Stopping and starting an application server
  - Application servers and associated components
  - Models and cloning
  - Enterprise application security

21.1 Introduction to XML and XMLConfig

The XMLConfig tool offers the WebSphere administrator the ability to interact with the administrative respository, possibly modifying or extracting configuration data. XMLConfig makes full use of the eXtensible Markup Language (XML), adhering to grammar and hierarchical conventions.

With XML documents coded to the WebSphere Application Server Configuration Markup Language syntax (WASCML), it is possible to invoke an action on a specified resource. Starting or stopping an application server is a common example.

As grammar and structure are of concern when coding XML documents, over 100 Document Type Definitions (DTDs) are cataloged within WebSphere. These are typically referenced at the start of any XML document with the inclusion of the <!DOCTYPE> tag.

21.2 XMLConfig components

Whilst the XMLConfig tool is actually a Java class it is seldomly invoked directly. Rather, located under the <WAS_HOME>/bin directory, either `XMLConfig.bat` or `XMLConfig.sh` are available for Windows and UNIX platforms respectively. Both these files share the same function of exporting the classpath prior to invoking the Java class.

The `com.ibm.websphere.xmlconfig.XMLConfig` java class arguments are as follows:

```
com.ibm.websphere.xmlconfig.XMLConfig      { ( -import <xml data file> )
||     [ ( -export <xml output file> [-partial <xml data file>] ) }
-adminNodeName <primary node name>  [ -nameServiceHost <host name> [
-nameServicePort <port number> ]   [-traceString <trace spec>
[-traceFile <file name>]]   [-substitute
<"key1=value1[;key2=value2;[...]]">]}
```

The <WAS_HOME>/bin/xmlconfig.dtd Document Type Definition (DTD) file contains the XML specifications that must be adhered to when invoking XMLConfig. These specifications ensure that XML import data meets the WebSphere WASCML syntax. If an element or attribute is incorrectly defined in an XML import file, an exception / error will occur. However, as XMLConfig import XML can contain nested elements, it is possible that the foremost objects will be created before the error is reached.

Additional Document Type Definition (DTD) catalogs can be found under the <WAS_HOME>/web/xml/grammar/dtd subdirectories. These are provided not for XMLConfig, but for generic XML support within WebSphere.

Typically, `XMLConfig.bat/sh` is invoked on the command line against the WebSphere administrative primary node. The import option can be substituted for either export or partial (export), prior to specifying the actual XML file.

The following example imports the createappserver.xml file on node itsonode:

```
./XMLConfig.sh -adminNodeName itsonode -import createappserver.xml
```

WebSphere administrators are also given the opportunity to import and export XML configuration data via the drop-down menu in the administrative console, as shown in Figure 734 on page 905. Both input and output are the same as if executed with the `XMLConfig` command.

21.3 XMLConfig new features

Prior to WebSphere V3.5, XMLConfig shipped only as a technology preview. Now, XMLConfig ships supporting several new features, offering the administrator an alternative method for configuring and managing both WebSphere Standard and Advanced Editions. In contrast to the WebSphere Administrative Console and the WebSphere Control Program (WSCP), XMLConfig is biased towards configuration. Similarly, XMLConfig is not an interactive tool and cannot be used to retrieve status information from WebSphere. However, the overhead of rigorously editing detailed XML, is worth it when variable substitution is used, enabling multiple servlets or EJBs to be quickly deployed.

The new XMLConfig features supported with WebSphere V3.5 are:

1. Model/clone support

   Now supported are the createclone, associateclone and disassociate XMLConfig actions. As demonstrated in Figure 725 on page 896, cloning is achievable only once a WebSphere model is established.

2. Security

   Implementing WebSphere general security is now possible with the XMLConfig tool. In addition, method group creation, EJB or URI method group mapping and method group permissions are all possible.

3. Enterprise applications

   Administrators can quickly create an enterprise application, shown in Figure 728 on page 899, for implementing security on a specific application server and associated elements.

4. StopForRestart

   Applicable to WebSphere node objects only. Effectively stops a node, as the XMLConfig action suggests, for a restart.

5. Command line and programmatic variable substitution support

   Allows users to quickly substitute variables from the XMLConfig command line to a specified XML file. Extremely useful for deploying multiple servlets or EJBs.

6. JDBC driver install/uninstall support

   Provides a one-step method for configuring and installing additional JDBC drivers, as required.

21.4 XML: a suitable markup language for WebSphere

Those not familiar with XML should recognize that it considerably contrasts with other markup languages, such as HTML. XML offers the user the scope to expand or enhance the actual markup tags of a document. Unlike HTML, where a fixed set of standardized function tags are employed, this enhancement or design freedom does not lie with the simple creation of an XML document. Rather, it requires the design and construction of a Document Type Definition (DTD) file to actually specify the underlying XML syntax and structure. Subsequent XML documents can then be coded, adhering to the constraints and validity set forth in the DTD specification.

As XML is fast emerging as a Web-based technology for transferring data prior to presentation at the client, WebSphere now ships with over 100 DTD catalogs. However, with XMLConfig we are only concerned with the xmlconfig.dtd DTD found in the <WAS_HOME>/bin directory. It is this file that maintains the XML specifications, governing structure and syntax when invoking XMLConfig functions on the WebSphere administrative database.

XML in part is a hierarchical based metalanguage, embracing elements, entities and attributes in a logical fashion. This is also true of WebSphere, which utilizes the concept of an object for each resource found under the administrative domain. Visually, the WebSphere Administrative Console best demonstrates this concept, with the WebSphere administrative domain being at the top of the hierarchy and the individual servlets at the lowermost points.

Using the WebSphere Administrative Console in the Topology quickly enables the administrator to recognize the differing elements and attributes that constitute the component parts of WebSphere. Familiarization with this structure or hierarchy is paramount when editing XML documents, as it enables the WebSphere administrator to quickly identify an object and understand the corresponding attributes.

In conclusion, XMLConfig offers an alternative method for configuring and administrating WebSphere. However, it does not directly replace the administrative console or the WebSphere Control Program (WSCP). With the use of variable substitution, XMLConfig is a powerful tool for deploying multiple EJBs and servlets, avoiding the lengthy menu-driven configuration necessary with the administrative console for each EJB or servlet.

21.5 Customizing XML for the WebSphere XMLConfig tool

Common to all XML is the schema or syntax that adheres to the specifications defined in the DTD. WebSphere XML is no exception to this rule, only being valid if it adheres to the constraints stipulated in the xmlconfig.dtd file.

At the simplest level, XML elements are constructed in a hierarchical or tree-like structure. Indeed, each element is defined by a tag and associated end tag. This concept is further extended since elements can be nested, forming the various branches of a tree. Each element can also have an associated attribute, which in turn, further describes the element.

```
<websphere-sa-config>
   <parent name="pname" action="valid-action">
      <child name="cname" action="valid-action"/>
   </parent>
</websphere-sa-config>
```

It is not surprising that the XML representation of the WebSphere topology tree is similar to that experienced with the navigation of the administrative console topology tree. This is evident in the following excerpt, which performs a create action on the web-application “ITSO2_web_app”, but only after first locating the respective node, application-server, and servlet-engine.

```
<websphere-sa-config>
  <node name="riscwas2" action="locate">
    <application-server name="Default Server" action="locate">
      <servlet-engine name="Default Servlet Engine" action="locate">
        <web-application name="ITSO2_web_app" action="create">
         ...
         ...
         </web-application>
      </servlet-engine>
    </application-server>
  </node>
</websphere-sa-config>
```

The locate action is used to select the specified element and effectively serves to guide us to the next nested object. Once the servlet-engine named “Default Servlet Engine” is located, we can create a web-application called “ITSO2_web_app”. The actual creation details have been omitted.

21.5.1 XMLConfig elements

Throughout the examples provided in this chapter you will see two common elements that never change:

```
<?xml version="1.0"?>
<!DOCTYPE websphere-sa-config
SYSTEM"$XMLConfigDTDLocation$$dsep$bin$dsep$xmlconfig.dtd">
```

Here, the first line specifies the XML version and the second line the Document Type Definition (DTD) file that governs the XML syntax and structural validity of any following XML markup. Since WebSphere is a cross-platform product, variable substitution will automatically supplement the correct values for the $XMLConfigDTDLocation$ the <WAS_HOME>, $dsep$ the directory separator and $psep$ the path delimiter.

XML elements are defined with the use of tags. Each element has a start and end tag, with the end tag being prefixed with a "/" forward slash. Figure 713 highlights the validity of nested tags, only creating a web-application once the node, application-server and servlet-engine are correctly located. The actual web-application specifics have been omitted in this case.

```
<websphere-sa-config>
  <node name="riscwas2" action="locate">
    <application-server name="ITSO App Server" action="locate">
      <servlet-engine name="ITSO Servlet Engine" action="locate">
        <web-application name="ITSO Web Application" action="create">
              ...
              ...
        </web-application>
      </servlet-engine>
    </application-server>
  </node>
</websphere-sa-config>
```

Figure 713. Nested XML tags

Each element requires a unique name to distinguish itself from any peers at the same level in the topology tree. However, as each branch of the topology tree is independent, the uniqueness towards the ends of the branches is not so critical. For example, using the administrative console wizard to create a full-blown application server with servlet engine and EJB container will always set the name of the EJB container to Default Container.

21.5.2 XMLConfig actions

Figure 713 on page 882 also introduces the concept of element actions, with locate and create being briefly introduced to configure a new Web application under an existing servlet engine, shown in bold type.

Valid element actions are: create | update | delete | locate | export | start | stop | ping | createclone | associateclone | disassociateclone | enable | disable | restart | StopForRestart. As expected the resulting function from each is as their name suggests. However, update is typically specified in preference to create, as it will default to the create action if the element specified does not already exist. If the element does however exist, the attributes will be updated.

Not all actions are valid for all types of elements.

There are two possible ways to determine which attributes are valid for each respective element or what elements are valid at the various levels in the XML hierarchy:

1. Consulting the xmlconfig.dtd DTD found in the <WAS_HOME>/bin directory will provide the definitive answer, although the xmlconfig.dtd file is a complex document and not that user-friendly. For example, valid attributes for a DataSource are:

   ```
   <!ELEMENT data-source ( database-name? , jdbc-driver-name? ,
   minimum-pool-size? , maximum-pool-size? , connection-timeout? ,
   idle-timeout? , orphan-timeout? )*>
   ```

2. If a similar element or object in WebSphere terminology already exists in your WebSphere configuration, an XMLConfig export can be consulted. However, if an object attribute is null, the element attribute name is not necessarily exported. An example is the <data-source name=""/> found in an EJB Container; see in Figure 719 on page 888.

Note

It is important to note that element names in XML are both case-sensitive and white-space-sensitive; for example, "ITSO App Server" is not the same as "itso app server", nor is "ITSO App Server" the same as "ITSOAppServer".

In the examples that follow in this chapter, new lines start with a "<" and terminate with a carriage return only after a ">" or "/>".

21.6 XMLConfig examples and uses

The following section details the most common XMLConfig examples.

21.6.1 Starting and stopping an application server

The first example provided, as shown in Figure 714, demonstrates how to start the "Default Server" application server that resides on a node named "riscwas2". You will have to modify both the application-server name and the node name values to perform this action on your system. Then run:

```
XMLConfig.sh -adminNodeName riscwas2 -import itsoStartDefault.xml
```

```
<?xml version="1.0"?>
<!DOCTYPE websphere-sa-config SYSTEM
"$XMLConfigDTDLocation$$dsep$bin$dsep$xmlconfig.dtd">

<websphere-sa-config>
  <node name="riscwas2" action="update">
    <application-server name="Default Server" action="start">
    </application-server>
  </node>
</websphere-sa-config>
```

Figure 714. itsoStartDefault.xml

Figure 715 shows with a simple change of the application-server action keyword characteristic that the itsoStartDefault.xml file can easily be modified to produce the itsoStopDefault.xml file. Then run:

```
XMLConfig.sh -adminNodeName riscwas2 -import itsoStopDefault.xml
```

```
<?xml version="1.0"?>
<!DOCTYPE websphere-sa-config SYSTEM
"$XMLConfigDTDLocation$$dsep$bin$dsep$xmlconfig.dtd">

<websphere-sa-config>
  <node name="riscwas2" action="update">
    <application-server name="Default Server" action="stop">
    </application-server>
  </node>
</websphere-sa-config>
```

Figure 715. itsoStopDefault.xml

21.6.2 Creating a new JDBC driver

With XMLConfig it is possible to quickly configure and install a new JDBC driver. In Figure 716 we create a new DB2 JDBC 2.0 driver called “anotherJDBCDriver”. Those familiar with the WebSphere Administrative Console topology tree will recall that JDBC drivers reside under the WebSphere administrative domain. For that reason, the jdbc-driver creation takes place immediately after the <websphere-sa-config> tag.

```
<?xml version="1.0"?>
<!DOCTYPE websphere-sa-config SYSTEM
"$XMLConfigDTDLocation$$dsep$bin$dsep$xmlconfig.dtd">

<websphere-sa-config>
<jdbc-driver name="anotherJDBCDriver" action="create">
    <implementation-class>com.ibm.db2.jdbc.app.DB2Driver
    </implementation-class>
    <url-prefix>jdbc:db2</url-prefix>
    <jta-enabled>false</jta-enabled>
    <install-info>
      <node-name>riscwas2</node-name>
      <jdbc-zipfile-location>/home/db2inst1/sqllib/java12/db2java.zip
      </jdbc-zipfile-location>
    </install-info>
  </jdbc-driver>
</websphere-sa-config>
```

Figure 716. itsoJDBCDriver.xml

Users may choose any arbitrary name that does not already exist within the WebSphere administrative database for the jdbc-driver name. The implementation class and the url-prefix need to reflect that used by the selected database. Currently DB2, Oracle, Sybase and InstantDB are supported by WebSphere V3.5.

The XML provided in Figure 716 also performs the action of installing the JDBC driver, starting at line <install-info>. Users will have to customize these values for their respective systems.

Install the JDBC driver with:

```
XMLConfig.sh -adminNodeName riscwas2 -import itsoJDBCDriver.xml
```

21.6.3 Creating a new DataSource

Once a suitable JDBC driver has been installed, a DataSource can be configured to use that driver. This is demonstrated in Figure 717. As the location of the DataSource is similar to that of the JDBC driver, underneath the WebSphere administrative domain, the data-source create action is implemented directly after the <websphere-sa-config> tag. Figure 717 creates a data-source named “ITSO DataSource”, where the actual database name is “itso”, using the jdbc-driver-name from Figure 716 on page 885. All other values are the defaults.

Create the DataSource with:

```
XMLConfig.sh -adminNodeName riscwas2 -import itsoDataSource.xml
```

```
<?xml version="1.0"?>
<!DOCTYPE websphere-sa-config SYSTEM
"$XMLConfigDTDLocation$$dsep$bin$dsep$xmlconfig.dtd">

<websphere-sa-config>
<data-source name="ITSO DataSource" action="create">
    <database-name>itso</database-name>
    <jdbc-driver-name>anotherJDBCDriver</jdbc-driver-name>
    <minimum-pool-size>1</minimum-pool-size>
    <maximum-pool-size>10</maximum-pool-size>
    <connection-timeout>120000</connection-timeout>
    <idle-timeout>180000</idle-timeout>
    <orphan-timeout>1800000</orphan-timeout>
</data-source>
</websphere-sa-config
```

Figure 717. itsoDataSource.xml

21.6.4 Creating a new application server

Figure 718 on page 887 creates a new application server named “ITSO App Server”. Since the application server exists under a node, we first specify the locate action on the node element. This locates the node called “riscwas2” before creating our application server.

You will recall that it is valid to specify the update action, rather than the create action, as update will revert to create if the object does not yet exist in the administrative database.

```
<?xml version="1.0"?>
<!DOCTYPE websphere-sa-config SYSTEM
"$XMLConfigDTDLocation$$dsep$bin$dsep$xmlconfig.dtd">

<websphere-sa-config>
  <node name="riscwas2" action="locate">
    <application-server name="ITSO App Server" action="update">
      <executable>java</executable>
      <command-line-arguments/>
      <environment/>
      <user-id></user-id>
      <group-id></group-id>
      <working-directory></working-directory>
      <umask>18</umask>
      <stdin></stdin>
      <stdout>/usr/WebSphere/AppServer/logs/ITSOASstdout.log</stdout>
      <stderr>/usr/WebSphere/AppServer/logs/ITSOASstderr.log</stderr>
      <process-priority>20</process-priority>
      <maximum-startup-attempts>2</maximum-startup-attempts>
      <ping-interval>60</ping-interval>
      <ping-timeout>200</ping-timeout>
      <ping-initial-timeout>300</ping-initial-timeout>
      <trace-specification></trace-specification>
      <trace-output></trace-output>
      <transaction-log-file></transaction-log-file>
      <olt-enabled>false</olt-enabled>
      <system-properties/>
      <debug-enabled>false</debug-enabled>
      <transaction-timeout>120</transaction-timeout>
<transaction-inactivity-timeout>60000</transaction-inactivity-timeout>
      <thread-pool-size>20</thread-pool-size>
      <security-enabled>false</security-enabled>
    </application-server>
  </node>
</websphere-sa-config>
```

Figure 718. itsoAS.xml

When using XMLConfig in Figure 718, the only values you need to alter are the parent node name, the application-server name and the stdout and stderr log file names. All the other elements can be further customized, but are provided here with their default values.

21.6.5 Creating a new EJB container

Extending an application server to accommodate an EJB container is a necessary action if you are going to deploy enterprise beans. Figure 719 creates an EJB container named “ITSO Container”, only after first locating the node named “riscwas2” and the application-server named “ITSO App Server”.

With an EJB container it is possible to set the DataSource and user ID and password on the container object itself. EJBs then deployed in the container will then inherit these values, unless they have their own DataSource and user ID and password defined.

```
<?xml version="1.0"?>
<!DOCTYPE websphere-sa-config SYSTEM
"$XMLConfigDTDLocation$$dsep$bin$dsep$xmlconfig.dtd">

<websphere-sa-config>
  <node name="riscwas2" action="locate">
    <application-server name="ITSO App Server" action="locate">
      <container name="ITSO Container" action="update">
        <user-id>itso</user-id>
        <password>itsoitso</password>
        <cache-config>
          <size>2047</size>
          <soft-limit>2000</soft-limit>
          <hard-limit>2047</hard-limit>
          <sweep-interval>1000</sweep-interval>
          <passivation-directory></passivation-directory>
        </cache-config>
        <data-source name="ITSO DataSource"/>
      </container>
    </application-server>
  </node>
</websphere-sa-config>
```

Figure 719. itsoCon.xml

If you choose not to set the user ID and password, then replace <user-id>itso</user-id> with <user-id></user-id> and <password>itsoitso</password> with <password></password>.

If you choose not to configure the DataSource on the container then drop the <data-source name="ITSO DataSource"/> line entirely.

21.6.6 Creating a new servlet engine

Shown in Figure 720 is the XML necessary to create a servlet engine beneath the newly created application server “ITSO App Server”. As the XML implements an OSE transport queue for the servlet engine, it is imperative that -1 is specified for the transport-port element. This will enable WebSphere to choose the next available free port for the protocol. Alternatively, if a port number is known to be free, it can be substituted here. It is also necessary to specify a unique queue-name for the servlet engine. This can be checked against the current values in use, found in the queues.properties file under <WAS_HOME>/temp directory.

```
<?xml version="1.0"?>
<!DOCTYPE websphere-sa-config SYSTEM
"$XMLConfigDTDLocation$$dsep$bin$dsep$xmlconfig.dtd">
<websphere-sa-config>
  <node name="riscwas2" action="locate">
    <application-server name="ITSO App Server" action="locate">
      <servlet-engine name="ITSO Servlet Engine" action="update">
      <maximum-connections>25</maximum-connections>
      <transport-port>-1</transport-port>
      <transport-type name="ose">
      <ose-transport>
         <link-type>local</link-type>
         <log-file-mask trace="false" inform="false" warning="false"
         error="true"/>
         <queue-name>ibmoselink2</queue-name>
         <clone-index>1</clone-index>
         <native-log-file>native.log</native-log-file>
      </ose-transport>
      </transport-type>
      </servlet-engine>
    </application-server>
  </node>
</websphere-sa-config>
```

Figure 720. itsoSE.xml

Creating a servlet engine with the XML provided in Figure 720 will also automatically generate a User Profile Manager and Session Manager under the servlet engine and a RemoteSRP bean under the associated EJB container, as created in Figure 719 on page 888.

Note that if you use Servlet 2.2/JSP 1.1 support, see 21.6.8.1, “Creating a new servlet engine for Servlet 2.2/JSP 1.1” on page 891.

21.6.7 Creating a new Web application

The XML provided in Figure 721 constructs a Web application called "ITSO Web Application" below the parent servlet engine object "ITSO Servlet Engine". The document root and classpath correlate directly with the location of the web and servlet directories on the local operating system. Configuration of the Web application path is achieved by setting the root-uri. Any values here needs to be prefixed by the virtual host name.

```
<?xml version="1.0"?>
<!DOCTYPE websphere-sa-config SYSTEM
"$XMLConfigDTDLocation$$dsep$bin$dsep$xmlconfig.dtd">

<websphere-sa-config>
  <node name="riscwas2" action="locate">
    <application-server name="ITSO App Server" action="locate">
     <servlet-engine name="ITSO Servlet Engine" action="locate">
      <web-application name="ITSO Web Application" action="update">
         <description>ITSO Web Application</description>
         <document-root>/usr/WebSphere/AppServer/hosts/default_host/IT
         SOWebApp/web</document-root>
         <classpath>
         <pathvalue=""/>
         </classpath>
         <error-page></error-page>
         <filter-list/>
         <group-attributes/>
         <auto-reload>true</auto-reload>
         <reload-interval>9000</reload-interval>
         <enabled>true</enabled>
         <root-uri>default_host/webapp/ITSOWebApp</root-uri>
         <shared-context>false</shared-context>
         <shared-context-jndi-name>SrdSrvltCtxHome</shared-context-jnd
         i-name>
      </web-application>
      </servlet-engine>
    </application-server>
  </node>
</websphere-sa-config>
```

Figure 721. itsoWebApp.xml

Note that if you use Servlet 2.2/JSP 1.1 support, see 21.6.8.2, "Creating a new Web application for servlet 2.2/JSP 1.1" on page 891.

21.6.8 Supporting Servlet 2.2 and JSP 1.1 APIs

Since WebSphere V3.5.2 supports Servlet 2.2/JSP 1.1, additional attributes needs to added in <servlet-engine> and <web-application> for Servlet2.2/JSP1.1 support.

21.6.8.1 Creating a new servlet engine for Servlet 2.2/JSP 1.1

To create a new servlet engine for Servlet 2.2/JSP1.1 support, you need to specify <servlet-mode>, for example,

```
<servlet-engine>
   <servlet-mode> [compliance or compatibility mode] </servlet-mode>
   <!-- servlet-mode takes an integer, please specify 0 for
   JSP1.1/Servlet2.2 compliance and 1 for WebSphere 3.5 Compatibility mode
   -->
</servlet-engine>
```

21.6.8.2 Creating a new Web application for servlet 2.2/JSP 1.1

To create a new Web application for Servlet 2.2/JSP1.1 support, you need to specify <error-page-j2ee>, <mime-mapping>, <welcome-file-list>, and <tag-lib>, for example,

```
<web-application>
   <error-page-j2ee>
      <error-code/> | <exception-type/>
      <location>
   </error-page-j2ee>
   <mime-mapping>
      <extension/>
      <mime-type/>
   </mime-mapping>
   <welcome-file-list>
      <welcome-file/>
      <welcome-file/>
      ......
   </welcome-file-list>
   <tag-lib>
      <tag-lib-uri/>
      <tag-lib-location/>
   </tag-lib>
</web-application>
```

21.6.9 Creating a new servlet

XMLConfig is a convenient method for deploying servlets under a Web application in WebSphere. Figure 722 demonstrates the addition of the JSP 1.0 processor servlet to the Web application “ITSO Web Application”. For each subsequent servlet to be deployed under the ITSO Web Application, the code between the <servlet></servlet> tags needs only to differ. The uri-paths inherit the root-uri prefix as defined on the parent Web application object.

Servlets that you may choose or indeed need to add, in addition to your own, include the Error Reporting Facility servlet, the File Serving Enabler, the Auto-Invoker and the JSP 1.0 Processor.

Install the servlet with:

```
XMLConfig.sh -adminNodeName riscwas2 -import itsoServlet2a.xml
```

```
<?xml version="1.0"?>
<!DOCTYPE websphere-sa-config SYSTEM
"$XMLConfigDTDLocation$$dsep$bin$dsep$xmlconfig.dtd">

<websphere-sa-config>
  <node name="riscwas2" action="locate">
    <application-server name="ITSO App Server" action="locate">
      <servlet-engine name="ITSO Servlet Engine" action="locate">
        <web-application name="ITSO Web Application" action="locate">
          <servlet name="jsp10" action="update">
            <description>JSP 1.0 support servlet</description>
            <code>com.sun.jsp.runtime.JspServlet</code>
            <init-parameters/>
            <load-at-startup>true</load-at-startup>
            <debug-mode>false</debug-mode>
            <uri-paths>
              <uri value="*.jsp"/>
              <uri value="*.jsv"/>
              <uri value="*.jsw"/>
            </uri-paths>
            <enabled>true</enabled>
          </servlet>
        </web-application>
      </servlet-engine>
    </application-server>
  </node>
</websphere-sa-config>
```

Figure 722. itsoServlet2a.xml

21.6.10 Creating a new EJB

XMLConfig allows users to quickly install both deployed and deployable EJBs into a selected EJB container. WebSphere will first convert any deployable EJBs to the deployed state, before their installation to the selected container. The XML for this scenario is shown in Figure 723. Compared to EJB deployment with the administrative console, XMLConfig EJB deployment is a one-step process. Since XMLConfig will handle the deployment of a deployable EJB, it is necessary to specify the location for the resulting deployed EJB. This location is configured with the use of the <deployed-jar-directory> tags. This line can remain when the jar-file specified is a deployed EJB. It is, however, imperative that the correct JNDI home name is set for both deployed and deployable EJBs under the <home-name> element.

```
<?xml version="1.0"?>
<!DOCTYPE websphere-sa-config SYSTEM
"$XMLConfigDTDLocation$$dsep$bin$dsep$xmlconfig.dtd">

<websphere-sa-config>
  <node name="riscwas2" action="update">
   <deployed-jar-directory>/usr/WebSphere/AppServer/deployedEJBs</deplo
   yed-jar-directory>
    <application-server name="ITSO App Server" action="locate">
      <container name="ITSO Container" action="locate">
        <ejb name="Counter" action="update">
         <jar-file>/usr/WebSphere/AppServer/deployableEJBs/Counter.jar
         </jar-file>
          <home-name>Counter</home-name>
          <user-id></user-id>
          <password></password>
          <create-db-table>false</create-db-table>
          <find-for-update>true</find-for-update>
          <minimum-pool-size>5</minimum-pool-size>
          <maximum-pool-size>500</maximum-pool-size>
          <primary-key-check>true</primary-key-check>
          <db-exclusive-access>false</db-exclusive-access>
        </ejb>
       </container>
    </application-server>
  </node>
</websphere-sa-config
```

Figure 723. itsoDeployableEJB.xml

21.6.11 XMLConfig variable substitution

With variable substitution it is possible to quickly supplement a value into an otherwise static XML document when invoking the actual `XMLConfig` command. This has two practical uses:

1. With the creation a generic XML document, such as the EJB deployment example in Figure 723 on page 893, it would be convenient to specify the EJB WebSphere object name, the JNDI home name and the associated JAR file at the time of executing the `XMLConfig` command. This way, multiple EJBs could be deployed without editing the XML document each time.
2. It offers the WebSphere administrator the ability to archive XML exports, without the security risk of publishing an unencrypted WebSphere password. Variable substitution is actioned on the server-password, the ltpa-password, ldap-bindpwd and on each enterprise application where security has been enabled.

To convert the itsoEJB.xml file as provided in Figure 723 on page 893 to use variable substitution, simply replace the following lines:

```
<ejb name="Counter" action="update">
```

for

```
<ejb name="$ejbname$" action="update">
```

```
<jar-file>/usr/WebSphere/AppServer/deployableEJBs/Counter.jar</jar-file>
```

for

```
<jar-file>/usr/WebSphere/AppServer/deployableEJBs/$jarfile$</jar-file>
```

```
<home-name>Counter</home-name>
```

for

```
<home-name>$homename$</home-name>
```

XMLConfig can now be invoked specifying differing EJB WebSphere object names, EJB JAR files and JNDI home names.

```
./XMLConfig.sh -adminNodeName riscwas2 -import itsoEJB3.xml -substitute
"ejbname=Container;jarfile=Container.jar;homename=Container"
```

21.6.12 XMLConfig model and clone support

WebSphere V3.5 XMLConfig now supports the createclone, associateclone and disassociateclone actions. Administrators will recall that cloning only supersedes the action of first creating a model reference. With the administrative console it is possible to recursively convert an application server to a model and then create an initial clone from the Model Properties menu.

Although the application server specifics have been omitted in Figure 724, the XML demonstrates the effective encapsulation of the application-server between the model <attributes> and </attributes> tags. As the XML will be used to create a model application server, rather than an actual application server, the create action is only performed on the <model> element. Finally, the <mode-full-name> specifies a reference that subsequent clones will use to locate their respective model counterparts. This is a hierarchical value that concatenates each sub-element name to the previous parent model-full-name.

```
<?xml version="1.0"?>
<!DOCTYPE websphere-sa-config SYSTEM
"$XMLConfigDTDLocation$$dsep$bin$dsep$xmlconfig.dtd">

<websphere-sa-config>
<model name="ITSO2ASModel" action="create">
  <type>Application Server</type>
   <attributes>
    <application-server name="ITSO2 App Server">
      ...
      ...
    </application-server>
   </attributes>
  <model-full-name>/ModelHome:ITSO2ASModel/</model-full-name>
   ...
</model>
</websphere-sa-config>
```

Figure 724. itsoModel.xml

Models, similar to JDBC drivers and DataSources, are positioned beneath the WebSphere administrative domain. For this reason model creation takes place immediately after the <websphere-sa-config> tag. WebSphere V3.5 PTF 2 extends XMLConfig support, allowing users to create a model with numerous EJBs deployed per EJB container. Similarly, PTF 2 supports XMLConfig export and import options, when models contain deployed EJBs.

21.6.12.1 Creating a new clone

The newly supported createclone action is demonstrated in Figure 726. Here, a cloned application server named “ITSO AS Clone3”, is created under the node “riscwas2”. The various subelements of the application server are also cloned in the XML, with the cloned servlet engine, cloned Web application, and cloned servlet directly lifted to form Figure 726 on page 897.

```
<?xml version="1.0"?>
<!DOCTYPE websphere-sa-config SYSTEM
"$XMLConfigDTDLocation$$dsep$bin$dsep$xmlconfig.dtd">

<websphere-sa-config>
<node name="riscwas2" action="update">

   <application-server name="ITSO AS Clone3" action="createclone">
    <model-full-name>/ModelHome:ITSOModel/</model-full-name>

          <container name="ITSO Container Clone3" action="createclone">
          <model-full-name>/ModelHome:ITSOModel/ModelHome:ITSOContainer
          /</model-full-name>

          <ejb name="Counter" action="createclone">
          <model-full-name>/ModelHome:ITSOModel/ModelHome:ITSOContainer
          /ModelHome:Counter/</model-full-name>
          </ejb>
          </container>
          ...
          (see Figure 726 on page 897 for this section)
          ...
    </application-server>
  </node>
</websphere-sa-config>
```

Figure 725. itsoClone.xml

The attribute values for each cloned element are obtained from the original model reference with the use of the <model-full-name> tags, as shown in Figure 725. The exception to this rule is the servlet engine, which by virtue of the function that it provides in WebSphere, needs to be configured listening on a different OSE port number from that of any peer.

When cloning a servlet engine it is vital that the OSE transport port is modified to the next available free port number, as shown in Figure 726. Similarly, the queue-name and clone-index values must be incremented in order to avoid clashing with any existing parameters found in the <WAS_HOME>/temp/queues.properties file. After XMLConfig is used to create a clone, it is necessary to stop and start the parent model to update this file.

```
<servlet-engine name="ITSO Servlet Engine Clone3" action="createclone">
   <model-full-name>/ModelHome:ITSOModel/ModelHome:ITSO Servlet
   Engine/</model-full-name>
   <maximum-connections>25</maximum-connections>
   <transport-port>8995</transport-port>
   <transport-type name="ose">
      <ose-transport>
      <link-type>local</link-type>
      <log-file-mask trace="false" inform="false" warning="false"
      error="true"/>
      <queue-name>ibmoselink3</queue-name>
      <clone-index>3</clone-index>
      <native-log-file>/usr/WebSphere/AppServer/logs/ITSOServletEngineC
      lone3.244_native.log</native-log-file>
      </ose-transport>
   </transport-type>

      <web-application name="ITSO Web Application Clone3"
      action="createclone">
      <model-full-name>/ModelHome:ITSOModel/ModelHome:ITSO Servlet
      Engine/ModelHome:ITSO Web Application/</model-full-name>

         <servlet name="file" action="createclone">
         <model-full-name>/ModelHome:ITSOModel/ModelHome:ITSO Servlet
         Engine/ModelHome:ITSO Web
         Application/ModelHome:file/</model-full-name>
         </servlet>
      </web-application>
</servlet-engine>
```

Figure 726. itsoClone.xml: servlet engine, Web application and servlet

The cloned session manager, user profile manager, and remoteSRP bean have been omitted from Figure 725 on page 896 and Figure 726.

21.6.12.2 Clone disassociation and association

Disassociating a clone from a model is the action of creating an independent application server, void of any control from the model. This is potentially useful if an administrator wishes to delete a model and associated clones, but wishes to keep one application server with associated elements for further use. Clone association is the reverse of disassociation, and can be used to affiliate the stand-alone application server back with the model.

Figure 727 demonstrates the disassociation of an application server clone named "ITSO App Server Clone4" from the model "ITSOModel". For each of the elements that constitute the application server, such as the EJB container and EJB, it is necessary to specify the model reference with the use of the <model-full-name> tags. This will generate a free-standing application server, again void of any control from the model.

```
<?xml version="1.0"?>
<!DOCTYPE websphere-sa-config SYSTEM
"$XMLConfigDTDLocation$$dsep$bin$dsep$xmlconfig.dtd">

<websphere-sa-config>
<node name="riscwas2" action="update">
   <application-server name="ITSO App Server Clone4"
   action="disassociateclone">
   <model-full-name>/ModelHome:ITSOModel/</model-full-name>
      <container name="ITSO Container Clone4"
      action="disassociateclone">
      <model-full-name>/ModelHome:ITSOModel/ModelHome:ITSO
      Container/</model-full-name>
         <ejb name="Counter" action="disassociateclone">
         <model-full-name>/ModelHome:ITSOModel/ModelHome:ITSO
         Container/ModelHome:Counter/</model-full-name>
         </ejb>
      </container>
      ...
      ...
   </application-server>
</node>
</websphere-sa-config>
```

Figure 727. itsoDisClone.xml

21.6.13 XMLConfig and security

XMLConfig now ships supporting the creation of enterprise applications, thus allowing the WebSphere administrator to provide security on a previously defined application server. The figures that follow in this section highlight the XML necessary to implement security on one such application server. Not discussed here is the enablement of WebSphere general security, which must be undertaken prior to creating the enterprise application example.

The following steps are required: 1. Enterprise application creation; 2. New method group creation; 3. EJB and URI method group mapping; and finally 4. Method group permission assignment.

In Figure 728, an enterprise application named "ITSO Ent App" is created in the WebSphere administrative domain. For each EJB or URI object that exists under the previously defined "ITSO Web Application" Web application, an element needs to be created. The latter can be a servlet, JSP or HMTL file. In this case, the URI /webapp/ITSOWebApp will satisfy HTTP requests for the file serving servlet.

```
<?xml version="1.0"?>
<!DOCTYPE websphere-sa-config SYSTEM
"$XMLConfigDTDLocation$$dsep$xmlconfig.dtd">

<websphere-sa-config>
  <enterprise-application name="ITSO Ent App" action="create">
    <ejb name="Counter"/>
    <uri name="/webapp/ITSOWebApp"/>
    <web-application name="ITSO Web Application"/>
  </enterprise-application>
  <enterprise-application-security action="update">
    <enterprise-application name="ITSO Ent App"/>
    <realm-name>ITSO</realm-name>
    <challenge-type ssl-enabled="false">
      <basic-challenge/>
    </challenge-type>
  </enterprise-application-security>
</websphere-sa-config>
```

Figure 728. itsoEntApp.xml

It is also possible to configure WebSphere security so that applications run with the effective authentication credentials of a specific user. This, if used, would be configured under the <enterprise-application-security> tag.

21.6.13.1 Creating a new method-group

Method-groups are used by WebSphere to associate an individual or collection of EJB methods / HTTP actions to a specific permission directive. For example, one method-group can hold read permissions, while another can write permissions and both can contain any number of objects.

The XML in Figure 729 was used to create an additional method-group called “ITSOMethods”.

```
<?xml version="1.0"?>
<!DOCTYPE websphere-sa-config SYSTEM
"$XMLConfigDTDLocation$$dsep$bin$dsep$xmlconfig.dtd">
<websphere-sa-config>
   <method-group>ITSOMethods</method-group>
</websphere-sa-config>
```

Figure 729. itsoMethodG.xml

21.6.13.2 EJB method group mapping

Next, if security is to be implement on an EJB, it is necessary to associate each EJB method with a WebSphere method group. Users can specify methods exactly what EJB methods are defined on the EJB object prior to using XMLConfig. Figure 730 shows the association between the EJB method “ejbCount” and the “ITSOMethods” method-group.

```
<?xml version="1.0"?>
<!DOCTYPE websphere-sa-config SYSTEM
"$XMLConfigDTDLocation$$dsep$xmlconfig.dtd">

<websphere-sa-config>
  <ejb-security>
    <ejb name="Counter"/>
      <method-group-mapping method="ejbCount"
      method-group="ITSOMethods"/>
      ...
      ...
      ...
      <run-as-mode-mapping method="*" run-as-mode="system"/>
   </ejb-security>
</websphere-sa-config>
```

Figure 730. itsoEJBMeth.xml

In WebSphere V3.5.2, users also can specify all the methods which should belong to a particular method group. This would not require the users to know (or specify) all the EJB methods in advance if users want to add al the methods to a mehod-group. Figure 731 shows the association between the "Counter" enterprise bean and the "ITSOMethodsAll" method-group.

```
<?xml version="1.0"?>
<!DOCTYPE websphere-sa-config SYSTEM
"$XMLConfigDTDLocation$$dsep$xmlconfig.dtd">

<websphere-sa-config>
  <ejb-security>
    <ejb name="Counter"/>
      <method-group-mapping-all method-group="ITSOMethodsAll"/>
      ...
      ...
      ...
      <run-as-mode-mapping method="*" run-as-mode="system"/>
   </ejb-security>
</websphere-sa-config>
```

Figure 731. tsoEJBMethAll.xml

21.6.13.3 URI method group mapping

WebSphere provides a set of predefined methods for dealing with HTTP requests, reflecting the possible actions that can be performed by any Web browser. Similarly, a set of predefined method-groups are configured to manage these HTTP methods. Figure 732 on page 902 shows the correlation between such HTTP method-group maps being applied to the URI objects: "/webapp/ITSOWebApp/" and "/webapp/ITSOWebApp/*.jsp".

The URI names in Figure 732 on page 902 reflect the URI a client will enter into their Web browser. The URI can be more specific than that shown in the example, thus limiting the URI requests down to individual servlets, JSPs or HTML pages.

```
<?xml version="1.0"?>
<!DOCTYPE websphere-sa-config SYSTEM
"$XMLConfigDTDLocation$$dsep$xmlconfig.dtd">

<websphere-sa-config>
   <uri-security>
      <uri name="/webapp/ITSOWebApp/"/>
      <method-group-mapping method="HTTP_GET"
      method-group="ReadMethods"/>
      <method-group-mapping method="HTTP_POST"
      method-group="ReadMethods"/>
      <method-group-mapping method="HTTP_PUT"
      method-group="WriteMethods"/>
      <method-group-mapping method="HTTP_DELETE"
      method-group="RemoveMethods"/>
   </uri-security>
   <uri-security>
      <uri name="/webapp/ITSOWebApp/*.jsp"/>
      <method-group-mapping method="HTTP_GET"
      method-group="ReadMethods"/>
      <method-group-mapping method="HTTP_POST"
      method-group="ReadMethods"/>
      <method-group-mapping method="HTTP_PUT"
      method-group="WriteMethods"/>
      <method-group-mapping method="HTTP_DELETE"
      method-group="RemoveMethods"/>
   </uri-security>
</websphere-sa-config>
```

Figure 732. itsoUri.xml

21.6.13.4 Method group permissions

The final step when configuring WebSphere enterprise application security is to actually specify the permissions on each method-group. Once established, the permissions will hold for each member of the method-group, be it an EJB method or a URI method (HTTP action).

```
<?xml version="1.0"?>
<!DOCTYPE websphere-sa-config SYSTEM
"$XMLConfigDTDLocation$$dsep$xmlconfig.dtd">

<websphere-sa-config>
  <permission app-name="ITSO Ent App" method-group="ITSOMethods">
    <access-id>*AllUsers</access-id>
  </permission>
  <permission app-name="ITSO Ent App" method-group="ReadMethods">
    <access-id>*AllUsers</access-id>
  </permission>
  <permission app-name="ITSO Ent App" method-group="WriteMethods">
    <access-id>*AllUsers</access-id>
  </permission>
  <permission app-name="ITSO Ent App" method-group="RemoveMethods">
    <access-id>*AllUsers</access-id>
  </permission>
  <permission app-name="ITSO Ent App" method-group="CreateMethods">
    <access-id>*AllUsers</access-id>
  </permission>
</websphere-sa-config>
```

Figure 733. itsoPermiss.xml

In Figure 733, the security permissions for each method-group are defined, based on the authentication mechanism defined under the WebSphere general security policy. Each method-group shown in the example has been set to allow all authenticated users permission to access the underlying EJB or URI methods. Alternatively, method groups can grant permission to specific users or groups, or waive authentication entirely.

Note

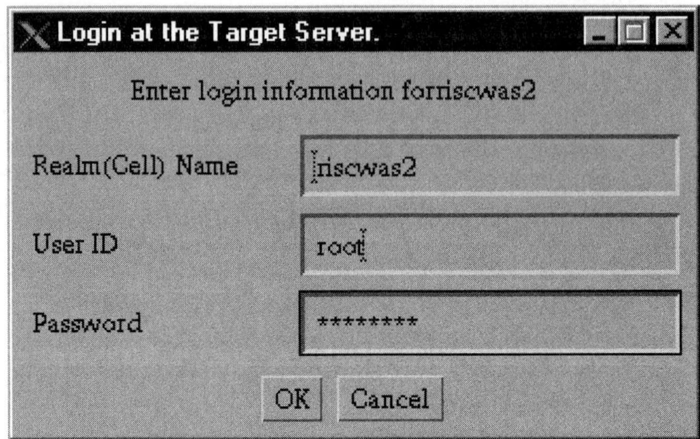

Enabling WebSphere general security will prompt users with a GUI login box for the server-password each time the XMLConfig command is run.

One possible workaround for disabling the GUI login challenge box when executing XMLConfig commands is to edit the sas.client.props file, found under the <WAS_HOME>/properties directory. Change com.ibm.CORBA.loginSource from prompt to properties and modify the loginUserid / loginPassword respectively.

21.6.14 Starting point for generating XML for use with XMLConfig

Because the majority of the examples provided in this chapter can be replicated using the administrative console, a suggested starting point when in doubt is to create a like object via the administrative console. Take a full XML export before and after issuing the command, as shown in Figure 734 on page 905, or with XMLConfig.

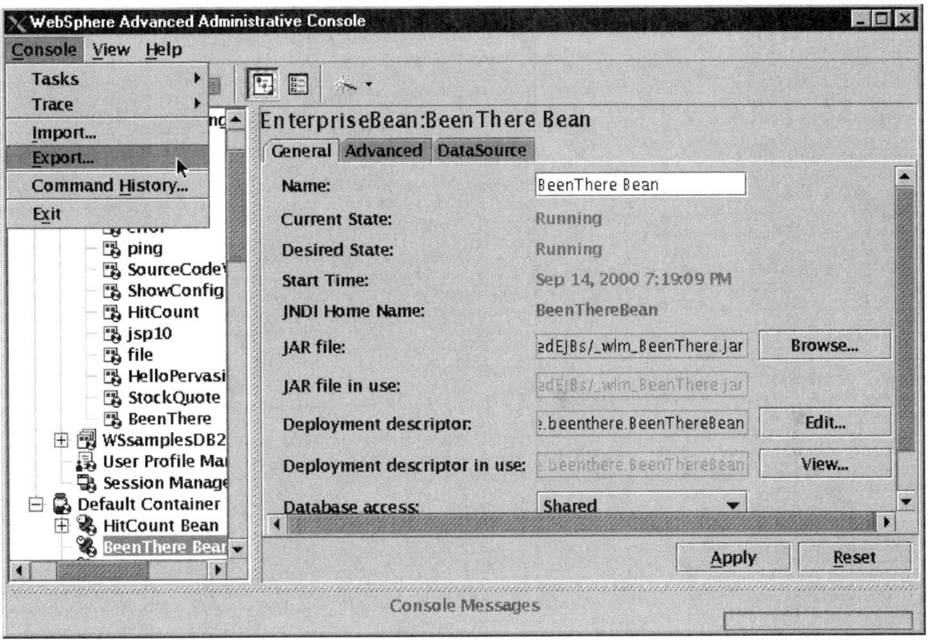

Figure 734. Administrative console XML export

Chapter 22. WebSphere sample programs

WebSphere V3.5 now ships with a full suite of samples that offer the WebSphere administrator a starting point upon which to build. For new administrators, deploying the samples will provide familiarization with the necessary configuration steps, and a template or topology hierarchy against which custom application servers and associated elements can be compared.

These samples cover JSPs, servlets, and JavaBeans and are available on all platforms. WebSphere Advanced Edition, except when deployed on Linux, offers an additional set of EJB samples. Finally, WebSphere V3.5 PTF 2 extends sample support beyond the original DB2 prerequisite, to Oracle and Sybase databases.

22.1 How to obtain the samples?

One guaranteed way of obtaining the samples is to select the **Samples** option during the WebSphere Application Server Custom Installation step, as shown in Figure 735. It is also necessary to select the **Configure default server** option, since the samples require such an application server for installation.

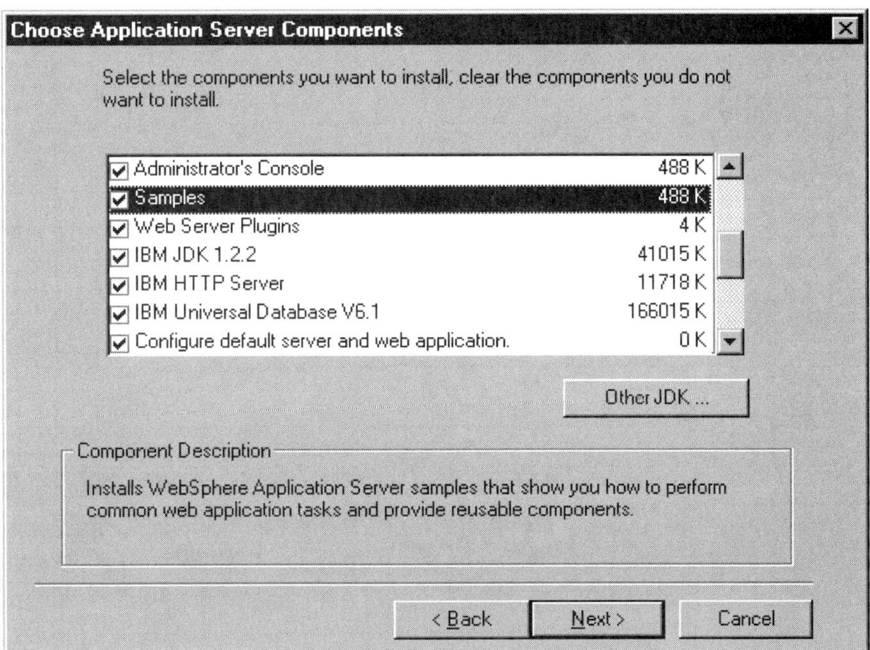

Figure 735. Component selection window during custom installation

22.2 WebSphere samples matrix

There are three distinct groups of samples that ship with WebSphere V3.5, each being deployed under the Default Server application server when installed. Each has a different Web application name.

The first, the examples Web application, is implemented as an integral part of the Default Server application server, and includes a number of samples for initially testing the integrity of the overall WebSphere V3.5 install. The second Web application, the WSsamplesIDB_app sample set, is based on the InstantDB database and is available across all supported platforms. Finally, the WSsamplesDB2_app Web application sample set is available on all platforms except Linux and can be installed on both the Standard and Advanced Editions of WebSphere V3.5. The only difference is that WebSphere Standard Edition will not support the EJB samples.

Table 46. WebSphere V3.5 samples matrix

Platform	Standard	Advanced	IDB	DB2	DB2 EJB	Oracle	Oracle EJB	Sybase	Sybase EJB
Linux	●		✓						
		●	✓						
AIX	●		✓	✓		✓		✓	
		●	✓	✓	✓	✓	✓	✓	✓
Solaris	●		✓	✓		✓		✓	
		●	✓	✓	✓	✓	✓	✓	✓
HP-UX	●		✓	✓		✓		✓	
		●	✓	✓	✓	✓	✓	✓	✓
Windows	●		✓	✓		✓		✓	
		●	✓	✓	✓	✓	✓	✓	✓

WebSphere V3.5 PTF2 extends the WSsamplesDB2_app sample set to support Oracle and Sybase databases. Applying PTF2 as a delta install, however, does not automatically change the WSsamplesDB2_app Web application name to reflect the new Oracle and Sybase support. Users can, nevertheless, modify the Web application name manually.

22.3 WebSphere samples installation

For most WebSphere administrators the installation of either the WSsamplesIDB_app Web application or the WSsamplesDB2_app Web application will appear transparent, being available the first time the administrative console is launched, as shown in Figure 738 on page 911.

The actual specifications for the Web applications are imported from two individual XML documents, invoked by a directive in the initial_setup.config file, found under the <WAS_HOME>/properties directory. The same initial_setup.config file is also responsible for importing the Default Server application server specifications into the WebSphere administrative database.

By default, administrators installing WebSphere V3.5 Advanced Edition and selecting the samples option will find the WSsamplesDB2_app Web application in their WebSphere topology, except on Linux. Likewise, administrators selecting the samples on a WebSphere V3.5 Standard Edition install will find the WSsamplesIDB_app Web application in their WebSphere topology.

However, WebSphere V3.5 Advanced Edition users are not restricted to just installing the WSsamplesDB2_app samples. Nor are Standard Edition users restricted to just the WSsamplesIDB_app samples. The only exception is Linux-based installs, where only the WSsamplesIDB_app samples ship regardless of the WebSphere ddition. Table 46 on page 908 documents the possible sample set support by platform, with extended support for Oracle and Sybase databases being applicable only once WebSphere V3.5 PTF2 is installed.

To enable both the WSsamplesDB2_app and the WSsamplesIDB_app samples on the same WebSphere V3.5 Advanced Edition install, users need to edit the initial_setup.config file, found under the <WAS_HOME>/properties directory. This step needs to be undertaken before the administrative server is started for the first time. On UNIX-based installs this is the action of executing the <WAS_HOME>/bin/startupServer.sh script. Locate the line that starts `<!--sample...`, and un-comment it, as shown in Figure 736 on page 910. The actual directory structure may, of course, be different from that shown in the example, depending on the given platform.

```
...
<config-file>/opt/WebSphere/AppServer/hosts/default_host/WSsamples_app/
WSsamples_app_create.xml</config-file>

<!--sampleIDB<config-file>/opt/WebSphere/AppServer/hosts/default_host/W
SsamplesID_app/WSsamplesIDB_app_create.xml</config-file>sampleIDB -->
...
```

Figure 736. initial_setup.config, before - WebSphere Advanced Edition

```
...
<config-file>/opt/WebSphere/AppServer/hosts/default_host/WSsamples_app/
WSsamples_app_create.xml</config-file>

<config-file>/opt/WebSphere/AppServer/hosts/default_host/WSsamplesID_ap
p/WSsamplesIDB_app_create.xml</config-file>
...
```

Figure 737. initial_setup.config, after - WebSphere Advanced Edition

Enabling the WSsamplesIDB_app samples on WebSphere V3.5 Advanced Edition also requires that the InstantDB database JAR files are added to the administrative server classpath. In the admin.config file, found in the <WAS_HOME>/bin/ directory, locate the com.ibm.ejs.sm.adminserver.classpath property, and add the following to the idb.jar file:

```
...
com.ibm.ejs.sm.adminserver.classpath=/opt/WebSphere/AppServer/lib/idb.j
ar:/opt/WebSphere/AppServer/...
...
```

For WebSphere V3.5 Standard Edition users wishing to enable the WSsamplesDB2_app samples, albeit without the EJB support, the principles of modifying the initial_setup.config file are exactly the same. This time, the comments are removed from around the WSsamples_app entry.

Once the administrative server, and indeed, the administrative console have been started, users will have to configure a JDBC driver and data source to run with the database samples included with the WSsamplesDB2_app Web application.

22.4 WebSphere samples location

Common to all Web applications is the logical framework of the underlying operating system directory structure that contains the same JSPs, servlets, Javabeans, and HTML pages that WebSphere uses:

- For the **examples** Web application you will find these under:

```
<WAS_HOME>/hosts/default_host/examples
```

- For the **WSsamplesDB2_app** Web application you will find these under:

```
<WAS_HOME>/hosts/default_host/WSsamples_app
```

- For the **WSsamplesIDB_app** Web application you will find these under:

```
<WAS_HOME>/hosts/default_host/WSsamplesIDB_app
```

The path is further subdivided between servlet and web directories, which correlate directly with the classpath and document root used by the Web application.

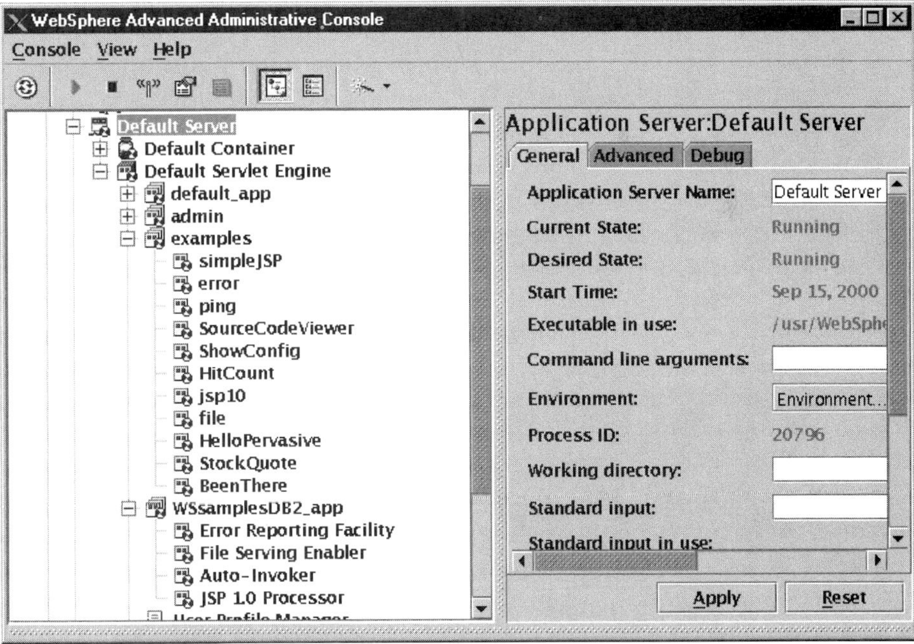

Figure 738. WebSphere Advanced Edition - WSsamplesDB2_app Web application

22.5 WebSphere WSsamplesDB2_app Web application

For WebSphere WSsamplesDB2_app Web application users there is now a redesigned HTML page that introduces the samples gallery. Here the samples are logically grouped by type and enable the user to quickly invoke a sample via a suitable browser.

Where:

```
http://<your_server>/WSsamples/index.html
```

There are three distinct categories of samples, with each category being slightly more complex.

- Level 1 - simple, no database required
- Level 2 - database required
- Level 3a - Enterprise JavaBeans - deployment
- Level 3b - Integrated YourCo example

With the exception of the Level 1 samples, it is necessary to configure a database and database source within WebSphere. WebSphere V3.5 PTF 2 extends sample support beyond the original DB2 prerequisite, to Oracle and Sybase databases, see Figure 739 on page 913 for database configuration details.

As a possible starting point for learning WebSphere programming, you may choose to modify the sample Java files provided under the WSsamplesDB2_app Web application home.

All the samples obviously require the Default Server to be operational.

22.6 Database configuration

The majority of the steps necessary to create a database and database source are documented at the WSsamples Web page (`http://<host_name>/WSsamples/index.html` or `http://<host_name>/WSsamplesIDB/indexhtml`). However, for added clarity the following remarks may prove useful.

The WSsamplesDB2_app samples, by default, uses the user ID wsdemo, with a password of wsdemo1 when accessing DB2. It is therefore necessary to create a user account and password on the system where the DB2 server is installed. Those not familiar with DB2 should note that authentication is performed against local operating system credentials.

With WebSphere V3.5 PTF2 and extended support for Oracle and Sybase databases. Part of the setup now includes creating a user ID of wsdemo with a password of wsdemo1 with sufficient authority, but no more, to populate the SAMPLE database, (or tablespace on Oracle).

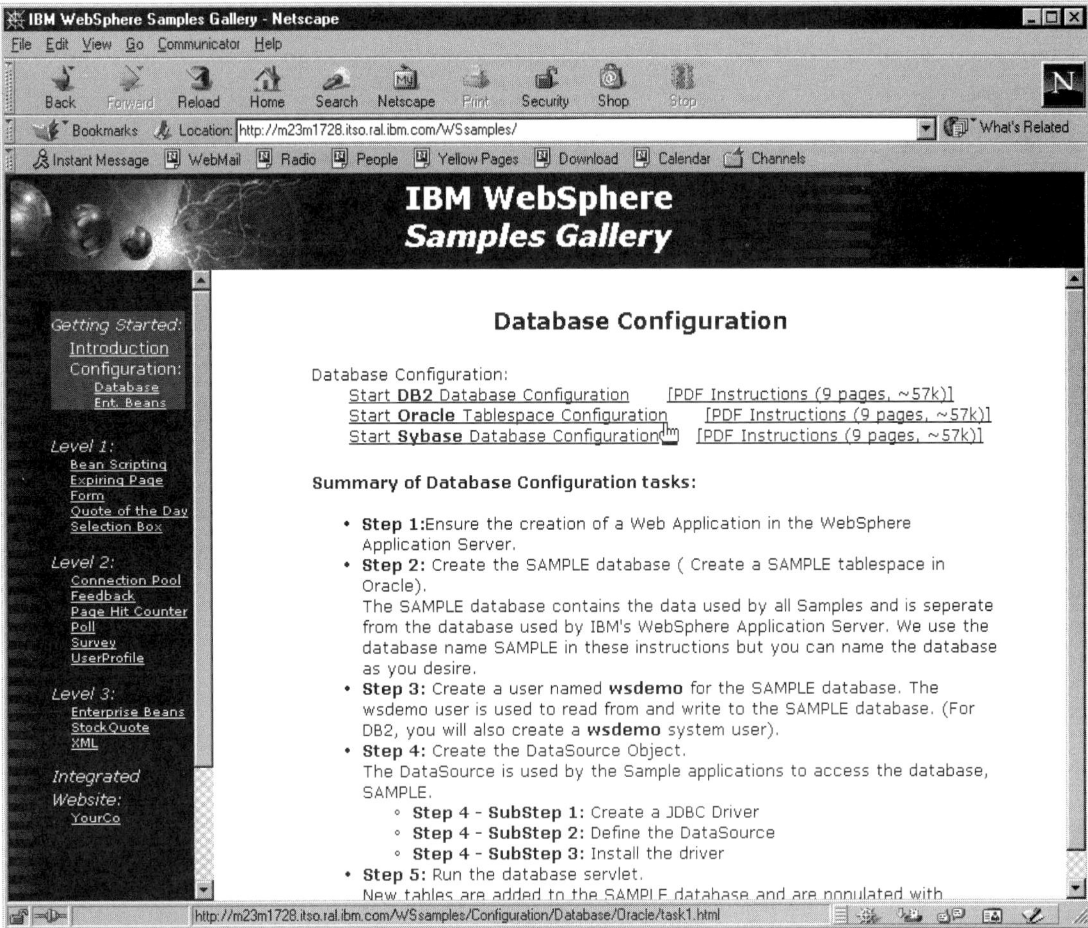

Figure 739. Sample database support ships with WebSphere V3.5.2

22.6.1 Checking database connectivity

It is a good practice to check database connectivity prior to configuring any WebSphere JDBC driver and data source.

```
#su - db2inst1
$db2
db2 =>connect to SAMPLE user wsdemo using wsdemo1
Database Connection Information

 Database server        = DB2/6000 7.1.0
 SQL authorization ID   = WSDEMO
 Local database alias   = SAMPLE

db2 =>
```

22.6.2 Defining a JDBC driver

The initial step in configuring database connectivity is to define the JDBC driver in WebSphere. This is achieved by changing the topology view to Type, selecting **JDBC Drivers** and with a right-click of the mouse button choosing **Create**, as shown in Figure 740.

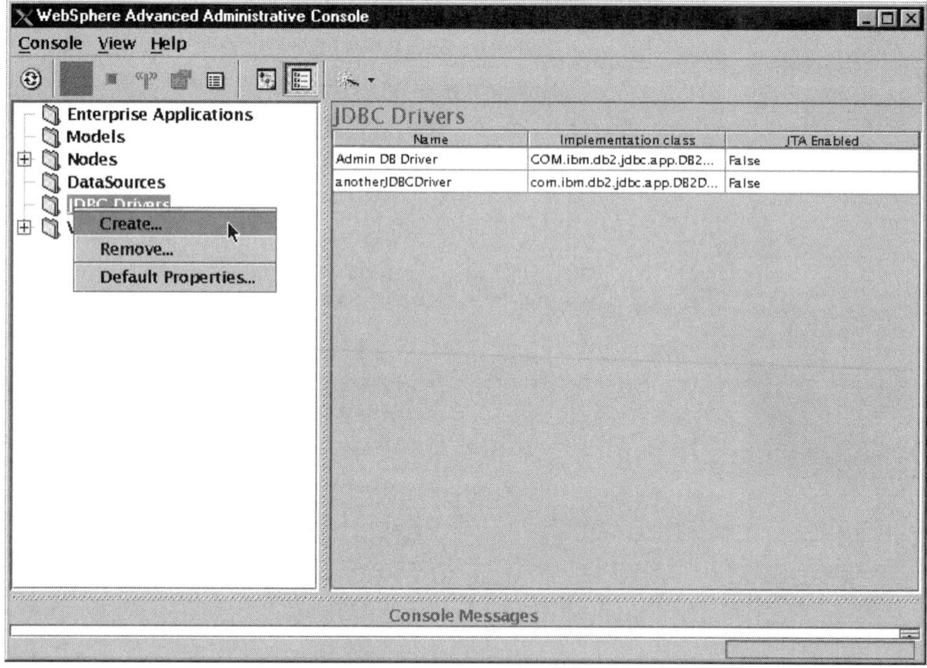

Figure 740. Defining a JDBC driver

Figure 740 also shows any previously configured JDBC drivers. Here, the two JDBC drivers, Admin DB Driver and anotherJDBCDriver, are both configured using the same DB2 JDBC implementation class.

Other options available here when defining an additional JDBC driver are Oracle, Sybase and InstantDB. Implementation classes are:

- com.ibm.db2.jdbc.app.DB2Driver
- oracle.jdbc.driver.OracleDriver
- com.ibm.as400.access.AS400JDBCDriver
- com.sybase.jdbc2.jdbc.SybDriver
- jdbc.idbDriver

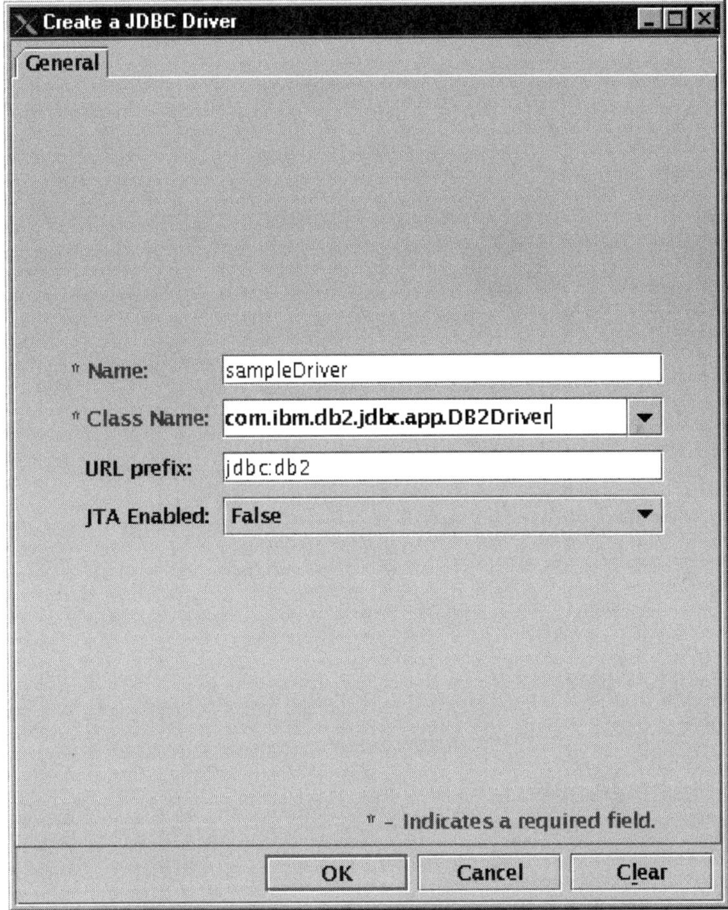

Figure 741. Creating a JDBC driver for the WSsamplesDB2_app

After selecting an arbitrary name for the JDBC driver and com.ibm.db2.jdbc.app.DB2Driver for the implementation class, click **OK** as shown in Figure 741. This action will update the JDBC Drivers window, where the newly created driver will be seen alongside the driver for the WebSphere administration database, albeit with a different name.

22.6.3 Creating a data source

With WebSphere V3.5 the preferred manner for interacting with a database is via a JDBC 2.0 data source. This is a shift away from using the Connection Manager APIs, which will be removed in future releases. However, the use of data sources enables connection pooling utilizing the IBM implementation of the class.

To create the necessary data source for the WSsamplesDB2_app Web application, change the Topology view to tree in the administrative console and select **DataSources**. With a right-click of the mouse button choose **Create** and proceed by defining the various fields. This is demonstrated in Figure 742.

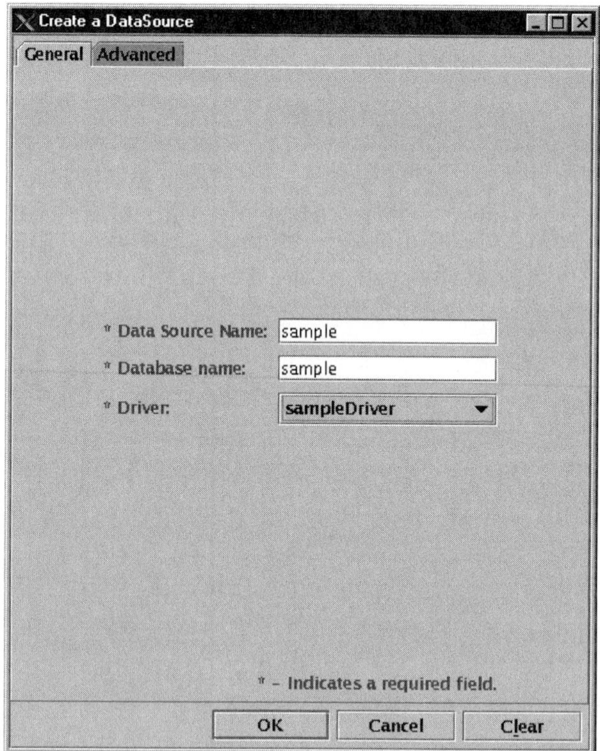

Figure 742. Creating a data source for the WSsamplesDB2_app

Note

Ensure that the data source name configured here is indeed "sample", since all of the compiled Java class samples have been hard coded with jdbc/sample.

The database name should reflect the actual name of the database within DB2. The DB2 command `list database directory` can be used to verify valid databases. For other databases please refer to the vendor-specific commands.

The Driver filed is obviously the JDBC Driver as configured in 22.6.2, "Defining a JDBC driver" on page 914.

When selected the Advanced tab, offers the user the opportunity to vary some of the connection pool attributes when required. For the WSsamplesDB2_app sample set, these values can be left unchanged.

22.6.4 Installing the driver

The final step in configuring database connectivity for the WSsamplesDB2_app Web application is to actually install the driver. This is achieved by selecting the JDBC driver, as created in Figure 741 on page 915, from the WebSphere Administrative Console Topology view and right-clicking the mouse button choosing the **Install** option. This will launch the configuration window as shown in Figure 743 on page 918.

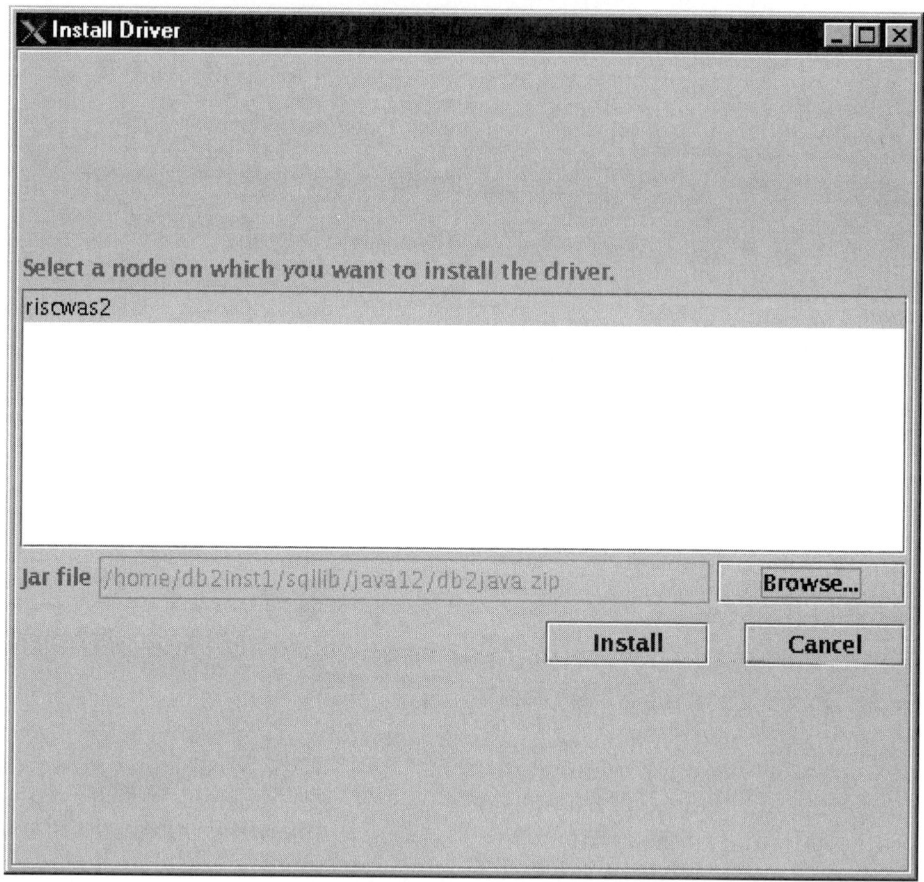

Figure 743. JDBC driver installation for the WSsampleDB2_app samples

Proceed by selecting the node on which the driver is to be installed. Then specify the JAR or ZIP file containing the actual classes for the database. Further documentation on configuring JDBC drivers is provided in Chapter 10, "JDBC 2.0 support" on page 371, but typically with the installation of a database or database client the respective JDBC classes are simultaneously installed.

Note

It is now necessary to stop and start the Default Server application server.

If you followed the database configuration instructions from the HTML gallery samples page, you simply need to complete step 6 (step 5 if PTF 2 is installed) to create the tables within the sample database. Alternatively, complete step 6 from the following URL:

```
http://<your_server>/WSsamples/Configuration/Database/DB2/task6.html
```

Completing step 6 (step 5 if PTF 2 is installed) finally creates the database tables required for the Level 2 samples.

> **Note**
>
> The HTML form in step 6 prompts for a DB2 user ID and password with sufficient privileges to actually create the necessary tables on the SAMPLE database. The wsdemo user typically does not have these privileges.

You are now set to evaluate the WSsamplesDB2_app Web application Level 2 samples.

22.7 WSsamplesDB2_app User Profile sample

The User Profile sample provided with the Level 2 samples requires the additional configuration of the User Profile Manager. This demonstrates the WebSphere UserProfile class and the ability to quickly submit user data into a database.

From the administrative console Topology view, select the User Profile Manager from under the Default Server application server. Highlight the DataSource tab and specify the newly created sample DataSource, setting the user ID to wsdemo and the password to wsdemo1. Finally, check the **Enable** tab in the properties window and select **Yes** for User Profile enablement.

22.8 Sample Enterprise JavaBeans configuration

The Enterprise JavaBeans samples build upon the database configuration steps explored with the Level 2 samples. To this end, you must have the JDBC driver and the sample data source properly configured and functioning prior to deploying the EJBs in this section. Then, with the successful deployment of all the EJBs, you will be able to run the YourCo Integrated Website demonstration from the following URL:

```
http://<your_server>/WSsamples
```

The majority of the steps necessary to successfully deploy the EJBs are documented under the WSsamples Web page (`http://<host_name>/WSsamples/index.html`). However, step-by-step guidance is provided in the following pages.

The starting point for this section is the configuration of a suitable container, into which we will deploy the sample EJBs. Fortunately, the Default Server application server already has an EJB container suitably defined for this use.

From the administrative console Topology view, select the **Default Container** EJB container object and highlight the DataSource tab in the properties window. This is shown in Figure 744. The DataSource filed needs to reference the data source called "sample" previously configured for the Level 2 samples as shown in Figure 745 on page 921.

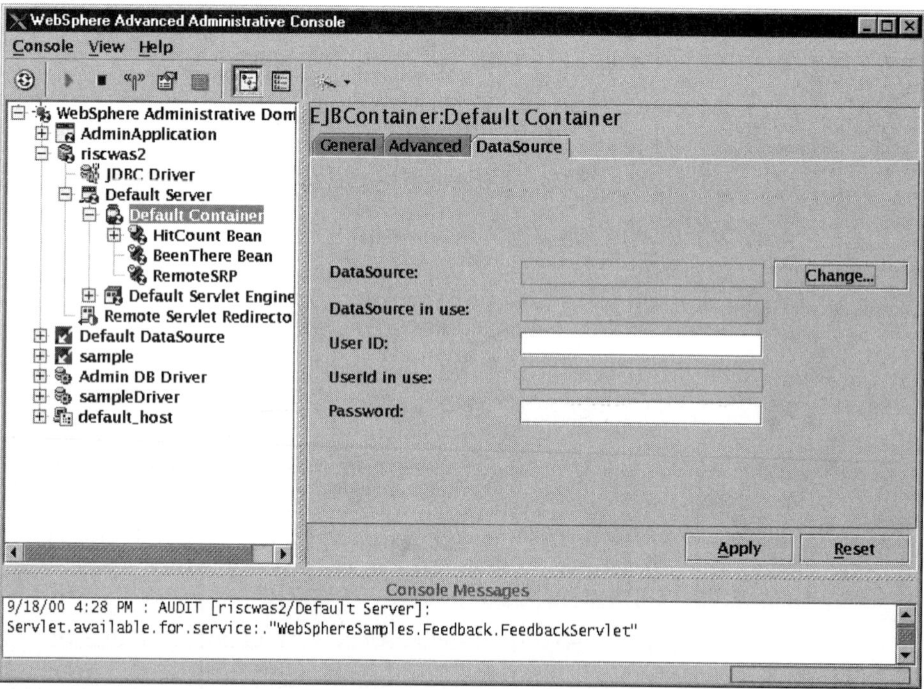

Figure 744. EJB Container configuration

With the exception of the Access, Hello, and Transfer beans, the EJBs provided with this sample utilize container-managed persistence (CMP). Those familiar with EJBs will also recall that beans themselves can manage their own persistence, hence bean-managed persistence (BMP).

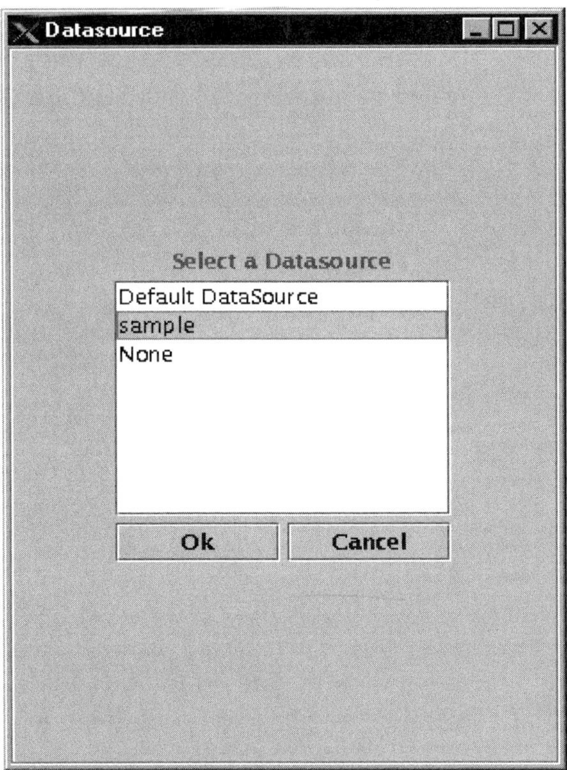

Figure 745. EJB Container data source selection

By specifying the data source on the EJB container object, each individual EJB deployed within the container will inherit the containers data source attributes. Alternatively, an individual EJB can override the container attributes, if the data source, user ID, password or attribute is specifically set on the bean itself. The HitCount bean within the Default Container is an example of this.

Note

Depending on your database authentication, it may be necessary to specify an alternative user ID and password in the EJB container DataSource configuration window.

In which case, set the data source attributes on the Default Container to:

- DataSource: sample

- User ID: wsdemo
- Password: wsdemo1

Configuring an individual EJB involves several steps and starts with selecting the Default Container object, right-clicking the mouse button and choosing the **Create -> EnterpriseBean** option as depicted in Figure 746.

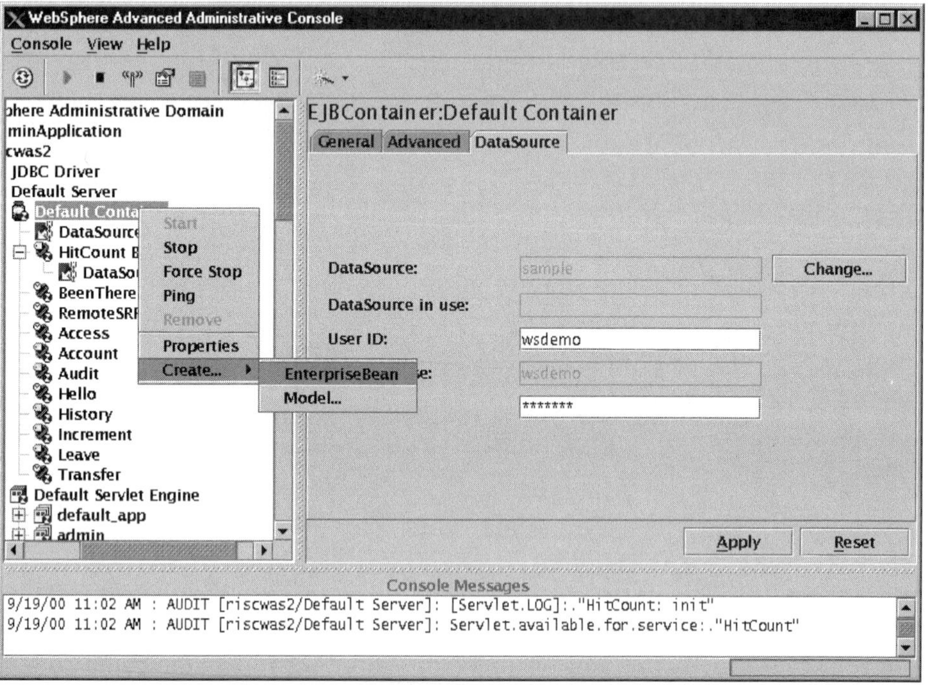

Figure 746. Creating an Enterprise Bean

Proceed by using the **Browse** button to locate the actual deployable JAR file. It is generally a good idea to leave the Name [classname] field blank, as this will automatically be updated in the JAR file selection process.

While all the EJBs provided for the WSsamplesDB2_app sample have already been made deployable, they have yet to be deployed and installed into the Default Container. In EJB terminology, deployable actually refers to the various Java classes that constitute an EJB JAR file and the creation of the ".ser" deployment descriptor. This is typically undertaken in a development environment, such as VisualAge for Java or with the WebSphere JETACE tool. However, it is still necessary to deploy the actual deployable EJBs within WebSphere.

During the WebSphere deployment process, additional supporting classes are added into the respective JAR files, which in turn are renamed and copied into the deployedEJBs directory found under the <WAS_HOME>/. The original, unaltered JAR file remains in the deployableEJBs directory, again found under the <WAS_HOME>/.

The following EJBs need to be deployed for the WSsamplesDB2_app samples:

> Account.jar, Audit.jar, History.jar, Increment.jar, Leave.jar, Access.jar, Hello.jar and Transfer.jar

In each case the .jar was omitted for the Name [classname] field.

By clicking the **Browse** option under the General window while creating an EnterpriseBean, locate the respective JAR file as demonstrated in Figure 747.

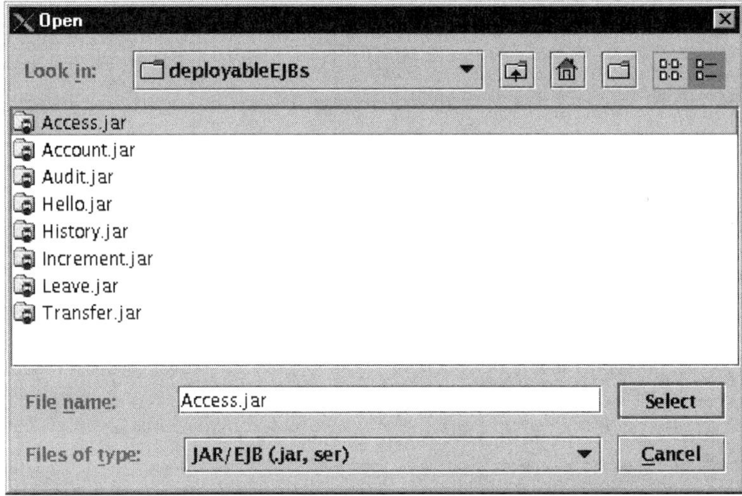

Figure 747. Locating the deployable EJB

Select and then double-click the appropriate JAR file (Access.jar). This will display the various ".ser" deployment descriptor files within the EJB. Figure 748 on page 924 shows the selection of the deployment descriptor.

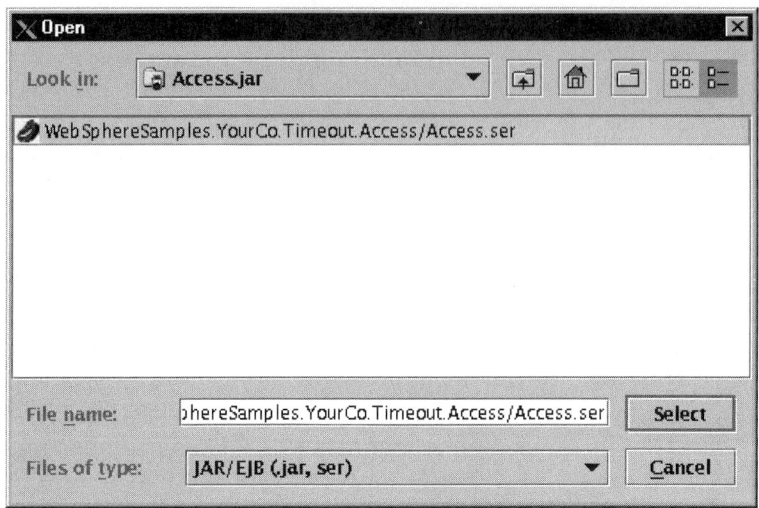

Figure 748. Selecting the appropriate EJB deployment descriptor

Finally, double-click the appropriate deployment descriptor (Access.ser) represented by a virtual bean icon. Users will find that with all the WSsamplesDB2_app samples there is only one deployment descriptor ".ser" per EJB.

Immediately the option prompts for the selection of either Deploy and Enable WLM or Deploy Only, the difference being solely with the inclusion, or not, of Work Load Management (WLM) support. In the case of the WSsamplesDB2_app samples it is sufficient to select **Deploy Only** as shown in Figure 749.

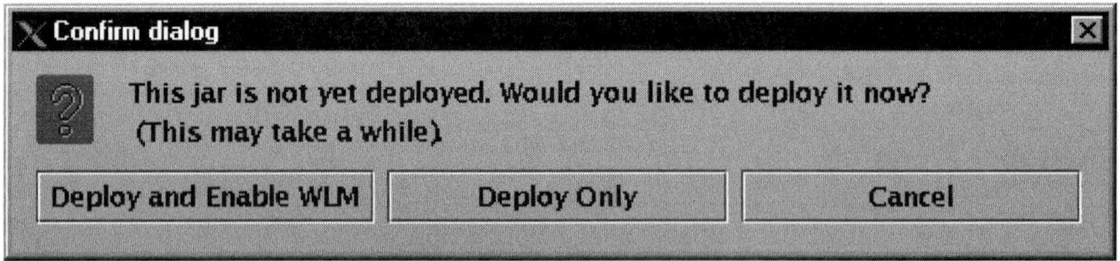

Figure 749. Confirming the EJB deployment

Deployment will now occur. On completion the user should click **OK** for both the window indicating that the bean was deployed successfully and the window indicating that the EnterpriseBean object was created properly.

These steps need to be repeated for all of the EJBs in the WSsamplesDB2_app sample set. Each time an EJB is successfully deployed, an object will be created under the Default Container Topology tree.

In order to activate the newly deployed EJBs, you can just stop and start the Default Container. Alternatively, if the Default Container is already running, individual EJBs can be started independently of one another.

If you followed the Enterprise Bean Configuration instructions from the HTML gallery samples page, you simply need to complete step 3 to populate the EJBLEAVEBEANTBL database table. This will set the starting sick, vacation and personal leave time for the YourCo Timeout sample. Alternatively, complete step 3 from the URL below:

```
http://<your_server>/WSsamples/Configuration/EJBeans/task3.html
```

Note

The actual database tables are created during step 6 of the Level 2 samples implementation. If at any time the sample database is dropped, you will need to rerun step 6 with the appropriate database privileges prior to populating the tables with the canned data.

You are now set to evaluate the WSsamplesDB2_app Level 3 samples. Here, four of the deployed EJBs are invoked from under the Enterprise Beans link, while the remaining four constitute the EJBs deployed within the YourCo integrated Web site example.

22.9 WebSphere Standard Edition samples

In contrast to the WSsamplesDB2_app sample set, the samples bundled with the WSsamplesIDB_app Web application require no further configuration other than ensuring that the Default Server application server is functional for WebSphere V3.5 Standard Edition users. Users should, however, ensure that the fully qualified system host name is defined in the host aliases list, under the default_host virtual host. Omitting this value may impact the servlets' (not just those included with the samples) ability to work dependably.

By choosing the samples option at the time the WebSphere V3.5 Standard Edition is installed, either by default with the Quick Installation option or by specific selection with the Custom Installation option, a separate Web application named WSsamplesIDB_app is created under the Default Server Topology tree.

WebSphere V3.5 Advanced Edition users will recall that they need to edit the initial_setup.config file and add the InstantDB database idb.jar file to the administrative server classpath prior to starting the administrative server for the first time, before running with the WSsamplesIDB_app samples.

The WSsamplesIDB_app samples can be invoked directly or from the redesigned HTML page (`http://<your_server>/WSsamplesIDB/index.html`) that introduces the samples gallery.

22.10 Sample InstantDB configuration

The Level 2 samples provided with WSsamplesIDB_app Web application use the compact, Java-based relational database InstantDB for demonstrating WebSphere database connectivity. Unlike the WSsamplesDB2_app Web application, no further configuration is necessary to evaluate the database samples, once the Default Server application server is started.

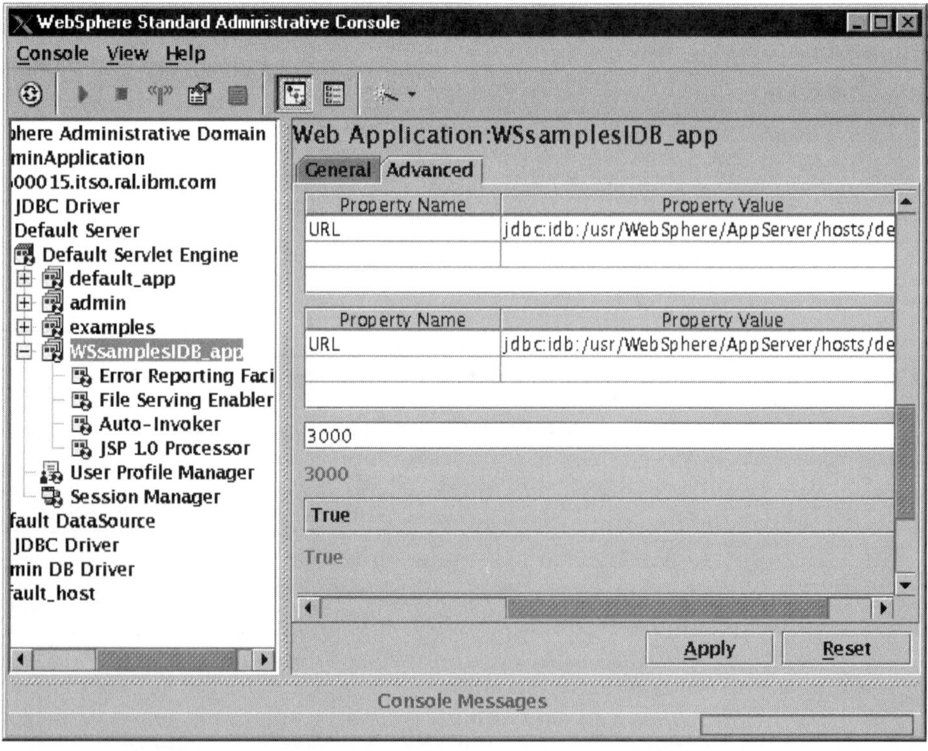

Figure 750. WSsamplesIDB_app Web application - InstantDB URL config

Although the InstantDB database is provided mainly for the purpose of accommodating the administrative database with WebSphere Standard Edition, it also offers the possibility for demonstrating the WebSphere Standard Edition database samples. To this end, both the database file structure and the (.prp) properties file are independent from those used by the WebSphere administrative database.

The InstantDB sample database is provided for demonstration purposes only.

Details are provided on how to effectively drop the database and restore the initial data for the WSsamplesIDB_app Web application from the following URL:

```
http://<your_server>/WSsamplesIDB/Configuration/Database/DBConfig.html
```

InstantDB is a compact, Java-based database, based on a pseudo file structure. To restore the original database content to that found after WebSphere Standard Edition is initially installed, first locate and recursively delete the sample directory under:

```
<WAS_HOME>/hosts/default_host/WSsamplesIDB_app/servlets/WebSphereSamples/Database
```

Then, unjar the jar_of_sampleIDB.jar file to recreate a new pseudo sample file structured database.

```
jar -xvf jar_of_sampleIDB.jar
```

22.11 Standard and Advanced Edition samples listing

In this section are detailed the various examples and samples that now ship with WebSphere V3.5 Standard and Advanced Editions.

22.11.1 The examples Web application

Table 47 on page 928 lists the samples provided in the Web application called “examples”. Users will recall that the examples Web application is installed as an integral part of the Default Server application server. Included in this listing are the file and jsp10 servlets, which enable HTML page serving and JSP support for this Web application respectively. The full Web path URL for each sample can be found defined under the virtual host default_host tree. Alternatively, users can invoke the samples from:

```
http://<your_server>/webapp/examples/index.html
```

Table 47. Web application examples

Examples	Description
simpleJSP	A simple JSP servlet
error	Calls the response.sendError() method
ping	Base line response time checker
SourceCodeViewer	Allows remote viewing of source code residing on the classpath
ShowConfig	Displays the current servlet engine configuration
HitCount	HitCount servlet - install verification
jsp10	JSP 1.0 support servlet
file	Enables file serving from this Web application
HelloPervasive	Hello Pervasive servlet - pervasive computing
StockQuote	Stock Quote servlet - pervasive computing

Users should note that the EJB increment demonstration within the HitCount sample and the BeenThere EJB WLM sample are not supported with WebSphere V3.5 Standard Edition.

For WebSphere V3.5 Advanced Edition users, the HitCount example ships with an associated EJB that is automatically installed within the Default Container EJB container. However, users must first specify either a datasource on the Default Container or on the EJB itself, before the sample can be used to store EJB incremental count data. Configuring the Default DataSource as the data source in this instance is acceptable for demonstration purposes.

Likewise, the BeenThere example needs further configuration before it can be evaluated. Users should consult the associated HTML ReadMe page, which describes the necessary steps involved in creating a model and number of clones to demonstrate workload management.

22.11.2 The WSsamplesIDB_app Web application

Both WebSphere V3.5 Standard and Advanced Editions support the samples that ship with the WSsampleIDB_app Web application. The full Web path URL for each sample can be found defined under the virtual host default_host tree. Alternatively users can invoke the samples from:

`http://<your_server>/WSsamplesIDB/index.html`

Table 48. WSsamplesIDB_app Web application

WSsamplesIDB_app	Description
Expiring Page	A JSP and Java servlet example that uses the callPage method
Form	An HTML form example that uses a Java servlet to store data in a bean, prior to displaying the output via a JSP
Quote of the Day	This example uses a Java servlet to load a bean with strings from a flat file, prior to randomly displaying the output via a JSP
Selection Box	Similar to the Form example, but the output JSP presents the data as a selectable menu
Feedback	Builds upon the Form example, but has an additional bean that updates the InstantDB database with input data, before displaying all the database entries via a JSP
Page Hit Counter (db)	This example uses a JSP and Java servlet to increment a counter on each invocation, the counter value being stored in the InstantDB database
Poll (db)	With the use of a Java servlet, poll questions are extracted from InstantDB, stored in a bean and then displayed via a JSP, and a further servlet and bean update InstantDB, before displaying the current tally via a JSP
Survey (db)	Similar to the Form example, but an additional Java servlet and bean update InstantDB, while a final JSP displays all the database submissions
YourCo (db)	The YourCo integrated Website demonstrates all of the above samples, deploying them collectively in a fictitious company Web site

Although no EJB support is shipped with WebSphere V3.5 Standard Edition, the examples depicted with a (db) demonstrate database connectivity.

22.11.3 The WSsampleDB2_app Web application

The WSsampleDB2_app Web application samples consist of servlets, JSPs, JavaBeans, and when installed on WebSphere V3.5 Advanced Edition, EJBs.

Prior to installing WebSphere V3.5 PTF 2, all of the database-dependent samples will work only on systems with DB2. WebSphere V3.5 PTF2 extends the WSsamplesDB2_app sample set to support Oracle and Sybase databases.

The WSsampleDB2_app Web application is not available on the Linux platform.

For ease of use, these samples are provided with an associated Web page from where the samples can be invoked and configured from the following URL:

```
http://<your_server>/WSsamples/index.html.
```

22.11.3.1 Level 1 samples

Use these samples to evaluate the simple principles of servlet, JSP and JavaBeans technology. No database configuration is required.

Table 49. Level1 samples

WSsampleDB2_app	Description: Level 1 samples
Expiring Page	A JSP and Java servlet example that uses the callPage method
Form	A HTML form example that uses a Java servlet to store data in a bean, prior to displaying the output via a JSP
Quote of the Day	This example uses a Java servlet to load a bean with strings from a flat file, prior to randomly displaying the output via a JSP
Selection Box	Similar to the Form example, but the output JSP presents the data as a selectable menu

22.11.3.2 Level 2 samples

These samples require the additional configuration of a database to work. Users should refer to necessary steps outlined in this chapter for configuring a JDBC driver and data source prior to evaluating these samples.

Table 50. Level 2 samples

WSsampleDB2_app	Description: Level 2 samples
Connection Pool (db)	Demonstrates the integral database connection pooling mechanism, thus avoiding the overhead of settingup a new connection for each database request

WSsampleDB2_app	Description: Level 2 samples
Feedback (db)	Builds upon the Form example, but has an additional bean that updates the InstantDB database with input data, before displaying all the database entries via a JSP
Page Hit Counter (db)	With the use of a Java servlet, poll questions are extracted from InstantDB, stored in a bean and then displayed via a JSP, and a further servlet and bean update InstantDB before displaying the current tally via a JSP
Survey (db)	Similar to the Form example, but an additional Java servlet and bean update InstantDB, while a final JSP displays all the database submissions
User Profile (db)	Demonstrates the possible use of the User Profile Manager, enabling a Java servlet to quickly store user information in the database; potentially useful for creating a customized registration page

The User Profile sample provided with the Level 2 samples requires the additional configuration of the User Profile Manager. This demonstrates the WebSphere UserProfile class and the ability to quickly submit user data into a database.

22.11.3.3 Level 3 samples

The final, and most complex samples, provided with WebSphere V3.5 Advanced Edition demonstrate EJB technology. Users are required to first complete the configuration steps necessary for the Level 2 examples, that is, they must configure a suitable JDBC driver and datasource. Only then may the EJB samples be deployed within WebSphere and evaluated.

Table 51. Level 3 samples

WSsampleDB2_app	Description: Level 3 samples
Enterprise Bean: Hello	A simple EJB sample that uses a Java servlet to access a stateless session enterprise bean
Enterprise Bean: Increment	A simple EJB sample that uses a Java servlet to access a persistent entity enterprise bean
Enterprise Bean: Account (db)	Similar to the Increment EJB sample above, but the persistent data is stored in the database

WSsampleDB2_app	Description: Level 3 samples
Enterprise Bean: Transfer (db)	Coupled with the Account enterprise bean sample, the transfer stateless session bean that manipulates the transfer of funds between accounts, requires database configuration
YourCo	The YourCo integrated Website demonstrates all of the above samples, deploying them collectively in a fictitious company Web site; in contrast to the WebSphere Standard Edition, these samples include EJB support

Chapter 23. Problem determination

This chapter outlines the tools available in WebSphere Application Server that can be utilized for problem determination. We examine and explain the log files that WebSphere uses as well as the trace facility provided in WebSphere. This chapter includes a discussion of which components to trace in given situations, and examples of using a trace. In addition, as of V3.5.2 WebSphere supports the Log Analyzer, which is useful for problem determination. See Chapter 24, "Log Analyzer" on page 975 for detailed information on this tool. Lastly we discuss the Object Level Trace (OLT) debugging facility and provide examples of its use.

23.1 The problem determination process

In summary the key points to consider in the problem determination process are as follows:

1. Validate your installation (Validate configuration in the admin.config and setupCmdLine. Verify you have correct product pre-reqs.)
2. What is your topology? For example, platforms, number of servers, database, Web server, and setup.
3. What is your application doing? For example, application structure, application components (servlets/JSPs/EJBs/databeans/connectors etc.), and back-end systems.
4. Do you have a simple test case to reproduce the problem?
5. Collect server logs and appropriate trace.
6. Collect server configuration through XMLConfig export.
7. Analyze logs, trace, and test case.
8. Isolate to appropriate product component.
9. Collect additional, more targeted, trace as necessary.
10. Identify and correct the problem.

23.1.1 Messages, logs and traces

Messages, logs, and traces are important diagnostic tools for investigating the behavior of WebSphere Application Server product code, including application servers and administrative servers. The WebSphere implementation of these items are defined as follows:

- *Messages* provide high-level view of important events, such as successful completions and fatal errors. The performance impact of messages is minimal to none, and they should always be enabled.

- *Logs* provide information about administrative and application servers as they initialize and run. They have a low-to-medium impact on performance, and should be left enabled; after an error or problem condition occurs, logs can be reviewed for clues as to what happened.
- *Traces* are collections of data from trace statements placed throughout the WebSphere product code. As the code executes, tracing information is sent to a specified file or stream, so that the administrator and IBM support personnel can analyze it.

23.2 Messages

Message events are generated by IBM WebSphere Application Server code in response to system events occurring in the application server environment. They are always collected. The administrator can decide whether to look at them.

There are four main types of message, as described in Table 52.

Table 52. Message types

Message	Explanation
audit	Indicates a significant event, for example the starting of a service.
warning	Indicates the occurrence of a problem that does not prevent continued system function, but which none the less should be investigated and remedied.
terminate	Indicates that a process has terminated normally.
fatal	Indicates that a process has encountered a fatal error and has terminated abnormally. When a process terminates in this way, the trace service writes its internal ring buffer to a local file.

Messages are displayed in the console messages area, and are also written to a file called "tracefile" in the <WAS_HOME>/logs directory by default. If desired, you can specify an alternative file necessary by updating the entry for the "com.ibm.ejs.sm.adminServer.traceFile" property in the <WAS_HOME>/bin/admin.config file.

WebSphere messages are Java exceptions. These messages are either errors, such as a virtual machine error, or runtime exceptions such as a ClassCastException. The messages are issued because a method in a WebSphere component generated an exception or an error, or because a called method threw an exception.

23.3 The format of log and trace files

For WebSphere versions prior to 3.5.2, log and trace file entries are formatted as follows:

[Timestamp] TID COMPONENT LEVEL MESSAGE ARGUMENTS

As of WebSphere V3.5.2, log and trace file entries are written in the following format:

[Timestamp] TID COMPONENT LEVEL MID MESSAGE ARGUMENTS

[Timestamp] – This is the timestamp of the message, with the elapsed time since process start and the fully qualified date, time and time zone, to millisecond precision
TID – Thread ID, the hash code of the thread emitting this message
COMPONENT – The short name of the component emitting this message
LEVEL – Level of the message, one of the following:

- > Entry to a method (debug)
- < Exit a method (debug)
- A Audit
- W Warning
- X Error
- E Event (debug)
- D Debug (debug)
- T Terminate (exits process)
- F Fatal (exits process)

MID - Message ID, with prefix pointing to the component that issued the message. Message prefix to component table as follows:

- ADGU Administrative GUI
- ADMS Administrative server
- ALRM Alarm
- CM20 2.0 Connection Manager
- CNTR EJB Container
- CONM Connection Manager
- DBMN Database Manager
- EJSW EJB Workload Management
- JSPG JavaServer Pages
- NMSV JNDI - Name Services
- PLGN Web server Plugins and Native code
- SECJ Security Application
- SESN Session and User Profiles
- SMTL WebSphere Systems Management Utilities
- SRVE Servlet Engine

TRAS Tracing Component
WCMD WebSphere Systems Management Commands
WINT Request Interceptors
WJTI Java Transaction Implementation
WJTS Java Transaction Service
WOBA WebSphere Object Adapter
WPRS WebSphere Persistence
WSVR WebSphere Server Runtime
WTRN WebSphere Transactions
WTSK WebSphere Systems Management TASKS
XMLM XML Component

MESSAGE – the text of message
ARGUMENTS – Option message arguments

Here is an example of a warning message in WebSphere V3.5.1:

```
[00.07.11 22:47:12:191 EDT] 53ccc3c5 ActiveEJBCont W Could not create bean
table
```

Here is an example of an auditing message in WebSphere V3.5.2:

```
[00.10.09 14:31:23:000 EDT] f0aef5c2 AdminServer   A ADMS0002I:
Initializing WebSphere Administration server
```

23.4 WebSphere log files

WebSphere keeps logs. Both logs entries and trace entries (discussed in the next section) have the same format.

WebSphere V3.5 generates runtime log files in the <WAS_HOME>/logs directory (by default).

Table 53 describes the files. Logs produced when installing WebSphere are created in platform-specifc locations; these are also described in Table 53. If you are deploying on HP-UX platforms you should note the special treatment of installation logs on that platform.

Table 53. Log and trace files

File Name	Description
(Windows)wssetup.log	It is created during the install process and records the installation information.

File Name	Description
(AIX/Solaris) WebSphere.instl or wsas.install.log	It is created during the install process and records the installation information. A native install generates the WebSphere.instl and a Java GUI install generates the wsas.install.log. Files located in directory /tmp.
(HP-UX) swagent.log	The installation information on HP is placed in the HP system log, swagent.log. It is located in directory /opt/var/adm/sw. Note: swagent is the system log instead of WebSphere log. It will be replaced when installing another product that needs it.
(Windows)wasdb2.log	It is created when running <server root>\bin\createdb2.bat to configure DB2 database was. Usually, it will be run when restarting machine for the first time after installing WebSphere with DB2 as the administrative database.
tracefile	Startup message for administrative server
nanny.trace	Use the nanny trace to monitor the administrative server events.
adminserver_stderr.log	Error message from administrative server.
stdout.log and stderr.log	Created by application servers and Servlet Redirectors. When you create a new application server or Servlet Redirector, the default setting of standard output and standard error are stdout.log and stderr.log. We suggest that you specify the file name as a unique name, such as <application server name>_stdout.log/stderr.log. stdout.log contains System.out messages from the application server or Servlet Redirector and stderr.log contains System.err messages from it.

File Name	Description
native log file (out-of-process logs)	There are two types of out-of-process logs: those created for administrative server and those created for application servers. These logs contain error and informational messages generated from the native code portion of the out-of-process engine. This information reflects server startup and server status change requests (start/stop/restart). You may verify the log file setting by clicking Setting on the Advanced panel of ServletEngine properties. The physical file name is in the form: <file name setting>.was-oop.<date>-<time>-<year>
plug-in trace file	Contains trace data from the native Web server plug-in. For example, the file name of the plug-in for IBM HTTP Server is: trace.log.ibmhttp.<date>-<time>-<year>
activity.log	This log file is new in WebSphere V3.5.2. It is used by the log analyzer. It is a binary file so you cannot read it with a text editor.

There will be additional log files produced by your chosen Web server. You will need to refer to the product-specific configuration to locate and interpret those files.

23.4.1 Sample output of log files

Several different outputs from log files are provided below as examples.

23.4.1.1 Sample output of tracefile

The message `WebSphere Administration server open for e-business` tells you that the administrative server has started.

```
[00.10.31 20:54:25:764 EST] d30d6e94 AdminServer   A ADMS0002I:
Initializing WebSphere Administration server
[00.10.31 20:54:25:844 EST] e8f46e97 DrAdminServer A SMTL0018I: DrAdmin
available on port 1,195
[00.10.31 20:55:00:514 EST] d30d6e94 AdminServer   A ADMS0024I:
WebSphere Administration server open for e-business
[00.10.31 23:48:56:546 EST] b6316e81 ActiveServerP A ADMS0008I: Starting
server: "Test"
[00.10.31 23:48:57:348 EST] b6316e81 ActiveServerP A ADMS0032I: Started
server: "Test" (pid "2440")
[00.11.01 24:05:25:268 EST] b6346e81 ActiveServerP A ADMS0029I: Stopped
server: "Test" (pid "2440")
```

23.4.1.2 Sample output of adminserver_stderr.log

We can see error messages from the administrative server:

```
Full thread dump Classic VM (J2RE 1.2.2 IBM build cn122-20000725a,
native threads):

"P=312644:O=1:StandardRT=16:LocalPort=1204:RemoteHost=9.24.104.166:Remo
tePort=1203:" (TID:0x140e658, sys_thread_t:0xb327c0, state:R, native
ID:0x163) prio=5
   at java.net.SocketInputStream.socketRead(Native Method)
   at java.net.SocketInputStream.read(SocketInputStream.java(Compiled
Code))
   at com.ibm.rmi.iiop.Message.readFully(Message.java(Compiled Code))
   at com.ibm.rmi.iiop.Message.createFromStream(Message.java(Compiled
Code))
   at com.ibm.CORBA.iiop.IIOPConnection.createInputStream(Unknown
Source)
   at com.ibm.CORBA.iiop.StandardReaderThread.run(Unknown Source)

"P=312644:O=1:StandardRT=15:LocalPort=1063:RemoteHost=kenueno:RemotePor
t=1201:" (TID:0x140e738, sys_thread_t:0xb321d0, state:R, native
ID:0x160) prio=5
   at java.net.SocketInputStream.socketRead(Native Method)
   at java.net.SocketInputStream.read(SocketInputStream.java(Compiled
Code))
   at com.ibm.rmi.iiop.Message.readFully(Message.java(Compiled Code))
   at com.ibm.rmi.iiop.Message.createFromStream(Message.java(Compiled
Code))
   at com.ibm.CORBA.iiop.IIOPConnection.createInputStream(Unknown
Source)
   at com.ibm.CORBA.iiop.StandardReaderThread.run(Unknown Source)

"P=312644:O=1:StandardRT=14:LocalPort=900:RemoteHost=kenueno:RemotePort
=1200:" (TID:0x140e780, sys_thread_t:0xb31bd0, state:R, native ID:0x4c)
prio=5
   at java.net.SocketInputStream.socketRead(Native Method)
   at java.net.SocketInputStream.read(SocketInputStream.java(Compiled
Code))
   at com.ibm.rmi.iiop.Message.readFully(Message.java(Compiled Code))
   at com.ibm.rmi.iiop.Message.createFromStream(Message.java(Compiled
Code))
   at com.ibm.CORBA.iiop.IIOPConnection.createInputStream(Unknown
Source)
   at com.ibm.CORBA.iiop.StandardReaderThread.run(Unknown Source)

"P=312644:O=1:StandardRT=13:LocalPort=1064:RemoteHost=kenueno:RemotePor
t=1199:"
```

23.4.1.3 Sample output of the default_server_stdout.log

Each application server can specify the stdout log file.

```
[00.10.16 17:03:10:849 EDT] d1f5d3e3 DrAdminServer A SMTL0018I: DrAdmin
available on port 2,803
[00.10.16 17:03:12:881 EDT] d0e953e3 ServletEngine A IBM WebSphere
Application Server - Web Container.  Copyright IBM Corp. 1998-2000
[00.10.16 17:03:13:112 EDT] d0e953e3 ServletEngine A Servlet
Specification Level: 2.2 - WebSphere 3.5 Compatibility Mode
[00.10.16 17:03:13:152 EDT] d0e953e3 ServletEngine A Supported JSP
Specification Levels: 1.1, 1.0, 0.91
[00.10.16 17:03:14:243 EDT] d0e953e3 ServletHost   A Loading group:
"default_app"
[00.10.16 17:03:14:844 EDT] d0e953e3 ServletInstan A SRVE0048I: Loading
servlet: "ErrorReporter"
[00.10.16 17:03:15:595 EDT] d0e953e3 WebGroup     A SRVE0091I: [Servlet
LOG]: "ErrorReporter: init"
[00.10.16 17:03:15:675 EDT] d0e953e3 ServletInstan A SRVE0130I: Servlet
available for service: "ErrorReporter"
[00.10.16 17:03:15:856 EDT] d0e953e3 ServletInstan A SRVE0048I: Loading
servlet: "invoker"
[00.10.16 17:03:16:046 EDT] d0e953e3 WebGroup     A SRVE0091I: [Servlet
LOG]: "invoker: init"
[00.10.16 17:03:16:146 EDT] d0e953e3 ServletInstan A SRVE0130I: Servlet
available for service: "invoker"
[00.10.16 17:03:16:356 EDT] d0e953e3 ServletInstan A SRVE0048I: Loading
servlet: "jsp10"
[00.10.16 17:03:16:527 EDT] d0e953e3 WebGroup     A SRVE0091I: [Servlet
LOG]: "jsp10: init"
[00.10.16 17:03:16:797 EDT] d0e953e3 ServletInstan A SRVE0130I: Servlet
available for service: "jsp10"
[00.10.16 17:04:58:313 EDT] b416d3ec ServletInstan A SRVE0048I: Loading
servlet: "snoop"
[00.10.16 17:04:58:503 EDT] b416d3ec WebGroup     A SRVE0091I: [Servlet
LOG]: "snoop: init"
[00.10.16 17:04:58:583 EDT] b416d3ec ServletInstan A SRVE0130I: Servlet
available for service: "snoop"
```

23.4.1.4 Sample output of the default_server_stderr.log

Each application server can specify the stdout log file.

```
Scratch dir for the JSP engine is:
C:\WebSphere\AppServer\temp\default_host\default_app
IMPORTANT: Do not modify the generated servlets
Scratch dir for the JSP engine is:
C:\WebSphere\AppServer\temp\default_host\admin
IMPORTANT: Do not modify the generated servlets
```

```
Scratch dir for the JSP engine is:
C:\WebSphere\AppServer\temp\default_host\examples
IMPORTANT: Do not modify the generated servlets
Scratch dir for the JSP engine is:
C:\WebSphere\AppServer\temp\default_host\WSsamplesDB2_app
IMPORTANT: Do not modify the generated servlets
```

23.4.1.5 Sample output of IBM HTTP Server plugin trace file

You can specify the trace level such as TRACE, INFORM, ERROR, and WARNING in the <WAS_HOME>/properties/bootstrap.properties file. This log file is very useful when you have problems configuring OSE Remote.

```
Tue Oct 24 14:42:35 2000 - 000001d0 000000eb - Error -
sysmgmt_queue_for_uri : Error returned from sysmgmt_vhost_for_aliasport
rc=9
Tue Oct 24 14:42:35 2000 - 000001d0 000000eb - Error -
sysmgmt_is_servlet_uri : failure in sysmgmt_queue_for_uri rc=9
```

23.5 The trace facility

WebSphere includes a comprehensive trace facility, which allows trace to be enabled for every Java class in the system. This section describes that facility.

23.5.1 Trace basics

The WebSphere trace facility allows customers or service personnel to follow the execution of Java code in the application server. It is selected on a Java component basis. The facility is provided for error reporting and problem diagnosis.

Trace can be collected from any of the WebSphere processes; an administrative server, an application server or a client such as the administrative console or WSCP.

Trace events are stored in a memory buffer called the *ring buffer*, and can be dumped to disk at any time. A destination file can also be declared to which the trace information is written in real time. If you don't specify a trace output file, the destination file will contain the ring buffer when dumped. Otherwise, there is a complete trace and a dump is not needed.

The ring buffer is a circular memory buffer, which means that once the end of the buffer is reached, trace events at the beginning of the buffer will be overwritten. The default size of the ring buffer is 8KB. This can be modified on a per process basis.

Tracing provides a lot of detail, but it can also drain performance. You should enable tracing only when you have reason to do so.

The trace subsystem does not trace user code (such as servlets or EJB components) unless System.err.println or System.out.println statements are added to the code. Output from the println statements then appears either in the <Application Server>_stdout or <Application Server>_stderr logs.

Since a trace is just another log, a WebSphere Application Server log entry and a trace entry will have the same format.

The following traces are available in WebSphere Application Server:

- tracefile
- nanny trace (UNIX)
- DrAdmin

View Figure 751 for a description of the log and trace points in Version 3.5 WebSphere:

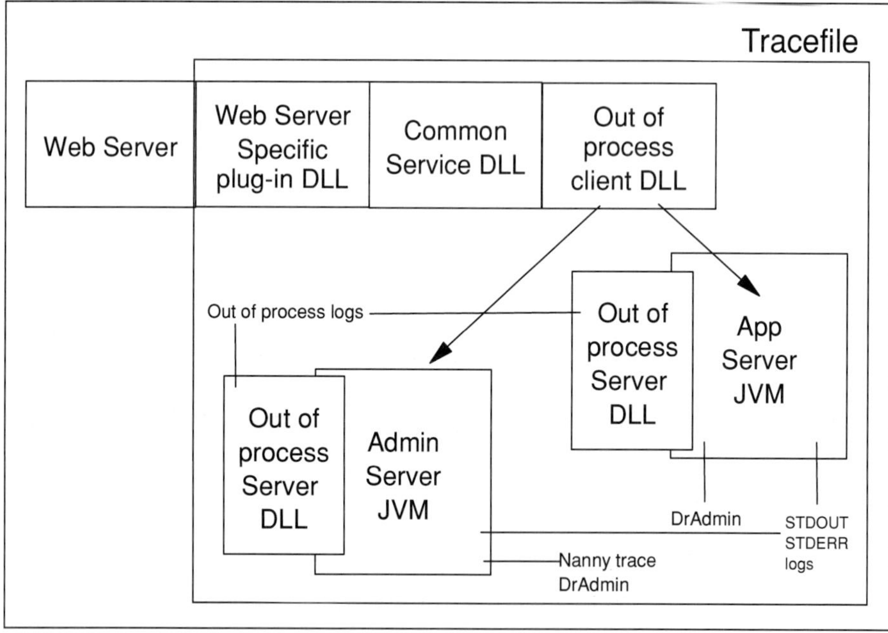

Figure 751. Logs and traces

23.5.2 Trace string format

A component is selected for tracing by setting a trace string, which contains the name of one or more components to trace and the level of information desired. The trace information for that component or components is then collected by the application server until the trace string is changed.

A trace string is created using the syntax

```
<component1>=<level>=[enabled|disabled]:<component2>=<level>=[enabled|disa
bled]
```

The component should contain the full name of the component, such as `com.ibm.servlet.engine.ServletHost`. A wildcard can be used to specify all components with a certain prefix, for instance `com.ibm.ejs.*` would refer to all components with a `com.ibm.ejs` prefix.

There are four possible levels of trace as shown in Table 54.

Table 54. Trace levels

Level	Meaning
entryExit	Entering and exiting functions
event	State changes
debug	Detailed debugging information
all	All of the above

23.5.3 Enabling a trace for the administrative console

You can enable a trace for the administrative console in two different ways.

1. To enable a trace through the GUI, from the WebSphere Administrative Console, select **Console -> Trace**.
2. Invoke the script used to start the administrative console:
   - `adminclient.sh` on UNIX
   - `adminclient.bat` on Windows

   with the following arguments:
   - Debug switch: -v on Windows, debug on UNIX
   - Name of the host on which administrative server is running: hostName
   - Port used to connect to administrative server: port

The debug switch sets the following trace string for the administrative console:

```
com.ibm.*=all=enabled
```

Change `javaw` in the script to `java` to see trace output in standard out.

23.5.4 Enabling trace for the administrative server

Note: Tracing the administrative server will have a severe impact on performance.

To trace administrative server startup and shutdown problems on a Windows platform:

1. Use a text editor to open the file <WAS_HOME>\bin\admin.config.
2. Add these lines:

   ```
   com.ibm.ejs.sm.adminServer.traceOutput=stdout
   com.ibm.ejs.sm.adminServer.traceString=aTraceString
   ```

   where `aTraceString` is the string component. An example is:

   ```
   com.ibm.ejs.sm.*-all=enabled
   ```

   Note: If you specified that your trace output be sent to a trace file when the administrative server is started, the trace file will be overridden each time you retry the startup. To preserve trace output from one retry to the next, specify that trace output be sent to stdout:

   a. Edit the file <WAS_HOME>\bin\admin.config
   b. Add the line:

      ```
      com.ibm.ejs.sm.adminServer.traceOutput=stdout
      ```

   c. Restart the administrative server. Stdout will append the traceoutput to the <WAS_HOME>\logs\tracefile.

To trace administrative server problems on UNIX:

1. Use a text editor to open the file <WAS_HOME>/bin/admin.config.
2. Add these lines:

   ```
   com.ibm.ejs.sm.adminServer.traceOutput=stdout
   com.ibm.ejs.sm.adminServer.traceString=aTraceString
   ```

   where `aTraceString` is the string component. An example is:

   ```
   com.ibm.ejs.sm.*=all=enabled
   ```

23.5.5 Setting trace as an application server property

An application server instance contains a Trace Specification field, into which a trace string can be typed directly. There is also a Trace Specification in Use field, which shows the current trace string in use. Figure 752 on page 945 shows an application server that has no current trace, and we are typing in a trace string to trace all of `com.ibm`.

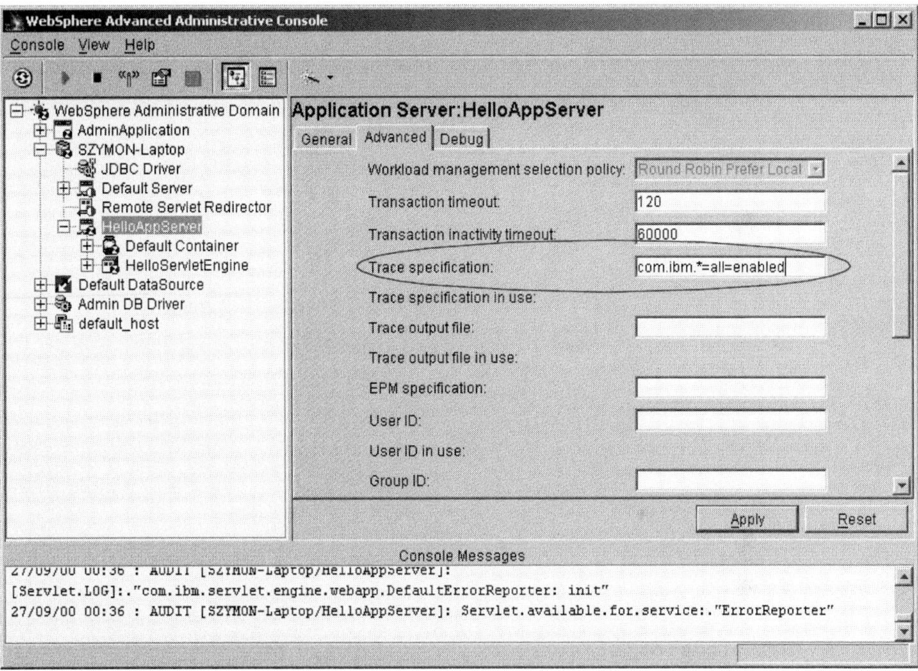

Figure 752. Trace property

Click **Apply** to update the properties, and then stop and restart the application server. It is important to restart the server; the application server will only read the Trace Specification field when it starts.

Once the application server has restarted, the Trace Specification in Use field will show the trace string that was typed in; WebSphere is now storing trace into the ring buffer according to that trace string.

The application server also has field for Trace output file and Trace output file in use. This field should contain the name of a file to which the trace output is written. You may use the names “stderr” and “stdout” to redirect the trace to the standard error or standard output of the server.

23.5.6 Using the Trace Administrative Console

The Trace Administrative Console enables dynamic setting of trace on a node (administrative server process) or an application server.

Right-click the server name in the administrative console and choose **Trace**, as shown in Figure 753 on page 946.

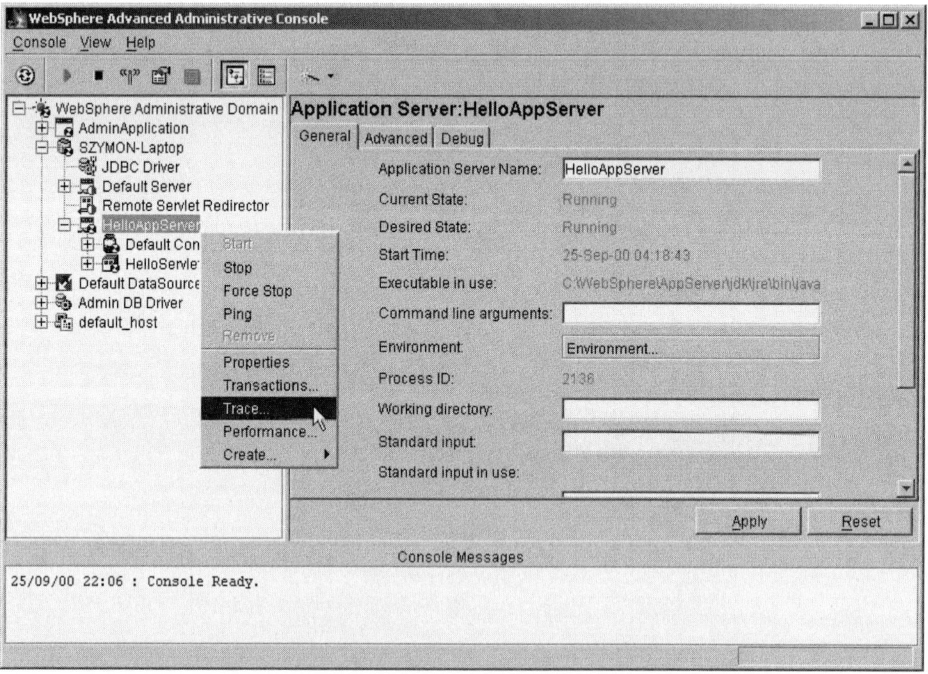

Figure 753. Configure trace in the administrative console

This will bring up the Trace Administration window, shown in Figure 754 on page 947.

The Trace Administration window contains fields for setting the size of the ring buffer and giving a file name to which the buffer is to be dumped.

It also contains white space for displaying component hierarchies. In this space are two entries, Components and Groups; each of these is the head of a hierarchy of entries that can be traced.

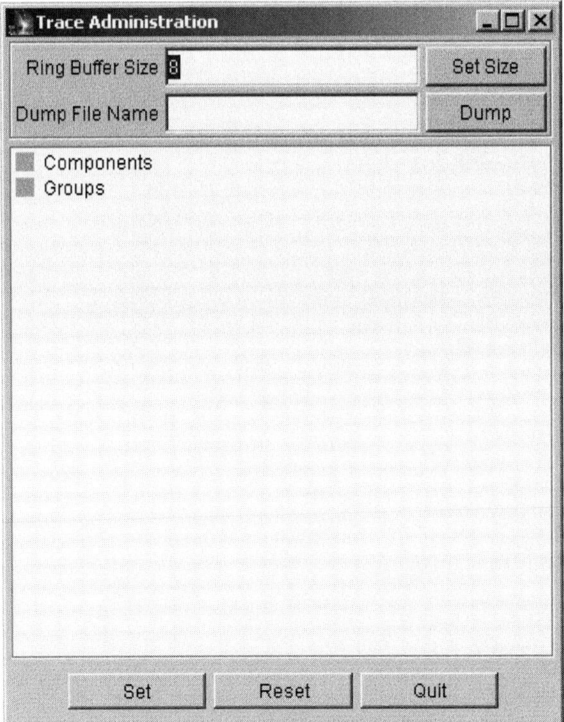

Figure 754. The Trace Administration window

To the left of each entry is a gray box. The gray color of the box means that, currently, a trace is not being collected for any of the subcomponents of that entry; if any subcomponent were being traced, the box would be pink. Double-click the box to the left of the title to open up the hierarchy.

The Components hierarchy includes all of the internal Java classes. The Groups hierarchy contains groups of components, grouped by the part of WebSphere that they will give information on. Figure 755 on page 948 shows a part of the component hierarchy in the Trace Administration window.

Navigate to the entry that represents the component you want to trace, and left click once to select it, then right click. A menu will appear, giving a choice of levels of trace to collect from that component.

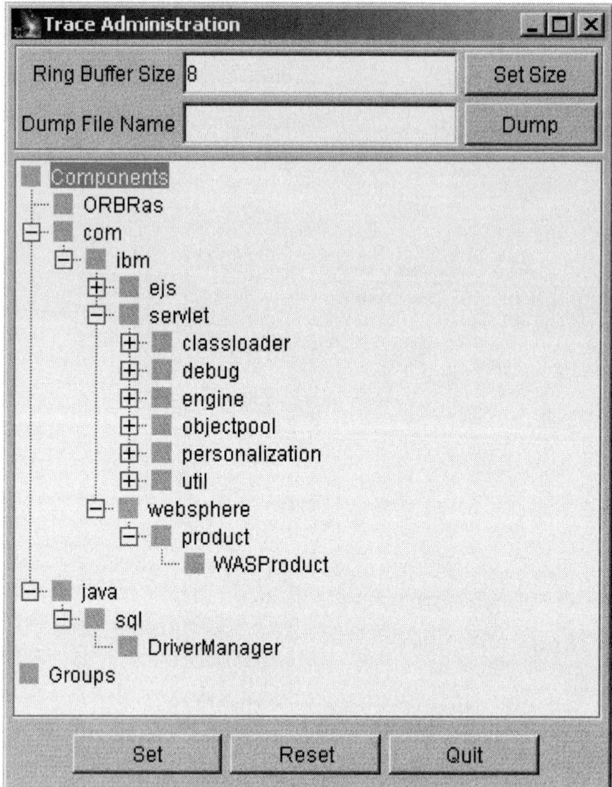

Figure 755. The component hierarchy

Figure 756 on page 949 shows the menu when right-clicking the com.ibm.servlet.classloader component. Note that we have opened the com.ibm.servlet.classloader hierarchy by clicking the plus sign in the hierarchy.

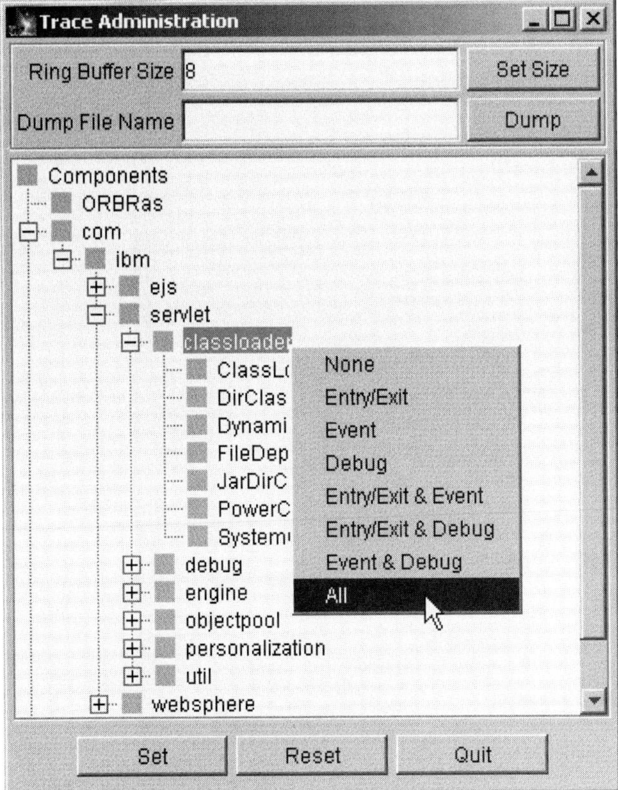

Figure 756. Set the trace level to All

Clicking the **All** level will highlight the components and subcomponents as shown in Figure 757 on page 950.

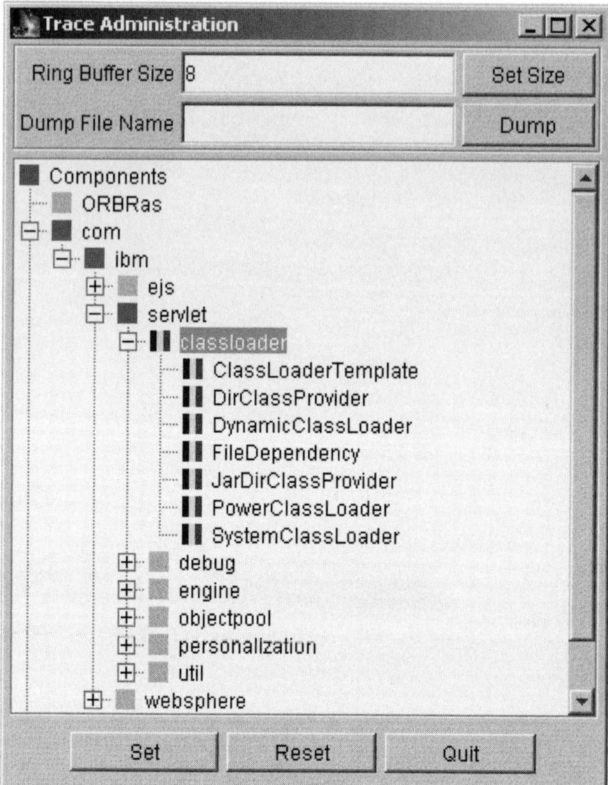

Figure 757. com.ibm.servlet.classloader=all=enabled

The box has now changed as follows:

1. All of the parent components of the trace mask com.ibm.servlet.classloader, namely com, com.ibm and com.ibm.servlet, and the Components field itself, have a pink box instead of the grey box, to show that a subcomponent is being traced.
2. The com.ibm.servlet.classloader component and all of its subcomponents have boxes split into three colors; blue on the left, yellow in the middle and red on the right. These colors stand in turn for entryExit level trace, event level trace, and debug level trace.

Now click the **com.ibm.servlet.debug** component and right click to bring up the menu. Select **entryExit level trace**. The grey box next to the component will change to contain a blue stripe on the left-hand side, indicating that entryExit level trace is enabled on this component. The color of the boxes next to the parent components com, com.ibm and com.ibm.servlet will not change because they are already pink, indicating that subcomponents of them are already being traced.

Use the same method to turn on event level trace on com.ibm.servlet.engine, debug level trace on com.ibm.servlet.objectpool, both entryExit and debug level trace on com.ibm.servlet.personalization and event and debug level trace on com.ibm.servlet.util. The final view will appear as in Figure 758.

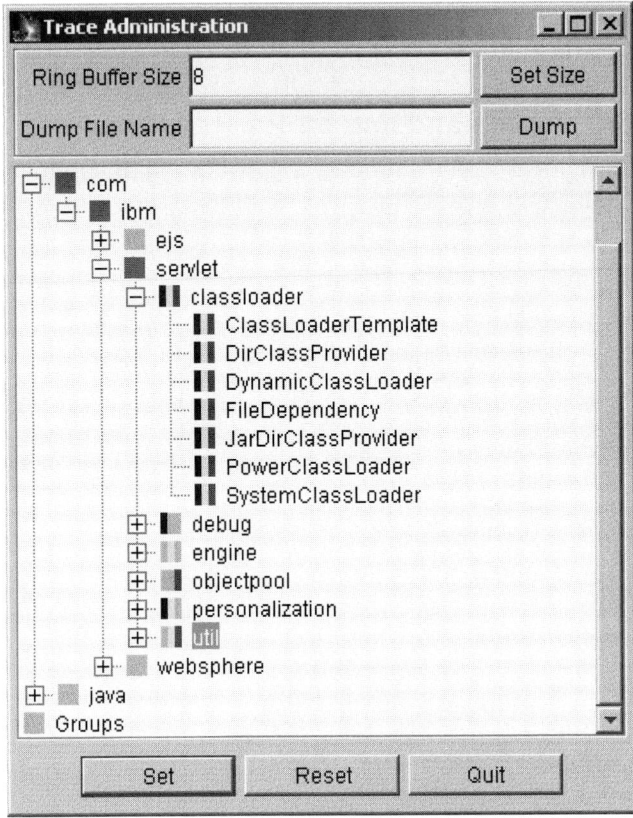

Figure 758. The final view of Trace Administration window

In summary, we have turned on the following trace:

```
*=all=disabled
com.ibm.servlet.classloader.*=all=enabled
com.ibm.servlet.debug.*=entryExit=enabled
com.ibm.servlet.engine.*=event=enabled
com.ibm.servlet.objectpool.*=debug=enabled
com.ibm.servlet.personalization.*=entryExit=enabled
com.ibm.servlet.personalization.*=event=enabled
```

```
com.ibm.servlet.util.*=event=enabled
com.ibm.servlet.util.*=debug=enabled
```

Click **Set** to make this the current trace string.

Once a trace string has been set using the Trace Administration window, the ring buffer can be dumped at any time.

Simply bring up the Trace Administration window again and type a file name into the Dump File Name box, then click **Dump** to write the contents of the ring buffer to that file.

23.5.7 Setting trace as a command line option

Most WebSphere programs support a -traceString option that allows you to specify the startup trace string.

23.5.8 Important trace packages

The following is a list of components that are commonly traced, and the information that can be gleaned by tracing that component.

com.ibm.ejs.container.*
EJB Container Runtime
Trace EJB problems
(for example, to determine the root cause of
TransactionRolledBackException, specify
com.ibm.ejs.container.EJSContainer=event=all)

com.ibm.ejs.sm.beans.*
Administrative server repository object trace
Trace Admininistrative server problems

com.ibm.ejs.sm.client.*
Administrative GUI Code
Trace client-side administrative problems

com.ibm.ejs.sm.active.*
Active objects of the admin system

Trace problems transferring configuration from the administrative database to active server

com.ibm.servlet.engine.*
Servlet Engine
Java Plug-in Code

com.ibm.servlet.personalization.*
HTTP Session
User Profile

com.ibm.servlet.classloader.*
Dynamic Classloading for Web applications

com.ibm.servlet.engine.ejs.*
Servlet Redirector

com.ibm.servlet.engine.oselistener.systemsmgmt.*
Automatic configuration of plugin config files (queues, rules, vhosts)

com.ibm.websphere.xmlconfig.*
XMLConfig tool

com.ibm.ejs.persistance.*
EJB Persistance Layer

com.ibm.ejs.security.*
WebSphere Security

com.ibm.ejs.csi.*, com.ibm.websphere.csi.*
Container Server Interface

com.ibm.ejs.cm.*
Connection Pooling Manager
Data Sources

com.ibm.ejs.sm.server.*
Administrative server Process
Managed Server Process

com.ibm.ejs.sm.util.process.*
Process Management Code

com.ibm.ejs.sm.util.db.*
Admin Database Manager
Trace SQL calls to the administrative database

23.5.9 Trace examples

Below are some trace examples.

23.5.9.1 Sample output of trace: com.ibm.ejs.container

We obtained the following trace when we accessed the HitCountBean EJB.

```
[00.11.01 23:30:38:720 EST] bf20d22b EJSContainer  > preInvoke
[00.11.01 23:30:38:750 EST] bf20d22b ContainerTx   > enlist
                                 ContainerManagedBean0(BeanId(IncBean,
com.transarc.jmon.examples.Inc.IncKey@84f11c53), state = CACHED_SHARED)
[00.11.01 23:30:38:750 EST] bf20d22b ContainerTx   < enlist
                                 true
[00.11.01 23:30:38:750 EST] bf20d22b EJSContainer  < preInvoke
[00.11.01 23:30:38:750 EST] bf20d22b EJSContainer  > postInvoke
[00.11.01 23:30:38:750 EST] bf20d22b ContainerTx   > beforeCompletion
[00.11.01 23:30:38:760 EST] bf20d22b ContainerTx   < beforeCompletion
[00.11.01 23:30:38:780 EST] bf20d22b ContainerTx   > afterCompletion
                                 true

com.ibm.ejs.container.ContainerTx@66c2d223
[00.11.01 23:30:38:780 EST] bf20d22b ContainerTx   < afterCompletion
[00.11.01 23:30:38:780 EST] bf20d22b EJSContainer  < postInvoke
```

23.5.9.2 Sample output of trace: com.ibm.servlet.engine

We obtained the following trace when we accessed the ping servlet.

```
[00.11.01 23:44:41:762 EST] bf30d22b SQEventListen D Run in thread
[00.11.01 23:44:41:762 EST] bf30d22b SQEventListen > ServiceRunnable.run
[00.11.01 23:44:41:762 EST] bf30d22b SQEventListen D Event is service
[00.11.01 23:44:41:762 EST] bf30d22b OSEListenerDi > service
[00.11.01 23:44:41:762 EST] bf30d22b SRPConnection > init
[00.11.01 23:44:41:762 EST] bf30d22b SRPConnection D resetting
SRPConnection Object
[00.11.01 23:44:41:762 EST] bf30d22b SRPConnection > resetObject
[00.11.01 23:44:41:762 EST] bf30d22b SRPConnection < resetObject
[00.11.01 23:44:41:762 EST] bf30d22b SRPConnection < init
[00.11.01 23:44:41:762 EST] bf30d22b ServletReques > dispatchByURI
                                 "/webapp/examples/ping"
[00.11.01 23:44:41:762 EST] bf30d22b ServletReques D
Worker#10-RequestProcessor.dispatch():com.ibm.servlet.engine.srp.Servle
tRequestProcessor@af2bd22b
[00.11.01 23:44:41:762 EST] bf30d22b ServletReques D Attempt to locate
cached invocation for: localhost:80/webapp/examples/ping
[00.11.01 23:44:41:762 EST] bf30d22b InvocationCac > get
                                 "localhost:80/webapp/examples/ping"
[00.11.01 23:44:41:762 EST] bf30d22b InvocationCac < get
```

23.5.9.3 Sample output of trace: com.ibm.ejs.security

The following is the sample output of the WebSphere Security trace.

```
[00.10.26 08:32:13:131 EDT] b1f603c7 SecurityColla <
performAuthorization
```

```
[00.10.26 08:32:13:932 EDT] f32883d3 SecurityColla >
SetUnauthenticatedCredIfNeeded
[00.10.26 08:32:13:932 EDT] f32883d3 SecurityColla <
SetUnauthenticatedCredIfNeeded :false
[00.10.26 08:32:13:932 EDT] f32883d3 SecurityColla >
performAuthorization
[00.10.26 08:32:13:932 EDT] f32883d3 SecurityColla D
methodInfo.getMethodName() : dumpRingBuffer
[00.10.26 08:32:13:932 EDT] f32883d3 SecurityColla D
methodInfo.getHomeName() : TraceServiceHome
[00.10.26 08:32:13:932 EDT] f32883d3 SecurityColla D
methodInfo.isHome(): false
[00.10.26 08:32:13:932 EDT] f32883d3 SecurityColla D Resource IS
protected.
[00.10.26 08:32:13:932 EDT] f32883d3 SecurityColla D resolvedMethodName
= dumpRingBuffer
[00.10.26 08:32:13:932 EDT] f32883d3 SecurityColla D invokedCred is
null: true
[00.10.26 08:32:13:932 EDT] f32883d3 SecurityColla D receivedCreds is
null: false
[00.10.26 08:32:13:932 EDT] f32883d3 SecurityColla > check authorization
[00.10.26 08:32:13:932 EDT] f32883d3 SecurityColla D Invoking principal
is System principal; Access allowed
[00.10.26 08:32:13:932 EDT] f32883d3 SecurityColla <
performAuthorization
```

23.5.10 Nanny trace

On UNIX platforms, the nanny process starts the administrative server. The nanny.maxtries parameter in the <WAS_HOME>/bin/admin.config file tells the nanny process how many times it should attempt to restart the administrative server.

On Windows platforms, the nanny service is part of the IBM WS AdminServer service that is registered with the operating system. Starting the IBM WS AdminServer service invokes adminservice.exe. If the service does not start, verify:

- The service was installed and is available by clicking **Start -> Settings -> Control Panel -> Services**
- The user ID under which WebSphere Application Server was installed has service privileges

If the nanny process fails to start the Admin Server on UNIX or if the IBM WS AdminServer service does not start on Windows platforms, you can bypass the nanny function and just start the administrative server:

1. Navigate to the <WAS_HOME>/bin/debug directory.
2. Invoke adminserver.sh on UNIX or adminserver.bat on Windows platforms.

Note: Starting the administrative server without using the nanny function means that nothing is monitoring the administrative server. If it fails in this state, nothing will restart it.

A nanny trace is available only on UNIX platforms.

On Windows platforms, use the Event log to view entries related to the WebSphere nanny service.

1. Select **Start -> Programs -> Administrative Tools**
2. Select **Event Viewer**
3. View events related to the WebSphere Application Server

23.5.11 Using DrAdmin

DrAdmin is a TCP/IP service that allows modification of the trace settings of a running process without using the administrative console. It also allows modification of the ring buffer size and dumping of the ring buffer, and it enables you to request a Java stack trace of a remote Java process. DrAdmin can be very useful when attempting to determine what is ocurring in a process that appears to be hung or is looping.

As each WebSphere server starts, it dumps its DrAdmin port to standard output, and reports a line similar to the following:

```
28/09/00 04:23 : AUDIT [SZYMON-Laptop/__adminServer]: DrAdmin available
on port 3,071
```

This provides the port number that the DrAdmin service is listening on for that process. (Use the last occurance in the log.)

You can then use the following commands:

1. To dump the threads to the ringbuffer:

```
java com.ibm.ejs.sm.util.debug.DrAdmin -serverPort <port number>
-dumpThreads
```

2. To dump the ringbuffer to a file:

```
java com.ibm.ejs.sm.util.debug.DrAdmin -serverPort  <port number>
-dumpRingBuffer threadDump.txt
```

Note: When setting the classpath, DrAdmin is in admin.jar.

The easiest way to run DrAdmin is to make a copy of your adminserver.bat (Windows) or adminserver.sh (UNIX) file, called dradmin.bat or dradmin.sh, and change the following line (the following example is for Windows):

```
%JAVA_HOME%\bin\java -DDER_DRIVER_PATH=%DER_DRIVER_PATH% -Xmx128m
-Xminf0.15 -Xmaxf0.25 com.ibm.ejs.sm.server.AdminServer -bootFile
%WAS_HOME%\bin\admin.config %restart% %1 %2 %3 %4
```

to

```
%JAVA_HOME%\bin\java com.ibm.ejs.sm.util.debug.DrAdmin %1 %2 %3 %4 %5 %6
%7 %8 %9
```

You can then run the dradmin.bat or dradmin.sh file using the following syntax:

```
Usage:
  java com.ibm.ejs.sm.util.debug.DrAdmin [options]

where options include:
  -help  shows this help message
  -serverHost <Server host name> [Defaults to localhost]
  -serverPort <Server port number> [required]
  -setTrace <Trace specification>
  -setRingBufferSize <Number of ringBuffer entries in K>
  -dumpRingBuffer <File to dump to> [default]
  -dumpState <dumpString>
  -stopServer
  -stopNode
  -dumpThreads
```

The WSCP `DrAdmin remote` command can also be used to invoke DrAdmin on a remote server, using the following syntax:

```
DrAdmin remote <server port>

The following options are available for remote

[-serverHost <string>]          Server host name
[-setTrace <string>]            Process the trace specification
[-setRingBufferSize <string>]   Set number of ringbuffer entries in K
[-dumpRingBuffer <string>]      Dump ring buffer to the specified file
[-dumpState <string>]           Process the dump specification
[-stopServer]                   Stop the server
[-stopNode]                     Stop the node
[-dumpThreads]                  Dump the server threads
```

23.6 Object level trace (OLT) and the IBM distributed debugger

Object Level Trace (OLT) is a distributed object tracing and debugging facility. It allows users to see their object interactions, and allows them to debug distributed code. OLT/Debugger is distributed in the sense that the trace and debug GUIs can run on a separate machine on the network from where the code is running. It is also distributed in the sense that you can trace and debug objects that exist in different address spaces and invoke each other.

OLT consists of two components: a debugger and a tracing facility. The debugger works like most debuggers. You can step through source code, set breakpoints, inspect variables and perform other actions. The trace presented by Object Level Trace is not like WebSphere's internal trace facility. The tracing facility is an object-level view of the interactions between the objects deployed in your application server. For example, if you traced a servlet that called another servlet in your application server, in the OLT GUI you would see a representation of both servlets and arrows between them showing the method call relationships.

In order to trace or debug a servlet, you must enable the application server where that servlet is deployed. OLT and debug enablement is done at the application server level. This means that all servlets and JSPs deployed in that server will be OLT enabled. The settings on the application server can be done through WebSphere Administrative Console.

23.6.1 Installing OLT and the distributed debugger

The IBM distributed debugger is not installed by default with WebSphere. However, it is contained on the CD. Therefore, you can select it when you install WebSphere. Or navigate to the OLT subdirectory on the disk and run setup.exe. Ensure that when installing you select the **Full Install** option to install all OLT/debugger support, including the OLT GUI and the Debugger GUI, as shown in Figure 759 on page 959.

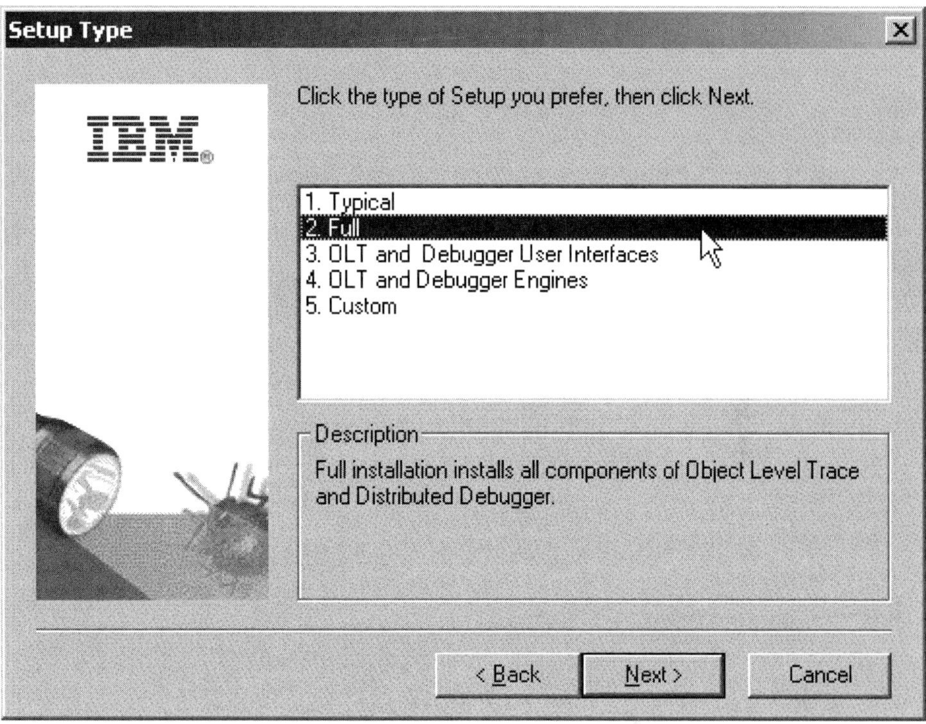

Figure 759. Choose the full install of OLT

23.6.2 Running OLT

In order to trace or debug Java code running in an application server, the following steps must be carried out *in order*.

1. Configure an application server's properties for OLT and debugging, and start the server
2. Start the OLT executable on the machine where you want to view OLT, or debug output
3. Request a resource or application deployed in the application server

23.6.2.1 Preparing your application for debugging

Before debugging your code, you must recompile your code with the debug information (use the -g option). To do so, please use the following command:

```
javac -g myclass.java
```

23.6.2.2 Enable OLT for an application server

Before tracing or debugging code running on an application server, you must enable tracing or debugging on the server.

1. Start the administrative server.
1. Start the WebSphere Administrative Console.
2. Click your application server.
3. Click the **Debug** tab.
4. To enable debugging, select the **Debug enabled** option. This starts the server in a debuggable JVM.
5. To enable OLT, select the **Object Level Tracing** option.
6. Click **Apply** to apply the changes.
7. Restart the application server.

Figure 760 shows the application server debug tag with both the debug and OLT options selected.

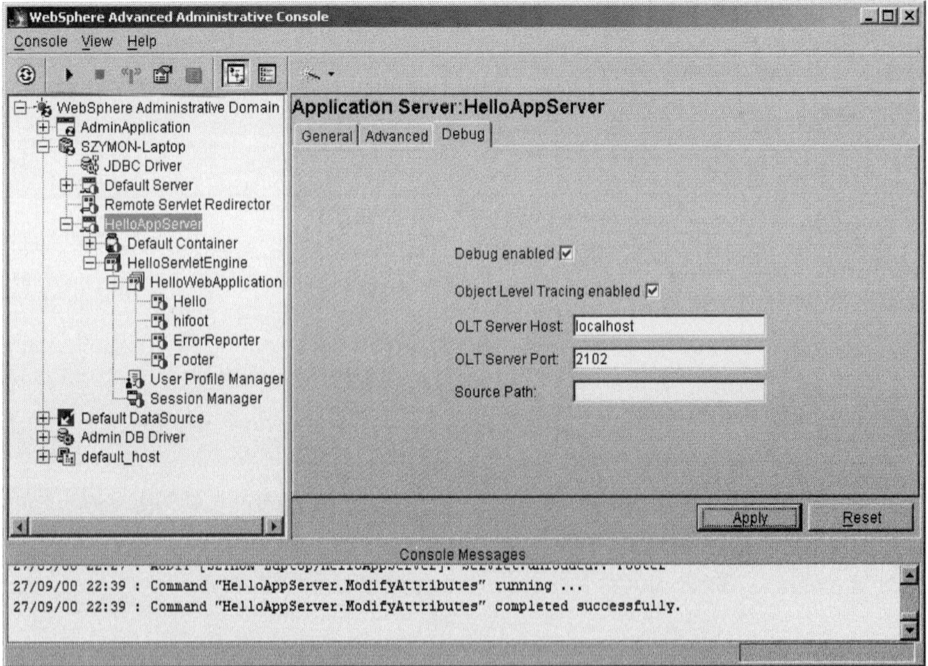

Figure 760. The application server: Debug tab

23.6.2.3 Running OLT

OLT creates a graphical trace of your distributed application. You can use this trace to analyze performance and isolate communication errors. In addition, you can set method breakpoints on the trace, prior to running OLT in conjunction with the debugger. Even if your ultimate goal is to debug your application, you should first create a trace by running OLT in trace only mode, then set method breakpoints and rerun OLT in trace and debug mode.

When you start Object Level Trace, the default settings assume that your client application is to run on the same workstation as OLT. You may, however, want to trace a client application that is run from a different workstation. In that case, follow the steps below to start the OLT components on separate machines.

23.6.2.4 Running OLT locally

To run OLT on the same machine as your application server, you simply need to invoke the command. From a command line, enter `olt`. The Object Level Trace Viewer window appears as depicted in Figure 761.

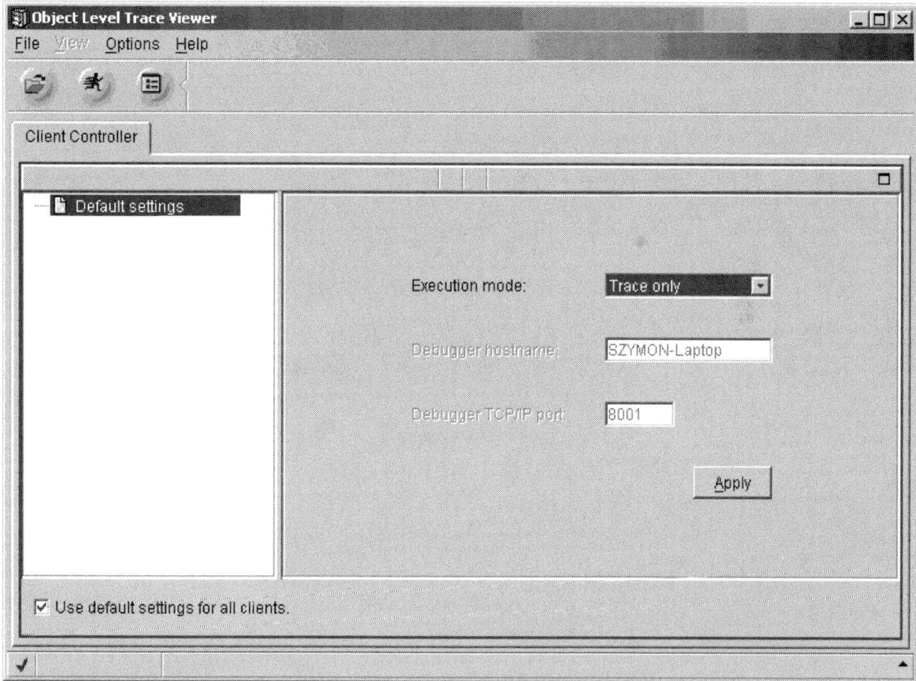

Figure 761. The OLT GUI

> **Note**
>
> On Windows NT, do not close the OLT command prompt window until you have finished tracing and debugging.

23.6.2.5 Running OLT from a remote workstation

Running OLT on a remote workstation is simple. On the machine where you intend to monitor the trace, invoke the `olt` command to bring up the OLT window as shown in Figure 761 on page 961.

Enable the application server for a remote OLT workstation

Before tracing or debugging code running on an application server, you must enable tracing or debugging on the server.

1. Start the administrative server.
2. Start the WebSphere Administrative Console.
3. Click your application server.
4. Click the **Debug** tab.
5. To enable debugging, select the **Debug enabled** option. This starts the server in a debuggable JVM.
6. To enable OLT, select the **Object Level Tracing enabled** option.
7. Change the OLT Server Host name to the remote OLT workstation host name.
8. Click **Apply** to apply the changes.
9. Restart the application server.

Figure 762 on page 963 shows the application server Debug tab with both the debug and OLT options selected.

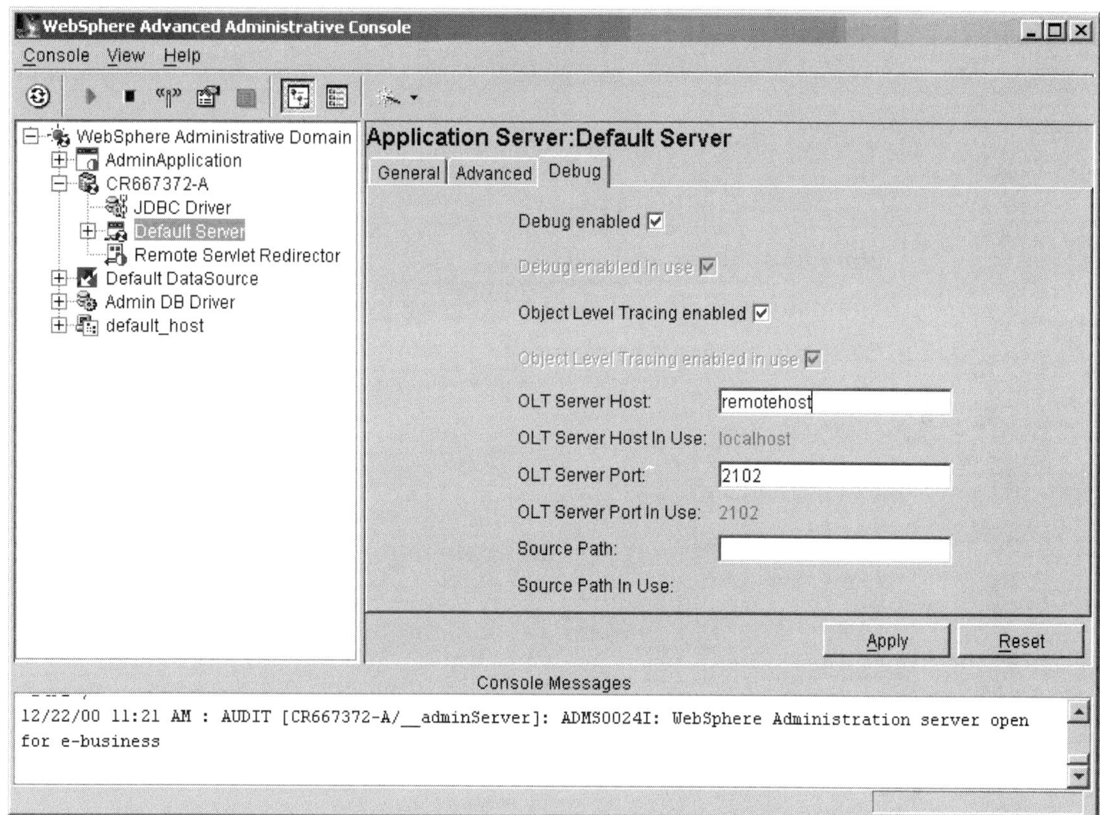

Figure 762. The application server: Debug tab

23.6.3 Object level trace - tracing a servlet

Start OLT then run the client that you want to trace as normal (in our case, we access a servlet with our browser).

When your client calls objects (in our case, we access servlets with our browser) on the application server (or multiple servers), some trace lines and event symbols should appear as shown in Figure 763.

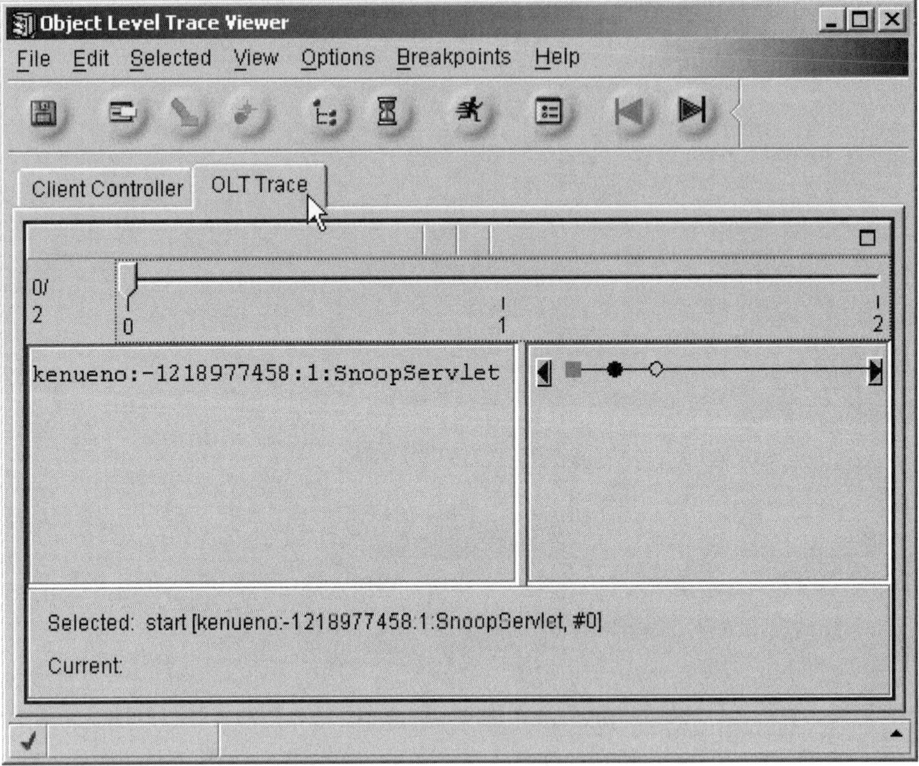

Figure 763. The OLT output of the snoop servlet

Even if you have not set the online mode, when your client calls objects, the OLT Trace tab will appear on the window.

For demonstration purposes, we use the chainer servlet example in Chapter 5, “Servlet support” on page 137. This servlet, called hifoot, is a chainer servlet that chains two other servlets together, the HelloWorldServlet that outputs the message “Hello, world”, and the FooterServlet that outputs a footer containing a copyright message. We will examine the interaction between the servlets. For this example, we have only turned on tracing, not debugging.

We call the servlet by typing the URL in our browser window. Figure 764 on page 965 contains the output of the hifoot chainer servlet.

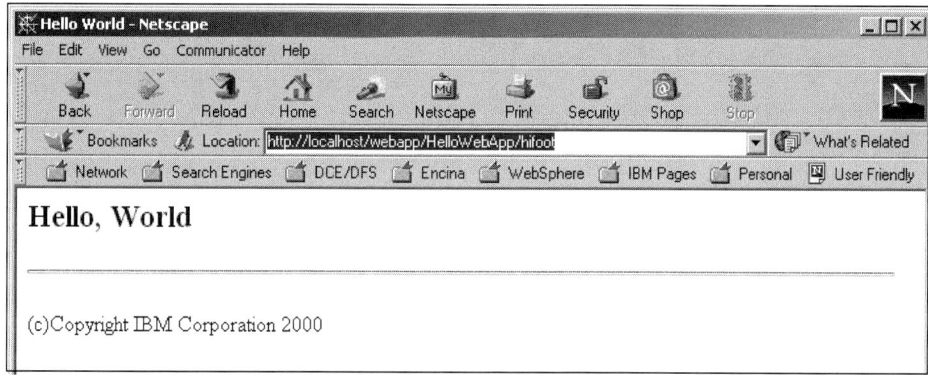

Figure 764. The output of the hifoot servlet

Once the servlet has run, we can see the interaction between the servlets in the object level trace viewer window. Figure 765 shows the viewer window after running the servlet.

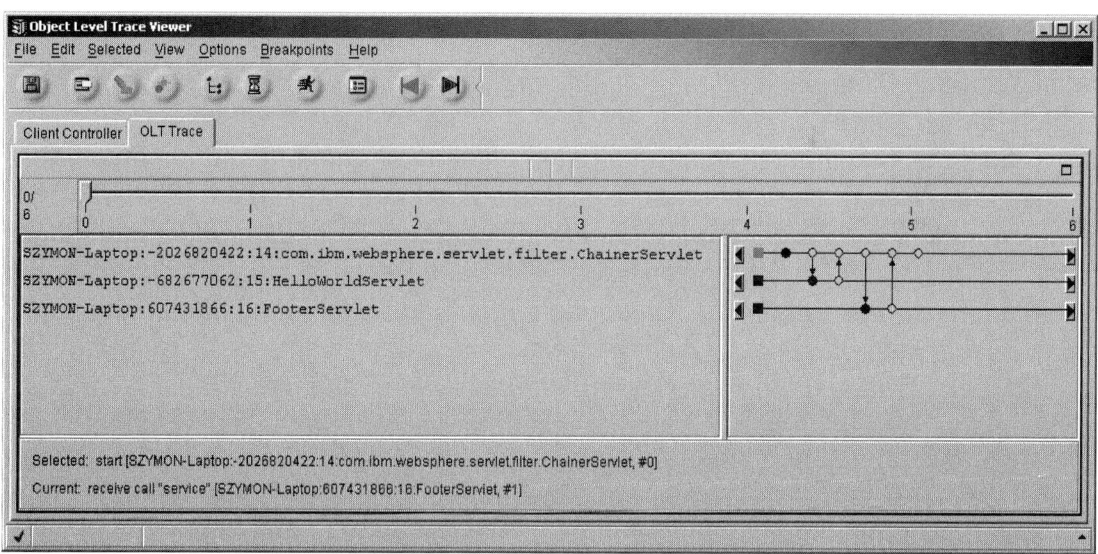

Figure 765. The OLT output of the hifoot servlet

The OLT Trace tab is split into four sections. The top section shows a slider with a sequence of events for the currently selected trace line. This slider enables scrolling the event focus along the trace. In this interaction there are six visible events. If you want to see the timeline you need to go to the real-time display by either selecting the hour-glass toolbar or by clicking **File -> Preferences -> OLT -> Display** and selecting the **Real-time** radio button in the Display style section and clicking the **OK** button. The middle pane on the left shows information about the objects being traced, in this case the servlets. The information is in the format:

```
HostName:ProcessId:ObjectId:ObjectName
```

The middle pane on the right shows the interaction between the objects, and the bottom pane gives information about the selected event. The two middle panes together represent trace lines: horizontal lines connecting a sequence of events or method calls running under a single execution thread. Each trace line represents either an object, servlet or EJB residing on the application server, or the client application or servlet which initiated the method call. Figure 766 shows a closeup of the interaction pane.

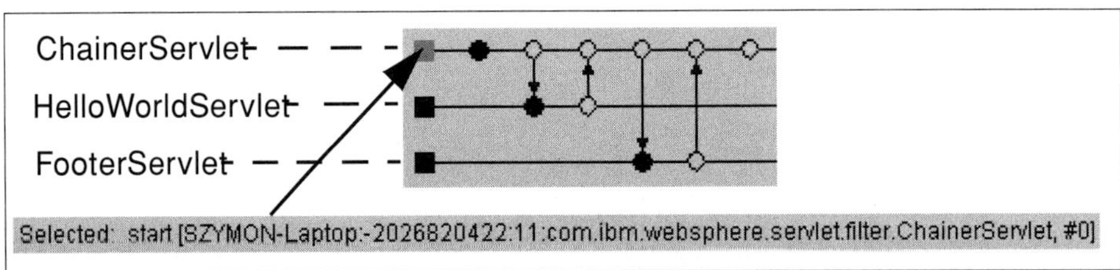

Figure 766. Interaction between servlets

The circles represent entries into and exits from methods. The filled circles are those on which breakpoints can be set. The selected event is colored in green, and this event is represented on the Selected status line at the bottom.

Selecting each of the events in turn, moving left to right and following the arrows between the trace lines, we can see the interaction between the servlets. Here is a summary of the events, taken from the status lines when choosing the events in turn. The format presented is type of call, name of call, object, event number (for that object).

```
oneway call "service" com.ibm.websphere.servlet.filter.ChainerServlet #1
call "service" com.ibm.websphere.servlet.filter.ChainerServlet #2
receive call "service" HelloWorldServlet #1
reply "doGet" HelloWorldServlet #2
receive reply "doGet" com.ibm.websphere.servlet.filter.ChainerServlet #3
call "service" com.ibm.websphere.servlet.filter.ChainerServlet #4
receive call "service" FooterServlet #1
reply "doGet" FooterServlet #2
receive reply "doGet" com.ibm.websphere.servlet.filter.ChainerServlet #5
reply "doGet" com.ibm.websphere.servlet.filter.ChainerServlet #6
```

23.6.4 Setting method breakpoints on the trace

Once the application has finished running, you can use the trace to set method breakpoints on debuggable events (debuggable events are represented by filled circles).

You can set a method breakpoint on any debuggable server event. You cannot set a method breakpoint on an application exception event, or an event that is waiting for its partner to arrive (these events are represented by an unfilled circle with an X through it).

To set a method breakpoint, select the filled circle that represents the object method of servlet, EJB, or JSP that you want to debug. From the circle's pop-up menu, select **Add to Method Breakpoint List** as shown in Figure 767.

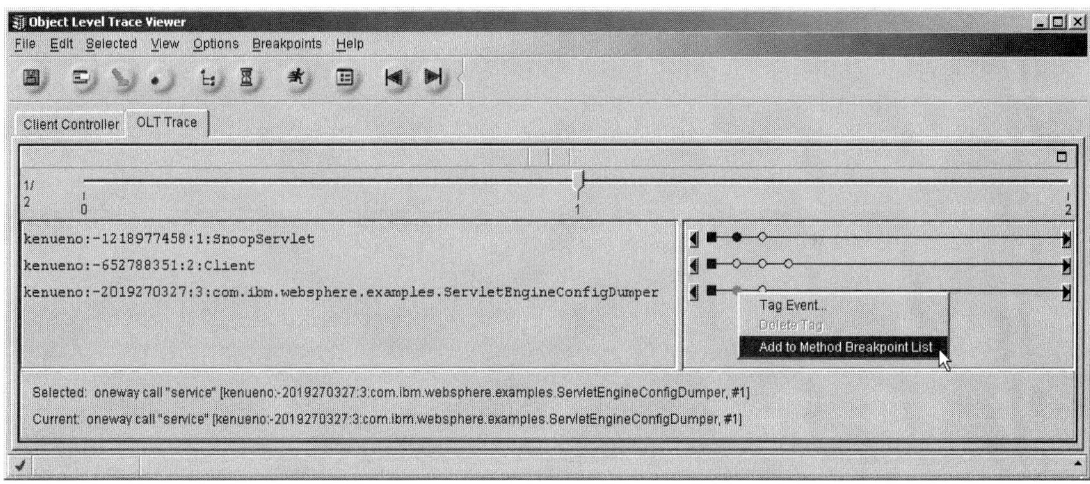

Figure 767. Add to Method Breakpoint List

Alternatively, you can manually enter breakpoint information using the Create Method Breakpoints dialog box, by selecting **Breakpoints -> Create Method Breakpoints** as shown in Figure 768 on page 968.

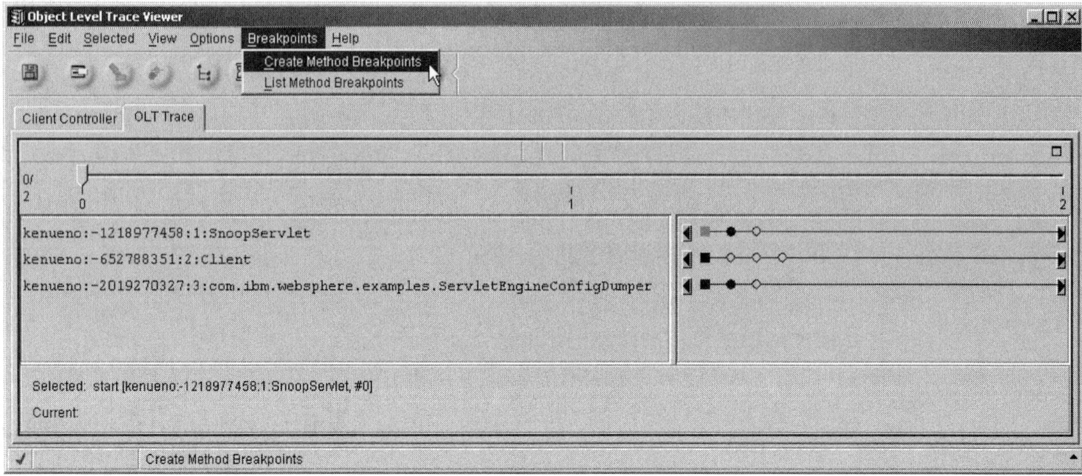

Figure 768. Create method breakpoints

Select the Server host name, Object name, and Method name from the drop-down list as shown in Figure 769. Click **Create** then click **OK**.

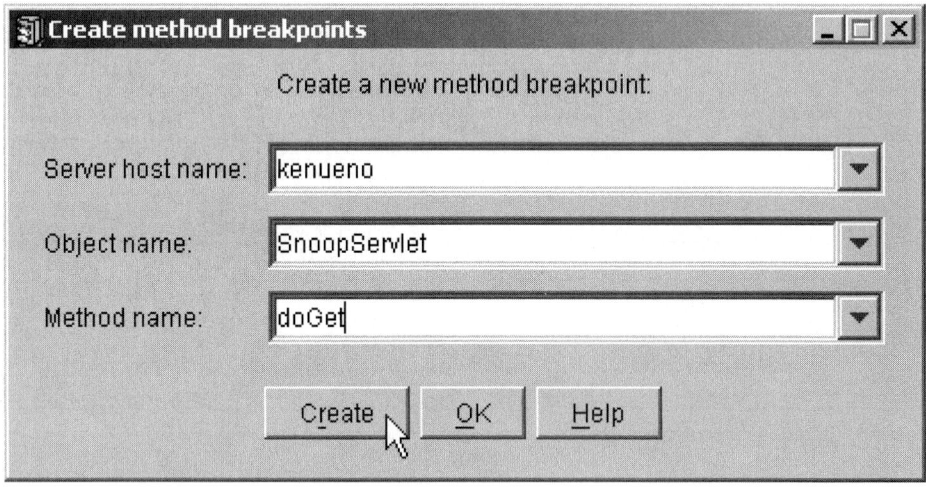

Figure 769. Create a new method breakpoint

23.6.5 Running the debugger from OLT

You can debug business objects, servlets, or EJBs using Object Level Trace. You should already have created a trace (by running OLT in "Trace only" mode) and set method breakpoints on the trace. To run the debugger, you must select **Trace and debug** from the Execution mode option on the Client Controller tab of the OLT viewer as shown in Figure 770.

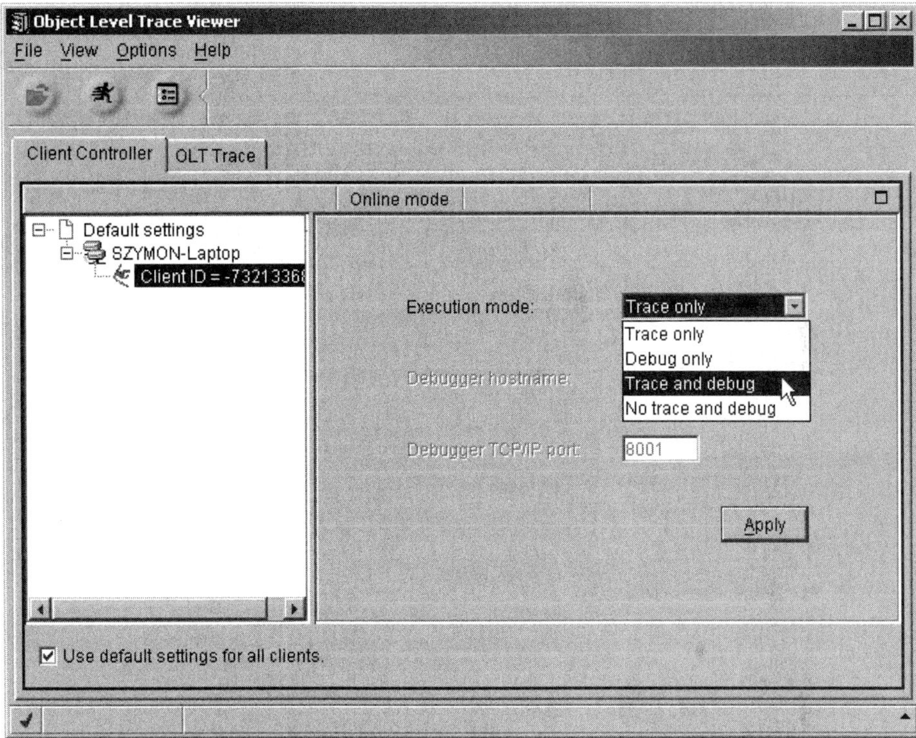

Figure 770. Choose Trace and debug mode

The value of the Debugger hostname determines where the debugger daemon should be started and where the debugger GUI will open. If the Debugger hostname points to the localhost, the daemon will be automatically started on the first client registering with the OLT, which is expected to execute in the “Trace and debug” or “Debug only” mode. Otherwise, if the Debugger hostname points to a remote host, the daemon has to be started on that host manually by executing the following command:

```
idebug -qdaemon -quiport=8001
```

To verify if the daemon is started check if the jdebug_sui process is running.

The location of the OLT Debugger Daemon determines where the debugger interface opens when OLT encounters your first method breakpoint. When you start OLT, the Debugger Daemon automatically starts on the same machine (assuming that you have not changed your Remote Debugger settings to point to another machine).

As your application runs, trace lines and symbols are added to the OLT Viewer. When OLT encounters a method breakpoint, the debugger automatically attaches to the process and finds the method on which you set the breakpoint. At the same time, the debugger interface opens wherever the OLT Debugger Daemon is running. Figure 771 on page 970 shows the debugger attached to the HelloWorldServlet.

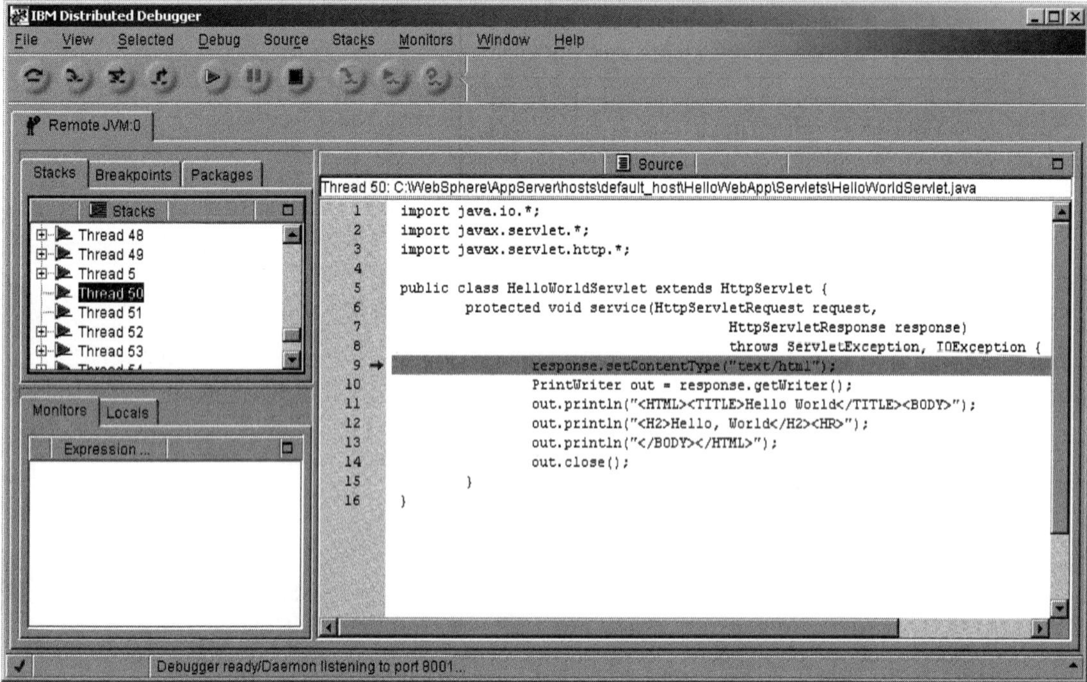

Figure 771. The debugger

The debugger here is at the beginning of the service method of the HelloWorldServlet.

Once you have stepped through the object method call, servlet, or EJB, your application runs until the next method breakpoint, or the end of the program, is reached. Alternatively, you can step the debugger out of the server-side function and into your client code. This opens a second debugger pane, which points to the client code, immediately past the server call. Thus, you are able to debug both server and client seamlessly, as if they were one application.

Note that when debugging Java classes, make sure that any source files for your classes are accessible from the system CLASSPATH environment variable. That is, if the source for my.package.MyClass resides in x:\source\my\package\MyClass.java, you must add x:\source to the CLASSPATH. Otherwise, you will not be able to view the source. Even the snoop servlet is not in the class path; therefore, IBM Distributed Debugger prompts for the correct source location as shown in Figure 772 on page 971.

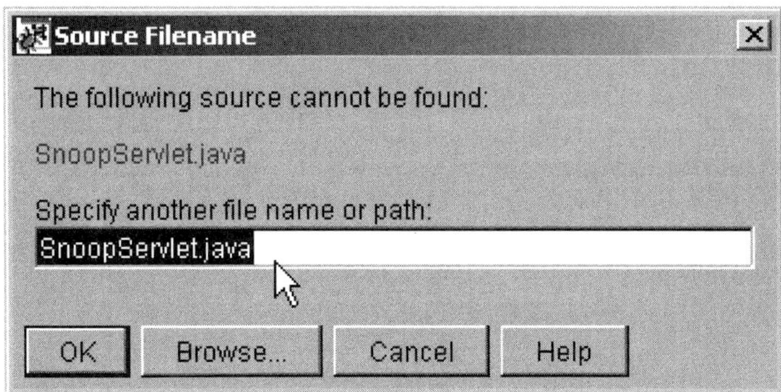

Figure 772. Cannot find the SnoopServlet.java source file

If you click **Cancel** from this window, the debugger will continue debugging without being able to show the source file.

Click **Browse...** to locate the source file. Select the source file and click **Open** as shown in Figure 773.

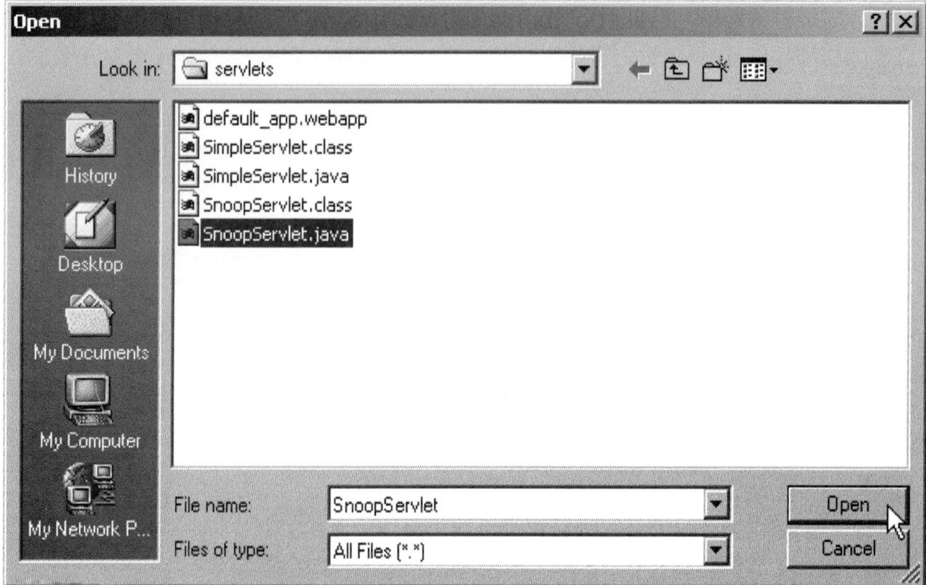

Figure 773. Select the SnoopServlet.java

Then go back to the Source Filename window. The source file name and path are specified as shown in Figure 774 on page 972. Click **OK** and the debugger will resume debugging at the first debuggable line of the snoop servlet.

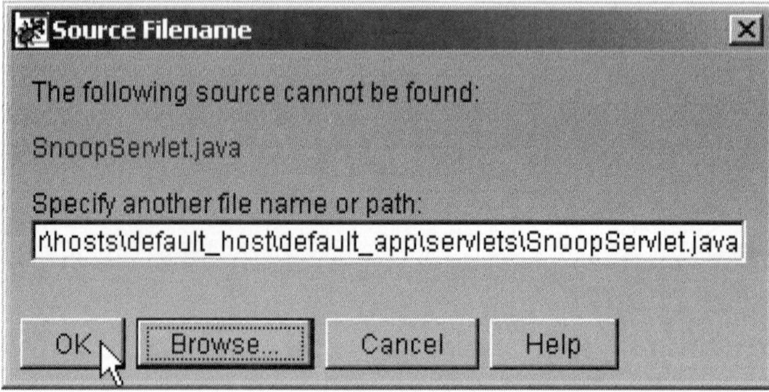

Figure 774. Location of the snoop servlet source file

23.6.6 Platforms supported for OLT and Distributed Debugger

Table 55 shows the current platforms supported for OLT and IBM Distributed Debugger.

Table 55. Current platforms supported for OLT and IBM Distributed Debugger

	AIX	AS/400	Solaris	Windows	HP-UX	Linux	Linux/390
OLT Tracing support	✓	✓	✓	✓	✓	✓	✓
Java Debugging support		✓		✓		limited functionality	limited functionality

Chapter 24. Log Analyzer

WebSphere V3.5.2 provides a new problem determination tool, the Log Analyzer.

The Log Analyzer is a GUI tool that permits the customer to view an activity.log file for errors and sort log entries based on severity, process ID, thread ID, etc. More importantly, this tool has a simple XML database behind it that permits the customer to analyze errors and offers additional information such as why the errors occurred and how to recover from them.

This chapter takes an in-depth look at the Log Analyzer. Note that this is a technology preview product of WebSphere V3.5.2. For this redbook, most of the Log Analyzer testing was done while using the WebSphere Advanced Edition.

24.1 Log Analyzer overview

The infrastructure for the Log Analyzer is part of WebSphere V3.5.2. However, the tool itself is not. The Log Analyzer is available for download. See 24.2, "Downloading and installing the Log Analyzer" on page 977 for detailed information.

A new message logging service has been added in WebSphere V3.5.2. This logging service will log messages to a shared file. This file is a binary file located in the <WAS_HOME>/logs directory and is named "activity.log". <WAS_HOME> is the WebSphere Application Server install directory. The activity.log cannot be easily viewed using a text editor. The preferred tool to view this file is the Log Analyzer.

The Log Analyzer takes one or more activity or trace logs, merges all the data and displays the entries in sequence. It analyzes error conditions in the log entries to provide error message explanations.

As shown in Figure 775 on page 976, the Log Analyzer's main window has three panes:

- Logs pane (left)

  All of the log entries are displayed in the logs pane in hierarchical order.

  The background color may help you quickly identify the ones that have high severity errors. After invoking the Analyzer or Advanced Analyze actions, an icon appears in front of the log entry to show which kind information can be obtained.

- Record pane (upper right)

  When you select an entry under the unit of work in the Logs pane, you see detailed information about the entry in the Record pane.

  Each entry in the activity log has many fields that you may check on the record pane.

- Analysis pane (lower right)

  In the Analysis pane, the Symptom page is the only one currently supported.

  For the Symptom page, the Log Analyzer provides a database of information to help you recover from some common errors. As a part of the Analyze action, if such recovery information is found in the database for the selected log entry, the information is displayed.

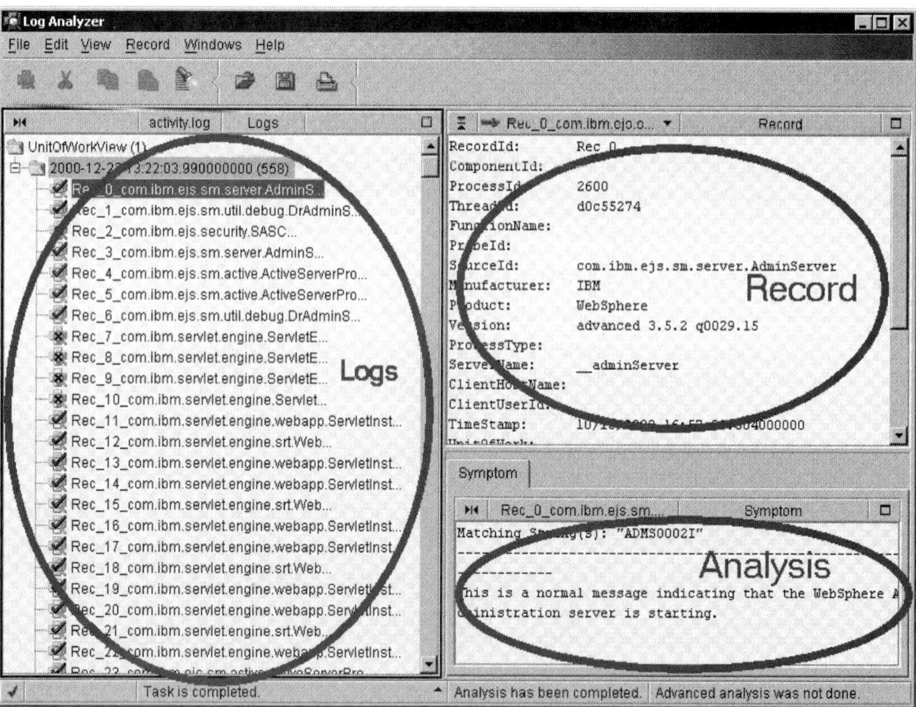

Figure 775. The main window of Log Analyzer

There is a status line at the bottom of the window showing the status of actions.

24.2 Downloading and installing the Log Analyzer

The Log Analyzer for WebSphere Application V3.5.2 technology preview is available for Web download from the following FTP site:

```
ftp://ftp.software.ibm.com/software/websphere/info/tools/loganalyzer/
```

To install the Log Analyzer, download the logbr.zip or logbr.tar.Z file appropriate for the target platform and unzip/untar it under the directory <WAS_HOME> where WebSphere Application Server V3.5.2 has been installed.

24.3 Using the Log Analyzer to view the activity.log

To view the activity log called "activity.log", execute the waslogbr script file (waslogbr.bat for Windows or waslogbr for UNIX), which is found in the <WAS_HOME>/bin directory. This starts the Log Analyzer graphical user interface (GUI) as shown in Figure 776.

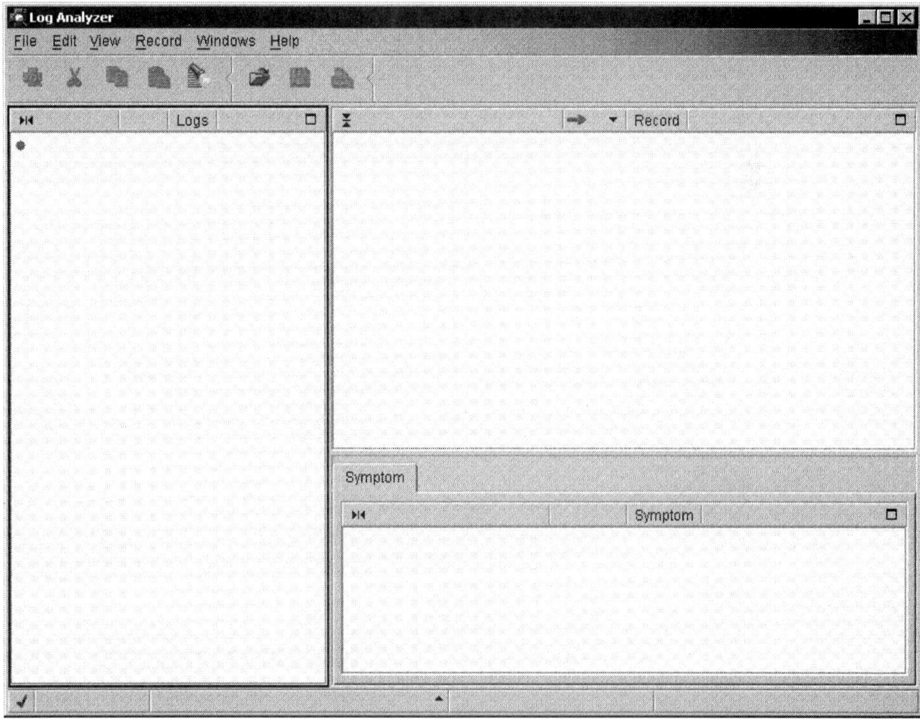

Figure 776. Using the Log Analyzer to view the activity.log

Then from the GUI, select **File->Open** as shown in Figure 777.

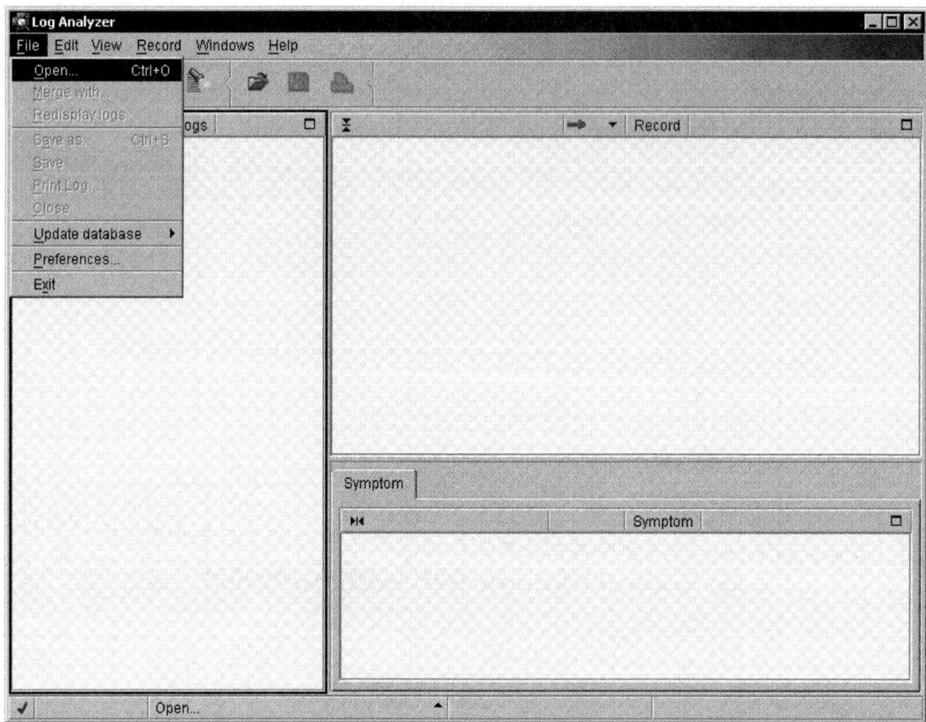

Figure 777. Open the activity.log #1

Then navigate to the directory containing the activity.log. Select the activity.log file and then select **Open** as shown in Figure 778.

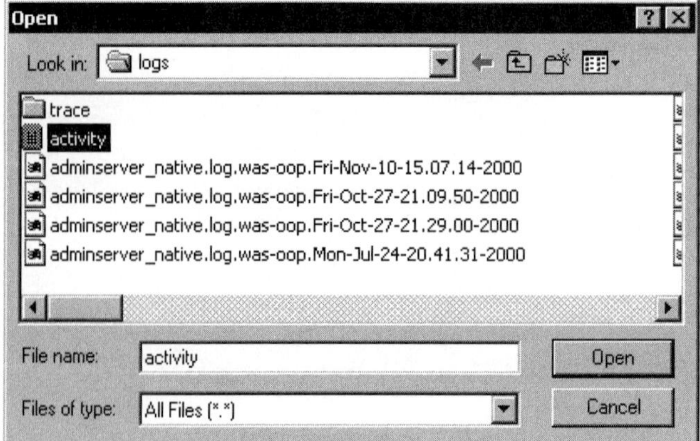

Figure 778. Open the activity.log #2

Now you will see the UnitOfWorkView folder on the Log Analyzer Logs pane and in that folder you probably can see a couple of folders (in our case, 2000-12-23 12:50:15.976000000) as shown in Figure 779.

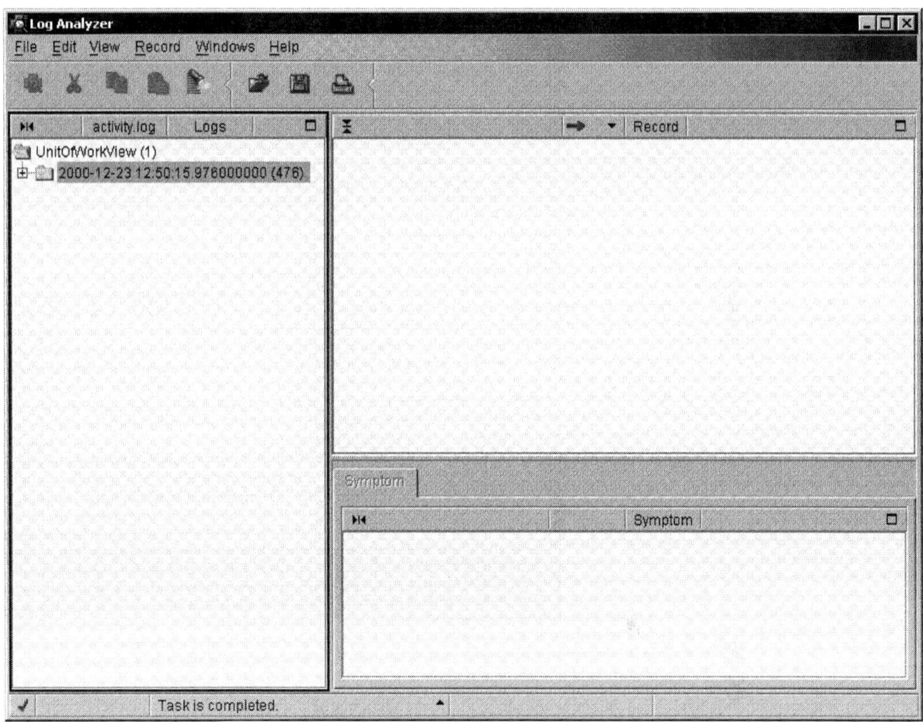

Figure 779. The UnitOfWorkView folder

24.4 Using showlog to view the activity.log

The Log Analyzer cannot be used to view remote files. If the platform on which you are running WebSphere Application Server does not support the use of a GUI, you should transfer the file in binary to the system on which you are running the administrative console and use the Log Analyzer tool there. In cases where this is not practical or inconvenient, an alternate tool named "showlog" is provided to view the activity.log.

The `showlog` script file (`showlog.bat` for Windows or `showlog` for UNIX) is found in the <WAS_HOME>/bin directory. Invoking `showlog` with no parameters will display usage instructions.

```
C:\>cd \WebSphere\AppServer\bin

C:\WebSphere\AppServer\bin>showlog
This program dumps a Websphere binary log file to standard out or a file.
Usage: showlog binaryFilename [outputFilename]
where:
        binaryFilename  represents the name of the input binary log file

        outputFilename  represents the name of the output file


C:\WebSphere\AppServer\bin>
```

To direct the activity log contents to stdout, use the invocation `showlog activity.log`.

```
C:\WebSphere\AppServer\bin>showlog C:\WebSphere\AppServer\logs\activity.log
$LANG = en_US
$CODESET = Cp1252
---------------------------------------------------------------
ComponentId:
ProcessId:        273
ThreadId:         f36a6af0
FunctionName:
ProbeId:
SourceId:         com.ibm.ejs.sm.server.AdminServer
Manufacturer:     IBM
Product:          WebSphere
Version:          advanced 3.5.2 ptf2b0041.07
ProcessType:
ServerName:       __adminServer
ClientHostName:
ClientUserId:
TimeStamp:        2000-10-19 18:22:29.461000000
UnitOfWork:
Severity:         3
Category:         AUDIT
FormatWarning:
PrimaryMessage:
ExtendedMessage: ADMS0002I: Initializing WebSphere Administration server
RawDataLen:       0
---------------------------------------------------------------
ComponentId:
ProcessId:        273
ThreadId:         17e86af1
FunctionName:
ProbeId:
SourceId:         com.ibm.ejs.sm.util.debug.DrAdminServer
Manufacturer:     IBM
Product:          WebSphere
Version:          advanced 3.5.2 ptf2b0041.07
ProcessType:
ServerName:       __adminServer
ClientHostName:
ClientUserId:
TimeStamp:        2000-10-19 18:22:29.582000000
UnitOfWork:
Severity:         3
Category:         AUDIT
FormatWarning:
PrimaryMessage:
ExtendedMessage: SMTL0018I: DrAdmin available on port 1177
RawDataLen:       0
---------------------------------------------------------------
ComponentId:
ProcessId:        273
ThreadId:         f36a6af0
FunctionName:
ProbeId:
SourceId:         com.ibm.ejs.sm.server.AdminServer
Manufacturer:     IBM
Product:          WebSphere
```

To dump the activity.log to a text file that can be viewed using a text editor use the invocation `showlog -d3 activity.log   textFileName`.

```
C:\WebSphere\AppServer\bin>showlog -d3 C:\WebSphere\AppServer\logs\activity.log C:\log

C:\WebSphere\AppServer\bin>dir C:\log.txt
 Volume in drive C has no label.
 Volume Serial Number is 2858-D36D

 Directory of C:\

10/19/00  06:37p                 1,778 log.txt
               1 File(s)          1,778 bytes
                            47,035,904 bytes free

C:\WebSphere\AppServer\bin>
C:\WebSphere\AppServer\bin>type c:\log.txt
$LANG = en_US
$CODESET = Cp1252
---------------------------------------------------------------
ComponentId:
ProcessId:       273
ThreadId:        f36a6af0
FunctionName:
ProbeId:
SourceId:        com.ibm.ejs.sm.server.AdminServer
Manufacturer:    IBM
Product:         WebSphere
Version:         advanced 3.5.2 ptf2b0041.07
ProcessType:
ServerName:      __adminServer
ClientHostName:
ClientUserId:
TimeStamp:       2000-10-19 18:22:29.461000000
UnitOfWork:
Severity:        3
Category:        AUDIT
FormatWarning:
PrimaryMessage:
ExtendedMessage: ADMS0002I: Initializing WebSphere Administration server
RawDataLen:      0
---------------------------------------------------------------
ComponentId:
ProcessId:       273
ThreadId:        17e86af1
FunctionName:
ProbeId:
SourceId:        com.ibm.ejs.sm.util.debug.DrAdminServer
Manufacturer:    IBM
Product:         WebSphere
Version:         advanced 3.5.2 ptf2b0041.07
ProcessType:
ServerName:      __adminServer
ClientHostName:
ClientUserId:
TimeStamp:       2000-10-19 18:22:29.582000000
```

24.5 Configuring the activity.log

There are four parameters that you can configure for the activity.log: size of activity.log, port number on which the logging service is listening, enabling shared logging, and the output format of the ring buffer. The first two are described in the following sections, and the output format is discussed in 24.8, "Using the Log Analyzer to view the ring buffer dump" on page 996. Enabling shared logging is not discussed.

24.5.1 Specify the size of activity.log

The activity.log will grow to a predetermined size and then will wrap. The default size is 1 MB.

A property named "SHARED_LOG_LENGTH" can be specified to change the size of this log.

To change this property, edit the file named <WAS_HOME>/properties/logging.properties. The size of the log is specified in KBytes. For example, to change the log size to 2 MB, enter the line `SHARED_LOG_LENGTH=2048` (without any spaces). If an invalid size is entered, the default size is used.

```
# The SHARED_LOG_LENGTH property in Kbytes. Default value is 1 meg.
# Following example would set the log length to 2 meg
#SHARED_LOG_LENGTH=2048
```

Figure 780. SHARED_LOG_LENGTH property in the logging.properties

The size change will take effect at the next server startup.

24.5.2 Specify the port on which the logging service is listening

The logging service starts automatically at server startup. This logging service requires the use of a dedicated port. The default port used is 1707. If there are multiple installations or administrative instances of WebSphere on a physical machine, each instance should use a different port.

A property named SHARED_LOG_LOCK_PORT is provided to change the port value. To change this property, edit the file named <WAS_HOME>/properties/logging.properties.

```
# The Port used to implement the shared log lock. Default value is 1707
#SHARED_LOG_LOCK_PORT=1708
```

Figure 781. SHARED_LOG_LOCK_PORT property in the logging.properties

For example to change the port to 1708, add the line `SHARED_LOG_LOCK_PORT=1708`.

Note: If the port number is changed, all servers in the affected installation or instance, including the administrative server, must be cycled for the change to take effect. The recommended procedure for changing the port for an installation or instance is to stop all servers including the administrative server, change the port value and then restart the servers.

If the port is in use by another application, the logging service may not be able to start or may not function correctly and the activity.log file will not be created or updated correctly. The command `netstat` can be used to determine if another application is using a given port. However, if another application dynamically binds to, uses and releases the port, this may not be detected by `netstat`. In this case the following set of heuristic checks may be performed to diagnose the port conflict. First check to see if the activity.log file has been created, and check the timestamp of the file. Also, you can check the <WAS_HOME>/logs/<server_name>_stderr.log, <WAS_HOME>/logs/adminserver_stderr.log or <WAS_HOME>/logs/tracefile for a stack trace that looks like the following:

```
        java.lang.Exception: Unable to obtain Shared Log Lock on port1707
   at
com.ibm.ejs.ras.SharedLogBase.acquireHostLock(SharedLogBase.java:187)
   at com.ibm.ejs.ras.SharedLogWriter.<init>(SharedLogWriter.java:130)
   at
com.ibm.ejs.ras.SharedLogWriter.getInstance(SharedLogWriter.java:100)
   at com.ibm.ejs.ras.Tr.initialize(Tr.java:241)
   at com.ibm.ejs.sm.server.ManagedServer.main(ManagedServer.java:121)
```

24.6 Display log entries in different groupings

All of the log entries are displayed in the logs pane in hierarchical order.

The logs pane displays log entries by unit of work (UOW) by default.

To help you quickly identify problems, you can display the log entries in different groupings by setting the sort fields in the Preferences Logs page. To configure the sort fields, from the Log Analyzer window select **File -> Preferences...** as shown in Figure 782.

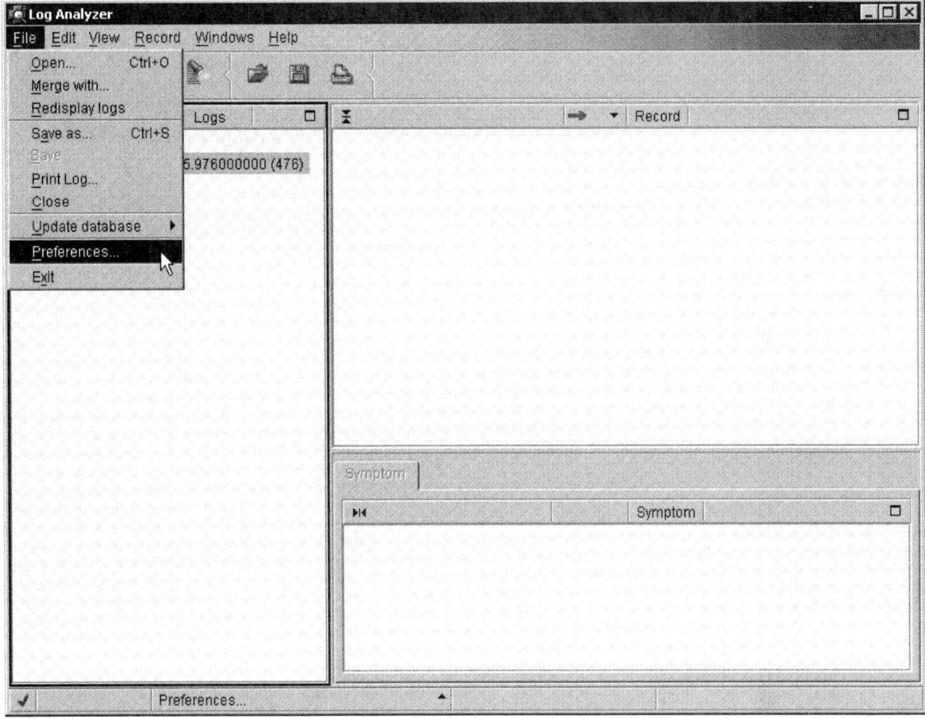

Figure 782. Configure the preferences

Then you will get the Analyzer Preferences windows. You can specify two filters. By default, UnitOf Work is specified as the Primary sort field as shown in Figure 783 on page 986.

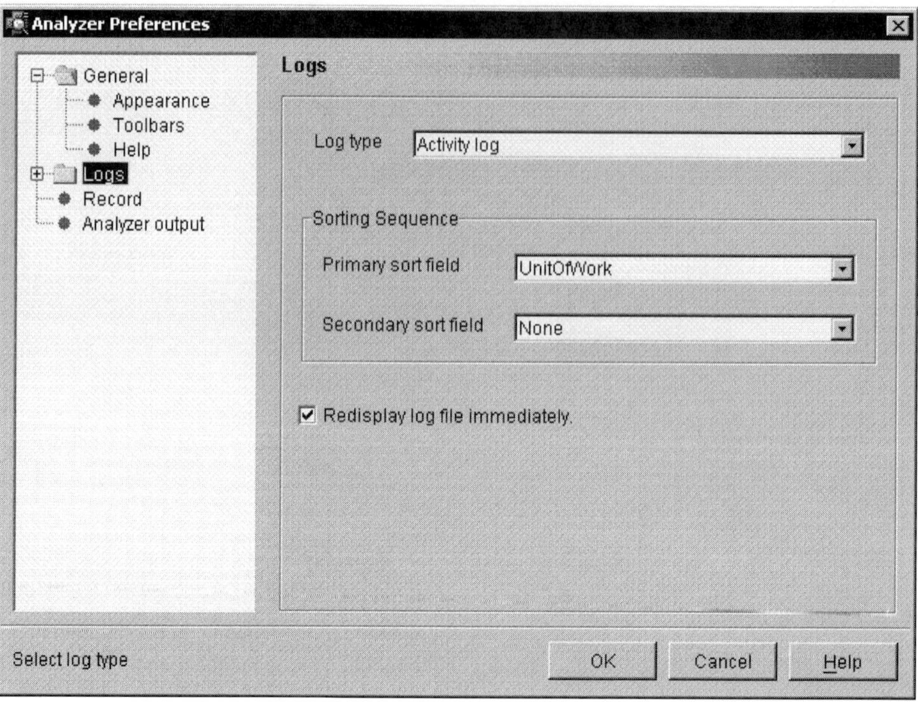

Figure 783. Log filtering

You may change the sorting sequence setting to select the most appropriate hierarchy for the problem you are solving. We will show you two sorting examples below.

24.6.1 Sorting by ServerName

For the first example, we set Primary sort field to ServerName on the Logs page of Analyzer Preferences, as shown in Figure 784 on page 987.

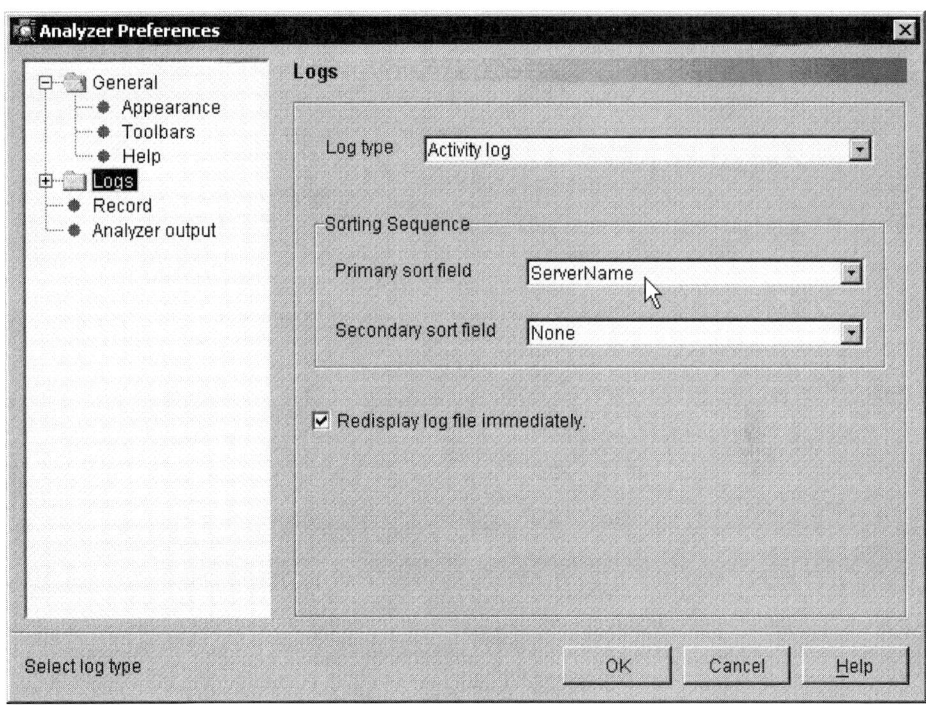

Figure 784. Logs page of Log Analyzer's Preferences

After clicking **OK**, the Logs pane changed as shown in Figure 785 on page 988.

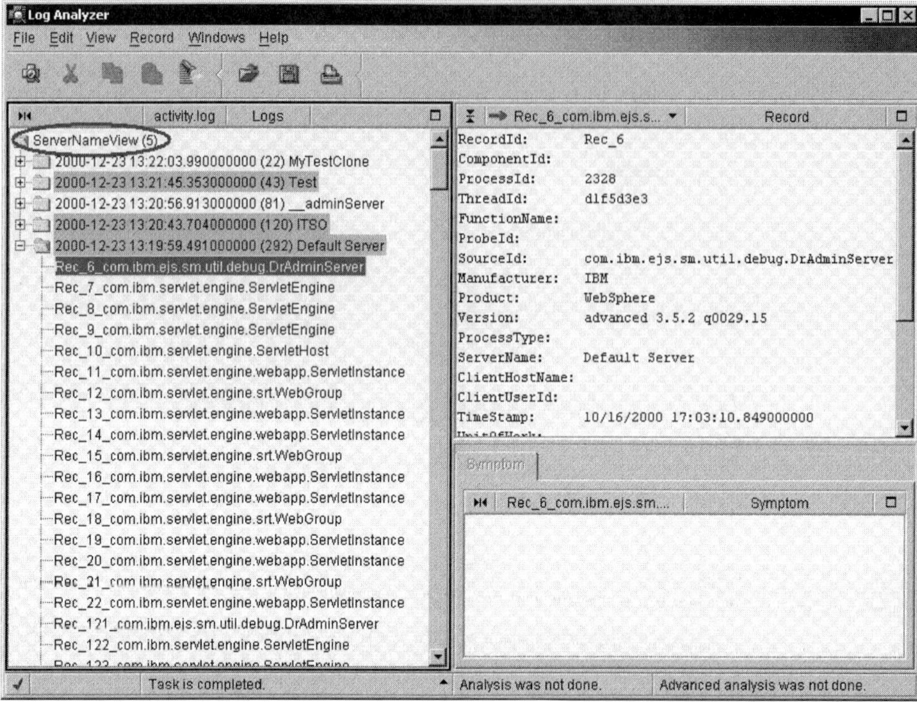

Figure 785. Logs pane after changing the sort field setting

The folders are sorted to show the servers with the latest timestamp at the top of the list. The entries within each server are listed in the reverse sequence, that is the first (earliest) entry for that server is displayed at the top of the list. If you have merged several logs in the Log Analyzer, all the log entries are merged in timestamp sequence within each server folder, as if they all came from the same log.

Each folder line has the following format:

Last timestamp + (+ Number of entries +) + Sort field identification name

For example:

2000-12-23 13:19:59.491000000 (292) Default Server

Every log entry is assigned an entry number, Rec_nnnn, when a log is opened in the Log Analyzer.

If more than one file is opened in the Log Analyzer (merged files), the Rec_nnnn identification will not be unique because the number is relative to the entry sequence in the original log file and not to the merged data that the Log Analyzer is displaying.

However, with the concatenation of the class name, it is likely this identification will be unique. This Rec_nnnn appears in the title and the first line (RecordId) in the Records pane.

24.6.2 Sorting by ProcessId

As the second example, we specified the ProcessId for the Primary sort field as shown in Figure 786.

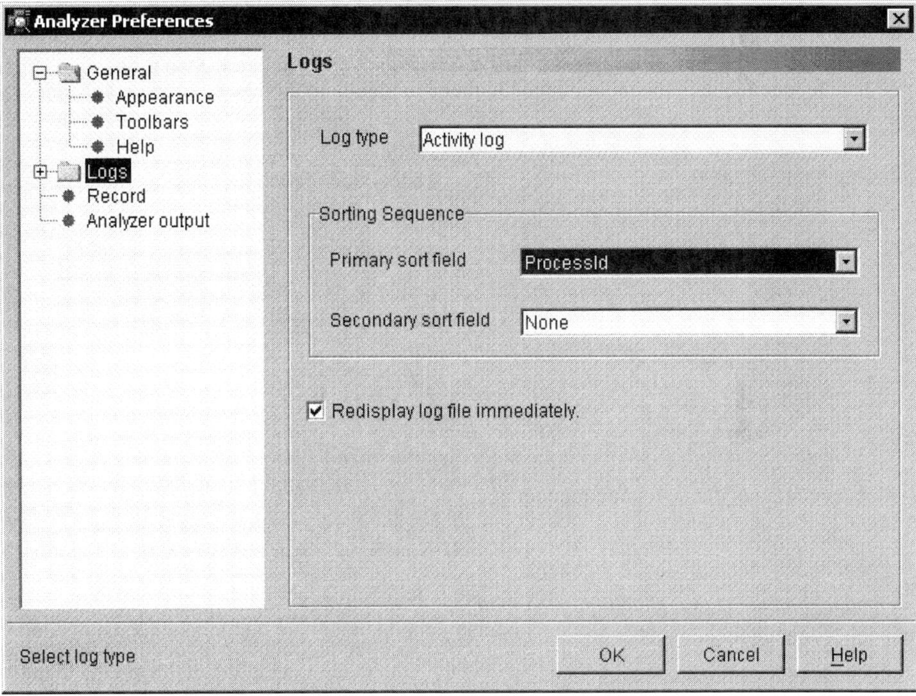

Figure 786. Sorting by process ID

Then click **OK**. You will see "ProcessIdView" on the Logs pane as shown in Figure 787 on page 990.

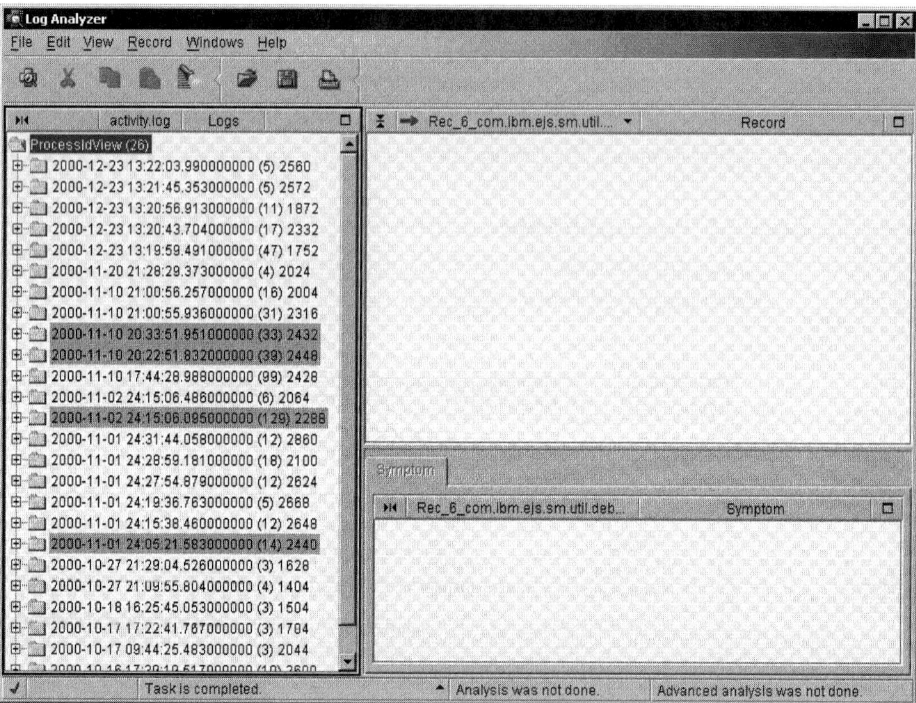

Figure 787. ProcessIdView

In Figure 787, you can see many folders under the ProcessIdView folder. That means that the activity.log includes many processes' information.

Let us open the ninth folder which has process ID 2432's information. Click the folder **2000-11-10 20:33:51.951000000 (33) 2432** to open it. Note that "2432" indicates the process ID and "(33)" means that there are 33 entries in it.

You will see the entries on the Logs pane as shown in Figure 788 on page 991.

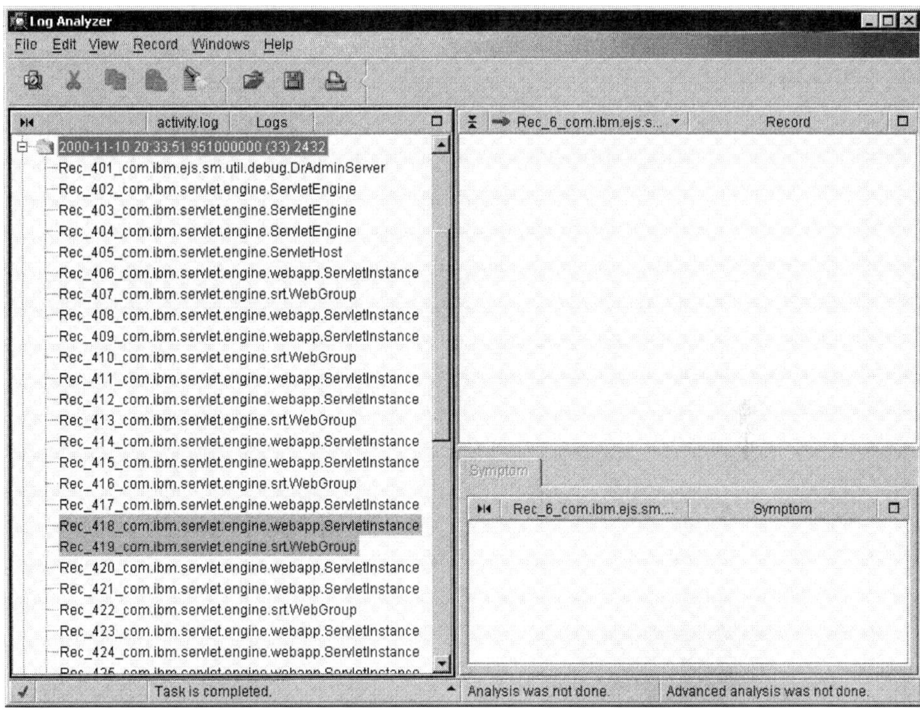

Figure 788. Analyzing by ProcessId #1

On the Logs pane, you can see a couple of entries that have a pink colored background. It means that it has a severity 1 error. Let us select the entry with record number 418 (Rec_418).

When we selected the entry the background of the entry became red and detailed information appeared on the Record pane (in our case, Rec_418) as shown in Figure 789 on page 992.

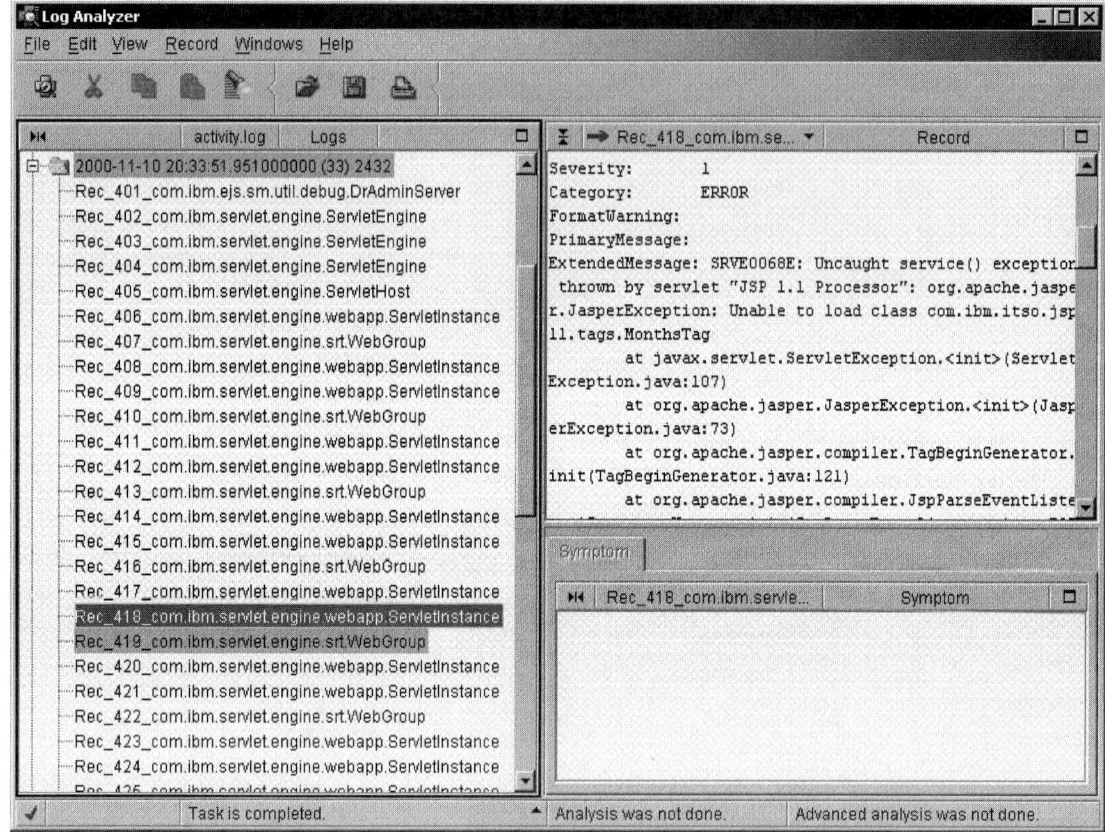

Figure 789. Analyzing by ProcessId #2

24.7 Analyze action

The Log Analyzer tool has a very powerful Analyze action that retrieves and displays additional documentation on known errors and error messages in the Analysis pane.

You can invoke the Analyze action from the root folder, any folder, or any selected log entry. If you invoke the Analyze function for the root folder, then all the entries in the log will be analyzed.

From the Logs pane, right click the folder that you want to analyze and click **Analyze** as shown in Figure 790 on page 993.

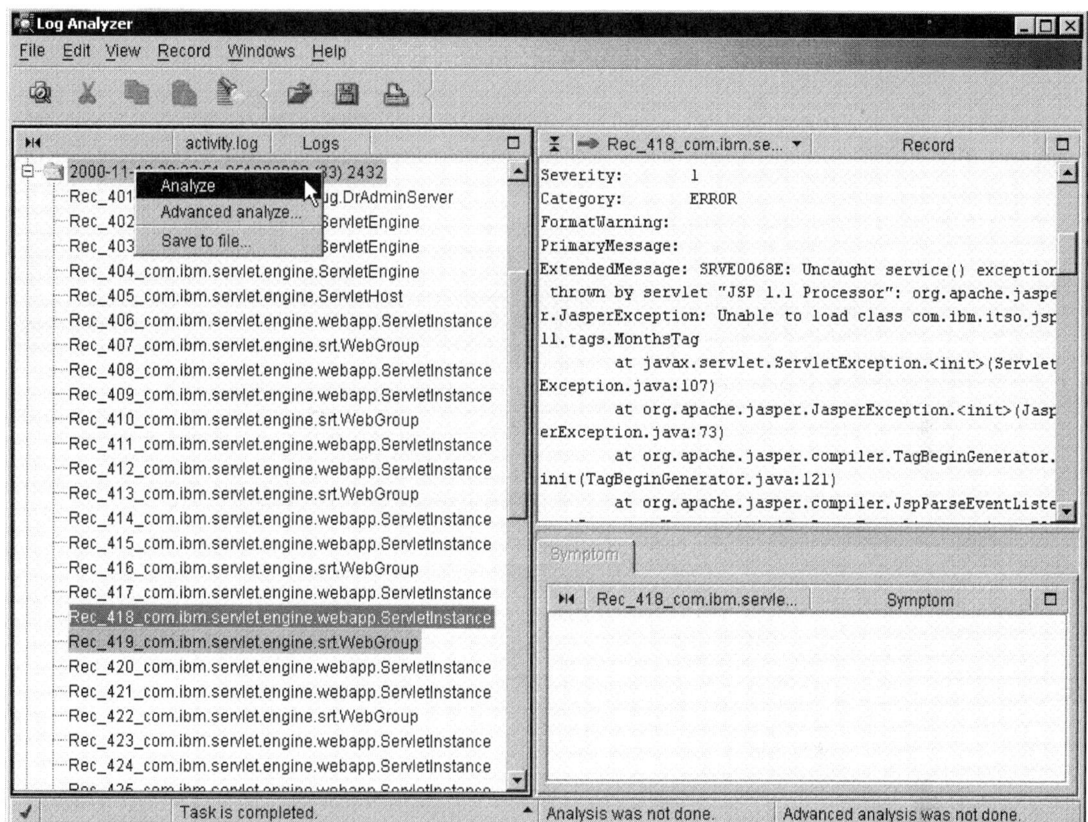

Figure 790. The Analyze action

After the Analyze action has been invoked, each log entry that was analyzed has one icon to indicate the analysis information as shown in Figure 791 on page 994.

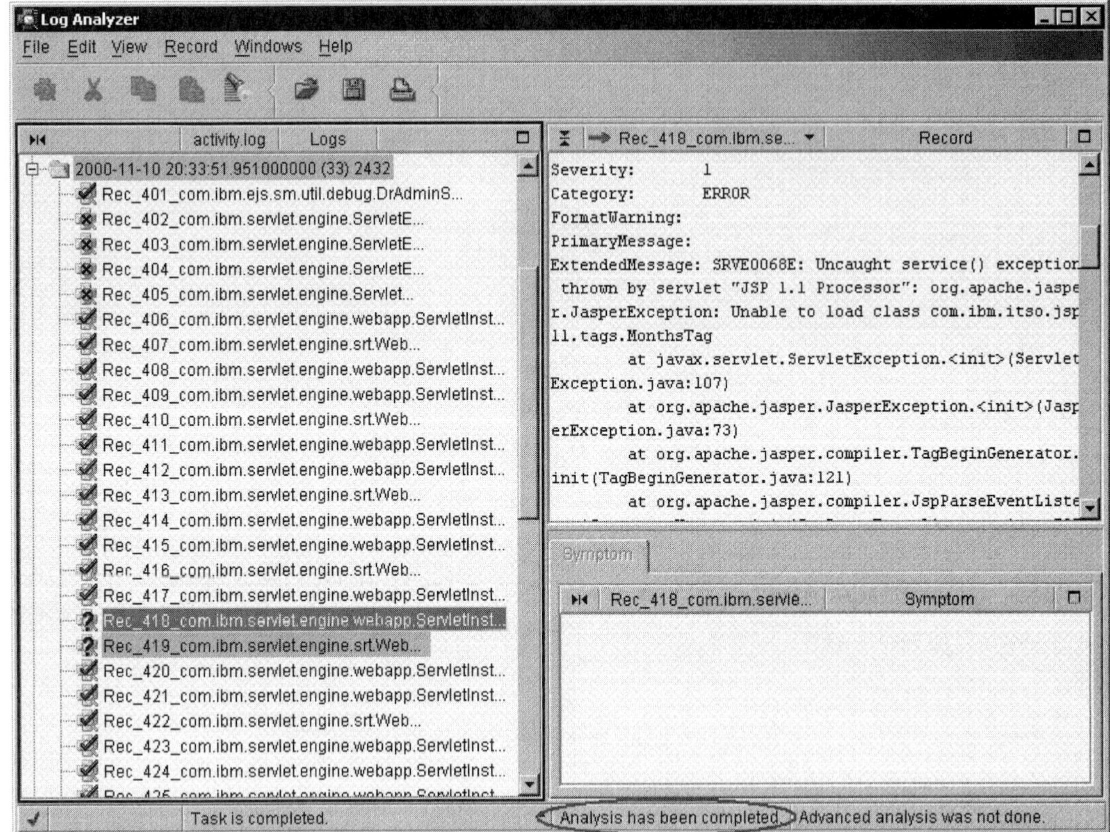

Figure 791. Analyzing log entries

Then, select an entry and you will see a description in the Symptom tab as shown in Figure 792 on page 995.

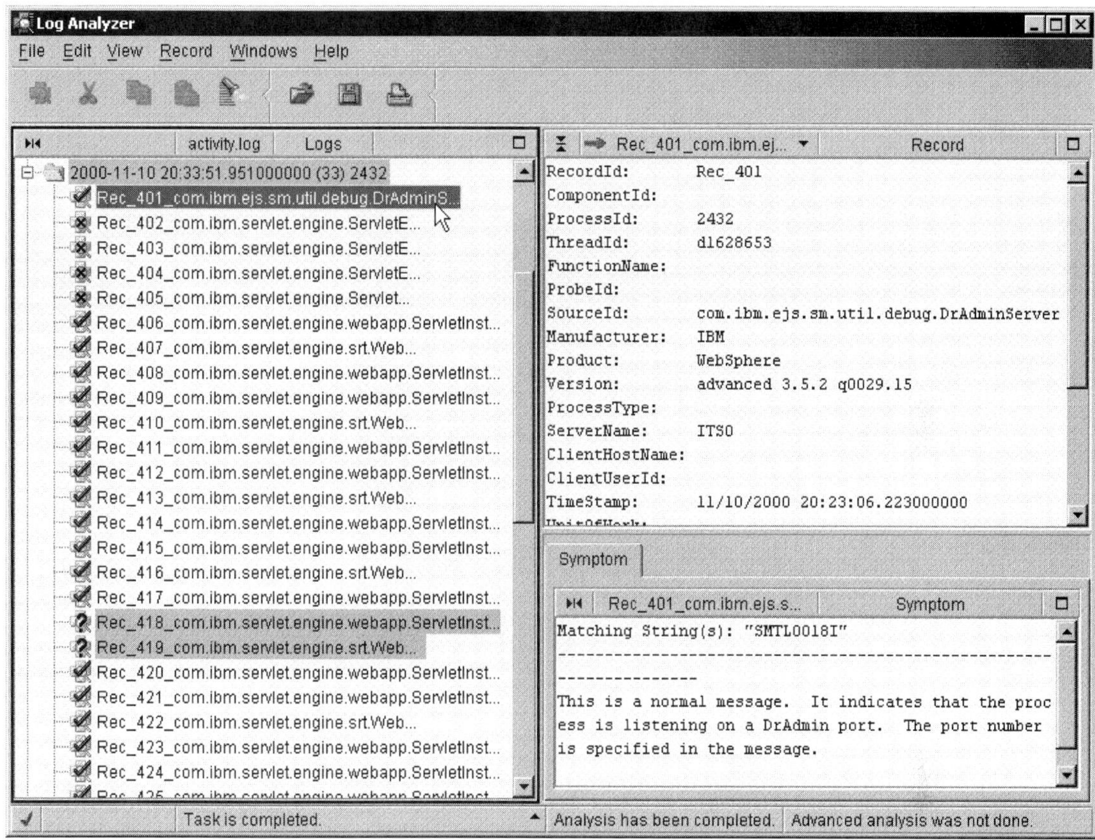

Figure 792. Symptom tab

Four different icons are supported:

indicates that the entry has some analysis information in one or more pages in the Analysis pane.

indicates that the error has been cascaded and that the real cause for the error is in the previous or next error record.

indicates that the entry has either a severity 1 or 2 error but no additional analysis information is available for it.

indicates that the entry has a severity 3 error and it has no analysis information.

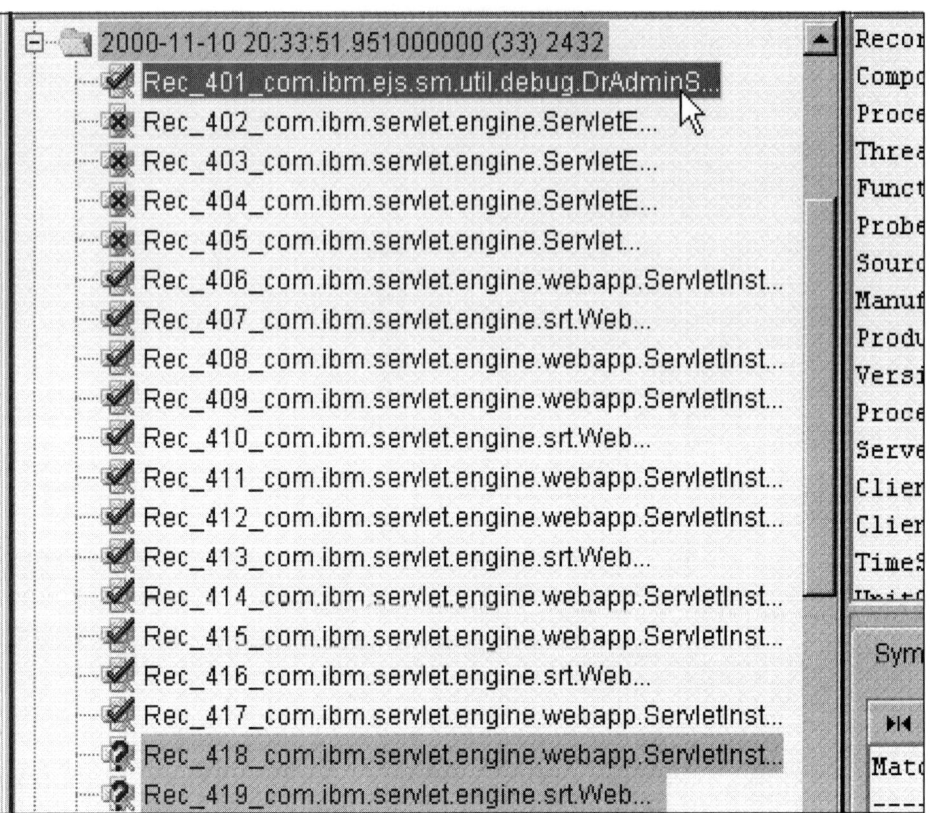

Figure 793. Icons indicate different entries

24.8 Using the Log Analyzer to view the ring buffer dump

The ring buffer dump file can be viewed using a text editor, or it can be viewed using the Log Analyzer.

In order to use the Log Analyzer to read the ring buffer trace file, the file has to be dumped into the activity log format. To do this, you need to modify the file <WAS_HOME>\properties\logging.properties before you dump the ring buffer trace. Uncomment (remove the # sign) in the last line:

```
#TRACE_OUTPUT_FORMAT=basic
```

and replace `basic` with `advanced` as in the following:

```
TRACE_OUTPUT_FORMAT=advanced
```

This will give you the ring buffer trace file in the activity log format.

```
$LANG = en_US
$CODESET = Cp1252
----------------------------------------------------------------
ComponentId:
ProcessId: 2072
ThreadId: d3530505
FunctionName:
ProbeId:
SourceId: com.ibm.ejs.sm.server.ManagedServer
Manufacturer: IBM
Product: WebSphere
Version: advanced 3.5.2 q0029.15
ProcessType:
ServerName: Default Server
ClientHostName:
ClientUserId:
TimeStamp: 2001-01-02 13:30:09.692000000
UnitOfWork:
Severity: 3
Category: EVENT
FormatWarning:
PrimaryMessage:
ExtendedMessage: Version : 3.5.2
RawDataLen: 0
----------------------------------------------------------------
ComponentId:
ProcessId: 2072
ThreadId: d3530505
FunctionName:
ProbeId:
SourceId: com.ibm.ejs.sm.server.ManagedServer
Manufacturer: IBM
Product: WebSphere
Version: advanced 3.5.2 q0029.15
ProcessType:
ServerName: Default Server
ClientHostName:
ClientUserId:
TimeStamp: 2001-01-02 13:30:09.692000001
UnitOfWork:
Severity: 3
Category: EVENT
FormatWarning:
```

Figure 794. Ring buffer trace file in log analyzer format

To view this file using the Log Analyzer, execute the waslogbr script file (waslogbr.bat or waslogbr), which is found in the <WAS_HOME>/bin directory. This starts the Log Analyzer GUI.

From the GUI select **File->Open**, then navigate to the directory containing the ring buffer dump file (in our case, ringbuffer.dump). Select the file and then select **Open**. On the Logs pane, you will see the file name that you selected (in our case, ringbuffer.dump).

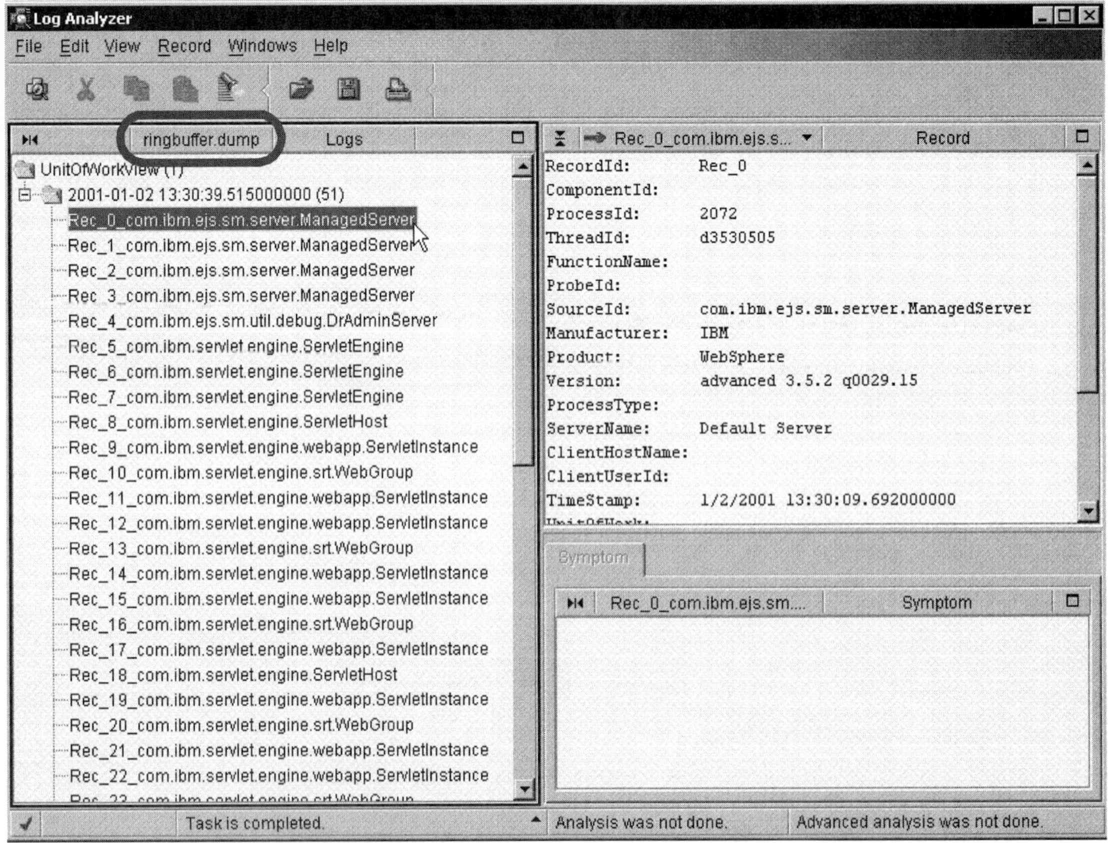

Figure 795. Viewing the ring buffer dump with Log Analyzer

Note that if a tracefile is generated by specifying a trace specification and trace output file on the Advanced tab for the application server in the WebSphere Administrative Console, the tracefile generated is not compatible with the Log Analyzer. Attempting to use the Log Analyzer to display that file will result in an error.

24.9 Updating the symptom database

The symptom database included in the Log Analyzer package that you downloaded contains entries for some common problems. IBM will make new versions of the symptom database with additional entries available for downloading at the FTP site from time to time.

In the <WAS_HOME>/bin/ivblogbr.properties file, there is a line that indicates the URL of the FTP site. The default setting is as follows:

```
ftp://ftp.software.ibm.com/software/websphere/info/tools/loganalyzer/sympt
oms/adv/symptomdb.xml
```

You can update the symptom database either by downloading it from the FTP site and then replacing the old one (<WAS_HOME>/symptoms/adv/symptomdb.xml) with it manually or using the Log Analyzer GUI function. To use the Log Analyzer GUI function, select **File -> Update database -> Adv Symptom Database** as shown in Figure 796 on page 1000.

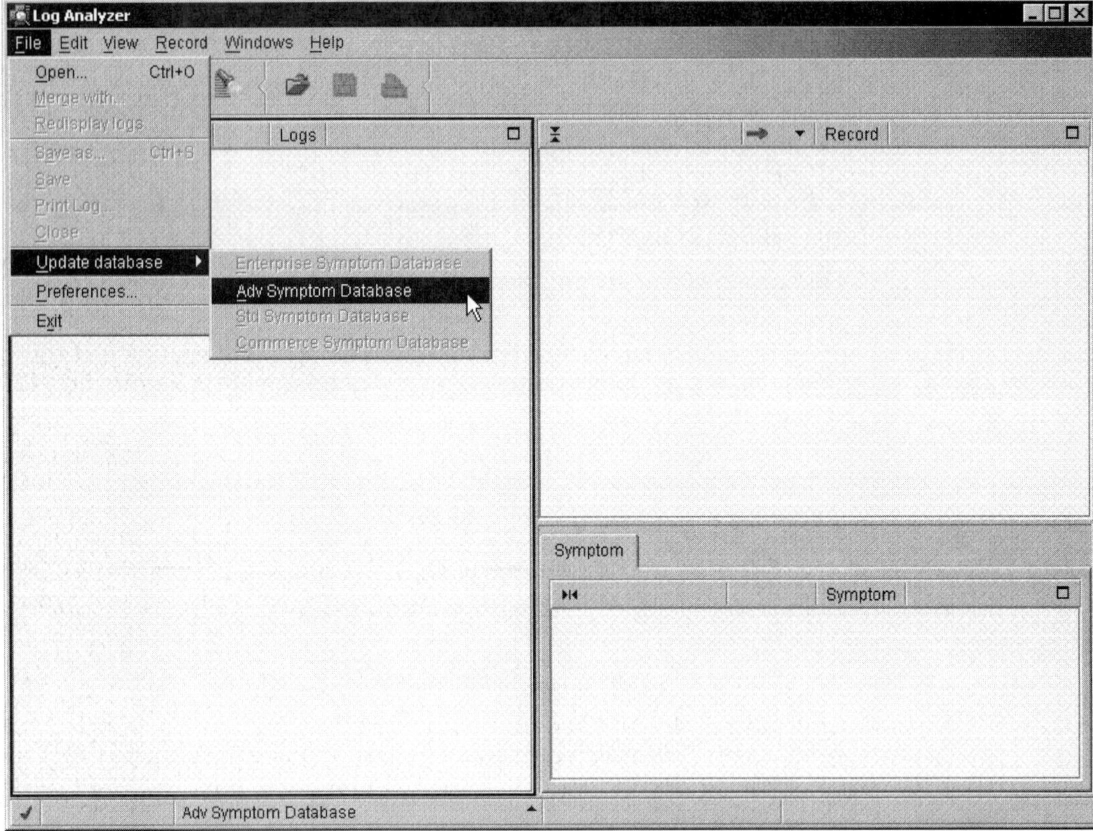

Figure 796. Update the symptom database

If you are trying to update the symptom database using the Log Analyzer GUI function on a machine behind a firewall, you will need to add the proxy definition in the command that launches the Log Analyzer.

If your organization uses an FTP proxy server, do the following:

- For Windows NT: Modify the <WAS_HOME>\bin\waslogbr.bat file and add the text shown in *Italics* below:

```
%JAVA_HOME%\bin\java -DIVB_HOME=%USERPROFILE%/logbr ^
 ......
 -Dftp.proxyHost=proxy_host -Dftp.proxyPort=port_number ^
 ......
```

- For UNIX: Modify the file <WAS_HOME>/bin/waslogbr and add the text shown in *Italics* below:

```
$JAVA_HOME/bin/java -ms10m -mx255m -DIVB_HOME=$HOME/logbr \
```

```
......
-Dftp.proxyHost=proxy_host -Dftp.proxyPort=port_number \
......
```

If your organization uses a SOCKS proxy server, do the following:

- For Windows NT: Modify the file <WAS_HOME>\bin\waslogbr.bat and add the text shown in *Italics* below:

  ```
  %JAVA_HOME%\bin\java -DIVB_HOME=%USERPROFILE%/logbr ^
  ......
  -DsocksProxyHost=proxy_host -DsocksProxyPort=port_number ^
  ......
  ```

- For UNIX: Modify file <WAS_HOME>/bin/waslogbr and add the text shown in *Italics* below:

  ```
  $JAVA_HOME/bin/java -ms10m -mx255m -DIVB_HOME=$HOME/logbr \
  ......
  -DsocksProxyHost=proxy_host -DsocksProxyPort=port_number \
  ......
  ```

If necessary, ask your system administrator for the name of the FTP or SOCKS proxy host and its port on your network.

24.10 Saving logs as an XML file

If you intend to look at the same Log Analyzer data again at a later time, you may want to save the data as an XML file.

From the Log Analyzer window, select **File -> Save** as depicted in Figure 797 on page 1002.

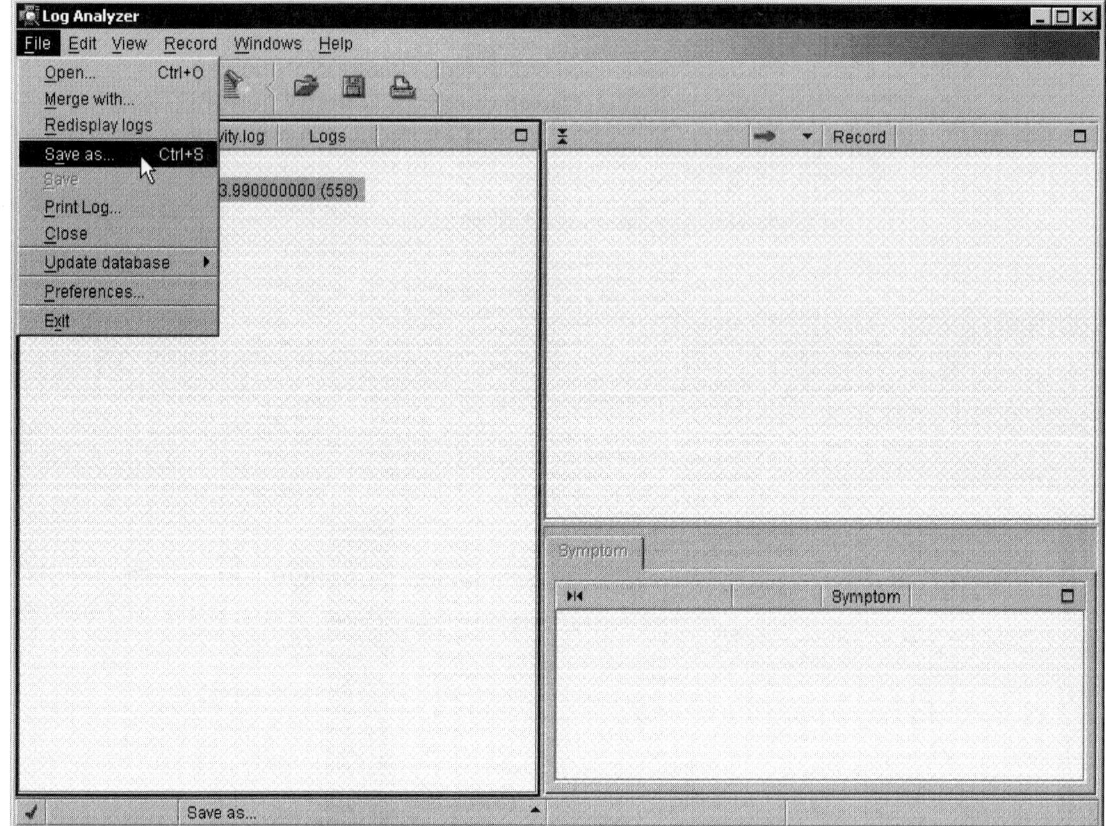

Figure 797. Saving the log file as an XML file

Then you specify the location and file name to save the log as an XML file or a text file, as shown in Figure 798 on page 1003, and click **Save**.

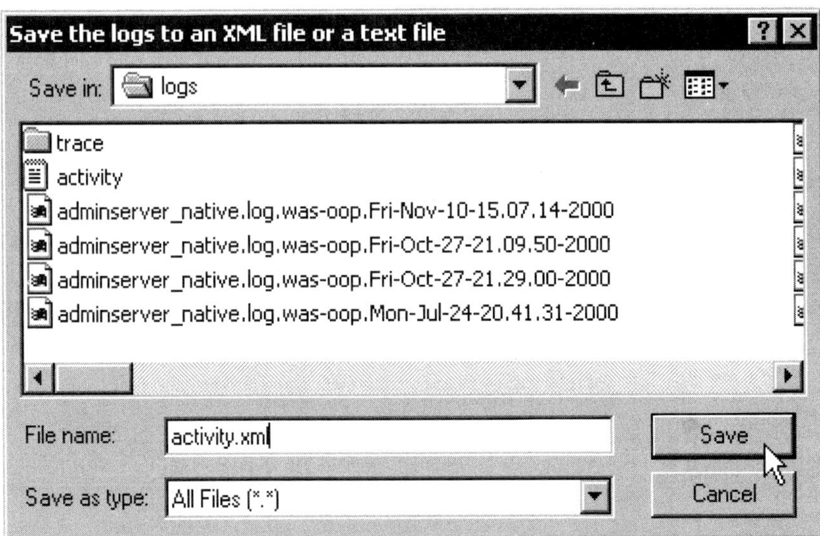

Figure 798. Saving the log file to an XML file or a text file

We specified the XML format to save our log and we can see the file that was saved as an XML file as shown in Figure 799 on page 1004.

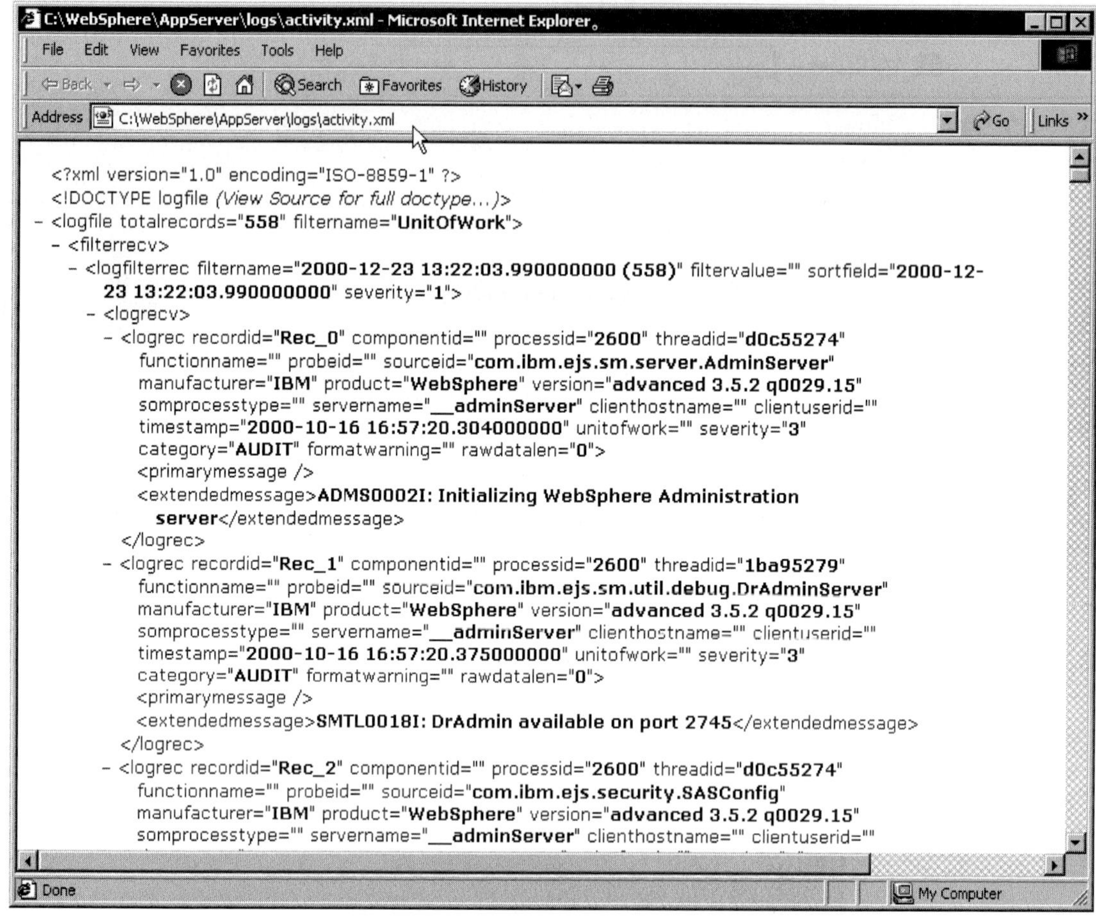

Figure 799. The log file saved as an XML file

Also, you can open the XML log file with the Log Analyzer as shown in Figure 800 on page 1005.

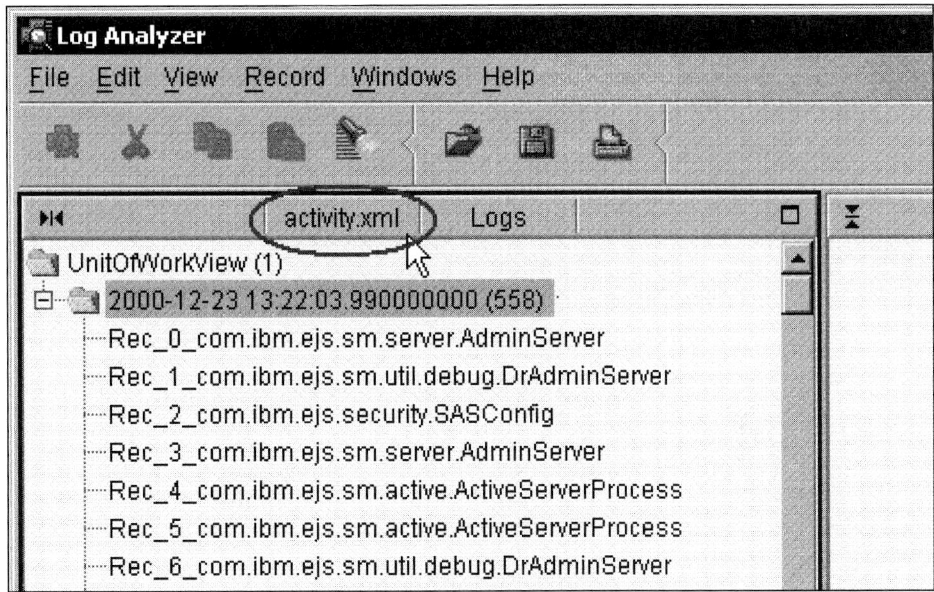

Figure 800. Open the log file that is saved as an XML file

Note that you can save the data in a text format, as shown in Figure 801 on page 1006.

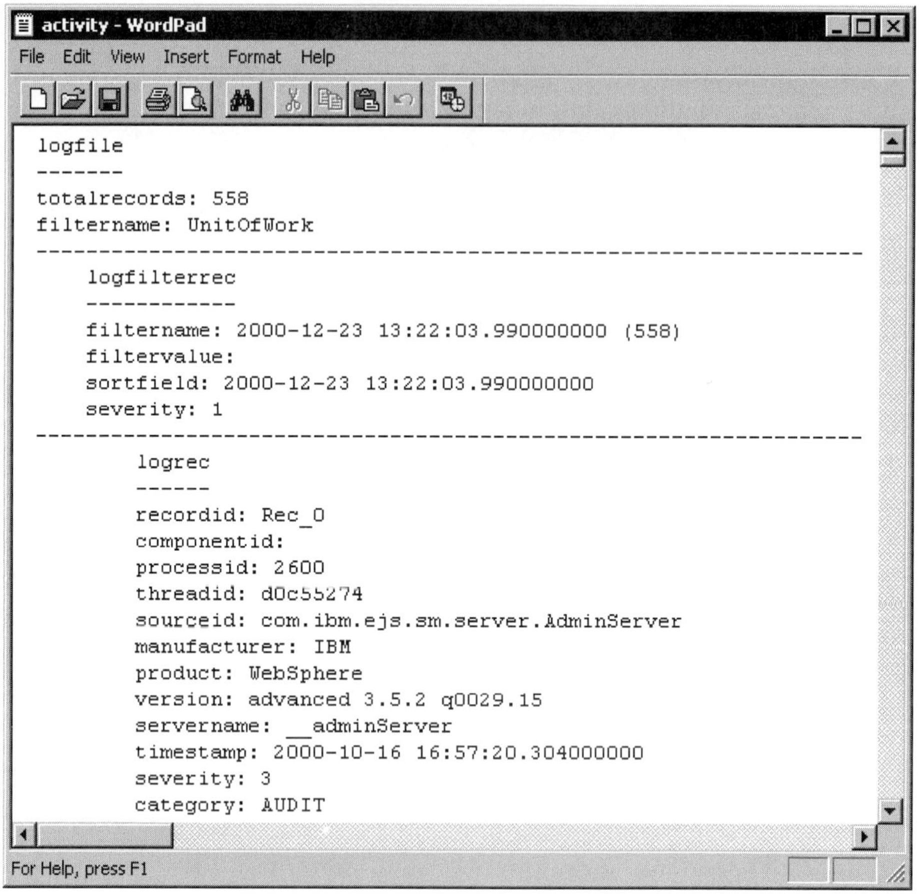

activity - WordPad

File Edit View Insert Format Help

```
logfile
-------
totalrecords: 558
filtername: UnitOfWork
-----------------------------------------------------------------
    logfilterrec
    ------------
    filtername: 2000-12-23 13:22:03.990000000 (558)
    filtervalue:
    sortfield: 2000-12-23 13:22:03.990000000
    severity: 1
-----------------------------------------------------------------
        logrec
        ------
        recordid: Rec_0
        componentid:
        processid: 2600
        threadid: d0c55274
        sourceid: com.ibm.ejs.sm.server.AdminServer
        manufacturer: IBM
        product: WebSphere
        version: advanced 3.5.2 q0029.15
        servername: __adminServer
        timestamp: 2000-10-16 16:57:20.304000000
        severity: 3
        category: AUDIT
```

For Help, press F1

Figure 801. Can save the log file as a text file

But you cannot open it with the Log Analyzer. You will get the error message as shown in Figure 802.

Figure 802. Cannot load the log file which was saved as a text file

Any retrieved Symptom information is also saved. If logs are merged in the Log Analyzer, the saved file contains entries of all the merged logs in the sequence that is shown in the Logs pane.

You can also do selective saves by making multiple selections of folders and/or entries in the Logs pane.

Chapter 25. Resource Analyzer

The Resource Analyzer is a stand-alone performance monitor for WebSphere Application Server Advanced Edition. The Resource Analyzer Console can be brought up on Windows or UNIX machines, and it can connect across platforms to the WebSphere Administrative Server running locally or on a remote machine.

This chapter takes an in-depth look at the new Resource Analyzer. Note that this is a technology preview product of WebSphere V3.5. For this redbook, most of the Resource Analyzer testing was done while connected to the WebSphere Administrative Server Advanced Edition. The version of Resource Analyzer did not work with Standard Edition when we tested.

25.1 About Resource Analyzer

The Resource Analyzer retrieves performance data by periodically polling the WebSphere Administrative Server. Data is collected continuously and retrieved as needed from within the Analyzer. The level of data to collect is specified by using the WebSphere Administrative Console. The Analyzer's graphical user interface is used to retrieve and view the data in a table or a chart, or to store the data in a log file.

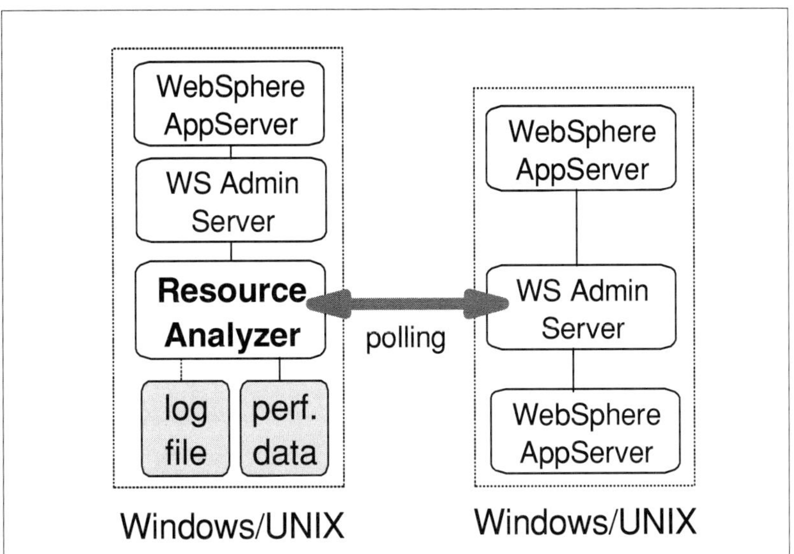

Figure 803. Resource Analyzer V3.5 block diagram

25.1.1 Performance data organization

Resource Analyzer organizes performance data in a hierarchy of groups. A group is a set of statistics, or counters, associated with a particular resource of the WebSphere. Groups can have subgroups. Counters, which measure an aspect of the running system, may or may not belong to one or more groups.

For example, the enterprise beans performance category is considered a root group. Subgroups (descendants) of this group are container instances. Each container instance represents the set of counters for that container. Counters for containers include the number of method calls and their average response time for all enterprise beans in the container. Enterprise beans residing in a container belong to a subgroup whose name is the remote class name of the enterprise bean. In Figure 804, the bean 2 group belongs to both the container 1 and container 2 groups.

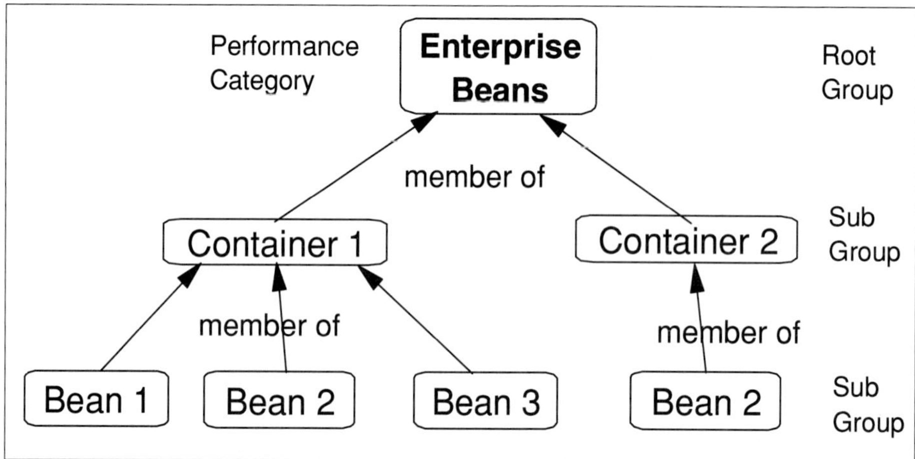

Figure 804. Example hierarchy of Enterprise Beans Performance group

When performance data is displayed for a group, the information is organized and displayed as families. A family is simply a view of all similar objects. Family tables show multiple resources of the same type and their counters.

25.2 What is collected and analyzed?

The Resource Analyzer provides a wide range of performance data for two kinds of resources:

- WebSphere resources, which include servlets and enterprise beans

- WebSphere runtime resources, which include the Java Virtual Machine (JVM) memory, application server thread pools, and database connection pools

Performance data includes:

- Numerical data
- Statistical data
- Load data

This data is reported for individual resources and aggregated for multiple resources. Numerical data could be such things as memory size or cache size. Statistical data are things like response times of an EJB method. Average size of a database connection pool is an example of load data.

The Analyzer collects and reports performance data for the following resources of WebSphere Application Server:

- WebSphere runtime
  - Reports memory used by a process as reported by the JVM. Examples are the total memory available and the amount of free memory for the JVM.
- Object Request Broker (ORB) thread pools
  - Reports information about the pool of threads an application server uses to process remote methods. Examples are the number of threads created and destroyed, the maximum number of pooled threads allowed, and the average number of active threads in the pool.
- Database connection pools
  - Reports usage information about connection pools for a database. Examples are the average size of the connection pool (number of connections), the average number of threads waiting for a connection, the average wait time in milliseconds for a connection to be granted, and the average time the connection was in use.
- Enterprise beans
  - Reports load values, response times, and lifecycle activities for enterprise beans. Examples include the average number of active beans and the average number of methods being processed concurrently.
- Enterprise bean methods

- Reports information about an enterprise bean's remote interfaces. Examples include the number of times a method was called and the average response time for the method.

- Enterprise bean object pools
  - Reports information on the size and usage of a cache of bean objects. Examples include the number of calls attempting to retrieve an object from a pool and the number of times an object was found available in the pool.
- Transactions
  - Reports transaction information for the container. Examples include the average number of active transactions, the average duration of transactions, and the average number of methods per transaction.
- Servlet engines
  - Reports usage information for Web applications, servlets, JavaServer Pages (JSPs), and HTTP sessions. Examples include the average number of concurrent requests for a servlet, the amount of time it takes for a servlet to perform a request, the number of loaded servlets in a Web application, and the average number of concurrently active HTTP sessions.

25.3 Resource Analyzer functionality

Depending on what is being measured, the Resource Analyzer can perform the following functions:

- View performance data in real time
- View performance data over specified time intervals
  - Data can be displayed in intervals showing performance during the last minute, the last 5 minutes, the last 10 minutes, and the last 20 minutes.
- Record current performance data in a log, and replay performance data from previous sessions
- Compare data for a single resource to an aggregate or group of resources on a single node
- View the data in chart form, allowing comparisons of one or more statistical values for a given resource on the same chart

Given all this data, the Resource Analyzer can be used to do the following:

- Monitor real-time performance, such as response times for servlet requests or enterprise bean methods

- Detect trends by analyzing snapshots of data over time
- Determine the efficiency of the resources within a given configuration
  - These resources could be the amount of allocated memory, the size of database connection pools, and the size of a cache for enterprise bean objects.
- Gauge the load on application servers
- Gauge the load on servlet engines

Note

Data collection and reporting will affect the performance of your distributed applications. Although performance data is automatically collected at all times, it is not reported by default. You must explicitly enable data-reporting for those aspects of your system to be monitored.

When data reporting is enabled, the types of data displayed depend on user-defined instrumentation levels.

25.4 Levels of data collection

Instrumentation levels can be changed by using the WebSphere Advanced Administrative Console as follows:

- To change levels for a running application server, use the Performance dialog box.
- To change levels for a stopped application server, use the EPM specification property.

25.4.1 Using the EPM specification property

The EPM specification input field is visible in the Advanced tab of an application server's property sheet. This is shown in Figure 805 on page 1014.

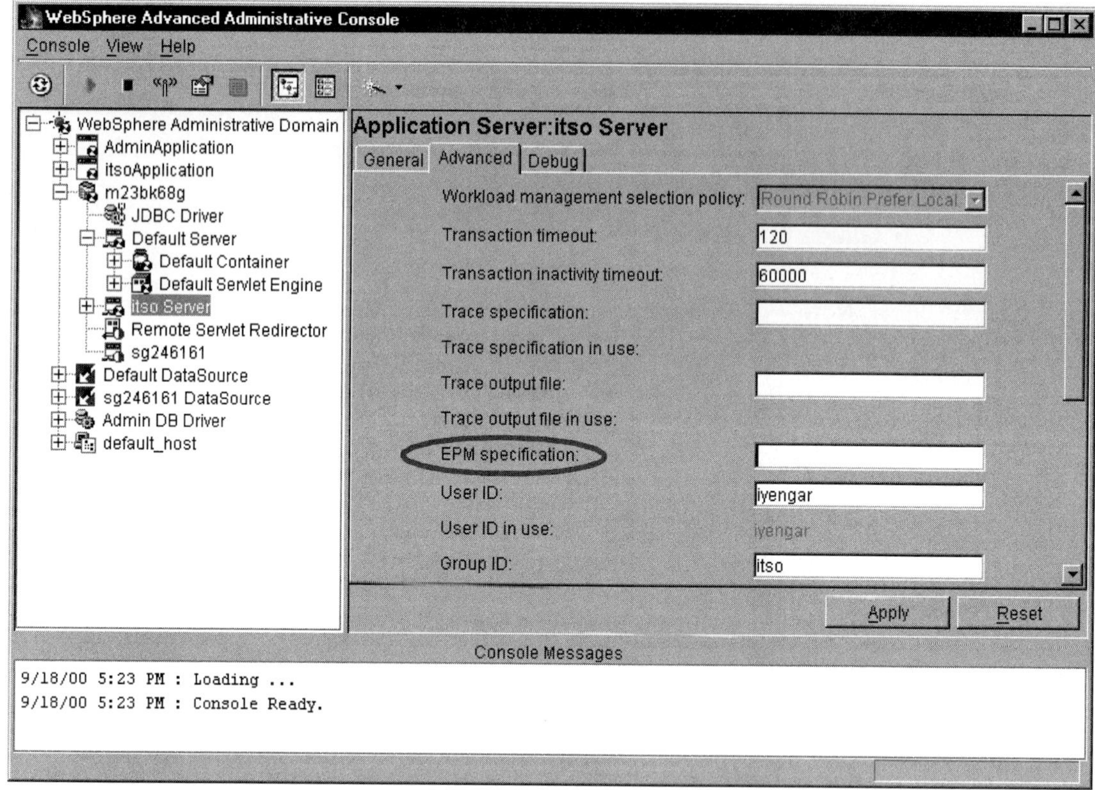

Figure 805. EPM specification

The property value can be one of two formats. The first format sets the instrumentation level for all performance modules; the second sets the level for individual modules.

```
epm=<LEVEL>
```

```
epm.module_name=MODULE_NAME
```

where:

`LEVEL` is none, low, medium, or high

`MODULE_NAME` is one of the following: beanData, beanMethodData, orbThreadPool, connectionMgr, objectPools, transactionData, servletEngine.

Multiple specifications can be separated by a colon as in the following example:

```
epm.beanData=medium:epm.transactionData=high
```

25.4.2 Using the Performance dialog

To view the Performance dialog box, right-click an application server and select the **Performance...** option as shown in Figure 806.

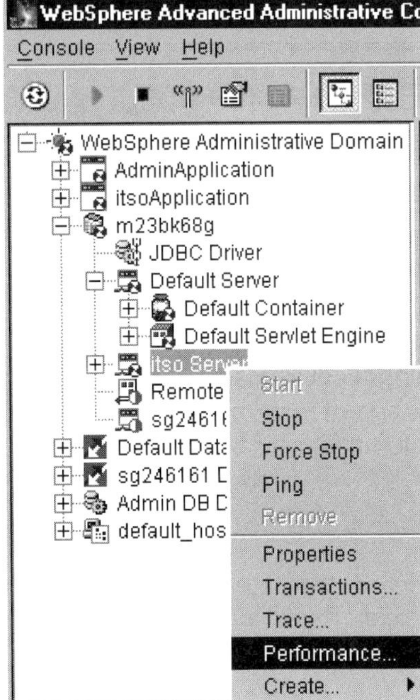

Figure 806. Performance option

By default nothing is set in the Performance dialog box and the icon box next to the Performance modules is pink in color as shown in Figure 807.

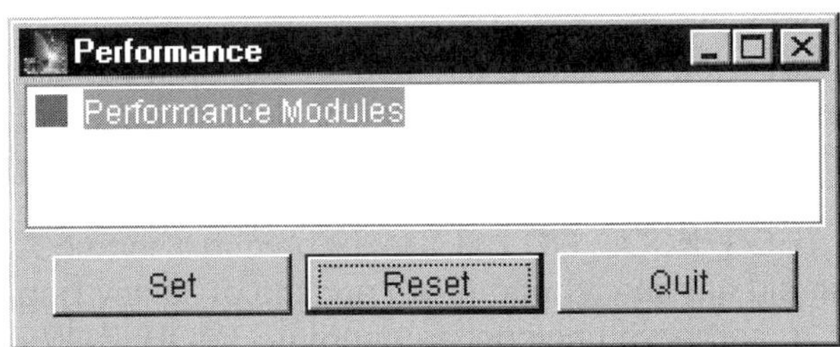

Figure 807. Initial setting in the Performance dialog box

In the Performance dialog box, the instrumentation level can be set for each performance category and each resource instance. The current instrumentation level is represented by a small box icon with color stripes as shown in Figure 808.

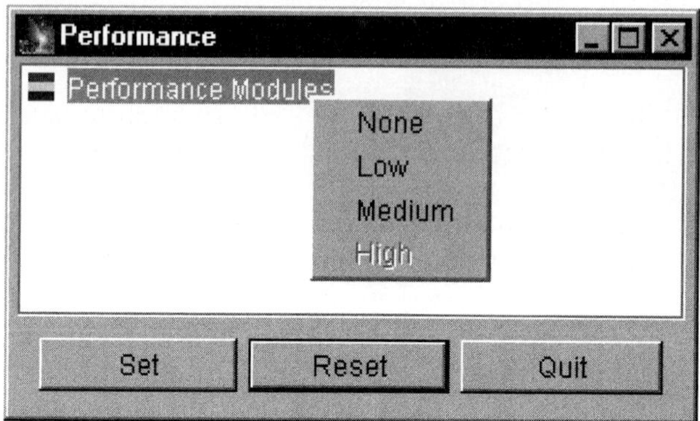

Figure 808. Performance dialog box shown with high impact counter setting

The color key is as follows:

- Grey -- No data is being collected.
- Blue -- Counters that have a low impact on performance are being collected.
- Yellow -- Counters that have a medium impact or lower are being collected.
- Red -- Counters that have a high impact or lower are being collected.

25.5 Resource Analyzer requirements

Before installing the Resource Analyzer the following software prerequisites need to be met:

- IBM JDK 1.2
- IBM WebSphere Application Server V3.5
- JCChart classes (included in chart.jar that comes with WebSphere Application Server V3.5 install)

You will also need an unzip utility because Resource Analyzer is distributed as a zip file.

25.6 Starting the Resource Analyzer

The Resource Analyzer is a GUI and it looks the same on all platforms. See Figure 809 on page 1018. To start the resource analyzer:

- On UNIX platforms, invoke the `ra.sh` shell script.
- On Windows platforms, run the `ra.bat` batch file.

These files can be found in the directory <RA_HOME>/ra/bin, where RA_HOME is the Resource Analyzer installation directory.

Before running either script, edit the script to change the environment variable WAS_HOME to the location of the root directory where WebSphere is installed.

By default, Resource Analyzer looks for the WebSphere Administrative Server on the host machine where the Analyzer is started. If the administrative server is running on another machine, specify that host name and port number.

The command usage to invoke the Resource Analyzer on Windows NT or Windows 2000 systems:

```
ra.bat [host_name [port_number]]
```

Where:

`[host_name]` is where the WebSphere Administrative Server is running

`[port_number]` is the port to connect to the administrative server

The default values are localhost and port 900.

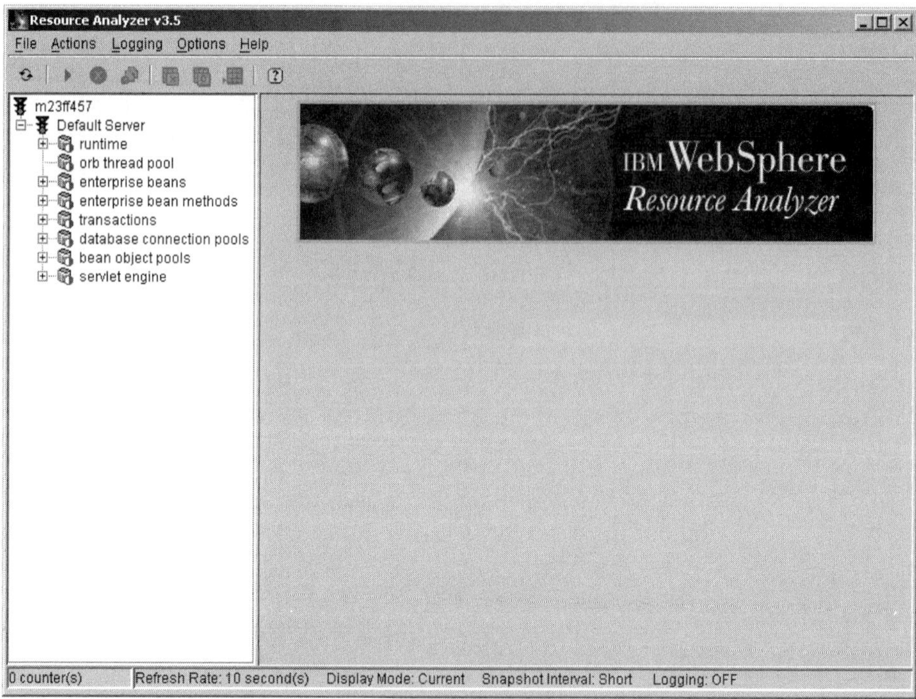

Figure 809. Resource Analyzer V3.5 GUI on Windows 2000

Due to memory requirements, it is recommended that you run the Resource Analyzer on a separate machine from the WebSphere Administrative Server.

Note

The Resource Analyzer does not require the WebSphere Administrative Server to be running. The Analyzer can be run in logging mode to view data from previously logged sessions.

Note

When Global Security is set via the WebSphere Administrative Console, the epm service within Resource Analyzer, by default, does not have the authority to connect to the administrative server. The following warning is displayed:

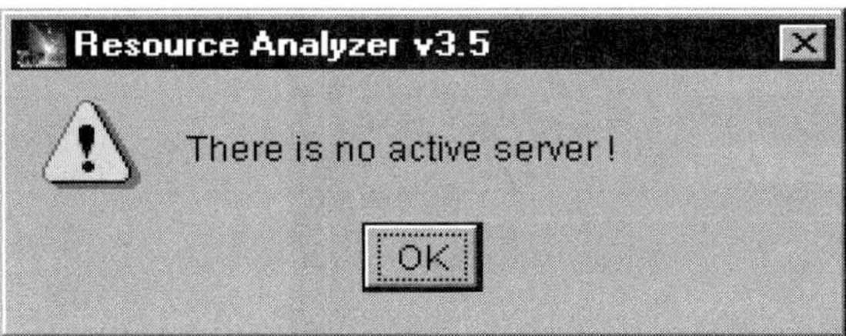

And the WebSphere Administrative Console Messages window displays the following error message:

```
9/6/00 9:56 AM : AUDIT [m23bk68g/__adminServer]: Authorization failed for
??? while invoking (Home)EpmServiceHome create
.
```

25.7 Working with the analyzer

When Resource Analyzer is invoked via the `ra` command, a status window as seen in Figure 810 pops up displaying the various resources that the Analyzer is obtaining.

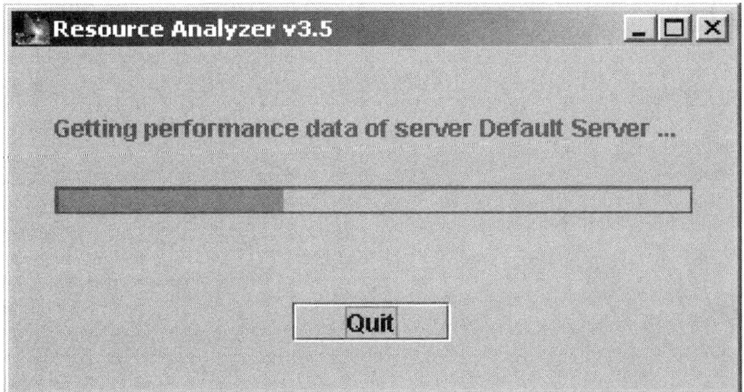

Figure 810. Resource Analyzer V3.5 status window upon startup

Eventually the Resource Analyzer Console is displayed. It has the same look and feel as the WebSphere Administrative Console with a navigation pane on the left and a workspace pane on the right.

If the WebSphere Administrative Server is running on the node that Resource Analyzer was launched on, the Resource Analyzer Console comes up without any warnings. In the navigation frame there will be a green icon next to the node name, indicating that the administrative server is active on that node. If the administrative server is inactive, a warning message will be displayed (Figure 811).

Click **OK** for the console to be fully displayed. The icon next to the node name will be red indicating that the administrative server is not running.

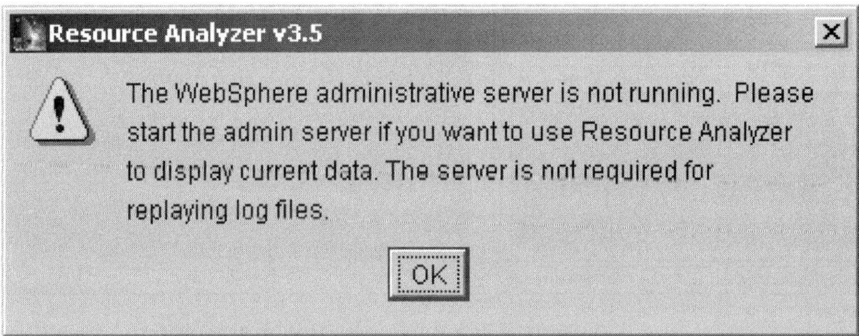

Figure 811. A warning message from the Resource Analyzer

The tree structure in the navigation pane of the Resource Analyzer Console should look quite similar to the tree structure in the WebSphere Administrative Console. The Resource Analyzer Console looks the same on Windows NT, Windows 2000 and UNIX platforms.

25.7.1 Starting the analysis of a resource

Select any resource and click the **Run** icon to start real-time analysis of that resource as shown in Figure 812 on page 1021.

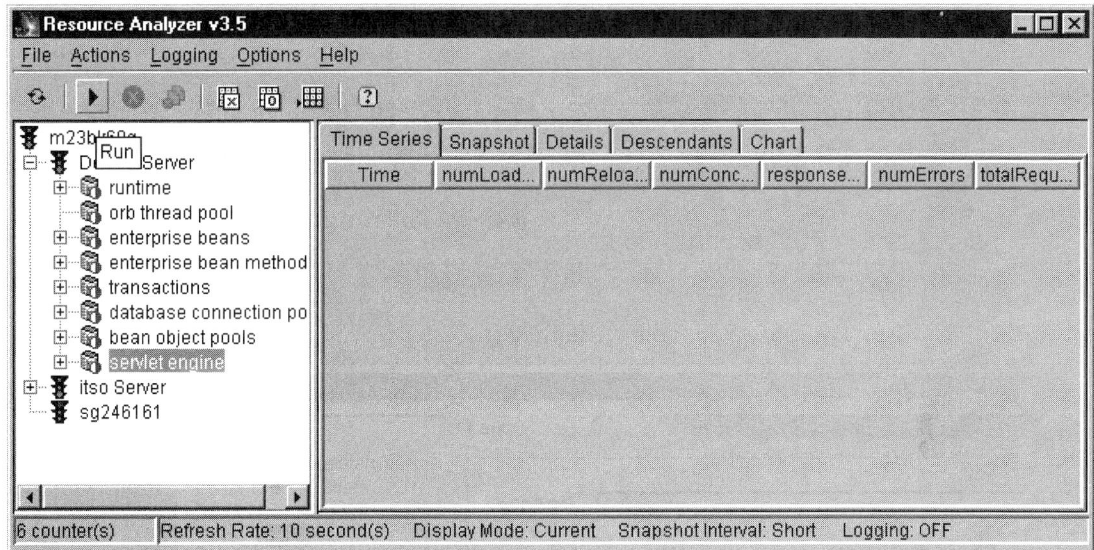

Figure 812. The Run icon highlighted in the Resource Analyzer console

The values are displayed in tabular or chart form and are refreshed every 10 seconds.

25.7.2 Setting the Refresh Rate

This refresh rate can be modified in the Resource Analyzer Console by clicking **Main Menu-->Options-->Set Refresh Rate....** as shown in Figure 813.

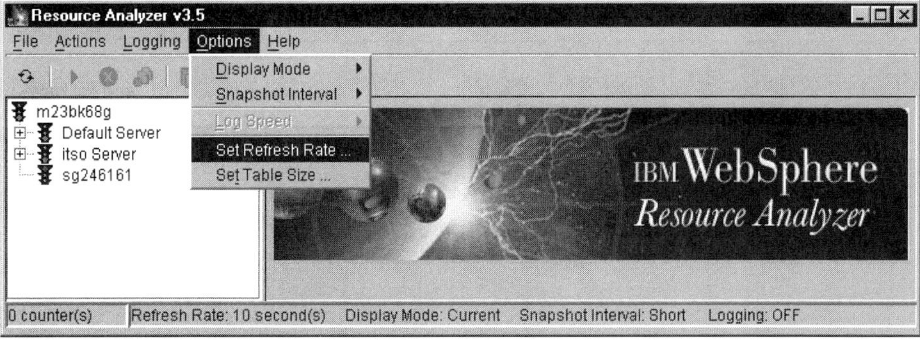

Figure 813. The menu option to set the refresh rate

25.7.3 Setting the Table Size

The size of the table where the analyzed records are stored can also be customized. The default table size is 40 rows. To change the table size click **Main Menu-->Options-->Set Table Size....** as shown in Figure 814.

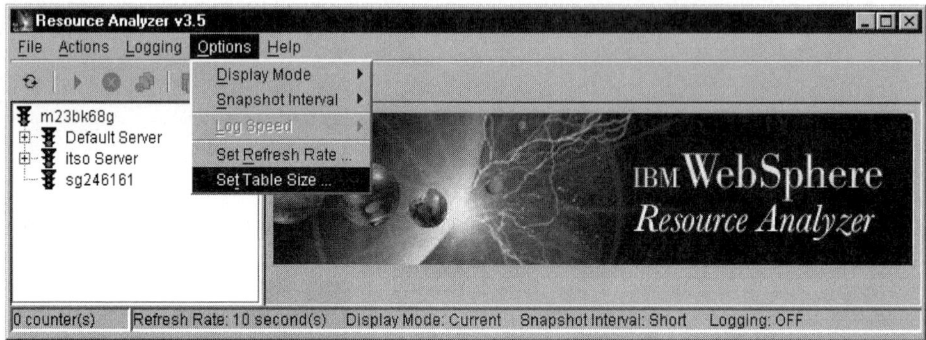

Figure 814. The menu option to set the table size

25.7.4 Viewing the analyses in chart form

The chart shown in Figure 815 on page 1023 was generated by selecting servlet engine and clicking the **Run** icon. It shows the initial configuration of the Default Server as it was set up with a typical WebSphere installation.

The number of loaded servlets = 15 and the number of ReLoads = 4. There are no concurrent requests or errors to report. Actually there are no requests, hence the total requests is zero and the total response time is zero.

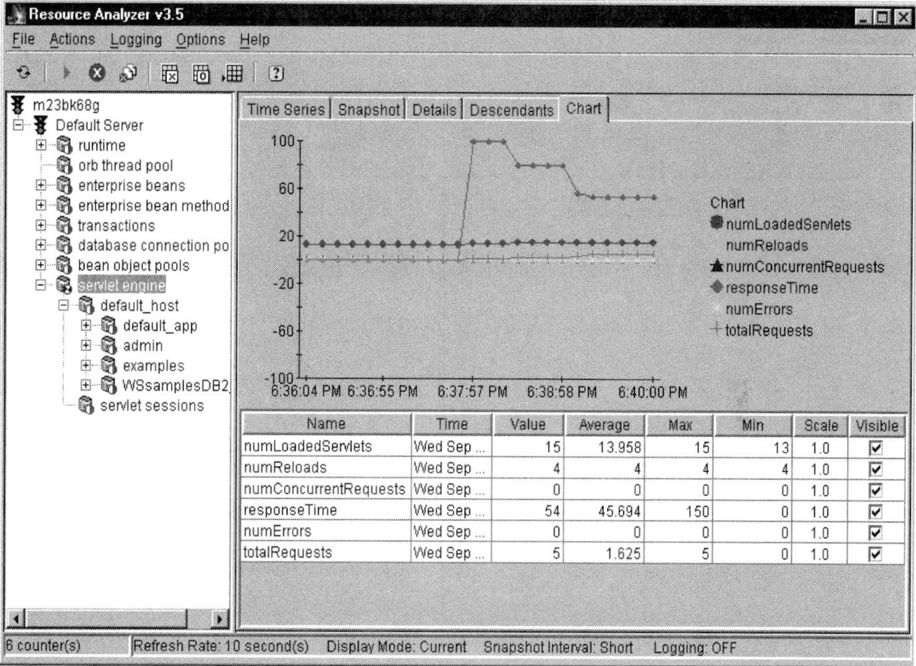

Figure 815. The resources of the default servlet engine

The sequence of events and time spikes, charted in Figure 815, is as follows:

1. The initial spike in response time to 100 occurred when the snoop servlet was first invoked in a browser.
2. The second spike to 80 was when the Hello servlet was first invoked.
3. The third spike to 56 was on a reload of the Hello servlet.
4. The snoop servlet was re-invoked via the URL.
5. The fourth spike to 54 was on a reload of the snoop servlet.

And those five servlet requests show up as Total number of Requests. All these values are captured in the Time Series tab.

25.7.5 Logging function in the analyzer

The Resource Analyzer offers the option to write to a log file. By default logging is turned OFF. To enable logging, click **Main Menu --> Logging --> Start...** as shown in Figure 816 on page 1024.

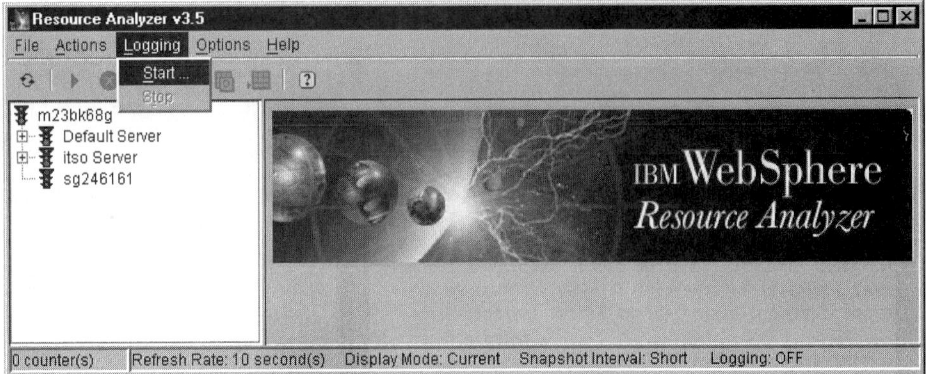

Figure 816. To start logging in the Resource Analyzer

When **Start...** is selected, a Save file window is displayed as shown in Figure 817. Specify the location and name of the log file. Once you click **Save**, logging will be turned ON. Resource Analyzer log files are stored as .lra files.

Figure 817. Saving a log file in Resource Analyzer V3.5

These log files cannot be viewed by text editors. They are legible only when opened via the Resource Analyzer Console.

Click **Main Menu --> File --> Open Log File...** as shown in Figure 818.

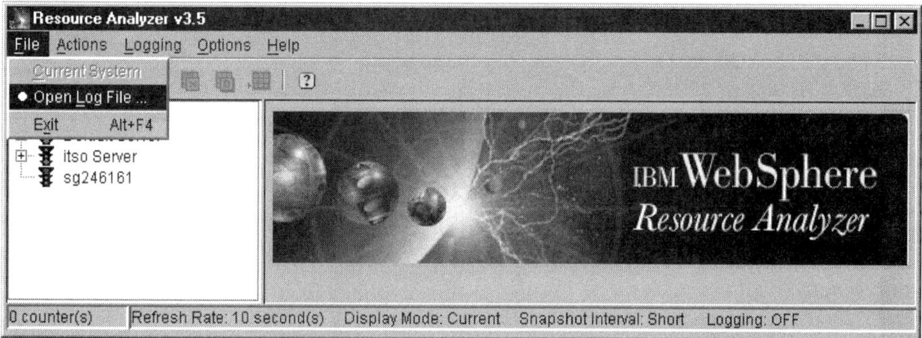

Figure 818. To open a saved Resource Analyzer log file (.lra)

When you select **Open Log File...** the file selection dialog window pops up. Specify the .lra file and click **Open** as shown in Figure 819.

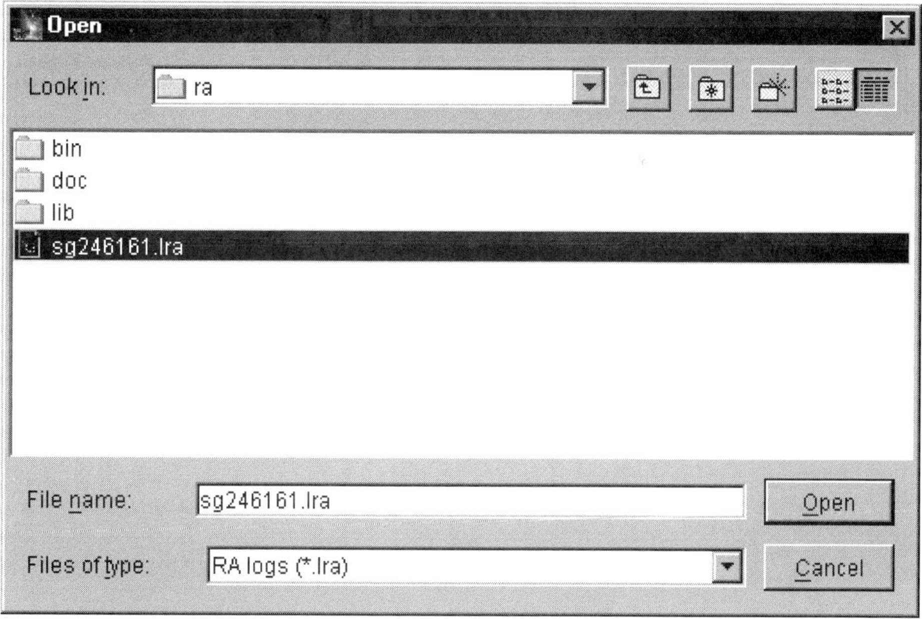

Figure 819. Resource Analyzer log file (.lra) selection dialog

Once the log file is loaded, it can be played. When the end of the log file is reached a message is displayed (Figure 820 on page 1026) indicating the same. At this point the log file can be rewound and replayed.

You do not need the WebSphere Administrative Server running to play these log files.

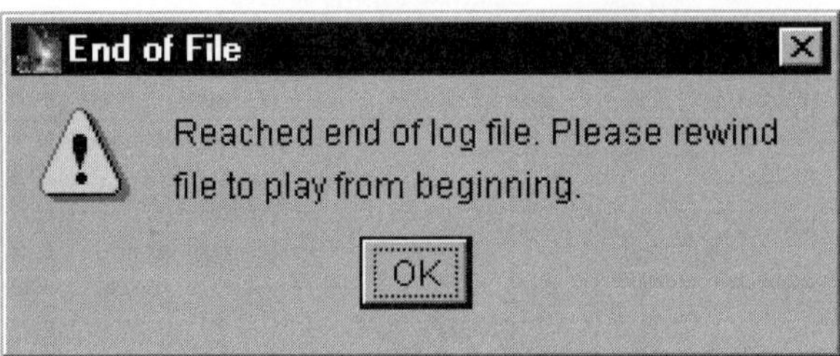

Figure 820. Message to rewind Resource Analyzer V3.5 log file

The log files can be replayed at varying speeds. Log speeds can be 1x, 5x, 20x or 60x the normal speed.

25.8 Resource Analyzer with WebSphere V3.5.2

At the time of writing this book, the Resource Analyzer for WebSphere V3.5 failed to collect statistics when using WebSphere V3.5.2. In addition, the EPM specification level was by default set to none, which is a change from prior versions of WebSphere. The directions below address both the failure to collect servlet statistics and the need to explicitly set an EPM specification level.

The failure to collect servlet statistics manifests itself as the default_host not being displayed under the servlet engine in two places:

1. From WebSphere Administrative Console, you select **application server** (in our case, DefaultServer) and make sure it started. Right click and select **Performance**, double-click **Performance Modules**, and expand **servlet engine**.

   At this point, you should (but do not) see default_host if you are using the DefaultServer.

2. From Resource Analyzer GUI, expand **DefaultServer** -> expand **servlet engine**.

   At this point, you should (but do not) see default_host.

In this section, we describe the workaround to solve this issue. If you don't see the above problem, you may not need to apply the following workaround. The problem may have been fixed.

Note

The Resource Analyzer for WebSphere V3.5 is a technology preview. Therefore, the workaround that we describe in this section is not supported by IBM.

To use the Resource Analyzer with WebSphere V3.5.2, do the following steps:

1. Create a directory for this workaround:

   <WAS_HOME>/fixes/com/ibm/servlet/

2. Get the product file appserver.properties:

   a. Copy <WAS_HOME>/lib/ibmwebas.jar to a temporary directory, such as /tmp directory.

   b. From that temporary directory, expand the ibmwebas.jar as follows:

   ```
   <WAS_HOME>/jdk/bin/jar -xvf ibmwebas.jar
   ```

   c. Change directory:

   ```
   cd com/ibm/servlet
   ```

   d. Copy appserver.properties to:

   <WAS_HOME>/fixes/com/ibm/servlet/

   You can now remove the contents of your /tmp directory.

3. Update appserver.properties:

   a. Change directory:

   ```
   cd <WAS_HOME>/fixes/com/ibm/servlet/
   ```

   b. Use a text editor to edit appserver.properties:

      1. Before any changes, you will see the two lines:

      ```
      #listeners.application=com.ibm.servlet.engine.EPMApplicationListe
      ner com.ibm.servlet.debug.OLTServletManager
      listeners.application=
      ```

      2. Uncomment the first line (remove the "#")

      3. Comment out the second line (add a "#")

      4. Save the file

4. To enable WebSphere to see the file appserver.properties (directions below are for Windows NT), edit the <WAS_HOME>/bin/admin.config and add:

<WAS_HOME>/fixes

to the beginning of the com.ibm.ejs.sm.adminserver.classpath.

```
com.ibm.ejs.sm.adminServer.disableEPM=true
com.ibm.ejs.sm.adminServer.jarFile=C\:/WebSphere/AppServer/lib/repository.jar,C\:/WebSp
com.ibm.ejs.sm.adminserver.classpath=C\:/WebSphere/AppServer/fixes;C\:/WebSphere/AppSer
```

Note that we recommend that you make a backup before you change the admin.config file.

If you start WebSphere with <WAS_HOME>\bin\debug\adminserver.bat, then edit the adminserver.bat file and replace the first classpath line with:

```
set WAS_CP=%WAS_HOME%\fixes
set WAS_CP=%WAS_CP%;%WAS_HOME%\lib\ibmwebas.jar
```

5. Start the administrative server.
6. Start the administrative console.
7. Enable EPM. You can do this in the following two ways:
   a. Right-click a running application server (in our case, Default Server) in the administrative console (it must be running): Select **Performance..** as shown in Figure 821 on page 1029.

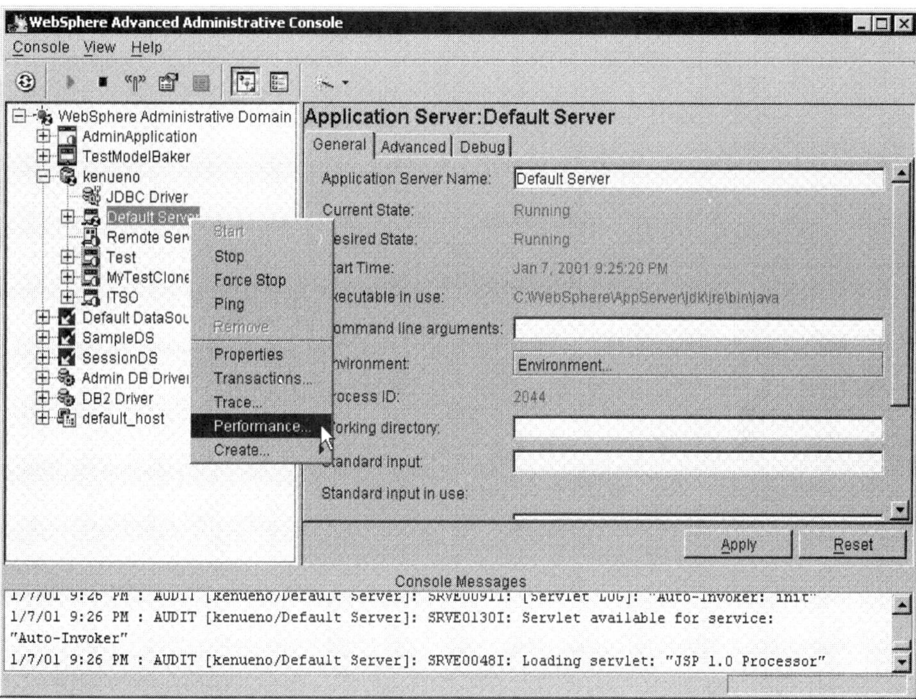

Figure 821. Enabling the EPM

Then you can specify an EPM specification.

Figure 822. Performance window

If you specify an EPM spec with the dialog as shown in Figure 822, then stop the application server. This setting is saved in the EPM spec automatically. (Additional information about setting the EPM specification level is covered in 25.4, “Levels of data collection” on page 1013.)

b. Alternatively, you can specify the EPM specification for example, `epm=low`, on the Advanced tab for the application server as shown in Figure 823 on page 1031. Be sure to click **Apply** to save your change.

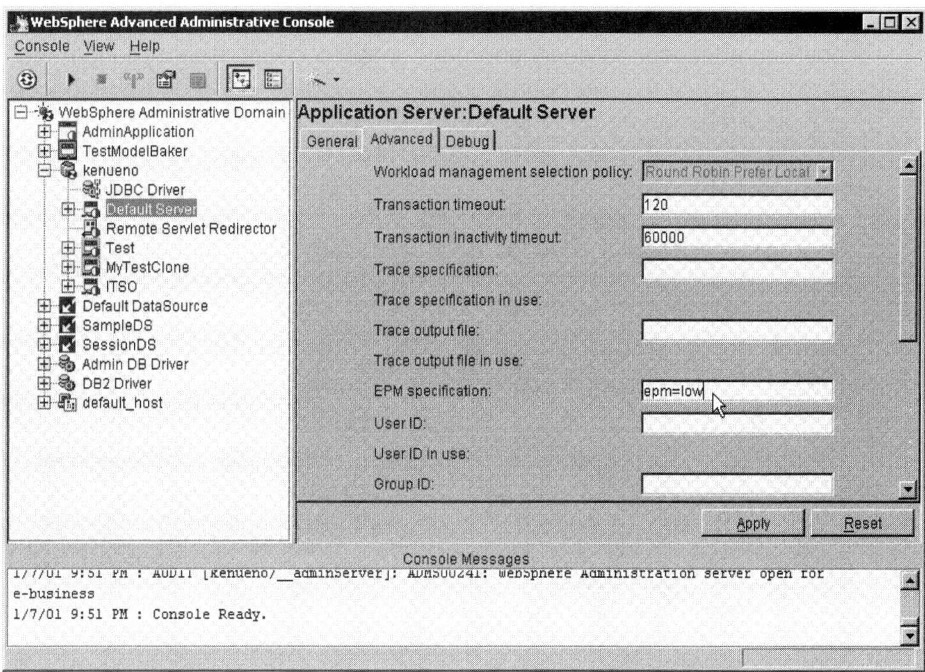

Figure 823. Specifying the EPM specification

If the application server has been running, you need to stop and restart it.

Now, the Resource Analyzer can collect statistics with WebSphere V3.5.2 as shown in Figure 824 on page 1032.

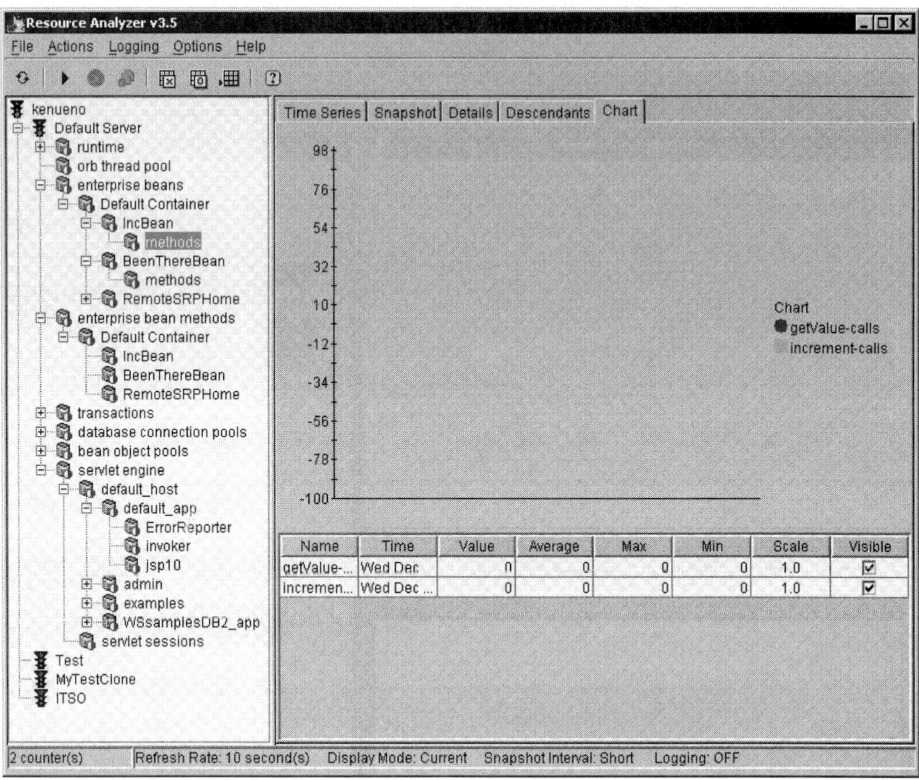

Figure 824. The Resource Analyzer is working with WebSphere V3.5.2

25.9 Resource Analyzer documentation

Most of this information can be found in the Resource Analyzer Help files. Even though there was an older version of the Resource Analyzer, the WebSphere V3.5 Resource Analyzer is considered a technology preview product. There is even a feedback option in the Help menu.

Chapter 26. Migration

As new versions of WebSphere are released, there is a need to migrate existing WebSphere installations. WebSphere V3.5 has a tool called the Migration Assistant that helps to upgrade from WebSphere V3.0.2.x to WebSphere V3.5.

What about upgrading an existing WebSphere V3.0.2.x configuration data? What are the prerequisites for WebSphere V3.5? The Installation Migration Assistant handles these issues and walks the user through the upgrade process.

Can a WebSphere V2.0.3.x installation be migrated? What about existing WebSphere applications? This chapter will take a look at the migration tool in particular and some general migration issues.

26.1 About the Migration Assistant

On the Windows platform, if the installation program detects Version 3.0.2.x of WebSphere, it automatically invokes the Migration Assistant. But one may choose to use XMLConfig or WSCP instead or even skip the migration process.

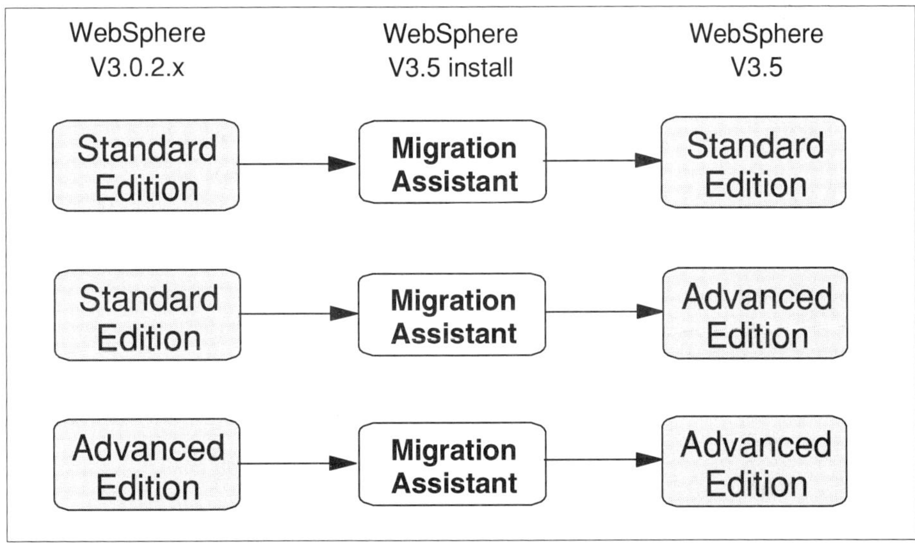

Figure 825. Migration paths using the WebSphere 3.5 Migration Assistant

On AIX and Solaris you have to manually invoke migration.sh. This shell script is found in <WAS_HOME>/bin.

Note

Migration Assistant does not exist on HP-UX because WebSphere V3.5 is the premier release on that platform.

26.2 Main steps in WebSphere migration

The migration process is interlaced with automated steps, targeted documentation, and some manual steps. The main steps in the migration process can be characterized as:

- Back up current configuration and user files
- Uninstall existing WebSphere V3.0.2.x
- Migrate prerequisites
- Install WebSphere V3.5
- Restore configuration and user files
- Post-migration tasks
- Modify/migrate user applications as needed

26.3 Migration Assistant panels

The best advice during the migration process would be to read all the windows/panels thoroughly. The Welcome window (See Figure 826 on page 1035) even has an option to skip migration entirely and proceed with a new WebSphere V3.5 installation.

Clicking the **Details** button brings up the InfoCenter pointing to the Migration Section. It is advisable to read the InfoCenter documentation.

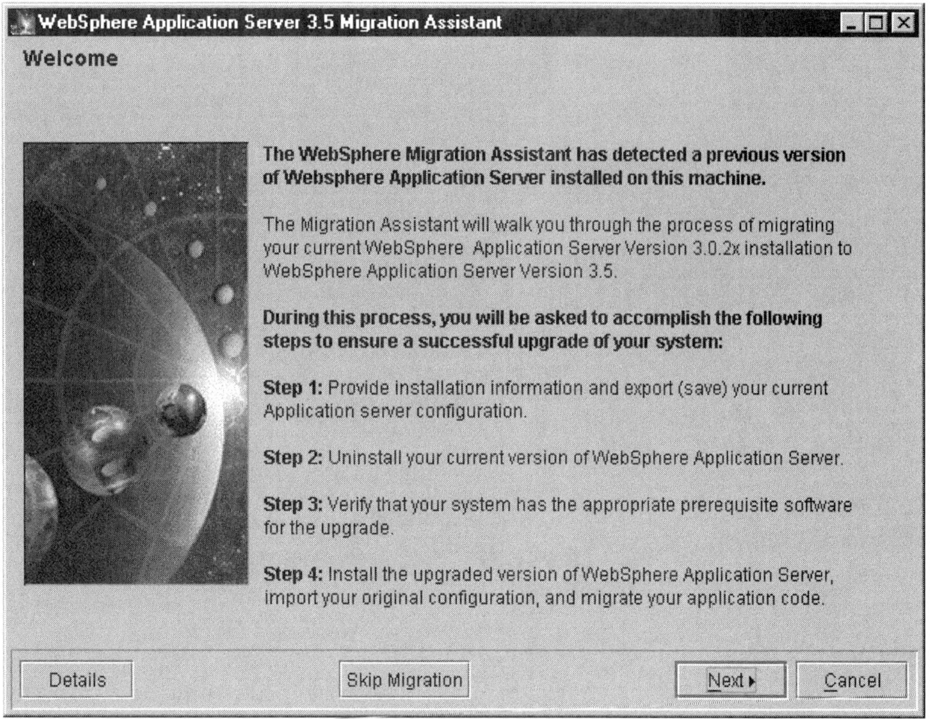

Figure 826. Welcome window of Migration Assistant

Before clicking **Next**, ensure that the WebSphere Administrative Server is running. If it is not running, start it now and then click **Next**.

On the following window enter information about the current WebSphere V3.0.2.x installation as shown in Figure 827 on page 1036 and click **Next**.

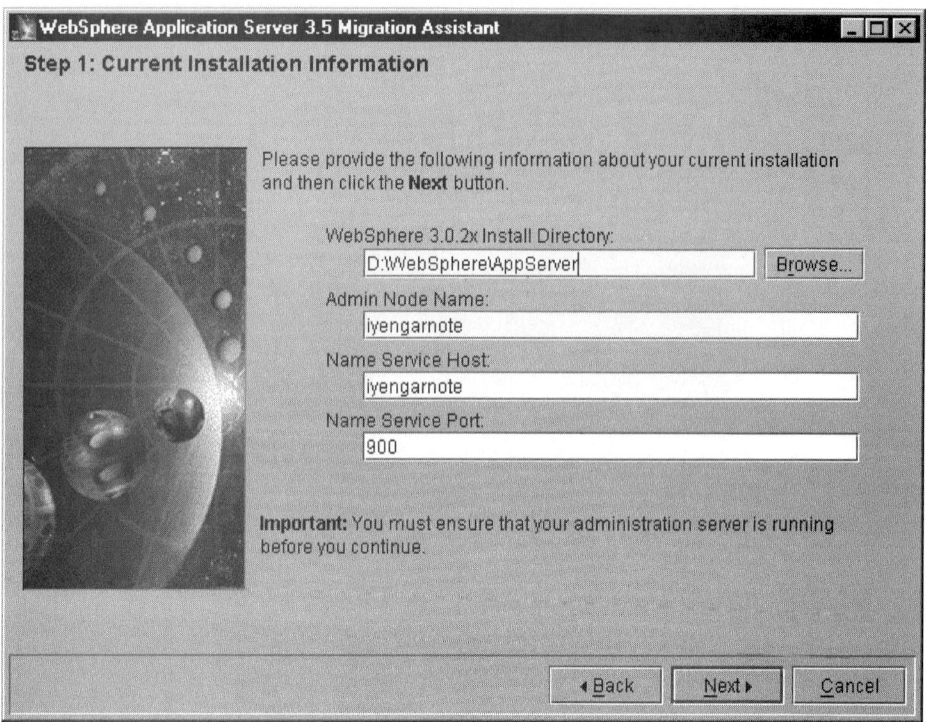

Figure 827. Information about existing WebSphere 3.0.2.x installation

Now you get an opportunity to save your WebSphere configuration. Specify the fully qualified path and filename to save your Backup Directory as shown in Figure 828 on page 1037.

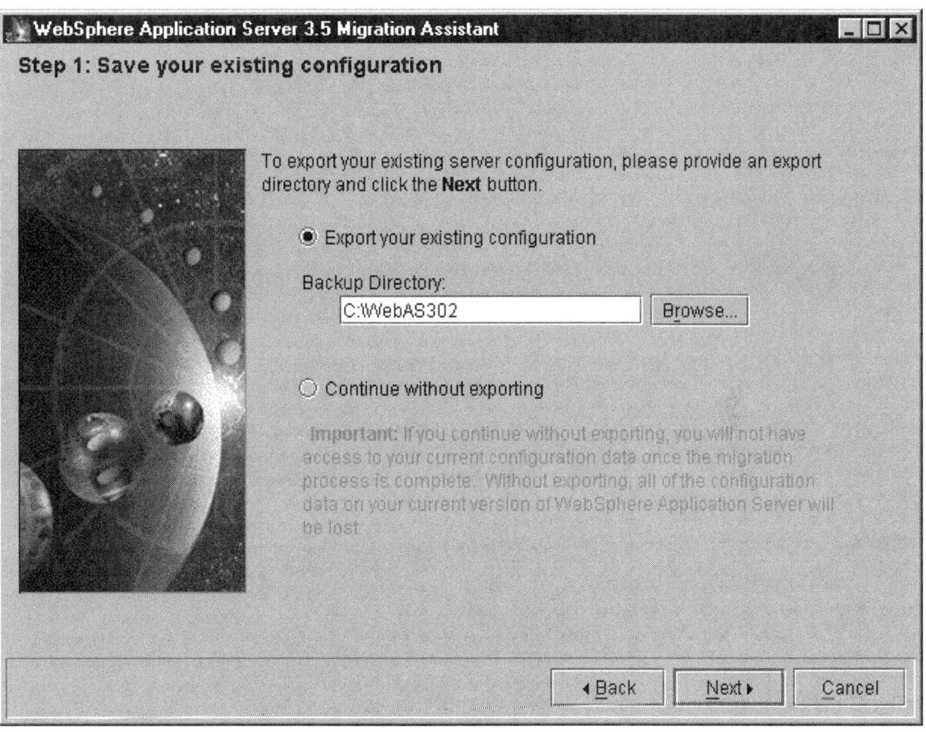

Figure 828. Window to specify the location of Backup Directory

When you click **Next**, the Export XML Config window is displayed as shown in Figure 829. This step could take a while depending on the original WebSphere configuration.

Figure 829. Export XML status window

After the configuration is exported without any problems, the completion window is displayed. This completes Step 1. Click **Next** to start the uninstall process. The Uninstall window is displayed as shown in Figure 830 on page 1038.

Before you click the **Uninstall** button, remember to stop the WebSphere Administrative Server.

Do not click **Next** until after the uninstall process is complete. When the Uninstall Complete window is displayed, on Windows NT, go ahead and reboot. The Migration Assistant picks up where it left off. Remember to:

- Back up the WebSphere administrative database and any other related database
- Drop the WebSphere V3.0.2.x administrative database

Note

WebSphere V3.0.2.x administrative database should be dropped because it is not compatible with that of WebSphere V3.5.

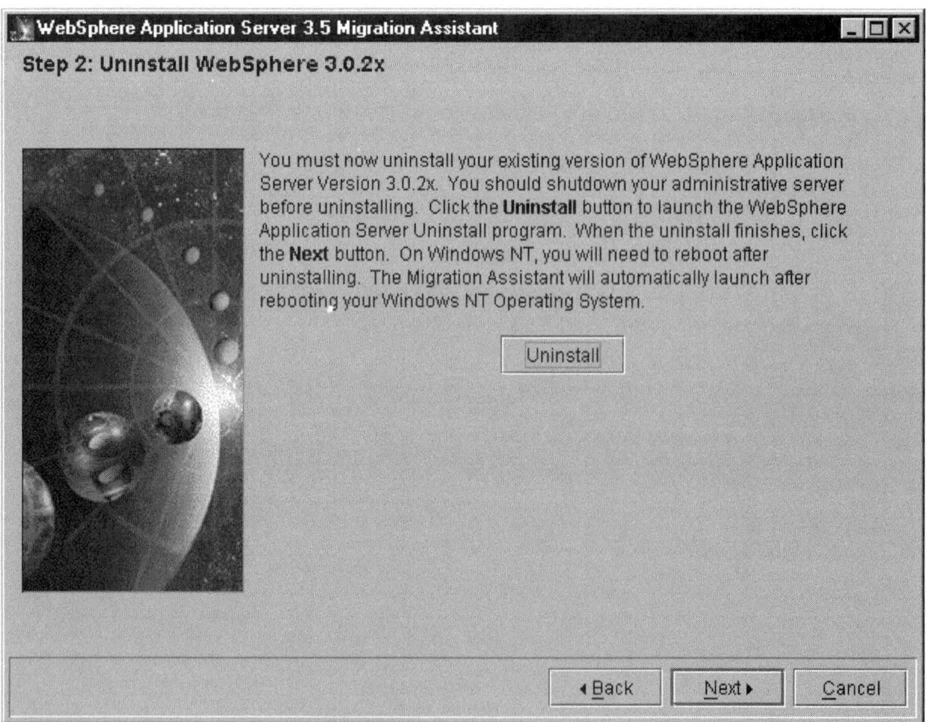

Figure 830. WebSphere 3.0.2.x uninstall window

This completes Step 2. You see the Uninstall Complete window as shown in Figure 831 on page 1039.

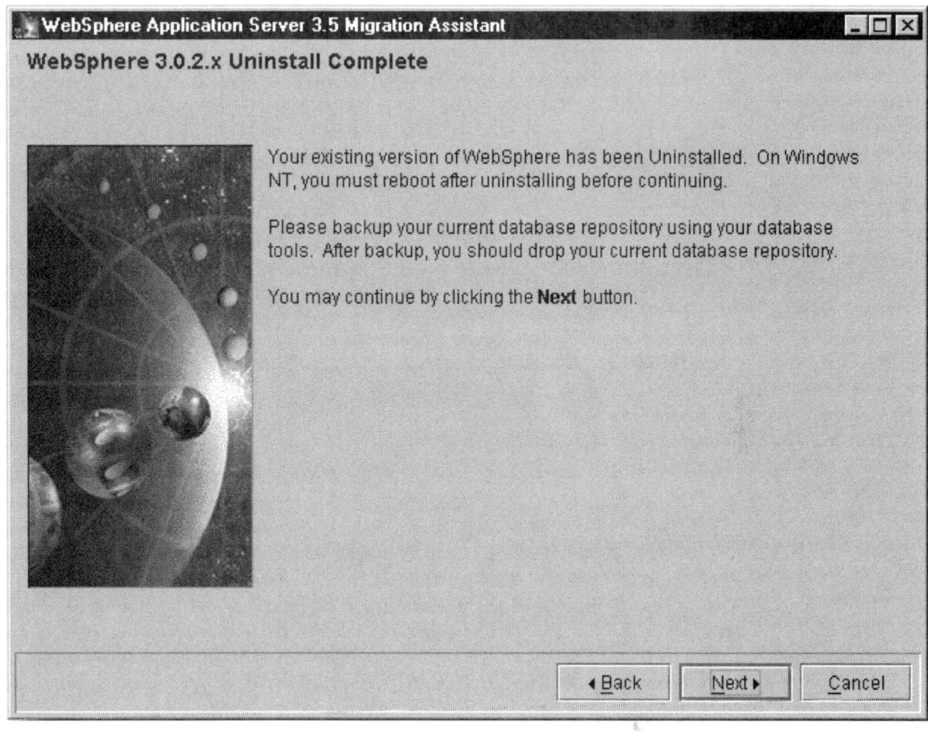

Figure 831. WebSphere 3.0.2.x uninstall completion window

WebSphere requires verification starts. The JDK and IBM HTTP Server will be upgraded automatically by the Migration Assistant. Any other Web server and the database used for the WebSphere administrative database would have to be manually upgraded.

Note

Upgrade the WebSphere administrative database as required by WebSphere V3.5 before proceeding with the installation.

In the following four windows, make note of the prerequisites and keep clicking **Next**. Clicking **Details** actually tries to bring up the following URL:

```
http://www.ibm.com/software/webservers/appserv/doc/v35/prereq.html
```

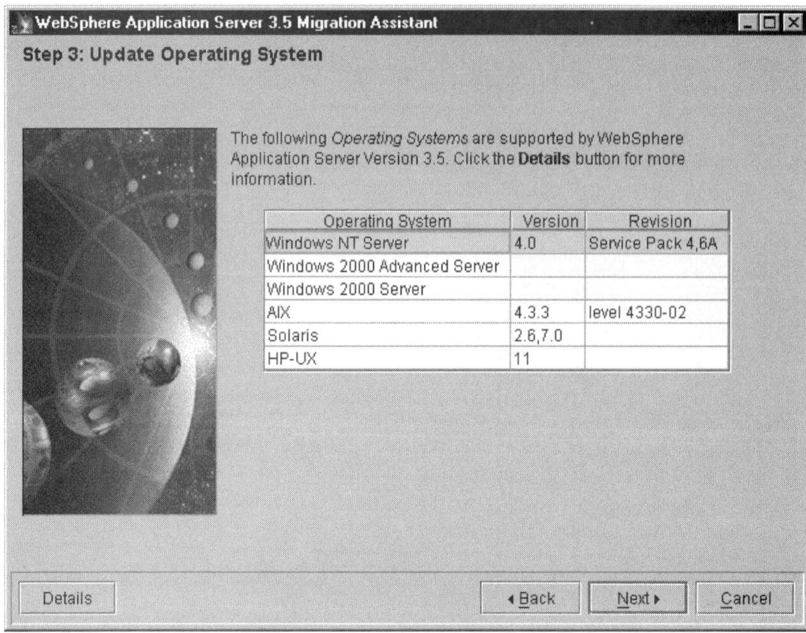

Figure 832. The operating system prerequisites for WebSphere V3.5

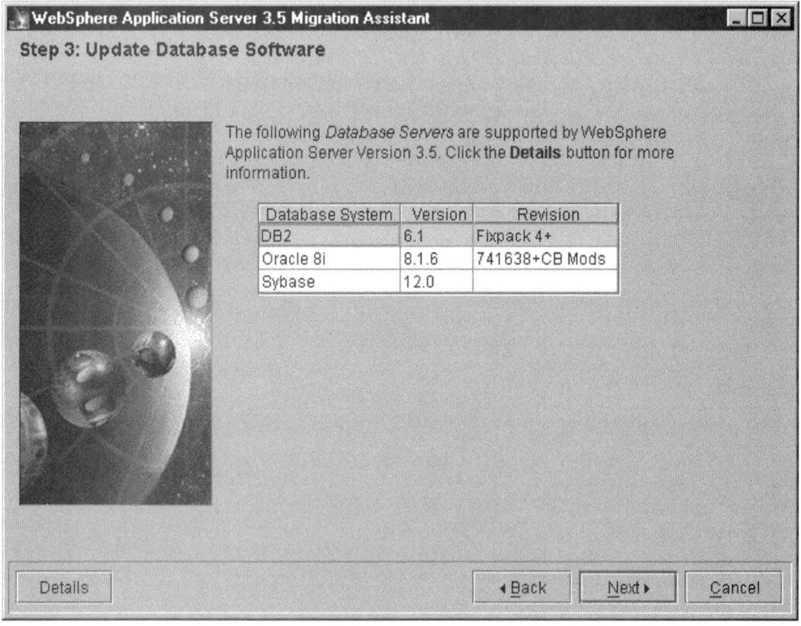

Figure 833. The administrative database prerequisites for WebSphere V3.5

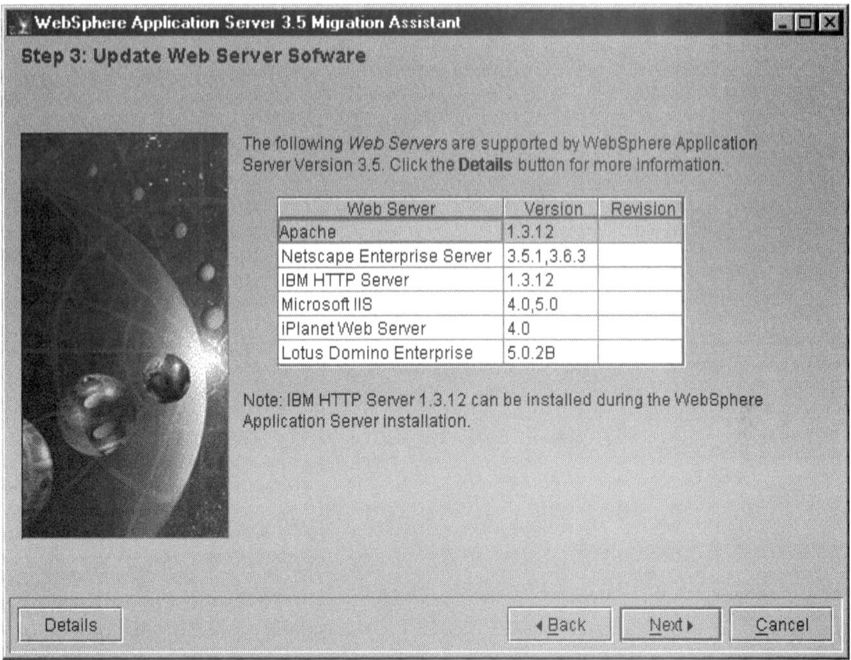

Figure 834. The Web server prerequisites for WebSphere V3.5

This completes Step 3.

The Migration Assistant is set to install WebSphere V3.5. Click the **Install** button to launch the installation program as shown in Figure 835 on page 1042.

Do not click **Next** until the installation is complete.

Note

If you inadvertently click **Next** and get an error message, just select **Cancel** in the error window.

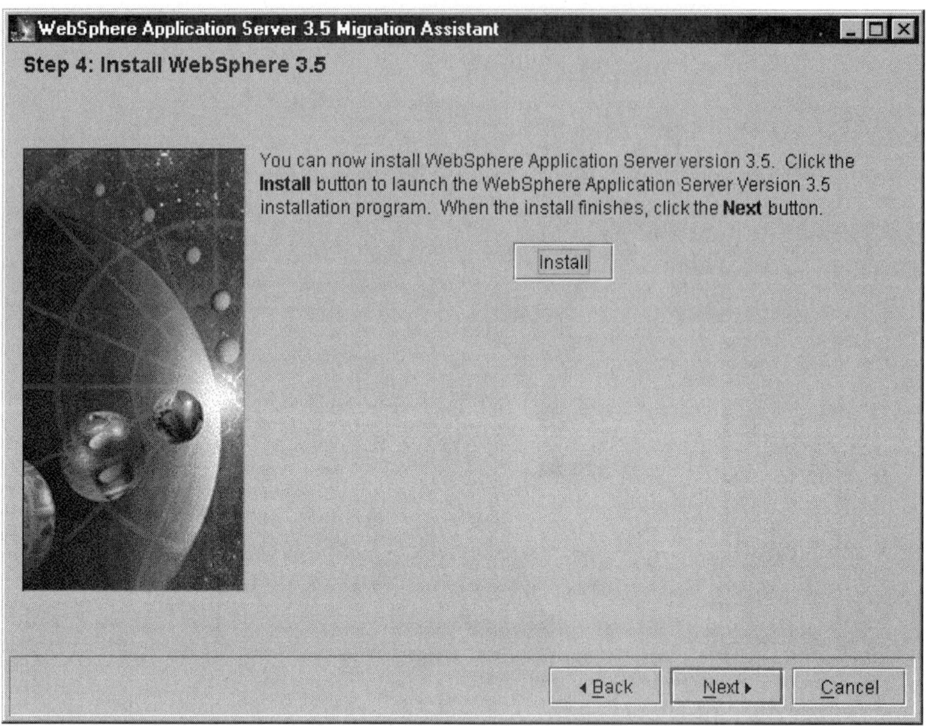

Figure 835. Migration Assistant ready to install WebSphere V3.5

Clicking **Install** launches the normal installation process. Refer to Appendix A, "Installation steps" on page 1049 for details.

When the Installation Complete window is displayed as shown in Figure 836 on page 1043, start the WebSphere Administrative Server. Then click **Next**.

Note

If you click **Next** before starting the WebSphere Administrative Server, do not worry, the following window also has an option to start the administrative server.

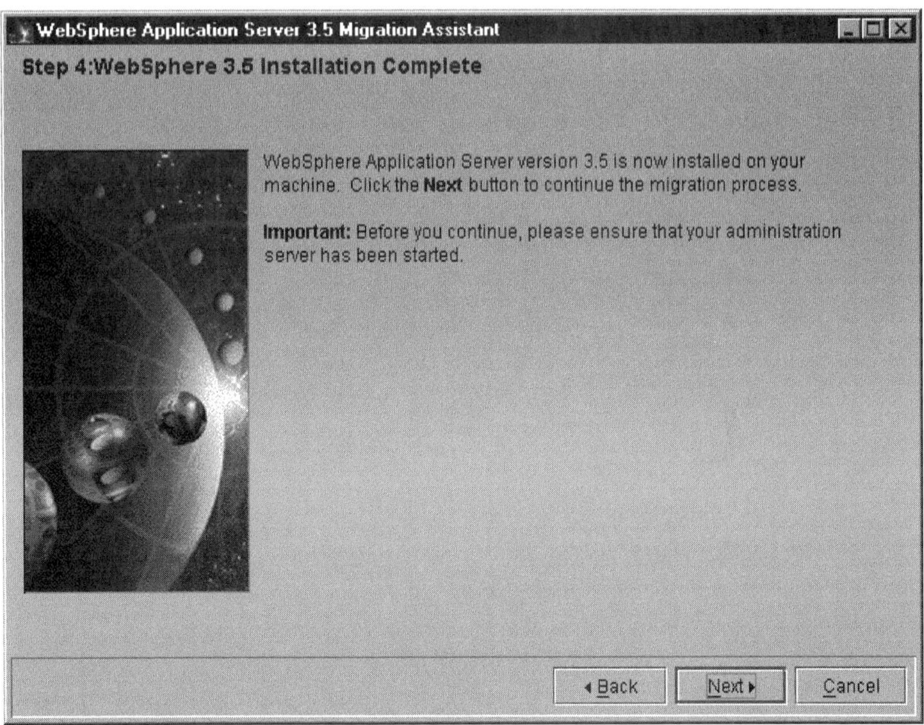

Figure 836. WebSphere Installation completion window

If the original server configuration was saved, the last thing left to do is to import the server configuration into the WebSphere V3.5 administrative database. Make sure the administrative server is running. On the Import Original Server Configuration window, specify the fully qualified path name of the new installation directory and click **Next** as shown in Figure 837 on page 1044.

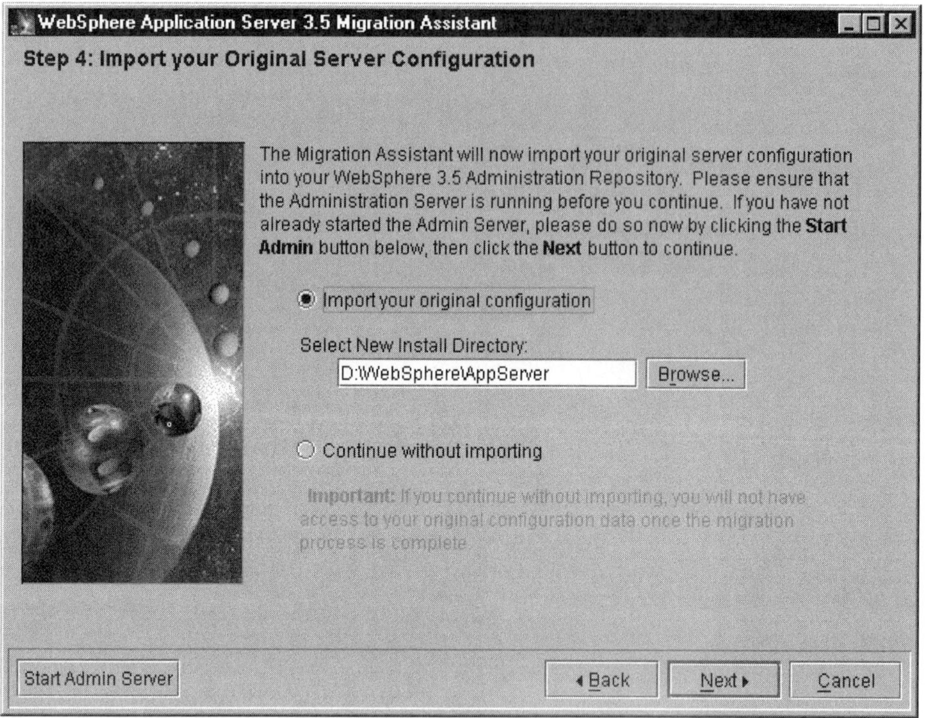

Figure 837. Specify original server configuration details

When you click **Next**, the Import XML Config window is displayed. The rotation of the planets goes on for quite some time depending on the original WebSphere configuration.

If you get an error during restoration of the original configuration, you can click **Back** and retry or click **Next** and fix things manually. View the migration.log file in the backup directory to get details of the error.

If all goes well, the Migration Assistant completion window is displayed, at which point you can click **Finish** as depicted in Figure 838 on page 1045.

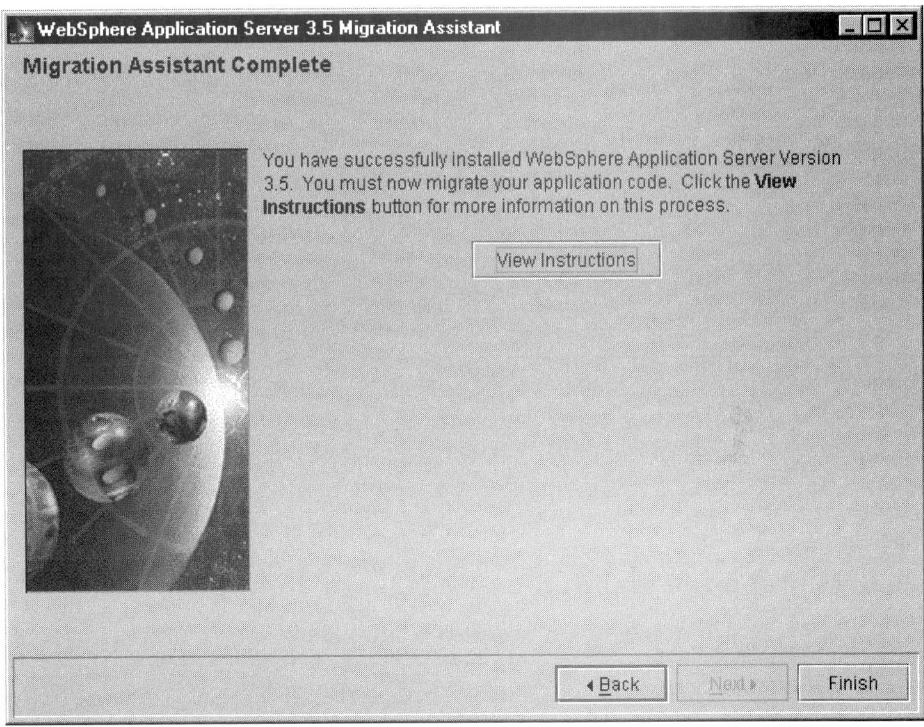

Figure 838. WebSphere V3.5 Migration Assistant completion window

Some post-migration things to do:

- Check the migration.log file to make sure there are no errors.
- If the WebSphere Administrative Server is not running, start it.
- Test the new WebSphere configuration by invoking showCfg servlet or snoop servlet.
- Migrate your applications, starting with re-deployment of your EJBs.

26.4 Files that are saved during migration

As we have seen the WebSphere administrative database information is saved. This is done behind the scenes using XMLConfig. Along with that the following user files are saved:

- Servlets
- Hosts
- Java classes

- Deployed and deployable EJBs

The following system files are also saved:

- Properties
- admin.config
- setupCmdLine

26.5 What is left to be done?

All EJBs need to be re-deployed because the Migration Assistant does not know where the source code is.

There are some Java package name changes attributed to the JDK 1.2 in the area of transaction and data source support. These changes are to javax.sql.* and javax.transaction.* packages.

26.6 Migration of WebSphere V2.0.3.x to WebSphere V3.5

There have been extensive changes by way of improvements going from WebSphere V2.0.3.x to WebSphere V3.5. Along with WebSphere Application Server code changes, there are issues of newer versions of Java APIs pertaining to JDK 1.2. That precludes solely relying on an automated tool like Migration Assistant.

In reality there is not a straight migration path from WebSphere V2.0.3.x to V3.5. The upgrade has to be accomplished in steps and it has to be done manually. The overall steps remain the same as outlined in 26.2, "Main steps in WebSphere migration" on page 1034. You can choose one of two paths:

- V2.0.3.x --> V3.0.2.x --> V3.5
  - To go from WebSphere V2.0.3.x to V3.0.2.x follow the section entitled Migration in the *WebSphere V3.0.2.x Getting Started Guide*.
  - Use the WebSphere V3.5 Migration Assistant to upgrade from WebSphere V3.0.2 to V3.5.
- V2.0.3.x -----> V3.5
  - Back up the V2.0.3.x configuration files.
  - Uninstall WebSphere V2.0.3.x.
  - Install WebSphere V3.5.
  - Manually modify/update all application files and configuration settings.

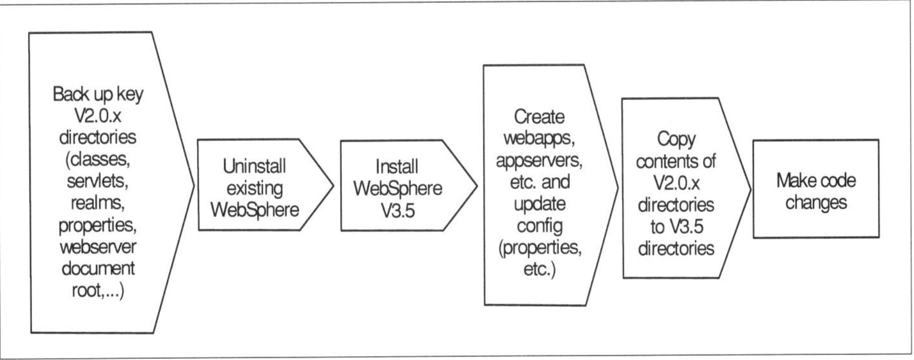

Figure 839. Steps to upgrade from WebSphere V2.0.x to WebSphere V3.5

Review the section on Migration (Article 3.4) in the InfoCenter. One of the tables from that section is summarized here.

Table 56. WebSphere migration from V2.x and V3.0.2.x to V3.5

Functional Area	WebSphere V3.5 support	Need to migrate from V3.0.2.x?	Need to migrate from V2.0.x?
EJBs	EJB1.0+	No*	Yes
Servlets	Servlet 2.1 + IBM extension	No	Yes
JSPs	JSP 1.0 recommended JSP .91 supported	See details in InfoCenter*	See details in InfoCenter*
XML	XML 2.0.x	No*	No*
JDBC and DB connection	JDBC 2.0	No	Yes
User Profiles	IBM user profile APIs	No	Yes
Sessions	IBM session APIs	No	Yes
Security	IBM security	No	No
Transactions	Java 1.2	Yes	Yes

All the caveats as indicated by the asterisks are available in the InfoCenter.

26.7 Migration Assistant documentation

At the end of the migration process when the Migration Assistant Completion window is displayed, click the **View Instructions** button to bring up WebSphere InfoCenter pointing to the Migrating APIs and Specification Section. More information can be found in the InfoCenter regarding migration and interoperability.

Note

WebSphere V3.0.2.x and WebSphere V3.5 ORB Interoperability is supported.

Appendix A. Installation steps

This chapter provides general information of installation about the WebSphere Application Server V3.5 with other related products, such as Web servers and database servers. When you install WebSphere together with other related products, please refer to the products' installation manuals.

Since there are many combinations of WebSphere configurations, we chose the Windows NT platform for this chapter. We describe a simple configuration (in most cases using the default settings) and do not consider such issues as security and performance. You could refer to this chapter for your system development environment but we recommend you consult more detailed documentation for your production system environment.

IBM will frequently update the information of hardware and software requirements for WebSphere on the IBM WebSphere Web site, since new versions of software which WebSphere supports are released every day. Therefore, we will not discuss them in this chapter. To obtain the most current information please refer to the IBM WebSphere Web site.

```
http://www-4.ibm.com/software/webservers/appserv/doc/v35/idx_aas.htm
```

A.1 Planning

Before you start installing WebSphere, there are several topics to consider. We assume that you have already decided upon your operating system, Web server, and DB server products.

A.1.1 Web server location

First, you should consider where you will install your Web server. There are two choices:

- Install it on the same node as WebSphere will be installed
- Install it on a different node from where WebSphere will be installed

Please refer to Chapter 16, "Topologies selection" on page 771 for detailed information. In this chapter, we will install the Web server and WebSphere on the same node.

A.1.2 Database server location

More importantly you need to consider where you will install the DB server for the WebSphere administrative database (and probably for your EJB persistence and HttpSession persistence depending on your application). There are two choices for database server location as well as Web server location:

- Install it on the same node as WebSphere will be installed
- Install it on a different node from where WebSphere will be installed

For your production environment, we recommend that the WebSphere administrative database reside on a remote database server. Even in the simple “single WebSphere machine” configuration such as no clones, or no clustering, the WebSphere administrative database resides on a remote database server. There are several reasons why this represents good practice.

First, most enterprises have already invested in a high availability solution for their database server, and the configuration repository represents a single point of failure in WebSphere, so it pays to make this highly available.

Second, the database that houses the configuration repository should be backed up on a regular basis, just as application data is. Housing the repository on the same server as the application data usually simplifies this task since appropriate DBA procedures such as database backup processes are already defined for this machine.

Additionally, the database server is typically sized and tuned for database performance, which may differ from the optimal configuration for the application server (in fact on many UNIX servers, installing the database involves modification of the OS kernel).

Lastly, if one places both the database and application server on the same machine, then under high load you have two processes, the application server and the database server, competing for increasingly scarce resources (CPU and memory), so in general one can expect significantly better performance by separating the application server from the database server.

In this chapter, we will configure the administrative database on a remote database server that is separate from the WebSphere node.

A.1.3 Java GUI installation or native installation

WebSphere V3.5 supports two different installation procedures. One is a Java GUI installation and the other is a native installation. The native installation has two modes: interactive and silent. On the UNIX platform, WebSphere supports all three installation modes. However, on the Windows platform, WebSphere doesn’t support the Java GUI installation. Note that the native installations on UNIX and Windows are slightly different. On UNIX, the native installation does not mean "GUI" installation. It is a character-based installation. However, on Windows, the WebSphere installation program uses the Install Shield with the native installation interactive mode.

Table 57. Java GUI installation and native installation support

	UNIX	Windows
Java GUI	✓	
Native: Interactive	✓ (character based)	✓ (Install Shield based)
Native: Silent	✓	✓

A.1.3.1 Java GUI installation

There are three options for Java GUI installation as follows:

- Quick: Everything you need for initial evaluation purposes or for lightweight "proof of concept" applications intended to run on single node server configurations, including IBM HTTP Server, InstantDB, and JDK1.2.2.
- Full: Everything you need to support production level, highly scalable applications intended to run on server from single node configurations to complex multi-node configurations, including IBM HTTP Server, DB2 V6.1 Fix Pack 4, and JDK 1.2.2.
- Custom: You may choose to install specific components of the total install package, or specify the use of other supported databases and Web servers.

A.1.3.2 Native installation

Instead of using a Java GUI installation program, you can install the WebSphere Application Server with a native installation. We provide only a brief description below. Please refer to the online manual for detailed information.

There are two options for a native installation:

- Interactive: You need to answer several questions while installing WebSphere.

  Note: On the Windows platform, the interactive mode of a native installation with the Install Shield looks similar to the Java GUI installation.
- Silent (non-interactive): To complete a silent installation, you modify parameters in a response file and then run the installation program for

WebSphere Application Server, supplying the setup or installation file as a command-line parameter.

On UNIX, with a native installation, there are several benefits:

- Remote installation: You can easily install WebSphere from a remote machine.
- Multiple-node installations: It's very easy to install WebSphere on several nodes that are configured identically.

There are a couple of restrictions with a native installation on UNIX:

- No prerequisite checking: You need to verify the required software level by yourself before you install WebSphere.
- Cannot use a system management utility, such as SMIT or SAM.

A.2 Installation steps overview

There are four major steps in installing WebSphere Application Server:

- Configure the operating system
- Install the Web server
- Install the database server and create the administrative database
- Install the WebSphere

A.2.1 Configure operating system

Before you install WebSphere and required software, you need to make sure that you configure your operating system properly. There are a couple of points which you should verify:

- Configuring network: You need to have at least one network interface configured. We recommend that you configure and verify network connectivity, including name resolution.
- Applying required patches: You should apply appropriate patches on your operating system. Please refer to the IBM WebSphere Web site to obtain information about the latest required patches.
- Having enough disk space: You should make sure if you have enough disk space for WebSphere installation.

A.2.2 Install Web server

After you configure the operating system, the next step is the installation of the Web server. We don't discuss the installation of Web server here. Please refer to the product's manual. After you install the Web server, you should verify whether it's working. For example, access the URL (such as `http://<servet_name>/)` with a Web browser on the remote machine.

We recommend that if you will be using an SSL (HTTPS) connection, you should verify the SSL configuration as well. Once you verify HTTP and HTTPS connections at this point, it will help you when you get any HTTP (or HTTPS) connection problems after you install the WebSphere.

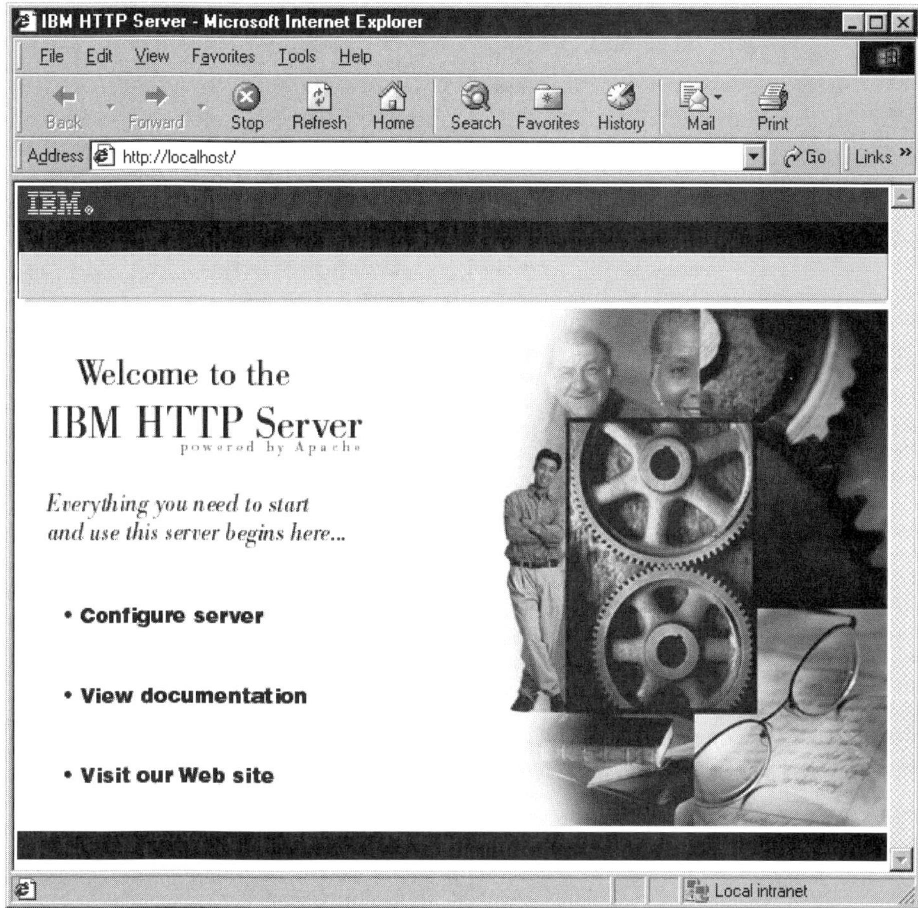

Figure 840. Verify Web server installation (IBM HTTP Server 1.3.12)

A.2.3 Install DB server and create an administrative database

The third step is the installation of the database server. Please refer to the database product's manual to install and configure the database server. The WebSphere installation manual also gives you detailed information. There are three steps you should do at this stage:

1. Install the database server software
2. Configure the administrative database
3. Verify the database connectivity

If you will create the administrative database on the remote database server node (this is the common configuration in the production system environment as we discussed A.1.2, "Database server location" on page 1049), you should configure and verify the remote database connectivity. You can find some information about the remote database connectivity for Sybase in Appendix B, "Remote Sybase connectivity" on page 1083. If you use DB2, refer to *WebSphere Scalability: WLM and Clustering using WebSphere Application Server Advanced*, SG24-6153.

Database server installation must be done before you install WebSphere Application Server. Since the database is used for the administrative database, WebSphere will not function without a database server.

In this chapter, we use DB2 and Oracle as the WebSphere administrative database.

A.2.3.1 Install DB2 server

Follow these steps to install DB2 UDB on the remote database node.

1. If you have the WebSphere Application Server CDs, find the DB2 UDB installation files on one of the WebSphere Application Server CDs. Run setup.exe in the \DB2 subdirectory.

   If you have the CD for DB2 UDB, run the setup.exe file.

   If you downloaded DB2 UDB, unzip the DB2 zip file to a temporary directory using an option that recreates the directory structure. Then, run the setup.exe file from the directory.
2. Select **Next**, choose the **Enterprise Edition**, and then select **Next**.
3. Check **Typical installation**, keep the default installation directory (C:\SQLLIB), and click **Next**.

   Note that if you are familiar with DB2, you don't have to select the Typical installation and you can specify which installation directory you prefer, depending on your system environment. For the purposes of this redbook, we select and configure very simple settings which are not appropriate for the production system environment.

4. Overwrite the default user name and password with your own user ID and password. Consider using the same user ID and password specified during the Web server installation. This will make it the DB2 administration ID as well. Note that DB2 requires a password of 8 or fewer characters.
5. Select **Next**, and continue with the installation.
6. After the product installs, restart your system.

Apply Fix Pack

If you installed the DB2 V6.1 from a WebSphere Application Server CD, you do not need to go further. DB2 V6.1 Fix Pack 4 was installed when you installed the base UDB product.

If you did not install the DB2 V6.1 from the WebSphere Application Server CD, download the DB2 V6.1 Fix Pack 4 from the product Web site or obtain a CD that holds the Fix Pack.

Next, do the following:

1. From the Services panel of the Control Panel, stop the services DB2 - DB2 and DB2 -DB2DAS00. If you have the Netfinity Support Manager or other monitoring agents you may need to stop these as well, since they can lock DB2.
2. If necessary, unzip the Fix Pack file into a temporary directory. Delete the DB2 installation directory if you wish.
3. Run `setup.exe`.
4. Click **Next**, then **Next** again and complete the installation.

When the installation finishes, restart your computer and log in as the user you have been using to configure the software.

After your system restarts, the DB2 First Steps and Control Center dialogs may display. At this point, you may create the database called "sample" used by the WebSphere Application Server samples. To create the database sample, click **Create the SAMPLE database** in the DB2 First Steps dialog and then click **Yes** in the confirmation dialog.

If you receive an error message stating that the database was not created, go to the Services dialog accessible from a Control Panel and ensure that the status for the DB2-DB2 service is Started. The startup type for the DB2-DB2 service should be Automatic and the hardware profile should be Enabled. Once you start the DB2-DB2 service, try creating the database sample again.

After you finish, close the DB2 dialogs.

Note: DB2 6.1 Fix Pack 4, 5 (not on AIX), and DB2 7.1 Fix Pack 1 are supported for WebSphere Application Server's administrative database. In order to check the Fix Pack level, execute the `db2level` command from your window. The following displays DB2 6.1 Fix Pack 5 in Windows NT. "DB2 V6.1.0.27" denotes DB2 V6.1 Fix Pack 5.

```
Microsoft(R) Windows NT(TM)
(C) Copyright 1985-1996 Microsoft Corp.

C:\>db2level
DB21085I  Instance "DB2" uses DB2 code release "SQL06010" with level identifier

"01060104" and informational tokens "DB2 v6.1.0.27", "s000729" and "WR21202".


C:\>
```

DB2 editions and versions

When using DB2 for the administrative database, WebSphere Application Server V3.5.2 requires DB2 V6.1 Fix Pack 4 or 5 or DB2 V7.1 Fix Pack 1. Also WebSphere requires the Enterprise edition of DB2. If you did not install a supported version of DB2 or you are using the Personal or WorkgroupEdition, the prereq checker reports that the wrong version of DB2 is installed and aborts the installation.

Create administrative database

In order for WebSphere to store the administrative configuration, you must create a database on the database server node. The database name must be the same one (or alias) as you will use for the JDBC URL entry name during the WebSphere Application Server installation. If you are using DB2 and not familiar with its remote connectivity, refer to *WebSphere Scalability: WLM and Clustering using WebSphere Application Server Advanced*, SG24-6153.

You can create the database by selecting **Start -> Programs -> DB2 for Windows NT -> Command Line Processor**.

- Enter `create database was`
- Enter `update db cfg for was using applheapsz 256`

- Enter `quit` to leave Command Line Processor (CLP)

Please refer to the WebSphere online manual and DB2 command reference for detailed information.

A.2.3.2 Install and configure DB2 client

In order to access the remote administrative database, you need to install the DB2 clients on the WebSphere node. After the installation of the DB2 clients, you need to configure the client to allow DB2 server communication. You can use the Control Center to configure remote database connections. You can also configure it by using the Client Configuration Assistant (CCA) in Windows NT. In this section, we use the Client Configuration Assistant. You can start the Client Configuration Assistant by selecting **Start -> Programs -> DB2 for Windows NT -> Client Configuration Assistant**.

Click **Add** to configure connections and the Add Database SmartGuide panel will appear to guide you through the addition of the new database. If you want to search the network for remote database, select the **Search the network** and then click **Next**.

On the Target Database tab, select the database on the remote server you want to use (in our case, WAS) and then click **Next**.

In the Alias tab, enter the database alias name. In our case, we specify WAS.

Click **Done** to finish the Add Database SmartGuide. You can verify the connection to your database server.

Click **Test Connection** button. Enter a user ID and password to access the remote database.

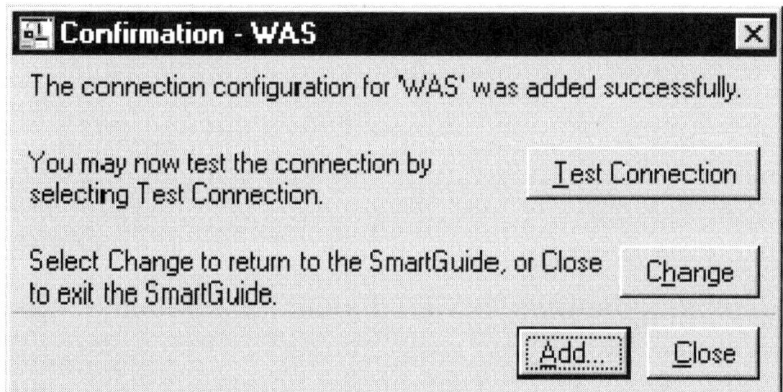

Figure 841. Verification of the server connection

If everything is successful, you will get the DB2 Message panel as shown in Figure 842. Click **OK**.

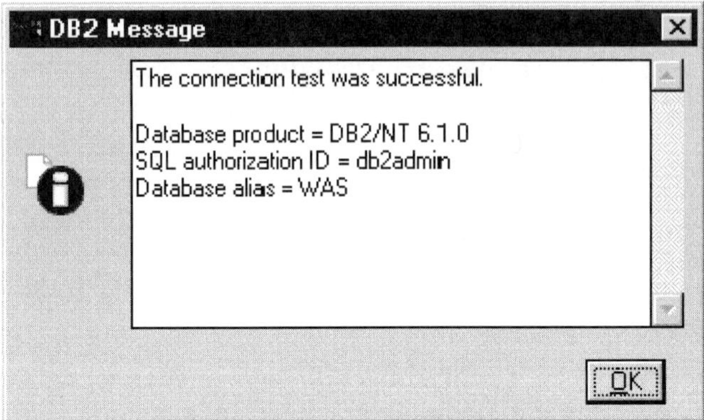

Figure 842. Successful remote database connection

Note that when you install the WebSphere, you specify the alias which you configured in the above step as the WebSphere administrative database database name. If you are not familiar with DB2 remote connectivity, please refer to the DB2 manual or *WebSphere Scalability: WLM and Clustering using WebSphere Application Server Advanced*, SG24-6153.

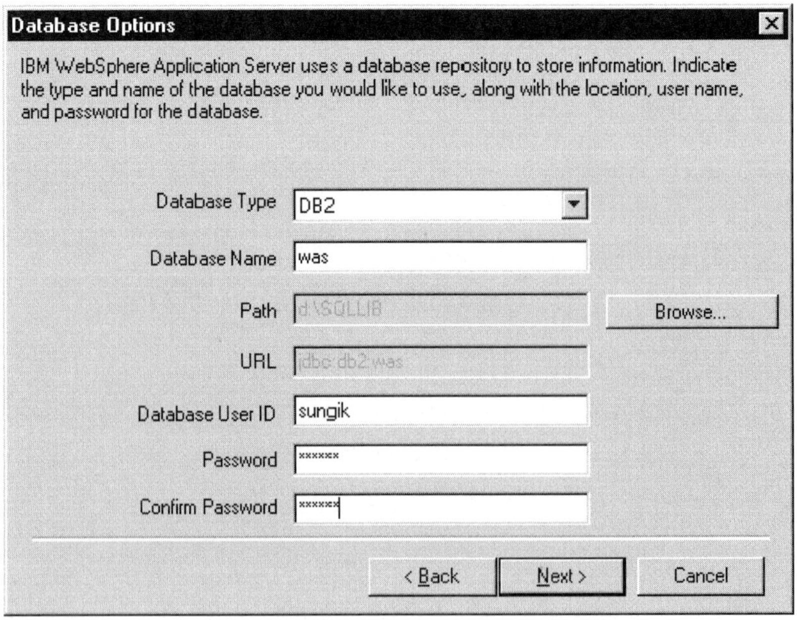

Figure 843. Database options window

A.2.3.3 Install Oracle server

It is important to note that Oracle 8i 8.1.6 is the only version supported for the WebSphere administrative database. Oracle 8.0.5 or 8.1.5 is not supported.

These steps cover how to install the Oracle 8i Release 2 (formerly Oracle 8.1.6), then create and configure a database. For detailed information on installation, see the Oracle documentation and the Oracle Web site.

To install the Oracle 8i:

1. Insert the Oracle CD into your database server machine's CD drive.
2. On the main Oracle dialog, select **Install/Deinstall Products**.
3. On the Welcome dialog, select **Next**.
4. On the File Locations dialog, verify the destination for Oracle 8i and click **Next**.
5. On the Available Products dialog, select **Oracle8i Enterprise Edition 8.1.6.0.0** and click **Next**.
6. On the Installation Types dialog, select **Typical** and then **Next**.
7. On the Database Identification dialog, for the Global Database Name type in `orcl.<hostname>` and then select **Next**.
8. On the Summary dialog, select **Install**.
9. After installation, on the database Configuration Assistant Alert dialog, click **OK**.
10. On the End of Installation dialog, click **Exit**.

Completing the above steps installs the Oracle 8i code and creates a global database named orcl.<hostname.domain>.

Configuring an Oracle 8i database

To use an Oracle database with WebSphere Application Server, you must configure the database:

1. Add the following line to the initialization file: `open_cursors = 200`

   On Windows NT, the initialization file is typically located at \orant\Database\Initxxx.ora, where xxx is your SID (example, orcl).

2. Using a Services panel, stop and restart the Oracle services OracleServiceORCL and OracleOraHome81TNSListener.
3. Define a WebSphere administration ID with database authority by entering the commands below. In the first command, `system` is the ID and `manager` is the default password.

```
sqlplus system/manager
create user EJSADMIN identified by xxxxxxxx;
grant connect, resource, dba to EJSADMIN;
quit
```

where xxxxxxxx is the password for EJSADMIN.

4. If needed, define an ID to deploy entity beans:

```
sqlplus system/manager
create user EJB identified by EJB;
grant connect, resource, dba to EJB;
quit
```

Note

If you are using the Advanced Edition and do not want EJSADMIN to have DBA authority, do not enter the commands above but, instead, complete the following two steps.

First, enter the commands:

```
sqlplus system/manager
create user EJSADMIN identified by EJSADMIN quota 100M on SYSTEM;
create user EJB identified by EJB quota 100M on USERS;
grant connect, resource to EJSADMIN;
grant connect, resource to EJB;
quit
```

Second, after you start the WebSphere Administrative Console, edit the data source for the HitCount bean (select **Default Server -> Default -> Container -> HitCount Bean -> DataSource**) so the user ID and password

5. Test access to the new database using the EJSADMIN user ID:

```
sqlplus ejsadmin/ejsadmin
```

After a message displays indicating a successful connection, enter `exit`.

A.2.3.4 Install Oracle client and configure remote access

WebSphere V3.5 supports two Oracle JDBC drivers, thin driver and OCI driver. For remote database connectivity, you should have one of them on the WebSphere node.

Using Oracle thin driver

If you want to use Oracle thin JDBC driver, you don't have to install Oracle client on the machine to access the remote database.

However, before you start the WebSphere Administrative Server, you need to have the classes12.zip file on the WebSphere node. You can download the classes12.zip file (or FTP or copy it from the Oracle server node) in your system. For example, you can copy the classes12.zip file under your <was>/lib directory.

If you install Oracle client on the WebSphere node, you can find the classes12.zip under the <install_drive>:\Oracle\Ora81\jdbc\lib directory.

Note that the place of the classes12.zip is specified in the <WAS_HOME>/bin/admin.config file. We will discuss this in Appendix A.2.5, "Post configuration" on page 1075.

Note that WebSphere does not use the Oracle client for the remote database connectivity. Therefore, you don't need to install it on the WebSphere node. However, if you would like to verify the remote database connectivity before you install the WebSphere, you need to install the Oracle client on the WebSphere node.

Using the Oracle OCI driver

In order to use the Oracle OCI JDBC driver, you need to install the Oracle client on the WebSphere node. Then you need to configure tnsnames.ora and sqlnet.ora files under the <install_drive>:\Oracle\ora81\network\admin directory on the WebSphere node. You also need to configure the listener.ora file on the database server node.

```
# TNSNAMES.ORA Network Configuration File: E:\Oracle\Ora81\network\admin\tnsnames.ora
# Generated by Oracle configuration tools.

EXTPROC_CONNECTION_DATA.RALEIGH.IBM.COM =
  (DESCRIPTION =
    (ADDRESS_LIST =
      (ADDRESS = (PROTOCOL = IPC)(KEY = EXTPROC0))
    )
    (CONNECT_DATA =
      (SID = PLSExtProc)
      (PRESENTATION = RO)
    )
  )

VISHY2.RALEIGH.IBM.COM =
  (DESCRIPTION =
    (ADDRESS_LIST =
      (ADDRESS = (PROTOCOL = TCP)(HOST = VISHY2)(PORT = 1521))
    )
    (CONNECT_DATA =
      (SERVICE_NAME = vishy2)
    )
  )
```

Figure 844. tnsnames.ora

```
# SQLNET.ORA Network Configuration File: E:\Oracle\Ora81\network\admin\sqlnet.ora
# Generated by Oracle configuration tools.

NAMES.DEFAULT_DOMAIN = raleigh.ibm.com

SQLNET.AUTHENTICATION_SERVICES= (NTS)

NAMES.DIRECTORY_PATH= (TNSNAMES)
```

Figure 845. sqlnet.ora

listener - Notepad

File Edit Search Help

```
# LISTENER.ORA Network Configuration File: E:\Oracle\Ora81\network\admin\listener.ora
# Generated by Oracle configuration tools.

WAS =
  (DESCRIPTION_LIST =
    (DESCRIPTION =
      (ADDRESS_LIST =
        (ADDRESS = (PROTOCOL = TCP)(HOST = VISHY2)(PORT = 1521))
      )
      (ADDRESS_LIST =
        (ADDRESS = (PROTOCOL = IPC)(KEY = EXTPROC0))
      )
    )
  )

SID_LIST_WAS =
  (SID_LIST =
    (SID_DESC =
      (SID_NAME = PLSExtProc)
      (ORACLE_HOME = E:\Oracle\Ora81)
      (PROGRAM = extproc)
    )
    (SID_DESC =
      (GLOBAL_DBNAME = vishy2)
      (ORACLE_HOME = E:\Oracle\Ora81)
      (SID_NAME = was)
    )
  )
```

Figure 846. listener.ora

A.2.4 WebSphere installation

Now, you are ready to install the WebSphere. This chapter describes general information of the installation of WebSphere Application Server V3.5. When you install the WebSphere, please refer to its installation manuals to obtain step-by-step instructions.

1. If Web server is running on your system, stop the Web server before proceeding with the following WebSphere installation.
2. Insert the WebSphere Application Server V3.5 CD. Run `\nt\setup.exe`. Note that you will need 100 MB free in your temp directory (usually on the C drive) even if you are installing on another drive, because the installation shield package unpacks to the temp directory.
3. Select a language and click **OK**.
4. Click **Next** to get past the introductory page as shown in Figure 847 on page 1064.

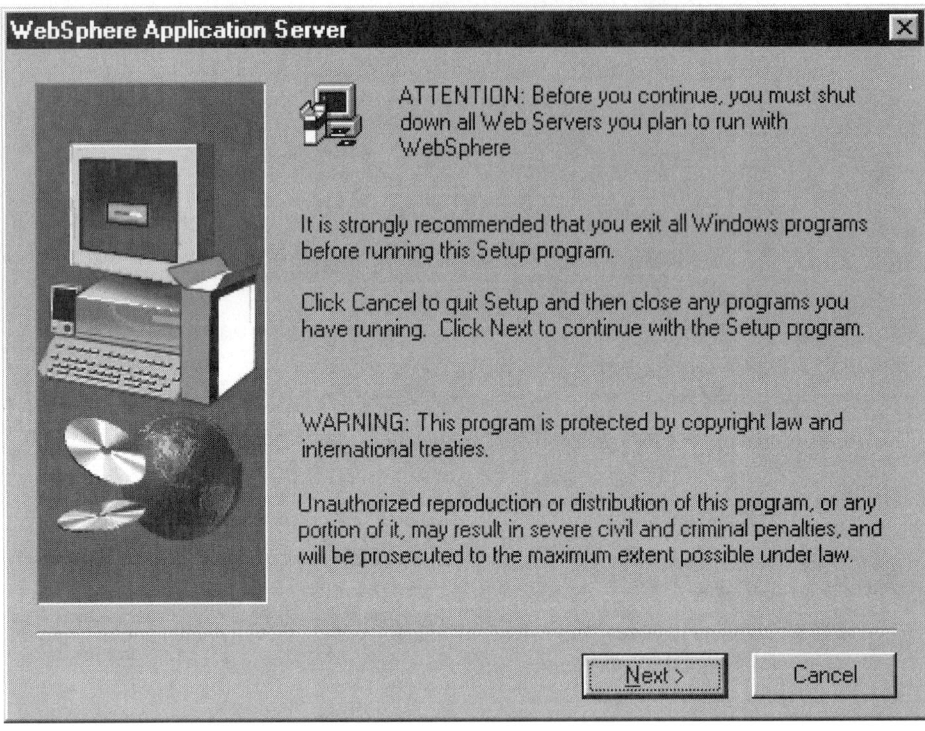

Figure 847. The introductory window

5. If WebSphere is already installed on your system, the Previous Installation Detected window appears.

   In order to back up and uninstall the existing WebSphere, click **Backup and Uninstall**. In order to install the WebSphere in a different directory, click **Next**.

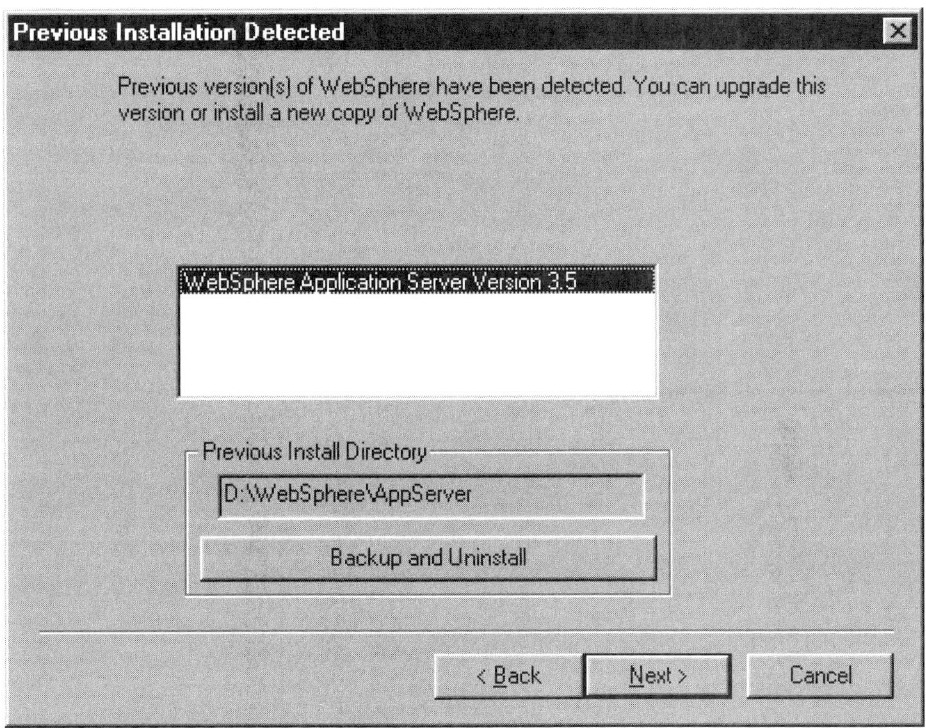

Figure 848. Previous Installation Detected window

6. Clicking **Quick Installation** installs IBM HTTP Server 1.3.12, InstantDB, and IBM JDK 1.2.2.

   Clicking **Custom** or **Full Installation** installs IBM HTTP Server 1.3.12, IBM DB2 Universal Database V6.1 with Fix Pack 4, and IBM JDK 1.2.2.

   Select **Custom Installation** and then click **Next**.

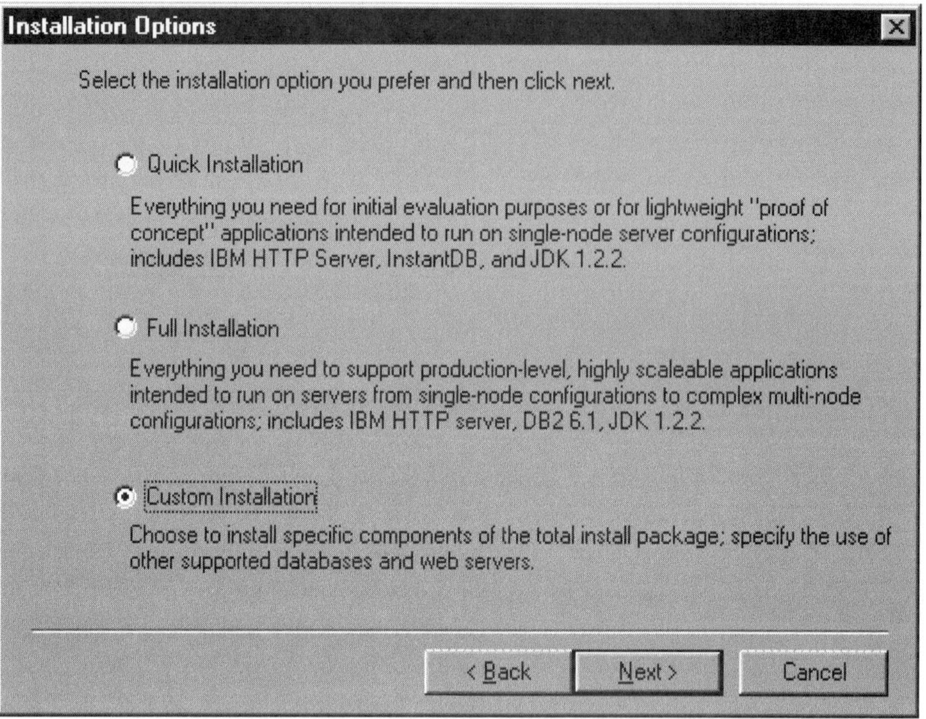

Figure 849. Installation Options window

7. If you selected **Quick Installation** or **Full Installation**, the Security Option window will appear.

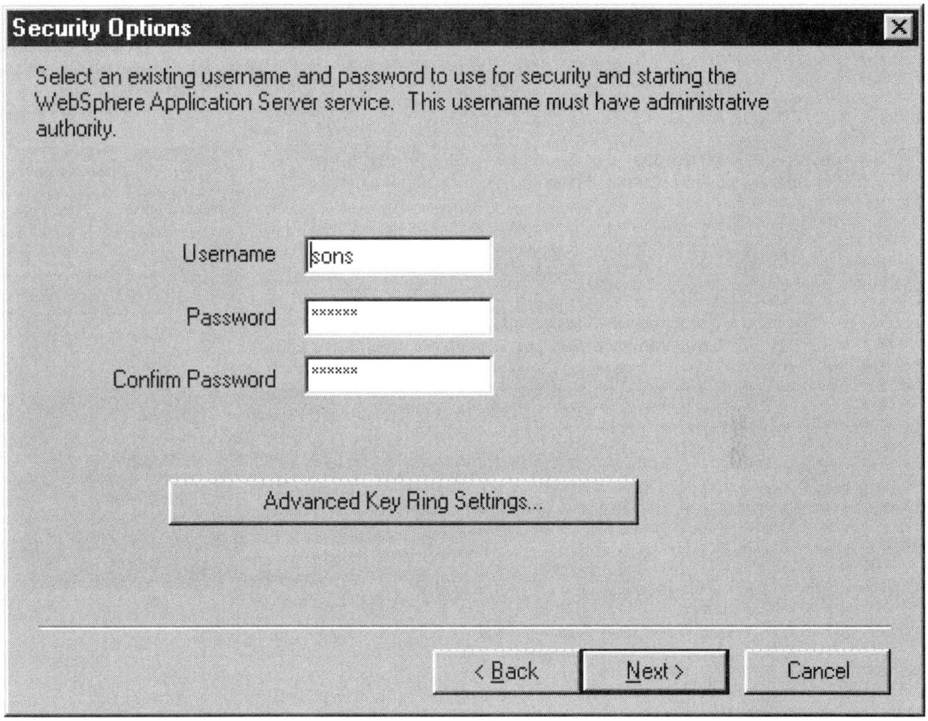

Figure 850. Security Options window

If you selected **Custom Installation** then the Choose Application Server Components window will appear. Select components you want. Figure 851 on page 1068 shows the default settings. Since we have already installed a database and Web server, we unchecked IBM HTTP Server and IBM Universal Database V6.1. In our case, we also selected **Configure default server and web application**, which you cannot see on the Choose Application Server Components window in Figure 851 on page 1068.

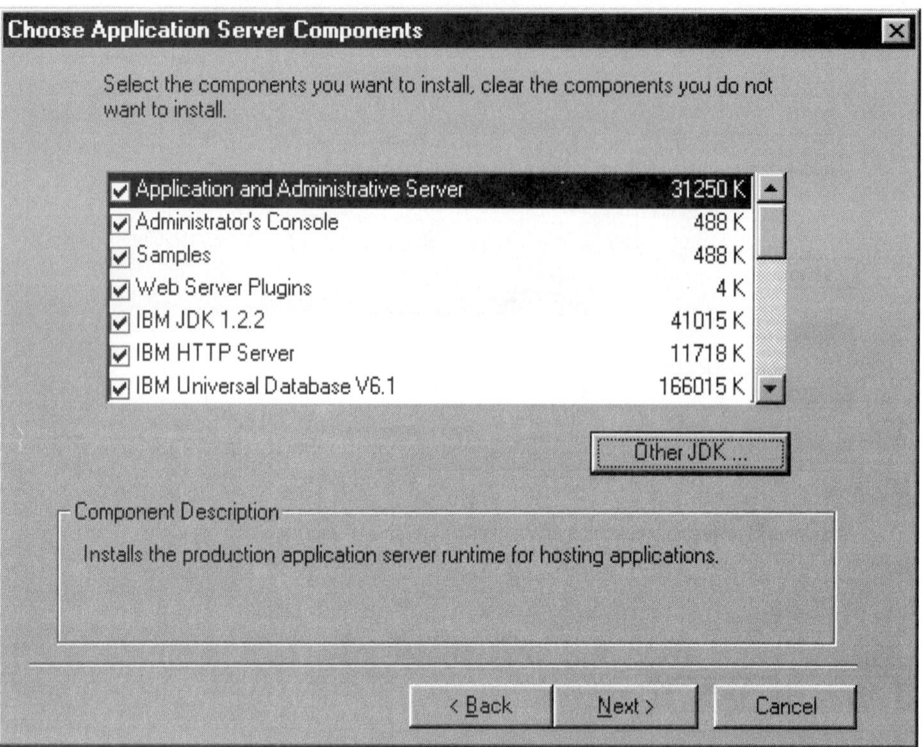

Figure 851. Choose Application Server Components window

Clicking the **Other JDK...** button displays the Select Java Development Kit window and will let you select another JDK directory.

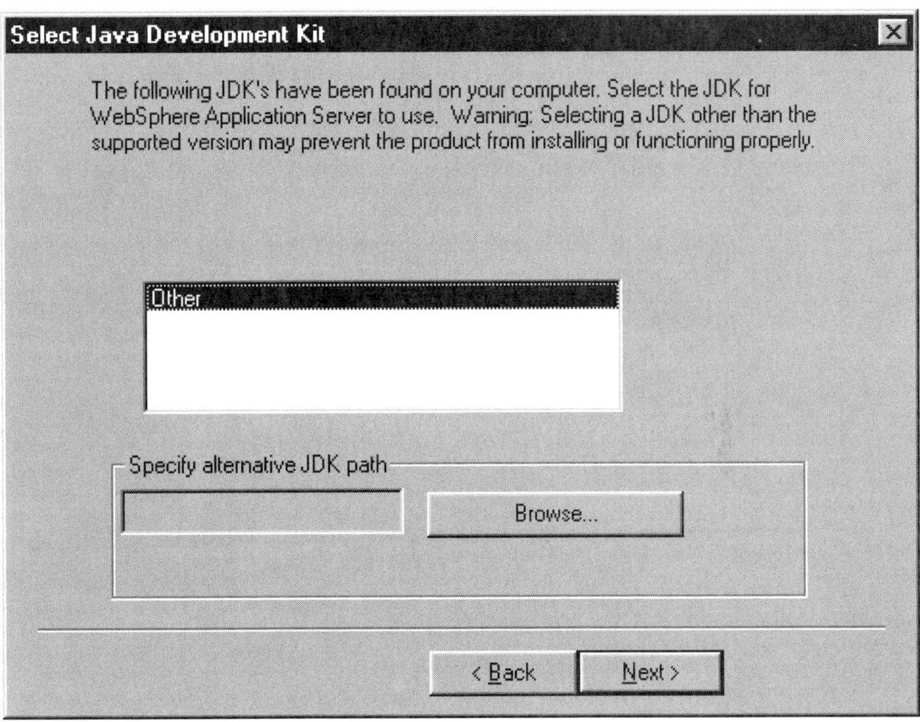

Figure 852. Select Java Development Kit window

Click **Back** to exit the window. Click **Next** if you specified the other JDK destination directory.

8. Click **Next**.
9. On the Choose Web Server Plugins window, select **IBM HTTP Server V1.3.12**. WebSphere Application Server V3.5 provides only IBM HTTP Server 1.3.12. You must separately buy and install the other supported Web servers. Then click **Next**.
10. Fill in the entries in the Security Options window. In Windows NT and Windows 2000, Username must be an existing user ID that has administrative privileges. If you do not need special key ring files, click **Next**.

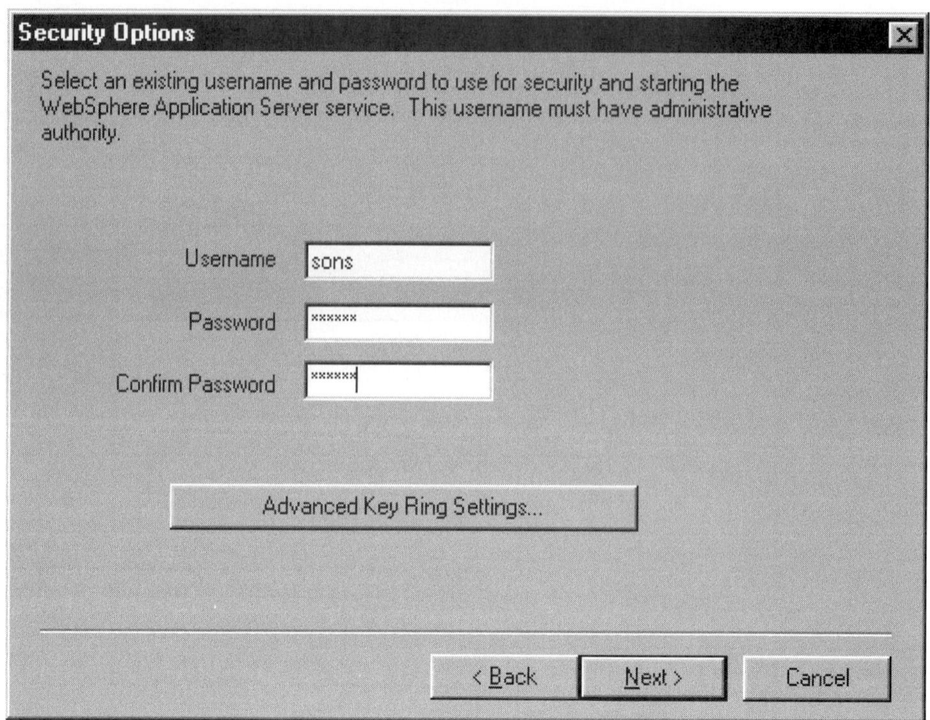

Figure 853. Security Options window

If you need special key ring files, click **Advanced Key Ring Settings**, specify Client Key Ring and Server Key Ring files and passwords, and then click **Next**.

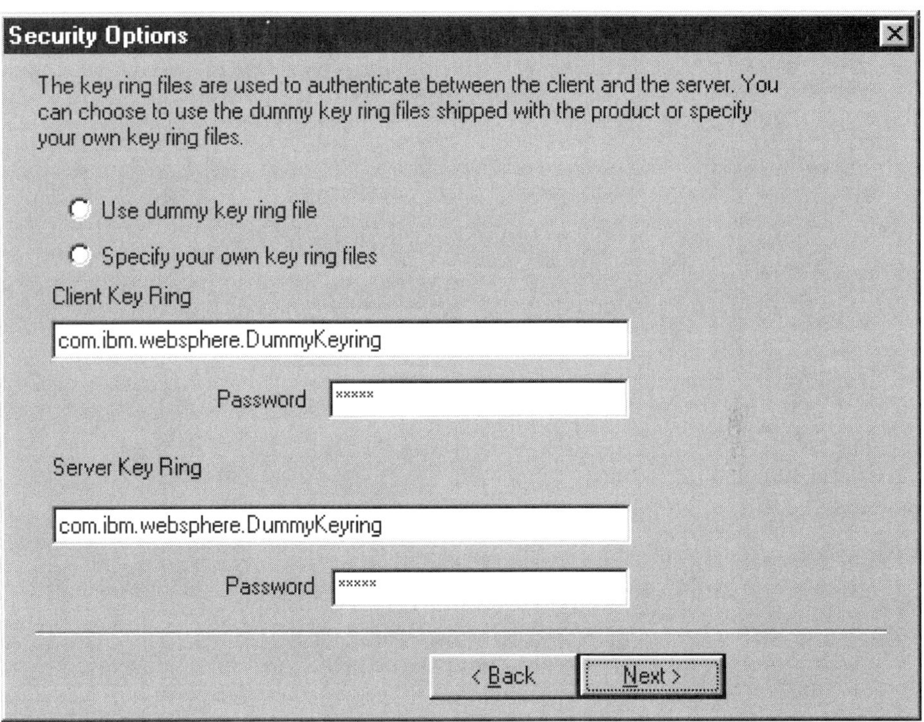

Figure 854. Security Options - Key Ring Files option

After the Security Options window reappears, click **Next** to move to the Product Directory window.

11.Specify the WebSphere destination directory and click **Next**.

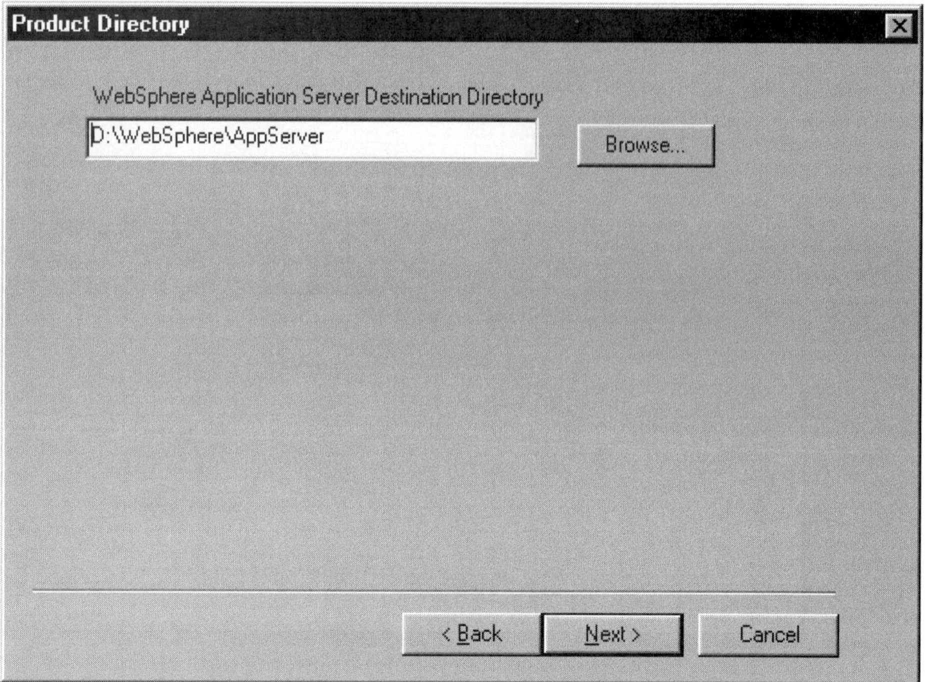

Figure 855. Product Directory window

12.On the Database Options window:

a. If you use DB2 for the administrative database:

- Select **DB2** for Database Type.
- Enter the name of the database for the Database Name. The default `was` is pre-written. You should specify the proper database alias for the administrative database.
- For Path, specify the path of the DB2 clients program.
- For URL, specify the database access URL. jdbc:db2:was is the default. If you use a different database alias for the administrative database, switch `was` to the appropriate alias.
- Enter the database user ID and password. You need to use the user ID and password that have proper privilege for the administrative database.

Then click **Next**.

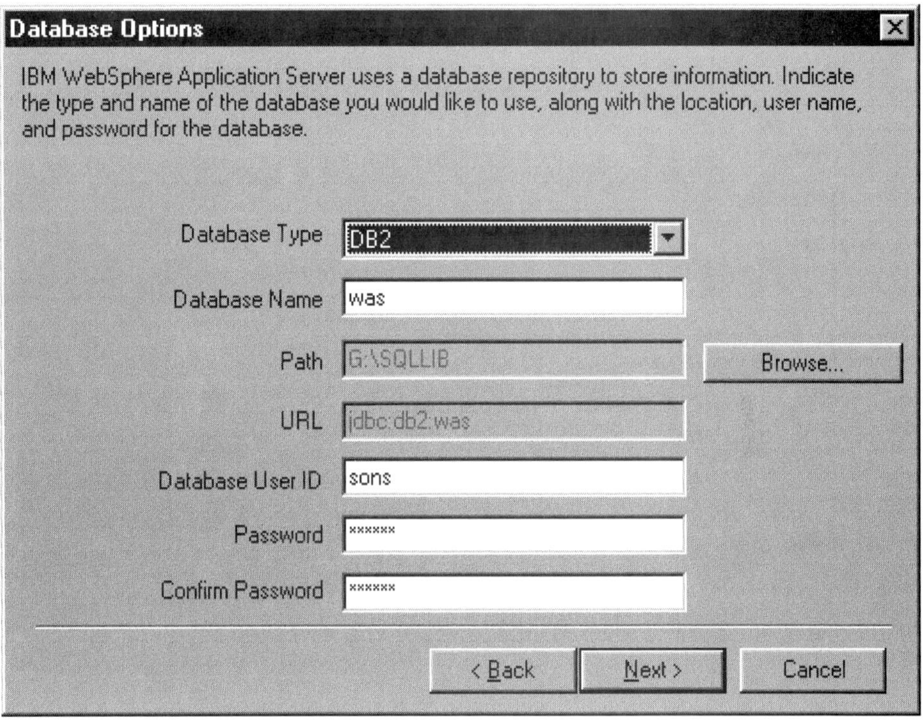

Figure 856. Database Options window - DB2

b. If you use Oracle as the administrative database:

- Select **Oracle** for Database Type.
- You should consult with your local database administrator to get the correct database name. The default database name is `orcl`.
- For Path, specify the path for the database program.
- For URL, specify the URL for accessing the database. The format is jdbc:oracle:thin:@<DB server name>:<port number>:<DB name>. For example, we specify `jdbc:oracle:thin:@SONS:1521:orcl`.
- For User ID, specify your user name. Note that if you use an invalid user ID to install the WebSphere, it will not successfully register the WebSphere Administrative Server to the Windows NT services database. If you have already installed the Oracle 8i, ensure that you specify the user name specified when configuring Oracle 8i for use with WebSphere Application Server (EJSADMIN).

- Enter your password and confirm it. If you have already installed the Oracle 8i, ensure that you specify the password specified when installing Oracle 8i.

Then click **Next**.

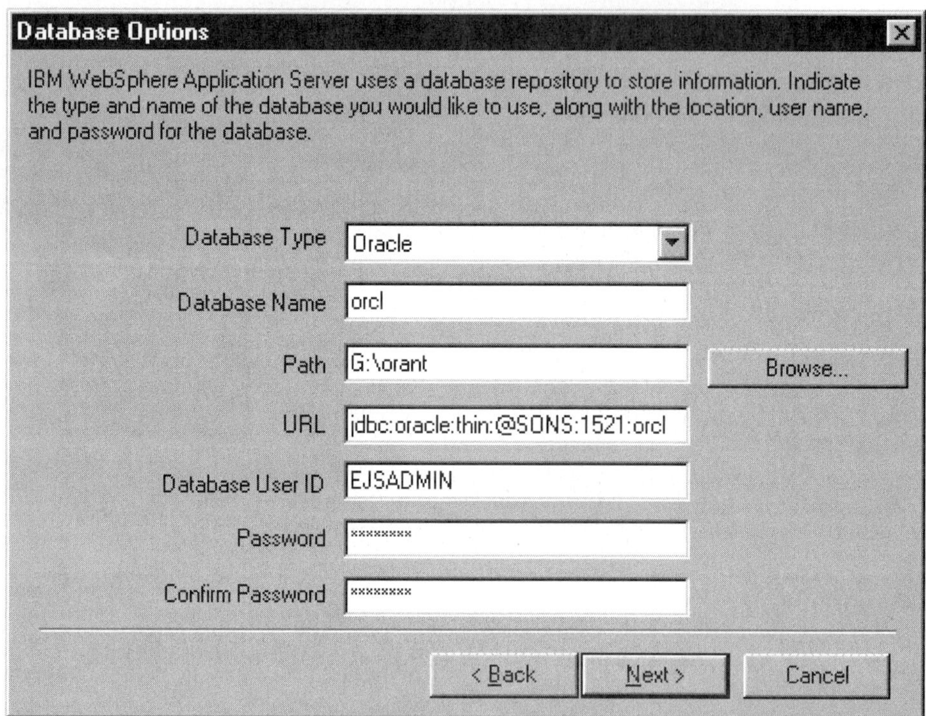

Figure 857. Database Options window - Oracle

13. On the Select Program Folder window, specify a new folder name. By default, IBM WebSphere\Application Server V3.5 is prespecified. Click **Next** to begin installation.

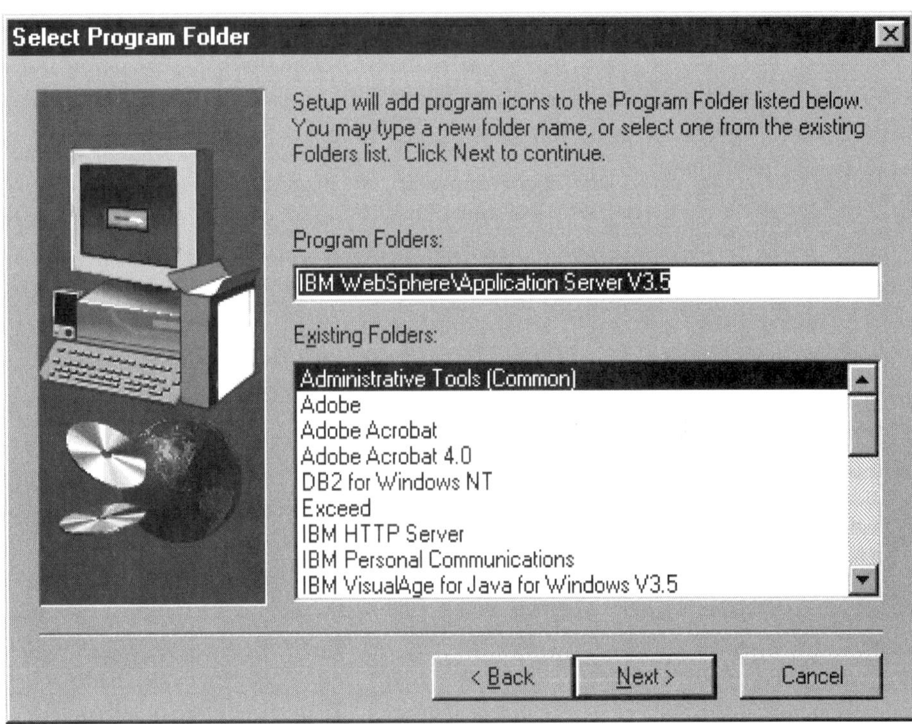

Figure 858. Select Program Folder window

14.Click **OK** and it will finish updating the files and installing.

15.The next page points you to the README and, if you are installing the samples, states where the samples have been installed. For the most recent version of the README or release notes, go to Library section of the product Web site at `http://www.ibm.com/software/webservers/appserv/`.

Click **Finish**, and choose to restart.

In Windows NT or Windows 2000, if you have not created DB2 database for the administrative database, DB2 CLP will automatically start and create a database for the administrative database after rebooting. However, if you have not created catalogs on the DB2 client node (WebSphere node), it might not work.

A.2.5 Post configuration

Post configuration refers to any activities to run WebSphere after the completion of the installation. You should do the following steps:

1. Start the database server
2. Modify the administrative database configuration on the WebSphere node
3. Start the administrative server
4. Start the administrative console
5. Start Web server

A.2.5.1 Start database server

WebSphere stores its configuration to the database and it is important to start database server before starting the WebSphere Administrative Server.

DB2

DB2 will automatically start when the machine is rebooted (by default).

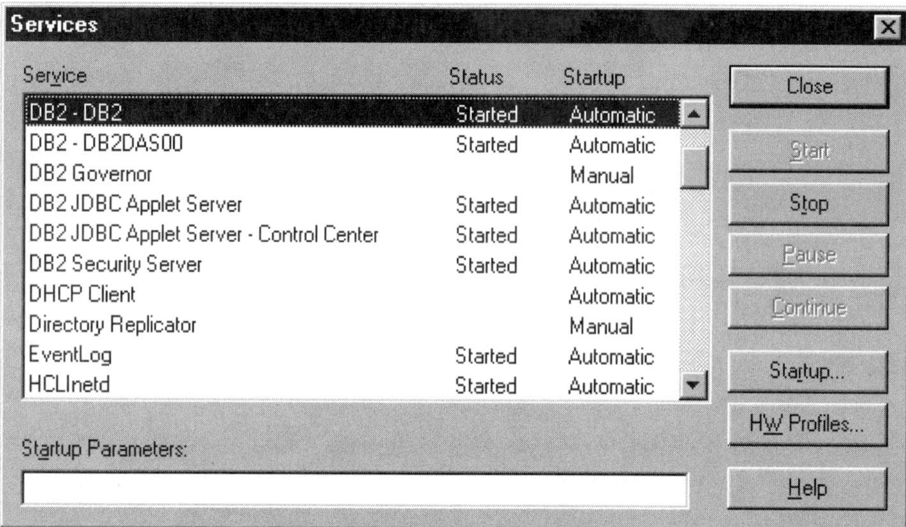

Figure 859. DB2 started in Windows NT

Oracle

Oracle will automatically start services (by default). Note that the service name of Oracle server includes the Oracle database name. For example, in our case, the database name is ORCL and the service name is OracleServiceORCL as shown in Figure 860 on page 1077.

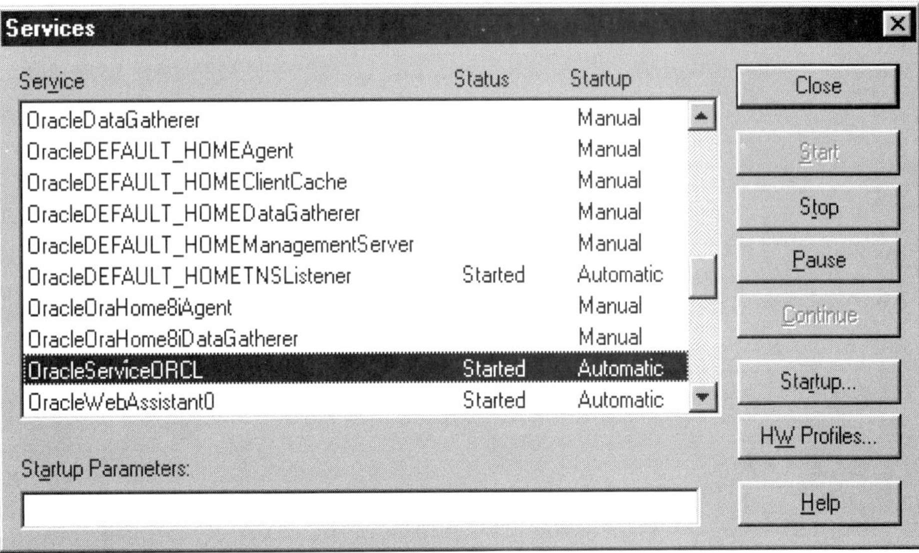

Figure 860. Oracle service started in Windows NT

A.2.5.2 Configure remote access for the administrative database

Before you start WebSphere, you should configure remote database connectivity for the administrative database.

Configuration for using Oracle thin driver

You should modify two files, <WAS_HOME>/bin/admin.config and startupServer as follows:

- Modify the admin.config, for example:

```
com.ibm.ejs.sm.adminserver.classpath=.....
...;C\:/WebSphere/AppServer/lib/classes12.zip;
com.ibm.ejs.sm.adminServer.dbUser=EJSADMIN
com.ibm.ejs.sm.adminServer.dbPassword=EJSADMIN
com.ibm.ejs.sm.adminServer.dbUrl=jdbc\:oracle\:thin\:@sons\:1521\:orcl
```

- Modify the setupCmdLine.bat file, for example:

```
SET DB2DRIVER=C:\Oracle\Ora81\jdbc\lib\classes12.zip
```

Configuration for using the Oracle OCI driver

You must modify your <WAS_HOME>/bin/admin.config file which the following parameter:

```
com.ibm.ejs.sm.adminServer.dbUrl=jdbc\:oracle\:oci8\:@SONS
```

A.2.5.3 Start the administrative server

Check if the WebSphere Application Server is already running.

In Windows NT, check Services under your Control Panel to make sure IBM WS AdminServer is not started and no Java processor is running from the processor tab of the Windows NT Task Manager.

There are three ways to start the WebSphere Administrative Server:

1. Open the Control Panel and select **Services**. If you scroll down you should see IBM WS AdminServer. Start the service by selecting **IBM WS AdminServer** and then selecting **Start**.

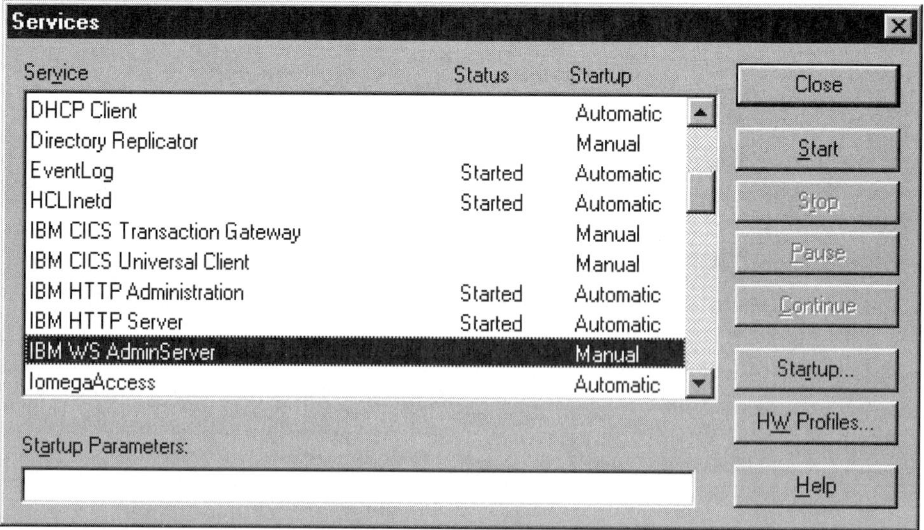

Figure 861. Start WebSphere Administrative Server in Windows NT

2. Select **Start -> Programs -> IBM WebSphere -> Application Server V3.5 -> Start Admin Server**.
3. Run the <WAS_HOME>/bin/debug/adminserver.bat file. Note that if you start the administrative server with the adminserver.bat file, you won't get the file called tracefile in the <WAS_HOME>/logs directory.

A.2.5.4 Start the administrative console

There are two ways to start the administrative console:

1. Select **Start -> Programs -> IBM WebSphere -> Application Server V3.5 -> Administrator's Console**.
2. Run <WAS_HOME>\bin\adminclient.bat file.

Remote administrative console

You can also start the administrative console of the WebSphere Application Server remotely. You must do this under the <was>/bin directory. The following is an example where the server is a remote Solaris machine and the administrative console is running from a Windows NT machine.

```
C:\WebSphere\AppServer\bin>adminclient sungiksun
Remote AdminServer sungiksun will be accessed on the default port (900).

C:\WebSphere\AppServer\bin>
```

A.2.5.5 Start an application server

You start your application server. When you start the Default Server application server under your node, you will also start the servlet engine and EJB container.

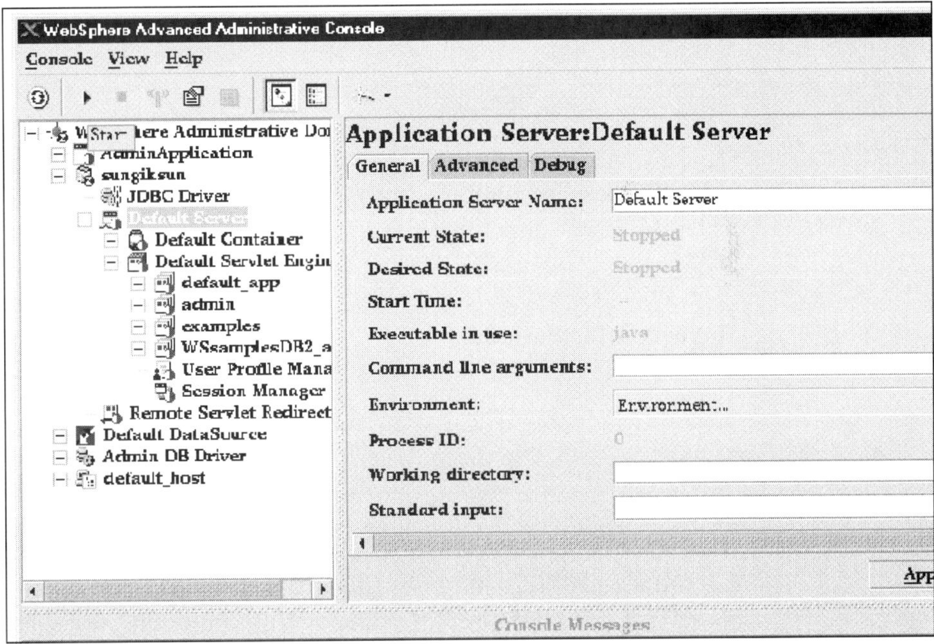

Figure 862. Starting the Default Server

Select **Default Server** under the machine node and then click the **Start** button (marked as an arrow on the menu bar).

A.2.5.6 Verify if the servers are working

So far we have started the WebSphere Administrative Server and application server under it. We need to start the Web server to handle HTTP requests from the client. In some cases, Web server may already be started. To see if the Web server is started, check the Service panel. If your Web server is not started, start it.

After the verification that your Web server is running, verify whether the Default Servlet servlet engine is working by accessing http://<server_name>/servlet/snoop.

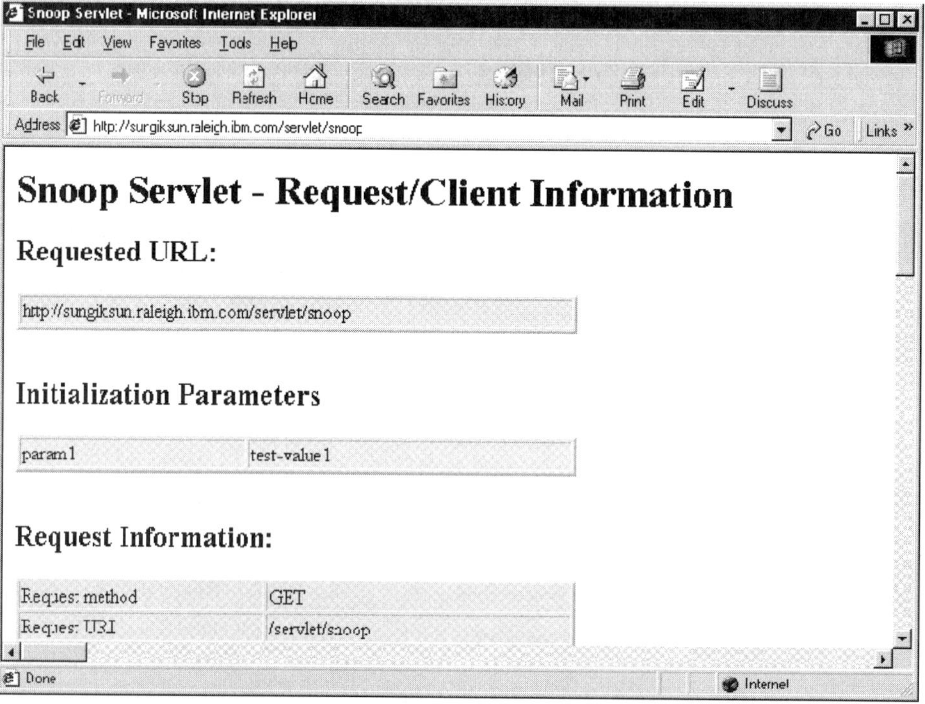

Figure 863. Verification of WebSphere's servlet engine running

You can also verify whether the Default Container EJB container is working. We will skip it in this chapter. Please refer to the InfoCenter.

A.2.6 Fix Pack installation

At the time this document is written, Fix Pack 2 is available. You can download the Fix Pack from the IBM WebSphere Support Web site. Before installing the Fix Pack, you must stop the Web server and WebSphere.

After downloding the zip file, unzip it to a temporary directory. From the directory, execute install script file. Then answer any questions which you will be asked, such as:

- Do you wish to update the WebSphere Application Server samples?
- Enter your Web server's doc root path.
- Do you wish to update the IBM HTTP Server 1.3.12?
- Enter the directory where the IBM HTTP Server 1.3.12 is installed.

A.3 Uninstallation of WebSphere Application Server

This section describes how to uninstall the product. If you want to migrate WebSphere V3.02 to V3.5, please refer to Chapter 26, "Migration" on page 1033.

You can uninstall the previously installed the WebSphere Application Server by selecting **Start -> Programs -> IBM WebSphere ->Application Server V3.5 -> Uninstall WebSphere Application Server**. After the completion of the uninstallation, you need to reboot the machine.

Appendix B. Remote Sybase connectivity

The details in this chapter are specific to the ramifications of installing WebSphere V3.5 Advanced Edition, when the Sybase ASE database for the administrative database is located remotely. Not discussed here are the necessary operating system parameters or possible WebSphere component selection issues that are more general to WebSphere as a whole. The WebSphere InfoCenter documentation provides a comprehensive description for installing WebSphere V3.5 with Sybase V12, albeit all on the same system.

B.1 Sybase jConnect Client

Remote Sybase connectivity is provided with the Sybase jConnect Client. Once configured with an appropriately installed Sybase database, jConnect will support both the WebSphere administrative database and the creation of subsequent Sybase JDBC datasources.

Sybase V12 supports both jConnect 4.2 and jConnect 5.2, with both versions available on the Sybase install media. However, users must install jConnect 5.2 for the JDBC 2.0 support required by WebSphere V3.5.

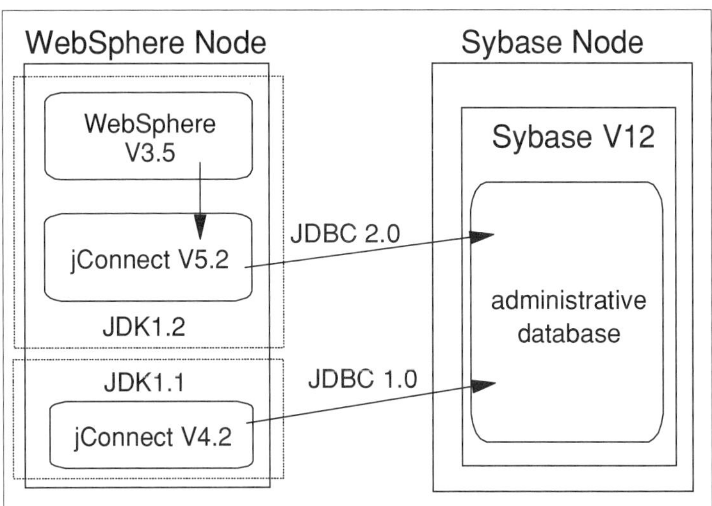

Figure 864. Remote Sybase jConnect connectivity

Steps for installing the Sybase jConnect Client:

1. Create a user called “sybase” and a group called “sybase”.

2. Extend or create a suitable file system (in our case, we created /usr/sybase file system and it was 180 MB).
3. Change the ownership of the newly created file system (in our case, we changed it to user: sybase, group: sybase).
4. As the user sybase, ensure that the JAVA_HOME environmental variable is set correctly [JDK 1.1.8 acceptable], and launch the Sybase install program from the Sybase install media.
5. Selecting a custom install, choose both jConnect 4.2 and jConnect 5.2 components. Note that you don't have to select jConnect 4.2 for WebSphere. In B.1.2, "Checking Sybase jConnect connectivity with jConnect 4.2" on page 1085, we discuss the reason why we installed it in our environment.

B.1.1 Remote WebSphere V3.5 installation with Sybase ASE

By default the WebSphere installation script, install.sh, located on the mountable CD-ROM media, calls the installation prerequisite checker to verify that all required prerequisites are satisfied. This will fail without modification, as the Sybase ASE database is installed remotely. To overcome this restriction, copy the prereq.properties file, also located on the mountable CD-ROM media, to a writeable filesystem such as /tmp. Here, edit the first stanza, [WAS], changing prereq_checker=1 to prereq_checker=0. To invoke install.sh using the newly modified prereq.properties file, run:

```
./install.sh /prereqfile /tmp/prereq.properties
```

The installation now proceeds no different from that of a regular WebSphere V3.5 install, with users choosing the desired WebSphere components via the Custom Installation option menu.

Once the Database options dialog box is reached, the database type should be set to Sybase. Database name, user ID and password should correspond with those defined on the Sybase remote ASE database for the WebSphere administrative database. The DB Home field is the main Sybase installation directory on the local system. Finally, the database URL should reflect the remote WebShere Sybase database "was" table / instance.

jdbc:sybase:Tds:<remote_hostname>:<port>/was

Figure 865 on page 1085 shows such an example, with the database URL taking the form jdbc:sybase:Tds:ken:4100/was.

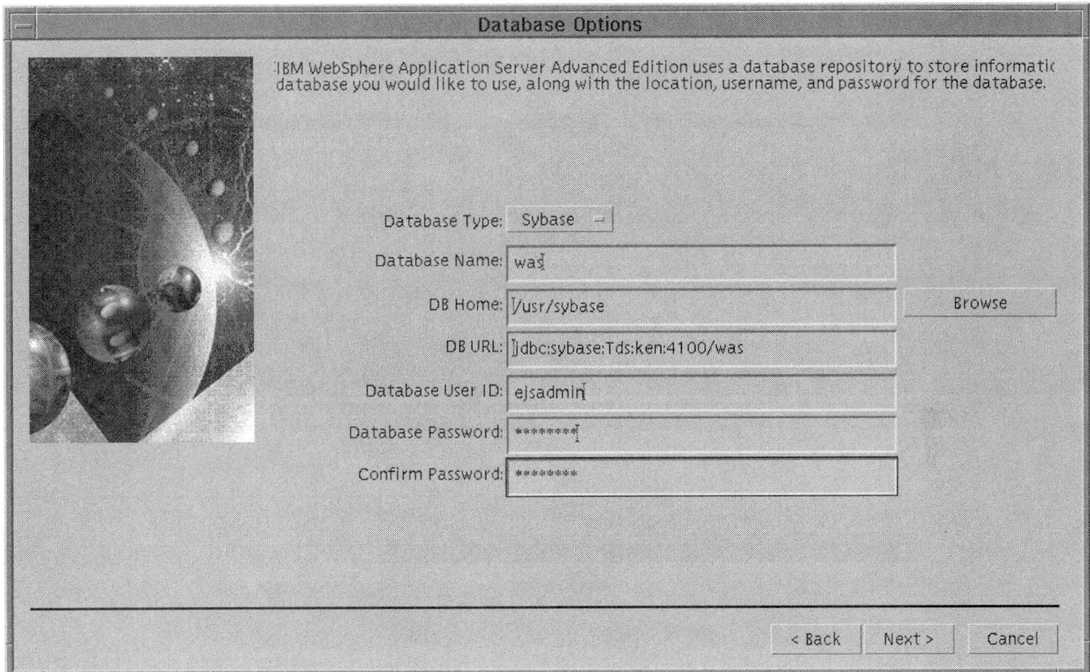

Figure 865. Database Options: remote Sybase settings

B.1.2 Checking Sybase jConnect connectivity with jConnect 4.2

Note: the following steps are not necessary to install WebSphere 3.5.

For our test environment both versions of jConnect were actually installed. JDK 1.2 is a prerequisite for jConnect 5.2. However, AIX 4.3.3 does not include the JDK 1.2.

This way, the native JDK 1.1.8 that ships with AIX 4.3.3 can be used with jConnect 4.2 to test Sybase remote network connectivity initially before we install WebSphere.

Then the JDK 1.2 that ships as part of WebSphere V3.5 can effectively be used, as required, with jConnect 5.2 after we install WebSphere.

In other words, prior to installing WebSphere V3.5, it is possible to check the Sybase database network connectivity with jConnect 4.2. As previously mentioned, jConnect 5.2 will not work unless the native operating system JDK installed is at Version 1.2 or higher.

Change to the user sybase and, if not already exported, export the environmental variables JDBC_HOME and CLASSPATH, as shown below in Figure 866.

```
#su - sybase
$ export JDBC_HOME=/usr/sybase/jConnect-4_2
$ export CLASSPATH=/usr/jdk_base/lib/classes.zip:$JDBC_HOME/classes
```

Figure 866. Environmental variables

Next, invoke the IsqlApp java class, as found under the <SYBASE_HOME>/jConnect-4_2/classes directory, specifying the user ID, password, remote host name of the Sybase database, and the remote Sybase listener port number, as shown in Figure 867.

```
$java IsqlApp -Usa -Psybase -Sjdbc:sybase:Tds:itso:4100

Enter a query:
1 > select @@version

------------------ Result set 1 -----------------------

Columns:
[ 1]    Adaptive Server Enterprise/12.0/P/SWR 8772 ESD 1/RS6000/AIX
4.3.2/1580/32bit/FBO/Tue Dec  7 09:14:03 1999

Enter a query:
1 >
```

Figure 867. Sybase jConnect 4.2 IsqlApp.class

In Figure 867 the host name of the remote Sybase database is “itso”. On a successful connection, the “select @@version” SQL query is issued requesting the Sybase ASE version details.

Appendix C. XML sample programs

This appendix contains instructions for setting up and running the CD Catalog XML example introduced in 13.3, “An XML example” on page 543 and discussed throughout Chapter 13, “XML and WebSphere” on page 539. Instructions are presented for configuring the Web application under WebSphere, running a Web client, and running the Java client.

All the Java source code, XML, XSL, and other files are provided to allow further study and experimentation with the sample.

C.1 Instructions for setting up and running the XML demo: Web Client

1. Create a Web application by selecting **Wizards ->Create a Web Application** as shown in Figure 868.

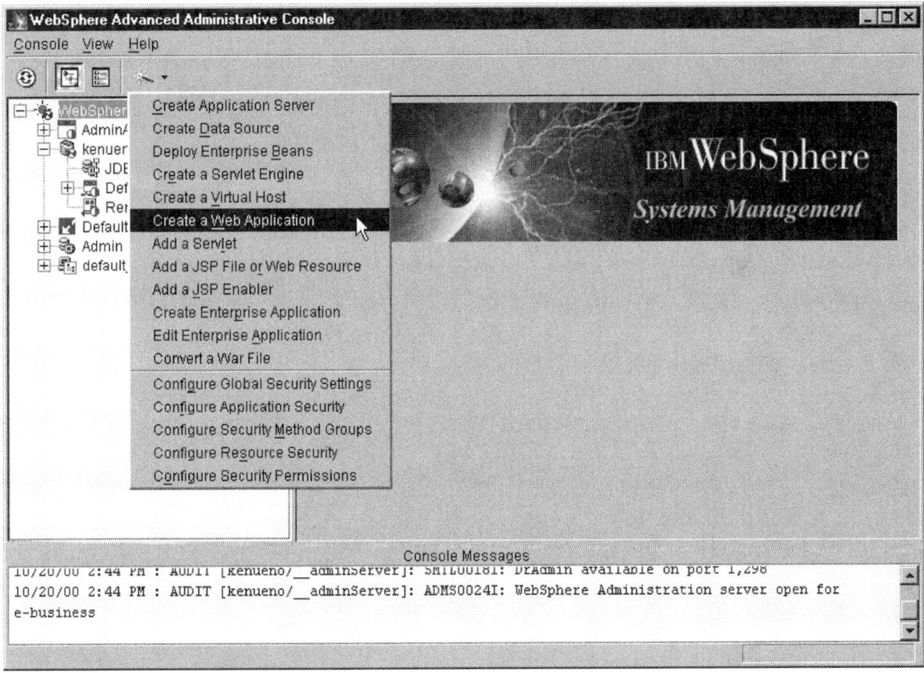

Figure 868. Creating a Web application for XMLDemo

2. In the Create Web Application window, specify XMLDemo for the Web Application Name and check **Enable File Servlet**, **Serve Servlets by Classname**, and **Enable JSP 1.0** as shown in Figure 869 on page 1088.

Then click **Next**.

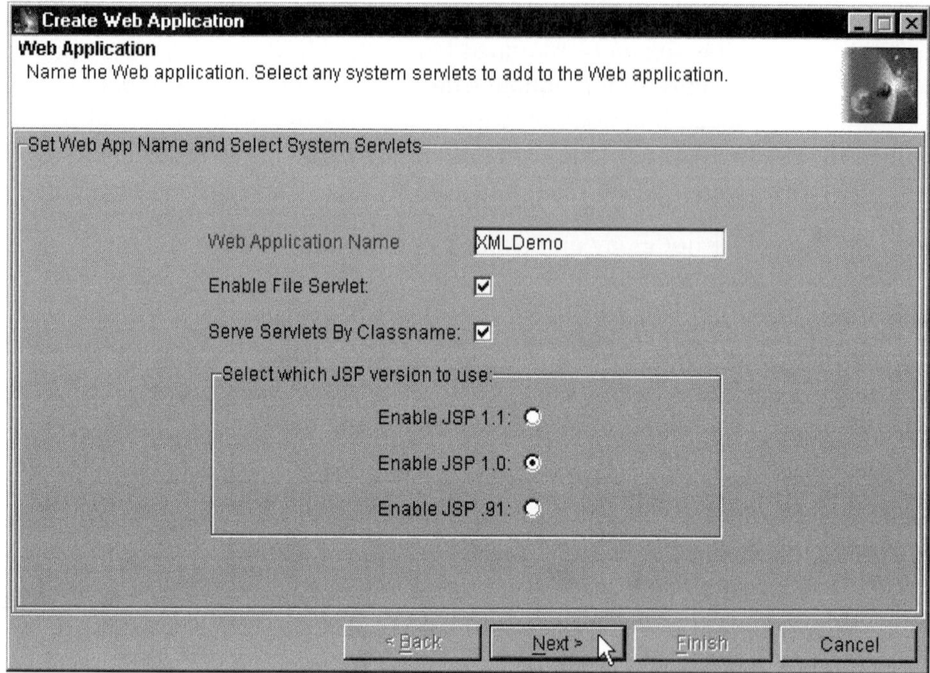

Figure 869. Create Web application: set Web application name

3. In the next window, choose a servlet engine, for example the Default Servlet Engine and click **Next** as shown in Figure 870 on page 1089.

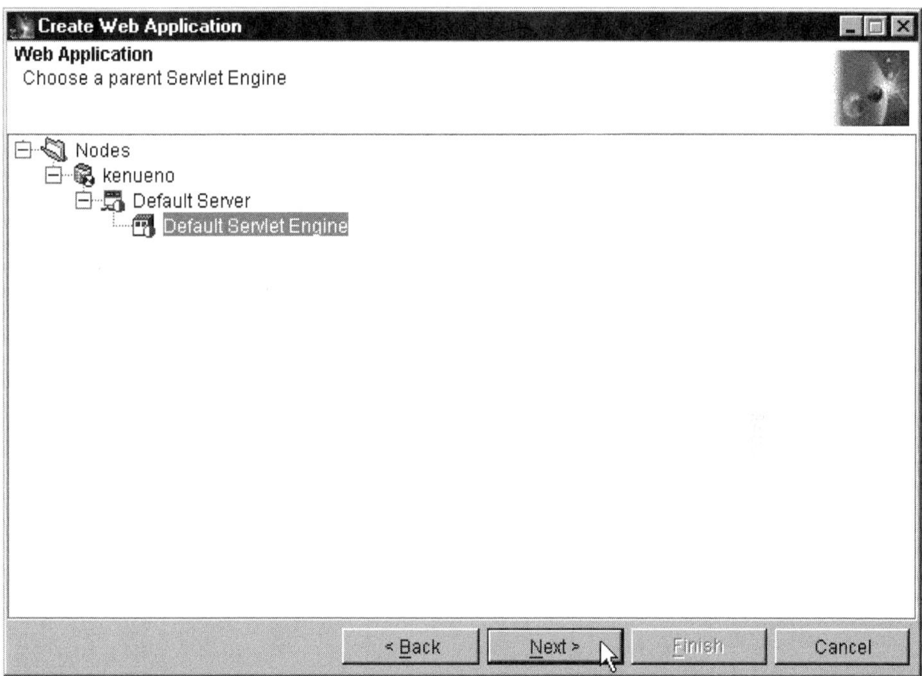

Figure 870. Create Web application: choose a parent servlet engine

4. In the next window, accept “virtual host = default_host” and “Web Application Path = /webapp/XMLDemo” as shown in Figure 871 on page 1090. Then click **Next**.

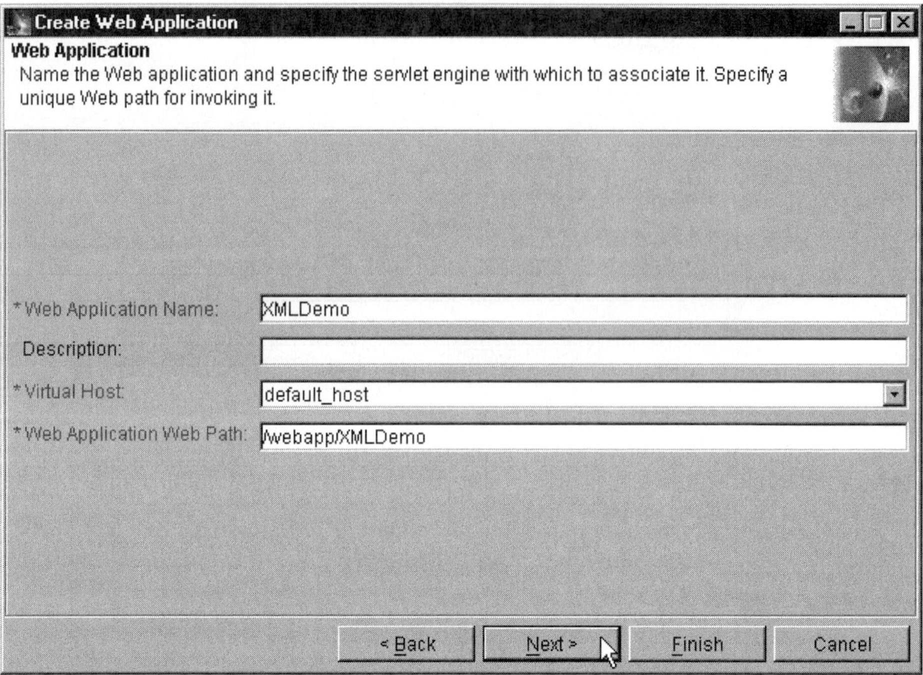

Figure 871. Create Web application: specify virtual host and Web path

5. In the next window, for our demonstration, you just click **Finish** as shown in Figure 872 on page 1091.

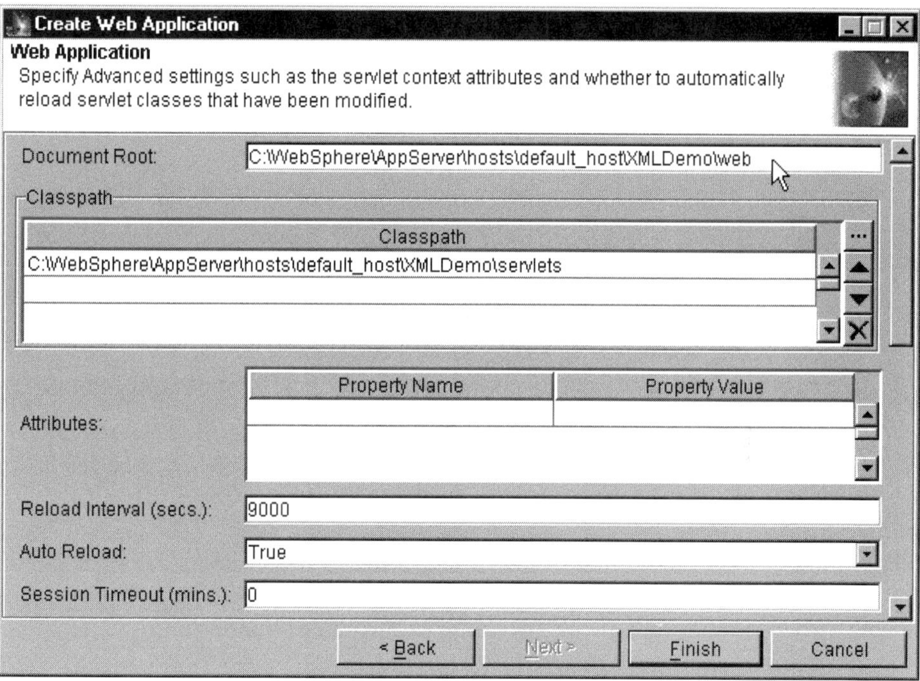

Figure 872. Create Web application: specify advanced settings

6. On the administrative console, you will see the XMLDemo Web application that you created as shown in Figure 873 on page 1092.

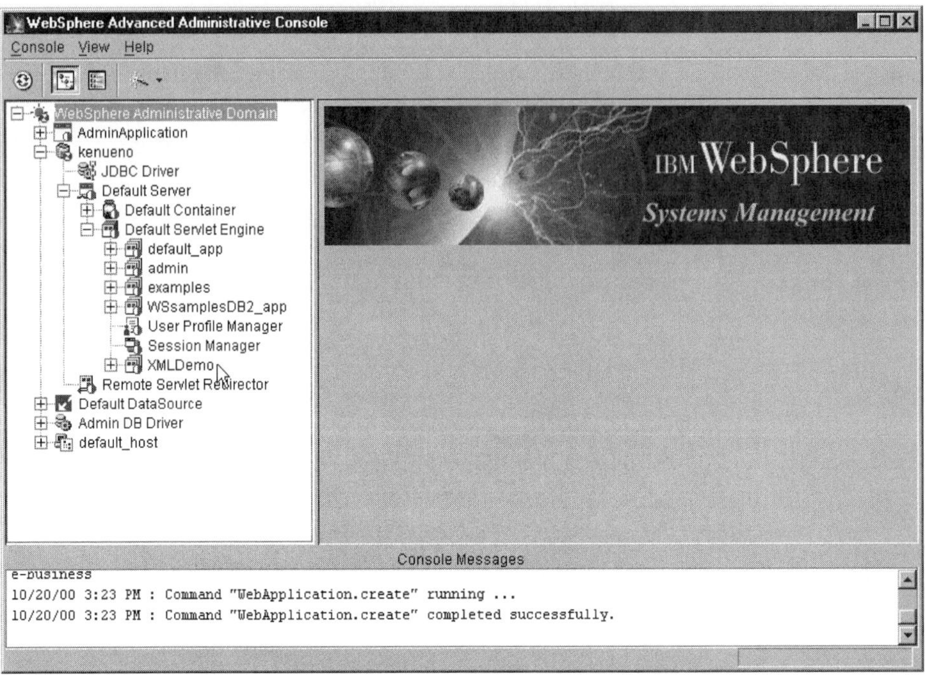

Figure 873. New Web application called XMLDemo

7. Copy the XMLDemo.zip file into the C:\tmp directory (or suitable directory for your system).
8. Unzip XMLDemo.zip into the <WAS_HOME>/hosts/default_host directory preserving the paths.

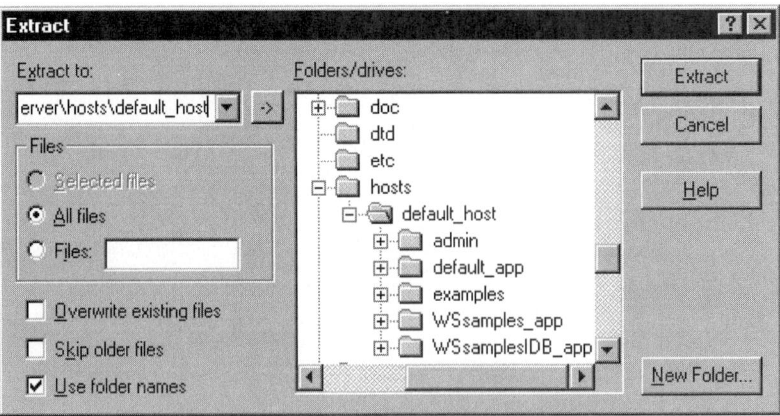

Figure 874. Extract XMLDemo.zip

It will create the XMLDemo directory and three subdirectories, so that files end up in the following directories:

- XMLDemo\servlets\com\ibm\redbook\SG246161\cdorganizer

  (The corresponding Java files end up there too, but they are not needed to run the example.)

  - CDJBean.class
  - CDListJBean.class
  - CDOXMLServlet.class
  - TrackJBean.class
  - TrackListJBean.class

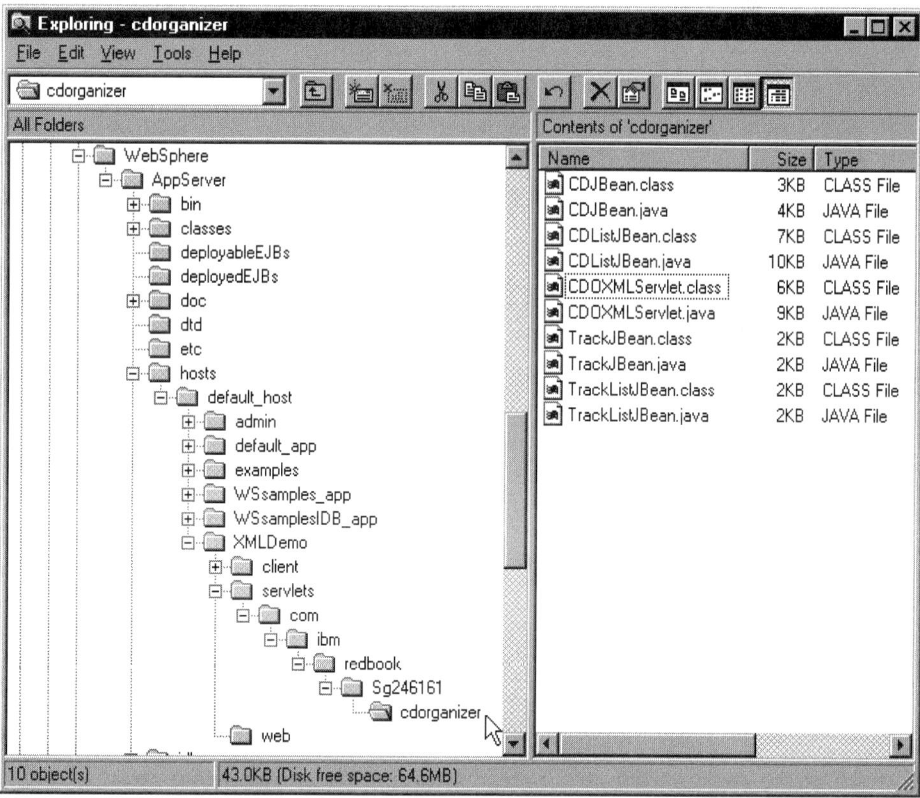

Figure 875. \XMLDemo\servlets\com\ibm\redbook\SG246161\cdorganizer directory

- XMLDemo\client\com\ibm\redbook\SG246161\cdorganizer\client

  (The corresponding Java files end up there too, but they are not needed to run the example.)

- CDOXMLClient.class
- SAXCatalogPrint.class

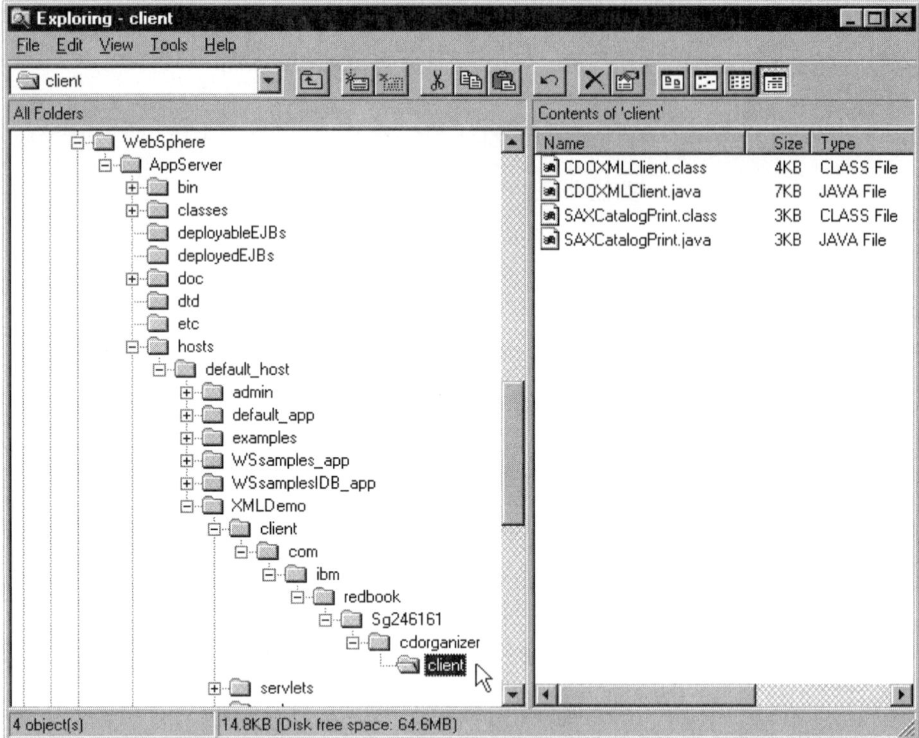

Figure 876. \XMLDemor\client\com\ibm\redbook\SG246161\cdorganizer\client directory

- XMLDemo\client\

  (These are batch files to run the client; you might need to change the paths inside them for your system.)

  - CDOXMLClientSetup.bat
  - runCDOXMLClient.bat

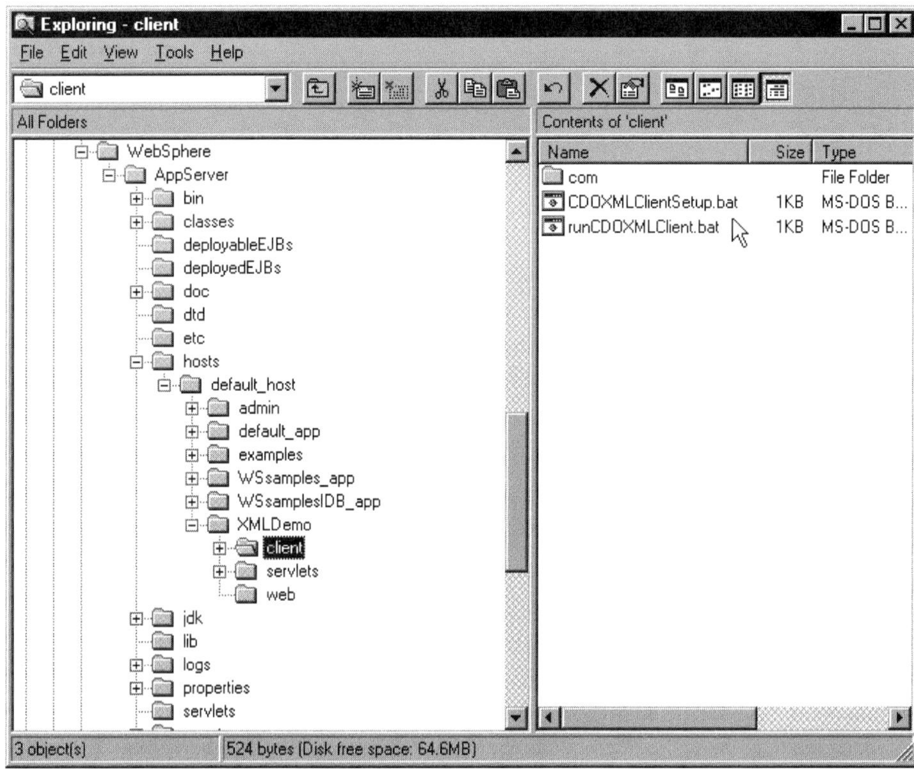

Figure 877. \XMLDemo\client directory

- XMLDemo\web
  - cdlist-nofor.xsl
  - cdlist.css
  - cdlist.dtd
  - cdlist.xsl
  - cdlist1.xml
  - cdlist1.xsl
  - cdlist2.xml
  - cdlist3.xml
  - cdlist4.xml
  - CDOXML.html
  - XMLCatalog.jsp

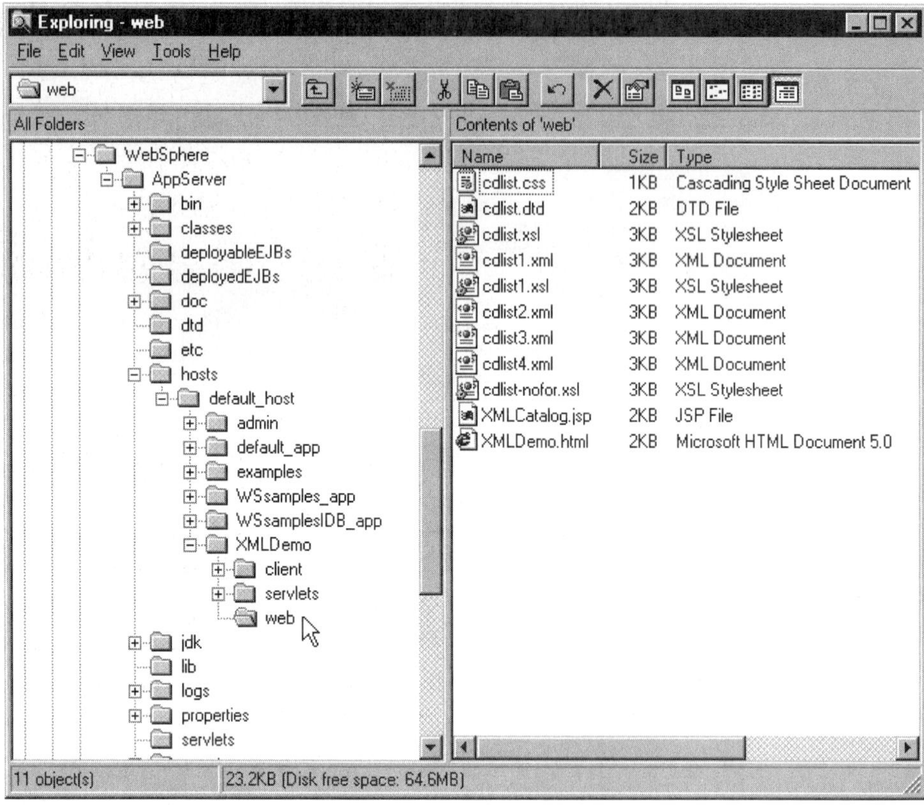

Figure 878. \XMLDemo\web directory

9. Start the Web application (in our case, XMLDemo) by selecting **XMLDemo Web Application -> Restart Web App** as shown in Figure 879 on page 1097.

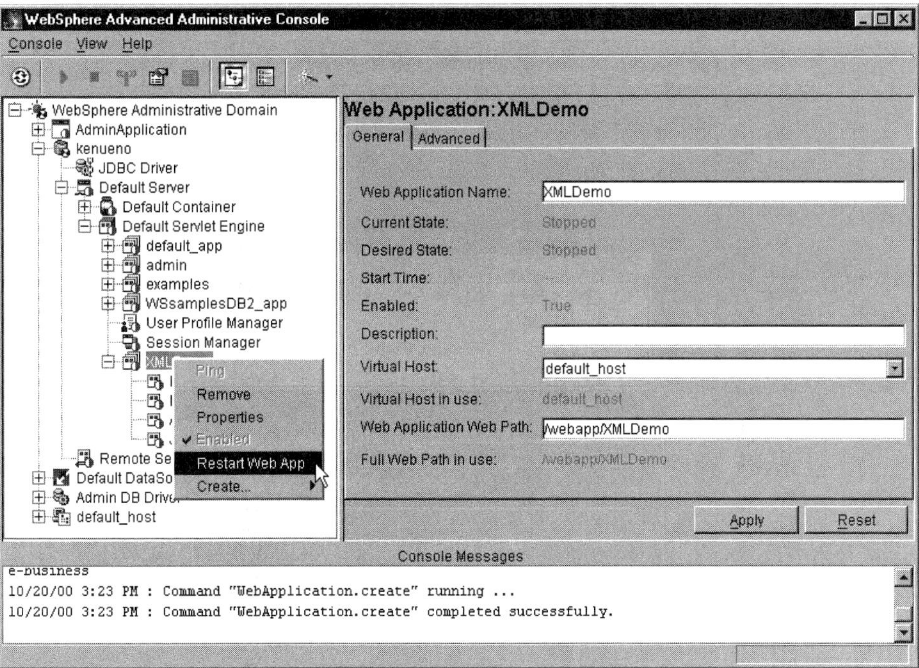

Figure 879. Start XMLDemo Web application

10.Start your HTTP Server if is not running.

11.Browse the following URI.

`http://localhost/webapp/XMLDemo/XMLDemo.html`

Then you will see the CD Catalog XML Example home page as shown in Figure 880 on page 1098.

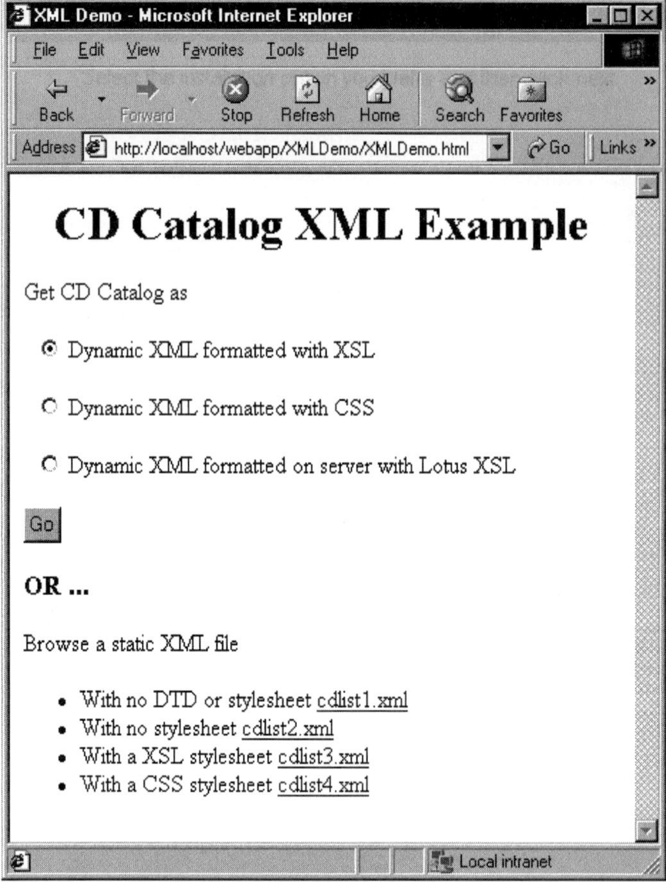

Figure 880. XMLDemo home page

12.Select **Dynamic XML formatted with XSL** and click **Go**. Then you will get the result as shown in Figure 881 on page 1099.

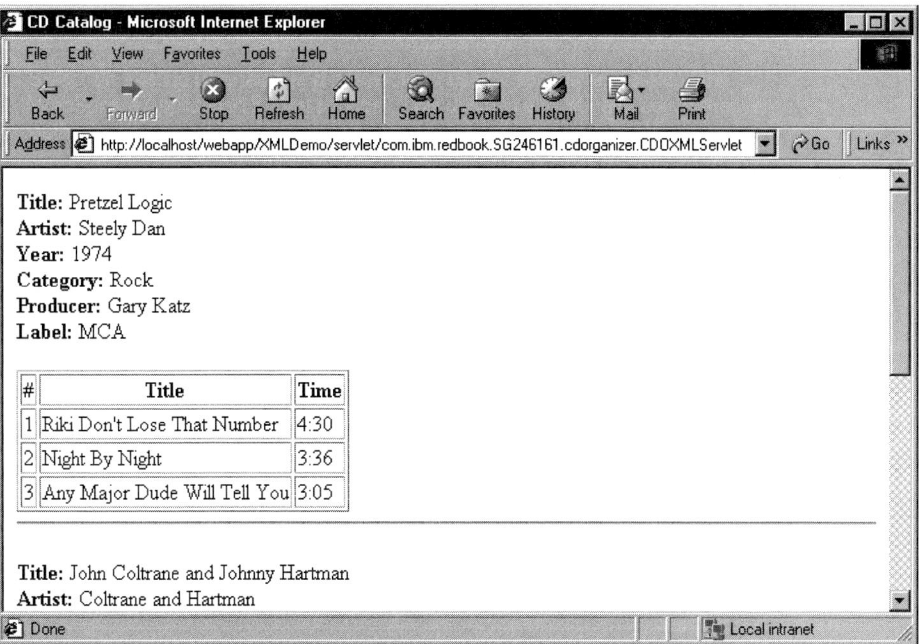

Figure 881. The output of Dynamic XML formatted with XSL

13.Select **Dynamic XML formatted with CSS** and click **Go**. Then you will get the result as shown in Figure 882 on page 1100.

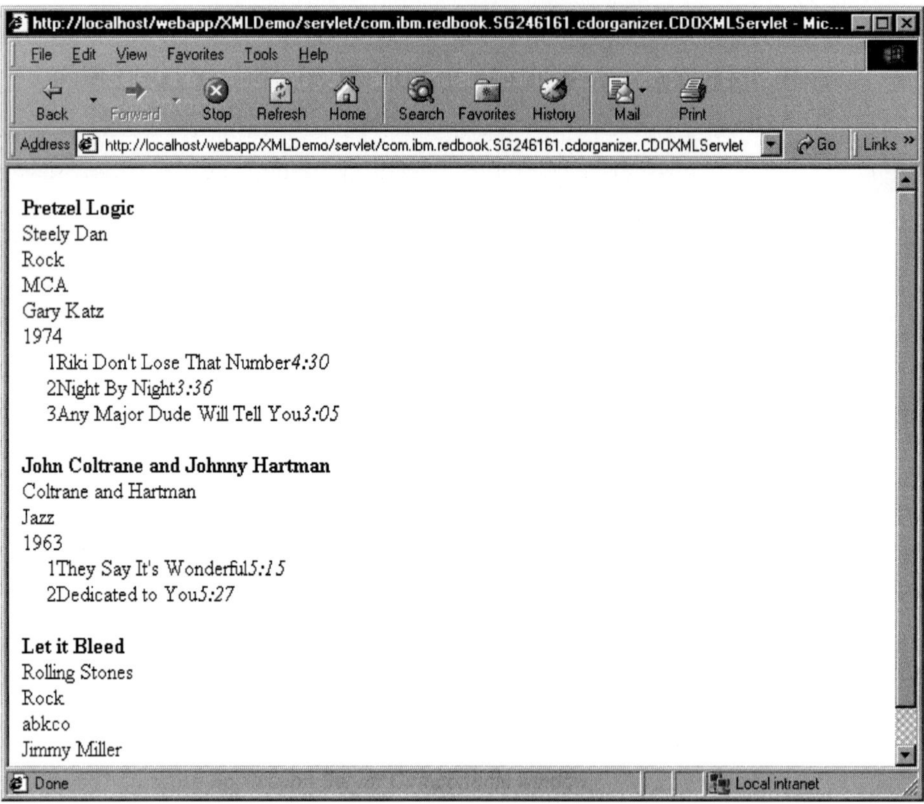

Figure 882. The output of Dynamic XML formatted with CSS

14. Select **Dynamic XML formatted on server with Lotus XSL** and click **Go**. Then you will get the result as shown in Figure 883 on page 1101.

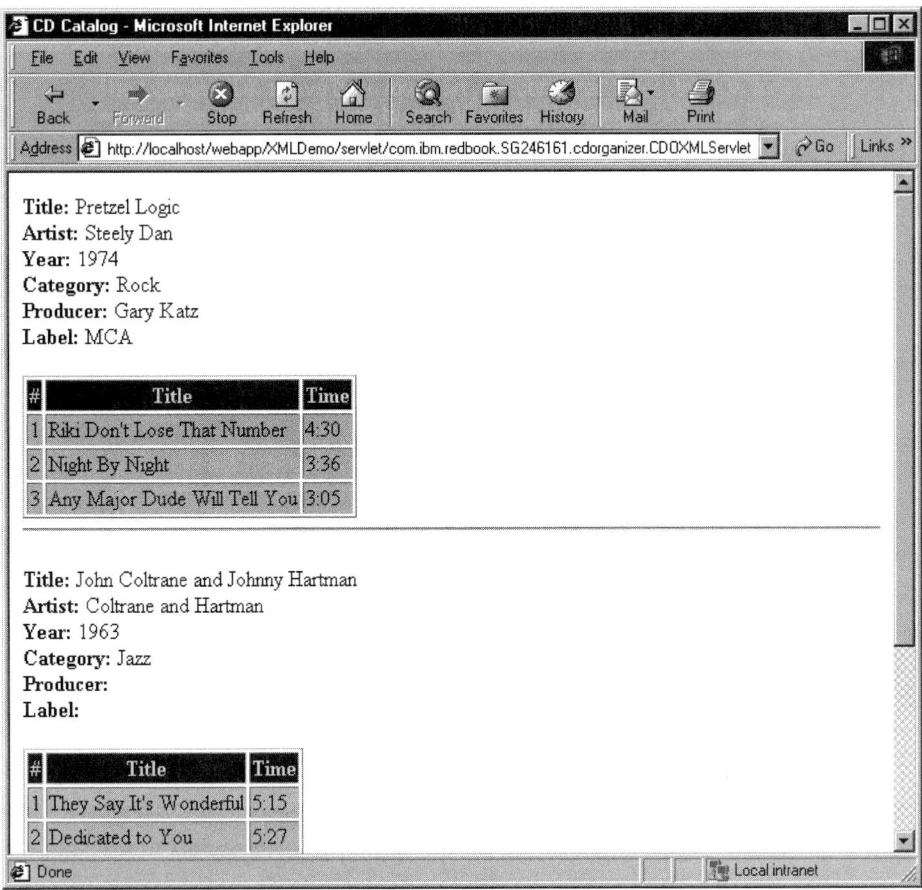

Figure 883. The output of Dynamic XML formatted with Lotus XSL

C.2 Instructions for setting up and running the XML demo: Java Client

1. To run the client make sure the paths in the CDOXMLClientSetup.bat batch file is correct for your system.

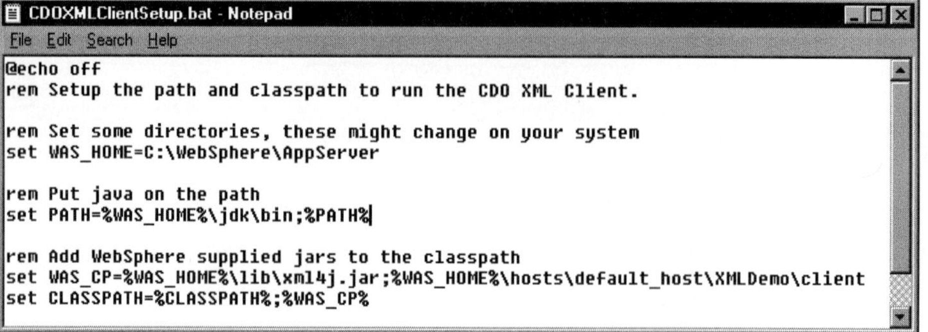

Figure 884. CDOXMLClientSetup.bat file

2. Then cd to C:\WebSphere\AppServer\hosts\default_host\XMLDemo\client (or wherever you put it).
3. Then run CDOXMLClientSetup once to set up the environment.

```
C:\>cd  C:\WebSphere\AppServer\hosts\default_host\XMLDemo\client

C:\WebSphere\AppServer\hosts\default_host\XMLDemo\client>CDOXMLClientSetup
```

4. Then issue `runCDOXMLClient` to run the CDOXMLClient one or more times.

```
C:\WebSphere\AppServer\hosts\default_host\XMLDemo\client>runCDOXMLCli
Retrieve and display CD Catalog using
  S - SAX
  D - DOM
===>S

**********
CD Catalog
**********

CD
===========================
id: 1
title: Pretzel Logic
artist: Steely Dan
category: Rock
label: MCA
producer: Gary Katz
date: 1974
track-number: 1
track-title: Riki Don't Lose That Number
running-time: 4:30
track-number: 2
track-title: Night By Night
running-time: 3:36
track-number: 3
track-title: Any Major Dude Will Tell You
running-time: 3:05


.............
.............

CD
===========================
id: 2
title: Let it Bleed
artist: Rolling Stones
category: Rock
label: abkco
producer: Jimmy Miller
date: 1969

***** End of CD Catalog *****
C:\WebSphere\AppServer\hosts\default_host\XMLDemo\client>
```

```
C:\WebSphere\AppServer\hosts\default_host\XMLDemo\client>runCDOXMLClient
Retrieve and display CD Catalog using
  S - SAX
  D - DOM
===>D

**********
CD Catalog
**********

CD
===========================
id: 1
title: Pretzel Logic
artist: Steely Dan
category: Rock
label: MCA
producer: Gary Katz
date: 1974
track-number: 1
track-title: Riki Don't Lose That Number
running-time: 4:30
track-number: 2
track-title: Night By Night
running-time: 3:36
track-number: 3
track-title: Any Major Dude Will Tell You
running-time: 3:05

...............
...............

CD
===========================
id: 2
title: Let it Bleed
artist: Rolling Stones
category: Rock
label: abkco
producer: Jimmy Miller
date: 1969
C:\WebSphere\AppServer\hosts\default_host\XMLDemo\client>
```

Appendix D. JNDI sample programs

This appendix contains instructions for setting up and running the LDAP Login JNDI example introduced in 9.4, “JNDI sample application” on page 353 and discussed throughout Chapter 9, “Using JNDI to access LDAP” on page 347. Instructions are presented for configuring the Web application under WebSphere, running a Web client.

D.1 JNDI sample files

All the Java source code, JSP, HTML files, and other files are provided to allow further study and experimentation with the sample.

1. HTML files and JSP files
   - LdapLogin.html
   - LdapLoginError.jsp
   - LdapNoSearchResult.jsp
   - LdapRegisterError.jsp
   - LdapRegisterResult.jsp
   - LdapSearchError.jsp
   - LdapSearchMenu.jsp
   - UserNotAllowed.jsp
2. Java files
   - Java Classes
     - com.ibm.itso.websphere.jndi.LDAPAccess
     - com.ibm.itso.websphere.jndi.LoginServlet
     - com.ibm.itso.websphere.jndi.RegistrationServlet
     - com.ibm.itso.websphere.jndi.SearchServlet
   - Jar file and property file
     - LdapSample.jar
     - ldap.properties

D.2 Deploy JNDI sample program to default_app

To deploy our sample program, you need to copy the Java source code, JSP, HTML files, and other files.

D.2.1 Copy HTML files and JSP files

Check the document root of default_app.

The default value on Windows NT should be:

<IBM HTTP Server install_root>\htdocs

The default value on AIX should be:

<IBM HTTP Server install_root>/htdocs/en_US

Create directory "ldap" in the document root, and copy *.html and *.jsp to it.

So, it will be:

<Document Root>\ldap\LdapLogin.html

<Document Root>\ldap\LdapLoginError.jsp

<Document Root>\ldap\LdapNoSearchResult.jsp

<Document Root>\ldap\LdapRegisterError.jsp

<Document Root>\ldap\LdapRegisterResult.jsp

<Document Root>\ldap\LdapSearchError.jsp

<Document Root>\ldap\LdapSearchMenu.jsp

<Document Root>\ldap\UserNotAllowed.jsp

D.2.2 Copy java files

Check the classpath of default_app; the default should be:

<WAS_HOME>\hosts\default_host\default_app\servlets

<WAS_HOME>\servlets

Copy LdapSample.jar and ldap.properties to classpath of default_app, for example, <WAS_HOME>\hosts\default_host\default_app\servlets.

So, it will be:

<WAS_HOME>\hosts\default_host\default_app\servlets\LdapSamples.jar

<WAS_HOME>\hosts\default_host\default_app\servlets\ldap.properties

D.2.3 Add servlets to default_app

1. Start WebSphere Administrative Console
2. Add LoginServlet

   Click the **Wizards** button and select **Add a Servlet**, then the wizard for adding a servlet displays. Follow next steps:

   a. Do you want to select an existing servlet JAR file or directory that contains servlet classes?

      Select **No** option and click **Next** to continue.

   b. Please select a Web Application to contain this servlet

      Select **WebSphere Administrative Domain --> Nodes --> <node name for local machine> --> Default Server --> Default Servlet Engine --> default_app**

      Put cursor to default_app and the Next button becomes active. Click **Next** to continue.

   c. Select the type of servlet you want to configure:

      Select **Create User-Defined Servlet** then click **Next** to continue.

   d. Specify the properties of the servlet:

      Servlet Name: LoginServlet

      Web Application: default_app

      Servlet Class Name: com.ibm.itso.websphere.jndi.LoginServlet

      Servlet Web Path List:

         Click **Add** button

         Input /servlet/LoginServlet

         Click **OK** button to return to the wizard

      Then click **Next** to continue.

   e. Specify Init Parameters:

      Init Parm Name: propertiesFilePath

      Init Parm Value:

      <WAS_HOME>\hosts\default_host\default_app\servlets\ldap.properties

      Then click **Finish**.

3. Add RegistrationServlet

   a. Repeat steps a to c above, refer to step “Add LoginServlet“

b. Specify the properties of the servlet:

   Servlet Name: RegistrationServlet

   Web Application: default_app

   Servlet Class Name: com.ibm.itso.websphere.jndi.RegistrationServlet

   Servlet Web Path List:

   Click **Add** button

   Input /servlet/RegistrationServlet

   Click **OK** button to return to the wizard

   Then click **Next** to continue.

c. Specify Init Parameters:

   Init Parm Name: propertiesFilePath

   Init Parm Value: <WAS_HOME>\hosts\default_host\default_app\servlets\ldap.properties

   Then click **Finish**.

4. Add SearchServlet

   a. Repeat steps a to c above, refer to step "Add LoginServlet"

   b. Specify the properties of the servlet:

   Servlet Name: SearchServlet

   Web Application: default_app

   Servlet Class Name: com.ibm.itso.websphere.jndi.SearchServlet

   Servlet Web Path List:

   Click **Add** button

   Input /servlet/SearchServlet

   Click **OK** button to return to the wizard

   Then click **Next** to continue.

   Then click **Finish**.

D.3 Run the JNDI sample

1. Start administrative server.
2. Start the Default Server, make sure that default_app is started.
3. Start a browser and access the following URI:

`http://<Valid_default_host_Alias>/ldap/LdapLogin.html`

(Where `Valid_default_host_Alias` is any valid alias for the default host.)

If you have no user ID and password, input your information on the bottom of the page, then click **Submit** to register.

If you have a user ID and password, input them on the top of the page, then click **Submit** to log in.

If you log in successfully, you may get a page to input your last name to retrieve the information. Input it, then click **Submit**.

Appendix E. Big3 application

This chapter contains instructions for setting up and running the Big 3 example introduced in Chapter 11, “Enterprise Java Services” on page 393 and Chapter 12, “Transactions” on page 503. Instructions are presented for configuring the Web application under WebSphere, running a Web client, and running the Java client.

All the Java source code, XML, XSL, and other files are provided to allow further study and experimentation with the sample.

E.1 Big3 - small insurance application

Big3 has a simple presentation and business logic. It also contains enough components for testing various configurations.

Big3 business logic consists of:

- Three Enterprise JavaBeans:
  - processClaim - the session bean
  - policy container-managed entity bean - the company's policy holder information
  - claim container-managed entity bean - the list of claims
- Presentation logic:
  - Servlet/HTML
  - Java client

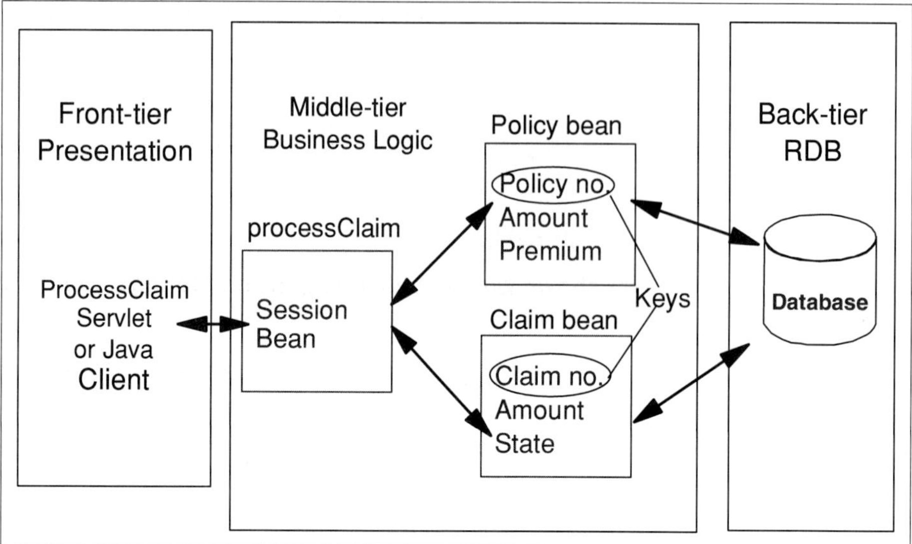

Figure 885. Big3 application components

The processClaim session bean can be invoked by a stand-alone Java application, a servlet, JSP, or HTML. The processClaim session bean creates the Policy and the Claim enterprise JavaBeans.

The Policy bean holds the customer policy data:

- Policy number (key field)
- Policy amount
- Policy premium

The Claim bean contains customer claim data:

- Claim number
- Amount of claim
- State

When an insurance company employee is using the Big3 application to view and modify customer information, the ProcessClaim servlet sends a request to the processClaim bean. This bean manages session information. If the customer has a claim, the business logic computes a new premium.

Once new claim or policy information is entered and committed, it is written to the database. In this example, both the policy and the claim data reside in the same database. It is possible to create separate databases for policy and claim data. The separate databases may or may not reside on the same physical node.

The information on Tier 1 and the processClaim bean are not persistent. The Policy and Claim bean information is persistent.

E.2 Object interaction diagram

Figure 886 shows what is happening inside the Big3 application when the client requests processClaim.

The client can be either servlet/HTML-based, or a Java client.

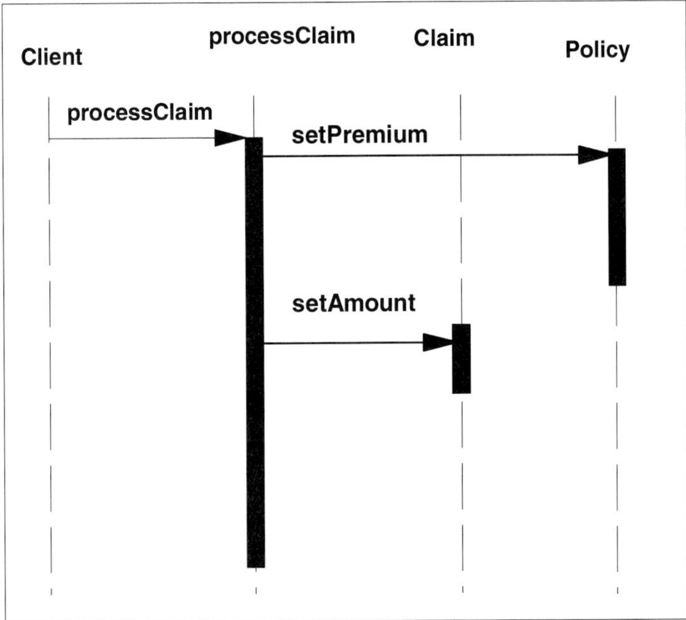

Figure 886. Big3 object interaction diagram

E.3 Install Big3

Let's install the Big3 application, assuming everything is on driver C: (update drives letters as necessary if your configuration is different):

1. Extract big3.zip to c:\

   \big3 to be installed in C: on your computer.

2. Copy c:\big3\big3deployed.jar to c:\WebSphere\AppServer\deployedEJBs directory.
3. Create c:\WebSphere\AppServer\hosts\default_host\Big3WebApp\servlets directory.
4. Copy c:\big3\big3servlets.jar to servlets directory created in step 3.
5. Create c:\IBM HTTP Server\htdocs\Big3 directory.
6. Copy c:\big3\html*.html files to the Big3 directory created in step 5.
7. Edit c:\big3\xml\Big3ServerForNTwithDefaultDatasource.xml and change the node name="lakemichigan" to your host name. Also check if the transport-port 8993 is used by existent application servers, such as the default server. If so, you need to change it to the one that is not used. Also, if the queue name ibmoselink1 is used by existent application servers, such as the default server, you need to change it to the one that is not used. We assume that WebSphere is installed on the C: drive. If you installed it on a different drive, you also need to specify an appropriate drive. We also assume that DB2 is used for the CMP. Please specify an appropriate DB URL for the database that you use.
8. Run XMLConfig -import c:\big3\xml\Big3ServerForNTwithDefaultDatasource.xml -adminNodeName YOUR_HOSTNAME.

E.4 Test the configuration

After you install the Big3, follow the steps to verify the configuration:

1. Start the Big3Server
2. Test the Java client
   a. From the c:\big3 directory, run RunClient 1234 1234 10 YOUR_HOSTNAME
   b. From the c:\big3 directory, run RunClientWithRetry 10 1234 1234 100 80 YOUR_HOSTNAME
3. Test the Web client
   a. Select location `http://YOUR_HOSTNAME/Big3/index.html`
   b. Click the **Submit** button
   c. The bottom of the output should show the message: `Claim Processed`
   d. You can also select `http://YOUR_HOSTNAME/Big3/verify.html` for performance testing.

E.5 Big3 application directory structure

The big3.zip file contains the Big3 sample N-tier EJB application and related files. After you extract the file, you will see the following the directory structure.

- C:\big3 - Big3 Application Home Directory
  - big3deployed.jar - Deployed EJBs exported from VisualAge for Java
  - big3client.jar - EJB client interfaces and stubs exported from VisualAage for Java
  - big3servlet.jar - big3 servlet class files
  - RunClient.bat - bat file to execute big3.client.Main on Windows NT
  - RunClientWithRetry.bat - bat file to execute big3.client.MainRetry on Windows NT
  - RunWlmClient.bat - bat file to execute big3.client.Main on Windows NT multiple times for WLM verification
  - GetClientClasspath.bat - bat file used be RunClient to set client classpath

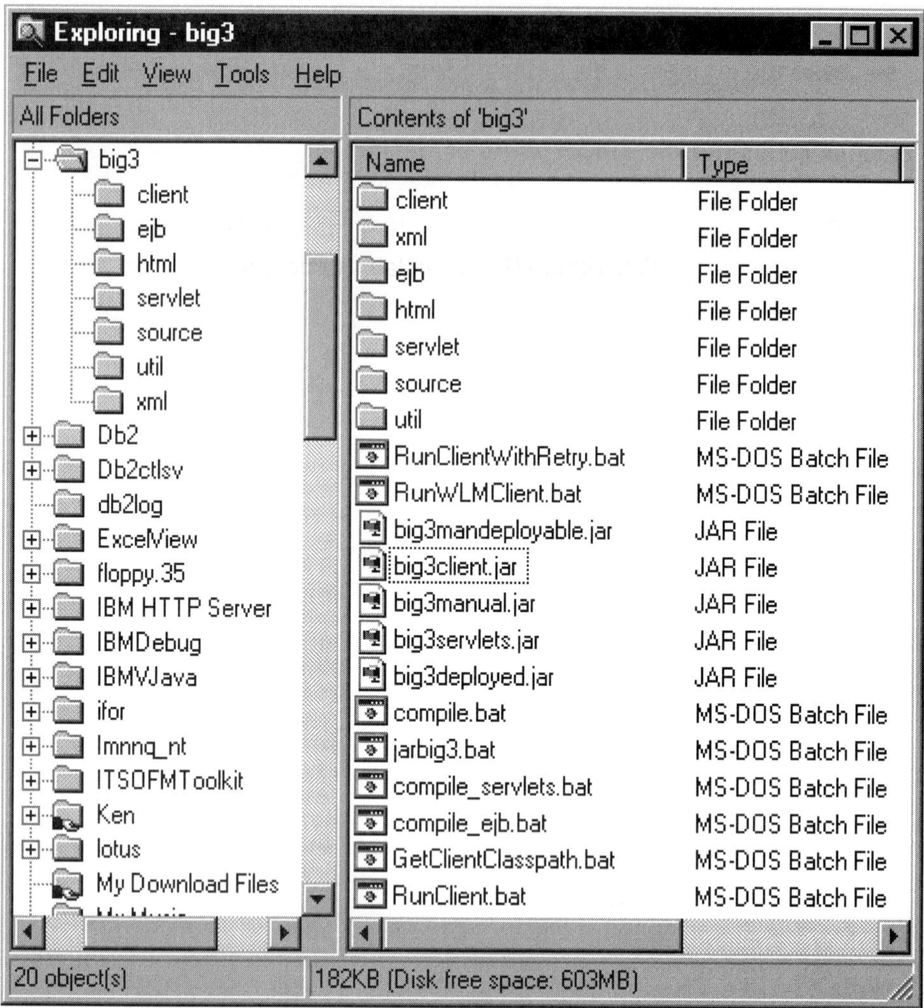

Figure 887. \big3 folder

- C:\big3\ejb - Big3 compiled .class files and Java source files for big3 EJBs
  - C:\big3\ejb\Claim.class
  - C:\big3\ejb\ClaimBean.class
  - C:\big3\ejb\ClaimBeanFinderHelper.class
  - C:\big3\ejb\ClaimHome.class
  - C:\big3\ejb\ClaimKey.class
  - C:\big3\ejb\Policy.class

- C:\big3\ejb\PolicyBean.class
- C:\big3\ejb\PolicyBeanFinderHelper.class
- C:\big3\ejb\PolicyHome.class
- C:\big3\ejb\PolicyKey.class
- C:\big3\ejb\ProcessClaim.class
- C:\big3\ejb\ProcessClaimBean.class
- C:\big3\ejb\ProcessClaimHome.class

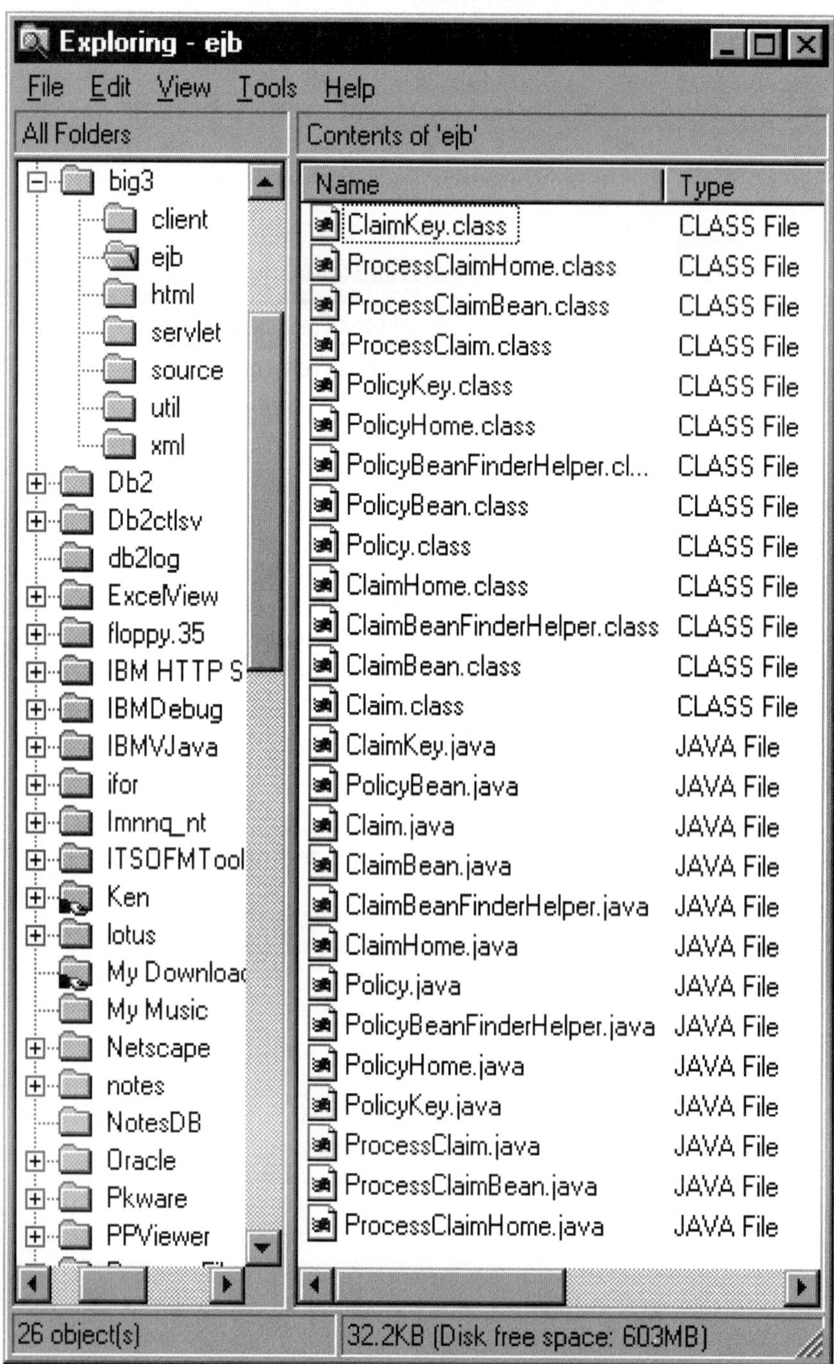

Figure 888. \big3\ejb folder

- C:\big3\client - Big3 JavaClient Directory (Java source file and class file for the big3 main Java client)

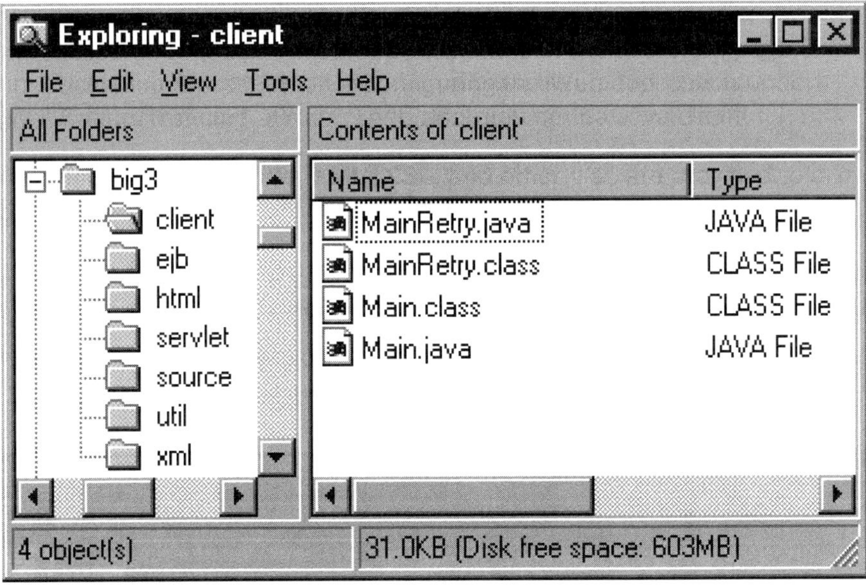

Figure 889. \big3\client folder

- C:\big3\html - Big3 .html files directory (Big3 HTML files)

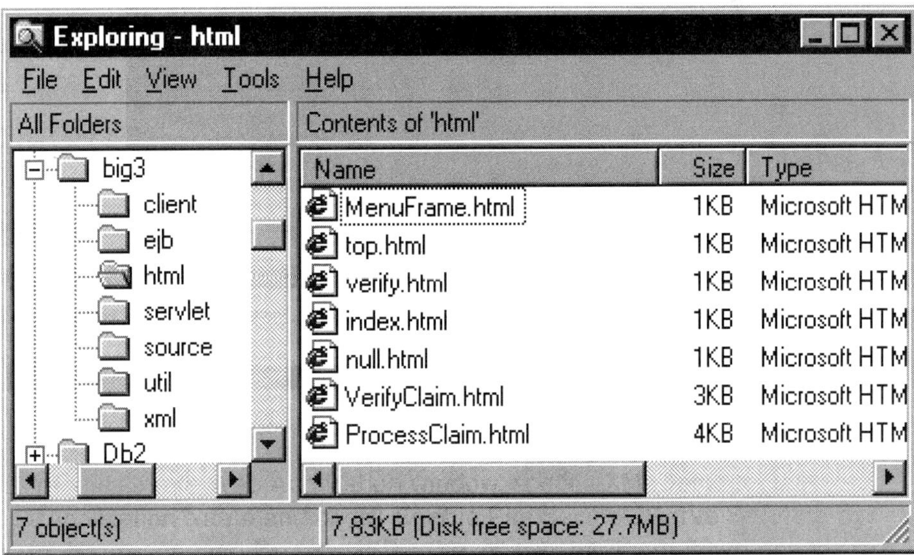

Figure 890. \big3\html folder

- C:\big3\servlet - Big3 servlets (Java source files and class files for the Big3 servlets)

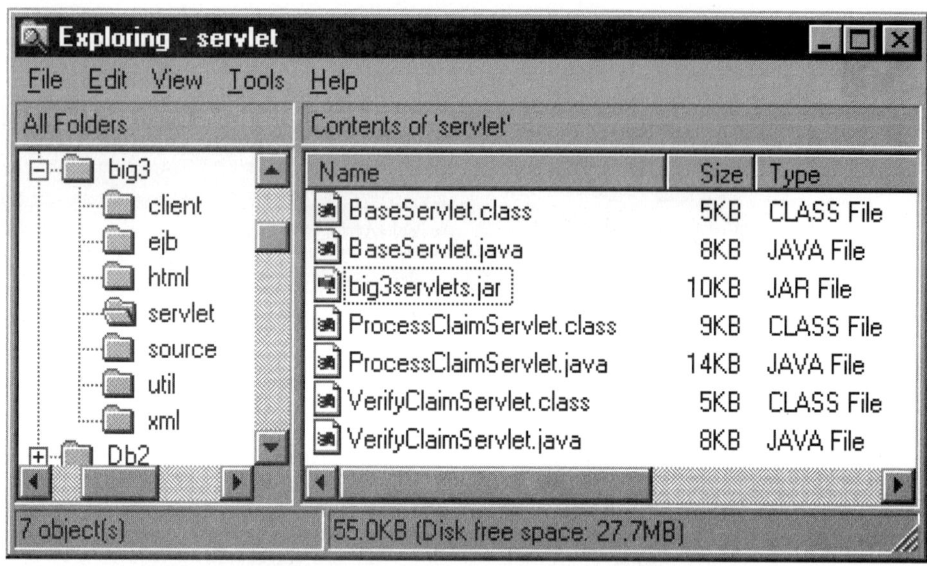

Figure 891. \big3\servlet folder

- C:\big3\source - Big3 .java files in .zip format (contains source.zip of Big3 EJBs, servlets, util, and client)

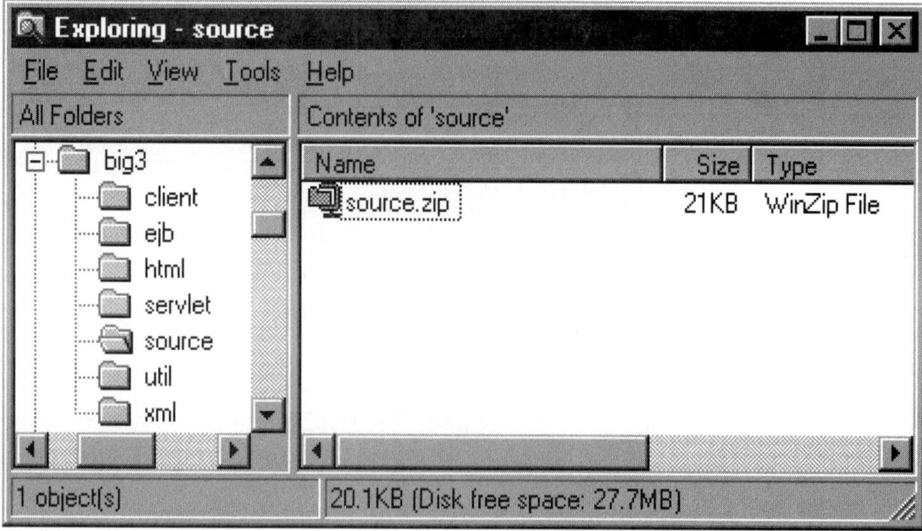

Figure 892. \big3\source folder

- C:\big3\util - Big3 NamingContextHelper .class file (Java source file and class files NamingContextHelper - used to cache InitialContext and EJB homes)

  The NamingContextHelper caches both Initial Contexts and Objects found in those Initial Contexts. Caching in this way can improve performance.

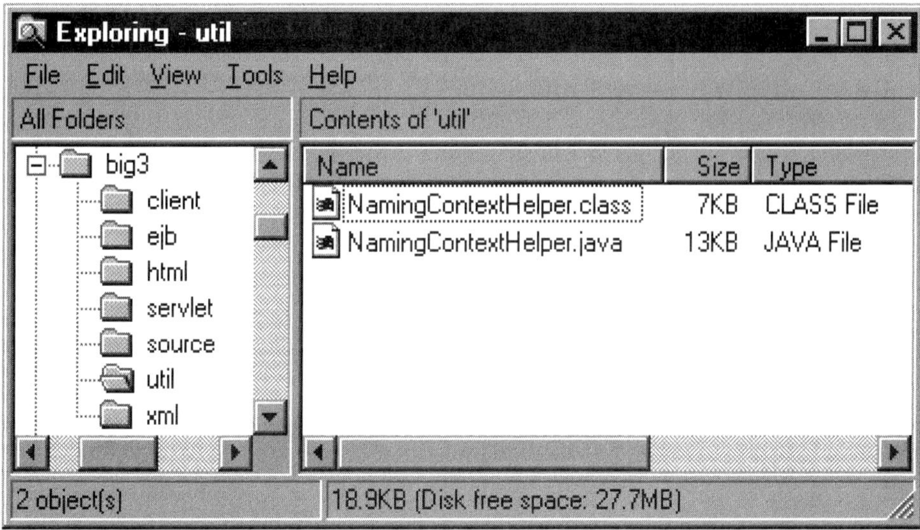

Figure 893. \big3\util folder

- \xml -XML Config Files to import

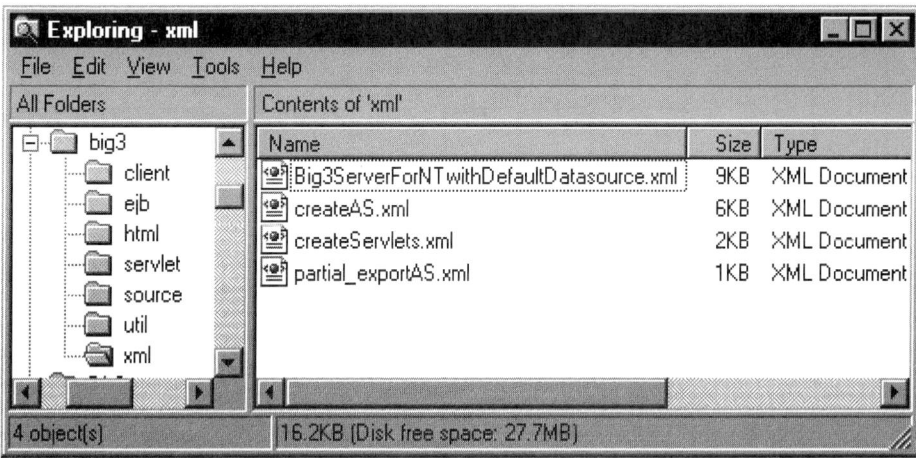

Figure 894. \big3\xml folder

Appendix F. The admin.config file definitions

This chapter contains the definitions of the admin.config file. The admin.config file contains many administrative server properties you can set. In addition, you might want to pass the administrative server some generic Java command line arguments.

Directives in the <WAS_HOME>/bin/admin.config file are similar to their counterparts on the Java command line for the administrative server. The command line argument name is appended to a standard package name for the administrative server. For example the command line argument -lsdPort becomes com.ibm.ejs.sm.adminServer.lsdPort in the admin.config file.

Table 58 on page 1123, Table 59 on page 1126, Table 60 on page 1127, Table 61 on page 1128, Table 62 on page 1128, Table 63 on page 1128, and Table 64 on page 1128 show the list of parameters that you can specify in the admin.config file. Note that you should only update this file if necessary before you update it. We recommend that you make a backup to recover from unexpected results of modification.

Table 58. List of parameters in the admin.config file: com.ibm.ejs.sm.adminServer package

Property	Default value	Description
agentMode	false	This property enables the use of an administrative agent rather than a full service administrative server. This property has no value and should be specified as follows: com.ibm.ejs.sm.adminServer.agentMode=true. If you later want to run a full service administrative server, you must comment out this property (or remove it from the admin.config).
bootstrapHost		Host name running the bootstrap service.
bootstrapPort	900	Port number that the ORB is listening on. The administrative console connects to this port.
classpath		Location of WebSphere Application Server libraries and files. Never edit this except for WebSphere patches or when updating the classpath to add JDBC driver to the administrative database.
dbDriver		This is the classname of the database JDBC driver.
dbPassword		This is the password for logging onto the database server.

Property	Default value	Description
dbSchema		This is the database schema for the administrative database. Note that this value should ONLY be modified in the case such as IBM Produce Support requires.
dbUrl		JDBC URL that is used for the administrative database.
dbUser		This is the name of the user logging onto the database server.
diagThreadPort	-1 = next available port	This property allows you to specify the port on which the DrAdmin thread listens for the administrative server. DrAdmin is a tool that allows you to dynamically enable and disable tracing for the administrative server or any application server (without needing to use the administrative console). Every time you start a server (administrative server or application server), the DrAdmin thread is started and the port on which it is listening is output as an Audit message event to the console and to the standard output file for the server. The default is to use the next available port. This property allows you to control the port and is mainly used in DMZ configurations.
disableAutoServerStart	false	Disable automatic starting of the application server. Setting this to true will start the node without starting any application server(s).
disableEPM	true	Used by the Resource Analyzer in V3.5. Used to disable Enterprise Performance Monitoring.

Property	Default value	Description
initializer		Property used for specifying initializer classes. The value for this property is a comma-delimited list of package qualified class names. The intiializer classes must implement com.ibm.ejs.sm.server.AdminServiceInitializer. This interface has an initialize method and a terminate method. Each time the administrative server starts up, the initialize methods are invoked, and when it shuts down (gratefully) the terminate methods are invoked. Invocation of the methods on the classes are based on the order in which the classes are specified for the property. Some examples of initializers are: com.ibm.ejs.security.Initializer com.ibm.servlet.engine.ejs.ServletEngineAdminIniti alizer com.ibm.servlet.config.InitialSetupInitializer
logFile		Path to the log file.
lsdHost		Host name running the Location Service Daemon.
lsdPort	9000	Port number that the naming service is listening on.
managedServerClassPath		Application server uses this classpath instead of inheriting from the administrative server.
nameServiceJar		Paht of the ame service bean JAR file.
nodeName		Node name to use in the WebSphere configuration. WebSphere will create a default node name equal to the result of the hostname command. But often (as is the case with SP nodes) one wants the node name to resolve a name associated with a NIC other than the primary. This can be achieved by adding the following directive to the top of <WAS_ROOT>/bin/admin.config before starting the admin server for the first time and populating the admin repository: com.ibm.ejs.sm.adminServer.nodeName=someSpe cificNodeName.
primaryNode		Primary node name.

Property	Default value	Description
seriousEventLogSize	1000	Specifies how many serious event records to keep. They are stored in the administrative database. If your database is becoming too full, set this size to the minimum value that is reasonable for your environment.
traceFile		Path to the admin server trace file.
traceOutput		Path to the trace output file.
traceString	off	Trace is collected on cumulative options in string.
tranInactivityTimeOut		This property allows you to set the transaction inactivity timeout for the administrative server. It is specified in milliseconds and defaults to 60 seconds. This property is equivalent to the Transaction inactivity timeout property for application servers (found on the Advanced tab of the properties sheet for the application server in the administrative console).
tranTimeout	600 seconds	Transaction timeout in seconds.
wlm		Enable WLM for administrative server.

Table 59. List of parameters in the admin.config file: com.ibm.ejs.util.process.Nanny package

Property	Default value	Description
adminServerJVMArgs		Java command line arguments. To learn the acceptable command line arguments for the administrative server: 1.Open the file adminserver.[bat|sh] in the bin directory Java command line of the product_installation_root. 2.Note the Java command for starting the server. 3.At a command prompt, issue the command with no arguments, or wrong arguments. A syntax message will be displayed, listing the acceptable commands.
errtraceFile		This is on Windows and not UNIX.
maxtries	3	Number of times the nanny process tries to restart WebSphere.
path		Location of executables in WebSphere Application Server, HTTP server, and database server

Property	Default value	Description
traceFile		Path to the nanny process tracefile.

Table 60. List of parameters in the admin.config file: com.ibm.CORBA package

Property	Default value	Description
BootstrapHost		Administrative server's host name.
BootstrapPort		Administrative server's bootstrap port number.
CommTrace	true	Turns on administrative server communication tracing.
ConfigURL		Path to the security property file for the administrative server.
ConnTrace		Shows connections made by ORB.
Debug		Turns on administrative server debug.
EnableApplicationOLT		Enable the Object Level Trace.
iiop.noLocalCopies	true	Toggle to turn on no local copies optimization. Prevents unnecessary serialization on local JVM. This parameter should be specified in the com.ibm.ejs.sm.util.process.Nanny.adminServerJvm Args line with the UtilClass parameter as follows: -Djavax.rmi.CORBA.UtilClass=com.ibm.CORBA.iiop .Util -Dcom.ibm.CORBA.iiop.noLocalCopies=true
ListenerPort		Specific port number WebSphere should listen on rather than a dynamic one. Useful in firewall configuration. Each app server has its own listening port, which by default is random, but can be fixed to a value using the -Dcom.ibm.CORBA.ListenerPort= property for its JVM. This is an unsecured port.
LocalHost	IP	Property that tells WebSphere the host name to reference. Sets the machine name/IP address for the node.
LSDSSLPort		Encrypted port for location service daemon. Used for security.
OLTApplicationHost		The remote OLT workstation host name for this parameter.
OLTApplicationPort		The port number which the remote OLT Server is listening on.

Property	Default value	Description
requestTimeout		ORB communication timeout in seconds. Useful to free WebSphere when transaction times out.
SSLPort	9001	Secure Socket Layer port number.

Table 61. List of parameters in the admin.config file: com.ibm.ejs.wlm package

Property	Default value	Description
RefreshInterval	300	The number of seconds that elapse between the administrative server updates of the model/clone information to the application servers.

Table 62. List of parameters in the admin.config file: install.initial package

Property	Default value	Description
config	false	Valid values are true or false. If set to true, the initial default configuration will be deployed. Once the default configuration is deployed, the system sets this to false. If you delete your repository and wish to redeploy your default configuration, set this value to true.
config.file		This is the path to the XML file for installing the initial default configuration.

Table 63. List of parameters in the admin.config file: server package

Property	Default value	Description
root		Main path of WebSphere.

Table 64. List of the parameters n the admin.config file: com.ibm.ws.jdk package

Property	Default value	Description
path		Location of JDK used by WebSphere.

Appendix G. Using the additional material

This redbook also contains additional material in CD-ROM format and Web material. See the appropriate section below for instructions on using or downloading each type of material.

G.1 Using the CD-ROM

The CD-ROM that accompanies this redbook contains the following:

Folder name	*Description*
JSP11Samples	Sample programs used in Chapter 6
SessionSamples	Sample programs used in Chapter 7
Servlet22Samples	Sample programs used in Chapter 8
JNDISamples	Sample programs used in Chapter 9
Big3	Sample programs used in Chapter 11 and 12
XMLSamples	Sample programs used in Chapter 13
DeploymentSamples	Sample programs used in Chapter 14

G.1.1 How to use the CD-ROM

You can access the contents of the CD-ROM in the CD-ROM root directory. Alternatively, you can create a subdirectory (folder) on your workstation and copy the contents of the CD-ROM into this folder.

G.2 Locating the additional material on the Internet

The CD-ROM material associated with this redbook is also available in softcopy on the Internet from the IBM Redbooks Web server. Point your Web browser to:

`ftp://www.redbooks.ibm.com/redbooks/SG246161`

Alternatively, you can go to the IBM Redbooks Web site at:

ibm.com/redbooks

Select the **Additional materials** and open the directory that corresponds with the redbook form number.

G.3 Using the Web material

The additional Web material that accompanies this redbook includes the following:

Folder name	*Description*
JSP11Samples	Sample programs used in Chapter 6
SessionSamples	Sample programs used in Chapter 7
Servlet22Samples	Sample programs used in Chapter 8
JNDISamples	Sample programs used in Chapter 9
Big3	Sample programs used in Chapter 11 and 12
XMLSamples	Sample programs used in Chapter 13
DeploymentSamples	Sample programs used in Chapter 14

G.3.1 How to use the Web material

Create a subdirectory (folder) on your workstation and copy the contents of the Web material into this folder.

Appendix H. Special notices

This publication is intended to help IT specialists to design and configure scalable Web application server using WebSphere Application Server Standard and Advanced Editions V3.5. The information in this publication is not intended as the specification of any programming interfaces that are provided by WebSphere Application Server. See the PUBLICATIONS section of the IBM Programming Announcement for WebSphere Application Server for more information about what publications are considered to be product documentation.

References in this publication to IBM products, programs or services do not imply that IBM intends to make these available in all countries in which IBM operates. Any reference to an IBM product, program, or service is not intended to state or imply that only IBM's product, program, or service may be used. Any functionally equivalent program that does not infringe any of IBM's intellectual property rights may be used instead of the IBM product, program or service.

Information in this book was developed in conjunction with use of the equipment specified, and is limited in application to those specific hardware and software products and levels.

IBM may have patents or pending patent applications covering subject matter in this document. The furnishing of this document does not give you any license to these patents. You can send license inquiries, in writing, to the IBM Director of Licensing, IBM Corporation, North Castle Drive, Armonk, NY 10504-1785.

Licensees of this program who wish to have information about it for the purpose of enabling: (i) the exchange of information between independently created programs and other programs (including this one) and (ii) the mutual use of the information which has been exchanged, should contact IBM Corporation, Dept. 600A, Mail Drop 1329, Somers, NY 10589 USA.

Such information may be available, subject to appropriate terms and conditions, including in some cases, payment of a fee.

The information contained in this document has not been submitted to any formal IBM test and is distributed AS IS. The use of this information or the implementation of any of these techniques is a customer responsibility and depends on the customer's ability to evaluate and integrate them into the customer's operational environment. While each item may have been reviewed by IBM for accuracy in a specific situation, there is no guarantee that the same or similar results will be obtained elsewhere. Customers attempting to adapt these techniques to their own environments do so at their own risk.

Any pointers in this publication to external Web sites are provided for convenience only and do not in any manner serve as an endorsement of these Web sites.

The following terms are trademarks of the International Business Machines Corporation in the United States and/or other countries:

IBM ®	DB2
WebSphere	TXSeries
VisualAge	SecureWay
Redbooks	Redbooks Logo
RS/6000	Netfinity
AIX	Home Director
AS/400	

The following terms are trademarks of other companies:

Tivoli, Manage. Anything. Anywhere.,The Power To Manage., Anything. Anywhere.,TME, NetView, Cross-Site, Tivoli Ready, Tivoli Certified, Planet Tivoli, and Tivoli Enterprise are trademarks or registered trademarks of Tivoli Systems Inc., an IBM company, in the United States, other countries, or both. In Denmark, Tivoli is a trademark licensed from Kjøbenhavns Sommer - Tivoli A/S.

C-bus is a trademark of Corollary, Inc. in the United States and/or other countries.

Java and all Java-based trademarks and logos are trademarks or registered trademarks of Sun Microsystems, Inc. in the United States and/or other countries.

Microsoft, Windows, Windows NT, and the Windows logo are trademarks of Microsoft Corporation in the United States and/or other countries.

PC Direct is a trademark of Ziff Communications Company in the United States and/or other countries and is used by IBM Corporation under license.

ActionMedia, LANDesk, MMX, Pentium and ProShare are trademarks of Intel Corporation in the United States and/or other countries.

UNIX is a registered trademark in the United States and other countries licensed exclusively through The Open Group.

SET, SET Secure Electronic Transaction, and the SET Logo are trademarks owned by SET Secure Electronic Transaction LLC.

Other company, product, and service names may be trademarks or service marks of others.

Appendix I. Related publications

The publications listed in this section are considered particularly suitable for a more detailed discussion of the topics covered in this redbook.

I.1 IBM Redbooks

For information on ordering these publications see "How to get IBM Redbooks" on page 1137.

- *The XML Files: Using XML and XSL with IBM WebSphere 3.0*, SG24-5479
- *Servlet and JSP Programming with IBM WebSphere Studio and VisualAge for Java*, SG24-5755
- *WebSphere Scalability: WLM and Clustering using WebSphere Application Server Advanced*, SG24-6153
- *Domino and WebSphere Together*, SG24-5955
- *Developing Enterprise JavaBeans with VisualAge for Java*, SG24-5429
- *Design and Implement Servlets, JSPs, and EJBs for IBM WebSphere Application Server*, SG24-5754
- *WebSphere V3 Performance Tuning Guide*, SG24-5657

I.2 IBM Redbooks collections

Redbooks are also available on the following CD-ROMs. Click the CD-ROMs button at **ibm.com**/redbooks for information about all the CD-ROMs offered, updates and formats.

CD-ROM Title	Collection Kit Number
IBM System/390 Redbooks Collection	SK2T-2177
IBM Networking Redbooks Collection	SK2T-6022
IBM Transaction Processing and Data Management Redbooks Collection	SK2T-8038
IBM Lotus Redbooks Collection	SK2T-8039
Tivoli Redbooks Collection	SK2T-8044
IBM AS/400 Redbooks Collection	SK2T-2849
IBM Netfinity Hardware and Software Redbooks Collection	SK2T-8046
IBM RS/6000 Redbooks Collection	SK2T-8043
IBM Application Development Redbooks Collection	SK2T-8037
IBM Enterprise Storage and Systems Management Solutions	SK3T-3694

I.3 Other resources

These publications are also relevant as further information sources:

- *Transaction Processing: Concepts and Techniques*, by Jim Gray and Andreas Reuter, Morgan Kaufmann Publishers, 1992, ISBN 1558601902
- *Design Patterns: Elements of Reusable Object-Oriented Software*, by Erich Gamma et al, Addison-Wesley, 1995, ISBN 0201633612
- *Tcl and the Tk Toolkit*, by John K. Ousterhout, Addison-Wesley, 1994, ISBN 020163337X

I.4 Referenced Web sites

These Web sites are also relevant as further information sources:

- `http://www.w3.org/` *XML-related specifications*
- `http://xml.apache.org/` *Xerces XML parser and Xalan XSL parser*
- `http://www.oasis-open.org/` *International consortium for industry specifications based on XML*
- `http://alphaworks.ibm.com/` *XML4J parser and Lotus XML*
- `http://www.ibm.com/developer/xml/` *Articles and information of interest to XML developers*
- `http://www-4.ibm.com/software/webservers/appserv/whitepapers.html` *WebSphere white paper*
- `http://www.ibm.com/software/webservers/appserv/library.html` *WebSphere documentation*
- `http://www.ibm.com/software/webservers/appserv/doc/v35/prereq.html` *WebSphere V3.5 pre-requirement*
- `http://www-4.ibm.com/software/webservers/appserv/doc/v35/idx_aas.htm` *WebSphere Application Server documentation*
- `http://www.ibm.com/software/webservers/appserv/` *WebSphere Application Server Web site*
- `http://dev.scriptics.com/` *Tcl developer Web site*
- `http://dev.scriptics.com/software/java/` *JACL Web site*

How to get IBM Redbooks

This section explains how both customers and IBM employees can find out about IBM Redbooks, redpieces, and CD-ROMs. A form for ordering books and CD-ROMs by fax or e-mail is also provided.

- **Redbooks Web Site ibm.com/redbooks**

  Search for, view, download, or order hardcopy/CD-ROM Redbooks from the Redbooks Web site. Also read redpieces and download additional materials (code samples or diskette/CD-ROM images) from this Redbooks site.

  Redpieces are Redbooks in progress; not all Redbooks become redpieces and sometimes just a few chapters will be published this way. The intent is to get the information out much quicker than the formal publishing process allows.

- **E-mail Orders**

  Send orders by e-mail including information from the IBM Redbooks fax order form to:

	e-mail address
In United States or Canada	pubscan@us.ibm.com
Outside North America	Contact information is in the "How to Order" section at this site: http://www.elink.ibmlink.ibm.com/pbl/pbl

- **Telephone Orders**

United States (toll free)	1-800-879-2755
Canada (toll free)	1-800-IBM-4YOU
Outside North America	Country coordinator phone number is in the "How to Order" section at this site: http://www.elink.ibmlink.ibm.com/pbl/pbl

- **Fax Orders**

United States (toll free)	1-800-445-9269
Canada	1-403-267-4455
Outside North America	Fax phone number is in the "How to Order" section at this site: http://www.elink.ibmlink.ibm.com/pbl/pbl

This information was current at the time of publication, but is continually subject to change. The latest information may be found at the Redbooks Web site.

IBM Intranet for Employees

IBM employees may register for information on workshops, residencies, and Redbooks by accessing the IBM Intranet Web site at http://w3.itso.ibm.com/ and clicking the ITSO Mailing List button. Look in the Materials repository for workshops, presentations, papers, and Web pages developed and written by the ITSO technical professionals; click the Additional Materials button. Employees may access MyNews at http://w3.ibm.com/ for redbook, residency, and workshop announcements.

IBM Redbooks fax order form

Please send me the following:

Title	**Order Number**	**Quantity**

First name | Last name

Company

Address

City | Postal code | Country

Telephone number | Telefax number | VAT number

☐ Invoice to customer number

☐ Credit card number

Credit card expiration date | Card issued to | Signature

We accept American Express, Diners, Eurocard, Master Card, and Visa. Payment by credit card not available in all countries. Signature mandatory for credit card payment.

Index

Symbols

Numerics

A

B

C

D

E

F

G

N

O

P

Q

R

S

T

U

V

W

X

Y

Z

IBM Redbooks review

Your feedback is valued by the Redbook authors. In particular we are interested in situations where a Redbook "made the difference" in a task or problem you encountered. Using one of the following methods, **please review the Redbook, addressing value, subject matter, structure, depth and quality as appropriate.**

- Use the online **Contact us** review redbook form found at **ibm.com**/redbooks
- Fax this form to: USA International Access Code + 1 845 432 8264
- Send your comments in an Internet note to redbook@us.ibm.com

Document Number **Redbook Title**	SG24-6161-00 WebSphere V3.5 Handbook
Review	
What other subjects would you like to see IBM Redbooks address?	
Please rate your overall satisfaction:	O Very Good O Good O Average O Poor
Please identify yourself as belonging to one of the following groups:	O Customer O Business Partner O Solution Developer O IBM, Lotus or Tivoli Employee O None of the above
Your email address: The data you provide here may be used to provide you with information from IBM or our business partners about our products, services or activities.	O Please do not use the information collected here for future marketing or promotional contacts or other communications beyond the scope of this transaction.
Questions about IBM's privacy policy?	The following link explains how we protect your personal information. **ibm.com**/privacy/yourprivacy/

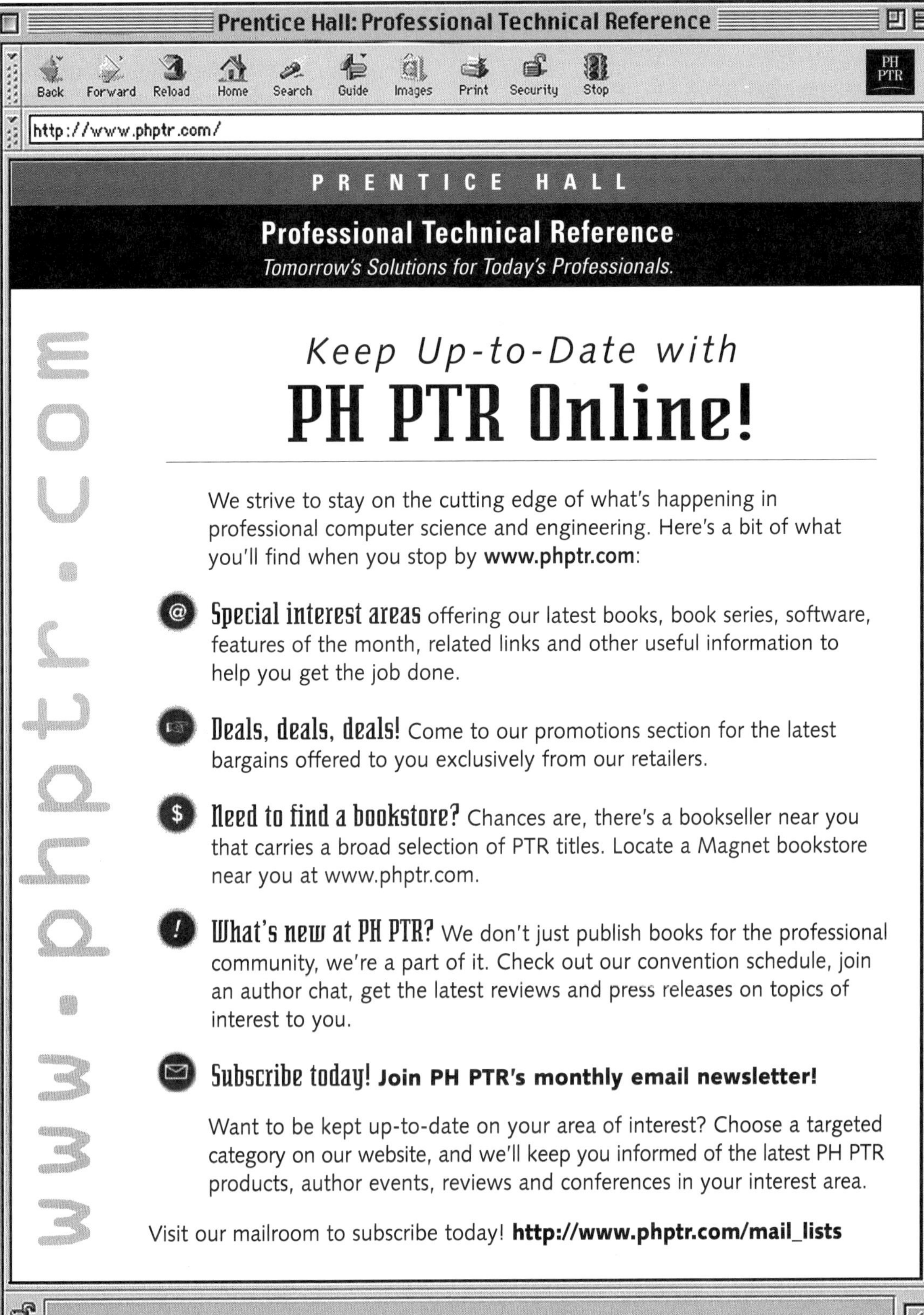

Prentice Hall: Professional Technical Reference
Back Forward Reload Home Search Guide Images Print Security Stop
PH PTR
http://www.phptr.com/
PRENTICE HALL
Professional Technical Reference
Tomorrow's Solutions for Today's Professionals.
www.phptr.com
Keep Up-to-Date with
PH PTR Online!
We strive to stay on the cutting edge of what's happening in professional computer science and engineering. Here's a bit of what you'll find when you stop by www.phptr.com:
Special interest areas offering our latest books, book series, software, features of the month, related links and other useful information to help you get the job done.
Deals, deals, deals! Come to our promotions section for the latest bargains offered to you exclusively from our retailers.
Need to find a bookstore? Chances are, there's a bookseller near you that carries a broad selection of PTR titles. Locate a Magnet bookstore near you at www.phptr.com.
What's new at PH PTR? We don't just publish books for the professional community, we're a part of it. Check out our convention schedule, join an author chat, get the latest reviews and press releases on topics of interest to you.
Subscribe today! Join PH PTR's monthly email newsletter!
Want to be kept up-to-date on your area of interest? Choose a targeted category on our website, and we'll keep you informed of the latest PH PTR products, author events, reviews and conferences in your interest area.
Visit our mailroom to subscribe today! http://www.phptr.com/mail_lists

LICENSE AGREEMENT AND LIMITED WARRANTY

READ THE FOLLOWING TERMS AND CONDITIONS CAREFULLY BEFORE OPENING THIS SOFTWARE MEDIA PACKAGE. THIS LEGAL DOCUMENT IS AN AGREEMENT BETWEEN YOU AND PRENTICE-HALL, INC. (THE "COMPANY"). BY OPENING THIS SEALED SOFTWARE MEDIA PACKAGE, YOU ARE AGREEING TO BE BOUND BY THESE TERMS AND CONDITIONS. IF YOU DO NOT AGREE WITH THESE TERMS AND CONDITIONS, DO NOT OPEN THE SOFTWARE MEDIA PACKAGE. PROMPTLY RETURN THE UNOPENED SOFTWARE MEDIA PACKAGE AND ALL ACCOMPANYING ITEMS TO THE PLACE YOU OBTAINED THEM FOR A FULL REFUND OF ANY SUMS YOU HAVE PAID.

1. **GRANT OF LICENSE:** In consideration of your payment of the license fee, which is part of the price you paid for this product, and your agreement to abide by the terms and conditions of this Agreement, the Company grants to you a nonexclusive right to use and display the copy of the enclosed software program (hereinafter the "SOFTWARE") on a single computer (i.e., with a single CPU) at a single location so long as you comply with the terms of this Agreement. The Company reserves all rights not expressly granted to you under this Agreement.

2. **OWNERSHIP OF SOFTWARE:** You own only the magnetic or physical media (the enclosed software media) on which the SOFTWARE is recorded or fixed, but the Company retains all the rights, title, and ownership to the SOFTWARE recorded on the original software media copy(ies) and all subsequent copies of the SOFTWARE, regardless of the form or media on which the original or other copies may exist. This license is not a sale of the original SOFTWARE or any copy to you.

3. **COPY RESTRICTIONS:** This SOFTWARE and the accompanying printed materials and user manual (the "Documentation") are the subject of copyright. You may not copy the Documentation or the SOFTWARE, except that you may make a single copy of the SOFTWARE for backup or archival purposes only. You may be held legally responsible for any copying or copyright infringement which is caused or encouraged by your failure to abide by the terms of this restriction.

4. **USE RESTRICTIONS:** You may not network the SOFTWARE or otherwise use it on more than one computer or computer terminal at the same time. You may physically transfer the SOFTWARE from one computer to another provided that the SOFTWARE is used on only one computer at a time. You may not distribute copies of the SOFTWARE or Documentation to others. You may not reverse engineer, disassemble, decompile, modify, adapt, translate, or create derivative works based on the SOFTWARE or the Documentation without the prior written consent of the Company.

5. **TRANSFER RESTRICTIONS:** The enclosed SOFTWARE is licensed only to you and may not be transferred to any one else without the prior written consent of the Company. Any unauthorized transfer of the SOFTWARE shall result in the immediate termination of this Agreement.

6. **TERMINATION:** This license is effective until terminated. This license will terminate automatically without notice from the Company and become null and void if you fail to comply with any provisions or limitations of this license. Upon termination, you shall destroy the Documentation and all copies of the SOFTWARE. All provisions of this Agreement as to warranties, limitation of liability, remedies or damages, and our ownership rights shall survive termination.

7. **MISCELLANEOUS:** This Agreement shall be construed in accordance with the laws of the United States of America and the State of New York and shall benefit the Company, its affiliates, and assignees.

8. **LIMITED WARRANTY AND DISCLAIMER OF WARRANTY:** The Company warrants that the SOFTWARE, when properly used in accordance with the Documentation, will operate in substantial conformity with the description of the SOFTWARE set forth in the Documentation. The Company does not warrant that the SOFTWARE will meet your requirements or that the operation of the SOFTWARE will be uninterrupted or error-free. The Company warrants that the media on which the SOFTWARE is delivered shall be free from defects in materials and workmanship under normal use for a period of thirty (30) days from the date of your purchase. Your only remedy and the Company's only obligation under these limited warranties is, at the Company's option, return of the warranted item for a refund of any amounts paid by you or replacement of the item. Any replacement of SOFTWARE or media under the warranties shall not extend the original warranty period. The limited warranty set forth above shall not apply to any SOFTWARE which the Company determines in good faith has been subject to misuse, neglect, improper installation, repair, alteration, or damage by you. EXCEPT FOR THE EXPRESSED WARRANTIES SET FORTH ABOVE, THE COMPANY

DISCLAIMS ALL WARRANTIES, EXPRESS OR IMPLIED, INCLUDING WITHOUT LIMITATION, THE IMPLIED WARRANTIES OF MERCHANTABILITY AND FITNESS FOR A PARTICULAR PURPOSE. EXCEPT FOR THE EXPRESS WARRANTY SET FORTH ABOVE, THE COMPANY DOES NOT WARRANT, GUARANTEE, OR MAKE ANY REPRESENTATION REGARDING THE USE OR THE RESULTS OF THE USE OF THE SOFTWARE IN TERMS OF ITS CORRECTNESS, ACCURACY, RELIABILITY, CURRENTNESS, OR OTHERWISE.

IN NO EVENT, SHALL THE COMPANY OR ITS EMPLOYEES, AGENTS, SUPPLIERS, OR CONTRACTORS BE LIABLE FOR ANY INCIDENTAL, INDIRECT, SPECIAL, OR CONSEQUENTIAL DAMAGES ARISING OUT OF OR IN CONNECTION WITH THE LICENSE GRANTED UNDER THIS AGREEMENT, OR FOR LOSS OF USE, LOSS OF DATA, LOSS OF INCOME OR PROFIT, OR OTHER LOSSES, SUSTAINED AS A RESULT OF INJURY TO ANY PERSON, OR LOSS OF OR DAMAGE TO PROPERTY, OR CLAIMS OF THIRD PARTIES, EVEN IF THE COMPANY OR AN AUTHORIZED REPRESENTATIVE OF THE COMPANY HAS BEEN ADVISED OF THE POSSIBILITY OF SUCH DAMAGES. IN NO EVENT SHALL LIABILITY OF THE COMPANY FOR DAMAGES WITH RESPECT TO THE SOFTWARE EXCEED THE AMOUNTS ACTUALLY PAID BY YOU, IF ANY, FOR THE SOFTWARE.

SOME JURISDICTIONS DO NOT ALLOW THE LIMITATION OF IMPLIED WARRANTIES OR LIABILITY FOR INCIDENTAL, INDIRECT, SPECIAL, OR CONSEQUENTIAL DAMAGES, SO THE ABOVE LIMITATIONS MAY NOT ALWAYS APPLY. THE WARRANTIES IN THIS AGREEMENT GIVE YOU SPECIFIC LEGAL RIGHTS AND YOU MAY ALSO HAVE OTHER RIGHTS WHICH VARY IN ACCORDANCE WITH LOCAL LAW.

ACKNOWLEDGMENT

YOU ACKNOWLEDGE THAT YOU HAVE READ THIS AGREEMENT, UNDERSTAND IT, AND AGREE TO BE BOUND BY ITS TERMS AND CONDITIONS. YOU ALSO AGREE THAT THIS AGREEMENT IS THE COMPLETE AND EXCLUSIVE STATEMENT OF THE AGREEMENT BETWEEN YOU AND THE COMPANY AND SUPERSEDES ALL PROPOSALS OR PRIOR AGREEMENTS, ORAL, OR WRITTEN, AND ANY OTHER COMMUNICATIONS BETWEEN YOU AND THE COMPANY OR ANY REPRESENTATIVE OF THE COMPANY RELATING TO THE SUBJECT MATTER OF THIS AGREEMENT.

Should you have any questions concerning this Agreement or if you wish to contact the Company for any reason, please contact in writing at the address below.

Robin Short
Prentice Hall PTR
One Lake Street
Upper Saddle River, New Jersey 07458

About the CD-ROM

The CD-ROM contains sample programs (source codes, Java class files, and others). You can access the contents of the CD-ROM by pointing your Windows Explorer to the CD-ROM drive. Alternatively, you can create a subdirectory (folder) on your workstation and copy the contents of the CD-ROM into this folder. For more information about the CD-ROM, see Appendix G, on page 1129, and the file readme.txt on the CD.

Technical Support

Prentice Hall does not offer technical support for this software. However, if there is a problem with the media, you may obtain a replacement copy by emailing us with your problem at:

disc_exchange@prenhall.com